Hotels and Bed & Breakfast 2002

GW00708116

Guide to inspected properties
Great Britain & Ireland

Goodwood Marriot Hotel

Hotels and
Bed & Breakfast
2002

Guide to inspected properties
Great Britain & Ireland

First published 2002
Copyright © RAC 2002

Published by BBC Worldwide Limited
Woodlands, 80 Wood Lane, London W12 0TT
Telephone: 020 8433 2000
Fax: 020 8433 3752

ISBN 0-563-53482-6

Publisher: Adam Waddell
Group Advertising Sales Manager: Phil Greenaway
Advertising Sales Executive: Paul Bentley

Editorial, production and repro: Thalamus Publishing
    Oliver Frey
    John Bowen
    Warren Lapworth
    Neil Williams
    Joanne Dovey
Regional maps: Roger Kean

This book contains mapping sourced from Ordnance Survey

Set in 8pt Helvetica Neue 55
Printed and bound in Spain by Cayfossa-Quebecor, Barcelona

RAC Motoring Services
1 Forest Road
Feltham
Middlesex
TW13 7RR
RAC Hotel Services
Telephone: 020 8917 2840
Fax: 020 8917 2813
Email: hotelservices@rac.co.uk

Contents

Welcome

to RAC Hotels and Bed & Breakfast 2002

What's your idea of the perfect getaway?
A romantic hideaway in Cornwall…
a penthouse suite overlooking the Thames…
a cosy bed & breakfast in Cork…
or a castle in the Highlands of Scotland?
Whatever you're after, you'll find it listed here.

RAC Hotels and Bed & Breakfast 2002 offers you a simple way to find the accommodation you're looking for. Whether you want gourmet cuisine, a homely atmosphere or sophisticated style, we have just the place for you. And you can stay for a week, a weekend, or just overnight…. it's up to you.

All our accommodation has been visited by an RAC inspector, providing you with complete reassurance. And they've also been classified according to our ratings and awards scheme, which is designed to bring you the information you need to make the right choice.

The guide is easy to use too. Overleaf, you'll find an outline of the symbols and abbreviations used throughout. And all the accommodation is ordered by region, so you can go straight to the pages you need. If you're looking for somewhere really special, you'll find our award-winning properties listed on pages 19 to 26.

But it's more than just a listing of accommodation. In the pages introducing each region, there are ideas on things to see and do when you visit, and at the back of the book you'll find useful Ordnance Survey maps which pinpoint where RAC inspected properties are located.

We hope you'll enjoy all that the guide has to offer… making your stay special wherever you go.

How to use this guide

Windermere, Cumbria

40 Gilpin Lodge Country House Hotel
Gold Ribbon Winner

★★★ ℜ ℜ ℜ
Crook Road, Windermere, Cumbria, LA23 3NE
Tel: 01539 488818 Fax: 01539 488058
Email: hotel@gilpin-lodge.co.uk
Web: www.gilpin-lodge.co.uk
Children minimum age: 7

This friendly, relaxing, elegant hotel is set in
20 acres of country gardens, moors and
woodland. Opposite Windermere golf course.
Sumptuous bedrooms. Exquisite food.
A Pride of Britain Hotel.
14 beds SB £80 DB £90 HBS £105 HBD £65
B £12.50 L £10 D £35.
CC: MC Vi Am DC Swi Delt
♿ 🖨 🍳 💻 ☎ 📠 P🅿 🐾 🍴
How to get there: Leave M6 at Junction 36.
Take A590/A591 to roundabout north of Kendal,
then B5284 for 5 miles.
See advert on this page

Regional index
Shows the order of the property's listing
within its regional section. See beginning of
regional section for full alphabetical list of
properties in that region.

Town and county
The guide is broken down into 12 regional
sections. Within each region, towns are
listed alphabetically.

Property name

Classification and relevant awards
For information on RAC ratings, please turn
to page 11. For more information on RAC
Awards, please turn to page 15.

Address and contact details
Please note, for properties in the Republic
of Ireland, telephone and fax numbers are
shown with the international dialling code.
To dial from the UK, drop the (0). To dial from
within the Republic, drop the +353 from
the number.

**Description of the property
and picture**
Not all properties listed have opted for these
two items.

**Number of ensuite rooms
and room prices**
For further details see page 9.

Meal prices
For further details see page 9.

Credit Cards accepted

Other information
These symbols (explained opposite) give you
further information on the property,
bedrooms and general facilities.

How to find the property

Advertisement nearby
This indicates that there is an advertisement
for the property nearby with more detail.

What the symbols mean

Classifications

★ Hotel classification (from 1 to 5 Stars) or Townhouse classification (from 4 to 5 Stars).

♦ Guest Accommodation classification (from 1 to 5 Diamonds).
Travel Accommodation is denoted by the name only and does not carry a Star or Diamond rating.

❖ A small number of properties joined the scheme just before the guide went to print so we have been unable to confirm their classification. This symbol indicates that a property is awaiting inspection.

Awards

For further information on RAC's Awards, please see page 15.

 Gold Ribbon Award

 Blue Ribbon Award

Little Gem   Little Gem Award

🍴 Dining Award (from 1 to 5 quality grades)

✗ Sparkling Diamond Award

🦌 Warm Welcome Award

Facilities

🐕 Dogs welcome (including guide dogs)

🦮 Guide dogs only welcome

⬆ Lift

🅿 Off-street parking

🅿 Secure off-street parking

⋮ Meeting/conference facilities

🔔 Licensed for the performance of wedding ceremonies

Room information

♿ Bedrooms with wheelchair access. For details of accommodation which offers disabled access, see page 704

☕ Tea/coffee-making facilities in all rooms

▢ TV in all rooms

☎ Telephone in all rooms

💻 Computer connection available

❄ Air conditioning in all rooms

🛏 Four-poster beds available

🚭 Non-smoking rooms available. Some properties may be 100% non-smoking, so smokers are advised to enquire in advance whether smoking rooms are available

Children

🧒 Children welcome (any minimum age restrictions are shown beneath contact details)

🐴 Supervised creche facility

🍼 Baby listening service

🍴 Children's meal menu

👨‍👩‍👧 Family bedrooms sleeping four or more persons

Sports and leisure facilities

🏊 Indoor swimming pool

🏊 Outdoor swimming pool

🏋 Gymnasium

SPA Health spa

👁 Beauty salon

🎱 Billiards/snooker/pool

🎮 Games room

🎾 Tennis

🏌 Golf

🐎 Horse riding

🎣 Fishing

Licensing information

🍾 Property is licensed for the sale of alcohol

Pricing information

SB   Rate for single room with breakfast

DB   Rate for double/twin room with breakfast (based on double occupancy)

HBS Rate for single room half board

HBD Rate for double/twin room half board (prices shown per person)

B   Price for breakfast (minimum)

L   Price for table d'hôte lunch (minimum)

D   Price for table d'hôte dinner (minimum)

Note: All room prices quoted in this guide are approximate and include VAT and service where applicable. Prices may range according to season and are based on what hoteliers have told us they expect to charge for 2002. Please check before booking. Although properties in Eire have been asked to quote rates in £ Sterling, there may be some cases where rates were quoted in Irish Punts or Euros and have been converted by the publisher into Sterling. Please check the exact rate when booking.

Cancellation policies, terms & conditions may apply.
Meal prices are also approximate and show the minimum price for a meal on the menu. We advise that you check with the Hotel or Guest Accommodation prior to booking a table.

Payment methods

Credit cards accepted as shown:

MC	Mastercard
Vi	Visa
Amex	American Express
DC	Diners Club
Swi	Switch
Delta	Delta
JCB	Japan Card Bank

If no credit cards are listed under the property's entry, cash is accepted or cheques to a given amount with a cheque guarantee card. Please check at the time of booking.

Only at Campanile & Kyriad Hotels-Restaurants

All en-suite rooms
from £ 38.50
per room

Enjoy a meal at our
Café Bistro Restaurants
- All you can eat Buffets
- A 3-course Bistro Menu at £11.95
- Full English and Continental Breakfast £5.95

Special weekend rate from £ 29.95*
(Fri-Sat-Sun)

Basildon:	01268 530 810
Birmingham:	0121 359 33 30
Cardiff:	029 20 549 044
Coventry:	024 76 622 311
Dartford:	01322 278 925
Doncaster:	01302 370 370
Glasgow:	opening soon in 2002
Hull:	01482 325 530
Leicester:	opening soon in 2002
Liverpool:	0151 709 8104
Manchester:	0161 833 1845
Milton Keynes:	01908 649 819
Redditch:	01527 510 710
Rotherham:	01709 700 255
Runcorn:	01928 581 771
Wakefield:	01924 201 054
Washington:	0191 416 5010
Clarine Birmingham:	0121 454 6514
Kyriad Burnley:	01282 421 551

CENTRAL RESERVATION
☎ : 0207 519 50 45
FAX: 0208 814 08 87
www.envergure.fr

* Offer subject to availability in participating hotels. This discount is not applicable with any other promotional offers.

Création Groupe Envergure (08/01) - SA au capital de 566.720.700 FF - 309 071 342 RCS Meaux.

GROUPE ENVERGURE
Hôteliers et Restaurateurs

900 HOTELS & RESTAURANTS EN EUROPE

RAC Ratings

From simplicity to luxury, it's your choice

The RAC Hotel and Guest Accommodation Scheme is designed to provide you with an objective, comprehensive guide to accommodation in the UK and Ireland. It enables you to choose exactly the type of property that suits you, your style and your budget.

Hotels and Guest Accommodation are graded annually following a visit from an RAC inspector (see page 28), who follows strict guidelines to ensure that standards of quality are maintained.

Star Ratings for Hotels – What to expect

★ Hotel

One Star Hotels have everything you need for a pleasant stay, including polite, courteous staff, informal service, and at least one dining area serving simple, tasty meals (although lunch may not always be served), as well as a small range of wines. Most of the bedrooms will have an ensuite bath or shower room, as well as a television, and should be well-maintained, clean and comfortable.

Last orders for dinner no earlier than 6.30pm

★★ Hotel

Two Star Hotels are usually small to medium sized, with smart, well-presented staff offering informal service. You can expect to enjoy a wider range of food and drink, with at least one restaurant or dining room open to residents for breakfast and dinner. Rooms should be comfortable and well-equipped with an ensuite bath or shower room and with a television in-room.

Last orders for dinner no earlier than 7.00pm

★★★ Hotel

At this level, you should find the reception and lounges more spacious, with a receptionist on duty. Staff should be professionally presented and may wear uniforms, responding to your requests promptly and efficiently. You can also expect a restaurant which serves residents and non-residents, as well as a wide selection of drinks served throughout the day and evening in the bar or lounge. All bedrooms should have ensuite bath or shower rooms and offer good standards of comfort, with extra touches like remote-control television, hairdryer, direct-dial telephone, toiletries in the bathroom and room service. There is also some provision for business travellers, like fax or email services.

Last orders for dinner no earlier than 8.00pm

Langshott Manor, Horley

RAC Ratings

★★★★ Hotel

At this level, you'll find the reception and lounge areas have good quality furnishings and décor, with smartly dressed, uniformed staff and a 24-hour reception. These Hotels pride themselves on offering top quality food and drink, taking a more serious approach to cuisine. You can expect at least one restaurant open to both residents and non-residents, with meals served seven days a week, an extensive choice of dishes and a comprehensive wine list. Drinks should also be available throughout the day and evening. Extra services like porterage, express checkout facilities (where appropriate), newspapers delivered to rooms, 24-hour room service and dry cleaning should also be available. Your room should be spacious and well-designed, with an ensuite bathroom including a fixed shower, remote control television, direct-dial telephone and a range of high quality toiletries.

Last orders for dinner no earlier than 9.00pm

★★★★★ Hotel

The whole Hotel should be spacious and luxurious, with impressive interior design, immaculate furnishings and attention to the very smallest detail. You should enjoy flawless service which, while it meets your every need, is never intrusive. The staff should be multilingual, professional and attentive, escorting you to your room on arrival, and there should be an efficient luggage handling system in place to ensure minimum delay. A doorman should greet you as you arrive, and there should be a full concierge service. You should also have access to at least one restaurant, with a high quality menu and a wine list which complements the style of cooking. Staff should show a real enthusiasm for and commitment to food and wine, and there should be a range of drinks and cocktails served in the bar or lounge, with table service also available.

You can expect an elegant, spacious room, with remote-control television, direct-dial telephone at the bedside and desk, a range of luxury toiletries, bath sheets and robes, as well as an ensuite bathroom with fixed shower.

Last orders for dinner no earlier than 10.00pm

Townhouse Accommodation

If you want to stay in a town or city but would prefer a more personal level of service, a Townhouse is ideal. These properties can offer you a greater level of privacy than an Hotel, while still providing luxuriously furnished bedrooms and suites. High quality room service is usually offered rather than public rooms or formal dining rooms usually associated with Hotels. They are usually in areas well-served by restaurants, and fall broadly into the four and five Star classification.

Culloden Hotel, Holywood, Co. Down

Diamond ratings for Guest Accommodation – What to expect

If you're looking for accommodation where service is on a personal level, you might like to choose a property in this classification. It includes guest houses, farmhouses, inns, restaurants with rooms and bed and breakfasts.

In the UK and Ireland, our bed and breakfasts in particular are known for offering a style and warmth envied around the world.

These properties are graded according to the Guest Accommodation Scheme, which assesses the accommodation at five levels of quality, or 'Diamonds'. One Diamond represents the simplest type of accommodation, while five Diamonds is the most luxurious.

The Diamond rating takes into account the level of general comfort, the style and quality of the furnishings and décor, the service shown by the staff, the friendliness of the atmosphere and the quality of the meals.

At all Diamond levels, cleanliness, good housekeeping, guest care and quality are of the highest importance. You can expect to find the following minimum standards at a Guest Accommodation property:

• A comfortable, modern room with fittings in good condition, and adequate storage and seating

• Sufficient hot water

• Bedding and towels changed at least once a week during your stay, with extra pillows and blankets available

• Wholesome, tasty, well-presented meals, including a full cooked breakfast (unless otherwise advertised)

• A professional welcome and departure with a properly prepared bill

Travel Accommodation

Ideal for an overnight stay, properties in this category usually provide budget or lodge accommodation in purpose-built units. They are becoming increasingly popular in major cities, but are usually conveniently located close to main roads, airports and motorways. They may be sited within motorway service areas. Many of the lodges now also provide meeting facilities and are geared up to meet the needs of business travellers. Your room should be well-fitted, ensuite and provide consistent standards which meet your expectations regardless of the location.

❖ Awaiting inspection

If a property joined the scheme just before the deadline for entries to this guide closed, they will carry this symbol.

Ivyleigh House, Portlaoise

RAC Awards

If you're looking for somewhere really special, choose one of our award-winning Hotels, Townhouses or Guest Accommodation properties.

These exceptional establishments are committed to delivering top quality service, with those little touches that make all the difference.

RAC Dining Award

The RAC Dining Award is particularly sought after. At properties displaying the Dining Award symbol below, you can expect a commendable dining experience and quality food.

This Award was introduced in 2000 after lengthy market research, and focuses not just on good food but the entire dining experience... from the quality and presentation of the food on the plate to the ambience and the knowledge of those serving you. It is awarded to Hotels, Townhouses and Guest Accommodation properties that serve meals.

The Awards are given following an incognito visit by one of our RAC inspectors, who are all professionally qualified with wide experience in the industry and trained to high RAC standards. Dinner, breakfast and room service (where appropriate) are taken into account when considering this Award.

There are no set criteria for a Dining Award, as each establishment is different, but the emphasis is on the quality of cooking. Our inspectors consider the whole dining experience, including the surroundings, the warmth of welcome, table appointments and the quality of the wine list.

The Dining Award is given starting at grade one, a high achievement in itself, through to grade five, representing superlative standards.

This grade of Award recognises establishments that produce above average meals, with tasty, carefully prepared food. The menu should be created with care and enthusiasm, and only fresh ingredients should be used. You can expect to enjoy warm, friendly service in simple, comfortable surroundings.

At this grade, you should expect a more serious approach to cooking, with a higher degree of technical skill and a combination of good quality ingredients enhancing the natural flavour of the food. The menu should have a selection of imaginative dishes as well as more traditional combinations, presented in comfortable surroundings by knowledgeable staff.

At this grade you should enjoy cooking of the highest national standard, with well developed technical skill, an imaginative menu and first class ingredients. Dishes should have balance, depth of flavour and flair, and the chef will probably choose to make their own bread, pasta and so on. The surroundings may be more sophisticated, and you should enjoy more professional service.

HATTON COURT

Nestling within its own extensive grounds in the heart of the rolling Cotswold countryside, Hatton Court is conveniently located for visits to 'Regency' Cheltenham Spa, the cathedral city of Gloucester and for exploring the many unspoilt picturesque villages of the Cotswolds.

Built in the 17th Century, careful and extensive refurbishment combines modern day standards of comfort and sophistication with the charm and character of a bygone age. However long your stay, you can be assured of unsurpassed service in the splendid and spacious surroundings of Hatton Court.

Hatton Court, Upton Hill, Upton St Leonards, Nr Cheltenham Tel: 01452 617412
Email: res@hatton-court.co.uk

THE SNOOTY FOX

The Snooty Fox has all the traditional friendliness and charm of a 16th Century coaching inn, whilst offering all present day standards of comfort and service. Great care has been taken in the restoration of this attractive building, which occupies a prime site in the historic market town of 'Royal' Tetbury.

Ideally placed as a centre for touring the Cotswolds, many delightful stately homes, ornate gardens and sleepy villages are all within a short distance of the hotel. Also conveniently located for visits to Cirencester, Cheltenham Spa and Bath.

The Snooty Fox, Market Place, Tetbury
Tel: 01666 502436
Email: res@snooty-fox.co.uk

www.hatton-hotels.co.uk

THE CASTLE INN

The Castle Inn must surely have the most perfect of settings, lying as it does in the heart of one of England's prettiest villages, enjoying simple tranquillity of an age long gone and yet only minutes from the national communications network.

Set in the market place of Castle Combe, this famous hostelry can trace its origins back to the 12th Century and many features of the original construction remain today. Heavy oak beams adorn its interior, retaining original character combined with the comforts of careful modernisation.

The Castle Inn, Castle Combe
Tel: 01249 783030
Email: res@castle-inn.co.uk

CHÂTEAU LA CHAIRE

Rozel Valley, on the north eastern tip of Jersey, is one of the most beautiful locations on the island. Tucked away amongst the unspoilt scenery of the valley's sunny slopes, The Château is surrounded by five acres of terraced gardens which look down on the bay and its bustling fishing community.

Built in 1843, the elegant proportions of the Château have been enhanced and transformed into one of the finest hotels within the UK. It has been awarded with many accolades including three AA Red Stars, an RAC Gold Ribbon and two prestigious Rosette dining awards. You can be assured of impeccable standards in an unsurpassed setting at Château la Chaire.

Château la Chaire, Jersey Tel:01534 863354
Email: res@chateau-la-chaire.co.uk

RAC Awards

RAC RAC RAC RAC

At this grade, you can indulge in innovative and exciting cuisine prepared by a highly accomplished chef, with a menu distinguished by flair and imagination. Dishes should be faultlessly presented, resulting in a memorable and noteworthy meal. Surroundings may be luxurious, with a depth of quality, comfort and style.

RAC RAC RAC RAC RAC

Only establishments offering superlative standards of cuisine are given a grade five Dining Award, offering the very highest level of quality in all areas. Flavours will be intense, daring and exciting with ingredients cooked to perfection and a harmonious combination of flavours. Menus may be innovative or classic, but will always be created using luxury ingredients, and served by immaculately uniformed and exceptionally competent staff. Chefs who receive this award are likely to be at the cutting edge of gastronomy and at the top of their profession, making for a truly memorable dining experience.

Hotel Awards

Only Hotels and Townhouses that truly exceed the standards required by RAC are awarded our Gold and Blue Ribbons. At these properties, you can expect a commitment to getting it right first time… every time.

Our Gold and Blue Ribbon Awards are given annually following an overnight, incognito inspection and can be achieved at all Star levels.

Gold Ribbon Award

Hotels and Townhouses that achieve this accolade are at the very pinnacle within their Star rating, and in many cases represent the 'cutting edge' of excellence in hotel keeping. They offer superlative standards of comfort, hospitality, food, service, customer care and guest awareness, and have that 'special something' that really makes them stand out from the crowd.

Blue Ribbon Award

The familiar RAC Blue Ribbon is given to those Hotels and Townhouses that continue to promote very high quality standards. The majority are personally owned and managed with professionalism, individual attention and boundless dedication. At any one of these properties, you will enjoy superior standards in comfort, service, hospitality and food.

A full listing of award winners for 2001-2002 can be found on pages 19 to 26.

Sheen Falls Lodge, Kenmare

RAC Awards

Guest Accommodation Awards

The following awards are made specifically to Guest Accommodation properties and recognise those which put comfort and hospitality first. Guest Accommodation includes small hotels, bed and breakfasts, guest houses, farmhouses, restaurants with rooms and inns.

Little Gem Award

Little Gem

This prestigious award is given to those properties that achieve the very height of excellence within the Guest Accommodation scheme. They will invariably be personally owned and managed with great dedication and enthusiasm, and really 'hit the spot' when it comes to hospitality.

At these properties, you can expect all-round quality in décor and furnishings, a warm welcome, genuine customer care and attention to detail, as well as high quality home cooked breakfasts and dinners (if served), all adding up to a memorable stay. A full listing of Little Gem Award winners can be found on pages 25 to 26.

Sparkling Diamond Award

This Award is made to those properties which achieve excellent standards when it comes to guest comfort, focusing on cleanliness and hygiene.

Warm Welcome Award

As the name implies, this Award is made to those properties that achieve the very highest levels of hospitality, making you feel at home from the moment you arrive to the time you depart.

Kirkton House, Cardross

Award Winners 2001–2002

Gold Ribbon Winners

This Award is given to those Hotels and Townhouses which consistently demonstrate a commitment to superlative standards of customer care, service and accommodation.

Ashdown Park Hotel, Forest Row

Gold Ribbon Hotels

Channel Islands

Chateau la Chaire Hotel, Jersey ★★★ p699

Longueville Manor Hotel, Jersey ★★★★ p698

England

Alexander House, Turners Hill ★★★ p114

Ashdown Park Hotel, Forest Row ★★★★ p112

Athenaeum Hotel & Apartments, London ★★★★ p47

Bath Priory, Bath ★★★★ p188

Buckland Manor, Broadway ★★★ p364

Calcot Manor, Tetbury ★★★ p395

Capital Hotel, London ★★★★ p52

Castle House, Hereford ★★★ p377

Chewton Glen Hotel, New Milton ★★★★★ p143

Claridge's, London ★★★★★ p41

Cliveden Hotel, Taplow ★★★★★ p166

Congham Hall Hotel, King's Lynn ★★★ p312

Four Seasons Hotel, London ★★★★★ p42

Gilpin Lodge Country House Hotel, Windermere ★★★ p522

Goring Hotel, London ★★★★ p53

Gravetye Manor Hotel, East Grinstead ★★★ p105

Hartwell House Hotel, Restaurant & Spa, Aylesbury ★★★★ p82

Hintlesham Hall, Ipswich ★★★★ p311

Holbeck Ghyll Country House Hotel, Windermere ★★★ p522

Hotel on The Park, Cheltenham ★★★ p368

Langshott Manor, Horley ★★★ p114

Le Manoir aux Quat'Saisons, Great Milton ★★★★ p116

Little Barwick House, Barwick Village ★ p290

Lords of the Manor, Upper Slaughter ★★★ p396

Lower Slaughter Manor, Lower Slaughter ★★★ p380

Lucknam Park Hotel, Colerne ★★★★ p188

Cliveden Hotel, Taplow

Award Winners 2001–2002

Mandarin Oriental Hyde Park,
London ★★★★★ p44

Manor House Hotel,
Castle Combe ★★★★ p212

Middlethorpe Hall Hotel, York ★★★ p456

New Hall, A Country House Hotel,
Sutton Coldfield ★★★★ p393

Northcote Manor, Umberleigh ★★★ p282

Priory Hotel, Wareham ★★★ p282

Queensberry Hotel, Bath ★★★ p190

Sharrow Bay Hotel, Howtown ★★★ p513

South Lodge Hotel,
Lower Beeding ★★★★ p114

Stapleford Park Hotel,
Melton Mowbray ★★★★ p342

Stock Hill House Hotel,
Gillingham ★★★ p224

Ston Easton Park, Ston Easton ★★★★ p188

Summer Lodge, Evershot ★★★ p217

The Berkeley, London ★★★★★ p45

The Castle at Taunton, Taunton ★★★ p267

The Connaught, London ★★★★★ p41

Tylney Hall Hotel, Basingstoke

The Dorchester Hotel, London ★★★★★ p45

The George Hotel, Yarmouth,
Isle of Wight ★★★ p127

The Halkin Hotel, London ★★★★ p53

The Landmark London,
London ★★★★★ p46

The Lanesborough Hotel,
London ★★★★★ p42

The Lygon Arms, Broadway ★★★★ p364

The Ritz, London ★★★★★ p46

The Savoy, London ★★★★★ p46

Thornbury Castle Hotel, Thornbury ★★★ p271

Tylney Hall Hotel, Basingstoke ★★★★ p123

Buckland Manor, Broadway

Ireland

Mount Juliet Hotel, Thomastown

The Old Rectory Country House Hotel, Conwy

Scotland

Wales

Gold Ribbon Townhouses

Award Winners 2001–2002

Blue Ribbon Winners

This Award is given to Hotels and Townhouses which consistently demonstrate a commitment to high standards.

Devonshire Arms, Bolton Abbey

Blue Ribbon Hotels

Channel Islands

Hougue Du Pommier, Guernsey ★★ p696

The Atlantic Hotel, Jersey ★★★★ p697

England

Beechleas, Wimborne Minster ★★ p288

Beetle & Wedge,
Moulsford-on-Thames ★★ p142

Bindon Country House Hotel,
Wellington ★★★ p267

Boscundle Manor House, Tregrehan ★★ p262

Broadoaks Country House,
Windermere ★★ p524

Brockencote Hall,
Chaddesley Corbett ★★★ p366

Cavendish Hotel, Baslow ★★★ p328

Charingworth Manor,
Chipping Campden ★★★ p369

Chester Grosvenor,
Chester ★★★★★ p484

Cotswold House,
Chipping Campden ★★★ p369

Crathorne Hall, Crathorne ★★★★ p455

Devonshire Arms, Bolton Abbey ★★★ p411

Donnington Valley Hotel,
Newbury ★★★★ p144

Eastwell Manor, Ashford ★★★★ p81

Feversham Arms Hotel, Helmsley ★★★ p422

Four Seasons Hotel Canary Wharf,
London ★★★★★ p43

Hob Green Hotel, Harrogate ★★★ p412

Horsted Place Sporting Estate & Hotel,
Uckfield ★★★ p136

Island Hotel, Isles of Scilly ★★★ p223

Lainston House, Winchester ★★★★ p170

Leeming House, Ullswater ★★★★ p507

Lindeth Fell Country House Hotel,
Bowness-on-Windermere ★★ p513

Linthwaite House Hotel,
Bowness-on-Windermere ★★★ p511

St Martins on The Isle, Isles of Scilly

Linthwaite House Hotel, Bowness-on-Windermere

Ireland

Swinside Lodge, Newlands

Award Winners 2001–2002

Scotland

Balbirnie House Hotel, Fife ★★★★ p612

Banchory Lodge, Banchory ★★★ p578

Highland Cottage,
Tobermory, Isle of Mull ★★ p607

Ladyburn, Maybole ★★ p612

Loch Torridon, Torridon ★★★ p623

Norton House, Edinburgh ★★★ p588

Raemoir House Hotel, Banchory ★★★ p578

The Westin-Turnberry Resort,
Turnberry ★★★★★ p624

Balbirnie House Hotel, Fife

Wales

Celtic Manor Resort, Newport ★★★★★ p558

Fairyhill, Swansea ★★ p563

Hotel Maes-y-Neuadd, Talsarnau ★★ p564

Hotel Portmeirion, Portmeirion ★★★ p560

St Davids Hotel & Spa, Cardiff ★★★★★ p538

Blue Ribbon Townhouses

22 Jermyn Street, London ★★★★★ p40

Dorset Square Hotel, London ★★★★ p46

Durley House, London ★★★★★ p42

The Cliveden Townhouse,
London ★★★★★ p41

The Pelham Hotel, London ★★★★ p53

St Davids Hotel & Spa, Cardiff

Little Gem Winners

This Award is given to those Guest Accommodation properties that excel in the all-round quality they show in hospitality, cleanliness and attention to detail.

Little Gem

England

Cambridge Lodge Hotel, Cambridge ♦♦♦♦ p298

Clow Beck House, Darlington ♦♦♦♦♦ p415

Coniston Lodge, Coniston ♦♦♦♦♦ p490

Croyde Bay House Hotel, Croyde ♦♦♦♦♦ p215

Hanchurch Manor Country House, Stoke-on-Trent ♦♦♦♦♦ p388

Lower Brook House, Lower Blockley ♦♦♦♦♦ p370

Lydgate House, Dartmoor ♦♦♦♦♦ p251

May Cottage, Thruxton ♦♦♦♦ p80

Moor View House, Okehampton ♦♦♦♦♦ p233

Northam Mill, Taunton ♦♦♦♦ p269

Number Twenty-Eight, Ludlow ♦♦♦♦♦ p380

Pinnacle Point, Eastbourne ♦♦♦♦♦ p108

Rowanfield Country House, Ambleside ♦♦♦♦♦ p473

Tasburgh House Hotel, Bath

Sawrey House Country Hotel & Restaurant, Near Sawrey ♦♦♦♦♦ p493

Seaview Moorings, St Marys ♦♦♦♦♦ p230

Shallowdale House, Ampleforth ♦♦♦♦♦ p406

Tasburgh House Hotel, Bath ♦♦♦♦ p196

The Ayrlington, Bath ♦♦♦♦♦ p194

The Castleton Hotel, Swanage ♦♦♦♦ p265

The Cobbles Restaurant with Rooms, Mildenhall ♦♦♦♦ p314

The County Hotel, Bath ♦♦♦♦♦ p193

The Moorlands, Pickering ♦♦♦♦♦ p431

The Nurse's Cottage, Sway ♦♦♦♦♦ p166

The Old Coach House, Blackpool ♦♦♦♦♦ p478

The Penfold Gallery, Steyning ♦♦♦♦♦ p164

Three Choirs Vineyards, Newent ♦♦♦♦♦ p382

Widbrook Grange, Bradford-on-Avon ♦♦♦♦♦ p206

Sychnant Pass House, Conwy

Award Winners 2001–2002

The Nurse's Cottage, Sway

Scotland

Brown's Hotel, Haddington ♦♦♦♦ p602

Craigadam, Castle Douglas ♦♦♦♦♦ p581

Dorstan Hotel, Edinburgh ♦♦♦♦ p591

Ettrickshaws Country House Hotel, Ettricksbridge ♦♦♦♦♦ p619

Gruline Home Farm, Isle of Mull ♦♦♦♦♦ p607

Kirkton House, Cardross ♦♦♦♦♦ p602

St Andrews B & B, St Andrews ♦♦♦♦♦ p621

The Pines, Grantown-on-Spey ♦♦♦♦♦ p601

Ireland

Ahernes Seafood Restaurant & Accommodation, Youghal ♦♦♦♦♦ p689

Ballywarren Country House, Cong ♦♦♦♦♦ p645

Castle Farm, Cappagh ♦♦♦♦♦ p662

Churchtown House, Rosslare ♦♦♦♦♦ p682

Coursetown Country House, Athy ♦♦♦♦♦ p637

Earls Court House, Killarney ♦♦♦♦♦ p672

Ivyleigh House, Portlaoise ♦♦♦♦♦ p680

Mal Dua House, Clifden ♦♦♦♦♦ p644

Mount Royd Country Home, Carrigans ♦♦♦♦ p641

Rathcoursey House, near Midleton ♦♦♦♦♦ p678

Trinity Lodge, Dublin ♦♦♦♦ p659

Wales

Sychnant Pass House, Conwy ♦♦♦♦♦ p545

Ivyleigh House, Portlaoise

Relax and Unwind

Take the stress out of finding an hotel with RAC Hotel Reservations

On the move and looking for an hotel or a cosy B&B? Look no further than RAC Hotel Reservations.

With just one phone call, RAC Hotel Reservations gives you unique access to over 3500 quality hotels and B&Bs throughout the UK & Ireland. Each one is inspected, rated and the best ones awarded on your behalf by our team of discerning inspectors for quality and service.

We'll not only source the perfect hotel or B&B to suit your pocket and your needs, we'll also source the latest deals and make the booking for you, completely free of charge*.

So if you are looking for somewhere to relax and unwind, whether on business or leisure, call us now.

Call **0870 603 9109** and quote RAC 04
or visit **www.rac.co.uk/hotels**

*Calls will be charged at National rates

*A to B – we **RAC** to it*

RAC

How we grade our hotels

When you see an RAC sign outside an Hotel or any of the other type of accommodation featured in this guide, it doesn't just mean they belong to the RAC scheme.

It also means that one of our team of inspectors has actually slept in one of their beds and eaten their breakfast… testing it out on your behalf. So we have first-hand experience of what it is like to stay in the accommodation you are about to enjoy.

RAC inspectors are trained professionals who visit each property on a regular basis, checking up on every detail of the service… from the first impression formed at booking, right up until they leave. They also observe the service received by others, to ensure they form a well-rounded opinion.

How an inspection works

All properties are inspected on an annual basis. RAC inspectors arrive unannounced as 'mystery guests', to ensure that they receive no special treatment. This helps them form a completely objective opinion of the accommodation.

Working to strict standards, the inspectors carry out an assessment of the establishment, deciding which rating should be given… and whether or not it is worthy of an award.

The inspection process is carefully controlled to ensure consistency, and a uniform approach is used in all inspections. Once completed, the inspector provides the owner or manager with a full and detailed report in person… so they will know exactly where they are doing well, and where there is room for improvement.

Our promise to you

When you choose an RAC Hotel or Guest Accommodation, you can rest assured that the property has been inspected and graded according to our ratings and awards scheme, providing you with an objective, reliable assessment.

What does it take to be an RAC inspector?

RAC inspectors are special people. They have a strong background in the hospitality industry, an eye for detail and a knack for getting on with others. They try to place themselves in the shoes of a whole variety of guests, to ensure that everyone's needs are taken into account.

They also need to keep up to date with the latest developments in the industry… so they can advise on everything from menu selection to improvements in technology.

Making the most of RAC services

RAC offers you a range of services to help ensure your holiday arrangements run smoothly. From our Hotel booking service to traffic news, insurance to route planning, we've got it covered.

Booking an Hotel or B&B

If you can't decide where to stay, why not ask the experts? In one phone call, RAC Hotel Reservations can help you find a place to stay that meets your needs. We have over 3,000 RAC inspected Hotels and Guest Accommodation properties, so if your first choice doesn't have availability, we can recommend the next best alternative. And we can also source the latest special offers, ensuring you get a great deal. Plus, we can help you with bookings abroad, although obviously these properties won't be RAC inspected. To make a booking, simply call 0870 603 9109 quoting RAC 04.

If you prefer to book online, visit RAC HotelFinder at www.rac.co.uk/hotels

Here, you can check availability, make a booking, view the latest special offers and find out more about thousands of RAC Hotels and Guest Accommodation throughout the UK and Ireland.

Travelling to your accommodation

RAC offers you a range of motoring services to help you get safely to your destination… with the least amount of hassle.

RAC Traffic Alert 1740 brings you up to the minute traffic information over the phone for motorways and major A roads. Simply dial 1740 from any mobile phone.

There's also online assistance at www.rac.co.uk, where you can access our free pan-European route planner, with live UK traffic updates.

Booking tips:

- Book as early as possible, especially for peak periods (June – September) and public holidays

- If booking via RAC Hotel Reservations (see left), please have your credit card handy as this may be required to guarantee your booking

- Always check what the property's cancellation policy is. If you do have to cancel your booking, ensure you give as much notice as possible to avoid cancellation charges. If you wish to be protected against a booking cancellation outside the cancellation terms, you might like to consider taking out RAC Travel Insurance.
  Call 0800 55 00 55 to find out more.

Making the most of RAC services

Travelling to Ireland and abroad

Going abroad? The help you need is just a click away at the RAC website. You can apply online for competitively-priced travel insurance. There's even advice on driving in Europe, European Motoring Assistance (should you break down at the side of the road) and much, much more.

Please visit www.rac.co.uk or
call RAC Travel Sales on 0800 55 00 55

Queries or complaints?

If you have any queries or feel dissatisfied with the level of service you have received at any RAC inspected properties, please first speak to the manager or owner directly at the time of your complaint so they have an opportunity to put things right straight away. If this approach doesn't work, please write to us, and we will take up the issue the next time we inspect the property. We value your feedback and will do everything we can to ensure your comments are taken seriously.

Please write to us, including all details and any relevant correspondence, at the following address:

RAC Hotel Services
1 Forest Road
Feltham
TW13 7RR

Please note: RAC will not obtain compensation for complaints or enter into any correspondence.

Never far Away

Over 200 locations across the UK & Ireland

- Over 200 locations nationwide
- Consistent quality accommodation
- Conveniently located
- Most major cities
- All major motorway networks
- Prices are per room per night
- All rooms are ensuite
- Luxury beds
- Tea & coffee making facilities
- Most rooms can sleep a family of four

Travelodge

Call our Reservation Sales Centre on
08700 850 950 or book on-line at www.travelodge.co.uk

London

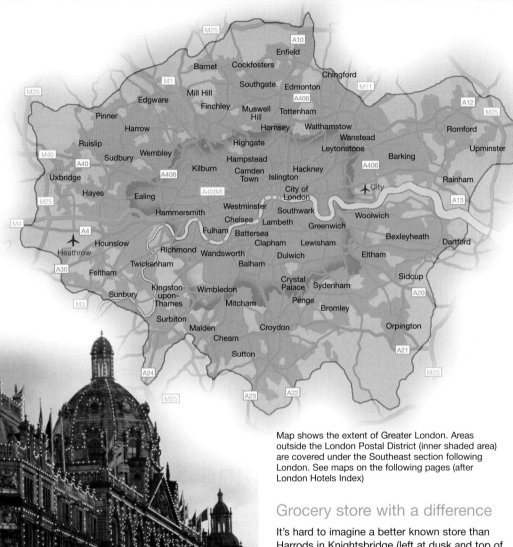

Map shows the extent of Greater London. Areas outside the London Postal District (inner shaded area) are covered under the Southeast section following London. See maps on the following pages (after London Hotels Index)

Grocery store with a difference

It's hard to imagine a better known store than Harrods in Knightsbridge (left at dusk and top of the page at night). Founded largely as a tea importer by Charles Henry Harrod in 1849, the store expanded until there were over 80 departments by 1902. The current building was completed in 1911, by which time Harrods had established itself as the world's foremost department store. For window shopping or the real thing, check out www.harrods.com

● Visit Shakespeare's past at the reconstructed Globe Theatre in Southwark, the premier venue for the bard's later works.

Home of the Beefeaters

The Tower of London (below) has served as palace, arsenal, mint, menagerie and record office, and now houses collections from the Royal Armouries within the White Tower. For Tower information go to www.hrp.org.uk or call 020 7709 0765.

London's famous West End is one of the world's great shopping centres, enclosed between Oxford Street (below) on the north, Regent's Street on the west, Charing Cross Road on the east and Trafalgar Square to the south. Shaftesbury Avenue, running diagonally through the area, houses many of the West End's theatres, Bond Street offers commercial art galleries and elegant jewellers, and the square mile of Soho boasts endless restaurants to suit every type of palate.

The vast British Airways London Eye (above), four times wide than the dome of St Paul's Cathedral, carries 32 passenger pods up to a height of 443 feet (135m). Make bookings on 0870 5000 600
or at www.british-airways.com/londoneye.

● Several tour buses operate around the city, leaving from key tourist spots at regular intervals.

● The Thames Flood Barrier at Woolwich Reach is nearly 20 years old, a remarkable piece of engineering, at a third of a mile long it is the world's largest moveable flood barrier.

● The South Bank Art Centre — now the venue of the Festival Hall, Hayward Gallery, National Film Theatre and the Royal National Theatre — was opened in 1951 as the venue for the Festival of Britain.

London Hotels

If you know the name of the hotel or guest accommodation use this page index in conjunction with the postcode map on the following page to see where it is located. Properties are listed alphabetically with their postcode and corresponding page number.

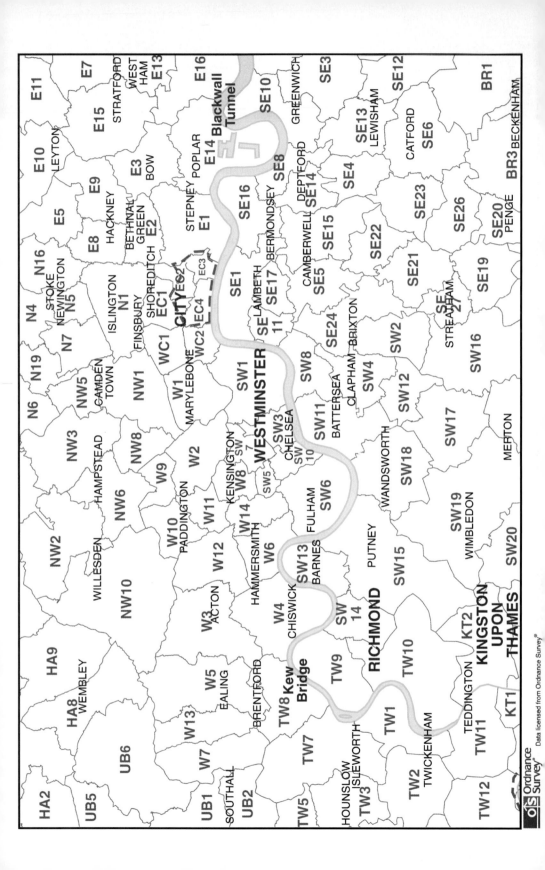

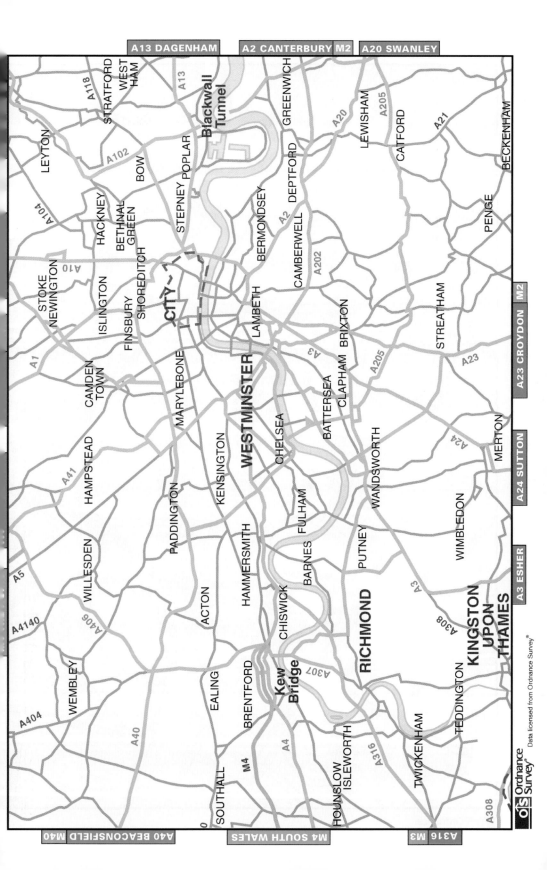

● denotes location of RAC Inspected property/properties

London

22 Jermyn Street

★ ★ ★ ★ ★ Townhouse
22 Jermyn Street, St. James's,
London, SW1Y 6HL
Tel: 020 7734 2353 Fax: 020 7734 0750
Email: office@22jermyn.com
Web: www.22.jermyn.com

22 Jermyn Street has a superb location, an
enviable reputation for first class service, wide
ranging facilities for business and leisure
travellers and is the winner of many prestigious
hotel awards.
18 bedrs DB £246.75 B £12.65
CC: MC Vi Am DC Swi Delt JCB

How to get there: From Hyde Park Corner take
the underpass leading to Piccadilly. Turn right
onto Duke Street, left into King Street onto St.
James' Square. Take left again at Charles II
Street. Left into Lower Regent Street and left
again on Jermyn Street.

41 Buckingham Palace Road

★ ★ ★ ★ ★ Townhouse
41 Buckingham Palace Road,
London, SW1W 0PS
Tel: 020 7300 0041 Fax: 020 7300 0141
Email: book41@rchmail.com
Web: www.redcarnationhotels.com
18 bedrs HBS £346 HBD £173
CC: MC Vi Am DC Swi Delt JCB

How to get there: Just five minutes walk from
Victoria train station. Situated on Buckingham
Palace Road opposite The Royal Mews,
Buckingham Palace.

51 Buckingham Gate

★ ★ ★ ★ ★ Townhouse
Buckingham Gate, London, SW1E 6AF
Tel: 020 7769 7766 Fax: 020 7963 8385
Email: info@51-buckinghamgate.co.uk
Web: www.51-buckinghamgate.co.uk
82 bedrs DB £358 B £13 L £15 D £15
CC: MC Vi Am DC Swi JCB

How to get there: Walk down Victoria Sreet and
turn left into Buckingham Gate. A short walk from
Buckingham Palace and St. James' Station.
See advert on facing page

Brown's Hotel

★ ★ ★ ★ ★
Albemarle Street, London, W1S 4BP
Tel: 020 7518 4792 Fax: 020 7518 4141
Email: reservations@brownshotel.com
Web: www.brownshotel.com
118 bedrs SB £310 DB £360 B £17 L £25 D £36
CC: MC Vi Am DC Swi

How to get there: From Hyde Park Corner into
Piccadilly, then left into Dover Street.

Charlotte Street Hotel

★ ★ ★ ★ ★ Townhouse
15-17 Charlotte Street, London, W1T 1RJ
Tel: 020 7806 2000 Fax: 020 7806 2002
Email: charlotte@firmdale.com
Web: www.firmdale.com
Situated north of Soho, this luxurious boutique
hotel is decorated in a fresh modern English
style, and is perfectly appointed with the
modern traveller in mind: even the bathrooms
have mini colour televisions.
52 bedrs SB £219.12 DB £256.12 B £13.50
L £15 D £25
CC: MC Vi Am Swi Delt JCB

How to get there: From Oxford Street, turn into
Rathbone Place, which leads onto Charlotte
Street. Hotel is on left.

Claridge's
Gold Ribbon Winner

★ ★ ★ ★ ★ ★ ® ® ®
Brook Street, Mayfair, London, W1A 2JQ
Tel: 020 7629 8860 Fax: 020 7499 2210
Email: info@claridges.co.uk
Web: www.savoygroup.com
203 bedrs SB £428 DB £480 B £22 L £29.50
D £29.50 CC: MC Vi Am DC Swi Delt

Cliveden Town House
Blue Ribbon Winner

★ ★ ★ ★ ★ Townhouse ®
26 Cadogan Gardens, London, SW3 2RP
Tel: 020 7730 6466 Fax: 020 7730 0236
Email: reservations@clivedentownhouse.co.uk
Web: www.clivedentownhouse.co.uk

A perfect balance of luxury, service, privacy and
location. At the very centre of fashionable
London. Combining the grandeur of the past
with the luxuries and conveniences of today.
35 bedrs SB £164.50 DB £293.75 B £14.50
L £7.50 D £12.50 CC: MC Vi Am DC Swi Delt

How to get there: From M4, follow signs to
Central London. After Natural History Museum,
road veers left, becoming Brompton Road. Take
fourth right turn at lights into Beauchamp Place.
Turn right into Cadogan Square and fifth left into
Gardens.

Connaught Hotel
Gold Ribbon Winner

★ ★ ★ ★ ★ ® ® ®
16 Carlos Place, Mayfair, London, W1K 2AL
Tel: 020 7499 7070 Fax: 020 7495 3262
Email: info@the-connaught.co.uk
Web: www.savoygroup.com
92 bedrs SB £435 DB £528
CC: MC Vi Am DC Swi Delt

London

Conrad London

★★★★★★ ® ®

Chelsea Harbour, London, SW10 0XG
Tel: 020 7823 3000 Fax: 020 7351 6525
Email: lonch_gm@hilton.com
160 bedrs B £16.50 L £16 D £21
CC: MC Vi Am DC Swi Delt JCB

⚓ & ⎏ 🛏 ⊗ ⌨ ☎ ❄ ℄ ⅃ P 🐕 👤 ♱ 🛏 ☷ ∰ ⊞
🍴 ℥

How to get there: A4; then Earl's Court Road
going south. Right into King's Road, left down
Lot's Road and hotel is straight ahead over
roundabout.

Covent Garden Hotel
Gold Ribbon Winner

★★★★★ Townhouse ® ®

10 Monmouth Street, London, WC2H 9HB
Tel: 020 7806 1000 Fax: 020 7806 1100
Email: covent@firmdale.com
Web: www.firmdale.com
Located in the heart of theatreland, this
luxurious boutique hotel combines dramatically-
designed interiors, superb service and the best
that modern design and technology can offer.
58 bedrs SB £236.75 DB £285.50 B £13.50
L £15 D £25
CC: MC Vi Am Swi Delt

⎏ ⧉ ⊗ ⌨ ☎ ❄ ℄ ⅃ 👤 ♱ ⊗ 🐕 ☷ ∰ 🍴
How to get there: Nearest tube is Covent
Garden. Walk to the end of Neal Street
(opposite tube) and turn left onto Monmouth
Street. Hotel is on right.

Durley House
Blue Ribbon Winner

★★★★★ Townhouse

115 Sloane Street, London, SW1X 9PJ
Tel: 020 7235 5537 Fax: 020 7259 6977
Email: durley@firmdale.com
Web: www.firmdale.com
Situated in Sloane Street, this all-suite hotel
comprises 11 elegantly-furnished apartments.
Perfect for Knightsbridge shopping, playing
tennis in the private garden or entertaining in
the privacy of your own suite.
11 bedrs SB £346.62 DB £346.62 L £8 D £8
CC: MC Vi Am Swi Delt

⎏ ⧉ 🛏 ⊗ ⌨ ☎ ❄ ℄ 🐕 ☷ ∰ ⌘
How to get there: From Knightsbridge turn
down Sloane Street, away from Hyde Park and
Durley House is on right 100 yards before
Sloane Square.

Four Seasons Hotel Park Lane
Gold Ribbon Winner

★★★★★ ® ® ®

Hamilton Place, Park Lane,
London, W1A 1AZ
Tel: 020 7499 0888 Fax: 020 7493 1895/6629
Web: www.fourseasons.com

With distinctive charm and warmth, set back
from Park Lane, and in the heart of Mayfair
overlooking Hyde Park, the Four Seasons Hotel
is unrivalled in its service and setting. The result
– a highly acclaimed hotel with handsomely-
appointed spacious rooms.
220 bedrs
CC: MC Vi Am DC Swi

⚓ ⎏ ⊗ ⌨ ☎ ❄ ℄ ⅃ P 🐕 👤 ♱ ☷ ∰ 🍴
How to get there: Set back from Park Lane in
Hamilton Place. Closest tubes are Hyde Park
Corner and Green Park. Well-situated for
Victoria and Paddington stations.

Four Seasons Hotel Canary Wharf
Blue Ribbon Winner

★★★★★ ® ®

Westferry Circus, Canary Wharf,
London, E14 8RS
Tel: 020 75101999 Fax: 020 75101998
Web: www.fourseasons.com
142 bedrs
CC: MC Vi Am DC Swi Delt JCB

⚓ & ⎏ 🛏 ⊗ ⌨ ☎ ❄ ℄ P 🐕 👤 ℄ ♱ 🐕 ⊗ ☷
∰ ℥ 🍴 ⌘ ℥

Lanesborough
Gold Ribbon Winner

★★★★★ ® ® ®

Hyde Park Corner, London, SW1X 7TA
Tel: 020 7259 5599 Fax: 020 7259 5606
Email: info@lanesborough.com
Web: www.lanesborough.com

One of London's pre-eminent hotels, The Lanesborough represents a revival of traditional hospitality. Originally a country retreat, the hotel captures the style and elegance of a private 19th century residence.
95 bedrs SB £348.38 DB £471.75 B £18.50 L £15 D £32 CC: MC Vi Am DC Swi Delt
How to get there: Follow signs to Hyde Park Corner.

Le Méridien Grosvenor House

★★★★★★
86–90 Park Lane, London, W1K 7TN
Tel: 020 7499 6363 Fax: 020 7493 3341
Email: grosvenor.reservations@forte-hotels.com
Web: www.lemeridien-grosvenorhouse.com
567 bedrs B £17.50 L £42.50 D £42.50
CC: MC Vi Am DC Swi Delt
How to get there: Situated on Park Lane, in the heart of Mayfair, overlooking Hyde Park.

Le Méridien Piccadilly

★★★★★
21 Piccadilly, London, W1V 0BH
Tel: 020 7734 8000 Fax: 020 7437 3574
Email: lmpiccrcs@forte-hotels.com
Web: www.lemeridien-hotels.com

266 bedrs
CC: MC Vi Am DC Swi Delt
How to get there: From M4, directly to Cromwell Road, through Knightsbridge and on to Piccadilly. Underground – Piccadilly Circus (Piccadilly & Bakerloo Lines), two minutes walk.

Le Méridien Waldorf

★★★★★★
Aldwych, London, WC2B 4DD
Tel: 0870 400 8484 Fax: 020 7836 7244
Web: www.lemeridien-waldorf.com
292 bedrs SB £347 DB £358.75 HBS £365.50 HBD £377.25 B £15 L £18.50 D £18.50
CC: MC Vi Am DC Swi Delt JCB
How to get there: Nearest underground stations are Covent Garden and Holborn. Charing Cross railway is 1/2 mile. Waterloo and Eurostar 3/4 mile.

London Marriott Hotel, County Hall

★★★★★
County Hall, London, SE1 7PB
Tel: 020 7591 1599 Fax: 020 7591 1128
Web: www.marriott.com/marriott/lonch

This unique five star hotel, situated in the historic GLC building of County Hall, offers 200 air-conditioned and quiet bedooms and is easily accessible from both Waterloo and Westminster stations.
200 bedrs SB £330.32 DB £330.32 B £15.95 L £25 D £30
CC: MC Vi Am DC Swi Delt JCB
How to get there: The hotel entrance is on the south side of Westminster Bridge; nearest underground stations are Westminster and Waterloo, both five minutes' walk.

London

Mandarin Oriental Hyde Park
Gold Ribbon Winner

★★★★★★ ⓡⓡⓡⓡ
66 Knightsbridge, London, SW1X 7LA
Tel: 020 7235 2000 Fax: 020 7235 4552
Email: reserve-molon@mohg.com
Web: www.mandarinoriental.com
200 bedrs SB £346.62 DB £346.62 B £18.95
CC: MC Vi Am DC Swi Delt
How to get there: Situated in the heart of Knightsbridge.

One Aldwych
Blue Ribbon Winner

★★★★★★ ⓡⓡⓡ
1 Aldwych, London, WC2B 4RH
Tel: 020 7300 1000 Fax: 020 7300 1001
Email: reservations@onealdwych.com
Web: www.onealdwych.com

Bang in the middle where the City meets the West End, One Aldwych incorporates sleek contemporary design, cutting-edge technology and professional, friendly service.
105 bedrs B £13.50 L £16.75 D £18.75
CC: MC Vi Am DC Swi Delt JCB
How to get there: At the point where The Aldwych meets The Strand, opposite Waterloo Bridge and close to Covent Garden.

Renaissance London Chancery Court

★★★★★★ ⓡⓡ
252 High Holborn, London, WC1V 7EN
Tel: 020 7829 9888 Fax: 020 7829 9889
Email: sales.chancerycourt
@renaissancehotels.com
Web: www.renaissancehotels.com/loncc
357 bedrs DB £335 B £17.95 L £18.50 D £35

CC: MC Vi Am DC Swi Delt
How to get there: By Holborn tube station, which runs through both the West End and The City.

Royal Garden Hotel
Blue Ribbon Winner

★★★★★★ ⓡⓡⓡⓡ
2-24 Kensington High Street, London, W8 4PT
Tel: 020 7937 8000 Fax: 020 7361 1991
Email: sales@royalgardenhotel.co.uk
Web: www.royalgardenhotel.co.uk

Situated in the heart of Kensington, overlooking Hyde Park and Kensington Gardens, The Royal Garden Hotel offers contemporary accommodation, three bars, two restaurants, health club and 24 hour business centre.
396 bedrs SB £290.12 DB £374.62 B £14
L £9.50 D £25 CC: MC Vi Am DC Swi Delt JCB
How to get there: On Kensington High Street (A315), between Kensington Church Street and Kensington Palace Gardens.

Sheraton Park Tower Hotel

★★★★★★ ⓡⓡⓡ
101 Knightsbridge, London, SW1X 7RN
Tel: 020 7235 8050 Fax: 020 7235 8231
Email: reservations_central_london
@starwoodhotels.com
Web: www.sheraton.com

In a superb location in the heart of Knightsbridge just a short stroll from Harrods, The Sheraton Park Tower boasts newly-renovated luxury suites and Butler floors, and the award-winning fish restaurant One-o-One. 289 bedrs CC: MC Vi Am DC Swi Delt

The Berkeley
Gold Ribbon Winner

★ ★ ★ ★ ★ ® ® ® ®

Wilton Place, London, SW1X 7RL
Tel: 020 7235 6000 Fax: 020 7235 4330
Email: info@the-berkeley.co.uk
Web: www.savoygroup.co.uk

Perfectly placed for shopping in Knightsbridge, The Berkeley is a showcase for some of England's leading interior designers. Facilities include the popular new Blue Bar and roof-top swimming pool.
204 bedrs SB £430 DB £530 B £18 L £20 D £25
CC: MC Vi Am DC

How to get there: 200 yards down Knightsbridge from Hyde Park Corner, on left hand side.

The Carlton Tower

★ ★ ★ ★ ★ ® ®

Cadogan Place, London, SW1X 9PY
Tel: 020 7235 1234 Fax: 020 7235 9129
220 bedrs CC: MC Vi Am DC Swi Delt JCB

The Dorchester
Gold Ribbon Winner

★ ★ ★ ★ ★ ® ® ® ®

Park Lane, London, W1A 2HJ
Tel: 020 7629 8888 Fax: 020 7409 0114
Email: reservations@dorchesterhotel.com
Web: www.dorchesterhotel.com
250 bedrs SB £377.88 DB £430.75 B £19.50
L £29.50 D £39.50
CC: MC Vi Am DC Swi Delt

How to get there: The Dorchester is located on Park Lane, opposite Hyde Park, approximately halfway between Marble Arch and Hyde Park Corner.
See advert below

London

The Landmark London
Gold Ribbon Winner

★★★★★
222 Marylebone Road, London, NW1 6JQ
Tel: 020 7631 8000 Fax: 020 7631 8080
Email: reservations@thelandmark.co.uk
Web: www.landmarklondon.co.uk

With some of the largest bedrooms in London, the Landmark London seamlessly integrates the elegance and grandeur of British Victorian style with the luxury and facilities of a world-class five-star hotel.
299 bedrs SB £332 DB £381 HBS £362
HBD £220.50 B £18.50 L £21 D £32
CC: MC Vi Am DC Swi Delt
How to get there: In front of Marylebone main line station and underground, also fronting Marylebone Road near Madame Tussaud's. Easy access to M40 and M4.

The Milestone Hotel & Apartments
Gold Ribbon Winner

★★★★★ Townhouse
1 Kensington Court, London, W8 5DL
Tel: 020 7917 1234 Fax: 020 7917 1133
Email: guestservices@milestone.redcarnationhotels.com
Web: www.redcarnationhotels.com

The Milestone, a Victorian architectural showpiece built in the 1880s, is a five-star intimate boutique hotel and offers a history rich in tradition, style and unparalleled attention to detail and service.
57 bedrs SB £310 DB £327.50 B £13.50
L £15.50 D £36.50 CC: MC Vi Am DC Swi Delt
How to get there: Directly opposite Kensington Palace, The Milestone is about 400 yards from High Street Kensington underground station.

The Ritz
Gold Ribbon Winner

★★★★★
150 Piccadilly, London, W1V 9DG
Tel: 020 7300 2308/9 Fax: 020 7493 2687
Email: enquire@theritzlondon.com
Web: www.theritzlondon.com
133 bedrs SB £382 DB £465 B £23.50 L £36
D £52 CC: MC Vi Am DC Swi Delt
How to get there: Located on Piccadilly, next to Green Park, a few steps from Bond Street. From Victoria station, north on Victoria Line to Green Park. Ritz 100 yards away.

The Savoy
Gold Ribbon Winner

★★★★★
The Strand, London, WC2R 0EU
Tel: 020 7836 4343 Fax: 020 7240 6040
Email: info@the-savoy.co.uk
Web: www.savoy-group.com
234 bedrs SB £308.50 DB £363.50 B £18.50
L £13 D £13 CC: MC Vi Am DC Swi
How to get there: Between Aldwych and Trafalgar Square on The Strand.

Athenaeum Hotel & Apartments
Gold Ribbon Winner

★★★★★ ♟ ♟ ♟
116 Piccadilly, London, W1J 7BJ
Tel: 020 7499 3464 Fax: 020 7493 1860
Email: info@athenaeumhotel.com
Web: www.athenaeumhotel.com

A luxurious family owned hotel in the heart of Mayfair, the Athenaeum offers traditional warmth and hospitality. In addition to the well appointed rooms, the Edwardian style apartments adjacent to the hotel offer an ideal home away from home.
157 bedrs SB £330 DB £375 B £14.50 L £14 D £15
CC: MC Vi Am DC Swi Delt
How to get there: Located on Piccadilly in the heart of Mayfair overlooking Green Park. Nearest tube is Green Park or Hyde Park corner.

Beaufort

★★★★ Townhouse
33 Beaufort Gardens, Knightsbridge, London, SW3 1PP
Tel: 020 7584 5252 Fax: 020 7589 2834
Email: thebeaufort@nol.co.uk
Web: www.thebeaufort.co.uk
28 bedrs SB £182.12 DB £252.63
CC: MC Vi Am DC Swi Delt JCB
How to get there: Off Brompton Road, Knightsbridge, between Harrods and Beauchamp Place.

Berkshire Hotel

★★★★★ ♟ ♟ ♟
350 Oxford Street, London, W1N 0BY
Tel: 020 7629 7474 Fax: 020 7629 8156
CC: MC Vi Am DC Swi JCB

Berners Hotel

★★★★★ ♟ ♟
Berners Street, London, W1A 3BE
Tel: 020 7666 2000 Fax: 020 7666 2001
Email: berners@berners.co.uk
Web: www.thebernershotel.co.uk
216 bedrs SB £206 DB £247 HBS £220
HBD £137.50 B £12.95 L £12.95 D £10.25
CC: MC Vi Am DC Swi Delt
How to get there: Located just off Oxford Street opposite Wardour Street and between Oxford Circus and Tottenham Court Road underground stations.

Chesterfield Mayfair

★★★★★ ♟ ♟
35 Charles Street, Mayfair, London, W1J 5EB
Tel: 020 7514 5609 Fax: 020 7409 1726
Email: reservations@chesterfield.
redcarnationhotels.com
Web: www.redcarnationhotels.com
110 bedrs SB £245 DB £268.60 HBS £257.50
HBD £281 B £13.50 L £12.50 D £12.50
CC: MC Vi Am DC Swi Delt JCB
How to get there: From Green Park station, turn to Berkeley Street, straight to Berkeley Square. The first street on the left is Charles Street.

Copthorne Tara Hotel London Kensington

★★★★
Scarsdale Place, Wrights Lane, Kensington, London, W8 5SR
Tel: 020 7872 2000 Fax: 020 7937 7100
Email: sales.tara@mill-cop.com
Web: www.millennium-hotels.com
834 bedrs SB £240 DB £255 B £15 L £19 D £19
CC: MC Vi Am DC JCB
How to get there: From M25, take exit 15 towards Earls Court. Scarsdale Place is just off Kensington High Street.

London

Crowne Plaza London St. James Hotel

★★★★★ ⓡ ⓡ
41-54 Buckingham Gate, London, SW1E 6AF
Tel: 020 7834 6655 Fax: 020 7630 7587
Email: reservations@cplansi.co.uk
Web: www.london.crowneplaza.com
342 bedrs DB £285 B £13 L £10 D £15
CC: MC Vi Am DC Swi JCB

How to get there: Walk down Victoria Street and turn left into Buckingham Gate. A short walk from Buckingham Palace and St. James' Station.
See advert below

Cumberland Hotel

★★★★
1A Great Cumberland Place, Marble Arch, London, W1A 4RF
Tel: 0870 400 8701 Fax: 020 7724 4621
Email: rm1001@forte-hotels.com
Web: www.thecumberland.co.uk
894 bedrs CC: MC Vi Am DC Swi Delt

How to get there: Situated on Oxford Street overlooking Marble Arch and Hyde Park. Underground: Central Line, Marble Arch Station.

Crowne Plaza London St. James Hotel

This beautifully-renovated hotel in the heart of Westminster offers 3 superb restaurants, 2 bars, a fully-equipped gym, luxurious treatments in the Shiseido Qi Salon and meeting facilities.

Buckingham Gate, London SW1E 6AF
Tel: 020 7834 6655   Fax: 020 7630 7587
reservations@cplansi.co.uk
www.london.crowneplaza.com

Dorset Square Hotel

Blue Ribbon Winner

★★★★ Townhouse ⓡ
39 Dorset Square, London, NW1 6QN
Tel: 020 7723 7874 Fax: 020 7724 3328
Email: dorset@firmdale.com
Web: www.firmdale.com
Just like a grand country house in town. Located in Marylebone. Bond Street, Regent's Park. West End theatres and the City's business centre are all within easy reach.
38 bedrs SB £126.90 DB £94 B £11.75 L £15
D £25
CC: MC Vi Am Swi Delt

How to get there: Nearest underground station is Baker Street. Or, proceed from M40 onto A40 (Euston Road). Take left hand lane off flyover. Turn left on Gloucester Place. Dorset Square is 1st left.

Flemings Mayfair

★★★★ ⓡ
Half Moon Street, Mayfair, London, W1J 7BH
Tel: 020 7499 2964 Fax: 020 7629 4063
Email: guest@flemings-mayfair.co.uk
Web: www.flemings-mayfair.co.uk
121 bedrs SB £214.58 DB £265.83 B £16 L £15
D £24.50
CC: MC Vi Am Swi Delt JCB

How to get there: The nearest underground station is Green Park. From the station to the hotel is three minutes' walking distance.

Harrington Hall

★★★★ ⓡ ⓡ
5-25 Harrington Gardens, London, SW7 4JW
Tel: 020 7396 9696 Fax: 020 7396 9090
Email: harringtonsales@compuserve.com
Web: www.harringtonhall.co.uk
200 bedrs SB £197.75 DB £219.50 B £10.50
L £17 D £22.95
CC: MC Vi Am DC Swi Delt

How to get there: 100 yards from Gloucester Road underground station (Piccadilly, Circle and District lines). One mile from M4 and A4.

Plan your route

Visit www.rac.co.uk for RAC's interactive route planner, including up to the minute traffic reports.

Holiday Inn London – Kensington South

★★★★

97 Cromwell Road, London, SW7 4DN
Tel: 020 7370 5757 Fax: 020 7373 1448
Email: forumlondon@interconti.com
Web: www.forum-london.interconti.com
910 bedrs B £10.25 L £15 D £25
CC: MC Vi Am DC Swi Delt

Hotel Russell

★★★★

Russell Square, London, WC1B 5BE
Tel: 020 7837 6470 Fax: 020 7837 2857
Web: www.principalhotels.co.uk
356 bedrs
CC: MC Vi Am DC Swi Delt

How to get there: Two minute walk from Russell Square tube station, within one mile of Euston, King's Cross and St. Pancras main line rail stations.

Jurys Clifton Ford Hotel

★★★★

Welbeck Street, London, W1M 8DN
Tel: +353(0)1 6070000 Fax: +353(0)1 6316999
Email: bookings@jurysdoyle.com
Web: www.jurysdoyle.com
255 bedrs SB £216 DB £232 B £16 D £25
CC: MC Vi Am DC Swi Delt

How to get there: Located 18 miles from London Heathrow. Paddington Station two miles and Bond tube ¼ mile. Just five minute walk from Bond and Oxford Streets.

Jurys Great Russell Street

★★★★

16-22 Great Russell Street, London, WC1B 3NN
Tel: +353(0)1 6070000 Fax: +353(0)1 6316999
Email: bookings@jurysdoyle.com
Web: www.jurysdoyle.com
169 bedrs SB £231 DB £247 B £13
CC: MC Vi Am

How to get there: Take the Picadilly line (Blue Line) to Holborn. Walk from Holborn: turn left outside station, walk up New Oxford Street, turn right at Dominion Theatre. Hotel is 2nd on right hand side.

Jurys Kensington Hotel

★★★★

109-113 Queen's Gate, South Kensington, London, SW7 5LR
Tel: +353(0)1 6070000 Fax: +353(0)1 6316999
Email: bookings@jurysdoyle.com
Web: www.jurysdoyle.com
173 bedrs SB £215 DB £230 B £14.95 D £16.50
CC: MC Vi Am DC Swi Delt

How to get there: Located 13 miles/21 kms from London Heathrow. South Kensington tube five minutes walk. Victoria station 1½ miles.

Kingsway Hall

★★★★★

Great Queen Street, Covent Garden, London, WC2B 5BZ
Tel: 020 7309 0909 Fax: 020 7309 9696
Email: kingswayhall@compuserve.com
Web: www.kingswayhall.co.uk
170 bedrs SB £230 DB £240 B £15.25
CC: MC Vi Am DC Swi Delt

London Bridge Hotel

★★★★★

8-18 London Bridge Street, London, SE1 9SG
Tel: 020 7855 2200 Fax: 020 7855 2233
Email: sales@london-bridge-hotel.co.uk
Web: www.london-bridge-hotel.co.uk
138 bedrs SB £195.95 DB £206.90 B £10.95
L £15 D £25
CC: MC Vi Am DC Swi JCB

How to get there: Directly opposite London Bridge station. Rail and underground links — Jubilee and Northern lines.

London Marriott Hotel Grosvenor Square

★★★★★

Grosvenor Square, London, W1K 6JP
Tel: 020 7493 1232 Fax: 020 7491 3201
Web: www.marriott.com
221 bedrs SB £227.45 DB £302.15 B £15.95
CC: MC Vi Am DC Swi

London

London Marriott Hotel Maida Vale

★★★★

Plaza Parade, Maida Vale, London, NW6 5RP
Tel: 020 7543 6000 Fax: 020 7543 2100
Email: marriottmaidavale@btinternet.com
Web: www.marriott.com/lonwh
223 bedrs SB £119 DB £119 B £13.50 L £18
D £25
CC: MC Vi Am DC Swi

How to get there: On A5 Edgware Road where
Kilburn High Road meets Maida Vale.

London Marriott Hotel Marble Arch

★★★★

134 George Street, London, W1H 6DN
Tel: 020 7723 1277 Fax: 020 7402 0666
Email: salesadmin.marblearch
          @marriotthotels.co.uk
Web: www.marriotthotels.co.uk/lonma
240 bedrs B £15.95 L £20 D £26
CC: MC Vi Am DC Swi JCB

How to get there: Close to Marble Arch and
Edgware Road tube stations; 15 minutes from
Paddington Station.

London Marriott Hotel Regents Park

★★★★

128 King Henry's Road, London, NW3 3ST
Tel: 020 7722 7711 Fax: 020 7586 5822
Web: www.marriotthotels.com/lonrp
303 bedrs SB £160 DB £175 HBS £185
HBD £112.50 B £16.95 L £16 D £18
CC: MC Vi Am DC Swi JCB

How to get there: Short taxi journey from King's
Cross or Euston stations; accessible from A1,
M1, M40 and M25.

Lowndes Hyatt Hotel

★★★★ Townhouse

21 Lowndes Street, London, SW1X 9ES
Tel: 020 7823 1234 Fax: 020 7235 1154
Email: lowndes@hyattintl.com
Web: www.london.hyatt.com
78 bedrs SB £244 DB £262 B £14 L £19 D £27
CC: MC Vi Am DC Delt

Millennium Bailey's Hotel

★★★★★

140 Gloucester Road, Kensington,
London, SW7 4QH
Tel: 020 7373 6000 Fax: 020 7370 3760
Email: sales.bailey's@mill-cop.com
Web: www.millennium-hotels.com
212 bedrs SB £263 DB £276 B £13
CC: MC Vi Am Swi

How to get there: Opposite Gloucester Road
underground station, serviced by Piccadilly,
Circle and District lines. 40 minutes to London
Heathrow and Gatwick airports.

Millennium Gloucester Hotel Kensington

★★★★

4-18 Harrington Gardens, London, SW7 4LH,
Tel: 020 7373 6030 Fax: 020 7373 0409
Email: sales.gloucester@mill-cop.com
Web: www.millenium-hotels.com
610 bedrs SB £263 DB £276 B £13
CC: MC Vi Am DC Swi

How to get there: Next to Gloucester Road
underground station, served by Piccadilly, Circle
and District lines. 40 minutes to London
Heathrow airport.

Millennium Hotel London Knightsbridge

★★★★★

17 Sloane Street, Knightsbridge, London,
SW1A 9NU
Tel: 020 7235 4377 Fax: 020 7235 3705
Email: reservations@mill-cop.com
Web: www.millennium-hotels.com
222 bedrs SB £275 DB £285 B £8 L £28 D £50
CC: MC Vi Am DC Swi Delt

How to get there: From the M4 take the A4
towards Central London, go past Harrods and
Sloane Street is on the right.

Millennium Hotel London Mayfair

Grosvenor Square, London, W1K 2HP
Tel: 020 7629 9400 Fax: 020 7629 7736
Email: reservations@mill-cop.com
Web: www.millenium-hotels.com

The elegant and luxurious Millennium Mayfair is situated in London's prestigious Grosvenor Square. The hotel is just five minutes walk from Oxford Street and Hyde Park.
348 bedrs SB £317 DB £358 B £18 L £18.50 D £21.50
CC: MC Vi Am DC Swi Delt

How to get there: Situated on Grosvenor Square, which can be reached via Park Lane or Berkeley Square.

Montcalm Hotel

Great Cumberland Place, London, W1H 7YW
Tel: 020 7402 4288 Fax: 020 7724 9180
Email: montcalm@montcalm.co.uk
Web: www.nikkohotels.com
120 bedrs B £15.95 L £20 D £20
CC: MC Vi Am DC Swi JCB

How to get there: Heathrow Express Service, Paddington and Baker Street stations all within a mile radius. Two-minute walk from Marble Arch underground station.

Park Lane Hotel

Piccadilly, London, W1Y 8BX
Tel: 020 7499 6321 Fax: 020 7499 1965
CC: MC Vi Am DC Swi JCB

Royal Horseguards

Whitehall Court, London, SW1A 2EL
Tel: 020 7839 3400 Fax: 020 7930 4010
Email: royal.horseguards@thistle.co.uk
Web: www.thistlehotels.com
280 bedrs
CC: MC Vi Am DC Swi Delt

How to get there: Two minutes from Charing Cross and 10 minutes from Victoria and Waterloo stations. Nearest underground station is Embankment.

Royal Lancaster Hotel

Lancaster Terrace, London, W2 2TY
Tel: 020 7262 6737 Fax: 020 7724 3191
CC: MC Vi Am DC Swi Delt JCB

Rubens at The Palace

39 Buckingham Palace Road,
London, SW1W 0PS
Tel: 020 7834 6600 Fax: 020 7828 5401
Email: jraggett@rubens.redcarnationhotels.com
Web: www.redcarnationhotels.com
173 bedrs
CC: MC Vi Am DC Swi Delt

How to get there: Three minutes walk from Victoria tube station. From Gatwick airport, take Gatwick Rail Express to Victoria and then a short walk to the hotel.

Rydges Kensington Plaza

61 Gloucester Road, Kensington,
London, SW7 4PE
Tel: 020 7584 8100 Fax: 020 7823 9175
Email: kph@sales-kenplaza.demon.co.uk
Web: www.rydges.com
89 bedrs SB £125 DB £170 B £8.50 L £4.50 D £8.50
CC: MC Vi Am DC Swi Delt JCB

How to get there: 100 yards from Gloucester Road tube station, near the corner of Gloucester and Cromwell roads.
See advert on following page

London

Rydges Kensington Plaza

Rydges Kensington Plaza is an elegant 4-star hotel reflecting all the best of the Victorian era. Lovingly restored in 2000, the hotel offers guests the best in modern services and facilities set in the welcoming ambience of London's past.

Located in the heart of Kensington within walking distance of Kensington Palace, Hyde Park, Knightsbridge and Earls Court,

Rydges Kensington Plaza is 100 metres from Gloucester Road tube, which services the Piccadilly, Circle and District lines.

61 Gloucester Road London SW7 4PE
Tel: 020 7584 8100   Fax: 020 7823 9175
kph@sales-kenplaza.demon.co.uk
www.rydges.com

Swallow International

★★★★★ ⓡ ⓡ
147 Cromwell Road, London, SW5 0TH
Tel: 020 7973 1000 Fax: 020 7244 8194
Email: international@swallow-hotels.co.uk
Web: www.swallowhotels.com
238 bedrs SB £139   DB £153 B £14 L £14 D £18
CC: MC Vi Am DC
⌶⌶ ☺ ▭ ☎ ✳ ☏ ▣ ⓢ ⚿ ⦙⦙⦙ ▦▦▦ ⴲ ⌧
How to get there: Hotel is on A4 opposite Cromwell Road Hospital. Turn right at Knaresborough Place, left into Collingham Place, and left at lights to front of hotel.

It's easier online

See the road ahead

The Capital

Gold Ribbon Winner

★★★★★ ⓡ ⓡ ⓡ ⓡ
22-24 Basil Street, Knightsbridge, London, SW3 1AT
Tel: 020 7589 5171 Fax: 020 7225 0011
Email: reservations@capitalhotel.co.uk
Web: www.capitalhotel.co.uk
48 bedrs SB £235 DB £312 B £12.50 L £26. 50 D £65 CC: MC Vi Am DC Swi Delt
⌶⌶ 🛏 ▭ ☎ ✳ ▣ ⚿ ✵ ⦙⦙⦙ ▦▦▦
How to get there: Heading west, turn left by side of Harrods, left again and straight on into Basil Street.

The Fox Club

★★★★ Townhouse
46 Clarges Street, Mayfair, London, W1Y 7PJ
Tel: 020 7495 3656 Fax: 020 7495 3656
Email: foxclub@clubhaus.com
Web: www.clubhaus.com
9 bedrs
CC: MC Vi Am Swi Delt
🛏 ▭ ☎ ✳ ☏ ⚿ ▦▦▦
How to get there: From Green Park underground station, turn right towards Hyde Park. Take third street on right.

The Goring

Gold Ribbon Winner

★★★★★ ℞ ℞ ℞
Beeston Place, Grosvenor Gardens,
London, SW1W 0JW
Tel: 020 7396 9000 Fax: 020 7834 4393
Email: reception@goringhotel.co.uk
Web: www.goringhotel.co.uk

Operated by four generations of the Goring
Family since it opened in 1910 The Goring
remains a bastion of elegance and
sophistication yet exemplifies all the best and
most advanced advantages of modern
technology and comfort.
74 bedrs SB £245 DB £315 B £12.50 L £27
D £39 CC: MC Vi Am DC Swi
⚑ ⊪ ⊗ ▭ ☎ ❋ ✆ P☏ ⚘ ⊂ ♁ ⌒ ♨ ♨♨

The Halkin

Gold Ribbon Winner

★★★★ ℞ ℞ ℞
Halkin Street, Belgravia, London, SW1X 7DJ
Tel: 020 7333 1000 Fax: 020 7333 1100
Email: sales@halkin.co.uk
Web: www.halkin.co.uk

The Halkin continues to set the standard in
contemporary luxury hotels. Great emphasis is
placed upon guest comfort and the highest
levels of personal yet unobtrusive service and
cuisine are legendary.

41 bedrs SB £365 DB £383 B £18 L £25 D £47
CC: MC Vi Am DC Swi Delt
⊪ ⚸ ▭ ☎ ❋ ✆ ⚘ ⌒ ♨♨
How to get there: Located between Belgrave
Square and Grosvenor Place. Access via
Chapel Street into Headfort Place and left into
Halkin Street.

The Montague

★★★★ ℞
15 Montague Street, London, WC1B 5BJ
Tel: 020 7637 1001 Fax: 020 7637 2506
Email: bookmt@rchmail.com
Web: www.redcarnationhotels.com

Close to Covent Garden and adjacent to the
British Museum, The Montague offers period
elegance and luxury furnishings. Ideal for leisure
as well as business needs with truly personal
service.
104 bedrs SB £185 DB £225 HBS £210
HBD £235 B £14.50 L £17.50 D £20
CC: MC Vi Am DC Swi Delt
⚑ ♿ ⊪ ✎ ⚸ ⊗ ⊜ ▭ ☎ ✆ ⚘ ⌒ ♨ ♨♨ SPA
How to get there: Located in Montague Street
just off Russell Square, close to British
Museum. Five minutes' walk from Russell
Square underground.

The Pelham Hotel

Blue Ribbon Winner

★★★★ Townhouse ℞ ℞
15 Cromwell Place, London, SW7 2LA
Tel: 020 7589 8288 Fax: 020 7584 8444
Email: pelham@firmdale.com
Web: www.firmdale.com
Steps away from South Kensington museums
and underground, this luxury townhouse is
managed in a traditional manner offering the
highest standards of comfort and service.
51 bedrs SB £189.75 DB £238.50 B £13.50
L £15 D £25 CC: MC Vi Am Swi Delt JCB
⊗ ▭ ☎ ❋ ✆ ⚘ ⌒ ♨ ♨♨
How to get there: Opposite South Kensington
tube station.

London

The Rembrandt

★★★★★ ®
11 Thurloe Place, Knightsbridge,
London, SW7 2RS
Tel: 020 7589 8100 Fax: 020 7225 3476
Email: rembrandt@sarova.co.uk
Web: www.sarova.com
195 bedrs SB £205 DB £245 B £12.95 L £17.95
D £17.95
CC: MC Vi Am DC Swi Delt JCB

How to get there: Follow A4 (Cromwell Road)
into Central London. The Rembrandt is opposite
Victoria & Albert Museum. Nearest tube South
Kensington.

The Stafford

Blue Ribbon Winner

★★★★★ ® ® ®
St. James's Place, London, SW1A 1NJ
Tel: 020 7493 0111 Fax: 020 7493 7121
Email: info@thestaffordhotel.co.uk
Web: www.thestaffordhotel.co.uk
81 bedrs SB £230 DB £250
CC: MC Vi Am DC Swi Delt

Washington Mayfair Hotel

★★★★
5-7 Curzon Street, London, W1J 5HE
Tel: 020 7499 7000 Fax: 020 7409 7183
Email: sales@washington-mayfair.co.uk
Web: www.washington-mayfair.co.uk.
173 bedrs SB £245.95 DB £256.90
HBS £275.85 HBD £158.15 B £11.95 L £11.95
D £13.95 CC: MC Vi Am DC Swi Delt

How to get there: Five minutes' walk from Green
Park station. West along Piccadilly, right into
Clarges Street; Curzon Street is at the end.

Westbury

★★★★★ ® ® ®
Bond Street, London, W1S 2YF
Tel: 020 7629 7755 Fax: 020 7495 1163
Email: westburyhotel@compuserve.com
Web: www.westbury-london.co.uk
254 bedrs SB £287 DB £303 HBS £306
HBD £162.50 B £11.75 L £ 16.50 D £19.50
CC: MC Vi Am DC Swi Delt

How to get there: On Bond Street, Mayfair.
Underground: Bond Street, Green Park, Oxford
Circus, Piccadilly Circus.
See advert below

The Westbury

The Westbury is one famous name
that is surrounded by others.

Centrally located in London,
Bond Street, it has Versace,
Tiffany's, Armani and Sotheby's
as neighbours.

From the moment you walk through
the door, you'll see the difference.

The welcome is as warm as the
service is well informed.

**Bond Street,
London W1S 2YF**

Tel: 020 7629 7755   Fax: 020 7495 1163   Email: westburyhotel@compuserve.com
Website: www.westbury-london.co.uk

Basil Street Hotel

★★★ ®
Knightsbridge, London, SW3 1AH
Tel: 020 7581 3311 Fax: 020 7581 3693
Email: info@thebasil.com
Web: www.thebasil.com

Situated in Knightsbridge — a few steps from
Harrods, this 80-bedroom hotel offers a
traditional style and service that draws people
back time after time. Restaurant open every day.
80 bedrs SB £174 DB £255 B £11 L £15.50
D £21 CC: MC Vi Am Swi Delt JCB
⫫ ☆ ⊕ ⊑ ☎ ☏ ▣ ☞ ☃ ♯ ❦ ♨ ♨
How to get there: One-minute walk from
Knightsbridge Underground Station. The Hotel
is located between Harrods and Sloane Street.

Bonnington in Bloomsbury

★★★
92 Southampton Row, London, WC1B 4BH
Tel: 020 7242 2828 Fax: 020 7831 9170
Email: sales@bonnington.com
Web: www.bonnington.com

Recently refurbished, independent hotel, ideally
situated for London's major attractions. Offers a
warm welcome to all guests. 'Waterfalls'
restaurant. 'Malt' bar and extensive conference
facilities.

215 bedrs SB £117 DB £149 B £7.85 L £12
D £19.75
CC: MC Vi Am DC Swi Delt
⫣ ⫫ ☆ ⊕ ⊑ ☎ ❄ ☃ ❀ ♯ ❦ ♨ ♨
How to get there: M40 Euston Road, opposite
station. Turn south into Upper Woburn Place,
past Russell Square into Southampton Row.
Bonnington on left.

Hogarth

★★★★ ® ®
Hogarth Road, Kensington, London, SW5 0QQ
Tel: 020 7370 6831 Fax: 020 7373 6179
Email: hogarth@marstonhotels.com
Web: www.marstonhotels.com

MARSTON HOTELS

86 bedrs SB £115 DB £149 B £12 L £10 D £20
CC: MC Vi Am DC Swi Delt
⫫ ☆ ⊕ ⊑ ☎ ☏ ▣ ☃ ❀ ♯ ❦ ♨ ♨
How to get there: Two-minute walk from Earl's
Court underground station.

Jurys Inn London

★★★
60 Pentonville Road, Islington, London, N1 9LA
Tel: +353(0)1 6070000 Fax: +353(0)1 6316999
Email: bookings@jurysdoyle.com
Web: www.jurysdoyle.com
229 bedrs B £8 D £15.95
CC: MC Vi Am DC Swi Delt
⫣ ⫫ ☆ ⊕ ⊑ ☎ ❄ ☏ ☃ ♯ ❦ ♨ ♨
How to get there: Located 25 miles from
London Heathrow Airport. London City 15 miles.
Euston Mainline 15 minutes walk and Angel
tube three minutes walk.

Mandeville Hotel

★★★
Mandeville Place, London, W1H 2BE
Tel: 020 7935 5599 Fax: 020 7935 9588
Email: info@mandeville.co.uk
Web: www.mandeville.co.uk
166 bedrs SB £145.50 DB £195 B £7.50 L £16
D £19
CC: MC Vi Am DC Swi Delt JCB
⫫ ☆ ⊕ ⊑ ☎ ☏ ☃ ♨ ♨

London

Novotel London Tower Bridge

★★★

10 Pepys Street, London, EC3N 2NR
Tel: 020 7265 6000 Fax: 020 7265 6060
Email: h3107@accorhotels.com
Web: www.accorhotels.com
203 bedrs SB £167 DB £199 B £9 L £4.50 D £12
CC: MC Vi Am DC Swi

How to get there: A half-minute from Tower Hill tube station. From M25, to Central London via the A13 to the City.

Novotel London Waterloo

★★★

113 Lambeth Road, Waterloo, London, SE1 7LS
Tel: 020 7793 1010 Fax: 020 7793 0202
Email: h1785@accor-hotels.com
Web: www.novotel.com
187 bedrs SB £147 DB £179 HBS £165
HBD £115 B £12 L £18.95 D £18.95
CC: MC Vi Am DC Swi Delt

How to get there: Located on the south bank of Lambeth Bridge, on Lambeth Road, opposite Lambeth Palace.

Novotel London West

★★★

Hammersmith International Centre,
1 Shortlands, Hammersmith, London, W6 8DR
Tel: 020 8741 1555 Fax: 020 8741 2120
Email: h0737@accor-hotels.com
Web: www.novotel.com
629 bedrs SB £145 DB £165 B £8.95 L £11.
D £12
CC: MC Vi Am DC Swi Delt

How to get there: Exit A4 at Hammersmith; follow signs for Earl's Court; turn left just before rejoining A4.

Need help booking?

RAC Hotel Reservations will find the accommodation that's right for you – and book it too.
Call today on 0870 603 9109 and quote 'Guide 2002'

Paragon Hotel

★★★

47 Lillie Road, London, SW6 1UD
Tel: 020 7385 1255 Fax: 020 7381 4450
Email: sales@paragonhotel.co.uk
Web: www.paragonhotel.co.uk
503 bedrs SB £135 DB £165 HBS £150
HBD £195 B £9.50 L £12.50 D £14.50
CC: MC Vi Am DC Swi Delt

How to get there: Opposite Earl's Court Exhibition Centre between Warwick Road and North End Road, close to West Brompton and Earl's Court tube stations.

Quality Hotel Westminster

★★★

82-83 Eccleston Square, London, SW1V 1PS
Tel: 020 7834 8042 Fax: 020 7630 8942
Email: admin@gb614.u-net.com
Web: www.choicehotels.com
107 bedrs SB £115.75 DB £130.75
HBS £133.75 HBD £74.38 B £5.75 L £5.20 D £18
CC: MC Vi Am DC Swi Delt

How to get there: Situated close to Victoria rail, coach and tube stations.

Saint Georges

★★★★

Langham Place, Regent Street, London, W1B 2QS
Tel: 020 7580 0111 Fax: 020 7436 7997
Email: saintgeorgeshotel@hotmail.com
Web: www.cairnhotelgroup.com
86 bedrs SB £177 DB £209
CC: MC Vi Am DC Swi Delt JCB

How to get there: M40, Euston Road, turn right at Regents Park into Portland Place. This leads onto Langham Place with the hotel on the left.

Strand Palace Hotel

★★★

372 The Strand, London, WC2R 0JJ
Tel: 0870 400 8702 Fax: 020 7936 2077
Email: reservations@strandpalacehotel.co.uk
Web: www.strandpalacehotel.co.uk
785 bedrs SB £124 DB £138 HBS £141
HBD £86 B £10.95 L £8.95 D £10.95
CC: MC Vi Am DC Swi Delt

How to get there: In the heart of theatreland on The Strand. Closest station is five minutes walk — Charing Cross.

The
CLARENDON
HOTEL
BLACKHEATH, LONDON

Conference & Banqueting

Restaurant

Honeymoon Suite

The finest Georgian Hotel in South East London

Montpelier Row, Blackheath, London SE3 0RW Tel: 020 8318 4321 www.clarendonhotel.com

The Gresham Hyde Park

★★★
66 Lancaster Gate, London, W2 3NZ
Tel: 020 726 25090 Fax: 020 772 31244
Email: hotel@gresham-hydeparkhotel.com
Web: www.gresham-hotels.com

GRESHAM HOTELS

188 bedrs B £10 L £15 D £21
CC: MC Vi Am DC Swi Delt JCB
Lↄ ⁂⊙⊜☐☎⁂⌕⌘⁂⁂'Y'
How to get there: Located on Lancaster Gate off Bayswater Road one mile from Marble Arch in between Lancaster Gate Station and Queensway Station (Central line).

Clarendon Hotel

★★
8-16 Montpelier Row, Blackheath, London, SE3 0RW
Tel: 020 8318 4321 Fax: 020 8318 4378
Email: relax@clarendonhotel.com
Web: www.clarendonhotel.com
183 bedrs SB £70 DB £80 HBS £87.50
HBD £57.50 B £7.50 L £10.50 D £17.50
CC: MC Vi Am DC Swi Delt

How to get there: Situated just off the A2 on Blackheath. Close to major motorways (M2/M25/A20) – M25 junctions two and three.
See advert on previous page

Comfort Inn Kensington

★★
22/32 West Cromwell Road, Kensington, London, SW5 9QJ
Tel: 020 7373 3300 Fax: 020 7835 2040
Email: admin@gb043.u-net.com
Web: www.choicehotels.com
125 bedrs SB £115.75 DB £140.75
HBS £133.75 HBD £79.38 B £10.75 D £18
CC: MC Vi Am DC Swi Delt
Lↄ⊙⊜☐☎⁂⌕⌘⁂⁂
How to get there: Located on West Cromwell Road. Continuation of A4(M) main arterial road into London from West.

Regents Park Hotel

★★
154-156 Gloucester Place, Marylebone, London, NW1 6DT
Tel: 020 7258 1911 Fax: 020 7258 0288
Email: rph-reservation@usa.net
Web: www.regentsparkhotel.com
29 bedrs SB £80 DB £99 B £3.50 L £7. D £10
CC: Vi Am DC Swi Delt JCB
⁂⊜☐☎⌕⌘⁂⁂
See advert left

Sleeping Beauty Motel

Travel Accommodation
543 Lea Bridge Road, Leyton, London, E10 7EB
Tel: 020 8556 8080 Fax: 020 8556 8080
Children minimum age: 4
84 bedrs
CC: MC Vi Am DC Swi Delt
⁂Lↄ⊜☐☎⁂⌘⁂⁂'Y'
How to get there: Ten minutes' walking distance from Walthamstow Central underground station.

Travelodge London (Battersea)

Travel Accommodation
Southampton House, 200 York Road, Battersea,
London, SW11 3SA
Tel: 08700 850 950
Web: www.travelodge.co.uk
80 bedrs B £4.25
CC: MC Vi Am DC Swi Delt

Travelodge London (City)

Travel Accommodation
1 Harrow Place, London, E1 7DB
Tel: 08700 850 950
Web: www.travelodge.co.uk
142 bedrs B £4.25
CC: MC Vi Am DC Swi Delt

Travelodge London (Docklands)

Travel Accommodation
A13, Coriander Avenue, East India Dock Road,
London, E14 2AA
Tel: 08700 850 950
Web: www.travelodge.co.uk
232 bedrs B £4.25
CC: MC Vi Am DC Swi Delt

Travelodge London (Kew Bridge)

Travel Accommodation
Tel: 08700 850 950
Web: www.travelodge.co.uk
Opens August 2002
111 bedrs B £4.25
CC: MC Vi Am DC Swi Delt

Travelodge London (Park Royal)

Travel Accommodation
A40, Western Avenue, Acton, London, W3 0TE
Tel: 08700 850 950
Web: www.travelodge.co.uk
64 bedrs B £4.25
CC: MC Vi Am DC Swi Delt

Benvenuti

◆◆◆◆
217 Court Road, Eltham, SE9 4TG
Tel: 020 8857 4855 Fax: 020 8265 5635

Four Seasons Hotel

◆◆◆◆
173 Gloucester Place, Regent's Park,
London, NW1 6DX
Tel: 020 7724 3461 Fax: 020 7402 5594
Web: www.4seasonshotel.co.uk
28 bedrs SB £95 DB £115
CC: MC Vi Am DC Swi Delt JCB

St. George Hotel

◆◆◆◆
49 Gloucester Place, Marble Arch,
London, W1U 8JE
Tel: 020 7486 8586 Fax: 020 7486 6567
Email: reservations@stgeorge-hotel.net
Web: www.stgeorge-hotel.net
19 bedrs SB £85 DB £125
CC: MC Vi Am DC Swi Delt JCB

How to get there: A short walk from Oxford
Street and Baker Street. Nearest tube is Marble
Arch.

The Claverley Hotel

◆◆◆◆
13-14 Beaufort Gardens, Knightsbridge,
London, SW3 1PS
Tel: 020 7589 8541 Fax: 020 7584 3410
Email: reservations@claverleyhotel.co.uk
Web: www.claverleyhotel.co.uk

An intimate, elegant designer-hotel located on a
quiet tree-lined cul-de-sac in prestigious
Knightsbridge, a two-minute stroll from Harrods.
All room rates include full English breakfast and
V.A.T.
30 bedrs SB £110 DB £140
CC: MC Vi Am DC Swi JCB

How to get there: Exit Knightsbridge tube at
Brompton Road. Third street on the left past
Harrods.

London

The Willett

32 Sloane Gardens, Sloane Square,
London, SW1W 8DJ
Tel: 020 7824 8415 Fax: 020 7730 4830
Email: willett@eeh.co.uk
Web: www.eeh.co.uk

Your home-from-home in London's charming
Sloane Gardens. A quiet retreat of terracotta
terraces, seemingly far away from the workaday
world yet close to everything that makes this
part of Chelsea renowned.
19 bedrs SB £79 DB £117
CC: MC Vi Am DC Swi Delt JCB

How to get there: Take A315 Knightsbridge to
Sloane Street. Hotel is in Sloane Square.

Windermere Hotel

142-144 Warwick Way, Victoria,
London, SW1V 4JE
Tel: 020 7834 5163 Fax: 020 7630 8831
Email: windermere@compuserve.com
Web: www.windermere-hotel.co.uk

An intimate, boutique hotel renowned for its
friendly and personalised service. Well-equipped
and individually-designed bedrooms. English
breakfast and dinner are served in the elegant
licensed restaurant. Parking available.
22 bedrs SB £84 DB £104 HBS £99 HBD £59.50

CC: MC Vi Am Swi Delt

How to get there: Turn left opposite Victoria
coach station, take first right into Hugh Street.
Proceed along to Alderney Street. Hotel is
directly opposite on corner of Alderney Street
and Warwick Way.

Anchor Hotel

10 West Heath Drive, London, NW11 7QH
Tel: 020 8458 8764 Fax: 020 8455 3204
Email: res@anchor-hotel.co.uk
Web: www.anchor-hotel.co.uk
11 bedrs SB £45 DB £65 CC: MC Vi Am Swi Delt

How to get there: One minute walk from
Golders Green tube station, or by car take North
Circular Road (A406) onto A598 Finchley Road.
At tube turn left, then take first right.

Atlas-Apollo Hotel

18-30 Lexham Gardens, Kensington,
London, W8 5JE
Tel: 020 7835 1155 Fax: 020 7370 4853
Email: reservations@atlas-apollo.com
Web: www.atlas-apollo.com
93 bedrs SB £75 DB £100
CC: MC Vi Am Swi Delt JCB

How to get there: Equidistant from Earl's Court
and Gloucester Road underground stations,
between Sainsbury's and the Cromwell Hospital
on the A4.

Averard Hotel

10 Lancaster Gate, Hyde Park, London, W2 3LH
Tel: 020 7723 8877 Fax: 020 7706 0860
Email: sales@averard.com
Web: www.averard.com

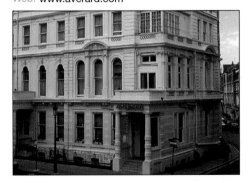

Excellently located, friendly family hotel in an interesting Victorian building with original public rooms and period style paintings, sculptures and other features
52 bedrs SB £70 DB £95
CC: MC Vi Am DC Swi Delt

How to get there: From Lancaster Gate underground station, right onto Bayswater Road, cross main traffic lights. After Swan pub, turn right to Lancaster Gate.

Central Hotel

♦♦♦
35 Hoop Lane, London, NW11 8BS
Tel: 020 8458 5636 Fax: 020 8455 4792
30 bedrs SB £55 DB £75
CC: MC Vi Am DC Swi Delt

How to get there: From M1, take North Circular Road East, turn right onto A598. After one mile, turn into Hoop Lane at Golders Green.

Craven Gardens Hotel

♦♦♦
16 Leinster Terrace, London, W2 3ES
Tel: 020 7262 3167 Fax: 020 7262 2083
Email: craven@dircon.co.uk
Children minimum age: 13
43 bedrs SB £70 DB £85
CC: MC Vi Am DC Swi Delt JCB

See advert right

Garth Hotel

♦♦♦
64-76 Hendon Way, Cricklewood, London, NW2 2NL
Tel: 020 8209 1511 Fax: 020 8455 4744
Email: enquiry@garthhotel.co.uk
Web: www.grth-hotel.co.uk
57 bedrs SB £75 DB £90 B £5 L £9 D £13.50
CC: MC Vi Am DC Swi Delt

Georgian Hotel

♦♦♦
87 Gloucester Place, London, W1V 6JF
Tel: 020 7486 3151 Fax: 020 7486 7535
Email: info@georgian-hotel.demon.co.uk
Web: www.londoncentralhotel.com
Children minimum age: 5
19 bedrs SB £75 DB £90
CC: MC Vi Am

This first class Victorian-designed hotel is ideally situated for visitors to the area. The hotel offers a high standard of rooms, equipped with colour satellite TV, direct-dial telephone, hairdryer. Facilities and services include a bar, cocktail lounge, room service, laundry service, car hire, and safe deposit boxes.

Craven Gardens Hotel
16 Leinster Terrace, London W2 3ES
Tel: 020 7262 3167 Fax: 020 7262 2083

London

How to get there: Close to Baker Street tube and Paddington station.

Grange Lodge Hotel

♦♦♦
48-50 Grange Road, Ealing, London, W5 5BX
Tel: 020 8567 1049 Fax: 020 8579 5350
Email: enquiries@londonlodgehotels.com
Web: www.londonlodgehotels.com
14 bedrs SB £37 DB £50
CC: MC Vi DC Swi Delt

How to get there: 10 minutes from Junction two of M4. Just off the A406 (North Circular Road) at crossroads of A4020 (Ealing Common).

Grove Hill Hotel

♦♦♦
38 Grove Hill, South Woodford, London, E18 2JG
Tel: 020 8989 3344 Fax: 020 8530 5286
23 bedrs SB £41 DB £58 B £5
CC: MC Vi Am DC Swi Delt JCB
How to get there: The hotel is close to South Woodford underground station, and directly off the A11, close to M11 and A406.

Hart House Hotel

◆◆◆

51 Gloucester Place, London, W1H 3PE
Tel: 020 7935 2288 Fax: 020 7935 8516
Email: reservations@harthouse.co.uk
Web: www.harthouse.co.uk

A highly recommended, clean and comfortable hotel run by the Bowden family for the last 32 years. It is in the heart of London's West End just off Oxford Street. Ideal for all tourist attractions.
15 bedrs SB £70 DB £105
CC: MC Vi Am Swi Delt
How to get there: Just off Oxford Street, behind Selfridges. Close to Marble Arch and Baker Street underground stations.

La Gaffe

La Gaffe is a welcoming family run hotel with charm and character. Located in historic Hampstead, four minutes from Hampstead Tube and three minutes from Hampstead Heath. All rooms are ensuite and the hotel boasts an award winning Italian Restaurant.

101-107 Heath Street, London NW3 6SS
Tel: 020 7435 8965   Fax: 020 7794 7592
Email: la-gaffe@msn.com
Website: www.lagaffe.co.uk

Henley House

◆◆◆

30 Barkston Gardens, Earls Court, London, SW5 0EN
Tel: 020 7370 4111 Fax: 020 7370 0026
Email: reservations@henleyhousehotel.com
Web: www.henleyhousehotel.com

Henley House is a small but very charming boutique-style hotel. The cosy and comfortable rooms are rich in decor and style with much attention paid to detail.
20 bedrs SB £72 DB £91
CC: MC Vi Am DC Swi Delt JCB
How to get there: From A4 turn down Earl's Court Road (A3220). Barkston Gardens is 2nd left after tube station.

Kandara Guest House

◆◆◆

68 Ockendon Road, Islington, London, N1 3NW
Tel: 020 7226 5721 Fax: 020 7226 3379
Email: admin@kandara.co.uk
Web: www.kandara.co.uk
11 bedrs SB £41 DB £54 CC: MC Vi Delt
How to get there: From A1 at Highbury Corner; along Canonbury Road; turn left onto Essex Road; Ockendon Road is 5th turning on right.

La Gaffe

◆◆◆

107-111 Heath Street, Hampstead, London, NW3 6SS
Tel: 020 7435 8965 Fax: 020 7794 7592
Email: la-gaffe@msn.com
Web: www.lagaffe.co.uk
18 bedrs SB £65 DB £90 B £3.50 L £5 D £10
CC: MC Vi Am Swi
How to get there: Hotel three minutes from Hampstead underground, three miles from Kings Cross and 18 miles from Heathrow.
See advert left

Langorf Hotel and Apartments

20 Frognal, Hampstead, London, NW3 6AG
Tel: 020 7794 4483 Fax: 020 7435 9055
Email: langorf@aol.com
Web: www.langorfhotel.com
36 bedrs SB £82 DB £98
CC: MC Vi Am DC Swi Delt
◫◷▢☎📞✂💇🛎👬

How to get there: Three miles north of Oxford Street. Three miles south of M1 Junction 1. Off the A41 Finchley Road.

Mitre House Hotel

178-184 Sussex Gardens, Hyde Park,
London, W2 1TU
Tel: 020 7723 8040 Fax: 020 7402 0990
Email: reservations@mitrehousehotel.com
Web: www.mitrehousehotel.com
70 bedrs SB £70 DB £80
CC: MC Vi Am DC Delt
♿◫◷▢☎📵✂💇👬

How to get there: One block north of Hyde Park, Paddington Station and buses to major sights. Heathrow Express to airport in 15 mins.
See advert on following page and back cover

New England Hotel

20 St. Georges Drive, Victoria, London, SW1V 4BN
Tel: 020 7834 8351 Fax: 020 7834 9000
Email: stay@newenglandhotel.com
Web: www.newenglandhotel.com

Privately owned hotel renowned for its blend of warm, friendly hospitality and high standards in a fantastic London location. It boasts an enviable high level of repeat business and pleasure clientele. Close to all major attractions.
25 bedrs SB £55 DB £69
CC: MC Vi Am DC Swi Delt
◫◷▢☎📞✂💇

How to get there: From Victoria station go onto Wilton Road and right at Warwick Way junction. Second left onto St. Georges Drive and the New England is on your left. See map on website.
See advert below

London

Park Lodge Hotel

◆◆◆

73 Queensborough Terrace, Bayswater,
London, W2 3SU
Tel: 020 7229 6424 Fax: 020 7221 4772
Email: smegroup.kfc@cwcom.net
SB £70 DB £85
CC: MC Vi Am DC Swi

Sidney Hotel

◆◆◆

68/76 Belgrave Road, Victoria,
London, SW1V 2BP
Tel: 020 7834 2738 Fax: 020 7630 0973
Email: reservations@sidneyhotel.com
Web: www.sidneyhotel.com
82 bedrs SB £78 DB £97
CC: MC Vi Am DC Swi Delt JCB

How to get there: Centrally situated near
Victoria Station, from station take Wilton Road,
go straight to third traffic light, turn left, hotel
situated on your right.
See advert below

Swiss Cottage Hotel

◆◆◆

4 Adamson Road, Swiss Cottage,
London, NW3 3HP
Tel: 020 7722 2281 Fax: 020 7483 4588
Email: reservations@swisscottagehotel.co.uk
Web: www.swisscottagehotel.co.uk
59 bedrs SB £95 DB £110
CC: MC Vi Am DC Swi Delt JCB

How to get there: From Swiss Cottage
underground leave at exit two and walk straight
ahead; hotel is one minute's walk.

It's easier online

 For all your motoring and travel
needs, visit www.rac.co.uk

Plan your route

 Visit www.rac.co.uk for RAC's
interactive route planner, including
up to the minute traffic reports.

London

Swiss House Hotel

♦ ♦ ♦

171 Old Brompton Road, South Kensington,
London, SW5 0AN
Tel: 020 7373 9383 Fax: 020 7373 4983
Email: recep@swiss-hh.demon.co.uk
Web: www.swiss-hh.demon.co.uk

"Excellent value for money" has always been
our motto. This hotel knows guests' priorities
and aims to meet them all. Clean and friendly
atmosphere.
15 bedrs SB £50 DB £89
CC: MC Vi Am DC Swi Delt JCB
⊗ ☎ ☐ ☎ 🕏 ⚡ ✦
How to get there: From M4 turn right into Earls
Court Road. Down the road, turn left onto Old
Brompton Road and hotel is situated after the
first set of lights on the right hand side.

The Diplomat Hotel

♦ ♦ ♦

2 Chesham Street, Belgravia, London, SW1X 8DT
Tel: 020 7235 1544 Fax: 020 7259 6153
Email: diplomat.hotel@btinternet.com
Web: www.btinternet.com/~diplomat.hotel

The Diplomat is situated in Belgravia, the most
exclusive and sought-after neighbourhood in
London. It is within easy walking distance of
Harrods and the fashionable Knightsbridge and
Chelsea shops.
26 bedrs SB £95 DB £140 L £6.00 D £6.00
CC: MC Vi Am DC Swi JCB
🕏 ⋕ ⊗ ☐ ☎ 🅿 🕏 ⚡ ⚑ ✦ ⁙
How to get there: Victoria, Knightsbridge and
Sloane Square underground stations all within
10 minutes walk.

The Victoria Inn

♦ ♦ ♦

65-67 Belgrave Road, Victoria,
London, SW1V 2BG
Tel: 020 7834 0182 Fax: 020 7931 0201
Email: info@victoriainn.co.uk
Web: www.victoriainn.co.uk
43 bedrs SB £69 DB £89
CC: MC Vi Am DC Swi Delt JCB
⋕ ⊗ ☐ ☎ 🕏 ✦
How to get there: From Victoria Station, take
Wilton Road, turn left into Belgrave Road; hotel
is on the left after 500m.

White Lodge Hotel

♦ ♦ ♦

1 Church Lane, Hornsey, London, N8 7BU
Tel: 020 8348 9765 Fax: 020 8340 7851

16 bedrs SB £30 DB £40
CC: MC Vi
⊗ ☎ ☐ 🕏 ⚡ ✦
How to get there: Church Lane faces Tottenham
Lane. Hotel next door to police station.

126 Worcester House Hotel

 ◆ ◆ ◆

38 Alwyne Road, Wimbledon,
London, SW19 7AE
Tel: 020 8946 1300 Fax: 020 8946 9120
Email: janet@worcesterhouse.demon.co.uk
Web: www.worcesterhousehotel.co.uk
9 bedrs SB £49.50 DB £70
CC: MC Vi Am Swi Delt

How to get there: A3 at Wimbledon take A219.
Follow road through village. Left off Wimbledon
Hill Road. Hotel at end on left-hand corner.

127 Abbey Lodge Hotel

◆ ◆

51 Grange Park, Ealing, London, W5 3PR
Tel: 020 8567 7914 Fax: 020 8579 5350
Email: enquiries@londonlodgehotels.com
Web: www.londonlodgehotels.com
Closed Christmas/New Year
16 bedrs SB £47 DB £59 B £inc
CC: MC Vi DC Swi Delt

How to get there: From M4 junction 2, A406 to
second set of lights. Turn left into A4020,
following Ealing Common to end, turn left, third
right into Grange Park.

128 Ashley Hotel

◆ ◆

15 Norfolk Square, Paddington, London, W2 1RU
Tel: 020 7723 3375 Fax: 020 7723 0173
Email: ashhot@btinternet.com
53 bedrs SB £36.50 DB £75 CC: MC Vi Swi Delt

How to get there: Use Paddington Station as
your landmark: hotel is a two minute walk away.

129 Barry House Hotel

◆ ◆

12 Sussex Place, Hyde Park, London, W2 2TP
Tel: 020 7723 7340 Fax: 020 7723 9775
Email: hotel@barryhouse.co.uk
Web: www.barryhouse.co.uk

Providing family-like care. Friendly, comfortable
B&B with en-suite bedrooms. English breakfast
included in competitive rates. Central location
close to Paddington Station.
18 bedrs SB £40 DB £80
CC: MC Vi Am DC Swi Delt

How to get there: Come out of Paddington
station, walk into London Street to the traffic
lights. Cross over into Sussex Place.

130 Caswell

◆ ◆

25 Gloucester Street, London, SW1V 2DB
Tel: 020 7834 6345 Fax: 020 7834 4900
Email: manager@hotellondon.co.uk
Web: www.hotellondon.co.uk
Children minimum age: 6
17 bedrs CC: MC Vi Swi Delt

How to get there: Caswell Hotel is
approximately eight minutes walk from Victoria
Station — just off Belgrove Road.

131 Edward Lear Hotel

◆ ◆

30 Seymour Street, London, W1H 5WD
Tel: 020 7402 5401 Fax: 020 7706 3766
CC: MC Vi

132 Haddon Hall Hotel

◆ ◆

39/40 Bedford Place, Russell Square,
London, WC1B 5JT
Tel: 020 7636 2474 Fax: 020 7580 4527
33 bedrs SB £69 DB £95
CC: MC Vi Am DC Swi Delt JCB

133 Hamilton House Hotel

◆ ◆

60 Warwick Way, Victoria, London, SW1V 1SA
Tel: 020 7821 7113 Fax: 020 7630 0806
Email: info@hamiltonhousehotel.com
Web: www.hamiltonhousehotel.com
40 bedrs SB £69 DB £85
CC: MC Vi Swi Delt

London

134 Hotel Orlando

◆ ◆

83 Shepherds Bush Road, London, W6 7LR
Tel: 020 7603 4890 Fax: 020 7603 4890
Email: hotelorlando@btconnect.com
Web: www.hotelorlando.co.uk

A family-run business of 22 years, this privately-owned 14 room hotel in a Victorian terrace is within easy walking distance of Hammersmith underground station, ideal for easy connection to central London and Heathrow Airport.
14 bedrs SB £40 DB £52
CC: MC Vi Am Swi Delt
🛏🖥☎🐾
How to get there: Situated between Hammersmith Underground Station and Shepherds Bush Underground Station. Five minutes walk either way.

135 Lincoln House Hotel

◆ ◆

33 Gloucester Place, Marble Arch,
London, W1U 8HY
Tel: 020 7486 7630 Fax: 020 7486 0166
Email: reservations@lincoln-house-hotel.co.uk
Web: www.lincoln-house-hotel.co.uk

Georgian B&B hotel in London, with modern comforts and en-suite rooms. Close to Oxford Street shopping, theatreland and nightlife. Recommended by famous guide books.
23 bedrs SB £69 DB £89
CC: MC Vi Am DC Swi Delt JCB
🛏🖥☎🐾
How to get there: Out of Marble Arch station, turn left, then second turning on the left into Portman Street. The continuation is Gloucester Place.

136 Merlyn Court Hotel

◆ ◆

2 Barkston Gardens, London, SW5 0EN
Tel: 020 7370 1640 Fax: 020 7370 4986
Email: london@merlyncourt.demon.co.uk
Web: www.smoothhound.co.uk/
hotels/merlyn.html

Comfortable, good value, family-run hotel in a central location off a quiet Edwardian square in Kensington. Family rooms are available. Easy access to Olympia and Earls Court exhibition halls, train stations and motorways.
17 bedrs SB £30 DB £55
CC: MC Vi Swi Delt JCB
🛏☎🐾
How to get there: Very central, easy links to airports and motorways (M4, M40, M1). Nearest underground station is Earl's Court.

Making a booking?

Don't forget to mention RAC Hotels and Bed & Breakfast 2002.

137 Parkwood Hotel

4 Stanhope Place, London, W2 2HB
Tel: 020 7402 2241 Fax: 020 7402 1574
Email: prkwd@aol.com
Web: www.parkwoodhotel.com
14 bedrs SB £73 DB £93
CC: MC Vi Swi Delt

How to get there: Marble Arch nearest tube station.

138 Ramsees Hotel

32-36 Hogarth Road, Earl's Court,
London, SW5 0PU
Tel: 020 7370 1445 Fax: 020 7244 6835
Email: ramsees@rasool.demon.co.uk
Web: www.ramseeshotel.com
67 bedrs SB £36 DB £48
CC: MC Vi Am DC Swi Delt
How to get there: From A4, turn down Earl's Court Road. At Lloyd's Bank on left, turn down Hogarth Road.

Trochee Hotel
Wimbledon ⓡⓐⓒ ♦♦

52 Ridgeway Place

21 Malcolm Road

The Trochee is a private bed and breakfast hotel offering a warm and homely atmosphere in a delightful part of London.

Situated in quiet tree-lined streets, the hotel is in two buildings, each with own lounge and dining room. All bedrooms have colour TV, hair dryer and tea/coffee making facilities, some ensuite rooms available. Close to Wimbledon town centre and the All England Tennis Club.

52 Ridgeway Place, London SW19 4SW
Tel: 020 8946 9425   Fax: 020 946 1579
21 Malcolm Road, London SW19 4AS
Tel: 020 8946 1579   Fax: 020 8746 1579

139 Rasool Court Hotel

19/21 Penywern Road, Earls Court,
London, SW5 9TT
Tel: 020 7373 8900 Fax: 020 7244 6835
Email: rasool@rasool.demon.co.uk
Web: www.rasoolcourthotel.com
57 bedrs SB £36 DB £48
CC: MC Vi Am DC Swi Delt
How to get there: A4 towards central London; then turn onto Earls Court Road. Underground station on right, take next right onto Penywern Road.

140 Trochee Hotel

52 Ridgeway Place, Wimbledon,
London, SW19 4SW
Tel: 020 8946 9425 Fax: 020 8785 4058
Web: www.trocheehotel.co.uk
15 bedrs SB £61 DB £67
CC: MC Vi Am
How to get there: From Wimbledon station, turn right and take second left into Worple Road. Take third right into Ridgway Place.

141 Trochee Hotel

21 Malcolm Road, Wimbledon,
London, SW19 4AS
Tel: 020 8946 9425 Fax: 020 8946 1579
Web: www.trocheehotel.co.uk
17 bedrs SB £41 DB £57
CC: MC Vi Am
See advert left

142 Wimbledon Hotel

78 Worple Road, Wimbledon, SW19 4HZ
Tel: 020 8946 9265 Fax: 020 8946 9265
14 bedrs SB £55 DB £65
CC: MC Vi Am DC Swi Delt
How to get there: From M25, take A3 to London, Kingston. Take Merton exit, turn left at next traffic lights, keep to right in U-turn.

London

143 Forest View Hotel

227 Romford Road, Forest Gate, London, E7 9HL
Tel: 020 8534 4844 Fax: 020 8534 8959
Children minimum age: 2
20 bedrs SB £35.85 DB £63.45 HBS £48.65
HBD £76.25 D £12.80
CC: MC Vi Swi Delt JCB

How to get there: From North Circular Road,
turn off at Ilford and turn left into Romford Road
(A118). Follow road to Forest Gate.

144 Kensington House Hotel

15-16 Prince of Wales Terrace, London, W8 5PQ
Tel: 0207 9372345 Fax: 0207 3686700
Email: reservations@kenhouse.com
Web: www.kenhouse.com
41 bedrs SB £145 DB £170 B £5.75 L £4.95
D £8.95
CC: MC Vi Am DC Swi Delt JCB

How to get there: Just off Kensington High
Street, corner of Prince of Wales Terrace and
Victoria Road, which is opposite Kensington
Palace.

145 Shaftesbury Hotel

65/73 Shaftesbury Avenue, London, W1V 7AA
Tel: 020 7434 4200 Fax: 020 7437 1717
CC: MC Vi Am DC Swi Delt JCB

146 Kensington Guest House

72 Holland Park Avenue, Holland Park,
London, W11 3QZ
Tel: 020 7229 9233 Fax: 020 7221 1077
Web: www.hotelondon.co.uk
6 bedrs DB £60
CC: MC Vi Am Swi Delt

How to get there: Two doors from Holland Park
tube station, three miles from central London on
the continuation of the Bayswater Road, near
A40(M).

Travelling abroad?

Two ways we can look after you.

If you're going abroad, don't forget to protect yourself against illness, accidents and your car breaking down. With our Travel Insurance and European Motoring Assistance, you'll have the reassurance of knowing we'll be there when you need us.

Travel Insurance

You'll be covered for the costs of illness, accident, delays and loss of belongings.

- Choose between Standard and Extra Cover
- Choose from single trip or annual cover
- Cover for medical expenses of up to £10 million
- Upgrade for winter sports available.

European Motoring Assistance

If you're taking your car to the continent, you can't afford to be without this valuable cover. In the event of a breakdown, one phone call will bring us to your rescue.

- Choose from 2 levels of cover: Standard Cover (worth up to £2,500 of assistance) Additional Cover (worth up to £3,500 of assistance)
- You're covered as soon as you leave home.

Call 0800 55 00 55

Lines open 8am to 9pm Mon to Fri, 9am to 5pm on Sat

and quote A006

A to B - we RAC to it

Southeast

Kettering
Huntingdon
Wellingborough
Newmarket
Warwick
Bury
St Edmunds
WARWICKSHIRE
Northampton
Cambridge
NORTHAMPTON-
Stratford-
SHIRE
SUFFOLK
upon-Avon
Ipswich
Evesham
Bedford
Banbury
Milton
BEDFORD-
Broadway
Keynes
SHIRE
Felixstowe
Stow-on
BUCKING-
Harwich
the Wold
HAMSHIRE
Luton
Bishop's
Stansted
Colchester
Aylesbury
Dunstable
Luton
Stortford
ESSEX
Hemel
HERTFORDSHIRE
Hertford
Clacton-on-Sea
Oxford
Hempstead
St Albans
Chelmsford
Cirencester
OXFORDSHIRE
Hatfield
Southend-on-Sea
Swindon
LONDON
City
Sheerness
Maidenhead
Margate
BERKSHIRE
Heathrow
Gravesend
Rochester
Reading
Bracknell
Chatham
Ramsgate
Marlborough
Newbury
Woking
Maidstone
Canterbury
WILTSHIRE
SURREY
Sevenoaks
Basingstoke
Aldershot
Reigate
Dover
Andover
Farnham
Guildford
Dorking
KENT
Gatwick
Ashford
Crawley
Tunbridge
Folkstone
Salisbury
Winchester
Horsham
Wells
Eastleigh
Petersfield
Uckfield
Southampton
WEST SUSSEX
EAST SUSSEX
Lewes
Chichester
Worthing
Hastings
Portsmouth
Brighton
Newhaven
Bognor
Eastbourne
Bournemouth
Regis
Newport

Glasgow
Edinburgh
Newcastle
Belfast
Dublin
Manchester
Birmingham
Cardiff
London

At Legoland Windsor –
one of Britain's premier
theme parks –you can
assemble Lego robots, play video games, see
recreations of famous landmarks and people,
tower over a model village and watch plays in
Imagination Theatre.
www.lego.com/eng/legoland/windsor or call
08705 040404 for tickets.

Hampton Court Palace

Although extensively developed by Cardinal Thomas Wolsey in the early 1500s, he was expelled from Hampton Court Palace by its infamous resident, Henry VIII, after failing to persuade the Pope to grant the king's divorce. The palace's six tours include Henry's Great Hall and Chapel Royal, William III's apartments and a Renaissance gallery, and there are special events throughout the year. For information go to www.hrp.org.uk or call 020 8781 9500.

Crown copyright: Historic Royal Palaces

Gardener's delight

The Royal Botanical Gardens, Kew (below), is a dizzying and unsurpassed array of plants and displays, arranged by style and theme and spread over 300 acres, much more than can be viewed in a single visit. Paintings of plants are on display in two galleries and a museum is dedicated to plant life and its cultivation. Queen Charlotte's Cottage is a charming part of the gardens; the 17th-century Kew Palace is closed to visitors at present but hopes to re-open in 2002. www.rbgkew.org.uk or 020 8332 5622.

● Hitchin British Schools, Hitchin, Hertfordshire, has a unique set of buildings telling the story of elementary education from 1810 to 1969, including a Lancasterian Monitorial Classroom of 1837 and a Galleried Classroom of 1853. See the web site for further details at www.hitchinbritishschools.org.uk or telephone 01462 452697.

© Dover Bronze Age Boat Trust

Pride of place in Dover Museum goes to a Bronze Age boat (above), the oldest known seagoing vessel in the world. One of England's oldest museums, it has some quaint artefacts that reflect changing attitudes, but focuses on paintings and exhibits about local history and lifestyles. See www.dover.gov.uk/museum/ or call 01304 201066.

● Walkers can follow the 80-mile South Downs Way across chalk uplands between Buriton, near Petersfield, and Beachy Head. Visit www.nationaltrails.gov.uk or call 023 9259 7618.

● Cyclists and walkers are well served by the New Forest; the lucky may spy wild deer, others just the now-domesticated ponies.

● The Isle of Thanet, a popular invasion point, became part of the mainland around 2,000 years ago and is now home to the traditional resorts of Margate, Broadstairs and Ramsgate.

● Fans of the turf are spoiled for choice, with the likes of Goodwood, Ascot, Epsom and Sandown Park only some of the more popular of the race courses.

© Elizabeth Fowler

● Established in the late 19th century using birthday money, the Walter Rothschild Zoological Museum in Tring, Hertfordshire, has a stunning collection of 4,000 preserved animals, with a unique Victorian atmosphere. Discover the bizarre, beautiful and rare at www.nhm.ac.uk/museum/tring or call 020 7942 6171.

© National Motor Museum, Beaulieu

Over 40 historic buildings dating from the 15th century to the Victorian period have been lovingly rebuilt at Weald & Downland Open Air Museum (above), north of Chichester, West Sussex. These striking exhibits include a pair of medieval shops, market hall, Tudor farmstead and working watermill, set among period gardens and woodland. Go to www.wealddown.co.uk or call 01243 811348.

The turrets of Herstmonceux Castle in Hailsham (below) were designed to impress — this 15th-century brick castle, one of the first in England, was built as a country home, rather than a defensive works. Walled gardens, parkland, a science centre and guided tours also make it a good picnic destination. For more information, go to www.herstmonceux-castle.com or phone 01323 834444.

Getting into gear

The National Motor Museum at Beaulieu houses over 250 vehicles, from the 1890s to the 1990s, on four, two, and occasionally three wheels, from the 1964 landspeed holder Bluebird right down to the Sinclair C5. A 1930s garage has been recreated using period artefacts (above), an interactive gallery shows how engines work and remote-controlled cars and driving simulators keep things fun for younger visitors. Visit www.beaulieu.co.uk or call 01590 612345.

Accommodation index

Hotels and Guest Accommodation are indexed by their order of appearance within this region, not by the page. To locate an establishment, note the number to the right of the listing and then find it on the establishment's name bar, as shown here

37 The Turning Mill Hotel

Abingdon, Oxfordshire

1 Abingdon Four Pillars

★★★

Marcham Road, Abingdon,
Oxfordshire, OX14 1TZ
Tel: 01235 553456 Fax: 01235 554117
Email: abingdon@four-pillars.co.uk
Web: www.four-pillars.co.uk
62 bedrs SB £97.75 DB £116.50 HBS £113.75
HBD £74.25 B £5.75 L £5.75 D £15.95
CC: MC Vi Am DC Swi Delt JCB

How to get there: From A34 take junction for
A415 towards Abingdon. At Abingdon, hotel is
on right of roundabout.

2 Heritage Hotels – The Upper Reaches

★★★★ ℞

High Street Abingdon, Thames Street,
Abingdon, Oxfordshire, OX14 3JA
Tel: 0870 400 8101 Fax: 01235 555182
Email: heritagehotels_abingdon.upper_reaches
@forte-hotels.com
Web: www.heritage-hotels.com
31 bedrs
CC: MC Vi Am DC Swi Delt

How to get there: Upon reaching Abingdon
town centre, turn from Stratton Way into Stert
Street (A415). Follow road towards Dorchester.
Stop just before bridge and turn left.

Aldershot, Hampshire

3 Potters International Hotel

★★★

1 Fleet Road, Aldershot, Hampshire, GU11 2ET
Tel: 01252 344000 Fax: 01252 311611
97 bedrs SB £120 DB £140 L £14.50 D £17.50
CC: MC Vi Am DC Swi Delt

Alfriston, East Sussex

4 Heritage Hotels – The Star Inn

★★★★ ℞

High Street, Alfriston, East Sussex, BN26 5TA
Tel: 0870 400 8102 Fax: 01323 870922
Web: www.heritage-hotels.com
37 bedrs SB £70 DB £140 HBS £85 HBD £170

B £12 L £7 D £17
CC: MC Vi Am DC Swi Delt

How to get there: Located in the centre of
Alfriston, which is accessed via the A27
between Brighton and Eastbourne.

5 White Lodge Country House Hotel

★★★

Sloe Lane, Alfriston, East Sussex, BN26 5UR
Tel: 01323 870265 Fax: 01323 870284
Email: sales@whitelodge-hotel.com
Web: www.whitelodge-hotel.com
19 bedrs SB £60 DB £120 HBS £75 HBD £75
B £6.50 L £11.50 D £21.50
CC: MC Vi Swi Delt

Alton, Hampshire

6 Alton Grange Hotel

★★★★ ℞ ℞

London Road, Alton, Hampshire, GU34 4EG
Tel: 01420 86565 Fax: 01420 541346
Email: info@altongrange.co.uk
Web: www.altongrange.co.uk
Children minimum age: 5
Closed December 23 to January 3

Owned and run by the resident owners, this
warm and friendly country house hotel has 35
individually-designed bedrooms and offers New
World fusion cuisine in Truffles restaurant or on
the fragrant sun-terrace.
31 bedrs SB £79.50 DB £97.50 HBS £107
HBD £76.25 B £9.95 L £18.50 D £27.50
CC: MC Vi Am DC Swi Delt JCB

How to get there: Leave M3 at J-4. Take A331
then A31 in Farnham/Winchester direction. Turn
right after seven miles at roundabout (signed
B3004 to Alton/Bordon). Hotel is 350 yards on
left.

Southeast

7 Travelodge Alton

Travel Accommodation
A31 Northbound, Winchester Road, Four Marks,
Near Alton, Hampshire, GU34 5HZ
Tel: 08700 850 950
Web: www.travelodge.co.uk
31 bedrs B £4.25
CC: MC Vi Am DC Swi Delt

Amersham, Buckinghamshire

8 Heritage Hotels – The Crown

★★★★ ₹ ₹
16 High Street, Amersham,
Buckinghamshire, HP7 0DH
Tel: 01494 721541 Fax: 01494 431283
Email: heritagehotels_amersham.crown
        @forte-hotels.com
Web: www.heritage-hotels.com
37 bedrs SB £60 DB £120
B £12.50 L £13.95 D £20.95
CC: MC Vi Am DC Swi Delt
How to get there: From M25 Junction 18, take
A404. Follow signs for Old Amersham. At Tesco
roundabout, go straight ahead, past pelican
crossing. The Crown is on left.

Andover, Hampshire

9 Fifehead Manor Hotel

★★★★ ₹ ₹
Middle Wallop, Stockbridge,
Hampshire, SO20 8EG
Tel: 01264 781565 Fax: 01264 781400
17 bedrs
CC: MC Vi Am Swi Delt
How to get there: Located on A343, six miles
from Andover and 12 miles from Salisbury.

10 White Hart Hotel

★★★
12 Bridge Street, Andover, Hampshire, SP10 1BH
Tel: 01264 352266 Fax: 01264 323767

It's easier online

For all your motoring and travel
needs, www.rac.co.uk

11 May Cottage

Little Gem

♦ ♦ ♦ ♦ ⚞ ☞
Thruxton, near Andover, Hampshire, SP11 8LZ
Tel: 01264 771241 Fax: 01264 771770
Children minimum age: 5

Georgian house set in picturesque tranquil
village with old inn. Stonehenge, Salisbury,
Winchester and stately homes and gardens all
nearby. Pretty, secluded garden with private
parking. A non-smoking establishment.
3 bedrs DB £55 CC: None accepted
How to get there: From A303, take turning
marked 'Thruxton (village only)'. May Cottage is
located almost opposite The George Inn.

12 Bourne Valley Inn

✚
Upper Link, St. Mary Bourne, Andover,
Hampshire, SP11 6BT
Tel: 01264 738361 Fax: 01264 738126
Email: bournevalley@wessexinns.fsnet.co.uk
9 bedrs SB £45 DB £55 HBS £60 HBD £42.50
B £5 L £5 D £10 CC: MC Vi Am Swi Delt
How to get there: Situated on the B3058 four
miles north-east of Andover, just off the A303.

See the road ahead

Just dial 1740* from any mobile
phone to get up-to-the-minute
RAC traffic information on
motorways and major A roads.
Try it now! *Calls to 1740 are charged
at premium rate.

Arundel, West Sussex

13 Comfort Inn Arundel

★★

Junction A27/A284, Crossbush, Arundel,
West Sussex, BN17 7QQ
Tel: 01903 840840 Fax: 01903 849849
Email: admin@gb642.u-net.com
Web: www.choicehotels.com
53 bedrs SB £58.25 DB £58.25 HBS £69
HBD £34.50 B £8.75 D £10.75
CC: MC Vi Am DC Swi Delt

How to get there: Go to junction of A27/A284
trunk road to the east of Arundel.

Ascot, Berkshire

14 Heritage Hotels – The Berystede

★★★★★

Bagshot Road, Ascot, Berkshire, SL5 9JH
Tel: 01344 623311 Fax: 01344 872301
Email: heritagehotels_ascot.berystede
         @forte-hotels.com
90 bedrs
CC: MC Vi Am DC Swi

How to get there: From Ascot, take A330 for
Brockenhurst.

Ashford, Kent

15 Eastwell Manor

Blue Ribbon Winner

★★★★

Eastwell Park, Boughton Lees, Ashford,
Kent, TN25 4HR
Tel: 01233 213000 Fax: 01233 635530
Email: eastwell@btinternet.com
Web: www.eastwellmanor.co.uk
62 bedrs SB £170 DB £200 HBS £202
HBD £132 B £11 L £16.50 D £32
CC: MC Vi Am DC Swi Delt

How to get there: Leave M20 at Junction 9.
Take A28 to Canterbury, then follow A251
towards Faversham. Hotel is 2¹/₂ miles on left-
hand side.
See advert right

16 London Beach Hotel and Golf Club

★★★

Ashford Road, St. Michaels, Tenterden, Ashford,
Kent, TN20 6SP
Tel: 01580 766279 Fax: 01580 763884
Email: enquiries@londonbeach.com
Web: www.londonbeach.com
27 bedrs CC: MC Vi Am Swi Delt

How to get there: Leave M20 at J9, follow signs
for Tenterden; hotel ¹/₂ mile before Tenterden.

17 Travelodge Ashford

Travel Accommodation
Eureka Leisure Park, Ashford, Kent, TN25 4BN
Tel: 08700 850 950
Web: www.travelodge.co.uk
67 bedrs B £4.25 CC: MC Vi Am DC Swi Delt

Plan your route

Visit www.rac.co.uk for RAC's
interactive route planner, including
up to the minute traffic reports.

Southeast

18 Croft Hotel

♦ ♦ ♦

Canterbury Road, Kennington, Ashford,
Kent, TN25 4DU
Tel: 01233 622140 Fax: 01233 635271
Email: crofthotel@btconnect.com

Small family-run hotel set in two acres of
grounds near to Canterbury, Leeds Castle,
Ashford International and Channel Tunnel. Dover
20 minutes.
27 bedrs SB £45 DB £58 HBS £56 HBD £40
D £11 CC: MC Vi Am Swi Delt
How to get there: From M20 Junction nine or
10, follow A28 signs to Canterbury. Croft Hotel
is on right.

Ashurst, Hampshire

19 Busketts Lawn Hotel

★ ★

174 Woodlands Road, Woodlands, Ashurst,
Hampshire, SO40 7GL
Tel: 02380 292272 Fax: 02380 292487
Email: enquiries@buskettslawnhotel.co.uk
Web: www.buskettslawnhotel.co.uk

A delightful family-run country house hotel in a
two-acre garden set in a quiet forest location.

Facilities include a Victorian four-poster suite
and a seasonal outdoor pool, with golf and
riding nearby.
14 bedrs SB £45 DB £85 HBS £63.50 HBD £61
L £6.50 D £18.50
CC: MC Vi Am DC Swi Delt JCB
How to get there: Accessible from J2 M27.
Woodlands is one mile from the A35 Ashurst
and 1 mile from A336 Netley Marsh.

Aylesbury, Buckinghamshire

20 Hartwell House

Gold Ribbon Winner

★ ★ ★ ★
Oxford Road, near Aylesbury,
Buckinghamshire, HP17 8NL
Tel: 01296 747444 Fax: 01296 747450
Email: info@hartwell-house.com
Web: www.hartwell-house.com
Children minimum age: 8
46 bedrs SB £162.50 DB £270 HBS £185
HBD £185 B £17.50 L £22 D £46
CC: MC Vi Swi Delt
How to get there: In Aylesbury, take A418
towards Oxford. Hartwell House is two miles
along this road on the right-hand side.

Baldock, Hertfordshire

21 Travelodge Baldock

Travel Accommodation
A1, Great North Road, Hinxworth, near Baldock,
Hertfordshire, SG7 5EX
Tel: 08700 850 950
Web: www.travelodge.co.uk
40 bedrs B £4.25
CC: MC Vi Am DC Swi Delt

Banbury, Oxfordshire

22 Heritage Hotels – Whately Hall

★★★★

Banbury Cross, Banbury, Oxfordshire, OX16 0AN
Tel: 0870 400 8104 Fax: 01295 271736
Email: heritagehotels_banbury.whately_hall
@forte-hotels.com
Web: www.heritage-hotels.com
72 bedrs SB £100 DB £110 HBS £120 HBD £85
B £12.95 L £12.95 D £23.50
CC: MC Vi Am DC Swi Delt JCB
How to get there: M40 take junction 11. Follow
A422 to Chipping Norton till Banbury Cross.
Hotel is just before on the right.

23 Lismore Hotel

★★

61 Oxford Road, Banbury, Oxfordshire, OX16 9AJ
Tel: 01295 267661 Fax: 01295 269010
23 bedrs SB £55 DB £75 HBS £70 HBD £45
B £7.50 D £16.50
CC: MC Vi Am DC Swi Delt
How to get there: From Banbury Cross in town
centre, follow road south. Take fourth turning left
into Old Parr Road, then first right into car park.

24 La Madonette Country Guest House

♦♦♦♦

North Newington Road, Banbury,
Oxfordshire, OX15 6AA
Tel: 01295 730212 Fax: 01295 730363
Email: lamadonett@aol.com
Web: www.lamadonette.co.uk

17th-century millhouse, peacefully situated in
rural surroundings on outskirts of Banbury. Well
located for Cotswolds, Stratford-upon-Avon,
Oxford and Silverstone. Licensed. Gardens,
outdoor pool.
5 bedrs SB £45 DB £65 CC: MC Vi DC Swi Delt

How to get there: From M40 Junction 11, follow
signs to Banbury Cross. Take B4035 for
approximately two miles, turn right for North
Newington, then 1/4 mile on right before village.

25 Easington House Hotel

♦♦♦

50 Oxford Road, Banbury, Oxfordshire, OX16 9AN
Tel: 01295 270181 Fax: 01295 269527
13 bedrs SB £55 DB £65 CC: MC Vi DC Swi Delt

26 The Unicorn Inn

♣

Market Place, Deddington, Banbury,
Oxfordshire, OX15 0SE
Tel: 01869 338838 Fax: 01869 338592
6 bedrs SB £45 DB £55 B £5 L £6 D £6
CC: MC Vi Am DC Swi Delt

Barton-on-Sea, Hampshire

27 Cliff House Hotel

★★★

Marine Drive West, New Milton, Barton-on-Sea,
Hampshire, BH25 7QL
Tel: 01425 619333 Fax: 01425 612462
Children minimum age: 10
9 bedrs CC: MC Vi Am Swi Delt

How to get there: Turn off A35 on B3058 to New
Milton. Turn right at roundabout on A337, then
left onto Sea Road at Barton-on-Sea. Hotel is at
end of Sea Road on cliff top.

Basildon, Essex

28 Chichester Hotel

★★★

Old London Road, Wickford, Basildon,
Essex, SS11 8UE
Tel: 01268 560555 Fax: 01268 560580
Web: www.chichester-essex.co.uk
33 bedrs SB £84 DB £93 B £5.95 L £9.50
D £10.75 CC: MC Vi Am DC

How to get there: Exit M25 at Junction 29. Turn
east on A127 (signposted Southend on Sea).
After 13 miles, turn north on the A130, after one
mile turn west on the A129, after 1/4 mile turn
right at hotel sign.

Southeast

29 Campanile

Travel Accommodation
Burches, Basildon, Essex, SS14 3AE
Tel: 01268 530810 Fax: 01268 286710
Web: www.campanile.fr

Campanile hotels offer comfortable and convenient budget accommodation and a traditional French style Bistro providing freshly-cooked food for breakfast, lunch and dinner. All rooms ensuite with tea/coffee making facilities, DDT and TV with pay-per-view channels.
97 bedrs SB £43.90 DB £54.85 B £5.95 L £4.95 D £5.95
CC: MC Vi Am DC Swi Delt

How to get there: Exit J29 M25, follow A127 then A176 towards Basildon and Billericay. Left at first roundabout and also at second, then first left.

30 Travelodge Basildon

Travel Accommodation
Festival Leisure Park, Festival Way, Basildon, SS14 3WB
Tel: 08700 850 950
Web: www.travelodge.co.uk
60 bedrs B £4.25
CC: MC Vi Am DC Swi Delt

Basingstoke, Hampshire

31 Hanover International Hotel & Club Basingstoke

★★★★★ ® ® ®
Nately Scures, Hook, Hampshire, RG27 9JS
Tel: 01256 764161 Fax: 01256 768341
Web: www.hanover-international.com
Closed December 26-30

HANOVER INTERNATIONAL
HOTELS & CLUBS

Surrounded by mature woodland, this elegant hotel with superb leisure club is conveniently located within a mile of the M3.
100 bedrs SB £135 DB £145 B £12.25 L £14.25 D £23
CC: MC Vi Am DC Swi Delt

How to get there: From M3 Junction 5, take the A287 to Basingstoke/Newnham. Turn left at crossroads onto the A30, and the hotel is 400 yards on the right hand side.

32 Hampshire Centre Court

★★★★ ®
Centre Drive, Basingstoke, Hampshire, RG24 8FY
Tel: 01256 816664 Fax: 01256 816727
Email: hampshirec@marstonhotels.com
Web: www.marstonhotels.com

MARSTON HOTELS

50 bedrs SB £119 DB £149 HBS £59.50 HBD £59.50 B £12 L £15 D £22.50
CC: MC Vi Am DC Swi Delt

How to get there: Leave M3 at Junction 6. Follow A33 for Reading. Turn right at Chineham Centre roundabout. Hotel 1/4 mile on left.

33 Romans Country House Hotel

★★★★ ⓡ ⓡ

Little London Road, Silchester, Basingstoke,
Hampshire, RG7 2PN
Tel: 0118 970 0421 Fax: 0118 970 0691
Email: romanhotel@hotmail.com
25 bedrs SB £95 DB £105 B £7.50 L £10 D £18
CC: MC Vi Am DC Swi Delt JCB

How to get there: Leave M3 at Junction six and
follow signs on A340 to Tadley/Aldermarston. At
Pamber end, follow hotel signs to Silchester.
See advert right

34 Travelodge Basingstoke

Travel Accommodation
Stag & Hounds, Winchester Road, Basingstoke,
Hampshire, RG22 5HN
Tel: 08700 850 950
Web: www.travelodge.co.uk
32 bedrs B £4.25
CC: MC Vi Am DC Swi Delt

Battle, East Sussex

35 Powder Mills

★★★★ ⓡ

Powdermill Lane, Battle, East Sussex, TN33 0SP
Tel: 01424 775511 Fax: 01424 714540
Email: powdc@aol.com
Web: www.powdermills.co.uk
40 bedrs SB £75 DB £99 HBS £90 HBD £72.50
B £10 L £15.50 D £25.50
CC: MC Vi Am DC Swi Delt

How to get there: Through the town of Battle,
towards Hastings. Take first turning right after
Battle Abbey, Powder Mills one mile down lane.

36 Little Hemingfold Hotel

♦ ♦ ♦ ⓡ

Telham, Battle, East Sussex, TN33 0TT
Tel: 01424 774338 Fax: 01424 775351
Closed 2 January to 11 February
12 bedrs
CC: MC Vi Am DC Swi Delt

How to get there: 1¹/₂ miles south of Battle on
A2100 towards Hastings. Look out for blue Hotel
sign adjacent to sign depicting sharp bend. Turn
down track to left of road for ¹/₂ miles.

Romans
Country House Hotel

RAC ★★★
RAC Dining Award ⓡⓡ

Country House set in the tranquil village of
Silchester, ideal for conferences and short
break holidays. Gourmet restaurant. Real log
fire in the oak panelled lounge. Leisure centre
with Tennis, Gymnasium, Sauna and unique
outdoor pool heated to a steaming 30° C year
round.

**Little London Road, Silchester,
Basingstoke, Hampshire RG7 2PN**
Tel: 01189 700421   Fax: 01189 700691
Email: romanhotel@hotmail.com

Beaconsfield, Buckinghamshire

37 Chequers Inn

★★ ⓡ

Kiln Lane, Wooburn Common, Beaconsfield,
Buckinghamshire, HP10 0JQ
Tel: 01628 529575 Fax: 01628 850124
Email: info@chequers-inn.com
Web: www.chequers-inn.com
17 bedrs SB £97.50 DB £102.50
B £7.50 L £17.95 D £21.95
CC: MC Vi DC Swi

How to get there: Leave M40 at Junction 2.
Follow signs to Beaconsfield. Take A40 towards
High Wycombe, left into Broad Lane, stay on
road. Hotel on left.
See advert on following page

Southeast

The Chequers Inn

Lovely 17th-century country inn with 17 pretty ensuite bedrooms. Exceptional award-winning restaurant and delicious bar meals. Close to Marlow, Henley and Windsor and ideal for exploring the Thames Valley or visiting London. 3 miles from M40 (J2) and 6 miles from M4 (J7). Conference Room • Weekend Breaks • Horse Racing Weekends

Kiln Lane, Wooburn Common,
Beaconsfield, Bucks HP10 0JQ
Tel: 01628 529575   Fax: 01628 850124
Email: info@chequers-inn.com
Website: www.chequers-inn.com

Beaulieu, Hampshire

38 Beaulieu Hotel

★★★
Beaulieu Road, Lyndhurst, Hampshire, SO42 7YQ
Tel: 0238 029 3344 Fax: 0238 029 2729
Email: beaulieu@carehotels.co.uk
Web: www.carehotels.co.uk
18 bedrs DB £120 HBD £81.50 B £7.50 L £5 D £7.50
CC: MC Vi Am Swi Delt
How to get there: From M27, follow signs to Lyndhurst, then Beaulieu on B3056. Beaulieu Hotel is approximately three miles along the road.

39 Master Builders House Hotel

★★★★ 👝 👝
Bucklers Hard, Beaulieu, Hampshire, SO42 7XB
Tel: 01590 616253 Fax: 01590 616297
Email: res@themasterbuilders.co.uk
Web: www.themasterbuilders.co.uk
25 bedrs SB £120 DB £165 HBS £155 HBD £117.50 B £12.50 L £25 D £35
CC: MC Vi Am Swi

Bedford, Bedfordshire

40 Bedford Swan Hotel

★★★
The Embankment, Bedford,
Bedfordshire, MK40 1RW
Tel: 01234 346565 Fax: 01234 212009
Email: info@bedfordswanhotel.co.uk
Web: www.bedfordswanhotel.co.uk

This beautiful hotel, situated in the centre of Bedford, overlooking the river Ouse, has 110 bedrooms, nine conference rooms, indoor pool, superb restaurant and public areas.
110 bedrs SB £93.95 DB £107.40 HBD £60 B £8.95 L £11.50 D £16.50
CC: MC Vi Am DC Swi Delt
How to get there: From M1 take A421 to Bedford, A6 to town centre. Cross the River Ouse; hotel immediately to the right.

41 Woodlands Manor

★★★★ 👝
Green Lane, Clapham, Bedford,
Bedfordshire, MK41 6EP
Tel: 01234 363281 Fax: 01234 272390
Email: woodlands.manor@pageant.co.uk
Web: www.pageant.co.uk
33 bedrs SB £75 DB £85 HBS £65 HBD £130 B £7.50 L £7.95 D £25.95
CC: MC Vi Am Swi Delt
How to get there: North on A6 from Bedford towards Kettering; first turning on right in village of Clapham.

Bexhill-on-Sea, East Sussex

42 Park Lodge Hotel

◆◆◆
16 Egerton Road, Bexhill-on-Sea,
East Sussex, TN39 3HH
Tel: 01424 216547

Bexleyheath, Kent

43 Bexleyheath Marriott Hotel

★★★★ ℞
1 Broadway, Bexleyheath, Kent, DA6 7JZ
Tel: 020 8298 1000 Fax: 020 8298 1234
Email: bexleyheath@marriotthotels.co.uk
142 bedrs SB £115 DB £131
B £13 L £14 D £19.75
CC: MC Vi Am DC Swi Delt

How to get there: The Bexleyheath Marriott is located just off the A2 and only minutes from Junction two of the M25.

Bicester, Oxfordshire

44 Travelodge Bicester

Travel Accommodation
M40 J10, Northampton Road, Ardley, Bicester, Oxfordshire, OX6 9RD
Tel: 08700 850 950
Web: www.travelodge.co.uk
98 bedrs B £4.25
CC: MC Vi Am DC Swi Delt

45 Westfield Farm

♦♦♦♦ ✱ ℞
The Fenway, Steeple Aston, Bicester, Oxfordshire, OX25 4SS
Tel: 01869 340591 Fax: 01869 347594
Email: info@westfieldmotel.u-net.com
Web: www.oxlink.co.uk/accom/westfield-farm/
9 bedrs SB £55 DB £75
CC: MC Vi Am DC Swi Delt

How to get there: Eight miles south of Banbury on A4260, turn first left into Steeple Aston. Hotel ½ mile, entrance on right.

Bickley, Kent

46 Glendevon House Hotel

♦♦♦
80 Southborough Road,
Bickley, Kent, BR1 2EN
Tel: 020 8467 2183

Billingshurst, West Sussex

47 Travelodge Billingshurst

Travel Accommodation
A29 Northbound, Stane Street, Five Oaks,
Billingshurst, West Sussex, RH14 9AE
Tel: 08700 850 950
Web: www.travelodge.co.uk
26 bedrs B £4.25
CC: MC Vi Am DC Swi Delt

Bishop's Stortford, Hertfordshire

48 Down Hall Country House Hotel

★★★★ ℞
Hatfield Heath, near Bishop's Stortford,
Hertfordshire, CM22 7AS
Tel: 01279 731441 Fax: 01279 730416
Email: reservations@downhall.co.uk
Web: www.downhall.co.uk

Victorian mansion of notable historic interest. Set in 110 acres of its own grounds of lawns, parkland and woodland. 103 en-suite bedrooms, plenty of parking and conference facilities for up to 250 people.
103 bedrs SB £120 DB £148
CC: MC Vi Am DC Swi Delt JCB

How to get there: Exit M11 at Junction 8. Take A1250 through Bishop's Stortford then A1060 to Hatfield Heath. Follow signs to Down Hall.
See advert on following page

Southeast

Down Hall
Country House

RaC
★★★★

Mid-Victorian stone mansion of notable historic interest. Set in 110 acres of its own grounds of lawns, parkland and woodland. 103 ensuite bedrooms, plenty of parking and conference facilities for up to 250 people.

Hatfield Heath, Bishop's Stortford, Essex CM22 7AS
Tel: 01279 731441   Fax: 01279 730416
Email: reservations@downhall.demon.co.uk

49 The Cottage

◆ ◆ ◆ ◆

71 Birchanger Lane, Birchanger, Bishop's Stortford, Hertfordshire, CM23 5QA
Tel: 01279 812349 Fax: 01279 815045
Closed Christmas to New Year

17th century listed house set in large mature garden. Quiet and peaceful village setting yet near M11 junction 8, Stansted airport and Bishop's Stortford.
16 bedrs SB £50 DB £70
CC: MC Vi Swi Delt JCB

How to get there: Leave M11 at Junction 8. Take A120 west for one mile. Take B1383 north towards Newport and Saffron Waldon, then first right into Birchanger Lane.

50 George Hotel

◆ ◆ ◆

1 North Street, Bishop's Stortford, Herts, CM23 2LQ
Tel: 01279 504128 Fax: 01279 655135
Email: enquiries@stanstedhotels.net
Web: www.stanstedhotels.net
30 bedrs SB £30 DB £55
CC: MC Vi Swi

51 The Old Post Office B&B

◆ ◆ ◆

Church End, Broxted, Great Dunmow, Essex, CM6 2BU
Tel: 01279 850050 Fax: 01279 850050
3 bedrs SB £35 DB £60
CC: MC Vi DC Swi Delt JCB

How to get there: Exit M11 at Stansted airport junction.

Bonchurch, Isle of Wight

52 Bonchurch Manor Hotel

★ ★ ★

Bonchurch Shute, Bonchurch, Isle of Wight, PO38 1NU
Tel: 01983 852868

Botley, Hampshire

53 MacDonald Botley Park

★ ★ ★ ★

Winchester Road, Boorley Green, Botley, Hampshire, SO32 2UA
Tel: 01489 780888 Fax: 01489 789242
Email: info@botleypark.macdonald-hotels.co.uk
Web: www.macdonald-hotels.co.uk
         /botleypark-hotels
100 bedrs SB £110 DB £120 HBS £130
HBD £80 B £12.50 L £15 D £20
CC: MC Vi Am DC Swi Delt

How to get there: From J11 of M3, 15 minutes: from J7 of M27, five minutes.

Bracknell, Berkshire

54 Coppid Beech Hotel

★★★★ ⍩

John Nike Way, Bracknell, Berkshire, RG12 8TF
Tel: 01344 303333 Fax: 01344 301200
Email: welcome@coppid-beech-hotel.co.uk
Web: www.coppidbeech.com
205 bedrs SB £175 DB £195 B £12.50 L £14.95
D £24.95 CC: MC Vi Am DC Swi Delt JCB

How to get there: Leave M4 at Junction 10. Take A329(M) to Wokingham. After three miles take first exit to Coppid Beech roundabout. Take first exit and in 300 yards the hotel is on the right.

55 Travelodge Bracknell

Travel Accommodation

London Road, Binfield, Bracknell,
Berkshire, RG42 2AA
Tel: 08700 850 950
Web: www.travelodge.co.uk
35 bedrs B £4.25 CC: MC Vi Am DC Swi Delt

Brentwood, Essex

56 Marygreen Manor Hotel

★★★★★ ⍩ ⍩

London Road, Brentwood, Essex, CM14 4NR
Tel: 01277 225252 Fax: 01277 262809
Email: info@marygreenmanor.co.uk
Web: www.marygreenmanor.co.uk
44 bedrs SB £135.50 DB £147.50 B £12
L £16.50 D £30
CC: MC Vi Am Swi Delt

How to get there: Exit the M25 at Junction 28. Take A1023, after two minutes the hotel is on right.
See advert below

57 Heybridge Hotel

★★★ ⍩

Roman Road, Ingatestone, Essex, CM4 9AB
Tel: 01277 353288 Fax: 01277 353288
22 bedrs SB £103 DB £124 HBS £121.80
HBD £80.80 B £11 L £16 D £16
CC: MC Vi Am DC Swi

Southeast

58 Travelodge Brentwood

Travel Accommodation
A127, Halfway House, East Hornden,
Brentwood, Essex, CM13 3LL
Tel: 08700 850 950
Web: www.travelodge.co.uk
22 bedrs B £4.25
CC: MC Vi Am DC Swi Delt

Brighton, East Sussex

59 Old Ship Hotel

★★★★
Kings Road, Brighton, East Sussex, BN1 1NR
Tel: 01273 329001 Fax: 01273 820718

60 Kings Hotel

★★★
139–141 Kings Road, Brighton,
East Sussex, BN1 2NA
Tel: 01273 820854 Fax: 01273 828309
Email: kingshotel@vienna-group.co.uk
Web: www.viennagroup.co.uk
84 bedrs SB £70 DB £110 HBS £80 HBD £65
B £7 D £12
CC: MC Vi Am DC Swi Delt

How to get there: From London or M25, take
M23/A23 to Brighton. Follow signs for the
seafront. On reaching Brighton Pier roundabout
take third exit and drive west. Hotel is opposite
West Pier.

61 Quality Hotel Brighton

★★★
West Street, Brighton, East Sussex, BN1 2RQ
Tel: 01273 220033 Fax: 01273 778000
Email: admin@gb057.u-net.com
Web: www.choicehotels.com
138 bedrs SB £105.75 DB £120.75
HBS £114.50 HBD £64.75 B £10.75 D £8.75
CC: MC Vi Am DC Swi Delt
How to get there: Follow A23 into Brighton.
Follow seafront/town centre signs and take
A259 to Hove/Worthing. Hotel off seafront, turn
right into West Street.

62 Travelodge Brighton

Travel Accommodation
A23, 165-167 Preston Road, Brighton,
East Sussex, BN1 6AN
Tel: 08700 850 950
Web: www.travelodge.co.uk
94 bedrs B £4.25
CC: MC Vi Am DC Swi Delt

63 Adelaide Hotel

♦♦♦♦ ✕
51 Regency Square, Brighton,
East Sussex, BN1 2FF
Tel: 01273 205286 Fax: 01273 220904
Email: adelaide@pavilion.co.uk
12 bedrs SB £41 DB £68
CC: MC Vi Am DC Swi Delt

How to get there: Regency Square is opposite
the West pier, off the main seafront.

64 Arlanda Hotel

♦♦♦♦
20 New Steine, Brighton, East Sussex, BN2 1PD
Tel: 01273 699300 Fax: 01273 600930
Email: arlanda@brighton.co.uk
Closed Christmas
16 bedrs SB £48 DB £120
CC: MC Vi Am DC Swi Delt
How to get there: From the Palace Pier,
Brighton, travel 400 yards east on Marine
Parade. Hotel is in New Steine on left.

65 Ascott House Hotel

♦♦♦♦ ✕
21 New Steine, Marine Parade, Brighton,
East Sussex, BN2 1PD
Tel: 01273 688085 Fax: 01273 623733
Email: ascotthouse@supanet.com
Web: www.ascotthousehotel.com
Children minimum age: 2
12 bedrs SB £36 DB £70
CC: MC Vi Swi Delt

How to get there: Follow A23 to the seafront.
Turn left at the roundabout in front of Palace
Pier. Take ninth turning on left off Marine Parade.

66 Fyfield House Hotel

◆ ◆ ◆ ◆ ⚘

26 New Steine, Brighton, East Sussex, BN2 1PD
Tel: 01273 602770 Fax: 01273 602770
Email: fyfield@aol.com
Web: www.fyfield/newsteinehotels.com
Closed Christmas
9 bedrs SB £45 DB £90
CC: MC Vi Am DC Swi Delt

How to get there: Town centre, at the Palace Pier, take A259 east. Eighth turning into the square, which has a one-way system.

67 Hotel Twenty One

◆ ◆ ◆ ◆ ⚘

21 Charlotte Street, Marine Parade, Brighton, East Sussex, BN2 1AG
Tel: 01273 686450 Fax: 01273 695560
Email: the21@pavilion.co.uk
Web: www.smoothhound.co.uk/hotels/21.html
8 bedrs SB £35.50 DB £60
CC: MC Vi Swi Delt

How to get there: From Palace Pier turn left onto A259. After ¾ mile, turn left onto Charlotte Street. Hotel Twenty One is on left-hand side.

68 Paskins Town House

◆ ◆ ◆ ◆

18/19 Charlotte Street, Brighton, BN2 1AG
Tel: 01273 601203 Fax: 01273 621973
Email: welcome@paskins.co.uk
Web: www.paskins.co.uk
19 bedrs SB £35 DB £75 B £9.95
CC: MC Vi Am DC Swi Delt JCB

How to get there: At Brighton pier, turn left. Paskins Hotel is on 11th road on right.

69 Regency Hotel

◆ ◆ ◆ ◆ ⚘ ⚑

28 Regency Square, Brighton, East Sussex, BN1 2FH
Tel: 01273 202690 Fax: 01273 220438
Email: enquiries@regencybrighton.co.uk
Web: www.regencybrighton.co.uk
Children minimum age: 6

Once the home of Jane, Dowager Duchess of Marlborough, this 1820 townhouse is now a small, smart hotel. Direct sea views. Car parking (500) under square. London one hour (train).
13 bedrs SB £65 DB £100
CC: MC Vi Am DC Swi Delt

How to get there: Regency Square is off the coastal road (Kings Road) directly opposite the West Pier.

70 Trouville

◆ ◆ ◆ ◆ ⚘

11 New Steine, Marine Parade, Brighton, East Sussex, BN2 1PB
Tel: 01273 697384
Closed Christmas and January
8 bedrs SB £29 DB £59
CC: MC Vi Am Delt JCB

How to get there: Take A23 to Palace Pier. Turn left onto A259. New Steine is the first square on left, after approx 300 yards.

71 Allendale Hotel

◆ ◆ ◆ ⚑

3 New Steine, Brighton, East Sussex, BN2 1PB
Tel: 01273 675436 Fax: 01273 602603

Southeast

72 Brighton Marina House Hotel

8 Charlotte Street, Brighton,
East Sussex, BN2 1AG
Tel: 01273 605349 Fax: 01273 679484
Email: rooms@jungs.co.uk
Web: www.s-h-systems.co.uk/hotels/brightma
10 bedrs SB £25 DB £45 HBS £45 HBD £37.50
D £19.50
CC: MC Vi Am DC

How to get there: At Brighton pier turn up
Marine Parade (A259). After second traffic
lights, take fifth left (Charlotte Street).

73 Cavalaire House

34 Upper Rock Gardens, Brighton,
East Sussex, BN2 1QF
Tel: 01273 696899 Fax: 01273 600504
Email: welcome@cavalaire.co.uk
Web: www.cavalaire.co.uk
Children minimum age: 5
Closed mid-January to mid-February
11 bedrs SB £25 DB £52
CC: MC Vi Am DC Swi Delt

How to get there: Follow signposts to town
centre/seafront. At Brighton Pier roundabout,
take A259 Rottingdean. At second set of lights,
turn left into Lower Rock Gardens. Hotel up hill.

74 Genevieve Hotel

18 Maderia Place, Brighton,
East Sussex, BN2 1TN
Tel: 01273 681653

75 Rowland House

21 St. George's Terrace, Kemp Town,
Brighton, East Sussex, BN2 1JJ
Tel: 01273 603639
Email: info@rowland-house.co.uk
Web: www.rowland-house.co.uk
Closed Christmas
11 bedrs SB £25 DB £45
CC: MC Vi Am Swi Delt

How to get there: From train station 20 minutes,
from bus station 10 minutes.

76 Melford Hall

41 Marine Parade, Brighton,
East Sussex, BN2 1PE
Tel: 01273 681435 Fax: 01273 624186
Children minimum age: 2
SB £30 DB £60
CC: MC Vi Am DC Swi Delt

How to get there: 400 yards from Brighton pier
on sea front towards signs for Marina or
Newhaven.

77 The Garth

28 Cornwall Gardens, Brighton,
East Sussex, BN1 6RJ
Tel: 01273 561515 Fax: 01273 561515
Email: mike-edwards@mistral.co.uk
Children minimum age: 5
3 bedrs SB £25 DB £45
CC: None accepted

How to get there: A23 into Brighton becomes
London Road; after one mile turn left into
Varndean Road; Cornwall Gardens is first right.

Broadstairs, Kent

78 Devonhurst Hotel

Eastern Esplanade, Broadstairs, Kent, CT10 1DR
Tel: 01843 863010 Fax: 01843 868940
Email: info@devonhurst.co.uk
Web: www.devonhurst.co.uk
Children minimum age: 5
9 bedrs SB £34.50 DB £59 HBS £49 HBD £88
D £14.50
CC: MC Vi Am DC Swi Delt JCB

How to get there: Follow main high street to the
bottom, bearing left into Albion Street. Take
third right into Dickens Road, then Eastern
Esplanade.

79 Oakfield Private Hotel

11 The Vale, Broadstairs, Kent, CT10 1RB
Tel: 01843 862506 Fax: 01843 600659
Email: info@oakfield-hotel.com
Web: www.oakfield-hotel.com
Children minimum age: 12
10 bedrs SB £26 DB £52 HBS £38 HBD £38
CC: MC Vi Am DC Swi Delt JCB
How to get there: Halfway down High Street,
turn right into Queens Road, then take the third
right. Hotel is 25 yards on right.

80 Bay Tree Hotel

12 Eastern Esplanade, Broadstairs,
Kent, CT10 1DR
Tel: 01843 862502 Fax: 01843 860589
Children minimum age: 10
11 bedrs SB £28 DB £56 HBS £42 HBD £42
D £14
CC: MC Vi Swi Delt
How to get there: Situated on clifftop Eastern
Esplanade. Follow main road through town,
turning right into Rectory Road on leaving
Broadstairs.

Brockenhurst, Hampshire

81 New Park Manor Hotel

★★★★ ⓡ ⓡ ⓡ
Brockenhurst, Hampshire, SO42 7QH
Tel: 01590 623467 Fax: 01590 62268
Email: enquiries@newparkmanorhotel.co.uk
Web: www.newparkmanorhotel.co.uk

24 bedrs SB £85 DB £110 HBS £95 HBD £70
B £10 L £14 D £27.50
CC: MC Vi Am DC Swi Delt

How to get there: Leave M27 at Junction 1.
Follow A337 to Lyndhurst and Brockenhurst.
Hotel sign and private drive on right midway
between Lyndhurst and Brockenhurst.

82 Rhinefield House

★★★★ ⓡ ⓡ
Rhinefield Road, Brockenhurst,
Hampshire, SO42 7QB
Tel: 01590 622922 Fax: 01590 622800
Email: rhinefield-house@arcadianhotels.co.uk
Web: www.arcadianhotels.co.uk
34 bedrs SB £110 DB £150 HBS £130 HBD £90
B £12.50 L £17.95 D £27.50
CC: MC Vi Am DC Swi Delt
How to get there: J1 M27 A337 to Lyndhurst;
then A35 west to Christchurch. Turn left after
2¹/₂ miles into Ornamental Drive, signposted
Rhinefield House.

83 Watersplash Hotel

★★★ ⓡ
The Rise, Brockenhurst, Hampshire, SO42 7ZP
Tel: 01590 622344 Fax: 01590 624047
Email: bookings@watersplash.co.uk
Web: www.watersplash.co.uk
23 bedrs SB £55 DB £76 HBS £77 HBD £60
B £4.50 L £9.95 D £22
CC: MC Vi Am Swi Delt

84 Cottage Hotel

Sway Road, Brockenhurst, Hampshire, SO42 7SH
Tel: 01590 622296 Fax: 01590 623014
Email: terry-eisner@compuserve.com
Web: www.cottagehotel.org
Children minimum age: 10
Closed December to February
7 bedrs SB £55 DB £95
CC: MC Vi Swi Delt
How to get there: From Lyndhurst on A337, turn
right at Carey's Manor into Grigg Lane.
Continue ¹/₂ a mile to crossroads, straight over
and Cottage is next to the war memorial.

Making a booking?

Don't forget to mention RAC
Hotels and Bed & Breakfast 2002.

Southeast

85 The Rose and Crown

◆◆◆

Lyndhurst Road, Brockenhurst,
Hampshire, SO42 7RH
Tel: 01590 622225 Fax: 01590 623056
Email: roseandcrown.brockenhurst@
eldridge-pope.co.uk
Web: www.eldridge-pope-inns.co.uk
14 bedrs SB £55 DB £65 B £7 L £3 D £7
CC: MC Vi Am Swi Delt

How to get there: From M27 take A337 through
Lyndhurst towards Lymington. Rose and Crown
is on the left when entering Brockenhurst.

Bromley, Kent

86 Bromley Court

★★★

Bromley Hill, Bromley, Kent, BR1 4JD
Tel: 020 8464 5011 Fax: 020 8460 0899
Email: bromleyhotel@btinternet.com
Web: www.bromley-hotel.co.uk
115 bedrs SB £100 DB £115 B £6.95 L £12
D £15
CC: MC Vi Am DC Swi Delt

How to get there: Exit J4 M25, A21 to Bromley.
Follow road to Bromley Hill; private drive
opposite Mercedes garage off A21.

Broxbourne, Herts

87 Cheshunt Marriott Hotel

★★★

Halfhide Lane, Turnford, Broxbourne,
Herts, EN10 6NG
Tel: 01992 451245 Fax: 01992 461611

Buckingham, Buckinghamshire

88 Buckingham Four Pillars Hotel

★★★

A421 Buckingham Ring Road,
Buckingham, MK18 1RY
Tel: 01280 822622 Fax: 01280 823074

89 Villiers Hotel

★★★ ♖ ♖ ♖

3 Castle Street, Buckingham,
Buckinghamshire, MK18 1BS
Tel: 01280 822444 Fax: 01280 822113
Email: villiers@villiershotel.demon.co.uk
46 bedrs SB £105 DB £120 B £6.95 L £12 D £25
CC: MC Vi Am DC Swi Delt

How to get there: From Junction nine on M40 or
Junction 13 on M1, take A421 to Buckingham.
Hotel is situated in Castle Street.

Burford, Oxfordshire

90 Travelodge Burford

Travel Accommodation
A40, Bury Barn, Burford, Oxfordshire, OX18 4JF
Tel: 08700 850 950
Web: www.travelodge.co.uk
40 bedrs B £4.25 CC: MC Vi Am DC Swi Delt

Burley, Hampshire

91 Moorhill House Hotel

★★★

Burley, near Ringwood, Hampshire, BH24 4AG
Tel: 01425 403285 Fax: 01425 403715
Email: moorhill@carehotels.co.uk
Web: www.carehotels.co.uk
24 bedrs SB £60 DB £120 HBS £81.50
HBD £81.50 B £7.50 D £21.50
CC: MC Vi Am Swi Delt

How to get there: From M27, take A31 to Burley.
Bear left at War Memorial, right past Queens
Head. Moorhill House is signposted on right.

Cadnam, Hampshire

92 Bartley Lodge Hotel

★★★★ ♖

Lyndhurst Road, Cadnam, Hampshire, SO40 2NR
Tel: 02380 812248 Fax: 02380 812075
Email: bartley@carehotels.co.uk
Web: www.carehotels.co.uk
31 bedrs SB £60 DB £120 HBS £81.50
HBD £81.50 B £7 L £5 D £21.50 CC: MC Vi Am

See advert on facing page

Camberley, Surrey

93 Heritage Hotels — Frimley Hall

★★★

Lime Avenue, off Portsmouth Road, Camberley,
Surrey, GU15 2BG
Tel: 0870 4008224 Fax: 01276 691253
Email: heritagehotels_camberley.frimley_hall
@forte-hotels.com
Web: www.heritage-hotels.com
86 bedrs SB £65 DB £90 HBS £75 HBD £55
B £13.50 L £7.50 D £19.50
CC: MC Vi Am DC Swi Delt
How to get there: From M3 Junction 3, pick up
A30 towards Camberley for one mile, then A325
towards Farnham. Conifer Drive one mile on right.

94 Camberley Guest House

♦ ♦ ♦ ✸

116 London Road, Camberley, Surrey, GU15 3TJ
Tel: 01276 24410 Fax: 01276 65409
Closed Christmas
7 bedrs CC: MC Vi DC
How to get there: Situated on main A30, parallel
to M3. From London, exit 3, from south coast
take exit 4. Hotel in town centre of Camberley.

Canterbury, Kent

95 Heritage Hotels — The Chaucer

★★★

Ivy Lane, Canterbury, Kent, CT1 1TT
Tel: 0870 400 8106 Fax: 01227 450397
42 bedrs SB £80 DB £112.60 HBS £100
HBD £60 B £12 L £6.95 D £15
CC: MC Vi Am DC Swi Delt
How to get there: Leave M2 at Junction 7.
Follow signs to Canterbury. At fifth roundabout
turn right. Hotel is on left.

96 Canterbury Hotel

★★

71 New Dover Road, Canterbury, Kent, CT1 3DZ
Tel: 01227 450551 Fax: 01227 780145
Email: canterbury.hotel@btinternet.com
Web: www.canterbury-hotel-appartments.co.uk
Children minimum age: 6
23 bedrs SB £55 DB £75 HBS £66 HBD £51
B £7 D £16.50 CC: MC Vi Am DC Swi Delt
How to get there: On A2 — New Dover Road.

Bartley Lodge Hotel

Grade II listed country house hotel set in
8 acres of grounds and gardens directly
adjoining the New Forest.

31 delightfully furnished bedrooms,
excellent cuisine, indoor leisure centre
with pool, sauna, fitness room and two
hard-surface tennis courts.

Cadnam, New Forest SO40 2NR

Tel: 023 8028 3717   Fax: 023 8028 3719
Email: bartley@carehotels.co.uk
Website: www.carehotels.co.uk

97 Thanington Hotel

140 Wincheap, Canterbury, Kent, CT1 3RY
Tel: 01227 453227 Fax: 01227 453225
Email: thanington@lineone.net
Web: www.thanington-hotel.co.uk
Closed Christmas
15 bedrs SB £55 DB £75
CC: MC Vi Am DC Swi Delt JCB
How to get there: Located on Canterbury-to-
Ashford A28 outside city walls, ten
minutes' walk from city centre

Chawston, Bedfordshire

98 Travelodge Chawston

Travel Accommodation
A1, Chawston, Bedfordshire, MK44 3QT
Tel: 08700 850 950
Web: www.travelodge.co.uk
40 bedrs B £4.25
CC: MC Vi Am DC Swi Delt

Southeast

Chelmsford, Essex

99 Atlantic Hotel

★★★

New Street, Chelmsford, Essex, CM1 1PP
Tel: 01245 268168 Fax: 01245 268169
Email: book@atlantichotel.co.uk
Web: www.atlantichotel.co.uk

59 bedrs SB £63.95 DB £82.90 B £5.95 L £10
D £20 CC: MC Vi Am DC Swi Delt
点 ⊗ ☺ ⛃ ☎ ✳ ⛏ ⬛ ❀ ░ ⁂ ⁑
How to get there: A1016 to Chelmsford and
signs to station. Over two mini-roundabouts, turn
left then right. At traffic lights left into New St.
See advert on facing page

100 County Hotel

★★★ ⊛

29 Rainsford Road, Chelmsford, Essex, CM1 2QA
Tel: 01245 455700 Fax: 01245 492762
Email: sales@countyhotel-essex.co.uk
Web: www.countyhotel-essex.co.uk
36 bedrs CC: MC Vi Am DC Swi Delt
⬡ 点 ☺ ⛃ ☎ ⛏ ⬛ ❀ ⼁ ⁂ ⁑
How to get there: From M25 Junction 28, take
A12 to Chelmsford. From town centre, take road
to rail station. Pass station, under bridge, hotel
on left after traffic lights.

101 Ivy Hill Hotel

★★★

Writtle Road, Margaretting, Essex, CM4 0EH
Tel: 01277 353040 Fax: 01277 355038
Email: sales@ivyhillhotel.co.uk
Web: www.ivyhillhotel.co.uk
33 bedrs SB £100 DB £125 HBS £90
HBD £52.50 B £6. L £20.95 D £20.95
CC: MC Vi Am DC Swi Delt
⬡ 点 ⛁ ☺ ⛃ ☎ ⬛ ❀ ⼁ ✤ ⁂ ⁑ ⚲ ⚘
How to get there: Eight miles east of the M25
on the A12. Take the second exit on the B1002
for Margaretting.

102 Beechcroft Hotel

♦ ♦ ♦

211 New London Road, Chelmsford,
Essex, CM2 0AJ
Tel: 01245 352462 Fax: 01245 347833
Email: enquiries@beechcrofthotel.com
Web: www.beechcrofthotel.com
19 bedrs SB £36 DB £52 CC: MC Vi Swi Delt
⛡ ⊗ ☺ ⛃ ⬛ ❀ ⚘
How to get there: Exit J28 M25 onto A12; then
A414. Cross three mini-roundabouts, first left at
next one. Hotel is on right after first traffic lights.

103 Tanunda Hotel

♦ ♦ ♦

217-219 New London Road, Chelmsford,
Essex, CM2 0AJ
Tel: 01245 354295 Fax: 01245 345503
20 bedrs SB £36 DB £60
CC: MC Vi Am DC Swi Delt
点 ☺ ⛃ ☎ ❀ ⁂ ⁑

Chenies, Hertfordshire

104 Bedford Arms Hotel

★★★ ⊛

Chenies, near Rickmansworth,
Hertfordshire, WD3 6EQ
Tel: 01923 283301 Fax: 01923 284825
Email: info@bedfordarms-hotel-chenies.com
Web: www.bedfordarms-hotel-chenies.com
10 bedrs SB £168.50 DB £182 B £13.50 L £25
D £25 CC: MC Vi Am DC Swi Delt
⛁ ⚘ ⊗ ☺ ⛃ ☎ ⬛ ❀ ⚯ ⼁ ⁂ ⁑
How to get there: 2 miles from M25 J18 on A404,
Amersham direction. Signposted Chenies, on right.

Chichester, West Sussex

105 Marriott Goodwood Park Hotel
& Country Club

★★★★ ⊛

Goodwood, Chichester, West Sussex, PO18 0QB
Tel: 01243 775537 Fax: 01243 520120
Web: www.marriotthotels.com/pmegs
94 bedrs SB £76 DB £92 HBS £91 HBD £61
CC: MC Vi Am DC Swi Delt
⬡ ⛁ ⚘ ⊗ ☺ ⛃ ☎ ⛏ ⬛ ❀ ⼁ ⚽ ⁂ ⁑ SPA ⚷
⚲ ⚞ ⛋
How to get there: Just off the A285 three miles
north of Chichester. Follow signs for Goodwood;
once in area, Marriott Hotel is signposted

106 Millstream Hotel

★★★★ ⊞ ⊞

Bosham Lane, Bosham, Chichester,
West Sussex, PO18 8HL
Tel: 01243 573234 Fax: 01243 573459
Email: info@millstream-hotel.co.uk
Web: www.millstream-hotel.co.uk

Beautifully-appointed country house dating from
1701, set in a picturesque sailing village. Bar,
sitting-room, restaurant and a bedroom
designed for wheelchair access, all on ground
floor. Locally renowned award-winning
restaurant.
35 bedrs SB £75 DB £120 HBS £70 HBD £70
B £9 L £12.50 D £23.50
CC: MC Vi Am DC Swi Delt

How to get there: From Chichester or Havant
take the A259 to Bosham. From Swan
roundabout follow brown signs south to hotel.

107 Ship Hotel

★★★★ ⊞ ⊞

North Street, Chichester, West Sussex, PO9 1NH
Tel: 01243 778000 Fax: 01243 788000
Email: bookings@shiphotel.com
Web: www.shiphotel.com
34 bedrs CC: MC Vi Am DC Swi Delt

How to get there: Follow signs to Chichester
Festival Theatre, until Northgate roundabout,
then turn into North Street. Hotel on left, car
park at rear.

108 Aberlands House Hotel

♦♦♦♦

Merston, Chichester, West Sussex, PO20 6DY
Tel: 01243 532675 Fax: 01243 788884
7 bedrs
CC: MC Vi Swi Delt

Atlantic Hotel

The Atlantic is a brand new hotel, with original
and forward-looking ideas. Our aim is to
provide an efficient and reliable service in a
smart and stylish surrounding with a real
emphasis on value. The New Street Brasserie
is our informal restaurant, serving classic yet
modern cuisine at affordable prices.

**New Street, Chelmsford, Essex
CM1 1PP**
Tel: 01245 268168   Fax: 01245 268169
Email: book@atlantichotel.co.uk
Website: www.atlantichotel.co.uk

109 The Vestry

♦♦♦♦ ⊞

23 Southgate, Chichester,
West Sussex, PO19 1ES
Tel: 01243 773358 Fax: 01243 530633
Email: vestry.chichester@eldridge-pope.co.uk
11 bedrs SB £60 DB £85 B £7.50 L £6.50 D £8.50
CC: MC Vi Swi Delt

How to get there: From the A27 join the
Chichester ring road and follow signs for
Southgate. The Vestry is on South Street.

Chinnor, Oxfordshire

110 Peacock Hotel

★★ ⊞

Henton, Chinnor, Oxfordshire, OX9 4AH
Tel: 01844 353519 Fax: 01844 353891

Southeast

Chipping Norton, Oxfordshire

111 Southcombe Lodge

♦ ♦ ♦ ✷

Southcombe, Chipping Norton,
Oxfordshire, OX7 5QH
Tel: 01608 643068 Fax: 01608 642948
Email: georgefindlysouthcombelodge
@tinyworld.co.uk
6 bedrs SB £35 DB £54
CC: None accepted

How to get there: On A44 from Oxford to
Chipping Norton, next to Chipping Norton golf
course.

Clacton-on-Sea, Essex

112 Le Vere Private Hotel

♦ ♦ ♦

15 Agate Road, Marine Parade West,
Clacton-on-Sea, Essex, CO15 1RA
Tel: 01255 423044 Fax: 01255 423044
6 bedrs SB £30 DB £47.50 HBS £40
HBD £32.50 D £12
CC: MC Vi Am DC Swi Delt JCB

How to get there: Go to seafront. From London
Road, turn right. Cross the lights. Agate Road is
next turn on right; hotel is halfway up on left, a
pink and white building.

Colchester, Essex

113 Five Lakes Hotel Golf Country Club

★ ★ ★ ★ ★ 🏮 🏮

Colchester Road, Tolleshunt Knights, Maldon,
Essex, CM9 8HX
Tel: 01621 868888 Fax: 01621 869696
Email: enquiries@fivelakes.co.uk
Web: www.fivelakes.co.uk

Set in 320 acres including two golf courses.
Spacious and innovative in design with extensive
leisure, health, beauty and sporting facilities.
Easily accessible from A12, M25 and M11.
114 bedrs
CC: MC Vi Am DC Swi Delt

How to get there: Take the A12 in the direction
of Kelvedon, then follow the brown and white
'Five Lakes' tourist board signage.

114 Butterfly Hotel

★ ★ ★

A12/A120 Junction, Old Ipswich Road,
Colchester, Essex, CO7 7QY
Tel: 01206 230900 Fax: 01206 231095
Email: colbutterfly@lineone.net
Web: www.butterflyhotels.co.uk
50 bedrs SB £83.50 DB £92 HBS £98.50
HBD £61 B £8.50 L £15 D £15
CC: MC Vi Am DC Swi Delt

How to get there: Situated north of Colchester
by the A12/A120 Ardleigh junction.

115 George

★ ★ ★

116 High Street, Colchester, Essex, CO1 1TD
Tel: 01206 578494 Fax: 01206 761732
Email: colcgeorge@aol.com
47 bedrs
CC: MC Vi Am DC Swi Delt

How to get there: Follow signs for Colchester
Town Centre. Once on the High Street, the hotel
is ¹/₂ mile down on the left-hand side.

116 Maison Talbooth Hotel

Blue Ribbon Winner

★ ★ ★ 🏮 🏮 🏮

Stratford Road, Dedham, Colchester,
Essex, CO7 6HN
Tel: 01206 322367 Fax: 01206 322752
Email: maison@talbooth.co.uk
Web: www.talbooth.com

Tranquility is the essence of this Victorian house with its imposing views over the Stow valley. Its restaurant is the renowned Le Talbooth, a short distance away along the riverbank.
10 bedrs SB £120 DB £155 HBD £100 L £16.50 D £22 CC: MC Vi Am DC Swi Delt

117 Marks Tey Hotel

★★★
London Road, Marks Tey, Colchester, Essex, CO6 1DU
Tel: 01206 210001 Fax: 01206 212167
Email: info@marksteyhotel.co.uk
Web: www.marksteyhotel.co.uk

This modern hotel and leisure club, ideally located close to the historic Roman town of Colchester, features 110 bedrooms, 12 conference and training rooms, superb restaurant and lounge bar.
110 bedrs SB £87.95 DB £102.90 HBD £56 B £8.95 L £11.50 D £16.50
CC: MC Vi Am DC Swi Delt

How to get there: From A12, take A120. At roundabout, take third exit to Colchester, at next roundabout first exit, Copford/Colchester. Hotel on left.

118 Rose & Crown Hotel

★★★★ ⍩ ⍩
East Street, Colchester, Essex, CO1 2TZ
Tel: 01206 866677 Fax: 01206 866616
CC: None accepted

119 Travelodge Colchester

Travel Accommodation
A12, London Road, Feering, Colchester, Essex, CO5 9EP
Tel: 08700 850 950
Web: www.travelodge.co.uk
39 bedrs B £4.25
CC: MC Vi Am DC Swi Delt

Cranbrook, Kent

120 Southgate — Little Fowlers

Rye Road, Hawkhurst, near Cranbrook, Kent, TN18 5DA
Tel: 01580 752526 Fax: 01580 752526
Email: susan.woodard@southgate.uk.net
Web: www.southgate.uk.net/
2 bedrs SB £40 DB £55
CC: None accepted

How to get there: From centre of Hawkhurst village by traffic lights take A268 Rye Road. After approx. ¼ mile, turn into signposted driveway. We are between Queens and Tudor Court-hotels.

Crawley, West Sussex

121 Travelodge Crawley

Travel Accommodation
Off A23, Church Road, Lowfield Heath, Crawley, West Sussex, RH11 0PQ
Tel: 08700 850 950
Web: www.travelodge.co.uk
186 bedrs B £4.25
CC: MC Vi Am DC Swi Delt

122 Waterhall Country House

◆◆◆
Prestwood Lane, Ifield Wood, near Crawley, West Sussex, RH11 0LA
Tel: 01293 520002 Fax: 01293 539905
Email: waterhallcountryhouse@lineone.net
Web: www.smoothhound.co.uk/hotels/waterhall
11 bedrs SB £35 DB £45
CC: MC Vi Am Swi Delt JCB

How to get there: Exit J10 M23, A2011 Crawley Avenue. Right at third roundabout into Ifield Avenue. Continue for two miles, Prestwood Lane on left.

Crowborough, East Sussex

123 Plough and Horses

◆ ◆ ◆ ◆

Walshes Road, Crowborough,
East Sussex, TN6 3RE
Tel: 01892 652614 Fax: 01892 652614
15 bedrs CC: MC Vi Swi Delt

⟨icons⟩

How to get there: A26 Tunbridge Wells to
Crowborough. First left at Boars Head
roundabout. Cross junction with Crowborough
Hill to the end of Tollwood Road.

Croydon, Surrey

124 Coulsdon Manor

★ ★ ★ ★ 🐾 🐾 🐾

Coulsdon Court Road, Old Coulsdon, Croydon,
Surrey, CR5 2LL
Tel: 020 8668 0414 Fax: 020 8668 3118
Email: coulsdonmanor@marstonhotels.com
Web: www.marstonhotels.com

MARSTON HOTELS

35 bedrs SB £115 DB £149 HBS £82.50
HBD £82.50 B £12 L £16.50 D £28
CC: MC Vi Am DC Swi Delt

⟨icons⟩

How to get there: Follow M2 towards Croydon.
Drive through Coulsdon on A23. Take turning right
into Stoats Nest Road. Hotel is one mile on right.

125 Croydon Park Hotel

★ ★ ★ ★

7 Altyre Road, Croydon, Surrey, CR9 5AA
Tel: 020 8401 0900 Fax: 020 8286 7676
Email: reservations@croydonparkhotel.co.uk
Web: www.croydonparkhotel.co.uk

The hotel has an excellent reputation as a 4-star
leisure destination, offering extensive facilities
and a prime location, with easy access by train
to London Victoria and Gatwick Airport.
211 bedrs SB £122 DB £137 HBS £139.95
HBD £86.45 B £10.50 L £17.95 D £17.95
CC: MC Vi Am DC Swi Delt

⟨icons⟩

How to get there: Enter Croydon on A235
Brighton Road. Follow signs to Fairfield Halls. At
major roundabout system, take first left exit into
Fairfield Road. Take first left into Altyre Road.

126 Selsdon Park Hotel

★ ★ ★ ★ ★ 🐾 🐾

Assington Road, Sanderstead, South Croydon,
Surrey, CR2 8YA
Tel: 020 8657 8811 Fax: 020 8651 6171
Email: selsdonpark@principalhotels.co.uk
Web: www.principalhotels.co.uk
204 bedrs
CC: MC Vi Am DC Swi Delt

⟨icons⟩

How to get there: On A2022 10 minutes from
East Croydon railway station, 15 minutes from
M25 Junction 6, 13 miles from Central London.

127 Hayesthorpe Hotel

★ ★

48-52 St. Augustine Avenue, South Croydon,
Surrey, CR2 6JJ
Tel: 020 8688 8120 Fax: 020 8680 1099
Email: hayesthorpe@ukonline.co.uk
Web: www.hayesthorpe.co.uk
Closed Christmas
25 bedrs SB £50 DB £55 HBS £67.50 HBD £40
D £12.50
CC: MC Vi Am DC Swi Delt

⟨icons⟩

How to get there: Take A23 to Croydon. Turn left
at Hilton Hotel into Waddon Way. Proceed to
roundabout, turn right and take first left into St.
Augustine Avenue.

128 Kirkdale Hotel

♦♦♦♦ ✆

22 St. Peters Road, Croydon, Surrey, CR0 1HD
Tel: 020 8688 5898 Fax: 020 8680 6001
Email: enquiries@kirkdalehotel.co.uk
Web: www.kirkdalehotel.co.uk
Closed Christmas to New Year

A character Victorian building with 19 rooms located very close to Croydon's bustling business, shopping and restaurant area. The hotel has awards for friendly service, lovely breakfast and 'Croydon in Bloom'.
19 bedrs SB £55 DB £75
CC: MC Vi DC Swi Delt JCB
How to get there: Leave M25 at Junction seven and follow signs for Croydon (9 miles). A few minutes from East and South Croydon stations.

Dartford, Kent

129 Rowhill Grange Hotel

★★★★★ ☕ ☕ ☕

Wilmington, Dartford, Kent, DA2 7QH
Tel: 01322 615136 Fax: 01322 615137
Email: admin@rowhillgrange.com
Web: www.rowhillgrange.com
Children minimum age: 5

With nine acres of mature gardens and the finest health spa in the south, Rowhill Grange is ideal for business or pleasure — just two miles from the M25.

38 bedrs HBS £134 HBD £99 B £8.95 L £19.95 D £29.95 CC: MC Vi Am DC Swi Delt

How to get there: Leave M20 junction 1 / M25 Junction three to Swanley. Follow B2175 through three roundabouts to Hextable on B258. Hotel is 1½ miles on left opposite garage.

130 Travelodge Dartford

Travel Accommodation
Charles Street, Off Crossways Boulevard, Dartford, Kent, DA2 6QQ
Tel: 08700 850 950
Web: www.travelodge.co.uk
65 bedrs B £4.25 CC: MC Vi Am DC Swi Delt

Deal, Kent

131 Kilgour House

♦♦♦♦ ✖

22 Gilford Road, Deal, Kent, CT14 7DJ
Tel: 01304 368311
Email: kilgourhouse@hotmail.com
Web: www.kilgourhouse.com
5 bedrs SB £22.50 DB £40 CC: None accepted

Dorchester-on-Thames, Oxfordshire

132 George Hotel

★★★★ ☕ ☕

High Street, Dorchester-on-Thames, Oxfordshire, OX10 7HH
Tel: 01865 340404 Fax: 01865 341620
17 bedrs SB £65 DB £85 B £10 L £15 D £25
CC: MC Vi Am Swi Delt

133 White Hart

★★★

High Street, Dorchester-on-Thames, Oxfordshire, OX10 7HN
Tel: 01865 340074 Fax: 01865 341082
Email: whitehartdorches@aol.com
Web: oxford-restaurants-hotels.co.uk
23 bedrs SB £70 DB £80 B £7 L £8 D £20
CC: MC Vi Am DC Swi Delt
How to get there: Just off A415/A4074 (from M40 Junction 6). Nearest rail station: Didcot.

Southeast

Dorking, Surrey

134 Heritage Hotels – Burford Bridge

★★★★ ℞

At the foot of Boxhill, Dorking,
Surrey, RH5 6BX
Tel: 0870 4008283 Fax: 01306 880386
Web: www.heritage-hotels.com
57 bedrs SB £175 DB £175 HBS £110 HBD £65
B £13.50 L £15 D £20
CC: MC Vi Am DC Swi

How to get there: Junction nine of M25, four
miles south on A24. Two miles north of Dorking.

135 Gatton Manor Hotel

★★★ ℞

Standon Lane, Ockley, near Dorking,
Surrey, RH5 5PQ
Tel: 01306 627555 Fax: 01306 627713
Email: gattonmanor@enterprise.net
Web: www.gattonmanor.co.uk
18 bedrs
CC: MC Vi Am DC Swi Delt

How to get there: Situated off A24/A29 between
Horsham and Dorking.

136 Heritage Hotels – White Horse

★★★

High Street, Dorking,
Surrey, RH4 1BE
Tel: 0870 400 8282 Fax: 01306 887241
Email: heritagehotels_dorking-
white_horse@fortehotels.com
Web: www.heritage-hotels.com
78 bedrs B £12.50 L £7.50 D £14.95
CC: MC Vi Am DC Swi

How to get there: Take Junction nine off M25 —
six miles south on A24, located on the High
Street in Dorking.

137 Travelodge Dorking

Travel Accommodation
A25, Reigate Road, Dorking,
Surrey, RH4 1QD
Tel: 08700 850 950
Web: www.travelodge.co.uk
54 bedrs B £4.25
CC: MC Vi Am DC Swi Delt

Dover, Kent

138 Churchill

★★★

Dover Waterfront, Dover, Kent, CT17 9BP
Tel: 01304 203633 Fax: 01304 216320
Email: enquiries@churchill-hotel.com
Web: www.churchill-hotel.com
66 bedrs SB £68 DB £97 HBS £76.50
HBD £59.50 B £9 L £12.50 D £18.95
CC: MC Vi Am DC Swi Delt

How to get there: From A20 follow signs for
Hoverport, turn left onto seafront, hotel is 800
yards along.

139 Wallett's Court Country House

★★★ ℞ ℞

Westcliffe, St. Margaret's Bay, Dover,
Kent, CT15 6EW
Tel: 01304 852424 Fax: 01304 853430
Email: wc@wallettscourt.com
Web: www.wallettscourt.com

Set in the heart of White Cliffs Country, this
17th-Century hotel with highly acclaimed
restaurant and spa is simply beautiful. Relaxed
and secluded, yet only three miles from Dover.
16 bedrs SB £75 DB £90 HBS £102.50
HBD £72.50 B £6 L £13.50 D £27.50
CC: MC Vi Am DC Swi Delt

How to get there: From M2/A2 or M20/A20, signs
A258 Deal. On A258, first right for Westcliffe, St.
Margaret's-at-Cliffe. Hotel one mile on right.

140 East Lee Guest House

108 Maison Dieu Road, Dover, Kent, CT16 1RT
Tel: 01304 210176 Fax: 01304 206705
Email: eastlee@eclipse.co.uk
Web: www.eastlee.co.uk
4 bedrs DB £50 CC: MC Vi Swi Delt

How to get there: Approaching from M20/A20, at York Street roundabout, turn left and proceed straight over next roundabout. Turn right at Dover town hall. At end of street, turn right into Maison Dieu Road.

141 Number One Guest House

1 Castle Street, Dover, Kent, CT16 1QH
Tel: 01304 202007 Fax: 01304 214078
Email: res@number1guesthouse.co.uk
Web: www.number1guesthouse.co.uk
3 bedrs DB £48 CC: None accepted

How to get there: Just off A20 turn right to castle on corner before Castle Hill. A2 one mile, two minutes from port, 10 minutes from tunnel

142 Tower House

Priory Hill, Dover, Kent, CT17 0AE
Tel: 01304 208212 Fax: 01304 208212
Email: enquiries@towerhouse.net
Web: www.towerhouse.net
2 bedrs DB £50
CC: None accepted

How to get there: M20 — B2011 to Dover; turn left at roundabout, then third turning left at main traffic lights to top of Priory Hill.

143 Ardmore Private Hotel

18 Castle Hill Road, Dover, Kent, CT16 1QW
Tel: 01304 205895 Fax: 01304 208229
Email: res@ardmoreph.co.uk
Web: www.ardmoreph.co.uk
Closed Christmas
4 bedrs DB £50
CC: MC Vi Swi Delt

How to get there: On A258 next to Dover Castle. Follow signs for castle from all roads to Dover. 10 minutes to Channel Tunnel, close to ports.

144 Gateway Hovertel

Snargate Street, Dover,
Kent, CT17 9BZ
Tel: 01304 205479 Fax: 01304 211504
Email: dspeters@hovertel.fsnet.co.uk
Closed closed Christmas & New Year
27 bedrs DB £50
CC: MC Vi Am DC Swi Delt JCB

How to get there: Follow M20/A20 into Dover over Hoverport roundabout on the left overlooking marine close to ferry and cruise terminals.

145 Hubert House Guest House

9 Castle Hill Road, Dover,
Kent, CT16 1QW
Tel: 01304 202253 Fax: 01304 210142
Email: huberthouse@btinternet.com
Web: www.huberthouse.co.uk
Closed October
6 bedrs SB £35 DB £50
CC: MC Vi Swi Delt JCB

How to get there: Situated on the A258 Deal road at the bottom of Castle Hill, close to Dover town centre.

146 Pennyfarthing

109 Maison Dieu Road, Dover,
Kent, CT16 1RT
Tel: 01304 205563 Fax: 01304 204439
Email: pennyfarthing.dover@btinternet.com
6 bedrs SB £26 DB £44
CC: None accepted

147 St. Martins Guest House

17 Castle Hill Road, Dover,
Kent, CT16 1QW
Tel: 01304 205938 Fax: 01304 208229
Email: res@stmartinsgh.co.uk
Web: www.stmartinsgh.co.uk
Closed Christmas
6 bedrs SB £35 DB £48
CC: MC Vi Swi Delt

How to get there: On the A258. Follow signs to Dover Castle from all roads to Dover. 10 minutes from Channel Tunnel, minutes from ports.

Southeast

148 Whitmore Guest House

◆ ◆ ◆ 🍴 🍷

261 Folkestone Road, Dover, Kent, CT17 9LL
Tel: 01304 203080 Fax: 01304 240110
Email: whitmoredover@aol.com
Web: www.smoothhound.co.uk/hotels/whitmore
Closed Christmas
4 bedrs SB £25 DB £44
CC: MC Vi Swi Delt JCB

How to get there: Leave M20/A20 at junction
with B2011. Take first exit off roundabout at
bottom of slip road (Folkestone Road). Guest
house three miles on right.

Dunkirk, Kent

149 Travelodge Dunkirk

Travel Accommodation
A2 Northbound, Gate Restaurant, Dunkirk,
Kent, ME13 9LN
Tel: 08700 850 950
Web: www.travelodge.co.uk
40 bedrs B £4.25
CC: MC Vi Am DC Swi Delt

Dunstable, Bedfordshire

150 Hanover International Hotel Dunstable

★ ★ ★ 🅡

Church Street, Dunstable, Bedfordshire, LU5 4RT
Tel: 01582 662201 Fax: 01582 696422
Email: info@hanover-dunstable.fsnet.co.uk
Web: www.hanover-international.com

HANOVER INTERNATIONAL
HOTELS & CLUBS

An original hotel with many exquisite features
offering old English charm. Close to Whipsnade,
Woburn and other local attractions.
68 bedrs SB £109 DB £119
CC: MC Vi Am DC Swi Delt
How to get there: Off Junction 11 of the M1.
Follow signs to Dunstable town centre. Pass
under bridge, hotel 200m further, opposite the
Priory church on the right.

Dymchurch, Kent

151 Waterside Guest House

◆ ◆ ◆ ◆ 🍴

15 Hythe Road, Dymchurch, Kent, TN29 0LN
Tel: 01303 872253 Fax: 01303 872253
Email: info@watersideguesthouse.co.uk
Web: www.watersideguesthouse.co.uk

Comfortable accommodation with excellent
cuisine. Overlooking Romney Marsh. Sandy
beach close by. Ideal for exploring Kent and
East Sussex. Ashford International station and
Channel tunnel approx 20 minutes away.
5 bedrs SB £30 DB £45 HBS £37 HBD £29.50
D £4.50
CC: MC Vi Swi Delt
How to get there: From M20 take Junction 11.
Follow signs to Hythe. Turn right onto A259.
Hotel approximately seven miles on right-hand
side.

East Grinstead, West Sussex

152 Gravetye Manor Hotel

Gold Ribbon Winner

★★★

Vowels Lane, near East Grinstead,
West Sussex, RH19 4LJ
Tel: 01342 810567 Fax: 01342 810080
Email: info@gravetyemanor.co.uk
Web: www.gravetyemanor.co.uk
Children minimum age: 7
18 bedrs SB £160 DB £200 B £14 L £56 D £56
CC: MC Vi Swi Delt

How to get there: Leave M23 at Exit 10, and
take A264 towards East Grinstead. After two
miles, at roundabout, take third exit (B2028)
towards Turners Hill.

153 Woodbury House

★★★

Lewes Road, East Grinstead,
West Sussex, RH19 3UD
Tel: 01342 313657 Fax: 01342 314801
Email: stay@woodburyhouse.com
Web: www.woodburyhouse.com
13 bedrs SB £85 DB £95 HBS £95 HBD £120
B £7.50 L £13.50 D £17.95
CC: MC Vi Am DC Swi Delt

How to get there: Take the M25 then M23,
leaving at Junction 10. Take the A264 to East
Grinstead and A22 towards Eastbourne. Hotel is
¹/₂ mile south of town centre.

Eastbourne, East Sussex

154 Grand Hotel

★★★★★ ℞ ℞

King Edward's Parade, Eastbourne,
East Sussex, BN21 4EQ
Tel: 01323 412345 Fax: 01323 412233
Email: reservations@grandeastbourne.co.uk
Web: www.grandeastbourne.co.uk

England's finest resort hotel, The Grand Hotel in
Eastbourne reflects the glories of Victorian
architecture. Recently restored, this magnificent
hotel offers award-winning cuisine, health club
and conscientious, friendly service.
152 bedrs SB £130 DB £165 HBS £150
HBD £125.50 CC: MC Vi Am DC Swi Delt

How to get there: Located at west end of
Eastbourne seafront.

155 Chatsworth

★★★

Grand Parade, Eastbourne,
East Sussex, BN21 3YR
Tel: 01323 411016 Fax: 01323 643270
Email: stay@chatsworth-hotel.com
Web: www.chatsworth-hotel.com
47 bedrs SB £55 DB £85 HBS £58 HBD £98
B £9.50 L £7.50 D £18.50
CC: MC Vi Am DC Swi Delt

How to get there: M23 towards Brighton; A27 to
Polegate; A22 to Eastbourne. Follow seafront
signs. Hotel between pier and bandstand.

156 Hydro Hotel

★★★

Mount Road, Eastbourne, East Sussex, BN20 7HZ
Tel: 01323 720643 Fax: 01323 641167
Email: sales@hydrohotel.co.uk
Web: www.hydrohotel.co.uk

An elegant traditional hotel offering the highest
standards of cuisine and service. Situated in a
unique garden setting with panoramic sea views.
84 bedrs SB £65 DB £125 HBS £75 HBD £75
B £8.50 L £9.95 D £18.50
CC: MC Vi Am Swi

How to get there: Proceed along King Edwards
Parade to the Grand Hotel. Note sign Hydro
Hotel. Proceed up South Cliff and the Hydro
Hotel signs are visible.

Southeast

157 Lansdowne Hotel

★★★

King Edward's Parade, Eastbourne,
East Sussex, BN21 4EE
Tel: 01323 725174 Fax: 01323 739721
Email: the.lansdowne@btinternet.com
Web: www.the.lansdowne.btinternet.co.uk
Closed 1–18 January
112 bedrs SB £55 DB £87 HBS £67.50
HBD £66 B £8.75 L £13.95 D £17.95
CC: MC Vi Am DC Swi Delt JCB

How to get there: M23, A23, A27, A22 or A259
to Eastbourne. Hotel at west end of seafront
(B2103) facing Western Lawns.
See advert on facing page

158 Mansion Hotel

★★★

Grand Parade, Eastbourne,
East Sussex, BN21 3YS
Tel: 01323 727411 Fax: 01323 720665
95 bedrs SB £38 DB £76 HBS £53 HBD £53
B £7.75 L £6.95 D £12.95
CC: MC Vi Swi Delt JCB

How to get there: M25 leave at junction seven
to Gatwick — Via M23 join A27 — Lewes
heading to Eastbourne. Follow signs to seafront.
We are between the pier and bandstand.

159 Princes Hotel

★★★

Lascelles Terrace, Eastbourne,
East Sussex, BN21 4BL
Tel: 01323 722056 Fax: 01323 727469
Email: princes-hotel@btconnect.com
Web: www.princes-hotel.co.uk
Closed January

A friendly family-run hotel situated in a beautiful
unspoilt Victorian terrace adjacent to seafront,
close to the theatres and a short level walk from
main shopping area.
45 bedrs SB £34 DB £60 HBS £40 HBD £37.50
D £14.50
CC: MC Vi Am DC Swi Delt

160 Wish Tower Hotel

★★★

King Edward's Parade, Eastbourne,
East Sussex, BN21 4EB
Tel: 01323 722676 Fax: 01323 721474
Email: wishtower@british-trust-hotels.com
Web: www.british-trust-hotels.com

Sea front location. Friendly and welcoming
hotel. Close to town centre. Easy walking
distance of the famous Prom and Victorian pier.
Traditional seaside conference and leisure break
hotel overlooking the Promenade and 'Carpet
Gardens'.
61 bedrs SB £30 DB £60 HBS £40 HBD £40
B £8 L £5.95 D £18
CC: MC Vi DC Swi Delt JCB

161 York House Hotel

★★★

Royal Parade, Eastbourne,
East Sussex, BN22 7AP
Tel: 01323 412918 Fax: 01323 646238
Email: frontdesk@yorkhousehotel.co.uk
Web: www.yorkhousehotel.co.uk
88 bedrs SB £45 DB £90 HBS £61 HBD £61
B £9 L £12.50 D £16
CC: MC Vi Am DC Swi Delt

How to get there: On Eastbourne seafront, 1/4 of
a mile east of the pier.

162 Congress Hotel

★★
31–37 Carlisle Road, Eastbourne,
East Sussex, BN21 4JS
Tel: 01323 732118 Fax: 01323 720016
Closed January to February

Located by main theatres in a level area.
Ramped entrance, so accessible for wheelchair
users. Family owned and managed — 'Service
our aim'.
62 bedrs SB £30 DB £60 HBS £33 HBD £33
B £5 D £10 CC: MC Vi Swi Delt

How to get there: Opposite Congress Theatre,
approx 150 yards from the seafront. Follow
signs for 'Theatres'.

163 Langham Hotel

★★
Royal Parade, Eastbourne,
East Sussex, BN22 7AH
Tel: 01323 731451 Fax: 01323 646623
Email: info@langhamhotel.co.uk
Web: www.langhamhotel.co.uk
Closed January
87 bedrs SB £50 DB £80 HBS £63 HBD £107
B £5.50 L £9.50 D £13.50
CC: MC Vi Am Swi Delt

How to get there: Follow Eastbourne seafront
signs from A27, A22 and A259. Hotel is ³/₄ of a
mile east of the pier near Redoubt Gardens.

164 Lathom Hotel

★★
Howard Square, Eastbourne,
East Sussex, BN21 4BG
Tel: 01323 641986 Fax: 01323 416405
45 bedrs CC: MC Vi
How to get there: 25 yards from seafront,
between bandstand and Wish Tower Slopes.
Turn right at TGWU Hotel.

Lansdowne Hotel

Traditional, privately owned seafront hotel
close to theatres, shops and Conference
Centre. Established since 1912. Attractive
Regency Bar. Elegant lounges and foyer
facing sea. 22 lock-up garages. English
cuisine. 112 ensuite bedrooms. Leisure Breaks
November–mid-May. Duplicate/Social Bridge
Weekends. Golfing holidays all year. A warm
welcome awaits you!

King Edward's Parade, Eastbourne, East Sussex BN21 4EE

Tel: 01323 725174   Fax: 01323 739721
Email: the.lansdowne@btinternet.com
Web: www.the.lansdowne.btinternet.co.uk

165 New Wilmington Hotel

★★
25 Compton Street, Eastbourne,
East Sussex, BN21 4DU
Tel: 01323 721219 Fax: 01323 745255
Email: info@new-wilmington-hotel.co.uk
Web: www.new-wilmington-hotel.co.uk
40 bedrs SB £42 DB £78 HBS £53 HBD £48
B £7.50 L £4 D £13
CC: MC Vi Am Swi Delt

How to get there: Follow signs to seafront,
keeping sea on left. At Wilmington Gardens turn
right. At end of road turn left.

166 Oban

★★
King Edward's Parade, Eastbourne,
East Sussex, BN21 4DS
Tel: 01323 731581 Fax: 01323 721994
Closed December to March
31 bedrs SB £28 DB £56 HBS £43 HBD £98
B £6.95 L £2 D £15 CC: MC Vi Swi Delt

How to get there: The Oban is on the seafront,
facing the Wish Tower, minutes from the Winter
Garden, theatres, tennis and bandstand.

Southeast

167 West Rocks Hotel

★★

Grand Parade, Eastbourne,
East Sussex, BN21 4DL
Tel: 01323 725217 Fax: 01323 720421
Children minimum age: 3
Closed mid-November to 1 March
45 bedrs SB £40 DB £56 HBS £53.50
HBD £41.50 B £7.50 L £13.50
CC: MC Vi Am DC Swi Delt JCB

How to get there: On Grand Parade midway
between central band stand and Wish Tower.

168 Pinnacle Point
Little Gem

♦♦♦♦♦

Foyle Way, Upper Duke's Drive, Eastbourne,
East Sussex, BN20 7XL
Tel: 01323 726666 Fax: 01323 743946
Web: www.pinnaclepoint.co.uk
Children minimum age: 12
Closed Christmas and New Year
3 bedrs SB £60 DB £100 CC: None accepted

How to get there: On Eastbourne sea front, at
the foot of the downs on the seaward side.

169 Brayscroft Hotel

♦♦♦♦

13 South Cliff Avenue, Eastbourne,
East Sussex, BN20 7AH
Tel: 01323 647005 Fax: 01323 720705
Email: brayscroft@hotmail.com
Web: www.brayscrofthotel.co.uk
Children minimum age: 14
5 bedrs SB £29.50 DB £59 HBS £41.50
HBD £41.50 D £12 CC: MC Vi Swi Delt JCB

How to get there: B2103 (Grand Parade) from
pier towards Beachy Head. Past Grand Hotel,
take right incline up South Cliff, then first right.

170 Chalk Farm Hotel

♦♦♦♦

Coopers Hill, Willingdon, Eastbourne,
East Sussex, BN20 9JD
Tel: 01323 503800 Fax: 01323 520331
8 bedrs CC: MC Vi Am DC Swi Delt

How to get there: Take A22 London-Eastbourne
road into Eastbourne, past Polegate traffic
lights. At next major traffic lights turn right into
Coopers Hill. Hotel 200 yards on right.

171 Bay Lodge Hotel

♦♦♦

61–62 Royal Parade, Eastbourne,
East Sussex, BN22 7AQ
Tel: 01323 732515 Fax: 01323 735009
Email: beryl@mnewson.freeserve.co.uk
12 bedrs SB £25 DB £50 HBS £33 HBD £33
B £4 D £8
CC: MC Vi Am Swi Delt

172 Sheldon Hotel

♦♦♦

9–11 Burlington Place, Eastbourne,
East Sussex, BN21 4AS
Tel: 01323 724120 Fax: 01323 430406
24 bedrs SB £31 DB £62
HBS £39 HBD £39
CC: MC Vi Am DC Swi Delt

How to get there: From pier, travel west towards
bandstand. Turn right by side of Cavendish
Hotel. Sheldon Hotel is 150m on left.

173 Sherwood Hotel

♦♦♦

7 Lascelles Terrace, Eastbourne,
East Sussex, BN21 4BJ
Tel: 01323 724002 Fax: 01323 439989
Email: sherwood-hotel@supanet.com
Web: www.sherwood-hotel-eastbourne.co.uk
14 bedrs SB £25 DB £25
HBS £32 HBD £32
B £3.50 D £7
CC: None accepted

How to get there: From A22 follow directions to
town west and theatres. Lascelles Terrace runs
between Devonshire Park and seafront.

Eastleigh, Hampshire

174 Travelodge Southampton (Eastleigh)

Travel Accommodation
A335, Ham Farm, Tyford Road, Eastleigh,
Hampshire, SO50 4LF
Tel: 08700 850 950
Web: www.travelodge.co.uk
61 bedrs B £4.25
CC: MC Vi Am DC Swi Delt

175 13 Camelia Grove

Fair Oak, near Eastleigh, Hampshire, SO50 7GZ
Tel: 02380 692822
2 bedrs SB £16.50 DB £33
CC: None accepted

How to get there: M3 J11. Left onto B3354,
through Twyford to Fair Oak. Up Mortimer Lane
on left, fourth turning on left.

Egham, Surrey

176 Runnymede Hotel & Spa

★★★★★ ℞ ℞ ℞
Windsor Road, Egham, Surrey, TW20 0AG
Tel: 01784 436171 Fax: 01784 436340
Email: info@runnymedehotel.com
Web: www.runnymedehotel.com

There's much more to life at the Runnymede:
renowned friendly service, private spa, tennis,
two restaurants, award-winning cuisine, river
terrace; Windsor, Eton, Savill Gardens, the
Thames — and much more.
180 bedrs SB £175.95 DB £227.90 HBS £88
HBD £88 B £13.95 L £19.95 D £26.95
CC: MC Vi Am DC Swi Delt

How to get there: Leave M25 at Junction 13.
Take A308 to Egham/Windsor. The Runnymede
is on the right at the entrance to Runnymede
Meadows.

Emsworth, Hampshire

177 Brookfield Hotel

★★★ ℞ ℞
Havant Road, Emsworth, Hampshire, PO10 7LF
Tel: 01243 373363 Fax: 01243 376342
40 bedrs
CC: MC Vi Am DC Swi Delt

How to get there: From A3(M), take M27 to
Chichester eastbound. At Emsworth turn off
onto A259 Havant road.

178 Travelodge Emsworth

Travel Accommodation
A27 Eastbound, Emsworth,
Hampshire, PO10 7RB
Tel: 08700 850 950
Web: www.travelodge.co.uk
36 bedrs B £4.25
CC: MC Vi Am DC Swi Delt

179 Jingles Hotel

♦ ♦ ♦
77 Horndean Road, Emsworth,
Hampshire, PO10 7PU
Tel: 01243 373755 Fax: 01243 373755
14 bedrs SB £29.50 DB £54 HBS £39.50
HBD £37 B £7.25 L £12.50 D £14
CC: MC Vi Am Swi Delt

How to get there: From A259 in Emsworth, head
north on the B2148 towards Rowlands Castle
for approximately one mile.

Enfield, Middlesex

180 West Lodge Park Hotel

★★★★ ℞ ℞
Cockfosters Road, Hadley Wood,
Hertfordshire, EN4 0PY
Tel: 020 8216 3900 Fax: 020 8216 3937
Email: info@westlodgepark.com
Web: www.westlodgepark.com
59 bedrs SB £110 DB £155 B £11 L £22 D £35
CC: MC Vi Am DC Swi Delt

How to get there: Exit J24 M25. Follow A111
towards Cockfosters. After one mile hotel is on
left-hand side.

Southeast

181 Royal Chace Hotel

★★★★

The Ridgeway, Enfield, Middlesex, EN2 8AR
Tel: 020 8884 8181 Fax: 020 8884 8150
Web: www.royal-chace.com
92 bedrs SB £110 DB £125 B £9.50 D £19.95
CC: MC Vi Am DC Swi Delt

How to get there: Leave M25 at Junction 24. Take A1005 towards Enfield. The Royal Chace Hotel is situated three miles along on right-hand side.

182 Oak Lodge Hotel

★★

80 Village Road, Enfield, Middlesex, EN1 2EU
Tel: 020 8360 7082
Email: oaklodge@fs.mail.net
Web: www.oaklodgehotel.co.uk
7 bedrs SB £79 DB £89.50 HBS £125 HBD £75
B £10.50 L £15 D £20
CC: MC Vi Am DC Swi Delt

How to get there: Leave M25 at junction 25. Turn right at 11th set of lights south along A10. Turn right at next lights into A105. Hotel ¼ mile on right.

183 The Enfield Hotel

★★

52 Rowan Tree Road, Enfield, Middlesex, EN2 8PW
Tel: 020 8366 3511 Fax: 020 8366 2432
Web: www.meridianleisure.com
34 bedrs SB £85 DB £95 HBS £105 HBD £67.50
B £5.75 L £4.25 D £3.25
CC: MC Vi Am DC Swi Delt

How to get there: M25 J24, A1005 pass hospital on left. At mini-roundabout straight across, third turning left, Bycullar road next left.

184 Epsom Downs Hotel

♦♦♦

9 Longdown Road, Epsom, Surrey, KT17 3PT
Tel: 01372 740643 Fax: 01372 723259
11 bedrs SB £75 DB £85 B £5
CC: MC Vi Am Swi Delt

How to get there: One mile from town centre.

185 Solent Hotel

★★★★★

Solent Business Park, Whiteley, Fareham, Hampshire, PO15 7AJ
Tel: 01489 880000 Fax: 01489 880007
Email: solent@shireinns.co.uk
Web: www.shireinns.co.uk
111 bedrs SB £130 DB £158 B £10.50 L £15
D £28.50
CC: MC Vi Am DC Swi Delt

How to get there: Leave M27 at Junction nine to Whiteley. Turn left at first roundabout. Hotel on your right.

186 Bembridge House

♦♦♦♦

Osborn Road, Fareham, Hampshire, PO16 7DS
Tel: 01329 317050 Fax: 01329 317050
Email: ian@bembridgehouse.freeserve.co.uk
Web: www.bembridgehouse.co.uk

Character rooms in lovingly-restored Victorian residence, in own quiet grounds. In town centre conservation area, minutes' walk from Ferneham Hall, shopping precinct and many varied restaurants. A ten-minute walk from the station. Gargantuan breakfasts. Cheerful welcome. Most needs satisfied!
5 bedrs SB £40 DB £50
CC: MC Vi Swi Delt JCB

How to get there: Exit M27 J11. Follow signs to Fareham town centre, then Ferneham Hall. Bembridge House is almost directly opposite.

Making a booking?

Don't forget to mention RAC Hotels and Bed & Breakfast 2002.

187 Avenue House Hotel

◆ ◆ ◆

22 The Avenue, Fareham, Hampshire, PO14 1NS
Tel: 01329 232175 Fax: 01329 232196
Children minimum age: 10
19 bedrs
CC: MC Vi Am DC
[symbols]
How to get there: M27 Junction nine
(signposted Fareham West), A27 to Fareham.
After five minutes, Fareham village on right,
hotel 300 yards further on left.

Faringdon, Oxfordshire

188 Faringdon Hotel

★ ★

1 Market Place, Faringdon, Oxfordshire, SN7 7HL
Tel: 01367 240536 Fax: 01367 243250

20 bedrs SB £60 DB £70 B £5 D £10
CC: MC Vi Am DC Swi Delt
[symbols]
How to get there: Nearest bus/railway stations
Swindon 12 miles Oxford 18 miles. M40 20
miles M4 14 miles. Faringdon is on A420.

Farnborough, Hampshire

189 Falcon Hotel

★ ★ ★

68 Farnborough Road, Farnborough,
Hampshire, GU14 6TH
Tel: 01252 545378 Fax: 01252 522539
Email: falcon@meridianleisure.com
Web: www.meridianleisure.com
30 bedrs SB £86 DB £99
B £10.95 L £14.95 D £19.95
CC: MC Vi Am DC Swi Delt JCB
[symbols]

Farnham, Surrey

190 Bishop's Table Hotel

★ ★ ★ ♔ ♔ ♔

27 West Street, Farnham, Surrey, GU9 7DR
Tel: 01252 710222 Fax: 01252 733494
Email: welcome@bishopstable.com
Web: www.bishopstable.com
Closed 26 December to 4 January
17 bedrs SB £95 DB £120 B £14.50 L £10.50
D £15
CC: MC Vi Am DC
[symbols]
How to get there: Take M3 Junction 4, follow
'Birdworld' signs and Farnham town centre
signs. Located nextdoor to library.

191 Heritage Hotels – The Bush Hotel

★ ★ ★

The Borough, Farnham, Surrey, GU10 4QQ
Tel: 0870 400 8225 Fax: 01252 733530
83 bedrs
CC: MC Vi Am DC Swi Delt
[symbols]
How to get there: Follow signs to town centre.
At lights turn left and immediate right into hotel
car park on South Street.

Faversham, Kent

192 Travelodge Faversham

Travel Accommodation
A299, Thanet Way, Faversham, Kent, ME8 9EL
Tel: 08700 850 950
Web: www.travelodge.co.uk
40 bedrs B £4.25 CC: MC Vi Am DC Swi Delt
[symbols]

Fleet, Hampshire

193 Lismoyne Hotel

★ ★ ★

Church Road, Fleet, Hampshire, GU13 8NA
Tel: 01252 628555 Fax: 01252 811761
62 bedrs SB £95 DB £145 HBS £110
HBD £87.50 B £9.95 L £14.95 D £18.95
CC: MC Vi Am DC Swi
[symbols]
How to get there: Approach town on B3013.
Cross over railway bridge and continue to town
centre. Pass through traffic lights and take
fourth right. Hotel ¼ mile on left.

Southeast

Folkestone, Kent

194 Clifton Hotel

★★★

The Leas, Clifton Gardens, Folkestone,
Kent, CT20 2EB
Tel: 01303 851231 Fax: 01303 223949
Email: reservations@thecliftonhotel.com
Web: www.thecliftonhotel.com
80 bedrs
CC: MC Vi Am DC Swi Delt

How to get there: From M20 Junction 13, The
Clifton Hotel is ¼ mile west of town centre on
A259.

195 Lighthouse Inn & Restaurant

111 Old Dover Road, Capel le Ferne,
near Folkestone, Kent, CT18 7HT
Tel: 01303 223300 Fax: 01303 256501
Web: www.the-lighthouse-inn.fsnet.co.uk
4 bedrs SB £40 DB £60
CC: MC Vi Am Swi Delt

How to get there: M20/A20 leave B2011 Capel
le Ferne, Old Dover Road (cliff top road,
overlooking the sea).

Fontwell, Sussex

196 Travelodge Fontwell

Travel Accommodation
A27/A29, Arundel Road, Fontwell,
Sussex, BN18 0SB
Tel: 08700 850 950
Web: www.travelodge.co.uk
63 bedrs B £4.25
CC: MC Vi Am DC Swi Delt

Fordingbridge, Hampshire

197 Ashburn Hotel

★★

Station Road, Fordingbridge,
Hampshire, SP16 1JP
Tel: 01425 652060 Fax: 01425 652150

Forest Row, East Sussex

198 Ashdown Park Hotel & Country Club
Gold Ribbon Winner

★★★★

Wych Cross, Forest Row, East Sussex, RH18 5JR
Tel: 01342 824988 Fax: 01342 826206
Email: reservations@ashdownpark.com
Web: www.ashdownpark.com

A stunning 186-acre country house hotel,
Ashdown Park offers log fires, gourmet cuisine,
fine wines, panoramic views, golf, beautiful
bedrooms and a luxurious country club. Ideal for
relaxation and indulgence.
107 bedrs SB £130 DB £165 HBS £150
HBD £112.50 B £13.75 L £23 D £37
CC: MC Vi Am DC Swi Delt

How to get there: M23 J10. Take A264 to East
Grinstead. Take A22 to Eastbourne through
Forest Row. Continue on Forest Row for two
miles. At Wych Cross turn left to Hartfield.
Ashdown Park is ¾ of a mile on the right.

Frimley Green, Surrey

199 Lakeside International Hotel

★★★

Wharf Road, Frimley Green, Surrey, GU16 6JR
Tel: 01252 838000 Fax: 01252 837857

Gatwick Airport

200 Copthorne Hotel
Effingham Park Gatwick

★★★★

West Park Road, Copthorne, West Sussex,
RH10 3EU
Tel: 01342 714994 Fax: 01342 713661
Email: sales.effingham@mill-cop.com
Web: www.millennium-hotels.com

Former stately home set in 40 acres of peaceful parkland. Superb leisure facilities including a nine-hole golf course. Close to many local attractions. Weekend break rates also available. 122 bedrs SB £158.95 DB £172.90 B £13.95 CC: MC Vi Am DC Swi Delt

How to get there: Leave M23 at Junction 10, taking A264 towards East Grinstead. At second roundabout, turn left onto B2028. Hotel is on the right.

201 Copthorne Hotel London Gatwick

★★★★★ R R

Copthorne Road, Copthorne,
West Sussex, RH10 3PG
Tel: 01342 348800 Fax: 01342 348822
Email: coplgw@mill-cop.com
Web: www.millennium-hotels.com

Traditional, welcoming country house hotel built around a 16th century farmhouse in 100 acres of gardens. Ideal for many local attractions. Weekend break rates also available. 227 bedrs SB £158.95 DB £172.90 B £13.95 L £18.95 D £21.50 CC: MC Vi Am DC Swi Delt

How to get there: Leave M23 at Junction 10, taking A264 towards East Grinstead. At first roundabout, take third exit which is the hotel entrance.

202 Le Méridien London Gatwick

★★★★ R

North Terminal, Gatwick Airport,
West Sussex, RH6 0PH
Tel: 01293 567070 Fax: 01293 567739
Email: reservations.gatwick@lemeridien-hotels.com
Web: www.lemeridien-gatwick.com
494 bedrs B £13.95 L £16 D £19.95
CC: MC Vi Am DC Swi Delt

How to get there: M23 exit nine towards Gatwick. At roundabout proceed straight across. Next roundabout second exit. Hotel entrance on right.

203 Renaissance London Gatwick Hotel

★★★★

Povey Cross Road, Horley,
Surrey, RH6 0BE
Tel: 01293 820169 Fax: 01293 820259
Email: rhi.lgwbr.reservations.mgr
        @renaissancehotels.com
Web: www.renaissancehotels.com

Friendly modern hotel with luxurious accommodation. Also benefitting from three dining venues and an extensively-equipped health club. Conference facilities and private dining available. 24-hour airport shuttle transfer. 254 bedrs SB £125 DB £140 B £12.50 L £16.50 D £18.50 CC: MC Vi Am DC Swi Delt

How to get there: M23 J9, follow signs for North Terminal. At roundabout, take last exit, turn left at next one and hotel is 500 yards on the left.

Southeast

204 South Lodge Hotel
Gold Ribbon Winner

★★★★★ ⓡⓡⓡⓡ

Brighton Road, Lower Beeding,
West Sussex, RH13 6PS
Tel: 01403 891711 Fax: 01403 891766
Email: enquiries@southlodgehotel.co.uk
Web: www.exclusivehotels.co.uk
43 bedrs SB £185 DB £225 HBS £225
HBD £157.50 B £15 L £20 D £40
CC: MC Vi Am DC Swi Delt

How to get there: From Gatwick, take M23
southbound. Turn off onto B2110 to Handcross.
Follow road to Leonardslee Gardens. Turn left
and the hotel is on right.

205 Alexander House Hotel
Gold Ribbon Winner

★★★ ⓡⓡⓡ

Turners Hill, West Sussex, RH10 4QD
Tel: 01342 714914 Fax: 01342 717328
Email: info@alexanderhouse.co.uk
Web: www.alexanderhouse.co.uk

Beautiful 17th century mansion. 15 luxury
ensuite rooms including four-poster suites. Set
amidst 135 acres of mature gardens and
parkland. Excellent Anglo/French cuisine
together with impeccable service guarantees a
memorable stay.
15 bedrs SB £135 DB £165 HBD £105 B £8
L £17 D £34
CC: MC Vi Am DC Swi Delt

206 Langshott Manor
Gold Ribbon Winner

★★★ ⓡⓡⓡ

Langshott, Horley, near Gatwick, Surrey, RH6 9LN
Tel: 01293 786680 Fax: 01293 783905
Email: admin@langshottmanor.com
Web: www.langshottmanor.com

'Europe's most civilised airport hotel' two miles
and 400 years from Gatwick Airport. An
Elizabethan manor house providing the best in
hospitality and cuisine, yet with the most
modern services.
15 bedrs SB £155 DB £175 HBS £180
HBD £120 B £12.50 L £24.95 D £37.50
CC: MC Vi Am DC Swi Delt

How to get there: From Horley, take A23
towards Redhill. At roundabout with Shell petrol
station, take third exit into Ladbroke Road.
Langshott is ³/₄ mile on right.

207 Stanhill Court Hotel

★★★ ⓡ

Stan Hill, Charlwood, Surrey, RH6 0EP
Tel: 01293 862166 Fax: 01293 862773
Email: enquiries@stanhillcourthotel.co.uk
Web: www.stanhillcourthotel.co.uk

The Victorians excelled at building baronial
mansions and Stanhill Court Hotel is a fine
example of their skills. 35 acres of glorious
countryside. Restaurant 1881 for fine dining.
14 bedrs SB £130 DB £150 B £12.25 L £29.75

D £32.50 CC: MC Vi Am DC Swi Delt

How to get there: On leaving Charlwood village, pass the Rising Sun pub on your right, pass T.H. Gorringe on left. Take next right (NOT Gatwick Zoo). Pass 40mph sign. Stanhill Court signposted.

208 Lawn Guest House

♦ ♦ ♦ ♦ ✎

30 Massets Road, Horley, Surrey, RH6 7DF
Tel: 01293 775751 Fax: 01293 821803
Email: info@lawnguesthouse.co.uk
Web: www.lawnguesthouse.co.uk

Luxury Victorian house set in a mature garden, five minutes to Gatwick, two minutes to the centre of Horley, and close to mainline rail station. Holiday parking. No smoking.
12 bedrs DB £55
CC: MC Vi Am Swi Delt

How to get there: M23 Junction 9. A23 towards Redhill. At third roundabout (Esso on left), take third exit. After 200 yards, turn right into Massetts Road. Lawn 400 yards on left.

209 Melville Lodge

♦ ♦ ☏

15 Brighton Road, Horley, Surrey, RH6 7HH
Tel: 01293 784951 Fax: 01293 785669
Email: melvillelodge.guesthouse@tesco.net
6 bedrs
CC: MC Vi

How to get there: From M25, take M23 to Gatwick, exit Junction 9. At South Terminal roundabout take second exit, at North Terminal roundabout fourth exit. At third roundabout third exit.

Gillingham, Kent

210 Travelodge Gillingham

Travel Accommodation
M2 J4/5, Rainham, Gillingham, Kent, ME8 8PQ
Tel: 08700 850 950
Web: www.travelodge.co.uk
58 bedrs B £4.25
CC: MC Vi Am DC Swi Delt

Godalming, Surrey

211 Kings Arms and Royal Hotel

★ ★

High Street, Godalming, Surrey, GU7 1DZ
Tel: 01483 421545 Fax: 01483 415403
18 bedrs SB £60 DB £66
CC: MC Vi Am Swi Delt

Gosport, Hampshire

212 Belle Vue Hotel

★ ★ ★

39 Marine Parade East, Lee-On-The-Solent, Gosport, Hampshire, PO13 9BW
Tel: 023 9255 0258 Fax: 023 9255 2624
Email: information@bellevue-hotel.co.uk
Web: www.bellevue-hotel.co.uk
Closed Christmas
27 bedrs SB £64.50 DB £89
B £9.50 L £19.50 D £19.50
CC: MC Vi Am DC Swi Delt

How to get there: From the M27 (Junction nine or 11), follow signs to Gosport, then Lee-On-The-Solent. The hotel is situated on the seafront just past shops.

Grays, Essex

213 Travelodge Grays

Travel Accommodation
A1306, Arterial Road West, Thurrock, Grays, Essex, RM16 3BG
Tel: 08700 850 950
Web: www.travelodge.co.uk
66 bedrs B £4.25
CC: MC Vi Am DC Swi Delt

Southeast

Great Milton, Oxfordshire

214 Le Manoir Aux Quat'Saisons
Gold Ribbon Winner

★★★★★ Ⓡ Ⓡ Ⓡ Ⓡ
Church Road, Great Milton,
Oxfordshire, OX44 7PD
Tel: 01844 278881 Fax: 01844 278847
Email: lemanoir@blanc.co.uk
Web: www.manoir.com
32 bedrs SB £260 DB £260 L £45 D £89
CC: MC Vi Am DC Swi Delt

How to get there: From London, leave M40 at
Junction 7. Turn towards Wallingford. Le Manoir
is signposted on the right two miles further on.

Hailsham, East Sussex

215 Travelodge Hailsham

Travel Accommodation
A22/A267, Boship Roundabout, Hellingly,
near Hailsham, East Sussex, BN27 4DT
Tel: 08700 850 950
Web: www.travelodge.co.uk
58 bedrs B £4.25
CC: MC Vi Am DC Swi Delt

Harlow, Essex

216 Swallow Churchgate

★★★ Ⓡ
Churchgate Street Village, Old Harlow,
Essex, CM17 0JT
Tel: 01279 420246 Fax: 01279 437720
Email: oldharlow.swallow@whitbread.com
Web: www.swallowhotels.co.uk
85 bedrs B £9.75 L £5.50 D £25
CC: MC Vi Am DC Swi

How to get there: Leave M11 at Junction 7.
Take A414 to Harlow. At fourth roundabout turn
right, onto B183. Follow signs to Churchgate
Street.

Harpenden, Hertfordshire

217 Hanover International Hotel Harpenden

★★★ Ⓡ
1 Luton Road, Harpenden, Hertfordshire, AL5 2PX
Tel: 01582 760271 Fax: 01582 460819
Email: davidhunter9@virgin.net
Web: www.hanover-international.com

HANOVER INTERNATIONAL
HOTELS & CLUBS

An attractive hotel that retains many original
features and offers excellent attention to detail.
Transport links are superb via the M1 and M25
motorways.
60 bedrs SB £105 DB £125
B £11.95 L £9.95 D £15
CC: MC Vi Am DC Swi Delt JCB

How to get there: Close to the town centre on
the left-hand side of Luton Road if coming from
Junction nine of M1, or right-hand side when
coming from Junction 10.

Harrow, Middlesex

218 Cumberland Hotel

★★★ Ⓡ
St. John's Road, Harrow, Middlesex, HA1 2EF
Tel: 020 8863 4111 Fax: 020 8861 5668
Email: reception@cumberlandhotel.co.uk
Web: www.cumberlandhotel.co.uk
84 bedrs SB £98 DB £110
B £5.50 L £10.95 D £15.50
CC: MC Vi Am DC Swi Delt

How to get there: Leave M1 at Junction 5. Take
A41 and then A409 to Harrow town centre. Hotel
is 1, St. John's Road (reached via Lyon Road).
See advert on facing page

219 Grim's Dyke

★★★★ ® ®

Old Redding, Harrow Weald, Middlesex, HA3 6SH
Tel: 020 8385 3100 Fax: 020 8954 4560
Email: reservations@grimsdyke.com
Web: www.grimsdyke.com
44 bedrs SB £125 DB £152 B £10 L £19 D £19
CC: MC Vi Am DC Swi Delt

How to get there: From north, leave M1 at
Junction 5. Take A41 towards A409 Harrow.
After Kiln Nursery on right, turn right. Hotel is
300 yards on right.
See advert below right

220 Quality Harrow Hotel

★★★ ®

12/22 Pinner Road, Harrow, Middlesex, HA1 4HZ
Tel: 020 8427 3435 Fax: 020 8861 1370
Email: info@harrowhotel.co.uk
Web: www.harrowhotel.co.uk
50 bedrs
CC: MC Vi Am DC Swi Delt

How to get there: Situated at junction of A312
and A404 on A404, leaving Harrow towards
Pinner and Rickmansworth.

221 Crescent Hotel

♦ ♦ ♦

58-62 Welldon Crescent, Harrow,
Middlesex, HA1 1QR
Tel: 020 8863 5491 Fax: 020 8427 5965
Email: jivraj@crsnthtl.demon.co.uk
Web: www.crsnthtl.demon.co.uk
21 bedrs SB £50 DB £65
CC: MC Vi Am DC Swi Delt JCB

How to get there: In centre of Harrow. Five
minutes from Harrow-on-the-Hill underground.

222 Hindes Hotel

♦ ♦ ♦

8 Hindes Road, Harrow, Middlesex, HA1 1SJ
Tel: 020 8427 7468 Fax: 020 8424 0673
Email: reception@hindeshotel.com
Web: www.hindeshotel.com
14 bedrs SB £39 DB £50
CC: MC Vi Am DC Swi Delt

How to get there: Leave M1 at Junction 5,
follow Harrow signs (A409). Or leave M4/A40 at
exit A312 and follow signs.

Southeast

223 Central Hotel

◆ ◆

6 Hindes Road, Harrow, Middlesex, HA1 1SJ
Tel: 020 8427 0893 Fax: 020 8424 8797
Email: central@hindeshotel.com
15 bedrs SB £39 DB £50
CC: MC Vi Am DC Swi Delt
How to get there: Hindes Road is off Station
Road (A409), in town centre. Hotel is opposite
entrance to Tesco superstore in central Harrow.

Harwich, Essex

224 Pier at Harwich

★★★★

The Quay, Harwich, Essex, CO12 3HH
Tel: 01255 241212 Fax: 01255 551922
Email: reception@thepieratharwich.com
Web: www.thepieratharwich.com
14 bedrs SB £62.50 DB £80 B £5.50 L £15
D £18.50 CC: MC Vi Am DC Swi Delt
How to get there: From A12, follow A120 down
to the quay (18 miles). Hotel opposite lifeboat
station.

225 Cliff Hotel

★★

Marine Parade, Dovercourt, Harwich,
Essex, CO12 3RE
Tel: 01255 503345 Fax: 01255 240358
Web: www.thecliffhotelharwich.co.uk
26 bedrs SB £55 DB £65 HBS £71.50 HBD £46
B £4 L £11.95 D £14.95
CC: MC Vi Am DC Swi Delt
How to get there: Leave A120 at Harwich
International. At roundabout take last exit to
Dovercourt, left at next mini-roundabout. 10th
turning right to seafront, right 200 yards along.

226 Tower Hotel

★★

Main Road, Dovercourt, Harwich,
Essex, CO12 3PJ
Tel: 01255 504952 Fax: 01255 504952
Email: admin@towerharwich.fsnet.co.uk
14 bedrs SB £50 DB £60 B £6 L £6 D £6
CC: MC Vi Am DC Swi Delt
How to get there: On the main road towards
Dovercourt and Harwich.

227 New Farm House

◆ ◆ ◆ ◆

Spinnel's Lane, Wix, Manningtree,
Essex, CO11 2UJ
Tel: 01255 870365 Fax: 01255 870837
Email: newfarmhouse@which.net
Web: www.newfarmhouse.com
11 bedrs SB £32 DB £50 HBS £44 HBD £37
B £7 D £12
CC: MC Vi Swi Delt
How to get there: Seven miles from Harwich,
from A120 follow signs to Wix. At village
crossroads, take Bradfield Road. Go under
bridge and take next right.

Haslemere, Surrey

228 Lythe Hill Hotel

★★★★★

Haslemere, Surrey, GU27 3BQ
Tel: 01428 651251 Fax: 01428 644131
Email: lythe@lythehill.co.uk
Web: www.lythehill.co.uk
41 bedrs SB £110 DB £149
B £8 L £24 D £40
CC: MC Vi Am DC Swi Delt
How to get there: Situated one mile east of
Haslemere on B2131.

Hastings, East Sussex

229 Eagle House Hotel

◆ ◆ ◆ ◆

12 Pevensey Road, St. Leonards,
East Sussex, TN38 0JZ
Tel: 01424 430535 Fax: 01424 437771
Email: eaglehouse@cwcom.net
Web: www.eaglehousehotel.com

Town centre hotel with car park. A Victorian house in period style. All bedrooms en-suite; restaurant overlooking walled garden. Near the main London road, but in a quiet residential area. 19 bedrs SB £33 DB £52 HBS £57.95 HBD £50.95 B £5 L £10.95 D £24
CC: MC Vi Am DC Swi Delt

How to get there: Follow signs to St. Leonards, Landan Road. At the church opposite office building Ocean House, turn sharp right into Pevensey Road.

Hatfield, Hertfordshire

230 Quality Hotel Hatfield

★★★
Roehyde Way, Hatfield, Hertfordshire, AL10 9AF
Tel: 01707 275701 Fax: 01707 266033
Email: admin@gb059.u-net.com
Web: www.choicehotels.com
76 bedrs SB £115.75 DB £125.75 B £10.75
CC: MC Vi Am DC Swi Delt

How to get there: Exit Junction three of A1(M). Follow signs for University of Hertfordshire. Hotel on Roehyde Way, 1/2 mile from junction roundabout.

Havant, Hampshire

231 Langstone Hotel

★★★
Northney Road, Hayling Island, Havant, Hampshire, PO11 0NQ
Tel: 023 9246 5011 Fax: 023 9246 6468
Email: info@langstonehotel.co.uk
Web: www.langstonehotel.co.uk

This modern hotel and leisure club, ideally located overlooking Langstone harbour and estuary, features 100 bedrooms, 11 conference and training rooms, a superb restaurant and lounge bar.

100 bedrs SB £93.95 DB £107.40 HBD £60 B £8.95 L £11.50 D £16.50
CC: MC Vi Am DC Swi Delt

How to get there: Leave A3(M) or A27 and follow signs to Havant/Hayling Island. A3023 across the bridge and turn immediate left.

232 Green Cottage

◆◆◆
23 Park Lane, Bedhampton, Havant, Hampshire, PO9 3HG
Tel: 023 9247 5670
Closed December and January
2 bedrs SB £25 DB £45
CC: None accepted

How to get there: From M27/A27/A3M follow signs to Bedhampton to B2177. At lights turn left into Hulbert Road, immediately right into Park Lane.

Hayes, Middlesex

233 London Heathrow Marriott Hotel

★★★★
Bath Road, Hayes, Middlesex, UB3 5AN
Tel: 020 8990 1100 Fax: 020 8990 1110
Web: www.marriotthotels.com/lhrhr
390 bedrs SB £149 DB £174
CC: MC Vi Am DC Swi Delt JCB

How to get there: Exit J4 M4, follow signs for Heathrow terminals 123; turn onto A4; hotel is on left.

234 Comfort Inn Heathrow

★★★
Shepiston Lane, Hayes, Middlesex, UB3 IBL
Tel: 020 85736162 Fax: 020 8848 1057
Email: info@comfortheathrow.com
Web: www.comfortheathrow.com
184 bedrs SB £118.50 DB £127
B £9.50 L £8 D £14.75
CC: MC Vi Am DC Swi

How to get there: Exit J4 M4; follow signs for Hayes, which brings you to Shepiston Lane. Hotel one mile on right beside Fire Station.

235 Shepiston Lodge Guest House

31 Shepiston Lane, Hayes, Middlesex, UB3 1LJ
Tel: 020 8573 0266 Fax: 020 8569 2536
Email: shepistonlodge@aol.com
Web: www.shepistonlodge.co.uk
22 bedrs SB £45 DB £60 L £5 D £5
CC: MC Vi Am Swi Delt JCB

How to get there: Exit J4 M4, follow signs for Hayes. 50 yards from Comfort Inn and Hayes fire station, in Shepiston Lane.

Hayling Island, Hampshire

236 Cockle Warren Cottage

36 Seafront, Hayling Island,
Hampshire, PO11 9HL
Tel: 023 9246 4961 Fax: 023 9246 4838
5 bedrs SB £40 DB £70 B £5
CC: MC Vi Swi Delt JCB

How to get there: On Hayling Island, follow signs to seafront, passing through Mengham Village. Take road to the left signed with brown signposts.

237 Broad Oak Hotel

Copse Lane, Hayling Island,
Hampshire, PO11 0QB
Tel: 023 9246 2333 Fax: 023 9246 2487

238 Redwalls

66 Staunton Avenue, Hayling Island,
Hampshire, PO11 0EW
Tel: 023 9246 6109
Email: daphne@redwalls66.freeserve.co.uk
Web: www.redwalls.co.uk
3 bedrs SB £30 DB £40 CC: None accepted

How to get there: Follow main road across island signposted Beachlands. Turn right into seafront road. Staunton Avenue is fourth on the right.

Making a booking?

Don't forget to mention RAC Hotels and Bed & Breakfast 2002.

Haywards Heath, West Sussex

239 Oakfield Cottage

Brantridge Lane, Staplefield, Haywards Heath, West Sussex, RH17 6JR
Tel: 01444 401121 Fax: 01444 401121
Email: joyoakfieldcot@aol.com
2 bedrs SB £25 DB £45
CC: None accepted

How to get there: Handcross (N) take B2110 (Turners Hill), after two miles turn right and right again into Brantridge Lane. Property 1¹/₂ miles on right-hand side.

Headcorn, Kent

240 Four Oaks Bed & Breakfast

Four Oaks Road, Headcorn, near Ashford, Kent, TN27 9PB
Tel: 01622 891224 Fax: 01622 890630
Email: info@fouroaks.uk.com
Web: www.fouroaks.uk.com

Restored, 500-year-old farmhouse in quiet rural location. Close to Leeds Castle, Sissinghurst gardens and mainline rail services. London one hour, Eurolink 30 minutes.
3 bedrs SB £25 DB £38
CC: MC Vi

How to get there: South from Maidstone on A274, right at Weald of Kent Golf Club. One mile on right.

It's easier online

For all your motoring and travel needs, www.rac.co.uk

Heathrow Airport, Middlesex

241 Le Méridien Heathrow

★★★★

Bath Road, Heathrow, Middlesex, UB7 0DU
Tel: 0870 400 8899 Fax: 020 8283 2001
Email: excelsior@lemeridien.co.uk
Web: www.lemeridien.com
828 bedrs SB £146.87 DB £146.87
B £14.95 L £18 D £20.95
CC: MC Vi Am DC Swi Delt JCB

How to get there: Exit J5 M4, follow signs for A4 London. Hotel is on the left as the slip road joins the A4.

242 Renaissance London Heathrow Hotel

★★★★ ♐

Bath Road, Hounslow, Middlesex, TW6 2AQ
Tel: 020 8897 6363 Fax: 020 8897 1113
Email: 106047.3556@compuserve.com
Web: www.renaissancehotels.com/lhrbr
648 bedrs SB £203 DB £203 HBS £215
HBD £113.50 B £12 L £12.50 D £17.50
CC: MC Vi Am DC Swi Delt JCB

243 Novotel London Heathrow

★★★

M4 Junction 4, Cherry Lane, West Drayton,
Middlesex, UB7 9HB
Tel: 01895 431431 Fax: 01895 431221
Email: h1551@accor-hotels.com
178 bedrs SB £125.00 DB £135.00
B £10.95 L £16.95 D £18.95
CC: MC Vi Am DC Swi Delt

How to get there: Junction 4 of M4, follow signs for Uxbridge A408. Keep to left lane, take second exit off the island onto Cherry Lane, signposted West Drayton. Hotel entrance on left.

244 Osterley Four Pillars Hotel

★★★

764 Great West Road, Isleworth,
Middlesex, TW7 5NA
Tel: 020 8568 7781 Fax: 020 8569 7819
Email: osterley@four-pillars.co.uk
Web: www.@four-pillars.co.uk
Closed 25–30 December
61 bedrs SB £98.75 DB £119.50 HBS £114.70
HBD £75.70 B £5.75 L £5.75 D £15.95
CC: MC Vi Am DC Swi Delt

How to get there: J3 M4; follow signs for A4. Pass Osterley tube station; hotel is one mile on left.

245 St. Giles Hotel

★★★

Hounslow Road, Feltham, Middlesex, TW14 9AD
Tel: 020 8817 7000 Fax: 020 8817 7002
Email: book@stgiles.com
Web: www.stgiles.com
300 bedrs SB £120 DB £130 B £10.50 L £10
D £12 CC: MC Vi Am DC Swi Delt

How to get there: Take A312 to Feltham, then A244 to town centre. Hotel is visible after 600 yards, opposite the train station.

246 Stanwell Hall Hotel

★★ ♐

Town Lane, Stanwell, Staines,
Middlesex, TW19 7PW
Tel: 01784 252292 Fax: 01784 245250
Web: www.stanwell-hall.co.uk
Closed 24–29 December
18 bedrs SB £80 DB £100 B £10.50 L £18 D £18
CC: MC Vi Am DC Swi Delt

How to get there: M25 at Junction 14. Follow signs to Heathrow Terminal 4. At roundabout, right to Staines. Traffic lights turn left to Stanwell. At mini roundabout turn right. Hotel on right.

Hemel Hempstead, Hertfordshire

247 Travelodge Hemel Hempstead

Travel Accommodation
Wolsey House, Wolsey Road,
Hemel Hempstead, Hertfordshire, HP2 4SF
Tel: 08700 850 950
Web: www.travelodge.co.uk
53 bedrs B £4.25 CC: MC Vi Am DC Swi Delt

Need help booking?

RAC Hotel Reservations will find the accommodation that's right for you – and book it too.
Call today on 0870 603 9109 and quote 'Guide 2002'

Southeast

248 Hyde Lane Farm

◆◆◆

Hyde Lane, Hemel Hempstead,
Hertfordshire, HP3 8SA
Tel: 019232 67380
2 bedrs SB £35
CC: None accepted

How to get there: Situated in quiet country lane.
Easy access to M1 and M25 Watford, St.
Albans and Hemel Hempstead.

Hertford, Hertfordshire

249 Heritage Hotels – The White Horse

★★★ ⓡ

Hertingfordbury, Hertford,
Hertfordshire, SG14 2LB
Tel: 0870 400 8114 Fax: 01992 550809

250 Salisbury Arms Hotel

★★

Fore Street, Hertford, Hertfordshire, SG14 1BZ
Tel: 01992 583091 Fax: 01992 552510
31 bedrs
CC: MC Vi Am DC Swi Delt

How to get there: Situated in the centre of
Hertford, off the A414 on Fore Street.

Hickstead, West Sussex

251 Travelodge Hickstead

Travel Accommodation
A23, Junction A23/A2300, Hickstead,
West Sussex, RH17 5NX
Tel: 08700 850 950
Web: www.travelodge.co.uk
55 bedrs B £4.25
CC: MC Vi Am DC Swi Delt

High Wycombe, Buckinghamshire

252 Bird in Hand

◆◆◆

West Wycombe Road, High Wycombe,
Buckinghamshire, HP11 2LR
Tel: 01494 523502 Fax: 01494 459449
6 bedrs DB £60 L £4 D £5
CC: MC Vi DC Swi Delt

How to get there: The Bird in Hand is on the
A40 West Wycombe to Oxford road, just a few
minutes from the town centre.

253 Blue Flag

◆◆◆

Marlow Road, Cadmore End, High Wycombe,
Buckinghamshire, HD14 3PF
Tel: 01494 881183 Fax: 01494 882269
17 bedrs SB £89 DB £99.50 B £8.50 L £5 D £8
CC: MC Vi Am DC Swi Delt

254 Clifton Lodge Hotel

◆◆◆

210 West Wycombe Road, High Wycombe,
Buckinghamshire, HP12 3AR
Tel: 01494 440095 Fax: 01494 536322
Email: hotelaccom@lineone.net
Web: www.cliftonlodgehotel.com
32 bedrs SB £69 DB £80 B £6.50 L £10 D £15
CC: MC Vi Am DC Swi Delt

How to get there: Clifton Lodge is situated on
the A40 West Wycombe Road, one mile from
the M40 and the centre of High Wycombe.

255 Drake Court Hotel

◆◆

141 London Road, High Wycombe,
Buckinghamshire, HP11 1BT
Tel: 01494 523639 Fax: 01494 472696
20 bedrs SB £38 DB £48 D £7
CC: MC Vi Am DC Swi Delt JCB

How to get there: Approx 1¹/₂ miles from M40
on A40 London Road ¹/₂ mile from town centre
towards London and Beaconsfield.

Hindhead, Surrey

256 Devils Punch Bowl

◆ ◆ ◆

London Road, Hindhead, Surrey, GU26 6AG
Tel: 01428 606565 Fax: 01428 605713
31 bedrs SB £69 DB £89 HBS £85 HBD £58.50
B £8.95 L £3.95 D £6.95
CC: MC Vi Am Swi Delt JCB

How to get there: 12 miles south of Guildford on the A3 main road to Portsmouth.

Hitchin, Hertfordshire

257 Firs Hotel & Restaurant

★ ★

83 Bedford Road, Hitchin, Hertfordshire, SG5 2TY
Tel: 01462 422322 Fax: 01462 432051
Email: info@firshotel.co.uk
Web: www.firshotel.co.uk
30 bedrs SB £52 DB £62 D £10
CC: MC Vi Am DC Swi Delt JCB

How to get there: Exit M1 at J10; A505 to Hitchin. Exit A1 at J8; A602 to Hitchin. Follow directions for Bedford. Hotel is outside Hitchin town centre on A600.

258 Redcoats Farmhouse Hotel

◆ ◆ ◆ ◆

Redcoats Green, near Hitchin,
Hertfordshire, SG4 7JR
Tel: 01438 729500 Fax: 01438 723322
Email: sales@redcoats.co.uk
Web: www.redcoats.co.uk
12 bedrs SB £85 DB £95 B £8.50 L £16 D £35
CC: MC Vi Am DC Swi

How to get there: Leave A1(M) at Junction 8, follow road to village of Little Wymondley. At end of village turn left at roundabout into Blakemore End Road (to Redcoats Green).

259 Tudor Oaks Lodge

◆ ◆ ◆

Taylors Road, Astwick, near Hitchin,
Hertfordshire, SG5 4AZ
Tel: 01462 834133 Fax: 01462 834133
Web: www.thetudoroakslodge.co.uk
Children minimum age: 6

15th-century lodge around secluded courtyard. Ensuite rooms, fresh food daily from bar snacks to à la carte. Real Ales.
13 bedrs SB £49.50 DB £62 B £8 L £8.50 D £10
CC: MC Vi Am DC Swi Delt

How to get there: Conveniently placed by the side of the A1, one mile north past Junction 10. Within easy reach of Letchworth, Baldock and Stevenage.

Hook, Hampshire

260 Tylney Hall Hotel
Gold Ribbon Winner

★ ★ ★ ★ ♚ ♚ ♚
Rotherwick, Hook, Hampshire, RG27 9AZ
Tel: 01256 764881 Fax: 01256 768141
Email: sales@tylneyhall.com
Web: www.tylneyhall.com

Set in manicured, historic gardens, Tylney Hall is a perfect location — elegant lounges, stunning views, fine leisure facilities, exquisite bedrooms and a breathtaking setting. A tranquil, romantic country house of distinction.
110 bedrs SB £130 DB £165 HBS £150
HBD £112.25 B £13.50 L £16 D £25
CC: MC Vi Am DC Swi Delt JCB

How to get there: M3 J5, A287 to Basingstoke, over A30 into Old School Road. Left at T-junction, right at crossroads, one mile along.

Southeast

Horsham, West Sussex

261 Ye Olde King's Head Hotel

★★

Carfax, Horsham,
West Sussex, RH12 1EG
Tel: 01403 253126 Fax: 01403 242291
42 bedrs SB £85 DB £98
CC: MC Vi Am DC Swi Delt

How to get there: At junction of The Carfax (town centre) and East Street. Follow brown tourist signs.

Horton-cum-Studley, Oxfordshire

262 Studley Priory Hotel

★★★★ ⚜ ⚜ ⚜

Horton-cum-Studley, Oxfordshire, OX33 1AZ
Tel: 01865 351203 Fax: 01865 351613
Email: res@studley-priory.co.uk
Web: www.studley-priory.co.uk

STUDLEY PRIORY

18 bedrs SB £110 DB £150 HBS £150 HBD £90
B £9 L £20 D £29.50
CC: MC Vi Am DC Swi Delt JCB

How to get there: Click onto website www.studley-priory.co.uk

Hounslow, Middlesex

263 Master Robert Hotel

★★★

Great West Road, Hounslow,
Middlesex, TW5 0BD
Tel: 020 8570 6261 Fax: 020 8569 4016
Email: stay@masterrobert.co.uk
Web: www.masterrobert.co.uk
96 bedrs SB £109 DB £133 HBS £129
HBD £86.50 B £9.25
CC: MC Vi Am DC Swi Delt

See advert on facing page

264 Travelodge Hounslow (Heston)

Travel Accommodation
M4 J2/3, Phoenix Way, Hounslow,
Middlesex, TW5 9NB
Tel: 08700 850 950
Web: www.travelodge.co.uk
209 bedrs B £4.25
CC: MC Vi Am DC Swi Delt

Hove, East Sussex

265 Courtlands Hotel

★★★

15–27 The Drive, Hove,
East Sussex, BN3 3JE
Tel: 01273 731055 Fax: 01273 328295

Situated in Hove's premier street, our ensuite rooms are ideal for both business and leisure visitors. Private car park and indoor swimming pool are available.
67 bedrs CC: MC Vi Am DC Swi Delt

How to get there: From A23 follow signs to Hove. Second turning at roundabout, follow Dyke Road, then Upper Drive and The Drive.

266 Imperial Hotel

★★★

First Avenue, Hove, East Sussex, BN2 2GU
Tel: 01273 777320 Fax: 01273 777310
Email: info@imperial-hove.com
Web: www.imperial-hove.com
76 bedrs SB £70 DB £100 B £7.95 L £16.50
D £16.50 CC: MC Vi Am DC Swi Delt
How to get there: Enter Brighton on A23,
proceed to seafront. Turn right (west) onto
A259. First Avenue one mile on right.

267 Langfords Hotel

★★★★

Third Avenue, Hove, East Sussex, BN3 2PX
Tel: 01273 738222 Fax: 01273 779426
Email: langfords@pavilion.co.uk
60 bedrs CC: MC Vi Am DC Swi Delt
How to get there: From A23 follow signs to
Hove. Turn left on seafront road (A259). Continue
east until you reach third avenue on left.

268 Princes Marine Hotel

★★★

153 Kingsway, Hove, East Sussex, BN3 2WE
Tel: 01273 207660 Fax: 01273 325913
Email: princemarine@bestwestern.co.uk
Web: www.brighton.co.uk/hotels/princes

Seafront hotel with well-equipped ensuite
bedrooms. Rooftop function suites, seaview
restaurant and bar. Large private car park.
Situated close to all attractions, bowling greens
and the King Alfred Leisure Centre. Open for
Christmas and New Year.
48 bedrs CC: MC Vi Am DC Swi Delt
How to get there: From M23, go straight to
seafront. Turn right at Palace Pier. Continue
along main seafront road. Hotel is 200 yards
west of King Alfred swimming pool.

Master Robert Hotel

Set in gardens two miles west of London on the
A4 and 15 minutes' drive from Heathrow Airport,
the Master Robert combines comfort with ideal
location. All bedrooms offer ensuite facilities with
satllite TV, trouser press, hair dryer, telephone,
hospitality tray. A la carte restaurant serves lunch
and dinner. The adjoining cocktail bar is an ideal
place to relax. Meeting and banqueting facilities
available from 3 to 130 people. Free car parking.

Great West Road, Hounslow, TW5 0BD
Tel: 020 8570 6261   Fax: 020 8569 4016

stay@masterrobert.co.uk
www.masterrobert.co.uk   ★★★

269 St. Catherine's Lodge Hotel

★★

Sea Front, Kingsway, Hove,
East Sussex, BN3 2RZ
Tel: 01273 778181 Fax: 01273 774949

A traditional seafront hotel, situated opposite
the leisure centre, with an abundance of
character throughout, particularly in the
Regency restaurant.
40 bedrs
CC: MC Vi Am DC Swi Delt
How to get there: St. Catherine's Lodge is
south-facing on the main A259 Seafront Road in
Hove. Near the King Alfred leisure centre.

Southeast

Hungerford, Berkshire

270 Marshgate Cottage Hotel

♦ ♦ ♦ ♦

Marsh Lane, Hungerford,
Berkshire, RG17 0QX
Tel: 01488 682307 Fax: 01488 685475
Email: reservations@marshgate.co.uk
Web: www.marshgate.co.uk
10 bedrs SB £36.50 DB £60
CC: MC Vi Swi Delt

How to get there: M4 J14. From High Street,
turn into Church Street. ¹/₂ a mile along, turn
right into Marsh Lane. Hotel is at end.

Hythe, Kent

271 Hythe Imperial Hotel

★★★★★ ⓡ ⓡ

Prince's Parade, Hythe,
Kent, CT21 6AE
Tel: 01303 267441 Fax: 01303 264610
Email: hytheimperial@marstonhotels.com
Web: www.marstonhotels.com

100 bedrs SB £115 DB £149 HBS £82.50
HBD £82.50 B £12 L £15 D £27
CC: MC Vi Am DC Swi Delt

How to get there: Leave M20 southbound at
Junction 11. Take A261 to Hythe. When in
Hythe follow signs to Folkestone. Turn right into
Twiss Road.

272 Stade Court Hotel

★★★ ⓡ

West Parade, Hythe, Kent, CT21 6DT
Tel: 01303 268263 Fax: 01303 261803
Email: stadecourt@marstonhotels.com
Web: www.marstonhotels.com

42 bedrs SB £69 DB £110 HBS £59.50
HBD £59.50 B £11 L £10.92 D £22
CC: MC Vi Am DC Swi Delt

How to get there: Leave M20 southbound at
Junction 11. Follow A261 to Hythe. When in
Hythe, turn right into Stade Street (by canal).

Ilford, Essex

273 Travelodge Ilford

Travel Accommodation

A12, The Beehive, Beehive Lane, Gants Hill,
Ilford, Essex, IG4 5DR
Tel: 08700 850 950
Web: www.travelodge.co.uk
32 bedrs B £4.25 CC: MC Vi Am DC Swi Delt

274 Travelodge Ilford (Central)

Travel Accommodation

A118, Winston Way, Ilford, Essex,
Tel: 08700 850 950
Web: www.travelodge.co.uk
Opens April 2002
86 bedrs B £4.25
CC: MC Vi Am DC Swi Delt

275 Park Hotel

♦ ♦ ♦

327 Cranbrook Road, Ilford, Essex, IG1 4UE
Tel: 020 8554 9616 Fax: 020 8518 2700
Email: parkhotelilford@netscapeonline.co.uk
Web: www.the-park-hotel.co.uk
20 bedrs SB £44.50 DB £55
CC: MC Vi Swi Delt

How to get there: Opposite Valentines Park, five
minutes walk from Gants Hill underground and
Ilford railway stations.

It's easier online

For all your motoring and travel
needs, www.rac.co.uk

Ask the experts

To book a Hotel or Guest
Accommodation, or for help
and advice, call RAC Hotel
Reservations on 0870 603 9109
and quote 'Guide 2002'

276 Woodville Guest House

10–12 Argyle Road, Ilford, Essex, IG1 3BQ
Tel: 020 8478 3779 Fax: 020 8478 6282
Email: cass@woodville-guesthouse.co.uk

Very friendly family-run business. Comfortable bedrooms, beamed dining room, garden and terrace make this a delightful stay. Most rooms ensuite. All rooms with Sky TV. Families with children particularly welcome. Two minutes from station. 20 minutes from city.
16 bedrs SB £35.00 DB £40.00
CC: None accepted
How to get there: Leave M25 for M11 southbound to A406. Leave at Ilford Junction. Past Ilford station, take second left off Cranbrook Road into Beal Road, then second left into Argyle Road.

277 Cranbrook Hotel

24 Coventry Road, Ilford,
Essex, IG1 4QR
Tel: 020 8554 6544 Fax: 020 8518 1463

Isle of Wight

278 Burlington Hotel

★★★
Bellevue Road, Ventnor, Isle of Wight, PO38 1DB
Tel: 01983 852113 Fax: 01983 853862
Children minimum age: 3
Closed November to March
24 bedrs SB £32 DB £64 HBS £40 HBD £40
B £8 D £15
CC: MC Vi Swi Delt

279 Country Garden Hotel

★★★★ ®
Church Hill, Totland Bay, Isle of Wight, PO39 0ET
Tel: 01983 754521 Fax: 01983 754521
Email: countrygardeniow@cs.com
Web: www.thecountrygardenhotel.co.uk
Children minimum age: 12
Closed January
16 bedrs SB £43 DB £78 HBS £52 HBD £48
B £8.50 D £18.50 CC: MC Vi Swi Delt
How to get there: Eight minutes' drive west from Yarmouth.

280 Eversley Hotel

★★★
Park Avenue, Ventnor, Isle of Wight, PO38 1LB
Tel: 01983 852244 Fax: 01983 856534
Email: eversleyhotel@yahoo.co.uk
Web: www.eversleyhotel.com
Closed January
30 bedrs SB £38 DB £70 HBS £50 HBD £50
B £5.50 D £15
CC: MC Vi Swi Delt

281 George Hotel
Gold Ribbon Winner

★★★★ ® ® ® ®
Quay Street, Yarmouth, Isle of Wight, PO41 0PE
Tel: 01983 760331 Fax: 01983 760425
Email: res@thegeorge.co.uk
Web: www.thegeorge.co.uk
Children minimum age: 10
17 bedrs SB £125 DB £165 HBS £115
HBD £110 B £13.50 L £18 D £25
CC: MC Vi Am Swi Delt JCB
How to get there: Situated in Yarmouth, between pier and castle.

282 Holliers Hotel

★★★
Church Road, Old Village, Shanklin,
Isle of Wight, PO37 6NU
Tel: 01983 862764 Fax: 01983 867314
Email: holliers@i12.com
Web: www.holliers.i12.com
30 bedrs SB £50 DB £65
HBS £66.95 HBD £49.45
CC: MC Vi Am Swi Delt
How to get there: Holliers Hotel is situated on the main A3055.

Southeast

283 Keats Green Hotel

★★★

3 Queens Road, Shanklin,
Isle of Wight, PO37 6AN
Tel: 01983 862742 Fax: 01983 868572
Email: enquiries@keatsgreenhoteliow.co.uk
Web: www.keatsgreenhoteliow.co.uk
Closed January to March

Comfort and enjoyment with a combination of space, location and friendly personal service from Geraldine and Lloyd Newton makes Keats Green Hotel an unbeatable destination for your holiday.
33 bedrs SB £28 DB £56 HBS £37 HBD £74
D £15 CC: MC Vi Swi Delt JCB

How to get there: Driving from Lake take A3055 towards Ventnor (Queens Road). Hotel is approx 400 yards on left.

284 Luccombe Hall Hotel

★★★

Luccombe Road, Shanklin,
Isle of Wight, PO37 6RL
Tel: 01983 862719 Fax: 01983 863082
Email: reservations@luccombehall.co.uk
Web: www.luccombehall.co.uk
35 bedrs CC: MC Vi Swi

How to get there: From Shanklin, take B3020 towards Ventnor. Take road towards Luccombe. Turn left at top. Hotel 100 yards on right.

285 New Holmwood

★★★

Queens Road, Egypt Point, Cowes,
Isle of Wight, PO31 8BW
Tel: 01983 292508 Fax: 01983 295020
Web: www.newholmwoodhotel.co.uk
26 bedrs SB £72 DB £85 HBS £88.50 HBD £59
B £7.50 L £9.50 D £16.50
CC: MC Vi Am DC Swi Delt

286 Sentry Mead

★★★★

Madeira Road, Totland Bay,
Isle of Wight, PO39 0BJ
Tel: 01983 753212 Fax: 01983 753212

287 Shanklin Manor House Hotel

★★★

Church Road, Old Village, Shanklin,
Isle of Wight, PO37 6XQ
Tel: 01983 862777 Fax: 01983 863464
Web: www.hotelsiow.co.uk
Children minimum age: 5
44 bedrs SB £41 DB £76 HBS £49 HBD £92
B £7.50 D £16
CC: MC Vi Swi Delt

288 Aqua Hotel

★★

17 The Esplanade, Shanklin,
Isle of Wight, PO37 6BN
Tel: 01983 863024 Fax: 01983 864841
Email: info@aquahotel.co.uk
Web: www.aquahotel.co.uk
Closed November to March
22 bedrs SB £25 DB £50 HBS £35 HBD £70
B £5 L £5 D £10
CC: MC Vi Am DC Swi Delt JCB

How to get there: Turn down Hope Road from Arthurs Hill, North Road or Atherley Road. Drive down to seafront until you arrive at the hotel.

289 Bay House Hotel

★★

8 Chine Avenue, Shanklin,
Isle of Wight, PO37 6AG
Tel: 01983 863180 Fax: 01983 868934
Email: bay-house@netguides.co.uk
Web: www.bayhouse-hotel.co.uk

Located in a quiet position with one of the finest views over the bay, this family-run hotel, serving exceptional cuisine, is just a five-minute walk to the old village and beach.

21 bedrs SB £26 DB £52 HBS £32 HBD £32

CC: MC Vi Swi Delt

How to get there: Follow A3055 from Sandown to traffic lights. Take Queen's Road to the end, then turn left into Chine Avenue.

290 Braemar Hotel

★★

1 Grange Road, Shanklin,
Isle of Wight, PO37 6NN
Tel: 01983 863172 Fax: 01983 863172
Closed January

11 bedrs SB £25 DB £50 HBS £36 HBD £72

CC: MC Vi Am Swi Delt

291 Clarendon Hotel & Wight Mouse Inn

★★

Newport Road, Chale, Isle of Wight, PO38 2HA
Tel: 01983 730431 Fax: 01983 730431
Email: info@wightmouseinns.co.uk
Web: www.wightmouseinns.co.uk

12 bedrs SB £58.50 DB £78 HBS £84 HBD £56
B £2.50 L £2.60 D £2.80

CC: MC Vi Swi Delt

How to get there: On the Military Road B3055.

292 Farringford

★★

Bedbury Lane, Freshwater Bay,
Isle of Wight, PO40 9PE
Tel: 01983 752500 Fax: 01983 756575
Email: enquiries@farringford.co.uk
Web: www.farringford.co.uk

Alfred Lord Tennyson's home for almost 40 years, now a well-appointed hotel set in 33 acres of parkland incorporating a nine hole par 3 golf course and poolside bistro.

18 bedrs SB £47.50 DB £95 HBS £65 HBD £65
B £8 L £14 D £21.95

CC: MC Vi Am Swi Delt

How to get there: Take A3054 towards Freshwater. Turn left to Norton Green, left at roundabout to Freshwater Bay, then right onto Bedbury Lane.

293 Fernbank Hotel

★★

Highfield Road, Shanklin, Isle of Wight, PO37 6PP
Tel: 01983 862790 Fax: 01983 864412
Email: enquiries@fernbankhotel.com
Web: www.fernbankhotel.com
Children minimum age: 5
Closed Christmas to New Year

20 bedrs SB £32 DB £64 HBS £46 HBD £46
B £6 L £8 D £14

CC: MC Vi Swi Delt

294 Hambledon Hotel

★★

11 Queens Road, Shanklin,
Isle of Wight, PO37 6AW
Tel: 01983 862403 Fax: 01983 867894
Email: enquiries@hambledon-hotel.co.uk
Web: www.hambledon-hotel.co.uk

12 bedrs SB £25 DB £50 HBS £35 HBD £70

CC: MC Vi Swi Delt

How to get there: Please call to request a map.

295 Heatherleigh Hotel

★★

17 Queens Road, Shanklin,
Isle of Wight, PO37 6AW
Tel: 01983 862503 Fax: 01983 862503
Email: aghardy@madasafish.com
Web: www.heatherleigh.co.uk

7 bedrs SB £25 DB £50 HBS £35.50 HBD £71
B £5 D £10.50

CC: MC Vi Swi

How to get there: On entering Shanklin, follow signs for Beach Lift. Heatherleigh is just 100 yards from cliff walk and lift.

Southeast

296 Hillside Hotel

★★

Mitchell Avenue, Ventnor,
Isle of Wight, PO38 1DR
Tel: 01983 852271 Fax: 01983 852271
Email: rac@hillside-hotel.co.uk
Children minimum age: 5
Closed Christmas
12 bedrs SB £24 DB £48 HBS £35 HBD £35
B £2.50 D £10 CC: MC Vi Swi Delt

How to get there: Take B2257 off A3055 at
junction between Leeson Hill and St. Bonipace
Road — hotel is 500 yards on right, from tennis
courts.

297 Malton House Hotel

★★

8 Park Road, Shanklin, Isle of Wight, PO37 6AY
Tel: 01983 865007 Fax: 01983 865576
Email: couvoussis@totalise.co.uk
15 bedrs CC: MC Vi

How to get there: From Sandown on A3055,
enter Shanklin. At the traffic lights (Hope Road),
go straight up hill. Take third road on the left.

298 Melbourne-Ardenlea Hotel

★★

Queens Road, Shanklin, Isle of Wight, PO37 6AP
Tel: 01983 862283 Fax: 01983 862865
Email: melbourne-ardenlea@virgin.net
Web: www.hotel-isleofwight.co.uk
Closed November to February

Long-established, family-run hotel in pleasant
gardens, giving personal service. Centrally
situated in peaceful area, yet close to all of
Shanklin's amenities.
53 bedrs SB £39 DB £78 HBS £46 HBD £46
D £15 CC: MC Vi Am Swi Delt

How to get there: From Sandown, bear left at
Fiveways Crossroads towards Ventnor. Hotel is
150 yards on right after passing church spire.

299 Montrene

★★

Avenue Road, Sandown, Isle of Wight, PO36 8BN
Tel: 01983 403722 Fax: 01983 405553
Email: montrenehotel@ic24.net
Web: www.montrene.co.uk
Closed January
41 bedrs SB £35 DB £70 HBS £43 HBD £43
CC: MC Vi Swi Delt

How to get there: Travel from Ryde via Brading,
under railway bridge. Keep to left at roundabout.
Hotel at end on right. Look out for yellow sign.

300 Orchardcroft

★★

Victoria Avenue, Shanklin, Isle of Wight, PO37 6LT
Tel: 01983 862133 Fax: 01983 862133
Email: nicklaffan@hotmail.com
Web: www.orchardcroft-hotel.co.uk
Children minimum age: 1
Closed January to March
16 bedrs SB £26 DB £52 HBS £38 HBD £76
B £5 D £12
CC: MC Vi Swi Delt

How to get there: From Newport on Sandown
road, turn right to Shanklin through Godshill into
Victoria Avenue. Orchardcroft is first hotel on left.

301 Sandpipers Country House Hotel

★★

Entrance through main car park, Freshwater
Bay, Isle of Wight, PO40 9QX
Tel: 01983 758500 Fax: 01983 754364
Email: sandpipers@fatcattrading.demon.co.uk
Web: www.fatcattrading.co.uk
12 bedrs SB £23.50 DB £47 HBS £35.50
HBD £35.50 B £3 L £3 D £6.75
CC: MC Vi Swi Delt

How to get there: Enter Freshwater Bay, drive
into main council park. Drive between two brick
pillars at the back to enter private car park.

302 Villa Mentone

★

11 Park Road, Shanklin, Isle of Wight, PO37 6AY
Tel: 01983 862346 Fax: 01983 862130
30 bedrs SB £40 DB £60 HBS £55 HBD £90
B £5 L £9 D £15 CC: None accepted

How to get there: Follow A3055 to Sandown,
then Shanklin. Follow Beach Lift signs.

303 Denewood Hotel

◆ ◆ ◆ ◆ ✕

7 Victoria Road, Sandown,
Isle of Wight, PO36 8AL
Tel: 01983 402980 Fax: 01983 402980
Email: holiday@denewoodhotel.co.uk
15 bedrs CC: MC Vi Swi Delt

304 Empress of the Sea

◆ ◆ ◆ ◆ ℞

10 Luccombe Road, Shanklin,
Isle of Wight, PO37 6RQ
Tel: 01983 862178 Fax: 01983 868636
Email: empress.sea@btopenworld.com
Web: www.empressofthesea.com
15 bedrs SB £50 DB £100 HBS £60 HBD £60
B £5 D £10
CC: MC Vi Am DC Swi Delt JCB

How to get there: Follow signs to Shanklin,
towards Ventnor. Turn onto Priory Road off
Church Road opposite Big Mead and arrive right.

305 Lake Hotel

◆ ◆ ◆ ◆ ✕

Shore Road, Lower Bonchurch, Ventnor,
Isle of Wight, PO38 1RF
Tel: 01983 852613
Email: richard@lakehotel.co.uk
Web: www.lakehotel.co.uk
Children minimum age: 3
Closed November to February
20 bedrs SB £30 DB £60 HBS £40 HBD £76
B £6 D £10
CC: None accepted

How to get there: The Lake Hotel is situated
opposite Bonchurch Pond, within easy reach of
Shanklin.

306 Lincoln Hotel

◆ ◆ ◆ ◆ ℘

30 Littlestairs Road, Shanklin,
Isle of Wight, PO37 6HS
Tel: 01983 861167 Fax: 01983 862147
Web: www.geocities.com/lincoln_hotel
Children minimum age: 6
Closed December to February
9 bedrs SB £18 DB £36 CC: None accepted

How to get there: Follow main Newport to
Sandown road. Turn right towards Shanklin.
Over bridge, first road on left.

307 Rockstone Cottage

◆ ◆ ◆ ◆ ✕ ℘

Colwell Chine Road, Freshwater,
Isle of Wight, PO40 9NR
Tel: 01983 753723 Fax: 01983 753721
Email: enquiries@rockstonecottage.co.uk
Web: www.rockstonecottage.co.uk

Children minimum age: 7
Built 1790, full of character, lovely gardens.
Lounge, licensed bar. 300 yards from Colwell
Bay's sandy beach. Lovely walks along sea
front, over downs. Nearby leisure centre, golf,
horse riding etc.
5 bedrs SB £33 DB £46
CC: None accepted

How to get there: From Yarmouth over bridge
for one mile. At Colwell Bay Inn, turn right.
Cottage is on right hand side.

308 Rooftree Hotel

◆ ◆ ◆ ◆

26 Broadway, Sandown,
Isle of Wight, PO36 9BY
Tel: 01983 403175 Fax: 01983 407354
Web: www.netguides.co.uk
9 bedrs SB £34 DB £62
HBS £41 HBD £31 D £14
CC: MC Vi Am DC Swi Delt
How to get there: The Broadway is the Isle of
Wight's main A-road. Hotel is on the corner of
Melville Street. From the rail station, turn right
and immediately left. Turn right onto the
Broadway, hotel up on left.

Southeast

309 St. Catherine's Hotel

1 Winchester Park Road, Sandown,
Isle of Wight, PO36 8HJ
Tel: 01983 402392 Fax: 01983 402392
Email: stcathhotel@hotmail.com
Web: www.isleofwight-holidays.co.uk
19 bedrs CC: MC Vi Swi Delt

How to get there: By car from Fishbourne to
Sandown, turn right at mini roundabout up
Broadway. St. Catherine's is at top of hill on left,
on corner of Broadway and Winchester Park Rd.

310 St. Leonard's Hotel

22 Queens Road, Shanklin,
Isle of Wight, PO37 6AW
Tel: 01983 862121 Fax: 01983 868895
Email: info@wight-breaks.co.uk
Web: www.wight-breaks.co.uk
Children minimum age: 3
7 bedrs SB £23 DB £46 HBS £33 HBD £33
CC: MC Vi Swi Delt

How to get there: Approach Shanklin on A3054.
At Fiveways lights take left-hand fork (signed
Ventnor). Hotel is on right after 1/4 mile.

311 The Lodge

Main Road, Brighstone, Isle of Wight, PO30 4DJ
Tel: 01983 741272 Fax: 01983 741144
Email: paul@thelodgebrighstone.com
Web: www.thelodgebrighstone.com
7 bedrs DB £50 CC: None accepted

How to get there: Leave Newport via Carisbrooke.
Take B3323 then B3399 to Brighstone. Proceed
through village, past Three Bishops Pub. The
Lodge is 1/2 mile on left-hand side.

312 Albert Cottage Hotel

York Avenue, East Cowes,
Isle of Wight, PO32 6BD
Tel: 01983 299309 Fax: 01983 299957
Email: james@scully-syer.fsnet.co.uk
Web: www.albertcottagehotel.co.uk
14 bedrs SB £55 DB £72 HBS £67 HBD £42
B £5 L £11 D £18 CC: MC Vi Am Swi Delt

How to get there: Situated very close to
Osbourne House in York Avenue.

313 Belmore Private Hotel

101 Station Avenue, Sandown,
Isle of Wight, PO36 8HD
Tel: 01983 404189 Fax: 01983 405942
Email: iowbelmore@talk21.com
Web: www.islandbreaks.co.uk/belmore
Children minimum age: 5
Closed 25–26 December
9 bedrs SB £17 DB £34 HBS £23 HBD £23
CC: MC Vi

How to get there: From Fishbourne car ferry,
turn left at traffic lights, take 3055 road to
Sandown. Driving along Broadway, turn left at
antique shop. Belmore is on left, past
Conservative Club.

314 Brackla Hotel

7 Leed Street, Sandown, Isle of Wight, PO36 9DA
Tel: 01983 403648 Fax: 01983 402887
Email: web@brackla-hotel.co.uk
Web: www.brackla-hotel.co.uk
Children minimum age: 3.
Closed October/March
14 bedrs SB £25 DB £50
CC: MC Vi Swi Delt

How to get there: Leed Street is situated off
main Brading to Shanklin road (A3055).

315 Georgian House Guest House

22 George Street, Ryde, Isle of Wight, PO33 2EW
Tel: 01983 563588
Email: d.cooke1@ntlworld.com
Web: www.georgian-guesthouse.co.uk
6 bedrs SB £23 DB £36
CC: None accepted

How to get there: George Street is opposite
Bus/Railway Station and Hovercraft terminal.
Hotel is 100 yards up George Street on right
hand side.

316 Latton House

♦ ♦ ♦ ℮

Madeira Road, Totland Bay,
Isle of White, PO39 0BJ
Tel: 01938 754868 Fax: 01983 754868
Children minimum age: 12.
Closed Christmas
4 bedrs SB £30 DB £52 HBS £46 HBD £42
D £16 CC: None accepted
⊗⊗⌷☐**P**♨ℍ

How to get there: A3054 from Yarmouth Ferry
Terminal towards Freshwater/Totland. Straight
on at first roundabout, right at next.

317 Little Span Farm

♦ ♦ ♦

Rew Lane, Wroxall, Ventnor,
Isle of Wight, PO38 3AU
Tel: 01983 852419 Fax: 01983 852419
Email: info@spanfarm.co.uk
Web: www.spanfarm.co.uk

Little Span Farm is working arable/sheep farm
situated in an area of outstanding natural
beauty, close to Ventnor and Shanklin beaches
and tourist attractions. Ideal for walking, cycling
or family holidays.
4 bedrs DB £40 CC: None accepted
✿⊗⌷☐**P**♨ℍ

How to get there: From B3327 to Wroxall turn
into West Street (by Post Ofice); drive out into
countryside around sharp bend. First farm on
right.

318 Mount House Hotel

♦ ♦ ♦ ⋊

20 Arthurs Hill, Shanklin, Isle of Wight, PO37 6EE
Tel: 01983 862556 Fax: 01983 867551
Closed January
9 bedrs SB £19 DB £38 HBS £26 HBD £52 D £8
CC: MC Vi Swi Delt
✿⌷☐**P**♨ℍ♨ᴍ

How to get there: Hotel is on the main road
from Sandown to Shanklin (A3055), on the
corner between Clarance Road and Arthurs Hill.

319 Richmond Hotel

♦ ♦ ♦

23 Palmerston Road, Shanklin,
Isle of Wight, PO37 6AS
Tel: 01983 862874 Fax: 01983 862874
Email: richmondhotel.shanklin@virgin.net
Web: www.richmondhotel-shanklin.co.uk
Closed November to February

Ideally situated to Shanklin old village, theatre
and beach, we offer a friendly welcome. A
comfortable home atmosphere and excellent
cooking — in fact, we are the missing ingredient
to your holiday.
10 bedrs SB £23 DB £46 HBS £33 HBD £66
CC: MC Vi Swi Delt
⊗⊗⌷☐**P**♨♨℃ℍ♨ᴍ

How to get there: Turn off Shanklin High Street
opposite Boots. Hotel facing you.

320 Shangri-La Hotel

♦ ♦ ♦ ℮

30 Broadway, Sandown, Isle of Wight, PO36 9BY
Tel: 01983 403672 Fax: 01983 403672
Email: shangrilahotel@aol.com
Web: www.shangrilahotel.co.uk
14 bedrs SB £20 DB £40 HBS £29 HBD £29
CC: MC Vi Swi Delt JCB
♿⊗⌷☐**P**♨ℍ♨ᴍ℮⚹

How to get there: On A3055. Turn left at traffic
lights from Newport Road. Hotel is on right after
approx ³/₄ mile.

321 White House Hotel

♦ ♦ ♦

7 Park Road, Shanklin, Isle of Wight, PO37 6AY
Tel: 01983 862776 Fax: 01983 865980

Southeast

322 Channel View Hotel

◆◆

4-8 Royal Street, Sandown,
Isle of Wight, PO36 8LP
Tel: 01983 402347 Fax: 01983 404128

Kidlington, Oxfordshire

323 Bowood House

◆◆◆

238 Oxford Road, Kidlington,
Oxfordshire, OX5 1EB
Tel: 01865 842288 Fax: 01865 841858
Email: bowoodhouse@kidlingtontotalserve.co.uk
Web: www.2stay.com/uk/hotels/bowood.html
20 bedrs SB £47.50 DB £59.50
HBS £59.50 HBD £36 D £9.50
CC: MC Vi Am Swi Delt JCB
How to get there: From south, M40 J8 onto
A40, at roundabout follow signs for Kidlington.
From north, M40 J9, A34, signs for Kidlington.

Kingston-upon-Thames, Surrey

324 The Kingston Lodge

★★★

94 Kingston Hill, Kingston-upon-Thames,
Surrey, KT2 7NP
Tel: 020 8541 4481 Fax: 020 8547 1013
Email: james.lever@forte-hotels.com
Web: www.heritage-hotels.com
84 bedrs SB £65 DB £125
HBS £75 HBD £75
B £8.50 L £9.95 D £18.50
CC: MC Vi Am Swi
How to get there: M25 Junction 10 to A3, up to
Robin Hood roundabout, after 14½ miles. Sharp
left onto Kingston Hill. Hotel 1½ miles on left.

325 Hotel Antoinette

★★

26 Beaufort Road, Kingston-upon-Thames,
Surrey, KT1 2TQ
Tel: 020 8546 1044 Fax: 020 8547 2595
Email: hotelantoinette@btconnect.com
Web: www.hotelantoinette.co.uk

Well-established family-owned hotel situated
close to London and many tourist attractions.
Comfortable accommodation, inviting
atmosphere and large car park. Brasserie
restaurant. Landscaped gardens.
100 bedrs SB £55 DB £65 B £8.50 D £12
CC: MC Vi Am Swi
How to get there: From Junction nine of M25
follow A243 to Kingston/Surbiton. At Surbiton
take second right after railway bridge, Maple
Road, then turn left at third set of traffic lights.

326 Travelodge Kingston

Travel Accommodation
Tel: 08700 850 950
Web: www.travelodge.co.uk
Opens September 2002
72 bedrs B £4.25
CC: MC Vi Am DC Swi Delt

Leatherhead, Surrey

327 Bookham Grange

★★

Little Bookham Common, Bookham,
Leatherhead, Surrey, KT23 3HS
Tel: 01372 452742 Fax: 01372 450080
Email: bookhamgrange@easynet.co.uk
Web: www.bookham-grange.co.uk
27 bedrs SB £70 DB £90
HBS £85 HBD £60
L £15 D £15
CC: MC Vi Am DC Swi
How to get there: Exit nine of M25 into
Leatherhead and A246 towards Guildford. In
Bookham, turn right into High Street, straight on
into Church Road and first right after Bookham
Station.

Leighton Buzzard

328 Travelodge Leighton Buzzard

Travel Accommodation
A5, Watling Street, Hockliffe, Leighton Buzzard,
Bedfordshire, LU7 9NB
Tel: 08700 850 950
Web: www.travelodge.co.uk
28 bedrs B £4.25
CC: MC Vi Am DC Swi Delt

Lewes, East Sussex

329 Shelleys Hotel

★★★★ 🐾 🐾
High Street, Lewes, East Sussex, BN7 1XS
Tel: 01273 472361 Fax: 01273 483152
Email: info@shelleys-hotel-lewes.com
Web: www.shelleys-hotel-lewes.com
19 bedrs SB £115 DB £172 HBS £118.50
HBD £86.50 B £10.25 L £8.50 D £25
CC: MC Vi Am DC Swi Delt

How to get there: From A23 London to Brighton
road, turn on A27 north of Brighton, signposted
Lewes. Hotel in High Street.

330 White Hart Hotel

★★★
High Street, Lewes, East Sussex, BN7 1XE
Tel: 01273 476694 Fax: 01273 476695
52 bedrs SB £62 DB £89 B £4 L £7.50 D £7.50
CC: MC Vi Am DC Swi Delt

How to get there: Hotel is in the town centre,
facing the law courts. The A27 Eastbourne to
Brighton Road skirts Lewes.
See advert right

331 Berkeley House Hotel

◆ ◆ ◆ ◆ ⚭
2 Albion Street, Lewes, East Sussex, BN7 2ND
Tel: 01273 476057 Fax: 01273 479575
Email: rp.berkeleyhse@lineone.net
Web: www.berkeleyhousehotel.co.uk
Closed Christmas
5 bedrs SB £40 DB £50
CC: MC Vi Am DC Swi Delt JCB

How to get there: Albion Street is a turning off
School Hill, which is part of the High Street in
the town centre.

332 Millers

◆ ◆ ◆ ◆
134 High Street, Lewes, East Sussex, BN7 1XS
Tel: 01273 475631 Fax: 01273 486226
Email: millers134@aol.com
Web: hometown.aol.com/millers134
Closed Christmas to New Year, Bonfire Night
2 bedrs SB £51 DB £57
CC: None accepted

How to get there: Situated on the High Street —
but be aware of the consecutive numbering.

Liphook, Hampshire

333 Travelodge Liphook

Travel Accommodation
A3 North, Liphook Bypass, Liphook,
Hampshire, GU30 7TT
Tel: 08700 850 950
Web: www.travelodge.co.uk
40 bedrs B £4.25
CC: MC Vi Am DC Swi Delt

White Hart Hotel

A charming 16th-century coaching inn which
has been magnificently extended to comprise
an indoor leisure complex with pool, sauna,
steam room and gym. Accommodation is
available in the main house or in our
contemporary annexe.

This privately owned, family run hotel offers a
friendly and lively though relaxed atmosphere.

High Street, Lewes,
East Sussex BN17 1XE
Tel: 01273 476694 Fax: 01273 476695

Southeast

Little Horsted, East Sussex

334 Horsted Place Sporting Estate & Hotel
Blue Ribbon Winner

★★★

Little Horsted, Uckfield, East Sussex, TN22 5TS
Tel: 01825 750581 Fax: 01825 750459
Email: hotel@horstedplace.co.uk
Web: www.horstedplace.co.uk
Children minimum age: 8
20 bedrs SB £125 DB £250 B £9.50 L £12.95
D £32 CC: MC Vi Am DC Swi Delt

How to get there: Exit M23 Jct 10 to East
Grinstead then A22 to Uckfield/Eastbourne. Hotel
is one mile south of Uckfield on A26 to Lewes.

Littlehampton, West Sussex

335 Travelodge Littlehampton

Travel Accommodation
A259, Worthing Road, Rustington,
Littlehampton, West Sussex, BN17 6JN
Tel: 08700 850 950
Web: www.travelodge.co.uk
36 bedrs B £4.25 CC: MC Vi Am DC Swi Delt

336 Rustington House Hotel

◆◆◆◆

Broadmark Lane, Rustington, Littlehampton,
West Sussex, BN16 2HH
Tel: 01903 771198
Email: rustingtonhousehotel@yahoo.com
Web: www.rustingtonhousehotel.com
Closed November
8 bedrs SB £39 DB £69 B £6.50
CC: MC Vi Swi Delt

How to get there: Follow signs for Rustington.
At traffic lights, look for tourist signs pointing to
hotel; Property is 400 yards on right from traffic
lights.
See advert on facing page

Need help booking?

RAC Hotel Reservations will find
the accommodation that's right
for you – and book it too.
Call today on 0870 603 9109
and quote 'Guide 2002'

Luton, Bedfordshire

337 Travelodge Luton

Travel Accommodation
641 Dunstable Road, Luton,
Bedfordshire, LU4 8RQ
Tel: 08700 850 950
Web: www.travelodge.co.uk
140 bedrs B £4.25
CC: MC Vi Am DC Swi Delt

338 Leaside Hotel & Restaurant

◆◆◆

72 New Bedford Road, Luton,
Bedfordshire, LU3 1BT
Tel: 01582 417643 Fax: 01582 734961
Closed 25–26, 31 December
16 bedrs SB £40 DB £55
B £8.50 L £19.50 D £19.50
CC: MC Vi Am DC Swi Delt JCB

How to get there: Situated near town centre
approx three miles from airport. Access to the
car park is via Old Bedford and Villa roads.

Lymington, Hampshire

339 Passford House Hotel

★★★

Mount Pleasant, Lymington,
Hampshire, SO41 8LS
Tel: 01590 682398 Fax: 01590 683494

340 Stanwell House

★★★

14–15 High Street, Lymington,
Hampshire, SO41 9AA
Tel: 01590 677123 Fax: 01590 677756
Email: sales@stanwellhousehotel.co.uk
Web: www.stanwellhousehotel.co.uk
29 bedrs SB £85 DB £110
HBS £110 HBD £80
B £6.50 L £9 D £25
CC: MC Vi Am DC Swi Delt

How to get there: Take Junction 1 M27, then
A397 Lyndhurst and Brockenhurst into
Lymington High Street. Hotel halfway along.
See advert on facing page

341 Britannia House

Mill Lane, Lymington, Hampshire, SO41 9AY
Tel: 01590 672091
Email: enquiries@britannia-house.com
Web: www.britannia-house.com
Children minimum age: 12

This luxurious 1870 character guest house
provides every comfort, yet only two minutes'
walk from picturesque Lymington marinas, shops
and restaurants. A traditional full English breakfast
is served in the cosy farmhouse kitchen.
3 bedrs SB £55 DB £75
CC: MC Vi Am Swi Delt JCB

How to get there: M27 west J1, A337 through
Lyndhurst and Brockenhurst: Britannia House is
in Lymington centre, corner of Station Street
and Mill Lane.

342 Efford Cottage

Everton, Lymington, Hampshire, SO41 0JD
Tel: 01590 642315 Fax: 01590 641030
Email: effordcottage@aol.com
Web: www.effordcottage.co.uk
Children minimum age: 14
3 bedrs DB £50
CC: None accepted

How to get there: Two miles west of Lymington
on A337 on the eastern edge of village of
Everton.

343 The Angel Inn

108 High Street, Lymington,
Hampshire, SO41 9AP
Tel: 01590 672050 Fax: 01590 671661
Web: www.eldridge-pope-inns.co.uk
12 bedrs SB £35 DB £70 L £3 D £7.95
CC: MC Vi Swi Delt

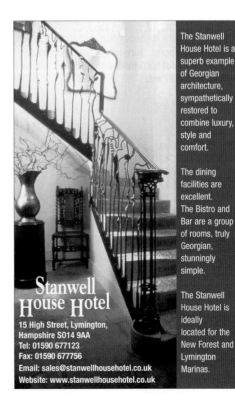
Southeast

Lyndhurst, Hampshire

344 Forest Lodge Hotel

★★★

Pikes Hill, Romsey Road, Lyndhurst,
Hampshire, SO43 7AS
Tel: 023 8028 3677 Fax: 023 8028 2940
Email: forest@carehotels.co.uk
Web: www.carehotels.co.uk
28 bedrs SB £60 DB £120 HBS £81.50
HBD £81.50 B £7.50 L £5 D £21.50
CC: MC Vi Am Swi Delt

How to get there: Exit M27 at J1. Take A337,
and after approximately three miles turn right
into Pikes Hill. Forest Lodge is on left.
See advert on this page

345 Knightwood Lodge

★

Southampton Road, Lyndhurst,
Hampshire, SO43 7BU
Tel: 023 8028 2502 Fax: 023 8028 3730
Web: www.knightwoodlodge.co.uk
18 bedrs SB £47.50 DB £90 HBS £62.50
HBD £120 L £4.95 D £17.95
CC: MC Vi Am DC Swi Delt JCB

How to get there: From Junction 1 of M27, take
A337 for Lyndhurst. Turn left at traffic lights in
Lyndhurst. Hotel is ¼ mile along A35
Southampton Road.

346 Little Hayes

◆◆◆◆

43 Romsey Road, Lyndhurst,
Hampshire, SO43 7AR
Tel: 023 8028 3816
5 bedrs DB £56
CC: MC Vi Swi Delt JCB

How to get there: From Junction 1 of M27, take
A337 signposted Lyndhurst. Little Hayes is on
right as you enter village.

347 Lyndhurst House

◆◆◆◆

35 Romsey Road, Lyndhurst,
Hampshire, SO43 7AR
Tel: 023 8028 2230 Fax: 023 8028 2230
Email: lyndhursthouse@aol.com
Web: www.newforest.demon.co.uk/lynho.html
Children minimum age: 10

5 bedrs SB £35 DB £48
CC: MC Vi

How to get there: M27 Junction 1, A337 to
Lyndhurst. Approx ¼ mile inside 30mph limit, on
right-hand side, laying back off road.

348 Penny Farthing Hotel

◆◆◆◆

Romsey Road, Lyndhurst, Hampshire, SO43 7AA
Tel: 023 8028 4422 Fax: 023 8028 4488
Email: stay@pennyfarthinghotel.co.uk
Web: www.pennyfarthinghotel.co.uk
Closed Christmas

A cheerful small hotel, ideally situated in the
village of Lyndhurst. Offering licensed bar,
bicycle store, comfortable ensuite rooms with
colour TV, telephone and tea/coffee making
facilities and large car park. Ideal base for
touring New Forest.
15 bedrs SB £45 DB £68 B £6.50
CC: MC Vi Am DC Swi Delt

How to get there: Leave M27 at Junction 1.
Take A337 to Lyndhurst. Hotel is on left as you
enter village.

Maidenhead, Berkshire

349 Monkey Island

★★★★★ 🛎🛎

Bray-on-Thames, Maidenhead,
Berkshire, SL6 2EE
Tel: 01628 623400 Fax: 01628 784732
Email: monkeyisland@btconnect.com
Web: www.monkeyisland.co.uk
26 bedrs SB £120 DB £150 HBS £160
HBD £105 B £8 L £24.50 D £35
CC: MC Vi Am DC Swi Delt

How to get there: J8/9 M4 to Maidenhead
central, second exit roundabout Windsor A308,
second left Bray village, right Old Mill lane.
Signposted to Hotel.

350 Thames Hotel

★★★
Raymead Road, Maidenhead, Berkshire, SL6 8NR
Tel: 01628 628721 Fax: 01628 773921
Email: reservations@thameshotel.co.uk
Web: www.thameshotel.co.uk

Idyllically situated on the banks of the River Thames. The hotel has 35 ensuite rooms, many with superb views of the river.
35 bedrs SB £103 DB £121 B £8 D £15
CC: MC Vi Am DC Swi Delt

How to get there: Leave M4 at Junction 7. Signed to Maidenhead. Over bridge and turn right at mini roundabout. Hotel is 200 yards on left.

351 The Inn on The Green

♦♦♦♦
The Old Cricket Common, Cookham Dean, Berkshire, SL6 9NZ
Tel: 01628 482638 Fax: 01628 487474
Email: enquiries@theinnonthegreen.com
Web: www.theinnonthegreen.com
9 bedrs SB £100 DB £120 HBS £120 HBD £80
B £10 L £13.95 D £17.95
CC: MC Vi Am Swi Delt
How to get there: First left after Marlow Bridge. After 1½ miles take first right, then first left, first left again, then turn left at the war memorial.

352 Clifton Guest House

♦♦♦
21 Crauford Rise, Maidenhead, Berkshire, SL6 7LR
Tel: 01628 620086 Fax: 01628 623572
Email: clifton@aroram.freeserve.co.uk
Web: www.cliftonguesthouse.co.uk
20 bedrs SB £40 DB £65
CC: MC Vi Am Swi Delt JCB

The
Forest Lodge
Hotel

The Forest Lodge Hotel is situated on the outskirts of the village of Lyndhurst and still retains much of its Georgian architecture.

Forest Lodge offers 28 delightfully furnished bedrooms along with an indoor leisure facility consisting of swimming pool, sauna and fitness room.

Pikes Hill, Lyndhurst, Hants SO43 7AS
Tel: 02380 283677   Fax: 02380 282940
Email: forest@carehotels.co.uk
Website: www.carehotels.co.uk

How to get there: From M4 Junction 8/9, follow A308 to Maidenhead Central and on towards Marlow. Crauford Rise is off Marlow Road.

Maidstone, Kent

353 Marriott Tudor Park Hotel & Country Club

★★★★
Ashford Road, Bearsted, Maidstone, Kent, ME14 4NQ
Tel: 01622 734334 Fax: 01622 735260
Web: www.marriotthotels.com/tdmgs
120 bedrs SB £110 DB £118 HBS £102
HBD £77 B £13 L £16.95 D £25
CC: MC Vi Am DC Swi Delt JCB
How to get there: Exit J8 M20; take Lenham exit at first roundabout, and Bearsted exit at second. Tudor Park is 1½ miles on the left.

Plan your route

Visit www.rac.co.uk for RAC's interactive route planner, including up to the minute traffic reports.

Southeast

354 Grange Moor Hotel

★★

St. Michael's Road, Maidstone, Kent, ME16 8BS
Tel: 01622 677623 Fax: 01622 678246
Email: reservations@grangemoor.co.uk
Closed 26–30 December
51 bedrs SB £48 DB £54 B £5.50 D £15
CC: MC Vi Swi Delt

How to get there: From Maidstone town centre approx. One mile to A26 Tonbridge road; turn left just after church.

355 Ringlestone Inn and Farmhouse Hotel

◆◆◆◆◆

Ringlestone Hamlet, near Harrietsham, Maidstone, Kent, ME17 1NX
Tel: 01622 859900 Fax: 01622 859966
Email: bookings@ringlestone.com
Web: www.ringlestone.com
3 bedrs SB £97 DB £123 B £6 L £6.50 D £7.95
CC: MC Vi Am DC Swi Delt

How to get there: Exit J8 M20 to A20 south. Take Hollingsbourne turn and go through village to top of the hill. Turn right at crossroads.

Westover Hall

RaC ★★★

RAC Dining Award ®®®

ETC Gold Award

A Grade II Listed Victorian Mansion on the edge of the New Forest, 200 yards from the beach with stunning uninterrupted views across to the Needles and Isle of Wight. Magnificent oak panelled interior with stained glass windows and antique furniture. Family owned and run with a relaxed friendly atmosphere. Excellent cuisine. Individually furnished, luxurious bedrooms, many with sea view, all ensuite.
A fascinating and unusual hotel.

Park Lane, Milford-on-Sea, Lymington, Hampshire SO41 0PT
Tel: 01590 643044 Fax: 01590 644490
Email: westoverhallhotel@barclays.net
Website: www.westoverhallhotel.com

Margate, Kent

356 Greswolde

◆◆◆◆ ⚔

20 Surrey Road, Cliftonville, Kent, CT9 2LA
Tel: 01843 223956 Fax: 01843 223956
Email: j.bearl@freeuk.co.uk
Children minimum age: 10
5 bedrs SB £28 DB £40 CC: MC Vi

How to get there: From London, M2 then A299 then A28. From Dover, A256 then A254. At seafront, turn left at clock tower. Continue past harbour for ½ mile. Surrey Road is on right.

Marlow, Buckinghamshire

357 Danesfield House Hotel and Spa

★★★★ ®®®

Henley Road, Marlow, Buckinghamshire, SL7 2EY
Tel: 01628 891010 Fax: 01628 890408
Email: sales@danesfieldhouse.co.uk
Web: www.danesfieldhouse.co.uk

Built at the turn of the century, the hotel stands in 65 acres of grounds overlooking the River Thames. Luxurious extensive spa includes 50 treatments, 20m pool, fitness studio etc.
87 bedrs SB £175 DB £225
B £12.50 L £24.50 D £26.50
CC: MC Vi Am DC Swi Delt

How to get there: Leave M4 at Junction 8/9 or M40 at Junction four and take A404 to Marlow. Then take A4155 towards Henley.

358 Heritage Hotels – The Compleat Angler

★★★★ ♛ ♛

Marlow Bridge, Marlow,
Buckingamshire, SL7 1RG
Tel: 0870 400 8100 Fax: 01628 486388
Email: heritagehotels_marlow.compleat_angler
@forte-hotels.com
Web: www.heritage-hotels.com
64 bedrs SB £229 DB £263
B £15.50 L £23.50 D £34.50
CC: MC Vi Am DC Swi Delt

How to get there: From A404, at the first roundabout follow signs for Bisham. Hotel is on right immediately before Marlow Bridge.

359 Holly Tree House

◆◆◆◆ ✕

Burford Close, Marlow Bottom,
Buckinghamshire, SL7 3NF
Tel: 01628 891110 Fax: 01628 481278
Email: hollytreeaccommodation@yahoo.co.uk
Closed Christmas to New Year
5 bedrs SB £69.50 DB £84.50
CC: MC Vi Am DC Swi Delt

How to get there: Leave M4 at Junction 8/9 and take A404 towards High Wycombe. Take Marlow turn to second mini-roundabout. Turn right. Proceed until sign indicates Marlow Bottom. Take second on left.

Milford-on-Sea, Hampshire

360 Westover Hall

Blue Ribbon Winner

★★★★ ♛ ♛ ♛

Park Lane, Milford-on-Sea, Hampshire, SO41 0PT
Tel: 01590 643044 Fax: 01590 644490
Email: westoverhallhotel@barclays.net
Web: www.westoverhallhotel.com
Children minimum age: 10

A grade II listed Victorian mansion on the edge of the New Forest, 200 yards from the beach with stunning uninterrupted views to The Needles and Isle of Wight. Family owned and run with a relaxed, friendly atmosphere.
14 bedrs SB £70 DB £120 HBS £95 HBD £85
B £12 L £6.50 D £29.50
CC: MC Vi Am DC Swi Delt

How to get there: Leave M27 at Junction 1. Follow A337 via Lyndhurst, Brockenhurst, Lymington, Pennington then Everton where you take B3058 to Milford-on-Sea.
See advert on facing page

Milton Keynes, Buckinghamshire

361 Moore Place Hotel

★★★ ♛ ♛

The Square, Aspley Guise, near Milton Keynes,
Buckinghamshire, MK17 8DW
Tel: 01908 282000 Fax: 01908 281888
Email: info@mooreplace.co.uk
Web: www.mooreplace.co.uk

Moore Place is a charming Georgian Manor in a delightful village location. The award-winning restaurant overlooks a beautiful courtyard garden with rockery and waterfall.
54 bedrs SB £100 DB £120 HBS £125 HBD £85
B £11 L £13.50 D £21
CC: MC Vi Am DC Swi Delt

How to get there: Exit M1 at Junction 13. Take A507 and then follow signs to Aspley Guise. Moore Place is on left-hand side in the village.

Making a booking?

Don't forget to mention RAC Hotels and Bed & Breakfast 2002.

Southeast

362 Quality Hotel & Suites Milton Keynes

★★★
Monks Way, Two Mile Ash, Milton Keynes,
Buckinghamshire, MK8 8LY
Tel: 01908 561666 Fax: 01908 568303
Email: admin@gb616.u-net.com
Web: www.choicehotels.com
88 bedrs SB £116.75 DB £126.75 HBS £132.75
HBD £71.38 B £11.95 L £3.50 D £16
CC: MC Vi Am DC Swi Delt

How to get there: Exit M1 at Junction 14, follow
until the A5. Go north and take next exit and
follow signs for A422, Two Mile Ash.

363 Swan Revived Hotel

★★ ♖
High Street, Newport Pagnell,
Buckinghamshire, MK16 8AR
Tel: 01908 610565 Fax: 01908 210995
Email: swanrevived@btinternet.com
Web: www.swanrevived.co.uk
42 bedrs SB £48 DB £64 HBS £64 HBD £45
B £8.50 L £5 D £16
CC: MC Vi Am DC Swi Delt

How to get there: From M1 Junction 14 take
A509 to Newport Pagnell (1.³/₄ miles). The hotel
is on the high street opposite the post office.

364 Campanile

Travel Accommodation
40 Penn Road, Fenny Stratford, Bletchley,
Milton Keynes, MK2
Tel: 01908 649819 Fax: 01908 649818
Web: www.envergure.fr

Typical Campanile bistro

Campanile hotels offer comfortable and
convenient budget accommodation and a
traditional French style Bistro providing freshly-
cooked food for breakfast, lunch and dinner. All
rooms ensuite with tea/coffee making facilities,

DDT and TV with Sky channels.
80 bedrs SB £48.90 DB £54.85 B £5.95
CC: MC Vi Am DC Swi Delt

How to get there: Follow A5 south, towards
Dunstable. At Little Chef roundabout, take
fourth exit, on right to Fenny Stratford. Take first
left turn.

365 Travelodge Milton Keynes

Travel Accommodation
V6, 199 Grafton Gate, Milton Keynes,
Buckinghamshire, MK9 1AL
Tel: 08700 850 950
Web: www.travelodge.co.uk
80 bedrs B £4.25 CC: MC Vi Am DC Swi Delt

366 Travelodge Milton Keynes (Bedford)

Travel Accommodation
A421, Beancroft Road, Marston Moretaine,
Milton Keynes, Bedfordshire, MK43 0PZ
Tel: 08700 850 950
Web: www.travelodge.co.uk
54 bedrs B £4.25 CC: MC Vi Am DC Swi Delt

367 Shire Motel

Open Pastures, Buckingham Road,
Deanshanger, Northants, MK19 6JV
Tel: 01908 262925 Fax: 01908 263642
Email: shiremotel@hotmail.com
Web: www.shiremotel.co.uk
47 bedrs SB £45 DB £60 HBS £55 HBD £37.50
B £5 D £5.10
CC: MC Vi Am Swi Delt JCB
How to get there: M1 junction 14 take A509 to
Milton Keynes, follow A5 till roundabout
showing A422 to Buckingham. We are at
Deanshanger on Buckingham Road.
See advert on facing page

Morden, Surrey

368 Travelodge Morden

Travel Accommodation
A24, Epsom Road, Morden, Surrey, SM4 5PH
Tel: 08700 850 950
Web: www.travelodge.co.uk
32 bedrs B £4.25 CC: MC Vi Am DC Swi Delt

Moulsford-on-Thames, Oxfordshire

369 Beetle & Wedge

Blue Ribbon Winner

★★◈◈
Ferry Lane, Moulsford-on-Thames,
Oxfordshire, OX10 9JF
Tel: 01491 651381 Fax: 01491 651376

On the banks of the Thames in an idyllic
location overlooking the water meadows, The
Beetle and Wedge, which is run by the owners,
has two award-winning restaurants and
beautiful accommodation.
10 bedrs SB £99 DB £175 HBS £175 HBD £125
B £17.50 L £15 D £35 CC: MC Vi Am DC Swi Delt

How to get there: From M4 Junction 12 take the
A4 south. At the second roundabout head
towards Wallingford, through Streatley to
Moulsford. Right at Ferry Lane.

New Alresford, Hampshire

370 Swan Hotel

★★
11 West Street, New Alresford,
Hampshire, SO24 9AD
Tel: 01962 732302 Fax: 01962 735274
Email: swanhotel@btinternet.com
23 bedrs CC: MC Vi

New Milton, Hampshire

371 Chewton Glen Hotel
Gold Ribbon Winner

★★★★★◈◈◈
Christchurch Road, New Milton,
Hampshire, BH25 6QS
Tel: 01425 275341 Fax: 01425 272310
Email: reservations@chewtonglen.com
Web: www.chewtonglen.com
Children minimum age: 6

Chewton Glen is the only privately owned hotel
in the UK with RAC 5-Star Rating plus Gold
Ribbon, together with three RAC Dining Awards,
and voted Best Country House Hotel in the
World by the American magazine, Gourmet, in
2000.
62 bedrs SB £295 DB £315 HBS £365
HBD £210 B £20 L £35 D £55
CC: MC Vi Am DC Swi Delt

How to get there: On A35 from Lyndhurst, drive
10 miles and turn left at staggered junction.
Follow brown tourist signs for hotel through
Walkford.

Southeast

Newbury, Berkshire

372 Vineyard at Stockcross
Blue Ribbon Winner

★★★★★ ℝ ℝ ℝ ℝ
Stockcross, Newbury, Berkshire, RG20 8JU
Tel: 01635 528770 Fax: 01635 528398
Email: general@the-vineyard.co.uk
Web: www.the-vineyard.co.uk

The Vineyard blends charm and elegant surroundings and exquisite furniture with beautiful art and sculptures. All guest rooms and suites are individually named after wines.
31 bedrs SB £146 DB £266 HBD £163 B £15.75 L £18 D £49 CC: MC Vi Am DC Swi Delt
How to get there: Exit J13 M4. Take A34 southbound and take exit to Stockcross. At next roundabout take the second exit. The Vineyard is ¼ mile on right.

373 Donnington Valley Hotel & Golf Course
Blue Ribbon Winner

★★★★ ℝ ℝ
Old Oxford Road, Donnington, Newbury, Berkshire, RG14 3AG
Tel: 01635 551199 Fax: 01635 551123
Email: general@donningtonvalley.co.uk
Web: www.donningtonvalley.co.uk

A luxurious privately owned 4-star hotel surrounded by its own 18-hole golf course. Superb food in the 'Wine Press' restaurant with an extensive wine list.
58 bedrs SB £152.50 DB £165 HBS £177.50 HBD £107.50 B £12.50 L £16 D £20
CC: MC Vi Am DC Swi Delt
How to get there: Leave M4 at Junction 13. Take A34 southbound to Newbury. Leave at first exit signed Donnington Castle. Take first right, then left. Hotel is one mile on right.

374 Regency Park Hotel

★★★★ ℝ
Bowling Green Road, Thatcham, Newbury, Berkshire, RG18 3RP
Tel: 01635 871555 Fax: 01635 871571
Email: info@regencyparkhotel.co.uk
Web: www.regencyparkhotel.co.uk

Recently refurbished luxury hotel renowned for its high standards of service. Extensive indoor leisure facilities with pool and gymnasium. Executive standard bedrooms and award-winning restaurant.
82 bedrs SB £125 DB £170 HBS £145 HBD £115 B £105 L £15.50 D £19.50
CC: MC Vi Am DC Swi Delt
How to get there: From Newbury take A4 signed Thatcham/Reading. At second roundabout follow signs to Cold Ash. Hotel one mile on left.

375 Travelodge Newbury

Travel Accommodation
Tothills Service Area, Newbury Bypass, A34 Trunk Road, Newbury, Berkshire, RG20 9ED
Tel: 08700 850 950
Web: www.travelodge.co.uk
40 bedrs B £4.25
CC: MC Vi Am DC Swi Delt

376 Bacon Arms Hotel

♦ ♦ ♦
Oxford Street, Newbury, Berkshire, RG14 1JB
Tel: 01635 31822 Fax: 01635 552496
Email: baconarms.newbury
@eldridge-pope.co.uk
Web: www.eldridge-pope.co.uk
14 bedrs SB £75 DB £85 B £5 L £6.95 D £10
CC: MC Vi Am DC Swi Delt JCB
How to get there: From town centre head along London Road past clock tower monument onto Oxford Street. We are on the right.

377 Queens Hotel

♦ ♦ ♦

8 The Market Place, Newbury,
Berkshire, RG14 5BD
Tel: 01635 47447 Fax: 01635 569626

378 The Swan Public House

♦ ♦ ♦

Station Road, Thatcham, Newbury,
Berkshire, RG19 4QL
Tel: 01635 871847 Fax: 01635 871851
6 bedrs SB £50 DB £60 L £6 D £6
CC: MC Vi Am Swi Delt
How to get there: Exit J12 M4 towards
Newbury. After nine miles turn left at Sony
roundabout; the Swan is about ¹/₂ mile on.

Newick, East Sussex

379 The Pilgrims Rest At The Bull Inn

♦ ♦ ♦

The Bull Inn, The Green, Newick,
East Sussex, BN8 4LA
Tel: 01825 722055
CC: None accepted

Newport Pagnell, Buckinghamshire

380 Courtyard by Marriott Milton Keynes

★ ★ ★

London Road, near Moulsoe, Newport Pagnell,
Buckinghamshire, MK16 0JA
Tel: 01908 613688 Fax: 01908 617335
Email: general.miltonkeynes@whitbread.com
Web: www.go.marriott.com/uk
49 bedrs SB £110 DB £118 B £3.95 L £8 D £10
CC: MC Vi Am DC Swi Delt JCB

381 Thurstons

♦ ♦ ♦

90 High Street, Newport Pagnell,
Buckinghamshire, MK16 8EH
Tel: 01908 611377 Fax: 01908 611394
8 bedrs
CC: MC Vi Am
How to get there: Located in the middle of
town centre in High Street, just off M21
Junction 14.

North Weald, Essex

382 Travelodge North Weald

Travel Accommodation
Epping Road, Tylers Green, North Weald,
Essex, CM16 6BJ
Tel: 08700 850 950
Web: www.travelodge.co.uk
60 bedrs B £4.25
CC: MC Vi Am DC Swi Delt

Old Harlow, Essex

383 Green Man Hotel

★ ★ ★

Mulberry Green, Old Harlow, Essex, CM17 0ET
Tel: 01279 442521 Fax: 01279 626113

Oxford, Oxfordshire

384 Cotswold Lodge Hotel

★ ★ ★ ★ ★ ® ®

66a Banbury Road, Oxford, Oxfordshire, OX2 6JP
Tel: 01865 512121 Fax: 01865 512490
Web: www.cotswoldhotel.co.uk

Beautiful Victorian building, half a mile from the
city centre in a quiet Conservation Area.
Recently refurbished to a very high standard.
Award-winning restaurant. Bar with log fires,
ample parking.
49 bedrs SB £125 DB £175 HBS £150
HBD £112.50 B £9.50 L £12.50 D £17
CC: MC Vi Am DC Swi Delt JCB
How to get there: From A40 ring road north of
Oxford, take A4165 into city. Cotswold Lodge is
on Banbury Road, two miles into city on left.

Southeast

385 Heritage Hotels – The Randolph

★★★★★ ⓡ ⓡ

Beaumont Street, Oxford, Oxfordshire, OX1 2LN
Tel: 0870 4008200
Email: heritagehotels_oxford.randolph
@forte-hotels.com
Web: www.heritage-hotels.com
119 bedrs SB £163.95 DB £200 HBS £190
HBD £220 B £15 L £10.95 D £20
CC: MC Vi Am DC Swi Delt

386 Oxford Belfry

★★★★ ⓡ

Milton Common, Thame, Oxfordshire, OX9 2JW
Tel: 01844 279381 Fax: 01844 279624
Email: oxfordbelfry@marstonhotels.com
Web: www.marstonhotels.com

130 bedrs SB £115 DB £149 HBS £69.50
HBD £69.50 B £12 L £16.50 D £28
CC: MC Vi Am DC Swi Delt

How to get there: Leave M40 northbound at
Junction 7. Travelling southbound leave at
Junction 8a. Hotel situated on A40, 1½ miles
from either junction.

387 Oxford Spires Four Pillars Hotel

★★★★

Abingdon Road, Oxford, Oxfordshire, OX1 4PS
Tel: 01865 324324 Fax: 01865 324325
Email: spires@four-pillars.co.uk
Web: www.four-pillars.co.uk
115 bedrs SB £151.95 DB £194.90 HBS £175.90
HBD £121.40 B £9.95 L £15.95 D £23.95
CC: MC Vi Am DC Swi Delt JCB

How to get there: Exit J9 M40 A34 towards
Oxford; then A423 turn left; left next
roundabout, hotel one mile on the right.
See advert above right

388 Oxford Thames Four Pillars Hotel

★★★★

Henley Road, Sandford-on-Thames, Oxford,
Oxfordshire, OX4 4GX
Tel: 01865 334444 Fax: 01865 334400
Email: thames@four-pillars.co.uk
Web: www.four-pillars.co.uk
60 bedrs SB £151.95 DB £194.90 HBS £175.90
HBD £121.40 B £9.95 L £15.95 D £23.95
CC: MC Vi Am DC Swi Delt JCB

How to get there: J9 M40 A34 towards Oxford.
Take A423 exit, then follow A4074 to Sandford.
At T-junction, turn right; hotel is on left.

389 Heritage Hotels – Eastgate Hotel

★★★ ⓡ

Merton Street, Oxford, Oxfordshire, OX1 4BE
Tel: 0870 400 8201 Fax: 01865 791681
Email: heritagehotels_oxford.eastgate
@forte-hotels.com
Web: www.heritage-hotels.com
64 bedrs SB £85 DB £160 HBS £105 HBD £90
B £10.50 L £5.95 D £10.95
CC: MC Vi Am DC Swi Delt

390 Balkan Lodge Hotel

★★

315 Iffley Road, Oxford, Oxfordshire, OX4 4AG
Tel: 01865 244524 Fax: 01865 251090
13 bedrs SB £68.50 DB £78.50
CC: MC Vi Swi Delt

391 Foxcombe Lodge Hotel

★★

Fox Lane, Boars Hill, Oxford,
Oxfordshire, OX1 5DP
Tel: 01865 326326 Fax: 01865 730628
Email: res@foxcombe.demon.co.uk
Web: www.circlehotels.co.uk
19 bedrs SB £50 DB £85 HBS £68 HBD £60
B £8.50 L £12.50 D £18.50
CC: MC Vi Am DC Swi Delt JCB

How to get there: At Hinksey Hill junction
A34/A4142 follow signs for Wooton. At top of
hill (½ mile) turn right. Hotel one mile on left.

392 Palace Hotel

★★

250–250a Iffley Road, Oxford,
Oxfordshire, OX4 1SE
Tel: 01865 727627 Fax: 01865 200478
Web: www.oxlink.co.uk/oxford/hotels/theplace
8 bedrs SB £69 DB £80 HBS £72.50 HBD £90
B £5.80 D £7.50 CC: MC Vi Am Swi Delt

How to get there: From city centre take A4158;
property is ½ a mile on the right-hand side.

393 Victoria Hotel

★★

180 Abingdon Road, Oxford,
Oxfordshire, OX1 4RA
Tel: 01865 724536 Fax: 01865 794909
Web: www.localhost/hotels/victoria
20 bedrs SB £65.50 DB £82.50
CC: MC Vi Swi Delt

394 Travelodge Oxford

Travel Accommodation
A34/A44, Peartree Roundabout,
Woodstock Road, Oxford, Oxfordshire, OX2 8JZ
Tel: 08700 850 950
Web: www.travelodge.co.uk
150 bedrs B £4.25 CC: MC Vi Am DC Swi Delt

395 Chestnuts Guest House

♦ ♦ ♦ ♦ ♦

45 Davenant Road, off Woodstock Road,
Oxford, Oxfordshire, OX2 8BU
Tel: 01865 553375 Fax: 01865 553375
Email: stay@chestnutguesthouse.co.uk
Children minimum age: 10
6 bedrs SB £50 DB £70
CC: MC Vi Am DC Swi Delt JCB

How to get there: Leave A40/A34 at Peartree
roundabout for Woodstock Road, then
Woodstock/A414 second left and A40 West off
Woodstock Road roundabout.

396 Eltham Villa

♦ ♦ ♦ ♦

148 Woodstock Road, Yarnton, Oxford,
Oxfordshire, OX5 1PW
Tel: 01865 376037 Fax: 01865 376037
Children minimum age: 5
Closed Christmas to New Year
6 bedrs
CC: MC Vi Swi Delt

How to get there: On the A44 between Oxford
and Woodstock, minutes from Blenheim Palace.

397 Galaxie Hotel

♦ ♦ ♦ ♦

180 Banbury Road, Oxford, Oxfordshire, OX2 7BT
Tel: 01865 515688 Fax: 01865 556824
Email: info@galaxie.co.uk
Web: www.galaxie.co.uk
32 bedrs
CC: MC Vi Swi Delt

How to get there: Situated one mile north of the
City of Oxford on the Banbury Road.

398 Marlborough House Hotel

♦ ♦ ♦ ♦

321 Woodstock Road, Oxford,
Oxfordshire, OX2 7NY
Tel: 01865 311321 Fax: 01865 515329
Email: enquiries@marlbhouse.win-uk.net
Web: www.oxfordcity.co.uk/hotels/marlborough
Children minimum age: 5
16 bedrs SB £69 DB £80
CC: MC Vi Am DC Swi Delt

How to get there: Located in north Oxford, six
miles from Junction 9, M40. 1½ miles from city
centre.

Southeast

399 Pickwick's

15/17 London Road, Headington,
Oxfordshire, OX3 7SP
Tel: 01865 750487 Fax: 01865 742208
Email: pickwicks@x-stream.co.uk
Web: www.pickwicks.oxfree.com
Closed Christmas and New Year
15 bedrs SB £40 DB £65
CC: MC Vi Am DC Swi Delt

How to get there: From M40 and Oxford ring road, follow city centre directions through Headington. Pickwicks is on the right after one mile.

400 Acorn Guest House

260–262 Iffley Road, Oxford,
Oxfordshire, OX4 1SE
Tel: 01865 247998 Fax: 01865 247998
Children minimum age: 9
Closed Christmas to New Year
12 bedrs SB £29 DB £52
CC: MC Vi Am Swi Delt JCB

How to get there: From Oxford ring road, follow A4158 north towards city centre. From roundabout go one mile; hotel is on left, just after Motorworld VW garage on right.

401 Bath Place Hotel

4/5 Bath Place, Holywell Street, Oxford,
Oxfordshire, OX1 3SU
Tel: 01865 791812 Fax: 01865 791834
Email: bathplace@compuserve.com
Web: www.bathplace.co.uk
Closed Christmas & New Year
14 bedrs SB £90 DB £95
CC: MC Vi Am DC Swi Delt

How to get there: Follow signs to the city centre, the hotel is 100 yards from Mansfield Road and Parks Road.

402 Coach and Horses

Stadhamton Road, Chislehampton,
Oxfordshire, OX44 7UX
Tel: 01865 890255 Fax: 01865 891995
Email: david-mcphillips@lineone.net
Web: www.coachhorsesinn.co.uk
Closed 26–30 December

A charming 16th-century oak-beamed inn and free house set in splendind Oxfordshire countryside. Excellent reputation for food and service.
9 bedrs SB £49.50 DB £60 L £5 D £10
CC: MC Vi Am DC Swi Delt

403 River Hotel

17 Botley Road, Oxford, Oxfordshire, OX2 0AA
Tel: 01865 243475 Fax: 01865 724306
Web: www.riverhotel.co.uk
Closed Christmas and New Year

Originally a master builder's home built in the 1870s, having been a small hotel for many years, now independently run by proprietor and staff, offering well-equipped bedrooms, most with en-suite facilities. Excellent location by River Thames at Osney Bridge. Easy walk to city.
20 bedrs SB £60 DB £70
CC: MC Vi

How to get there: For Botley Road, exit A420 west off ring road (A34). One mile towards city and rail station. Hotel on right beside Osney Bridge.

404 The Talkhouse

Wheatley Road, Stanton St. John, near Oxford,
Oxfordshire, OX33 1EX
Tel: 01865 351648 Fax: 01865 351085
Email: talkhouse@stantonstjohn.fsnet.co.uk
4 bedrs SB £40 DB £60 B £4.95 L £5.50 D £8.95
CC: MC Vi Am Swi Delt
How to get there: Find Oxford ring road
intersection with A40 — the Headington
roundabout. The last exit (crematorium)
continue to T-junction and turn right.

Pagham, West Sussex

405 Inglenook Hotel

★★★

253–255 Pagham Road, Pagham,
West Sussex, PO21 3QB
Tel: 01243 262495 Fax: 01243 262668
Email: reception@the-inglenook.com
Web: www.the-inglenook.com
18 bedrs SB £50 DB £90 HBS £60 HBD £57.50
B £8.50 L £11.95 D £16.95
CC: MC Vi Am DC Swi Delt
How to get there: Ten minutes from A27,
travelling south, signposted Pagham.
See advert below right

Pangbourne, Berkshire

406 George Hotel

★★★

The Square, Pangbourne, Berkshire, RG8 7AJ
Tel: 01189 842237 Fax: 01189 844354
Email: info@georgehotelpangbourne.co.uk
Web: www.georgehotelpangbourne.co.uk
26 bedrs B £7 L £7 D £15
CC: MC Vi Am DC Swi Delt
How to get there: Leave M4 at Junction 12.
Follow signs for A340 towards Pangbourne. On
arrival in village, turn right at mini roundabout.
Hotel 50 yards on left.

Pevensey, East Sussex

407 Providence Cottage

45 Coast Road, Pevensey, Pevensey Bay,
East Sussex, BN24 6LP
Tel: 01323 769993
2 bedrs DB £35 HBD £25
CC: None accepted
How to get there: From A22 Polegate turn onto
A27; at roundabout turn onto A259, then first
left Wallsend Road, and first left again onto
coast road.

408 Priory Court Hotel

❖

Castle Road, Pevensey, East Sussex, BN24 5LG
Tel: 01323 763150 Fax: 01323 769030
Email: priorycourthotel@aol.com
10 bedrs SB £45 DB £60 B £6 L £6 D £15
CC: MC Vi DC Swi Delt JCB
How to get there: At the roundabout at junction
of A27 and A259, follow sign for Pevensey.

Southeast

Portsmouth, Hampshire

409 Portsmouth Marriott Hotel

★★★★

Southampton Road, Portsmouth,
Hampshire, PO6 4SH
Tel: 023 9238 3151 Fax: 023 9238 8701
Email: reservations.portsmouth
@marriotthotels.co.uk
Web: www.marriotthotels.co.uk
HBS £149 HBD £89.50
B £11 L £12.95 D £12.95
CC: MC Vi Am DC Swi Delt JCB

How to get there: The hotel is located adjacent to the M27 motorway at junction 12, five minutes from Portsmouth city centre.

410 Queen's Hotel

★★★

Clarence Parade, Southsea, Portsmouth,
Hampshire, PO5 3LJ
Tel: 023 9282 2466 Fax: 023 9282 1901
Email: bestwestqueens@aol.com
Web: www.queenshotel-southsea.co.uk
100 bedrs SB £59.75 DB £91.50 HBS £74.50
HBD £60.25 B £9.75 L £14.75 D £19.75
CC: MC Vi Am DC Swi Delt

How to get there: Leave M27 for M275 to Portsmouth. Follow signs to Southsea seafront. Hotel is opposite war memorial.

411 Sandringham Hotel

★★

7 Osborne Road, Southsea,
Hampshire, PO5 3LR
Tel: 023 9282 6969 Fax: 023 9282 2330
Email: reception@sandringham-hotel.co.uk
Web: www.sandringham-hotel.co.uk
44 bedrs SB £30 DB £48 HBS £40.95
HBD £32.95 B £3.95 L £7.95 D £9.95
CC: MC Vi Am DC Swi

How to get there: At end of M275 follow signs for sea front and hovercraft. At Southsea Common turn left; hotel is 300 yards on left.

Plan your route

Visit www.rac.co.uk for RAC's interactive route planner, including up to the minute traffic reports.

412 Travelodge Portsmouth

Travel Accommodation
Kingston Crescent, Portsmouth,
Hampshire, PO2 8QJ
Tel: 08700 850 950
Web: www.travelodge.co.uk
78 bedrs B £4.25
CC: MC Vi Am DC Swi Delt

413 Uppermount House Hotel

♦ ♦ ♦ ♦ ⚄

The Vale, off Clarendon Road, Southsea,
Portsmouth, Hampshire, PO5 2EQ
Tel: 023 9282 0456 Fax: 023 9282 0456

An attractive, family-run Victorian villa with rooms of character, some with four-poster or canopy beds. Within easy walking distance of the city centre.
12 bedrs SB £28 DB £50 HBS £34.50
HBD £37.50
CC: MC Vi Swi Delt JCB

How to get there: Exit M275; head for D-Day musem. Turn down road opposite. Drive over crossroad; right at T-junction and take first right.

414 Abbeville Hotel

♦

26 Nettlecombe Avenue, Portsmouth,
Hampshire, PO4 0QW
Tel: 023 9282 6209
Closed Christmas/New Year
10 bedrs SB £23 DB £46
CC: None accepted

How to get there: Left at South Parade pier, then first left into Granada Road, first right into Bembridge Crescent; hotel on second corner on left.

Princes Risborough, Buckinghamshire

415 Rose & Crown

★★

Wycombe Road, Saunderton, Princes
Risborough, Buckinghamshire, HP27 9NG
Tel: 01844 345299 Fax: 01844 343140
Email: tim@rosecrowninn.com
Undergoing refurbishment for 2002, The Rose
and Crown will be upgraded substantially. The
newly refurbished restaurant and bar serve
excellent food ranging from traditional to
contemporary styles.
15 bedrs SB £73.25 DB £87 B £7.50 L £3.50
D £5.95 CC: MC Vi Am Swi Delt
꙾꙾꙾꙾꙾꙾꙾꙾꙾꙾꙾
How to get there: Situated on the A4010
midway between High Wycombe and Aylesbury.

Purley, Surrey

416 Aries Guest House

◆◆◆

38 Brighton Road, Coulsdon,
Surrey, CR5 2BA
Tel: 020 8668 5744 Fax: 0208668 5744
Email: enquiries@arieshouse.co.uk
Web: www.arieshouse.co.uk
5 bedrs SB £26 DB £40 B £3.50
CC: MC Vi Am Swi Delt
꙾꙾꙾꙾꙾꙾꙾꙾
How to get there: On the A23 between Purley and
Coulsdon — 400 yards north of Coulsdon
shopping centre and Smitham rail station.

Ramsgate, Kent

417 Grove End Hotel

◆◆◆

2 Grange Road, Ramsgate, Kent, CT11 9NA
Tel: 01843 587520 Fax: 01843 853666

Reading, Berkshire

418 Millennium Madejski Hotel Reading

★★★★ ☃ ☃ ☃
Madejski Stadium, Junction 11 M4,
Reading, Berkshire, RG2 0FL
Tel: 0118 925 3500 Fax: 0118 925 3501
Email: sales.reading@mill-cop.com
Web: www.millennium-hotels.com

Prestigious hotel with superb luxury facilities
ideally located in royal Berkshire for business
trips and leisure weekends. Nearby attractions
include Legoland and Windsor Castle.
140 bedrs SB £218.95 DB £232.90
HBS £243.95 HBD £141.45 B £13.95 L £15 D £25
CC: MC Vi Am DC Swi Delt JCB
꙾꙾꙾꙾꙾꙾꙾꙾꙾꙾꙾꙾꙾꙾꙾꙾꙾
How to get there: Take the M4 junction 11.
Follow the A33 towards Reading. Follow signs
to the Madejski Stadium. One mile from M4.

419 Renaissance Reading Hotel

★★★★

Oxford Road, Reading, Berkshire, RG1 7RH
Tel: 0118 958 6222 Fax: 0118 959 7842
Web: www.renaissancehotels.com/lhrlr
196 bedrs SB £145 DB £145 HBS £75 HBD £45
B £9.95 L £10.95 D £10.95
CC: MC Vi Am DC Swi Delt JCB
꙾꙾꙾꙾꙾꙾꙾꙾꙾꙾꙾꙾꙾꙾꙾꙾꙾꙾
How to get there: Exit J11 M4, follow A33 to
Reading town centre where hotel is signposted
from inner distribution road.

420 Copper Inn Hotel

★★★ ☃ ☃
Church Road, Pangbourne-on-Thames,
Berkshire, RG8 7AR
Tel: 0118 9842244 Fax: 0118 9845542
Email: reservations@copper-inn.co.uk
Web: www.copper-inn.co.uk
Ideal for a peaceful stay. The award-winning
restaurant will take you for a walk through
flavours and fresh produce, and the staff will
make you feel at home.
22 bedrs SB £95 DB £120 B £7.50 L £12.95
D £21.95 CC: MC Vi Am DC Swi
꙾꙾꙾꙾꙾꙾꙾꙾꙾꙾꙾꙾꙾꙾꙾
How to get there: Exit M4 J12 for Theale, then
follow A340 to Pangbourne Hotel on left.

Southeast

421 Courtyard by Marriott Reading

★★★

Bath Road, Padworth, Reading,
Berkshire, RG7 5HT
Tel: 0118 971 4411 Fax: 0118 971 4442
Web: www.marriotthotels.com/lhrrd
50 bedrs SB £130 DB £140 B £8.50 L £10 D £15
CC: MC Vi Am DC Swi JCB

How to get there: Exit J12 M4, A4 to Newbury.
Hotel is on the left after 3½ miles. Reading
station approx seven miles.

422 Hanover International Hotel Reading

★★★

Pingewood, Reading, Berkshire, RG30 3UN
Tel: 0118 950 0885 Fax: 0118 939 1996
Email: reading@hanover-international.com
Web: www.hanover-international.com

HANOVER INTERNATIONAL
HOTELS & CLUBS

Stunning modern hotel in a spectacular lakeside
setting, convenient for London, Windsor Castle,
Legoland, M4, Heathrow and Gatwick.
Extensive indoor and outdoor leisure facilities,
including watersports.
81 bedrs SB £139 DB £139
B £12.50 L £10 D £19.50
CC: MC Vi Am DC Swi Delt

How to get there: M4 Junction 11, A33 south
(Basingstoke). Right at first roundabout then
second right. Follow lane for two miles, through
traffic lights. Hotel on left.

423 Mill House Hotel

★★ 🐾

Old Basingstoke Road, Swallowfield, Reading,
Berkshire, RG7 1PY
Tel: 01189 883124 Fax: 01189 885550
Email: info@themillhousehotel.co.uk
Web: www.themillhousehotel.co.uk
Closed 25 December to 3 January

12 bedrs SB £72.50 DB £90 HBS £90
HBD £62.50 B £8.50 L £12.50 D £22.50
CC: MC Vi Am DC Swi Delt

How to get there: On M4, J11, take A33 to
Basingstoke. At roundabout 1st exit, two miles
RHS. M3 J5, signs to Reading, B3349 to
Swallowfield.

424 Rainbow Corner Hotel

★★

132–138 Caversham Road, Reading,
Berkshire, RG1 8AY
Tel: 0118 955 6902 Fax: 0118 958 6500
Email: info@rainbowhotel.co.uk
Web: www.rainbowhotel.co.uk
24 bedrs SB £81.50 DB £98 HBS £95 HBD £62
B £6.50 D £11.95
CC: MC Vi Am DC Swi

How to get there: On A329, one mile from
Reading town centre. Signposted
Caversham/Henley.

425 Travelodge Reading

Travel Accommodation
A33 Southbound, Reading,
Berkshire, RG2 0JE
Tel: 08700 850 950
Web: www.travelodge.co.uk
80 bedrs B £4.25
CC: MC Vi Am DC Swi Delt

426 Travelodge Reading (Central)

Travel Accommodation
Oxbourne House, 58-60 Oxford Road,
Reading, Berkshire, RG1 7LT
Tel: 08700 850 950
Web: www.travelodge.co.uk
80 bedrs B £4.25
CC: MC Vi Am DC Swi Delt

427 Travelodge Reading (East)

Travel Accommodation
M4, Burghfield, Reading, Berkshire, RG30 3UQ
Tel: 08700 850 950
Web: www.travelodge.co.uk
86 bedrs B £4.25
CC: MC Vi Am DC Swi Delt

428 Travelodge Reading (West)

Travel Accommodation
M4, Burghfield, Reading, Berkshire, RG30 3UQ
Tel: 08700 850 950
Web: www.travelodge.co.uk
102 bedrs B £4.25
CC: MC Vi Am DC Swi Delt

429 The Highwayman

◆◆◆◆🍷
Exlade Street, Checkendon, near Reading,
Berkshire, RG8 0UA
Tel: 01491 682020 Fax: 01491 682229
Children minimum age: 5
4 bedrs SB £55 DB £70 B £5 L £14.95 D £18.65
CC: MC Vi Am Swi Delt

How to get there: Take A4074 Reading/Oxford
road; at Woodcote/Checkenden junction follow
signs for Exlade Street to The Highwayman.

Redhill, Surrey

430 Ashleigh House Hotel

◆◆◆◆ ✂
39 Redstone Hill, Redhill, Surrey, RH1 4BG
Tel: 01737 764763 Fax: 01737 780308
Closed Christmas and New Year
8 bedrs SB £40 DB £56 CC: MC Vi

How to get there: Gatwick 15 minutes by car, 10
minutes by train. London 30 minutes by train.

Reigate, Surrey

431 Reigate Manor Hotel

★★★
Reigate Hill, Reigate,
Surrey, RH2 9PF
Tel: 01737 240125 Fax: 01737 223883
50 bedrs
CC: MC Vi Am DC Swi Delt

How to get there: Leave M25 at Junction eight
and head south on A217. Hotel is one mile on
right.

Richmond, Surrey

432 The Bingham Hotel

❖
61/63 Petersham Road, Richmond,
Surrey, TW10 6UT
Tel: 020 8940 0902 Fax: 020 8948 8737

Ringwood, Hampshire

433 Tyrrells Ford Country House Hotel

★★★
Avon, New Forest,
Hampshire, BH23 7BH
Tel: 01425 672646 Fax: 01425 672262
Email: tyrrellsford@aol.com
16 bedrs SB £75 DB £120
HBS £95 HBD £170
B £10 L £17.95 D £25
CC: MC Vi Am Swi Delt JCB

How to get there: Tyrrells Ford from M3/M27 at
Ringwood; follow B3347 for three miles.

434 Travelodge Ringwood

Travel Accommodation
A31, St. Leonards, Ringwood,
Hampshire, BH24 2NR
Tel: 08700 850 950
Web: www.travelodge.co.uk
Opens March 2002
31 bedrs B £4.25
CC: MC Vi Am DC Swi Delt

Southeast

435 The Original White Hart

◆ ◆ ◆
Market Place, Ringwood,
Hampshire, BH24 1AW
Tel: 01425 472702 Fax: 01425 471993
Email: originalwhitehart.ringwood
@eldridge-pope.co.uk
15 bedrs SB £45 DB £55 B £5 L £6.50 D £8.50
CC: MC Vi Swi Delt

Rochester, Kent

436 Bridgewood Manor

★★★★★ 🎗 🎗 🎗
Bridgewood Roundabout, Walderslade Woods,
Chatham, Kent, ME5 9AX
Tel: 01634 201333 Fax: 01634 201330
Email: bridgewoodmanor@marstonhotels.com
Web: www.marstonhotels.com

100 bedrs SB £115 DB £149 HBS £69.50
HBD £69.50 B £12 L £15.50 D £28
CC: MC Vi Am DC Swi Delt

How to get there: Leave M2 at Junction three or
M20 at Junction 6. Follow A229 towards
Rochester. At Bridgewood roundabout take third
exit.

437 Royal Victoria & Bull Hotel

★
High Street, Rochester,
Kent, ME1 1PX
Tel: 01634 846266 Fax: 01634 832312
Email: enquiries@rvandb.co.uk
Web: www.rvandb.co.uk
28 bedrs SB £57.50 DB £72.50
B £5.75 L £5.45 D £10
CC: MC Vi Am DC Swi Delt JCB

How to get there: Follow A2 into Rochester. Go
across bridge and get into middle lane. After
lights, turn right into Northgate at first dual
carriageway intersection. Turn right into High
Street: hotel is on left.

Romsey, Hampshire

438 Heritage Hotels – The White Horse

★★★
Market Place, Romsey,
Hampshire, SO51 8ZJ
Tel: 0870 400 8123 Fax: 01794 517485

Ruislip, Middlesex

439 The Barn Hotel

★★★
West End Road, Ruislip,
Middlesex, HA4 6JB
Tel: 01895 636057 Fax: 01895 638379
Email: info@thebarnhotel.co.uk
Web: www.thebarnhotel.co.uk
59 bedrs SB £135 DB £170 HBS £150
HBD £105 B £12 L £15 D £15
CC: MC Vi Am DC Swi Delt JCB

How to get there: A40 exit Ruislip/Polish War
memorial. Left into West End Road (A4180).
Continue two miles, turn right on mini-
roundabout.
See advert on facing page

Rye, East Sussex

440 Flackley Ash

★★★
Peasmarsh, near Rye,
East Sussex, TN31 6YH
Tel: 01797 230651 Fax: 01797 230510
Email: flackleyash@marstonhotels.com
Web: www.marstonhotels.com

45 bedrs SB £79 DB £119
HBS £76 HBD £76
B £10 L £12 D £26
CC: MC Vi Am DC Swi Delt

How to get there: Leave M25 at Junction 5, take
A21 signposted Tunbridge Wells. Take A268
towards Rye. Hotel on left when entering
Peasmarsh.

441 Rye Lodge Hotel

★★★ ℞

Hilder's Cliff, Rye, East Sussex, TN31 7LD
Tel: 01797 223838 Fax: 01797 223585
Email: info@ryelodge.co.uk
Web: www.ryelodge.co.uk

Attractive ensuite rooms. Every amenity. Room service — breakfast in bed! Delicious candlelit dinners in the elegant, marble-floored terrace room. Relaxed atmosphere. Indoor swimming pool, spabath, sauna — really caring service.
18 bedrs SB £59.50 DB £90
HBS £60 HBD £62.50 D £23.50
CC: MC Vi Am DC Swi Delt JCB
♿ ⚞ ☕ ▯ ☎ ▣☎ 🐕 ♫ ⚶ 🏔 SPA 🔲
How to get there: Follow town centre signs to Landgate Arch (ancient monument); through Landgate Arch — hotel is 100 yards on right.

442 The Mermaid Hotel

★★★ ℞ ℞

Mermaid Street, Rye, East Sussex, TN31 7EY
Tel: 01797 223065 Fax: 01797 225069

443 Benson Hotel

◆◆◆◆◆ ℞ ⚙ ℘

15 East Street, Rye, East Sussex, TN31 7JY
Tel: 01797 225131 Fax: 01797 225512
Web: www.bensonhotel.co.uk

Situated in the heart of historic Rye, Benson offers sumptuous period-style bedrooms, most four-posters, with all-modern conveniences, attractive lounge, conservatory and terrace overlooking the River Rother and Romney Marshes.
4 bedrs SB £60 DB £94 CC: MC Vi Swi Delt
✉ ⚙ ▯ ☎ ▣ 🏔
How to get there: For East Street, follow town centre signs. Pass through landgate and after 300 yards take first left. Hotel 75 yards up hill on left.

444 Jeake's House

◆◆◆◆◆ ⚙ ℘

Mermaid Street, Rye, East Sussex, TN31 7ET
Tel: 01797 222828 Fax: 01797 222623
Email: jeakeshouse@btinternet.com
Web: www.jeakeshouse.com
Children minimum age: 11
12 bedrs SB £32.50 DB £79
CC: MC Vi Swi Delt
✉ ⚶ ⚙ ▯ ☎ ▣☎ 🍴 ⚶ 🏔
How to get there: Approach Rye from A259 or A2070. Follow town centre signs. From High Street turn right into West Street, which leads to Mermaid Street.
See advert on following page

Southeast

Jeake's House

17th-century Jeake's House stands on the most famous cobbled street in Rye's medieval town centre. Each stylishly restored bedroom with brass, mahogany or Four-Poster bed creates a very special atmosphere, combining traditional elegance with modern comforts.

Breakfast served in the galleried dining room is traditional or vegetarian and the roaring fire and timeless atmosphere will combine to make your stay truly memorable.

There is a comfortable drawing room and book-lined bar. Private car park nearby.

RaC
◆◆◆◆◆
✳☒☂

Mermaid Street, Rye, Eest Sussex
TN31 7ET
Tel: 01797 222828   Fax: 01797 222623
Email: jeakeshouse@btinternet.com
Website: www.jeakeshouse.com

---

445 White Vine House

◆◆◆◆◆ ✳☒☂
High Street, Rye, East Sussex, TN31 7JF
Tel: 01797 224748 Fax: 01797 223599
Email: irene@whitevinehouse.freeserve.co.uk

Tudor town house in the heart of ancient Rye with comfortable bedrooms, oak beams, stone fireplaces, books and paintings. Excellent breakfasts. Ideal for antique hunting, castles and gardens.
7 bedrs SB £50 DB £90 B £5 L £4.40
CC: MC Vi Am DC Swi Delt
🍷📠🐾⊗☺🖵♨🏠🐾👬
How to get there: At Rye follow signs to town centre and enter under Landgate Arch. Follow road into High Street and hotel is on right.

446 Durrant House Hotel

◆◆◆◆ ✳☒
Market Street, Rye, East Sussex, TN31 7LA
Tel: 01797 223182 Fax: 01797 226940
Email: kingslands@compuserve.com
Web: www.durrnthouse.com

A charming listed building located in the heart of Rye. It has six individually decorated bedrooms, all equipped to a high standard, including four-poster and triple rooms. Informal atmosphere.
7 bedrs D £18 CC: MC Vi Swi Delt
📠🐾⊗☺🖵♨🎬🐾👬
How to get there: Follow signs for town centre. Pass through the Landgate up to the High Street, then first left up East Street.

447 Hope Anchor Hotel

◆ ◆ ◆ ◆

Watchbell Street, Rye, East Sussex, TN31 7HA
Tel: 01797 222216 Fax: 01797 223796
Email: info@hotel-rye.freeserve.co.uk
Web: www.rye-tourism.co.uk/hopeanchor
12 bedrs SB £50 DB £90
CC: MC Vi DC Swi Delt

448 Old Borough Arms

◆ ◆ ◆ ◆ ✗

The Strand, Rye, East Sussex, TN31 7DB
Tel: 01797 222128 Fax: 01797 222128
Email: oldborougharms@btinternet.com
9 bedrs SB £30 DB £60 CC: MC Vi Swi Delt

How to get there: 20 minutes from Junction 10 of M20. Hotel is on corner of Mermaid Street, one block away from the A259.

449 Strand House

◆ ◆ ◆ ◆ ✗

The Strand, Tanyard's Lane, Winchelsea, Rye, East Sussex, TN36 4JT
Tel: 01797 226276 Fax: 01797 224806
Email: strandhouse@winchelsea98.fsnet.co.uk
Web: www.smoothhound.co.uk/
    hotels/strand.html
Children minimum age: 2
Closed Christmas
10 bedrs SB £38 DB £64
CC: MC Vi Swi Delt JCB

How to get there: From Rye take A259 towards Hastings. Property is first house on left side after passing village sign, set back from road, approx 1½ miles from Rye.

Travelling abroad by car?

European Motoring Assistance can help you out of a sticky situation abroad. Buy online at www.rac.co.uk or call RAC Travel Sales on 0800 55 00 55.

One click does it all

For the latest special offers and online booking, plus detailed information on over 3,000 RAC inspected properties, visit www.rac.co.uk/hotels

---

450 Magnolia House

◆ ◆ ◆ ✗

15 Udimore Road, Rye, East Sussex, TN31 7DS
Tel: 01797 222561 Fax: 01797 227525
Web: www.magnoliaguesthouse.co.uk

Licensed premises, situated a few minutes' level walk to Medieval Rye. A family-run guest house with spacious accommodation.
6 bedrs SB £25 DB £50 HBS £35 HBD £27.80
L £4.95 D £5.50
CC: MC Vi Am DC Swi Delt JCB

How to get there: Going out of Rye on the B2089 to Battle: just over the river bridge on the right.

Saffron Walden, Essex

451 Crown House

★ ★ ⓡ

Great Chesterford, Saffron Walden,
Essex, CB10 1NY
Tel: 01799 530515 Fax: 01799 530683
Web: www.virtualhotels.com
18 bedrs CC: MC Vi Am Swi

How to get there: Close to M11 Junction 9, on B1383 (old A11), one mile from Stump Cross roundabout.

Sandwich, Kent

452 Bell Hotel

★ ★ ★ ⓡ

The Quay, Sandwich, Kent, CT13 9EF
Tel: 01304 613388 Fax: 01304 615308
Email: hotel@princes-leisure.co.uk
Web: www.princes-leisure.co.uk
33 bedrs SB £78.75 DB £105 B £8 L £13.75
D £13.75 CC: MC Vi Am DC Swi Delt

See advert on following page

Southeast

The Bell Hotel

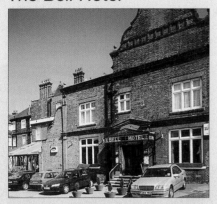

Situated in the heart of classic championship golf links country, The Bell Hotel enjoys an international reputation for its hospitality and cuisine. Exclusive golf breaks combine the traditional comforts of this 3-star hotel with golf at the famous Prince's Golf Club.

The Quay, Sandwich, Kent CT13 9EF
Tel: 01304 613388   Fax: 01304 615308
hotel@princes-leisure.co.uk
www.princes-leisure.co.uk

Hempstead House

• Private Victorian Country House Hotel set in three acres of beautifully landscaped gardens.
• Individually designed luxurious guest suites.
• Award winning restaurant serving classic English and French cuisine.
• Spacious, elegant reception and conference rooms.
• Outdoor heated swimming pool and floodlit terraces.

 ♦♦♦♦♦

London Road, Bapchild,
Sittingbourne, Kent ME9 9PP
Tel: 01795 428020   Fax: 01795 436362
Email: info@hempsteadhouse.co.uk
Website: www.hempsteadhouse.co.uk

Sedlescombe, East Sussex

453 Brickwall Hotel

★★★
The Green, Sedlescombe,
East Sussex, TN33 0QA
Tel: 01424 870253 Fax: 01424 870785
Email: reception@brickwallhotel.totalserve.co.uk
26 bedrs SB £60 DB £88 HBS £75 HBD £67.50
B £9 L £12.50 D £20
CC: MC Vi Am DC Swi Delt JCB

How to get there: The Brickwall Hotel is situated in the village of Sedlescombe on the B2244, three miles east of Battle.

Sevenoaks, Kent

454 No 4 Old Timbertop Cottages

♦♦♦♦
Bethel Road, Sevenoaks, Kent, TN13 3UE
Tel: 01732 460506 Fax: 01732 464484
Email: anthony@ruddassociates.co.uk
Closed Christmas to New Year
Delightful self-contained cottage, sleeping 4. Twin bedroom, bath/shower, sitting-room with sofabed, TV, fully-fitted kitchen, patio garden and parking.
1 bedrs SB £40 DB £55
CC: None accepted
How to get there: Directions will be given by e-mail, fax or telephone.

455 Bramber

♦♦♦
45 Shoreham Lane, Riverhead, Sevenoaks, Kent, TN13 3DX
Tel: 01732 457466 Fax: 01732 457466
Children minimum age: 7
2 bedrs SB £26.50 DB £45
CC: None accepted
How to get there: A25 Riverhead roundabout towards Maidstone; up a slight incline, then turn first right; Bramber is the middle chalet bungalow and garage on the right.

It's easier online

For all your motoring and travel needs, www.rac.co.uk

456 Moorings Hotel

♦ ♦ ♦

97 Hitchen Hatch Lane, Sevenoaks,
Kent, TN13 3BE
Tel: 01732 452589 Fax: 01732 456462
Email: theryans@mooringshotel.co.uk
Web: www.mooringshotel.co.uk
23 bedrs SB £43 DB £65 B £5 L £5 D £7.50
CC: MC Vi Am DC Swi Delt
点⊗⊜□☎📞📠🐾⌇⍔⏷⛓️⋔⋔⋔
How to get there: Follow signs for Sevenoaks
from M25 Junction 5. For one mile, head
towards Sevenoaks and Riverhead. At the
roundabout, turn right and after one mile turn
left into Hitchen Hatch Lane opposite railway
station.

Shepperton, Middlesex

457 Warren Lodge Hotel

★★★

Church Square, Shepperton,
Middlesex, TW17 9JZ
Tel: 01932 242972 Fax: 01932 253883
Email: info@warrenlodgehotel.co.uk
Web: www.warrenlodgehotel.co.uk

Pretty riverside hotel with gardens and river
terrace. Well-appoointed bedrooms, some with
river view. Good English and continental cuisine.
Weekend rates available.
50 bedrs SB £91 DB £109
B £7.50 L £11.95 D £15.95
CC: MC Vi Am DC Swi Delt JCB
⊜□☎P⍔⛓️⋔⋔⋔
How to get there: From J11 M25 Chertsey, take
B375 to Shepperton. At roundabout at bottom
of High Street take sign for Church Square.

Sittingbourne, Kent

458 Hempstead House

♦ ♦ ♦ ♦ ♦ ⍟ ✗

London Road, Bapchild, Sittingbourne,
Kent, ME9 9PP
Tel: 01795 428020 Fax: 01795 436362
Email: info@hempsteadhouse.co.uk
Web: www.hempsteadhouse.co.uk
14 bedrs SB £70 DB £80 HBS £92.50
HBD £62.50 B £5 L £6.95 D £22.50
CC: MC Vi Am DC Swi Delt JCB
🚁🗄️🐈⊗⊜□☎📞P⍔🕯️🐎⏷⛓️⋔⋔⋔
🏇
How to get there: 1¹/₂ miles east of
Sittingbourne along main A2.
See advert on facing page

459 Beaumont

♦ ♦ ♦ ✗

74 London Road, Sittingbourne, Kent, ME10 1NS
Tel: 01795 472536 Fax: 01795 425921
Email: beaumont74@aol.com
Web: www.thebeaumont.co.uk
9 bedrs SB £49 DB £55 B £5
CC: MC Vi Am DC Swi Delt
点🗄️🐈⊗⊜□☎📞P⍔⋔⋔⋔
How to get there: From M2 or M20, take A249
north towards Sheerness. Take A2 exit, turn
right at roundabout and follow A2 for one mile
towards Sittingbourne.

Slough, Berkshire

460 Copthorne Hotel Slough Windsor

★★★★

Cippenham Lane, Slough, Berkshire, SL1 2YE
Tel: 01753 516222 Fax: 01753 516237
Email: sales.slough@mill-cop.com
Web: www.millenium-hotels.com
219 bedrs SB £193.50 DB £257 B £13.50
L £20.50 D £21.50 CC: MC Vi Am DC Swi
点�🏋️🐈⊜□☎❄️📞P⍔⏷⛓️🦢🌴⋔⋔⋔ 🆂🅿🅰
🍴✓
How to get there: Exit M4 J6. Follow A355
Slough. Turn left at roundabout. The hotel is on
the left.

Making a booking?

Don't forget to mention RAC
Hotels and Bed & Breakfast 2002.

Southeast

461 Slough/Windsor Marriott

★★★★ 🛏

Ditton Road, Langley, Slough, Berkshire, SL3 8PT
Tel: 01753 544244 Fax: 020 7591 1528
Web: www.marriott.com/lhrsl
382 bedrs B £9.95 L £16 D £16
CC: MC Vi Am DC Swi Delt

462 Courtyard by Marriott Slough/Windsor

★★★

1 Chuch Street, Chalvey, Slough,
Berkshire, SL1 2NH
Tel: 01753 551551 Fax: 01753 553333
Web: www.courtyard.com/slwin
150 bedrs SB £155 DB £159 HBS £175
HBD £97.50 B £7.50 L £7.50 D £12
CC: MC Vi Am DC Swi Delt

How to get there: J6 M4 towards Slough central.
First roundabout; take last exit and turn right.

Sonning-on-Thames, Berkshire

463 French Horn Hotel

★★★ 🛏 🛏 🛏

Sonning-on-Thames, Berkshire, RG4 6TN
Tel: 01189 692204 Fax: 01189 442210
Email: thefrenchhorn@compuserve.com
Web: www.thefrenchhorn.co.uk
Closed 25–31 December
20 bedrs SB £110 DB £130 L £27 D £40
CC: MC Vi Am DC Swi Delt

How to get there: Turn off A4 between
Maidenhead and Reading take the B478 through
Sonning. We are situated on the Northern bank.

Southampton, Hampshire

464 Marriott Meon Valley Hotel

★★★★ 🛏

Sandy Lane, Shedfield, Southampton,
Hampshire, SO32 2HQ
Tel: 01329 833455 Fax: 01329 834411
Web: www.marriotthotels.com/scugs
113 bedrs SB £99 DB £109 HBS £103 HBD £73
B £14.45 L £19.95 D £22
CC: MC Vi Am DC Swi Delt JCB

465 Novotel Southampton

★★★

1 West Quay Road, Southampton,
Hampshire, SO15 1RA
Tel: 023 8033 0550 Fax: 023 8022 2158
Email: h1073@accor-hotels.com
Web: www.novotel.com
121 bedrs SB £79 DB £88.50
B £9.50 L £13.50 D £17.50
CC: MC Vi Am DC Swi Delt

How to get there: From M3 to M27
Bournemouth direction, then Junction three of
M271 Southampton Docks. At the end turn left
on A35.

466 Elizabeth House Hotel

★★

43–44 The Avenue, Southampton,
Hampshire, SO17 1XP
Tel: 023 8022 4327 Fax: 023 8022 4327
Email: mail@elizabethhousehotel.com
Web: www.elizabethhousehotel.com
21 bedrs SB £47.50 DB £57.50 B £6 L £3 D £8
CC: MC Vi Swi Delt JCB

How to get there: From M3, take A33 towards
town centre. Hotel on left after common but
before main traffic lights.

467 The Star Hotel & Restaurant

★★

26 High Street, Southampton,
Hampshire, SO14 2NA
Tel: 023 8033 9939 Fax: 023 8033 5291

468 Travelodge Southampton

Travel Accommodation
144 Lodge Road, Southampton,
Hampshire, SO14 6QR
Tel: 08700 850 950
Web: www.travelodge.co.uk
52 bedrs B £4.25
CC: MC Vi Am DC Swi Delt

469 Acacia Lodge Guest House

Providence Hill, Bursledon, Southampton,
Hampshire, SO31 8AT
Tel: 023 8056 1155 Fax: 023 8056 1161
Email: petekenway@aol.com
5 bedrs SB £25 DB £50
CC: None accepted

How to get there: Exit J8 M27; follow signs for
Southampton East and Hamble. Take first exit
off roundabout.

470 Landguard Lodge

21 Landguard Road, Southampton,
Hampshire, SO15 5DL
Tel: 023 8063 6904 Fax: 023 8063 2258
Email: landguardlodge@141.com
Web: www.landguardlodge.co.uk
Children minimum age: 5
10 bedrs SB £29 DB £45
CC: MC Vi Am Swi Delt

How to get there: North of railway station,
between Hill Lane and Shirley Road.

471 Botleigh Grange Hotel

Hedge End, Southampton,
Hampshire, SO30 2GA
Tel: 01489 787700 Fax: 01489 788535

Southend-on-Sea, Essex

472 Balmoral Hotel

★★
32–36 Valkyrie Road, Westcliff-on-Sea,
Essex, SS0 8BU
Tel: 01702 342947 Fax: 01702 337828
Email: enquiries@balmoralsouthend.com
Web: www.balmoralsouthend.com
32 bedrs SB £45 DB £69
HBS £55 HBD £89
B £6.95 L £4.95 D £9.95
CC: MC Vi Am Swi Delt
See advert on this page

473 Mayflower Hotel

6 Royal Terrace, Southend-on-Sea,
Essex, SS1 1DY
Tel: 01702 340489
Closed Christmas
23 bedrs SB £25.85 DB £39.95
CC: None accepted
How to get there: Along sea front to pier; up
pier hill into Royal Terrace; The Mayflower Hotel
is on the right side.

474 Terrace Hotel

8 Royal Terrace, Southend-on-Sea,
Essex, SS1 1DY
Tel: 01702 348143 Fax: 01702 348143
Children minimum age: 3
9 bedrs SB £21 DB £36
CC: None accepted
How to get there: Proceed along seafront. Turn
up Pier Hill opposite. The Pier Hill runs into
Royal Terrace.

Southeast

475 Tower Hotel and Restaurant

♦ ♦ ♦

146 Alexandra Road, Southend-on-Sea,
Essex, SS1 1HE
Tel: 01702 348635 Fax: 01702 433044
Email: tower.rest@virgin.net
32 bedrs
CC: MC Vi Am DC Swi Delt

How to get there: Turn off A13 into Milton Road,
turn left into Cambridge Road and take third
right at mini-roundabout into Wilson Road.
Hotel on right at crossroads.

St. Albans, Hertfordshire

476 Sopwell House Hotel,
Country Club & Spa

★★★★ ⬮ ⬮ ⬮

Cottonmill Lane, Sopwell, St. Albans,
Hertfordshire, AL1 2HQ
Tel: 01727 864477 Fax: 01727 844741
Email: enquiries@sopwellhouse.co.uk
Web: www.sopwellhouse.co.uk

An elegant Georgian country house hotel,
minutes away from M1 and M25 and 20 minutes
from London by train. For meetings,
accommodation, leisure and dining.
128 bedrs SB £137.50 DB £190 HBS £162.95
HBD £120.45 B £12.95 L £15.95 D £25
CC: MC Vi Am DC Swi Delt

How to get there: M25 J22 to A1081 St. Albans,
or M1 J8 to M10 and A414.

Making a booking?

Don't forget to mention RAC
Hotels and Bed & Breakfast 2002.

477 Quality Hotel St. Albans

★★★

232-236 London Road, St. Albans,
Hertfordshire, AL1 1JQ
Tel: 01727 857858 Fax: 01727 855666
Email: st.albans@quality-hotels.net
Web: www.quality-hotels.net
43 bedrs SB £85 DB £110
B £8 L £2.80 D £14.25
CC: MC Vi Am DC Swi Delt

How to get there: Leave M25 at Junction 22.
Follow A1081 to St. Albans. After three miles,
hotel is on left-hand side.

478 St. Michael's Manor

★★★★ ⬮ ⬮

Fishpool Street, St. Albans,
Hertfordshire, AL3 4RY
Tel: 01727 864444 Fax: 01727 848909
Email: smmanor@globalnet.co.uk
Web: www.stmichaelsmanor.com
Closed 27-29 December

23 individually styled bedrooms enjoy a unique
blend of award-winning lakeside gardens,
architectural splendour and unparalleled
service. Just 10 minutes walk from the Abbey
and city centre. Easy access to London,
Heathrow and Luton airports, and the M25 and
M1.
23 bedrs SB £125 DB £160
B £16.50 L £18.50 D £37.50
CC: MC Vi Am DC Swi Delt

How to get there: Leave M25 at Junction 21a.
Go through Chiswell Gn. Turn left at King Harry
pub and right at roundabout. Past Waitrose,
turn right again at next roundabout and next
right then left.

479 Ardmore House Hotel

♦ ♦ ♦

54 Lemsford Road, St. Albans,
Hertfordshire, AL1 3PR
Tel: 01727 859313 Fax: 01727 859313
Email: info@ardmorehousehotel.com
Web: www.ardmorehousehotel.altodigital.co.uk
40 bedrs SB £55 DB £80 CC: MC Vi Am Swi Delt
⬧🎐☺🍳🖵☎🅿🖇🍵🎬📺♻️⛲ 🛏
How to get there: M25 Junction 22, A1081 to St.
Albans. London Colney roundabout, take A1081
(London Road). Two sets of traffic lights: right at
2nd mini-roundabout. Hotel 800 yards on right.
See advert right

St. Leonards on Sea, East Sussex

480 Royal Victoria Hotel

★ ★ ★

Marina, St. Leonards on Sea,
East Sussex, TN38 0BD
Tel: 01424 445544 Fax: 01424 721995

Staines, Middlesex

481 **Heritage Hotels – The Thames Lodge**

★ ★ ★ ⓡ

Thames Street, Staines, Middlesex, TW18 4SJ
Tel: 0870 400 8121 Fax: 01784 454858
Web: www.heritage-hotels.com
78 bedrs SB £79.50 DB £119 HBS £89.50
HBD £69.50 B £11.95 L £14.95 D £21
CC: MC Vi Am DC Swi Delt JCB
♿🐕☺🍳🖵☎📞🅿🖇🍵🎬♻️⛲ 🛏
How to get there: Leave M25 at junction 13. Take
A30 to London. At Crooked Billet roundabout,
follow signs for Staines town centre.

Stansted Airport, Essex

482 Vintage Court Hotel

★ ★ ★

Vintage Corner, Puckeridge, near Ware,
Hertfordshire, SG11 1SA
Tel: 01920 822722 Fax: 01920 822877
30 bedrs SB £67.95 DB £76.90 HBS £87.90
HBD £58.40 B £8.95 L £5.50 D £19.95
CC: MC Vi Am DC Swi Delt
⬧🐕☺🍳🖵☎📞🅿🎬♻️⛲ 🛏 ♿
See advert right

Ardmore House Hotel

Large Edwardian
house set in the
conservation area of
St. Albans, but in
close proximity to the
main city station for
London and easy
walking distance of
the town centre.
With a wide choice of
ensuite Single, Twin,
Double or Family
Rooms, we can offer
comfortable
accommodation to
suit all requirements,
including a
four-poster bedded
room. Large Breakfast
Room overlooking the
Garden, Residents'
Bar and Evening
Dining Room.

54 Lemsford Road, St. Albans,
Hertfordshire AL1 3PR
Tel: 01727 859313   Fax: 01727 859313
info@ardmorehousehotel.com
www.ardmorehousehotel.altodigital.co.uk

Vintage Court Hotel

Family owned, professionally managed hotel
set in peaceful Hertfordshire with spacious,
tastefully furnished ensuite bedrooms.
Self-contained banqueting suite for up to
150 guests. Conference facilities include
three large lecture rooms.

Vintage Corner, Puckeridge, near
Ware, Hertfordshire SG11 1SA
At the junction of A10 & A120
Tel: 01920 822722   Fax: 01920 822877

Southeast

Stevenage, Hertfordshire

483 Novotel Stevenage

★★★

Knebworth Park, Stevenage,
Hertfordshire, SG1 2AX
Tel: 01438 346100 Fax: 01438 723872
Email: h0992@accor-hotels.com
Web: www.novotel.com
100 bedrs SB £99 DB £109
CC: MC Vi Am DC Swi

How to get there: Hotel is situated on Junction seven of A1(M) motorway, at entrance to Knebworth Park.

Steyning, West Sussex

484 The Old Tollgate Restaurant and Hotel

★★★

The Street, Bramber, Steyning,
West Sussex, BN44 3WE
Tel: 01903 879494 Fax: 01903 813399
Email: otr@fastnet.co.uk
Web: www.oldtollgatehotel.com
31 bedrs SB £79.65 DB £87.30 HBS £101.60
HBD £131.20 B £6.65 L £14.65 D £21.95
CC: MC Vi Am DC Swi Delt

How to get there: From A24 or A27, take A283 signposted to Steyning, then follow signposts to Bramber. Brown tourist signs advertise hotel.

485 Penfold Gallery Guest House | Little Gem

♦ ♦ ♦ ♦ ♦

30 High Street, Steyning,
West Sussex, BN44 3GG
Tel: 01903 815595 Fax: 01903 816686
Email: johnturner57@cs.com
Web: artyguesthouse.co.uk
Children minimum age: 12

A medieval dwelling full of architectural interest, the Penfold Gallery has the beautiful backdrop of the South Downs. Personal attention to all guests. Creative cooking. Non-smoking.
3 bedrs SB £48 DB £78
HBS £72 HBD £63 D £24
CC: MC Vi Swi

How to get there: Leave A27 at junction with A283 and follow signs to Steyning. The Penfold Gallery Guest House is east of the mini-roundabout in the High Street.

486 Springwells Hotel

♦ ♦ ♦ ♦

9 High Street, Steyning, West Sussex, BN44 3GG
Tel: 01903 812446 Fax: 01903 879823
Email: contact@springwells.co.uk
Web: www.springwells.co.uk
Closed Christmas to New Year

A former Georgian Merchant House in a picturesque village. All rooms are individually furnished with TV and telephone; the bar and adjoining conservatory lead to a patio and outdoor heated swimming pool.
11 bedrs SB £33 DB £56 B £6.95
CC: MC Vi Am DC

Stockbridge, Hampshire

487 The George Inn

♦ ♦ ♦ ♦

The Crossroads, Nether Wallop,
near Stockbridge, Hampshire, SO20 8EG
Tel: 01264 781224 Fax: 01264 782830
2 bedrs SB £40 DB £55
CC: MC Vi Am Swi Delt JCB

How to get there: On A353 between Salisbury and Andover, on crossroads with B3084.

488 Carbery

♦ ♦ ♦

Salisbury Hill, Stockbridge,
Hampshire, SO20 6EZ
Tel: 01264 810771 Fax: 01264 811022
Closed three weeks around Christmas

Carbery Guest House is two minutes' walk from
the old market village of Stockbridge
overlooking the River Test in one acre of
landscaped gardens.
11 bedrs SB £29 DB £55 HBS £43.50 HBD £42
D £14.50 CC: MC Vi Swi Delt

How to get there: Hotel at Salisbury end of
Stockbridge on A30.

Stokenchurch, Buckinghamshire

489 Kings Arms Hotel

★ ★ ★

Oxford Road, Stokenchurch,
Buckinghamshire, HP14 3TA
Tel: 01494 609090 Fax: 01494 484582

Streatley-on-Thames, Berkshire

490 The Swan at Streatley

★ ★ ★ ★ ★ ⏣ ⏣

Streatley-on-Thames, Berkshire, RG8 9HR
Tel: 01491 878800 Fax: 01491 872554
Email: sales@swan-diplomat.co.uk
Web: www.swan-diplomat.co.uk
46 bedrs SB £117.50 DB £157 HBS £144.50
HBD £105.50 B £8 L £17.50 D £24.50
CC: MC Vi Am DC Swi Delt

How to get there: Leave M4 at Junction 12, take
exit towards Theale, then take A340 to
Pangbourne. Once there take A329 to Streatley.

491 The Bull at Streatley

♦ ♦ ♦

Reading Road, Streatley, Reading,
Berkshire, RG8 9JJ
Tel: 01491 872392 Fax: 01491 875231
Email: bull.streatley@eldridge-pope.co.uk
6 bedrs DB £70 L £8.95 D £8.95
CC: MC Vi Am DC Swi Delt JCB

How to get there: On the junction of A329 and
B4009 in Streatley.

Surbiton, Surrey

492 Pembroke Lodge Guest House

♦ ♦ ♦ ⌇

35 Cranes Park, Surbiton, Surrey, KT5 8AB
Tel: 020 8399 8636 Fax: 020 8390 0731
6 bedrs SB £35 DB £48
CC: None accepted

Sutton Scotney, Hampshire

493 Travelodge Sutton Scotney (North)

Travel Accommodation
A34, Winchester Bypass, Sutton Scotney,
Hampshire, SO21 3JY
Tel: 08700 850 950
Web: www.travelodge.co.uk
31 bedrs B £4.25
CC: MC Vi Am DC Swi Delt

494 Travelodge Sutton Scotney (South)

Travel Accommodation
A34, Winchester Bypass, Sutton Scotney,
Hampshire, SO21 3JY
Tel: 08700 850 950
Web: www.travelodge.co.uk
40 bedrs B £4.25
CC: MC Vi Am DC Swi Delt

Southeast

Sutton, Surrey

495 Thatched House Hotel

★★
135 Cheam Road, Sutton, Surrey, SM1 2BN
Tel: 020 8642 3131 Fax: 020 8770 0684
32 bedrs SB £70 DB £85 HBS £80 HBD £52.50
B £7.50 L £10.95 D £13.50
CC: MC Vi DC Swi Delt JCB

How to get there: M25 at Junction 8. A217
towards Sutton. At junction with A232, turn right.
Hotel is 500 yards on right, before town centre.

496 Eaton Court Hotel

◆◆
49 Eaton Road, Sutton, Surrey, SM2 5ED
Tel: 020 8643 6766 Fax: 020 8642 4580
Email: manager@eatoncourthotel.co.uk
Web: www.eatoncourthotel.co.uk
Children minimum age: 3
Closed two weeks over Christmas
13 bedrs SB £35 DB £55
CC: MC Vi Am DC Swi Delt

How to get there: Leave M25 at Junction 8. Take
A217 to Sutton, then B2230. Take first right after
BP filling station into Cedar Road. Turn right into
Eaton Road and hotel is number 49.

Swanley, Kent

497 Hillview Guest House

◆◆◆◆
Wood Street, Swanley Village, Kent, BR8 8DX
Tel: 01322 666612
3 bedrs SB £35 DB £50 CC: MC Vi

How to get there: Exit J3 M25 A20, follow signs
to Brands Hatch. Second left into Button Street;
at T-junction turn left, then first left.

Sway, Hampshire

498 The Nurse's Cottage
Little Gem

◆◆◆◆◆ 🍴🍴 ✕ 🍴
Station Road, Sway, Lymington,
Hampshire, SO41 6BA
Tel: 01590 683402 Fax: 01590 683402
Email: nurses.cottage@lineone.net
Web: www.hants.gov.uk/tourist/hotels

Children minimum age: 10
Closed two weeks in March, three in November.

One of the New Forest's most highly acclaimed
guest accommodations, selected universally by
the UK's leading hospitality guides. Open to
non-residents for breakfast, afternoon tea,
dinner and Sunday luncheon. Booking essential.
3 bedrs SB £60 DB £100 HBS £72.50
HBD £62.50 B £6.75 L £15.50 D £18.25
CC: MC Vi Am Swi Delt JCB

How to get there: Off B3055 in village centre,
next to post office.
See advert on facing page

Taplow, Berkshire

499 Cliveden House
Gold Ribbon Winner

★★★★★ ⓡⓡ ⓡⓡ ⓡ
Taplow, Berkshire, SL6 0JF
Tel: 01628 668561 Fax: 01628 661837
Email: reservations@clivedenhouse.co.uk
Web: www.clivedenhouse.co.uk

Set in 376 acres of the National Trust's finest
gardens, a mere 20 minutes from Heathrow,
Cliveden boasts 39 magnificent rooms, the
Michelin-starred 'Waldo's' restaurant and the
beautiful Pavilion spa on the banks of the Thames.
39 bedrs DB £375 B £12 L £21.50 D £42
CC: MC Vi Am DC Swi Delt

How to get there: From Junction seven of M4,
follow brown National Trust signs to Taplow.
From M40 Junction 2, follow signs to Taplow.

Thame, Oxfordshire

500 Spread Eagle Hotel

★★★★ ⚝ ⚝

16 Cornmarket, Thame, Oxfordshire, OX9 2BR
Tel: 01844 213661 Fax: 01844 261380
Email: enquiries@spreadeaglehotelthame.co.uk
Web: www.spreadeaglehotelthame.co.uk

Carefully-modernised former coaching inn, set in town centre. Large car park. Good centre for visiting Oxford and the Vale of Aylesbury. Hospitality is the speciality.
33 bedrs SB £96.55 DB £112.30 HBS £109.95 HBD £70 B £10 L £18 D £25
CC: MC Vi Am DC

How to get there: In town centre of Thame, on A418 between Aylesbury and Oxford. Leave M49 at Junction six southbound, Junction eight northbound. Car park at rear of hotel.

501 Travelodge Thame

Travel Accommodation
A418/B4011, Thame, Oxfordshire, OX9 3XA
Tel: 08700 850 950
Web: www.travelodge.co.uk
31 bedrs B £4.25
CC: MC Vi Am DC Swi Delt

Thatcham, Berkshire

502 Travelodge Thatcham

Travel Accommodation
Oxford Road, Hermitage, Thatcham, Berkshire, RG18 9XX
Tel: 08700 850 950
Web: www.travelodge.co.uk
64 bedrs B £4.25
CC: MC Vi Am DC Swi Delt

Southeast

Toddington, Bedfordshire

503 Travelodge Toddington

Travel Accommodation
M1, Toddington, Bedfordshire, LU5 6HR
Tel: 08700 850 950
Web: www.travelodge.co.uk
66 bedrs B £4.25
CC: MC Vi Am DC Swi Delt

Tonbridge, Kent

504 Langley Hotel

★★
18–20 London Road, Tonbridge, Kent, TN10 3DA
Tel: 01732 353311 Fax: 01732 771471
Email: the.langley@virgin.net
Web: www.rbhotels.co.uk
34 bedrs
CC: MC Vi Am Swi Delt

How to get there: Leave M25 at Junction five
and take A21 southbound, then B245 through
Hildenborough. Hotel is on left as you approach
Tonbridge.

Spa Hotel

Situated in 14 acres of beautiful grounds,
paddocks and stables, the Spa has 71 ensuite
bedrooms. The Chandelier Restaurant offers
French cuisine, with an English influence,
complemented by an international wine list.
Extensive Health and Beauty facilities are
available. The Spa is very accessible and is
within easy reach of the M25, Tunbridge Wells
railway station and both Gatwick and
Heathrow airports.

Langton Road, Mount Ephraim,
Tunbridge Wells, Kent TN4 8XJ
Tel: 01892 520331   Fax: 01892 510575
Email: info@spahotel.co.uk
Website: www.spahotel.co.uk

Tring, Hertfordshire

505 Pendley Manor

★★★★
Cow Lane, Tring, Hertfordshire, HP23 5QY
Tel: 01442 891891 Fax: 01442 890687
Email: info@pendley-manor.co.uk

Grade II Listed luxury country house hotel, 71
bedrooms, many with four-poster beds.
Excellent conference facilities, all meeting rooms
have natural light. Award-winning restaurant with
new magnificent leisure complex.
74 bedrs CC: MC Vi Am DC Swi Delt

How to get there: From M25 take A41 to Tring.
From Tring exit, take A4251 towards
Berkhamsted for 200 yards, first left, Cow Lane,
hotel on right-hand side.

506 Old Forge

◆◆◆◆
5 High Street, Ivinghoe, Leighton Buzzard,
Berkshire, LU7 9EP
Tel: 01296 668122 Fax: 01296 668122
Children minimum age: 6
6 bedrs SB £48 DB £60 CC: MC Vi Am Swi Delt

How to get there: Situated less than 30 minutes
from the M1 motorway (Junctions eight or 11).
Five minutes from Tring railway station.

Tunbridge Wells, Kent

507 Royal Wells Inn Hotel

★★★
Mount Ephraim, Tunbridge Wells, Kent, TN4 8BE
Tel: 01892 511188 Fax: 01892 511908
Email: info@royalwells.co.uk
Web: www.royalwells.co.uk
18 bedrs SB £75 DB £110 HBS £95 HBD £75
B £9 L £12 D £25
CC: MC Vi Am DC Swi Delt JCB

508 Spa Hotel

★★★★ ☕ ☕

Mount Ephraim, Tunbridge Wells, Kent, TN4 8XJ
Tel: 01892 520331 Fax: 01892 510575
Email: info@spahotel.co.uk
Web: www.spahotel.co.uk
71 bedrs SB £92.50 DB £119.50 HBS £78
HBD £78 B £10.25 L £22 D £25
CC: MC Vi Am DC Swi

How to get there:M25 at Junction 5 and join
A21. Take fourth exit for A26 Tunbridge Wells.
Fork right onto A264. Hotel is ¹/₂ a mile on right.
See advert left

509 Russell Hotel

★★

80 London Road, Tunbridge Wells, Kent, TN1 1DZ
Tel: 01892 544833 Fax: 01892 515846
Email: sales@russell-hotel.com
Web: www.russell-hotel.com
25 bedrs SB £70 DB £90 HBS £88 HBD £60.50
CC: MC Vi Am Swi Delt

How to get there: In the centre of Tunbridge
Wells, opposite the common on the main
London Road.

Uckfield, East Sussex

510 Buxted Park Hotel

★★★★★ ☕

Buxted, Uckfield, East Sussex, TN22 4AY
Tel: 01825 732711 Fax: 01825 732770

511 Hooke Hall

◆ ◆ ◆ ◆ ◆

250 High Street, Uckfield, East Sussex, TN22 1EN
Tel: 01825 761578 Fax: 01825 768025
Email: a.percy@virgin.net
Children minimum age: 12
Closed Christmas
10 bedrs SB £57.50 DB £75 B £5.50
CC: MC Vi

How to get there: Hooke Hall is at the northern
end of the High Street, set back from the road.

Wallingford, Oxfordshire

512 George Hotel

★★★

High Street, Wallingford, Oxfordshire, OX10 0BS
Tel: 01491 836665 Fax: 01491 825359
Email: info@george-hotel-wallingford.com
Web: www.george-hotel-wallingford.com
39 bedrs SB £102.50 DB £123 HBS £120
HBD £158 B £8.50 L £12.50 D £17.50
CC: MC Vi Am DC Swi Delt

513 Springs Hotel

★★★★ ☕ ☕

Wallingford Road, North Stoke, Wallingford,
Oxfordshire, OX10 6BE
Tel: 01491 836687 Fax: 01491 836877
Email: info@thespringshotel.co.uk
Web: www.thespringshotel.co.uk
31 bedrs SB £90 DB £100
B £9.50 L £5 D £25
CC: MC Vi Am DC Swi Delt

Waltham Abbey, Essex

514 Waltham Abbey Marriott Hotel

★★★★

Old Shire Lane, Waltham Abbey, Essex, EN9 3LX
Tel: 01992 717170 Fax: 01992 711841
Web: www.marriott.co.uk
162 bedrs CC: MC Vi Am DC Swi Delt

How to get there: Located at J-26 on M25, 15
minutes from Central London.

Southeast

Vintage Court Hotel

Family owned, professionally managed hotel set in peaceful Hertfordshire with spacious, tastefully furnished ensuite bedrooms. Self-contained banqueting suite for up to 150 guests. Conference facilities include three large lecture rooms.

Vintage Corner, Puckeridge, near Ware, Hertfordshire SG11 1SA
At the junction of A10 & A120
Tel: 01920 822722   Fax: 01920 822877

Ware, Hertfordshire

515 Marriott Hanbury Manor

★★★★★
Ware, Hertfordshire, SG12 0SD
Tel: 01920 487722
Email: reservations.hanburymanor
@marriotthotels.co.uk
Web: www.marriotthotels.com/stngs
161 bedrs SB £160 DB £200 HBS £200
HBD £140 B £16 L £25 D £30
CC: MC Vi Am DC Swi Delt

How to get there: Exit J25 M25 and take A10 north. Hotel is situated 12 miles from M25 just past the Thundridge village sign.

Need help booking?

RAC Hotel Reservations will find the accommodation that's right for you – and book it too. Call today on 0870 603 9109 and quote 'Guide 2002'

516 Vintage Court Hotel

★★★
Vintage Corner, Puckeridge, near Ware, Hertfordshire, SG11 1SA
Tel: 01920 822722 Fax: 01920 822877
30 bedrs SB £67.95 DB £76.90 HBS £87.90
HBD £58.40 B £8.95 L £5.50 D £19.95
CC: MC Vi Am DC Swi Delt

How to get there: At the junction of the A10 and A120.
See advert on following page

Watford, Hertfordshire

517 White House Hotel

★★★★
Upton Road, Watford, Hertfordshire, WD1 7EL
Tel: 01923 237316 Fax: 01923 233109
Email: info@whitehousehotel.co.uk
Web: www.whitehousehotel.co.uk
59 bedrs SB £93.50 DB £153 HBS £108.50
HBD £84 B £9.50 L £17.95 D £17.95
CC: MC Vi Am DC Swi Delt

How to get there: Follow signs to town centre ring road. Take centre lane past lights at Market Street. Upton Road is on left.
See advert on facing page

Welwyn, Hertfordshire

518 Quality Hotel Welwyn

★★★
The Link, Welwyn, Hertfordshire, AL6 9XA
Tel: 01438 716911 Fax: 01438 714065
Email: admin@gb623.u-net.com
Web: www.choicehotels.com
96 bedrs SB £100.75 DB £109.95 HBS £115.45
HBD £62.23 B £10.95 L £3.50 D £14.50
CC: MC Vi Am DC Swi Delt

How to get there: The hotel can be found just off the A1(M) at Junction 6. There is a railway station at Welwyn Garden City.

Plan your route

Visit www.rac.co.uk for RAC's interactive route planner, including up to the minute traffic reports.

Wembley, Middlesex

519 Adelphi Hotel

◆◆◆

4 Forty Lane, Wembley, Middlesex, HA9 9EB
Tel: 020 8904 5629 Fax: 020 8908 5314
Email: enquiry@adelphihotel.fsnet.co.uk
Web: www.hoteladelphi.co.uk

All rooms are well-equipped and furnished to a high standard; en-suite rooms with tea- and coffee-making facilities and direct-dial phones. Easy access to Wembley Stadium complex and main North London routes.
13 bedrs SB £38 DB £48
CC: MC Vi Am DC Swi Delt

How to get there: 10 minutes from Wembley Park tube, about 1½ miles from M1, 500 yards from A406. A40, M25, A1 quite near.

520 Arena Hotel

◆◆◆

6 Forty Lane, Wembley, Middlesex, HA9 9EB
Tel: 020 8908 0670 Fax: 020 8908 2007
Email: enquiry@arenahotel.fsnet.co.uk
Web: www.arena-hotel.co.uk
13 bedrs SB £49 DB £59
CC: MC Vi Am DC Swi Delt

How to get there: Two miles from M1 junction with North Circular road (A406).

521 Elm Hotel

◆◆◆

Elm Road, Wembley, Middlesex, HA9 7JA
Tel: 020 8902 1764 Fax: 020 8903 8365
Email: info@elmhotel.co.uk
Web: www.elmhotel.co.uk
33 bedrs SB £48 DB £65 B £5
CC: MC Vi Swi Delt

How to get there: Wembley Central Station 150 yards (main line and Tube). From North Circular (A406), turn west. Turn right at Woolwich Building Society, Elm Road first left.

Southeast

West Drayton, Middlesex

522 Travelodge West Drayton

Travel Accommodation
Sipson Road, West Drayton, Middlesex, UB7 0DU
Tel: 08700 850 950
Web: www.travelodge.co.uk
288 bedrs B £4.25 CC: MC Vi Am DC Swi Delt

Westcliff-on-Sea, Essex

523 Rose House Hotel

♦ ♦ ♦
21–23 Manor Road, Westcliff-on-Sea,
Essex, SS0 7SR
Tel: 01702 341959 Fax: 01702 390918
21 bedrs SB £27.50 DB £50 HBS £34 HBD £32
B £5 D £7 CC: MC Vi

See advert on this page

Weybridge, Surrey

524 Oatlands Park Hotel

★★★★★ ®
146 Oatlands Drive, Weybridge, Surrey, KT13 9HB
Tel: 01932 847242 Fax: 01932 842252
Email: info@oatlandsparkhotel.com
Web: www.oatlandsparkhotel.com
144 bedrs SB £140 DB £200 B £13.50 L £24
D £29 CC: MC Vi Am DC Swi Delt
⊕ & ⊔ ⊿ ⊗ ⊜ ▯ ☎ ☏ ▣ ⊠ ⅋ ♯ ⊷ ⬚ ⫙ 'Y'
Q ♈
How to get there: From Weybridge centre, follow
road up Monument Hill to mini roundabout. Turn
left into Oatlands Drive. Hotel 500 yards on left.

525 Ship Hotel

★★★
Monument Green, Weybridge, Surrey, KT13 8BQ
Tel: 01932 848364 Fax: 01932 857153
Email: info@peelhotel.com
Web: www.peelhotel.com
39 bedrs SB £139.50 DB £171 HBS £162
HBD £108 B £11.50 L £14.50 D £22.50
CC: MC Vi Am DC Swi Delt
⊗ ⊜ ▯ ☎ ▣ ⊠ ⅋ ⊷ ⬚ ⫙
How to get there: From M25 Junction 11, take
A317 to Weybridge. Straight over two
roundabouts to T-junction: turn left into High
Street. Hotel approx 300 yards on left.

Wheatley, Oxfordshire

526 Travelodge Wheatley

Travel Accommodation
A40, Old London Road, Wheatley,
Oxfordshire, OX33 1JH
Tel: 08700 850 950
Web: www.travelodge.co.uk
36 bedrs B £4.25 CC: MC Vi Am DC Swi Delt

Winchester, Hampshire

527 Lainston House Hotel
Blue Ribbon Winner

★★★★★ ® ® ®
Sparsholt, Winchester, Hampshire, SO21 2LT
Tel: 01962 863588 Fax: 01962 776672
Email: enquiries@lainstonhouse.com
Web: www.exclusivehotels.co.uk

Set in 63 acres of gardens and parkland. The
ideal location for long weekends or a few days
away. Individually styled bedrooms and award-
winning 'Avenue Restaurant' combine to make
this 17th Century House Hotel a luxurious place
to stay.
50 bedrs SB £115 DB £180 HBS £150 HBD £125
B £15 L £14 D £35 CC: MC Vi Am DC Swi Delt
⊕ & ⊿ ⊀ ▯ ☎ ☏ ▣ ⊠ ⅋ ♯ ⊷ ⬚ ⫙ 'Y' Q
⊷
How to get there: Travelling south on A34 take
B3420 (Winchester), turn right into Harestock
Road. Travel one mile in direction of
Stockbridge B3049, travel ½ mile, sign on brow
of hill 'Lainston next turning on left'.

528 The Wessex Hotel

★★★★

Paternoster Row, Winchester,
Hampshire, SO23 9LQ
Tel: 0870 4008126 Fax: 01962 849617
Email: mail@wessexhotel.co.uk
Web: www.wessexhotel.co.uk
94 bedrs SB £74 DB £150 HBS £89 HBD £89
B £3 L £5 D £10 CC: MC Vi Am DC Swi Delt

How to get there: Leave M3 at Junction nine
and head towards Winnall. Go straight over
main roundabout. Turn left, stay in left lane. Turn
right at King Alfred's statue roundabout. Turn
left into Colebrook Street. Hotel on right.

529 Shawlands

◆ ◆ ◆ ◆

46 Kilham Lane, Winchester,
Hampshire, SO22 5QD
Tel: 01962 861166 Fax: 01962 861166
Email: kathy@pollshaw.u-net.com
Children minimum age: 5

Attractive, modern house in quiet elevated
position overlooking countryside. One mile from
city centre. Colour TV, hairdryers and welcome
tray in bedrooms. Breakfast includes homemade
bread and preserves with fruit from garden.
5 bedrs SB £30 DB £40 CC: MC Vi Swi Delt

How to get there: A3090 from Winchester. Over
roundabout, right at second set of lights.

See the road ahead

Just dial 1740* from any mobile
phone to get up-to-the-minute
RAC traffic information on
motorways and major A roads.
Try it now! *Calls to 1740 are charged
at premium rate.

530 Wykeham Arms

◆ ◆ ◆ ◆

75 Kingsgate Street, Winchester,
Hampshire, SO23 9PE
Tel: 01962 853834 Fax: 01962 854411
Email: doreen@wykehamarms.sfnet.co.uk
Children minimum age: 14
14 bedrs SB £45 DB £79.50 L £5 D £12.95
CC: MC Vi Am DC Swi Delt

How to get there: Immediately south of the
cathedral by Kingsgate, at junction of Canon
Street and Kingsgate Street.

531 Old Barn Cottage

◆ ◆ ◆

Onslebury, near Winchester,
Hampshire, SO21 1LU
Tel: 01962 777410 Fax: 01962 777755
Closed Christmas
1 bedrs SB £20 DB £35 CC: None accepted

How to get there: Follow tourist signs for
Marwell Zoo. Pass entrance, keep left for three
km. House on right between Ship Inn and
church.

532 Stanmore Hotel

◆ ◆ ◆

Stanmore Lane, Winchester,
Hampshire, SO22 4BL
Tel: 01962 852720 Fax: 01962 850467

533 The Winchester Royal

◆

St. Peter Street, Winchester,
Hampshire, SO23 8BS
Tel: 01962 840840 Fax: 01962 841582

534 Travelodge Winchester

Travel Accommodation
A303, Barton Stacey, Winchester,
Hampshire, SO21 3NF
Tel: 08700 850 950
Web: www.travelodge.co.uk
20 bedrs B £4.25 CC: MC Vi Am DC Swi Delt

Southeast

Windsor, Berkshire

535 Heritage Hotels – The Castle Hotel

★★★ ®
High Street, Windsor, Berkshire, SL4 1LJ
Tel: 01753 851011 Fax: 01753 856930
Email: heritagehotels_windsor.castle
@forte-hotels.com
Web: www.heritage-hotels.com

Originally a Coaching Inn, the Hotel has grown over the years and now boasts 111 luxury bedrooms. Many executive rooms look towards Windsor Castle, and two restaurants offer a unique blend of cuisine and ambience.
111 bedrs SB £171 DB £201 HBS £75 HBD £60 B £12.50 L £9.95 D £22.95
CC: MC Vi Am DC Swi Delt

How to get there: Leave M4 at Junction six and follow the signs for Windsor Castle. The hotel is on the left at the top of High Street.

536 Netherton Hotel

♦ ♦ ♦
96–98 St. Leonard's Road, Windsor, Berkshire, SL4 3NU
Tel: 01753 855508 Fax: 01753 621267
Email: netherton@btconnect.com
Web: www.nethertonhotel.co.uk

The Netherton Hotel is situated ideally for many local attractions. All rooms en-suite, many having been recently refurbished. Only seven miles from Heathrow and two miles from M4.

20 bedrs DB £70 CC: MC Vi Swi Delt

How to get there: From M4, Junction 6, take A355 to large roundabout. Take second exit into Goslar Way. Continue over and take first left immediately after traffic lights.

537 Oscar Hotel

♦ ♦ ♦
65 Vansittart Road, Windsor, Berkshire, SL4 5DB
Tel: 01753 830613 Fax: 01753 833744
Email: info@oscarhotel.com
Web: www.oscarhotel.com
13 bedrs SB £60 DB £80
CC: MC Vi Am DC Swi Delt JCB

How to get there: M4 J6 to Windsor, first slip road to roundabout, left, then first right into Vansittart Road.

538 Park Farm

♦ ♦ ♦ ⍟
St. Leonards Road, Windsor, Berkshire, SL4 3EA
Tel: 01753 866823 Fax: 01753 850869
Email: stay@parkfarm.com
Web: www.parkfarm.com
4 bedrs SB £40 DB £59 CC: None accepted
How to get there: From M4 (Junction 6), head towards Windsor. At roundabout with traffic lights, take third exit. At T-junction, turn right. Park Farm is on left.

539 Clarence Hotel

♦ ♦
9 Clarence Road, Windsor, Berkshire, SL4 5AE
Tel: 01753 864436 Fax: 01753 857060
Web: www.clarence-hotel.co.uk
20 bedrs SB £56 DB £67
CC: MC Vi Am DC Swi Delt JCB
How to get there: Leave M4 at Junction four and follow dual carriageway towards Windsor. Turn left at roundabout onto Clarence Road.

Witney, Oxfordshire

540 Witney Four Pillars Hotel

★★★
Ducklington Lane, Witney, Oxfordshire, OX8 7TJ
Tel: 01993 779777 Fax: 01993 703467
Email: witney@four-pillars.co.uk
Web: www.four-pillars.co.uk

83 bedrs SB £97.75 DB £116.50 HBS £113.75
HBD £74.25 B £5.75 L £5.75 D £15.95
CC: MC Vi Am DC Swi Delt JCB

How to get there: A40 towards Cheltenham; 2nd
exit for Witney A415; hotel is on the left.

541 The Bird In Hand

♦♦♦♦

Whiteoak Green, Hailey, Witney,
Oxfordshire, OX29 9XP
Tel: 01993 868321 Fax: 01993 868702
Email: birdinhand@heavitreeinns.co.uk
16 bedrs SB £49.50 DB £58 HBS £67 HBD £46
L £2.95 D £2.95 CC: MC Vi DC Swi Delt JCB

Woburn, Bedfordshire

542 Bedford Arms

★★★

George Street, Woburn, Milton Keynes,
Bedfordshire, MK17 9PX
Tel: 01525 290441 Fax: 01525 290432
53 bedrs CC: MC Vi Am Swi Delt

How to get there: Leave M1 at Junction 13 and
follow signs to Woburn.

Woodstock, Oxfordshire

543 Heritage Hotels – The Bear

★★★★ ℞℞

Park Street, Woodstock, Oxfordshire, OX20 1SZ
Tel: 0870 4008202 Fax: 01993 813380
Email: heritagehotels_woodstock.bear@forte-
hotels.com
Web: www.heritage-hotels.com
54 bedrs SB £135 DB £175 HBS £90 HBD £90
B £14.50 L £14.50 D £19.50
CC: MC Vi Am DC Swi Delt

How to get there: From London, take M40 to
Oxford and leave at Junction 8. Then take A40
to Oxford North. Take A44 to Woodstock and
turn left into town centre.

544 The Feathers

Blue Ribbon Winner

★★★★ ℞℞℞

Market Street, Woodstock,
Oxfordshire, OX20 1SX
Tel: 01993 812291 Fax: 01993 813158
Email: enquiries@thefeathers.co.uk
Web: www.feathers.co.uk

17th-century country town house. Situated in
the heart of Woodstock, nestled by the gates of
Blenheim Palace. A comfortable friendly
atmosphere pervades throughout with charm
and character
20 bedrs SB £115 DB £155 HBS £135
HBD £92.50 B £14.75 L £17.50 D £35
CC: MC Vi Am DC Swi Delt JCB

How to get there: Exit J8 M40. Take A40
towards Oxford; A44 towards Woodstock. Take
2nd left into town centre, first hotel on left.

It's easier online

For all your motoring and travel
needs, www.rac.co.uk

Ask the experts

To book a Hotel or Guest
Accommodation, or for help
and advice, call RAC Hotel
Reservations on 0870 603 9109
and quote 'Guide 2002'

Southeast

545 Gorselands Hall

Boddington Lane, North Leigh, Witney,
Oxfordshire, OX29 6PU
Tel: 01993 882292 Fax: 01993 883629
Email: hamilton@gorselandshall.com
Web: www.gorselandshall.com

Lovely old Cotswold stone country house with
oak beams and flagstone floors in delightful
rural location. Large secluded garden. Ideal for
Blenheim Palace, Oxford and Cotswolds. Lovely
river walks nearby.
6 bedrs SB £35 DB £50
CC: MC Vi Am Swi Delt
How to get there: Gorselands Hall is 150 yards
from A4095 between North Leigh and Long
Hanborough. Four miles from Woodstock, nine
miles from Oxford.

Worthing, West Sussex

546 Beach Hotel

★★★

Marine Parade, Worthing,
West Sussex, BN11 3QJ
Tel: 01903 234001 Fax: 01903 234567
Email: thebeachhotel@btinternet.com
Web: www.thebeachhotel.co.uk
83 bedrs SB £59.75 DB £95 HBS £71.75
HBD £59.50 B £9.50 D £19.50
CC: MC Vi Am DC Swi Delt
How to get there: Just off the A27 by road.

547 Best Western Berkeley

★★★

86-95 Marine Parade, Worthing,
West Sussex, BN11 3QD
Tel: 01903 820000 Fax: 01903 821333
Email: berkeley@wakefordhotels.co.uk
Web: www.wakefordhotels.co.uk/berkeley

84 bedrs SB £75 DB £110 HBS £90 HBD £140
CC: MC Vi Am DC Swi
How to get there: Follow the signs to Worthing
seafront. Travel west from the pier for ½ mile.

548 The Windsor Hotel

★★★

14/20 Windsor Road, Worthing,
West Sussex, BN11 2LX
Tel: 0800 980 4442 Fax: 01903 210763
Email: enquiries@thewindsor.co.uk
Web: www.thewindsor.co.uk
30 bedrs SB £70 DB £85 B £9.95 D £16,95
CC: MC Vi Am DC Swi Delt JCB
How to get there: Westbound; follow Hotels
East signs until directed down Windsor Road.
Eastbound; coast road until tourist sign directs
you down Windsor Road.

549 Cavendish

★★

115/116 Marine Parade, Worthing,
West Sussex, BN11 3QG
Tel: 01903 236767 Fax: 01903 823840
Email: thecavendish@mistral.co.uk
Web: www3.mistral.co.uk/thecavendish
17 bedrs SB £47.50 DB £70 HBS £60 HBD £95
B £7.50 L £12.50 D £12.50
CC: MC Vi Am Swi Delt
How to get there: From the A27 or A24, follow
signs to seafront. Hotel 600 yards from Pier West.

550 Bonchurch House Hotel

♦♦♦♦

1 Winchester Road, Worthing,
West Sussex, BN11 4DJ
Tel: 01903 202492 Fax: 01903 202492
Email: bonchurch@enta.net
Web: www.smoothhound.co.uk/hotels
/bonchurc.html
Children minimum age: 3
Bonchurch is a home-from-home small hotel.
Resident proprietors. Ideally situated close to
seafront, shops and entertainment.
7 bedrs SB £25 DB £50 B £5
CC: MC Vi Swi Delt JCB
How to get there: When entering Worthing,
follow road sign A259 to Littlehampton and
tourist direction signage 'Hotels West'. Hotel
situated on junction betwen Richmond and
Wykeham Road.

Commission-free
foreign currency

Your journey can get off to a flying start, thanks to a commission free service RAC has organised with currency experts, Travelex.

Forget standing in long queues, just order your commission free currency and travellers cheques from the comfort of your home and your order will be delivered to your door.

Call RAC Travel Sales
0800 55 00 55
quoting GUI1

Travelex

A to B - we RAC to it

Southwest

Glasgow • • Edinburgh

• Newcastle

Belfast •

Dublin • • Manchester

Birmingham •

Cardiff • London •

Cirencester •
Stroud •
Monmouth
Swindon • Newbury •
M4
M5
Marlborough •
Chepstow • S GLOUCESTER-SHIRE M4
Chipenham •
A338
Andover
M4
Newport • Bristol Bath
WILTSHIRE
A303
N SOMERSET BATH & NE SOMERSET
Winchester
A38
Frome Sallsbury •
Weston-super-Mare •
A37
Shepton Mallet •
Glastonbury •
Shaftesbury •
A31
A350
Bridgwater •
Blandford Forum
Poole Bournemouth
Minehead •
SOMERSET Yeovil
DORSET
Taunton • A303
A37
A39
Dorchester •
Barnstaple •
Bridport A35
A361
DEVON Weymouth •
Bideford •
Lyme Regis
M5
Exeter • Sidmouth
A386
Okehampton • Exmouth •
Bude •
Teignmouth •
Launceston • A38 Torquay •
A30 Tavistock • Paignton •
Dartmouth •
Liskeard •
Plymouth •
Wadebridge •
Bodmin •
CORNWALL
Newquay • St Austel •
A30
Truro •
St Ives • Falmouth •
Helston •
Penzance •

● Portsmouth and its Royal Naval Base, Naval Museum and moored ships (HMS Victory and HMS Warrior) is the perfect location for those with nautical interests.

The most glorious sight in the City of Wells, Wells Cathedral (right) contains over 300 statues in niches in the West front. Associated with Europe's first completely gothic cathedral is the Bishop's Palace, defended by moat and wall since the 14th century.

Established in 1959, Bennetts Water Gardens (above) near Weymouth specialises in water lilies, displayed and grown in a series of small lakes. This tranquil setting also has an educational nature trail and a tropical house containing exotic plants. www.waterlily.co.uk or 01305 785150 for further information.

● Horse World, near Bristol, is a rescue centre and retirement home for over 200 ponies, horses and donkeys. Originally established nearly 50 years ago as a sanctuary for ex-working horses, it now has a museum, film presentation and nature trail – and of course, lots of horses to meet, in the fields and during the twice-daily "Parade of Horses". www.horseworld.org.uk or 01275 540173.

● Ferries from Bournemouth and Poole take you to Brownsea Island, site of a castle and a haven for red squirrels and other wildlife.

● Fans of the great age of steam, and its most infamous route in particular, should visit the Steam Museum of the Great Western Railway in Swindon.

Salcombe Bay in Devon (above) is one of the Southwest's many attractive beaches.

● Irresistible to children and the young at heart, The Dinosaur Museum in Dorchester has wonderful hands-on displays and models of the terrible lizards, as well as the traditional fossil displays and reassembled skeletons. Computerised displays and a model of a dinosaur evolved into humanoid form keep up the excitement. For more details, go to www.dinosaur-museum.org.uk or call 01305 269880.

Following the trail

The River Parrett Trail passes through the gentle hills of the Dorset and Somerset borders and across the wetlands of the Somerset Levels and Moors. Follow the entire 50-mile length of the river or just walk a section, taking in orchards, limestone cottages, medieval churches and patterns of water courses. Learn more at www.riverparrett-trail.org.uk or get a trail guide via 01935 462462.

The Eden Project, based in a sheltered crater-shaped valley in St Austell, Cornwall, is dominated by two vast domed conservatories known as Biomes (above). Made from inflatable panels of incredibly strong triple-glazed transparent foil, the Biomes hold a range of 2,000 exotic plant types and habitats — including rainforests, Mediterranean, South African and Californian settings — in temperatures up to 28°C (80°F). Go to www.edenproject.co.uk or call 01726 811911.

● Use a cobbled path at low tide or boat at high tide to reach St Michael's Mount, granite island base of an eighth-century Cornish monastery which later became a fortress.

Developed from the owner's aviaries of injured and rescued birds, Screech Owl Sanctuary near Indian Queens, Cornwall (above), was established in 1990 to nurse sick birds of prey back to health, homing those who cannot be returned to the wild. Visitors can see 34 species of owl; indoor presentations even allow you to touch tame birds. Call 01726 860182 or see www.owlsanct.freeserve.co.uk.

● The peak of Glastonbury Tor commands stunning views and is the site of a ruined 14th-century church known as St Michael's Tower.

● Keen walkers can follow part of the Southwest Coast Path — at 630 miles, the UK's longest footpath. Running from Minehead to Poole, it is marked on Ordnance Survey maps, or see www.westcountry-walking-holidays.com

The great Roman temple and Baths in Bath (above) are one of the country's finest ancient monuments. Hot water from Britain's only thermal springs still flows through the heart of this 2,000-year-old site. The everyday life of a Roman spa is revealed in the ancient gifts offered at the temple here. More information at www.romanbaths.co.uk or 01225 477785.

Spectacular subterranean caves are abundant below the Mendip Hills in Somerset, notably at Cheddar Gorge and, six miles away, Wookey Hole (below), formed by the flow of the River Axe. The tour of the latter focuses on the story of an evil witch turned to stone, an eerie tale in unearthly surroundings, which once were the home of Celts. www.wookey.co.uk or 01749 672243 for more information.

● Wiltshire has the infamous Neolithic circles of Stone Henge and Avebury.

● The 702-foot Clifton Suspension Bridge at Bristol, designed by Isambard Kingdom Brunel, was first proposed in 1753 but not completed until 1864.

© Patrick Cooke

The spectacular valley gardens of Mapperton House, Beaminster, Dorset (above), are surrounded by wooded landscape. This beautiful 16th century manor house, open to the public on June and July weekdays, is adjoined by All Saints church, originally medieval. Visit www.mapperton.com or phone 01308 862645.

Accommodation index

Hotels and Guest Accommodation are indexed by their order of appearance within this region, not by the page. To locate an establishment, note the number to the right of the listing and then find it on the establishment's name bar, as shown here

(37) The Turning Mill Hotel

Dart Valley Railway runs between Totnes and
Buckfastleigh in Devon.

Almondsbury, South Gloucestershire

1 Abbotts Way Guest House

♦♦♦♦ ✕

Gloucester Road, Almondsbury, Bristol, BS32 4JB
Tel: 01454 613134 Fax: 01454 613134
6 bedrs SB £31 DB £50
CC: MC Vi Am DC Swi Delt

How to get there: From M4/M5 junction at Lamondsbury, travel two miles north. Guest house on left. From M5 north, leave at Junction 14. Follow A38 for Bristol: guest house seven miles on right.

Axminster, Devon

2 Fairwater Head Hotel

★★★★ ℞ ℞

Hawkchurch, Devon, EX13 5TX
Tel: 01297 678349 Fax: 01297 678459
Email: j.c.lowe@btinternet.com
Closed January
20 bedrs SB £84 DB £148 HBS £92 HBD £164
B £8 L £14 D £25
CC: MC Vi Am DC Swi Delt

How to get there: 2½ miles from A35 and 14 miles from Crewkerne on the B3165. Signposted to hotel locally from B3165.

Barnstaple, Devon

3 The Imperial Hotel

★★★★ ℞

Taw Vale Parade, Barnstaple, Devon, EX32 8NB
Tel: 01271 345861 Fax: 01271 324448
Email: info@brend-imperial.co.uk
Web: www.brend-imperial.co.uk

With luxury refurbishment now completed The Imperial is Barnstaple's premier hotel and the only 4-star. The hotel overlooks the River Taw and Barnstaple.
63 bedrs SB £79 DB £95 HBS £101
HBD £69.50 B £10 L £12.50 D £22
CC: MC Vi Am DC Swi Delt

How to get there: Leave M5 at Junction 27 and take A361 to Barnstaple. Follow signs to town centre passing Tesco. Proceed straight over next two roundabouts. River is on left, hotel on right.
See advert on following page

4 Barnstaple Hotel

★★★

Braunton Road, Barnstaple, Devon, EX31 1LE
Tel: 01271 376221 Fax: 01271 324101
Email: info@barnstaplehotel.co.uk
Web: www.brend-hotels.co.uk

On the coastal side of Barnstaple, offering easy access to North Devon's beaches and Exmoor. The hotel has a superb health and leisure complex.
60 bedrs SB £59.50 DB £79 HBS £79 HBD £58
B £9.50 L £11 D £18.50
CC: MC Vi Am DC Swi Delt

How to get there: Take A361 Braunton/Ilfracombe road from Barnstaple. Hotel is located on left approximately one mile from town centre.

Southwest

IN THE HEART OF NORTH DEVON

The luxurious Imperial Hotel, stands in its own
manicured grounds on the banks of the River Taw.
Boasting all the elegance and style of a beautiful hotel
it provides first class service with the finest of wines
and superb cuisine, with ensuite bedrooms,
satellite TV and a lift to all floors.

In a central location with free resident parking,
The Imperial is the perfect base from which to explore
the historic market town of Barnstaple, Englands oldest
borough and many time 'Britain in Bloom' winner, or the
idyllic surroundings of places like Clovelly,
Lynmouth and Saunton.

FOR A FREE COLOUR BROCHURE, PLEASE CONTACT:

THE IMPERIAL HOTEL
RAC ★★★★
TAW VALE PARADE, BARNSTAPLE, NORTH DEVON EX32 8NB.
TEL: (01271) 345861 FAX: (01271) 324448
www.brend-imperial.co.uk e-mail: info@brend-imperial.co.uk

Brend Hotels
The Westcountry's Leading Hotel Group

5 Park Hotel

★★★
New Road, Taw Vale, Barnstaple,
Devon, EX32 9AE
Tel: 01271 372166 Fax: 01271 323157
Email: info@parkhotel.co.uk
Web: www.brend-hotels.co.uk

With the whole of North Devon on your
doorstep, the Park Hotel combines luxury with
excellent value. Overlooking park and the River
Taw, and an easy walk to the town centre.
42 bedrs SB £56.50 DB £65 HBS £74 HBD £50
B £9.50 L £10 D £18.50
CC: MC Vi Am DC Swi Delt

How to get there: Leave M5 at Junction 27 and
take A361 to Barnstaple. Follow signs to town
centre, passing Tesco. Proceed straight ahead
at next two roundabouts. Rock Park is on left,
the hotel entrance on right.

6 Royal and Fortescue Hotel

★★★★ 🄰 🄰
Boutport Street, Barnstaple, Devon, EX31 3HG
Tel: 01271 342289 Fax: 01271 340102
Email: info@royalfortescue.co.uk
Web: www.brend-hotels.co.uk

A former coaching inn, recent refurbishment has
retained this historic charm whilst adding fine
modern facilities. Lord Fortescue's restaurant,
elegant balls, beautiful bedrooms and the
adjacent bar and brasserie "62 Jut Bank" are all
at your disposal.
50 bedrs SB £56.50 DB £65 HBS £74.50
HBD £51 B £9.50 L £10 D £18.50
CC: MC Vi Am DC Swi Delt

How to get there: Located in the town centre at
the junction of High Street and Boutport Street.

7 Downrew House

★★ 🄰
Bishops Tawton, Barnstaple, Devon, EX32 0DY
Tel: 01271 342497 Fax: 01271 323947
Email: downrew@globalnet.co.uk
Web: www.downrew.co.uk
12 bedrs SB £55 DB £80 HBS £70 HBD £55
B £7.50 L £14.95 D £22.50
CC: MC Vi Am DC Swi Delt

How to get there: Situated three miles south of
Barnstaple off A377. Signposted opposite
garage in Bishops Tawton. Hotel at top of lane.

8 Rising Sun Inn

Umberleigh, near Barnstaple,
North Devon, EX37 9DU
Tel: 01769 560447 Fax: 01769 560764
Email: risingsuninn@btinternet.com
Web: www.risingsuninn.com

Ideal for touring, eight miles from busy
Barnstaple, this quiet 13th-century inn
overlooks the Taw River. Chas and Heather offer
warm hospitality, comfortable accommodation
and award-winning food.
9 bedrs SB £46 DB £80 HBS £62 HBD £56
B £5.50 L £2.95 D £4.95 CC: MC Vi Swi Delt

How to get there: Junction of A377 and B3227,
opposite Umberleigh Bridge.

Bath, Bath & NE Somerset

9 Royal Crescent Hotel

Blue Ribbon Winner

16 Royal Crescent, Bath,
Bath & NE Somerset, BA1 2LS
Tel: 01225 823333 Fax: 01225 339401
Email: reservations@royalcrescent.co.uk
Web: www.royalcrescent.co.uk
45 bedrs DB £255 HBD £340 B £17.50 L £18.50
D £30
CC: MC Vi Am DC Swi Delt

How to get there: Guests are provided with
precise directions when making reservations.
See advert below

Southwest

10 The Bath Spa Hotel

★★★★★ ® ® ®
Sydney Road, Bath,
Bath & NE Somerset, BA2 6JF
Tel: 0870 4008222 Fax: 01225 444006
Email: fivestar@bathspa.u-net.com
Web: www.bathspahotel.com
102 bedrs SB £175 DB £230 HBS £140
HBD £140 B £14.75 L £17.50 D £35
CC: MC Vi Am DC Swi Delt

How to get there: Leave M4 at Junction 18.
Take A46 to Bath. At 1st roundabout turn right
onto A4. Follow signs for city centre. Turn left
onto A36 at lights. At mini roundabout turn right,
then next left into Sydney Place. Hotel is 200
yards up hill on right.

11 Combe Grove Manor Hotel & Country Club

★★★★★ ® ®
Brassknocker Hill, Monkton Combe, Bath,
Bath & NE Somerset, BA2 7HS
Tel: 01225 834644 Fax: 01225 834961
Email: richard.williams@combegrovemanor.com
Web: www.combegrovemanor.com
40 bedrs SB £110 DB £110 HBS £130
HBD £150 B £7.50 L £18 D £28
CC: MC Vi Am DC Swi Delt

How to get there: From Bath city centre follow
signs for the university. Go past the university
for 1½ miles; hotel entrance is on the left.

12 Lucknam Park Hotel
Gold Ribbon Winner

★★★★★ ® ® ®
Colerne, Chippenham, Wiltshire, SN14 8AZ
Tel: 01225 742777 Fax: 01225 743536
Email: reservations@lucknampark.co.uk
Web: www.lucknampark.co.uk
41 bedrs SB £173 DB £231 HBS £195
HBD £140 B £18 L £25 D £45
CC: MC Vi Am DC Swi Delt

How to get there: Westbound, leave M4 at
Junction 17. Take A350 to Chippenham, A420
to Ford, turn left to Colerne, and right at
crossroads to the hotel.
See advert on facing page

13 Ston Easton Park
Gold Ribbon Winner

★★★★ ® ® ®
Ston Easton, Bath,
Bath & NE Somerset, BA3 4DF
Tel: 01761 241631 Fax: 01761 241377
Email: stoneastonpark@stoneaston.co.uk
Web: www.stoneaston.co.uk
Children minimum age: 7
23 bedrs SB £130 DB £185 HBS £225
HBD £145 L £16 D £39.50
CC: MC Vi Am DC Swi Delt JCB

See advert on this page

14 The Bath Priory
Gold Ribbon Winner

★★★★ ® ® ® ®
Weston Road, Bath,
Bath & NE Somerset, BA1 2XT
Tel: 01225 331922 Fax: 01225 448276
Email: bathprioryhotel@compuserve.com
Web: www.thebathpriory.co.uk

Set in four acres of landscaped gardens, the
Bath Priory offers visitors comfort, peace and
privacy as well as luxurious health and leisure
spa facilities. Open daily for lunch and dinner.
28 bedrs SB £145 DB £230 HBS £175
HBD £142.50 B £18 L £25 D £45
CC: MC Vi Am DC Swi Delt JCB

How to get there: Situated in the north-west
corner of the city, the Bath Priory Hotel is a 15-
minute walk from the city centre.

15 Windsor Hotel

★★★★ ®

69 Great Pulteney Street, Bath,
Bath & NE Somerset, BA2 4DL
Tel: 01225 422100 Fax: 01225 422550
Email: sales@bathwindsorhotel.com
Web: www.bathwindsorhotel.com
Children minimum age: 12
14 bedrs SB £85 DB £135 B £7 L £10 D £25
CC: MC Vi Am DC Swi Delt JCB

How to get there: M4 J18, A46 to Bath, A4. Turn
onto A36, ¹⁄₄ of a mile, right at roundabout,
second right into Great Pulteney Street.
See advert on following page

16 Abbey Hotel

★★★ ® ®

North Parade, Bath,
Bath & NE Somerset, BA1 1LF
Tel: 01225 461603 Fax: 01225 447758
Email: ahres@compasshotels.co.uk
Web: www.compasshotels.co.uk

Privately owned and operated, and situated in
the heart of Bath near the Abbey and Roman
Baths. Recently refurbished to the standard one
expects from a good three-star hotel
60 bedrs SB £80 DB £125 HBS £90
HBD £72.50 B £9.50 L £11.50 D £22
CC: MC Vi Am DC Swi Delt

How to get there: In city centre, close to Bath
Abbey and railway station.

See the road ahead

Just dial 1740* from any mobile
phone to get up-to-the-minute
RAC traffic information on
motorways and major A roads.
Try it now! *Calls to 1740 are charged
at premium rate.

Southwest

17 Heritage Hotels – The Francis

★★★ ℞
Queen Square, Bath,
Bath & NE Somerset, BA1 2HH
Tel: 0870 400 8223 Fax: 01225 319715
Email: heritagehotels-bath.francis
@forte-hotels.com
Web: www.heritage-hotels.com
95 bedrs SB £75 DB £150 HBS £90 HBD £85
B £13.50 L £7.50 D £21.95
CC: MC Vi Am DC Swi Delt JCB
⊪ 🖊 🛎 🕸 🖂 🖥 ☎ 📞 Ⓟ🐾 🛁 ⌇℃ 🏧 🛌 🛏

How to get there: Exit the M4 at Junction 18
and proceed along the A46 to Bath city centre.
Proceed to end of George Street and turn left
into Queen Square. The Francis is on the south
side of the square.

18 Lansdown Grove Hotel

★★★★ ℞ ℞
Lansdown Road, Bath,
Bath & NE Somerset, BA1 5EH
Tel: 01225 483888 Fax: 01225 483838
Email: lansdown@marstonhotels.com
Web: www.marstonhotels.com

50 bedrs SB £109 DB £135 HBS £75 HBD £75
B £12 L £12.50 D £22
CC: MC Vi Am DC Swi Delt
🔺 ♿ ⊪ 🖊 🕸 🛎 🖂 🖥 ☎ 📞 Ⓟ🐾 🛁 ⌇℃ 🏧 🛌 🛏

How to get there: Leave M4 at Junction 18.
Follow A46 towards Bath city centre. Take
Broad Street. Follow signs for Lansdown and
Bath Races.

19 Queensberry Hotel & Olive Tree Restaurant   Gold Ribbon Winner

★★★★ ℞ ℞ ℞
Russel Street, Bath,
Bath & NE Somerset, BA1 2QF
Tel: 01225 447928 Fax: 01225 446065
Email: enquiries@bathqueensberry.com
Web: www.bathqueensberry.com
Closed Christmas

A luxury privately owned townhouse in Georgian
Bath, minutes from Royal Crescent, Roman
Baths and Pump Rooms. The Olive Tree
restaurant is nationally renowned for informal
contemporary British cooking.
29 bedrs SB £90 DB £120 B £9.50 L £14.50
D £24 CC: MC Vi Swi Delt
♿ ⊪ 🖊 🛎 🖂 ☎ 📞 Ⓟ🐾 🛁 ⌇℃ 🏧 🛌

How to get there: Exit M4 J-18. A46 to city
centre. Right fork at mini-roundabout after 2nd
lights, right at next lights. Second left, first right.

20 George's Hotel

★★
2-3 South Parade, Bath,
Bath & NE Somerset, BA2 4AA
Tel: 01225 464923 Fax: 01225 425471
Email: info@georgeshotel.co.uk
Web: www.georgeshotel.co.uk
19 bedrs SB £65 DB £75
CC: MC Vi Am Swi Delt
♿ 🖊 🖥 🖂 ☎ 🛁 ⌇℃ 🛌 🛏

How to get there: In city centre between Abbey
and stations, next to public car park.

21 Limpley Stoke Hotel

★★
Lower Limpley Stoke, Bath, Bath & NE
Somerset, BA3 6HZ
Tel: 01225 723333 Fax: 01225 722400

22 Old Mill Hotel

★★

Tollbridge Road, Batheaston, Bath,
Bath & NE Somerset, BA1 7DE
Tel: 01225 858476 Fax: 01225 852600
Email: oldmill@batheaston.freeserve.co.uk
Web: www.oldmillbath.co.uk

Riverside hotel with breathtaking views but only
1¹/₂ miles from centre of Bath. Unique
waterwheel restaurant. All rooms recently
refurbished. Free car parking. Private fishing.
27 bedrs
CC: MC Vi Am Swi Delt

How to get there: Exit 18 on M4 towards Bath
(A46). Turn left after nine miles to Batheaston.
Old Mill is located by the tollbridge, ¹/₂ miles
from the A46.

23 Wentworth House Hotel

★★

106 Bloomfield Road, Bath,
Bath & NE Somerset, BA2 2AP
Tel: 01225 339193 Fax: 01225 310460
Email: stay@wentworthhouse.co.uk
Web: www.wentworthhouse.co.uk
Children minimum age: 5
18 bedrs SB £50 DB £75 HBS £60 HBD £48
B £5.50 L £5 D £7
CC: MC Vi Am DC Swi Delt

How to get there: Exit J18 M4 into city, A36 for
Bristol, then A367 Exeter/Wells for one mile.
Turn right just past 'The Bear' pub.
See advert on following page

Southwest

Wentworth House Hotel

An imposing Victorian mansion 15 minutes walk from the city. Set in a peaceful location with large gardens, sun terraces and superb views. Heated swimming pool. Licensed restaurant, and cocktail bar. Golf and walks nearby. Lovely rooms, some with 4 poster beds, and conservatories. Special offer short breaks available. Large carpark.

106 Bloomfield Road, Bath BA2 2AP
Tel: 01225 339193   Fax: 01225 310460
Email: stay@wentworthhouse.co.uk
Website: www.wentworthhouse.co.uk

24 Woolverton House Hotel

★★ ⏱

Woolverton, Bath, NE Somerset, BA3 6QS
Tel: 01373 830415 Fax: 01373 831243
Email: mail@bathhotel.com
Web: www.bathhotel.com
Children minimum age: 10

12 bedrs SB £49.50 DB £63.50 HBS £64.50 HBD £93.50 B £4.95 L £9.50 D £11.95
CC: MC Vi Delt
⛪ ⊘ ⌚ ▢ ☎ ☏ ▣▤ ♨ ♿ ⚟ ⚌ ⚏ ⚲
How to get there: Located on the A36, eight miles south of Bath in direction of Warminster. See advert below

Dorian House

Enter an atmosphere of period charm, c.1880. All ensuite bedrooms feature telephone, TV, tea and coffee. Traditional solid oak four-poster beds, panoramic views over Bath or our beautiful garden. Ten minutes' walk to the centre.

1 Upper Oldfield Park, Bath BA2 3JX
Tel: 01225 426336   Fax: 01225 444699
dorian.house@which.net
www.dorianhouse.co.uk

Woolverton House Hotel

Situated close to the historic city of Bath in a lovely countryside setting, a warm welcome, good food and excellent wines await you at Woolverton House. Delightful gardens, parking, and comfortable rooms to a high standard at affordable prices.

Woolverton, bath BA3 6QS
Tel: 01373 830415   Fax: 01373 831243
mail@bathhotel.com
www.bathhotel.com

25 Travelodge Bath

Travel Accommodation
1 York Buildings, George Street, Bath,
Bath & NE Somerset, BA1 3EB
Tel: 08700 850 950
Web: www.travelodge.co.uk
66 bedrs B £4.25 CC: MC Vi Am DC Swi Delt

26 Travelodge Beckington

Travel Accommodation
A36, Trowbridge Road, Beckington, Bath,
Bath & NE Somerset, BA3 6SF
Tel: 08700 850 950
Web: www.travelodge.co.uk
40 bedrs B £4.25
CC: MC Vi Am DC Swi Delt

27 Athole Guest House

◆ ◆ ◆ ◆ ◆ ✵
33 Upper Oldfield Park, Bath,
Bath and NE Somerset, BA2 3JX
Tel: 01225 334307 Fax: 01225 320009
Email: bookings@atholehouse.co.uk
Web: www.atholehouse.co.uk
3 bedrs SB £45 DB £65
CC: MC Vi Am Swi Delt JCB
How to get there: From M4 follow signs for
through traffic/Radstock/Wells into Wells Road.
Take first turning on right.

28 Cheriton House

◆ ◆ ◆ ◆ ◆ ✵ ✦
9 Upper Oldfield Park, Bath,
Bath & NE Somerset, BA2 3JX
Tel: 01225 429862 Fax: 01225 428403
Email: cheriton@which.net
Web: www.cheritonhouse.co.uk
Children minimum age: 12
10 bedrs SB £48 DB £66
CC: MC Vi Am DC Swi Delt
How to get there: South of city centre, just off
A367.

29 County Hotel

Little Gem

◆ ◆ ◆ ◆ ◆ ✵ ✦
18/19 Pulteney Road, Bath,
Bath & NE Somerset, BA2 4EZ
Tel: 01225 425003 Fax: 01225 466493
Email: reservations@county-hotel.co.uk
Web: www.county-hotel.co.uk
Children minimum age: 13.
Closed Christmas
22 bedrs SB £70 DB £98
CC: MC Vi Am DC Swi Delt
How to get there: Follow A46. Before reaching
city centre, turn left at traffic lights following
signposts for Exeter on A36. Turn right to
Holborne Museum on left and proceed over
roundabout. Hotel 50m on right.

30 Dorian House

◆ ◆ ◆ ◆ ◆ ✵ ✦
1 Upper Oldfield Park, Bath,
Bath & NE Somerset, BA2 3JX
Tel: 01225 426336 Fax: 01225 444699
Email: dorian.house@which.net
Web: www.dorianhouse.co.uk
8 bedrs SB £42. DB £55
CC: MC Vi Am Swi Delt JCB
How to get there: Exit M4 J-18, A46, A4 to
Bath. Follow A36 signposted Bristol. Left on
A367. First right is Upper Oldfield Park.
See advert on facing page

31 Oldfields Hotel

◆ ◆ ◆ ◆ ◆ ✵ ✦
102 Wells Road, Bath,
Bath & NE Somerset, BA2 3AL
Tel: 01225 317984 Fax: 01225 444471
Email: info@oldfields.co.uk
Web: www.s-h-
systems.co.uk/hotels/oldfiel2.html
Closed December 20 to February
14 bedrs SB £48 DB £70 B £6
CC: MC Vi Am Swi Delt
How to get there: From M4 Junction 18, take
A46 to Bath. Take A4 into city. Take A36 Bristol
Road, then A367 (Wells Road). Oldfields is 1/3 of
a mile up hill on right.
See advert on following page

Southwest

Oldfields Hotel

Elegant and traditional bed-and-breakfast, situated 10 minutes' walk from the city centre, with private parking. Oldfields has 14 bedrooms, all ensuite, a large breakfast choice from buffet and menu, all included in the room rates.

Oldfields is the ideal place from which to visit Bath and the surrounding area.

102 Wells Road, Bath BA2 3AL
Tel: 01225 317984   Fax: 01225 444471
info@oldfields.co.uk
www.s-h-systems.co.uk/hotels/oldfiel2.html

32 The Ayrlington

Little Gem

♦♦♦♦♦ ⚒

25 Pulteney Road, Bath, NE Somerset, BA2 4EZ
Tel: 01225 425495 Fax: 01225 469029
Email: mail@ayrlington.com
Web: www.ayrlington.com
Closed Christmas to New Year

Conveniently located close to Bath city centre, this small, tranquil, luxury hotel boasts an elegant interior, excellent views, private parking, and access to the nearby golf course.
12 bedrs DB £75 CC: MC Vi Am Swi Delt

How to get there: M4 Junction 18, A46 then A4 into city. Left at lights (signed A36), right at end of road. Over roundabout, hotel 100 yards on right.
See advert on facing page

33 Ashley Villa Hotel

♦♦♦♦ ⚒ ☂

26 Newbridge Road, Bath,
Bath & NE Somerset, BA1 3JZ
Tel: 01225 421683 Fax: 01225 313604
Email: ashleyvilla@clearface.co.uk
Web: www.ashleyvilla.co.uk

Friendly, family-run hotel with relaxing informal atmosphere. Close to city centre, private car park, bar, restaurant, lovely gardens and outdoor pool. Premier rooms include four-poster and large family accommodation.
18 bedrs SB £49 DB £69 HBS £64 HBD £49.50 L £6.50 D £15
CC: MC Vi Am Swi Delt

How to get there: Leaving Bath on A4 Bristol, take Upper Bristol Road west onto left fork. At second set of traffic lights turn into Newbridge Road. Hotel 200m on right.

34 Brompton House

♦♦♦♦ ⚒

St. John's Road, Bath,
Bath & NE Somerset, BA2 6PT
Tel: 01225 420972 Fax: 01225 420505
Email: bromptonhouse@btinternet.com
Web: www.bromptonhouse.co.uk
Children minimum age: 15
16 bedrs SB £48 DB £70
CC: MC Vi Am Swi Delt

How to get there: Leave M4 at Junction 18, take A46 for 12 miles. Then take A4 for city centre, then A36. Turn into St. Johns Road, Brompton House is adjacent to church.
See advert on facing page

Plan your route

Visit www.rac.co.uk for RAC's interactive route planner, including up to the minute traffic reports.

Southwest

35 Cholwell Hall

♦ ♦ ♦ ♦ ⚄

Clutton, Somerset, BS39 5TE
Tel: 01761 452380
Email: info@cholwellhall.co.uk
Web: www.cholwellhall.co.uk

Fine country house in glorious Mendip countryside, 10 miles from Bath, Bristol and Wells. Enjoy the two acre grounds, huge rooms and lovely views. Ample parking, non-smoking. Ring for brochure.

3 bedrs DB £60 CC: None accepted

⊗ ☕ 🖵 🄿📞 🛁 ♨ ⛲ ⚓

How to get there: Bristol – A37 South, 11 miles. Bath – A4 one mile, then Corston, Marksbury, Chelwood. Our entrance A37 southern edge of Clutton.

Brompton House

Charming Georgian house (former rectory 1777). Family owned and run. Car park and beautiful secluded gardens. 6 minutes level walk to main historic sights and restaurants. 16 tastefully furnished and fully equipped ensuite bedrooms. Delicious choice of breakfasts. No smoking.

St. John's Road, Bath BA2 6PT
Tel: 01225 420972   Fax: 01225 420505
Email: bromptonhouse@btinternet.com
Website: www.bromptonhouse.co.uk

The Ayrlington

24/25 Pulteney Road, Bath BA2 4EZ
Tel: 01225 425495 Fax: 01225 469029
Email: mail@ayrlington.com Web: www.ayrlington.com

RɑC AA, ETC ♦ ♦ ♦ ♦ ♦

A handsome listed Victorian house set in a splendid walled garden with exceptional views of the Abbey. Bath's centre and historic sites are just a five-minute level stroll away. The elegant interior is a graceful blend of English and Asian antiques, artwork and fine fabrics. All bedrooms have an individual theme and are beautifully furnished, some with 4 poster beds and spa baths. The Hotel has a residents' bar, private parking and is entirely non smoking.

Closed 23rd December to 7th January

36 Gainsborough

Weston Lane, Bath,
Bath & NE Somerset, BA1 4AB
Tel: 01225 311380 Fax: 01225 447411
Email: gainsborough_hotel@compuserve.com
Web: www.gainsboroughhotel.co.uk
17 bedrs SB £49 DB £62
CC: MC Vi Am Swi

How to get there: We are on the north-west side
of the city, west of Royal Crescent and Circus
near the R.U.H. hospital.
See advert below

37 Laura Place Hotel

♦♦♦♦

3 Laura Place, Great Pulteney Street, Bath,
Bath & NE Somerset, BA2 4BH
Tel: 01225 463815 Fax: 01225 310222
Children minimum age: 8.
Closed December 22 to March 1
8 bedrs SB £60 DB £72 CC: MC Vi Am

How to get there: From A4 via Bathwick Street,
along Henrietta Street. Laura Place is a square
with a central fountain.

The Gainsborough
RAC ♦♦♦

A spacious comfortable country house set in
our own attractive grounds, where we provide
a relaxing and informal atmosphere for your
stay. All the sights and shops are a pleasant
walk via the park. Our 17 tastefully furnished
bedrooms are fully equipped and ensuite.
A small friendly bar, two sun terraces, a
private car park and warm welcome awaits.

Weston Lane, Bath BA1 4AB
Tel: 01225 311380   Fax: 01225 447411
Website: www.gainsboroughhotel.co.uk

38 Oakleigh House

19 Upper Oldfield Park, Bath, Somerset, BA2 3JX
Tel: 01225 315698 Fax: 01225 448223
Email: oakleigh@which.net
Web: www.oakleigh-house.co.uk
3 bedrs SB £50 DB £80
CC: MC Vi Am DC Swi Delt

How to get there: Take A367 from centre of
Bath, then first turning on right. Oakleigh is
100m on right.

39 Sydney Gardens

♦♦♦♦

Sydney Road, Bath,
Bath & NE Somerset, BA2 6NT
Tel: 01225 464818 Fax: 01225 484347
Email: pete@sydneygardens.co.uk
Web: www.sydneygardens.co.uk
Children minimum age: 10.
Closed Christmas to January
6 bedrs CC: MC Vi Am Swi Delt

How to get there: From M4 Junction 18, follow
A46. Turn left at sign for Exeter-Warminster
(A36), cross river, turn right at Sydney Gardens,
then next left.

40 Tasburgh House Hotel
Little Gem

♦♦♦♦

Warminster Road, Bath, NE Somerset, BA2 6SH
Tel: 01225 425096 Fax: 01225 463842
Email: hotel@bathtasburgh.co.uk
Web: www.bathtasburgh.co.uk

Charming Victorian mansion in seven acres of
lovely gardens and meadowpark – along the
Kennet and Avon Canal. Spectacular views and
convenient for the city centre. Gourmet evening
meals. Personal, caring service. Country house
comforts in a city setting.

12 bedrs SB £57 DB £82 HBS £82 HBD £66
B £8.50 D £25
CC: MC Vi Am DC Swi Delt

How to get there: Follow signs for A36 to
Warminster from city centre. Hotel stands on
north side of A36, adjacent to Bathampton Lane
junction, approx ¹/₂ a mile from Bathwick Street
roundabout and Sydney Gardens.

41 Bonheur B & B

♦ ♦ ♦ ⌖

52 Box Road, Bathford, Bath,
Bath & NE Somerset, BA1 7QH
Tel: 01225 859537 Fax: 01225 859537
Email: bonheur@waitrose.com
Web: www.visitus.co.uk/bath/hotel/bonheur
5 bedrs SB £35 DB £55
CC: MC Vi Swi Delt

How to get there: From Bath, follow A4 to
Bathford. Take Box/Chippenham road. Bonheur
is 200m past Dunsford Landrovers.

42 Edgar Hotel

♦ ♦ ♦

64 Great Pulteney Street, Bath,
Somerset, BA2 4DN
Tel: 01225 420619 Fax: 01225 466916
Web: www.edgar-hotel.co.uk
16 bedrs SB £50 DB £75
CC: MC Vi Swi Delt JCB

43 Lamp Post Villa

♦ ♦ ♦

3 Crescent Gardens, Bath,
Bath & NE Somerset, BA1 2NA
Tel: 01225 331221 Fax: 01225 426783
Closed Christmas
4 bedrs SB £35 DB £55
CC: MC Vi Am Swi Delt

How to get there: On A4 Bristol road, in western
side of city centre close to Victoria Park.

44 Orchard Lodge

♦ ♦ ♦

Warminster Road, Bathampton, Bath,
Bath & NE Somerset, BA2 6XG
Tel: 01225 466115 Fax: 01225 446050
Email: orchardlo@aol.com
Web: www.orchardlodgebath.co.uk
14 bedrs SB £48 DB £73

CC: MC Vi Am DC Swi Delt

How to get there: On the main A36 Warminster
Road at Bathampton, 1¹/₂ miles from city centre.

Bideford, Devon

45 Royal Hotel

★ ★ ★

Barnstaple Street, Bideford, Devon, EX39 4AE
Tel: 01237 472005 Fax: 01237 478957
Email: info@royalbideford.co.uk
Web: www.brend-hotels.co.uk

The Royal Hotel overlooks ancient Bideford
Bridge and the River Torridge and is a good
base for exploring the countryside and coastline
of North Devon.
31 bedrs SB £54.50 DB £65 HBS £73
HBD £51.50 B £9.50 L £10 D £18.50
CC: MC Vi Am DC Swi Delt

How to get there: At the eastern end of old
Bideford bridge.

46 Hoops Country Inn and Hotel

★ ★ ★ ℞ ℞

Horns Cross, near Clovelly, Bideford,
Devon, EX39 5DL
Tel: 01237 451222 Fax: 01237 451247
Email: reservations@hoopsinn.co.uk
Web: www.hoopsinn.co.uk
Children minimum age: 12.
Closed Christmas Day
12 bedrs
CC: MC Vi Am DC Swi Delt JCB

How to get there: Exit J27 M5, follow directions
for Barnstaple; bypass Barnstaple, take A39.
Hoops is midway between Bideford and
Clovelly

Southwest

47 Riversford Hotel

★★

Limers Lane, Bideford, Devon, EX39 2RG
Tel: 01237 474239 Fax: 01237 421661

Blandford Forum, Dorset

48 Crown Hotel

★★★★

West Street, Blandford Forum, Dorset, DT11 7AJ
Tel: 01258 456626 Fax: 01258 451084
32 bedrs SB £68 DB £82 B £7.50 L £15.95
D £15.95 CC: MC Vi Am DC Swi

How to get there: Located in the centre of
Blandford Forum, by the River Stour.

Boscastle, Cornwall

49 Wellington Hotel

★★★

Old Road, Boscastle, Cornwall, PL35 0AQ
Tel: 01840 250202 Fax: 01840 250621
Email: vtobutt@enterprise.net
Web: www.wellingtonboscastle.co.uk
Children minimum age: 7

A listed 16th-century Coaching Inn situated in
glorious National Trust countryside in an area of
outstanding natural beauty, with picturesque
Elizabethan Harbour nearby. Excellent Anglo-
French Georgian restaurant.
17 bedrs SB £31 DB £54 HBS £45 HBD £41
B £6.50 L £5.50 D £17.50
CC: MC Vi Am DC Swi Delt

Bournemouth, Dorset

50 Bournemouth Highcliff Marriott Hotel

★★★★

105 St. Michael's Road, Westcliff, Bournemouth,
Dorset, BH2 5DU
Tel: 01202 557702 Fax: 01202 292734
Email: reservations.bournemouth
@marriotthotels.co.uk
Web: www.marriotthotel.com/bohbm
152 bedrs SB £63 DB £96 HBS £87 HBD £70
B £11.45 L £11.50 D £26
CC: MC Vi Am DC Swi

How to get there: Follow signs for BIC When on
Westcliff Road turn into St. Michael's Road;
hotel is on the left at seafront.

51 Norfolk Royale Hotel

★★★★

Richmond Hill, Bournemouth, Dorset, BH2 6EN
Tel: 01202 551521 Fax: 01202 299729
Email: norfolkroyale@englishrosehotels.co.uk
Web: www.englishrosehotels.co.uk

95 bedrs SB £105 DB £145 HBS £67.50
HBD £67.50 B £9.95 L £12.50 D £22.50
CC: MC Vi Am DC Swi Delt

How to get there: M3 from London area then
A27 via A33. Take A31 to Wessex Way and at
A34 junction left into Richmond Hill.
See advert on facing page

52 Bay View Court Hotel

★★★

35 East Overcliff Drive, East Cliff, Bournemouth,
Dorset, BH1 3AH
Tel: 01202 294449 Fax: 01202 292883
Email: enquiry@bayviewcourt.co.uk
Web: www.bayviewcourt.co.uk
64 bedrs SB £42 DB £84 HBS £50 HBD £100
B £12 D £18
CC: MC Vi Am Swi Delt

How to get there: Turn off A338 at St. Paul's
roundabout. Head for clifftop.

53 Burley Court Hotel

★★★

Bath Road, Bournemouth, Dorset, BH1 2NP
Tel: 01202 552824 Fax: 01202 298514
Email: info@burleycourthotel.co.uk
Web: www.burleycourthotel.co.uk
Closed early January
38 bedrs
CC: MC Vi Swi Delt

How to get there: Leave A338 at St. Pauls roundabout. Take third exit at next two roundabouts. Burley Court is the first hotel after the crossing.

54 Chesterwood

★★★

East Overcliff Drive, East Cliff, Bournemouth, Dorset, BH1 3AR
Tel: 01202 558057 Fax: 01202 556285
Email: enquiry@chesterwoodhotel.co.uk
Web: www.chesterwoodhotel.co.uk
50 bedrs SB £44 DB £88 HBS £54 HBD £54
B £12 L £7.95 D £18
CC: MC Vi Am Swi Delt

How to get there: Go along A338 in to Bournemouth. Follow signs for East Cliff. Situated on cliff top between the two piers.

55 Chine

★★★ ®

25 Boscombe Spa Road, Bournemouth, Dorset, BH5 1AX
Tel: 01202 396234 Fax: 01202 391737
Email: reservations@chinehotel.co.uk
Web: www.chinehotel.co.uk

Attractive Victorian Hotel with award-winning cuisine, located in three acres of mature gardens with direct access to the beach. Indoor and outdoor pools, jacuzzi, outdoor hot-tub, sauna and trymnasium.

The Norfolk Royale Hotel

An Edwardian hotel with country house atmosphere in the heart of the resort. Its leisure spa includes a pool, spa bath, steam room and sauna together with a garden. All rooms have direct dial telephone and TV and are comfortably furnished to a high standard. A secure underground carpark is available.

Richmond Hill, Bournemouth BH2 6EN
Tel: 01202 551521   Fax: 01202 299729
norfolkroyale@englishrosehotels.co.uk
www.englishrosehotels.co.uk

89 bedrs SB £55 DB £110 HBS £70 HBD £70
B £9 L £15 D £19 CC: MC Vi Am DC Swi Delt

How to get there: On A338, follow signs for town centre. Take first exit at St. Pauls roundabout, then second exit, then first exit. Turn right into Boscome Spa Road.

56 Cliffeside

★★★

East Overcliff Drive, Bournemouth, Dorset, BH1 3AQ
Tel: 01202 555724 Fax: 01202 314534
Email: mail@cliffesidehotel.uk.com
Web: www.arthuryoung.co.uk
62 bedrs SB £49 DB £98 HBS £57 HBD £57
B £5 L £3 D £18.95 CC: MC Vi Swi Delt

How to get there: Five minutes from A338. Follow signs to the East Cliff.

Plan your route

Visit www.rac.co.uk for RAC's interactive route planner, including up to the minute traffic reports.

Southwest

57 Cumberland Hotel

★★★

East Overcliff Drive, Bournemouth,
Dorset, BH1 3AF
Tel: 01202 290722 Fax: 01202 311394
Email: reservations@cumberlandhotel.uk.com
Web: www.arthuryoung.co.uk
Children minimum age: six months
102 bedrs SB £49 DB £98 HBS £57 HBD £57
B £7.95 L £8.95 D £18.95
CC: MC Vi Swi Delt

How to get there: Take A338 to Bournemouth,
turn left at first roundabout. At next, take 3rd
exit, at next take 2nd exit, at next take 2nd exit
to T-junction. Turn left. Hotel 200m on left.

58 Durley Hall Hotel

★★★

Durley Chine Road, Bournemouth,
Dorset, BH2 5JS
Tel: 01202 751000 Fax: 01202 757535
Email: sales@durleyhall.co.uk
Web: www.durleyhall.co.uk
81 bedrs SB £52 DB £104 HBS £67 HBD £67
B £9.50 L £10.25 D £18.50
CC: MC Vi Am DC Swi Delt

How to get there: Approaching on the A338
Wessex Way, follow signs to the West Cliff and
Bournemouth International Centre.

59 East Anglia Hotel (Best Western)

★★★

6 Poole Road, Bournemouth, Dorset, BH2 5QX
Tel: 01202 765163 Fax: 01202 752949
Email: info@eastangliahotel.com
Web: www.eastangliahotel.com
70 bedrs SB £49 DB £90 HBS £61 HBD £57
CC: MC Vi Am DC Swi Delt

How to get there: From A338, take exit
signposted BIC & West Cliff. Take 3rd exit at
next roundabout into Poole road. Hotel is on
right.

60 Elstead Hotel

★★★

Knyveton Road, Bournemouth, Dorset, BH1 3QP
Tel: 01202 293071 Fax: 01202 293827
Email: info@the-elstead.co.uk
Web: www.the-elstead.co.uk

50 en-suite rooms, many refurbished. Set in a
quiet tree-lined avenue with superb leisure
complex. Good fresh home-cooked food and
friendly attentive service offered.
50 bedrs SB £55 DB £89 HBS £67.50
HBD £58.50 B £9.50 D £18.50
CC: MC Vi Am Swi Delt

How to get there: From A338 follow signs to
Bournemouth. Turn into St. Paul's Road off the
main Wessex way. Turn first left into Knyveton
Road.

61 Heathlands

★★★

12 Grove Road, East Cliff, Bournemouth,
Dorset, BH1 3AY
Tel: 01202 553336 Fax: 01202 555937
Email: info@heathlandshotel.com
Web: www.heathlandshotel.com

115-bedroom hotel located on the East Cliff
within easy walking distance to sandy beaches,
cosmopolitan town centre and award-winning
gardens. The hotel is justly proud of its reputation
for fine cuisine and friendly, efficient staff.
115 bedrs CC: MC Vi Swi Delt

How to get there: Follow signs to East Cliff. At
roundabout, turn into Gervis Road.

Southwest

62 Hotel Courtlands

★★★

16 Boscombe Spa Road, Bournemouth,
Dorset, BH5 1BB
Tel: 01202 302442 Fax: 01202 309880
Email: ajms@themail.co.uk
Web: hotelcourtlands.co.uk
58 bedrs SB £45 DB £89 HBS £58 HBD £55
B £8.50 L £2.95 D £13.50
CC: MC Vi Swi Delt

How to get there: A338 to Bournemouth,
turning off at Asda roundabout onto
Christchurch Road. Right into Boscombe Spa
Road: hotel on right.

63 Hotel Miramar

★★★

East Overcliff Drive, Bournemouth,
Dorset, BH1 3AL
Tel: 01202 556581 Fax: 01202 291242
Email: sales@miramar-bournemouth.com
Web: www.miramar-bournemouth.com

Situated atop the prestigious East Cliff.
Magnificent views overlooking landscaped
gardens and Bournemouth Bay. An elegant
hotel with traditional English interior.
44 bedrs SB £70 DB £130 HBS £85 HBD £80
B £8.50 L £10 D £20.95
CC: MC Vi Am Swi Delt

How to get there: Turn into St. Paul's Road off
the main Wessex Way roundabout. Turn right at
the next roundabout. Take third exit at the next
roundabout and second at the next. Hotel 50m
on right.

64 Hotel Piccadilly

★★★

Bath Road, Bournemouth, Dorset, BH1 2NN
Tel: 01202 552559 Fax: 01202 298235
45 bedrs SB £62 DB £94 HBS £72 HBD £114
B £6.50 L £5 D £18.95
CC: MC Vi Am DC Swi Delt

How to get there: From A338, follow signs for
Lansdowne and take Bath Road off Lansdowne
roundabout.

65 Mayfair Hotel

★★★

27 Bath Road, Bournemouth, Dorset, BH1 2NW
Tel: 01202 551983 Fax: 01202 298459
Email: info@themayfair.com
Web: www.themayfair.com
40 bedrs SB £40 DB £80 HBS £49 HBD £98
B £6,95 D £13.95
CC: MC Vi Am DC Swi Delt

How to get there: Take A338 southbound to first
roundabout. Take last exit off, and at next
roundabout 3rd exit off into Bath Road.

66 Pavilion Hotel

★★★

Bath Road, Bournemouth, Dorset, BH1 2NS
Tel: 01202 291266 Fax: 01202 559264
44 bedrs SB £32 DB £64 HBS £41 HBD £82
B £6.50 L £7.50 D £14
CC: MC Vi Am DC Swi Delt JCB

How to get there: Along A338 first left exit at
Bournemouth Station roundabout; third exit at
St. Swithins roundabout onto Holdenhurst
Road; next roundabout Bath Road.

67 Quality Hotel Bournemouth

★★★

8 Poole Road, Bournemouth, Dorset, BH2 5QU
Tel: 01202 763006 Fax: 01202 766168
Email: admin@gb641.u-net.com
Web: www.qualityinn.com/hotel/gb64154 bedrs
CC: MC Vi Am DC Swi Delt

How to get there: Take A338 into Bournemouth.
Exit at Town Centre West, take right-hand exit
onto Poole Road.

68 Queens Hotel

★★★★

Meyrick Road, East Cliff, Bournemouth,
Dorset, BH1 3DL
Tel: 01202 554415 Fax: 01202 294810
Email: mail@queenshotel.uk.com
Web: www.arthuryoung.co.uk
109 bedrs SB £62.50 DB £105 HBS £72.50
HBD £62.50 B £6.95 L £8.95 D £17.95
CC: MC Vi Am DC Swi Delt

How to get there: Follow signs into
Bournemouth from the A338 to Landsdowne or
East Cliff. The Queens Hotel is situated one
road back from seafront.

69 Trouville

★★★

5 Priory Road, Westcliff, Bournemouth,
Dorset, BH2 5DH
Tel: 01202 552262 Fax: 01202 293324
Email: mail@trouvillehotel.uk.com
Web: www.arthuryoung.co.uk
77 bedrs SB £57.50 DB £115 HBS £70.50
HBD £141 B £8.95 D £18.95
CC: MC Vi Am DC Swi Delt

How to get there: Leave M3 for M27
Bournemouth. On entering Bournemouth, follow
directions for Bournemouth International Centre.
At roundabout turn second left. Hotel is on right.

70 Winterbourne Hotel

★★★

Priory Road, Bournemouth, Dorset, BH2 5DJ
Tel: 01202 296366 Fax: 01202 780073
Email: reservations@winterbourne.co.uk
Web: www.winterbourne.co.uk

Enjoying a prime position on the West Cliff with
magnificent sea views. Adjacent to the

Bournemouth International Centre and within 400m of pier, beaches and town centre.
41 bedrs SB £36 DB £64 HBS £46 HBD £42 B £7 L £2.50 D £14.50
CC: MC Vi Am Swi Delt

How to get there: Follow signs to Bournemouth International centre (BIC). Exit Wessex Way to the BIC. As you approach the BIC, Winterbourne is halfway down hill (Priory Road).

71 Arlington Hotel

★★
Exeter Park Road, Lower Gardens, Bournemouth, Dorset, BH2 5BD
Tel: 01202 552879 or 553012 Fax: 01202 298317
Email: enquiries@arlingtonbournemouth.co.uk
Web: www.arlingtonbournemouth.co.uk
Children minimum age: 2.
Closed early January
28 bedrs SB £32.50 DB £65 HBS £39.75 HBD £79.50 B £6.50 D £12.50
CC: MC Vi Am Swi Delt

How to get there: Follow all signs to Bournemouth International Centre, Town Centre, Pier, Beach. Exeter Park Road runs behind Royal Exeter Hotel.

72 Chinehurst Hotel

★★
Studland Road, Westbourne, Bournemouth, Dorset, BH4 8JA
Tel: 01202 764583 Fax: 01202 762854
Children minimum age: 2
30 bedrs
CC: MC Vi Swi Delt
How to get there: From A338/A35, take 3rd junction off Frizzel roundabout into The Avenue. Turn left at lights, then right at roundabout into Alumhurst Road. Take last turning left into Studland Road.

73 County Hotel

★★
Westover Road, Bournemouth, Dorset, BH1 2BT
Tel: 01202 552385 Fax: 01202 297255
48 bedrs
CC: MC Vi Am DC Swi Delt

How to get there: Entering by A338 from Ringwood, turn left at Railway Station. Turn right at next roundabout, straight over next two roundabouts. Hotel on left at 3rd roundabout.

74 Croham Hurst Hotel

★★
9 Durley Road, West Cliff, Bournemouth, Dorset, BH2 5JH
Tel: 01202 552353 Fax: 01202 311484

75 Fircroft Hotel

★★
Owls Road, Bournemouth, Dorset, BH5 1AE
Tel: 01202 309771 Fax: 01202 395644
Email: info@fircrofthotel.co.uk
Web: www.fircrofthotel.co.uk
50 bedrs SB £25 DB £50 HBS £36 HBD £72
CC: MC Vi Am DC Swi Delt

How to get there: Off A338 over flyover. Next exit head for Boscombe Pier. The hotel is situated on corner of St. John's Road and Owls Road.

76 Grange Hotel

★★
Overcliff Drive, Southbourne, Bournemouth, Dorset, BH6 3NL
Tel: 01202 433093 Fax: 01202 424228
Web: www.bournemouthgrangehotel.co.uk
31 bedrs SB £29.50 DB £59 B £9.50 L £2.50 D £15.50 CC: MC Vi Swi Delt
How to get there: Follow Overcliff Drive to clifftop.

77 Russell Court Hotel

★★
Bath Road, Bournemouth, Dorset, BH1 2EP
Tel: 01202 295819 Fax: 01202 293457
Email: russellcrt@aol.com
Web: www.enterprisehotel.co.uk
56 bedrs SB £63.50 DB £107 HBS £69.50 HBD £59.50 B £5.95 L £4 D £14.95
CC: MC Vi Am DC Swi Delt
How to get there: Follow onto the A31 at the end of the M27. Turn left just past Ringwood onto A338 for Bournemouth. Turn off at roundabout for town centre. At next roundabout turn right and follow signs for BIC. Hotel on left on Bath Road.

Southwest

78 St. George Hotel

★★

West Cliff Gardens, Bournemouth,
Dorset, BH2 5HL
Tel: 01202 556075 Fax: 01202 557330

79 Tower House Hotel

★★

West Cliff Gardens, Bournemouth,
Dorset, BH2 5HP
Tel: 01202 290742 Fax: 01202 553505
Email: towerhousehotel.macartney@fsnet.co.uk
32 bedrs SB £30 DB £60 HBS £39 HBD £39
B £6 L £7.50 D £10
CC: MC Vi Am DC Swi Delt JCB
🛗 🐾 🖥 ☎ 📞 P🅿 🎥 ⊓ 🏊 ⅲ

80 Ullswater Hotel

★★

West Cliff Gardens, Bournemouth,
Dorset, BH2 5HW
Tel: 01202 555181 Fax: 01202 317896
Email: enq@ullswater.uk.com
Web: www.ullswater.uk.com

A family-run hotel, centrally situated close to all
amenities. Comfortable and tastefully furnished
with an emphasis on good food and personal
service.
42 bedrs SB £27 DB £54 HBS £32 HBD £64
B £5.50 L £7.50 D £11.50
CC: MC Vi Am Swi
🛗 🐾 🖥 ☎ P🅿 🎥 ⊓ 🏊 ⅲ ⅲ ℮ ♿
How to get there: From any major route into
Bournemouth, follow the signs for the West Cliff.
The Ullswater Hotel is situated in West Cliff
Gardens, just off the main West Cliff Road.

81 Whitehall Hotel

★★

Exeter Park Road, Bournemouth,
Dorset, BH2 5AX
Tel: 01202 554682 Fax: 01202 554682
49 bedrs SB £30 DB £60 HBS £44 HBD £88
B £5 D £14
CC: MC Vi Am DC Swi Delt JCB
🛗 🐾 🖥 ☎ 🎥 ⊓ 🏊 ⅲ

82 Boltons Hotel

♦♦♦♦ 🎥 ♟

9 Durley Chine Road South, Westcliff,
Bournemouth, Dorset, BH2 5JT
Tel: 01202 751517 Fax: 01202 751629
12 bedrs SB £38.50 DB £80 HBS £50 HBD £50
B £6.95 D £12.50
CC: MC Vi Swi
♿ 🐾 🖥 ☎ P🅿 ⊓ 🏊 ⅲ ⅲ ⚓

83 Durley Court Hotel

♦♦♦♦ 🎥

5 Durley Road, West Cliff, Bournemouth,
Dorset, BH2 5JQ
Tel: 01202 556857 Fax: 01202 554455
Email: durleycourthotel@lineone.net
Children minimum age: 5
16 bedrs SB £30 DB £56 HBS £39 HBD £37
B £5 D £9
CC: MC Vi Swi Delt JCB
🖥 🖥 P🅿 ⊓ 🏊 ⅲ

84 The Lodge At Meyrick Park

♦♦♦♦

Central Drive, Bournemouth, Dorset, BH2 6LH
Tel: 01202 786000 Fax: 01202 786020

85 Tudor Grange Hotel

♦♦♦♦ 🎥

31 Gervis Road, Bournemouth, Dorset, BH1 3EE
Tel: 01202 291472 Fax: 01202 311503
Email: info@tudorgrangehotel.co.uk
Web: www.tudorgrangehotel.co.uk
Closed 24 December to 2 January
12 bedrs SB £28.35 DB £54.70
CC: MC Vi Am Swi Delt
🖥 ☎ P🅿 🎥

86 Carisbrooke Hotel

♦ ♦ ♦

42 Tregonwell Road, Bournemouth,
Dorset, BH2 5NT
Tel: 01202 290432 Fax: 01202 310499
Email: all@carisbrooke58.freeserve.co.uk
Web: www.carisbrooke.co.uk
22 bedrs SB £18 DB £50 HBS £26.75
HBD £33.75
CC: MC Vi Am Swi Delt
♿ ⬛ 🐾 ⊗ ☕ ⬛ ☎ 🅿 🔆 ♨ ⛱ 👥
How to get there: A338 Bournemouth, signs for
BIC and Westcliffe. Past roundabout, third left,
second hotel on right.

87 Hotel Washington

♦ ♦ ♦ ✖

3 Durley Road, West Cliff, Bournemouth,
Dorset, BH2 5JQ
Tel: 01202 557023

88 Ravenstone Hotel

♦ ♦ ♦

36 Burnaby Road, Alum Chine, Westbourne,
Bournemouth, Dorset, BH4 8JG
Tel: 01202 761047 Fax: 01202 761047
Email: holidays@ravenstone36.freeserve.co.uk
Web: www.ravenstone36.freeserve.co.uk
Closed November to March

Situated in quiet road, yet close to wooded
chine and safe sandy beach. Easy access to
Bournemouth and Poole town centres. Same
owner since 1986.
9 bedrs SB £22 DB £40 HBS £30 HBD £28 D £8
CC: MC Vi Swi Delt
☕ ⬛ 🅿 🔆 👥 ◖
How to get there: Follow A338 to Westbourne,
then signs for Alum Chine. From Alumhurst
Road, turn left into Beaulieu Road. Then turn
right into Burnaby Road.

Bovey Tracey, Devon

89 Edgemoor

★ ★ ★ ♟ ♟

Lowerdown Cross, Haytor Road, Bovey Tracey,
Devon, TQ13 9LE
Tel: 01626 832466 Fax: 01626 834760
Email: edgemoor@btinternet.com
Web: www.edgemoor.co.uk
Children minimum age: 10.
Closed New Year
16 bedrs SB £57.50 DB £95 B £3.95 L £14.75
D £19.95
CC: MC Vi Am Swi Delt JCB
♿ ⬛ 🐾 ⊗ ☕ ⬛ ☎ 🅿 🔆 ♨ ♨ ⛱ 👥
How to get there: From A38, take A382 towards
Bovey Tracey. Then take B3387 towards Haytor
and Widecombe. Fork left after ¼ miles. Hotel is
then ½ miles on right.

90 Coombe Cross Hotel

★ ★

Coombe Lane, Bovey Tracey, Devon, TQ13 9EY
Tel: 01626 832476 Fax: 01626 835298
Email: info@coombecross.co.uk
Web: www.coombecross.co.uk
Closed January
23 bedrs SB £45 DB £70 HBS £60 HBD £50
B £10.95 D £22.95
CC: MC Vi Am Swi Delt
♿ 🐾 ⊗ ☕ ⬛ ☎ 🅿 🔆 ♨ ♨ ⛱ 👥 ⛱ 👥 🍸 ◖ ⬛
How to get there: From A38, travel NW on A382
to Bovey Tracey centre. Go up High Street past
church – hotel 400m on left.

Box, Wiltshire

91 The Spinney

♣

Lower Kingsdown Road, Box,
Wiltshire, SN13 8BA
Tel: 01225 742019

Bradford-on-Avon, Wiltshire

92 Leigh Park Hotel

★ ★ ★

Leigh Road West, Bradford-on-Avon,
Wiltshire, BA15 2RA
Tel: 01225 864885 Fax: 01225 862315

Southwest

93 Widbrook Grange
Little Gem

◆◆◆◆◆ 🏠 ⚡ 🍴

Trowbridge Road, Bradford-on-Avon,
Wiltshire, BA15 1UH
Tel: 01225 863173 Fax: 01225 862890
Email: widgra@aol.com

An elegant yet homely Georgian farmhouse set in extensive beautiful gardens and surrounded by tastefully converted stable bedrooms. Relax in the indoor pool or just enjoy the peace and tranquility.
20 bedrs SB £95 DB £110 D £27.50
CC: MC Vi Am DC Swi Delt JCB
♿ 🖨 ☺ 🐾 ☎ 🚶 🛏 🍴 🖥

Battleborough Grange Hotel

Surrounded by mellow Somerset countryside, the hotel is just one mile from M5, making it a convenient location for both business and leisure guests. Bedrooms are well equipped and some offer extensive views of the historic Iron Age fort of Brent Knoll. Public rooms include a convivial bar, conservatory restaurant and extensive function facilities.
Civil ceremonies also available.

Bristol Road, Highbridge,
Somerset TA9 4HJ

Tel: 01278 760208   Fax: 01278 760208
Website: www.battleboroughgrange.com

Brent Knoll, Somerset

94 Battleborough Grange Hotel

★★
Bristol Road, Brent Knoll, Somerset, TA9 4HJ
Tel: 01278 760208 Fax: 01278 760208
Email: info@battleboroughgrangehotel.co.uk
Web: www.battleboroughgrangehotel.co.uk
15 bedrs SB £53 DB £70 HBS £70 HBD £52.50
B £7.50 L £4.95 D £15
CC: MC Vi Am DC Swi Delt
🏠 🖨 ☺ 🖵 ☎ 🚶 P 🅿 🐾 ⚡ 🍴 🛏 🍴 🖥 🛏
How to get there: Exit J22 M5. Take A38 towards Weston-Super-Mare for one mile. 300 yards from Garden World on left.
See advert below left

Bridgwater, Somerset

95 Walnut Tree Hotel

★★★ 🏠
North Petherton, Bridgwater, Somerset, TA6 6QA
Tel: 01278 662255 Fax: 01278 663946
Email: sales@walnut-tree-hotel.co.uk
Web: www.walnut-tree-hotel.co.uk
32 bedrs SB £62 DB £72 HBS £63 HBD £86
B £8.50 L £6.50 D £14.50
CC: MC Vi Am DC Swi Delt
🏠 ♿ 🖨 ☺ 🖵 ☎ ❄ 🚶 P 🅿 🐾 ⚡ 🍴 🛏 🍴 🖥 🛏
How to get there: Exit J24 M5; follow signs for North Petherton. Hotel is opposite the Church.

96 Admirals Table

◆◆◆
Bristol Road, Dunball, Bridgwater,
Somerset, TA6 4TN
Tel: 01278 685671
13 bedrs SB £46 DB £50 B £5.95
CC: MC Vi Am Swi Delt JCB
♿ 🐾 ☺ 🖵 🖵 ☎ 🚶 P 🅿 🐾 🍴 🛏 🖥 🛏
How to get there: From M5 J23 (west) to Bridgwater, 3rd exit at roundabout. At next roundabout, 1st exit onto A38, 100 yards on left.

Bridport, Dorset

97 Haddon House Hotel

★★★

West Bay, Bridport, Dorset, DT6 4EL
Tel: 01308 423626 Fax: 01308 427348
Web: www.haddonhousehotel.co.uk
12 bedrs DB £65 CC: MC Vi Am DC

How to get there: At the Crown Inn roundabout take the B3157 West Bay road, travel to mini roundabout. Hotel on righthandside of road.

98 Roundham House Hotel

★★★

Roundham Gardens, Bridport, Dorset, DT6 4BD
Tel: 01308 422753 Fax: 01308 421500
Email: cyprencom@compuserve.com
Web: www.roundhamhouse.co.uk
Children minimum age: 7.
Closed January to February
8 bedrs SB £35 DB £60 HBS £50 HBD £88
B £10 D £17.95 CC: MC Vi Swi Delt

How to get there: From A35, enter Bridport, find the 'Crown Inn roundabout', take signpost to West Bay. 2nd turning left into Roundham Gardens.

99 Betchworth House

♦♦♦♦

Main Street, Chideock, Dorset, DT6 6JW
Tel: 01297 489478 Fax: 01297 489932
Children minimum age: 10
5 bedrs SB £30 DB £50 CC: MC Vi Swi Delt

How to get there: Located on A35, two miles from Bridport and six miles from Lyme Regis.

Bristol

100 Aztec Hotel

★★★★

Aztec West Business Park, Almondsbury,
Bristol, BS12 4TS
Tel: 01454 201090 Fax: 01454 201593
Email: aztec@shireinns.co.uk
Web: www.shireinns.co.uk
128 bedrs SB £154 DB £174
CC: MC Vi Am DC Swi

How to get there: Close to M4/M5 intersection. M5 at Junction 16. Follow signs for Aztec West.

101 Bristol Marriott Hotel City Centre

★★★★

2 Lower Castle Street, Old Market,
Bristol, BS1 3AD
Tel: 0117 929 4281 Fax: 0117 927 6377
Web: www.marriotthotels.com/brsdt
289 bedrs SB £138 DB £151 B £13.50 L £10
D £17.95 CC: MC Vi Am DC Swi Delt

How to get there: From the M4 junction 19 for M32, stay on M32 until T-junction moving into the leftmost lane. Take the third exit off the roundabout, bear right into Lower Castle Street.

102 Bristol Marriott Royal Hotel

★★★★

College Green, Bristol, BS1 5TA
Tel: 0117 925 5100 Fax: 0117 925 1515
Email: reservations.bristolroyal
@marriotthotels.co.uk
Web: www.whitbread.com
Children minimum age: 14
242 bedrs SB £149 DB £159 HBS £169
HBD £104.50 B £10.50 L £15 D £20
CC: MC Vi Am DC Swi Delt

How to get there: Hotel is centrally placed next to Bristol Cathedral. Follow signs for city centre.

103 Jurys Bristol Hotel

★★★★

Prince Street, Bristol, BS1 4QF
Tel: +353(0)1 6070000 Fax: +353(0)1 6316999
Email: bookings@jurysdoyle.com
Web: www.jurysdoyle.com
Children minimum age: 12
191 bedrs SB £144.50 DB £154 B £9.50
L £14.50 D £17.95 CC: MC Vi Am DC Swi Delt

How to get there: Situated along River Quayside in the centre of City.

104 Alveston House Hotel

★★★

Thornbury, Bristol, BS12 2LA
Tel: 01454 415050 Fax: 01454 415425
Email: info@alvestonhousehotel.co.uk
Web: www.alvestonhousehotel.co.uk
30 bedrs CC: MC Vi Am DC Swi Delt

How to get there: 3½ miles north of M4/M5 junction on main A38 at Alveston.

Southwest

105 Avon Gorge Hotel

★★★

Sion Hill, Bristol, BS8 4LD
Tel: 0117 973 8955 Fax: 0117 923 8125
Email: info@avongorge-hotel-bristol.com
Web: www.peelhotel.com
76 bedrs SB £107 DB £117 B £9.95 L £16.50
D £16.50 CC: MC Vi Am DC Swi Delt

How to get there: From M5, use Junction 19, signposted Clifton; go over suspension bridge, turn right. From M4, use Junction 19 and take M32 to city; follow signs to Clifton and bridge.

106 Berkeley Square Hotel

★★★

15 Berkeley Square, Clifton, Bristol, BS8 1HB
Tel: 0117 925 4000 Fax: 0117 925 2970
Email: berkeley@cliftonhotels.com
Web: www.cliftonhotels.com

Bristol's most highly rated three-star hotel is situated in a magnificent Georgian Square in the heart of the city, and with just 41 bedrooms offers an exceptionally warm, friendly and personal service.
42 bedrs SB £96 DB £117 HBS £111
HBD £73.50 L £15 D £15
CC: MC Vi Am DC Swi Delt JCB

107 Henbury Lodge Hotel

★★★★ ℜ

Station Road, Henbury, Bristol, BS10 7QQ
Tel: 0117 950 2615 Fax: 0117 950 9532
Email: enquiries@henburylodge.com
Web: www.henburylodge.com
21 bedrs SB £53 DB £86 B £6.50 L £6.50
D £19.75
CC: MC Vi Am DC Swi Delt JCB

How to get there: From M5 Junction 17, follow A4018 to 3rd roundabout. Turn right. At T-junction, turn right. Hotel is 200m up on corner.

108 Best Western Glenroy Hotel

★★

Victoria Square, Clifton, Bristol, BS8 4EW
Tel: 0117 973 9058 Fax: 0117 973 9058
Email: admin@glenroyhotel.demon.co.uk
Web: www.glenroyhotel.demon.co.uk
Closed Christmas
44 bedrs SB £62 DB £82 HBS £74 HBD £53
D £10 CC: MC Vi Am DC Swi Delt JCB

How to get there: From M5 Junction 19, follow signs for Clifton. Proceed over bridge and turn right into Clifton Down, turn left into Merchants Road.

109 Clifton Hotel

★★

St. Paul's Road, Clifton, Bristol, BS8 1LX
Tel: 0117 973 6882 Fax: 0117 974 1082
Email: clifton@cliftonhotels.com
Web: www.cliftonhotels.com

59 bedrs SB £74 DB £84 HBS £89 HBD £57
CC: MC Vi Am DC Swi Delt

110 Rodney Hotel

★★

4 Rodney Place, Clifton, Bristol, BS8 4HY
Tel: 0117 973 5422 Fax: 0117 946 7092
Email: rodney@cliftonhotels.com
Web: www.cliftonhotels.com

Town house forming part of a Georgian Terrace. Sympathetically renovated and converted.
31 bedrs SB £69 DB £83 HBS £84 HBD £56.50 L £10 D £15 CC: MC Vi Am DC Swi Delt JCB
 ❄☻🕮💻☎📞🛎📶🏃

111 Seeley's Hotel

★★
17-27 St. Paul's Road, Clifton, Bristol, BS8 1LX
Tel: 0117 9738544 Fax: 0117 9732406
Email: admin@seeleys.demon.co.uk
Web: www.seeleyshotel.co.uk
Closed Christmas and New Year

Located in the beautiful suburb of Clifton, the Seeley's Hotel offers 54 tastefully furnished en-suite bedrooms, lounge bar, excellent restaurant, three conference suites, sauna, award-winning garden, and car park.
54 bedrs SB £65 DB £80 HBS £77.05 HBD £52.05 B £5 D £12.05
CC: MC Vi Am DC Swi
🖂❄☻🕮💻☎📞🅿🛎🏃📶🏃🍴
How to get there: From city centre proceed up Park Street towards Clifton. Head towards BBC studios on Whiteladies Road and turn left opposite into St. Pauls Road.

112 Travelodge Bristol

Travel Accommodation
Anchor Road, Bristol, BS21 5TT
Tel: 08700 850 950
Web: www.travelodge.co.uk
56 bedrs B £4.25 CC: MC Vi Am DC Swi Delt
❄☻💻🛎

113 Travelodge Bristol (Severnview)

Travel Accommodation
M48 J1, Aust, Bristol, BS12 3BH
Tel: 08700 850 950
Web: www.travelodge.co.uk
50 bedrs B £4.25 CC: MC Vi Am DC Swi Delt
❄☻💻🛎

114 Travelodge Bristol (Cribbs Causeway)

Travel Accommodation
A4018, Lamb & Flag Harvester, Cribbs Causeway, Bristol, BS10 7TL
Tel: 08700 850 950
Web: www.travelodge.co.uk
56 bedrs B £4.25 CC: MC Vi Am DC Swi Delt
❄☻💻🛎

115 Downs View Guest House

◆◆◆
38 Upper Belgrave Road, Clifton, Bristol, BS8 2XN
Tel: 0117 973 7046
Email: bookings@downsviewguesthouse.co.uk
Web: www.downsviewguesthouse.co.uk
Closed Christmas and New Year
15 bedrs SB £35 DB £50 CC: MC Vi Swi JCB
❄☻☻💻🛎
How to get there: Exit J17 M5, follow signs to Zoo; on left after five miles. From centre, top of Whiteladies Road, turn left.

116 Oakfield Hotel

◆◆◆
52/54 Oakfield Road, Bristol, BS8 2BG
Tel: 0117 973 5556 Fax: 0117 974 4141
27 bedrs SB £30 DB £40 HBS £37.50 HBD £27.50 CC: None accepted
🏃❄☻💻🅿🛎📶🏃

117 Washington Hotel

◆◆◆
St. Paul's Road, Clifton, Bristol, BS8 1LX
Tel: 0117 973 3980 Fax: 0117 973 4740
Email: washington@cliftonhotels.com
Web: www.cliftonhotels.com
Closed Christmas

Tasteful conversion of Georgian buildings situated close to shops and amenities.
46 bedrs SB £53 DB £67
CC: MC Vi Am DC Swi Delt JCB
🏃❄☻💻☎📞🅿🛎

118 Westbourne Hotel

40-44 St. Pauls Road, Clifton, Bristol, BS8 1LR
Tel: 0117 973 4214
Email: westbournehotel@bristol8.fsworld.co.uk
Web: www.westbournehotel-bristol.co.uk

31 bedroom family-owned hotel in the heart of Clifton. Close to shopping centres and historical places of interest. A bar and restaurant are on site and the hotel also has a secluded beer garden.
31 bedrs SB £52 DB £65 B £3.50 L £4.50 D £4.50
CC: MC Vi Am DC Swi Delt JCB

119 Tortworth Court Four Pillars Hotel

Tortworth, Wotton-under-Edge, South Gloucestershire, GL12 8HH
Tel: 01454 263000 Fax: 01454 263001
Email: bristol@four-pillars.co.uk
Web: www.four-pillars.co.uk
189 bedrs SB £151.95 DB £194.90
HBS £175.90 HBD £121.40 B £9.95 L £15.95
D £23.95
CC: MC Vi Am DC Swi Delt JCB

How to get there: J14 M5 onto B4509, past visitors' centre, take next right. Hotel is on right approximately ½ a mile.
See advert below left

Brixham, Devon

120 The Smugglers Haunt Hotel

★

Church Hill, Brixham, Devon, TQ5 8HH
Tel: 01803 853050 Fax: 01803 858738
Email: enquiries@smugglershaunt-hotel-devon.co.uk
Web: www.smugglershaunt-hotel-devon.co.uk
14 bedrs SB £31 DB £52 HBS £37 HBD £32
D £6.95
CC: MC Vi Am DC Swi Delt JCB

121 Brookside Guest House

160 New Road, Brixham, Devon, TQ5 8DA
Tel: 01803 858858
5 bedrs SB £16 DB £18
CC: None accepted

How to get there: Approaching Brixham on A3022 take left fork for town centre (New Road); Property is 6th on right.

122 Harbour View Hotel

65 King Street, Brixham, Devon, TQ5 9TH
Tel: 01803 853052
8 bedrs SB £25 DB £40
CC: MC Vi Swi Delt JCB

How to get there: A3022 Brixham road to town centre/harbour, left at lights, right at T-junction. Hotel is on right of inner harbour.

Bude, Cornwall

123 Hartland Hotel

★★★

Hartland Terrace, Bude, Cornwall, EX23 8JY
Tel: 01288 355661 Fax: 01288 355664
Web: www.hartlandhotel.co.uk
Closed December to February
28 bedrs SB £46 DB £78 HBS £64 HBD £58
B £8.50 D £20
CC: None accepted

How to get there: Turn left into Hartland Terrace
from main street (opposite Boots). Hotel
signposted in main street.

124 Camelot Hotel

★★ ₨

Downs View, Bude, Cornwall, EX23 8RE
Tel: 01288 352361 Fax: 01288 355470
Email: stay@camelot-hotel.co.uk
Web: www.camelot-hotel.co.uk

Overlooking Bude Golf Course. A short walk from
beaches and town centre. Elegantly refurbished
to a high standard with first class, friendly service
and superb freshly-prepared food.
24 bedrs SB £51 DB £82 HBS £70 HBD £60
D £19
CC: MC Vi Am Swi Delt JCB

How to get there: Follow one-way system past
post office. Stay in left lane; Camelot is at
bottom of hill on left.

Making a booking?

 Don't forget to mention RAC
Hotels and Bed & Breakfast 2002.

125 Cliff Hotel

♦ ♦ ♦ ♦ ₨ ✕

Maer Down Road, Bude, Cornwall, EX23 8NG
Tel: 01288 353110 Fax: 01288 353110
Web: www.cliffhotel.co.uk
Closed November to March
15 bedrs SB £29.50 DB £39.50 HBS £33.50
HBD £21.75 L £2.85 D £13.50
CC: MC Vi Swi

How to get there: Through High Street, past
post office on left. Second left. First right to
crossroads. Straight on, hotel on left hand side.

126 Coombe Barton Inn

♦ ♦ ♦

Crackington Haven, Cornwall, EX23 0JG
Tel: 01840 230345 Fax: 01840 230788
6 bedrs SB £30 DB £50 B £5 L £8 D £12
CC: MC Vi Swi Delt

How to get there: Head south on A39 from
Bude for eight miles. Turn off right at Wainhouse
Corner. Follow road down to the beach.

Budleigh Salterton, Devon

127 Long Range Hotel

♦ ♦ ♦ ₨

5 Vales Road, Budleigh Salterton,
Devon, EX9 6HS
Tel: 01395 443321 Fax: 01395 445220
Email: longrange@eclipse.co.uk
7 bedrs
CC: MC Vi Swi Delt

How to get there: From Exeter approach
Budleigh Salterton. Turn left at traffic lights.
Continue to T-junction, turn left. Take first right
and first right again. Hotel on left.

Carkeel

128 Travelodge Saltash

Travel Accommodation
A38, Callington Road, Carkeel,
Cornwall, PL12 6LF
Tel: 08700 850 950
Web: www.travelodge.co.uk
53 bedrs B £4.25
CC: MC Vi Am DC Swi Delt

Southwest

Castle Combe, Wiltshire

129 Manor House Hotel
Gold Ribbon Winner

★★★★★ ℞ ℞ ℞

Castle Combe, Chippenham, Wiltshire, SN14 7HR
Tel: 01249 782206 Fax: 01249 782159
Email: enquiries@themanorhouse.co.uk
Web: www.exclusivehotels.co.uk

The picturesque Manor House Hotel and Golf Club at Castle Combe, near Bath, makes the perfect destination to indulge yourself in a relaxing few days of sheer luxury.
46 bedrs B £10 L £12.95 D £35
CC: MC Vi Am DC Swi Delt JCB

How to get there: Hotel is just off the B4039 between junctions 17 and 18 of the M4. Once in the village of Castle Combe, the hotel entrance is beside the bridge.
See advert on facing page

130 Castle Inn

★★★

Castle Combe, Wiltshire, SN14 7HN
Tel: 01249 783030 Fax: 01249 782315
Email: res@castle-inn.co.uk
Web: www.castle-inn.co.uk

THE CASTLE INN

11 bedrs
CC: MC Vi Am DC Swi Delt JCB

Plan your route

Visit www.rac.co.uk for RAC's interactive route planner, including up to the minute traffic reports.

Chagford, Devon

131 Three Crowns Hotel

★★

High Street, Chagford, Devon, TQ13 8AJ
Tel: 01647 433444 Fax: 01647 433117
Email: threecrowns@msn.com
Web: www.chagford-accom.co.uk

A warm and friendly 13th-century inn situated in a picturesque village within Dartmoor. Oak beams, four-poster beds. Noted for good food and ale.
18 bedrs SB £42.50 DB £65 HBS £60 HBD £99
B £5.50 L £4.95 D £17.50
CC: MC Vi Swi Delt

132 Great Tree Hotel

◆◆◆◆ ℞ ✕ ℞

Sandy Park, near Chagford, Devon, TQ13 8JS
Tel: 01647 432491 Fax: 01647 432562
Email: nigel@greattree.co.uk
Web: www.greattree.co.uk

A delightfully quiet and secluded location in 25 acres of woods and gardens dedicated to nature conservation. A lovely, unpretentious and homely atmosphere.
10 bedrs CC: MC Vi Am DC Swi Delt

How to get there: Take the A30 to Whiddon Down roundabout. Drive south down A382 for 2½ miles.

Chideock, Dorset

133 Chimneys

Main Street, Chideock, Bridport, Dorset, DT6 6JH
Tel: 01297 489368
Email: chimneys@ chideock.co.uk
5 bedrs SB £30 DB £46
CC: None accepted

How to get there: Found on A35 in Chideock Village.

Chippenham, Wiltshire

134 Travelodge Chippenham (LeighDelamere)

Travel Accommodation
M4, Chippenham, Wiltshire, SN14 6LB
Tel: 08700 850 950
Web: www.travelodge.co.uk
69 bedrs B £4.25
CC: MC Vi Am DC Swi Delt

135 White Hart Inn

Ford, Chippenham, Wiltshire, SN14 8RP
Tel: 01249 782213 Fax: 01249 783075
Email: whitehart.ford@eldridge-pope.co.uk
11 bedrs SB £65 DB £88 B £8.95 L £5.50
D £10.95
CC: MC Vi Am Swi Delt

How to get there: M4 J18, A46 Bath. First roundabout, left at A420 Chippenham, six miles. From London J17 to Chippenham, A420 Bristol, five miles to Ford.

Christchurch, Dorset

136 The Avonmouth Hotel

★★★
95 Mudeford, Mudeford, Christchurch, Dorset, BH23 3NT
Tel: 0870 400 8120 Fax: 01202 479004

Southwest

137 Waterford Lodge Hotel

★★★ ♚ ♚
87 Bure Lane, Friars Cliff, Christchurch, Dorset, BH23 4DN
Tel: 01425 278801 Fax: 01425 279130
Email: waterford@bestwestern.co.uk
Web: www.waterfordlodge.com
18 bedrs CC: MC Vi Am DC Swi Delt

How to get there: Two miles east of Christchurch on A337, turn south towards Mudeford and hotel is half a mile on left.

Cirencester, Gloucestershire

138 The Black Horse

17 Castle Street, Cirencester,
Gloucestershire, GL7 1QD
Tel: 01285 653187
4 bedrs SB £45 DB £50 B £5
CC: MC Vi Am DC Swi Delt

How to get there: Head for town centre, pass
church and go across traffic lights, hotel on left.

Clevedon, North Somerset

139 Walton Park Hotel

1 Wellington Terrace, Clevedon, North
Somerset, BS21 7BL
Tel: 01275 874253 Fax: 01275 343577

Combe Martin, Devon

140 Blair Lodge Hotel

Moory Meadow, Seaside, Combe Martin,
Devon, EX34 0DG
Tel: 01271 882294
Children minimum age: 10

Blair Lodge is a small, quiet, family-run hotel
overlooking Combe Martin bay, with an
excellent reputation for its very high standards
and good value.
10 bedrs SB £21 DB £46 D £12
CC: None accepted

How to get there: Leave M5 at Junction 27 and
take A361 towards Barnstaple. On roundabout
near South Molton join A399 to Combe Martin.

Corsham, Wiltshire

141 Methuen Arms Hotel

High Street, Corsham, Wiltshire, SN13 0HB
Tel: 01249 714867 Fax: 01249 712004
25 bedrs SB £55 DB £75 HBS £68 HBD £44.50
B £7.95 L £9.95 D £9.95
CC: MC Vi Am Swi Delt JCB

How to get there: On A4 between Chippenham
and Bath. Follow signs for town centre.

Crediton, Devon

142 Lower Burrow Coombe

Cheriton Fitzpaine, Crediton, Devon, EX17 4JS
Tel: 01363 866220
Closed December to February
3 bedrs SB £22 DB £34
CC: None accepted

How to get there: M5 to Tiverton; follow signs to
Exeter. At Bickleigh take the A3072 towards
Crediton; three miles on right, sign for the farm.

Cricklade, Wiltshire

143 White Hart Hotel

High Street, Cricklade, Swindon, SN6 6AA
Tel: 01793 750206 Fax: 01793 750650
Web: www.the-whitehart-hotel.co.uk
13 bedrs
CC: MC Vi DC Swi Delt

How to get there: A419, Swindon six miles,
Cirencester four miles. Junction 15 M4, then
A419 to Cirencester. Approximately nine miles.

Croyde, Devon

144 Kittiwell House Hotel

★★

St. Marys Road, Croyde, Devon, EX33 1PG
Tel: 01271 890247 Fax: 01271 890469

Kittiwell House is a thatched 16th-century hotel
with 12 en-suite bedrooms and an award-
winning restaurant. Situated in the seaside village
of Croyde. Ideal for golfers, walkers and surfers.
12 bedrs SB £49 DB £78 HBS £69 HBD £59
B £7.50 D £21.50
CC: MC Vi Swi Delt

How to get there: M5 at Junction 27. Take A361
to Barnstaple. Continue on A361 to Braunton.
Turn left at traffic lights in Braunton. In centre of
Croyde, turn right into St. Mary's road for 500m.
Kittiwell House is behind Manor House pub.

145 Croyde Bay House Hotel

Little Gem

♦♦♦♦♦

Moor Lane, Croyde, Devon, EX33 1PA
Tel: 01271 890270
Closed December to February
7 bedrs DB £80 HBD £55
CC: MC Vi Am Swi Delt

How to get there: Leave M5 at Junction 27.
Follow A361 to Barnstaple, then signs for
Braunton. Left in Braunton to Croyde village.
Left in centre of Croyde, then left again into
Moor Lane. Follow road into slipway ³/₄ miles.

Cullompton, Devon

146 Manor House Hotel

★★

2/4 Fore Street, Cullompton, Devon, EX15 1JL
Tel: 01884 32281
10 bedrs
CC: MC Vi Am DC Swi Delt

147 Waterloo Cross Inn

♦♦♦

Waterloo Cross, Uffculme, Cullompton,
Devon, EX15 3ES
Tel: 01884 840328 Fax: 01884 840908
10 bedrs SB £45.95 DB £56.90 B £4.95
CC: MC Vi Am Swi Delt

How to get there: M5 J27, A38 Wellington/-
Willand. Inn is situated 500m on the right.

Dartmouth, Devon

148 Heritage Hotels – The Dart Marina

★★★★

Sandquay, Dartmouth, Devon, TQ6 9PH
Tel: 01803 832580 Fax: 01803 835040
Email: heritagehotels_dartmouth.dart_marina
        @forte-hotels.com
Web: www.heritage-hotels.com
50 bedrs SB £45 DB £90 HBS £60 HBD £60
B £12 L £7.50 D £18.50 ΩCC: MC Vi Am DC
Swi Delt

How to get there: Take A3122 from Totnes and
follow signs for 'Dart Marina'. Hotel overlooks
the marina itself, beside the 'Higher Ferry'.

149 Royal Castle Hotel

★★★★

11 The Quay, Dartmouth, Devon, TQ6 9PS
Tel: 01803 833033 Fax: 01803 835445
Email: enquiry@royalcastle.co.uk
Web: www.royalcastle.co.uk

Two bars serving choice bar meals, ales and
wines. Adam room restaurant specialising in
local seafood. 25 luxuriously appointed en-suite
bedrooms to choose from.
25 bedrs SB £53.45 DB £109.90 HBS £66.45
HBD £139.90 B £6.50 L £8 D £15.50
CC: MC Vi Am Swi Delt

How to get there: Leave M5,take A38 to Totnes.
Once in Totnes, turn right towards Dartmouth at
first lights. The hotel is in the town centre.

Southwest

Dawlish, Devon

150 Langstone Cliff Hotel

★★★

Dawlish Warren, Dawlish, Devon, EX7 0NA
Tel: 01626 868000 Fax: 01626 868006
Email: rac@langstone-hotel.co.uk
Web: www.langstone-hotel.co.uk
68 bedrs SB £56 DB £96 HBS £70 HBD £62
B £8 L £10 D £16
CC: MC Vi Am DC Swi Delt

How to get there: From M5 Junction 30, follow A379 for Dawlish. Turn left at Harbour for Dawlish Warren. At beach turn right up hill. Hotel 500m.
See advert on facing page

Devizes, Wiltshire

151 Bear Hotel

★★★

The Market Place, Devizes, Wiltshire, SN10 1HS
Tel: 01380 722444 Fax: 01380 722450
Closed 25 and 26 December
24 bedrs SB £60 DB £88
CC: MC Vi Am Swi Delt

How to get there: From Junction 15 of M4 at Chippenham, follow signs to Devizes. Hotel is in the town centre.

Dorchester, Dorset

152 The Wessex Royale Hotel

★★★★

High West Street, Dorchester, Dorset, DT1 1UP
Tel: 01305 262660 Fax: 01305 251941
Email: info@wessex-royale-hotel.com
Web: www.wessex-royale-hotel.com
23 bedrs SB £59 DB £79 HBS £75 HBD £109
B £5.99 L £4.99 D £15
CC: MC Vi Am DC Swi Delt JCB

153 Junction Hotel

♦♦♦

42 Great Western Road, Dorchester, Dorset, DT1 1UF
Tel: 01305 268826 Fax: 01305 751947

Dulverton, Devon

154 Jubilee House

♦♦♦♦

Highaton Farm, West Anstey, South Molton, Devon, EX36 3PJ
Tel: 01398 341312 Fax: 01398 341323
Email: denton@exmoorholiday.co.uk
Web: www.exmoorholiday.co.uk
4 bedrs SB £19.50 DB £50 D £12
CC: MC Vi Am DC Swi Delt JCB

How to get there: Situated on B3227 midway between South Molton/Bampton. Take turning to West Anstey/Yeo Mill at side of the Jubilee Inn. Jubilee House is 400m along lane on right.

Dunster, Somerset

155 Heritage Hotels – The Luttrell Arms

★★★

32-36 High Street, Dunster, Somerset, TA24 6SG
Tel: 0870 400 8110 Fax: 01643 821567
Web: www.heritage-hotels.com
28 bedrs SB £70 DB £110 HBS £85 HBD £70
B £10 L £15 D £24.50
CC: MC Vi Am DC Swi Delt JCB

How to get there: Follow Dunster village sign from A39. Hotel is on the left in the High Street.

Evercreech, Somerset

156 Pecking Mill Inn

♦♦♦

A371, Evercreech, Shepton Mallett, Somerset, BA4 6PG
Tel: 01749 830336 Fax: 01749 831316
Email: peckingmill@peckingmill.freeserve.co.uk
6 bedrs SB £35 DB £55 L £3.95 D £10
CC: MC Vi Swi Delt

How to get there: Four miles south-east of Shepton Mallett on A371, one mile from Bath & West Showground. Nine miles north of Wincanton.

Evershot, Dorset

157 Summer Lodge
Gold Ribbon Winner

★★★★ ® ® ®

Evershot, Dorset, DT2 0JR
Tel: 01935 83424 Fax: 01935 83005
Email: reservations@summerlodgehotel.com
Web: www.summerlodgehotel.com
17 bedrs SB £95 DB £135 HBS £125
HBD £97.50 B £12.50 L £12.50 D £24.75
CC: MC Vi Am DC Swi Delt JCB

How to get there: Exit J8 M3, A303, then A37
towards Dorchester, then Evershot, Summer Lane.

Exeter, Devon

158 Heritage Hotels – The Southgate

★★★★ ®

Southernhay East, Exeter, Devon, EX1 1QF
Tel: 0870 400 8333 Fax: 01392 413549
Email: tony.aspden@macdonald-hotels.co.uk
Web: www.heritage-hotels.com
110 bedrs SB £127.95 DB £140.90 HBS £93
HBD £68 B £12.95 L £8.50 D £10
CC: MC Vi Am DC Swi Delt

How to get there: M5 junction 30 A379 to
Exeter. Follow signs to city centre. After two
miles hotel is on your right.

159 Manor House Hotel & Golf Course

★★★★ ® ®

Moretonhampstead, Devon, TQ13 8RE
Tel: 01647 445000 Fax: 01647 440355
Email: reception@principalhotels.co.uk
Web: www.principalhotels.co.uk
90 bedrs SB £90 DB £120 HBS £99 HBD £89
B £11.50 L £12.50 D £24.95
CC: MC Vi Am DC Swi

160 Woodbury Park Hotel Golf
& Country Club

★★★★

Woodbury Castle, Woodbury, Exeter,
Devon, EX5 1JJ
Tel: 01395 233382 Fax: 01395 234701
Email: woodburypark@eclipse.co.uk
Web: www.woodburypark.co.uk

One of the UK's top sporting retreats. This
luxurious hotel, set in idyllic Devonshire
countryside, offers the best of everything with
the renowned warmth and hospitality of the
West country.
57 bedrs SB £98 DB £128 HBS £120.95
HBD £75.98 B £6.50 D £22.90
CC: MC Vi Am Swi Delt

How to get there: Exit M5 J30. Follow A376,
then A3052 towards Sidmouth; then join B3180
where hotel is signed.

Southwest

161 Barton Cross Hotel

★★★★ ☻ ☻

Huxham, Stoke Canon, Exeter, Devon, EX5 4EJ
Tel: 01392 841245 Fax: 01392 841942

162 Devon Hotel

★★★

Exeter bypass, Matford, Exeter, Devon, EX2 8XU
Tel: 01392 259268 Fax: 01392 413142
Email: info@devonhotel.co.uk
Web: www.brend-hotels.co.uk

Luxurious standards of comfort, personal
service and fine wine in the hotel's bar and
brasserie 'Carriages'. The Devon Hotel is
conveniently located within easy reach of the
M25 and Exeter city centre.
41 bedrs SB £59 DB £82 HBS £77 HBD £59
B £10 L £11 D £18
CC: MC Vi Am DC Swi Delt
How to get there: Leave M5 at Junction 30.
Take 3rd exit, signposted Torquay. On old Exeter
bypass at Matford.

163 Queen's Court Hotel

★★★★ ☻

6-8 Bystock Terrace, Exeter, Devon, EX4 4HY
Tel: 01392 272709 Fax: 01392 491390
Email: sales@queenscourt-hotel.co.uk
Web: www.queenscourt-hotel.co.uk
18 bedrs SB £65 DB £75 B £3.50 L £5 D £7.50
CC: MC Vi Am DC Swi Delt
How to get there: In city centre between Central
and St. David's stations; opposite clock tower
on far side of square.

164 The White Hart Hotel

★★★

66 South Street, Exeter, Devon, EX1 1EE
Tel: 01392 279897 Fax: 01392 230169
Closed Christmas for accommodation
55 bedrs SB £61 DB £94 B £8 L £5.50 D £10
CC: MC Vi Am DC Swi Delt
How to get there: From junction 30 (Granada
Services) follow signs for City Centre A379 on
to the B3182 Topsham Road into South Street
See advert on facing page

165 Fingle Glen Hotel Golf & Country Club

★★

Old Tedburn Road, Tedburn St. Mary, Exeter,
Devon, EX6 6AF
Tel: 01647 61817
CC: None accepted

166 Great Western Hotel

★★

St. David's Station Approach, Exeter, EX4 4NU
Tel: 01392 274039 Fax: 01392 425529
Email: reception@greatwesternhotel.co.uk
Web: www.greatwesternhotel.co.uk
37 bedrs SB £42 DB £66 HBS £52 HBD £43
B £6.50 L £14 D £14
CC: MC Vi Am DC Swi Delt

167 Red House Hotel

★★

2 Whipton Village Road, Whipton, Exeter,
Devon, EX4 8AR
Tel: 01392 256104 Fax: 01392 666145
Email: red.house.hotel@eclipse.co.uk
12 bedrs SB £44 DB £58 HBS £54 HBD £39
B £6.95 L £5.95 D £14.95
CC: MC Vi Am DC Swi Delt
How to get there: The hotel is on the B3212
Pinhoe to Exeter road.

168 Travelodge Exeter

Travel Accommodation

M5, Sandygate, Exeter, Devon, EX2 7HF
Tel: 08700 850 950
Web: www.travelodge.co.uk
102 bedrs B £4.25
CC: MC Vi Am DC Swi Delt

Southwest

---

169 St. Andrews Hotel

◆ ◆ ◆ ◆ ※ ❧

28 Alphington Road, Exeter, Devon, EX2 8HN
Tel: 01392 276784 Fax: 01392 250249
Closed Christmas to New Year

St. Andrews is a long-established, family-run hotel offering a high standard of comfort and service in a friendly relaxing atmosphere. Excellent home cooking.
17 bedrs
CC: MC Vi Am DC Swi Delt
占⊗⊜☐☎📞🄿❊✒🅷❤♔
How to get there: Leave M5 at Junction 31, signposted Exeter. Follow signs to city centre and Marsh Barton along Alphington Road (A377). St. Andrews is on the left.

170 Hotel Gledhills

◆ ◆ ◆ ※

32 Alphington Road, Exeter, Devon, EX2 8HN
Tel: 01392 430469 Fax: 01392 430469
Email: hotelgledhills@netscapeonline.co.uk
Web: www.uk-explorer.co.uk/gledhills
Closed Christmas
12 bedrs SB £25 DB £49
CC: MC Vi Swi Delt
❊⊗⊜☐🄿❊♔
How to get there: Leave M5 at Junction 31 and take A30 for Okehampton. After one mile, take road to Exeter city centre. Follow signs to centre and road becomes Alphington Road. Gledhills is on the left.

171 Park View Hotel

♦ ♦ ♦ ✕

8 Howell Road, Exeter, Devon, EX4 4LG
Tel: 01392 271772
Email: philbatho@parkviewhotel.freeserve.co.uk
Web: www.parkviewhotel.freeserve.co.uk

Family-run in a peaceful setting overlooking
park, close to city centre. All rooms tastefully
decorated to high standards. Dining room
opens onto attractive garden with pond and
waterfall feature.
14 bedrs SB £32 DB £49 CC: MC Vi Swi Delt
How to get there: M5 J29, follow A3015 to city
centre until clocktower. Take fourth exit (Elm
Grove Road). At end, turn left into Howell Road.
Park View 100m on right.

172 Telstar Hotel

♦ ♦ ♦

75-77 St. David's Hill, Exeter, Devon, EX4 4DW
Tel: 01392 272466 Fax: 01392 272466
Email: reception@telstar-hotel.co.uk
Web: www.telstar-hotel.co.uk
20 bedrs SB £22 DB £45
CC: MC Vi Swi Delt
How to get there: Drive through city centre from
A30 or Junction 30 of M5. Hotel is between city
centre and St. David's station.

173 Braeside

♦ ♦

21 New North Road, Exeter, Devon, EX4 4HF
Tel: 01392 256875 Fax: 01392 256875
7 bedrs SB £21 DB £36 HBS £29 HBD £26
CC: MC Vi Swi Delt
How to get there: M5 J29 follow all signs to
town centre, through to New North Road. We
are between the clock tower and the prison.

Exmouth, Devon

174 Royal Beacon Hotel

★ ★ ★ ⓡ

The Beacon, Exmouth, Devon, EX8 2AF
Tel: 01395 264886 Fax: 01395 268890
Email: reception@royalbeaconhotel.co.uk
Web: www.royalbeaconhotel.co.uk

Former Georgian posting house overlooking the
sea, with 25 guest rooms, spacious lounge and
bar, and a charming restaurant featuring
superbly prepared fresh local cuisine.
25 bedrs SB £45 DB £85 HBS £57 HBD £55
B £6 L £11 D £15
CC: MC Vi Am DC Swi Delt

175 Manor Hotel

★ ★

The Beacon, Exmouth, Devon, EX8 2AG
Tel: 01395 272549 Fax: 01395 225519
Web: www.manorexmouth.co.uk
40 bedrs SB £28 DB £50 HBS £37.50
HBD £34.50 D £9.50
CC: MC Vi Swi Delt JCB
How to get there: From M5 take A376 to
Exmouth: signs for seafront, then left at T-
junction at end of Imperial Road.

Falmouth, Cornwall

176 Budock Vean – The Hotel On The River

★★★★★ ® ®

Mawnan Smith, near Falmouth,
Cornwall, TR11 5LG
Tel: 01326 252100 Fax: 01326 250892
Email: relax@budockvean.co.uk
Web: www.budockvean.co.uk
Children minimum age: 7.
Closed 2 – 25 January

Friendly, peaceful, family-run 4-star hotel in 65
acres with sub-tropical gardens, golf course,
large indoor pool, boat, jetty, health spa and
award-winning restaurant.
57 bedrs SB £53 DB £106 HBS £63 HBD £63
B £11 L £10 D £25.50
CC: MC Vi DC Swi Delt
⊕ ⊔ 🖾 ✿ ⊗ 🖵 ☎ P 🖻 ⊮ C ⋔ 🐾 ⋕⋕ ⋔⋔ SPA
⚲ ⌕ 🖻 🖗 🖾

How to get there: From A39 Truro to Falmouth
road, follow brown tourist signs to Trebah
Garden. Continue for half a mile past Trebah to
the hotel.

177 Royal Duchy Hotel

★★★★ ® ®

Cliff Road, Falmouth, Cornwall, TR11 4NX
Tel: 01326 313042 Fax: 01326 319420
Email: info@royalduchy.co.uk
Web: www.brend-hotels.co.uk

Falmouth's Only 4-star Hotel

Situated in a prime location on Falmouth's seafront,
The Royal Duchy Hotel enjoys panoramic views
across Falmouth's famous bay.
Renowned cuisine is matched by the hotel's lavish
accommodation. Every bedroom enjoys private
bathroom en-suite, colour television with satellite
reception and direct dial telephone. A lift provides
easy access to all floors.
Facilities include heated indoor swimming pool
complex with sauna, solarium, spa bath
and family games room.

RAC ★★★★

FOR A FREE COLOUR BROCHURE & BREAKS TARIFFS,
PLEASE CONTACT: Mr D. Rebum,
The Royal Duchy Hotel, Cliff Road, Falmouth, Cornwall TR11 4NX
Tel: (01326) 313042 Fax: (01326) 319420
www.royalduchy.co.uk
Email: info@royalduchy.co.uk

The Westcountry's Leading Hotel Group

Brend Hotels

On the seafront, Falmouth's only 4-star hotel is
renowned for award-winning cuisine, warm
attentive service and luxurious accommodation.
43 bedrs SB £62 DB £116 HBS £74 HBD £70
B £6.75 L £1.50 D £24
CC: MC Vi Am DC Swi Delt
⊕ & ⊔ 🕱 ⊗ 🖵 ☎ 🖀 P🖻 ⊮ C ⋔ 🐾 ⋕⋕ ⋔⋔ ℂ
⚲ 🖾

How to get there: Situated at the castle end of
the seafront on the left-hand side.
See advert above

178 Falmouth Beach Resort Hotel

★★★

Gyllyngvase Beach, Seafront, Falmouth,
Cornwall, TR11 4NA
Tel: 01326 310500 Fax: 01326 319147
Email: info@falmouthbeachhotel.co.uk
Web: www.falmouthbeachhotel.co.uk
123 bedrs
CC: MC Vi Am Swi Delt
⊕ & ⊔ 🖾 ✿ ⊗ 🖵 ☎ 🖀 P 🖻 ⊮ C ⋔ 🐾 ⋕⋕
⋔⋔ SPA ⵙ ℂ ⌕ 🖾

See advert on following page

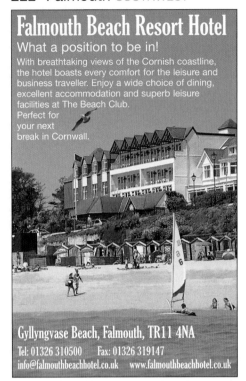

179 Falmouth Hotel

★★★
Castle Beach, Falmouth, Cornwall, TR11 4NZ
Tel: Freephone 0800 0193121 Fax: 01326 319533
Email: info@falmouthhotel.com
Web: www.falmouthhotel.com
Closed Christmas and New Year

Set in extensive landscaped gardens with panoramic views of Falmouth Bay. The Falmouth is the epitomy of Victorian grandeur and comfort with an emphasis on fine dining and gracious living.
69 bedrs SB £52.30 DB £94.25 HBS £69.30 HBD £64.13 CC: MC Vi Am DC Swi Delt

How to get there: Upon entering Falmouth from any direction, follow signs for the seafront. Located at the castle end of Cliff Road.

180 Green Lawns Hotel

★★★★ ♖ ♖
Western Terrace, Falmouth, Cornwall, TR11 4QJ
Tel: 01326 312734 Fax: 01326 211427
Email: info@greenlawnshotel.com
Web: www.greenlawnshotel.com
39 bedrs SB £55 DB £110 HBS £75 HBD £75 B £8 L £5 D £20
CC: MC Vi Am DC Swi Delt

How to get there: Follow A39 to Falmouth. Continue to main beaches; hotel is on right by mini-roundabout.
See advert left

181 Greenbank

★★★

Harbourside, Falmouth, Cornwall, TR11 2SR
Tel: 01326 312440 Fax: 01326 211362
Email: sales@greenbank-hotel.com
Web: www.greenbank-hotel.com

On the water's edge of one of the world's largest natural harbours, The Greenbank provides the ideal base from which to explore Cornwall's spectacular gardens and historical sites of interest.
60 bedrs SB £57 DB £98 HBS £72 HBD £65 L £10 D £18
CC: MC Vi Am DC Swi Delt

How to get there: Approach Falmouth from Penryn. Follow the Greenbank sign from roundabout along North Parade. Hotel is ½ a mile past Marina on left.

182 Gyllyngdune Manor Hotel

★★★

Melvill Road, Falmouth, Cornwall, TR11 4AR
Tel: 01326 312978 Fax: 01326 211881
34 bedrs
CC: MC Vi Am DC Swi Delt

How to get there: Take A39 to Falmouth. Follow signs for hotels, beaches and docks. Join Melvill Road at Western Terrace. Hotel approx ½ a mile on right.

183 Bosanneth Hotel

◆◆◆◆ ✵ ✇

Gyllyngvase Hill, Falmouth, Cornwall, TR11 4DW
Tel: 01326 314649 Fax: 01326 314649
Email: bosanneth.falmouth@tinyworld.co.uk
Web: www.bosannethhotel.com
Children minimum age: 5.
Closed 1 December – 28 February
8 bedrs SB £25 DB £50 HBS £40 HBD £80
CC: None accepted

How to get there: Enter Falmouth on A39, follow signs for beaches. Take Dracaena Avenue, Western Terrace, Melvill Road. Turn right after rail bridge into Gyllyngvase Hill.

184 Chellowdene

◆◆◆◆ ✵

Gyllyngvase Hill, Falmouth, Cornwall, TR11 4DN
Tel: 01326 314950
Closed October to March
6 bedrs DB £20 HBD £30 CC: None accepted

How to get there: Take A39 into Falmouth. Follow road signed Beaches, Gyllyngvase Beach. Chellowdene 60m from main beach.

185 Ivanhoe Guest House

◆◆◆◆ ✇

7 Melvill Road, Falmouth, Cornwall, TR11 4AS
Tel: 01326 319083 Fax: 01326 319083
Email: ivanhoe@enterprise.net
Children minimum age: 5
6 bedrs SB £20 DB £44 CC: None accepted

How to get there: A39 to Falmouth, follow signs to the docks. Road becomes Melvill Road and Ivanhoe is near the end on the right.

186 Rathgowry Hotel

◆◆◆◆ ✵

Gyllyngvase Hill, Gyllyngvase Beach, Falmouth, Cornwall, TR11 4DN
Tel: 01326 313482
Email: a.ranford@virgin.net
Closed October to March
10 bedrs SB £23 DB £46 HBS £32 HBD £64 D £9
CC: None accepted

How to get there: Falmouth on A39. head for beaches along Dracaena Avenue, Western Terrace, Melville Rd; turn right into Gyllynvase Hill.

187 Trevaylor Hotel

◆◆◆◆

8 Pennance Road, Falmouth, Cornwall, TR11 4EA
Tel: 01326 313041 Fax: 01326 316899
Email: stay@trevaylor.co.uk
Web: www.trevaylor.co.uk
9 bedrs SB £19.50 DB £39 HBS £29 HBD £58 B £3 D £9.50 CC: MC Vi Swi Delt

How to get there: Take signs for the beaches. Go along Western Terrace, Green Lawns Hotel on right, turn right at mini-roundabout.

Southwest

188 Tudor Court Hotel

♦ ♦ ♦ ♦ ⚡ ☕

55 Melvill Road, Falmouth, Cornwall, TR11 4DF
Tel: 01326 312807 Fax: 01326 312807
Email: peterb@tudor-court-hotel.freeserve.co.uk
Web: www.cornwall-online.co.uk/
　　　tudor-court-hotel
Children minimum age: 6
10 bedrs SB £24 DB £46
CC: MC Vi Am DC
🚫 ☕ 🖵 🅿 🐾 ♨ 🎣 ♒ 🍴

How to get there: From Truro, continue on main road and head for docks. Hotel on right-hand side of Melvill Road.

189 Gyllyngvase House Hotel

♦ ♦ ♦

Gyllyngvase Road, Falmouth,
Cornwall, TR11 4GH
Tel: 01326 312956 Fax: 01326 316166
Email: gyllyngvase@btinternet.com
Web: www.smoothhound.co.uk/
　　　hotels/gyllyngv.html
Closed Christmas
15 bedrs SB £29.50 DB £59 HBS £52 HBD £52
CC: MC Vi Am DC Swi Delt
⚓ ☕ 🖵 ☎ 🅿 ♨ 🎣 🍴

How to get there: From A30, follow signs to Truro, then from Truro to Falmouth. Follow sign to beaches and dock. Hotel is on the corner of Gyllyngvase and Melvill roads.

Fowey, Cornwall

190 Fowey Hotel

★ ★ ★ ★ ℞ ℞

The Esplanade, Fowey, Cornwall, PL23 1HX
Tel: 01726 832551 Fax: 01726 832125
Email: fowey@richardsonhotels.co.uk
30 bedrs CC: MC Vi Am Swi
♿ ♨ 🍷 🐾 🚫 ☕ 🖵 ☎ 🅿 ♨ 🎣 ♒ ♒ 🍴

How to get there: Continue along A390. Just past Lostwithiel, take left turn for Fowey. Follow signs from roundabout.

Frome, Somerset

191 Mendip Lodge Hotel

★ ★ ★

Bath Road, Frome, Somerset, BA11 2HP
Tel: 01373 463223 Fax: 01373 463990

192 The Sun Inn

♦ ♦ ♦

6 Catherine Street, Frome, Somerset, BA11 1DA
Tel: 01373 471913
6 bedrs SB £30 DB £55 CC: MC Vi Swi Delt
🚫 ☕ 🖵 ♨ 🍴

Gillingham, Dorset

193 Stock Hill House

Gold Ribbon Winner

★ ★ ★ ★ ℞ ℞ ℞ ℞

Stock Hill, Gillingham, Dorset, SP8 5NR
Tel: 01747 823626 Fax: 01747 825628
Email: reception@stockhillhouse.co.uk
Web: www.stockhillhouse.co.uk
Children minimum age: 7

Set in 11 acres, this hotel has an impressive beech-lined driveway. Bedrooms are luxurious and individually-styled. There is a sumptuously-furnished lounge for you to relax in, and our cuisine shows a blend of Austrian and international influences.
8 bedrs HBS £120 HBD £120 B £15 L £22
D £35 CC: MC Vi Swi
🏊 🚫 🖵 ☎ 🅿 ♨ 🎣 ♒ 🍴 🍴 ⚲

How to get there: Three miles off the A303 , situated on the B3081. One mile from Gillingham rail station.

Plan your route

Visit www.rac.co.uk for RAC's interactive route planner, including up to the minute traffic reports.

Making a booking?

Don't forget to mention RAC Hotels and Bed & Breakfast 2002.

Glastonbury, Somerset

194 Southtown House

◆ ◆ ◆

West Pennard, Glastonbury, Somerset, BA6 8NS
Tel: 01458 834552 Fax: 01458 834494
Email: trelawny@tesco.net
Children minimum age: 8
2 bedrs SB £25 DB £50
CC: None accepted

How to get there: From Glastonbury A361 east
into West Pennard. Turn right at sign for village
hall, 1/2 mile left into Southtown, 1/4 mile to the
property, which is stone and slate.

Helston, Cornwall

195 Nansloe Manor Hotel

★ ★ ☬ ☬ ☬

Meneage Road, Helston, Cornwall, TR13 0SB
Tel: 01326 574691 Fax: 01326 564680
Email: info@nansloe-manor.co.uk
Web: www.nansloe-manor.co.uk
Children minimum age: 10
7 bedrs SB £59 DB £110 HBS £84 HBD £80
B £10 L £13 D £24.95
CC: MC Vi Swi Delt JCB

How to get there: 300m on the left from
Helston/Lizard roundabout A394/A3083.

Holford, Somerset

196 Alfoxton Park Hotel

★ ★

Holford, Somerset, TA5 1SG
Tel: 01278 741211
Closed December to March
18 bedrs SB £40 DB £80 HBS £53 HBD £53
D £18
CC: MC Vi Am DC Swi Delt

Honiton, Devon

197 The Deer Park Country Hotel

★ ★ ★ ☬

Buckerell Village, Honiton, Devon, EX14 0PG
Tel: 01404 41266 Fax: 01404 46598

Ilfracombe, Devon

198 Arlington Hotel

★ ★

Sommers Crescent, Ilfracombe, Devon, EX34 9DT
Tel: 01271 862002 Fax: 01271 862803
Email: bookings@devoniahotels.co.uk
Web: www.devoniahotels.co.uk
32 bedrs SB £26.00 DB £52.00 HBS £33.00
HBD £33
CC: MC Vi Am Swi Delt

How to get there: Leave M5 at Junction 27.
Take A361 to Barnstaple, then to Ilfracombe.
Straight across two sets of traffic lights, then
left-hand fork and first left.

199 Darnley Hotel

★ ★ ☬

3 Belmont Road, Ilfracombe, Devon, EX34 8DR
Tel: 01271 863955 Fax: 01271 864076
Email: darnleyhotel@yahoo.co.uk
Web: www.northdevon.co.uk/darnley
10 bedrs SB £25 DB £42 HBS £34.50
HBD £30.50 L £1.50 D £9.50
CC: MC Vi Am DC Swi Delt JCB

How to get there: On entering Ilfracombe turn
left up Church Hill, first left into Belmont Road;
hotel is approx. 50 yards on left.

200 Elmfield Hotel

★ ★

Torrs Park, Ilfracombe, Devon, EX34 8AZ
Tel: 01271 863377 Fax: 01271 866828
Email: elmfieldhotel@aol.com
Web: www.elmfieldhotelilfracombe.co.uk
Closed November to March
13 bedrs SB £40 DB £80 HBS £45 HBD £90
B £8 D £16
CC: MC Vi Swi Delt

How to get there: Take A361 from Barnstaple, at
first lights in Ilfracombe turn left, at second
lights turn left, 10 metres left again, hotel at top
of hill on the left.
See advert on following page

Southwest

Elmfield Hotel

Stands in an acre of gardens, with a heated indoor swimming pool, jacuzzi, sauna, solarium, and car park. For that special occasion two rooms have four-poster beds. The Hotel has an excellent reputation for its English and Continental cuisine and has received a Dining Award from the RAC.

Torrs Park, Ilfracombe,
North Devon EX34 8AZ
Tel: 01271 863377   Fax: 01271 866828
Website: www.northdevon.co.uk/
elmfieldhotel

201 Ilfracombe Carlton Hotel

★★

Runnacleave Road, Ilfracombe, Devon, EX34 8AR
Tel: 01271 862446 Fax: 01271 865379
Closed January to February

Lovely Victorian-style hotel. Central location adjacent to coastal walks, beach, gardens and theatre. We aim to please – somewhere special for you!
48 bedrs SB £27.50 DB £50 HBS £35 HBD £35
B £12.50 D £13.50
CC: MC Vi Am Swi Delt

How to get there: From M5 Junction 27, take A361 to Barnstaple, then A361 to Ilfracombe. Turn left at lights (seafront), and left again.

202 St. Brannocks House

★★

61 St. Brannocks Road, Ilfracombe,
Devon, EX34 8EQ
Tel: 01271 863873 Fax: 01271 863873
Email: stbrannocks@aol.com
Web: www.stbrannockshotel.co.uk
12 bedrs SB £24 DB £48 HBS £34 HBD £34
D £10
CC: MC Vi Am Swi Delt

How to get there: Leave M5 at Junction 27. Take A361 through Barnstaple to Ilfracombe. The hotel is on A361 on left as you approach town.

203 St. Helier

★★

Hillsborough Road, Ilfracombe, Devon, EX34 9QQ
Tel: 01271 864906 Fax: 01271 864906
Email: st_helier_hotel@yahoo.com
Closed October to April
10 bedrs SB £30 DB £54 HBS £38 HBD £35
B £4 D £12
CC: MC Vi Delt

How to get there: From M5, leave at Junction 27 taking A361 towards Barnstaple to Ilfracombe. Through High Street towards Combe Martin, hotel is on the left.

204 Tracy House Hotel

★★

Belmont Road, Ilfracombe, Devon, EX34 8DR
Tel: 01271 863933
9 bedrs
CC: MC Vi

How to get there: Approx. 200m from end of High Street. Ascend Chuch Hill from A361. Turn left into Belmont Road, property is fourth on left.

205 Cairn House Hotel

★

43 St. Brannocks Road, Ilfracombe,
Devon, EX34 8EH
Tel: 01271 863911 Fax: 01271 863911
10 bedrs SB £20 DB £40 HBS £30 HBD £30
D £10
CC: MC Vi DC Swi

How to get there: Leave M5 at Junction 27. Follow Tiverton bypass A361 to Barnstaple, and on to Ilfracombe. Go straight across Mullacott Cross roundabout: hotel 1¼ miles.

206 Torrs Hotel

Torrs Park, Ilfracombe, Devon, EX34 8AY
Tel: 01271 862334
Email: info@thetorrshotel.co.uk
Web: www.thetorrshotel.co.uk
Closed mid November to mid February
14 bedrs SB £22.50 DB £45 HBS £32.50
HBD £32.50 D £10 CC: MC Vi Am Swi Delt

How to get there: From Barnstaple (A361), turn
left at first set of traffic lights in Ilfracombe. At
second set turn left and then left again.

207 Westwell Hall Hotel

Torrs Park, Ilfracombe, Devon, EX34 8AZ
Tel: 01271 862792 Fax: 01271 862792
Email: westwellhall@btconnect.com
Closed December to March
10 bedrs SB £22 DB £44 HBS £34 HBD £68
CC: MC Vi Am DC Swi Delt JCB

How to get there: A361 from Barnstaple. Left at
both first and second traffic lights, then immediately left. Take second on right into Upper Torrs.

208 Avalon Hotel

♦ ♦ ♦ ♦ ☞

6 Capstone Crescent, Ilfracombe,
Devon, EX34 9BT
Tel: 01271 863325 Fax: 01271 866543
Email: christine@avalon-hotel.co.uk
Web: www.avalon-hotel.co.uk
Closed December to January
10 bedrs SB £30 DB £50 HBS £40 HBD £35
D £10 CC: MC Vi Am Swi Delt
How to get there: Seafront to harbour. Turn left
into Capstone when the Sandpiper Yellow pub
is in front of you; hotel is on right

209 Seven Hills Hotel

♦ ♦ ♦ ♦

Torrs Park, Ilfracombe, North Devon, EX34 8AY
Tel: 01271 862207
Email: seven.hills@hydrocomputers.force9.co.uk
Children minimum age: 1
9 bedrs SB £22.50 DB £45 HBS £32.50
HBD £30 D £10 CC: MC Vi Am Swi
How to get there: Left at traffic lights when
entering Ilfracombe from Barnstaple. Next left,
then immediate right, hotel is immediately in front.

210 Southcliffe Hotel

♦ ♦ ♦ ♦ ☜ ☞

Torrs Park, Ilfracombe, Devon, EX34 8AZ
Tel: 01271 862958
Children minimum age: 16.
Closed November to March
12 bedrs SB £40 DB £50 HBS £51 HBD £36
D £12
CC: MC Vi Swi Delt
How to get there: Take A361 to Ilfracombe. At
first set of lights, turn left into Wilder Road. At
the next set of lights, turn left again into Torrs
Park. The Southcliffe Hotel can be found on the
left hand side.

211 Strathmore Hotel

♦ ♦ ♦ ♦ ☜

57 St. Brannocks Road, Ilfracombe,
Devon, EX34 8EQ
Tel: 01271 862248 Fax: 01271 862243
Email: strathmore@ukhotels.com
Web: www.strathmoreukhotels.com

Relax in our delightful Victorian Hotel furnished
with lovely paintings and antiques. Enjoy a
hearty breakfast followed by a day of
sightseeing in Devon's beautiful countryside,
then sample a fabulous home-cooked dinner.
9 bedrs SB £29 DB £56 HBS £47.95
HBD £46.95 D £18.95
CC: MC Vi Swi Delt JCB
How to get there: Exit J27 M5, A361
Barnstaple/Ilfracombe. Straight across Mullacott
roundabout – hotel on left side after 1³/₄ miles.

Southwest

212 Capstone Hotel & Restaurant

◆◆◆

15/16 St. James' Place, Ilfracombe,
Devon, EX34 9BJ
Tel: 01271 863540 Fax: 01271 862277
Email: capstonehotel@ilfracombe2000.co.uk
Web: www.ilfracombe2000.co.uk.
    freeserve.co.uk
Closed November to Easter
12 bedrs SB £19.50 DB £39 HBS £28.50
HBD £28.50 B £5 L £4 D £5
CC: MC Vi Am Swi Delt

How to get there: Entering Ilfracombe, turn left
at lights. Follow seafront, past Landmark
Theatre, to St. James' Place. Look for bow-
windowed restaurant on left.

213 Greyven House

◆◆◆

4 St. James Place, Ilfracombe, Devon, EX34 9BH
Tel: 01271 862505 Fax: 01271 863928
Web: www.greyvenhouse.co.uk
Closed November to February
7 bedrs SB £18.50 DB £37 HBS £28.50
HBD £57 B £4 L £5 D £7
CC: MC Vi Am DC Swi Delt

How to get there: Take the seafront road into
Ilfracombe. Greyven House is 200m past the
Tourist Office on the left.

Ilminster

214 Travelodge Ilminster

Travel Accommodation
A303, Horton Cross, Ilminster,
Somerset, TA19 9PT
Tel: 08700 850 950
Web: www.travelodge.co.uk
32 bedrs B £4.25 CC: MC Vi Am DC Swi Delt

Instow, Devon

215 Commodore Hotel

★★★

Marine Parade, Instow, Devon, EX39 4JN
Tel: 01271 860347 Fax: 01271 861233
Email: admin@the-commodore.freeserve.co.uk
Web: www.commodore-instow.co.uk
20 bedrs SB £55 DB £105 HBS £68

HBD £137.50 B £9.50 L £14 D £22.50
CC: MC Vi Am Swi Delt

How to get there: Leave M5 at Junction 27,
onto North Devon Link Road. The turn-off for
Instow is signposted just before the Torridge
Bridge. Follow the signs for Instow to bring you
to Marine Parade.

Isles of Scilly

216 Island Hotel

Blue Ribbon Winner

★★★★ ⓡ ⓡ ⓡ
Tresco, Isles of Scilly, TR24 0PU
Tel: 01720 422883 Fax: 01720 423008
Email: islandhotel@tresco.co.uk
Closed November to February
48 bedrs SB £90 DB £220 HBS £90 HBD £125
B £9 L £12 D £33
CC: MC Vi Am DC Swi Delt

How to get there: Departure from Penzance
recommended via British International
Helicopters. Direct to Tresco Heliport for
collection. Departure St. Marys via boat to
Tresco for collection.
See advert on facing page

217 St. Martins on the Isle

Blue Ribbon Winner

★★★★ ⓡ ⓡ ⓡ
St. Martin's, Isles of Scilly, Cornwall, TR25 0QW
Tel: 01720 422092 Fax: 01720 422298
Email: stay@stmartinshotel.co.uk
Web: www.stmartinshotel.co.uk
Closed November – February

Warmed by the Gulf Stream, the island of St.
Martin's enjoys a microclimate far warmer than
the mainland and is the perfect destination for
those who appreciate an unspoilt, pollution-free
healthy outdoor environment, coupled with
outstanding food and service.

30 bedrs SB £95 DB £190 HBS £85 HBD £85
B £12 L £10 D £30
CC: MC Vi Am DC Swi Delt

How to get there: 20 minute helicopter journey
from Penzance, and then 20 minute boat trip to
St. Martin's from St. Mary's.

218 Star Castle Hotel

★★★★ 🏮 🏮 🏮

The Garrison, St. Mary's, Isles of Scilly, TR21 0JA
Tel: 01720 422317 Fax: 01720 422343
Closed mid-October to mid-March
34 bedrs SB £62 DB £106 HBS £72 HBD £63
B £6 L £3 D £23
CC: MC Vi Am Swi Delt

How to get there: A five-minute walk from the
quay. A courtesy car will collect all guests from
the airport.
See advert right

219 Hotel Godolphin

★★

St. Mary's, Isles of Scilly, Cornwall, TR21 0JR
Tel: 01720 422316 Fax: 01720 422252
Email: enquiries@hotelgodolphin.co.uk
Web: www.hotelgodolphin.co.uk
Closed November to March
31 bedrs SB £52 DB £114 HBS £62 HBD £67
B £8 D £20
CC: MC Vi Swi Delt

220 Tregarthen's Hotel

★★★ 🏮

Hughtown, St. Mary's, Isles of Scilly, TR21 0PP
Tel: 01720 422540 Fax: 01720 422089
Email: reception@tregarthens-hotel.co.uk
Web: www.tregarthens-hotel.co.uk
Closed October to March
33 bedrs SB £63 DB £110 HBS £73 HBD £130
B £9.50 D £24.50
CC: MC Vi Am DC Swi Delt

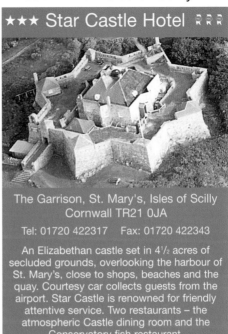
Southwest

221 Seaview Moorings
Little Gem

♦ ♦ ♦ ♦ ♦ ⌦ ⍾

The Strand, St. Mary's, Isles of Scilly, TR21 0PT
Tel: 01720 422327 Fax: 01720 422211
Children minimum age: 14
Alongside St. Mary's Harbour. Four luxury suites
of rooms all with sea views and an extensive
range of facilities for your comfort. Breakfast
menu to cater for all tastes.
4 bedrs
CC: None accepted

How to get there: Hotel is situated directly
opposite St. Mary's harbour quay.

222 Carnwethers Country House

♦ ♦ ♦ ♦ ⌦ ⍾

Pelistry Bay, St. Mary's, Isles of Scilly, TR21 0NX
Tel: 01720 422415 Fax: 01720 422415
Children minimum age: 12.
Closed October to April
9 bedrs HBS £62 HBD £52
CC: None accepted

How to get there: 2¹/₂ miles from Hughtown and
quay; two miles from St. Mary's heliport. Guests
are met by taxi or minibus.

Ivybridge, Devon

223 Sportsmans Inn

★★

Exeter Road, Ivybridge, Devon, PL21 0BQ
Tel: 01752 892280 Fax: 01752 690714
18 bedrs SB £40 DB £50 HBS £50 HBD £70
B £8 L £4 D £6
CC: MC Vi Am Swi Delt

How to get there: Just off A38, 10 miles from
Plymouth, centre of Ivybridge town.

Keynsham, Bristol

224 Grasmere Court

♦ ♦ ♦ ♦ ⍾ ⌦

22 Bath Road, Keynsham, Bristol, BS31 1SN
Tel: 01179 862662 Fax: 01179 862762
Email: grasmerecourthotel@supanet.com
Web: www.grasmerecourthotel.co.uk

Superior family-run hotel conveniently situated
between Bristol and Bath. The hotel has been
recently refurbished to a high standard. All
rooms are well-appointed with private facilities.
Free parking for all.
16 bedrs SB £49 DB £66 B £Inclusive D £15
CC: MC Vi Am Swi Delt

How to get there: Situated on main A4 road,
midway between the cities of Bristol and Bath.

Kingsbridge, Devon

225 Cottage Hotel

★★★ ⍩ ⍩

Hope Cove, Devon, TQ7 3HJ
Tel: 01548 561555 Fax: 01548 561455
Email: info@hopecove.com
Web: www.hopecove.com
Closed January
35 bedrs SB £23 DB £46 HBS £39 HBD £39
B £8.95 L £9.35 D £18.55 CC: Swi Delt

How to get there: From Kingsbridge take A381
towards Salcombe; Hope Cove signposted.
Continue towards Hope Cove, turn left for Inner
Hope. Hotel is on right.

Launceston, Cornwall

226 Hurdon Farm

♦ ♦ ♦ ♦ ⌦

Launceston, Cornwall, PL15 9LS
Tel: 01566 772955
Closed November to April
6 bedrs SB £21 DB £42 HBS £32.50 HBD £32.50
CC: None accepted

How to get there: A30 at first Launceston exit.
From Bodmin turn right, second exit off
roundabout. From Exeter take first exit from
roundabout, second right signed Trebullet.
Hurdon first right.

Lifton, Devon

227 Arundell Arms Hotel

★★★★ ⏚ ⏚ ⏚
Lifton, Devon, PL16 0AA
Tel: 01566 784666 Fax: 01566 784494
Email: reservations@arundellarms.com
Web: www.arundellarms.com
Closed Christmas
27 bedrs SB £76.50 DB £117 HBS £93
HBD £83 B £10 L £18 D £30
CC: MC Vi Am DC Swi

How to get there: Leave M5 at Junction 31.
Take A30 towards Launceston. Hotel is two
miles east of Launceston in Lifton village.

Lizard, Cornwall

228 Housel Bay Hotel

★★★ ⏚
Housel Cove, Lizard, Cornwall, TR12 7PL
Tel: 01326 290 417/917 Fax: 01326 290 359
Email: info@houselbay.com
Web: www.houselbay.com

Britain's most southerly mainland hotel and
restaurant located in a spectacular position
overlooking the western approaches. Secluded
sandy cove. Stylish cuisine. The Cornish coast
path runs through the hotel gardens.
21 bedrs SB £43 DB £86 HBS £60 HBD £60
B £7.50 L £7.50 D £17
CC: MC Vi Am Swi Delt

How to get there: At the Lizard sign post, take
the left fork. Follow hotel signs.

229 Parc Brawse House Hotel

◆ ◆ ◆ ◆
Penmenner Road, Lizard, Cornwall, TR12 7NR
Tel: 01326 290466 Fax: 01326 290466
Email: lindabrookes@cwcom.net
Web: www.cornwall-online.co.uk/parcbrawse
Closed November and January
7 bedrs SB £19 DB £38 HBS £30 HBD £61
B £4.95 D £10.50
CC: MC Vi Swi Delt

How to get there: In Lizard Village just past car
park on Green, turn right at newsagents on
corner. Hotel is 400m on right.

Looe, Cornwall

230 Klymiarven

★★★ ⏚
Barbican Hill, Looe, Cornwall, PL13 1BH
Tel: 01503 262333 Fax: 01503 262333
Email: klymiarven@cwcom.net
Web: www.klymiarven.co.uk
Closed January
14 bedrs
CC: MC Vi Swi

How to get there: From M5 South take A38
Plymouth-Liskeard road. After 10 miles take
A374 towards Looe, then B3253. Turn left after
Looe Garden Centre onto Barbican. Take tourist
bed sign Barbican Hill to Klymiarven.

231 Coombe Farm Hotel

◆ ◆ ◆ ◆ ⚹
Widegates, Looe, Cornwall, PL13 1QN
Tel: 01503 240223 Fax: 01503 240895
Email: coombe_farm@hotmail.com
Web: www.coombefarmhotel.co.uk
Closed November to February
10 bedrs SB £40 DB £70 HBS £57 HBD £53
D £17.50
CC: MC Vi Am Swi Delt
How to get there: Take M4/A38 to Plymouth and
A38 towards Liskeard. Take A387 to Looe at
Trerulefoot roundabout. Continue on A387 to
Hessenford, hotel one mile beyond on left.
See advert on following page

Southwest

Coombe Farm
Country House   Cornwall

Relax in a lovely country house in a wonderful setting with superb views down a wooded valley to the sea. Enjoy delicious food, candlelit dining, log fires, heated outdoor pool and warm, friendly hospitality.

Nearby golf course, horse-riding, glorious walks, beaches, National Trust houses, gardens and the Eden Project.

Widegates, Looe PL13 1QN

Te: 01503 240223   Fax: 01503 240895
Email: coombe_farm@hotmail.com

♦♦♦♦

LOSTWITHIEL
Hotel   RAC ★★★

GOLF & COUNTRY CLUB

Ideally located for all of Cornwall, this Country Club Hotel offers everything for leisure and relaxation. 18 ensuite bedrooms, games room, indoor swimming pool, gymnasium, tennis courts, golf course, fishing. Conference facilities for up to 150 persons.

Lower Polscoe, Lostwithiel, Cornwall PL22 0HQ

Tel: 01208 873550   Fax: 01208 873479
Email: reception@golf-hotel.co.uk
Website: www.golf-hotel.co.uk

---

232 Deganwy Hotel

♦♦♦♦

Station Road, Looe, Cornwall, PL13 1HL
Tel: 01503 262984
Email: deganwyhotel@aol.com
Closed November to December
8 bedrs SB £22 DB £32
CC: None accepted

How to get there: Situated in East Looe, 100m from East/West Looe Bridge, on the A387, opposite doctors' surgery.

233 Panorama Hotel

♦♦♦♦

Hannafore Road, Looe, Cornwall, PL13 2DE
Tel: 01503 262123 Fax: 01503 265654
Email: alan@looe.co.uk
Web: www.looe.co.uk
Children minimum age: 5
10 bedrs SB £25 DB £47 HBS £39 HBD £37 D £14.50
CC: MC Vi Swi Delt

How to get there: Hotel is in west Looe overlooking pier and beach.

Lostwithiel, Cornwall

234 Lostwithiel Hotel Golf & Country Club

★★★

Lower Polscoe, Lostwithiel, Cornwall, PL22 0HQ
Tel: 01208 873550 Fax: 01208 873479
Email: reception@golf-hotel.co.uk
Web: www.golf-hotel.co.uk
19 bedrs SB £42 DB £84 HBS £49 HBD £49 B £5 L £3 D £14.95
CC: MC Vi Am DC Swi Delt

How to get there: Off A390 eastern side of Lostwithiel. Tourist sign-posted.
See advert left

235 Royal Oak Inn

★★

Duke Street, Lostwithiel, Cornwall, PL22 0AH
Tel: 01208 872552 Fax: 01208 872552
6 bedrs SB £37.50 DB £63 B £5 L £5 D £7.50
CC: MC Vi Am DC Swi Delt JCB

How to get there: The hotel is in the centre of the town off the A390.

Lulworth Cove, Dorset

236 Cromwell House Hotel

 ★★

Lulworth Cove, Wareham 10 miles,
Dorset, BH20 5RJ
Tel: 01929 400253 Fax: 01929 400566
Email: catriona@lulworthcove.co.uk
Web: www.lulworthcove.co.uk
Closed Christmas

Lulworth Cove 200 yards, spectacular sea
views. Direct Access Dorset coastal footpath.
Swimming pool (May-October), home cooking,
fish specialities, bar, wine list. Group bookings
welcome. Special breaks. Open all year.
17 bedrs SB £42.50 DB £80 HBS £57.50
HBD £51.50 B £7 L £4.50 D £15
CC: MC Vi Am DC Swi Delt JCB

How to get there: London M3 to Winchester,
M27 to Ringwood, A31 to Bere Regis, B3501
south to West Lulworth, 200 yards after end of
West Lulworth on left high above main road
before you reach Lulworth Cove.

Lydford, Devon

237 Moor View House

Little Gem

Vale Down, Lydford, Okehampton,
Devon, EX20 4BB
Tel: 01822 820220 Fax: 01822 820220

Licensed Victorian country house in moorland.
Gardens, log fires, peace and quiet, lovely
views, ideal touring centre. NT property.
Reputation for good English food, sound wines.
4 bedrs SB £45 DB £65 HBS £60 HBD £95 D £20
CC: None accepted

How to get there: From M5 at Exeter A30 to
Sourton Cross, A386 Tavistock Moor View House
drive four miles on right, 8 miles before Tavistock.

Lyme Regis, Dorset

238 Alexandra

★★★

Pound Street, Lyme Regis, Dorset, DT7 3HZ
Tel: 01297 442010 Fax: 01297 443229
Email: enquiries@hotelalexandra.co.uk
Web: www.hotelalexandra.co.uk
Closed January
26 bedrs SB £50 DB £110 HBS £65 HBD £70
B £8 L £13 D £22.50
CC: MC Vi Am Swi

How to get there: Turn off M5 at Junction 25.
Take A358 to Axminster. Take B3261 to B3165
Lyme Regis. From M5, take A303 to reach A358.

239 Dower House

★★★★ (RAC) (RAC)

Rousdon, Lyme Regis, Dorset, DT7 3RB
Tel: 01297 21047 Fax: 01297 24748
Email: mdowerhouse@aol.com
Closed December to January

Tranquil country charm by the sea. Relax in our
award-winning gardens, swim in our heated
indoor pool. Voted best hotel in Dorset 2001 and
recommended by 'Which' Hotel Guide 2001.
9 bedrs
CC: MC Vi Am Swi Delt

How to get there: Dower House is three miles
outside of Lyme Regis on the A3052 between
Lyme Regis and Seaton.

Southwest

240 Kersbrook Hotel

◆ ◆ ◆ ◆

Pound Road, Lyme Regis, Dorset, DT7 3HX
Tel: 01297 442596 Fax: 01297 442596
Web: www.lymeregis.com/kersbrook-hotel
Closed November to March
10 bedrs CC: MC Vi Am Swi Delt

How to get there: The road that leads to the
harbour is Cobb Road. Pound Road is at the
top of Cobb Road crossroads.

241 Devon Hotel

◆ ◆ ◆

Uplyme, Lyme Regis, Dorset, DT7 3TQ
Tel: 01297 443231 Fax: 01297 445836
Email: thedevon.hotel@virgin.net
Web: www.lymeregis.com/devon-hotel
12 bedrs SB £35 DB £70 HBS £45 HBD £45
CC: MC Vi Swi Delt

How to get there: From A35, turn into Lyme
Road by Hunters Lodge pub. Hotel is on left
after one mile.

Lympsham, Somerset

242 Batch Country Hotel

★ ★

Batch Lane, Lympsham, Somerset, BS24 0EX
Tel: 01934 750371

Lynmouth, Devon

243 Tors Hotel

★ ★ ★

Lynmouth, Devon, EX35 6NA
Tel: 01598 753236 Fax: 01598 752544
Email: torshotel@torslynmouth.co.uk
Web: www.torslynmouth.co.uk
Closed January to February
33 bedrs SB £40 DB £70 HBS £55 HBD £50
B £6.95 L £16 D £25
CC: MC Vi Am DC Swi Delt

How to get there: Leave M5 at Junction 23.
Take A39 for Bridgwater. Travel west for 40
miles through Minehead and Porlock. Down
Countisbury Hill, the hotel is on left as you enter
Lynmouth.

244 Bath Hotel

★ ★

Seafront, Lynmouth, Devon, EX35 6EL
Tel: 01598 752238 Fax: 01598 752544
Email: bathhotel@torslynmouth.co.uk
Web: www.torslynmouth.co.uk
Closed December to January
24 bedrs SB £35 DB £58 HBS £44 HBD £76
B £6 L £3.50 D £17
CC: MC Vi Am DC Swi Delt

How to get there: On A39 from Minehead, on
entering Lynmouth turn right towards the sea.
Hotel on left by harbour.

Lynton, Devon

245 Sandrock Hotel

★ ★

Longmead, Lynton, Devon, EX35 6DH
Tel: 01598 753307 Fax: 01598 752665
Closed November to January

Family-run hotel with modern comforts. Ideal for
relaxing and exploring Exmoor's coastal beauty.
8 bedrs SB £26 DB £27 HBS £41 HBD £42
B £4.50 D £15 CC: MC Vi Am Swi Delt

How to get there: On arrival in Lynton, follow
signs to The Valley of Rocks.

246 Seawood

★ ℞

North Walk, Lynton, Devon, EX35 6HJ
Tel: 01598 752272 Fax: 01598 752272
Web: www.smoothhound.co.uk
Children minimum age: 12.
Closed November to April
12 bedrs SB £29 DB £58 HBS £46 HBD £46
D £16 CC: None accepted

How to get there: Turn right at St. Mary's
Church in Lynton High Street into the North
Walk and Seawood is second property on left.

Malmesbury, Wiltshire

247 Old Bell Hotel

★★★★

Abbey Row, Malmesbury, Wiltshire, SN16 0AG
Tel: 01666 822344 Fax: 01666 825145
Email: info@oldbellhotel.com
Web: www.oldbellhotel.com
31 bedrs SB £75 DB £100 HBS £96.75
HBD £71.75 B £10 L £11.75 D £21.75
CC: MC Vi Am DC Swi Delt

How to get there: Exit J17 M4, A429
Cirencester. After five miles, left to Malmesbury.
Left at Market Cross. Hotel next to Abbey.

248 The Old Rectory Country House Hotel

★★★★

Crudwell, near Malmesbury, Wiltshire, SN16
9EP
Tel: 01666 577194
Email: office@oldrectorycrudwell.co.uk
Web: www.oldrectorycrudwell.co.uk
13 bedrs SB £65 DB £88 B £10 L £15 D £17.95
CC: MC Vi Am DC Swi Delt JCB

How to get there: Eight miles from J17 off the
M4; follow A429 towards Cirencester; hotel is
opposite the Plough next to the church.

249 Mayfield House Hotel

★★★

Crudwell, Malmesbury, Wiltshire, SN16 9EW
Tel: 01666 577409 Fax: 01666 577977
Email: mayfield@callnetuk.com
24 bedrs SB £62 DB £82 B £4.95 L £5 D £18.50
CC: MC Vi Am DC Swi Delt

How to get there: Situated on the A429 between
Malmesbury and Cirencester. Seven miles north
of Junction 17 on the M4.

Marazion, Cornwall

250 Chymorvah Private Hotel

♦ ♦ ♦

Marazion, Cornwall, TR17 0DQ
Tel: 01736 710497 Fax: 01736 710508
Web: www.smoothhound.co.uk/hotels
/chymorvah.html
Closed Christmas and New Year
9 bedrs SB £26 DB £52 HBS £38 HBD £76
B £3.95 L £4.50 D £12

CC: MC Vi Swi Delt

How to get there: Take A30 at Marazion/St.
Michael's Mount roundabout, go through town,
travel eastwards towards Helston on A390 and
turn right after Fire Engine Inn.

Marlborough, Wiltshire

251 Ivy House Hotel

★★★★

Marlborough, Wiltshire, SN8 1HJ
Tel: 01672 515333 Fax: 01672 515338
Email: ivyhouse@btconnect.com

Overlooking Marlborough's famous High Street,
this hotel combines the luxuries of 3-star
accommodation, first-class food and friendly,
efficient service with the character of a listed
Georgian building.
30 bedrs
CC: MC Vi Am Swi Delt

How to get there: Take Junction 15 from M4
then A346 to Marlborough. Ivy House is situated
on A4 in the main high street of Marlborough.

252 Merlin Hotel

♦ ♦ ♦

High Street, Marlborough, Wiltshire, SN8 1LW
Tel: 01672 512151 Fax: 01672 515310
14 bedrs SB £45 DB £70
CC: MC Vi Swi Delt

How to get there: The Merlin Hotel is in the
middle of this historic High Street.

Making a booking?

 Don't forget to mention RAC
Hotels and Bed & Breakfast 2002.

Melksham, Wiltshire

253 Conigre Farm Hotel

 ★★ ®

Semington Road, Melksham, Wiltshire, SN12 6BZ
Tel: 01225 702229 Fax: 01225 707392
Email: conigrefarm.hotel@virgin.com
Web: www.c.fhotel.co.uk

A charming 400-year-old farmhouse set in award-winning gardens with a relaxed and warm atmosphere and a popular restaurant with a good local reputation. An ideal base for touring all local attractions.
8 bedrs SB £43 DB £62
CC: MC Vi Swi Delt
How to get there: Situated on the south side of Melksham, on the Semington road off the A350.

Mevagissey, Cornwall

254 The Fountain Inn

◆◆◆

Mevagissey, Cornwall, PL26 6QH
Tel: 01726 842320
Email: billymoore@ntlworld.com
Web: www.fountain-inn.cwc.net
5 bedrs SB £25 DB £50 L £2.50 D £7.25
CC: MC Vi Swi Delt JCB
How to get there: In center of village on south coast six miles from St. Austell.

See the road ahead

Just dial 1740* from any mobile phone to get up-to-the-minute RAC traffic information on motorways and major A roads. Try it now! *Calls to 1740 are charged at premium rate.

Midsomer Norton, Somerset

255 Pipers Pool

◆◆◆

Wells Road, Chilcompton, near Bath, Somerset, BA3 4ET
Tel: 01761 233803
Children minimum age: 5
2 bedrs SB £40 DB £60 HBS £55 HBD £40
CC: None accepted
How to get there: From Bristol, follow A37; past Ston Easton, turn left to Chilcompton. Pipers Pool is 2nd property after village shop on right.

Minehead, Somerset

256 Rectory House Hotel

★★ ®

Northfield Road, Minehead, Somerset, TA24 5QH
Tel: 01643 702611
7 bedrs SB £30 DB £60 HBS £42 HBD £42
D £19.50 CC: MC Vi
How to get there: From The Avenue turn into Martlet Road, then right into Northfield Road; hotel 180 yards on left, car park to rear.

257 Gascony Hotel

◆◆◆◆

50 The Avenue, Minehead, Somerset, TA24 5BB
Tel: 01643 705939 Fax: 01643 709926
Closed November to February
13 bedrs SB £28.50 DB £50 HBS £39.50
HBD £37 CC: MC Vi Swi Delt
How to get there: On main road between town centre and seafront.

258 Mayfair

◆◆◆◆

25 The Avenue, Minehead, Somerset, TA24 5AY
Tel: 01643 702719 Fax: 01643 702719
Email: info@hotelmayfair.com
Web: www.hotelmayfair.com
Closed October to March
13 bedrs SB £25 DB £50 HBS £37 HBD £37
B £5 D £12 CC: MC Vi Swi Delt
How to get there: Follow signs to town centre. Turn left towards seafront. Continue past hospital and church. Mayfair is the only hotel on left.

259 Rest and Be Thankful Inn

Wheddon Cross, near. Minehead, Exmoor,
Somerset, TA24 7DR
Tel: 01643 841222 Fax: 01643 841813
Email: enquiries@restandbethankful.co.uk
Web: www.restandbethankful.co.uk
Children minimum age: 11
5 bedrs SB £30 DB £60 HBS £39.50
HBD £39.50 B £6.25 L £3 D £5
CC: MC Vi Am DC Swi Delt JCB

How to get there: Nine miles south of Minehead.
Situated on crossroads of A396 (Minehead-
Tiverton road) and B3224 (Taunton-Exford).

260 Beverleigh

Beacon Road, Minehead, Somerset, TA24 5SE
Tel: 01643 708450
Email: beverleigh@talk21.com
3 bedrs SB £27.50 DB £44
CC: None accepted

How to get there: Off main shopping street, go
into Blenheim Road, then first left Martlet Road.
Cross straight into Burgundy Road and Beacon
Road. Park at North Hill Road.

261 Stockleigh Lodge

Exford, Exmoor, Somerset, TA24 7PZ
Tel: 01643 831500 Fax: 01643 831595
Email: myra@stockleighexford.freeserve.co.uk
Web: www.stockleighexford.freeserve.co.uk
9 bedrs SB £25 DB £50 HBS £40 HBD £80 D £15
CC: None accepted

How to get there: Exit M5 at Junction 25,
Taunton. Follow signs to Minehead on A358. At
Bishops Lydeard turn left onto B3224. Follow
signs to Exford. Take Simons Bath road out of
Exford. Lodge on right.

Nailsworth, Gloucestershire

262 Laurels at Inchbrook

Inchbrook, Nailsworth, Gloucestershire, GL5 5HA
Tel: 01453 834021 Fax: 01453 834021
Email: laurels@inchbrook.fsnet.co.uk
Web: www.smoothhound.co.uk/
      hotels/thelaure.html

6 bedrs SB £35 DB £50.50 HBS £42 HBD £40
B £7 D £15
CC: None accepted

How to get there: One mile north of Nailsworth,
three miles south of Stroud, tucked into the
Inchbrook Bends on the A46.

Newquay, Cornwall

263 Barrowfield Hotel

★★★

Hilgrove Road, Newquay, Cornwall, TR7 2QY
Tel: 01637 878878 Fax: 01637 879490
Email: booking@barrowfield.prestel.co.uk
83 bedrs SB £46 DB £92 HBS £60 HBD £60
CC: MC Vi Am Swi Delt

How to get there: Enter Newquay via seafront.
Turn left onto Hilgrove Road. Situated on right-
hand side.

264 Hotel Bristol

★★★

Narrowcliff , Newquay, Cornwall, TR7 2PQ
Tel: 01637 875181 Fax: 01637 879347
Email: info@hotelbristol.co.uk
Web: www.hotelbristol.co.uk

This stylish family-run clifftop hotel celebrates
75 years of service and hospitality in 2002.
Within easy driving distance of the Eden Project
and many other attractions. Getaway breaks
available all year.
74 bedrs SB £63.50 DB £107 HBS £73.50
HBD £63.50 B £9.50 L £12.50 D £21.50
CC: MC Vi Am DC Swi Delt JCB

How to get there: At Highgate Hill (A30), turn off
to A39 then A392. At Quintrell Downs take
A3058, keep straight on for 2½ miles.

Southwest

The Kilbirnie Hotel

The Kilbirnie occupies a position directly facing the sea and has all the modern amenities which once could wish to find. Centrally situated in town and with easy access to beaches. Excellent accommodation, cuisine and service. Heated indoor/outdoor swimming pools, sauna, solarium, hydro spa. Snooker room. Lift to all floors.

Narrowcliff, Newquay TR7 2RS

Tel: 01637 875155   Fax: 01637 850769
Email: enquirykilbirnie@aol.com
Website: www.kilbirniehotel.co.uk

265 Hotel Riviera

★★★
Lusty Glaze Road, Newquay, Cornwall, TR7 3AA
Tel: 01637 874251 Fax: 01637 850823
Web: www.hotelrivieranewquay.com
48 bedrs SB £45.00 DB £90.00 HBS £55.00
HBD £55 B £7.50 L £10.00 D £15.00
CC: MC Vi Am Swi Delt

See advert below

266 Kilbirnie Hotel

★★★
Narrowcliffe, Newquay, Cornwall, TR7 2RS
Tel: 01637 875155 Fax: 01637 850769
Email: enquirykilbirnie@aol.com
Web: www.kilbirniehotel.co.uk
65 bedrs SB £34 DB £68 HBS £42 HBD £42
B £5.50 D £14 CC: MC Vi Am DC Swi Delt

How to get there: Entering Quintrell Downs, turn right and take the seafront road for approx. three miles. Hotel is on left overlooking seafront.
See advert left

267 Trebarwith Hotel

★★★

Trebarwith Crescent, Newquay,
Cornwall, TR7 1BZ
Tel: 01637 872288 Fax: 01637 875431
Email: enquiry@trebarwith-hotel.co.uk
Web: www.trebarwith-hotel.co.uk
Closed November to March
41 bedrs SB £30 DB £60 HBS £35 HBD £35
B £7 L £3 D £14
CC: MC Vi Am Swi Delt

How to get there: From town centre turn left just
before bus station into Trebarwith Crescent.
Hotel is located at end of crescent.
See advert right

268 Great Western Hotel

★★

Cliff Road, Newquay, Cornwall, TR7 2PT
Tel: 01637 872010 Fax: 01637 874435
Web: www.chycor.co.uk/greatwestern
72 bedrs SB £35 DB £70 HBS £45 HBD £40
B £8 L £10 D £14
CC: MC Vi Am DC Swi Delt

How to get there: Take A30 'Indian Queens' to
Quintrell Downs roundabout. Turn right, over
level crossing, to seafront in Newquay. Hotel is
on right.

269 Philema Hotel

★★

Esplanade Road, Pentire, Newquay,
Cornwall, TR7 1PY
Tel: 01637 872571 Fax: 01637 873188
Email: info@philema.demon.co.uk
Web: www.smoothhound.co.uk/hotels/
    philema.html
Closed November to February
33 bedrs SB £25 DB £50 HBS £39 HBD £39
B £5 D £7.50
CC: MC Vi Swi Delt
How to get there: Follow A392 to roundabout;
turn left for Pentire Hotels. Continue down
Pentire Road. Hotel situated on corner.

Plan your route

Visit www.rac.co.uk for RAC's
interactive route planner, including
up to the minute traffic reports.

Trebarwith Hotel
"Probably the best views in Newquay"

There's more too! Gardens, sun terraces,
private beach entrance, large indoor pool.
All complemented by relaxing, comfortable,
friendly atmosphere, high standards of
housekeeping, excellent food and caring
hospitality. Extensive indoor leisure facilities,
entertainment, secure parking. Quiet, central
location, an oasis in the heart of Newquay!

Newquay,
Cornwall
TR7 1BZ
Tel:
01637 872288

Fax:
01637 875431

RƎC ★★★

Email: enquiries@trebarwith-hotel.co.uk
Website: Trebarwith-hotel.co.uk

270 Priory Lodge Hotel

◆◆◆◆ ✕

30 Mount Wise, Newquay, Cornwall, TR7 2BN
Tel: 01637 874111 Fax: 01637 851803
Closed January to February
26 bedrs SB £26 DB £52 HBS £38 HBD £76
B £4 L £2 D £10 CC: MC Vi Swi Delt
How to get there: Enter Newquay via seafront,
left onto B3282; 500m on right, black-and-white
telephone box in grounds

271 Windward Hotel

◆◆◆◆ ✕ ✦

Alexandra Road, Porth, Newquay,
Cornwall, TR7 3NB
Tel: 01637 873185 Fax: 01637 852436
Email: caswind@aol.com
Web: www.windwardhotel.co.uk
14 bedrs SB £33 DB £48 HBS £43 HBD £34
L £10 D £12 CC: MC Vi Am Swi Delt
How to get there: Join the A392 at Indian
Queens for seven miles. At the roundabout at
Quintell Downs, take the A3058 to Newquay,
then B3276 to Padstow at the double
roundabout. Hotel is on right after one mile.

Southwest

272 Carlton Hotel

◆ ◆ ◆

Towan Headland, 6 Dane Road, Newquay,
Cornwall, TR7 1HL
Tel: 01637 872658
Closed November to Easter
10 bedrs SB £22 DB £44
CC: None accepted
🐕 🖥 💻 🅿 🗱 🏃 ⌂ ✎ ⅲ
How to get there: Newquay on A30 onto A392,
down Higher Tower Road. Left at Red Lion. The
Carlton Hotel is at top of Dane Road.

273 Rolling Waves Hotel

◆ ◆ ◆ ✗

Alexandra Road, Porth, Newquay,
Cornwall, TR7 3NB
Tel: 01637 873236 Fax: 01637 873236
Email: enquiries@rollingwaves.co.uk
Web: www.rollingwaves.co.uk
9 bedrs SB £20 DB £40 HBS £27 HBD £27
CC: MC Vi Swi Delt
🔗 🐕 ⊗ 🖥 💻 🅿 🗱 🏃 ⌂ ✎ ⅲ
How to get there: From A30 turn into A3059
Newquay Road. On entering Newquay at first
roundabout turn right into B3276 to Padstow.
Hotel is on right past Porth beach.

Newton Abbot, Devon

274 Ilsington Country House Hotel

★ ★ ★ ℞
Ilsington Village, Newton Abbot,
Devon, TQ13 9RR
Tel: 01364 661452 Fax: 01364 661307
Email: hotel@ilsington.co.uk
Web: www.ilsington.co.uk

Set in a stunning rural location within Dartmoor
National Park with indoor swimming pool, spa
pool, gymnasium, sauna/steam room and
award-winning restaurant. All make this family-
owned hotel an ideal destination.
25 bedrs SB £74.50 DB £110 HBS £85 HBD £69
B £8.95 L £13.95 D £25.95
CC: MC Vi Am Swi Delt JCB
⌶ 🐕 ⊗ 💻 ☎ 🅿 🗱 🏃 ⌂ ✎ 🌀 ⅲ ⅲ SPA 'ꭨ' ✂
How to get there: Follow A38 towards
Plymouth. Take exit to Bovey Tracey, then third
exit from roundabout, first right to Ilsington.
Hotel five miles on, on right.

275 Passage House Hotel

★ ★ ★
Hackney Lane, Kingsteignton, Newton Abbot,
Devon, TQ12 3QH
Tel: 01626 355515 Fax: 01626 363336
Email: mail@passagehousehotel.co.uk
Web: www.passagehousehotel.co.uk
38 bedrs SB £69.50 DB £80 B £9.50 L £11.25
D £19.50
CC: MC Vi Am DC Swi Delt
⌶ ⊗ 🖥 💻 ☎ 📞 🅿 🗱 🏃 ⌂ ✎ 🌀 ⅲ ⅲ 'ꭨ' ✂
How to get there: Leave M5 at Junction 31 for
A380. Leave at A381 exit and follow racecourse
signs.

276 Barn Owl Inn

◆ ◆ ◆ ◆
Aller Mills, Kings Kerswell,
Newton Abbot, TQ12 5AN
Tel: 01803 872130 Fax: 01803 875279

North Petherton, Somerset

277 The Boat & Anchor Inn

🔶
Huntworth, North Petherton, Somerset, TA7 0AQ
Tel: 01278 662473 Fax: 01278 662473

Okehampton, Devon

278 Percy's Country Hotel & Restaurant
Blue Ribbon Winner

★★

Coombeshead Estate, Virginstow,
Devon, EX21 5EA
Tel: 01409 211236 Fax: 01409 211275
Email: info@percys.co.uk
Web: www.percys.co.uk
Children minimum age: 12

Percy's is the perfect venue for those wishing to unwind in a relaxed informal environment. Modern architectural excellence coupled with traditional Country House comfort and award-winning cuisine sets the scene for a most enjoyable and memorable stay.
8 bedrs SB £79.50 DB £99.50 HBS £112
HBD £82.50 B £8 L £12 D £32.50
CC: MC Vi Am Swi Delt
How to get there: From Launceston A388, right at St. Giles on the Heath, then 2 1/4 miles on the right.
See advert on following page

279 Travelodge Okehampton (West)

Travel Accommodation
A30/A386, Sourton Cross, Okehampton,
Devon, EX20 4LY
Tel: 08700 850 950
Web: www.travelodge.co.uk
42 bedrs B £4.25
CC: MC Vi Am DC Swi Delt

Ottery St. Mary, Devon

280 Tumbling Weir Hotel

★★

Canaan Way, Ottery St. Mary, Devon, EX11 1AQ
Tel: 01404 812752 Fax: 01404 812752
Email: sa3648@eclipse.co.uk

Thatched hotel with beautiful gardens and tranquil setting. Close proximity to Exeter, its airport and the coast. Imaginative a la carte menu and interesting lunches. Ideal for weddings and meetings.
11 bedrs SB £49 DB £74 HBS £71.50
HBD £56.50 B £6 L £5 D £15
CC: MC Vi Am Swi Delt

281 Pitt Farm

♦♦♦♦

Fairmile, Ottery St. Mary, Devon, EX11 1NL
Tel: 01404 812439 Fax: 01404 812439
Web: www.smoothhound.co.uk/hotels/pittfarm.html
Closed Christmas and New Year

This 16th-century thatched farmhouse nestles in the picturesque Otter Valley. Ideal centre for touring. Devon/Exeter 10 miles, Honiton six miles.
5 bedrs SB £20 DB £40 CC: MC Vi Swi
How to get there: Follow signs for Fairmile on A30. In Fairmile turn into B3176 towards Cadhay House. After 1/2 mile, Pitt Farm is on left. From Ottery St. Mary, take Fairmile Road. Farm one mile.

Southwest

PERCY'S

COUNTRY HOTEL & RESTAURANT

RELAX... TASTE... ENJOY

VIRGINSTOW, DEVON **WWW.PERCYS.CO.UK**

Padstow, Cornwall

282 Heritage Hotels – The Metropole

★★★★ ♟

Station Road, Padstow, Cornwall, PL28 8DB
Tel: 01841 532486 Fax: 01841 532867
Email: heritagehotels-padstow.metropole
@forte-hotels.com
Web: www.heritage-hotels.com
50 bedrs SB £64 DB £99 HBS £74 HBD £78
B £12.95 D £23 CC: MC Vi Am DC Swi Delt
How to get there: Follow A30 from Bodmin to
Wadebridge. Locate B3890 to Padstow. Take 2nd
on right (School Hill). The Metropole is on the left.

283 Treglos Hotel

Blue Ribbon Winner

★★★★ ♟ ♟

Constantine Bay, Padstow, Cornwall, PL28 8JH
Tel: 01841 520727 Fax: 01841 521163
Email: enquiries@treglos-hotel.co.uk
Web: www.treglos-hotel.co.uk
Closed mid-November to end February

Situated in an area of outstanding natural
beauty, this privately owned country house hotel
overlooks the spectacular North Cornwall
coastline and nearby Trevose golf course.
44 bedrs SB £55 DB £110 HBS £73 HBD £73
B £10.25 L £10.30 D £25 CC: MC Vi Swi Delt
How to get there: From Padstow follow signs to
St. Merryn, then Constantine Bay and brown
signs to Treglos.

284 Woodlands Country House

♦ ♦ ♦ ♦

Treator, Padstow, Cornwall, PL28 8RU
Tel: 01841 532426 Fax: 01841 532426
Web: www.padstow.com
Closed November to March
9 bedrs SB £25 DB £50 CC: None accepted
How to get there: Hotel is on B3276 between
Padstow and Trevone, ½ a mile from Padstow.

285 Bedruthan House Hotel

♦ ♦ ♦

Bedruthan Steps, St. Eval, Cornwall, PL27 7UW
Tel: 01637 860346 Fax: 01637 860763
Email: bedruthanhouse@excite.co.uk
Web: www.chycor.co.uk/hotels/bedruthan
Children minimum age: 3.
Closed December and January
6 bedrs SB £20.50 DB £41 HBS £28 HBD £28
L £7 D £8 CC: MC Vi Swi Delt
How to get there: On B3276 Coast Road
halfway between Newquay and Padstow.

Paignton, Devon

286 Redcliffe Hotel

★★★

Marine Drive, Paignton, Devon, TQ3 2NL
Tel: 01803 526397 Fax: 01803 528030
Email: redclfe@aol.com
Web: www.redcliffehotel.co.uk
65 bedrs SB £52 DB £104 HBS £60 HBD £60
B £8 L £11 D £17 CC: MC Vi Am DC Swi Delt
How to get there: Head for Paignton seafront.
Redcliffe Hotel is at the Torquay end of seafront,
on the sea side of the road.

287 Dainton Hotel

★★

95 Dartmouth Road, Three Beaches
Goodrington, Paignton, Devon, TQ4 6NA
Tel: 01803 550067 Fax: 01803 666339
Web: www.daintonhotel.com
11 bedrs SB £35 DB £60 HBS £45 HBD £40
B £4.50 L £5.95 D £5.95
CC: MC Vi Swi
How to get there: Follow Zoo sign after
entrance next right 'Penwill Way' at the bottom
turn right 400 yards on left is Dainton Hotel.

288 Preston Sands Hotel

★★

Marine Parade, Sea Front, Paignton,
Devon, TQ3 2NU
Tel: 01803 558718 Fax: 01803 522875
Children minimum age: 9
31 bedrs SB £25 DB £50 HBS £35 HBD £70
B £6.50 D £13 CC: MC Vi Am Swi Delt

Southwest

289 Sea Verge Hotel

★★

Marine Drive, Preston, Paignton, Devon, TQ3 2NJ
Tel: 01803 557795
Children minimum age: 9.
Closed November to March
12 bedrs DB £18 HBD £18 D £9.50
CC: None accepted

How to get there: On seafront overlooking Preston beach and Green.

290 Torbay Holiday Motel

★★

Totnes Road, Paignton, Devon, TQ4 7PP
Tel: 01803 558226 Fax: 01803 663375
Email: enquiries@thm.co.uk
Web: www.thm.co.uk
16 bedrs SB £37.50 DB £59 HBS £45.50
HBD £37.50 B £3 L £3.95 D £8
CC: MC Vi Swi

How to get there: Situated on the A385 Totnes road 2½ miles from Paignton.
See advert below

Torbay Holiday Motel
Paignton

Purpose-built motel on the A385
Totnes/Paignton road,
2 miles from Paignton.

Totnes Road, Paignton TQ4 7PP

Tel: 01803 558226   Fax: 01803 663375
Email: enquiries@thm.co.uk
Website: www.thm.co.uk

291 Roundham Lodge

♦♦♦♦♦

16 Roundham Road, Paignton, Devon, TQ4 6DN
Tel: 01803 558485 Fax: 01803 553090
Email: may@vega68.freeserve.co.uk
Web: www.smoothhound.co.uk/hotels/
roundl.html
Closed two weeks around Christmas
5 bedrs DB £40
CC: None accepted

How to get there: Just off Eastern Esplanade at mini-roundabout Sands Road. Turn left. Follow road round then second turning on right. Hotel on left hand side.

292 Redcliffe Lodge

♦♦♦

1 Marine Drive, Paignton, Devon, TQ3 2NJ
Tel: 01803 551394
Children minimum age: 16

The family-run hotel that offers a great friendly atmosphere with excellent cuisine and breathtaking sea views. If it is a fun-packed holiday you want, or just to unwind and relax, Paignton's the place to be.
17 bedrs SB £30 DB £48 HBS £25 HBD £56
CC: MC Vi Swi Delt

How to get there: At northern end of Paignton seafront, opposite Paignton Green and close to the beach.

293 Sealawn Hotel

♦♦♦

20 Esplanade Road, Paignton, Devon, TQ4 6BE
Tel: 01803 559031
Closed Christmas to New Year
12 bedrs CC: MC Vi Delt

How to get there: The Sealawn Hotel is situated between the pier and the multiplex cinema on Paignton seafront.

Par, Cornwall

294 Elmswood House Hotel

♦♦♦♦

73 Tehidy Road, Tywardreath, Par,
Cornwall, PL24 2QD
Tel: 01726 814221 Fax: 01726 814399
7 bedrs SB £27 DB £47 HBS £37 HBD £67 D £10
CC: None accepted

How to get there: Turn off A390 at junction for
Fowey. Follow road for three miles B3269 turn
left at junction for Tywardreath & Par. Hotel
opposite St. Andrew's Church.

Parkham, Devon

295 Penhaven Country House Hotel

★★★★ 🅡 🅡

Rectory Lane, Parkham, Devon, EX39 5PL
Tel: 01237 451711 Fax: 01237 451878
Email: reservations@penhaven.co.uk
Web: www.penhaven.co.uk
Children minimum age: 10
12 bedrs SB £70 DB £140 HBS £85 HBD £170
B £8 L £13 D £17
CC: MC Vi DC Swi Delt

How to get there: Turn left opposite Coach &
Horses at Horns Cross on A39. Follow signs to
Parkham, continue up hill to church then take
second left.

Penzance, Cornwall

296 Queens Hotel

★★★ 🅡

The Promenade, Penzance, Cornwall, TR18 4HG
Tel: 01736 362371 Fax: 01736 350033
Email: enquiries@queens-hotel.com
Web: www.queens-hotel.com

Voted 'Discover Britain's Hotel Of The Year'. An
elegant Victorian hotel enjoying pride of place

on the seafront promenade of Penzance with
majestic views which sweep across Mount's
Bay from St. Michael's Mount to the Lizard
Peninsula.
70 bedrs SB £45 DB £90 HBS £60 HBD £120
B £7.50 L £5.50 D £16.95
CC: MC Vi Am DC Swi Delt

How to get there: Follow signs for harbour and
Promenade. Follow to Promenade on seafront.
See advert on following page

297 Tarbert Hotel & Restaurant

★★ 🅡

11 Clarence Street, Penzance,
Cornwall, TR18 2NU
Tel: 01736 363758 Fax: 01736 331336
Email: reception@tarbert-hotel.co.uk
Web: www.tarbert-hotel.co.uk
Closed December and January

A superb example of a Georgian period hotel
where personal attention and high standards of
service are guaranteed. A warm welcome awaits
you.
12 bedrs SB £25 DB £50 HBS £38.50 HBD £40
B £7.50 D £13.75
CC: MC Vi Am Swi Delt JCB

How to get there: Approach Penzance via A30.
At first roundabout after Heliport take ring road,
signposted Land's End. At third roundabout turn
left, then right into Clarence Street.

298 Estoril Hotel

★

46 Morrab Road, Penzance, Cornwall, TR18 4EX
Tel: 01736 362468 Fax: 01736 367471
Email: estorilhotel@aol.com
Web: www.estorilhotel.co.uk
9 bedrs SB £29.50 DB £59
CC: MC Vi Swi

Southwest

The Queens Hotel

Penzance   RAC★★★

Elegant Victorian Hotel enjoying pride of place on the sea front promenade of Penzance with majestic views which sweep across Mounts Bay to St. Michael's Mount and Lizard Peninsula. Excellent restaurant with local seafood. Lands End, Minack Theatre, Tate Gallery within a short drive.

The Promenade, Penzance TR18 4HG

Tel: 01736 362371   Fax: 01736 350033

Email: enquiries@queens-hotel.com

Website: www.queens-hotel.com

299 Carlton Hotel

◆◆◆

Promenade, Penzance, Cornwall, TR18 4NW

Tel: 01736 362081

12 bedrs SB £18 DB £22

CC: MC Vi Am Swi JCB

How to get there: From Penzance Railway/Bus Station follow signs for seafront and harbour. Carlton is one mile on the right.

300 Keigwin Hotel

◆◆◆

Alexandra Road, Penzance, Cornwall, TR18 4LZ

Tel: 01736 363930 Fax: 0870 1673499

Email: info@keigwinhotel.co.uk

Web: www.keigwinhotel.co.uk

8 bedrs SB £15 DB £33 HBS £25.50 HBD £25.50 D £10.50

CC: MC Vi DC Swi Delt JCB

How to get there: Proceed straight along the seafront to a mini-roundabout, turn right into Alexandra Road: hotel is halfway along on right.

301 Mount Royal Hotel

◆◆◆

Chyandour Cliff, Penzance, Cornwall, TR18 3LQ

Tel: 01736 362233 Fax: 01736 362233

Email: mountroyal@talk21.com

Web: www.s-h-systems.co.uk/hotels/
     mountroyal.html

Closed November to February

7 bedrs CC: None accepted

How to get there: Situated on the main road entering Penzance on the old A30.

302 Penmorvah Hotel

◆◆◆

Alexandra Road, Penzance, Cornwall, TR18 4LZ

Tel: 01736 363711 Fax: 01736 363711

8 bedrs SB £18 DB £36 HBS £32 HBD £32

CC: MC Vi Am Swi Delt

How to get there: Approach Penzance promenade, turn right up Alexandra Road at mini-roundabout, hotel on right-hand side near top.

303 Woodstock

◆◆◆

29 Morrab Road, Penzance, Cornwall, TR18 4EZ

Tel: 01736 369049 Fax: 01736 369049

Email: woodstocp@aol.com

Web: www.cruising-america.com/woodstock

Children minimum age: 5

8 bedrs SB £15 DB £30

CC: MC Vi Am DC Swi Delt

How to get there: Enter Penzance past railway station and drive along sea front. Turn right after The Lugger Inn. Woodstock 200m on right.

Pewsey, Wiltshire

304 The Woodbridge Inn

◆◆◆

North Newnton (A345), Pewsey, Wiltshire, SN9 6JZ

Tel: 01980 630266 Fax: 01980 630266

Plan your route

Visit www.rac.co.uk for RAC's interactive route planner, including up to the minute traffic reports.

Plymouth, Devon

305 Copthorne Hotel Plymouth

★★★★

Armada Way, Plymouth, Devon, PL1 1AR
Tel: 01752 224161 Fax: 01752 670688
Email: sales.plymouth@mill-cop.com
Web: www.millennium-hotels.com
135 bedrs SB £136.95 DB £150.90
HBS £155.45 HBD £93.95
CC: MC Vi Am DC Swi Delt

How to get there: Follow signs for Plymouth and then Continental Ferryport. At the 4th roundabout the hotel is on the 1st left.

306 New Continental Hotel

★★★

Mill Bay Road, Plymouth, Devon, PL1 3LD
Tel: 01752 220782 Fax: 01752 227013
Email: newconti@aol.com
Web: www.newcontinental.co.uk
Closed December 24 to January 4
99 bedrs SB £92 DB £102 B £10 L £10.95
D £16.25 CC: MC Vi Am Swi Delt

How to get there: From A38, follow signs for city centre, Pavilions Conference Centre and Continental Ferryport. Hotel is adjacent to Pavilions Conference Centre in Millbay Road.

307 Novotel Plymouth

★★★

Marsh Mills Roundabout, 270 Plymouth Road, Plymouth, Devon, PL6 8NH
Tel: 01752 221422 Fax: 01752 223922
Email: h0508sb@accor-hotels.com
Web: www.accor-hotels.com
100 bedrs CC: MC Vi Am DC Swi Delt

How to get there: Located at the gateway to Plymouth, adjacent to A38. Exit the A38 at Marsh Mills junction (opposite Sainsbury's).

308 Strathmore Hotel

★★★

Elliot Street, The Hoe, Plymouth, Devon, PL1 2PR
Tel: 01752 662101 Fax: 01752 223690
54 bedrs CC: MC Vi Am Swi Delt

How to get there: Leave A38 at Plymouth, left at roundabout, follow city centre then Hoe/Barbican. Left into Athenaeum Street onto Elliot Street.

309 Camelot Hotel

★★

5 Elliott Street, Plymouth, Devon, PL1 2PP
Tel: 01752 221255 Fax: 01752 603660
Email: camelotuk@supanet.com
18 bedrs SB £39 DB £50 HBS £51 HBD £37
B £7.50 L £5.95 D £5.95
CC: MC Vi Am DC Swi Delt

How to get there: Leaving A38 at Plymouth, follow signs for city centre, the Hoe, Citadel Road, and then onto Elliot Street.

310 Invicta Hotel

★★

11/12 Osborne Place, Lockyer Street, The Hoe, Plymouth, Devon, PL1 2PU
Tel: 01752 664997 Fax: 01752 664994
Email: info@invictahotel.co.uk
Web: www.invictahotel.co.uk
Closed Christmas to New Year
23 bedrs SB £42 DB £52 HBS £55.50 HBD £38
D £10.50 CC: MC Vi Am Swi Delt

How to get there: From A38 head to city centre. Left at sign for The Hoe. After Barclays Bank, second left, Lockyer Street. Hotel opposite bowling green.

311 Langdon Court Hotel

★★★ ?

Down Thomas, Wembury, Plymouth, PL9 0DY
Tel: 01752 862358 Fax: 01752 863428
Email: enquiries@langdoncourt.co.uk
Web: www.langdoncourt.co.uk

Charming Tudor Manor, with unique 17th-century walled garden, glorious South Hams countryside, award-winning cuisine, six miles from Plymouth city centre and one mile from Wembury Beach. Civil Wedding Licence.
19 bedrs B £7.50 L £10 D £15
CC: MC Vi Am DC Swi Delt JCB

How to get there: Follow tourist signs to hotel from Elburton on A379 (Plymouth to Kingsbridge road). Approx. 6 miles from Plymouth city crntre.

Southwest

312 Drake Hotel

1 Windsor Villas, Lockyer Street, The Hoe,
Plymouth, Devon, PL1 2QD
Tel: 01752 229730 Fax: 01752 255092
Email: drakehotel@themutual.net
Web: www.drakehotel.themutual.net
Closed Christmas to New Year
35 bedrs SB £44 DB £56 HBS £56 HBD £80
B £5 D £13
CC: MC Vi Am DC Swi Delt JCB
How to get there: Follow signs to city centre.
Turn left at Theatre Royal. Take last left and first
right.

313 Imperial Hotel

Lockyer Street, The Hoe, Plymouth,
Devon, PL1 2QD
Tel: 01752 227311 Fax: 01752 674986
Closed December 24 to January 1
23 bedrs SB £49 DB £64 HBS £61 HBD £88 B £5
D £12
CC: MC Vi Am DC Swi Delt
How to get there: Head for city centre, at
Theatre Royal turn left up hill, turn left at traffic
lights then first right.

314 Victoria Court Hotel

64 North Road East, Plymouth, Devon, PL4 6AL
Tel: 01752 668133 Fax: 01752 668133
Email: victoria.court@btinternet.com
13 bedrs SB £42 DB £55 B £5.50 D £14.50
CC: MC Vi Am DC Swi Delt

315 Ashgrove Hotel

218 Citadel Road, The Hoe, Plymouth,
Devon, PL1 3BB
Tel: 01752 664046 Fax: 01752 252112
Email: ashgroveho@aol.com
Closed Christmas and New Year
9 bedrs SB £25 DB £40
CC: MC Vi Am Swi Delt
How to get there: From city centre, left at
Theatre Royal, right at traffic lights onto Nott
Street, then left at next lights (Walrus pub). Up
Athenaeum Street, turn right, Ashgrove on left.

316 Rosaland Hotel

32 Houndiscombe Lane, Plymouth,
Devon, PL4 6HQ
Tel: 01752 664749 Fax: 01752 256984
Email: manager@rosalandhotel.com
Web: www.rosalandhotel.com
9 bedrs SB £19 DB £34 HBS £31 HBD £29
CC: MC Vi Am Swi Delt
How to get there: Sainsbury's roundabout, first
exit. Left-hand lane to Mutley. Through next
three lights; right at fourth and again at fifth.

317 Headland Hotel

1a Radford Road, West Hoe, Plymouth,
Devon, PL1 3BY
Tel: 01752 660866 Fax: 01752 313339
Email: info@headlandhotelplymouth.co.uk
Web: www.headlandhotelplymouth.co.uk
Closed Christmas and New Year
29 bedrs SB £20 DB £30 B £2.50
CC: MC Vi Am Swi Delt
How to get there: From city centre, follow brown
sign "Pavilions". At mini-roundabout follow sign
for West Hoe & Seafront. Hotel is directly in
front.

Poole, Dorset

318 Haven

★★★★★

Sandbanks, Poole, Dorset, BH13 7QL
Tel: 01202 707333 Fax: 01202 708796
Email: reservations@havenhotel.co.uk
Web: www.havenhotel.co.uk

An exclusive hotel located on the tip of
Sandbanks peninsula. Stunning sea views,
award winning cuisine, first class service,
fabulous leisure and beauty spa facilities.

94 bedrs SB £85 DB £170 HBS £98 HBD £98
B £10 L £16 D £25
CC: MC Vi Am DC Swi Delt

How to get there: Take A31 towards
Bournemouth, A338 Wessex Way, onto B3065.
At Sandbanks Bay turn left, follow road to end
of peninsula, hotel is on left by Ferry Point.

319 Salterns

★★★★ ☾ ☾

38 Salterns Way, Lilliput, Poole, Dorset, BH14 8JR
Tel: 01202 707321 Fax: 01202 707488
20 bedrs SB £96 DB £140 HBS £116 HBD £96
B £15 L £25 D £30
CC: MC Vi Am DC Swi Delt

How to get there: From Poole, follow signs for
Sandbanks, at Lilliput turn right by Barclays
Bank into Saltern Way.
See advert below right

320 Sandbanks Hotel

★★★★ ☾ ☾

Banks Road, Poole, Dorset, BH13 7PS
Tel: 01202 707377 Fax: 01202 708885
Email: john@sandbankshotel.co.uk
Web: www.sandbankshotel.co.uk

On Blue Flag Award Golden Sands, the
Sandbanks is perfect for holidays and short
breaks. Special children's restaurant and play
facilities, waterside brasserie and leisure centre.
116 bedrs SB £73 DB £146 HBS £78 HBD £78
B £8.50 L £15.50 D £20.50
CC: MC Vi Am DC Swi Delt

How to get there: Take A31 towards
Bournemouth. Turn onto A338. At Liverpool
Victoria roundabout keep far left and take
B3065 to Sandbanks Beach. At T-junction, turn
left. Hotel 500m on left.

321 The Mansion House

★★★★ ☾ ☾ ☾

Thames Street, Poole, Dorset, BH15 1JN
Tel: 01202 685666 Fax: 01202 665709
Email: enquiries@themansionhouse.co.uk
Web: www.themansionhouse.co.uk

One of Dorset's most highly acclaimed hotels
and restaurants. A Georgian house set in a quiet
cobbled mews with an outstanding reputation
for cuisine and service. Located within five
minutes of the Channel ferries.
32 bedrs SB £65 DB £100 HBS £90 HBD £75
L £15.95 D £22.95
CC: MC Vi Am DC Swi Delt JCB

How to get there: Head for Channel ferry; at lifting
bridge left onto quayside; first road on the left.

Southwest

322 Norfolk Lodge Hotel

★★
1 Flaghead Road, Canford Cliffs, Poole,
Dorset, BH13 7JL
Tel: 01202 708614 Fax: 01202 708614
17 bedrs SB £59 DB £65 HBS £62 HBD £44.50
B £5 L £10 D £12
CC: MC Vi Am DC Swi Delt JCB
🐕🍵💻☎️🅿️🕯️🎋🕻♿️🍴

323 Shah of Persia Hotel

♦♦♦♦✑
173 Longfleet Road, Poole, Dorset, BH15 2HS
Tel: 01202 685346 Fax: 01202 679327
Web: www.eldridge-pope-inns.co.uk
15 bedrs SB £67.50 DB £85 B £7.50 L £6.70
D £7.20
CC: MC Vi Am Swi Delt
🔧🍵🍷💻☎️🕻🅿️🕯️♿️🍴
How to get there: Follow the signs for the A338
to Bournemouth, then the A35 to Poole. The
Shah of Persia is situated on left side of the
crossroads of the A35 and B3068 leading to
Poole town centre.

Porlock, Somerset

324 Oaks Hotel
Blue Ribbon Winner

★★ ♟ ♟
Porlock, Somerset, TA24 8ES
Tel: 01643 862265 Fax: 01643 863131
Email: info@oakshotel.co.uk
Web: www.oakshotel.co.uk
Children minimum age: 8
8 bedrs SB £65 DB £105 HBS £90 HBD £77.50
D £25 CC: MC Vi Swi Delt
🐕🍷🍵💻☎️🅿️🕯️🍴

325 Ship Inn

★
High Street, Porlock, Somerset, TA24 8QD
Tel: 01643 862507 Fax: 01643 863244

326 Andrews on the Weir

♦♦♦♦ ♟ ♟ ♟ ✕
Porlock Weir, Porlock, Somerset, TA24 8PB
Tel: 01643 863300 Fax: 01643 863311
Email: information@andrewsontheweir.co.uk
Web: www.andrewsontheweir.co.uk
Children minimum age: 12.
Closed two weeks in November and January.

Overlooking tiny Porlock Weir harbour, chef-
proprietor Andrew Dixon offers some of the
most exciting cuisine available around the West
Country. Quality is his philosophy, sourcing
fresh, local ingredients.
5 bedrs SB £50 DB £65 L £10.50 D £32.50
CC: MC Vi Am Swi Delt JCB
📠🐕🍷🍵💻🅿️🕯️🍴

Porlock Weir, Somerset

327 Anchor & Ship Hotel

★★★
Porlock Weir, Somerset, TA24 8PB
Tel: 01643 862753 Fax: 01643 862843
Email: anchorhotel@clara.net
Web: www.smoothhound.co.uk/hotels/
anchorho.html

Quiet, comfortable hotel at water's edge of
small picturesque harbour amidst Exmoor's
magnificent scenery and spectacular coastline,
near the north Devon border. Unspoilt rural
England. Superb food, attentive service. Special
offers available.
20 bedrs SB £60 DB £110 HBS £85 HBD £80
B £10.95 D £24.75
CC: MC Vi Am Swi Delt
🔧📠🐕🍵💻☎️🅿️🕯️🎋🕻♿️🛏️🍴
How to get there: M5 to Taunton, A358 Taunton
to Williton, A39 Williton to Porlock, then B3224
to Porlock Harbour.

Postbridge, Devon

328 Lydgate House

 Little Gem

♦♦♦♦♦
Postbridge, Dartmoor, Devon, PL20 6TJ
Tel: 01822 880209 Fax: 01822 880202
Email: lydgatehouse@email.com
Web: www.lydgatehouse.com
Children minimum age: 12

Refurbished Victorian country house set in 36 acres beside the East Dart River in the heart of the Dartmoor National Park, 500 yards from the road and overlooking the valley.
7 bedrs SB £35 DB £76 HBS £52 HBD £55
D £21 CC: MC Vi Swi Delt

How to get there: Between Moreton Hampstead and Princetown on B3212. Turn south just by bridge over East Dart. 400 yards down lane.

Redruth, Cornwall

329 Lyndhurst Guest House

♦♦♦
80 Agar Road, Illogan Highway, Redruth, Cornwall, TR15 3NB
Tel: 01209 215146 Fax: 01209 313625
Email: sales@lyndhurst-guesthouse.net
Web: www.lyndhurst-guesthouse.net
6 bedrs SB £19 DB £38 HBS £25 HBD £52
CC: MC Vi Swi Delt

How to get there: On the A3047, betwen Redruth and Pool by traffic lights at Railway Inn.

330 Tzitzikama Lodge

♦♦♦♦
Rock Road, Rock, Cornwall, PL27 6NP
Tel: 01208 862839
Email: tzitzikama.lodge@btinternet.com
Web: www.cornwall-online.co.uk/
  tzitzikama-lodge
8 bedrs SB £37.50 DB £55
CC: MC Vi Delt

How to get there: Follow the signs to Rock where we are in the centre of the village.

Salcombe, Devon

331 Thurlestone Hotel

★★★★★
Thurlestone, Devon, TQ7 3NN
Tel: 01548 560382 Fax: 01548 561069
Email: enquiries@thurlestone.co.uk
Web: www.thurlestone.co.uk
67 bedrs SB £50 DB £100 HBS £50 HBD £50
B £4 L £3.50 D £28
CC: MC Vi Am Swi

How to get there: At Buckfastleigh (A38) take A384 to Totnes then A381 to Kingsbridge. At roundabout take A379 to Churchston. At second roundabout turn left into B3197, then right into lane to Thurlestone.

332 Bolt Head

★★★
South Sands, Salcombe, Devon, TQ8 8LL
Tel: 01548 843751
Email: info@boltheadhotel.com
Web: www.boltheadhotel.com
Closed November to February
28 bedrs SB £62 DB £124 HBS £72 HBD £72
B £9.50 L £16.50 D £27
CC: MC Vi Am DC Swi Delt

How to get there: From M5, take A38 towards Plymouth. Then take A384/A381 towards Totnes/Kingsbridge. Then follow signs for South Sands and Salcombe.

Southwest

333 Soar Mill Cove Hotel

Blue Ribbon Winner

★★★★ ♖ ♖ ♖

Soar Mill Cove, Salcombe, Devon, TQ7 3DS
Tel: 01548 561566 Fax: 01548 561223
Email: info@makepeacehotels.co.uk
Web: www.makepeacehotels.co.uk
Closed January

21 bedrs SB £85 DB £170 HBS £116 HBD £116
B £15 L £15 D £29
CC: MC Vi Am Swi Delt JCB
How to get there: From Totnes, follow A381 to
Kingsbridge. Turn right towards Salcombe (on
A381). Four miles at Malborough, turn right to
Soar. After church, bear left.

334 Tides Reach Hotel

★★★★ ♖ ♖

South Sands, Salcombe, Devon, TQ8 8LJ
Tel: 01548 843466 Fax: 01548 843954
Email: enquire@tidesreach.com
Web: www.tidesreach.com
Children minimum age: 8
35 bedrs SB £90 DB £150 HBS £100 HBD £90
B £10.25 L £15 D £30
CC: MC Vi Am DC Swi Delt
How to get there: Leave A38 at Buckfastleigh.
Follow A384 to Totnes, then A381 to Salcombe.
Follow sandcastle symbol signs to South Sands.
See advert below left

335 Devon Tor Hotel

◆ ◆ ◆ ◆

Devon Road, Salcombe, Devon, TQ8 8HJ
Tel: 01548 843106 Fax: 01548 842425
Email: malcolmbarlow@devontor.freeserve.co.uk
Web: www.salcombeinformation.co.uk
6 bedrs SB £60 DB £60
CC: None accepted

336 Torre View Hotel

◆ ◆ ◆ ◆

Devon Road, Salcombe, Devon, TQ8 8HJ
Tel: 01548 842633 Fax: 01548 842633
Email: bouttle@torreview.eurobell.co.uk
Web: www.smoothhound.co.uk/hotels/
torreview.html
Children minimum age: 4.
Closed November to February
8 bedrs SB £32 DB £60 HBS £44 HBD £40 D
£14
CC: MC Vi Delt
How to get there: Arrive from Kingsbridge on
A381, continue ahead on Main Road, and
Devon Road branches off left. Hotel is situated
½ mile down Devon Road on left side.

Salisbury, Wiltshire

337 Heritage Hotels – The White Hart

★★★★ ♖

St. John Street, Salisbury, Wiltshire, SP1 2SD
Tel: 0870 4008125 Fax: 01722 412761
68 bedrs SB £105 DB £145 HBS £70 HBD £70
B £11.95 L £7.95 D £22

CC: MC Vi Am DC Swi Delt

How to get there: Take Ring Road, heading towards city centre and cathedral. Proceed into Exeter Street, and join St. John Street. Hotel is at the end of the road on right.

338 Red Lion

★★★

Milford Street, Salisbury, Wiltshire, SP1 2AN
Tel: 01722 323334 Fax: 01722 325756
Email: reception@the-redlion.co.uk
Web: www.the-redlion.co.uk

Traditional 13th-century coaching inn. Famous for its creeper-clad courtyard, charm and antique-filled rooms. An ideal touring base for a wealth of nearby attractions.
51 bedrs SB £97 DB £127 HBS £118 HBD £85 B £5.50 L £11.95 D £19
CC: MC Vi Am DC Swi Delt

339 Travelodge Amesbury (Stonehenge)

Travel Accommodation
A303, Countess Road, Amesbury, Salisbury, Wiltshire, SP4 7AS
Tel: 08700 850 950
Web: www.travelodge.co.uk
48 bedrs B £4.25
CC: MC Vi Am DC Swi Delt

340 Old Sub Deanery

◆◆◆◆◆

18 The Close, Salisbury, Wiltshire, SP1 2EB
Tel: 01722 336331
Email: old-subdeanery@amserve.net
1 bedrs DB £75
CC: None accepted

How to get there: Elegant period house, situated in the Cathedral Close.

341 Cricket Field House Hotel

◆◆◆◆

Wilton Road, Salisbury, Wiltshire, SP2 9NS
Tel: 01722 322595 Fax: 01722 322595
Email: cricketfieldhousehotel@btinternet.com
Web: www.cricketfieldhousehotel.com
Children minimum age: 14
14 bedrs SB £40 DB £55 D £14.95
CC: MC Vi Swi Delt

How to get there: Take A36 west from Salisbury to Wilton.

342 Stratford Lodge

◆◆◆◆

4 Park Lane, Salisbury, Wiltshire, SP1 3NP
Tel: 01722 325177 Fax: 01722 325177
Email: enquiries@stratfordlodge.co.uk
Web: www.stratfordlodge.co.uk
Children minimum age: 5
8 bedrs SB £50 DB £70 HBS £65 HBD £42.50
CC: MC Vi Am Swi Delt JCB

How to get there: A345 towards Salisbury. Right after Alldays shop. Park Lane is immediately on right. Stratford Lodge is second house on right.

343 Websters

◆◆◆◆

11 Hartington Road, Salisbury, Wiltshire, SP2 7LG
Tel: 01722 339779 Fax: 01722 339779
Email: websters.salis@eclipse.co.uk
Web: www.websters-bed-breakfast.com
Children minimum age: 12

Set on the end of a colourful terrace of Victorian houses in a quiet cul-de-sac, with off-street parking. Computer available for guests' use. Easy walk to Cathedral and rail station.
5 bedrs SB £32 DB £42 HBS £46 HBD £33 D £12
CC: MC Vi Swi Delt

How to get there: From city centre west towards Wilton. At St. Pauls roundabout take A360 Devizes road. 400m on left is Hartington Road.

Southwest

344 Byways House

♦♦♦

31 Fowler's Road, City Centre, Salisbury,
Wiltshire, SP1 2QP
Tel: 01722 328364 Fax: 01722 322146
Email: byways@bed-breakfast-salisbury.co.uk
Web: www.bed-breakfast-salisbury.co.uk
Closed Christmas and New Year

Attractive family-run Victorian house close to
cathedral in quiet area of city centre. Large car
park. Traditional English or vegetarian breakfasts.
Ideal for Stonehenge and Wilton House.
23 bedrs SB £33 DB £45
CC: MC Vi Swi Delt
How to get there: Arriving in Salisbury, follow
A36, then follow youth hostel signs until outside
hostel. Fowler's Road is opposite: Byways is a
big Victorian house on the left.

345 Cornmarket Inn

♦♦♦

29-32 Cheesemarket, Salisbury, Wiltshire, P1 1TL
Tel: 01722 412925 Fax: 01722 412927
8 bedrs
CC: MC Vi Am DC Swi Delt
How to get there: In Salisbury town centre.
Located on west side of market square, next to
public library.

346 Hayburn Wyke Guest House

♦♦♦

72 Castle Road, Salisbury, Wiltshire, SP1 3RL
Tel: 01722 412627 Fax: 01722 412627
Email: hayburn.wyke@tinyonline.co.uk
Web: www.hayburnwykeguesthouse.co.uk
7 bedrs SB £29 DB £40
CC: MC Vi Am Swi Delt
How to get there: Situated on Castle Road
(A345), half a mile north of city centre at the
junction with Stratford Road, by Victoria Park.

347 The Junipers

♦♦♦♥

3 Juniper Road, Firsdown, near Salisbury,
Wiltshire, SP5 1SS
Tel: 01980 862330 Fax: 01980 862071
Email: junipers.bb@tesco.net
Web: www.homepages.tesco.net/
~junipers.bb/junipers.bb/
2 bedrs DB £42
CC: None accepted
How to get there: A30 five miles north of
Salisbury, turn right before Little Chef into
Firsdown, then 2nd road on left is Juniper Road.

Saunton, Devon

348 Saunton Sands Hotel

★★★★ ♥♥

Saunton, Devon, EX33 1LQ
Tel: 01271 890212 Fax: 01271 890145
Email: info@sauntonsands.com
Web: www.sauntonsands.com

North Devon's premier 4-star hotel commands
spectacular views, and provides a wealth of
facilities.
92 bedrs SB £68 DB £136 HBS £80 HBD £80
B £10 L £11 D £25
CC: MC Vi Am DC Swi Delt
How to get there: From Barnstaple town centre
take A361 Braunton road. From Braunton follow
the Saunton sign.
See advert on facing page

Sennen, Cornwall

349 Homefields

◆◆◆◆ ✍

Mayon, Sennen, Cornwall, TR19 7AD
Tel: 01736 871418 Fax: 01736 871666
Email: homefields1bandb@aol.com
Web: www.homefieldsguesthouse.co.uk
Closed Christmas

A warm welcome awaits you at our small and friendly guesthouse overlooking Cape Cornwall. Close to beaches, with sea views. Good food, and pets are welcome.
5 bedrs SB £20.25 DB £45 CC: MC Vi Swi Delt
&🖙🐾⊗⛾🖵🄿✂🛏🕊👬
How to get there: Follow A30 from Penzance for eight miles to village of Sennen. Homefields is opposite the Post Office.

Sennen Cove, Cornwall

350 Old Success Inn

★★

Sennen Cove, Cornwall, TR19 7DG
Tel: 01736 871232 Fax: 01736 788354

Shaftesbury, Dorset

351 Royal Chase

★★★★ ℞ ℞

Salisbury Road, Shaftesbury, Dorset, SP7 8DB
Tel: 01747 853355 Fax: 01747 851969
Email: royalchasehotel@btinternet.com
Web: www.theroyalchasehotel.co.uk
33 bedrs SB £93 DB £117 HBS £114
HBD £79.50 B £8.50 L £5.95 D £21
CC: MC Vi Am DC Swi Delt
⟁&🐾⊗⛾🖵☎🄿❀✂🎯🕊👬👬♨
How to get there: On the outskirts of Shaftesbury on the roundabout joining the A30 and A350 Salisbury and Blandford roads.

352 Grove Arms Inn

◆◆◆◆ ✍

Ludwell, near Shaftesbury, Dorset, SP7 9ND
Tel: 01747 828328 Fax: 01747 828960
Email: grovearms@talk21.com
Web: www.grovearms.co.uk

Award-winning Grade II listed thatched property, refurbished in 1999 to high standard. Surrounded by beautiful countryside for walks and picturesque scenery. Good food and friendly welcome.
6 bedrs CC: MC Vi Swi
⊗⛾🖵🄿👬
How to get there: On main A30 Shaftesbury to Salisbury road.

Southwest

353 Grove House Hotel

◆◆◆◆ ⓡ ✕

Ludwell, Shaftesbury, Dorset, SP7 9ND
Tel: 01747 828365 Fax: 01747 828365

Friendly family-run guest house in village
location two miles east of Shaftesbury. Large
beautiful garden in peaceful countryside. All
rooms en-suite.
11 bedrs SB £31.50 DB £63
CC: MC Vi Swi Delt
❦⊘⌨🅿️❄️👕
How to get there: On A30 towards Salisbury.

Shepton Mallet, Somerset

354 Shrubbery Hotel

★★ⓡⓡ

17 Commercial Road, Shepton Mallet,
Somerset, BA4 5BU
Tel: 01749 346671 Fax: 01749 346581
11 bedrs
CC: MC Vi Am DC Swi Delt
📠❦⊘⌨☎️📞🅿️✕🎬🍴❄️🏓👕
How to get there: Situated in the town centre,
off A37 on main A371, next to police station.

355 Belfield House

◆◆◆ ✕

34 Charlton Road, Shepton Mallet,
Somerset, BA4 5PA
Tel: 01749 344353 Fax: 01749 344353
Email: andrea@belfield-house.co.uk
Web: www.belfield-house.co.uk
6 bedrs SB £19 DB £42
CC: MC Vi Swi Delt
❦⊘⌨🅿️✕🍴❄️
How to get there: On main A361 Wells/Frome
Road. Just 200 yards from main A37 junction,
opposite leisure centre.

356 43 Maesdown Road

◆◆ ✆

Evercreech, Shepton Mallet, Somerset, BA4 6LE
Tel: 01749 830721
Children minimum age: 5
3 bedrs SB £18 DB £35
CC: None accepted
♿🐾⊘⌨🅿️✕
How to get there: From Bath & West
Showground on A37, turn left, then first right for
village, one mile. First left after village name sign.

Sherborne, Dorset

357 Eastbury Hotel

★★★ⓡⓡ

Long Street, Sherborne, Dorset, DT9 3BY
Tel: 01935 813131 Fax: 01935 817296
Email: eastbury.sherbourne@virgin.net
Closed 1-7 January
15 bedrs SB £55 DB £91 HBS £71.25
HBD £61.50 B £10.95 L £3.50 D £17.95
CC: MC Vi Am Swi Delt
🔥📠⊛⊘⌨☎️🅿️✕🎬🍴❄️🏓👕
How to get there: On A30 travelling east, turn
right into North road. At crossroads straight
over; turn left into Long Street; Eastbury on the
right.

358 The Half Moon

◆◆◆◆ ✕

Half Moon Street, Sherbourne, Dorset, DT9 6LP
Tel: 01935 812017 Fax: 01935 815295
16 bedrs SB £54 DB £69
CC: MC Vi Am Swi Delt
⊘⌨☎️👕

359 Heritage Hotels – The Sherborne

✤

Horsecastles Lane, Sherborne, Dorset, DT9 6BB
Tel: 01935 813191 Fax: 01935 816493
Web: www.forte-heritage.com
59 bedrs
CC: MC Vi Am DC Swi Delt
🔥❦⊛⊘⌨☎️🅿️✕🍴🏓👕

Shipham, Somerset

360 Daneswood House Hotel

★★★★ ® ® ®

Cuck Hill, Shipham, Somerset, BS25 1RD
Tel: 01934 843145 Fax: 01934 843824
Email: info@daneswoodhotel.co.uk
Web: www.daneswoodhotel.co.uk
17 bedrs SB £89.50 DB £105.50 B £8.95
L £19.95 D £29.95
CC: MC Vi Am DC Swi

How to get there: One mile inland off A38
Bridgwater-Bristol road, at far side of village on
left.

Sidmouth, Devon

361 Belmont Hotel

★★★★★ ®

The Esplanade, Sidmouth, Devon, EX10 8RX
Tel: 01395 512555 Fax: 01395 579101
Email: info@belmont-hotel.co.uk
Web: www.brend-hotels.co.uk

Located on Sidmouth's famous esplanade, the
Belmont offers all the amenities you would
expect from a 4-star hotel, while retaining the
charm and character of its origin.
50 bedrs SB £62 DB £114 HBS £79 HBD £72
B £13.50 L £15 D £25
CC: MC Vi Am DC Swi Delt

How to get there: On Sidmouth seafront.
See advert on following page

362 Riviera

★★★★ ® ® ®
The Esplanade, Sidmouth, Devon, EX10 8AY
Tel: 01395 515201 Fax: 01395 577775
Email: enquiries@hotelriviera.co.uk
Web: www.hotelriviera.co.uk

A majestic Regency hotel, situated on the
Esplanade with panoramic sea views and a
splendid terrace overlooking Lyme Bay.
27 bedrs SB £79 DB £69 HBS £90 HBD £80
B £9.50 L £18 D £28
CC: MC Vi Am DC Swi

How to get there: M5 from London Exit 30
follow A3052. Hotel Riviera is situated in centre
of the Esplanade.
See advert on following page

363 Victoria Hotel

★★★★ ®
The Esplanade, Sidmouth, Devon, EX10 8RY
Tel: 01395 512651 Fax: 01395 579154
Email: info@victoriahotel.co.uk
Web: www.brend-hotels.co.uk

Overlooking the esplanade and the sea,
magnificent rooms, renowned cuisine and
superb leisure facilities make the Victoria one of
England's finest hotels.
61 bedrs SB £73 DB £134 HBS £88 HBD £82
B £12.50 L £16 D £27.50
CC: MC Vi Am DC Swi Delt

How to get there: Located on Sidmouth
seafront.
See advert on following page

Southwest

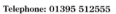

364 Bedford Hotel

★★★

The Esplanade, Sidmouth, Devon, EX10 8NR
Tel: 01395 513047 Fax: 01395 578563
Closed February
36 bedrs SB £60 DB £120 HBS £64 HBD £64
B £9.95 L £12.50 D £19.95
CC: MC Vi Swi Delt

How to get there: Centrally situated on
Sidmouth seafront
See advert right

365 Royal Glen Hotel

★★★

Glen Road, Sidmouth, Devon, EX10 8RW
Tel: 01395 513221 Fax: 01395 514922
Email: sidmouthroyalglen.hotel@virgin.net
Web: www.royalglenhotel.co.uk

In a secluded position close to the sea front,
this one-time royal residence will appeal to
those seeking old-world charm, comfort, good
catering and personal service.
32 bedrs SB £31 DB £62 HBS £46 HBD £46
B £7 D £16 CC: MC Vi Am Swi Delt

How to get there: Follow signs to seafront. Turn
right onto Esplanade. Turn right into your road
at the end of the Promenade.

366 Salcombe Hill House Hotel

★★★

Beatlands Road, Sidmouth, Devon, EX10 8JQ
Tel: 01395 514697 Fax: 01395 578310

367 Westcliff Hotel

★★★★

Manor Road, Sidmouth, Devon, EX10 8RU
Tel: 01395 513252 Fax: 01395 578203
Email: stay@westcliffhotel.co.uk
Web: www.westcliffhotel.co.uk
Children minimum age: 6.
Closed November to March
40 bedrs SB £68 DB £121.80 HBS £80.85
HBD £73.50 B £11.50 L £4.50 D £25
CC: MC Vi Swi Delt

How to get there: Turn right at Sidmouth seafront,
then right into Manor Road; first right into hotel.
See advert on previous page

368 Royal York & Faulkner Hotel

★★

Esplanade, Sidmouth, Devon, EX10 8AZ
Tel: 0800 220714 Fax: 01395 577472
Email: yorkhotel@eclipse.co.uk
Web: www.royalyorkhotel.net
Closed January
70 bedrs SB £30 DB £60 HBS £38 HBD £76
B £7 L £4.95 D £15 CC: MC Vi Swi Delt

How to get there: Hotel is situated in the centre
of Sidmouth's Esplanade.

369 Groveside

♦♦♦

Vicarage Road, Sidmouth, Devon, EX10 8UQ
Tel: 01395 513406
Email: groveside.sidmouth@virgin.net
Web: www.eastdevon.net/groveside
10 bedrs SB £24 DB £48
CC: None accepted

How to get there: From M5 or A303 follow signs
to Honiton, then signs to Sidmouth. Hotel is just
on the edge of town, to left on the main road.

South Cerney, Gloucestershire

370 The Eliot Arms Hotel

♦♦♦♦

Clarks Hay, South Cerney, Cirencester,
Gloucestershire, GL7 5UA
Tel: 01285 860215 Fax: 01285 861121
Email: eliotarms.cirencester
          @eldridge-pope.co.uk
11 bedrs SB £50 DB £60 L £4.95 D £7.95
CC: MC Vi Am Swi Delt

How to get there: From London M4 J15 follow
signs to Swindon A419, 2nd exit to Cirencester,
at Little Chef take 2nd exit to Spine Road jct.
Branch left and at roundabout take 1st exit for
B4696, then turn right for Watermark Leisure
Club. Hotel on left hand side.

South Molton, Devon

371 High Bullen Hotel

★★★★

Chittlehamholt, Devon, EX37 9HD
Tel: 01769 540561 Fax: 01769 540492
Email: info@highbullen.co.uk
Web: www.highbullen.co.uk
40 bedrs SB £57.50 DB £47.50 HBS £75
HBD £70 B £2.50 L £5.50 D £25
CC: MC Vi Swi Delt

How to get there: Leave M5 at Junction 27.
Take A361 to South Molton. Take B3226. After
five miles turn right up hill to Chittlehamholt.
High Bullen is 1/2 miles beyond village, on left.

St. Agnes, Cornwall

372 Rose-in-Vale Country House Hotel

★★★★

Mithian, St. Agnes, Cornwall, TR5 0QD
Tel: 01872 552202 Fax: 01872 552700
Email: reception@rose-in-vale-hotel.co.uk
Web: www.rose-in-vale-hotel.co.uk
Closed January and February
18 bedrs SB £57.50 DB £99 HBS £72.50
HBD £64.50 B £9.50 L £3.50 D £24.95
CC: MC Vi Swi Delt

373 Rosemundy House Hotel

★★

8 Rosemundy, St. Agnes, Cornwall, TR5 0UF
Tel: 01872 552101 Fax: 01872 554000
Email: info@rosemundy.co.uk
Web: www.rosemundy.co.uk
44 bedrs CC: MC Vi Swi Delt

How to get there: M5 and A38, left to
Oakhampton / Launceston A30 until Chiverton
roundabout (Little Chef), right for St. Agnes
(B3277). Right turn down Rosemundy Hill.

374 Penkerris

Penwinnick Road, St. Agnes, Cornwall, TR5 0PA
Tel: 01872 552262 Fax: 01872 552262
Email: info@penkerris.co.uk
Web: www.penkerris.co.uk

Creeper-clad Edwardian residence with garden in unspoilt Cornish village. A home-from-home with real food and comfortable rooms. Licensed. Ample parking. Cliff walks and beaches nearby.
9 bedrs SB £17.50 DB £30.50 HBS £27.50 HBD £50 D £10 CC: MC Vi Am Delt
How to get there: From roundabout at Chivertoncross on A30, take B3277 to St. Agnes itself. Penkerris is first on right after village sign and 30mph limit sign.

St. Austell, Cornwall

375 Carlyon Bay Hotel

★★★★ ⊕ ⊕
Sea Road, Carlyon Bay, St. Austell,
Cornwall, PL25 3RD
Tel: 01726 812304 Fax: 01726 814938
Email: info@carlyonbay.co.uk
Web: www.brend-hotels.co.uk

A superb hotel in a cliff-top location offering spectacular views. The hotel's 18-hole golf course runs along the clifftop adjacent to the hotel.

73 bedrs SB £74 DB £150 HBS £86 HBD £87
B £10.50 L £12 D £24
CC: MC Vi Am DC Swi Delt
See advert below

376 Cliff Head Hotel

★★★ ⊕
Sea Road, Carlyon Bay, St. Austell,
Cornwall, PL25 3RB
Tel: 01726 812345 Fax: 01726 815511
Email: cliffheadhotel@btconnect.com
Web: www.cornishriviera.co.uk/cliffhead
60 bedrs SB £45 DB £75 HBS £62 HBD £105
B £7.50 L £7.95 D £12.95
CC: MC Vi Am DC Swi Delt
How to get there: From Plymouth, take A390 to Dobwalls, then to St. Austell. Just before entering St. Austell, follow signs to Carlyon Bay.

377 The Porth Avallen Hotel

★★★ ⊕
Sea Road, Carlyon Bay, St. Austell,
Cornwall, PL25 3SG
Tel: 01726 812802 Fax: 01726 817097

Southwest

378 Boscundle Manor

Blue Ribbon Winner

★★★ ♖ ♖

Tregrehan, St. Austell, Cornwall, PL25 3RL
Tel: 01726 813557 Fax: 01726 814997
Email: stay@boscundlemanor.co.uk
Web: www.boscundlemanor.co.uk
Closed November to March

A small country house hotel with luxurious accommodation, extensive facilities including indoor and outdoor swimming pools, woodland walks and a golf practice area. Beautifully prepared fresh food with oustanding wine list.
12 bedrs SB £70 DB £120 HBS £90 HBD £80 D £20
CC: MC Vi Am Swi Delt JCB

How to get there: Two miles east of St. Austell, off A390 on road signposted 'Tregrehan'.

St. Ives, Cornwall

379 Chy-an-albany Hotel

★★★

Albany Terrace, St. Ives, Cornwall, TR26 2BS
Tel: 01736 796759 Fax: 01736 795584
Email: info@chyanalbanyhotel.com
Web: www.chynalbanyhotl.co.uk
40 bedrs SB £39 DB £78 HBS £51 HBD £102
B £7.50 D £14.95 CC: MC Vi Swi Delt

How to get there: A3074 road to St. Ives, through Carbis Bay, down Tregenna Hill past car sales; left hand fork at bottom of hill.

380 Porthminster

★★★

The Terrace, St. Ives, Cornwall, TR26 2BN
Tel: 01736 795221 Fax: 01736 797043
Email: reception@porthminster-hotel.co.uk
Web: www.porthminster-hotel.co.uk
Closed early January

43 bedrs SB £44 DB £88 HBS £59 HBD £118
B £9 L £8 D £16 CC: MC Vi Am DC Swi Delt

How to get there: Porthminster Hotel is on A3074.

381 Chy-An-Dour Hotel

★★

Trelyon Avenue, St. Ives, Cornwall, TR26 2AD
Tel: 01736 796436 Fax: 01736 795772
Email: chyndour@aol.com
Web: www.connexions.co.uk/chyandourhotel
23 bedrs SB £61 DB £70 HBS £77 HBD £51
B £6 D £16
CC: MC Vi Swi Delt

How to get there: From A30, take A3074 towards St. Ives. Hotel is on right 50m past Jet filling station.

382 Dean Court Hotel

♦♦♦♦ ♈

Trelyon Avenue, St. Ives, Cornwall, TR26 2AD
Tel: 01736 796023 Fax: 01736 796233
Email: deancourt@amserve.net
Children minimum age: 14
12 bedrs SB £37.50 DB £75 HBS £45 HBD £45
D £10
CC: MC Vi DC Swi Delt JCB

How to get there: From A30 take A3074 through Carbis Bay to St. Ives. Dean Court is located on the right side of Trelyon Avenue.

383 Longships Hotel

♦♦♦♦

Talland Road, St. Ives, Cornwall, TR26 2DF
Tel: 01736 798180 Fax: 01736 798180
25 bedrs SB £30 DB £60 HBS £36 HBD £72 B £5
D £10.50
CC: MC Vi Swi Delt

How to get there: Take left fork at Portminster Hotel. Follow Talland Area Accommodation sign. Hotel is first in Talland Road.

384 Regent Hotel

♦♦♦♦ ♓ ♈

Fern Lea Terrace, St. Ives, Cornwall, TR26 2BH
Tel: 01736 796195 Fax: 01736 794641
Email: enquiries@regenthotel.com
Web: www.regenthotel.com
9 bedrs SB £29.75 DB £63
CC: MC Vi Am DC Swi Delt JCB

385 Trewinnard

♦ ♦ ♦ ♦ ☕ ✗

4 Parc Avenue, St. Ives, Cornwall, TR26 2DN
Tel: 01736 794168 Fax: 01736 798161
Email: trewinnard@cwcom.net
Web: trewinnard-hotel-stives.co.uk
Children minimum age: 6.
Closed November to March
7 bedrs SB £23 DB £56
CC: MC Vi Swi Delt JCB
🛏 ⊗ ☺ 🖵 P ✂ ✦ 🎖

How to get there: Take A3074 to St. Ives. Turn left at Natwest Bank. Turn left at mini-roundabout, go past car park, and house is 150m on right.

St. Mawes, Cornwall

386 Idle Rocks Hotel

★ ★ ★ ☕ ☕

Harbourside, St. Mawes, Cornwall, TR2 5AN
Tel: 01326 270771 Fax: 01326 270062
Email: idlerocks@richardsonhotels.co.uk
Web: www.richardsonhotels.co.uk
28 bedrs CC: MC Vi Am Swi Delt
🛏 🐾 ⊗ ☺ 🖵 ☎ P ⊛ ✂ ✦ ⋔ ✦ ⠿ 🎖

How to get there: M5 onto A30, then onto A39, A390 and A3078. Hotel first on left in village.

387 Rosevine Hotel

Blue Ribbon Winner

★ ★ ★ ☕ ☕ ☕

Rosevine, Porthscatho, St. Mawes, Truro, Cornwall, TR2 5EW
Tel: 01872 580206 Fax: 01872 580230
Email: info@rosevine.co.uk
Web: www.rosevine.co.uk
Closed December to January, open Christmas only

17 bedrs SB £105 DB £140 HBS £135
HBD £190 B £8 L £8 D £28

CC: MC Vi Am Swi Delt
♿ 🐾 ⊗ ☺ 🖵 ☎ P ✂ ✦ ⋔ ✦ 🎖 ⠿ ⓔ ⎙

How to get there: When approaching St. Mawes on A3078, turn right at sign for Rosevine Hotel and Porthcurnic beach.

Stoke Gabriel, Devon

388 Gabriel Court Hotel

★ ★ ★ ☕

Stoke Hill, Stoke Gabriel, near Totnes, Devon, TQ9 6SF
Tel: 01803 782206 Fax: 01803 782333
Email: obeacom@aol.com
Web: www.gabrielcourthotel.co.uk
19 bedrs
CC: MC Vi Am DC Swi Delt
🐾 ☺ 🖵 ☎ 📞 P ⊛ ✂ ✦ ⋔ ✦ ⠿ 🎖 ⚲ ⚘

How to get there: Turn off A385 (between Totnes and Paignton) at Parkers Arms pub. Proceed towards Stoke Gabriel. On entering village, stay left and you will reach hotel.

Stourton, Wiltshire

389 Spread Eagle Inn

♦ ♦ ♦ ♦ ☕ ✗ ☕

Stourhead, Stourton, near Warminster, Wiltshire, BA12 6QE
Tel: 01747 840587 Fax: 01747 840954
5 bedrs SB £60 DB £85 B £5.95 L £5.95 D £15.95
CC: MC Vi Am DC Swi Delt JCB
🐾 ⊗ ☺ 🖵 ☎ P ✂ ✦ ⋔ ✦ ⠿ 🎖

Street, Somerset

390 The Wessex

★ ★ ★

High Street, Street, Somerset, BA16 0EF
Tel: 01458 443383 Fax: 01458 446589
Email: wessex@hotel-street.freeserve.co.uk
Web: www.wessexhotel.com
50 bedrs SB £56.50 DB £73 HBS £66.50
HBD £83 B £7.50 L £8.95 D £9.95
CC: MC Vi Am DC Swi
♿ ⠿ 🐾 ⊗ ☺ 🖵 ☎ P ⊛ ✂ ✦ ✦ ⠿ 🎖

How to get there: M5, Junction 23 to Bridgewater, Glastonbury and Street. From A303 follow B3151 to Street. Nearest railway station Castle Cary.

Southwest

Pines Hotel rac ★★★

Situated at the secluded end of Swanage Bay with marvellous panoramic sea views and private steps down to the beach. Long established reputation for our service and cuisine. Undoubtedly one of the finest views on the South Coast.

Burlington Road, Swanage,
Dorset BH19 1LT
Tel: 01929 425211   Fax: 01929 422075
reservations@pineshotel.co.uk
www.pineshotel.co.uk

391 The Birches

♦♦♦♦ ✹ ⚘

13 Housman Road, Street, Somerset, BA16 0SD
Tel: 01458 442902
Email: askins@ukonline.co.uk
Closed November to February
2 bedrs SB £30 DB £50 CC: None accepted

How to get there: From A39: B3151, 2nd right after Millfield traffic lights, first left. From A303: B3151, first left after 30 mph sign, then first right.

392 The Bear Inn

♦♦♦

High Street, Street, Somerset, BA16 0EF
Tel: 01458 442021 Fax: 01458 840007
25 bedrs B £4.25 L £3.30 D £3.30
CC: MC Vi Am Swi Delt

How to get there: We are two miles from Glastonbury just off the A39.

It's easier online

For all your motoring and travel needs, www.rac.co.uk

Swanage, Dorset

393 Pines Hotel

★★★ ℞

Burlington Road, Swanage, Dorset, BH19 1LT
Tel: 01929 425211 Fax: 01929 422075
Email: reservations@pineshotel.co.uk
Web: www.pineshotel.co.uk
48 bedrs SB £47 DB £94 HBS £59.50 HBD £119
B £10 L £13.50 D £20.50
CC: MC Vi Swi Delt JCB

How to get there: At seafront, left then 2nd right to end of road.
See advert on following page

394 Purbeck House Hotel

★★★

91 High Street, Swanage, Dorset, BH19 2LZ
Tel: 01929 422872 Fax: 01929 421194
Email: purbeckhouse@easynet.co.uk
Web: www.purbeckhousehotel.co.uk
Children minimum age: 2
18 bedrs SB £49 DB £88 HBS £64 HBD £67
B £7.95 L £4 D £21.95
CC: MC Vi Am DC Swi Delt

How to get there: Arrive in Swanage via Ferry. Head for town centre. Turn right at White Swan public house. Hotel on left.

395 Havenhurst

★★

3 Cranborne Road, Swanage, Dorset, BH19 1EA
Tel: 01929 424224 Fax: 01929 422173
17 bedrs SB £23.50 DB £47 HBS £42 HBD £42
B £5.50 L £9.50 D £16
CC: MC Vi Swi Delt

How to get there: Take A351 to Swanage along Victoria Avenue. Turn right at traffic lights. First right into Cranborne Road.

See the road ahead

Just dial 1740* from any mobile phone to get up-to-the-minute RAC traffic information on motorways and major A roads. Try it now! *Calls to 1740 are charged at premium rate.

396 The Castleton Hotel

Little Gem

◆ ◆ ◆ ◆

1 Highcliffe Road, Swanage, Dorset, BH19 1LW
Tel: 01929 423972 Fax: 01929 422901
Children minimum age: 8
Family run non-smoking hotel situated 150
yards from Swanage's Beach. All rooms en-
suite and decorated to high standard. Please
telephone for brochure and tariff.
9 bedrs SB £35 DB £70 HBS £53 HBD £52.50
D £17.95
CC: MC Vi DC Swi Delt
How to get there: A351 via Wareham to Swanage,
left at seafront. Follow road up hill towards
Studland. First road on right off of seafront.

397 Sandringham Hotel

◆ ◆ ◆

20 Durlston Road, Swanage,
Dorset, BH19 2HX
Tel: 01929 423076 Fax: 01929 423076
Email: silk@sandhot.fsnet.co.uk
11 bedrs SB £29 DB £58 HBS £41 HBD £41
B £6 D £12
CC: MC Vi Swi Delt JCB
How to get there: On entering Swanage, follow
signs to Durlston Country Park.

Swindon, Wiltshire

398 Blunsdon House Hotel

★ ★ ★ ★
The Ridge, Blunsdon, Swindon,
Wiltshire, SN26 7AS
Tel: 01793 721701 Fax: 01793 720625
Email: info@blunsdonhouse.co.uk
Web: www.blunsdonhouse.co.uk

Set in private grounds with stunning views of
the Cotswolds. Extensive leisure facilities
including indoor pool, two gyms, tennis and
squash courts, steam & sauna rooms, 9-hole
par-3 golf course and 'Secrets' beauty therapy
salon. Two restaurants, three bars. Discover
Blunsdon House Hospitality.
120 bedrs SB £98 DB £126.50 HBS £67.50
HBD £67.50 B £10 L £15 D £20
CC: MC Vi Am DC Swi Delt
How to get there: Leave M4 at Junction 15. take
A419 to Cirencester. After seven miles you
reach Broad Blunsdon. 200 yards past traffic
lights turn right into village.

399 Swindon Marriott Hotel

★ ★ ★ ★
Pipers Way, Swindon, Wiltshire, SN3 1SH
Tel: 01793 512121 Fax: 01793 513114
Email: reservations.swindon
        @marriotthotels.co.uk
Web: www.marriotthotels.com/swidt
153 bedrs B £13 L £15 D £17
CC: MC Vi Am DC Swi Delt

400 Chiseldon House Hotel

★ ★ ★
New Road, Chiseldon, Swindon,
Wiltshire, SN4 0NE
Tel: 01793 741010 Fax: 01793 741059
Email: chishoho@hotmail.com
Web: www.chiseldonhousehotel.co.uk
21 bedrs SB £80 DB £100 HBS £100 HBD £70
B £9 L £15 D £25 CC: MC Vi Am DC Swi Delt
How to get there: M4 J15, A346 south. ¾ of a
mile, right into New Road. Hotel is 300 yards on
the right.

Southwest

Stanton House Hotel

A Cotswold stone country house hotel set in the tranquil surroundings of beautiful Wiltshire countryside. The hotel has the unusual factor of having a Japanese restaurant and food shop. The ideal venue for a conference, wedding or simply just to get away from it all for a weekend break with a difference.

The Avenue, Stanton, Fitzwarren, Swindon, Wiltshire SN6 7SD
Tel: 01793 861777   Fax: 01793 861857
reception @stantonhouse.co.uk
www.stantonhouse.co.uk

401 Marsh Farm Hotel

★★★★ ® ®
Coped Hall, Wootton Bassett, Swindon, Wiltshire, SN4 8ER
Tel: 01793 848044 Fax: 01793 851528
Email: marshfarmhotel@btconnect.com
Web: www.marshfarmhotel.co.uk
Closed December 26 – 30

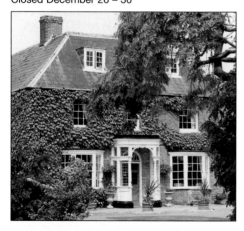

This beautiful grade two listed Victorian farm house has been tastefully restored and converted into a luxury country hotel. Reid's

Conservatory Restaurant, offers excellent cuisine and fine wines.
38 bedrs SB £100 DB £120 B £9.50 L £14.50 D £22.50 CC: MC Vi Am DC Swi Delt
How to get there: Leave M4 at J-16. Take A3102 towards Wootton Bassett, at 2nd roundabout turn right. Hotel is immediately on your left.

402 Stanton House Hotel

★★★ ®
The Avenue, Stanton, Fitzwarren, Swindon, Wiltshire, SN6 7SD
Tel: 01793 861777 Fax: 01793 861857
Email: reception@stantonhouse.co.uk
Web: www.stantonhouse.co.uk
86 bedrs SB £69 DB £109 B £13 L £15 D £15
CC: MC Vi Am DC Swi Delt JCB
How to get there: Exit J15 M4 northbound A419; at Honda, turn off to Highworth. After third roundabout, take left turning to Stanton Fitzwarren.
See advert left

403 The Pear Tree at Purton

Blue Ribbon Winner

★★★ ® ® ®
Church End, Purton, Swindon, Wiltshire, SN5 4ED
Tel: 01793 772100 Fax: 01793 772369
Email: relax@peartreepurton.co.uk
Web: www.peartreepurton.co.uk
Closed 26/12/02 to 30/12/02

This personally run Cotswold stone former vicarage is set in 7½ acres and surrounded on all sides by rolling Wiltshire farmland. Ideal for visiting the Cotswolds, Bath, Oxford and Swindon.
18 bedrs SB £110 DB £120 HBS £170 HBD £90 B £8.50 L £15.50 D £31.50
CC: MC Vi Am DC Swi Delt JCB
How to get there: From M4 J16 follow signs to Purton. At Spar grocers turn right. Hotel is ½ mile on left.

404 Villiers Inn

★★★

Moormead Road, Wroughton, Swindon,
Wiltshire, SN4 9BY
Tel: 01793 814744 Fax: 01793 814119
Email: hotels@villiersinn.co.uk
Web: www.villiersinn.co.uk
33 bedrs SB £79 DB £89 B £5 L £5 D £10
CC: MC Vi Am DC Swi Delt
How to get there: Leave M4 at Junction 15.
Take A346 to Chisledon, turn right onto B4005
towards Wroughton. Take A4361 to Swindon.
Hotel 100m on right.

405 Fir Tree Lodge

◆ ◆ ◆

17 Highworth Road, Stratton St. Margaret,
Swindon, Wiltshire, SN3 4QL
Tel: 01793 822372 Fax: 01793 822372
11 bedrs
CC: None accepted
How to get there: Opposite Rat Trap public
house. Follow 419 until A361 Highworth/Burford
turn. Turn at roundabout, approximately 100m
on right.

406 Fusion

24 High Street, Oldtown, Swindon,
Wiltshire, SN1 3EP
Tel: 01793 480083 Fax: 01793 431915
Closed Christmas Day, Boxing Day
19 bedrs DB £80 B £5 L £3 D £15
CC: MC Vi Am DC Swi Delt
How to get there: Off M4 junction 15 to old
town marked Bell Hotel.

Taunton, Somerset

407 Bindon Country House
Blue Ribbon Winner

★★★ 🏵 🏵 🏵
Langford Budville, Wellington,
Somerset, TA21 0RU
Tel: 01823 4000 70 Fax: 01823 4000 71
Email: stay@bindon.com
Web: www.bindon.com

Nestled amongst seven acres of stunning formal
and woodland gardens there is at once a sense
of calm... "Je trouve bien" ("I find well") is the
motto of the house.
12 bedrs SB £85 DB £105 HBD £75 B £10
L £12.95 D £29.95
CC: MC Vi Am DC Swi Delt
How to get there: Exit M5 at Junction 26, take
A38 to Wellington. Take B3187 to Langford
Budville, then follow hotel signs.

408 Castle Hotel
Gold Ribbon Winner

★★★★ 🏵 🏵 🏵 🏵
Castle Green, Taunton, Somerset, TA1 1NF
Tel: 01823 272671 Fax: 01823 336066
Email: reception@the-castle-hotel.com
Web: www.the-castle-hotel.com

Welcoming travellers to Somerset's county town
for 800 years, the Castle Hotel offers rare
standards of comfort and service and a restaurant
now rated one of the best in the country.
44 bedrs SB £110 DB £165 B £12.50 L £18
D £30
CC: MC Vi Am DC Swi Delt
How to get there: From M5, take Junction 25
and follow signs to town centre, then brown
signs to Castle Hotel.

Southwest

409 Holiday Inn M5 Junction 25

★★★

Deane Gate Avenue, Taunton, Somerset, TA1 2UA
Tel: 0870 400 9080 Fax: 01823 332266
Web: www.holiday-inn.com
99 bedrs SB £110.95 DB £122.90 HBS £125.95
HBD £76.45 B £11.95 L £12 D £15
CC: MC Vi Am DC Swi Delt JCB

How to get there: Exit J25 M5; follow signs
Blackbroom Business Park; hotel is on the right.

410 The Mount Somerset Hotel

★★★★

Lower Henlade, Taunton, Somerset, TA3 5NB
Tel: 01823 442500 Fax: 01823 442900
Email: info@mountsomersethotel.co.uk
Web: www.mountsomersethotel.com
11 bedrs SB £95 DB £155 HBS £120 HBD £205
B £9.95 L £19.95 D £25.95
CC: MC Vi Am Swi Delt

How to get there: Junction 25, M5, take A358
for Chard, turn right to Stoke St. Mary, left at T-
junction. Hotel on right.

411 Corner House Hotel

★★

Park Street, Taunton, Somerset, TA1 4DQ
Tel: 01823 284683 Fax: 01823 323464
Email: res@corner-house.co.uk
Web: www.corner-house.co.uk

THE CORNER HOUSE

29 bedrs SB £42 DB £62 B £4.95 L £7.95
D £19.95
CC: MC Vi Am Swi Delt

How to get there: On the corner of the A38
Wellington Road and Park Street.

See the road ahead

Just dial 1740* from any mobile
phone to get up-to-the-minute
RAC traffic information on
motorways and major A roads.
Try it now! *Calls to 1740 are charged
at premium rate.

412 Farthings Hotel and Restaurant

★★★

Hatch Beauchamp, Taunton, Somerset, TA3 6SG
Tel: 01823 480664 Fax: 01823 481118
Email: farthings1@aol.com
Web: www.farthingshotel.com

Relaxing Georgian house owned and run by
Stephen (your chef) and Hilary (your host)
Murphy. Log fires in winter, tranquil gardens in
summer, and always a wonderful dinner.
10 bedrs SB £64 DB £94 D £23.50
CC: MC Vi Am Swi Delt

How to get there: Exit J25 M5, A358 towards
Ilminster. Go 3¹/₂ miles, then turn left at sign for
Hatch Beauchmp. Farthings Hotel is one mile
from turn.

413 Travelodge Taunton

Travel Accommodation
Hankeridge Way, Riverside, Taunton,
Somerset, PA1 2LR
Tel: 08700 850 950
Web: www.travelodge.co.uk
48 bedrs B £4.25
CC: MC Vi Am DC Swi Delt

414 Elm Villa

♦♦♦♦♦

Staplegrove Road, Taunton, Somerset, TA2 6AJ
Tel: 01823 336165
Email: ferguson@elmvilla10.freeserve.co.uk
2 bedrs SB £35 DB £52
CC: None accepted

How to get there: From Taunton centre, house is
on A3027 near junction with A358 Minehead
road.

415 Meryan House Hotel

♦♦♦♦ ⓇⓇ ⁂

Bishops Hull, Taunton, Somerset, TA1 5EG
Tel: 01823 337445 Fax: 01823 322355
Email: meryanhouse@mywebpage.net
Web: www.mywebpage.net/meryanhouse
12 bedrs SB £49 DB £60 HBS £67 HBD £45
B £7 D £16 CC: MC Vi Swi Delt JCB

🔌🖨🐾🕮🖳🖵☎📞🅿📷🛁🎦🗚🏨🍴

How to get there: Take A38 out of Taunton for
about one mile, after crematorium turn right into
Bishops Hull Road. Hotel approximately 600
yards.

416 Northam Mill
Little Gem

♦♦♦♦ Ⓡ ⁂ 🍷

Water Lane, Stogumber, Taunton,
West Somerset, TA4 3TT
Tel: 01984 656916 Fax: 01984 656144
Email: bmsspicer@aol.com
Web: www.northam-mill.co.uk

Hidden for 300 years...Old Mill House four-acre
garden and river. Nestling in hidden quiet valley
between Quantock and Brendon Hills in West
Somerset. Idyllic. Five course daily-changing
menu. Own eggs, vegetables, bread, preserves.
Beamed library. Individually furnished, all ensuite. Luxury furnished garden suite.
6 bedrs SB £25.50 DB £51 HBS £42.85
HBD £30.60 B £9.50 D £22.50
CC: MC Vi Am Swi Delt

🔌🖨🐾🕮🖳🖵☎📷🗚🏨

How to get there: From Taunton on A358
towards Minehead, approx. 11 miles turn left to
Stogumber/Northam Mill. Follow all signs for
Northam Mill.

417 Rendy Farm

♦♦♦♦ ⁂

Oake, Taunton, Somerset, TA4 1BB
Tel: 01823 461160 Fax: 01823 461161

418 Salisbury House Hotel

♦♦♦♦ ⁂

14 Billetfield, Taunton, Somerset, TA1 3NN
Tel: 01823 272083 Fax: 01823 365978
Email: res.salisbury@btinternet.com
Web: www.salisburyhousehotel.com

Elegant Victorian town centre location near Vivary
Park. Just recently refurbished. All bedrooms are
en-suite, spacious & well-equipped with luxury
bathrooms and pocketed-sprung beds. TV &
hospitality tray. Large car park.
17 bedrs SB £38 DB £55 B £6
CC: MC Vi Swi Delt

🔌🖵🖳☎🅿🛁🗚🏨🍴

How to get there: Follow signs to Taunton town
centre. From east reach, bear left and go past
Sainsbury's and BP garage. Hotel is on right,
past church.

419 Stilegate

♦♦♦♦ ⁂🍷

Staple Close, West Quantoxhead, Williton,
Taunton, Somerset, TA4 4DN
Tel: 01984 639119 Fax: 01984 639119
Email: stilegate@aol.com
Web: www.members.aol.com/stilegate
3 bedrs SB £28 DB £48
CC: None accepted

🔌🖵🖳🅿📷🎦🍴🕮(🛁🍷

How to get there: Take A39 from Bridgwater to
Minehead. Take first left past Windmill Public
House, through West Quantoxhead. Take
second right into Staple Lane, first right into
Staple Close.

Southwest

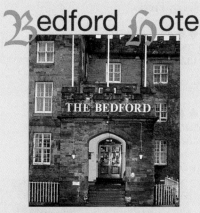

Bedford Hotel

Stunning historical building situated in the market town of Tavistock. One mile from the open moor. Renowned for its old fashioned hospitality and award winning 2AA Rosette restaurant.

★★★

1 Plymouth Road, Tavistock,
Devon PL19 8BB

Tel: 01822 613221   Fax: 01822 618034
Email: jane@bedford-hotel.co.uk
Website: www.warm-welcom-hotels.co.uk

Warm and intimate Browns, originally a C17 coaching inn was totally refurbished last year and now offers luxurious accommodation complemented by lively menus from the 2-rosette award-winning restaurant. Intimate wine bar, conservatory, courtyard garden, function/meeting room and ancient well!

80 West Street, Tavistock, Devon PL19 8AQ
Tel: 01822 618686   Fax: 01822 618646
Email: enquiries@brownsdevon.co.uk
Website: www.brownsdevon.co.uk

---

420 Chitcombe Farm

♦ ♦ ♦ ☕

Huish Champflower, Taunton, Somerset, TA4 2EL
Tel: 01398 371274 Fax: 01398 371111
Email: jekennen@hotmail.com
Web: www.chitcombefarm.co.uk
2 bedrs SB £25 DB £40 HBS £37 HBD £32 B £5
L £5 D £12.50 CC: None accepted

How to get there: From Taunton B3227 to Wiveliscombe; right in square to Huish Champflower. Left to Upton. Chitcombe Farm 2½ miles on right.

421 Lime House

♦ ♦ ♦ ✍

Linden Grove, Taunton, Somerset, TA1 1EF
Tel: 01823 274686
Children minimum age: 4
2 bedrs SB £25 DB £45 CC: None accepted

How to get there: J25 M5 follow signs for Cricket Ground/Market. Left at T-junction. 3rd turning right (Staplegrove Road), 2nd right (Linden Grove).

Tavistock, Devon

422 Bedford Hotel

★★★★ ℞ ℞

1 Plymouth Road, Tavistock, Devon, PL19 8BB
Tel: 01822 613221 Fax: 01822 618034
Email: jane@bedford-hotel.co.uk
Web: www.warm-welcome-hotels.co.uk
29 bedrs SB £47.50 DB £75 HBS £67.50
HBD £57.50 B £6.50 L £7.95 D £19.95
CC: MC Vi Am DC Swi Delt

How to get there: In the centre of Tavistock, opposite the parish church.
See advert above left

423 Browns Hotel

★★★ ℞

80 West Street, Tavistock, Devon, PL19 8AQ
Tel: 01822 618686 Fax: 01822 618646
Email: enquiries@brownsdevon.co.uk
Web: www.brownsdevon.co.uk
20 bedrs SB £55 DB £90 L £8.95 D £17.95
CC: MC Vi Am Swi Delt

How to get there: In town centre, on right hand side of West Street, which is one-way.
See advert left

424 The Horn of Plenty

★★★
Gulworthy, Tavistock, Devon, PL19 8JD
Tel: 01822 832528 Fax: 01822 832528
Email: enquiries@thehornofplenty.co.uk
Web: www.thehornofplenty.co.uk
Children minimum age: 10
Closed 25th and 26th December
10 bedrs SB £105 DB £115 L £18.50 D £40
CC: MC Vi Am Swi
How to get there: From Tavistock take the A390 towards Liskeard and Callington for three miles to the Gulworthy crossroads, take a right turn and follow the signs to The Horn of Plenty.

Thornbury, Gloucestershire

425 Thornbury Castle
Gold Ribbon Winner

★★★
Castle Street, Thornbury,
South Gloucestershire, BS35 1HH
Tel: 01454 281182 Fax: 01454 416188
Email: thornburycastle@compuserve.com
Web: www.thornburycastle.com
Closed four days in early January

Beautiful 16th century castle-palace, once owned by Henry VIII, offering 25 carefully restored bedchambers. Renowned for its fine food, the castle has three dining rooms, each baronial in style with open fires.
26 bedrs SB £105 DB £130 B £8.95 L £22.50 D £42.50
CC: MC Vi Am DC Swi Delt
How to get there: To Thornbury on A38. At traffic lights turn to town centre. Through High Street and left into Castle Street. Castle behind St. Mary's church (look for brown castle signage).
See advert above right

Thornbury Castle

This beautiful 16th-century castle, once owned by Henry VIII, stands in 15 acres of regal splendour. Surrounded by its vineyard and Tudor Garden, it is renowned for being one of the finest Country House Hotels in England. The recipient of many prestigious awards for its fine food and excellent accommodation.
Thornbury, Gloucestershire BS35 1HH
Tel: 01454 281182 Fax: 01454 416188
Email: thornburycastle@compuserve.com
Website: www.thornburycastle.com

Tintagel, Cornwall

426 Port William Inn

♦♦♦♦
Trebarwith Strand, Tintagel, Cornwall, PL34 0HB
Tel: 01840 770230 Fax: 01840 770936
Email: william@eurobell.co.uk
5 bedrs SB £60 DB £85
CC: MC Vi Am Swi Delt

Tiverton, Devon

427 Travelodge Tiverton

Travel Accommodation
M5 J27, Tiverton, Devon, EX16 7HD
Tel: 08700 850 950
Web: www.travelodge.co.uk
40 bedrs B £4.25 CC: MC Vi Am DC Swi Delt

428 The Fishermans Cot

♦♦♦♦
Bickleigh, Tiverton, Devon, EX16 8RN
Tel: 01884 855289 Fax: 01884 855241

429 Bridge Guest House

◆ ◆ ◆

23 Angel Hill, Tiverton, Devon, EX16 6PE
Tel: 01884 252804 Fax: 01884 252804
Web: www.smoothhound.co.uk/hotels/
    bridgegh.html
10 bedrs SB £26 DB £50 HBS £40 HBD £40 B £6
D £16 CC: None accepted

How to get there: Leave M5 at Junction 27.
Take A361 north for seven miles. Leave A361
into Tiverton. Bridge Guest House situated in
centre of town, by river.

430 Lodgehill Farm Hotel

◆ ◆ ◆

Tiverton, Devon, EX16 5PA
Tel: 01884 251200 Fax: 01884 242090
Email: lodgehill@dial.pipex.com
Web: www.lodgehill.co.uk
10 bedrs SB £35 DB £65 HBS £50 HBD £47.50
B £8.50 L £12.50 D £17.50
CC: MC Vi Swi Delt JCB

How to get there: Hotel is on A396 Bickleigh
road leaving Tiverton.

Torcross, Devon

431 Greyhomes Hotel

★

Torcross, Devon, TQ7 2TH
Tel: 01548 580220 Fax: 01548 580832
Email: howard@greyhomeshotel.co.uk
Web: www.greyhomeshotel.co.uk
Children minimum age: 5.
Closed November to March
6 bedrs SB £34 DB £56 B £6.95 D £17.50
CC: MC Vi

How to get there: Torcross is on A379 between
Kingsbridge and Dartmouth. Leave A379 and
enter village square. Pass shops and take
through-road up hill. Hotel second turning on left.

Tormarton, South Gloucestershire

432 Compass Inn – Tormarton

★ ★

Badminton, Tormarton,
South Gloucestershire, GL9 1JB
Tel: 01454 218242 Fax: 01454 218417

Torpoint, Cornwall

433 Whitsand Bay

★ ★

Portwrinkle, Crafthole, Torpoint,
Cornwall, PL11 3BU
Tel: 01503 230276 Fax: 01503 230329
Web: www.cornish-golf-hotels.co.uk
40 bedrs SB £42 DB £33 HBS £53 HBD £44
B £10.50 L £5 D £19.50
CC: MC Vi Am DC Swi Delt

How to get there: A38 past Plymouth. At
Trerulefoot roundabout, take A374 towards
Torpoint and follow signs after approx. 3 miles.

Torquay, Devon

434 The Imperial Hotel

★ ★ ★ ★ ★ ★

Park Hill Road, Torquay, Devon, TQ1 2DG
Tel: 01803 294301 Fax: 01803 298293
Email: imperialtorquay@paramount-hotels.co.uk
Web: www.paramount-hotels.co.uk
153 bedrs SB £102 DB £185 HBS £127.50
HBD £235 B £7.50 L £12 D £25
CC: MC Vi Am Swi

435 Palace Hotel

★ ★ ★ ★

Babbacombe Road, Torquay, Devon, TQ1 3TG
Tel: 01803 200200 Fax: 01803 299899
Email: info@palacetorquay.co.uk
Web: www.palacetorquay.co.uk
141 bedrs SB £71 DB £142 HBS £81 HBD £81
B £9.50 L £15 D £25
CC: MC Vi Am DC Swi Delt

How to get there: Exit M5 at Junction 30. Follow
signs on A380 to Newton Abbot, then signs to
Torquay and Babbacombe.
See advert on facing page

436 The Grand

★ ★ ★ ★

Seafront, Torquay, Devon, TQ2 6NT
Tel: 01803 296677 Fax: 01803 213462
Email: grandhotel@netsite.co.uk
Web: www.grandtorquay.co.uk

Set in its own grounds with panoramic views over Torbay. Award-winning cuisine, sumptuous surroundings, indoor and outdoor swimming pools and friendly, attentive staff.
110 bedrs SB £72 DB £126 HBS £97 HBD £88 L £7.50 D £25
CC: MC Vi Am DC Swi Delt
⊔⊥ ⚞ ⊗ ☺ ▢ ☎ 📞 P⚬ ☕ ✆ 🏛 ⚔ 🏊 ⚘ ⚘⚘ ⚙ ⚓
How to get there: At the end of the M5, take the A380 to Torquay seafront. At the seafront turn right, and The Grand is the first building on the right. Take first right, then left for hotel main entrance.

437 Belgrave Hotel

★★★
Sea Front, Torquay, Devon, TQ2 5HE
Tel: 01803 296666 Fax: 01803 211308
Email: info@belgrave-hotel.co.uk
Web: www.belgrave-hotel.co.uk
71 bedrs SB £42 DB £84 HBS £48 HBD £48
B £8.50 L £2.95 D £16 CC: MC Vi Am DC Swi Delt
⊔⊥ ⚞ ⊗ ☺ ▢ ☎ P⚬ ☕ ✆ 🏛 ⚘⚘ ⚘⚘ ⚓
How to get there: Follow signs to Torquay seafront. Turn left and go along seafront. Veer left up Shedden Hill and we are on the left.

438 Corbyn Head Hotel

★★★★ ⚘ ⚘
Seafront, Torquay, TQ2 6RH
Tel: 01803 213611 Fax: 01803 296152
Email: info@corbynhead.com
Web: www.corbynhead.com
50 bedrs SB £40 DB £80 HBS £50 HBD £50
B £10.50 L £15 CC: MC Vi Am DC Swi
♿ ⚞ ⊗ ☺ ▢ ☎ 📞 ☕ 🏛 ⚘ ⚘⚘ ⚘⚘ ⚓
How to get there: At sea front, turn right towards Livermead and Cockington. Hotel is situated just past Cockington Lane on right opposite Livermead beach.
See advert on following page

Southwest

439 Homers Hotel

★★★★ ♖ ♖

Warren Road, Torquay,
Devon, TQ2 5TN
Tel: 01803 213456 Fax: 01803 213458
Email: homers@tinyonline.co.uk
Web: www.homers-hotel.co.uk
Beautiful Victorian Villa high up on the cliffs with spectacular views across Torbay. Ideal location for sightseing Devon/Cornwall. Close to town, beach and theatre.
13 bedrs SB £45 DB £80 HBS £65 HBD £60
L £16 D £25
CC: MC Vi Am Swi Delt
🕭🖼🐾⊗🍺🖵☎🅿🛆🕯📶👬👪
How to get there: Follow signs for seafront. Turn left. Take hill in front of Belgrave Hotel, then first turn on right.

440 Hotel Gleneagles

★★★

Asheldon Road, Wellswood, Torquay,
Devon, TQ1 2QS
Tel: 01803 293637 Fax: 01803 295106
Email: hotelgleneagles@lineone.net
Web: www.hotel-gleneagles.com
Children minimum age: 14

Under ³/₄ of a mile from the harbour in a tree-lined avenue, overlooking Anstey's Cove, with path to the beach. All rooms are en-suite with balconies, TVs and telephones. Poolside restaurant.
41 bedrs SB £35 DB £70 HBS £41 HBD £40.50
B £7 L £5 D £15
CC: MC Vi Am Swi Delt
🕭🕮🐾⊗🍺🖵☎🅿🛆🕯📶👪👬🗻
How to get there: Babbacombe Road to St. Mathias Church, on right, 300 yards, Hollies Hotel on right. Turn right into Asheldon Road and hotel is on right.

441 Livermead Cliff Hotel

★★★

Seafront, Torquay, Devon, TQ2 6RQ
Tel: 01803 299666 Fax: 01803 294496
Email: enquiries@livermeadcliff.co.uk
Web: www.livermeadcliff.co.uk
64 bedrs SB £39.50 DB £79 HBS £49.50
HBD £45 B £9 L £9.95 D £16.95
CC: MC Vi Swi Delt
🕮🐾⊗🍺🖵☎📞🅿🛆🕯📶🍴👬👪👪🕯🗻
🍤
How to get there: From M5, take A379 to Torquay. Follow A3022 through town to seafront. Turn right, sign to Paignton. Hotel 600 yards seaward side.

442 Livermead House Hotel

★★★

Seafront, Torquay, Devon, TQ2 6QJ
Tel: 01803 294361 Fax: 01803 200758
Email: rewhotels@aol.com
Web: www.livermead.com
67 bedrs SB £45 DB £90 HBS £52 HBD £52
B £9.25 L £10.75 D £19.75
CC: MC Vi Am DC Swi Delt
🌊🕭🕮🐾⊗🍺🖵☎🅿🛆🕯📶👬👪🗻
How to get there: From Exeter, take A380 to Torquay then follow the signs for seafront.
See advert on facing page

443 Osborne Hotel

★★★★ ♖ ♖ ♖

Hesketh Crescent, Meadfoot, Torquay,
Devon, TQ1 2LL
Tel: 01803 213311 Fax: 01803 296788
Email: id@osborne-torquay.co.uk
Web: www.osborne-torquay.co.uk
29 bedrs
CC: MC Vi Am Swi
🕮🍺🖵☎🅿🛆🕯📶🍴👬👪👪🏹🕯🗻🔍🔲
🗻

444 Toorak Hotel

★★★★ ♖ ♖

Chestnut Avenue, Torquay, Devon, TQ2 5JS
Tel: 01803 400400 Fax: 01803 400140
Email: rheale@tlh.co.uk
Web: www.tlh.co.uk
92 bedrs
CC: MC Vi Am Swi Delt
🕮⊗🍺🖵☎🅿🛆🕯📶👬👪🕯🔍🔲🗻
How to get there: Immediately opposite the Riviera Centre, which is clearly signed from all major routes into the town.

Southwest

445 Abbey Court Hotel

★★

Falkland Road, Torquay, Devon, TQ2 5JR
Tel: 01803 297316 Fax: 01803 297316

446 Ansteys Cove Hotel

★★★

327 Babbacombe Road, Torquay,
Devon, TQ1 3TB
Tel: 0800 0284953 Fax: 01803 211150
Email: info@torquayengland.com
Web: www.torquayengland.com
Closed November to March
9 bedrs SB £29 DB £52 HBS £39 HBD £36 L £5
D £10
CC: MC Vi Am Swi Delt JCB

How to get there: Turn left onto B3199 at
Babbacombe. Turn right onto Babbacombe
Road. Hotel is on right opposite the Palace Hotel.

447 Ansteys Lea Hotel

★★

Babbacombe Road, Torquay, Devon, TQ1 2QJ
Tel: 01803 294843 Fax: 01803 214333
Email: stay@ansteys-lea.co.uk
Web: www.ansteys-lea.co.uk
24 bedrs SB £25 DB £50 HBS £35 HBD £35
CC: MC Vi Swi Delt

448 Apsley Hotel

★★

Torwood Gardens Road, Torquay,
Devon, TQ1 1EG
Tel: 01803 292058 Fax: 01803 215105
CC: None accepted

449 Burlington Hotel

★★

Babbacombe Road, Torquay, Devon, TQ1 1HN
Tel: 01803 210950 Fax: 01803 200189
Email: info@burlingtonhotel.co.uk
Web: www.torquayholidayhotels.co.uk
55 bedrs SB £37 DB £60 HBS £47 HBD £40
L £3 D £10 CC: MC Vi Swi Delt

How to get there: Take M5 to Exeter. Follow
signs to Torquay. At Torquay seafront turn left.
At clock tower turn left. Hotel ½ a mile on
right.

450 Bute Court Hotel

★★

Belgrave Road, Torquay, Devon, TQ2 5HQ
Tel: 01803 293771 Fax: 01803 213429
Email: bute-court-hotel@talk21.com
Web: www.bute-court-hotel.co.uk
45 bedrs SB £30 DB £60 HBS £35 HBD £35
B £4 D £8.50
CC: MC Vi Swi Delt

How to get there: Right at South Devon College,
passing Police station. Belgrave Road is 200
yards down on the right.

451 Cavendish Hotel

★★

Belgrave Road, Torquay, Devon, TQ2 5HN
Tel: 01803 293682 Fax: 01803 292802

452 Coppice Hotel

★★

Barrington Quay, Torquay, Devon, TQ1 2QJ
Tel: 01803 297786 Fax: 01803 211085
Closed November to January
40 bedrs
CC: None accepted

How to get there: Hotel is one mile on left from
harbour.

453 Crofton House Hotel

★★

Croft Road, Torquay, Devon, TQ2 5TZ
Tel: 01803 293761 Fax: 01803 211796
Email: james@croftonhouse.freeserve.co.uk
Web: www.crofton-house-hotel.co.uk
Closed January
36 bedrs SB £35 DB £70 HBS £45 HBD £90
B £5.95 D £9.95
CC: MC Vi Swi Delt

How to get there: Follow signs for town centre
into Belgrave Road, turn left into Lucius Street
at lights, and take first right into Croft Road.

454 Gresham Court Hotel

★★
Babbacombe Road, Torquay, Devon, TQ1 1HG
Tel: 01803 293007 Fax: 01803 215951
Email: greshamcourthotel@hotmail.com
Web: www.gresham-court-hotel.co.uk
Closed January
30 bedrs CC: MC Vi Am Swi Delt

How to get there: From harbourside, bear left at clocktower, signpost to Babbacombe. Hotel is on left near Torquay Musuem, approx ¹/₄ mile.

455 Howden Court Hotel

★★
23 Croft Road, Torquay, Devon, TQ2 5UD
Tel: 01803 294844 Fax: 01803 211356
SB £27.50 DB £45 HBS £41 HBD £36 B £6.25
D £12.75
CC: None accepted

456 Inglewood Hotel

★★
Belgrave Road, Torquay, Devon, TQ2 5HP
Tel: 01803 293800
Email: enquiry@theinglewoodhotel.co.uk
Web: www.theinglewoodhotel.co.uk
52 bedrs

How to get there: From M5 take A380 to Torquay; follow seafront signs; at seafront turn left, then first left; hotel is second on the left.

457 Norcliffe

★★
Seafront, Babbacombe Downs Road,
Torquay, TQ1 3LF
Tel: 01803 328456 Fax: 01803 328023
27 bedrs CC: MC Vi

How to get there: Join A380 Exeter-Newton Abbot. Continue along Newton Road. Turn left at traffic lights. Follow signs to TUFC. Turn left at Manor Road lights, right at crossroads. Turn left.

458 Roseland Hotel

★★
Warren Road, Torquay, Devon, TQ2 5TT
Tel: 01803 210950 Fax: 01803 200189
Email: info@burlingtonhotel.co.uk
Web: www.torquayholidayhotels.co.uk
40 bedrs SB £37 DB £60 HBS £47 HBD £40
L £3 D £10 CC: MC Vi Swi Delt

How to get there: At seafront turn left up Sheddon Hill and turn right at Warren Road.

459 Shedden Hall Hotel

★★
Shedden Hill, Torquay, Devon, TQ2 5TY
Tel: 01803 292964 Fax: 01803 295306
Email: sheddenhtl@aol.com
Web: www.sheddenhallhotel.co.uk
Children minimum age: 4.
Closed January
24 bedrs SB £35 DB £70 HBS £40 HBD £40
B £5.95 D £12.95 CC: MC Vi Am DC Swi Delt JCB

How to get there: From M5, take A380 and follow signs to Torquay seafront. Turn left at seafront traffic lights. At next set proceed up Sheden Hill.

460 Ashley Rise Hotel

★
18 Babbacombe Road, Torquay, Devon, TQ1 3SJ
Tel: 01803 327282
Email: ashleyrisehotel@ukonline.co.uk
Web: www.ashleyrisehotel.co.uk
25 bedrs CC: MC Vi Swi Delt JCB

How to get there: Follow signs to Babbacombe model village; at St. Marychurch turn left towards Torquay town centre; on to Babbacombe Road, third left.

461 Colindale Hotel

◆◆◆◆◆
20 Rathmore Road, Chelston, Torquay,
Devon, TQ2 6NZ
Tel: 01803 293947
Children minimum age: 6.
Closed Christmas to New Year
8 bedrs SB £25 DB £50 HBS £40 HBD £40 D £15
CC: MC Vi Swi Delt JCB

How to get there: From seafront head for Torquay station, Colindale Hotel is approx 300m past station, on left.

Southwest

462 Haldon Priors

♦ ♦ ♦ ♦ ✍

Meadfoot Sea Road, Torquay, Devon, TQ1 2LQ
Tel: 01803 213365 Fax: 01803 215577
Closed November to February
6 bedrs SB £38 DB £60 CC: None accepted
⊗ ⌘ ⌑ 𝗣 🐾 🔊 ⚘

How to get there: Pass Torquay Harbour on right. Turn left at the clocktower. Turn right at lights. Hotel on left, just before the beach.

463 Haytor Hotel

♦ ♦ ♦ ♦

Meadfoot Road, Torquay, Dexon, TQ1 2JP
Tel: 01803 294708 Fax: 01803 292511
Email: enq@haytorhotel.com
Web: www.haytorhotel.com
Children minimum age: 12

Elegant Georgian property set in over an acre of mature gardens. Ideal venue for short and long breaks both for pleasure and business. Delicious choice of breakfasts. No smoking.
15 bedrs SB £50 DB £50 HBS £65 HBD £40
CC: MC Vi DC Swi Delt JCB
♿ 📠 🕯 ⊗ ⌘ ⌑ ☎ 𝗣 🐾 🔊 ⚘ ⧗

How to get there: Left at seafront past Princess Theatre. Head for inner harbour to clocktower roundabout. Turn left, then right at lights.

464 Kingston House

♦ ♦ ♦ ♦ ✍

75 Avenue Road, Torquay, TQ2 5LL
Tel: 01803 212760 Fax: 01803 201425
Email: butto@kingstonhousehotel.co.uk
Children minimum age: 8
6 bedrs SB £22.50 DB £45 CC: None accepted
📠 ⊗ ⌘ ⌑ 𝗣 🐾

465 Lawnswood Guest House

♦ ♦ ♦ ♦

6 Scarborough Road, Torquay, Devon, TQ2 5UJ
Tel: 01803 403593
3 bedrs SB £16 DB £32 HBS £23 HBD £23

CC: None accepted
🕯 ⊗ ⌘ ⌑

How to get there: At sea front, bear left at second set of traffic lights after college into Belgrave Road. 2nd left after traffic lights.

466 Lindens Hotel

♦ ♦ ♦ ♦ ✍ ⚑

31 Bampfylde Road, Torquay, Devon, TQ2 5AY
Tel: 01803 212281
Closed November to December
7 bedrs SB £19 DB £38 HBS £27 HBD £27
CC: None accepted
🕯 ⊗ ⌘ ⌑ 𝗣 🐾 ⚘

How to get there: Fork right at rail station, across lights; Lindens is in first road on left.

467 Morley Hotel

♦ ♦ ♦ ♦ ✍ ⚑

16 Bridge Road, Torquay, Devon, TQ2 5BA
Tel: 01803 292955 Fax: 01803 290111
Email: morleyhotel@aol.com
Web: www.hotelstorquay.com
8 bedrs CC: MC Vi Swi Delt
♿ ⌘ ⌑ 𝗣 🐾 🕯 ⛲ ⚘ ⧗

How to get there: Approaching Torquay, turn right into Avenue Road. Proceed past traffic lights. Take first left into Bampfylde Road. Bridge Road is second left.

468 Seaway Hotel

♦ ♦ ♦ ♦ ✍

Chelston Road, Torquay, Devon, TQ2 6PU
Tel: 01803 605320 Fax: 01803 605320
13 bedrs CC: MC Vi Am Delt
🕯 ⌘ ⌑ 𝗣 🐾 🕯 ⚘ ⧗

How to get there: Chelston Road is the second turning on the right when leaving the seafront via Seaway Lane. Hotel is first property on left.

469 Banksea Hotel

♦ ♦ ♦ ✍

51 Avenue Road, Torquay, Devon, TQ2 5LE
Tel: 01803 213911 Fax: 01803 213911
Children minimum age: 8

Bob and Petra welcome you to The Banksea Licensed Hotel, noted for its friendly, relaxing and informal atmosphere, personal service, fine cuisine and cosy cellar bar. Chef proprietor.
5 bedrs SB £16 DB £32 HBS £23 HBD £23
CC: MC Vi Swi JCB

How to get there: From Exeter M5 onto A380 onto A3002 Torquay: signs to seafront, hotel on left hand side of road.

470 Briarfields Hotel

◆ ◆ ◆

84-86 Avenue Road, Torquay, Devon, TQ2 5LF
Tel: 01803 297844 Fax: 01803 297844
Email: briarfieldshotel@aol.com
Web: briarfields.co.uk
Closed December
10 bedrs SB £30 DB £36 CC: MC Vi Swi

How to get there: Approaching Torquay from Newton Abbot, bear right at the junction of Torre station and Halfords down Avenue Road. Hotel is situated halfway down on right.

471 Devon Court Hotel

◆ ◆ ◆

Croft Road, Torquay, Devon, TQ2 5UE
Tel: 01803 293603 Fax: 01803 213660

472 Glenwood

◆ ◆ ◆

Rowdens Road, Torquay, Devon, TQ2 5AZ
Tel: 01803 296318 Fax: 01803 296462
Email: enquiries@glenwood-hotel.co.uk
Web: www.glenwood-hotel.co.uk
Children minimum age: 7
10 bedrs SB £25 DB £50 HBS £34.50
HBD £34.50 B £5 D £9.50
CC: MC Vi Am DC Swi Delt JCB

How to get there: Bear right by traffic lights at rail station. After next set of lights in Avenue Road, turn left into Bampfylde Road. Take first left.

473 Hotel Patricia

◆ ◆ ◆

64 Belgrave Road, Torquay, Devon, TQ2 5HY
Tel: 01803 293339 Fax: 01803 293339
Email: hotelpatricia@aol.com
11 bedrs SB £23 DB £40 CC: MC Vi

How to get there: Turn into Belgrave Road from seafront; 250 yards on left hand side.

474 The Exton

◆ ◆ ◆

12 Bridge Road, Torquay, Devon, TQ2 5BA
Tel: 01803 293561
Email: extonhotel@lineone.net
Web: www.extonhotel.co.uk
5 bedrs SB £15 DB £30 HBS £23 HBD £23
CC: MC Vi Swi Delt JCB

How to get there: Bear right at Torre station (Avenue Road). Through lights, then left into Bampfylde, then first left into Rowdens.

475 Allerdale Hotel

Croft Road, Torquay, Devon, TQ2 5UD
Tel: 01803 292667 Fax: 01803 292667
Email: enquiry@allerdalehotel.co.uk
Web: www.allerdalehotel.co.uk
Closed January

A Victorian villa nestling in own spacious south-facing garden with path to seafront. Family-run hotel with all rooms en-suite, excellent choice menus. Centrally situated for all amenities. Parking.
20 bedrs SB £30 DB £60 HBS £40 HBD £50
B £5 L £12 D £18
CC: MC Vi Am Swi Delt

How to get there: Follow A380 to seafront. Turn left, next traffic lights take left fork (Sheddon Hill). First turning on left is Croft Road.

Totnes, Devon

476 Royal Seven Stars Hotel

★ ★

The Plains, Totnes, Devon, TQ9 5DD
Tel: 01803 862125 Fax: 01803 867925
16 bedrs SB £60 DB £74 B £7 L £9 D £18
CC: MC Vi Am DC Swi Delt

How to get there: Follow signs for Totnes from A38 for six miles, then signs for town centre.

Alverton Manor

- Banqueting & Conference facilities up to 200
- 34 Luxury bedrooms all ensuite
- Cornwall's most popular venue for wedding ceremonies
- Ideal for wedding receptions and special occasions
- Award winning Terrace Restaurant, à la carte & table d'hote menus
- Own 18-hole golf course within the historic Killiow Estate five minutes away by car
- Cornwall's centre of business

Tregolls Road, Truro TR1 1ZQ
Tel: 01872 276633   Fax: 01872 222989
Email: alverton@connexions.co.uk

The Brookdale Hotel

With the new Cornish Grill Restaurant and recently refurbished ensuite bedrooms, The Brookdale offers spacious accommodation with an excellent menu. Situated near the centre of Truro, easy access to all major routes, close to scenic parks, river walks and fine shopping facilities.Many of Cornwall's attractions are within 30 minutes drive—Eden Project, Tate Gallery, Lizard and Land's End.

Tregolls Road, Truro TR1 1JZ
Tel: 01872 273513   Fax: 01872 272400
brookdale@hotelstruro.com
www.hotelstruro.com

477 The Waterman's Arms

Bow Bridge, Ashprington, Totnes,
Devon, TQ9 7EG
Tel: 01803 732214 Fax: 01803 732314
15 bedrs SB £54 DB £69 L £4 D £4
CC: MC Vi Am Swi Delt

How to get there: From Totnes take Dartmouth/Kingsbridge road. At top of hill turn left, signposted The Waterman's Arms.

Trowbridge, Wiltshire

478 Hilbury Court Hotel

★★

Hilperton Road, Trowbridge, Wiltshire, BA14 7JW
Tel: 01225 752949 Fax: 01225 777990

Truro, Cornwall

479 Nare Hotel

★★★★

Carne Beach, Veryan, Truro, Cornwall, TR2 5PF
Tel: 01872 501111 Fax: 01872 501856
Email: office@narehotel.co.uk
Web: www.narehotel.co.uk
36 bedrs SB £76 DB £76 HBS £86 HBD £86
B £15 L £13 D £33 CC: MC Vi Swi

How to get there: From the M5 and A30, take the B3275. Turn right two miles after Ladock for Truro, left towards St. Mawes. Right onto A3078, over Veryan bridge and left after 1¹/₂ miles for Veryan. The hotel is one mile beyond the village.

480 Alverton Manor

★★★

Tregolls Road, Truro, Cornwall, TR1 1ZQ
Tel: 01872 276633 Fax: 01872 222989
Email: reception@alvertonmanor.demon.co.uk
34 bedrs SB £72 DB £109 HBS £84
HBD £66.50 B £9.75 L £3.70 D £23.50
CC: MC Vi Swi Delt

How to get there: North or east, travel west on M5. From Exeter passes through Cornwall on A30. Take A39, left at Carnon Downs service station.

See advert above left

481 The Brookdale Hotel

★ ★ ★

Tregolls Road, Truro, Cornwall, TR1 1JZ
Tel: 01872 273513 Fax: 01872 272400
Email: Brookdale@hotelstruro.com
Web: www.hotelstruro.com
30 bedrs SB £52 DB £70 HBS £64.50
CC: MC Vi Am Swi Delt
🐾☺☺☐☎📞▯🅿�♬😊♨♨♨▮▮▮
How to get there: On A39 approach road into
Truro, at lower end of Tregolls Road, 250m to
the east of the roundabout.
See advert on facing page

482 Carlton Hotel

★ ★

Falmouth Road, Truro, Cornwall, TR1 2HL
Tel: 01872 272450 Fax: 01872 223938
Email: reception@carltonhotel.co.uk
Web: www.carltonhotel.co.uk
Family-managed Victorian-styled hotel, five
minutes from city centre and ideal for holidays
and business trips. Cornish welcome
guaranteed.
29 bedrs SB £40 DB £53 HBS £50 HBD £36.50
B £5 L £5.50 D £10
CC: MC Vi Am DC Swi Delt
🐾☺☺☐☎🅿🗬♬♨♨♨▮▮▮🆂🅿🅰
How to get there: Take A39 to Truro. Proceed
across two roundabouts onto bypass. At top of
hill, turn right into Falmouth Road. Hotel is
100m on right.

483 Marcorrie Hotel

◆ ◆ ◆ ◆

20 Falmouth Road, Truro, Cornwall, TR1 2HX
Tel: 01872 277374 Fax: 01872 241666
Email: marcorrie@aol.com
Web: www.hotelstruro.com
12 bedrs SB £39.50 DB £49.50
CC: MC Vi Am Swi Delt
🐾☺☺☐☎📞▯🅿🗬ℭ♬😊▮▮▮
How to get there: At Falmouth junction on Truro
ring road, turn to city centre. Hotel is 400 yards

Southwest

Umberleigh, Devon

484 Northcote Manor Hotel
Gold Ribbon Winner

★★★★ ʀ ʀ ʀ

Burrington, near Umberleigh,
North Devon, EX39 9LZ
Tel: 01769 560501 Fax: 01769 560770
Email: rest@northcotemanor.co.uk
Web: www.northcotemanor.co.uk
Children minimum age: 10

The 18th century Manor and the grounds
located high above the Taw River Valley, offers
an atmosphere of timeless tranquility.
Professional, attentive but unobtrusive service
with excellent food is what Northcote Manor
aims to provide.
11 bedrs SB £99 DB £132 HBS £132
HBD £98.50 B £15 L £20 D £35
CC: MC Vi Am DC Swi Delt
How to get there: Do not enter Burrington
village: Entrance to Northcote Estate is on main
A377 Barnstaple/Exeter road opposite
Portsmouth Arms Pub and railway station.
See advert on previous page

Wadebridge, Cornwall

485 Roskarnon House Hotel

◆ ◆ ◆

Rock, near Wadebridge, Cornwall, PL27 6LD
Tel: 01208 862785
Closed October to March
12 bedrs SB £30 DB £55 HBS £40 HBD £75
CC: Am
How to get there: From Wadebridge, follow road
to Rock, Trebetherick, Polzeath and then to golf
course. Hotel situated on road to golf course.

Wareham, Dorset

486 Priory Hotel
Gold Ribbon Winner

★★★ ʀ ʀ ʀ

Church Green, Wareham, Dorset, BH20 4ND
Tel: 01929 551666 Fax: 01929 556485
Email: reception@theprioryhotel.co.uk
Web: www.theprioryhotel.co.uk
Children minimum age: 8
19 bedrs SB £85 DB £185 B £12.50 L £15
D £30.50 CC: MC Vi DC Swi Delt
How to get there: Wareham is on the A3451 to
the west of Poole: hotel is at southern end of
town between church and river.
See advert below

487 Springfield Country Hotel

★★★★ ʀ

Grange Road, Stoborough, Wareham,
Dorset, BH20 5AL
Tel: 01929 552177 Fax: 01929 551862
Email: enquiries@springfield-country-hotel.co.uk
Web: www.springfield-country-hotel.co.uk
48 bedrs SB £75 DB £110 HBS £89.50
HBD £74.50 B £9.50 L £10 D £19.50
CC: MC Vi Am DC Swi Delt
How to get there: Take A35 towards Wareham.
At end of dual carriageway take 1st exit off
roundabout (A351). At roundabout just outside
Wareham take 2nd exit. Straight over next
roundabout. After ³/₄ mile turn right. Hotel 300
yards on left.

488 Worgret Manor Hotel

★★

Worgret, Wareham, Dorset, BH20 6AB
Tel: 01929 552957 Fax: 01929 554804
Email: worgretmanor@freeserve.co.uk
Web: www.worgretmanor.freeserve.co.uk
11 bedrs SB £55 DB £80 HBS £70 HBD £55
B £5 D £14.95 CC: MC Vi Am DC Swi Delt
How to get there: Follow A351 from Poole to
Wareham, then signs for Wool on A352.

489 Travelodge Warminster

Travel Accommodation
A36, Warminster, Wiltshire, BA12 7RU
Tel: 08700 850 950
Web: www.travelodge.co.uk
31 bedrs B £4.25
CC: MC Vi Am DC Swi Delt

490 The George Inn

♦ ♦ ♦ ♦

Longbridge Deverill, Warminster,
Wiltshire, BA12 7DG
Tel: 01985 840396 Fax: 01985 841333

Wells, Somerset

491 Swan Hotel

★ ★ ★

Sadler Street, Wells, Somerset, BA5 2RX
Tel: 01749 836300 Fax: 01749 836301
Email: swan@bhere.co.uk
Web: www.bhere.co.uk

15th-century coaching hotel, with original four-poster beds and cheerful log fires, facing west front of Wells Cathedral. Traditional English food and an ideal location for touring.
50 bedrs SB £84.50 DB £108 HBD £69.50
B £9.50 L £4.95 D £19.95
CC: MC Vi Am DC Swi Delt

How to get there: Hotel faces the west front of Wells Cathedral in city centre.

Making a booking?

Don't forget to mention RAC
Hotels and Bed & Breakfast 2002.

492 White Hart Hotel

★ ★ ★

Sadler Street, Wells, Somerset, BA5 2RR
Tel: 01749 672056 Fax: 01749 671074
Email: info@whitehart-wells.co.uk
Web: www.whitehart-wells.co.uk

15th-century coaching hotel, situated directly opposite Wells Cathedral, offering comfortable accommodation and fine English food. Open fires and an ideal location make this family-run hotel an excellent choice.
15 bedrs SB £63 DB £80 HBS £72 HBD £57.50
B £7.50 L £8 D £15
CC: MC Vi Am Swi Delt
How to get there: Approaching Wells follow signs for Hotels and Deliveries. Hotel is the first one on the right as you enter Wells.

493 Bekynton House

♦ ♦ ♦ ♦

7 St. Thomas Street, Wells,
Somerset, BA5 2UU
Tel: 01749 672222 Fax: 01749 672222
Email: reservations@bekynton.freeserve.co.uk
Children minimum age: 5.
Closed Christmas and New Year
4 bedrs SB £38 DB £52
CC: MC Vi
How to get there: St. Thomas Street is the B3139 Wells to Radstock road, via The Horringtons; we are three doors from the Fountain Inn.

One click does it all

For the latest special offers and online booking, plus detailed information on over 3,000 RAC inspected properties, visit www.rac.co.uk/hotels

Southwest

494 Double Gate Farm

Godney, Wells, Somerset, BA5 1RX
Tel: 01458 832217 Fax: 01458 835612
Email: hilary@doublegate.demon.co.uk
Web: www.doublegatefarm.com
Closed Christmas to New Year

Award-winning farmhouse accommodation –
outdoor, sunshine breakfasts in summertime –
includes home-made bread and local produce.
Ideally situated for sightseeing, walking and
cycling. Golden retriever and two mischievous
moggies!
6 bedrs SB £30 DB £50 CC: MC Vi Swi Delt
How to get there: From Wells take A39 south. At
Polsham turn right. Continue approx three
miles. Farmhouse on left.

Weston-Super-Mare, Somerset

495 Beachlands Hotel

17 Uphill Road North, Weston-Super-Mare,
Somerset, BS23 4NG
Tel: 01934 621401 Fax: 01934 621966
Email: info@beachlandshotel.com
Web: www.beachlandshotel.com

This delightful family-run hotel, situated
overlooking the 18-hole golf course, only 300
yards from the sandy beach, benefits from
ample parking and an indoor heated swimming
pool and sauna.

24 bedrs SB £49.50 DB £85 HBS £68
HBD £58.75 B £8.50 L £13.50 D £12
CC: MC Vi Am DC Swi Delt
How to get there: Junction 21 on M5, follow
signs for beach. Hotel is 6½ miles from exit,
overlooking golf course 200 yards before beach.

496 Commodore Hotel

★★★
Beach Road, Sand Bay, Kewstoke,
Weston-Super-Mare, Somerset, BS22 9UZ
Tel: 01934 415778 Fax: 01934 636483

497 Arosfa

★★
Lower Church Road, Weston-Super-Mare,
Somerset, BS23 2AG
Tel: 01934 419523 Fax: 01934 636084
Email: reception@arosfahotel.co.uk
Web: www.arosfahotel.co.uk
46 bedrs SB £45 DB £65 HBS £55 HBD £50
B £6.50 L £5 D £16 CC: MC Vi Am DC Swi Delt
How to get there: From sea front take first right
past Winter Gardens; Hotel is 100m on left
beyond the college.

498 Dauncey's Hotel

★★
Claremont Crescent, Weston-Super-Mare,
Somerset, BS23 2ED
Tel: 01934 410180 Fax: 01934 410181
Email: david@daunceyshotel.fsnet.co.uk

Dauncey's has been run by the Hunt family for
40 years. Superb views across Weston Bay.
Well-appointed sea-view rooms. Open to non-
residents.
80 bedrs SB £33 DB £66 HBS £45 HBD £45
B £6.25 L £4.50 D £12 CC: MC Vi Swi Delt
How to get there: Situated at the north end of
the promenade, in a Victorian crescent.

499 Queenswood

★★

Victoria Park, Weston-Super-Mare,
Somerset, BS23 2HZ
Tel: 01934 416141 Fax: 01934 621759
Email: stay@queenswoodhotel.com
Web: www.queenswoodhotel.com
17 bedrs SB £48 DB £70 HBS £64.50
HBD £46.50 CC: MC Vi Am DC Swi Delt JCB

How to get there: The Queenswood is centrally
situated in a quite cul-de-sac just off the
seafront, in a slightly elevated position.

500 The Old Colonial

◆◆◆◆

30 Knightstone Road, Weston-Super-Mare,
Somerset, BS23 2AW
Tel: 01934 620739 Fax: 01934 645725

501 Wychwood Hotel

◆◆◆◆ ✠

148 Milton Road, Weston-Super-Mare,
Somerset, BS23 2UZ
Tel: 01934 627793
Closed Christmas
9 bedrs SB £30 DB £48 HBS £42 HBD £72 D £12
CC: MC Vi Delt

How to get there: From Junction 21 of M5
follow signs for town centre. Take third exit at
fifth roundabout and at second traffic lights turn
right into Milton Road – hotel 400 yards on right.

502 Baymead

◆◆◆

19-23 Longton Grove Road,
Weston-Super-Mare, Somerset, BS23 1LS
Tel: 01934 622951 Fax: 01934 620640
33 bedrs SB £26 DB £46 HBS £34.50
HBD £31.50 B £5 D £8.50
CC: None accepted

How to get there: Exit M5 at Junction 21. At
seafront, turn right, then right again into
Knightstone Road. Turn left into West Street. At
T-junction, turn left. Keep right, hotel on right.

Plan your route

 Visit www.rac.co.uk for RAC's
interactive route planner, including
up to the minute traffic reports.

503 Blakeney Guest House

◆◆◆

52 Locking Road, Weston-Super-Mare,
Somerset, BS23 3DN
Tel: 01934 624772
6 bedrs SB £16 DB £14 HBS £23 HBD £21
CC: MC Vi Am DC Swi Delt

How to get there: Leave M5 at Junction 21
heading south. Follow signs for tourism
accommodation into Weston-super-Mare.

504 L'Arrivee Guest House

◆◆◆

75 Locking Road, Weston-Super-Mare,
Somerset, BS23 3DW
Tel: 01934 625328 Fax: 01934 625328
Email: carolinetr@bun.co.uk
12 bedrs SB £22.50 DB £45 HBS £32 HBD £32
D £9.50 CC: MC Vi Swi Delt

How to get there: M5 at Junction 21. Follow
B3440 Locking Road signs. L'Arrivee is on the
right hand side 300 yards before Tesco store.

505 Oakover Guest House

◆◆◆ ✠

25 Clevedon Road, Weston-Super-Mare,
Somerset, BS23 1DA
Tel: 01934 620125
7 bedrs SB £19 DB £38 CC: MC Vi Swi Delt

How to get there: M5 Junction 21, follow signs
to Tropicana/seafront. Turn left into Clevedon
Road. Hotel is on left, just before traffic lights.

Weymouth, Dorset

506 Hotel Rembrandt

★★★

12-18 Dorchester Road, Weymouth,
Dorset, DT4 7JU
Tel: 01305 764000 Fax: 01305 764022
Email: reception@hotelrembrandt.co.uk
Web: www.hotelrembrandt.co.uk
75 bedrs SB £75 DB £98 HBS £85 HBD £56
B £6.95 L £4.95 D £14.95
CC: MC Vi Am DC Swi Delt

How to get there: From Dorchester, along A354,
straight on at Manor roundabout (by Safeway).
Hotel ³⁄₄ of a mile on left, 800 yards from
seafront.

Southwest

507 Hotel Rex

★★★★

29 The Esplanade, Weymouth,
Dorset, DT4 8DN
Tel: 01305 760400 Fax: 01305 760500
Email: rex@kingshotels.f9.co.uk
Web: www.kingshotel.co.uk
31 bedrs SB £49 DB £78 HBS £62 HBD £105
B £7 D £13.75
CC: MC Vi Am DC Swi Delt
How to get there: Take A354 to Weymouth.
Head towards seafront. Follow signs towards
ferry and harbour. The Rex overlooks beach and
harbour.

508 Best Western Hotel Prince Regent

★★

139 The Esplanade, Weymouth, Dorset, DT4 7NR
Tel: 01305 771313 Fax: 01305 778100
Email: hprwey@aol.com

Seafront location with magnificent views of the
bay and coastline. A short level stroll to town
centre and attractions. A good base to explore
Dorset.
50 bedrs SB £48 DB £68 HBS £58 HBD £44
B £6.50 D £13.75
CC: MC Vi Am DC Swi Delt
How to get there: At Dorchester, take A354 for
Weymouth. Follow signs for town centre. Turn
left at clock tower and proceed along
Esplanade.

509 Central Hotel

★★

15 Maiden Street, Weymouth, Dorset, DT4 8BB
Tel: 01305 760700 Fax: 01305 760300
Email: central@kingshotels.f9.co.uk
Web: www.kingshotels.co.uk

Closed 15 December to 2 March
29 bedrs SB £40 DB £67 HBS £46 HBD £39
D £8.50 CC: MC Vi Am Swi Delt
How to get there: Take A354 from Dorchester.
Head for seafront. At Marks & Spencer, take
small road called New Street to rear of hotel.

510 Crown Hotel

★★

51/52 St. Thomas Street, Weymouth,
Dorset, DT4 8EQ
Tel: 01305 760800 Fax: 01305 760300
Email: crown@kingshotels.f9.co.uk
Web: www.kingshotels.co.uk
86 bedrs SB £36 DB £66 HBS £45 HBD £41 L £6
CC: MC Vi Am Swi Delt
How to get there: From Dorchester, take the
A354 to Weymouth. When you reach the back
water on the left, follow this. Take the second
bridge over the water. Crown Hotel is on left.

511 Fairhaven Hotel

★★

37 The Esplanade, Weymouth, Dorset, DT4 8DH
Tel: 01305 760200
Email: fairhaven@kingshotels.f9.co.uk
Web: www.kingshotels.co.uk
Closed November to March
90 bedrs SB £40 DB £68 HBS £46 HBD £39
D £8.50
CC: MC Vi Am Swi Delt
How to get there: Take A354 to Weymouth.
Head towards seafront. Follow signs towards
Ferry. Fairhaven Hotel is 200 yards before Ferry
Terminal.

512 Birchfields

♦ ♦ ♦

22 Abbotsbury Road, Weymouth,
Dorset, DT4 0AE
Tel: 01305 773255 Fax: 01305 773255
Email: birchfieldshotel@lineone.net
Web: www.smoothhound.co.uk/hotels/
birchfields.html
Closed November to February
9 bedrs SB £18 DB £46 CC: MC Vi Swi Delt JCB
How to get there: From Jubilee Clock on
Esplanade, go down King Street. Take 2nd Exit
at Kings roundabout. Go over Swannery Bridge.
Take 2nd exit Westham roundabout onto
Abbotsbury Road. Birchfields 100m on right.

513 Concorde

♦♦♦

131 The Esplanade, Weymouth, Dorset, DT4 7EY
Tel: 01305 776900 Fax: 01305 776900
14 bedrs
CC: None accepted
How to get there: Hotel is situated on The
Esplanade.

514 Greenhill Hotel

♦♦♦

8 Greenhill, Weymouth, Dorset, DT4 7SQ
Tel: 01305 786026
Closed December to January
17 bedrs
CC: MC Vi Swi Delt
How to get there: Situated on Weymouth
promenade at Junction of A353 and A354.

515 Sandcombe Hotel

♦♦♦

8 The Esplanade, Weymouth, Dorset, DT4 8EB
Tel: 01305 786833
Email: ann.mcveigh@virgin.net
Web: www.resort-guide.co.uk/sandcombe
Children minimum age: 5
9 bedrs SB £20 DB £46
CC: None accepted
How to get there: Located on Esplanade
between beach and harbour. Near to Pavilion
theatre and Condor ferry port.

516 Trelawney Hotel

♦♦♦

1 Old Castle Road, Weymouth, Dorset, DT4 8QB
Tel: 01305 783188 Fax: 01305 783181
Email: trelawney@freeuk.com
Web: www.trelawneyhotel.com
10 bedrs SB £40 DB £66
CC: MC Vi Swi Delt JCB
How to get there: Approximately one mile from
town centre. Follow A354 towards Portland.
Hotel is 800 yards on left from 'Harbour'
roundabout.

517 Westwey Hotel

♦♦♦

62 Abbotsbury Road, Weymouth,
Dorset, DT4 0BJ
Tel: 01305 784564
Children minimum age: 3.
Closed December
9 bedrs SB £22 DB £44 CC: None accepted
How to get there: From Victorian clock esplanade
turn right into King Street. At roundabout take
second exit. At next roundabout take second exit
into Abbotsbury Road.

Whiddon Down, Oakhampton

518 Travelodge Okehampton (East)

Travel Accommodation
A30/A382, Merryeet Roundabout, Exeter Road,
Whiddon Down, Okehampton, Devon, EX20 2QT
Tel: 08700 850 950
Web: www.travelodge.co.uk
40 bedrs B £4.25 CC: MC Vi Am DC Swi Delt

Williton, Somerset

519 White House Hotel

★★ ♞ ♞

Long Street, Williton, Somerset, TA4 4QW
Tel: 01984 632306
Closed November to May
10 bedrs SB £55 DB £108 HBS £89 HBD £157
B £12 D £34 CC: None accepted
How to get there: On A39 in centre of village.

Southwest

Wimborne Minster, Dorset

520 Beechleas Hotel and Restaurant
Blue Ribbon Winner

★★⁣

17 Poole Road, Wimborne Minster,
Dorset, BH21 1QA
Tel: 01202 841684 Fax: 01202 849344
Email: beechleas@hotmail.com
Web: www.beechleas.com

A beautifully-restored Grade II listed Georgian
house with delightful walled garden, award-
winning restaurant, log fires in winter, sunny
conservatory in summer and a lovely ambience.
9 bedrs SB £69 DB £79 B £9.95 D £24.75

CC: MC Vi Am DC Swl Delt

How to get there: From A31 take road into
Wimbourne. From the centre, take A349 to
Poole. House is 100m on the right.

Winkleigh, Devon

521 Winkleigh Court

♦♦♦♦

Winkleigh, Devon, EX19 8HZ
Tel: 01837 83160 Fax: 01837 83162

Winsford, Somerset

522 Royal Oak Inn

★★★

Exmoor National Park, Winsford,
Somerset, TA24 7FE
Tel: 01643 851455 Fax: 01643 851009
Email: enquiries@royaloak-somerset.co.uk
Web: www.royaloak-somerset.co.uk

On the edge of Exmoor National park in the centre of an ancient riverside village, you will find a very charming place – a 12th-century thatched inn with open fireplaces and oak beams, two cheerful bars and comfortable en-suite rooms.

14 bedrs B £12.50 L £15
CC: MC Vi Am DC Swi Delt

How to get there: Take M5 south, exit at Junction 27. At Tiverton roundabout take A396 north for 20 miles through Exbridge and Bridgetown. Next turning left to Winsford.

Woolacombe, Devon

523 Watersmeet Hotel

★★★★

Mortehoe, Woolacombe, Devon, EX34 7EB
Tel: 01271 870333 Fax: 01271 870890
Email: info@watersmeethotel.co.uk
Web: www.watersmeethotel.co.uk
Closed January

Watersmeet enjoys panoramic sea views across Woolacombe Bay to Lundy Island. Award-winning cuisine and fine wines. Indoor and outdoor pools. Steps to private beach.

22 bedrs SB £83 DB £150 HBS £98 HBD £83
B £16.50 L £2.40 D £21

CC: MC Vi Am Swi Delt

How to get there: Leave M5 at Junction 27. Take A361 to Barnstaple. Follow signs for Woolacombe. Take Esplanade along seafront. The hotel is on left.

524 Woolacombe Bay Hotel

★★★★

Woolacombe, Devon, EX34 7BN
Tel: 01271 870388 Fax: 01271 870613
Email: woolacombe.bayhotel@btinternet.com
Web: www.woolacombe-bay-hotel.co.uk
Closed January to mid February
64 bedrs SB £60 DB £120 HBS £84 HBD £84
CC: MC Vi Am DC Swi Delt

How to get there: Leave M5 at Junction 27. Follow A361 to Mullacott Cross. Take B3343 to Woolacombe. Hotel in centre of village.
See advert on facing page

525 Headlands Hotel

★★

Beach Road, Woolacombe, Devon, EX34 7BT
Tel: 01271 870320 Fax: 01271 870320
Email: headhotel@lineone.net
Children minimum age: 4
13 bedrs SB £30 DB £60 HBS £42 HBD £84
B £5 D £12
CC: MC Vi Swi Delt

How to get there: Follow A361 from Barnstaple to Millacott Cross. Turn left. Follow road into Woolacombe. The Headlands is situated on right, just before seafront.

526 Lundy House Hotel

★★

Mortehoe, Woolacombe, North Devon, EX34 7DZ
Tel: 01271 870372 Fax: 01271 871001
Web: www.lundyhousehotel.co.uk
Closed January
8 bedrs CC: MC Vi Swi Delt

How to get there: In Woolacombe, proceed to the end of the Esplanade, and Lundy House is the 3rd property on the seaside.

Southwest

527 Crossways Hotel

The Seafront, Woolacombe,
North Devon, EX34 7DJ
Tel: 01271 870395 Fax: 01271 870395
Web: www.s-h-systems.co.uk/hotels/
    crossway.html
Closed November to February
9 bedrs SB £25 DB £50 HBS £30 HBD £30
L £1.50 D £5 CC: None accepted

How to get there: J27 M5. Follow A361 Barnstaple
towards Ilfracombe, left for Woolacombe. Turn
right at seafront. Hotel ½ a mile on right.

538 Cleeve House

North Morte Road, Mortehoe, Woolacombe,
Devon, EX34 7ED
Tel: 01271 870719 Fax: 01271 870719
Email: info@cleevehouse.co.uk
Web: www.cleevehouse.co.uk
Children minimum age: 10.
Closed November to March

A warm welcome awaits guests at this homely
hotel. The bedrooms are comfortable and well-
equipped with many thoughtful extras. The
ground floor bedroom has wheelchair access.
7 bedrs DB £64 HBD £49 B £6 D £17
CC: MC Vi Swi Delt

How to get there: In the village of Mortehoe, 50
yards on the left side of the lighthouse road
(North Morte Road).

Yelverton, Devon

529 Two Bridges Hotel

Two Bridges, Yelverton, Devon, PL20 6SW
Tel: 01822 890581 Fax: 01822 890575
Email: tb@warm-welcome-hotels.co.uk
Web: www.warm-welcome-hotels.co.uk

29 bedrs SB £52.50 DB £85 HBS £72.50
HBD £62.50 B £6.50 L £7.95 D £25
CC: MC Vi Am DC Swi Delt

How to get there: At junction of B3357
(Ashburton/Tavistock) and B3212
(Moretonhampstead/Yelverton).

Yeovil, Somerset

530 Little Barwick House
Gold Ribbon Winner

Barwick Village, near Yeovil, Somerset, BA22 9TD
Tel: 01935 423902 Fax: 01935 420908

A listed Georgian Dower House with a delightful
garden offers exceptional comfort and charm.
The restaurant, locally popular and nationally
renowned, serves superb food and interesting
wines at affordable prices – worth a detour!
6 bedrs SB £60 DB £93 HBS £78 HBD £66 B £7
L £12.50 D £21.95 CC: MC Vi Am Swi

How to get there: On A37 south from Yeovil, left
at first roundabout (by Red House pub) through
village. House signed left after 200 yards.

531 Travelodge Yeovil

Travel Accommodation
A303, Podimore, Yeovil, Somerset, BA22 8JG
Tel: 08700 850 950
Web: www.travelodge.co.uk
31 bedrs B £4.25 CC: MC Vi Am DC Swi Delt

Open and
shut case

Don't get caught out by unexpected legal costs

The availability of Legal Aid in all types of cases has all but disappeared. So what do you do if you or members of your family suffer injury after an accident? Visit a high street solicitor hoping that financial assistance will be available?

'No win No fee agreements' **Many solicitors and claims recovery firms may offer this facility but at what cost? In some instances they may ask you to pay up front for out of pocket expenses for reports and court fees. A GP's report may be just £50 but a specialist medical report may be £450. If your claim proceeds to court, Court fees may cost in excess of £100 and Barrister's fees commence at £100 per hour!**

A hefty insurance premium to underwrite your claim may be payable. **And as much as 30% may be deducted from the compensation awarded to you in lieu of their fees! That means if you were awarded £5000 for your injuries, you would receive only £3500! RAC's Legal Expenses Insurance ensures you receive your damages in full.**

RAC Legal Expenses Insurance is personal based and will cover you irrespective of the vehicle you are travelling in. **Further Cover may be obtained to protect your partner or your family!**

Does your existing policy cover the following benefits?

- Up to £50,000 legal expenses cover for non-fault accidents
- Up to £10,000 legal expenses cover for the defence of certain road traffic offences
- 24 hour legal helpline providing advice on most legal matters
- Cover driving/travelling in any vehicle
- Cover for passengers travelling with you
- Cover for you as a pedestrian

Consider the alternatives and ask yourself whether you would take the same comfort and peace of mind from these that RAC legal expenses insurance will provide you with?

Call now! Immediate cover is available from just **£15**

08705 533533

A to B – we RAC to it

East Anglia

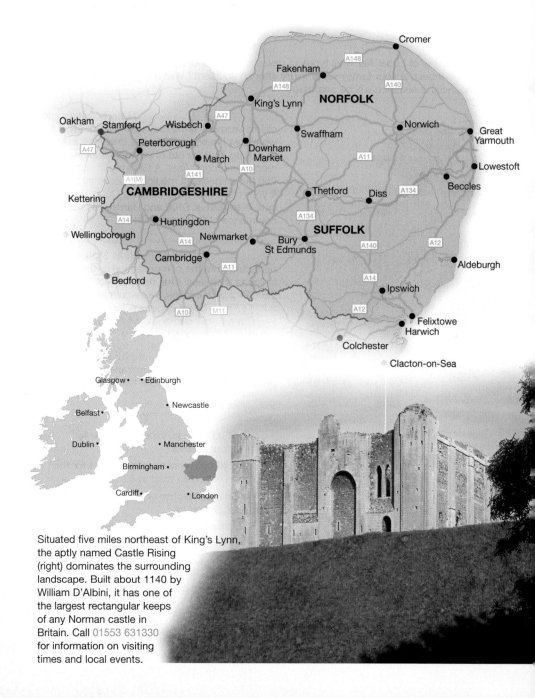

Cromer

A148

Fakenham

A148

A140

King's Lynn

NORFOLK

Oakham

Stamford

Wisbech

A47

Norwich

Great
Yarmouth

Peterborough

Swaffham

A47

Downham
Market

A11

Lowestoft

March

A141

A10

Beccles

A1(M)

CAMBRIDGESHIRE

Thetford

Diss

A134

Kettering

A134

Huntingdon

A14

Wellingborough

A14

Newmarket

SUFFOLK

Bury
St Edmunds

A140

A12

Cambridge

A11

Aldeburgh

Bedford

A14

Ipswich

A10

M11

A12

Felixtowe
Harwich

Colchester

Clacton-on-Sea

Glasgow •   • Edinburgh

• Newcastle

Belfast •

Dublin •   • Manchester

Birmingham •

Cardiff •   • London

Situated five miles northeast of King's Lynn,
the aptly named Castle Rising
(right) dominates the surrounding
landscape. Built about 1140 by
William D'Albini, it has one of
the largest rectangular keeps
of any Norman castle in
Britain. Call 01553 631330
for information on visiting
times and local events.

● In medieval times the coastal communities of East Anglia had stronger trading links with the Netherlands than with London. One consequence of this attachment to Holland are the windmills that can be seen dotted around the Norfolk countryside. Many windmills have been restored to full working order, such as at Billingford (01603 222705), Denver (01366 3840090), Great Bircham (01485 578393), Berney Arms at Halvergate Marsh (01604 730320). Seasonal closures and opening times vary, so it is best to telephone first, or check with local Tourist Information centres.

● At Cromer on the North Norfolk coast it is said that when you look out to sea there is no 'land' until the North Pole!

On the beach

Gorleston-on-Sea, across the mouth of the Yare from Great Yarmouth, in Norfolk has a secluded bay with sandy beaches stretching into the distance. Safe bathing, windsurfing, yachting and jet-skiing are all popular, but there is also a quieter side to Gorleston, with its early Victorian villas and a still-working inshore fishing fleet.

The Great Yarmouth area alone has 15 miles of beaches. Further south are the old fishing ports of Aldeburgh (below) and Southwold.

Boating on the River Ant; a great way to relax.

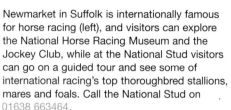

Newmarket in Suffolk is internationally famous for horse racing (left), and visitors can explore the National Horse Racing Museum and the Jockey Club, while at the National Stud visitors can go on a guided tour and see some of international racing's top thoroughbred stallions, mares and foals. Call the National Stud on 01638 663464.

● Colchester is England's oldest town (founded by the Romans in the 5th century BC). It makes an excellent base for visiting the surrounding countryside including the Stour valley, nearby towns such as Clacton-on-Sea and Ipswich, and has several interesting sights itself including its Dutch Quarter and massive castle keep, set in attractive parkland. Call 01206 282828 for the Visitor Information Centre.

In 1284, Cambridge became a centre of learning with the founding of the first colleges. In 1441, Henry VI rebuilt much of the city, and his centrepiece was the glorious King's College, with its magnificent chapel (right). Until 1873 only Eton students were allowed to study at the college, but in 1972 it became one of the first to admit women. The author E.M. Forster and the economist John Maynard Keynes are among its famous alumni. Call 01223 331212 or go to www.tourismcambridge.com.

● Cambridge university was allegedly founded in the1220s by scholars driven from Oxford.

The bosses at the junctions of Norwich Cathedral's magnificent vaulted ceiling (above) depict the story of the Bible.

The Butt and Oyster (above) is one of the best-known pubs in Suffolk. At high tide it is possible to serve drinks directly from the bar to the people aboard boats on the River Orwell.

Accommodation index

Hotels and Guest Accommodation are indexed by their order of appearance within this region, not by the page. To locate an establishment, note the number to the right of the listing and then find it on the establishment's name bar, as shown here

• At Sutton Hoo, the burial site of Anglo-Saxon King Raedwald, was discovered in 1939, with a second site found in 1991.

• Although East Anglia has a reputation for being flat, Suffolk has quite hilly terrain.

A haven for many species of birds, the Norfolk Broads (above) are among the most important wetlands in Europe.

37 The Turning Mill Hotel

The Bridge of Sighs in Cambridge is a beautiful sight while punting on the River Cam.

East Anglia

Abington, Cambridgeshire

1 Travelodge Abington

Travel Accommodation
A11, Fourwentways, Abington,
Cambridgeshire, CB1 6AP
Tel: 08700 850 950
Web: www.travelodge.co.uk
40 bedrs B £4.25 CC: MC Vi Am DC Swi Delt

Blakeney, Norfolk

2 Blakeney Hotel

★★★★

Quayside, Blakeney, Norfolk, NR25 7NE
Tel: 01263 740797 Fax: 01263 740795
Email: reception@blakeney-hotel.co.uk
Web: www.blakeney-hotel.co.uk
59 bedrs SB £60 DB £120 HBS £70 HBD £70
B £8.50 L £12.90 D £22.50
CC: MC Vi Am DC Swi

How to get there: The hotel is situated on the Quay at Blakeney and is signposted from the A149 coast road midway between Sheringham and Wells.

3 Blakeney Manor Hotel

★★

The Quay, Blakeney, Holt, Norfolk, NR25 7ND
Tel: 01263 740376 Fax: 01263 741116
Closed January 6-27

Located on Blakeney Quay overlooking National Trust marshland, this privately-owned 16th-century manor house has flint-faced barn conversions. Guests enjoy comfortable lounges, sunny courtyard, and dining in our popular restaurant.
37 bedrs SB £33 DB £66 HBS £38 HBD £38

B £7.50 L £6.95 D £17
CC: MC Vi Swi Delt

How to get there: Blakeney Quay is located off the A149 coast road between Cromer and Wells.

Bury St. Edmunds, Suffolk

4 Butterfly Hotel

★★★

Symonds Road, Moreton Hall Estate,
Bury St. Edmunds, Suffolk, IP32 7BW
Tel: 01284 705800 Fax: 01284 702545
Email: burybutterfly@lineone.net
Web: www.butterflyhotels.co.uk
65 bedrs SB £88 DB £96.50 HBS £105.50
HBD £65.75 B £8.50 L £15 D £17.50
CC: MC Vi Am DC Swi Delt

How to get there: Take A14 towards Bury St. Edmunds (Bury East exit).

Cambridge, Cambridgeshire

5 Gonville Hotel

★★★

Gonville Place, Cambridge,
Cambridgeshire, CB1 1LY
Tel: 01223 221111 Fax: 01223 315470
Email: info@gonvillehotel.co.uk
Web: www.gonvillehotel.co.uk
64 bedrs SB £109 DB £139 HBS £121.50
HBD £164 B £10.50 L £5.50 D £12
CC: MC Vi Am DC Swi Delt

How to get there: Exit M11 at junction 11. Take A1309 to city centre. At second mini-roundabout turn right into Lensfield Road. Straight on at main junction. Hotel 20 yards on right.

Making a booking?

Don't forget to mention RAC Hotels and Bed & Breakfast 2002.

Plan your route

Visit www.rac.co.uk for RAC's interactive route planner, including up to the minute traffic reports.

6 Arundel House Hotel

★★★ ♞ ♞

Chesterton Road, Cambridge,
Cambridgeshire, CB4 3AN
Tel: 01223 367701 Fax: 01223 367721
Email: info@arundelhousehotels.co.uk
Web: www.arundelhousehotels.co.uk
Closed Christmas

Beautifully located overlooking the River Cam
and open parkland, this elegant Victorian
terrace hotel offers some of the best food in the
area. Close to the city centre and University
colleges.
102 bedrs SB £67.50 DB £85 B £5.95 L £18.95
D £18.95
CC: MC Vi Am DC Swi Delt
⊗⊜⛝☎Ⓟ♨⛾☾♬⛩⛲⛲
How to get there: The hotel is situated in the
north of the city, overlooking the River Cam.
From M11 J13, follow signs to Cambridge until
mini-roundabout. Turn left then through traffic
lights. Hotel 400 yards on left.

7 Centennial Hotel

★★

63/71 Hills Road, Cambridge,
Cambridgeshire, CB2 1PG
Tel: 01223 314652 Fax: 01223 315443
Closed Christmas to New Year
39 bedrs SB £77 DB £93 HBS £92 HBD £59
CC: MC Vi Am DC Swi Delt
&⊗⊜⛝☎Ⓟ♨⛾☾⛲⛲
How to get there: Opposite botanical gardens,
conveniently near railway station and city
centre.

8 Cambridge Lodge Hotel

Little Gem

♦♦♦♦ ♞ ♞ ❦

139 Huntingdon Road, Cambridge,
Cambridgeshire, CB3 0DQ
Tel: 01223 352833 Fax: 01223 355166
Email: cambridge.lodge@btconnect.com
Web:
www.smoothound.co.uk/hotels/cambridge.html

Our mock-tudor hotel and restaurant prides
itself on providing a warm welcome to all. Fine
dining in our intimate beamed restaurant and
comfortable accommodation bring guests back
time after time.
15 bedrs SB £66 DB £82 B £8.25 L £15.50 D £22
CC: MC Vi Am DC Swi Delt
⊗⊜⛝☎Ⓟ♨⛲⛲
How to get there: J13 M11 turn right onto
Madingley Road, then left into Storeys Way.
From A14 onto A1307, then onto Huntingdon
Road.

9 Hills Guesthouse Cambridge

♦♦♦♦

157 Hills Road, Cambridge, CB2 2RJ
Tel: 01223 214216 Fax: 01223 214216

10 Lensfield Hotel

♦♦♦♦

53 Lensfield Road, Cambridge,
Cambridgeshire, CB2 1EN
Tel: 01223 355017 Fax: 01223 312022
Email: enquiries@lensfieldhotel.co.uk
Web: www.lensfieldhotel.co.uk
Closed Christmas
30 bedrs SB £55 DB £89 HBS £64 HBD £53.50
B £5 D £9
CC: MC Vi Am DC Swi Delt
⊗⊜⛝☎📞Ⓟ♨⛾☾⛲

How to get there: Take signposts to Cambridge centre and join city ring road. Approach hotel via Silver Street or Trumpington Street, turning into Lensfield Road.

11 Suffolk House

♦ ♦ ♦ ♦ ※
69 Milton Road, Cambridge,
Cambridgeshire, CB4 1XA
Tel: 01223 352016 Fax: 01223 566816
Children minimum age: 8

Friendly, non-smoking, family run establishment, within easy walking distance of city centre and colleges. All rooms ensuite with direct dial telephone. Pleasant secluded garden. Private car park.
8 bedrs SB £60 DB £75
CC: MC Vi Am Swi Delt JCB
⊗ 🕭 ▢ ☎ 🅿 ⸙
How to get there: 1¼ miles from A10/A14/ A1309 junction.

12 Ashtrees Guest House

♦ ♦ ♦ ※
128 Perne Road, Cambridge,
Cambridgeshire, CB1 3RR
Tel: 01223 411233 Fax: 01223 411233
Email: mandy@mhill22.fsnet.co.uk
Closed January
7 bedrs
CC: MC Vi
⊗ 🕭 ▢ 🅿 ⸙

How to get there: On city ring road between Trumpington and Newmarket Road. From M11 leave at Junction 11. From A14 westbound use A1303, eastbound B1047.

13 Assisi Guest House

♦ ♦ ♦
193 Cherry Hinton Road, Cambridge,
Cambridgeshire, CB1 7BX
Tel: 01223 246648 Fax: 01223 412900
Closed Christmas to New Year

Fine detached Victorian house ideally situated for the university and Addenbrooke's Hospital. Family run offering personal service, with spacious rooms all ensuite with colour TV, telephone and tea/coffee-making facilities. Large car park.
19 bedrs SB £35 DB £50
CC: MC Vi Am Swi Delt
& ⊗ 🕭 ▢ ☎ 🅿
How to get there: From the centre of Cambridge, take the Hills Road toward Addenbrooke's Hospital. Cherry Hinton Road is the first left after the railway station turning.

14 Brooklands

♦ ♦ ♦ ※
95 Cherry Hinton Road, Cambridge,
Cambridgeshire, CB1 7BS
Tel: 01223 242035 Fax: 01223 242035
Web: www.brooklandsguesthouse.co.uk
5 bedrs SB £30 DB £50
CC: MC Vi Am DC Swi Delt
✉ ⊗ 🕭 ▢ ☎ 🅿 ⸙

East Anglia

Chatteris, Cambridgeshire

15 Cross Keys Hotel

★ 🏃 🏃

12-16 Market Hill, Chatteris,
Cambridgeshire, PE16 6BA
Tel: 01354 693036 Fax: 01354 694454
Email: thefens@crosskeyshotel.fsnet.co.uk

This delightful 16th century inn offers old world
charm, traditional hospitality and friendly
service. Situated at the junction of the A141 and
A142 opposite the parish church in the heart of
the Fens.
12 bedrs SB £21.50 DB £32.50 HBD £44
B £5.50 L £9.50 D £12.50 CC: MC Vi Swi Delt JCB
🖾 🛏 ⊗ 🖭 🕾 🅿 🛎 ⅋ ℃ Ħ 🧺 ⠿ ⠿
How to get there: Enter into Chatteris on the A141
or A142. Hotel in the centre of the town, opposite
the parish church of St. Peter & St. Paul.

Clacton-on-Sea, Essex

16 The Sandrock Hotel

◆◆◆

1 Penfold Road, Marine Parade West,
Clacton-on-Sea, Essex, CO15 1JN
Tel: 01255 428215 Fax: 01255 428215

Well-presented small hotel in excellent position
very close to sea-front. High standards of
house-keeping and a friendly welcome. Good
home-cooking. Rear car park.

9 bedrs SB £35 DB £52 HBS £47 HBD £38
D £12 CC: MC Vi Am DC Swi Delt JCB
🚾 🛏 ⊗ 🖭 🅿 🛎 ⅋ ℃ 🧺 ⠿
How to get there: Take A120 to Clacton. Turn
right at the seafront. The Sandrock Hotel is in
the second turning on the right, past pier.

Cromer, Norfolk

17 Westgate Lodge Hotel

◆◆◆◆ ✕

Macdonald Road, Cromer, Norfolk, NR27 9AP
Tel: 01263 512840
Children minimum age: 3
11 bedrs
CC: MC Vi Swi Delt
🖭 🅿 ⠿ 🛎 ⠿⠿⠿
How to get there: Just off the main seafront
opposite the Putting Green.

18 Cliff Cottage Bed & Breakfast

◆◆◆

18 High Street, Overstrand, Norfolk, NR27 0AB
Tel: 01263 578179
Email: roymin@btinternet.com
2 bedrs DB £38 CC: None accepted
🛏 ⊗ 🖭 🅿
How to get there: Take B1159 Cromer to
Mundesley road. Turn left into Overstrand
village. Turn left again prior to Sea Marge Hotel.
Cottage at end.

19 Wellington Hotel

◆◆◆

Garden Street, Cromer, Norfolk, NR27 9HN
Tel: 01263 511075 Fax: 01263 511914
Closed Christmas
8 bedrs SB £27.50 DB £35 L £5
CC: MC Vi Swi Delt
⊗ 🖭 🛎 Ħ ⠿⠿⠿ 🍷
How to get there: Situated just above the pier
and beaches.

20 Anglia Court Hotel

◆◆

Seafront, Runton Road, Cromer,
Norfolk, NR27 9AR
Tel: 01263 512443 Fax: 01263 573104
Email: cward31567@aol.com
Web: www.smoothhound.co.uk/hotels/
angliaco.html
27 bedrs
CC: MC Vi Am DC Swi Delt

How to get there: From Norwich, enter Cromer on A140 and follow A149 for Sheringham. From King's Lynn enter Cromer on A148 and follow A149 to Sheringham.

Dereham, Norfolk

21 Yaxham Mill

♦ ♦ ♦

Norwich Road, Yaxham, Dereham,
Norfolk, NR19 1RP
Tel: 01362 693144 Fax: 01362 699801
Web: www.yaxham-mill.co.uk
8 bedrs SB £30 DB £39.50 B £2.99 L £2.99
D £5.95 CC: MC Vi Swi Delt

How to get there: A47 Dereham follow signs for Wynmondham until you reach Yaxham, continue on towards Mattishall, ½ mile on the right.

Downham Market, Norfolk

22 Castle Hotel

★ ★

High Street, Downham Market, Norfolk, PE38 9HF
Tel: 01366 384311 Fax: 01366 384311
Email: castle@castle-hotel.com
Web: www.castle-hotel.com
12 bedrs SB £59 DB £75 HBS £67 HBD £99
B £8.50 L £11.95 D £17.95 CC: MC Vi Am

How to get there: From M11 take A10 for Ely into Downham Market. At traffic lights straight over. Hotel on next corner.

Duxford, Cambridgeshire

23 Duxford Lodge Hotel

★ ★ ★ ★ 🏚 🏚 🏚

Ickleton Road, Duxford,
Cambridgeshire, CB2 4RU
Tel: 01223 836444 Fax: 01223 832271
Email: duxford@btclick.com
Web: www.touristnetuk.com/em/duxford
15 bedrs SB £57.50 DB £99 HBS £82.50
HBD £74.50 B £4.25 L £10 D £25
CC: MC Vi Am DC Swi Delt

How to get there: M11 at Junction 10 take A505 eastbound. Take 1st right turn. Hotel ½ a mile.
See advert above right

Duxford Lodge Hotel

Country House Hotel in beautiful grounds, ten minutes south of Cambridge off J10 M11. Ideal when visiting Duxford Air Museum. Near to Colleges, Newmarket races and 20 minutes from Stansted Airport. Private dining available. Ground floor rooms opening onto gardens. Minimum rates for Friday, Saturday and Sunday nights.

Duxford, Cambridgeshire, CB2 4RU
Tel: 01223 836444   Fax: 01223 832271
duxford@btclick.com
www.touristnetuk.com/em/duxford

Ely, Cambridgeshire

24 Travelodge Ely

Travel Accommodation
A10, Ely Bypass, Ely, Cambridgeshire, CB3 3NN
Tel: 08700 850 950
Web: www.travelodge.co.uk
39 bedrs B £4.25
CC: MC Vi Am DC Swi Delt

25 Nyton

♦ ♦ ♦

7 Barton Road, Ely, Cambridgeshire, CB7 4HZ
Tel: 01353 662459 Fax: 01353 666217
Email: nytonhotel@yahoo.co.uk
10 bedrs SB £45 DB £70 HBS £60 HBD £65
CC: MC Vi Am DC

How to get there: From A10, pass golf centre on right. Take first turning on right, signposted 'Cathedral Car Park'. Hotel is on right hand side, 200 yards into turning.

Fakenham, Norfolk

26 Wensum Lodge Hotel

★★ ®

Bridge Street, Fakenham, Norfolk, NR21 9AY
Tel: 01328 862100 Fax: 01328 863365
17 bedrs
CC: MC Vi Swi Delt

How to get there: Situated a few yards away
from town centre. Easily reached from Norwich
on A1067, King's Lynn on A148 and Swaffham
on A1065.

Felixstowe, Suffolk

27 Orwell Hotel

★★★ ®

Hamilton Road, Felixstowe, Suffolk, IP11 7DX
Tel: 01394 285511 Fax: 01394 670687
Email: office@orwellhotel.co.uk
Web: www.orwellhotel.co.uk
58 bedrs SB £65 DB £75 HBS £77.50
HBD £48.75 B £9.50 L £15.50 D £18
CC: MC Vi Am DC Swi Delt

How to get there: A14 to Felixstowe. Straight at
dock roundabout. Straight at second
roundabout. Right at third roundabout into
Beatrice Ave. Hotel at end.

28 Grafton Guest House

♦♦♦♦

The Grafton, 13 Sea Road, Felixstowe,
Suffolk, IP11 2BB
Tel: 01394 284881 Fax: 01394 279101

Fenstanton, Cambridgeshire

29 Travelodge Fenstanton

Travel Accommodation
A14, Cambridge Road, Fenstanton,
Cambridgeshire, PE18 9LP
Tel: 08700 850 950
Web: www.travelodge.co.uk
40 bedrs B £4.25
CC: MC Vi Am DC Swi Delt

Gorleston-on-Sea, Norfolk

30 The Pier Hotel

★★

Harbour Mouth, Gorleston-on-Sea,
Norfolk, NR31 6PL
Tel: 01493 662631 Fax: 01493 440263
Email: bookings@pierhotelgorleston.co.uk
Web: www.pierhotelgorleston.co.uk
19 bedrs SB £46 DB £55 HBS £52.50 HBD £80
B £6.50 L £10 D £11.50
CC: MC Vi Am DC Swi Delt

How to get there: From A12 Lowestoft or A47
Norwich three miles from Yarmouth. Ask for
Harbourmouth Gorleston-on-Sea.

Great Yarmouth, Norfolk

31 Cliff Hotel

★★★

Cliff Hill, Gorleston-on-Sea, Norfolk, NR31 6DH
Tel: 01493 662179 Fax: 01493 653617
Email: cliffhotel@aol.com
39 bedrs
CC: MC Vi Am DC Swi Delt

How to get there: From M11 take A11 to
Norwich, then A47 to Great Yarmouth. Hotel is at
north end of Gorleston's Upper Marine Parade.

32 Imperial Hotel

★★★ ®

North Drive, Great Yarmouth, Norfolk, NR30 1EQ
Tel: 01493 842000 Fax: 01493 852229
Email: imperial@scs-datacom.co.uk
Web: www.imperialhotel.co.uk
39 bedrs SB £69 DB £85 HBS £90 HBD £66
B £8.50 L £12.50 D £20.50
CC: MC Vi Am DC Swi

How to get there: Follow signs to seafront. Turn
left into North Drive. Hotel is 1/2 mile north of
Britannia Pier.

33 Star Hotel

★★★
Hall Quay, Great Yarmouth, Norfolk, NR30 1HG
Tel: 01493 842294 Fax: 01493 330215
40 bedrs SB £69 DB £90 HBS £80 HBD £55
B £6.50 L £5 D £14.95
CC: MC Vi Am DC Swi Delt JCB

How to get there: From A12 directly opposite
Haven Bridge. On entering Yarmouth from A47
take the third exit on first roundabout on right.

34 The Regency Dolphin Hotel

★★★
14-16 Albert Square, Great Yarmouth,
Norfolk, NR30 3JH
Tel: 01493 855070 Fax: 01493 853798
Email: regency@meridianleisure.com
Web: www.meridianleisure.com
42 bedrs
CC: MC Vi Am DC Swi Delt

How to get there: Follow signs to pleasure
beach along north drive. Turn right at the Sea
Life Centre. Follow road into Albert Square.

35 Burlington Palm Court Hotel

★★
North Drive, Great Yarmouth, NR30 1EG
Tel: 01493 844568 Fax: 01493 331848
Email: enquiries@burlington-hotel.co.uk
Web: www.burlington-hotel.co.uk
Closed December to January

This family-run hotel has views of the sea and
recreation grounds. There is ample car parking
and an indoor swimming pool.
70 bedrs
CC: MC Vi Am DC Swi Delt

How to get there: Follow signs for seafront.
Hotel is 600 yards from Britannia Pier, at the
quieter end of town.

36 Sandringham Hotel

★★
74-75 Marine Parade, Great Yarmouth,
Norfolk, NR30 2BU
Tel: 01493 852427 Fax: 01493 852336
24 bedrs SB £29.50 DB £56.50 HBS £37.50
HBD £70 B £5.50 L £6.50 D £9.50 CC: MC Vi

How to get there: From seafront, turn inland
opposite Britannia Pier.

37 Two Bears

★★
Southtown Road, Great Yarmouth,
Norfolk, NR31 0HU
Tel: 01493 603198 Fax: 01493 440486

38 Admiral House Hotel

◆◆◆◆
12a Nelson Road South, Great Yarmouth,
Norfolk, NR30 3JL
Tel: 01493 343712 Fax: 01493 843712

39 All Seasons Lodge Hotel

◆◆◆◆
55-56 Clarence Road, Gorleston,
Great Yarmouth, Norfolk, NR31 6DR
Tel: 01493 651111
CC: None accepted

40 Corner House Hotel

◆◆◆◆
Albert Square, Great Yarmouth,
Norfolk, NR30 3JH
Tel: 01493 842773
Email: accommodation
@thecornerhousehotel.co.uk
Web: www.thecornerhousehotel.co.uk
Closed October to March
8 bedrs SB £25 DB £50 HBS £32 HBD £32 B £6
D £10 CC: None accepted

How to get there: From A12/A47 south along
seafront. Opposite Wellington Pier & Winter
Gardens.

East Anglia

41 Alclive Hotel

♦♦♦

33-35 North Denes Road, Great Yarmouth,
Norfolk, NR30 4LU
Tel: 01493 844741
Closed October to April
20 bedrs SB £26 DB £46 HBS £30 HBD £27
CC: MC Vi Swi Delt
How to get there: Take the A47 to Great
Yarmouth. Turn left at roundabout onto A149.
Turn right at traffic lights. Take the first left into
Salisbury Road. Turn left at North Denes Road.

42 Anglia House Hotel

♦♦♦

56 Wellesley Road, Great Yarmouth,
Norfolk, NR30 1EX
Tel: 01493 844395
10 bedrs SB £15 DB £30 HBS £23 HBD £23 D £8
CC: None accepted
How to get there: Follow seafront signs. Left at
lights past Sainsbury's. Through traffic lights,
turn left. Opposite Wellesley Park.

43 Arch House

♦♦♦

14 Wellington Road, Great Yarmouth,
Norfolk, NR30 3AQ
Tel: 01493 854258
8 bedrs SB £17 DB £38 HBS £17 HBD £19
CC: None accepted

44 Armani Hotel

♦♦♦

14-15 Sandown Road, Great Yarmouth,
Norfolk, NR30 1EY
Tel: 01493 843870 Fax: 01493 843870
Email: armani-hotel@faxvia.net
Web: www.smoothhound.co.uk/hotels/
        armanih.html
Children minimum age: 3
22 bedrs SB £20 DB £20 HBS £28 HBD £28 D £8
CC: None accepted
How to get there: Follow signs to seafront. On
seafront turn left. Sandown Road is second turn
left opposite entrance to Waterways Garden.

45 Beaumont House

♦♦♦

52 Wellesley Road, Great Yarmouth,
Norfolk, NR30 1EX
Tel: 01493 843957 Fax: 01493 301241
Email: hotelbeaumont@virgin.net
14 bedrs SB £16 DB £32 HBS £23 HBD £23 D £7
CC: MC Vi Swi Delt
How to get there: Hotel is one street away from
beach, overlooking Wellesley Park recreation
ground.

46 Belvedere

♦♦♦ ❦

90 North Denes Road, Great Yarmouth,
Norfolk, NR30 4LN
Tel: 01493 844200

Open all year. Car parking. Ensuite rooms
available with central heating, colour TVs, tea
and coffee-making facilities. Own keys: access
at all times. Varied menu.
9 bedrs CC: None accepted
How to get there: At seafront, proceed north to
'Waterways' – turn left into Beaconsfield Road.
Turn right at mini roundabout. Hotel fifth
property on right.

47 Bonheur Hotel

♦♦♦ ❦

3 Norfolk Square, Great Yarmouth,
Norfolk, NR30 1EE
Tel: 01493 843042 Fax: 01493 745235
Email: en@bonheur-hotel.co.uk
Web: www.bonheur-hotel.co.uk
10 bedrs SB £20 DB £40 HBS £28 HBD £27.50
D £8 CC: MC Vi Am Swi Delt JCB

48 Bramalea Balmoral

◆◆◆

114–115 Wellesley Road, Great Yarmouth,
Norfolk, NR30 2AR
Tel: 01493 844722
15 bedrs SB £16 DB £32 HBS £22 HBD £22
CC: None accepted

How to get there: From bus station go left into
Regent Road; over traffic lights, turn left into
Wellesley Road. Property is 100 yards on right.

49 Cavendish House

◆◆◆

19/20 Princes Road, Great Yarmouth,
Norfolk, NR30 2DG
Tel: 01493 844829 Fax: 01493 843148

50 Chateau Hotel

◆◆◆

1 North Drive, Great Yarmouth,
Norfolk, NR30 1ED
Tel: 01493 859052
Closed October to March
11 bedrs SB £28.50 DB £46
CC: MC Vi Delt

How to get there: Opposite bowling greens on
seafront, just north of Britannia Pier.

51 Chequers Hotel

◆◆◆ ※

27 Nelson Road South, Great Yarmouth,
Norfolk, NR30 3JA
Tel: 01493 853091
Email: david@chequershotel.freeserve.co.uk
8 bedrs SB £18 DB £36 HBS £24 HBD £48
CC: None accepted

How to get there: Drive to seafront. Turn
opposite Wellington pier, then turn down Albert
Square. At T junction, Chequers is on opposite
corner.

52 Collingwood Hotel

◆◆◆

25/26 Princes Road, Great Yarmouth,
Norfolk, NR30 2DG
Tel: 01493 844398 Fax: 01493 844398
Web: www.smoothhound.co.uk/hotels/
collingwood.html
Children minimum age: 6
Closed December and January

19 bedrs SB £19 DB £20
CC: MC Vi Am Swi Delt

How to get there: Follow signs to the seafront.
Turn right. Princes Road is opposite the
Britannia Pier. Collingwood is the second hotel
on the left.

53 Dene House

◆◆◆

89 North Denes Road, Great Yarmouth,
Norfolk, NR30 4LW
Tel: 01493 844181 Fax: 01493 302359
Email: pulham@denehouse.fsbusiness.co.uk
8 bedrs SB £15 DB £30 HBS £22 HBD £44
CC: MC Vi Swi Delt

How to get there: Off A47, signs for seafront; at
traffic lights past Sainsbury's, left to
roundabout; straight on past six houses, on the
right.

54 Fairholme Hotel

◆◆◆

23-24 Princes Road, Great Yarmouth,
Norfolk, NR30 2DG
Tel: 01493 843447

55 Gai-Sejour

◆◆◆

21 Princes Road, Great Yarmouth,
Norfolk, NR30 2DG
Tel: 01493 843371
11 bedrs SB £14 DB £30 HBS £19 HBD £40 D £5
CC: None accepted

How to get there: Off Marine Parade, just
opposite Britannia Pier.

56 Hamilton Hotel

◆◆◆ ※

23/24 North Drive, Great Yarmouth,
Norfolk, NR30 4EU
Tel: 01493 844662 Fax: 01493 332123
Email: enquiries@hamilton-hotel.co.uk
Web: www.hamilton-hotel.co.uk
25 bedrs SB £32 DB £48 HBS £40 HBD £64
B £5 D £8
CC: MC Vi Swi Delt

How to get there: Follow signs for seafront. Turn
left at Brittania Pier Hotel 800 yards along the
seafront.

East Anglia

57 Hotel Victoria

2 Kings Road, Great Yarmouth,
Norfolk, NR30 3JW
Tel: 01493 843872 Fax: 01493 843872
35 bedrs SB £21 DB £36 HBS £29 HBD £26
CC: MC Vi Am Swi Delt

How to get there: Kings Road is opposite the model village, close to Wellington Pier. Second building in from seafront.

58 Kentville Guest House

5 Kent Square, Great Yarmouth,
Norfolk, NR30 2EX
Tel: 01493 844783
9 bedrs SB £15 DB £34 HBS £20 HBD £44
CC: None accepted

How to get there: Kent Square is just off the seafront. Take Standard Road (opposite Marina Leisure Centre). Hotel is in corner.

59 Kilbrannan

14 Trafalgar Road, Great Yarmouth,
Norfolk, NR30 2LD
Tel: 01493 850383
5 bedrs SB £17 DB £32
CC: None accepted

How to get there: Approach sea front past Britannia pier. Before the Marina Centre, turn right up Trafalgar Road. Kilbrannan is half way up.

60 Kingsley House

68 King Street, Great Yarmouth,
Norfolk, NR30 2PP
Tel: 01493 850948 Fax: 01493 850948
Email: brian.savoury@bt.internet.com
7 bedrs SB £18 DB £36 HBS £23 HBD £23
CC: None accepted

How to get there: Located at the southern end of King Street. Kingsley House is a short walk from seafront and town centre.

61 Lea-Hurst

117 Wellesley Road, Great Yarmouth,
Norfolk, NR30 2AP
Tel: 01493 843063
Email: jilltheleahurs@netscapeonline.co.uk
8 bedrs
CC: None accepted

How to get there: Take A47 to Great Yarmouth. Follow signs to seafront. Turn right at Britannia Pier onto Regent Road. Take first road on right (Wellesley Road). Lea-Hurst 30 yards on right.

62 Little Emily Hotel

18 Princes Road, Great Yarmouth,
Norfolk, NR30 2DG
Tel: 01493 842515
9 bedrs SB £15 DB £30 HBS £21 HBD £21
CC: None accepted

How to get there: Follow A12 into Great Yarmouth. Follow signs to seafront and Britannia Pier. Princes Road is immediately left, before pier.

63 Marine Lodge

19-20 Euston Road, Great Yarmouth,
Norfolk, NR30 1DY
Tel: 01493 331210 Fax: 01493 332040
Email: marinelodge@burlington-hotel.co.uk
Closed November to March
39 bedrs SB £32 DB £40 B £6
CC: MC Vi Am DC Swi Delt

How to get there: Marine Lodge is situated 300 yards north of the Britannia Pier on Great Yarmouth seafront.

64 Maryland

53 Wellesley Road, Great Yarmouth,
Norfolk, NR30 1EX
Tel: 01493 844409
Children minimum age: 2
7 bedrs SB £18 DB £34 HBS £28 HBD £27
CC: None accepted

How to get there: Follow seafront signs. Turn left at traffic lights into St. Nicholas Road. Go straight over traffic lights, turn left. 400 yards on left.

65 Raynscourt Hotel

♦ ♦ ♦

83 Marine Parade, Great Yarmouth,
Norfolk, NR30 2DJ
Tel: 01493 856554
Closed January to March
55 bedrs SB £28 DB £52 HBS £33.50
HBD £33.50 B £4.50 D £7.50
CC: MC Vi Am DC Swi Delt JCB

66 Richmond House

♦ ♦ ♦ ✍

113 Wellesley Road, Great Yarmouth,
Norfolk, NR30 2AR
Tel: 01493 853995
Children minimum age: 3
Closed Christmas
8 bedrs
CC: MC Vi

How to get there: Close to Britannia pier and
seafront.

67 Russell Private Hotel

♦ ♦ ♦ ✍ ♞

26 Nelson Road South, Great Yarmouth,
Norfolk, NR30 3JL
Tel: 01493 843788
Email: paul.mason@russell-private-hotel.co.uk
Web: www.russell-private-hotel.co.uk
Closed October to April
10 bedrs SB £20 DB £40 HBS £26 HBD £25
CC: MC Vi Delt

How to get there: Turn right past Wellington
Pier, onto Kings Road. Take next right onto
Nelson Road South. Hotel 150 yards on left.

68 Sandholme Hotel

♦ ♦ ♦

12-13 Sandown Road, Great Yarmouth,
Norfolk, NR30 1EY
Tel: 01493 300001 Fax: 01493 842161
Email: sandholme@lineone.net
Web: www.sandholme-hotel.co.uk
Children minimum age: 3
19 bedrs SB £20 DB £35 HBS £29 HBD £23.50
CC: MC Vi Am Swi Delt

How to get there: Follow seafront signs. When
sea is in front of you, turn left. At the Imperial
Hotel & Waterways turn left. The Sandholme is
50 yards on right.

69 Sedley House

♦ ♦ ♦

5 St. Georges Road, Great Yarmouth,
Norfolk, NR30 2JR
Tel: 01493 855409
Children minimum age: 10
7 bedrs SB £13 DB £26 CC: None accepted

How to get there: From A12, take bypass to
A47. Enter town via A47. Continue over
roundabout. Cross four sets of lights, turn left
after park. Sedley House is 50 yards on left.

70 Senglea Lodge

♦ ♦ ♦

7 Euston Road, Great Yarmouth,
Norfolk, NR30 1DX
Tel: 01493 859632
Email: info@senglealodge.freeserve.co.uk
Web: www.uk-bedandbreakfasts.com
7 bedrs SB £15 DB £30 HBS £21 HBD £21
CC: MC Vi Swi

How to get there: On entering Great Yarmouth
on the A47 or A12, go straight over 1st and 2nd
roundabouts. Take a left turn to seafront. Go
straight through traffic lights. Lodge on right
hand side.

71 Shemara Guest House

♦ ♦ ♦

11 Wellesley Road, Great Yarmouth,
Norfolk, NR30 2AR
Tel: 01493 844054 Fax: 01493 844054
Closed December
9 bedrs CC: None accepted

How to get there: Take A47 to Yarmouth, past
rail station. Follow signs for seafront. Take
fourth turning right. Wellesley Road is halfway
down on right.

72 Sienna Lodge

♦ ♦ ♦

17-18 Camperdown, Great Yarmouth,
Norfolk, NR30 3JB
Tel: 01493 843361
Closed November
14 bedrs SB £22 DB £44 HBS £28 HBD £28 D £8
CC: None accepted

How to get there: Turn off seafront opposite Sea
Life Centre into Camperdown. Sienna Lodge is
on the corner of Nelson Road South.

East Anglia

73 Siesta Lodge

53/54 York Road, Great Yarmouth,
Norfolk, NR30 2NE
Tel: 01493 843207
Email: siesta-lodge@aol.com
Web: www.siestalodge.co.uk
7 bedrs SB £15 DB £30 HBS £20 HBD £20 D £5
CC: None accepted

How to get there: Along the seafront going south, Marina centre on left and Maritime Museum on right, York Road is next right.

74 Southern Hotel

46 Queens Road, Great Yarmouth,
Norfolk, NR30 3JR
Tel: 01493 843313 Fax: 01493 853047
Email: southern.hotel@tinyonline.co.uk
Web: www.southernhotel.co.uk
Closed October to March
20 bedrs SB £24 DB £42 HBS £28 HBD £52
CC: None accepted

How to get there: Southern Hotel is situated close to Wellington Pier and Model Village on Great Yarmouth's Golden Mile.

75 Sunshine Lodge Hotel

73 Marine Parade, Great Yarmouth,
Norfolk, NR30 2DQ
Tel: 01493 842250 Fax: 01493 857521
Email: john@sunshinelodge.freeserve.co.uk
Web: www.sunshinelodge.freeserve.co.uk
11 bedrs SB £18 DB £36
CC: MC Vi Swi Delt

How to get there: Sunshine Lodge is on the sea front opposite the Britannia Pier and just before the Hollywood cinema.

76 The Ryecroft

91 North Denes Road, Great Yarmouth,
Norfolk, NR30 4LW
Tel: 01493 844015 Fax: 01493 856096
Email: theryecroft@aol.com
Web: www.ryecroft-guesthouse.co.uk
8 bedrs SB £19 DB £38 HBS £28 HBD £28
CC: MC Vi Swi Delt JCB

How to get there: Keep seafront on your right. After "Waterways" sign take left Beaconsfield Road and right at crossroad into North Denes Road. Ryecroft on right.

77 The Shrewsbury Guest House

9 Trafalgar Road, Great Yarmouth,
Norfolk, NR30 2LD
Tel: 01493 844788

78 Thelton House Hotel

60 Wellesley Road, Great Yarmouth,
Norfolk, NR30 1EX
Tel: 01493 843288
Email: thelton@lineone.net
7 bedrs SB £15 DB £30
CC: None accepted

79 Trevi Guest House

57 Wellesley Road, Great Yarmouth,
Norfolk, NR30 1EX
Tel: 01493 842821
9 bedrs SB £15 DB £30 HBS £21 HBD £21
CC: None accepted

How to get there: Follow signs to seafront. Proceed through traffic lights past Sainsbury's. Take first turning on left. Trevi Guest House is opposite the recreation ground.

80 Windy Shore Hotel

♦ ♦ ♦

29 North Drive, Great Yarmouth,
Norfolk, NR30 4EW
Tel: 01493 844145 Fax: 01493 852364
Email: hduffield@windyshore.freeserve.co.uk
Web: www.windyshorehotel.co.uk

Situated in one of the prettiest parts of the
seafront, overlooking the illuminated Venetian
waterways and rock gardens, The Windyshore
is the ideal seaview hotel with ample car
parking.
25 bedrs SB £23.50 DB £42.50 HBS £32.50
HBD £30 B £4 D £9.50
CC: None accepted
How to get there: Head towards the sea front,
turn left and head north along North Drive.

81 Woods End

♦ ♦ ♦

49 Wellesley Road, Great Yarmouth,
Norfolk, NR30 1EX
Tel: 01493 842229
8 bedrs SB £15 DB £30 HBS £21.50 HBD £21.50
CC: None accepted
How to get there: Overlooking Wellesley Park
and sea.

82 Charron Guest House

♦ ♦

151 Nelson Road Central, Great Yarmouth,
Norfolk, NR30 2HZ
Tel: 01493 843177 Fax: 01493 843177
Children minimum age: 2
Closed October to Easter
10 bedrs SB £18 DB £42 HBS £25 HBD £28
CC: None accepted

83 Chatsworth Hotel

♦ ♦

32 Wellesley Road, Great Yarmouth,
Norfolk, NR30 1EU
Tel: 01493 842890
17 bedrs
CC: None accepted

84 Gable End Hotel

♦ ♦

30 North Drive, Great Yarmouth,
Norfolk, NR30 4EW
Tel: 01493 842112

85 Hotel Elizabeth

1 Marine Parade, Great Yarmouth,
Norfolk, NR30 3AG
Tel: 01493 855551 Fax: 01493 853338
Email: enqiries@hotelelizabeth.co.uk
Web: www.hotelelizabeth.co.uk
53 bedrs
CC: MC Vi Am DC Swi Delt JCB
How to get there: From A47 or A12 as you
approach Great Yarmouth follow signs to
seafront. Hotel located opposite Sea Life Centre
and Wellington Pier Theatre.

Hethersett, Norfolk

86 Travelodge Hethersett

Travel Accommodation
A11, Thickthorn Service Area,
Norwich Road, Hethersett,
Norwich, Norfolk, NR9 3AU
Tel: 08700 850 950
Web: www.travelodge.co.uk
62 bedrs B £4.25
CC: MC Vi Am DC Swi Delt

East Anglia

Holt, Norfolk

87 Daubeney Hall Farm

◆ ◆ ◆ ◆

Lower Hall Lane, Sharrington, Norfolk, NR24 2PQ
Tel: 01263 861412
Email: ninaogier@hotmail.com
2 bedrs SB £23 DB £40 CC: None accepted

How to get there: At Fakenham, take A148
eastbound for nine miles. Turn right into lane for
Sharrington. Take first left past church.
Daubeney Hall is 100 yards on left.

88 Lawns Hotel

◆ ◆ ◆ ◆

26 Station Road, Holt, Norfolk, NR25 6BS
Tel: 01263 713390 Fax: 01263 710642
Email: info@lawnshotel.co.uk
Web: www.lawnshotel.co.uk
Children minimum age: 8
10 bedrs SB £37.50 DB £75 CC: MC Vi Swi Delt

How to get there: Situated 50m from town
centre War Memorial along Station Road.

Horning, Norfolk

89 Petersfield House Hotel

★ ★ ★

Lower Street, Horning, Norfolk, NR12 8PF
Tel: 01692 630741 Fax: 01692 630745
Email: reception@petersfieldhotel.co.uk
Web: www.petersfieldhotel.co.uk
18 bedrs SB £60 DB £80 HBS £67 HBD £52
B £7.50 L £13.95 D £16.95 CC: MC Vi Am DC

How to get there: From Norwich, take the
A1151 to Wroxham. Turn right at Hoveton,
taking A1062 to Horning. The hotel is in the
centre of the village.

Hunstanton, Norfolk

90 Caley Hall Motel

★ ★

Old Hunstanton, Hunstanton, Norfolk, PE36 6HH
Tel: 01485 533486 Fax: 01485 533348
38 bedrs SB £42 DB £64 HBS £60.75
HBD £50.75 D £18.75
CC: MC Vi Swi Delt

91 Lodge Hotel & Restaurant

★ ★ ★

Old Hunstanton Road, Hunstanton,
Norfolk, PE36 6HX
Tel: 01485 532896 Fax: 01485 535007
Email: reception@thelodge-hotel.co.uk
Web: www.thelodge-hotel.co.uk
22 bedrs SB £51 DB £98 HBS £72 HBD £70
B £7.50 L £10 D £22
CC: MC Vi Am Swi Delt

How to get there: From King's Lynn, take the
A149 to Hunstanton and on into Old
Hunstanton. Hotel on right-hand side.

Huntingdon, Cambridgeshire

92 Huntingdon Marriott Hotel

★ ★ ★ ★

Kingfisher Way, Hinchingbrooke Business Park,
Huntingdon, Cambridgeshire, PE29 6FL
Tel: 01480 446000 Fax: 01480 451111
Web: www.marriotthotels.com/cbghd
150 bedrs SB £125 DB £138 B £10 L £10 D £25
CC: MC Vi Am DC Swi Delt

How to get there: From A1/M6/M1 take A14
towards Cambridge. Pass Brampton racecourse.
Hotel is on right at next roundabout.

93 Lion Hotel

★ ★

High Street, Buckden, Huntingdon,
Cambridgeshire, PE18 5XA
Tel: 01480 810313 Fax: 01480 811070
15 bedrs SB £65 DB £85 B £5.50 L £12.50
D £16.75 CC: MC Vi Am Swi Delt

94 The Grange Hotel

◆ ◆ ◆

115 High Street, Brampton, Huntingdon,
Cambridgeshire, PE28 4RA
Tel: 01480 459516 Fax: 01480 459391
Email: enquiries@grangehotelbrampton.com
Web: www.grangehotelbrampton.com
8 bedrs SB £55 DB £70 CC: MC Vi Am Swi Delt

How to get there: Exit A14 Brampton
racecourse (B1514) towards Huntingdon. After
mini-roundabout, turn right into Grove Lane.
Hotel faces T-junction.

Ipswich, Suffolk

95 Hintlesham Hall

Gold Ribbon Winner

★★★★ ®®®

Hintlesham, near Ipswich, Suffolk, IP8 3NS
Tel: 01473 652334 Fax: 01473 652463
Email: reservations@hintlesham-hall.co.uk
Web: www.hintleshamhall.com

An uncommon blend of formality and relaxation
conjured by a friendly professional staff in a
glorious hotel and restaurant. A unique health
club and a top class golf club.
33 bedrs SB £94 DB £120 L £21 D £27
CC: MC Vi Am DC Swi

How to get there: Five miles west of Ipswich on
the A1071.

96 Courtyard by Marriott Ipswich

★★★

The Havens, Ransomes Europark, Ipswich,
Suffolk, IP3 9SJ
Tel: 01473 272244 Fax: 01473 272484
Email: reservations.ipswich@whitbread.com
Web: www.courtyard.com/ipwcy
60 bedrs SB £92 DB £99 HBS £110 HBD £67
CC: MC Vi Am DC Swi Delt

How to get there: Travelling east on the A14,
once over the Orwell bridge take the slip road
signposted Ransomes Europark. The hotel
faces you.

Plan your route

Visit www.rac.co.uk for RAC's
interactive route planner, including
up to the minute traffic reports.

97 Novotel Ipswich

★★★

Greyfriars Road, Ipswich, Suffolk, IP1 1UP
Tel: 01473 232400 Fax: 01473 232414
Web: www.novotel.com
100 bedrs SB £92 DB £103 HBS £108
HBD £135 B £11 L £14 D £16
CC: MC Vi Am DC Swi Delt JCB

How to get there: From the A12/A14, take the
A137 towards Ipswich Central for two miles.
After crossing river, hotel is visible ahead.

98 Swallow Belstead Brook Hotel

★★★ ®

Belstead Road, Ipswich, Suffolk, IP2 9HB
Tel: 01473 68241 Fax: 01473 681249
Email: sales@belsteadbrook.co.uk
Web: www.belsteadbrook.co.uk

This 16th-century former hunting lodge, found in
the suburbs, offers superb grounds, original
features and fine food which has won an RAC
Dining Award.
88 bedrs SB £99 DB £108.75 HBS £119.50
HBD £70 B £7.75 L £14.95 D £20.50
CC: MC Vi Am DC Swi Delt

How to get there: Just south of Ipswich, five
minutes from A12/A14 intersection.

99 Travelodge Ipswich

Travel Accommodation
A12 Southbound, Bentley Service Station,
Capel St. Mary, Ipswich, Suffolk, IP9 2JJ
Tel: 08700 850 950
Web: www.travelodge.co.uk
32 bedrs B £4.25
CC: MC Vi Am DC Swi Delt

East Anglia

King's Lynn, Norfolk

100 Butterfly Hotel

★★★

Beveridge Way, Hardwick Narrows Estate,
King's Lynn, Norfolk, PE30 4NB
Tel: 01284 705800 Fax: 01284 702545
Email: kingsbutterfly@lineone.net
Web: www.butterflyhotels.co.uk
50 bedrs SB £83.50 DB £92 HBS £98.50
HBD £61 B £8.50 L £15 D £15
CC: MC Vi Am DC Swi

How to get there: A10/A147 roundabout.

101 Congham Hall Hotel
Gold Ribbon Winner

★★★ ❀ ❀ ❀ ❀

Grimston, King's Lynn, Norfolk, PE32 1AH
Tel: 01485 600250 Fax: 01485 601191
Email: reception@conghamhallhotel.co.uk
Web: www.conghamhallhotel.co.uk
14 bedrs SB £85 DB £130 HBS £115
HBD £97.50 B £10 L £5 D £27.50
CC: MC Vi Am DC Swi Delt JCB

102 Kismet Bed & Breakfast

◆ ◆ ◆ ◆ ❀ ❀

Main Road, Terrington St. John, King's Lynn,
Norfolk, PE14 7RR
Tel: 01945 881364 Fax: 01945 881364
Children minimum age: 12

Centrally located between King's Lynn and
Wisbech in bypassed village. Well-decorated,
fully-equipped en-suite bedrooms. $\frac{1}{2}$-acre
garden, excellent parking, guests' lounge/diner.
Holders of RAC Warm Welcome and Sparkling
Diamond awards.
3 bedrs DB £50 CC: None accepted

How to get there: From King's Lynn take A47 to
Wisbech. Take 1st slip road off A47. Turn left,
and after 150 yards left again. Hotel is white
property 500 yards on left.

103 Guanock Hotel

◆ ◆ ◆

South Gates, King's Lynn, Norfolk, PE30 5QJ
Tel: 01553 772959 Fax: 01553 772959
Email: guanockhotel@faxvia/net
17 bedrs SB £22 DB £39 D £5
CC: MC Vi Am DC Swi Delt JCB

How to get there: From A47 A17 follow signs to
town centre. We are on right immediately after
passing through the south gates.

104 Twinson Lee

◆ ◆ ◆

109 Tennyson Road, King's Lynn,
Norfolk, PE30 5PA
Tel: 01553 762900 Fax: 01533 769944
Closed Christmas
3 bedrs SB £20 DB £40 HBS £26 HBD £28
CC: None accepted

105 Beeches Guest House

◆ ◆

2 Guanock Terrace, King's Lynn,
Norfolk, PE30 5QT
Tel: 01553 766577 Fax: 01553 776664
Closed Christmas
7 bedrs SB £25 DB £40 HBS £31.50 HBD £27
D £7.50
CC: MC Vi Am Swi Delt JCB

Lavenham, Suffolk

106 Heritage Hotels – The Swan

★★★★ ❀

High Street, Lavenham, Suffolk, CO10 9QA
Tel: 0870 4008116 Fax: 01787 248286
Email: heritagehotels_lavenham.swan
@forte-hotels.com
Web: www.heritage-hotels.com
51 bedrs SB £79 DB £158 HBS £94 HBD £188
B £14.95 L £13.95 D £27.95
CC: MC Vi Am DC Swi Delt

How to get there: Follow the A14, then A134
Sudbury and follow signs for Lavenham. The
hotel is situated on the High Street.

Leiston, Suffolk

107 White Horse Hotel

★

Station Road, Leiston, Suffolk, IP16 4HD
Tel: 01728 830694 Fax: 01728 833105
Email: whitehorse@globalnet.co.uk
Web: www.whitehorsehotel.co.uk
14 bedrs SB £37.50 DB £56
B £6 L £7.50 D £11.50
CC: MC Vi Am DC Swi Delt

Lolworth, Cambridgeshire

108 Travelodge Lolworth

Travel Accommodation
A14, Huntingdon Road, Lolworth,
Cambridgeshire, CB3 8DR
Tel: 08700 850 950
Web: www.travelodge.co.uk
20 bedrs B £4.25
CC: MC Vi Am DC Swi Delt

Lowestoft, Suffolk

109 Albany Hotel

♦ ♦ ♦

400 London Road South, Lowestoft,
Suffolk, NR33 0BQ
Tel: 01502 574394 Fax: 01502 581198
Email: geoffrey.ward@btclick.com
Web: www.albanyhotel-lowestoft.co.uk
8 bedrs
CC: MC Vi Swi Delt

How to get there: Situated on A12 northbound,
the hotel is approximately 350 yards on right
once you have entered the one-way system.

110 Hazeldene

♦ ♦ ♦

21 Marine Parade, Lowestoft, Suffolk, NR33 0QL
Tel: 01502 517 907
5 bedrs SB £22 DB £36
CC: None accepted

How to get there: Seafront location at South
Beach and opposite lifeguards' station. Five
minutes walk from town centre and railway
station.

March, Cambridgeshire

111 The Olde Griffin Inn

★ ★

High Street, March, Cambridgeshire, PE15 9JS
Tel: 01354 652517 Fax: 01354 650086
Web: www.smoothhound.co.uk/
       hotels/oldegrif.html
21 bedrs SB £45.00 DB £59.50
B £5.45 L £5.95 D £6.95
CC: MC Vi Am DC Swi Delt JCB

How to get there: Entering March from any
direction, the hotel is the biggest white building
in the middle of the High Street.

Mildenhall, Suffolk

112 Smoke House

★ ★ ★

Beck Row, Mildenhall, Suffolk, IP28 8DH
Tel: 01638 713223 Fax: 01638 712202
Email: enquiries@smoke-house.co.uk
Web: www.smoke-house.co.uk

Oak beams, log fires and a warm welcome
await you at the Smoke House. Facilities
include modern bedrooms, two bars, two
lounges and a restaurant. 96 bedrooms, all
ensuite.
96 bedrs SB £80 DB £105 HBS £92.50
HBD £57.50 B £9.50 L £15.95 D £15.95
CC: MC Vi Am DC Swi Delt

113 Travelodge Mildenhall

Travel Accommodation
A11, Five Ways Roundabout, Barton Mills,
Mildenhall, Suffolk, IP28 6AE
Tel: 08700 850 950
Web: www.travelodge.co.uk
40 bedrs B £4.25 CC: MC Vi Am DC Swi Delt

114 Cobbles Restaurant With Rooms — Little Gem

♦ ♦ ♦ ♦ 🍴 🍴 ✕ 🥂

38 Market Place, Mildenhall, Suffolk, IP28 7EF
Tel: 01638 717022 Fax: 01638 717022
Email: gordon@thecobbles.netlineuk.net
Web: www.cobblesrestaurant.co.uk
Children minimum age: 3
3 bedrs
CC: MC Vi Am Swi Delt
⊗ 🗐 🖵 🏂 🐾 ♨ ♙

How to get there: Exit A11 at Barton Mills roundabout, take A1101 to Mildenhall. At second mini-roundabout turn left, then take next left to Market Place.

Needham Market, Suffolk

115 Travelodge Needham Market

Travel Accommodation
A14/A140, Needham Market, Suffolk, IP6 8LP
Tel: 08700 850 950
Web: www.travelodge.co.uk
40 bedrs B £4.25
CC: MC Vi Am DC Swi Delt
🐾 🗐 🖵 🏂

Newmarket, Suffolk

116 Bedford Lodge Hotel

★★★
Bury Road, Newmarket, Suffolk, CB8 7BX
Tel: 01638 663175 Fax: 01638 667391

117 Rutland Arms Hotel

★★★
High Street, Newmarket, Suffolk, CB8 8NB
Tel: 01638 664251 Fax: 01638 666298
Email: gapleisure@rutlandarmshotel.com
Web: www.rutlandarmshotel.com

Old fashioned hospitality in the heart of Newmarket. As the home of racing, Newmarket has attracted the great and the good since the time of Charles II, and few have left the town without a visit to the historic Rutland Arms, one of the High Street's most striking buildings and one of Newmarket's finest establishments.
46 bedrs SB £72.50 DB £84.50 B £6.25
L £12.50 D £17.50
CC: MC Vi Am DC Swi Delt
⊗ 🗐 🖵 ☎ 📞 🅿 🏂 🍴 ♨ ♙

How to get there: From M11 take A11 (Junction 9) and signs to Newmarket town centre. Hotel is on the High Street.

118 Swynford Paddocks Hotel

★★★★ 🍴 🍴
Six Mile Bottom, Newmarket, Suffolk, CB8 0UE
Tel: 01638 570234 Fax: 01638 570283
Email: sales@swynfordpaddocks.com
Web: www.swynfordpaddocks.com
15 bedrs SB £110 DB £135 B £12.50 L £24.50
D £28.50
CC: MC Vi Am DC Swi Delt
⚙ 🐴 🗐 🖵 ☎ 🅿 🏂 🎍 🐾 ♨ ♙ ⚲

How to get there: From A14 take A1303 signposted Newmarket. After ³/₄ mile, turn right after Prince Albert pub. Continue for five miles to crossroads at Six Mile Bottom. Turn left.

Norwich, Norfolk

119 De Vere Dunston Hall

★★★★ 🍴 🍴
Ipswich Road, Norwich, Norfolk, NR14 8PQ
Tel: 01508 470444 Fax: 01508 470689
Email: dhreception@devere-hotels.com
130 bedrs SB £110 DB £150 HBS £115
HBD £95 B £13 L £7 D £16
CC: MC Vi Am DC Swi Delt
♿ 🛗 ⚙ ⊗ 🗐 🖵 ☎ 📞 🅿 🏂 🍴 🌳 ♨ ♙ 🍸 🎿 ⚲
🎱 💲

How to get there: On the A140 Ipswich Road, three miles south of Norwich centre, just off the A47.

120 Marriott Sprowston Manor Hotel & Country Club

★★★★ 🍴
Wroxham Road, Norwich, Norfolk, NR7 8RP
Tel: 01603 410871 Fax: 01603 423911

121 Annesley House Hotel

★★★

6 Newmarket Road, Norwich, Norfolk, NR2 2LA
Tel: 01603 624553 Fax: 01603 621577
Closed Christmas and New Year
26 bedrs
CC: MC Vi Am DC Swi Delt

How to get there: On A11, ¹/₂ mile from city centre on right-hand side.

122 Barnham Broom Hotel & Country Club

★★★★

Honingham Road, Barnham Broom, Norwich,
Norfolk, NR9 4DD
Tel: 01603 759393 Fax: 01603 758224
Email: enquiry@barnhambroomhotel.co.uk
Web: www.barnham-broom.co.uk
52 bedrs SB £90 DB £110 HBS £108.50
HBD £73.50 B £8.95 L £11.75 D £18.50
CC: MC Vi Am DC Swi Delt

How to get there: 10 miles west of Norwich, off A47/A11 trunk routes. Follow brown tourist signs bearing a white golf flag.

123 Oaklands Hotel

★★★

89 Yarmouth Road, Thorpe St. Andrews,
Norfolk, NR7 0HH
Tel: 01603 434471 Fax: 01603 700318
Email: reception@oaklands-hotel.co.uk
Web: www.oaklands.hotel.co.uk
38 bedrs SB £65 DB £75 HBS £75 HBD £42.50
B £7.50 L £7.50 D £17.95
CC: MC Vi Am Swi Delt

How to get there: Turn off the A47 onto the A1042. Then join the A1242 towards Norwich. The Oaklands is on the right hand side.

124 Quality Hotel Norwich

★★★

2 Barnard Road, Bowthorpe, Norwich,
Norfolk, NR5 9JB
Tel: 01603 741161 Fax: 01603 741500
Email: admin@gb619.u-net.com
Web: www.choicehotels.com
80 bedrs SB £100.75 DB £110.75 HBS £116.25
HBD £63.13 B £11.75 L £15.50 D £15.50
CC: MC Vi Am DC Swi Delt

How to get there: From A11, follow A47 towards Swaffham. Situated on A1074 Norwich/Cromer road. At double roundabout go straight over. Hotel next roundabout on right.

125 Swallow Nelson Hotel

★★★

Prince of Wales Road, Norwich,
Norfolk, NR1 1DX
Tel: 01603 760260 Fax: 01603 620008
132 bedrs SB £102.50 DB £123
B £8.50 L £11.50 D £16.95
CC: MC Vi Am DC Swi Delt JCB

How to get there: Follow signs to city centre and station. The hotel is situated opposite the railway station.

126 Hotel Wroxham

★★

The Bridge, Wroxham, Norwich,
Norfolk, NR12 8AJ
Tel: 01603 782061 Fax: 01603 784279
Email: enquiries@hotelwroxham.co.uk
Web: www.hotelwroxham.co.uk

Situated on the banks of the River Bure, in the capital of Broadland, only seven miles from Norwich on the A1151, the Hotel Wroxham is a riverside oasis catering for both the leisure and business visitor. Its unique 'Waterside Terrace Bar and Restaurant' serves a la carte, carvery and bar snack meals. Excellent wedding and conference facilities, riverside suites with balconies, private boat moorings and car parking.
18 bedrs SB £42.50 DB £65 HBS £52.50
HBD £37.50 L £5.95 D £6.95
CC: MC Vi Am Swi Delt

How to get there: Take A1151 from Norwich at Wroxham, 1st right after the River Bridge, then hard right again. Car park is on the right.

East Anglia

127 Travelodge Acle

Travel Accommodation
A47, Acle bypass, Acle, Norwich,
Norfolk, NR13 3BE
Tel: 08700 850 950
Web: www.travelodge.co.uk
40 bedrs B £4.25
CC: MC Vi Am DC Swi Delt
🏶🖥️🖵♿

128 Gables Guest House

♦♦♦♦

527 Earlham Road, Norwich, Norfolk, NR4 7HN
Tel: 01603 456666 Fax: 01603 250320
Closed December 20 to January 2

Friendly, family-run non-smoking guest house
with secluded gardens, high quality ensuite
rooms, illuminated car park at rear. Walking
distance to university. Close to city, research
park and hospital.
11 bedrs SB £40 DB £58
CC: MC Vi Swi Delt JCB
♿🏶⊗🖥️🖵☎️📞🅿️♿€🔥
How to get there: From southern bypass, take
B1108 Watton Road and follow signs for
University/City Centre. After Fiveways
roundabout, The Gables is 300 yards on the left.

129 Edmar Lodge

♦♦♦

64 Earlham Road, Norwich, Norfolk, NR2 3DF
Tel: 01603 615599 Fax: 01603 495599
Email: mail@edmarlodge.co.uk
Web: www.edmarlodge.co.uk

Edmar Lodge is a family run guest house where
you will find a warm welcome. Cable TV in
rooms. We are situated only 10 minutes walk
from city centre.
5 bedrs SB £28 DB £40
CC: MC Vi Am Swi Delt JCB
🏶⊗🖥️🖵🅿️♿🔥
How to get there: Ring road or A47 take B1108
into city. Edmar Lodge on the right towards city
just past controlled zone signs.

130 Kings Head Inn

♦♦♦

The Street, Acle, Norwich, Norfolk, NR13 3DY
Tel: 01493 750204 Fax: 01493 750713
Email: info@kingsheadinnacle.co.uk
6 bedrs SB £35.90 DB £54.85
B £4.50 L £5.95 D £7.95
CC: MC Vi Swi Delt
🏶🖥️🖵🅿️♿🔥♿🎿🎿
How to get there: From A11 or A140, join A47 to
Yarmouth. Continue to Acle, turn off into Acle,
Kings Head in centre.

131 Wedgewood House

♦♦♦🐾

42 St. Stephens Road, Norwich, Norfolk, NR1 3RE
Tel: 01603 625730 Fax: 01603 615035
Email: mail@wedgewoodhouse.co.uk
12 bedrs
CC: MC Vi Am DC Swi Delt
⊗🖥️🖵🅿️♿🎿
How to get there: Follow A1/Newmarket Road
towards city centre. Wedgewood House is on
right, opposite the hospital.

Peterborough, Cambridgeshire

132 Peterborough Marriott Hotel

★★★★

Alwalton Village, Lynch Wood, Peterborough,
Cambridgeshire, PE2 6GB
Tel: 01733 371111 Fax: 01733 238077
Web: www.marriotthotels.co.uk
157 bedrs SB £60 DB £70 HBS £74 HBD £49
B £11 L £15.50 D £19.75
CC: MC Vi Am Swi Delt JCB
❄️♿🏶⊗🖥️🖵☎️❄️📞🅿️♿🎿🔥♿☎️🎿🎿
🎿🍴🖵
How to get there: Turn off A1 at
Alwalton/showground/Chesterton. At T-Junction
turn left. Hotel is at next roundabout on your
left.

133 Bull Hotel

★★★
Westgate, Peterborough,
Cambridgeshire, PE1 1RB
Tel: 01733 561364 Fax: 01733 557304
Email: info@bull-hotel-peterborough.com
118 bedrs
CC: MC Vi Am DC Swi Delt

How to get there: From A1, follow city centre
signs. Boures Boulevard, St. John's Road. First
left at roundabout, New Road, right along
Northminster, hotel on left.

134 Butterfly Hotel

★★★
Thorpe Meadows, off Longthorpe Parkway,
Peterborough, Cambridgeshire, PE3 6GA
Tel: 01284 705800 Fax: 01284 702545
Email: peterbutterfly@lineone.net
Web: www.butterflyhotels.co.uk
70 bedrs SB £88 DB £96.50 HBS £103
HBD £63.25 B £8.50 L £15 D £17.50
CC: MC Vi Am DC Swi

135 Travelodge Peterborough

Travel Accommodation
A47/A1073
Tel: 08700 850 950
Web: www.travelodge.co.uk
42 bedrs B £4.25
CC: MC Vi Am DC Swi Delt

136 Travelodge Peterborough (Alwalton)

Travel Accommodation
A1 South, Alwalton, Peterborough,
Cambridgeshire, PE7 3UR
Tel: 08700 850 950
Web: www.travelodge.co.uk
32 bedrs B £4.25
CC: MC Vi Am DC Swi Delt

137 Thorpe Lodge Hotel

◆◆◆
83 Thorpe Road, Peterborough,
Cambridgeshire, PE3 6JQ
Tel: 01733 348759 Fax: 01733 891598

Southwold, Suffolk

138 28 Fieldstile Road

◆◆◆
28 Fieldstile Road, Southwold,
Suffolk, IP18 6LD
Tel: 01502 723588 Fax: 01502 723588
Open Easter to October
3 bedrs SB £35 DB £45
CC: None accepted

How to get there: Southwold. Cross mini-
roundabout, first left. Past church & hospital
towards seafront, No.28 left side with sign and
red door.

139 Anchor House

◆◆◆
19 North Road, Southwold,
Suffolk, IP18 6BG
Tel: 01502 725055 Fax: 01502 725055
1 bedrs SB £35 DB £50
CC: None accepted
How to get there: Take main road into
Southwold over 'Might's Bridge'. Take first left
into North Road. Anchor House is 10th property
on right.

East Anglia

St. Ives, Cambridgeshire

140 Dolphin Hotel

★★★

London Road, St. Ives, Huntingdon,
Cambridgeshire, PE27 5EP
Tel: 01480 466966 Fax: 01480 495597
Web: www.dolphinhotelcambs.co.uk

The Dolphin Hotel is a family-owned hotel on
the banks of the Great Ouse in the old market
town of St. Ives. Guests enjoy good food and
friendly efficient service. The large riverside
terrace is ideal for a refreshing drink or light
meal served in a relaxed atmosphere. The
terrace and waterside restaurant offer
panoramic views of the river and surrounding
120 acres of meadow land.
67 bedrs SB £80 DB £100
B £6 L £5.50 D £14.50
CC: MC Vi Am DC Swi Delt
How to get there: From A14, take A1096
towards St. Ives. Turn left at first roundabout,
then immediately right. The Dolphin is 800 yards
further on.

141 Oliver's Lodge Hotel

★★★

Needingworth Road, St. Ives,
near Cambridge, Cambridgeshire,
PE17 4JP
Tel: 01480 463252 Fax: 01480 461150
Email: reception@oliverslodge.co.uk
Web: www.oliverslodge.co.uk
17 bedrs
CC: MC Vi Am Swi Delt
How to get there: From M11/A1, take A14 then
A1096 to St. Ives. At 1st roundabout, go straight
across. At next roundabout, turn left and first
right. Hotel 500 yards down the road on right.

142 Slepe Hall Hotel

★★★

Ramsey Road, St. Ives,
Cambridgeshire, PE27 5RB
Tel: 01480 463122 Fax: 01480 300706
Email: mail@slepehall.co.uk
Web: www.slepehall.co.uk
16 bedrs SB £80 DB £95
B £7.50 L £12.50 D £15.50
CC: MC Vi Am DC Swi Delt
How to get there: Leave A14 on A1096. At
roundabout with Manchester Arms pub, take
A1123 towards Huntingdon. At traffic lights by
Toyota garage turn left. Slepe Hall 1/3 of a mile
on left.

Stowmarket, Suffolk

143 Travelodge Stowmarket

Travel Accommodation
A45 West, Westbound, Haughley, Stowmarket,
Suffolk, IP14 3PY
Tel: 08700 850 950
Web: www.travelodge.co.uk
40 bedrs B £4.25
CC: MC Vi Am DC Swi Delt

Sudbury, Suffolk

144 Mill Hotel

★★★

Walnut Tree Lane, Sudbury, Suffolk, CO10 1BD
Tel: 01787 375544 Fax: 01787 373027
56 bedrs SB £69.50 DB £99
B £8 L £15 D £25
CC: MC Vi Am DC Swi Delt
How to get there: From A12 Colchester take
A134 to Sudbury. Follow signs for A131. Pass
main square, 3rd on right.

145 Old Bull & Trivets Guesthouse

◆ ◆ ◆

Church Street, Sudbury, Suffolk, CO10 6BL
Tel: 01787 374120 Fax: 01787 379044
9 bedrs SB £47 DB £57 B £5 L £5 D £8
CC: MC Vi Am DC Swi Delt

Swaffham, Norfolk

146 Lydney House Hotel

★★

Norwich Road, Swaffham,
Norfolk, PE37 7QS
Tel: 01760 723355 Fax: 01760 721410
Email: rooms@lydney-house.demon.co.uk
Web: www.lydney-house.demon.co.uk
12 bedrs CC: MC Vi Am Swi

How to get there: Lydney House can be found
on Norwich Road, ¼ of a mile from traffic lights
in centre of town.

147 Horse & Groom

◆◆◆

40 Lynn Street, Swaffham, Norfolk, PE37 7AX
Tel: 01760 721567

Swavesey, Cambridgeshire

148 Travelodge Swavesey

Travel Accommodation
A14, Cambridge Road, Swavesey,
Cambridgeshire, CB4 5QA
Tel: 08700 850 950
Web: www.travelodge.co.uk
36 bedrs B £4.25 CC: MC Vi Am DC Swi Delt

Thetford, Norfolk

149 Lynford Hall Hotel

★★★

Lynford Hall, Mundford, near Thetford,
Norfolk, IP26 5HW
Tel: 01842 878351 Fax: 01842 878252
21 bedrs SB £79 DB £99 B £11 L £16 D £25
CC: MC Vi Am Swi Delt

How to get there: From A134 Mundford roundabout take A1065 to Swaffham. Take first right.

150 Comfort Inn Thetford

★★

Thetford Road, Northwold, near Thetford,
Norfolk, IP26 5LQ
Tel: 01366 728888 Fax: 01366 727121
Email: admin@gb632.u-net.com
Web: www.choicehotels.com

Children minimum age: 14
34 bedrs SB £62.75 DB £62.75 HBS £73.50
HBD £36.75 B £7.75 L £6.50 D £10.75
CC: MC Vi Am DC Swi Delt

How to get there: From Thetford roundabout
(A11/A134 north) follow A134 north for 12 miles
over a roundabout and past Northwold. Hotel
then on left.

Tivetshall St. Mary, Norfolk

151 Old Ram Coaching Inn

★★

Ipswich Road, Tivetshall St. Mary,
Norfolk, NR15 2DE
Tel: 01379 676794 Fax: 01379 608399
Email: theoldram@btinternet.com
Web: www.theoldram.com

Listed 17th century hotel, restaurant and free
house. Award winning food. Big on fish. Over-
60s' and children's menus. Superb
accommodation, meeting space. Ample car
parking.
11 bedrs SB £51.95 DB £70.90 HBS £55
HBD £85 B £6.95 L £9.95 D £11.95
CC: MC Vi Swi Delt

How to get there: On the A140, 15 minutes
south of Norwich and the A47 by-pass. Five
miles from the market town of Diss.

Walsingham, Norfolk

152 Old Rectory

◆◆◆

Waterden, Walsingham, Norfolk, NR22 6AT
Tel: 01328 823298
2 bedrs DB £50 CC: None accepted

How to get there: Take the B1355 Fakenham to
Burnham market road, turn right at Waterden
sign before the village centre of South Creake.
One mile up lane on left-hand side.

East Anglia

Wells-next-the-Sea, Norfolk

153 Kilcoroon

◆ ◆ ◆

Chancery Lane, Wells-next-the-Sea,
Norfolk, NR23 1ER
Tel: 01328 710270
Children minimum age: 10
3 bedrs DB £38
CC: None accepted

How to get there: At Wells town sign, turn
towards town centre. Third turning right onto
Buttlands, Kilcoroon situated left of Crown
Hotel.

154 Oyster Cottage Bed & Breakfast

◆ ◆ ◆

Oyster Cottage, 20 High Street, Wells-next-the-
Sea, Norfolk, NR23 1EP
Tel: 01328 711997 Fax: 01328 711910
Email: bb@oyster-cottage.co.uk
Web: www.oyster-cottage.co.uk
2 bedrs
CC: None accepted

How to get there: From town sign take Mill
Road to town centre, at junction by Barclays
Bank – High St. is on the right.

Wisbech, Cambridgeshire

155 Crown Lodge Hotel

★ ★ ⓡ

Downham Road, Outwell, Wisbech,
Cambridgeshire, PE14 8SE
Tel: 01945 773391 Fax: 01945 772668
Email: crownlodgehotel@hotmail.com
Web: www.smoothhound.co.uk/
     hotels/crownl.html

Situated on the banks of Well Creek, in the
village of Outwell, this family-run hotel offers a
warm, friendly atmosphere with excellent
standards of accommodation and cuisine.
10 bedrs SB £55 DB £70
B £8.45 L £12 D £16.50
CC: MC Vi Am DC Swi Delt JCB

How to get there: Situated on the A1122/A1101
Downham Market to Wisbech road.
Approximately five miles to Wisbech and seven
miles to Downham Market.

156 Rose & Crown

★ ★

Market Place, Wisbech,
Cambridgeshire, PE13 1DG
Tel: 01945 589800 Fax: 01945 474610
20 bedrs
CC: MC Vi Am DC Swi Delt

How to get there: From London, leave A1 at
Junction 10 and follow A47 to Wisbech. From
Suffolk, take A1101 and then A47 from King's
Lynn. The hotel is in the centre of Wisbech.

Woodbridge, Suffolk

157 Ufford Park Hotel

★ ★ ★ ⓡ

Yarmouth Road, Ufford,
Woodbridge,
Suffolk, IP12 1QW
Tel: 01394 383555 Fax: 01394 383582
Email: uffordparkltd@btinternet.com
Web: www.uffordpark.co.uk
50 bedrs SB £89 DB £105 HBS £95.95
HBD £66.45 B £9.95 L £4.95 D £17.95
CC: MC Vi Am DC Swi

Ask the experts

To book a Hotel or Guest
Accommodation, or for help
and advice, call RAC Hotel
Reservations on 0870 603 9109
and quote 'Guide 2002'

The easiest way to learn to drive

- Get a head start with the driving simulator

- Theory test training available

- Know your progress at every stage

- Mock theory and practical tests

- Manual, Automatic and Disability cars

- Save money with block booking discounts

- Instructor training available

- All major credit cards accepted

Call your local BSM centre on
08457 276 276

www.bsm.co.uk
Head Office: 1 Forest Road Feltham TW13 7RR

East Midlands

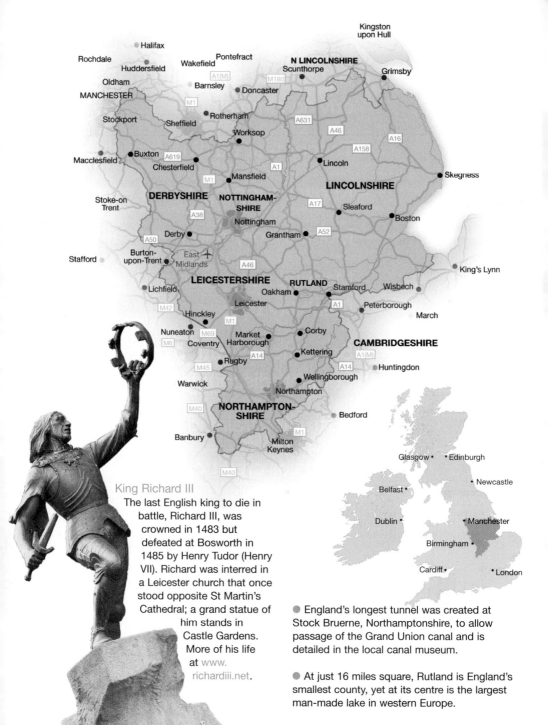

Halifax
Rochdale
Huddersfield
Oldham
MANCHESTER
Wakefield
Pontefract
Barnsley
A1(M)
M180
Doncaster
M1
Stockport
Sheffield
Rotherham
A631
Worksop
Buxton
A619
Chesterfield
Macclesfield
A1
Mansfield
M1
Stoke-on Trent
DERBYSHIRE
A38
Derby
A50
Burton-upon-Trent
East Midlands
Stafford
Lichfield
LEICESTERSHIRE
M42
Hinckley
Nuneaton
M69
M6
Coventry
Warwick
M45
Rugby
M40
Banbury
NORTHAMPTON-SHIRE
M40
Kingston upon Hull
N LINCOLNSHIRE
Scunthorpe
Grimsby
A46
A16
A158
Lincoln
Skegness
LINCOLNSHIRE
NOTTINGHAM-SHIRE
A17
Sleaford
Nottingham
Boston
Grantham
A52
King's Lynn
RUTLAND
Oakham
Stamford
Wisbech
A1
Peterborough
Leicester
March
Market Harborough
Corby
A14
Kettering
A1(M)
CAMBRIDGESHIRE
A14
Huntingdon
Wellingborough
Northampton
M1
Bedford
Milton Keynes

King Richard III

The last English king to die in battle, Richard III, was crowned in 1483 but defeated at Bosworth in 1485 by Henry Tudor (Henry VII). Richard was interred in a Leicester church that once stood opposite St Martin's Cathedral; a grand statue of him stands in Castle Gardens. More of his life at www.richardiii.net.

Glasgow • Edinburgh
• Newcastle
Belfast •
Dublin •
• Manchester
Birmingham •
Cardiff •
• London

● England's longest tunnel was created at Stock Bruerne, Northamptonshire, to allow passage of the Grand Union canal and is detailed in the local canal museum.

● At just 16 miles square, Rutland is England's smallest county, yet at its centre is the largest man-made lake in western Europe.

Robin Hood is still Nottingham's most famous son and biggest attraction. The statue of him (below) near the castle gatehouse is the most famous monument dedicated to the Sheriff of Nottingham's nemesis. For more on Hood and his haunts, see www.robinhood.co.uk.

● Simon de Montfort, Earl of Leicester (1239–65) and social reformer is celebrated in a number of places in the county. De Montfort Hall offers all types of music, opera, dance, musicals, shows and comedy. 0116 233 3113 or www.demontforthall.co.uk.

● The caverns of Blue John, Treak Cliff, Speedwell and Peak make Castleton, Derybyshire, the best area for show caves outside of the Mendips.

Part of the Peak District (below), Britain's first National Park, extends into north Derbyshire.

● The 11th-century St Martin's church was built over Roman foundations and later became Leicester's cathedral. The adjoining Guildhall was Leicester's town hall for 300 years and later a police station, but now houses a museum.

For three days every May Spalding in Lincolnshire (below) is host to a flower festival.

● The Galleries of Justice in Nottingham presents a history of crime and punishment, including the perpetrators, their restraints, enforcers and detection methods. You can be convicted in a Victorian courtroom and condemned to dank cells below! Call 0115 952 0555 or go to www.galleriesofjustice.org.uk.

Nottingham's grand Council House is topped by a 200-foot high dome (above) which houses a deep hour-bell. A mosaic coat of arms leads to Italian marble columns and steps to views of murals and a frieze inside the dome. Phone 0115 952 8323 to arrange a tour.

5, 4, 3, 2, 1...
The National Space Centre near Leicester celebrates space and space travel. Recreations of mission control and a space station, studies of astronaut training and satellite technology, and up-to-date reports on current space projects are upstaged by huge sections of rocket held in the centre's amazing translucent pupa-like tower. www.spacecentre.co.uk or 0870 607 7223.

Not everything Roman worked. The Jewry Wall (above) is part of an aqueduct to supply the public baths of Ratae Coritanorum (Leicester) with water, but it failed to do so. Roman relics are prevalent at the Jewry Wall Museum.

The religion of Jainism is based around six "substances" – soul, matter, motion, rest, space

and time. The Jain Centre in Leicester (left) is a place of pilgrimage for British followers of Jainism and a superlative piece of Indian architecture, decorated with unusual and intricate carvings.

There has been an inn on the site of the Trip To Jerusalem pub, Nottingham (above), since 1189; certainly the cellars built into the base of Castle Rock give the impression of an ancient site. So named because soldiers from the castle above visited before their trip to the Holy Land for the Third Crusade. Today it attracts those who enjoy unusual drinking establishments. Visit www.triptojerusalem.com.

● Newstead Abbey near Mansfield was the ancestral home of Lord Byron, romantic poet and unlikely participant in the Greek War of Independence. Visitors to the 12th-century house, a monastery until its dissolution by Henry VIII, can see Byron's apartment and manuscripts, first editions and memorabilia, and perhaps even the White Lady or Black Friar, the resident ghosts. www.newsteadabbey.co.uk or call 01623 455900 for more information.

● The Bakewell Show, Derbyshire, in August is a major agricultural event, its dog show and show jumping entrants often competing in Crufts and the Horse of the Year Show respectively.

● Lincolnshire once had many airfields; its aeronautic past is traced at Newark Air Museum, along with 54 planes and cockpits.

● The Heights of Abraham Country Park offers stunning views of the Derbyshire Dales, thanks to an alpine-style cable car system.

Accommodation index

Hotels and Guest Accommodation are indexed by their order of appearance within this region, not by the page. To locate an establishment, note the number to the right of the listing and then find it on the establishment's name bar, as shown here

(37) The Turning Mill Hotel

Alfreton, Derbyshire

1 Travelodge Alfreton

Travel Accommodation
A38/A61, Old Swanwick Colliery Road, Alfreton,
Derbyshire, DE55 1HJ
Tel: 08700 850 950
Web: www.travelodge.co.uk
60 bedrs B £4.25
CC: MC Vi Am DC Swi Delt

Alkmonton, Derbyshire

2 Dairy House Farm

◆ ◆ ◆ ◆ ⦰

Alkmonton, Longford, Derbyshire, DE6 3DG
Tel: 01335 330359 Fax: 01335 330359
Email: andy@dairyhousefarm.org.uk
Web: www.dairyhousefarm.org.uk

Red brick farmhouse with oak-beamed dining
room and lounge. Large inglenook fireplace.
Tranquil location, good home cooking and
colourful garden.
5 bedrs SB £25 DB £50 HBS £40 HBD £40
B £5 L £8 D £15
CC: None accepted
⊗ ⥁ ☐ P⦰ ⵜⵜⵜ ⫞
How to get there: Off A515 at Cubley: take road
to Alkmonton. Dairy House Farm is 1¹⁄₂ miles
south.

Ashbourne, Derbyshire

3 Callow Hall Hotel

★ ★ ★ ♞ ♞ ♞
Mappleton, Ashbourne, Derbyshire, DE6 2AA
Tel: 01335 300900 Fax: 01335 300512
Email: reservations@callowhall.co.uk
Web: www.callowhall.co.uk
Closed Christmas Day and Boxing Day

A unique atmosphere created in this family-run
country house hotel. Noted for its fine dining,
using the freshest of ingredients and superb
wine list. Victorian garden and woodland setting.
16 bedrs SB £85 DB £130 HBS £123 HBD £103
L £20.50 D £38.50
CC: MC Vi Am DC Swi
⫞ ⬚ ⥭ ⥁ ☐ ☎ ⬙ P⦰ ⵚ ⵏ ⪳ ⵜⵜⵜ ⵜⵜⵜ ⫞
How to get there: Follow A515 through
Ashbourne, after Market Square turn left past
Bowling Green pub. Take first right for
Mappleton, entrance on right after bridge.

4 Hanover International Hotel & Club Ashbourne

★ ★ ★
Derby Road, Ashbourne, Derbyshire, DE6 1XH
Tel: 01335 346666 Fax: 01335 346549
Email: hanoversale@ashbourneh.freeserve.co.uk
Web: www.hanover-international.com

HANOVER INTERNATIONAL
HOTELS & CLUBS

Attractively purpose-built hotel and leisure club
at the 'Gateway to Dovedale' with the highest
standards of traditional comfort and warm
friendly service.
50 bedrs SB £88 DB £103 B £8.95 L £5 D £15
CC: MC Vi Am DC Swi Delt
⟁ ⫞ ⛾ ⥭ ⊗ ⥁ ☐ ☎ ⬙ P ⵚ ⵏ ⪳ ⵜⵜⵜ ⵜⵜⵜ Ⓨ ⧇
How to get there: Take A52 to Ashbourne, first
roundabout turn right. Hotel approx ¹⁄₂ a mile on
the left.

5 Heritage Hotels – Peveril of the Peak

★★★

Thorpe, Ashbourne, Derbyshire, DE6 2AW
Tel: 0870 4008109 Fax: 01335 350507
Web: www.heritage-hotels.com
46 bedrs SB £105 DB £122 HBS £80 HBD £80
B £10.50 L £11.95 D £22
CC: MC Vi Am DC Swi Delt JCB

How to get there: Follow A515 from Ashbourne
towards Buxton. 1 mile out of Ashbourne turn
left, signposted Thorpe. Continue along this road
and hotel is situated in the village of Thorpe.

6 Dog and Partridge Country Inn

★★

Swinscoe, Ashbourne, Derbyshire, DE6 2HS
Tel: 01335 343183 Fax: 01335 342742
Email: dogpart@fsbdial.co.uk
Web: www.dogandpartridge.co.uk
29 bedrs SB £50 DB £70 HBS £65 HBD £50
B £10 L £5 D £15 CC: MC Vi Am DC Swi Delt

How to get there: Follow A52 from Ashbourne
towards Leek. Located on the left-hand side, 3
miles from Ashbourne.

7 Courtyard by Marriott Ashbourne

♦♦♦♦ ✕ ♟

Dairy House Farm, Alkmonton, Longford,
Ashbourne, Derbyshire, DE6 3DG
Tel: 01335 330187 Fax: 01335 330187
Email: andy@dairyhousefarm.org.uk
Web: www.dairyhousefarm.org.uk
Closed December

The Courtyard is situated in a tranquil location
and has been converted from early Victorian
cowsheds into tastefully well appointed
bedrooms, all rooms en-suite.
7 bedrs SB £30 DB £48 CC: MC Vi DC Swi Delt

How to get there: Follow signs of A50 for
Church Broughton. Follow signs of A515 for
Alkmonton. Follow signs of A52 for Longford.

8 Lichfield House

♦♦♦♦ ✕

Bridgeview, Mayfield, Ashbourne,
Derbyshire, DE6 2HN
Tel: 01335 344422/346146
Email: lichfieldhouse@barclays.net
Closed Christmas
3 bedrs SB £35 DB £60
CC: None accepted

How to get there: Take the A53 from Ashbourne
to Leek. Turn left onto B5032. Lichfield House is
the first house on left.

Ashby de la Zouch, Leicestershire

9 Fallen Knight Hotel

★★★★ ♖ ♖

Kilwardby Street, Ashby de la Zouch,
Leicestershire, LE65 2FQ
Tel: 01530 412230 Fax: 01530 417596
CC: MC Vi Am DC Swi
See advert below

East Midlands

Ashford-in-the-Water, Derbyshire

10 Rowdale

Ashford-in-the-Water, Bakewell,
Derbyshire, DE45 1NX
Tel: 01629 640260
Email: info@rowdale.co.uk
Web: www.rowdale.co.uk
5 bedrs SB £27.50 DB £50.00
CC: None accepted

How to get there: Turn off A6 at Ashford (2 miles
north of Bakewell), follow A6020, farm on left after
1¹/₂ miles, entrance 100 yards past buildings.

Ashover, Derbyshire

11 Old School Farm

Uppertown, Ashover, Derbyshire, S45 0JF
Tel: 01246 590813
Closed November to March
4 bedrs SB £22 DB £44 HBS £30 HBD £30
CC: None accepted

How to get there: Take A362 Chesterfield to
Matlock road. Turn onto the B5057 Darley Dale
road. Turn left to Uppertown.

Bakewell, Derbyshire

12 The Old Bakery

Church Street, Youlgrave, Bakewell,
Derbyshire, DE45 1UR
Tel: 01629 636887
Web: www.cresbrook.co.uk/youlgve/oldbakery
3 bedrs SB £22 DB £32
CC: None accepted

How to get there: A6 2 miles south of Bakewell
take B5056 to Youlgreave; Old Bakery 100m on
right after the church.

Barton-upon-Humber, Lincolnshire

13 Reeds Hotel

★★★

Far-Ings Road, Barton-upon-Humber,
Lincolnshire, DN18 5RG
Tel: 01652 632313 Fax: 01652 636361
Email: info@reedshotel.co.uk
Web: www.reedshotel.co.uk
35 bedrs SB £75 DB £98 HBS £89.95
HBD £56.98 B £9.95 L £11.95 D £11.95
CC: MC Vi Am DC Swi Delt

How to get there: Exit M180 onto A15 at
Barton-upon-Humber. Take first exit onto
A1077. Take first right, hotel is straight on.

Baslow, Derbyshire

14 Cavendish Hotel

Blue Ribbon Winner

★★★★

Church Lane, Baslow, Derbyshire, DE45 1SP
Tel: 01246 582311 Fax: 01246 582312
Email: info@cavendish-hotel.net
Web: www.cavendish-hotel.net
24 bedrs SB £107 DB £170 HBS £142
HBD £220 B £8.50 L £26 D £26
CC: MC Vi Am DC Swi Delt

Belper, Derbyshire

15 Shottle Hall Guest House

Shottle, Belper, Derbyshire, DE56 2EB
Tel: 01773 550203
Closed Christmas to New Year
9 bedrs SB £36 DB £68 B £6 D £15
CC: None accepted

How to get there: Off B5023, 200m north of
crossroads with A517 Belper-Ashbourne road.

Blyth, Nottinghamshire

16 Travelodge Blyth

Travel Accommodation
A1m/A614, Hilltop Roundabout, Blyth,
Nottinghamshire, S81 8HG
Tel: 08700 850 950
Web: www.travelodge.co.uk
38 bedrs B £4.25
CC: MC Vi Am DC Swi Delt

Boston, Lincolnshire

17 Comfort Inn Boston

★★
Bicker Bar roundabout, A17/A52 Junction,
Boston, Lincolnshire, PE20 3AN
Tel: 01205 820118 Fax: 01205 820228
Email: admin@gb607.u/net.com
Web: www.choicehotels.com
55 bedrs SB £57.25 DB £57.25 HBS £68
HBD £34 B £7.75 D £10.75
CC: MC Vi Am DC Swi Delt

Bourne, Lincolnshire

18 Angel Hotel

◆◆◆
Market Place, Bourne, Lincolnshire, PE10 9AE
Tel: 01778 422346 Fax: 01778 426113

14 bedrs SB £45 DB £55 HBS £40 HBD £45
B £5 L £3.95 D £5.95
CC: MC Vi Am DC Swi Delt JCB

Buxton, Derbyshire

19 Palace Hotel

★★★★
Palace Road, Buxton, Derbyshire, SK17 6AG
Tel: 01298 22001 Fax: 01298 72131
Email: palace@paramount-hotels.co.uk
Web: www.paramount-hotels.co.uk

The Palace is an historic Victorian hotel situated
within 5 acres of beautifully manicured gardens.
The magnificent features and friendly service
combine to ensure that your stay with us is truly
memorable.
122 bedrs SB £110 DB £125 HBS £128.50
HBD £81 B £8.50 L £6.95 D £11.95
CC: MC Vi Am Swi Delt JCB

20 Buckingham Hotel

★★★
1/2 Burlington Road, Buxton,
Derbyshire, SK17 9AS
Tel: 01298 70481 Fax: 01298 72186
Email: frontdesk@buckinghamhotel.co.uk
Web: www.buckinghamhotel.co.uk
37 bedrs SB £55 DB £75 HBS £70 HBD £55
B £7.50 L £12 D £15
CC: MC Vi Am DC Swi Delt JCB

How to get there: Lying opposite the Pavilion
Gardens car park at the junction of St. John's
Road (A53 Leek) and Burlington Road. See
website.

21 Lee Wood Hotel

★★★★ ☙ ☙
Manchester Road, Buxton, Derbyshire, SK17 6TQ
Tel: 01298 23002 Fax: 01298 23228
Email: leewoodhotel@btinternet.com
40 bedrs CC: MC Vi Am DC Swi Delt

How to get there: From North, leave M1 at
Junction 29, Chesterfield-Baslow-Buxton. From
South, Leave M1 at Junction 23A/24: take A50
for approx 19 miles then A515 to Buxton.

East Midlands

22 Grove Hotel

★★

Grove Parade, Buxton, Derbyshire, SK17 6AJ
Tel: 01298 23804 Fax: 01298 77906
Email: brewery@frederic-robinson.co.uk
Web: www.frederic-robinson.com
14 bedrs SB £35 DB £65
B £3.50 L £5.95 D £10.50
CC: MC Vi Swi

How to get there: Situated in town centre, opposite Spa Baths.

23 Hartington Hotel

★★

18 Broad Walk, Buxton, Derbyshire, SK17 6JR
Tel: 01298 22638 Fax: 01298 22638
Email: syl.mel@hartingtonhotel.co.uk
Web: www.hartingtonhotel.co.uk
Closed 10 days at Christmas
16 bedrs SB £40 DB £65 HBS £52.50 HBD £45
B £6.50 D £12.50
CC: MC Vi Am Swi JCB

How to get there: From A515 end of Buxton, turn left after Swan pub down Bath Road. Near the bottom, right into Hartington Road.

24 Netherdale Guest House

♦♦♦♦

16 Green Lane, Buxton, Derbyshire, SK17 9DP
Tel: 01298 23896 Fax: 01298 73771
Children minimum age: 10.
Closed November to January
10 bedrs SB £25 DB £50
CC: None accepted

How to get there: From London Road traffic lights, the hotel is 250m up Green Lane towards Pooles Cavern.

25 Hawthorn Farm Guest House

♦♦♦

Fairfield Road, Buxton, Derbyshire, SK17 7ED
Tel: 01298 23230 Fax: 01298 71322
Email: alan.pimblett@virgin.net
Web: www.hawthorn-farm.co.uk
10 bedrs SB £23 DB £52
CC: MC Vi Am DC Swi Delt JCB

How to get there: Hawthorn Farm is situated on the A6 towards Manchester on leaving Buxton.

26 Roseleigh Hotel

♦♦♦

19 Broad Walk, Buxton, Derbyshire, SK17 6JR
Tel: 01298 24904 Fax: 01298 24904
Email: enquiries@roseleighhotel.co.uk
Web: www.roseleighhotel.co.uk
14 bedrs SB £22 DB £48 B £5
CC: MC Vi Swi Delt

27 Westminster Hotel

♦♦♦

21 Broad Walk, Buxton, Derbyshire, SK17 6JR
Tel: 01298 23929 Fax: 01298 71121
Email: cecelia@westminsterhotel.demon.co.uk
Web: www.westminsterhotel.demon.co.uk
12 bedrs SB £35 DB £60
CC: MC Vi Swi Delt

How to get there: From A6 follow Macclesfield signs through traffic lights to next crossroads. Turn right to Bath Road, and second left to Hartington Road.

Castle Donington, Leicestershire

28 Donington Park Farmhouse Hotel

♦♦♦♦

Melbourne Road, Isley Walton, near Derby, Leicestershire, DE74 2RN
Tel: 01332 862409 Fax: 01332 862364
Email: info@parkfarmhouse.co.uk
Web: www.parkfarmhouse.co.uk
Closed Christmas
15 bedrs SB £69 DB £79 B £8 D £19
CC: MC Vi Am DC Swi Delt JCB

How to get there: From exit 23A or 24 on M1, proceed past East Midlands airport to Isley Walton. Turn right, hotel is ½ a mile on right.

Chesterfield, Derbyshire

29 Travelodge Chesterfield

Travel Accommodation
A61, Birmington Road, Chesterfield, Derbyshire, S41 9BE
Tel: 08700 850 950
Web: www.travelodge.co.uk
20 bedrs B £4.25
CC: MC Vi Am DC Swi Delt

Coalville, Leicestershire

30 Hermitage Park Hotel

★ ★ ★
Whitwick Road, Coalville,
Leicestershire, LE67 3FA
Tel: 01530 814814 Fax: 01530 814202
Email: hotel@hermitagepark.com
Web: www.hermitagepark.com

25 bedrs
CC: MC Vi Am Swi Delt
⟨icons⟩
How to get there: Exit Junction13/A42 or
Junction 22/M1 and take A511 to Coalville, then
follow tourism signs from A511 to Hermitage
Park Hotel.
See advert below right

Colsterworth, Lincolnshire

31 Travelodge Colsterworth

Travel Accommodation
A1 Northbound, New Fox, South Witham,
Colsterworth, Lincolnshire, NG33 5LN
Tel: 08700 850 950
Web: www.travelodge.co.uk
32 bedrs B £4.25
CC: MC Vi Am DC Swi Delt
⟨icons⟩

Coningsby, Lincolnshire

32 The Leagate Inn

◆ ◆ ◆ ◆ ℞
Leagate Road, Coningsby, Lincolnshire, LN4 4RS
Tel: 01526 342370 Fax: 01526 345468

Corby, Northamptonshire

33 Thatches-On-The-Green

◆ ◆ ◆ ◆ ⟨icons⟩
9 School Lane, Weldon, Corby,
Northamptonshire, NN17 3JN
Tel: 01536 266681 Fax: 01536 266659
Email: tom@thatches-on-the-green.fsnet.co.uk
Web: www.thatches-on-the-green.fsnet.co.uk
6 bedrs SB £35.25 DB £58.75
CC: MC Vi Swi
⟨icons⟩
How to get there: The house is to be found in
the centre of the village opposite the Woolpack
on the A43 next to the Weldon cricket ground.

Making a booking?

ⓘ Don't forget to mention RAC
Hotels and Bed & Breakfast 2002.

Plan your route

Visit www.rac.co.uk for RAC's
interactive route planner, including
up to the minute traffic reports.

East Midlands

Daventry, Northamptonshire

34 Hanover International Daventry

★★★★

Sedgemoor Way, Ashby Road, Daventry,
Northamptonshire, NN11 5SG
Tel: 01327 307000 Fax: 01327 706313
Email: conference@daventryhih.ndo.co.uk
Web: www.hanover-international.com

HANOVER INTERNATIONAL
HOTELS & CLUBS

Stylish and elegant, located in the Nene Valley
close to Silverstone, with a superb fully
equipped leisure club. The Waterside
Restaurant overlooks beautiful Drayton Water.
138 bedrs SB £115 DB £115 B £11.95 L £12.50
D £19.95
CC: MC Vi Am DC Swi Delt
How to get there: Junction 18 M1 on A361 to
Daventry, 5 miles from motorway on the edge of
town.

35 Hellidon Lakes Hotel, Golf & Country Club

★★★★

Hellidon, Daventry, Northamptonshire, NN11 6GG
Tel: 01327 262550 Fax: 01327 262559
Email: hellidon@marstonhotels.com
Web: www.marstonhotels.com

MARSTON HOTELS

71 bedrs SB £115 DB £149 HBS £73 HBD £73
B £12 L £14.50 D £24
CC: MC Vi Am DC Swi Delt

Derby, Derbyshire

36 Marriott Breadsall Priory Hotel & Country Club

★★★★ ℞

Moor Road, Morley, near Derby,
Derbyshire, DE7 6DL
Tel: 01322 832235 Fax: 01332 833509
112 bedrs SB £130 DB £150
CC: MC Vi Am DC Swi Delt

37 Hotel La Gondola

★★★★ ℞

220 Osmaston Road, Derby,
Derbyshire, DE23 8JX
Tel: 01332 332895 Fax: 01332 384512
Email: service@lagondola.co.uk
Web: www.lagondola.co.uk
20 bedrs SB £54.50 DB £61 HBS £67
HBD £42.50 B £7 L £7.25 D £13.50
CC: MC Vi Am DC Swi Delt

How to get there: Leave M1 at Junction 25. Take
A514 towards Melbourne. Hotel is 5 minutes from
city centre and 10 minutes from Derby station.

38 The International Hotel

★★★

Burton Road, Derby, Derbyshire, DE23 6AD
Tel: 01332 369321 Fax: 01332 294430

39 Travelodge Castle Donnington

Travel Accommodation
M1 J23a, Castle Donnington, Derby,
Derbyshire, DE74 2TN
Tel: 08700 850 950
Web: www.travelodge.co.uk
80 bedrs B £4.25
CC: MC Vi Am DC Swi Delt

40 Travelodge Derby

Travel Accommodation
Kings Way, Rowditch, Derby, Derbyshire, DE3 3LY
Tel: 08700 850 950
Web: www.travelodge.co.uk
40 bedrs B £4.25
CC: MC Vi Am DC Swi Delt

41 Rose & Thistle

◆◆◆
21 Charnwood Street, Derby,
Derbyshire, DE1 2GG
Tel: 01332 344103 Fax: 01332 291006
Email: rosethistle@gpanet.co.uk
13 bedrs SB £21.50 DB £40 CC: MC Vi Swi Delt

How to get there: M1 at Junction 24, A6 to Derby.
Follow inner ring road to Charnwood Street.

Dovedale, Derbyshire

42 Izaak Walton Hotel

★★★
Dovedale, Derbyshire, DE6 2AY
Tel: 01335 350555 Fax: 01335 350539
Email: reception@izaakwalton-hotel.com
Web: www.izaakwalton-hotel.com
30 bedrs SB £86 DB £112 B £9.50 L £15.95
D £26 CC: MC Vi Am DC Swi Delt

How to get there: Hotel is situated 5 miles NW
of Ashbourne. Take A515 towards Buxton. After
2 miles turn left on the B5054 to Thorpe,
Dovedale and Ilam. Hotel after 4 miles.

Finedon, Northamptonshire

43 Tudor Gate Hotel

★★★
35 High Street, Finedon,
Northamptonshire, NN9 5JN
Tel: 01933 680408 Fax: 01933 680745

Glossop, Derbyshire

44 Wind in the Willows Hotel

★★★
Derbyshire Level, Glossop, Derbyshire, SK13 7PT
Tel: 01457 868001 Fax: 01457 853354
Email: info@windinthewillows.co.uk
Web: www.windinthewillows.co.uk
Children minimum age: 8
12 bedrs SB £74 DB £99 B £9.50 D £25
CC: MC Vi Am DC Swi Delt

How to get there: 1 mile east of Glossop centre
on A57 to Sheffield. Turn right opposite Royal
Oak pub. Hotel 400 yards on right.

45 George Hotel

◆◆
34 Norfolk Street, Glossop,
Derbyshire, SK13 7QU
Tel: 01457 855449 Fax: 01457 857033
9 bedrs SB £25 DB £40 L £4 D £10
CC: MC Vi Swi Delt

How to get there: George Hotel is in the town
centre, opposite Glossop railway station.

46 Kings Clough Head Farm

◆◆
off Monks Road, Glossop, Derbyshire, SK13 6ED
Tel: 01457 862668
3 bedrs
CC: None accepted
How to get there: Situated near the A624
Glossop-Hayfield road.

Grantham, Lincolnshire

47 Grantham Marriott Hotel

★★★★
Swingbridge Road, Grantham,
Lincolnshire, NG31 7XT
Tel: 01476 593000 Fax: 01476 592592
Web: www.marriotthotels.com
90 bedrs SB £89 DB £99 B £12.50 L £10 D £15
CC: MC Vi Am DC Swi Delt

How to get there: From A1 north, take turn for
A607 Melton Mowbray. Hotel is at end of slip road
on left. From A1 south, take A607 turn and then
first right. First left and Hotel is straight ahead.

48 Travelodge Colsterworth

Travel Accommodation
A1, Colsterworth, Grantham,
Lincolnshire, NG35 5JR
Tel: 08700 850 950
Web: www.travelodge.co.uk
31 bedrs B £4.25
CC: MC Vi Am DC Swi Delt

It's easier online

For all your motoring and travel
needs, www.rac.co.uk

East Midlands

49 Travelodge Grantham

Travel Accommodation
A1, Gonerby Moor, Grantham,
Lincolnshire, NG32 2AB
Tel: 08700 850 950
Web: www.travelodge.co.uk
39 bedrs B £4.25
CC: MC Vi Am DC Swi Delt

50 Black Bull

Black Bull Farm, North Witham, Grantham,
Lincolnshire, NG33 5LL
Tel: 01476 860086 Fax: 01476 860796

Grindleford, Derbyshire

51 Maynard Arms Hotel

★★★★ ℞ ℞
Main Road, Grindleford, Derbyshire, S32 2HE
Tel: 01433 630321 Fax: 01433 630445
Email: info@maynardarms.co.uk
Web: www.maynardarms.co.uk
10 bedrs SB £69 DB £79 HBD £49.50 B £6.50
L £21.50 D £21.50
CC: MC Vi Am Swi Delt

How to get there: Situated on the B6521
running through Grindleford. Accessible from
M1 Junctions 29 and 33.

Hassop, Derbyshire

52 Hassop Hall

★★★★ ℞ ℞
Hassop, Bakewell, Derbyshire, DE45 1NS
Tel: 01629 640488 Fax: 01629 640577
Email: hassophallhotel@btinternet.com
Closed Christmas

The ancient seat of the Eyre family, in a tranquil
setting at the heart of the Peak District National
Park.
13 bedrs SB £87 DB £95 HBS £115
HBD £75.50 B £7.95 L £16.90 D £27.75
CC: MC Vi Am DC Swi Delt

How to get there: From Junction 29 on M1,
follow signs to Chesterfield town centre, then
take A619 to Baslow and A623 to Calver. Turn
left at traffic lights onto B6001. Hassop is 1 mile.

Hathersage, Derbyshire

53 George Hotel

★★★★ ℞ ℞
Main Road, Hathersage, Derbyshire, S32 1BB
Tel: 01433 650436 Fax: 01433 650099
Email: info@george-hotel.net
Web: www.george-hotel.net
19 bedrs SB £69.50 DB £99.50 HBS £89.50
HBD £69.75 B £5.50 L £10 D £15
CC: MC Vi Am DC Swi Delt
How to get there: Leave M1 at Junction 29.
Head west on A619 to Baslow, then north onto
B6001 to Hathersage.

Hayfield, Derbyshire

54 Pool Cottage

♦ ♦ ♦
Park Hall, Little Hayfield, High Peak,
Derbyshire, SK22 2NN
Tel: 01663 742463
Email: dean@poolcottage.fsbusiness.co.uk
Closed Christmas to 1st April

Beautiful and unusual Victorian greenhouse
conversion, south-facing house, set in secluded
National Trust woodland in Peak District
National Park near Kinder Scout, with wonderful
walks from the doorstep.

3 bedrs SB £20 DB £40 CC: None accepted

How to get there: Off A624 up unmade lane with a National Trust sign at entrance marked 'Park Hall Woods', then first on left.

Hinckley, Leicestershire

55 Hanover International Hotel & Club Hinckley

★★★★

A5 Watling Street, Hinckley,
Leicestershire, LE10 3JA
Tel: 01455 631122 Fax: 01455 635370
Email: sales@hanover-international.com
Web: www.hanover-international.com

HANOVER INTERNATIONAL
HOTELS & CLUBS

Unique, friendly modern hotel and extensive leisure club set in lovely countryside, with easy access to Midlands attractions, the NEC and motorway connections.
349 bedrs SB £115 DB £125 B £12.50 L £11.95 D £18.95 CC: MC Vi Am DC Swi Delt

How to get there: Hanover International is situated 300 yards from Junction 1 of M69 which links the M1 and M6.

56 Kings Hotel

★★

13–19 Mount Road, Hinckley,
Leicestershire, LE10 1AD
Tel: 01455 637193 Fax: 01455 636201
Email: kingshinck@aol.com
Web: www.kings-hotel.net
Children minimum age: 10
7 bedrs SB £69.50 DB £79.50 HBS £85 HBD £65 B £10 D £20
CC: MC Vi Am DC Swi Delt

How to get there: From Hinckley town centre, follow signs for hospital. Hotel is at the bottom end of the same road.

Holbeach, Lincolnshire

57 Cackle Hill House

Cackle Hill Lane, Holbeach,
Lincolnshire, PE12 8BS
Tel: 01406 426721 Fax: 01406 424659
Children minimum age: 10
3 bedrs SB £25 DB £40
CC: None accepted

How to get there: From A17 at Holbeach roundabout, take B1168 to Cackle Hill. Hotel ½ mile on right.

Kettering, Northamptonshire

58 Kettering Park Hotel

★★★★

Kettering Parkway, Kettering,
Northamptonshire, NN15 6XT
Tel: 01536 416666 Fax: 01536 416171
Email: kpark@shireinns.co.uk
Web: www.shireinns.co.uk
119 bedrs SB £130 DB £150 L £6 D £20
CC: MC Vi Am DC Swi

How to get there: Take Junction 9 on A14. Hotel is just off roundabout.

East Midlands

59 Travelodge Kettering (Westbound)

Travel Accommodation
A14 Westbound, A1/M1 Link Road, Kettering,
Northamptonshire
Tel: 08700 850 950
Web: www.travelodge.co.uk
40 bedrs B £4.25 CC: MC Vi Am DC Swi Delt

Leicester, Leicestershire

60 Leicester Stage Hotel

★★★
299 Leicester Road (A50), Wigston Fields,
Leicester, Leicestershire, LE18 1JW
Tel: 0116 288 6161 Fax: 0116 281 1874
Email: reservations@stagehotel.co.uk
Web: www.stagehotel.co.uk
75 bedrs CC: MC Vi Am DC Swi Delt

How to get there: From Junction 21 M1 outer
ring road southeast (A563) towards Oadby,
Wigston. Turn right towards Northampton A50.
Hotel ¼ mile on left.

61 Regency

★★★★
360 London Road, Leicester,
Leicestershire, LE2 2PL
Tel: 0116 2709634 Fax: 0116 2701375
Email: info@the-regency-hotel.com
Web: www.the-regency-hotel.com

Whatever the purpose of your stay, this
exquisitely restored Victorian town house hotel
will charm you with its grace and elegance.
32 bedrs SB £35 DB £54
CC: MC Vi Am Swi Delt

How to get there: Located on the main A6,
approximately ½ mile from the city centre.
Close to universities.

62 Red Cow Hotel

★★
Hinckley Road, Leicester Forest East, Leicester,
Leicestershire, LE3 3PG
Tel: 0116 238 7878 Fax: 0116 238 6539

Lincoln, Lincolnshire

63 Bentley Hotel & Leisure Club

★★★
Newark Road, South Hykeham, Lincoln,
Lincolnshire, LN6 9NH
Tel: 01522 878000 Fax: 01522 878001
Email: info@thebentleyhotel.uk.com
Web: www.thebentleyhotel.uk.com

Lincoln's newest, and the only hotel sporting a
smart leisure club. Indoor pool and large
conference facilities. Popular with both
corporate and leisure markets.
53 bedrs SB £62 DB £77 B £8.75 L £8.95
D £14.75 CC: MC Vi Am DC Swi Delt

How to get there: From A1, take A46 towards
Lincoln. After 10 miles, go straight over first
roundabout on Lincoln bypass. Hotel 50 yards
on left.

64 Branston Hall Hotel

★★★
Branston Park, Lincoln Road, Lincoln,
Lincolnshire, LN4 1PD
Tel: 01522 793305 Fax: 01522 790734
Email: brahal@enterprise.net
Web: www.scoot.co.uk/branston_hall
45 bedrs SB £59.50 DB £79.50 HBS £73.50
HBD £104.50 B £7.50 L £13.95 D £17.95
CC: MC Vi Am DC Swi Delt JCB

How to get there: Branston Hall Hotel is situated
on the B1188 3 miles south of Lincoln.
See advert on following page

65 Courtyard by Marriott Lincoln

★★★

Brayford Wharf North, Lincoln,
Lincolnshire, LN1 1YW
Tel: 01522 544244 Fax: 01522 516860
Web: www.marriotthotels.com
95 bedrs SB £90 DB £97 HBS £108
HBD £66.50 B £4.50 L £12.95 D £16.95
CC: MC Vi Am DC Swi Delt
⛨ 🐾 🝤 🖵 ☎ ✳ 🕿 **P**🔊 🕎 🌴 🛎 ♨ 🍴 'Y'
How to get there: A57 Lincoln central onto
Carkolme Road; first major traffic lights turn left,
then right onto Newlands. Follow signs for
Marriott Hotel.

66 Golf Hotel

★★★

The Broadway, Woodhall Spa, near Lincoln,
Lincolnshire, LN10 6SG
Tel: 01526 353535 Fax: 01526 353096
Web: www.principalhotels.co.uk
50 bedrs SB £65 DB £85 HBS £77 HBD £54.50
B £7.50 D £17.95
CC: MC Vi Am DC Swi Delt
⛨ 🦮 🝤 🖵 ☎ **P**🔊 🕎 🌴 ♨ 🍴 ⚗ 🔍
How to get there: Take B1189 to Metheringham,
then B1191 to Woodhall Spa. When
approaching Woodhall, The Golf Hotel is
situated on the main street, "The Broadway".

67 Grand Hotel

★★★

St. Mary's Street, Lincoln, Lincolnshire, LN5 7EP
Tel: 01522 524211 Fax: 01522 537661
Email: reception@thegrandhotel.uk.com
Web: www.thegrandhotel.uk.com

Family-owned for over 70 years and renowned
throughout the county for its excellent cuisine.
Situated in the heart of the city.
46 bedrs SB £54 DB £69 HBS £49.50
HBD £49.50 B £7.50 L £9 D £13.75
CC: MC Vi Am DC Swi Delt
🗲 🝤 🖵 ☎ **P**🔊 🕎 🌴 ♨ 🍴
How to get there: From A1 take A46. Follow
signs for Lincoln Central and then railway station.

68 Heritage Hotels – The White Hart

★★★

Bailgate, Lincoln, Lincolnshire, LN1 3AR
Tel: 01522 526222 Fax: 01522 531798
Email: heritagehotels-lincoln.whiteheart
@forte-hotels.com
Web: www.heritage-hotels.com
48 bedrs CC: MC Vi Am DC Swi Delt
◁ ⛨ 🗲 🐾 ⊗ 🝤 🖵 ☎ 🕿 **P**🔊 🕎 🌴 🛎 ♨ 🍴
How to get there: The White Hart is in Bailgate,
midway between the castle and the cathedral.

69 Castle Hotel

★★ 🍴

Westgate, Lincoln, Lincolnshire, LN1 3AS
Tel: 01522 538801 Fax: 01522 575457
Email: rac@castlehotel.net
Web: www.castlehotel.net
Children minimum age: 8
Professional service and a friendly, attentive
manner are abundant in this established
privately owned hotel. Bedrooms are
traditionally and individually decorated whilst
Knights restaurant has merited national and
regional awards.
19 bedrs SB £62 DB £84 HBS £77 HBD £57
B £6.50 D £17.90 CC: MC Vi Am DC Swi Delt JCB
🦮 🗲 🐾 ⊗ 🝤 🖵 ☎ 🕿 **P**🔊 🌴 ♨ 🍴
How to get there: Follow signs to 'Lawn Visitors
Centre'. At mini-roundabout, turn left. Hotel is
on left at end of Westgate.

70 Travelodge Lincoln

Travel Accommodation
A46, Thorpe On The Hill, Lincoln,
Lincolnshire, LN6 9AJ
Tel: 08700 850 950
Web: www.travelodge.co.uk
32 bedrs B £4.25 CC: MC Vi Am DC Swi Delt
🐾 🝤 🖵 🕎

71 Archers Lodge

♦ ♦ ♦ ♦

133 Yarborough Road, Lincoln,
Lincolnshire, LN1 1HR
Tel: 01522 520201 Fax: 01522 520201
Email: info@archerslodge.co.uk
Web: www.archerslodge.co.uk
3 bedrs SB £25 DB £40 HBS £32 HBD £27
CC: MC Vi Swi Delt
🐾 ⊗ 🝤 🖵 **P** 🕎
How to get there: Take A57 into Lincoln to main
traffic lights. Turn left, follow road through two
sets of lights. Halfway up on the right.

East Midlands

Branston Hall Hotel

Branston Hall offers beautiful ensuite accommodation in a characteristic and elegant Country House set in 88 acres of wooded park land and lakes. The Lakeside Restaurant offers table d'hôte, an extensive à la carte menu and an international wine list. Relax in our new indoor pool, jacuzzi or spa and take advantage of the hotel's peace and tranquility. We are 5 minutes from the centre of historic Lincoln. For more information or to request a brochure call us.

Branston Park, Branston, Lincoln LN4 1PD
Tel: 01522 793305   Fax: 01522 790734
Email: brahal@enterprise.net
Website: www.scoot.co.uk/branston_hall

Originally Leicestershire's most exclusive private club, created around the original 17th-century listed building. This award winning 4-star hotel is set amid 4 acres of beautiful landscaped gardens. Stay in one of our individually designed bedrooms, including 3 suites. Your stay will be enhanced by the hotel's two RAC and AA award-winning restaurants where you can choose between the intimate alcoves of the Shires Restaurant with its classical cuisine or the light conservatory atmosphere of the Orangery Brasserie with its selection of contemporary dishes.

Charnwood House
66 Leicester Road, Quorn LE12 8BB
Tel: 01509 415050   Fax: 01509 415557

72 Tennyson Hotel

◆ ◆ ◆ ◆
7 South Park, Lincoln, Lincolnshire, LN5 8EN
Tel: 01522 521624 Fax: 01522 521355
Email: tennyson.hotel@virgin.net
Web: www.tennysonhotel.com
Closed Christmas
8 bedrs SB £33 DB £45 B £5
CC: MC Vi Swi Delt
How to get there: South of the city, on the A15, 15 metres from the high street roundabout.

73 The Gables

◆ ◆ ◆ ◆
546 Newark Road, North Hykeham, Lincoln, Lincolnshire, LN6 9NG
Tel: 01522 829102 Fax: 01522 850497

74 Admiral Guest House

◆ ◆ ◆
16–18 Nelson Street, Lincoln, Lincolnshire, LN1 1PJ
Tel: 01522 544467 Fax: 01522 544467
Email: tony@admiral63.freeserve.co.uk
9 bedrs SB £22 DB £38 HBS £29 HBD £22.50
CC: MC Vi Swi Delt

How to get there: 5 minutes walk from the university situated on Carholme Road, close to the A57.

75 Bradford Guest House

◆ ◆ ◆
67 Monks Road, Lincoln, Lincolnshire, LN2 5HP
Tel: 01522 523947
5 bedrs SB £25 DB £40 HBS £32 HBD £54
B £1 D £7 CC: None accepted

How to get there: 300 yards east of Lindum Road/Silver Street junction.

76 Halfway Farm Motel

◆ ◆ ◆
A46 Swinderby, Lincoln, Lincolnshire, LN6 9HN
Tel: 01522 868749 Fax: 01522 868082
Closed Christmas to New Year
17 bedrs SB £35 DB £42
CC: MC Vi Am Swi Delt

How to get there: On A46 Newark to Lincoln road. Opposite disused RAF Swinderby airfield, five minutes from Lincoln bypass.

77 Pines Guest House

♦ ♦ ♦

104 Yarborough Road, Lincoln, LN1 1HR
Tel: 01522 532985 Fax: 01522 532985
Email: pines.guest.house@ntlworld.com
Web: www.smoothhound.co.uk
6 bedrs SB £17 DB £33 HBD £23 D £6
CC: None accepted
🔥🐾⊛🍽⏚ 🄿☎ 🛏♨ ♣ 🏛 ⏣
How to get there: West side of city. Accessible from Relief Road. A15 — A46, A158, A607, A57. Close to city centre and cathedral.

78 Old Rectory Guest House

♦ ♦

19 Newport, Lincoln, Lincolnshire, LN1 3DQ
Tel: 01522 514774
Closed Christmas and New Year
7 bedrs SB £20 DB £40 CC: None accepted
⊛🍽⏚ 🄿 ♨
How to get there: From A46 ring road turn off at Lincoln North roundabout. Straight over next one to Newport. We are at the south end.

79 Tennyson Court

♦ ♦

3 Tennyson Street, Lincoln, Lincolnshire, LN1 1LZ
Tel: 0800 980 5408 Fax: 01522 887997
Email: sales@tennyson-court.co.uk
Web: www.tennyson-court.co.uk
3 bedrs SB £34.90 DB £39.90
CC: None accepted
🔥⊛🍽⏚☎ 🄿☎ ♨ ♣
How to get there: Follow A57 into Lincoln, left onto Hewon Road, right at top onto West Parade, then next left is Tennyson Street.

80 South Park Guest House

❖

11 South Park, Lincoln, Lincolnshire, LN5 8EN
Tel: 01522 528243 Fax: 01522 524603
Email: enquiries@southpark-lincoln.co.uk
Web: www.southpark-lincoln.co.uk

Once a Victorian home, carefully refurbished to retain its original character whilst providing excellent guest accommodation with modern expectations of standards. Parking, ensuite, credit cards, near city, parks, shops and restaurants.
7 bedrs SB £25 DB £40 CC: MC Vi Am
🍽⊛🍽 🄿 ♨
How to get there: In the south of Lincoln follow the High Street to the bottom turning left at the roundabout. 100m on the left.

Loughborough, Leicestershire

81 Quorn Country Hotel

★★★★ 🄫 🄫 🄫

66 Leicester Road, Quorn,
Leicestershire, LE12 8BB
Tel: 01509 415050 Fax: 01509 415557
23 bedrs SB £91 DB £113 HBS £90 HBD £70
B £8.95 L £18 D £22.50
CC: MC Vi Am DC Swi Delt
⏏🔥🍽⊛🍽☎❄🄿♨℃🛏♣ 🏛 ♨ ⛵
How to get there: From A6 Loughborough to Leicester road, take exit for Quorn (Quorndon) village. Hotel near village hall and opposite police station.
See advert on facing page

82 Quality Hotel & Suites Loughborough

★★★

Junction 23, M1, New Ashby Road,
Loughborough, Leicestershire, LE11 0EX
Tel: 01509 211800 Fax: 01509 211868
Email: admin@gb613.u-net.com
Web: www.choicehotels.com
94 bedrs SB £111.95 DB £131.95 HBS £126.90
HBD £73.45 B £11.95 L £14.95 D £14.95
CC: MC Vi Am DC Swi Delt
⏏🔥🖨🐾⊛🍽⏚☎📞🄿☎♨℃🛏♣ 🏛 🏛
🍽⏣🄪
How to get there: From Junction 23 M1, follow A512 towards Loughborough town centre. Hotel is approx 800m on left-hand side.

East Midlands

83 Cedars Hotel

★★★

Cedar Road, Loughborough,
Leicestershire, LE11 2AB
Tel: 01509 214459 Fax: 01509 233573
Email: goodman@cedars01.freeserve.co.uk
Web: www.cedars01.freeserve.co.uk

Family-run hotel in quiet surroundings,
specialising in private functions. Cots available;
family rooms available. Rolls Royce available for
weddings at no extra charge on some packages.
36 bedrs SB £65 DB £80 L £11 D £11
CC: MC Vi Am DC Swi Delt

How to get there: Proceed along the A6 towards
Leicester turning left into Cedar Lane opposite
Loughborough crematorium.

84 Great Central Hotel

★★

Great Central Road, Loughborough,
Leicestershire, LE11 1RW
Tel: 01509 263405 Fax: 01509 264130
Email: reception@greatcentralhotel.co.uk
Web: www.greatcentralhotel.co.uk
22 bedrs CC: MC Vi Swi Delt

How to get there: Enter Loughborough on the
A6. Turn onto the A60 to Nottingham. Great
Central Road is first on the right.

85 De Montfort Hotel

♦ ♦ ♦

88 Leicester Road, Loughborough,
Leicestershire, LE11 2AQ
Tel: 01509 216061 Fax: 01509 233667
9 bedrs SB £28.35 DB £38.40 D £7
CC: MC Vi Am DC Swi Delt

How to get there: Situated on A6 Leicester
Road, 5 minutes from the town centre.

Market Harborough, Leicestershire

86 Sun Inn Hotel & Restaurant

★★★

Main Street, Marston, Trussell,
Leicestershire, LE16 9TY
Tel: 01858 465531 Fax: 01858 433155
Email: manager@suninn.com
Web: www.suninn.com
Closed Christmas and New Year
20 bedrs
CC: MC Vi Am DC Swi Delt

How to get there: Exit J20 M1, A4304. Marston
Trussell is between Theddingworth and
Lubenham. By rail, Market Harborough is 3
miles away.

87 Travelodge Desborough

Travel Accommodation
A6 Southbound, Harborough Road,
Desborough, near Market Harborough,
Northamptonshire, NN14 2UG
Tel: 08700 850 950
Web: www.travelodge.co.uk
32 bedrs B £4.25
CC: MC Vi Am DC Swi Delt

Markfield, Leicestershire

88 Travelodge Markfield

Travel Accommodation
A50/M1, Littleshaw Lane,
Markfield, LE6 0PP
Tel: 08700 850 950
Web: www.travelodge.co.uk
60 bedrs B £4.25
CC: MC Vi Am DC Swi Delt

Matlock, Derbyshire

89 Riber Hall

★★★★ ♖ ♖
Matlock, Derbyshire, DE4 5JU
Tel: 01629 582795 Fax: 01629 580475
Email: info@riber-hall.co.uk
Web: www.riber-hall.co.uk
Children minimum age: 10

Renowned historic and tranquil country manor house set in peaceful rolling Derbyshire hills. Gourmet cuisine — AA two rosettes, RAC two Dining Awards. Privately owned and proprietor-run for 30 years.
14 bedrs SB £97 DB £129 HBS £128.50
HBD £190.50 B £8 L £13 D £28.50
CC: MC Vi Am DC Swi Delt JCB
How to get there: One mile off A615 at Tansley, signed to Riber.

90 The New Bath Hotel

★★★
New Bath Road, Matlock Bath,
Derbyshire, DE4 3PX
Tel: 0870 400 8119 Fax: 01629 580268
Email: heritagehotels_bath.matlock.new_bath
@forte-hotels.com
Web: www.heritage-hotels.com
55 bedrs SB £64 DB £128 HBS £79 HBD £79
B £10.95 L £3.95 D £21.95
CC: MC Vi Am DC Swi Delt JCB
How to get there: Leave M1 at Junction 28. Follow A38, then A610. Proceed to Little Chef restaurant at Ambergate. Turn right. Hotel is approximately 20 minutes along A6 on left.

91 Hillview

◆◆◆
80 New Street, Matlock, Derbyshire, DE4 3FH
Tel: 01629 583662
Email: hillview@quista.net
Children minimum age: 5
Closed November to Easter
3 bedrs SB £20 DB £40
CC: None accepted
How to get there: From Matlock centre (A6, Crown Square), proceed up the hill, take fourth right into New Street. Hillview is on the corner.

92 Jackson Tor House

◆◆◆
76 Jackson Road, Matlock, Derbyshire, DE4 3JQ
Tel: 01629 582348 Fax: 01629 582348
Email: jacksontorhotel@uk2.net
29 bedrs SB £20 DB £35
HBS £29 HBD £29 D £8.95
CC: MC Vi Am Swi Delt

93 The Coach House, Home Farm

◆◆◆
Main Road, Lea, near Matlock,
Derbyshire, DE4 5GJ
Tel: 01629 534346
Email: barbarahobson@coachhouselea.co.uk
Web: www.coachhouselea.co.uk
3 bedrs DB £45 B £5.95 L £6.50 D £6.50
CC: MC Vi Swi Delt
How to get there: From A6 Cromford follow road to Crich. After a mile, turn left at Leabridge for Lea and Riber. The Coach House is ³/₄ mile on left.

Melbourne, Derbyshire

94 Melbourne Arms

◆◆◆
92 Ashby Road, Melbourne,
Derbyshire, DE73 1ES
Tel: 01332 864949

East Midlands

Melton Mowbray, Leicestershire

95 Stapleford Park Hotel
Gold Ribbon Winner

★★★★ ♔ ♔ ♔

Stapleford, Melton Mowbray,
Leicestershire, LE14 2EF
Tel: 01572 787522 Fax: 01572 787651
Web: www.stapleford.co.uk

Neither words nor pictures can adequately
describe this most imposing of Grade I Listed
15th–18th-century stately homes. Set in 500
acres of parkland, Stapleford Park boasts a
trout lake and private 18-hole championship
golf course.
51 bedrs SB £210 DB £210 D £44
CC: MC Vi Am DC Swi

How to get there: From Melton Mowbray, follow
ring road and signs for Grantham. Stay in left-
hand lane until Grantham Road turns left: don't
turn left, but drive through traffic lights. Follow
signs for B676 Stapleford. After 4 miles, turn
right at Stapleford signpost.

Newark, Nottinghamshire

96 Travelodge Newark

Travel Accommodation
A1, North Muskham, Newark,
Nottinghamshire, NG23 6HT
Tel: 08700 850 950
Web: www.travelodge.co.uk
30 bedrs B £4.25 CC: MC Vi Am DC Swi Delt

It's easier online

For all your motoring and travel
needs, www.rac.co.uk

Northampton, Northamptonshire

97 Northampton Marriott

★★★★

Eagle Drive, Northampton,
Northamptonshire, NN4 7HW
Tel: 01604 768700 Fax: 01604 702485
Email: northampton@marriotthotels.co.uk
Web: www.marriott.com
120 bedrs SB £110 DB £130 B £13 L £15
D £22.75 CC: MC Vi Am DC Swi

How to get there: From M1 exit at Junction 15
and take A508 /A45 to Northampton. Take slip
road to Delapre golf/Brackmills.

98 Courtyard by Marriott Daventry

★★★

High Street, Flore, near Northampton,
Northamptonshire, NN7 4LP
Tel: 01327 349022 Fax: 01327 349017
Email: reservations.daventry@whitbread.com
Web: www.courtyard.com/bhxmk
53 bedrs SB £85 DB £92 HBS £102 HBD £63
B £8.50 L £8.50 D £10 CC: MC Vi Am DC Swi Delt

99 Courtyard by Marriott Northampton

★★★

Bedford Road, Northampton,
Northamptonshire, NN4 7YF
Tel: 01604 622777 Fax: 01604 635454
Web: www.marriotthotels.com
104 bedrs SB £94 DB £105 HBS £113 HBD £66
B £11.50 L £8 D £12
CC: MC Vi Am DC Swi Delt JCB

How to get there: Exit J15 M1 follow A508 1
mile, then A428 to Bedford; hotel 200m on left.

100 Quality Hotel Northampton

★★★

Ashley Way, Westone Favell, Northampton,
Northamptonshire, NN3 3EA
Tel: 01604 739955 Fax: 01604 415023
Email: admin@gb070.u-net.com
Web: www.choicehotels.com
66 bedrs SB £105.75 DB £115.75 HBS £123.70
HBD £66.85 B £10.75 L £7.95 D £17.95
CC: MC Vi Am DC Swi Delt

How to get there: Exit M1 at Junction 15. Take
A508 to Nipton and A45 to Wellingborough, then
A43 to Kettering and Weston Favell turn-off.

101 Travelodge Dunston

Travel Accommodation
A45, Upton Way, Dunston, Northampton,
Northamptonshire, NN5 6EG
Tel: 08700 850 950
Web: www.travelodge.co.uk
62 bedrs B £4.25
CC: MC Vi Am DC Swi Delt

Nottingham, Nottinghamshire

102 Bestwood Lodge Hotel

★★★
Bestwood Country Park, Arnold, Nottingham,
Nottinghamshire, NG5 8NE
Tel: 0115 920 3011 Fax: 0115 967 0409
Web: www.bestwestern.co.uk
39 bedrs SB £75 DB £90 B £10 D £18.50
CC: MC Vi Am DC Swi Delt

103 Novotel Nottingham/Derby

★★★
Bostock Lane, Long Eaton,
Derbyshire, NG10 4EP
Tel: 0115 946 5111 Fax: 0115 946 5900
Email: h0507@accor-hotels.com
Web: www.novotel.com
108 bedrs SB £52.50 DB £52.50
B £7 L £ 8.99 D £16
CC: MC Vi Am DC Swi

How to get there: Between Nottingham and
Derby, take Junction 25 of the M1. Direction
Long Eaton.

104 Strathdon Hotel

★★★★
Derby Road, Nottingham,
Nottinghamshire, NG1 5FT
Tel: 0115 941 8501 Fax: 0115 948 3725
Email: info@strathdon-hotel-nottingham.com
Web: www.strathdon-hotel-nottingham.com
68 bedrs SB £79.50 DB £114 HBS £95.50
HBD £75 B £9.50 L £11 D £16
CC: MC Vi Am DC Swi Delt
How to get there: Located in the centre of
Nottingham; from M1 J26 take A610, or from
J25 take A52, both into centre.

105 Westminster Hotel

★★★
312 Mansfield Road, Nottingham,
Nottinghamshire, NG5 2EF
Tel: 0115 955 5000 Fax: 0115 955 5005
Email: mail@westminster-hotel.co.uk
Web: www.westminster-hotel.co.uk
72 bedrs SB £83.50 DB £107 HBS £98.50
HBD £137 B £7.50 L £5 D £15
CC: MC Vi Am DC Swi Delt

How to get there: M1 J-26, take A610 to
Nottingham centre. Left onto A6130. Signs for
A60 north (Mansfield Road).
See advert on following page

106 Haven

★★
Grantham Road (A52), Whatton,
Nottinghamshire, NG13 9EU
Tel: 01949 850800 Fax: 01949 851454
33 bedrs SB £40 DB £55 B £6 L £4.99 D £6
CC: MC Vi Am DC Swi Delt

How to get there: Halfway between Nottingham
and Grantham, on A52 between Bingham and
Bottesford

107 Travelodge Ilkeston

Travel Accommodation
M1, Ilkeston, Nottingham,
Nottinghamshire, NG9 3PL
Tel: 08700 850 950
Web: www.travelodge.co.uk
35 bedrs B £4.25
CC: MC Vi Am DC Swi Delt

108 Travelodge Nottingham

Travel Accommodation
Riverside Retail Park, Queens Drive,
Nottingham, Nottinghamshire, NG2 1RT
Tel: 08700 850 950
Web: www.travelodge.co.uk
61 bedrs B £4.25
CC: MC Vi Am DC Swi Delt

East Midlands

Plan your route

Visit www.rac.co.uk for RAC's
interactive route planner, including
up to the minute traffic reports.

109 Andrews Private Hotel

◆ ◆ ◆

310 Queens Road, Beeston,
Nottingham, NG9 1JA
Tel: 0115 925 4902 Fax: 0115 925 4902
Children minimum age: 9
10 bedrs
CC: None accepted

How to get there: Leave M1 at Junction 25.
Take A52 for Nottingham. Over two
roundabouts, turn right at second set of lights
onto B6006. Turn right at fourth lights, hotel
200m on right.

110 Royston Hotel

◆ ◆ ◆ ⚹

326 Mansfield Road, Nottingham,
Nottinghamshire, NG5 2EF
Tel: 0115 962 2947 Fax: 0115 956 5018

Oakham, Rutland

111 Old Wisteria Hotel

★ ★ ★ 🄰

4 Catmose Street, Oakham, Rutland, LE15 6HW
Tel: 01572 722844 Fax: 01572 724473
Email: enquiries@wisteriahotel.co.uk
Web: www.wisteriahotel.co.uk

A welcoming country house ambience. Intimate
lounge bar and restaurant. Private dining and
meeting rooms. Friendly and attentive service. A
minute's drive into rolling countryside.
25 bedrs SB £65 DB £85 HBS £80 HBD £57.50
B £6.50 L £7.50 D £15
CC: MC Vi Am DC Swi Delt

How to get there: Hotel in Oakham town at
junction A606/A6003. From A1 North join B668.
From A1 South join A606. From Nottingham or
Kettering join A6003.

Redmile, Nottinghamshire

112 Peacock Inn

◆ ◆ ◆ 🄰 🄰

Church Corner, Main Street, Redmile,
Nottinghamshire, NG13 0GA
Tel: 01949 842554
10 bedrs SB £60 DB £70 B £8.95 L £5.95 D £8.95
CC: MC Vi Am DC Swi Delt JCB

How to get there: Off A1 M1. Along A52 to
Redmile. We are in the village of Redmile by the
church.

Retford, Nottinghamshire

113 Travelodge Retford

Travel Accommodation
A1 Northbound, Markham Moor, Retford,
Nottinghamshire, DN22 0QU
Tel: 08700 850 950
Web: www.travelodge.co.uk
40 bedrs B £4.25
CC: MC Vi Am DC Swi Delt

Rushden, Northamptonshire

114 Travelodge Rushden

Travel Accommodation
A45 East, Rushden,
Northamptonshire, NN10 9AP
Tel: 08700 850 950
Web: www.travelodge.co.uk
40 bedrs B £4.25
CC: MC Vi Am DC Swi Delt

Westminster Hotel

RAC ★★★

Conveniently located for Nottingham's tourist attractions, its celebrated shopping centre and wealth of sporting venues, our family owned and run hotel is decorated and equipped to the highest standards. Included in our 72 rooms are 2 Four Poster bedded rooms and also 19 Superior rooms which are air conditioned and offer the added attraction of king-size beds, dedicated PC/Fax connection points and, in the bathroom, the luxury of a shower unit which provides a relaxing steam shower. Dinner in the informal atmosphere of our highly acclaimed restaurant, where excellent food and good wines are sensibly priced, will simply add to the enjoyment of your stay. The hotel also has 5 meeting rooms including a function suite for up to 60, all of which are air conditioned.

Best Western

312 Mansfield Road, Nottingham NG5 2EF
Tel: 0115 955 5000   Fax: 0115 955 5005
Email: mail@westminster-hotel.co.uk
Website: www.westminster-hotel.co.uk

The Westminster Hotel Ltd. Registered Office: 312 Mansfield Road, Nottingham NG5 2EF. Registered in England No. 2311762

Scunthorpe, Lincolnshire

115 Hanover International Scunthorpe

★★★

Rowland Road, Scunthorpe,
North Lincolnshire, DN16 1SU
Tel: 01724 842223 Fax: 01724 280646

HANOVER INTERNATIONAL
HOTELS & CLUBS

This small, friendly hotel set in the heart of the garden town of Scunthorpe is an ideal base to explore an area of rural tranquility and natural beauty.
38 bedrs
CC: MC Vi Am DC Swi Delt

How to get there: Leave M180 at Junction 3. Turn right at roundabout. At next roundabout take third exit, take second left into Brumby Wood Lane. Go straight over next roundabout. Hotel is on right.

116 Forest Pines Hotel

★★★★ ℞

Ermine Street, Broughton, Brigg,
North Lincolnshire, DN20 0AQ
Tel: 01652 650770 Fax: 01652 650495
Email: enquiries@forestpines.co.uk
Web: www.forestpines.co.uk

Set in woodland grounds, the hotel offers everything for the discerning guest including golf and leisure/beauty facilities. AA rosette-awarded restaurant. Ideally situated for the historic city of Lincoln.
86 bedrs SB £90 DB £100
CC: MC Vi Am DC Swi Delt JCB

How to get there: Exit J4 M180. Hotel is 200 metres to the north at junction of A18 and A15.

Shepshed, Leicestershire

117 The Grange Courtyard

◆◆◆◆

The Grange, Forest Street, Shepshed,
Leicestershire, LE12 9DA
Tel: 01509 600189 Fax: 01509 600189
Email: linda.lawrence@thegrangecourtyard.co.uk
Web: www.thegrangecourtyard.co.uk
Children minimum age: 8
10 bedrs SB £55 DB £75 D £7.50
CC: MC Vi Swi

How to get there: Exit J23 M1, A512 towards Ashby. 3/4 of a mile, traffic lights, turn right. 3/4 of a mile, turn right at petrol station into Forest Street.

Skegness, Lincolnshire

118 Crown Hotel

★★★

Drummond Road, Skegness,
Lincolnshire, PE25 3AB
Tel: 0500 007274 Fax: 01754 610847

119 Vine Hotel

★★★

Vine Road, Skegness,
Lincolnshire, PE25 3DB
Tel: 01754 763018 Fax: 01754 769845
Email: vinehotel@bateman.co.uk
Web: www.skegness-resort.co.uk/vine
20 bedrs SB £55 DB £75
HBS £65 HBD £95
B £7.50 L £9.50 D £16.50
CC: MC Vi Am DC Swi Delt JCB

120 Crawford Hotel

South Parade, Skegness, Lincolnshire, PE25 3HR
Tel: 01754 764215 Fax: 01754 764215
Closed 1 November to December 24
20 bedrs SB £30.80 DB £49.40
HBS £37.70 HBD £65.40
CC: MC Vi DC Swi Delt JCB
How to get there: Hotel is on South Parade,
approached via Lumley Road to clock tower;
turn right onto South Parade.

121 The Saxby Hotel

Saxby Avenue, Skegness, Lincolnshire, PE25 3LG
Tel: 01754 763905 Fax: 01754 763905
Closed November — Easter
15 bedrs SB £24 DB £48 HBS £32 HBD £32
B £4 L £6 D £8
CC: MC Vi Swi Delt JCB

122 Seacroft Hotel

South Parade, Skegness, Lincolnshire, PE25 3EH
Tel: 01754 762301 Fax: 01754 761037
Web: www.friendlyhotel.co.uk
50 bedrs SB £28 DB £50 HBS £35 HBD £30
B £7 L £10 D £10
CC: MC Vi Am Swi Delt
How to get there: Keep the sea/beach on your
left. Our lawn is at the end of the promenade.

Sleaford, Lincolnshire

123 Carre Arms Hotel

1 Mareham Lane, Sleaford,
Lincolnshire, NG34 7JP
Tel: 01529 303156 Fax: 01529 303139
Email: enquiries@carrearmshotel.co.uk
Web: www.carrearmshotel.co.uk
13 bedrs SB £50 DB £70
B £9.50 L £11.50 D £15.50
CC: MC Vi Am Swi Delt
How to get there: 3 mins from Sleaford rail
station, easy access from Lincoln, Grantham
(A1), Boston (A15) and Newark (A1).

124 Travelodge Sleaford

A15/A17, Holdingham Roundabout, Sleaford,
Lincolnshire, NG34 8NP
Tel: 08700 850 950
Web: www.travelodge.co.uk
40 bedrs B £4.25
CC: MC Vi Am DC Swi Delt

South Normanton, Derbyshire

125 Renaissance Derby/Nottingham Hotel

Carter Lane East, South Normanton,
Derbyshire, DE55 2EH
Tel: 01773 812000 Fax: 01773 580032
Web: www.marriotthotels.co.uk
158 bedrs SB £95 DB £108
B £13.50 L £14.95 D £21
CC: MC Vi Am DC Swi Delt
How to get there: Exit M1 J28. Take A38
towards Mansfield and take first left down
Carter Lane East. Hotel is 100 yards on left.

Spalding, Lincolnshire

126 Cley Hall Hotel

22 High Street, Spalding, Lincolnshire, PE11 1TX
Tel: 01775 725157 Fax: 01775 710785
Email: cleyhall@enterprise.net
Web: www.cleyhallhotel.com
12 bedrs
CC: MC Vi Am DC Swi Delt
How to get there: Into Spalding, Junction
A151/A16 MacDonald's roundabout, follow road
towards town. Keep the river on the right. 500m
from town centre.

127 Travelodge Spalding

A17 Wisbeck Road, Long Sutton Bypass, Long
Sutton, Spalding, Lincolnshire, PE12 9AG
Tel: 08700 850 950
Web: www.travelodge.co.uk
40 bedrs B £4.25
CC: MC Vi Am DC Swi Delt

East Midlands

128 Travel Stop

◆ ◆

Locksmill Farm, 50 Cowbit Road, Spalding,
Lincolnshire, PE11 2RJ
Tel: 01775 767290 Fax: 01775 767716
Email: travelstopraclodg@btinternet.com
16 bedrs
CC: MC Vi Am

How to get there: Located on B1173, ³/₄ mile
from centre of Spading, by the side of the River
Welland.

Stamford, Lincolnshire

129 George of Stamford

Blue Ribbon Winner

★★★★ ☕ ☕ ☕
71 St. Martins, Stamford, Lincolnshire, PE9 2LB
Tel: 01780 750750 Fax: 01780 750701
Email: reservations@georgehotelofstamford.com
Web: www.georgehotelofstamford.com
47 bedrs SB £78 DB £105 B £9.50 L £7.50
D £7.50
CC: MC Vi Am DC Swi Delt

How to get there: North of Peterborough. From
A1, B1081 to Stamford at roundabout. Hotel
situated on left at first set of traffic lights.

130 Lady Anne's Hotel

★★
37–38 High Street, St. Martins Without,
Stamford, Lincolnshire, PE9 2LJ
Tel: 01780 470331
28 bedrs SB £52 DB £75
B £6.50 L £9.95 D £14.50
CC: MC Vi Am DC Swi Delt JCB

131 Rock Lodge

◆ ◆ ◆ ◆ ◆ ✗
1 Empingham Road, Stamford,
Lincolnshire, PE9 2RH
Tel: 01780 481758 Fax: 01780 481757
Email: rocklodge@innpro.co.uk
Web: www.innpro.co.uk
4 bedrs SB £50 DB £60
CC: Vi

How to get there: Leave A1 at A606, follow
signs to Stamford 1¹/₄ miles. Entrance on left at
junction of A606 and B1081

132 Candlesticks Hotel & Restaurant

◆ ◆

1 Church Lane, Stamford, Lincolnshire, PE9 2JU
Tel: 01780 764033 Fax: 01780 756071
Email: pinto@breathmail.net

A small family hotel run by Mr & Mrs Pinto for
25 years providing freshly cooked food and
luxury bedrooms with a fridge and Sky TV. Dine
in comfortable and elegant surroundings and
enjoy excellent cuisine at a price you can afford.
8 bedrs SB £35 DB £50. HBS £47. HBD £40
L £12.50 D £16.50
CC: MC Vi Am Swi Delt

How to get there: From A1 down St. Martins
High Street. Turn left into Church Street by St.
Martins Church.

Stretton, Leicestershire

133 Ram Jam Inn

★★★ ☕
Great North Road, Stretton, near Oakham,
Leicestershire, LE15 7QX
Tel: 01780 410776 Fax: 01780 410361
Email: rji@rutnet.co.uk
7 bedrs SB £56 DB £75
B £2.95 L £5.45 D £6.95
CC: MC Vi Am Swi Delt

How to get there: Travelling north on A1, look
for hotel sign. Through service station, just past
B668 turn off. Southbound, take B668 exit and
follow signs for Oakham.

Ask the experts

To book a Hotel or Guest
Accommodation, or for help
and advice, call RAC Hotel
Reservations on 0870 603 9109
and quote 'Guide 2002'

Sutton-on-Sea, Lincolnshire

134 Grange and Links Hotel

★★★

Sea Lane, Sandilands, Mablethorpe,
Lincolnshire, LN12 2RA
Tel: 01507 441334 Fax: 01507 443033
Email: grangelinks@ic24.net
Web: www.grangeandlinkshotel.com
23 bedrs SB £59.50 DB £78
B £7.50 L £6 D £20
CC: MC Vi Am DC Swi Delt

How to get there: From south, take A16 to
Spilsby and Ulceby Cross. From north, take A16
to Louth and Ulceby Cross, then A1104 to
Alford and A1111 to Sutton-on-Sea.

Thrapston, Northamptonshire

135 Travelodge Thrapston

Travel Accommodation
A14, Thrapston, Northamptonshire, NN14 4UR
Tel: 08700 850 950
Web: www.travelodge.co.uk
40 bedrs B £4.25
CC: MC Vi Am DC Swi Delt

Thrussington, Leicestershire

136 Travelodge Thrussington

Travel Accommodation
A46 South, Thrussington, Leicestershire, LE7 8TF
Tel: 08700 850 950
Web: www.travelodge.co.uk
32 bedrs B £4.25
CC: MC Vi Am DC Swi Delt

Tibshelf, Derbyshire

137 Tibshelf Travel Inn

Travel Accommodation
Tibshelf Motorway Services, M1 North Bound,
Tibshelf, Derbyshire, DE55 5TZ
Tel: 01773 591010 Fax: 01773 876609

Towcester

138 Travelodge Towcester

Travel Accommodation
A43 East, Brackley Road, Towcester,
Northamptonshire, NN12 7TQ
Tel: 08700 850 950
Web: www.travelodge.co.uk
33 bedrs B £4.25
CC: MC Vi Am DC Swi Delt

Uppingham, Leicestershire

139 Travelodge Uppingham

Travel Accommodation
A47, Glaston Road, Uppingham,
Rutland, LE15 8SA
Tel: 08700 850 950
Web: www.travelodge.co.uk
40 bedrs B £4.25
CC: MC Vi Am DC Swi Delt

140 Old Rectory

♦ ♦ ♦

Belton-in-Rutland, Uppingham,
Rutland, LE15 9LE
Tel: 01572 717279 Fax: 01572 717343
Email: bb@iepuk.com
Web: www.rutnet.co.uk/orb
5 bedrs SB £20 DB £38 B £7
CC: MC Vi Delt JCB

How to get there: From Leicester A47 take first
turn to Belton-in-Rutland village. Old Rectory is
on left after 400 yards.

East Midlands

141 Lake Isle

★★ ⬮ ⬮

16 High Street East, Uppingham,
Rutland, LE15 9PZ
Tel: 01572 822951 Fax: 01572 822951
Email: info@lakeislehotel.com
Web: www.lakeislehotel.com

Personally run 18th century hotel situated in pretty market town of Uppingham. Restaurant offers weekly changing menus with a wine list of more than 300 wines.
12 bedrs SB £55 DB £74
HBS £65 HBD £29.50 L £7 D £18.50
CC: MC Vi Am DC Swi Delt

How to get there: Via Queen Street to the rear of the property for parking. On foot, via Reeves Yard.

Weedon Bec, Northamptonshire

142 Globe Hotel

★★

High Street, Weedon Bec,
Northamptonshire, NN7 4QD
Tel: 01327 340336 Fax: 01327 349058
Email: the globeatweedon@hotmail.com
Web: www.theglobeatweedon.co.uk
18 bedrs SB £45 DB £55
B £3.95 L £3.95 D £7.95
CC: MC Vi Am Swi Delt

How to get there: From junction 16 M1 take Daventry road. For three miles on junction of A5 and A45.

Woodhall Spa, Lincolnshire

143 Petwood Hotel

★★★ ⬮

Stixwould Road, Woodhall Spa, Lincolnshire,
LN10 6QF
Tel: 01526 352411 Fax: 01526 353473
Email: reception@petwood.co.uk
Web: www.petwood.co.uk
50 bedrs SB £63 DB £126
HBS £80 HBD £80
B £9 L £13.50 D £20.50
CC: MC Vi Am DC Swi Delt

How to get there: From Sleaford, take A153 to Tattershall. Turn left onto B1192 to Woodhall Spa. From Lincoln, south on B1188 and B1191.

Worksop, Nottinghamshire

144 Charnwood Hotel

★★★ ⬮

Sheffield Road, Blyth, Worksop,
Nottinghamshire, S81 8HF
Tel: 01909 591610 Fax: 01909 591429
33 bedrs SB £65 DB £90
HBS £83 HBD £60
B £7.95 L £12.95 D £19.95
CC: MC Vi Am DC Swi Delt JCB

145 Lion Hotel

★★★

112 Bridge Street, Worksop,
Nottinghamshire, S80 1HT
Tel: 01909 477925 Fax: 01909 479038
45 bedrs SB £40 DB £55
HBS £78 HBD £98
B £5 L £10 D £15
CC: MC Vi Am DC Swi Delt JCB

146 Travelodge Worksop

Travel Accommodation
A57, St. Anne's Drive, Worksop,
Nottinghamshire, S80 3QD
Tel: 08700 850 950
Web: www.travelodge.co.uk
40 bedrs B £4.25
CC: MC Vi Am DC Swi Delt

Open and
shut case

Don't get caught out by unexpected legal costs

The availability of Legal Aid in all types of cases has all but disappeared. So what do you do if you or members of your family suffer injury after an accident? Visit a high street solicitor hoping that financial assistance will be available?

'No win No fee agreements' Many solicitors and claims recovery firms may offer this facility but at what cost? In some instances they may ask you to pay up front for out of pocket expenses for reports and court fees. A GP's report may be just £50 but a specialist medical report may be £450. If your claim proceeds to court, Court fees may cost in excess of £100 and Barrister's fees commence at £100 per hour!

A hefty insurance premium to underwrite your claim may be payable. And as much as 30% may be deducted from the compensation awarded to you in lieu of their fees! That means if you were awarded £5000 for your injuries, you would receive only £3500! RAC's Legal Expenses Insurance ensures you receive your damages in full.

RAC Legal Expenses Insurance is personal based and will cover you irrespective of the vehicle you are travelling in. Further Cover may be obtained to protect your partner or your family!

Does your existing policy cover the following benefits?

Consider the alternatives and ask yourself whether you would take the same comfort and peace of mind from these that RAC legal expenses insurance will provide you with?

Call now! Immediate cover is available from just £15

08705 533533

- Up to £50,000 legal expenses cover for non-fault accidents
- Up to £10,000 legal expenses cover for the defence of certain road traffic offences
- 24 hour legal helpline providing advice on most legal matters
- Cover driving/travelling in any vehicle
- Cover for passengers travelling with you
- Cover for you as a pedestrian

A to B - we RAC to it

West Midlands

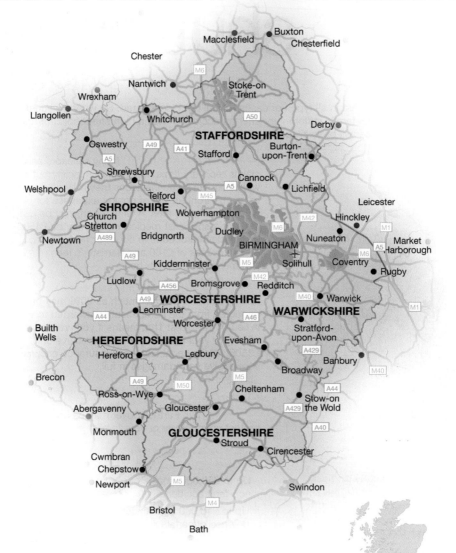

Macclesfield Buxton
Chesterfield
Chester
Nantwich Stoke-on-Trent
Wrexham
Llangollen Whitchurch A50 Derby
STAFFORDSHIRE
Oswestry A49 A41 Stafford Burton-upon-Trent
A5
Shrewsbury Cannock
Welshpool Telford A5 Lichfield
SHROPSHIRE Wolverhampton Leicester
Church Stretton Dudley Hinckley
Newtown A489 Bridgnorth **BIRMINGHAM** Nuneaton A5 Market Harborough
A49 M6
Kidderminster M5 Solihull Coventry
Ludlow A456 Bromsgrove Redditch Rugby
A49 M40 Warwick
Leominster **WORCESTERSHIRE**
A44 Worcester A46 **WARWICKSHIRE**
Builth Wells Stratford-upon-Avon
HEREFORDSHIRE Evesham A429
Hereford Ledbury Banbury
Broadway M40
Brecon A49 M50 M5
Ross-on-Wye Cheltenham A44
Abergavenny Gloucester Stow-on the Wold
A429 A40
Monmouth **GLOUCESTERSHIRE**
Cwmbran Stroud Cirencester
Chepstow
Newport M5 Swindon
Bristol M4
Bath

● There's much to entertain in the Birmingham area, with the NEC, National Indoor Arena, Symphony Hall, galleries, theatres (including the new Birmingham Hippodrome) and the new Millennium Point, which brings science and technology to vivid, interactive life and includes an IMAX cinema.

● Combine walking in the beautiful Forest of Dean, easily reached from most parts of the region, with art and entertainment by following the Forest of Dean Sculpture Trail.

Glasgow • • Edinburgh
• Newcastle
Belfast •
Dublin • • Manchester
Birmingham •
Cardiff •
• London

Shakespeare's County

The ghost of the Earl of Warwick may not agree, but all of Warwickshire's signs say it belongs to the Bard, and never more so than in his birthplace, Stratford-upon-Avon. Visitors can see his house (right), his wife Anne Hathaway's premarital cottage (below), or visit the three Royal Shakespeare Company (RSC) theatres: the Swan Theatre, The Other Place and the prime Royal Shakespeare Theatre, on the banks of the River Avon. Visit www.rsc.org.uk or phone the box office on 01789 403 403. And for further details try www.stratford.co.uk/birthplace or 01789 204016.

● Among the picturesque Malvern Hills and its towns is Malvern Link, where Edward Elgar composed much of his work.

● Book lovers are drawn to Hay-on-Wye and its many collectors' book shops, particularly during Hay Literary Festival in May.

● The Stoke-on-Trent area was the centre of the pottery industry for 200 years; names such as Wedgwood, Royal Doulton and Spode are celebrated in the Potteries Museum & Art Gallery.

Farming History

Acton Scott Historic Working Farm (right), on the A49 between Ludlow and Shrewsbury, presents a living tableau of 19th-century agricultural life. Visitors can see traditional farming techniques — indoor as well as outdoor — rural craftsmen, and old breeds of livestock. www.shropshire-cc.gov.uk/museum.nsf or call 01694 781306.

Royal Pump Rooms

Baths were first built near Leamington Spa's natural springs in 1784 and The Royal Pump Rooms (below) were opened in 1815 to meet demand for the water's therapeutic qualities. Fortunes eventually declined and now the Pump Rooms act as the historic site of the town's art gallery, museum and library. 01926 742762 or www.royal-pump-rooms.co.uk.

Fragments of the original Norman castle of 1068 remain, but most of today's Warwick Castle (above) was built in the 14th century. There's lots to excite, including battling knights and jousting competitions by day and banquets and candle-lit tours by night. Use the 24-hour info line, 0870 442 2000 or www.warwick-castle.co.uk.

● Tewkesbury Abbey, consecrated in 1121 on the site of an eighth-century Saxon monastery, is huge and features England's largest Norman tower at 148 feet tall.

Industrial Revolution

In 1709 Abraham Darby refined the iron smelting process in what is now known as Ironbridge Gorge, near Telford; 82 years later, Abraham Darby III created the iron bridge itself (below). The birthplace of the Industrial Revolution, the valley has seven museums detailing the development of iron, glass and china craftsmanship, yet nature still thrives on the gorge's sides. www.ironbridge.org.uk or 01952 432166 for more.

The 18th-century Broadway Tower (below) commands stunning views of the Cotswolds.

Accommodation index

Hotels and Guest Accommodation are indexed by their order of appearance within this region, not by the page. To locate an establishment, note the number to the right of the listing and then find it on the establishment's name bar, as shown here

37 The Turning Mill Hotel

Alcester, Warwickshire

1 Travelodge Alcester

Travel Accommodation
A435, Oversley Mill Roundabout, Birmingham
Road, Alcester, Warwickshire, B49 6AA
Tel: 08700 850 950
Web: www.travelodge.co.uk
40 bedrs B £4.25
CC: MC Vi Am DC Swi Delt
🐕 🕲 🖵 ☆

Balsall Common, West Midlands

2 Haigs Hotel

★ ★ ⍣ ⍣ ⍣
273 Kenilworth Road, Balsall Common,
West Midlands, CV7 7EL
Tel: 01676 533004 Fax: 01676 535132
Closed Christmas to New Year

Family-run hotel recently refurbished to a high
standard. Award-winning restaurant. Ideally
situated five miles from the NEC and at hub of
Midland motorways. Close to Warwick and
Stratford-upon-Avon.
23 bedrs
CC: MC Vi Am Swi Delt
🕭 🕲 🖵 ☎ 🍴 P🌐 ☆ 🏛 🏛
How to get there: Located close to Junction 4
M6, Junction 6 M42 and Junction 15 M40.
Close to Warwick and Stratford, only 10 minutes
from NEC/Birmingham Airport on A452.

Berkeley, Gloucestershire

3 Prince of Wales

★ ★ ★
Berkeley Road, Berkeley,
Gloucestershire, GL13 9HD
Tel: 01453 810474 Fax: 01453 511370
43 bedrs SB £70 DB £86
B £6.50 L £15 D £15
CC: MC Vi Am DC Swi Delt
🛏 🕲 🖵 ☎ P ☆ 🕃 🍴 🐾 🏛 🏛
How to get there: The hotel is situated on the
A38 which runs parallel with the M5 between
junctions 13 and 14.

Bewdley, Worcestershire

4 George Hotel

★ ★ ⍣
Load Street, Bewdley,
Worcestershire, DY12 2AW
Tel: 01299 402117 Fax: 01299 401269
Email: enquiries@georgehotelbewdley.co.uk
Web: www.georgehotelbewdley.co.uk
11 bedrs SB £47 DB £68 HBS £58 HBD £47.25
B £6.50 L £9.95 D £12.50
CC: MC Vi Swi Delt
 🍴 🐕 🕲 🖵 ☎ P🌐 ☆ 🕃 🍴 🏛 🏛
How to get there: Town centre location, 300m
from river. From M5 Junction 3, take A456 to
Bewdley. From M5 Junction 6, take A449 to
Kidderminster, then A456 to Bewdley. From M42
Junction 1, take A448 to Kidderminster then
A456 to Bewdley.

Bibury, Gloucestershire

5 The Catherine Wheel

◆ ◆ ◆
Arlington, Bibury near Cirencester,
Gloucestershire, GL7 5ND
Tel: 01285 740250 Fax: 01285 740779
Email: catherinewheel.bibury
@eldridge-pope.co.uk
4 bedrs SB £60 DB £120
L £4.95 D £7.95
CC: MC Vi Am Swi
🕭 🐕 🕲 🖵 P ☆ 🍴 🏛 ⍮
How to get there: Located seven miles from
Cirencester. Follow signs to Burford and Stow
from town centre along the B4425.

West Midlands

Birmingham

6 Birmingham Marriott Hotel

★ ★ ★ ★ ★ ⚇ ⚇ ⚇

12 Hagley Road, Birmingham,
West Midlands, B16 8SJ
Tel: 0121 452 1144 Fax: 0121 456 3442
Web: www.marriotthotels.com/bhxbh
98 bedrs SB £163.45 DB £177.90 HBS £195.80
HBD £121.45 B £12.45 L £16.50 D £32.50
CC: MC Vi Am DC Swi Delt JCB

How to get there: Approaching Five Ways Round-about from city centre, fourth exit into Calthorpe Road. Take slip road on right after the clock.

7 Burlington Hotel

★ ★ ★ ★ ⚇

6 Burlington Arcade, 126 New Street,
Birmingham, B2 4JQ
Tel: 0121 643 9191 Fax: 0121 628 5005
112 bedrs CC: MC Vi Am DC Swi Delt

8 Copthorne Hotel Birmingham

★ ★ ★ ★ ⚇

Paradise Circus, Birmingham,
West Midlands, B3 3HJ
Tel: 0121 200 2727 Fax: 0121 200 1197
Email: sales.birmingham@mill-cop.com
Web: www.millennium-hotels.com
212 bedrs SB £163.95 DB £183.95 B £13.95
L £15 D £18 CC: MC Vi Am DC Swi Delt

How to get there: Situated by Centenary Square, approximately 10 minutes from M6 Junction 6, follow city centre route (A38)

9 Birmingham Great Barr Hotel

★ ★ ★

Pear Tree Drive, Newton Road, Great Barr,
Bimingham, West Midlands, B43 6HS
Tel: 0800 373 853 Fax: 0121 357 9197
Email: sales@thegreatbarrhotel.co.uk
Web: www.thegreatbarrhotel.co.uk
105 bedrs SB £77.95 DB £93.95 HBS £95.45
HBD £64.45 B £8.95 L £12.95 D £17.50
CC: MC Vi Am DC Swi Delt

How to get there: Take M6 Exit 7, follow A34 to Birmingham. Turn right at Scott Arms traffic lights onto Newton Road. After 1¼ miles, turn right into Pear Tree Drive.

10 Comfort Inn Edgbaston, Birmingham

★ ★ ★

267 Hagley Road, Edgbaston,
Birmingham, West Midlands, B16 9NA
Tel: 0121 454 8071 Fax: 0121 455 6149
Email: admin@gb606.u-net.com
Web: www.choicehotels.com
166 bedrs SB £69.25 DB £69.25 HBS £83.75
HBD £41.88 B £9.75 D £14.50
CC: MC Vi Am DC Swi Delt

How to get there: From M6 take exit 6 and head for central Birmingham. Turn right onto ring road. Turn right onto A456 to Kidderminster (Hagley Road).

11 Jurys Inn Birmingham

★ ★ ★

245 Broad Street, Birmingham, B1 2HO
Tel: 0870 9072222 Fax: +353(0)1 631 6999
Email: bookings@jurysdoyle.com
Web: www.jurysdoyle.com
Closed 24-26 December inclusive
445 bedrs SB £73.50 DB £82
B £8.50 CC: MC Vi Am

How to get there: Jurys Inn Birmingham is situated approx. Eight miles from Birmingham International Airport, or one mile from New Street train station.

12 Novotel Birmingham Airport

★ ★ ★

Birmingham International Airport, Birmingham,
West Midlands, B26 3QL
Tel: 0121 782 7000 Fax: 0121 782 0445
Email: h1158@accor-hotels.com
Web: www.novotel.com
195 bedrs SB £116 DB £125
B £11.50 L £13.95 D £21
CC: MC Vi Am DC Swi Delt

How to get there: Leave M42 at Junction 6. Take A45 to Birmingham. Follow signs to airport terminal; the hotel is located immediately opposite terminal.

Making a booking?

Don't forget to mention RAC Hotels and Bed & Breakfast 2002.

13 Novotel Birmingham Centre

★★★
70 Broad Street, Birmingham, B1 2HT
Tel: 0121 643 2000 Fax: 0121 643 9796
Email: h1077@accor-hotels.com
Web: www.novotel.com
148 bedrs SB £109 DB £119
B £10.75 L £10 D £15
CC: MC Vi Am DC Swi Delt

How to get there: Exit M6 Junction 6, follow A38(M). Follow signs for Convention Centre; Novotel is 200m along street from Centre.

14 Portland Hotel

★★★
313 Hagley Road, Edgbaston, Birmingham, West Midlands, B16 9LQ
Tel: 0121 455 0535 Fax: 0121 456 1841
Email: sales@portland-hotel.demon.co.uk
Web: www.portland-birmingham.co.uk
63 bedrs SB £52.45 DB £62.95 HBS £66.95
HBD £91.95 B £7.95 L £13.95 D £13.95
CC: MC Vi Am DC Swi Delt

How to get there: Hotel is situated on A456, Hagley Road into Birmingham city centre from M5 Junction 3.

15 Quality Hotel

★★★
116 Hagley Road, Birmingham, West Midlands, B16 9NZ
Tel: 0121 454 6621 Fax: 0121 456 2935
Email: admin@gb605.u-net.com
Web: www.choicehotels.com
215 bedrs SB £94.75 DB £104.75 HBS £109.25
HBD £59.63 B £9.75 D £14.50
CC: MC Vi Am DC Swi Delt

How to get there: From M6 exit 6 and head for central Birmingham. Right onto ring road and right onto A456 to Kidderminster (Hagley Road).

16 Quality Sutton Court Hotel

★★★
66 Lichfield Road, Sutton Coldfield, West Midlands, B74 2NA
Tel: 0121 354 4991 Fax: 0121 355 0083
Email: reservations@sutton-court-hotel.co.uk
Web: www.sutton-court-hotel.co.uk.index.htm
59 bedrs SB £95 DB £118 HBS £112 HBD £153
B £9.50 D £17
CC: MC Vi Am DC Swi Delt

How to get there: Leave M42 at Junction 9. Take A446 toards Lichfield. Take A453 towards Sutton Coldfield, hotel is on left at second set of traffic lights.

17 Beechwood

★★
201 Bristol Road, Edgbaston, Birmingham, B5 7UB
Tel: 0121 440 2133 Fax: 0121 446 4549
20 bedrs CC: MC Vi Am DC Swi Delt

How to get there: From city centre, proceed on Bristol Road past traffic lights at McDonalds, hotel is on right, one mile from city centre.

18 Greswolde Park Hotel

★★
980 Warwick Road, Acocks Green, Birmingham, West Midlands, B27 6QG
Tel: 0121 706 4068 Fax: 0121 706 0649
Email: jeff@greswolde.freeserve.co.uk
Web: www.greswolde.freeserve.co.uk
10 bedrs
CC: MC Vi Swi Delt

How to get there: From M42 Junction 6 take A45 to Birmingham. Fork left to Acocks Green, left at island. Straight down to T-Junction, turn right. Second hotel on right.

West Midlands

It's easier online

For all your motoring and travel needs, www.rac.co.uk

See the road ahead

Just dial 1740* from any mobile phone to get up-to-the-minute RAC traffic information on motorways and major A roads. Try it now! *Calls to 1740 are charged at premium rate.

19 Heath Lodge Hotel

★★
117 Coleshill Road, Marston Green,
Birmingham, B37 7HT
Tel: 0121 779 2218 Fax: 0121 779 2218
Email: reception@heathlodgehotel.
　　　freeserve.co.uk
Web: www.heathlodgehotel.com
17 bedrs SB £54 DB £69
HBS £70 HBD £44.50 D £6.95
CC: MC Vi Am Swi Delt

20 Hotel Clarine

★★
229 Hagley Road, Birmingham,
West Midlands, B16 9RP
Tel: 0121 454 6514 Fax: 0121 456 2722
Email: reception@kyriadbirmingham.co.uk
Web: www.kyriadbirmingham.co.uk

Campanile hotels offer comfortable and
convenient budget accommodation and a
traditional French-style Bistro providing freshly
cooked food for breakfast, lunch and dinner. All
rooms en-suite with tea/coffee-making facilities,
DDT and TV with Sky channels.
27 bedrs
CC: MC Vi Am DC Swi Delt

How to get there: From M6 Junction 6 follow
A38 towards city centre. Over flyover and three
underpasses. At main traffic lights turn right.
Take second exit at roundabout. Hotel one mile
on right.

21 Woodlands Hotel & Restaurant

★★
379–381 Hagley Road, Edgbaston,
Birmingham, B17 8DL
Tel: 0121 420 2341 Fax: 0121 429 3935
Email: hotel@woodlands2000.freeserve.co.uk
Web: www.thewoodlandshotel.co.uk
20 bedrs SB £50 DB £64 HBS £62 HBD £43
B £5.50 D £12.50 CC: MC Vi Am Swi Delt JCB

22 Campanile

Travel Accommodation
Chester Street, Aston Locks,
Birmingham, B6 4BE
Tel: 0121 359 3330 Fax: 0121 359 1223

Campanile hotels offer comfortable and
convenient budget accommodation and a
traditional French-style Bistro providing freshly-
cooked food for breakfast, lunch and dinner. All
rooms ensuite with tea/coffee-making facilities,
DDT and TV with pay movie channels.
111 bedrs SB £48.90 DB £54.85 HBS £55
HBD £36.10 B £5.95 L £5.95 D £6.95
CC: MC Vi Am DC Swi Delt

How to get there: Junction 6 of M6, then A38.
Take second exit (ringroad), go left at roundabout,
then first left into Richard Street. From city centre,
take M6 direction then ring road.

23 Travelodge Birmingham (Central)

Travel Accommodation
230 Broad Street, Birmingham, B15 1AY
Tel: 08700 850 950
Web: www.travelodge.co.uk
136 bedrs B £4.25 CC: MC Vi Am DC Swi Delt

24 Travelodge Birmingham (Dudley)

Travel Accommodation
A461, Dudley Road, Brierley Hill, Birmingham,
West Midlands, DY5 1LQ
Tel: 08700 850 950
Web: www.travelodge.co.uk
32 bedrs B £4.25 CC: MC Vi Am DC Swi Delt

25 Travelodge Birmingham (East)

Travel Accommodation
1741 Coventry Road, Harry Ramsdens Site,
Yardley, Birmingham, B26 1DS
Tel: 08700 850 950
Web: www.travelodge.co.uk
40 bedrs B £4.25 CC: MC Vi Am DC Swi Delt

26 Travelodge Birmingham (South)

Travel Accommodation
M5, Illey Lane, Birmingham, B32 4AR
Tel: 08700 850 950
Web: www.travelodge.co.uk
62 bedrs B £4.25 CC: MC Vi Am DC Swi Delt

27 Travelodge Birmingham (Sutton Coldfield)

Travel Accommodation
A452 Chester Road, Boldmere Road,
Sutton Coldfield, Birmingham, B72 5UP
Tel: 08700 850 950
Web: www.travelodge.co.uk
32 bedrs B £4.25 CC: MC Vi Am DC Swi Delt

28 Central Guest House

◆◆◆
1637 Coventry Road, South Yardley,
Birmingham, West Midlands, B26 1DD
Tel: 0121 706 7757 Fax: 0121 706 7757
Email: mmou826384@aol.com
Web: www.centralguesthouse.com
5 bedrs SB £20 DB £40 HBS £20 HBD £20
CC: MC Vi Swi
How to get there: Situated four miles from NEC,
four miles from Birmingham city centre.

29 Comfort Inn Edgbaston

◆◆◆
Station Street, City Centre, Birmingham, B5 4DY
Tel: 0121 643 1134 Fax: 0121 643 3209
Email: comfort.inn@talk21.com
Closed 25–26 December
40 bedrs SB £60 DB £75 B £8
CC: MC Vi Am Swi Delt
How to get there: Leave M6 at Junction 6. Head
for city centre on A38M. Follow Queensway to
Bromsgrove. Turn onto Hill Street (near New
Street station).

30 La Caverna Restaurant and Hotel

◆◆◆
23-27 Coventry Road, Sheldon,
Birmingham, B26 3PG
Tel: 0121 743 7917 Fax: 0121 722 3307
19 bedrs SB £42 DB £59 L £17
CC: MC Vi Am DC Swi
How to get there: 3 miles from NEC and Airport,
close to junction of Coventry Road and Wells Rd.

31 Lyndhurst Hotel

◆◆◆
135 Kingsbury Road, Erdington,
Birmingham, B24 8QT
Tel: 0121 373 5695 Fax: 0121 373 5697
Email: info@lyndhurst-hotel.co.uk
Web: www.lyndhurst-hotel.co.uk
Closed Christmas

Popular family-run 14 bedroomed hotel, offering
comfortable ensuite rooms at reasonable prices.
Close to Aston University, University of Central
England, Aston Villa leisure centre and Star City
entertainment centre.
14 bedrs SB £42 DB £49
HBS £52 HBD £32.25 B £5 D £10
CC: MC Vi Am DC
How to get there: Exit J6 M6; A5127 to roundabout. Second left up Gravelly Hill. Right-hand
fork along Kingsbury road. Hotel on the right.

West Midlands

32 Tri-Star Hotel

◆◆◆

Coventry Road, Elmdon, Birmingham, B26 3QR
Tel: 0121 782 1010 Fax: 0121 782 6131

Ideally situated two miles from Junction 6 of the
M42, and 1½ miles from Birmingham
International Airport and the NEC, the hotel
maintains a homely atmosphere at moderate
charge. Licensed bar. Ample parking.
14 bedrs
CC: MC Vi Am DC Swi Delt
How to get there: 2 miles from Junction 6 of M42,
1½ miles from Birmingham International Airport,
train station and National Exhibition Centre.

33 Rollason Wood Hotel

◆◆

Wood End Road, Erdington,
Birmingham, B24 8BJ
Tel: 0121 373 1230 Fax: 0121 382 2578
Email: rollwood@globknet.co.uk

Friendly family-run hotel with 35 bedrooms.
Choose from economy, with shower, or fully ensuite. Licensed bar and à la carte restaurant.
Weekend and weekly reductions.
35 bedrs SB £18 DB £32 D £6
CC: MC Vi Am DC Swi Delt
How to get there: Exit M6 at Junction 6 and
take A5127 to Erdington. At island turn right
onto A4040. Hotel ¼ of a mile on left.

34 Briar Rose

✤

25 Bennetts Hill, Birmingham, B2 5RS
Tel: 0121 634 8100 Fax: 0121 634 8200

35 Crowne Plaza Birmingham NEC

✤

Pendigo Way, NEC, Birmingham, B40 1PS
Tel: 0121 781 4000 Fax: 0121 767 5029

Bourton-on-the-Water, Gloucestershire

36 Chester House Hotel

★★

Bourton-on-the-Water,
Gloucestershire, GL54 2BU
Tel: 01451 820286 Fax: 01451 820471
Email: juliand@chesterhouse.u-net.com
Web: www.bizare.demon.co.uk/chester
Closed December to January
22 bedrs
CC: MC Vi Am DC Swi Delt
How to get there: In centre of village. Take left
road bridge spanning river, which leads to hotel
car park.

37 Old New Inn

★★

High Street, Bourton-on-the-Water,
Gloucestershire, GL54 2AF
Tel: 01451 820467 Fax: 01451 810236
Email: reception@theoldnewinn.co.uk
Web: www.theoldnewinn.co.uk
9 bedrs SB £38 DB £76 HBS £53 HBD £53
B £8 L £10 D £12
CC: MC Vi Swi

38 The Kingsbridge Inn

◆◆◆

The Riverside, Bourton-on-the-Water,
Cheltenham, Gloucestershire, GL54 2BS
Tel: 01451 820371

Bridgnorth, Shropshire

39 Mill Hotel

★★★★
Alveley, near Bridgnorth,
Shropshire, WV15 6HL
Tel: 01746 780437 Fax: 01746 780850
Web: www.theaa.com/hotels/36837.html
21 bedrs SB £75.50 DB £100 HBS £99
HBD £73.50 B £8 L £12.75 D £23.50
CC: MC Vi Am DC Swi

How to get there: Situated just off main A442,
midway between Kidderminster and Bridgnorth.

40 Old Vicarage

Blue Ribbon Winner

★★★★ 🍷 🍷 🍷
Worfield, Bridgnorth, Shropshire, WV15 5JZ
Tel: 01746 716497 Fax: 01746 716552
Email: admin@the-old-vicarage.co.uk
Web: www.oldvicarageworfield.com

Rural, peaceful, country house hotel overlooking
rolling Shropshire countryside. Award-winning
wine list and restaurant, fourteen luxuriously
appointed bedrooms. A warm welcome assured
from David & Sarah Blakstad and their
dedicated team.
14 bedrs SB £75 DB £115 HBS £105 HBD £75
B £10.50 L £18.50 D £22.50
CC: MC Vi Am DC Swi Delt

How to get there: The Old Vicarage is one mile
from the A454 and two miles from the A442 to
the east of Bridgnorth — look for the brown
signs.

41 Parlors Hall Hotel

★★
Mill Street, Bridgnorth, Shropshire, WV15 5AL
Tel: 01746 761931 Fax: 01746 767058
13 bedrs SB £42 DB £54 B £6.50 L £5 D £15
CC: MC Vi Am Swi Delt JCB

See advert below

42 The Swan Inn

★★
Knowle Sands, Bridgnorth, WV16 5JL
Tel: 01746 763424 Fax: 01746 768507
Email: info@swaninnhotel.co.uk
Web: www.swaninnhotel.co.uk
6 bedrs DB £55 B £5 L £5 D £8
CC: MC Vi Swi Delt

How to get there: Follow Severn river on the
road to Highley, B4555, ½ mile outside
Bridgnorth.

West Midlands

Broadway, Worcestershire

43 The Lygon Arms
Gold Ribbon Winner

★★★★ ⓐⓑⓒ ⓐⓑⓒ ⓐⓑⓒ
Broadway, Worcestershire, WR12 7DU
Tel: 01386 854405 Fax: 01386 854470
Email: shancox@the-lygon-arms.co.uk
Web: www.the-lygon-arms.co.uk
The Lygon Arms, situated in the charming
village of Broadway, offers the perfect marriage
of old and new. Traditional hospitality and
seamless service blend effortlessly with modern
comforts and luxurious spa facilities.
69 bedrs SB £145 DB £240 HBS £185
HBD £160 B £10.50 L £25 D £39.50
CC: MC Vi Am DC Swi Delt JCB
How to get there: In the centre of Broadway
village, off the Broadway bypass.

44 Buckland Manor
Gold Ribbon Winner

★★★ ⓐⓑⓒ ⓐⓑⓒ ⓐⓑⓒ
Buckland, Broadway, Worcestershire, WR12 7LY
Tel: 01386 852626 Fax: 01386 853557
Email: enquire@bucklandmanor.com
Web: www.bucklandmanor.com
Children minimum age: 12

13th-century manor situated in the heart of the
Cotswolds, in glorious grounds. Superb food
and wines in award-winning restaurant. Luxury
bedrooms with antiques and four-poster beds.
13 bedrs SB £205 DB £215
B £15 L £28.50 D £45.50
CC: MC Vi Am DC Swi Delt
How to get there: Two miles south of Broadway,
on B4632.

45 Dormy House

★★★ ⓐⓑⓒ ⓐⓑⓒ ⓐⓑⓒ
Willersey Hill, Broadway,
Worcestershire, WR12 7LF
Tel: 01386 852711 Fax: 01386 858636
Email: reservations@dormyhouse.co.uk
Web: www.dormyhouse.co.uk
Closed Christmas

Meticulously converted 17th-century Cotswold
farmhouse combining traditional charm with all
the modern comforts. Leisure facilities include:
games room, gym, sauna/steam room, putting
green and croquet lawn.
49 bedrs SB £113 DB £156
B £10.50 L £20.50 D £32.50
CC: MC Vi Am DC Swi Delt
How to get there: Off A44 at top of Fish Hill. 1½
miles from Broadway, take turn signposted
Saintbury/picnic area. After ½ mile fork left.
Dormy House on left.
See advert on facing page

46 Leasow House Hotel

◆◆◆◆
Laverton Meadow, Broadway,
Worcestershire, WR12 7NA
Tel: 01386 584526 Fax: 01386 584596
Email: leasow@clara.net
Web: www.leasow.co.uk

Cotswold stone farmhouse in quiet countryside location near Broadway village. An ideal base for touring the Cotswolds and Stratford-upon-Avon.
7 bedrs
CC: MC Vi Am

How to get there: From Broadway take B4632 towards Winchcombe. After two miles turn right to Wormington and Dumbleton. Hotel is first on the right.

47 Windrush Guest House

♦ ♦ ♦ ♦ ⌖ ℉

Station Road, Broadway,
Worcestershire, WR12 7DE
Tel: 01386 853577 Fax: 01386 853790
Email: richard@broadway-windrush.co.uk
Web: www.broadway-windrush.co.uk
5 bedrs SB £30 DB £50 L £10 D £15
CC: MC Vi Am DC Swi Delt JCB

How to get there: Follow Broadway sign from roundabout on A44 (bypass). Windrush House is near start of Station Road, opposite junction with B4632.

Bromsgrove, Worcestershire

48 Hanover International Hotel & Club Bromsgrove

★★★★

Kidderminster Road, Bromsgrove,
Worcestershire, B61 9AB
Tel: 01527 576600 Fax: 01527 878981
Email: enquiries.hanover-bromsgrove@virgin.net
Web: www.hanover-international.com

HANOVER INTERNATIONAL
HOTELS & CLUBS

This magnificent hotel has a distinctive Mediterranean flavour and charm with an extensive leisure club and a wealth of local attractions in easy reach.
114 bedrs SB £135 DB £155
B £9.95 L £6 D £19.50
CC: MC Vi Am DC Swi Delt

How to get there: From Junction 4 or 5 M5 or Junction 1 M42, follow A38 into Bromsgrove centre. Follow signs to Kidderminster (A448). Hotel is ½ mile outside Bromsgrove.

49 Avoncroft Guest House

♦ ♦ ♦ ♦ ⌖

77 Redditch Road, Stoke Heath, Bromsgrove,
Worcestershire, B60 4JP
Tel: 01527 832819
4 bedrs SB £30 DB £45
CC: None accepted

How to get there: Exit J1 M42, A38 Bromsgrove South. After Safeway's, the house is on top of the hill on the right.

West Midlands

Burton upon Trent

50 Travelodge Burton upon Trent

Travel Accommodation
A38, Lichfield Rd,
Barton Under Needwood, Burton upon Trent,
Staffordshire, DE13 8ED
Tel: 08700 850 950
Web: www.travelodge.co.uk
20 bedrs B £4.25
CC: MC Vi Am DC Swi Delt

51 Travelodge Burton upon Trent (South)

Travel Accommodation
A38 Southbound, Lichfield Road,
Barton Under Needwood, Burton upon Trent,
Staffordshire, DE13 8EH
Tel: 08700 850 950
Web: www.travelodge.co.uk
40 bedrs B £4.25
CC: MC Vi Am DC Swi Delt

52 Queens Hotel

★★★
One Bridge Street, Burton upon Trent,
Staffordshire, DE14 1SY
Tel: 0870 4603 800 Fax: 01283 523823
Email: hotel@burton-conferencing.com
Web: www.burton-conferencing.com
38 bedrs SB £45 DB £59.50 HBS £59.50
HBD £44.50 B £6.95 L £7.50 D £14.95
CC: MC Vi Am Swi Delt
How to get there: Town centre on corner of
Bridge Street and High Street. From M42
Junction 11 take A444. From A38 follow town
centre.
See advert below left

53 Delter Hotel

◆ ◆ ◆ ✕
5 Derby Road, Burton upon Trent,
Staffordshire, DE14 1RU
Tel: 01283 535115 Fax: 01283 845261
Email: delterhotel@burtonontrenthotels.co.uk
Web: www.burtonontrenthotels.co.uk
6 bedrs SB £34 DB £47 HBS £46 HBD £69
D £12.50 CC: MC Vi Swi Delt
How to get there: From A511 turn into
Derby Road at roundabout. Hotel 50 yards on
left. Or, from A38 join A5121 Burton north,
straight over two roundabouts. Hotel ½ mile
on right.

Chaddesley Corbett, Worcestershire

54 Brockencote Hall
Blue Ribbon Winner

★★★★ ☆ ☆ ☆
Chaddesley Corbett, near Kidderminster,
Worcestershire, DY10 4PY
Tel: 01562 777876 Fax: 01562 777872
Email: info@brockencotehall.com
Web: www.brockencotehall.com
17 bedrs
CC: MC Vi Am DC Swi Delt
How to get there: From Exit 4 of M5 or Exit 1 of
M42, go into Bromsgrove and take A448
towards Kidderminster. Hotel is situated five
miles out of Bromsgrove, on left-hand side.

Cheltenham, Gloucestershire

55 Cheltenham Park Hotel

★★★★ ◉
Cirencester Road, Charlton Kings, Cheltenham,
Gloucestershire, GL53 8EA
Tel: 01242 222021 Fax: 01242 226935

56 Heritage Hotels – The Queen's

★★★★
Promenade, Cheltenham, GL50 1NN
Tel: 0870 400 8107 Fax: 01242 224145
Web: www.heritage-hotels.com
79 bedrs SB £125 DB £165
B £11 L £9 D £22
CC: MC Vi Am DC Swi Delt
How to get there: Follow town centre signs from
A40 (Oxford) or A46. Situated behind the town
hall.

57 Hotel Kandinsky

★★★★ Townhouse ◉ ◉
Bayshill Road, Cheltenham,
Gloucestershire, GL50 3AS
Tel: 01242 527788 Fax: 01242 226412
Email: kate@hotelkandinsky.com
Web: www.hotelkandinsky.com
48 bedrs
CC: MC Vi Am DC Swi Delt
How to get there: M5 Junction 11. A40 into
Cheltenham, following signs to centre. At third
roundabout take second exit. Hotel is on corner
of Bayshill and Parabola roads.

58 Carlton Hotel

★★★
Parabola Road, Cheltenham,
Gloucestershire, GL50 3AQ
Tel: 01242 514453 Fax: 01242 226487
Email: enquirie@thecarltonhotel.co.uk
Web: www.thecarltonhotel.co.uk
75 bedrs SB £65 DB £85 HBS £70 HBD £95
B £5.50 D £17.50
CC: MC Vi Am DC Swi Delt
How to get there: Follow signs to Town Hall. At
Town Hall, take middle lane, across traffic lights,
past Ladies' College, left at lights and first right
into Parabola Road.

59 Charlton Kings Hotel

★★★ ◉
London Road, Charlton Kings, Cheltenham,
Gloucestershire, GL52 6UU
Tel: 01242 231061 Fax: 01242 241900
Email: enquiries@charltonkingshotel.co.uk
Web: www.charltonkingshotel.co.uk

Small privately owned hotel set in an acre of
grounds. Most rooms have views of the
Cotswolds. Just a few minutes from Cheltenham
town centre and an ideal touring base.
14 bedrs SB £61 DB £105 HBS £79 HBD £65
B £10 L £8.95 D £15.95
CC: MC Vi Am Swi Delt
How to get there: First property on left as you
enter Cheltenham from Oxford on A40, or M5
junction 11 then A40 to Oxford.

60 George Hotel

★★★
St. Georges Road, Cheltenham,
Gloucestershire, GL50 3DX
Tel: 01242 235751 Fax: 01242 224359
Email: hotel@stayatthegeorge.co.uk
Web: www.stayatthegeorge.co.uk

Town centre, privately-owned Regency-style
hotel. Two-minute walk to fashionable shopping
areas, theatre and antique shops. Perfect for
both business and pleasurable breaks.
38 bedrs SB £70 DB £90 HBS £89.95
HBD £64.95 B £8.50 L £6.95 D £19.95
CC: MC Vi Am DC Swi Delt
How to get there: M5 at Junction 11 follow signs
to Cheltenham. Turn left at TGI Fridays. Turn
right into St. Georges Road. Hotel is on left.

West Midlands

61 Greenway

Blue Ribbon Winner

★★★★ ⓇⓇⓇ

Shurdington, Cheltenham, GL51 4UG
Tel: 01242 862352 Fax: 01242 862780
Email: greenway@btconnect.com
Children minimum age: 7
21 bedrs SB £99 DB £165 HBS £129
HBD £107.50 B £12 L £10 D £38.50
CC: MC Vi Am DC Swi Delt

How to get there: Located on the A46
Cheltenham to Stroud road, approx 1½ miles
from city centre.

62 Hotel on The Park

Gold Ribbon Winner

★★★ ⓇⓇⓇⓇ

Evesham Road, Cheltenham,
Gloucestershire, GL52 2AH
Tel: 01242 518898 Fax: 01242 511526
Email: stay@hotelonthepark.co.uk
Web: www.hotelonthepark.co.uk
Children minimum age: 8
12 bedrs SB £89 DB £129.50
HBS £109.25 HBD £82
CC: MC Vi Am DC Swi Delt

How to get there: Head for town centre, join
one-way system. Follow signs to Evesham. Join
Portland Street, which becomes Evesham Road.
Hotel is on left.

63 Prestbury House Hotel & Restaurant

★★★ Ⓡ

The Burgage, Prestbury, Cheltenham,
Gloucestershire, GL52 3DN
Tel: 01242 529533 Fax: 01242 227076
Email: sandjw@freenetname.co.uk
Web: www.prestburyhouse.co.uk

300-year-old manor house hotel and restaurant
(open to non-residents), set in five acres of

secluded grounds. Cheltenham centre is 1½
miles away. Full conference and wedding
reception facilities.
17 bedrs SB £60 DB £80 HBS £75 HBD £55
B £10 L £14 D £20 CC: MC Vi Am DC Swi

How to get there: Follow any sign for
Cheltenham Racecourse on entering
Cheltenham. Hotel is ½ mile from racecourse
entrance, signposted from Prestbury village.

64 Wyastone Hotel

★★★ Ⓡ

Parabola Road, Montpellier, Cheltenham Spa,
Gloucester, GL50 3BG
Tel: 01242 245549 Fax: 01242 522659
Email: reservations@wyastonehotel.co.uk
13 bedrs SB £55 DB £78 B £7.50 D £19
CC: MC Vi Swi Delt JCB

How to get there: Exit M5 J11; follow A40 to
town centre. Turn right second roundabout at
third exit. Take second exit to Bayshill Road;
Parabola Road bears off left.

65 Travelodge Cheltenham

Travel Accommodation
Golden Valley Roundabout, Hatherley Lane,
Cheltenham,
Tel: 08700 850 950
Web: www.travelodge.co.uk
Opens July 2002
80 bedrs B £4.25
CC: MC Vi Am DC Swi Delt

66 Lypiatt House

♦♦♦♦♦ Ⓡ

Lypiatt Road, Cheltenham,
Gloucestershire, GL50 2QW
Tel: 01242 224994 Fax: 01242 224996

67 Beaumont House Hotel

♦♦♦♦ Ⓡ

56 Shurdington Road, Cheltenham,
Gloucestershire, GL53 0JE
Tel: 01242 245986 Fax: 01242 520044
Email: rocking.horse@virgin.net
Web: www.smoothhound.co.uk/
hotels/beauchel.html
Children minimum age: 10
15 bedrs SB £52 DB £65
CC: MC Vi Am Swi Delt JCB

68 Moorend Park Hotel

◆◆◆◆

Moorend Park Road, Cheltenham,
Gloucestershire, GL53 0LA
Tel: 01242 224441 Fax: 01242 572413
Email: moorendpark@freeuk.com
Web: moorendpark.freeuk.com
Closed Christmas to New Year
9 bedrs SB £48 DB £62
CC: MC Vi Am Swi Delt JCB

How to get there: Located on the A46 off M5
Junction 11A.

69 Broomhill Guest House

◆◆◆

218 London Road, Cheltenham,
Gloucestershire, GL52 6HW
Tel: 01242 513086 Fax: 01242 513086
3 bedrs SB £25 DB £40 B £5
CC: Am DC

How to get there: On A40 (Oxford) and A435
(Cirencester) junction, opposite Holy Apostles
Church, Charlton Kings.

70 Strayleaves

◆◆◆

282 Gloucester Road, Cheltenham,
Gloucestershire, GL51 7AG
Tel: 01242 572303 Fax: 01242 572303
3 bedrs
CC: None accepted
How to get there: Turn left from rear entrance
of Cheltenham railway station. 300 yards,
second house on left. Look for Strayleaves
sign.

Chipping Campden, Gloucestershire

71 Charingworth Manor

Blue Ribbon Winner

★★★ ｒｒ

Chipping Campden, Gloucestershire, GL55 6NS
Tel: 01386 593555 Fax: 01386 593353
Email: charingworthmanor
@englishrosehotels.co.uk
Web: www.englishrosehotels.co.uk

26 bedrs SB £115 DB £180 HBD £84.50
L £37.50 D £37.50
CC: MC Vi Am DC Swi Delt
How to get there: From M40 leave at Junction
15. Take A429 towards Stow, then B4035
toward Chipping Camden. Charingworth Manor
is on the right.
See advert below

72 Cotswold House

Blue Ribbon Winner

★★★ ｒｒｒ

The Square, Chipping Campden,
Gloucestershire, GL55 6AN
Tel: 01386 840330 Fax: 01386 840310
Email: reception@cotswoldhouse.com
Web: www.cotswoldhouse.com
15 bedrs SB £85 DB £185
HBS £120 HBD £230
B £14.50 L £15 D £26.50
CC: MC Vi Am Swi Delt
How to get there: Leave M40 at Junction 15,
taking the A429 south towards Cirencester.
After 16 miles turn right onto B4035, signposted
Campden.

West Midlands

73 Seymour House Hotel

★★★ ®

High Street, Chipping Campden,
Gloucestershire, GL55 6AH
Tel: 01386 840429 Fax: 01386 840369
Email: enquiry@seymourhousehotel.com
Web: www.seymourhousehotel.com
15 bedrs SB £75 DB £110 HBS £95 HBD £75
B £7 L £9.75 D £18
CC: MC Vi Am Swi Delt

How to get there: Hotel to be found in town centre.

74 Three Ways House Hotel

★★★ ® ®

Mickleton, Chipping Campden,
Gloucestershire, GL55 6SB
Tel: 01386 438429 Fax: 01386 438118
Email: threeways@puddingclub.com
Web: www.puddingclub.com

Charming Cotswold village hotel with 41
individually-designed bedrooms, air-
conditioned and stylish restaurant.
Conveniently situated for Hidcote Manor
Garden and Stratford-upon-Avon. Seen on TV
as Home of the Pudding Club.
41 bedrs SB £67 DB £98 HBS £92 HBD £74
B £8 L £15 D £25
CC: MC Vi Am DC Swi Delt

How to get there: Situated on the B4632 in the centre of Mickleton village.

See the road ahead

Just dial 1740* from any mobile
phone to get up-to-the-minute
RAC traffic information on
motorways and major A roads.
Try it now! *Calls to 1740 are charged
at premium rate.

75 Lower Brook House

Little Gem

♦ ♦ ♦ ♦ ♦ ® ® ® ✕ ℰ

Lower Street, Blockley,
Gloucestershire, GL56 9DS
Tel: 01386 700286 Fax: 01386 700286
Email: lowerbrookhouse@cs.com
Web: www.lowerbrookhouse.co.uk
7 bedrs SB £65 DB £96
B £7.50 L £12.50 D £20
CC: MC Vi Swi Delt

How to get there: On the A44 between Moreton-
in-Marsh and Broadway take turning to Blockley.
Go down road and into valley and car park.
See advert on facing page

76 Nineveh Farm

♦ ♦ ♦ ♦ ✕ ℰ

Campden Road, Mickleton,
 Chipping Campden,
Gloucestershire, GL55 6PS
Tel: 01386 438923
Email: stay@ninevehfarm.co.uk
Web: www.ninevehfarm.co.uk
Children minimum age: 5
5 bedrs SB £40 DB £50
CC: MC Vi Swi Delt

How to get there: Close to Mickleton village,
three miles from Chipping Campden (B4081)
and eight miles from Stratford-upon-Avon
(B4632).

Chipping Sodbury, Gloucestershire

77 Sodbury House Hotel

♦ ♦ ♦ ♦ ✕

Badminton Road, Old Sodbury,
Gloucestershire, BS37 6LU
Tel: 01454 312847
Email: sodhousehotel@tesco.net
Web: www.visitus.co.uk
17 bedrs SB £50 DB £78
CC: MC Vi Am DC

How to get there: Located three miles from
junction 18 of M4, via A46, signposted Stroud.
At traffic lights, turn left (A432), signposted
Yate/Bristol.

Church Stretton, Shropshire

78 Travellers Rest Inn

◆ ◆ ◆

Upper Affcot, Church Stretton,
Shropshire, SY6 6RL
Tel: 01694 781275 Fax: 01694 781555
Email: reception@travellersrestinn.co.uk
Web: www.travellersrestinn.co.uk
12 bedrs SB £30 DB £55 L £5 D £7
CC: MC Vi Am DC Swi Delt

How to get there: Situated on west side of A49, five miles south of Church Stretton, near the villages of Bushmore and Wistanstow.

Cirencester, Gloucestershire

79 Corinium Hotel

★ ★ ®

12 Gloucester Street, Cirencester,
Gloucestershire, GL7 2DG
Tel: 01285 659711 Fax: 01285 885807
Email: info@coriniumhotel.co.uk
Web: coriniumhotel.co.uk
15 bedrs SB £65 DB £130 B £6.75
L £3.25 D £7.50 CC: MC Vi Am Swi Delt

How to get there: Quarter mile north of church in town centre car park off Spitalgate Lane turn towards town from traffic lights on A419

80 Fleece Hotel

★ ★

Market Place, Cirencester,
Gloucestershire, GL7 2NZ
Tel: 01285 658507 Fax: 01285 651017
Email: relax@fleecehotel.co.uk
28 bedrs SB £90.95 DB £114.90 HBS £49.50
HBD £49.50 B £6.95 L £11.95 D £13.95
CC: MC Vi Am Swi Delt JCB

How to get there: Follow signs for the town centre. The Fleece has a black-and-white Tudor front.

Ask the experts

To book a Hotel or Guest Accommodation, or for help and advice, call RAC Hotel Reservations on 0870 603 9109 and quote 'Guide 2002'

Lower Brook House

A 17th-century Country House by a babbling brook, set in an idyllic village. Little Gem Winner 2000 together with Warm Welcome, Sparkling Diamond and three Dining Awards. Seven tastefully appointed ensuite rooms filled with little luxuries to ensure a memorable visit. Good Food, Fine wines and Unique Hospitality.

Lower Street, Blockley,
Gloucestershire GL56 9DS
Tel: 01386 700286   Fax: 01386 700286
Email: lowerbrookhouse@cs.com
Website: www.lowerbrookhouse.co.uk

 Little Gem
◆◆◆◆◆

81 Wild Duck Inn

★ ★

Drakes Island, Ewen, Gloucestershire, GL7 6BY
Tel: 01285 770310 Fax: 01285 770924
Email: wduckinn@aol.com
11 bedrs SB £60 DB £80
B £6.50 L £5 D £6.95
CC: MC Vi Am Swi Delt

How to get there: From Cirencester take A429 towards Malmesbury and M4. At Kemble turn left to Ewen. The Wild Duck is in the centre of the village.

See advert on following page

82 Travelodge Cirencester

Travel Accommodation
Burford Road, Cirencester,
Tel: 08700 850 950
Web: www.travelodge.co.uk
43 bedrs B £4.25
CC: MC Vi Am DC Swi Delt

West Midlands

83 Jolifleur

London Road, Poulton, Cirencester,
Gloucestershire, GL7 5JG
Tel: 01285 850118 Fax: 01285 850118

84 The Bungalow

93 Victoria Road, Cirencester,
Gloucestershire, GL7 1ES
Tel: 01285 654179 Fax: 01286 656159
Email: cbeard7@compuserve.com
6 bedrs SB £35 DB £45 CC: None accepted
How to get there: From town centre, church is
on left, proceed to traffic lights. Turn right into
Victoria Road. The Bungalow is two-thirds down
road on left.

Codsall, Staffordshire

85 Moors Farm & Country Restaurant

Chillington Lane, Codsall, Staffordshire, WV8 1QF
Tel: 01902 842330 Fax: 01902 847878
Email: enquiries@moorsfarmhotel.co.uk

Web: www.moorsfarm-hotel.co.uk
Children minimum age: 4
6 bedrs CC: MC Vi Swi Delt

How to get there: Take the road from Codsall to
Codsall Wood. Turn right into Chillington Lane.
Right at T-junction. Entrance 200m on right.

Coleshill, Warwickshire

86 Old Barn Guest House

Birmingham Road, Coleshill,
Warwickshire, B46 1DP
Tel: 01675 463692 Fax: 01675 466275
9 bedrs SB £40 DB £68.50
CC: MC Vi Am DC Swi Delt JCB

How to get there: From M6 Junction 4, turn
onto A446 towards Coleshill. Turn left at island
onto B4114. Old Barn ¼ mile on the left.

It's easier online

For all your motoring and travel
needs, www.rac.co.uk

The Wild Duck Inn
An attractive 15th-century inn of great character

The Wild Duck is a mellow Cotswold stone Elizabethan Inn. A typical local English inn with a warm and welcoming ambience, rich in colours and hung with old oil portraits of English ancestors. Large open log fires burn in the bar and the oak-panelled residents' lounge in winter time.

The garden is secluded, delightful and perfect for 'alfresco' dining in the summer. The bar offers six real ales and the wine list is extensive and innovative.

The country-style dining room offers fresh seasonal food; game in winter and fresh fish delivered overnight from Brixham in Devon, which can include such exotic fare as parrot fish and tilapia.

There are nine bedrooms, two of which have four-poster beds and overlook the garden. All rooms have direct dial telephone, colour TV and tea/coffee-making facilities.

Within one mile, The Wild Duck is surrounded by the Cotswold Water Park, with over 80 lakes providing fishing, swimming, sailing, water and jet skiing. Polo at Cirencester Park is a regular event and every March Cheltenham holds the Gold Cup Race Meeting. Horse trials at Gatcombe Park and Badminton are also held annually.

Location: From M4 take Junction 17 and follow Cirencester, turn right at Kemble and follow signs to Ewen

Drakes Island, Ewen, Near Cirencester GL7 6BY
Tel: 01285 770310 / 770364   Fax: 01285 770924   Email: wduckinn@aol.com

Coln St. Aldwyns, Gloucestershire

87 New Inn At Coln
Blue Ribbon Winner

★★ Ⓡ Ⓡ Ⓡ
Coln St-Aldwyns, near Cirencester,
Gloucestershire, GL7 5AN
Tel: 01285 750651 Fax: 01285 750657
Email: stay@new-inn.co.uk
Web: www.new-inn.co.uk
Children minimum age: 10

An exceptional 16th-century coaching inn set in an idyllic Cotswold village. Wonderful food in bar and restaurant. Quality bedrooms and attentive, courteous staff. Great walking countryside.
14 bedrs SB £72 DB £99 HBS £95 HBD £71.50
B £8.50 L £18.50 D £23.50
CC: MC Vi Am Swi Delt

How to get there: From Burford (A40), take B4425 towards Bibury; turn left after Aldsworth.

Coventry, West Midlands

88 Marriott Forest of Arden Hotel and Country Club

★★★★ Ⓡ
Maxstoke Lane, Meriden,
West Midlands, CV7 &HR
Tel: 01676 522335 Fax: 01676 521176
Web: www.marriotthotels.com/cvtgs
214 bedrs SB £94 DB £118
HBS £114 HBD £79
B £12.50 L £16.50 D £26.50
CC: Vi Am DC Swi Delt JCB

How to get there: M42 J6, A45 towards Coventry. After one mile, left into Shepherds Lane. Hotel 1½ miles on the left.

89 Brooklands Grange Hotel and Restaurant

★★★★ Ⓡ Ⓡ
Holyhead Road, Coventry,
West Midlands, CV5 8HX
Tel: 02476 601601 Fax: 02476 601277
Email: lesley.jackson@virgin.net
Web: www.brooklands-grange.co.uk
31 bedrs SB £90 DB £105 B £12
CC: MC Vi Am DC Swi Delt

How to get there: On the A4114 near Allesley village roundabout, 1½ miles from city centre.

90 Courtyard by Marriott Coventry

★★★
A45 London Road, Ryton on Dunsmore,
Coventry, West Midlands, CV8 3DY
Tel: 02476 301585 Fax: 02486 301610
Web: www.courtytd.com/cvtcy
49 bedrs SB £89 DB £95 HBS £106
HBD £61.50 B £10.50 L £12.50 D £17
CC: MC Vi Am DC Swi Delt

How to get there: M6 J2 A46 towards Coventry airport. Hotel is on A45 on the south side of Coventry.

91 Heritage Hotels – The Brandon Hall

★★★
Brandon, Coventry, West Midlands, CV8 3FW
Tel: 0870 4008105 Fax: 0247 6544909
Email: heritagehotels_coventry.Brandon-Hall@forte-hotels.com
Web: www.heritage-hotls,com
60 bedrs SB £133 DB £146
B £12.95 L £14.95 D £25
CC: MC Vi Am DC Swi Delt

92 Novotel Coventry

★★★
Wilsons Lane, Lonford, Coventry,
West Midlands, CV6 6HL
Tel: 02476 365000 Fax: 02476 362422
Email: h0506@accor-hotels.com
Web: www.accorhotel.com
98 bedrs
CC: MC Vi Am DC Swi Delt

How to get there: Junction 3 M6, take B4113 towards Bedworth. At large roundabout take third exit; hotel is 20 yards on left.

West Midlands

93 Quality Hotel Stonebridge Manor

★★★

Birmingham Road, Allesley Village, Coventry,
West Midlands, CV5 9BA
Tel: 024 76403835 Fax: 024 76403081
78 bedrs SB £95 DB £105 HBS £110 HBD £60
B £9.75 L £12 D £15
CC: MC Vi Am DC Swi Delt JCB

94 Campanile

Travel Accommodation
4 Wigston Road, Walsgrave,
West Midlands, CV2 2SD
Tel: 02476 622311 Fax: 02476 602362

Typical Campanile bedroom

Campanile hotels offer comfortable and
convenient budget accommodation and a
traditional French-style Bistro providing freshly-
cooked food for breakfast, lunch and dinner. All
rooms en-suite with tea/coffee-making facilities,
DDT and TV with Sky channels.
47 bedrs SB £46.90 DB £52.95 HBS £53
HBD £32 B £5.95 L £4.95 D £6.50
CC: MC Vi Am DC Swi Delt

How to get there: The hotel is off M6 Junction
2. Take the A4600 for ³/₄ mile and turn right on
second roundabout.

Droitwich, Worcestershire

95 Travelodge Droitwich

Travel Accommodation
A38 Northbound, Rashwood, Dodderhill,
Droitwich, Worcestershire, WR9 8DA
Tel: 08700 850 950
Web: www.travelodge.co.uk
32 bedrs B £4.25
CC: MC Vi Am DC Swi Delt

96 The Old Farmhouse

◆◆◆◆◆

Hadley Heath, Ombersley, near Droitwich,
Worcestershire, WR9 0AR
Tel: 01905 620837 Fax: 01905621722
Email: judylambe@ombersley.demon.co.uk
Web: www.theoldfarmhouse.com
5 bedrs SB £30 DB £50
CC: None accepted

How to get there: Exit J6 M5 A449 towards
Kidderminster; turn right to Hadley; third house
one mile on right. From J5, take A38, A4133 for
one mile, then left to end of lane.

Dudley, West Midlands

97 Copthorne Hotel Merry Hill Dudley

★★★★

Level Street, Brierley Hill, Dudley,
West Midlands, DY5 1UR
Tel: 01384 482882 Fax: 01384 482773
Email: gill.talbot@mill-cop.com
Web: www.book.with-us.com

Modern 138-bedroom hotel in an attractive
waterfront setting in the heart of the Midlands.
Faradays bar & restaurant offers a wide range of
Mediterranean dishes.
138 bedrs SB £148.25 DB £171.50
HBS £163.25 HBD £201.50 B £13.25 L £7 D £14
CC: MC Vi Am DC Swi Delt

How to get there: Leave M5 at Junction 2.
Follow A4123 for Dudley. After 2¹/₂ miles follow
signs for A461 to Stourbridge/Merry Hill Centre.

Plan your route

Visit www.rac.co.uk for RAC's
interactive route planner, including
up to the minute traffic reports.

Eccleshall, Staffordshire

98 Glenwood

◆ ◆ ◆

Croxton, Stafford, Staffordshire, ST21 6PF
Tel: 01630 620238
3 bedrs SB £22 DB £40 CC: None accepted

How to get there: Leave M6 at Junction 14. Travel to Eccleshall. Take B5026 to Loggerheads. After three miles, enter the village of Croxton. The Cottage is on right.

Evesham, Worcestershire

99 Evesham Hotel

★ ★ ★ ★

Cooper's Lane, off Waterside, Evesham, Worcestershire, WR11 1DA
Tel: 01386 765566 Fax: 01386 765443
Email: reception@eveshamhotel.com
Web: www.eveshamhotel.com
40 bedrs SB £79 DB £108 B £7 L £10 D £21
CC: MC Vi Am DC Swi Delt

How to get there: Cooper's Lane runs off Waterside, the road that runs along the River Avon.

100 Northwick Hotel

★ ★ ★

Waterside, Evesham, Worcestershire, WR11 1BT
Tel: 01386 40322 Fax: 01386 41070
Email: enquiries@northwickhotel.co.uk
Web: www.northwickhotel.co.uk
31 bedrs SB £66 DB £90 HBS £70 HBD £55
B £7.50 L £14.50 D £22.50
CC: MC Vi Am DC Swi Delt

How to get there: M5 J9, follow signposts to Evesham for 11 miles, then follow road signposted to town centre. Turn right at bridge and follow signs for Northwick Hotel. Hotel is ½ a mile on right.

101 Mill at Harvington

Blue Ribbon Winner

★ ★ ★ ★

Anchor Lane, Harvington, Evesham, Worcestershire, WR11 8PA
Tel: 01386 870688 Fax: 01386 870688
Email: millatharvington@aol.com
Children minimum age: 10

Tastefully converted beautiful Georgian house and former baking mill, set in acres of parkland on the banks of the River Avon, ½ mile from the main road.
21 bedrs SB £65 DB £108 HBS £86 HBD £131
B £6.50 L £7.95 D £12
CC: MC Vi Am DC Swi Delt

How to get there: Turn south off the Norton/Bidford road opposite Harvington village, four miles northeast of Evesham. Hotel 600 yards on left.

102 Park View Hotel

◆ ◆ ◆

Waterside, Evesham, Worcestershire, WR11 6BS
Tel: 01386 442639
Email: mike.spires@btinternet.com
Web: www.superstay.co.uk
Closed Christmas and New Year
26 bedrs SB £25 DB £44 CC: MC Vi Am Swi Delt

How to get there: Hotel is ¼ of a mile southeast of the town centre on Waterside (B4035), which runs alongside the river.

Fownhope, Herefordshire

103 Green Man Inn

★ ★

Fownhope, Herefordshire, HR1 4PE
Tel: 01432 860243 Fax: 01432 860207
Web: www.smoothhound.co.uk/
hotels/greenman.html
20 bedrs SB £39.50 DB £67 HBS £47.50
HBD £95 B £6.25 L £7.50 D £10.95
CC: MC Vi Swi Delt

How to get there: From M50 take Ledbury road (A449). After 2 miles, left onto B4224 Fownhope for 5 miles. Green Man is in centre of village on left.

West Midlands

Gloucester, Gloucestershire

104 Kings Head Inn

 ◆ ◆ ◆

Birdwood, Huntley, Gloucestershire, GL19 3EF
Tel: 01452 750348 Fax: 01452 750348
6 bedrs SB £25 DB £40 B £4 L £4 D £4.50
CC: MC Vi Swi Delt

How to get there: Take A40 from Gloucester to
Ross-on-Wye. We are about six miles from
Gloucester on lefthandside with row of flag
poles on front of large car park.

105 The Little Thatch

 ◆ ◆ ◆

141 Bristol Road, Quedgeley, Gloucester,
Gloucestershire, GL2 4PQ
Tel: 01452 720687 Fax: 01452 724141
Email: info@thelittlethatch.co.uk
Web: www.yell.com
22 bedrs SB £44 DB £53 HBS £56 HBD £38.50
B £4.50 L £5 D £5
CC: MC Vi Am Swi Delt

How to get there: Exit J12 M5 and follow
directions to Severn Vale shopping centre
B4008 to Quedgeley. Just past Tesco
roundabout on the right.

Great Malvern, Worcestershire

106 Thornbury House Hotel

 ★ ★

16 Avenue Road, Great Malvern,
Worcestershire, WR14 3AR
Tel: 01684 572273 Fax: 01684 577042
Email: thornburyhousehotel@compuserve.com
17 bedrs SB £48 DB £72 HBS £58 HBD £50
B £8 D £5 CC: MC Vi Am DC Swi Delt JCB

How to get there: Follow signs for Great
Malvern Railway Station. Hotel is situated just
above the station.

Hampton in Arden, West Midlands

107 Cottage Guest House

 ◆ ◆ ◆

Kenilworth Road, Balsall Common,
Hampton in Arden, West Midlands, B92 0LW
Tel: 01675 442323 Fax: 01675 443323

Web: www.smoothhound.co.uk/cottage.html
9 bedrs SB £28 DB £44 B £10
CC: None accepted

How to get there: 3 miles from J6 M42; 3¹⁄₂ J4
M6; NEC three miles, Birmingham airport 3¹⁄₂
miles, National Motorcycle Museum three miles.

Hartlebury, Worcestershire

108 Yew Tree House

 ◆ ◆ ◆ ◆

Norchard, Crossway Green, Hartlebury,
Worcestershire, DY13 9SN
Tel: 01299 250921 Fax: 01299 250921
Email: paul@knightp.swinternet.co.uk
Web: www.yewtreeworcester.co.uk
4 bedrs SB £30 DB £50 CC: None accepted

How to get there: Take Norchard sign at
Crossway Green roundabout on A449, down
lane, round sharp left bend; Yew Tree House is
150 yards on the left.

Hay-on-Wye, Herefordshire

109 Old Black Lion

★ ★ ⌂ ⌂

26 Lion Street, Hay-on-Wye,
Herefordshire, HR3 5AD
Tel: 01497 820841
Web: www.oldblacklion.co.uk
Children minimum age: 5
10 bedrs SB £40 DB £75
B £7 L £5.95 D £8.95
CC: MC Vi Swi Delt

Henley-in-Arden, Warwickshire

110 Lapworth Lodge

 ◆ ◆ ◆

Bushwood Lane, Lapworth, Henley-in-Arden,
Warwickshire, B94 5PJ
Tel: 01564 783038 Fax: 01564 783635

Hereford, Herefordshire

111 Belmont Lodge & Golf Course

★★★
Belmont, Hereford, HR2 9SA
Tel: 01432 352666 Fax: 01432 358090
Email: info@belmontlodge.co.uk
Web: www.belmontlodge.co.uk
30 bedrs SB £52 DB £72
HBS £67 HBD £51
B £7.45 L £4.50 D £15
CC: MC Vi Am DC Swi Delt

How to get there: Situated southwest of Hereford on the A456 Hereford to Abergavenny road, 1½ miles from Hereford city centre.

112 Castle House
Gold Ribbon Winner

★★★★ ℞ ℞ ℞ ℞
Castle Street, Hereford,
Herefordshire, HR1 2NW
Tel: 01432 356321 Fax: 01432 365909
Email: info@castlehse.co.uk
Web: www.castlehse.co.uk
15 bedrs SB £90 DB £155
B £10.50 L £18.95 D £29.95
CC: MC Vi Am Swi Delt

How to get there: Follow signs for city centre, then city centre east. At the end of St. Owen Street, right into Ethelbert Street, then right into Castle Street.
See advert on this page

113 The Green Dragon

★★★
Forte Heritage, Broad Street, Hereford,
Herefordshire, HR4 9BG
Tel: 01432 272506 Fax: 01432 352139
83 bedrs
CC: MC Vi Am DC Swi Delt

114 Three Counties Hotel

★★★
Belmont Road, Hereford,
Herefordshire, HR2 7BP
Tel: 01432 299955 Fax: 01432 275114
Email: enquiries@threecountieshotel.co.uk
Web: www.threecountieshotel.co.uk

RAC ★★★

Castle HOUSE

RAC Dining Award ℞℞℞℞℞

Centrally located in the heart of rural Herefordshire, Castle House is a gracious and hospitable town house with just 15 rooms where guests can enjoy unashamed luxury and unrivalled attention. The award-winning restaurant promises to be an exquisite experience with impeccable service and outstanding cuisine.

Castle Street, Hereford HR21 2NW
Tel: 01432 356321   Fax: 01432 365909
info@castlehse.co.uk   www.castlehse.co.uk

Modern hotel with a relaxing atmosphere and beautiful scenery on the outskirts of the city. Bedrooms set by a quiet garden.
60 bedrs SB £63 DB £82.50
B £4.50 D £17.50
CC: MC Vi Am DC Swi Delt

How to get there: 1½ miles outside Hereford city on A465 — the main road to Abergavenny.

West Midlands

115 Aylestone Court Hotel

♦ ♦ ♦ ♦

Aylestone Hill, Hereford, Herefordshire, HR1 1HS
Tel: 01432 341891 Fax: 01432 267691
Email: ayleshotel@aol.com
Web: aylestonecourthotel.homestead.com
9 bedrs SB £65 DB £95
B £7.50 L £12.50 D £19.50
CC: MC Vi Am DC Swi Delt JCB

How to get there: Aylestone Court Hotel stands at the bottom of Aylestone Hill (A456), marked Hereford City Centre (opposite train station).

Kenilworth, Warwickshire

116 Peacock Hotel

★ ★ ★ ★ ℞ ℞

149 Warwick Road, Kenilworth,
Warwickshire, CV8 1HY
Tel: 01926 851156 Fax: 01926 864644
Email: peacockhotel@rafflesmalaysian.com
Web: www.peacockhotel.com

Small and luxurious hotel committed to providing outstanding quality and first class service at reasonable prices. Ideally located for weddings and functions with choice of three elegant restaurants, contemporary bar, gardens and ample parking. Weekend leisure breaks, optional tours and "in-house" coach service available.
15 bedrs SB £80 DB £100 HBS £89 HBD £59
B £3.95 L £3.95 D £9.75
CC: MC Vi Am DC Swi Delt

Making a booking?

Don't forget to mention RAC Hotels and Bed & Breakfast 2002.

Kidderminster, Worcestershire

117 Stone Manor

★ ★ ★ ★ ℞

Near Kidderminster, Stone,
Worcestershire, DY10 4PJ
Tel: 01562 777555 Fax: 01562 777834
Email: enquiries@stonemanorhotel.co.uk
Web: www.stonemanorhotel.co.uk
57 bedrs SB £96.25 DB £102.50 HBS £115.25
HBD £70.25 B £6.25 L £13.50 D £19
CC: MC Vi Am DC Swi Delt

How to get there: From south M40/M42 J1 to A38 and A448 to Kidderminster. From south M5 J6 onto A449, A450 and A448. From north M5 J3, A456 to A450 and A448.

118 Redfern Hotel

★ ★ ℞

Lower Street, Cleobury Mortimer,
Shropshire, DY14 8AA
Tel: 01299 270395 Fax: 01299 271011
Email: redfernhotel@btconnect.com
Web: www.redfern-hotel.co.uk
11 bedrs SB £55 DB £90 HBS £65 HBD £55
B £11 L £4.99 D £19.95 CC: MC Vi Swi Delt

How to get there: Midway between Ludlow and Kidderminster (11 miles) on A4117.

119 Travelodge Hartlebury

Travel Accommodation
A449 Southbound, Hartlebury, Near
Kidderminster, Hereford & Worcester, DY13 9SH
Tel: 08700 850 950
Web: www.travelodge.co.uk
32 bedrs B £4.25 CC: MC Vi Am DC Swi Delt

Kington, Herefordshire

120 Burton Hotel

★ ★

Mill Street, Kington, Herefordshire, HR5 3BQ
Tel: 01544 230323 Fax: 01544 230323
Email: burton@hotelherefordshire.co.uk
Web: www.hotelherefordshire.co.uk
15 bedrs SB £40 DB £60 HBS £47 HBD £41
B £5.50 L £6.50 D £16 CC: MC Vi Am

How to get there: 14 miles from Leominster on A44, driving due west. 3 miles from Welsh border.

Leamington Spa, Warwickshire

121 Angel Hotel

★★★
Regent Street, Leamington Spa,
Warwickshire, CV32 4NZ
Tel: 01926 881296 Fax: 01926 881296
Email: angelhotel143@hotmail.com
Web: www.the-angel-hotel.co.uk
50 bedrs SB £45 DB £60
B £6.50 L £12.50 D £16.50
CC: MC Vi Am DC Swi Delt

How to get there: Leamington Spa junction from M40, head for town centre. Turn off main parade opposite Barclay's Bank, up Holly Walk to Archway car park.

122 Courtyard by Marriott Leamington Spa

★★★
Olympus Avenue, Tachbrook Park, Leamington Spa, Warwickshire, CV34 6RJ
Tel: 01926 425522 Fax: 01926 881322
Web: www.courtyard.com/lspwa
91 bedrs B £10 L £12 D £14
CC: MC Vi Am DC Swi Delt JCB

123 Abbacourt

★★ 🍴🍴
40 Kenilworth Road, Leamington Spa,
Warwickshire, CV32 6JF
Tel: 01926 451755 Fax: 01926 886339
Email: abbacourt@maganto.freeserve.co.uk
23 bedrs
CC: MC Vi Am Swi

How to get there: The Abbacourt Hotel is located on the A452 Kenilworth road, five minutes walk from Leamington town centre.

124 Adams Hotel

★★
22 Avenue Road, Leamington Spa,
Warwickshire, CV31 3PQ
Tel: 01926 450742 Fax: 01926 313110
Email: adams22@tinyworld.co.uk
12 bedrs SB £58 DB £72 B £6.50 L £18 D £22
CC: MC Vi Am DC Swi Delt

How to get there: Situated on A452/A425 near Victoria Park.

Leominster, Herefordshire

125 Talbot Hotel

★★★
West Street, Leominster, Herefordshire, HR6 8EP
Tel: 01568 616347 Fax: 01568 614880
Email: talbot@bestwestern.co.uk

Original town centre 15th-century coaching house with beams and open fire. Set in the historic English/Welsh border town dating from the 7th-century. Ideal touring location, mid-Wales, Shrophire and Herefordshire.
20 bedrs SB £47 DB £68 HBS £64 HBD £48.50
B £3.50 L £11.50 D £13
CC: MC Vi Am DC Swi Delt JCB

How to get there: The Talbot Hotel is in the centre of Leominster, found when following the one-way traffic system.

Lichfield, Staffordshire

126 Angel Croft Hotel

★★
Beacon Street, Lichfield,
Staffordshire, WS13 1AA
Tel: 01543 258737 Fax: 01543 415605

127 Coppers End Guest House

◆◆◆
Walsall Road, Muckley Corner, Lichfield,
Staffordshire, WS14 0BG
Tel: 01543 372910 Fax: 01543 360423
6 bedrs SB £26 DB £40
HBS £31 HBD £46 B £4
CC: MC Vi Am DC Delt

West Midlands

Long Compton, Warwickshire

128 Ascott House Farm

♦♦♦♦ ※

Whichford, Shipston-on-Stour,
Warwickshire, CV36 5PP
Tel: 01608 684 655 Fax: 01608 684 539
Email: dp.haines.farms@farmline.com
Web: touristnetuk.com/wm/ascotthouse
Closed Christmas and New Year
3 bedrs SB £27 DB £44
CC: None accepted
🏠🕭🖵🅿🛎
How to get there: A3400 from Chipping Norton
to Long Compton. Turn right at end of village to
Whichford and Ascott. In Whichford ½ mile to
Ascott. In Ascott first right and first drive on
right.

Lower Slaughter, Gloucestershire

129 Lower Slaughter Manor
Gold Ribbon Winner

★★★ ®®®®

Lower Slaughter, Gloucestershire, GL54 2HP
Tel: 01451 820456 Fax: 01451 822150
Email: lowsmanor@aol.com
Web: www.lowerslaughter.co.uk
Children minimum age: 12
16 bedrs
CC: MC Vi Am DC Swi Delt
🖥🖵☎🅿🛎 ♨ ▦ ♣🔍⛳
How to get there: From A429 Cirencester to
Stow-on-the-Wold road, just two miles from
Stow, follow signs to The Slaughters just past
an Esso garage. Entering the village, the Manor
is on the right.

Ludlow, Shropshire

130 Dinham Hall

★★★ ®®

Dinham, Ludlow, Shropshire, SY8 1EJ
Tel: 01584 876464 Fax: 01584 876019
Email: info@dinhamhall.co.uk
Web: www.dinhamhall.co.uk
14 bedrs SB £70 DB £120 B £7.50 L £26 D £26
CC: MC Vi Am DC Swi Delt
⛲🖥🏠🕭🖵☎🅿🛎▦▥
How to get there: Turn left at Ludlow Castle:
Dinham Hall is 50m on left.

131 Travelodge Ludlow

Travel Accommodation
A49, Wooferton, Ludlow, Shropshire, SY8 4AL
Tel: 08700 850 950
Web: www.travelodge.co.uk
32 bedrs B £4.25
CC: MC Vi Am DC Swi Delt
🏠🕭🖵🛎

132 Number Twenty Eight
Little Gem

♦♦♦♦♦ ※℉

28 Lower Broad Street, Ludlow,
Shropshire, SY8 1PQ
Tel: 01584 876996 Fax: 01584 876860
Email: ross@no28.co.uk
Web: www.no28.co.uk
9 bedrs DB £75
CC: MC Vi Swi Delt
🏠🛇🕭🖵☎🛎▦

133 Chadstone Guest House

♦♦♦♦ ® ※℉

Aston Munslow, Craven Arms,
Shropshire, SY7 9ER
Tel: 01584 841675 Fax: 01584 841620
Email: chadstone.lee@btinternet.com
Web: www.chadstonebandb.co.uk
Children minimum age: 12

Friendly personal service, luxurious
accommodation, tastefully furnished with well-
equipped bedrooms. Spacious lounge and
attractive dining room with panoramic views of
the Shropshire countryside.
3 bedrs SB £26 DB £52
HBS £41 HBD £41 D £15
CC: None accepted
🛇🕭🖵🅿🛎▦
How to get there: Turn east off A49 onto B4368
in Craven Arms. In Aston Munslow, pass the
Swan Inn; Chadstone is 100m on right

134 The Church Inn

◆◆◆

Buttercross, Ludlow, Shropshire, SY8 1AW
Tel: 01584 872174 Fax: 01584 877146
Email: reception@thechurchinn.com
Web: www.thechurchinn.com
9 bedrs SB £30.50 DB £50 L £4 D £4
CC: MC Vi Am Swi Delt JCB
🐾🖰🖵☎📞🔌🛏😊🍴👬

135 The Hoopits

◆◆◆ ✗

Greete, Ludlow, Shropshire, SY8 3BS
Tel: 01584 879187
Email: thehoopits@talk21.com
Closed 14 December to 14 January
3 bedrs SB £22.50 DB £45 HBS £34.50
HBD £34.50 D £12 CC: None accepted
😊🍃📭
How to get there: A49 turn at sign for Clee Hill
and Caynham. Take turn signposted Tenbury
and Greete. Property is one mile, on left.

Lydney, Gloucestershire

136 George Inn

◆◆◆

High Street, St. Briavels, Lydney,
Gloucestershire, GL15 6TA
Tel: 01594 530228 Fax: 01594 530260
4 bedrs SB £35 DB £45 CC: MC Vi DC Swi Delt
🐾🖰🖵📭🍴👬
How to get there: Six miles from Chepstow on
the Lydney Road.

Malvern, Worcestershire

137 Malvern Hills Hotel

★★

Wynds Point, Malvern,
Worcestershire, WR13 6DW
Tel: 01684 540690 Fax: 01684 540327
Email: malhilhotl@aol.com
Web: www.malvernhillshotel.co.uk

A character bedroomed country house hotel set
amidst the tranquillity of the Malvern Hills, with
direct access for walking. Excellent cuisine and
real ales. Pets welcome.
14 bedrs SB £45 DB £75 HBS £64.50
HBD £114 B £6.50 L £13 D £19.50
CC: MC Vi Am DC Swi Delt JCB
♿🖰🐾😊🖵🖵☎📭🔌🛏😊🍴👬👪🖰
How to get there: On A449 Malvern to Ledbury
road at junction with B4232 (opposite car park
for British Camp Iron Age hill fort).

138 Mount Pleasant Hotel

★★

Belle Vue Terrace, Malvern,
Worcestershire, WR14 4PZ
Tel: 01684 561837 Fax: 01684 569968
14 bedrs
CC: MC Vi Am DC Swi Delt
🖰🖵☎📭🔌🍴👪👬

Moreton-in-Marsh, Gloucestershire

West Midlands

139 Crown Inn & Hotel

★★★

High Street, Blockley, Gloucestershire, GL56 9EX
Tel: 01386 700245 Fax: 01386 700247
Email: info@crown-inn-blockley.co.uk
Web: www.crown-inn-blockley.co.uk
24 bedrs SB £70 DB £99 B £9.95 L £10 D £20
CC: MC Vi Am DC Swi Delt
🖰🐾🖰🖵☎📭🔌🍴🛏👪👬
How to get there: Located off the A44
Oxford/Evesham road between Moreton-in-
Marsh and Broadway. Situated two miles from
Chipping Campden, two miles from Moreton.

140 Aston House

◆◆◆◆ ✗ 🐾

Broadwell, Moreton-in-Marsh,
Gloucestershire, GL56 0TJ
Tel: 01451 830475
Email: fja@netcomuk.co.uk
Web: www.netcomuk.co.uk/~nmfa/
     aston_house.html
Children minimum age: 10
Closed December and January
3 bedrs DB £46
CC: None accepted
🖰🖵☎📭🔌
How to get there: A429 from Stow-on-the-Wold
towards Moreton. After one mile turn right at
Broadnell/Donnington crossroads. First house
on left after 1/2 mile.

141 Farriers Cottage

44 Todenham, Moreton-in-Marsh,
Gloucestershire, GL56 9PF
Tel: 01608 652664 Fax: 01608 652668
Email: susanannwoolston@aol.com
Web: www.thefarrierscottage.co.uk
1 bedrs DB £45 CC: None accepted

How to get there: Leave Moreton northbound on
A429. Take first right after railway bridge to
Todenham. Cottage opposite church and pub,
after three miles.

Newcastle-under-Lyme, Staffordshire

142 Borough Arms Hotel

★★

King Street, Newcastle-under-Lyme,
Staffordshire, ST5 1HX
Tel: 01782 629421 Fax: 01782 712388

143 Comfort Inn Newcastle-under-Lyme

★★

Liverpool Road, Cross Heath,
Newcastle-under-Lyme,
Staffordshire, ST5 9DX
Tel: 01782 717000 Fax: 01782 713669
Email: admin@gb617.u-net.com
Web: www.choicehotels.com
68 bedrs SB £68.25 DB £68.25
HBS £80 HBD £40
B £8.75 D £11.75
CC: MC Vi Am DC Swi Delt

How to get there: From the M6, take Junction
16 and pick up A500 for Newcastle-under-
Lyme, then the A34.

Plan your route

Visit www.rac.co.uk for RAC's
interactive route planner, including
up to the minute traffic reports.

See the road ahead

Just dial 1740* from any mobile
phone to get up-to-the-minute
RAC traffic information on
motorways and major A roads.
Try it now! *Calls to 1740 are charged
at premium rate.

Newent, Gloucestershire

144 Three Choirs Vineyards
Little Gem

Newent, Gloucestershire, GL18 1LS
Tel: 01531 890223 Fax: 01531 890877
Email: info@threechoirs.com
Web: www.threechoirs.com

Set in 100 acres of rolling Gloucestershire
countryside, we offer peace and tranquillity in
which to enjoy our fine wines and excellent
food. All rooms have lovely views over the
vineyards.
8 bedrs SB £65 DB £85 HBS £90 HBD £62.50
L £12.50 D £20
CC: MC Vi Swi Delt JCB
How to get there: Follow brown tourist signs
from Newent or Dymock. On B4215, two miles
north of Newent

Nuneaton, Warwickshire

145 Travelodge Bedworth

Travel Accommodation
A444 North, Bedworth Bypass, Nuneaton,
Warwickshire, CV10 7TF
Tel: 08700 850 950
Web: www.travelodge.co.uk
40 bedrs B £4.25
CC: MC Vi Am DC Swi Delt

146 Travelodge Nuneaton

Travel Accommodation
A47, Yeoman Harvester, St. Nicholas Park Drive,
Nuneaton, Warwickshire, CV11 6EN
Tel: 08700 850 950
Web: www.travelodge.co.uk
28 bedrs B £4.25
CC: MC Vi Am DC Swi Delt

Oakamoor, Staffordshire

147 Ribden Farm

◆◆◆◆ ❋
Oakamoor, Stoke-on-Trent,
Staffordshire, ST10 3BW
Tel: 01538 702830 Fax: 01538 702830
Email: ribdenfarm@aol.com
Web: www.ribden.fsnet.co.uk
5 bedrs SB £36 DB £44
CC: MC Vi Swi Delt

How to get there: On the B5417 Cheadle to
Wardlow Road, on the right, ½ mile before
junction with A52. Ribden Farm is second farm
down drive.

Oswestry, Shropshire

148 Travelodge Oswestry

Travel Accommodation
A5/A483, Mile End Services, Oswestry,
Shropshire, SY11 4JA
Tel: 08700 850 950
Web: www.travelodge.co.uk
40 bedrs B £4.25
CC: MC Vi Am DC Swi Delt

Making a booking?

 Don't forget to mention RAC
Hotels and Bed & Breakfast 2002.

One click does it all

 For the latest special offers and
online booking, plus detailed
information on over 3,000
RAC inspected properties,
visit www.rac.co.uk/hotels

Painswick, Gloucestershire

149 Painswick Hotel

Blue Ribbon Winner

★★★★ ❦❦❦
Kemps Lane, Painswick,
Gloucestershire, GL6 6YB
Tel: 01452 812160 Fax: 01452 814059
Email: reservations@painswickhotel.com
Web: www.painswickhotel.com
19 bedrs SB £95 DB £120 HBS £100 HBD £95
B £8.50 L £13 D £27.50
CC: MC Vi Am Swi Delt JCB

How to get there: Follow A46 to Painswick,
turning into St. Mary's Street next to the church.
Follow the road around and turn right at The
March Hare. Hotel 200 yards on right.

150 Hambutts Mynd

◆◆◆
Edge Road, Painswick, Gloucestershire, GL6 6UP
Tel: 01452 812352 Fax: 01452 813862
Email: e.warland@aol.com
Web: www.accommodation.uk.net/
painswick.htm
Children minimum age: 10
Closed January
3 bedrs SB £28 DB £48
CC: MC Vi Swi

How to get there: Entering Painswick from
Cheltenham, turn right at end of church wall.
From Stroud, take first left after car park.

Redditch, Worcestershire

151 Quality Hotel Redditch

★★★
Pool Bank, Southcrest, Redditch,
Worcestershire, B97 4JS
Tel: 01527 541511 Fax: 01527 402600
Email: admin@gb646.u-net.com
Web: www.choicehotels.com
73 bedrs SB £95.75 DB £109.75 HBS £112.25
HBD £63.13 B £10.75 L £9.95 D £12.95
CC: MC Vi Am DC Swi Delt

West Midlands

152 Campanile

Travel Accommodation
Far Moor Lane, Winyates Green, Redditch,
Worcestershire, B98 0SD
Tel: 01527 510710 Fax: 01527 517269
Web: www.campanile.fr

Typical Campanile bistro

46 bedrs SB £43.45 DB £48.40 HBS £51
HBD £51 B £4.95 L £3.50 D £11.25
CC: MC Vi Am DC Swi Delt
&嫌⊗⊜☐☎📞🅿️⊛⌕ℎ♨♨♨
How to get there: Exit M42 J3 and head for
Redditch along the A435, then take the first exit
for Redditch.

Ross-on-Wye, Herefordshire

153 Chase Hotel

★★★ ®
Gloucester Road, Ross-on-Wye,
Herefordshire, HR9 5LH
Tel: 01989 763161 Fax: 01989 768330
Email: info@chasehotel.co.uk
Web: www.chasehotel.co.uk
Children minimum age: 12

Georgian Country House with extensive grounds
and gardens. The perfect rural location for
relaxation and comfort. Award-winning cuisine.
Event catering for up to 200 guests.
36 bedrs SB £70 DB £85 HBS £65 HBD £50
B £9.50 L £14.50 D £22.50
CC: MC Vi Swi Delt
⊿🖉⊗⊜☐☎🅿️⊛ℎ♨♨♨ 'Y'
How to get there: From M50 Junction 4, left for
Ross-on-Wye. A40 Gloucester at 2nd round-
about,right for town centre at third roundabout.
Hotel on left.

154 Chasedale Hotel

★★
Walford Road, Ross-on-Wye,
Herefordshire, HR9 5PQ
Tel: 01989 562423 Fax: 01989 567900
Email: chasedale@supanet.com
Web: www.chasedale.co.uk
10 bedrs SB £34.50 DB £69
HBS £46 HBD £46 D £15
CC: MC Vi DC Swi Delt
嫌⊗☐☎🅿️⊛⌕ℎ♨♨♨
How to get there: Half a mile south of Ross-
on-Wye, on B4234 Ross-to-Coleford road on
left.

155 Old Court Hotel

★
Symonds Yat West, Ross-on-Wye,
Herefordshire, HR9 6DA
Tel: 01600 890367 Fax: 01600 890964
Email: oldcourt@aol.com
Web: www.oldcourthotel.com
Children minimum age: 12
18 bedrs SB £48 DB £76 B £10 D £22
CC: MC Vi Am DC Swi Delt
⚘🖉嫌⊗☐☎📞🅿️♨♨♨⚲
How to get there: Follow sign for Symonds Yat
West from A40, midway between Ross-on-Wye
and Monmouth.

156 Rosswyn Hotel

★
High Street, Ross-on-Wye,
Herefordshire, HR9 5BZ
Tel: 01989 562733 Fax: 01989 567115
Email: rosswynhotel@talk21.com
8 bedrs SB £40 DB £60 B £5 L £4 D £12
CC: MC Vi Am Swi Delt
🖉嫌⊗☐☎🅿️⊛ℎ

157 Brynheulog

♦♦♦♦ ⚬
Howle Hill, Ross-on-Wye, Herefordshire, HR9 5SP
Tel: 01989 562051 Fax: 01989 562051
4 bedrs
&🖉嫌⊗⊜☐🅿️⊛⌕ℎ♨✿

158 Garth Cottage Hotel

♦ ♦ ♦ ♦

Symonds Yat East, Herefordshire, HR9 6JL
Tel: 01600 890364 Fax: 01600 890364
Children minimum age: 12
Closed November to March
4 bedrs DB £50 HBD £83 D £16.50
CC: None accepted
⊗ ☺ **P** 🛏 ⁂
How to get there: From A40, leave at Little Chef
Whitchurch. Follow signs for Symonds Yat East
on B4229.

159 Inn On The Wye

♦ ♦ ♦

Kerne Bridge, Goodrich, near Ross-on-Wye,
Herefordshire, HR9 5QS
Tel: 01600 890872 Fax: 01600 890594
Web: www.theinnonthewye.co.uk
8 bedrs SB £36.50 DB £48 HBS £41.50
HBD £39 B £3.95 L £4.95 D £5.95
CC: MC Vi Am DC Swi Delt
⟨⟩ ♿ 📷 🐾 ⊗ ☺ 🖵 **P**🌷 🛏 🍴 ⁂ ⁂
How to get there: Three miles from Ross-on-
Wye on the B4228 near Kerne Bridge. London
two hours drive, Birmingham one hour, Cardiff
one hour.

160 The Whitehouse

♦ ♦ ♦

Wye Street, Ross-on-Wye,
Herefordshire, HR9 7BX
Tel: 01989 763572 Fax: 01989 763572
Children minimum age: 11
7 bedrs SB £35 DB £50
CC: MC Vi Am Swi Delt JCB
☺ 🖵 🛏 🍴 🍽 ⁂
How to get there: Halfway down Wye street
from Tourist Office, adjacent to river.

Rugby, Warwickshire

161 The Olde Coach House Inn

♦ ♦ ♦

Main Street, Ashby St. Ledgers, near Rugby,
Warwickshire, CV23 8DN
Tel: 01788 890349 Fax: 01788 891922

It's easier online

 For all your motoring and travel
needs, www.rac.co.uk

162 Travelodge Rugby

Travel Accommodation
A45, London Road, Dunchurch, Thurlaston,
near Rugby, Warwickshire, CV23 9LG
Tel: 08700 850 950
Web: www.travelodge.co.uk
40 bedrs B £4.25 CC: MC Vi Am DC Swi Delt
🍴 ☺ 🖵 🛏

Rugeley, Staffordshire

163 Cedar Tree Hotel

★ ★ ★

Main Road, Brereton, Rugeley,
Staffordshire, WS15 1DY
Tel: 01889 584241 Fax: 01889 575823
32 bedrs SB £42.50 DB £52.50 HBS £54
HBD £32.50 B £6.50 L £11.50 D £11.50
CC: MC Vi Am DC Swi Delt JCB
♿ 🐾 ☺ 🖵 ☎ 📞 **P**🌷 🛏 🍽 ⁂ ⁂
How to get there: The hotel is on the A51
towards Lichfield, approx one mile from Rugeley
town centre and seven miles from Lichfield.

164 Travelodge Rugeley

Travel Accommodation
A51/B5013, Western Springs Road, Rugeley,
Staffordshire, WS15 2AS
Tel: 08700 850 950
Web: www.travelodge.co.uk
32 bedrs B £4.25
CC: MC Vi Am DC Swi Delt
🍴 ☺ 🖵 🛏

Shrewsbury, Shropshire

165 Prince Rupert Hotel

★ ★ ★ ★

Butcher Row, Shrewsbury, Shropshire, SY1 1UQ
Tel: 01743 499955 Fax: 01743 357306
Email: post@prince-rupert-hotel.co.uk
Web: www.prince-rupert-hotel.co.uk
70 bedrs SB £85 DB £105 HBS £70 HBD £55
B £7.50 L £5 D £14
CC: MC Vi Am DC Swi Delt JCB
📶 📷 🐾 ☺ 🖵 ☎ 📞 **P**🌷 🛏 🍴 🍽 🌂 ⁂ ⁂ SPA
🍸 ⚲
How to get there: From the M54, follow signs
for town centre. Travel over English Bridge and
up the Wyle Cop. Turn sharp right into Fish
Street. Hotel is 200m ahead.

West Midlands

166 Abbots Mead Hotel

★★

9–10 St. Julians Friars, Shrewsbury,
Shropshire, SY1 1XL
Tel: 01743 235281 Fax: 01743 369133
Email: res@abbotsmeadhotel.co.uk
Web: www.abbotsmeadhotel.co.uk
16 bedrs SB £40 DB £56 HBS £55 HBD £43
B £5 D £15 CC: MC Vi Am Swi Delt

How to get there: M54, signs to town centre,
take first sharp turn left, over English Bridge (by
Corn House Wine Bar), hotel is on the left.

167 Nesscliffe Hotel

★★

Nesscliffe, Shrewsbury, Shropshire, SY4 1DB
Tel: 01743 741430 Fax: 01743 741104
Email: mike@wright70.fsnet.co.uk
8 bedrs SB £45 DB £55 B £6.50 L £4.50 D £6.95
CC: MC Vi Am Swi Delt

How to get there: On the A5 between Oswestry
and Shrewsbury.

168 Travelodge Shrewsbury

Travel Accommodation
A5/A49, Bayston Hill, Shrewsbury By Pass,
Shrewsbury, Shropshire, SY3 0DA
Tel: 08700 850 950
Web: www.travelodge.co.uk
40 bedrs B £4.25 CC: MC Vi Am DC Swi Delt

Solihull, West Midlands

169 Nailcote Hall Hotel

★★★★ 🍴🍴🍴
Nailcote Lane, Berkswell,
West Midlands, CV7 7DE
Tel: 024 76466174 Fax: 024 76470720
Email: info@nailcotehall.co.uk
Web: www.nailcotehall.co.uk

Charming Elizabethan house in 15 acres of
grounds. Relax in the Piano Bar Lounge, dine in
the award-winning Oak Room Restaurant or
Mediterranean Rick's. Swimming pool, gym,
steam room, solaium, tennis, 9-hole golf course.
38 bedrs
CC: MC Vi Am DC Swi Delt

170 Renaissance Solihull Hotel Birmingham

★★★★ 🍴🍴
651 Warwick Road, Solihull,
West Midlands, B91 1AT
Tel: 0121 7113000 Fax: 0121 7113963
Email: reservations.solihull@whitbread.com
Web: www.whitbread.com
179 bedrs DB £180
B £11.75 L £15.85 D £22.50
CC: MC Vi Am DC Swi Delt

How to get there: Leave Junction 5 of M42.
Take B4025 to Solihull town centre. Drive
through centre, over roundabout, hotel on right.

171 Arden Hotel

★★★
Coventry Road, Bickenhill, Solihull,
West Midlands, B92 0EH
Tel: 01675 443221 Fax: 01675 443221

172 Flemings Hotel

★★
141 Warwick Road, Olton, Solihull,
West Midlands, B92 7HW
Tel: 0121 706 0371 Fax: 0121 706 4494
Email: reservations@flemingshotel.co.uk
Web: www.flemingshotel.co.uk
70 bedrs SB £32 DB £56 HBS £32 HBD £56
B £5 L £5 D £7
CC: MC Vi Am DC Swi Delt

How to get there: M42 J5 onto A41 Seven Stars
Road turn right 100 yards past fourth set of
traffic lights.

Stafford, Staffordshire

173 Quality Hotel Stafford

★★★

Pinfold Lane, Penkridge, Stafford,
Staffordshire, ST19 5QP
Tel: 01785 712459 Fax: 01785 715532
Email: admin@gb067.u-net.com
Web: www.choicehotels.com
47 bedrs SB £95.75 DB £109.75 HBS £112.70
HBD £63.35 B £10.75 L £9.50 D £13.95
CC: MC Vi Am DC Swi Delt

How to get there: Exit at either Junction 12 or
13 of the M6 motorway. After approximately two
miles, at George and Fox pub turn into Pinfold
Lane. Hotel on left-hand side.

174 Abbey Hotel

★★

65–68 Lichfield Road, Stafford,
Staffordshire, ST17 4LW
Tel: 01785 258531 Fax: 01785 246875
Closed Christmas and New Year
17 bedrs SB £40 DB £60 B £9 D £12
CC: MC Vi Am Swi Delt

How to get there: M6 at Junction 13, towards
Stafford. Turn right at Esso garage to roundabout,
follow Silkmore Lane. At second roundabout take
second exit. Hotel ¼ mile on right.

175 Albridge Hotel

★

72 Wolverhampton Road, Stafford, ST17 4AW
Tel: 01785 254100 Fax: 01785 223895
9 bedrs CC: MC Vi Am DC Swi Delt

How to get there: Leave M6 at Junction 13.
Follow signs for Stafford, the town is 2 ³/₄ miles
on A449. Hotel is on left after Telegraph Inn,
opposite Victoria Wine.

176 Leonards Croft Hotel

◆◆◆

80 Lichfield Road, Stafford,
Staffordshire, ST17 4LP
Tel: 01785 223676
Closed Christmas
9 bedrs SB £30 DB £50 D £5 CC: MC Vi

How to get there: Leave M6 at Junction 13. Take
A449 and turn right at the Esso garage to
roundabout. Hotel is on A34 over bridge on right.

177 Offley Grove Farm

◆◆◆

Adbaston, near Eccleshall, Stafford,
Staffordshire, ST20 0QB
Tel: 01785 280205 Fax: 01785 280205
Email: accom@offleygrovefarm.freeserve.co.uk
Web: www.offleygrovefarm.co.uk
2 bedrs SB £22 DB £40 CC: None accepted

How to get there: From North; Exit J15 M6 onto
A519; follow signs for Eccleshall, Woodseaves,
Shebdon and Adbaston. From south; J10A M6,
M54, A41, A519 first left, travel a further 3¹/₂ miles.

Staunton-on-Wye, Herefordshire

178 The Portway Inn

◆◆◆

The Brecon Road, Staunton-on-Wye,
Herefordshire, HR4 7NH
Tel: 01981 500474

Stoke-on-Trent, Staffordshire

179 George Hotel

★★★★ 𝕽𝕽

Swan Square, Burslem, Stoke-on-Trent,
Staffordshire, ST6 2AE
Tel: 01782 577544 Fax: 01782 837496
Email: georgestoke@btinternet.com
Web: www.georgehotelstock.cwc.net
39 bedrs SB £70 DB £90 B £8.95 L £10.95
D £16.95 CC: MC Vi Am DC Swi Delt JCB

How to get there: From M6, take Junctions 15
or 16 onto A500. Turn left onto A53. At A50
junction turn left. Burslem is one mile further.

180 North Stafford

★★★

Station Road, Stoke-on-Trent,
Staffordshire, ST4 2AE
Tel: 01782 744477 Fax: 01782 744580
Email: stuart.mcmanus@principalhotels.co.uk
Web: www.principalhotels.co.uk
80 bedrs SB £105 DB £130 HBS £115 HBD £70
B £10 L £9.95 D £16.95 CC: MC Vi Am DC Swi

How to get there: Leave M6 at Junction 15. Join
A555 after ²/₃ mile. Follow signs for railway
station, hotel directly opposite.

West Midlands

181 Travelodge Stoke

Travel Accommodation
A500/A34 near M6 J16, Newcastle Road, Talke,
Stoke-on-Trent, Staffordshire, ST7 1UP
Tel: 08700 850 950
Web: www.travelodge.co.uk
62 bedrs B £4.25
CC: MC Vi Am DC Swi Delt

182 Hanchurch Manor Country House
Little Gem

Hanchurch, Stoke-on-Trent,
Staffordshire, ST4 8SD
Tel: 01782 643030 Fax: 01782 643035
Children minimum age: 12
5 bedrs SB £71.50 DB £82.50
CC: MC Vi

How to get there: Junction 15 M6 southbound
A519 Eccleshall through traffic lights for ³/₄ mile
under motorway bridge. Hotel driveway
immediately on right.

183 Corrie Guest House

13-15 Newton Street, Basford, Stoke-on-Trent,
Staffordshire, ST4 6JN
Tel: 01782 614838
Email: the.corrie@talk21.com
Web: thecorrie.com

A warm and friendly welcome awaits you at this
fine Victorian house, ideally situated for
shopping, Alton Towers, theatres, universities
and hospitals. In a quiet location between
Newcastle and Hanley.
8 bedrs SB £22 DB £38
CC: MC Vi Swi

How to get there: From M6 take Junction 15 or
16 onto A500 towards Stoke. Take the A53 exit
towards Newcastle-under-Lyme. Take the third
left turn.

184 Rhodes Hotel

42 Leek Road, Stoke-on-Trent,
Staffordshire, ST4 2AR
Tel: 01782 416320 Fax: 01782 416323
Email: rhodeshot42@aol.com
7 bedrs SB £20 DB £35
CC: MC Vi Delt

How to get there: Ten minutes drive from M6
Junctions 15/16. Close to Stoke-on-Trent
station, on A52 Stoke to Leek road.

185 L.Beez Guest House

46 Leek Road, Stoke-on-Trent,
Staffordshire, ST4 2AR
Tel: 01782 846727 Fax: 01782 846727

Family run, walking distance from Stoke railway
station. TV all rooms, tea/coffee facilities. High
standard of cleanliness and fire safety. Close to
all pottery factory shops, Staffordshire
University and Alton Towers.
5 bedrs SB £20 DB £35
CC: None accepted

How to get there: On A52 Stoke to Leek 10
minutes from M6/J15 250 yards Stoke railway
station. Opposite Post Office enquiry office.

Stone, Staffordshire

186 Travelodge Stafford

Travel Accommodation
M6, Stone, Staffordshire, ST15 0EU
Tel: 08700 850 950
Web: www.travelodge.co.uk
49 bedrs B £4.25
CC: MC Vi Am DC Swi Delt

Stow-on-the-Wold, Gloucestershire

187 Wyck Hill House Hotel

★★★★★ ♟ ♟
Burford Road, Stow-on-the-Wold, Cheltenham,
Gloucestershire, GL56 0ND
Tel: 01451 831936 Fax: 01451 832243
Email: wyck@wrensgroup.com
Web: www.wrensgroup.com
32 bedrs SB £110 DB £160 HBS £135
HBD £105 B £12.95 L £10.95 D £36.50
CC: MC Vi Am DC Swi Delt
How to get there: Three miles south of Stow-on-the-Wold on A424 towards Burford and Swindon.

188 Fosse Manor Hotel

★★★★ ♟ ♟
Stow-on-the-Wold, Cheltenham,
Gloucestershire, GL54 1JX
Tel: 01451 830354 Fax: 01451 832486
Email: enquiries@fossemanor.co.uk
Web: www.fossemanor.co.uk
Closed 21–29 December
21 bedrs SB £55 DB £98 HBS £78 HBD £78
B £8.50 L £12.50 D £26
CC: MC Vi Am DC Swi Delt
How to get there: One mile south of Stow-on-the-Wold on the A429 Warwick to Cirencester road.

189 Stow Lodge Hotel

★★★
The Square, Stow-on-the-Wold,
Gloucestershire, GL54 1AB
Tel: 01451 830485 Fax: 01451 831671
Email: chris@stowlodge.com
Web: www.stowlodge.com
Children minimum age: 5
Closed Christmas and early January

21 bedrs SB £60 DB £70
B £11 D £19
CC: MC Vi Swi Delt
How to get there: The hotel has entrances off the main market square and also the A429 in Stow-on-the-Wold

190 Limes

♦ ♦ ♦ ⚡
Tewkesbury Road, Stow-on-the-Wold,
Gloucestershire, GL54 1EN
Tel: 01451 830034 Fax: 01451 830034
Closed Christmas
5 bedrs SB £27 DB £43
CC: None accepted
How to get there: Off A429 towards Evesham & Broadway Road (A424). 300 yards on left.

Stratford-upon-Avon, Warwickshire

191 Heritage Hotels – The Shakespeare

★★★★ ♟ ♟
Chapel Street, Stratford-upon-Avon,
Warwickshire, CV37 6ER
Tel: 0870 400 8182 Fax: 01789 415411
Web: www.heritage-hotels.com
74 bedrs SB £130 DB £180
B £12.50 L £15 D £24
CC: MC Vi Am Swi Delt JCB None accepted

192 Stratford Manor

★★★★ ♟ ♟
Warwick Road, Stratford-upon-Avon,
Warwickshire, CV37 0PY
Tel: 01789 731173 Fax: 01789 731131
Email: stratfordmanor@marstonhotels.com
Web: www.marstonhotels.com

104 bedrs SB £115 DB £149 HBS £69.50
HBD £69.50 B £12 L £16.50 D £28
CC: MC Vi Am DC Swi Delt
How to get there: Leave M40 at Junction 15, follow A46 towards Stratford. Take A439 signposted Stratford town centre. Hotel one mile on left.

West Midlands

193 Stratford Victoria

★★★★ ®

Arden Street, Stratford-upon-Avon,
Warwickshire, CV37 6QQ
Tel: 01789 271000 Fax: 01789 271001
Email: stratfordvictoria@marstonhotels.com
Web: www.marstonhotels.com

102 bedrs SB £99 DB £135 HBS £73 HBD £73
B £12 L £14 D £24 CC: MC Vi Am DC Swi Delt
🏠♿⛵🛎🐾❄🖥️💻☎📞🅿️🐕🍴☕🎭🍖🎣🦞 ♨♨ 'Y'
How to get there: Exit M40 Junction 15, take
A46 then A3400. Turn right at traffic light into
Arden Street; hotel is 150 yards on right.

194 The Alveston Manor

★★★★

Clopton Bridge, Stratford-upon-Avon,
Warwickshire, CV37 7HP
Tel: 0870 400 8181 Fax: 01789 413333
Email: gm1209@forte-hotels.com
Web: www.heritage-hotels.com
113 bedrs SB £131.75 DB £180 HBS £99
HBD £99 B £12 L £14 D £21
CC: MC Vi Am DC Swi Delt
🏠♿🛎🐾❄🖥️☎📞🅿️🐕🍖♨♨♨
How to get there: M40 Junction 15. A46 then
A439 into Stratford. Follow one-way system
towards Banbury and Oxford. Hotel just over
bridge.

195 Welcombe Hotel

★★★★ ®®®

Warwick Road, Stratford-upon-Avon, CV37 0NR
Tel: 01789 295252 Fax: 01789 414666
Web: www.welcombe.co.uk
64 bedrs
CC: MC Vi Am DC Swi Delt
🏠🛎🖥️☎📞🅿️🐕🍖🎭🍖♨♨♨🏌️
How to get there: Leave M40 at Junction 15.
Follow A46 to Stratford-upon-Avon. Then take
the A439 for three miles. Hotel is on the right.

196 Grosvenor Hotel

★★★ ®

Warwick Road, Stratford-upon-Avon,
Warwickshire, CV37 6YT
Tel: 01789 269213 Fax: 01789 266087
Email: info@groshotelstratford.co.uk
Web: www.groshotelstratford.co.uk

This elegant grade II Georgian hotel, ideally
situated in the centre of Stratford-upon-Avon,
features 67 bedrooms, five conference rooms, a
lounge bar and superb restaurant.
67 bedrs SB £93.95 DB £107.90 HBD £60
B £8.95 L £11.50 D £16.50
CC: MC Vi Am DC Swi Delt
🏠♿❄🖥️☎📞🅿️🍖🎭🍖♨♨♨
How to get there: From M40, take Junction 15
and A439 (A46) into Stratford. Hotel is on
Warwick Road (A439) in the centre of Stratford.

197 Heritage Hotels – The Swan's Nest

★★★

Bridgefoot, Stratford-upon-Avon,
Warwickshire, CV37 7LT
Tel: 0870 400 8183 Fax: 01789 414547

198 Salford Hall

★★★★ ®®

Abbots Salford, Warwickshire, WR11 5UT
Tel: 01386 871300 Fax: 01386 871301
Email: reception@salfordhall.co.uk
Web: www.salfordhall.co.uk
Closed Christmas
33 bedrs CC: MC Vi Am DC Swi Delt
🏠🖥️🖥️☎📞🅿️🍖🎭🍖♨♨♨🎾🏌️
How to get there: From M40 Junction 15, take
A46 towards Stratford. After 12 miles, take road
signposted "Salford Priors, Abbots Salford."
Follow for 1½ miles and Salford Hall is on left.

199 Ambleside Guest House

♦♦♦ 🐾®

41 Grove Road, Stratford-upon-Avon,
Warwickshire, CV37 6PB
Tel: 01789 297239 Fax: 01789 295670
Email: peter@amblesideguesthouse.com
Web: www.amblesideguesthouse.com
8 bedrs SB £20 DB £40
CC: MC Vi Swi Delt JCB
🖥️❄🖥️🅿️🍖🐾
How to get there: Opposite Firs Park, five
minutes' walk from railway station.

200 Avon View Hotel

♦♦♦♦ ⊁ ♟

121 Shipston Road, Stratford-upon-Avon,
Warwickshire, CV37 9QL
Tel: 01789 297542 Fax: 01789 292936
Email: avon-view@lineone.net
10 bedrs SB £35 DB £60
HBS £48 HBD £42.50 D £13
CC: MC Vi Am DC Swi Delt
⏃⊗⊝⬜☎ ▣☀🐕⛺ 🏨 👪
How to get there: South of river on A3400, or
walk from river bridge along old tramway walk.

201 Eastnor House

♦♦♦♦ ⊁ ♟

33 Shipston Road, Stratford-upon-Avon,
Warwickshire, CV37 7LN
Tel: 01789 268115 Fax: 01789 551133
Email: enquirie@eastnorhouse.com
Web: www.eastnorhouse,com
9 bedrs SB £50 DB £70
CC: MC Vi Am Swi Delt
⊗⊝⬜☎🔌▣☀🐕🛶
How to get there: Located just south of the river
on the Shipston road (A3400) close to the
centre of Stratford.

202 Hampton Lodge Guest House

♦♦♦♦ 📺 ⊁ ♟

38 Shipston Road, Stratford-upon-Avon,
Warwickshire, CV37 7LP
Tel: 01789 299374 Fax: 01789 299374
Email: hamptonlodge@aol.com
Web: www.hamptonlodge.co.uk
7 bedrs SB £45.00 DB £63 D £16.50
CC: MC Vi Am Swi Delt JCB
⏃⊗⊝⬜☎▣☀🐕🛶
How to get there: M40 J15, take A46 then A439
to Stratford. Follow A3400 over River Avon. Turn
right into Shipston Road; Hampton Lodge on
left.

203 Hardwick House Guest House

♦♦♦♦ ⊁ ♟

1 Avenue Road, Stratford-upon-Avon,
Warwickshire, CV37 6UY
Tel: 01789 204307 Fax: 01789 296760
Email: hardwick@waveriver.co.uk
Web: www.stratford-upon-
avon.co.uk/hardwick.htm
Children minimum age: 2

A large Victorian house set in a quiet, mature,
tree-lined avenue, a few minutes walk from the
town centre. Non-smoking bedrooms. Large car
park.
14 bedrs SB £38 DB £65
CC: MC Vi Am Swi Delt
📠⊗⊝⬜▣☀🛶👪
How to get there: From M40 Junction 15 take
A46 then A439 to Stratford town centre. Turn
right after the 30mph sign into St. Gregory's
Road. Hardwick House is 200 yards on the right.

204 Melita Private Hotel

♦♦♦♦ ⊁

37 Shipston Road, Stratford-upon-Avon,
Warwickshire, CV37 7LN
Tel: 01789 292432 Fax: 01789 204867
Email: melita37@email.msn.com
Web: www.melitahotel.co.uk
Closed Christmas & New Year

Beautifully-appointed Victorian house offers a
friendly, cheerful service and excellent breakfast
menu. Ample parking, theatres and town centre
seven minute walk. Ensuite, non-smoking
bedrooms.
12 bedrs SB £49 DB £69
CC: MC Vi Am Swi Delt JCB
🐾⊗⊝⬜☎▣☀❄🛶👪
How to get there: On the A3400, south of town
centre. 150 yards from the Clopton Bridge.

West Midlands

205 Penryn Guest House

 ◆◆◆◆ ✗

126 Alcester Road, Stratford-upon-Avon,
Warwickshire, CV37 9DP
Tel: 01789 293718 Fax: 01789 266077
Email: penrynhouse@btinternet.com
Web: www.smoothhound.co.uk/
　　　hotels/penryn.html
7 bedrs SB £30 DB £50
CC: MC Vi Am DC Swi Delt JCB
&⊗⊜☐P☃Ⴕ🏊
How to get there: Leave M40 at Junction 15.
Follow signs to Stratford on A46. At third
roundabout (8 miles from motorway), turn left
onto A422 to Stratford town centre. Penryn one
mile on left, 800 metres from rail station.

206 Sequoia House Hotel

 ◆◆◆◆ ✗

51-53 Shipston Road, Stratford-upon-Avon,
Warwickshire, CV37 7LN
Tel: 01789 268852 Fax: 01789 414559
Email: info@sequoiahotel.co.uk
Web: www.stratford-upon-
avon.co.uk/sequoia.htm
Children minimum age: 5
23 bedrs
CC: MC Vi Am DC Swi Delt
⊗⊜☐☎P☃✗Ⴕ♨♨♨ iii
How to get there: On A3400 100m from the
Clopton bridge. From south, hotel on left. From
north, enter Stratford and follow signs for
Shipston A3400. Cross river, continue on A3400
and hotel is on right.

207 Victoria Spa Lodge

 ◆◆◆◆ ✗ 🍷

Bishopton Lane, Bishopton, Stratford-upon-
Avon, Warwickshire, CV37 9QY
Tel: 01789 267985 Fax: 01789 204728
Email: ptozer@victoriaspalodge.demon.co.uk
Web: www.stratford-upon-avon.co.uk/
　　　victoriaspa.htm

Explore the wonderful Cotswolds from this Grade
II listed lodge. Seven beautifully appointed
ensuite bedrooms, with all modern facilities.
Ample parking. Completely non-smoking.
7 bedrs SB £50 DB £65
CC: MC Vi Swi Delt
⊗⊜☐P☃Ⴕ🏊

208 Cymbeline House

 ◆◆◆

24 Evesham Place, Stratford-upon-Avon,
Warwickshire, CV37 6HT
Tel: 01789 292958 Fax: 01789 292958
Email: cymbelinebb-3-07-a@amserve.net
Closed Christmas
6 bedrs SB £18 DB £36
CC: None accepted
⊠🐾⊗⊜☐P☃Ⴕ

209 Ingon Bank Farm B&B

 ◆◆◆ ✗

Ingon Bank Farm, Warwick Road,
Stratford-upon-Avon, Warwickshire, CV37 0NY
Tel: 01789 292642 Fax: 01789 292642

Traditional farmhouse on a working farm, in a
quiet location two miles from Stratford-upon-
Avon. Comfortable ensuite bedrooms with all
facilities. Residents' lounge with open fire.
3 bedrs SB £25 DB £44
CC: None accepted
🐾⊗⊜☐P☃Ⴕ
How to get there: From Stratford, take A439
north towards Warwick for two miles. Hotel is
signposted on left, 350 yards north of the
Snitterfield turning.

210 Marlyn Hotel

3 Chestnut Walk, Stratford-upon-Avon,
Warwickshire, CV37 6HG
Tel: 01789 293752 Fax: 01789 293752
Email: evansmarlynhotel@aol.com
8 bedrs SB £22 DB £44 B £4.50 D £10.50
CC: MC Vi

How to get there: Town centre down High,
Chapel and Church streets, turn right into
Chesnut Walk; on right, opposite car parking
under trees.

211 Nando's Guest House

18 & 19 Evesham Place, Stratford-upon-Avon,
Warwickshire, CV37 6HT
Tel: 01789 204907 Fax: 01789 204907

Stroud, Gloucestershire

212 Travelodge Stonehouse

Travel Accommodation
A419, Eastington, Stonehouse, Near Stroud,
Gloucestershire, GL10 3SQ
Tel: 08700 850 950
Web: www.travelodge.co.uk
40 bedrs B £4.25
CC: MC Vi Am DC Swi Delt

213 The Crown Inn

Frampton Mansell, Stroud,
Gloucestershire, GL6 8JG
Tel: 01285 760601 Fax: 01285 760681
12 bedrs SB £44 DB £69 B £7.95
CC: MC Vi Am Swi Delt

How to get there: Take the A419 from Stroud to
Cirencester, come through Stroud and head
towards Cirencester up a windy steep hill (with
an airfield on right at top) 150 yards on left
turning Frampton Mansell.

214 Crown Inn

Bath Road, Inchbrook, Stroud,
Gloucestershire, GL5 5HA
Tel: 01453 832914 Fax: 01453 832914
Web: www.inchbrook.cwc.net
4 bedrs SB £30 DB £45
B £2.50 L £4.95 D £4.95
CC: MC Vi Swi

How to get there: On the A46 between Stroud
and Nailsworth.

215 Downfield Hotel

134 Cainscross Road, Stroud,
Gloucestershire, GL5 4HN
Tel: 01453 764496 Fax: 01453 753150
Email: messenger@downfieldotel.demon.co.uk
Web: www.downfieldotel.demon.co.uk
21 bedrs SB £40 DB £55
B £7 D £12
CC: MC Vi Am Swi Delt

How to get there: M5 exit 13 to A419; hotel 4 1/2
miles on left. M4 exit 15 to A419; hotel on right
just after Stroud ring road.

Sutton Coldfield, West Midlands

216 New Hall Country House
Gold Ribbon Winner

★★★★ ® ® ®
Walmley Road, Walmley,
Sutton Coldfield, B76 1QX
Tel: 0121 378 2442 Fax: 0121 378 4637
Email: newhall@thistle.co.uk
Web: www.newhallhotel.net
Children minimum age: 8
60 bedrs SB £165 DB £201
B £16.75 L £29.50 D £29.50
CC: MC Vi Am DC Swi Delt

West Midlands

217 Moor Hall Hotel

★★★★ ®

Moor Hall Drive, Four Oaks, Sutton Coldfield,
West Midlands, B75 6LN
Tel: 0121 308 3751 Fax: 0121 308 8974
Email: mail@moorhallhotel.co.uk
Web: www.moorhallhotel.co.uk

Country house hotel set in parkland yet within
easy reach of Birmingham and NEC. Restaurant
with RAC Dining Award, extensive conferencing
and leisure facilities. Ample free parking.
82 bedrs SB £110 DB £126 HBS £130 HBD £83
B £9.50 L £8.95 D £20 CC: MC Vi Am Swi

How to get there: Leave M42 at Junction 9.
Take A446 to Lichfield, A453 to Sutton
Coldfield, turn right at traffic lights into Weeford
Road and Moor Hall is on the left.

218 Reindeer Park Lodge

♦ ♦ ♦ ♦ ✿

Kingsbury Road, Leamarston, Sutton Coldfield,
West Midlands, B76 0DE
Tel: 01675 470811 Fax: 01675 470710

Symonds Yat, Herefordshire

219 Saracens Head Hotel

★★

Symonds Yat, Symonds Yat,
Herefordshire, HR9 6JL
Tel: 01600 890435 Fax: 01600 890034
Email: bookings@saracenshead.com
Web: www.saracenshead.com
Children minimum age: 9
Closed December to January
9 bedrs CC: MC Vi Swi Delt

How to get there: Leave A40 between Ross-on-
Wye and Monmouth at the Little Chef
restaurant. Follow signs to Symonds Yat East
for three miles.

Tamworth, Staffordshire

220 Travelodge Tamworth

Travel Accommodation
M42 J10, Green Lane, Tamworth,
Staffordshire, B77 5PS
Tel: 08700 850 950
Web: www.travelodge.co.uk
62 bedrs B £4.25
CC: MC Vi Am DC Swi Delt

Telford, Shropshire

221 Clarion, Madeley Court

★★★★ ® ®

Castlefields Way, Madeley Court, Telford,
Shropshire, TF7 5DW
Tel: 01952 680068 Fax: 01952 684275
Email: admin@gb068.u-net.com
Web: www.choicehotels.com
47 bedrs SB £121.75 DB £136.75
HBS £144.75 HBD £79.88
B £11.75 L £3.95 D £23
CC: MC Vi Am DC Swi Delt

How to get there: Leave M54 at Exit 4. Take
A442 towards Kidderminster to Castlefields
roundabout. Hotel is situated as you exit first left.

222 White House Hotel

★★ ®

Wellington Road, Muxton, Telford,
Shropshire, TF2 8NG
Tel: 01952 604276 Fax: 01952 670336
Email: james@whhotel.co.uk
Web: www.whhotel.co.uk
32 bedrs SB £62.50 DB £75
HBS £65 HBD £45
B £6 L £11.50 D £13.50
CC: MC Vi Am Swi Delt JCB

223 Travelodge Telford

Travel Accommodation
A5223, Whitchurch Drive, Shawbirch, Telford,
Shropshire, TF1 3QA
Tel: 08700 850 950
Web: www.travelodge.co.uk
40 bedrs B £4.25
CC: MC Vi Am DC Swi Delt

Tetbury, Gloucestershire

224 Calcot Manor

Gold Ribbon Winner

★★★ ⍩ ⍩ ⍩
near Tetbury, Gloucestershire, GL8 8YJ
Tel: 01666 890391 Fax: 01666 890394
Email: reception@calcotmanor.co.uk
Web: www.calcotmanor.co.uk

Charming Cotswold stone manor house
originally dating back to the 15th century.
28 bedrs SB £125 DB £155 L £15 D £25
CC: MC Vi Am DC Delt
How to get there: Three miles outside Tetbury,
on the crossroads of the A4135 and A46.

225 The Snooty Fox

★★★ ⍩
Market Place, Tetbury, Gloucestershire, GL8 8DD
Tel: 01666 502436 Fax: 01666 503479
Email: res@snooty-fox.co.uk
Web: www.snooty-fox.co.uk

THE SNOOTY FOX

12 bedrs SB £71.50 DB £95 HBD £30
B £7.95 L £5.95 D £9.95
CC: MC Vi Am DC Swi Delt JCB

226 Tavern House

◆◆◆◆ ⍩ ⍩
Willesley, Tetbury, Gloucestershire, GL8 8QU
Tel: 01666 880444 Fax: 01666 880254
Children minimum age: 10
4 bedrs SB £49.50 DB £69 B £7.95
CC: None accepted
How to get there: M4 J-118, A46, A433, four
miles. Willesley after Didmarton. Tavern House
on right.

Tutbury, Staffordshire

227 Ye Olde Dog & Partridge Hotel

★★★★ ⍩ ⍩
High Street, Tutbury, near Burton-upon-Trent,
Staffordshire, DE13 9LS
Tel: 01283 813030 Fax: 01283 813178
Email: info@yeoldedogandpartridge.co.uk
Web: www.dogandpartridge.net
20 bedrs SB £60 DB £75
B £8.50 L £10.80 D £12.25
CC: MC Vi Am Swi
How to get there: From Junction 24 off M1, take
A50 to Stoke-on-Trent. Take A511 toward
Burton-on-Trent (Scrofton, Foston, Hatton) and
follow signs for Tutbury.
See advert below

See the road ahead

Just dial 1740* from any mobile
phone to get up-to-the-minute
RAC traffic information on
motorways and major A roads.
Try it now! *Calls to 1740 are charged
at premium rate.

West Midlands

Upper Slaughter, Gloucestershire

228 Lords Of The Manor

Gold Ribbon Winner

★★★ ⓡ ⓡ ⓡ
Upper Slaughter, Gloucestershire, GL54 2JD
Tel: 01451 820243 Fax: 01451 820696
Email: lordsofthemanor@btinternet.com
Web: www.lordsofthemanor.com
Children minimum age: 9

A 17th-century former rectory set amidst eight acres of gardens. Comfortable surroundings and fine cuisine make it an ideal base to explore the Cotswolds.
27 bedrs
CC: MC Vi Am DC Swi Delt

Upton St. Leonards, Gloucestershire

229 Hatton Court Hotel

★★★★ ⓡ ⓡ
Upton Hill, Upton St. Leonards, Gloucester, Gloucestershire, GL4 8DE
Tel: 01452 617412 Fax: 01452 612945
Email: res@hatton-court.co.uk
Web: www.hatton-court.co.uk

HATTON COURT

45 bedrs SB £95 DB £115 HBS £120 HBD £75
B £11.50 L £14.50 D £27.50
CC: MC Vi Am DC Swi Delt

Ask the experts

To book a Hotel or Guest Accommodation, or for help and advice, call RAC Hotel Reservations on 0870 603 9109 and quote 'Guide 2002'

Upton-upon-Severn, Worcestershire

230 White Lion Hotel

★★★ ⓡ
High Street, Upton-upon-Severn, Worcestershire, WR8 0HJ
Tel: 01684 592551 Fax: 01684 593333
Email: info@whitelionhotel.demon.co.uk
Web: www.whitelionhotel.demon.co.uk
11 bedrs SB £53 DB £77
HBS £75 HBD £49.50
B £8.50 L £10 D £10
CC: MC Vi Am Swi Delt JCB

Uttoxeter, Staffordshire

231 Travelodge Uttoxeter

Travel Accommodation
A40/B5030, Ashbourne Road, Uttoxeter, Staffordshire, ST14 5AA
Tel: 08700 850 950
Web: www.travelodge.co.uk
32 bedrs B £4.25
CC: MC Vi Am DC Swi Delt

232 Oldroyd Guest House & Hotel

♦ ♦ ♦
18–22 Bridge Street, Uttoxeter, Staffordshire, ST14 8AP
Tel: 01889 562763 Fax: 01889 568916

Walsall, West Midlands

233 Quality Boundary Hotel

★★★
Birmingham Road, Great Barr, Walsall, West Midlands, WS5 3AB
Tel: 01922 633609 Fax: 01922 635727
Email: info@boundaryhotel.com
Web: www.boundaryhotel.com
94 bedrs SB £90 DB £170
L £7.95 D £10
CC: MC Vi Am DC Swi Delt

How to get there: Exit J7 M6; follow A34 for Walsall. Just over one mile on left.

234 Quality Hotel and Suites Walsall

★★★
20 Wolverhampton Road West, Bentley,
Walsall, West Midlands, WS2 0BS
Tel: 01922 724444 Fax: 01922 723148
Email: admin@gb622.u-net.com
Web: www.choicehotels.com
154 bedrs SB £106.75 DB £121.75 HBS
£121.25 HBD £68.13 B £11.75 L £5.95 D £14.50
CC: MC Vi Am DC Swi Delt

How to get there: Located at Junction 10 of M6.

235 Abberley Hotel

★★
29 Bescot Road, Walsall,
West Midlands, WS2 9AD
Tel: 01922 627413 Fax: 01922 720933
Email: abberley.hotel@virgin.net
Web: www.abberleyhotel.co.uk
28 bedrs
CC: MC Vi Am Swi Delt

How to get there: Leave M6 at Junction 9 and
take signs to Walsall. At traffic lights bear to left.
Hotel visible on right, 1/4 mile from junction.

236 Royal Hotel

★★
Ablewell Street, Walsall, West Midlands, WS1 2EL
Tel: 01922 621561 Fax: 01922 630028
28 bedrs SB £35 DB £49
CC: None accepted

Warley, West Midlands

237 Travelodge Oldbury

Travel Accommodation
A4123, Wolverhampton Road, Warley,
West Midlands, B69 7BH
Tel: 08700 850 950
Web: www.travelodge.co.uk
33 bedrs B £4.25
CC: MC Vi Am DC Swi Delt

It's easier online

For all your motoring and travel
needs, www.rac.co.uk

Warwick, Warwickshire

238 Chesford Grange

★★★★
Chesford Bridge, Kenilworth,
Warwickshire, CV8 2LD
Tel: 01926 515106 Fax: 01926 855272
Email: karen.everitt@principalhotels.co.uk
Web: www.principalhotels.co.uk
218 bedrs SB £130 DB £150
HBS £145 HBD £82.50
B £10.50 L £11.95 D £19.50
CC: MC Vi Am DC Swi Delt

How to get there: Exit M40 at Junction 15. Take
A46 toward Coventry and A452 slip road to
Leamington. Turn right at roundabout to
Leamington; hotel is 250 yards on right.

239 Glebe Hotel

★★★
Church Street, Barford, Warwick,
Warwickshire, CV35 8BS
Tel: 01926 624218 Fax: 01926 624625

240 Warwick Arms Hotel

★★
17 High Street, Warwick,
Warwickshire, CV34 4AT
Tel: 01926 492759 Fax: 01926 410587

241 Croft Guest House

♦♦♦♦
Haseley Knob, Warwick, Warwickshire, CV35 7NL
Tel: 01926 484447 Fax: 01926 484447
Email: david@croftguesthouse.co.uk
Web: www.croftguesthouse.co.uk
9 bedrs SB £34 DB £48
CC: MC Vi Am Swi Delt JCB

How to get there: From A46 follow A4177 for
four miles to second roundabout. Turn right (still
A4177). After 1/2 mile turn right to Haseley Knob
village.

West Midlands

242 King's Head Inn

♦ ♦ ♦ ⸙

39 Saltisford, Warwick, Warwickshire, CV34 4TD
Tel: 01926 775177 Fax: 01926 775166
Email: thekingsheadwarwick@hotmail.com
Web: www.thekingsheadwarwick.co.uk
9 bedrs SB £50 DB £60 B £4 L £6 D £11
CC: MC Vi Swi

How to get there: M40 Jct15 A429 Warwick, left at Bowling Green St., left at roundabout. We are on the left.

Westonbirt, Gloucestershire

243 Hare and Hounds

★★★

Westonbirt, Tetbury, Gloucestershire, GL8 8QL
Tel: 01666 880233 Fax: 01666 880241
Email: hareandhoundswbt@aol.com
Web: www.hareandhoundshotel.co.uk

Spacious, comfortable hotel in extensive gardens next to Westonbirt Arboretum, within easy reach of M4 and M5. Quality dining in the restaurant or bar. Conference and banquetting suite. Tennis and squash.
31 bedrs SB £76 DB £104 HBS £96
HBD £71.50 CC: MC Vi Am DC Swi Delt

How to get there: J17 M4 to Tetbury via Malmesbury; A433 for 2 miles to Westonbirt. Exit J13 M5, Stroud and A46 to Westonbirt turning.

Whitchurch, Shropshire

244 Dukes

♦ ♦ ♦ ♦ ⸙

Halghton, Whitchurch, Shropshire, SY13 3DU
Tel: 01948 830269
Email: gilberts@thedukes.fsbusiness.co.uk
3 bedrs SB £30 DB £54

CC: None accepted

How to get there: At Whitchurch, A525 for Wrexham. After six miles, turn left for Horseman's Green. Past houses, turn right for Halghton. Hotel is on right after ½ mile.

245 Roden View Guest House

♦ ♦ ♦ ♦ ⸙

Dobson Bridge, Whixall, Whitchurch, Shropshire, SY13 2QL
Tel: 01948 710320 Fax: 01948 710320
Email: rodenview@talk21.com
3 bedrs SB £20 DB £40 HBS £30 HBD £30
B £5 L £10 D £10 CC: None accepted

How to get there: From Whitchurch, B5476 for Wem. After 5 miles, pass Bull & Dog Pub. Take next right and travel for two miles, turn left at T-junction. Over canal bridge, Roden View on left.

Whittington, Shropshire

246 Ye Olde Boot Inn

★

Castle Street, Whittington, Shropshire, SY11 4DF
Tel: 01691 662250 Fax: 01691 662250
6 bedrs SB £35 DB £46 CC: MC Vi Swi Delt JCB

Wolverhampton, West Midlands

247 Connaught Hotel

★★★

Tettenhall Road, Wolverhampton, WV1 4SW
Tel: 01902 424433 Fax: 01902 710353
Email: conhotel@wolverhampton.co.uk
60 bedrs SB £50 DB £70 HBS £55 HBD £40
B £3.50 L £8.50 D £14.50
CC: MC Vi Am DC Swi Delt JCB

248 Novotel Wolverhampton

★★★

Union Street, Wolverhampton, WV1 3JN
Tel: 01902 871100 Fax: 01902 870054
Email: h1188@accor-hotels.com
Children minimum age: 16
132 bedrs SB £81 DB £90 HBS £97 HBD £61
B £10 L £13 D £16.50
CC: MC Vi Am DC Swi Delt

How to get there: Easy access from M6, M5 and M54. Follow signs to Wolverhampton town centre, then railway station. Hotel situated on St. George's ring road.

249 Quality Hotel Wolverhampton

★★★ ℞

Penn Road, Wolverhampton, WV3 0ER
Tel: 01902 429216 Fax: 01902 710419
Email: admin@gb069.u-net.com
Web: www.choicehotels.com
92 bedrs SB £98.75 DB £108.75 HBS £115.70
HBD £62.85 B £9.75 L £10.50 D £16.95
CC: MC Vi Am DC Swi Delt

How to get there: M6 Junction 10, A454 to Wolverhampton. Approach town centre, follow A449 Kidderminster signs. Hotel is ¼ mile on right.

250 Barons Court Hotel

★★

142 Gold Thorn Hill, Wolverhampton, WV2 3JE
Tel: 01902 341751 Fax: 01902 340033
Email: info@baronscourthotel.com
Web: www.baronscourthotel.com
Children minimum age: 10

This country house hotel situated near the centre of town retains its Edwardian charm and character. Original oak floors and beams. Graceful dining room, innovative menu.
17 bedrs CC: MC Vi Swi Delt

How to get there: Take A449 Kidderminster road from Wolverhampton ring road. At third set of traffic lights (1 mile) turn left into Goldthorn Hill.

251 Travelodge Birmingham North

Travel Accommodation
M6 J10a/11, Essington,
Wolverhampton, WV11 2AT
Tel: 08700 850 950
Web: www.travelodge.co.uk
64 bedrs B £4.25 CC: MC Vi Am DC Swi Delt

252 Fox Hotel

118 School Street, Wolverhampton, WV3 0NR
Tel: 01902 421680 Fax: 01902 711654
Email: sales@foxhotel.co.uk
Web: www.foxhotel.co.uk
33 bedrs SB £35 DB £55 HBS £45 HBD £37.50
B £5 L £4 D £8 CC: MC Vi Am DC Swi Delt JCB

How to get there: Situated on city centre ring road, clockwise on the right, anticlockwise on your left.

Worcester, Worcestershire

253 Heritage Hotels – The Giffard

★★★

High Street, Worcester, Worcestershire, WR1 2QR
Tel: 0870 400 8133 Fax: 01905 723458
102 bedrs CC: MC Vi Am DC Swi Delt

254 Manor Arms Country Inn & Hotel

♦♦♦

Abberley Village, Worcestershire, WR6 6BN
Tel: 01299 896507 Fax: 01299 896723
Email: themanorarms@btconnect.com
Web: www.themanorarms.co.uk
9 bedrs SB £38 DB £50
B £6 L £5 D £10 CC: MC Vi

How to get there: Leave A443 at Abberley and follow signs to 'Norman Church' and Abberley Village. As you enter the village the Manor Arms is located on the left, opposite the church.

Wotton-under-Edge, Gloucestershire

255 Burrows Court

♦♦♦

Nibley Green, North Nibley,
Gloucestershire, GL11 6AZ
Tel: 01453 546230 Fax: 01453 544536
Email: p.f.rackley@tesco.net
Web: www.burrowscourt.co.uk
Closed January to February
6 bedrs SB £36 DB £54 CC: MC Vi Delt

How to get there: From the A38 Bristol to Gloucester road, turn off at sign to Blanchworth, North Nibley, Stinchcombe. Hotel opposite North Nibley village sign.

West Midlands

Northeast

Durham, like many areas in the Northeast, is famous for its green spaces and places to unwind.

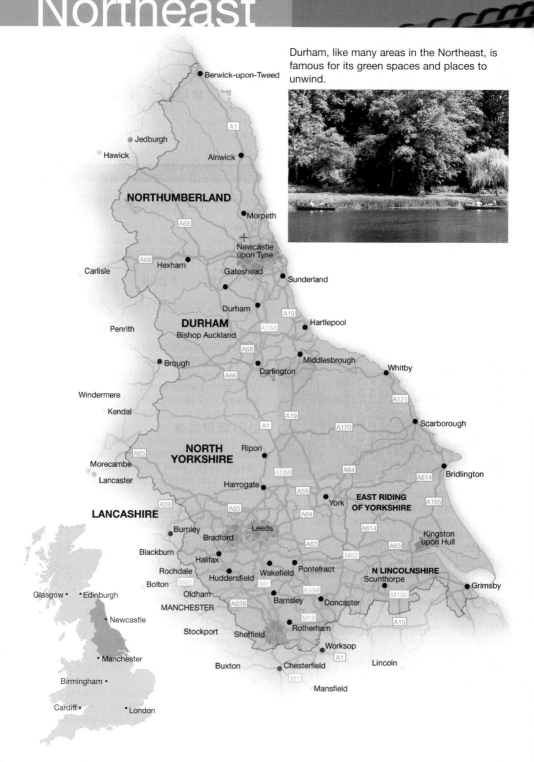

Berwick-upon-Tweed

A1

Jedburgh

Hawick

Alnwick

NORTHUMBERLAND

Morpeth

A68

Newcastle upon Tyne

Carlisle

A69 Hexham

Gateshead

Sunderland

Durham

A19

DURHAM

A1(M)

Hartlepool

Penrith

Bishop Auckland

A68

Brough

Middlesbrough

Whitby

Darlington

A66

A171

Windermere

Kendal

A19

Scarborough

A1

A170

NORTH YORKSHIRE

Ripon

A65

Morecambe

A1(M)

A64

A614

Bridlington

Lancaster

Harrogate

A59

York

EAST RIDING OF YORKSHIRE

A165

LANCASHIRE

A59

A65

A64

Burnley

Leeds

A614

Kingston upon Hull

Bradford

A63

M62

A63

Blackburn

Halifax

Rochdale

Wakefield Pontefract

N LINCOLNSHIRE

Scunthorpe

Grimsby

Bolton

M62

Huddersfield

M1

Oldham

A1(M)

M180

MANCHESTER

A628

Barnsley

Doncaster

A15

Stockport

M18

Rotherham

Sheffield

Worksop

A1

Buxton

Chesterfield

Lincoln

M1

Mansfield

Glasgow •Edinburgh

•Newcastle

•Manchester

Birmingham •

Cardiff •

•London

Swirle Pavillion (right) on Newcastle's quayside provides a striking contrast to the old Baltic Flour Mill. Once a small stream feeding into the Tyne, the area was filled with kilns for the making of lime, used in building. The Baltic Flour Mill has been converted into a visual arts centre, with artist's studios, workshops, galleries, and a cinema.

● Harrogate is famous for being a spa town, with its Royal Baths Assembly Rooms, where it is still possible to take a Turkish bath in Victorian surroundings.

● Holy Island (once known as Lindisfarne) was a centre of early Christianity in the Kingdom of Northumbria and in Britain as a whole. The island is reached by a causeway which is submerged at high tide.

The rejuvenation of the Northeast is complete with the opening of the new Gateshead Millennium Bridge (below). Linking Gateshead to Newcastle, the pedestrian bridge is a marvel of design and technology. You can watch it move live by webcam at www.tynebridgewebcam.com or better still, visit and see it for real!

Durham's cathedral (left) is one of the great buildings of Britain. This view is from the River Wear, which forms a horseshoe around the city.

● Historically, York was England's second city for centuries, until the Industrial Revolution created sudden growth in the likes of Birmingham and Manchester. It is famous for its Minster, medieval alleys, racecourse and excellent museums.

Britain's largest landmark sculpture, the Angel of the North (right), rises from the pit head baths site of the former Teams Colliery. Made from steel, the sculpture stands 20m (65ft), overlooking the A1. Its 54m (175ft) wing span is almost as big as a jumbo jet's. Commissioned by Gateshead Council, the Angel of the North was created by internationally renowned sculptor Antony Gormley.

● The Royal Armouries in Leeds was purpose-built to house the arms and armour collection from the Tower of London. Adult admission is £4.90, but free for children.

● Berwick-upon-Tweed changed hands between the Scots and English many times during the middle ages. A walk along the town's ramparts gives fine views out to sea in this historic border town.

● The National Museum of Photography, Film and Television in Bradford has free admission. Inside is Britain's largest cinema screen (an IMAX screen over 50 feet wide). Admission to the IMAX theatre is £5.80 for adults.

● Saltaire, just outside Bradford is a millworkers' village specially constructed in the 19th century to give workers a better life.

Monument Mall, Newcastle (right): a tasteful blend of the old and the new.

Durham market place (above) was the commercial heart of the ancient city.

Accommodation index

Hotels and Guest Accommodation are indexed by their order of appearance within this region, not by the page. To locate an establishment, note the number to the right of the listing and then find it on the establishment's name bar, as shown here

> 37 The Turning Mill Hotel

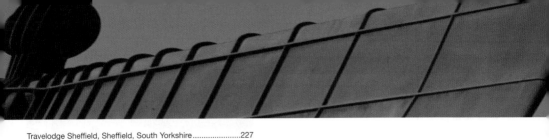

Alnwick, Northumberland

1 Katerina's Guest House

Sun Buildings, High Street, Rothbury,
Northumberland, NE65 7TQ
Tel: 01669 620691
Email: cath@katerinasguesthouse.co.uk
Web: www.katerinasguesthouse.co.uk

Charming no-smoking guesthouse in pretty
Rothbury village. Ideal centre for touring lovely
Northumberland hills, National Park, coastline,
Hadrian's Wall, Scottish Borders. Beautiful
rooms, all ensuite, with four-poster beds.
3 bedrs SB £30 DB £46 HBS £40.75
HBD £33.75 D £10.50 CC: None accepted

How to get there: From south use A1 A597 and
B6344, from Scotland use A587 and B6341.
Guest house is beyond shops, up the main street.

2 Hawkhill Farmhouse

Lesbury, Alnwick, Northumberland, NE66 3PG
Tel: 01665 830380 Fax: 01665 830093
Children minimum age: 10
Closed Christmas
3 bedrs DB £48 CC: None accepted

How to get there: Leave A1 for Alnwick. Yake
A1068 Alnmouth. Two miles second farm turn
right up tree-lined drive. You've arrived.

Ampleforth, North Yorkshire

3 Shallowdale House
Little Gem

West End, Ampleforth,
North Yorkshire, YO62 4DY
Tel: 01439 788325 Fax: 01439 788885
Email: stay@shallowdalehouse.demon.co.uk
Web: www.shallowdalehouse.demon.co.uk
Children minimum age: 12
Closed Christmas to New Year

Situated in glorious countryside, this stylish
country house boasts stunning views from every
room. A delightful place to stay, with delicious
freshly prepared food, tranquil atmosphere and
caring, attentive service.
3 bedrs SB £44 DB £64 HBS £66.50 HBD £55
D £22.50 CC: MC Vi Delt

How to get there: At the west end of
Ampleforth, on the turning to Hambleton.

Austwick, North Yorkshire

4 Austwick Country House Hotel

Austwick, Settle, North Yorkshire, LA2 8BY
Tel: 01524 251224 Fax: 01524 251796
Email: austwickh@cs.com

The Yorkshire Dales' best kept secret. A
Georgian Country House Hotel dating from
1750. Furnished with English and Oriental
Antiques. RAC award-winning restaurant. 12
exclusive ensuite bedrooms.
12 bedrs
CC: MC Vi Swi

How to get there: Follow A65 from Skipton to
Kendal. Three miles past Settle turn right at the
Cross Street Pub into the National Park. 3/4 mile
over bridge, hotel is on the left.

Bamburgh, Northumberland

5 Waren House Hotel

★★★

Waren Mill, Belford, Northumberland, NE70 7EE
Tel: 01668 214581 Fax: 01668 214484
Email: enquiries@warenhousehotel.co.uk
Web: www.warenhousehotel.co.uk
Children minimum age: 14

Traditional Country House Hotel in 6 acres
grounds on edge of Budle Bay and 2 miles from
Bamburgh Castle. Superb accommodation,
excellent food extensive reasonably price wine list.
10 bedrs SB £90 DB £120 HBS £100 HBD £78
B £15.50 D £18.45
CC: MC Vi Am DC Swi Delt JCB

How to get there: 14 miles south of Berwick-
upon-Tweed. Take B1342, off the A1, to Waren
Mill. Hotel on southwest corner of Bodle Bay.

6 Lord Crewe Arms

★★

Front Street, Bamburgh,
Northumberland, NE69 7BL
Tel: 01668 214243 Fax: 01668 214273
Email: lca@tinyonline.co.uk
Web: www.lordcrewe.com
Children minimum age: 5
Closed 1 December to 1 March
18 bedrs SB £40 DB £79 L £3.95 D £18
CC: MC Vi Swi Delt JCB

Barnard Castle, County Durham

7 Old Well Inn

♦♦♦

21 The Bank, Barnard Castle,
County Durham, DL12 8PH
Tel: 01833 690130 Fax: 01833 690140
Email: reservations@oldwellinn.co.uk
Web: www.oldwellinn.co.uk
10 bedrs SB £48 DB £60 B £5 L £3 D £8
CC: MC Vi Am Swi Delt

How to get there: Situated in the centre of
Barnard Castle below the Market Cross, in the
Antique Quarter.

Barnsley, South Yorkshire

8 Travelodge Barnsley

Travel Accommodation
A682/A635/A633, School Street, Stairfoot,
Barnsley, Yorkshire, S70 3PT
Tel: 08700 850 950
Web: www.travelodge.co.uk
32 bedrs B £4.25 CC: MC Vi Am DC Swi Delt

9 Tankersley Manor

♣

Church Lane, Tankersley, Barnsley,
South Yorkshire, S75 3DQ
Tel: 01226 744700 Fax: 01226 744505

Beadnell, Northumberland

10 Low Dover Bed & Breakfast

♦♦♦♦

Low Dover, Harbour Road, Beadnell,
Northumberland, NE67 5BJ
Tel: 01665 720291 Fax: 01665 720291
Email: kathandbob@lowdover.co.uk
Web: www.lowdover.co.uk
Children minimum age: 12

Virtually encompassed by the sea, superior
beachside accommodation. Ground floor suites,
each with private lounge and patio door
entrance. Enjoy breakfast with panoramic sea
views. Beautiful garden. Beach 50 metres. Also
self-catering. Superb webite.
2 bedrs DB £54 CC: MC Vi Swi Delt

How to get there: Follow signposts and go to
Beadnell Harbour. Low Dover is the last house
on the right, adjacent to the beach.

Northeast

Bedale, North Yorkshire

11 Elmfield Country House

◆◆◆◆◆

Arrathorne, Bedale, North Yorkshire, DL8 1NE
Tel: 01677 450558 Fax: 01677 450557
Email: stay@elmfieldhouse.freeserve.co.uk
Web: www.countryhouseyorkshire.co.uk
9 bedrs SB £35 DB £50 HBS £47 HBD £37 D £12
CC: MC Vi Swi Delt

How to get there: From A1, A684 into Bedale.
Follow A684 towards Leyburn after village of
Patrick Brompton. Right at crossroads towards
Richmond. Elmfield is 1½ miles on right.

12 Little Holtby

◆◆◆◆

Little Holtby, Leeming Bar, Northallerton,
North Yorkshire, DL7 9LH
Tel: 01609 748762 Fax: 01609 748822
Email: littleholtby@yahoo.co.uk
Web: www.littleholtby.co.uk
3 bedrs SB £30 DB £50 HBS £42.50 HBD £37.50
D £12.50 CC: None accepted

How to get there: 50 yards from A1 northbound, 2
miles from junction of A684 Northallerton/Bedale.

The
Blue Bell
Hotel

Perfectly situated between Northumberland's
magnificent coastline and superb National
Parks, the Hotel offers delightful ensuite
bedrooms, excellent cuisine in three individual
restaurants and merit awards for comfort,
hospitality and food. Short breaks for golf,
birdwatching and walking are available all year
round.

Market Place, Belford, NE70 7NE
Tel: 01668 213543   Fax: 01668 213787
Email: bluebell@gloabalnet.co.uk
Website: www.bluebellhotel.com

13 Southfield

◆◆◆

96 South End, Bedale, North Yorkshire, DL8 2DS
Tel: 01677 423510
4 bedrs SB £22 DB £44 CC: None accepted

How to get there: Take A1 to Bedale. Turn left at
'White Bear'. Hotel 400 yards on right, with
privet hedge and white stone front.

Belford, Northumberland

14 Blue Bell Hotel

★★★★

Market Square, Belford,
Northumberland, NE70 7NE
Tel: 01668 213543 Fax: 01668 213787
Email: bluebell@globalnet.co.uk
Web: www.bluebellhotel.com
17 bedrs SB £39 DB £78 HBS £49 HBD £49
B £7 L £7 D £23 CC: MC Vi Am Swi Delt

See advert below left

Bellingham, Northumberland

15 Riverdale Hall Hotel

★★★

Bellingham, Northumberland, NE48 2JT
Tel: 01434 220254 Fax: 01434 220457
Email: iben@riverdalehall.demon.co.uk
Web: www.riverdalehall.demon.co.uk

A stone-built 19th-century mansion with a
modern wing set in five acres of grounds
alongside the North Tyne River.
20 bedrs SB £48 DB £84 HBS £67 HBD £61
B £9.95 L £10.95 D £19.95
CC: MC Vi Am DC Swi Delt

How to get there: Turn off B6320 after bridge
onto C200. Hotel is 150 yards on left.

Berwick-upon-Tweed, Northumberland

16 Kings Arms Hotel

★★★

Hide Hill, Berwick-upon-Tweed,
Northumberland, TD15 1EJ
Tel: 01289 307454 Fax: 01289 308867
Email: kingsarmshotel@virgin.co.uk
Web: www.kings-arms-hotel.com
36 bedrs SB £69.50 DB £89.50 HBS £84.50
HBD £59.75 B £8.50 L £6.50 D £12.50
CC: MC Vi Am DC Swi

How to get there: Leave A1 from north or south
into town centre, then right at Guildhall and first
right into Hyde Hill.

17 Queen's Head Hotel

★

Sandgate, Berwick-upon-Tweed,
Northumberland, TD15 1EP
Tel: 01289 307852 Fax: 01289 307858
6 bedrs SB £35 DB £60 HBS £50 HBD £45
B £6.50 L £9.50 D £15
CC: MC Vi Swi

How to get there: Into town centre pass by town
hall next door to cinema at the bottom of the hill.

18 Number 40 Ravensdowne

◆◆◆◆

40 Ravensdowne, Berwick-upon-Tweed,
Northumberland, TD15 1DQ
Tel: 01289 306992 Fax: 01289 331606
Email: petedot@dmuckle.freeserve.co.uk
Web: www.secretkingdom.com/40/
ravensdowne.html
Closed Christmas, New Year
3 bedrs DB £40
CC: None accepted

How to get there: Down main street past Town
Hall clock into Woolmarket; turn left, and the
house is on the right.

One click does it all

For the latest special offers and
online booking, plus detailed
information on over 3,000
RAC inspected properties,
visit www.rac.co.uk/hotels

Beverley, Yorkshire

19 Tickton Grange

★★★★

Tickton, Beverley, Yorkshire, HU17 9SH
Tel: 01964 543666 Fax: 01964 542556
Email: maggy@tickton-grange.demon.co.uk
Web: www.ticktongrange.co.uk
17 bedrs SB £73.50 DB £92 B £8.50 L £15.95
D £25 CC: MC Vi Am DC Swi Delt

How to get there: Three miles from Beverley on
the A1035.

20 Manor House

★★★

Northlands, Walkington, Beverley, HU17 8RT
Tel: 01482 881645 Fax: 01482 866501
Email: derek@the-manor-house.co.uk
Web: www.the-manor-house.co.uk
Children minimum age: 12
7 bedrs SB £78.50 DB £97 B £5.50 D £15
CC: MC Vi Swi Delt

How to get there: Situated on the Newbald
Road between Walkington and Bishop Burton,
two miles west of Beverley.

Northeast

21 Eastgate Guest House

7 Eastgate, Beverley, HU17 0DR
Tel: 01482 868464 Fax: 01482 871899
16 bedrs SB £25 DB £38
CC: None accepted

How to get there: Very close to train and bus stations, within sight of Beverley Minster.
See advert on previous page

Bingley, West Yorkshire

22 Five Rise Locks Hotel and Restaurant

Beck Lane, off Park Road, Bingley,
West Yorkshire, BD16 4DD
Tel: 01274 565296 Fax: 01274 568828
Email: info@five-rise-locks.co.uk
Web: www.five-rise-locks.co.uk

Formerly a wealthy Victorian mill owner's house, now in the rural setting of the canal conservation area. Each bedroom is individually designed and tastefully furnished. Enjoy freshly-prepared food complemented by an imaginative wine list in elegant, yet relaxing surroundings.
9 bedrs SB £52 DB £62
B £7.50 L £10 D £10
CC: MC Vi Swi Delt JCB

How to get there: From Bingley, turn onto Park Road. Continue for ¼ of a mile. At crossroads sign turn left. Hotel on left.

Birtley, County Durham

23 Travelodge Washington (North)

Travel Accommodation
A1, Portobello, Birtley, County Durham, DH3 2SJ
Tel: 08700 850 950
Web: www.travelodge.co.uk
31 bedrs B £4.25 CC: MC Vi Am DC Swi Delt

24 Travelodge Washington (South)

Travel Accommodation
A1, Portobello, Birtley , County Durham, DH3 2SJ
Tel: 08700 850 950
Web: www.travelodge.co.uk
36 bedrs B £4.25
CC: MC Vi Am DC Swi Delt

Bishop Auckland, Co. Durham

25 Greenhead Country House Hotel

Fir Tree, Crook, Bishop Auckland, Co. Durham,
DL15 8BL
Tel: 01388 763143 Fax: 01388 763143
Email: info@thegreenheadhotel.co.uk
Web: www.thegreenheadhotel.co.uk
Children minimum age: 13

The Birbecks offer clean, comfortable accommodation set in acres of open countryside. Great hospitality ensuring guests' comfort. "Richly deserves the Warm Wellcome and Sparkling Diamond awards' — RAC report, 2000.
7 bedrs SB £42 DB £55
CC: MC Vi Am Swi Delt

How to get there: A1 to A68 into Fir Tree. Turn right at pub. Hotel 500 yards on the left.

26 Helme Park Hall Hotel

★★★

Near Fir Tree, Bishop Auckland,
Co Durham, DL13 4NW
Tel: 01388 730970 Fax: 01388 731799
Email: post@johnwheeler.co.uk
12 bedrs SB £46 DB £75 HBS £58.95
HBD £50.45 B £4.25 L £3.95 D £12.95
CC: MC Vi Am Swi Delt JCB

How to get there: Located on the A68 1½ miles
north of the intersection with the A689.
See advert on following page

Blanchland, Northumberland

27 Lord Crewe Arms Hotel

★★ ®

Consett, Blanchland, Northumberland, DH8 9SP
Tel: 01434 675251 Fax: 01434 675337

Bolton Abbey, North Yorkshire

28 Devonshire Arms
Blue Ribbon Winner

★★★★ ® ® ® ®
Bolton Abbey, near Skipton,
North Yorkshire, BD23 6AJ
Tel: 01756 718111 Fax: 01756 710564
Email: sales@thedevonshirearms.co.uk
Web: www.thedevonshirearms.co.uk

Owned by the Duke and Duchess of Devonshire,
The Devonshire Arms Country House Hotel offers
individually-designed bedrooms, award-winning
restaurants and a fully-equipped leisure club, all
in beautiful surroundings
41 bedrs SB £135 DB £185 HBD £117.50
L £10 D £45

CC: MC Vi Am DC Swi

How to get there: The Devonshire Arms is
situated five miles east of Skipton on the B6160,
just 250 yards north of the junction with the A59.

Boroughbridge, North Yorkshire

29 Crown Hotel

★★★★ ®
Horsefair, Boroughbridge,
North Yorkshire, YO51 9LB
Tel: 01423 322328 Fax: 01423 324512
Email: sales@crownboroughbridge.co.uk
Web: www.crownboroughbridge.co.uk

Former coaching inn with 37 bedrooms, all ensuite. Leisure facilities which include pool, gym
and beauty therapist. Large secure private car
park. Excellent conference facilities, bars and
restaurant.
37 bedrs
CC: MC Vi Am DC Swi Delt

How to get there: Leave A1(M) at Junction 48
and take road into Boroughbridge. Follow signs
into town; hotel is located on the T-junction. Car
park is at rear.

Northeast

HELME PARK HALL HOTEL
Country House & Restaurant

Nr. Fir Tree, Bishop Auckland,
Co. Durham DL13 4NW
Telephone: 01388 730970
Fax: 01388 731799

RAC
★★★

A Country House Hotel with a reputation for plentiful, quality food with service and accommodation of a high standard following the recent refurbishment by the new owners. Standing in a unique 2-acre setting with tremendous views, the hotel offers a tranquil break for both tourists and business people. The hotel is easily accessible and is close to many of County Durham's attractions, including Durham City. **WELL WORTH A VISIT.**

---

30 Rose Manor

★★★

Horsefair, Boroughbridge,
North Yorkshire, YO51 9LL
Tel: 01423 322245 Fax: 01423 324920
Email: rosemanorhotel@ukf.net
Web: www.rosemanorhotel.co.uk

Elegant country house hotel set in secluded grounds with large private car park. Within one mile of Boroughbridge exit on A1(M). Excellent conference and function facilities.
20 bedrs SB £79.50 DB £110
B £6.95 L £10.75 D £18 CC: MC Vi Am Swi Delt
How to get there: Within one mile of exit 48 on A1(M) Boroughbridge.

31 The Crown Inn

Roecliffe, Boroughbridge,
North Yorkshire, YO51 9LY
Tel: 01423 322578 Fax: 01423 324060
9 bedrs SB £35 DB £65 B £5 L £2.95 D £2.95
CC: MC Vi Swi Delt
How to get there: A1(M) J48, follow signs for Bar Lane and Roecliffe. The Crown is on the right at the end of the village.

Bradford, West Yorkshire

32 Hanover International Bradford

★★★★

Mayo Avenue, off Rooley Lane, Bradford,
West Yorkshire, BD5 8HZ
Tel: 01274 406606 Fax: 01274 406600
Email: sales@cedar-court.com
Web: www.hanover-international.com

131 bedrs SB £114.75 DB £124.50 HBS £134.25
HBD £81.75 B £7.50 L £10 D £19.50
CC: MC Vi Am DC

How to get there: Leave M62 at Junction 26.
Take M606 to Bradford. Take third exit A6177
Mayo Avenue off roundabout at end of M606.
Take first sharp right.

33 Marriott Hollins Hall Hotel
    & Country Club

★★★★

Hollins Hill, Baildon, Shipley, near Bradford,
West Yorkshire, BD17 7QW
Tel: 01274 530053 Fax: 01274 530187
Email: frontdesk.hollinshall@marriotthotels.co.uk
Web: www.marriotthotels.com/lbags
122 bedrs DB £119 HBD £72
CC: MC Vi Am DC Swi Delt JCB

Keep on moving

Sign up now for one month's free
trial of RAC Route Minder for
personalised traffic information.
Visit www.rac.co.uk/routeminder

34 Courtyard by Marriott Leeds/Bradford

★★★

The Pastures, Tong Lane, Bradford,
West Yorkshire, BD4 0RP
Tel: 0113 2854646
Web: www.marriotthotels.co.uk
53 bedrs SB £50 DB £70 HBS £66 HBD £52
B £10.95 L £12.50 D £18
CC: MC Vi Am DC Swi Delt

How to get there: Exit J27 M62, A650 towards
Bradford. At Save petrol station roundabout,
take third exit to Drighlington; first left is Tong
Lane.

35 Midland Hotel

★★★

Forster Square, Bradford,
West Yorkshire, BD1 4HU
Tel: 01274 735735 Fax: 01274 720003
Email: info@midland-hotel-bradford.com
90 bedrs CC: MC Vi Am DC Swi Delt

How to get there: Head towards Bradford city
centre, following signs for Forster Square
station. Hotel located 50 yards from station.

36 Novotel Bradford

★★★

Merrydale Road, Bradford, BD4 6SA
Tel: 01274 683683 Fax: 01274 651342
Email: h0510@accor-hotels.com
Web: www.novotel.com
127 bedrs SB £59.50 DB £68 HBS £73
HBD £87.10 B £5.50 L £10.50 D £10.50
CC: MC Vi Am DC Swi Delt

How to get there: Junction 26 M62, then Junction
2 M606. Right off sliproad and next right.

37 Quality Hotel Bradford

★★★

Bridge Street, Bradford, BD1 1JX
Tel: 01274 728706 Fax: 01274 736358
Email: admin@gb654.u-net.com
Web: www.choicehotels.com
57 bedrs SB £90.75 DB £105.75 HBS £107.25
HBD £61.13 B £10.75 D £16.50
CC: MC Vi Am DC Swi Delt

How to get there: From all directions, head for
city centre and Bradford Interchange. Hotel is
situated directly opposite the interchange.

Northeast

38 Travelodge Bradford

Travel Accommodation
1 Midpoint, Dick Lane, Pudsey, Bradford,
West Yorkshire, BD3 8QD
Tel: 08700 850 950
Web: www.travelodge.co.uk
48 bedrs B £4.25
CC: MC Vi Am DC Swi Delt

Bridlington, East Yorkshire

39 Expanse Hotel

★★★
North Marine Drive, Bridlington, YO15 2LS
Tel: 01262 675347 Fax: 01262 604928
Email: expanse@brid.demon.co.uk
Web: www.expanse.co.uk
48 bedrs
CC: MC Vi Am Swi Delt

40 New Revelstoke Hotel

★★★
1–3 Flamborough Road, Bridlington, YO15 2HU
Tel: 01262 672362 Fax: 01262 672362
Email: info@revelstokehotel.co.uk
Web: www.revelstokehotel.co.uk
25 bedrs SB £50 DB £39
HBS £62 HBD £52.50
B £3.95 L £9 D £12
CC: MC Vi Am DC Swi Delt JCB
How to get there: From the A1 or M1 motorway
to Howden, A614 to Bridlington. From the North
A165 to Bridlington. From Humberside airport
A15 to Humberside then take A165 to
Bridlington.

41 Marina Guest House

♦♦♦
8 Summerfield Road, Bridlington,
East Yorkshire, YO15 3LF
Tel: 01262 677138
7 bedrs SB £22.50 DB £35
HBS £29 HBD £24 B £17.50 D £24
CC: None accepted

How to get there: Second right along Marine
Drive after Spa theatre complex on the south
side of town.

42 The Ivanhoe Hotel

♦♦♦
63 Cardigan Road, Bridlington,
East Yorkshire, YO15 3JS
Tel: 01262 675983

43 Park View Hotel

♦♦
9–11 Tennyson Avenue, Bridlington,
East Yorkshire, YO15 2EU
Tel: 01262 672140 Fax: 01262 672140
16 bedrs SB £17 DB £34 HBS £23 HBD £23
CC: None accepted

Burnsall, North Yorkshire

44 Red Lion Inn

★★ ♙♙
By The Bridge, Burnsall,
North Yorkshire, BD23 6BU
Tel: 01756 720204 Fax: 01756 720292
Email: redlion@daelnet.co.uk
Web: www.redlion.co.uk
11 bedrs
CC: MC Vi Am DC Swi Delt

How to get there: From A59 Harrogate/Skipton
road at Bolton Abbey, take B6160. Head for
Burnsall/Grassington. Hotel is five miles down
this road.

Cleethorpes, Lincolnshire

45 Kingsway Hotel

★★★
Kingsway, Cleethorpes,
N.E.Lincolnshire, DN35 0AE
Tel: 01472 601122 Fax: 01472 601381
Web: www.kingsway-hotel.com
Children minimum age: 5
Closed Christmas
50 bedrs SB £68 DB £84 B £8 L £12.75 D £14.95
CC: MC Vi Am DC Swi Delt

46 Holmhirst Hotel

◆ ◆ ◆

3 Alexandra Road, Cleethorpes,
Lincolnshire, DN35 8LQ
Tel: 01472 692656 Fax: 01472 692656
Email: holmhirst@aol.com
Children minimum age: 3
8 bedrs
CC: MC Vi

How to get there: From M1, take M18, M180,
A180. Follow signs to Cleethorpes. Holmhirst
Hotel on the seafront near to pier gardens.

47 Mallow View

◆ ◆

9/11 Albert Road, Cleethorpes,
Lincolnshire, DN35 8LX
Tel: 01472 691297 Fax: 01472 691297
15 bedrs SB £15 DB £30
CC: None accepted

How to get there: Just off sea front, centre.

Cornhill-on-Tweed, Northumberland

48 Collingwood Arms Hotel

★ ★
Cornhill-on-Tweed,
Northumberland, TD12 4UH
Tel: 01890 882424 Fax: 01890 883644

Darlington, County Durham

49 Clow Beck House

Little Gem

◆ ◆ ◆ ◆ ◆
Monk End Farm, Croft-on-Tees, Darlington,
County Durham, DL2 2SW
Tel: 01325 721075 Fax: 01325 720419
Email: david@clowbeckhouse.co.uk
Web: www.clowbeckhouse.co.uk
Closed Christmas to New Year
13 bedrs SB £47.50 DB £80 D £9.00
CC: MC Vi Am Swi Delt

How to get there: Follow brown tourist signs
that are on all roads leading to Croft-on-Tees.

Doncaster, South Yorkshire

50 Regent Hotel

★ ★ ★
Regent Square, Doncaster, South Yorkshire,
DN1 2DS
Tel: 01302 364180 Fax: 01302 322331
Email: admin@theregenthotel.co.uk
Web: www.theregenthotel.co.uk

A charming Victorian building overlooking a
secluded Regency park. The hotel is ideally
situated within easy reach of Doncaster's
vibrant town centre and only minutes away from
the historic racecourse.
50 bedrs SB £75 DB £85 B £7.50 L £4.50
D £12.50 CC: MC Vi Am DC Swi Delt

How to get there: Follow brown signs to
racecourse. Turn into Bennetthorpe Road. After
1/2 mile, hotel is on right.

51 Wentbridge House Hotel

★ ★ ★
Wentbridge, near Pontefract,
West Yorkshire, WF8 3JJ
Tel: 01977 620444 Fax: 01977 620148
Email: info@wentbridgehouse.co.uk
Web: www.wentbridgehouse.co.uk

Beautiful and historic Georgian mansion built in
1700 and set in 20 acres of the Went valley.
Individually furnished bedrooms, superb
restaurants, award-winning food and fine wines.
18 bedrs SB £75 DB £100 B £7.50 L £12.50
D £25 CC: MC Vi Am DC Swi Delt
How to get there: Wentbridge House is 1/2 mile off
A1 and 4 miles south of the A1/A162 interchange.

Northeast

52 Campanile

Travel Accommodation
Bawtry Road, Doncaster Leisure Park,
South Yorkshire, DN4 7PD
Tel: 01302 370770 Fax: 01302 370813

Typical Campanile bistro

A lodge-style hotel situated close to the town
centre. Ideal for all people, from business and
leisure to conferences. Restaurant open to non-
residents.
50 bedrs SB £45.90 DB £51.85 HBS £52
HBD £34 B £5.95 L £2.95 D £6.50
CC: MC Vi Am DC Swi Delt
How to get there: Leave the M18 at Junction 3.
Follow tourist signs for Racecourse and Leisure
Park. Hotel is situated behind the Dome Leisure
Park.

53 Travelodge Doncaster

Travel Accommodation
A1, Great North Road, Carcroft, Doncaster,
South Yorks, DN6 8LR
Tel: 08700 850 950
Web: www.travelodge.co.uk
40 bedrs B £4.25
CC: MC Vi Am DC Swi Delt

54 Travelodge Doncaster

Travel Accommodation
M18 J5, Hatfield, Doncaster,
West Yorkshire, DN8 5GS
Tel: 08700 850 950
Web: www.travelodge.co.uk
40 bedrs B £4.25
CC: MC Vi Am DC Swi Delt

55 Canda Lodge

Hampole Balk Lane, Skellow, Doncaster,
South Yorkshire, DN6 8LF
Tel: 01302 724028 Fax: 01302 727999
4 bedrs SB £35 DB £40 CC: MC Vi Delt
How to get there: On A1 south take Skellow
exit, or northbound take Pontefract exit (A639),
then take A1 south.

Driffield, East Yorkshire

56 White Horse Inn

Main Street, Hutton Cranswick, Driffield,
East Yorkshire, YO25 9QN
Tel: 01377 270383/136 Fax: 01377 270383

An inn situated by the village pond and green,
with proprietor Clive Tomlinson offering you a
warm and friendly welcome. An ideal base for
touring the Yorkshire Wolds.
8 bedrs SB £29.50 DB £45 L £5 D £5
CC: MC Vi Am Delt
How to get there: Off M62 at Howden, A614 into
Driffield. A164 towards Beverley and 3 miles south
of Driffield left into Hutton Cranswick. Hotel 500
yards down main street on left, opposite green.

57 Blacksmiths Country Cottage
Guest House

Driffield Road, Kilham, near Driffield,
East Yorkshire, YO25 4SN
Tel: 01262 420624
Email: maxatblacksmiths@ukonline.co.uk
Web: www.blacksmiths-cottage.co.uk
Closed October to April
4 bedrs SB £34 DB £48 HBS £44 HBD £34
CC: None accepted
How to get there: Off the A164 Driffield to
Bridlington road.

Durham, Co. Durham

58 Durham Marriott Hotel, Royal County

★★★★ ® ®
Old Elvet, Durham, County Durham, DH1 3JN
Tel: 0191 386 6821 Fax: 0191 386 7238
Email: durhamroyalmarriott@whitbread.com
Web: www.marriotthotels.com/xvudm
139 bedrs SB £105 DB £125 B £13 L £7.50
D £18.95 CC: MC Vi Am DC Swi Delt
⚓ 🅖 ⅏ 📠 💢 🅦 ⊘ 🖰 🖳 ☎ 📞 🅿 🔥 ♨ 🕯 ♀ ♣ ⛲
🏌 SPA ᵞ 🎴
How to get there: Off A1(M) onto A690 to
Durham. Straight over first roundabout, at
second turn left. At traffic lights turn left and
hotel is on left.

59 Swallow Eden Arms Hotel

★★★ ®
Rushyford, County Durham, DL17 0LL
Tel: 01388 720541 Fax: 01388 721871
Email: edenarms.swallow@whitbread.com
Web: www.swallow-hotels.co.uk
45 bedrs SB £85 DB £115.00 HBS £103.95
HBD £70 D £20.00 CC: MC Vi Am DC Swi Delt
⚓ 📠 ⊘ 🖰 🖳 ☎ 📞 🅿 🔥 ♨ 🕯 ⛲ 🏌 SPA ᵞ 🎴
How to get there: Located two miles from
A1(M), leaving at J60 onto A689 to Bishop
Auckland.

60 Swallow Three Tuns Hotel

★★★★ ® ®
New Elvet, County Durham, DH1 3AQ
Tel: 0191 375 1504 Fax: 0191 384 2093
Email: threetuns.reservations@btinternet.com
Web: www.swallow-hotels.com
50 bedrs SB £102 DB £120 B £9.95 L £7.95
D £19.50 CC: MC Vi Am DC Swi Delt
💢 🅦 ⊘ 🖰 🖳 ☎ 📞 🅿 🔥 ♨ 🕯 ♀ ⛲ 🏌

61 Hallgarth Manor Hotel

★★
Pittington, Durham, County Durham, DH6 1AB
Tel: 0191 372 1188 Fax: 0191 372 1249
Email: sales@hallgarthmanorhotel.com
Web: www.hallgarthmanorhotel.com
23 bedrs B £6 L £13.50 D £17.95
CC: MC Vi Am DC Swi Delt
💢 🅦 ⊘ 🖰 🖳 ☎ 🅿 🔥 ♨ 🕯 ♀ ⛲ 🏌
How to get there: A1(M) Junction 62, A690
Sunderland. After ¹/₂ mile turn right. ¹/₂ mile to
crossroads — straight over. After one mile turn
left.
See advert right

62 Travelodge Durham

Station Lane, Gilesgate, Durham
Tel: 08700 850 950
Web: www.travelodge.co.uk
58 bedrs B £4.25
CC: MC Vi Am DC Swi Delt
🐕 ⊘ 🖳 ⛲

63 Ramside Hall Hotel

★★★
Carrville, Durham, County Durham, DH1 1TD
Tel: 0191 386 5282 Fax: 0191 386 0399
80 bedrs
CC: MC Vi Am DC Swi Delt
⚓ 🅖 ⅏ 📠 💢 🅦 ⊘ 🖳 ☎ 🅿 🔥 🕯 ♀ ⛲ 🏌 ⚗
How to get there: 400 yards from the A1M/
A690 Junction towards Sunderland. Turn right
just after railway bridge.

Making a booking?

Don't forget to mention RAC
Hotels and Bed & Breakfast 2002.

Northeast

Epworth, Humberside

64 Red Lion Hotel

★★
Market Place, Epworth, Humberside, DN9 1EU
Tel: 01427 872208 Fax: 01427 874330

Filey, North Yorkshire

65 Saxdale House

◆◆◆◆
Bartindale Road, Hunmanby,
North Yorkshire, YO14 0JD
Tel: 01723 892346 Fax: 01723 892400
Email: saxdale.house@virgin.net
Web: www.saxdale.co.uk
3 bedrs DB £44 HBD £34
CC: None accepted
How to get there: Exit A64 at Staxton, take
A1039 to Filey. Hunmanby first right after 30
mph sign; over crossroads, third property on the
right.

66 Seafield Hotel

◆◆◆
9-11 Rutland Street, Filey,
North Yorkshire, YO14 9JA
Tel: 01723 513715
14 bedrs SB £20 DB £40
HBS £26 HBD £26
B £4 D £6
CC: MC Vi Delt
How to get there: Follow signpost to Filey from
A64. At crossroads in town centre turn right.
Take second left into Rutland Street.

Gateshead, Tyne & Wear

67 Travelodge Newcastle (East)

Travel Accommodation
A194, Whitemare Pool, Wardley, Gateshead,
Tyne & Wear, NE10 8YB
Tel: 08700 850 950
Web: www.travelodge.co.uk
71 bedrs B £4.25
CC: MC Vi Am DC Swi Delt

Goathland, North Yorkshire

68 Inn on the Moor

★★
Goathland, North Yorkshire, YO22 5LZ
Tel: 01947 896296 Fax: 01947 896484
Email: innonthemoor@btconnect.com
Web: www.innonthemoor.com
Closed 24/12/00 to 2/1/01
25 bedrs
CC: MC Vi Am DC Swi Delt
How to get there: Situated off the main Whitby-
Pickering road (A169), 14 miles from Pickering
and nine miles from Whitby.

Goole, Humberside

69 Clifton

★★
155 Boothferry Road, Goole,
Humberside, DN14 6AL
Tel: 01405 761336 Fax: 01405 762350
Email: cliftonhotel@telinco.co.uk
Web: www.cliftonhotel.cwc.net
Closed Christmas
9 bedrs SB £44 DB £52 B £3.95 D £7.95
CC: MC Vi Am DC Swi Delt
How to get there: Leave M62 at Junction 36 and
follow Goole Town Centre signs. At second
traffic lights, turn right into Boothferry Road.
Hotel is 500 yards on left.

Grimsby, Lincolnshire

70 Travelodge Grimsby

Travel Accommodation
A180
Tel: 08700 850 950
Web: www.travelodge.co.uk
Opens September 2002
40 bedrs B £4.25
CC: MC Vi Am DC Swi Delt

Plan your route

Visit www.rac.co.uk for RAC's
interactive route planner, including
up to the minute traffic reports.

Halifax, West Yorkshire

71 The Rock Inn Hotel

★★★

Holywell Green, Halifax, West Yorkshire, HX4 9BS
Tel: 01422 379721 Fax: 01422 379110
Email: reservations@rockinnhotel.com
Web: www.rockinnhotel.com
30 bedrs SB £67 DB £70 B £8.95 L £6 D £15
CC: MC Vi Am DC Swi Delt

How to get there: 1½ miles from Junction 24 of M62 towards Blackley.

72 Travelodge Halifax

Travel Accommodation
Dean Clough Gate 9, Halifax,
West Yorkshire, HX3 5AX
Tel: 08700 850 950
Web: www.travelodge.co.uk
52 bedrs B £4.25
CC: MC Vi Am DC Swi Delt

73 Shibden Mill Inn

◆◆◆◆

Shibden Mill Fold, Shibden, Halifax,
West Yorkshire, HX3 7UL
Tel: 01422 365840 Fax: 01422 362971
Email: shibdenmillinn@zoom.co.uk
Web: www.shibdenmillinn.com

Shibden Mill Inn nestles in the fold of the Shibden valley overlooking Red Beck. The 17th century inn is steeped in history and has been sympathetically renovated by present owners.
12 bedrs SB £60 DB £72
CC: MC Vi Swi Delt

How to get there: Leave M62 at junction 26, follow A58 Halifax for 5½ miles, turn left onto Kell Lane, follow Shibden Mill Inn signs.

74 The Fleece Inn

◆◆◆

Ripponden Bank, Barkisland, Halifax,
West Yorkshire, HX4 0DJ
Tel: 01422 822598 Fax: 01422 822598
Children minimum age: 5
4 bedrs SB £35 DB £50 B £5 L £3 D £5
CC: MC Vi Swi

How to get there: M62 J22, A672 to Halifax. At traffic lights in Ripponden take first right onto B6113 to Elland.

Harrogate, North Yorkshire

75 Cedar Court Hotel

★★★★ ℞

Queen Building, Park Parade, Harrogate,
North Yorkshire, HG1 5AH
Tel: 01423 858585 Fax: 01423 504950
Email: cedarcourt@bestwestern.co.uk
Web: www.cedarcourthotels.co.uk

The Cedar Court, Harrogate's first hotel, dating back to 1671, and sympathetically restored after a multi-million pound investment. It offers all the modern facilities you would expect, whilst retaining the charm and hospitality of a bygone era.
100 bedrs SB £60 DB £80 HBS £65 HBD £45 B £9.95 L £14.50 D £18.50
CC: MC Vi Am DC Swi Delt

How to get there: Situated off Knaresborough Road in Harrogate, overlooking the 'Stray' parkland.

76 The Majestic Hotel

★★★★

Ripon Road, Harrogate,
North Yorkshire, HG1 2HU
Tel: 01423 568972 Fax: 01423 502283

Northeast

77 Balmoral Hotel

★★★

Franklin Mount, Harrogate,
North Yorkshire, HG1 5EJ
Tel: 01423 508208 Fax: 01423 530652
Email: info@balmoralhotel.co.uk
Web: www.balmoralhotel.co.uk
20 bedrs SB £72 DB £198 HBS £86 HBD £64
B £6.50 L £6 D £12.50
CC: MC Vi Am Swi Delt

How to get there: Follow signs for Harrogate
Conference Centre. On Kings Road. The
Balmoral is 500 yards past the centre on the
right-hand side.

78 Boar's Head Hotel

★★★★ 🐾 🐾 🐾
Ripley, Harrogate, North Yorkshire, HG3 3AY
Tel: 01423 771888 Fax: 01423 771509
Email: reservations@boarsheadripley.co.uk
Web: www.boarsheadripley.co.uk

Elegantly restored coaching inn provides
outstanding food, fine wines, friendly attentive
service with comfortable and relaxing
surroundings. In historic village location and
beautiful Dales countryside.
25 bedrs SB £99 DB £120 HBS £100 HBD £80
L £12.20 D £21.50
CC: MC Vi Am DC Swi Delt
How to get there: The Boar's Head is three
miles north of Harrogate on the A61, 10 minutes
from the A1.

79 Cutlers on the Stray

★★★★ 🐾
19, West Park, Harrogate,
North Yorkshire, HG1 1BL
Tel: 01423 524471 Fax: 01423 506728
Email: reception@cutlers.fsbuiness.co.uk
Web: www.cutlers-web.com

Overlooking Harrogate's famous Stray, Cutler's
on the Stray offers a unique recipe for delightful
accommodation in contemporary surroundings.
Our informal brasserie has an excellent
reputation for innovative food in a stylish,
informal atmosphere.
19 bedrs SB £79 DB £89 HBS £95.25
HBD £52.65
CC: MC Vi Am Swi Delt
How to get there: Follow the A59 or A61 to the
Prince of Wales roundabout; we are located 100
yards along West Park, direction town centre.

80 Grants Hotel & Chimney Pots Bistro

★★★ 🐾
3–13 Swan Road, Harrogate,
North Yorkshire, HG1 2SS
Tel: 01423 560666 Fax: 01423 502550
Email: enquiries@grantshotel-harrogate.com
Web: www.grantshotel-harrogate.com

Award-winning hotel situated in the heart of
Harrogate close to town centre and Valley
Gardens. Affiliated to Academy Health and
Leisure Club. Fine fresh food in Chimney Pot
Bistro.
42 bedrs SB £99 DB £110 B £7.50 L £6.50
CC: MC Vi Am DC Swi Delt JCB
How to get there: From south, take A61 past
Betty's tea room on left, down hill to traffic
lights, and straight across then 1st left into
Swan Road.

81 Harrogate Spa Hotel

★★★
West Park, Harrogate, North Yorkshire, HG1 1LB
Tel: 01423 564601 Fax: 01423 507508
71 bedrs
CC: MC Vi Am DC Swi Delt
↟↾ ⚥ ☺ ☐ ☎ Ⓟ ⚓ ⚑ ⚌ ⚌

How to get there: From A61 follow signs for city centre. Turn right into Albert Street and right into hotel.

82 Hob Green Hotel

Blue Ribbon Winner

★★★★ ⊛ ⊛
Markington, Harrogate, North Yorkshire, HG3 3PJ
Tel: 01423 770031 Fax: 01423 771589
Email: info@hobgreen.com
Web: www.hobgreen.com

Set in 800 acres of beautiful rolling countryside, a charming and elegant hotel known locally for its excellent restaurant. The main rooms, furnished with antiques, enjoy a stunning view of the valley below.
12 bedrs SB £85 DB £95
HBS £90 HBD £70
B £9 L £9.95 D £23.50
CC: MC Vi Am DC Swi Delt
◁ ⊠ ⚥ ☺ ☐ ☎ ⚓ Ⓟ ⚓ ⚓ ⌂ ⚌ ⚌

How to get there: Between Harrogate and Ripon on A61 turn towards Markington at Wormald Green, following brown information road signs.

83 Imperial Hotel

★★★
Prospect Place, Harrogate,
North Yorkshire, HG1 1LA
Tel: 01423 565071 Fax: 01423 500082
Email: imperial@british-trust-hotels.com
Web: www.british-trust-hotels.com

Centre of famous spa town of Harrogate, Victorian hotel with modern comforts — charm and style all of its own. Ideal for exploring North Yorkshire (Bronte country, historic houses and other attractions).
82 bedrs SB £75 DB £100 HBS £85 HBD £60
B £9.95 L £9.95 D £18
CC: MC Vi DC Swi Delt JCB
◁ ⚿ ↟ ⚥ ☺ ☐ ☐ ⚓ Ⓟ ⚓ ⌂ ⌂ ⚑ ⚌ ⚌

How to get there: Leave A1(M) at Junction 47. Follow signs for Harrogate. On reaching Harrogate, turn left at first roundabout, right at next. Hotel 250 yards on right.

84 Swallow St. George

★★★
1 Ripon Road, Harrogate,
North Yorkshire, HG1 2SY
Tel: 01423 561431 Fax: 01423 530037
Email: harrogate.swallow@whitbread.co.uk
Web: www.swallowhotels.com
90 bedrs SB £105 DB £130 B £9.95 L £13
D £19.95 CC: MC Vi Am DC Swi JCB
◁ ⚿ ↟↾ ⊠ ↟ ⚥ ☺ ☐ ☎ ⚓ Ⓟ ⚓ ⌂ ⌂ ⚑ ⚑
⚌ ⚌ ⚏ ♈ ⚐

How to get there: From A1 exit at Weatherby through Harrogate for Ripon A61. Other directions follow signs for Harrogate Conference Centre.

85 Ascot House Hotel

★★ ⊛
53 Kings Road, Harrogate,
North Yorkshire, HG1 5HJ
Tel: 01423 531005 Fax: 01423 503523
Email: admin@ascothouse.com
Web: www.ascothouse.com
Closed New Year
19 bedrs SB £53 DB £78 HBS £65 HBD £51
B £7.50 D £15.95 CC: MC Vi Am DC Swi Delt
◁ ⊠ ↟ ☺ ☐ ☎ Ⓟ ⚓ ⌂ ⌂ ⚑ ⚌ ⚌

How to get there: Follow signs for town centre and conference/exhibition centre. Hotel is on left as you drive up Kings Road, about 500 yards from conference centre.

Northeast

86 Alexa House Hotel

◆◆◆◆

26 Ripon Road, Harrogate,
North Yorkshire, HG1 2JJ
Tel: 01423 501988 Fax: 01423 504086
Email: alexahouse@msn.com
Web: www.alexahouse.co.uk
13 bedrs SB £50 DB £65 D £15
CC: MC Vi Swi Delt
How to get there: ½ mile from crossroads of
A59 and A61, towards Harrogate town centre.

87 Arden House Hotel

◆◆◆◆ ✗

69/71 Franklin Road, Harrogate,
North Yorkshire, HG1 5EH
Tel: 01423 509224 Fax: 01423 561170
Email: prop@ardenhousehotel.free-online.co.uk
Web: www.ardenhousehotel.co.uk
14 bedrs SB £32 DB £60 D £17
CC: MC Vi Am Swi Delt
How to get there: On entering Harrogate, follow
signs for Conference and Exhibition Centre. At
the Conference Centre on Kings Road, turn left
into Strawberry Dale Avenue, then left into
Franklin Road.

88 Ashley House Hotel

◆◆◆◆ ✗

36–40 Franklin Road, Harrogate,
North Yorkshire, HG1 5EE
Tel: 01423 507474 Fax: 01423 560858
Email: ron@ashleyhousehotel.com
Web: www.ashleyhousehotel.com

Only five minutes' walk from the town centre.
Comfortable, well-equipped bedrooms and a
cosy bar specialising in single malt whiskies. A
warm welcome and friendly service await you.
Contact Ron or Linda to reserve your room.
18 bedrs SB £42.50 DB £65
CC: MC Vi Am DC Swi Delt JCB

89 Shannon Court Hotel

◆◆◆◆ ✗

65 Dragon Avenue, Harrogate,
North Yorkshire, HG1 5DS
Tel: 01423 509858 Fax: 01423 530606
Email: shannon@hotels.harrogate.com
Web: www.harrogate.com/shannon
Closed Christmas to New Year
8 bedrs SB £30 DB £55
CC: MC Vi Swi
How to get there: Five minutes from town centre
in High Harrogate, off the Skipton Road (A59).

Hebden Bridge, West Yorkshire

90 Carlton Hotel

★★★

Albert Street, Hebden Bridge,
West Yorkshire, HX7 8ES
Tel: 01422 844400 Fax: 01422 843117
Email: ctonhotel@aol.com
Web: www.hebdenbridgecalton.co.uk
16 bedrs SB £56 DB £75
B £8 L £7 D £14.95
CC: MC Vi Am DC Swi Delt JCB
How to get there: Just off the A646 in the centre
of Hebden Bridge.

Helmsley, North Yorkshire

91 Feversham Arms Hotel

Blue Ribbon Winner

★★★★ ®®

1 High Street, Helmsley, York, YO62 5AG
Tel: 01439 770766 Fax: 01439 770346
Email: fevershamarms@hotmail.com
Web: www.feversham.com
17 bedrs SB £70 DB £90
HBS £90 HBD £65
B £10 L £15 D £20
CC: MC Vi Am Swi Delt
How to get there: From A1, take A168 dual
carriageway to Thirsk, then A170. Or, at A1
junction with A64, take A64 to York North
bypass, then B1363.
See advert on facing page

92 Heritage Hotels – The Black Swan

★★★★ ☖ ☖
Market Place, Helmsley,
North Yorkshire, YO62 5BJ
Tel: 01439 770466 Fax: 01439 770174
45 bedrs SB £72 DB £144
HBS £87 HBD £174
B £12 L £3.50 D £26.50
CC: MC Vi Am DC Swi Delt

How to get there: Entering Helmsley on the A170, the hotel is at the top of the Market Square

93 Pheasant Hotel

★★★
Harome, Helmsley, North Yorkshire, YO62 5JG
Tel: 01439 771241 Fax: 01439 771744
Children minimum age: 5
Closed December to February
12 bedrs SB £45 DB £90 H
BS £70 HBD £70
B £10 L £6.50 D £20
CC: MC Vi Am Swi Delt

How to get there: Leave Helmesley on A170 in direction of Scarborough. After ¼ of a mile, turn right signposted Harome. Hotel near church.

94 Crown Hotel

★★
Market Place, Helmsley,
North Yorkshire, YO62 5BJ
Tel: 01439 770297 Fax: 01439 771595
12 bedrs SB £35 DB £70 HBS £49 HBD £49
B £6.95 L £11 D £15.95
CC: MC Vi Swi Delt
How to get there: In the market square in the centre of Helmsley.

95 The Feathers

★★
Market Place, Helmsley,
North Yorkshire, YO6 5BH
Tel: 01439 770275 Fax: 01439 771101
Email: feathershotel@aol.com
Web: www.feathershotel.com
14 bedrs SB £45 DB £60 B £5 L £5 D £10
CC: MC Vi Swi
How to get there: On the A170 Thirsk to Scarborough road directly facing the Market Square.

Northeast

Hexham, Northumberland

96 Langley Castle Hotel

★★★★★

Langley-on-Tyne, Hexham,
Northumberland, NE47 5LU
Tel: 01434 688888 Fax: 01434 684019
Email: manager@langleycastle.com
Web: www.langleycastle.com
18 bedrs SB £99.50 DB £125
HBS £109.50 HBD £67.50
B £9.50 L £12.50 D £28.50
CC: MC Vi Am DC Swi Delt

How to get there: By car, follow A69 to Hagdon Bridge, then two miles south on A686 to Langley Castle.
See advert on previous page

97 Swallow George Hotel

★★★★

Chollerford, Hexham,
Northumberland, NE46 4EW
Tel: 01434 681611 Fax: 01434 681727
Email: chollerford.swallow@whitbread.com
Web: www.georgehotel-chollerford.com

This delightful country hotel with riverside gardens has excellent accommodation, a reputation for fine cuisine and full leisure facilities.
47 bedrs SB £60 DB £90.00 HBS £80 HBD £65
B £9.75 L £12.50 D £21.50
CC: MC Vi Am DC Delt

How to get there: From the A1 at Newcastle, turn onto A69 (Hexham). Pass Hexham, take A6079 to Chollerford.

98 Blackcock Inn

♦♦♦

Falstone, Kielder Water,
Northumberland, NE48 1AA
Tel: 01434 240200 Fax: 01434 240200
Email: blackcock@falstone.fsbusiness.co.uk
Web: www.smoothhound.co.uk/
hotels/black.html
4 bedrs SB £28 DB £50
B £3.50 L £3.95 D £5.95
CC: MC Vi Swi Delt

How to get there: Falstone can be accessed off the C200 road from Bellingham which can be accessed off the A68 or the B6320.

99 Rose & Crown Inn

♦♦♦

Main Street, Slaley, Hexham,
Northumberland, NE47 0AA
Tel: 01434 673263 Fax: 01434 673305
Email: rosecrowninn@supanet.com
Web: www.smoothhound.co.uk/
hotels/rosecrowninn
3 bedrs SB £27.50 DB £45
B £5.95 L £7.50 D £11.95
CC: MC Vi Am Swi Delt JCB

How to get there: From A68, take B6306. Rose & Crown Inn on left after approximately four miles.

Holmfirth, West Yorkshire

100 White Horse Inn

♦♦

Scholes Road, Jackson Bridge, Holmfirth,
Huddersfield, West Yorkshire, HO9 1LY
Tel: 01484 683940
Web: www.holme-valley.co.uk
5 bedrs SB £25 DB £40 B £2.90 L £3.50 D £3.95
CC: Vi Swi Delt

How to get there: Leave M1 southbound at Junction 39. Take A616 to Denby Dale. Or, from M1 northbound, leave at Junction 35A, and take A616 to Huddersfield.

Huddersfield, West Yorkshire

101 Bagden Hall

★★★

Wakefield Road, Scisset, Huddersfield,
West Yorkshire, HD8 9LE
Tel: 01484 865330 Fax: 01484 861001
Email: info@bagdenhall.demon.co.uk
Web: www.bagdenhall.demon.co.uk

Traditional country house hotel, set in 40 acres
of beautiful parkland and boasting a superb 9-
hole golf course.
17 bedrs SB £60 DB £80 HBS £79 HBD £59
B £7.50 L £8.95 D £18.95
CC: MC Vi Am DC Swi Delt

How to get there: Situated on the A636 between
Scissett and Denby Dale. Only 10 minutes drive
from J38 and J39 on the M1.

102 Briar Court Hotel

★★★

Halifax Road, Huddersfield,
West Yorkshire, HD3 3NT
Tel: 01484 519902 Fax: 01484 431812
Email: briarcourthotel@btconnect.com
Web: www.briarcourthotel.co.uk

Modern hotel, refurbished throughout with 48
bedrooms, Zanzibar Wine & Coffee Lounge and
conference and wedding facilities. Adjacent is
Da Sandro Ristorante — authentic Italian cuisine
served in an unrivalled atmosphere.
48 bedrs SB £65 DB £75 B £6 L £6 D £11
CC: MC Vi Am DC Swi Delt

How to get there: Briar Court Hotel is on A629,
300 yards from M62 Junction 24, also within
easy reach of M1.

103 George Hotel

★★★★

St. George Square, Huddersfield,
West Yorkshire, HD1 1JA
Tel: 01484 515444 Fax: 01484 435056
Email: info@brook-hotels.co.uk
Web: www.brook-hotels.co.uk
60 bedrs SB £90 DB £100 HBS £105 HBD £130
B £10 L £10.95 D £15.95
CC: MC Vi Am DC Swi Delt

How to get there: From M62, exit Junction 24
and follow signs for Huddersfield town centre.
Hotel is adjacent to train station.

104 Hanover International Huddersfield

★★★

Penistone Road, Kirkburton, Huddersfield,
West Yorkshire, HD8 0PE
Tel: 01484 607783 Fax: 01484 607961
Web: www.hanover-international.com

A former spinning mill full of charm and
character, the Brasserie 209 offers
contemporary cuisine in stylish surroundings.
Ideally situated for 'Last of the Summer Wine'
country.
47 bedrs
CC: MC Vi Am DC Swi Delt

Northeast

105 Huddersfield Hotel

★★★

33–47 Kirkgate, Huddersfield,
West Yorkshire, HD1 1QT
Tel: 01484 512111 Fax: 01484 435262
Email: enquiries@huddersfieldhotel.com
Web: www.huddersfieldhotel.com

60 bedrs SB £54 DB £70
B £5 L £6 D £12
CC: MC Vi Am DC Swi Delt

See advert on facing page

106 Dalton Bed & Breakfast

♦ ♦ ♦ ✠

2 Crossley Lane, Dalton, Huddersfield,
West Yorkshire, HD5 9SX
Tel: 01484 540091 Fax: 01484 540091
Email: jackie-vivion@ntlworld.com
3 bedrs SB £20 DB £40
CC: None accepted

How to get there: Hotel is situated two miles
south-east of town centre, three miles from M62
Junction 25, 13 miles from Junction 38 of M1.

Hull, East Yorkshire

107 Portland Hotel

★★★

Paragon Street, Hull, East Yorkshire, HU1 3PJ
Tel: 01482 326462 Fax: 01482 213460

108 Quality Hotel, Kingston-upon-Hull

★★★

Ferensway, Hull, East Yorkshire, HU1 3UF
Tel: 01482 325087 Fax: 01482 323172
Email: admin@gb611.u-net.com
Web: www.choicehotels.com
155 bedrs SB £100.75 DB £110.75 HBS
£117.25 HBD £63.63 B £10.75 L £4.95 D £16.50
CC: MC Vi Am DC Swi Delt

How to get there: M62 onto M63, onto Clive
Sullivan Way. Turn left at roundabout (A1079).
Follow signs for railway station. Hotel 200 yards
on left.

109 Willerby Manor

★★★ ℞

Well Lane, Willerby, Hull,
East Yorkshire, HU10 6ER
Tel: 01482 652616 Fax: 01482 653901
Email: info@willerbymanor.co.uk
Web: www.willerbymanor.co.uk
Closed Christmas
51 bedrs SB £82.75 DB £107.50 B £6.20 D £15
CC: MC Vi Am Swi Delt

How to get there: M62 runs into A63. Take exit
to Beverley and Humber Bridge. Follow until
you reach Willerby. At roundabout take third
exit, hotel signposted from next roundabout.

110 Comfort Inn Hull

★★

11 Anlaby Road, Hull, East Yorkshire, HU1 2PJ
Tel: 01482 323299 Fax: 01482 214730
Email: admin@gb631.u-net.com
Web: www.choicehotels.com
59 bedrs SB £60.25 DB £60.25 HBS £72.25
HBD £36.13 B £7.75 D £12
CC: MC Vi Am DC Swi Delt

111 Campanile

Beverley Road, Freetown Way, Hull,
East Yorkshire, HU2 9AN
Tel: 01482 325530 Fax: 01482 587538

Typical Campanile bedroom

The hotel is situated in the city centre of Hull.
Facilities include a French bistro restaurant and
conference facilities. Good access for the
disabled.
47 bedrs SB £46.90 DB £52.85
B £5.95 L £2.95 D £5.95
CC: MC Vi Am DC Swi Delt JCB
⚠ 🛏 🐾 ⊗ ⊙ 🖳 ☎ 📞 P🔧 🎿 ⌖ 🏌 ♨ 🍴
How to get there: From M62, A63 into Hull,
passing Humber Bridge. Pass a flyover, follow
signs for city centre A1079. At junction of
Freetown Way and Beverley Road, straight
across lights and turn right.

112 Earlsmere

♦ ♦ ♦
76–78 Sunny Bank, Spring Bank West, Hull,
East Yorkshire, HU3 1LQ
Tel: 01482 341977 Fax: 01482 473714
Email: su@earlsmerehotel.karoo.co.uk
9 bedrs SB £18 DB £32
CC: MC Vi DC Swi Delt
⚑ 🐾 ⊗ ⊙ 🖳 🎿 ⌖ 🏌 🍴

113 Rombalds Hotel & Restaurant

★★★ ☕ ☕
11 West View, Wells Road, Ilkley,
West Yorkshire, LS29 9JG
Tel: 01943 603201 Fax: 01943 816586
Email: reception@rombalds.demon.co.uk
Web: www.rombalds.co.uk

Standing between the town and the moors, this
elegantly-furnished hotel provides comfortable
lounges, well-equipped bedrooms and an
attractive restaurant service with award-winning
cuisine.
15 bedrs SB £55 DB £80
HBS £70.50 HBD £55.50
B £7.95 L £8.95 D £9.95
CC: MC Vi Am DC Swi Delt JCB
⚠ 🛏 🐾 ⊗ ⊙ 🖳 ☎ P🔧 🎿 ⌖ 🏌 ♨ 🍴 🍴
How to get there: On Leeds/Skipton A65, left at
second main lights, follow signs for Ilkley Moor.
Hotel 600 yards on left.

Northeast

Ingleton, North Yorkshire

114 Springfield Country House Hotel

Main Street, Ingleton, North Yorkshire, LA6 3HJ
Tel: 01524 241280 Fax: 01524 241280
Closed Christmas

Detached Victorian villa, large garden. Patio down to River Greta, with home-grown vegetables in season. Home cooking. Private fishing, car park. Pets welcome.
5 bedrs SB £23 DB £46 HBS £34 HBD £68 D £11
CC: MC Vi Am DC Delt

How to get there: On A65(T), 11 miles north-west of Settle. Springfield is 100 yards from A65(T).

Keighley, West Yorkshire

115 Dalesgate Hotel

★★

406 Skipton Road, Utley, Keighley,
West Yorkshire, BD20 6HP
Tel: 01535 664930 Fax: 01535 611253
Email: stephen.e.atha@btinternet.com
Web: www.dalesgate.co.uk
20 bedrs SB £45 DB £65 HBS £52 HBD £40
B £6.95 D £13.95
CC: MC Vi Am DC Delt

How to get there: From Keighley town centre follow the signs for Skipton. At roundabout go straight across. The hotel is in the village of Utley, 1½ miles on right on Skipton Road.

Knaresborough, North Yorkshire

116 Abbey Garth

♦♦♦♦

28 Abbey Road, Knaresborough,
North Yorkshire, HG5 8HX
Tel: 01423 862043 and 07811 615947
Web: www.gocities.com/abbey_garth
Children minimum age: 10
2 bedrs DB £50 CC: None accepted

How to get there: From A1(M), A59 to Knaresborough. At third traffic lights turn left to River Bridge, then left at Half Moon pub.

117 Newton House Hotel

♦♦♦♦

5–7 York Place, Knaresborough,
North Yorkshire, HG5 0AD
Tel: 01423 863539 Fax: 01423 869748
Email: newtonhouse@btinternet.com
Web: www.newtonhousehotel.com
12 bedrs SB £35 DB £55 HBS £52.50 HBD £90
D £17.50 CC: MC Vi Swi Delt JCB

How to get there: Take A59 turn-off A1(M), follow signs to Knaresborough. Hotel on right just before third set of traffic lights.

118 Yorkshire Lass

♦♦♦

High Bridge, Harrogate Road, Knaresborough,
North Yorkshire, HG5 8DA
Tel: 01423 862962 Fax: 01423 869091
Email: yorkshirelass@knaresborough.co.uk
Web: www.knaresborough.co.uk/yorkshirelass
6 bedrs SB £42.50 DB £49.50 HBS £52.50
HBD £29.75 B £6 L £6 D £12.50
CC: MC Vi Swi Delt

How to get there: On A59 between Knaresborough and Harrogate, opposite Mother Shipton's Cave.

Knottingley, West Yorkshire

119 Travelodge Knottingley

Travel Accommodation
A1/M62, Ferrybridge, Knottingley,
West Yorkshire, WF11 0AF
Tel: 08700 850 950
Web: www.travelodge.co.uk
36 bedrs B £4.25 CC: MC Vi Am DC Swi Delt

Lastingham, North Yorkshire

120 Lastingham Grange Hotel

★★★
Lastingham, North Yorkshire, YO62 6TH
Tel: 01751 417345 Fax: 01751 417358
Email: reservations@lastinghamgrange.com
Web: www.lastinghamgrange.com

The Grange, with ten acres of well-kept gardens and fields, is set on the edge of the moors in the historic village of Lastingham; a peaceful backwater.
12 bedrs SB £89 DB £168 HBS £115 HBD £105
B £10 L £10 D £32.75 CC: MC Vi Swi Delt JCB
🐾♨🖥☎🅿♿🎬🍴♥♦

Leeds, West Yorkshire

121 Travelodge Leeds (East)

Travel Accommodation
Colton Mill Business Park, Leeds,
Tel: 08700 850 950
Web: www.travelodge.co.uk
Opens June 2002
60 bedrs B £4.25 CC: MC Vi Am DC Swi Delt
🍴♨🖥♿

122 42 The Calls

★★★★★ Townhouse 🚗 🚗 🚗
Leeds, Yorkshire, LS2 7EW
Tel: 01132 440099 Fax: 01132 344100
Email: hotel@42thecalls.co.uk
Web: www.42thecalls.co.uk
Closed Christmas
41 bedrs CC: MC Vi Am DC Swi Delt
♿♨🐾♨🖥☎🅿♿🎬🍴♥♦♦
How to get there: Follow city centre signs onto the city centre loop. Turn left at junction 15. Number 42 is then immediately on your right.

123 Hotel Metropole

★★★★
King Street, Leeds, West Yorkshire, LS1 2HQ
Tel: 01132 450841 Fax: 01132 425156
Web: www.principalhotels.co.uk
118 bedrs SB £122 DB £149
B £7.95 L £9.95 D £18.95
CC: MC Vi Am DC Swi Delt
🐾♿♨🖥☎🅿♿🎬🍴♥♦
How to get there: Exit J2 off M62, or J47 off M1, then follow signs for city centre.

124 Le Méridien Queens

★★★★
City Square, Leeds, LS1 1PL
Tel: 0870 400 8696 Fax: 0113 242 5154
Email: queens.reservations@forte-hotels.com
Web: www.lemeridien.com
199 bedrs SB £127 DB £149 HBS £145
HBD £92 B £12.75 L £16.50 D £19.50
CC: MC Vi Am DC Swi Delt
🐾♿♨🖥☎🅿♿🎬🍴♥♦
How to get there: From M621 follow signs for Holbeck and City Centre. Continue under railway bridge and take first left towards Granary Wharf Market.

125 Leeds Marriott Hotel

★★★★
4 Trevelyan Square, Boar Lane, Leeds,
West Yorkshire, LS1 6ET
Tel: 0113 236 6366 Fax: 0113 236 6367
Web: www.marriotthotels.com/lbadt
244 bedrs B £11 L £15 D £19
CC: MC Vi Am Swi Delt
🐾♿♨🖥☎❄♨🍴♥♦♦🍷
How to get there: Follow signs for city loop and pick up brown tourist signs for city centre hotels, then Marriott Hotel signs.

126 Chevin Lodge Country Park Hotel

★★★
Yorkgate, Otley, West Yorkshire, LS21 3NU
Tel: 01943 467818 Fax: 01943 850335
Email: reception@chevinlodge.co.uk
Web: www.chevinlodge.co.uk
49 bedrs SB £65 DB £110 HBS £78 HBD £68
B £7.50 L £12.50 D £21.50
CC: MC Vi Am Swi Delt
🐾♿♨🖥☎🅿♿🍴♥♦♦🧖🍷📶
🍷🚣
How to get there: On a quiet rural road just off the A658 Leeds/Bradford airport to Harrogate road, two miles north of airport.

Northeast

127 Golden Lion Hotel

★★★
2 Lower Briggate, Leeds,
West Yorkshire, LS1 4AE
Tel: 0113 243 6454 Fax: 0113 242 9327
Email: info@goldenlionhotel-leeds.com
89 bedrs
CC: MC Vi Am DC Swi Delt

How to get there: Half mile from Junction 3 of
M621, towards city centre. On loop road
Junction 16. Five minutes walk from station.

128 Milford Hotel

★★★
A1 Great North Road, Peckfield,
Leeds, LS25 5LQ
Tel: 01977 681800 Fax: 01977 681245
Email: enquiries@mlh.co.uk
Web: www.mlh.co.uk
47 bedrs SB £71.95 DB £80.90
B £3595 L £3.95 D £12.95
CC: MC Vi Am DC Swi

How to get there: Situated on southbound
carriageway of A1 where A63 from Leeds joins
A1, and six miles north of A1/M62 intersection.

129 The Merrion

★★★
Merrion Centre, Wade Lane, Leeds,
West Yorkshire, LS2 8NH
Tel: 0113 243 9191 Fax: 0113 243 4444
Email: info@merrion-hotel-leeds.com
Web: www.merrion-hotel-leeds.com
109 bedrs SB £110.75 DB £138.50 HBS
£125.75 HBD £84.25
B £9.25 L £12 D £12
CC: MC Vi Am DC Swi Delt JCB

How to get there: Follow signs for city centre.
Join inner loop road and exit at Junction 7 into
Wade Lane.

130 Travelodge Leeds (Central)

Travel Accommodation
Blayds Court, Blayds Yard, Swinegate, Leeds,
West Yorkshire, LS1
Tel: 08700 850 950
Web: www.travelodge.co.uk
100 bedrs B £4.25
CC: MC Vi Am DC Swi Delt

131 Pinewood Hotel

◆◆◆◆
78 Potternewton Lane, Leeds,
West Yorkshire, LS7 3LW
Tel: 0113 2622561 Fax: 0113 2622561

A most comfortable, welcoming small hotel of
distinction. Rooms are attractively decorated
and well-furnished with many extra touches
enhancing guest comfort.
10 bedrs SB £38 DB £48
HBS £50.95 HBD £36.95 D £12.95
CC: MC Vi Am Delt

How to get there: Leave town centre on A61
towards Harrogate. After two miles, at the first
roundabout turn right. Hotel is 600 yards on left.

132 The Thorpe Park Hotel

♣
Century Way, Thorpe Park, Leeds, LS15
Tel: 0113 264 1000

Leeming Bar, North Yorkshire

133 White Rose Hotel

★★
Bedale Road, Leeming Bar, Northallerton,
North Yorkshire, DL7 9AY
Tel: 01677 422707 Fax: 01677 425123
Email: royston@whiterosehotel.co.uk
Web: www.whiterosehotel.co.uk
18 bedrs SB £42 DB £56
B £4.75 L £4.75 D £5.95
CC: MC Vi Am DC Swi Delt

How to get there: 12 miles south of Scotch
Corner, take A684 turning right for Northallerton.
We are $1/2$ a mile along on left.

134 The Lodge at Leeming Bar

Travel Accommodation
Bedale, Leeming Bar, North Yorkshire, DL8 1DT
Tel: 01677 422122 Fax: 01677 424507
Email: thelodgeatleemingbar@btinternet.com
Web: www.leemingbar.com
39 bedrs SB £49.50 DB £56 HBS £62 HBD £40
B £2.50 L £2.50 D £5
CC: MC Vi Am Swi Delt JCB

How to get there: Just off the A1 at the
Bedale/Northallerton junction 10 miles south of
Scotch Corner.

Levisham, North Yorkshire

135 Moorlands

Little Gem

◆ ◆ ◆ ◆ ◆ ※ ⍨

Levisham, Pickering, North Yorkshire, YO18 7NL
Tel: 01751 460229 Fax: 01751 460470
Email: ronaldoleonardo@aol.com
Web: www.moorlandslevisham.co.uk
Children minimum age: 15
Closed December to March

A beautifully-restored Victorian country house in
four acres of wooded gardens with stunning
views across the valley. Ideal base for walking,
cycling or touring the beautiful North York Moors.
7 bedrs SB £35 DB £70 CC: MC Vi

How to get there: A169 from Pickering, turn left.
Go through Lockton into Levisham. First house
on the right.

Leyburn, North Yorkshire

136 Wensleydale Heifer

★ ★ ⍨ ⍨

West Witton, Wensleydale,
North Yorkshire, DL8 4LS
Tel: 01969 622322 Fax: 01969 624183
9 bedrs SB £60 DB £80 HBS £75 HBD £60
B £8.50 L £4.95 D £7.95
CC: MC Vi Am DC Swi Delt

How to get there: The inn is on the A684 trans-
Pennine road from Leyburn to Hawes.

137 Golden Lion Hotel

★

Market Square, Leyburn, North Yorkshire, DL8 5AS
Tel: 01969 622161 Fax: 01969 623836
Email: annegoldenlion@aol.com
Web: www.thegoldenlion.co.uk
15 bedrs SB £25 DB £50
HBS £40 HBD £40
B £5 L £6.25 D £6.50
CC: MC Vi Am Swi Delt

How to get there: 8 miles from Leeming or
Scotch Corner exits from A1, centrally located
in town centre.

Liversedge, West Yorkshire

138 Healds Hall Hotel

★ ★ ⍨

Leeds Road, Liversedge,
West Yorkshire, WF15 6JA
Tel: 01924 409112 Fax: 01924 401895
Email: healdshall@ndirect.co.uk

18th-century family-run hotel with a nationally-
acclaimed award-winning restaurant, and an
exciting new modern bistro. Weddings are our
speciality. Conference facilities are self-contained.
24 bedrs SB £60 DB £78
HBS £76 HBD £55
B £5 L £6.95 D £6.95
CC: MC Vi Am DC Swi Delt JCB

How to get there: On A62 between Leeds and
Huddersfield. Near M1 Junction 40 and M62
Junction 26/27.

Northeast

Malham, North Yorkshire

139 Buck Inn

★★★
Malham, Skipton, North Yorkshire, BD23 4DA
Tel: 01729 830317 Fax: 01729 830670
10 bedrs
CC: MC Vi Am Swi Delt

How to get there: Take A65 Skipton–Settle. Turn right in Gargrove, signposted Malham. Follow this main road for seven miles to Malham. The Buck Inn is in the village centre.

Malton, North Yorkshire

140 Burythorpe House Hotel

★★★★ ⍨ ⍨
Burythorpe, Malton, North Yorkshire, YO17 9LB
Tel: 01653 658200 Fax: 01653 658204
Email: reception@burythorpehousehotel.com
Web: www.burythorpehousehotel.com
16 bedrs SB £50 DB £60
HBS £68.50 HBD £91
B £6.50 L £12.75 D £15.50
CC: MC Vi Swi Delt

How to get there: Situated on the outskirts of Burythorpe.

141 Green Man Hotel

★★★
15 Market Street, Malton,
North Yorkshire, YO17 7LY
Tel: 01653 600370 Fax: 01653 696006
Email: greenman@englishrosehotels.co.uk
Web: www.englishrosehotels.co.uk

![English Rose Hotels logo]

24 bedrs SB £60 DB £90
HBS £35.50 HBD £35.50
B £10 L £12.50 D £15.50
CC: MC Vi Am DC Swi Delt

How to get there: Follow A64 from A1/M1. Leave at exit for Malton at start of bypass. Turn first left after passing Talbot Hotel.

142 Talbot Hotel

★★
Yorkersgate, Malton, North Yorkshire, YO17 7AJ
Tel: 01653 694031 Fax: 01653 693355
Email: talbothotel@englishrosehotels.co.uk
Web: www.englishrosehotels.co.uk

A classic and comfortable inn, close to local attractions, which include Castle Howard and Eden Camp. A warm welcome awaits at this hotel with its ample free parking.
31 bedrs SB £49.50 DB £90 HBS £32.50
HBD £32.50 B £10 L £10 D £16.95
CC: MC Vi Am DC Swi Delt

How to get there: From A64 follow road into Malton: the hotel is on right.

143 Wentworth Arms

★
Town Street, Malton, North Yorkshire, YO17 0HD
Tel: 01653 692618 Fax: 01653 600061
Email: wentwortharms@btinternet.com
Children minimum age: 6
5 bedrs SB £25 DB £50
B £5 L £7.50 D £15 CC: MC Vi Am Swi Delt

How to get there: Turn off A64 onto A169 to Malton. Hotel is 400 yards on right

Mirfield, West Yorkshire

144 Travelodge Huddersfield

Travel Accommodation
A62, Mirfield, West Yorkshire, WF14 0BY
Tel: 08700 850 950
Web: www.travelodge.co.uk
27 bedrs B £4.25 CC: MC Vi Am DC Swi Delt

Morpeth, Northumberland

145 Linden Hall

★★★★ Ⓡ Ⓡ
Longhorsley, Morpeth,
Northumberland, NE65 8XF
Tel: 01670 500000 Fax: 01670 500001
Email: stay@lindenhall.co.uk
Web: www.lindenhall.co.uk

A magnificent grade II listed Georgian country
house set in 450 acres of park and woodland,
perfectly situated in beautiful Northumberland.
Facilities include a fully-equipped health centre
and an award-winning golf course.
50 bedrs SB £73 DB £104
B £9.50 L £15.50 D £24.50
CC: MC Vi Am DC Swi Delt
How to get there: Linden Hall is located off the
A697 between the villages of Longhorsley and
Longframlington.

146 The Cook and Barker Inn

◆◆◆◆ Ⓡ Ⓡ
Newton-on-the-Moor, Felton, Morpeth,
Northumberland, NE65 9JY
Tel: 01665 575234 Fax: 01665 575234
5 bedrs SB £37.50 DB £70 HBS £62.50
HBD £57.50 B £7.50 L £10 D £20
CC: MC Vi Am Swi Delt
How to get there: Heading north on the A1 from
Morpeth, travel about nine miles. The A1
merges back into dual carriageway; look for
signs for Newton-on-the-Moor.

Travelling abroad by car?

European Motoring Assistance
can help you out of a sticky
situation abroad. Buy online at
www.rac.co.uk or call RAC Travel
Sales on 0800 55 00 55.

Newcastle upon Tyne, Tyne & Wear

147 Copthorne Hotel Newcastle

★★★★★ Ⓡ Ⓡ
The Close, Quayside, Newcastle upon Tyne,
Tyne & Wear, NE1 3RT
Tel: 0191 222 0333 Fax: 0191 230 1111
Email: sales@newcastle@mill-cop.com
Web: www.millenniumhotels.com
156 bedrs SB £178.50 DB £217
B £13.50 L £12 D £18
CC: MC Vi Am DC Swi Delt JCB
How to get there: From A1, follow signs for city
centre (A184 and A189). Over the bridge, sharp
left, left at mini roundabout, then B1600.
Situated on the banks of the Tyne.

148 Newcastle Marriott Hotel Gosforth Park

★★★★ Ⓡ Ⓡ
High Gosforth Park, Gosforth,
Newcastle upon Tyne, Tyne & Wear, NE3 5HN
Tel: 0191 236 4111 Fax: 0191 236 8192
Email: marriott/hotels/whitbread
@whitbread.gosforthpark
Web: marriott.com/marriott/ncigf
178 bedrs SB £115 DB £125
B £11 L £18.50 D £26
CC: MC Vi Am DC Swi Delt
How to get there: Situated five miles north of
Newcastle on A1 Wideopen turn-off (A1056).
2nd exit at roundabout and hotel lies straight
ahead.

149 Newcastle Marriott Hotel Metrocentre

★★★★ Ⓡ
Metrocentre, Gateshead,
Tyne & Wear, NE11 9XF
Tel: 0191 493 2233 Fax: 0191 493 2030
Email: reservations,newcastle
@marriotthotels.co.uk
Web: www.marriotthotels.com/marriott/nclgh
150 bedrs SB £165 DB £175 HBS £190
HBD £105 B £13 L £15 D £20
CC: MC Vi Am DC Swi Delt JCB
How to get there: Situated on the A1 adjacent
to the Gateshead Metrocentre. From both north
and south, leave A1 at Metrocentre exit.

Northeast

150 The Vermont

Blue Ribbon Winner

★★★★★ ♜ ♜

Castle Garth, Newcastle, NE1 1RQ
Tel: 0191 233 1010 Fax: 0191 233 1234
Email: info@vermont-hotel.co.uk
101 bedrs
CC: MC Vi Am DC Swi Delt

How to get there: City Centre location by the high level bridge and the castle.

151 Novotel Newcastle

★★★

Ponteland Road, Kenton, Newcastle,
Tyne & Wear, NE3 3HZ
Tel: 0191 214 0303 Fax: 0191 214 0633
Email: h1118@accor-hotels.com
Web: www.novotel.com
126 bedrs CC: MC Vi Am DC Swi Delt

How to get there: From A1 take A696 junction. At roundabout take Kingston Park turnoff; at mini roundabout again take Kingston Park. Novotel on right.

152 Swallow Hotel

★★★

High Street, Gateshead, Tyne & Wear, NE8 1PE
Tel: 0191 477 1105 Fax: 0191 478 1638
Email: swallowgateshead@btconnect.com
Web: www.swallowhotelgateshead.com
103 bedrs SB £85 DB £105 B £6.95 L £10.75
D £19.75 CC: MC Vi Am DC Swi Delt

How to get there: From A1(M) take A184 to Gateshead. At Jet garage roundabout turn right, cross next 2 roundabouts and follow hotel signs.

153 Swallow Imperial Newcastle

★★★

Jesmond Road, Jesmond,
Newcastle upon Tyne, Tyne & Wear, NE2 1PR
Tel: 0191 231 5511 Fax: 0191 212 1069
Email: jesmond.swallow-hotels@whitbread.com
122 bedrs SB £90 DB £115 HBS £43 HBD £43
B £10.50 L £11.50 D £19.50
CC: MC Vi Am DC Swi Delt

How to get there: Just off A167. Follow signs for coast A1058.

154 The Caledonian

★★★

Osborne Road, Newcastle upon Tyne,
Tyne & Wear, NE2 2AT
Tel: 0191 281 7881 Fax: 0191 281 6241
89 bedrs SB £89 DB £99 HBS £101 HBD £62
B £8.95 L £4.99 D £15
CC: MC Vi Am DC Swi Delt

How to get there: From A1 follow Jesmond signs. Turn left into Osborne Road, OR from Tyne Tunnel follow Newcastle signs — A1058. Turn left into Osborne Road.

155 Cairn Hotel

★★

97 Osborne Road, Jesmond,
Newcastle upon Tyne, Tyne & Wear, NE2 2TA
Tel: 0191 281 1358 Fax: 0191 281 9031
Email: cairn-hotel@hotmail.com
Web: www.cairnhotelgroup.com
50 bedrs SB £59.50 DB £75 B £6 D £12.75
CC: MC Vi Am DC Swi Delt JCB

How to get there: Situated ½ mile from the city centre, in the area of Jesmond, minutes from a metro station.

See advert on facing page

156 Travelodge Newcastle (Central)

Travel Accommodation
Foster Street, Newcastle upon Tyne,
Tyne & Wear, NE1 2NH
Tel: 08700 850 950
Web: www.travelodge.co.uk
120 bedrs B £4.25
CC: MC Vi Am DC Swi Delt

157 Travelodge Newcastle (North)

Travel Accommodation
A1, Fisher Lane, Seaton Burn,
Newcastle upon Tyne, Tyneside, NE13 6EP
Tel: 08700 850 950
Web: www.travelodge.co.uk
40 bedrs B £4.25
CC: MC Vi Am DC Swi Delt

Otterburn, Northumberland

158 Butterchurn Guest House

♦ ♦ ♦ ♦

Main Street, Otterburn,
Northumberland, NE19 1NP
Tel: 01830 520585 Fax: 01830 520874
Email: keith@butterchurn.freeserve.co.uk
Web: www.butterchurn.freeserve.co.uk

Excellent ensuite quality accommodation.
Situated on the main scenic route to and from
Scotland. Central base to explore
Northumberland National Park, including Kielder
Water, Hadrian's Wall, Northumberland castles
and coastline.
7 bedrs SB £25 DB £40 CC: MC Vi Delt
🔸🔸🔸🔸🔸🔸🔸🔸🔸🔸
How to get there: The Butterchurn is in the
middle of Otterburn village, opposite the church,
on the A696.

Pateley Bridge, North Yorkshire

159 Roslyn Hotel

♦ ♦ ♦ 🐾

King Street, Pateley Bridge,
North Yorkshire, HG3 5AT
Tel: 01423 711374 Fax: 01423 711374
Email: roslynhotelatpateley@talk21.com
Web: www.nidderdale.co.uk/roslynhotel
6 bedrs SB £40 DB £50 HBS £51 HBD £36 D £11
CC: None accepted
🔸🔸🔸🔸🔸🔸
How to get there: Turn right off Main Street.
Hotel 250 yards on left-hand side of King Street.

Plan your route

Visit www.rac.co.uk for RAC's
interactive route planner, including
up to the minute traffic reports.

The Cairn Hotel

Situated in a select area of lively Jesmond,
with restaurants, bars and shops close by,
and minutes from central Newcastle. All
rooms ensuite with colour TV, tea and coffee
making facilities, and phones. The hotel has
a lively bar, also restaurant with snacks and
Table d'Hote menu available.

97 Osborne Road, Jesmond, Newcastle-upon-Tyne NE2 2TA

Tel: 0191 281 1358   Fax: 0191 281 9031
Email: cairn-hotel@hotmail.com
www.cairnhotelgroup.com

Peterlee, County Durham

160 Hardwicke Hall Manor Hotel

★ ★

Heslenden Road, Blackhall, Peterlee,
County Durham, TS27 4PA
Tel: 01429 836326 Fax: 01429 837676
15 bedrs SB £52.50 DB £62.50
HBS £71.45 HBD £81.45
B £9.95 L £11.95 D £18.95
CC: MC Vi Am DC Swi Delt JCB
🔸🔸🔸🔸🔸🔸🔸🔸🔸🔸🔸🔸🔸
How to get there: Leave A19 at Castle Eden
A181 and B1281. Follow B1281 for two miles;
hotel is on the left-hand side.

Ask the experts

To book a Hotel or Guest
Accommodation, or for help
and advice, call RAC Hotel
Reservations on 0870 603 9109
and quote 'Guide 2002'

Northeast

Blacksmiths Country Inn

Lovely 16th-century hostelry, fully refurbished but retaining all the ambience of years past. Cosy lounges, superb food and wine in wonderful surroundings. Quality ensuites, some ground floor, panoramic views, ideal walking base.

Hartoft End, Rosedale Abbey,
Pickering, North Yorkshire YO18 8EN
Tel: 01751 417331   Fax: 01751 417167
Email: blacksmiths.rosedale@virgin.net
Website: www.blacksmithsinn-
rosedale.co.uk

Pickering, North Yorkshire

161 Blacksmith's Country Inn

★★★★ ℝ ℝ

Hartoft End, Rosedale Abbey, Pickering,
North Yorkshire, YO18 8EN
Tel: 01751 417331 Fax: 01751 417167
Email: blacksmiths.rosedale@virgin.net
Web: www.blacksmithsinn-rosedale.co.uk
18 bedrs SB £43.50 DB £67 HBS £58.50
HBD £58.50 B £6 L £10 D £16
CC: MC Vi Swi Delt

How to get there: Head west from Pickering on the A170 towards Helmsley. After three miles turn right at Wrelton. Hartoft is signposted five miles.
See advert left

Need help booking?

ⓘ RAC Hotel Reservations will find the accommodation that's right for you – and book it too. Call today on 0870 603 9109 and quote 'Guide 2002'

Rogerthorpe Manor

Best Western

Rogerthorpe Manor is the ideal place to stay while on a business trip or perhaps a family weekend. All around there are fine walks in rolling countryside. Nearby there is excellent fishing and golf. The historic city of York is easily accessible as are many of the plethora of historic areas and fine buildings of North Yorkshire.
A relaxing step between London and Scotland – ideal to stop for race meetings at York, Doncaster, Pontefract, Wetherby, Ripon or Thirsk – whatever the occasion you are assured a warm welcome at Rogerthorpe Manor.

Rogerthorpe Manor
Country House Hotel
Thorpe Lane, Badsworth, Pontefract,
Yorkshire WF9 1AB
Tel: 01977 643839 Fax: 01977 645704
Email: ops@rogerthorpemanor.co.uk

162 Rose Cottage Farm

◆ ◆ ◆ ◆
Cropton, Pickering, North Yorkshire, YO18 8HL
Tel: 01751 417302
Web: www.smoothhound.co.uk

A 17th-century farmhouse; cruck beams, many
original features. Our aim is to provide good
food using our own produce, in a cosy informal
atmosphere. Easy access to moors and coast.
2 bedrs DB £40 HBD £32
CC: None accepted

How to get there: Leave A170 at Wrelton; follow
signs to Cropton. At the New Inn take first right;
Rose Cottage in centre of village.

Pontefract, West Yorkshire

163 Rogerthorpe Manor

★ ★ ★ ☜
Thorpe Lane, Badsworth, Pontefract,
West Yorkshire, WF9 1AB
Tel: 01977 643839 Fax: 01977 645704
Email: ops@rogerthorpemanor.co.uk
24 bedrs SB £80 DB £95
HBS £95 HBD £62.50
B £9.95 L £14.95 D £14.95
CC: MC Vi Am DC

See advert on facing page

164 Travelodge Pontefract

Travel Accommodation
A1 South, Wentbridge, Pontefract,
West Yorkshire, WF8 3JB
Tel: 08700 850 950
Web: www.travelodge.co.uk
56 bedrs B £4.25
CC: MC Vi Am DC Swi Delt

Redworth, County Durham

165 Redworth Hall Hotel
Blue Ribbon Winner

★ ★ ★ ★ ☜ ☜
Redworth, Newton Aycliffe,
County Durham, DL5 6NL
Tel: 01388 772442 Fax: 01388 775112
Email: redworthhall@paramount-hotels.co.uk
Web: www.paramount-hotels.co.uk
100 bedrs
CC: MC Vi Am DC Swi Delt

How to get there: Leave A1M at Junction 58.
Take A68 to Bishop Auckland roundabout.
Proceed straight on, hotel ¼ mile on left.

Richmond, North Yorkshire

166 Quality Hotel Scotch Corner

★ ★ ★
Junction A1/A66, Scotch Corner,
near Darlington, North Yorkshire, DL10 6NR
Tel: 01748 850900 Fax: 01748 825417
Email: admin@gb609.u-net.com
Web: www.choicehotels.com
90 bedrs SB £95.75 DB £105.75 H
BS £113.70 HBD £61.85
B £10 L £1.95 D £17.95
CC: MC Vi Am DC Swi Delt

How to get there: Situated off Scotch Corner
roundabout on the A1/A66 junction on the
northbound side of the A1.

167 Bridge House Hotel

★ ★
Catterick Bridge, Richmond,
North Yorkshire, DL10 7PE
Tel: 01748 818331 Fax: 01748 818331
Email: bridgehousehotel@hotmail.com
15 bedrs SB £45 DB £70
HBS £60 HBD £50
B £6.50 L £9.95 D £15
CC: MC Vi Am DC Swi Delt

How to get there: Take Catterick exit off the A1.
Approximately four miles south of Scotch
Corner, hotel opposite Catterick racecourse.

Northeast

168 Travelodge Scotch Corner

Travel Accommodation
A1(M), Middleton Tyas Lane, Scotch Corner,
Richmond, North Yorkshire, DL10 6PQ
Tel: 08700 850 950
Web: www.travelodge.co.uk
50 bedrs B £4.25
CC: MC Vi Am DC Swi Delt

169 Travelodge Skeeby

Travel Accommodation
A1 North, Scotch Corner, Skeeby,
Richmond, North Yorkshire, DL10 5EQ
Tel: 08700 850 950
Web: www.travelodge.co.uk
40 bedrs B £4.25
CC: MC Vi Am DC Swi Delt

Ripon, North Yorkshire

170 Unicorn Hotel

★★
Market Place, Ripon,
North Yorkshire, HG4 1BP
Tel: 01765 602202 Fax: 01765 690734
Email: admin@unicorn-hotel.co.uk
Web: www.unicorn-hotel.co.uk
Closed Christmas
33 bedrs SB £48 DB £68
HBS £58 HBD £88
B £7 L £7.95 D £14.95
CC: MC Vi Am DC Swi Delt
How to get there: Four miles from A1 on A61.
Located in market place, city centre.

171 Box Tree Cottages

♦♦♦
Coltsgate Hill, Ripon,
North Yorkshire, HG4 2AB
Tel: 01765 698006 Fax: 01765 698015
Email: riponbandb@aol.com
Web: www.boxtreecottages.com
4 bedrs SB £35 DB £50
CC: None accepted
How to get there: From Market Place take North
Street and Coltsgate Hill will be found 300 yards
on the left.

Romaldkirk, Co. Durham

172 Rose & Crown

Blue Ribbon Winner

★★★ ⓡ ⓡ ⓡ
Romaldkirk, Barnard Castle,
County Durham, DL12 9EB
Tel: 01833 650213 Fax: 01833 650828
Email: hotel@rose-and-crown.co.uk
Web: www.rose-and-crown.co.uk
Closed Christmas

An 18th-century stone-built traditional coaching
inn set on the middle green in one of Teesdale's
loveliest locations.
12 bedrs SB £62 DB £86 L £13.95 D £25
CC: MC Vi Swi Delt
How to get there: Six miles north-west from
Barnard Castle on B6277

Rotherham, South Yorkshire

173 Hellaby Hall

★★★★ ⓡ
Old Hellaby Lane, Hellaby, Rotherham,
South Yorkshire, S66 8SN
Tel: 01709 702701 Fax: 01709 702701
Web: www.grandheritage.com
52 bedrs SB £107.50 DB £135 HBS £60
HBD £60 B £12.50 L £12.50 D £21.95
CC: MC Vi Am DC Swi Delt JCB
How to get there: Exit J32 M1, then J1 M18.
Follow signs for A631 to Dawtry. On the left
after traffic lights.

174 Best Western Consort Hotel

★★★

Brampton Road, Thurcroft, Rotherham,
South Yorkshire, S66 9JA
Tel: **01709 530022** Fax: 01709 531529
Email: **info@consorthotel.com**
Web: **www.consorthotel.com**
27 bedrs SB **£72** DB **£82** HBS **£90** HBD **£58**
L **£5** D **£17** CC: **MC Vi Am DC Swi Delt**

175 Best Western Elton Hotel

★★★

Main Street, Bramley, Rotherham,
South Yorkshire, S66 2SF
Tel: **01709 545681** Fax: 01709 549100
Email: **bestwestern.eltonhotel@btinternet.com**
Web: **www.bestwestern.co.uk**
29 bedrs SB **£68.50** DB **£98** HBS **£88.50**
HBD **£69** B **£5.50** L **£12.50** D **£20**
CC: **MC Vi Am DC Swi Delt JCB**

How to get there: 1/4 mile from M18 Junction 1.
Follow A631 Rotherham. Turn right into
Ravenfield. Hotel at end of Bramley village.

176 Courtyard by Marriott Rotherham

★★★★ ℞

West Bawtry Road, Rotherham,
South Yorkshire, S60 4NA
Tel: **01709 830630** Fax: 01709 830549
100 bedrs CC: **MC Vi Am DC Swi Delt**

How to get there: Leave M1 at Junction 33 and
follow signs for Rotherham A630. Turn left at
next roundabout, hotel visible on right.

177 Brecon Hotel

★★

Moorgate Road, Rotherham,
South Yorkshire, S60 2AY
Tel: **01709 828811** Fax: 01709 513030

The Brecon's excellent reputation has been built
up since 1963, giving a friendly atmosphere
where all our staff care for your well-being.
21 bedrs SB **£48.50** DB **£57** D **£16.25**
CC: **MC Vi Am DC Swi Delt**

How to get there: Junction 33 of M1, follow
signs to Bawtry (A631). After ½ mile turn left at
traffic lights for A618. Hotel one mile on right.

178 Campanile

Travel Accommodation
Lowton Way off Denby Way, Hellaby Industrial
Estate, Rotherham, South Yorkshire, S66 8RY
Tel: **01709 700255** Fax: 01709 545169

Typical Campanile bistro

The Campanile offers its nationwide tradition of
a relaxed atmosphere in the Bistro Restaurant,
with comfortable rooms. Conference, business
or weekend stays all catered for.
52 bedrs SB **£44.45** DB **£49.40**
HBS **£51** HBD **£32.50**
B **£5.95** L **£3.50** D **£6.95**
CC: **MC Vi Am DC Swi Delt**

How to get there: Leave M18 at Junction 1, leave
M1 at Junction 32. At roundabout turn towards
Bawtry. Turn left at lights, then second left.

Roxby, Lincolnshire

179 The Fox Inn

◆ ◆

Roxby, Lincolnshire, TS13 5EB
Tel: **01947 840548**
2 bedrs SB **£20** DB **£40**
CC: **None accepted**

Northeast

Saltburn, Cleveland

180 Grinkle Park Hotel

★★★ ®

Grinkle Lane, Easington, Saltburn-by-the-Sea,
Cleveland, TS13 4UB
Tel: 01287 640515 Fax: 01287 641278
Email: grinkle.parkhotel@bass.com
Web: www.grinklepark.co.uk

Refurbished 19th century house. Set in 35 acres
of parkland. Drive lined with Rhododendrons
and Azaleas. Perfect location to get away from
it all.
20 bedrs
CC: MC Vi Am DC Swi Delt

How to get there: Situated nine miles from
Guisborough, signed left off the main A171
Guisborough to Whitby road.

Scarborough, North Yorkshire

181 Ambassador Leisure Hotel

★★★

Centre of The Esplanade, South Cliff,
Scarborough, North Yorkshire, YO11 2AY
Tel: 01723 362841 Fax: 01723 366166
Email: ambassadorinfo@scarboroughhotel.com
Web: www.scarboroughhotel.com

Stunning sea view Victorian hotel offering 59 en-
suite bedrooms with full facilities. Heated
swimming pool, spa, steam room and solarium.
Nightly entertainment. Lift. Free parking.
59 bedrs SB £28 DB £56
HBS £38 HBD £38
B £5 L £2 D £16.95
CC: MC Vi Am DC Swi Delt

How to get there: On A64, turn right at
roundabout opposite B&Q, turn right at next
roundabout, then immediately left down Avenue
Victoria to the cliff top.

182 Clifton Hotel

★★★

Queens Parade, Scarborough,
North Yorkshire, YO12 7HX
Tel: 01723 875691 Fax: 01723 364203
Email: cliftonhotel@englishrosehotels.co.uk
Web: www.englishrosehotels.co.uk

Overlooking the North Bay and close to Sea Life
Centre, Atlantic Water Park and Kinderland. Ensuite bedrooms with direct-dial phone, TV and a
welcome refreshment tray. The hotel offers
ample free car parking.
69 bedrs SB £55 DB £90 HBS £35.50
HBD £35.50 L £11.50 D £16.50
CC: MC Vi Am DC Swi Delt

How to get there: Follow A64 from A1/M1. Turn
left at Scarborough rail station and right at
Peasholm Park. Hotel is opposite Alexandra
Bowls Centre.

183 Crown Hotel

★★★

Esplanade, Scarborough,
North Yorkshire, YO11 2AG
Tel: 01723 357450 Fax: 01723 362271
Email: reservations@scarboroughhotel.com
Web: www.scarboroughhotel.com

Famous hotel (1835) perched on the esplanade
with exhilarating views of south bay, castle, and
harbour. Home to Scarborough's finest health
club and two excellent restaurants offering
friendly, professional service.
83 bedrs SB £48 DB £96 HBS £58 HBD £58
B £8.95 L £2.95 D £16.95
CC: MC Vi Am DC Swi Delt

How to get there: At south end of Valley Bridge
(A165), turn east across Valley Bridge Parade
onto Belmont Road. Continue to cliff top, hotel
on right.

184 East Ayton Lodge Country Hotel

★★★

Moor Lane, East Ayton, Scarborough,
North Yorkshire, YO13 9EW
Tel: 01723 864227 Fax: 01723 862680
Email: ealodgentl@cix.co.uk
Web: www.eastlaytonlodgehotel.com
30 bedrs SB £49 DB £65 HBS £71.50 HBD £60
L £9.95 D £22.50
CC: MC Vi Am Swi Delt

How to get there: 400 yards off the A170
Scarborough/Thirsk road in the village of East
Ayton, 3½ miles from Scarborough.

185 Hackness Grange

★★★★ ☕ ☕

North Yorkshire Moors National Park, Hackness,
North Yorkshire, YO13 0JW
Tel: 01723 882345 Fax: 01723 882391

Email: hacknessgrange@englishrosehotels.co.uk
Web: www.englishrosehotels.co.uk

A Georgian country house hotel with facilities
that include an indoor pool with jacuzzi, tennis
and pitch and putt golf. There are delightful
walks and the hotel enjoys an excellent
reputation for cuisine.
33 bedrs SB £77.50 DB £135 HBS £65.50
HBD £54.50 B £12.50 L £12.50 D £25
CC: MC Vi Am DC Swi Delt

How to get there: From A1/M1 take A64. On
entering Scarborough follow B1261 and follow
Hackness sign on right. Entering Hackness
village, turn left for hotel.

Northeast

186 Hotel St. Nicholas

★★★

St. Nicholas Cliff, Scarborough,
North Yorkshire, YO11 2EU
Tel: 01723 364101 Fax: 01723 500538
Email: stnicholas@british-trust-hotels.com
Web: www.british-trust-hotels.com

An ideal location for business or leisure. RAC 3-star hotel, which offers a range of superb conference rooms, leisure club with indoor swimming pool, security car parking and a choice of excellent cuisine complemented by the finest wines.
144 bedrs SB £71.50 DB £95 HBS £87.45
HBD £63.45 B £7.95 L £10 D £15.95
CC: MC Vi DC Swi Delt JCB

How to get there: Follow A64 into town centre. Turn right at first traffic lights, left at second lights. Go over small roundabout and take second turn on right.

187 Palm Court Hotel

★★★

St. Nicholas Cliff, Scarborough,
North Yorkshire, YO11 2ES
Tel: 01723 368161 Fax: 01723 371547
46 bedrs SB £41 DB £76 HBS £54.50
HBD £51.50 B £6 L £9.25 D £13.50
CC: MC Vi Am DC Swi Delt

How to get there: Follow the signs for the town centre, then the town hall. The hotel is en-route.

188 The Royal Hotel

★★★

St. Nicholas Street, Scarborough,
North Yorkshire, YO11 2HE
Tel: 01723 364333 Fax: 01723 500618
Email: royalhotel@englishrosehotels.co.uk
Web: www.englishrosehotels.co.uk

137 bedrs SB £57.50 DB £105 HBS £47.50
HBD £47.50 L £12.95 D £18.50
CC: MC Vi Am DC Swi Delt

See advert on previous page

189 Wrea Head Country Hotel

★★★

Off Barmoor Lane, Scalby, Scarborough,
North Yorkshire, YO13 0PB
Tel: 01723 378211 Fax: 01723 355936
Email: wreaheadhotel@englishrosehotels.co.uk
Web: www.englishrosehotels.co.uk

Peace and tranquillity, in landscaped woodlands on the edge of the North York Moors National Park describe this beautifully-decorated English country house, where fine wines and quality cuisine combine to create the perfect retreat.
20 bedrs SB £75 DB £120 HBS £59.50
HBD £49.50 L £12.50 D £25
CC: MC Vi Am DC Swi Delt

How to get there: Take A64 from A1/M1. On entering Scarborough, take A171 (Whitby Road). Pass Scalby and turn left. Hotel drive on left, after pond.

190 Bradley Court Hotel

★★

7–9 Filey Road, Scarborough,
North Yorkshire, YO11 2SE
Tel: 01723 360476 Fax: 01723 376661
Email: info@bradleycourthotel.co.uk
Web: www.bradleycourthotel.co.uk
40 bedrs
CC: MC Vi DC Swi Delt

How to get there: Follow A64 into Scarborough. Turn right at mini roundabout after B&Q. Follow road to next mini roundabout, turn left, hotel 50 yards further on.

191 Brooklands Hotel

★★

Esplanade Gardens, South Cliff, Scarborough,
North Yorkshire, YO11 2AW
Tel: 01723 376576 Fax: 01723 376576
Email: stay@brooklands-hotel.co.uk
Web: www.brooklands-hotel.co.uk
Closed January
63 bedrs SB £20 DB £40 HBS £25 HBD £50
B £5 D £10 CC: MC Vi Swi Delt

How to get there: From York A64, turn right at mini-roundabout after B&Q, right at mini-roundabout, left at Victoria Avenue, left at Esplanade, then second left.
See advert above right

192 Gridley's Crescent Hotel

★★★ ♞ ♞

The Crescent, Scarborough,
North Yorkshire, YO11 2PP
Tel: 01723 360929 Fax: 01723 354126
Email: reception@crescent-hotel.co.uk
Web: www.crescent-hotel.co.uk
Children minimum age: 6
20 bedrs SB £45 DB £82
B £9.50 L £10 D £16.50
CC: MC Vi Am Swi

How to get there: On arrival in Scarborough town centre, follow signs to Brunswick Centre, Museum & Art Gallery. At Brunswick Centre, turn right into The Crescent.

193 Red Lea Hotel

★★

Prince of Wales Terrace, South Cliff,
Scarborough, North Yorkshire, YO11 2AJ
Tel: 01723 362431 Fax: 01723 371230
Email: redlea@globalnet.co.uk
Web: www.redleahotel.co.uk
67 bedrs SB £37 DB £74 HBS £49 HBD £98
B £6 L £9 D £12 CC: MC Vi Am Swi Delt

How to get there: Follow signs for South Cliff. Hotel is located off the Esplanade near the cliff lift.

194 Ryndle Court Hotel

★★

47 Northstead Manor Drive, Scarborough,
North Yorkshire, YO12 6AF
Tel: 01723 375188 Fax: 01723 375188
Email: enquiries@ryndlecourt.co.uk
Web: www.ryndlecourt.co.uk
Closed November and January
14 bedrs SB £37 DB £60 HBS £47 HBD £78
B £6 L £9.50 D £10
CC: MC Vi Am DC Swi Delt JCB

How to get there: Follow signs marked 'North Bay and Leisure Parks' to Northstead Manor Drive.
See advert on following page

Northeast

195 Sunningdale Hotel

★★

105 Peasholm Drive, Scarborough,
North Yorkshire, YO12 7NB
Tel: 01723 372041 Fax: 01723 354691
Email: sunningdale@barclays.net
Web: www.sunningdale-scarborough.co.uk

Sunningdale is a modern family-run hotel, on the north side of Scarborough, opposite Peasholm Park, close to the North Bay and all its attractions.
11 bedrs SB £28 DB £56 HBS £36 HBD £36
D £9 CC: MC Vi Am Swi Delt JCB

How to get there: Drive into Scarborough and turn left at the rail station onto Northway. Follow this road down Columbus Ravine to Peasholm Park. Hotel is on left.

196 The New Southlands

★★

15 West Street, Scarborough,
North Yorkshire, YO11 2QW
Tel: 01723 361461 Fax: 01723 376035
Email: tony@slands.fsnet.co.uk
Web: www.epworth.co.uk
58 bedrs
CC: MC Vi Swi Delt

197 Ganton Greyhound

♦♦♦♦

Main Road, Ganton, near Scarborough,
North Yorkshire, YO12 4NX
Tel: 01944 710116 Fax: 01944 712705
Email: gantongreyhound@supanet.com
Web: www.gantongreyhound.com
18 bedrs SB £25 DB £55 B £6 L £6 D £7
CC: MC Vi Am DC Swi

How to get there: Alongside the A64 at Ganton, nine miles from Scarborough, 35 miles from York.
See advert left

198 Ashcroft Hotel

102 Columbus Ravine, Scarborough,
North Yorkshire, YO12 7QZ
Tel: 01723 375092
7 bedrs CC: MC Vi

How to get there: Hotel is in North Bay area, 500
yards up Columbus Ravine from Peasholm Park.

199 Blacksmiths Arms

High Street, Cloughton, Scarborough,
North Yorkshire, YO13 0AE
Tel: 01723 870244
11 bedrs SB £30 DB £52 CC: MC Vi Swi Delt

200 Clarence Gardens

4–5 Blenheim Terrace, Scarborough,
North Yorkshire, YO12 7HF
Tel: 01723 374884 Fax: 01723 374884
Closed November-March
24 bedrs SB £18.50 DB £37 HBS £26.50
HBD £26.50 D £8.50 CC: None accepted

How to get there: From top of the North Bay we
are approx. 700 yards from castle facing the sea.

201 Granby Hotel

Queen Street, Scarborough,
North Yorkshire, YO11 1HL
Tel: 01723 373031 Fax: 01723 373031
Closed October to March
25 bedrs SB £24.50 DB £43 HBS £31.50
HBD £28.50 B £4 D £7 CC: None accepted

How to get there: Follow signs for Scarborough
town centre and castle. Queen Street is off to
the right as you head towards the castle.

202 Hotel Levante

118 Columbus Ravine, Scarborough,
North Yorkshire, YO12 7QZ
Tel: 01723 372366
7 bedrs SB £20 DB £40 HBS £27 HBD £27

How to get there: From station turn onto
Northway which runs into Columbus Ravine. On
the left 100m before Peasholm Park.

203 Kenways Guest House

9 Victoria Park Avenue, Scarboough,
North Yorkshire, YO2 7TR
Tel: 01723 365757 Fax: 01723 365757
Web: www.homestead.com/
kenwaysguesthouse/index.html
7 bedrs SB £17.50 DB £35 HBS £23 HBD £23
B £3 D £5.50 CC: None accepted

How to get there: North Bay seafront to
roundabout, past Atlantis, first left up to
Peasholm Park Hotel. Victoria Park Avenue is to
the side.

204 Lincoln Hotel

112 Columbus Ravine, North Bay, Scarborough,
North Yorkshire, YO12 7QZ
Tel: 01723 500897 Fax: 01723 500897
Email: sandra@lincolnhotel.fsnet.co.uk
Web: www.lincolnhotel.fsnet.co.uk
8 bedrs SB £22 DB £44 HBS £30 HBD £30
CC: None accepted

How to get there: Follow tourist attraction signs
for North Bay; at Peasholm roundabout last exit
Columbus Ravine; hotel is approx 400 yards on
right–hand side.

205 Lynton Private Hotel

104 Columbus Ravine, Scarborough,
North Yorkshire, YO12 7QZ
Tel: 01723 374240
Email: watson@paul-cherryl.fsnet.co.uk
8 bedrs SB £20 DB £40
HBS £28 HBD £28 CC: MC Vi

How to get there: From the railway station take
Northway. Go straight on through two
roundabouts. The Lynton Hotel is on the left.

206 Olivers

34 West Street, South Cliff, Scarborough,
North Yorkshire, YO11 2QP
Tel: 01723 368717
Email: olivers@scarborough.co.uk
6 bedrs SB £25 DB £40 HBS £33 HBD £28.50

How to get there: Turn left off the Filey road
A165 into Granville Road, and Olivers is at the
end at 34 West Street

Northeast

207 Outlook Hotel

18 Ryndleside, Scarborough,
North Yorkshire, YO12 6AD
Tel: 01723 364900
Email: info@outlookhotel.co.uk
Web: www.outlookhotel.uk
Children minimum age: 5
10 bedrs DB £40 HBD £27 CC: None accepted

How to get there: Follow signs for North Bay; at
Peasholm Park proceed up hill on Northstead
Manor Drive; Ryndleside is first on left.

208 Parade Hotel

29 Esplanade, Scarborough,
North Yorkshire, YO11 2AQ
Tel: 01723 361285
Children minimum age: 2
Closed November to April
17 bedrs SB £28 DB £56 HBS £39
HBD £39 D £11 CC: MC Vi Swi Delt

How to get there: From centre A165 Filey Road,
across Valley Bridge, second left (Albion Road),
follow to Esplanade, hotel 100 yards on right.

209 Sefton Hotel

18 Prince of Wales Terrace, South Cliff,
Scarborough, North Yorkshire, YO11 2AL
Tel: 01723 372310
Closed November to February
14 bedrs SB £23 DB £46 HBS £28 HBD £28
B £3 L £5 D £8 CC: None accepted

210 The Phoenix

157 Columbus Ravine, Scarborough,
North Yorkshire, YO12 7QZ
Tel: 01723 368319 Fax: 01723 368319
Web: www.phoenix-scarborough.co.uk
8 bedrs DB £30 HBD £46 CC: MC Vi
How to get there: Head for North Bay, Peasholm
Park. Property 100 yards from park on right.

211 Tudor House Hotel

164/166 North Marine Road, Scarborough,
North Yorkshire, YO12 7HZ
Tel: 01723 361270

212 West Lodge Hotel

38 West Street, Scarborough,
North Yorkshire, YO11 2QP
Tel: 01723 500754
7 bedrs SB £19 DB £38 HBS £26
HBD £52 D £7 CC: MC Vi Delt

How to get there: From Railway Station, follow
sign for Filey over bridge. Church on the right.
West Street is opposite.

213 Wheatcroft Lodge

156-158 Filey Road, Scarborough,
North Yorkshire, YO11 3AA
Tel: 01723 374613
Email: wheatcroftlodge@bushinternet.com
Web: www.wheatcroft.scarborough.co.uk
Closed Christmas
Wheatcroft Lodge is situated close to South
Cliff Golf Course and offers warm hospitality,
excellent breakfasts, comfortable rooms, private
car park for all guests and reasonable prices.
7 bedrs SB £22.50 DB £45
CC: MC Vi Delt

How to get there: On the A165 Scarborough to
Bridlington Road two miles south of
Scarborough centre, near South Cliff Golf Club.

214 Willow Dene Hotel

110 Columbus Ravine, North Bay, Scarborough,
North Yorkshire, YO12 7QZ
Tel: 01723 365173
Children minimum age: 3
Closed November to February
10 bedrs SB £18 DB £36 HBS £24 HBD £24

How to get there: A64 to Falsgrave lights; right to
railway station, left through lights; two roundabouts on, left past church before Peasholm Park.

215 Newlands Hotel

80 Columbus Ravine, Scarborough,
North Yorkshire, YO12 7QU
Tel: 01723 367261
5 bedrs SB £15 DB £30 CC: None accepted
How to get there: A165 to the north of
Scarborough between Peasholm Park and the
town centre.

Scotch Corner, North Yorkshire

216 Vintage Hotel

◆ ◆ ◆

Scotch Corner, North Yorkshire, DL10 6NP
Tel: 01758 824424 Fax: 01758 826272
Closed Christmas to New Year

Family-run roadside hotel overlooking open
countryside. Open plan rustic style bar and
restaurant. Ideal overnight stop or base for
visiting Yorkshire Dales/Moors.
8 bedrs CC: MC Vi Am DC Swi Delt

How to get there: Leave A1 at Scotch Corner.
Take A66 towards Penrith, Vintage Hotel 200
yards on left.

Seaham, Co. Durham

217 Seaham Hall Hotel and Oriental Spa
Blue Ribbon Winner

★ ★ ★ ★ ® ® ®
Lord Byron's Walk, Seaham,
County Durham, SR7 7AG
Tel: 0191 516 1400 Fax: 0191 516 1410
Email: reservations@seaham-hall.com
Web: www.seaham-hall.com

An innovative hotel close to Newcastle,
Sunderland, Durham and the A1. Great food,
real service and quality design. The Oriental Spa
opens during 2002, combining the best of
Eastern and Western therapies.

19 bedrs SB £185 DB £195 B £9.50 L £27 D £39
CC: MC Vi Am DC Swi Delt

How to get there: Exit A1 J62. A19 south to
Seaham. B1410 into Seaham, straight over at
lights.

Seahouses, Northumberland

218 Bamburgh Castle Hotel

★ ★
Seahouses, Northumberland, NE68 7SQ
Tel: 01665 720283 Fax: 01665 720848
Email: bamburghcastlehotel@talk21.com
Web: www.bamburghcastlehotel.co.uk
Closed mid-January, two weeks
20 bedrs SB £41.95 DB £75.90 HBS £49.97
HBD £49.97 B £12 L £5 D £15.50
CC: None accepted

219 Olde Ship Hotel

★ ★ ®
9 Main Street, Seahouses,
Northumberland, NE68 7RD
Tel: 01665 720200 Fax: 01665 721383
Email: theoldeship@seahouses.co.uk
Web: www.seahouses.co.uk
Children minimum age: 10
Closed December to January

A stone's throw from the harbour, this friendly
family-run hotel has tremendous character, with
its cosy public areas and corridors adorned with
nautical and period memorabilia.
18 bedrs SB £40 DB £80 HBS £57.50
HBD £57.50 B £6 L £10.50 D £17.50
CC: MC Vi Swi Delt

How to get there: Five miles north of Alnwick on
A1. Take the B1340 to Seahouses. The hotel is
perched at the harbour top.

Northeast

Sedgefield, Cleveland

220 Hardwick Hall Hotel

★★★
Sedgefield, Cleveland, TS21 2EH
Tel: 01740 620253 Fax: 01740 622771
Web: www.hardwickhall.co.uk

52 bedrs SB £70 DB £90 HBS £86
HBD £48 B £10
CC: MC Vi Am DC Swi Delt

How to get there: Just north of the A117/A689
roundabout at Sedgefield, minutes from A1(M)
Junction 60 and A19.

Selby, North Yorkshire

221 The Royal Oak Inn-Hotel

♦♦♦
Main Street, Hirst Courtney, Selby,
North Yorkshire, YO8 8QT
Tel: 01757 270633 Fax: 01757 270333

Settle, North Yorkshire

222 Plough Inn

★★
Wigglesworth, North Yorkshire, BD23 4RJ
Tel: 01729 840243 Fax: 01729 840243
Web: www.the-plough-
        wigglesworth.freeserve.co.uk
12 bedrs
CC: MC Vi Swi Delt

How to get there: Take the B6478 of the A65 at
Long Preston and follow signs to Wigglesworth.

223 Golden Lion Hotel

♦♦♦♦
Duke Street, Settle, North Yorkshire, DO24 9DU
Tel: 01729 822203 Fax: 01729 824103
Email: bookings@goldenlion.yorks.net
Web: www.yorkshirenet.co.uk/stayat/goldenlion

17th-century coaching inn with open log fires
and welcoming atmosphere. 12 recently
refurbished bedrooms, 10 ensuite with
beautifully co-ordinated decoration. Wide range
of home-cooked food and Thwaite's ales.
12 bedrs SB £33 DB £62 HBS £45 HBD £88
B £6.50 L £9.25 D £9.25
CC: MC Vi Swi Delt JCB

How to get there: As you enter Settle town
centre from south, hotel is on right-hand side of
road, just before the market square.

Sheffield, South Yorkshire

224 Sheffield Marriott

★★★★
Kenwood Road, Sheffield,
South Yorkshire, S7 1NQ
Tel: 01142 583811 Fax: 01142 500138
Web: www.marriotthotels.com
115 bedrs SB £95 DB £120 B £11 L £15 D £25
CC: MC Vi Am DC Swi Delt

How to get there: Leave M1 at Junction 33.
Travel six miles to the city centre. Follow signs
for A61 South, to Netheredge Hotels.

225 Charnwood Hotel

★★★

10 Sharrow Lane, Sheffield,
South Yorkshire, S11 8AA
Tel: 0114 2589411 Fax: 0114 2555107
Email: king@charnwood.force9.co.uk
Closed Christmas to New Year

This charming Georgian residence has elegant
public areas and conference facilities, charming
bedrooms and two excellent restaurants.
Situated 1½ miles south-west of the city centre
and only 10 minutes by car from Derbyshire's
Peak District National Park.
22 bedrs SB £83 DB £98
B £7.75 L £15.25 D £15.25
CC: MC Vi Am DC Swi Delt

226 Novotel Sheffield

★★★

Arundel Gate, Sheffield, Yorkshire, S1 2PR
Tel: 0114 278 1781 Fax: 0114 278 7744
Email: h1348-gm@accor-hotels.com
144 bedrs SB £91.95 DB £102 HBS £106.95
HBD £66 B £9.95 L £4.95 D £11.50
CC: MC Vi Am DC Swi

How to get there: In the heart of the city, five
minutes from Junction 33 M1 via A57, Parkway.
10 minutes from Sheffield airport, close to rail
station.

227 Travelodge Sheffield

Travel Accommodation
A630 Ringroad Services, 340 Prince Of Wales
Road, Sheffield, South Yorkshire, S2 1FF
Tel: 08700 850 950
Web: www.travelodge.co.uk
60 bedrs B £4.25
CC: MC Vi Am DC Swi Delt

228 The Briary

♦♦♦♦♦

12 Moncrieffe Road, Nether Edge, Sheffield,
South Yorkshire, S7 1HR
Tel: 0114 255 1951 Fax: 0114 249 4745
Email: briaryguesthouse@hotmail.com
6 bedrs SB £40 DB £52
CC: MC Vi Am Swi Delt

How to get there: Turn right off A621 from
Abbeydale Road at Yorkshire Bank traffic lights,
up Sheldon Road to next lights, turn right onto
Moncrieffe Road.

229 Andrews Park Hotel

♦♦♦

48 Kenwood Road, Nether Edge, Sheffield,
South Yorkshire, S7 1NQ
Tel: 0114 2500111 Fax: 0114 2555423
Email: andrewsparkhotel@talk21.com
13 bedrs SB £48 DB £65 HBS £62 HBD £45
B £6.50 L £12 D £14.50
CC: MC Vi Am Swi Delt

How to get there: One mile from city centre.
Take A625 inner ring road. Hotel is located by
Ecclesall Road.

230 Etruria House Hotel

♦♦♦

91 Crookes Road, Broomhill, Sheffield,
South Yorkshire, S10 5BD
Tel: 01142 662241 Fax: 01142 670853
Email: etruria@waitrose.com
10 bedrs SB £38 DB £52
CC: MC Vi

How to get there: Leave M1 at Junction 33.
Follow A57 towards Glossop for two miles. At
traffic lights in Broomhill, turn right. Hotel 200
yards on left.

231 Hunter House Hotel

♦♦♦

685–691 Ecclesall Road, Sheffield,
South Yorkshire, S11 8TG
Tel: 0114 2662709 Fax: 0114 2686370
Email: ma@hhh.freeserve.co.uk
Web: www.hunterhousehotel.com
24 bedrs CC: MC Vi Am Swi Delt

How to get there: From Sheffield town centre
take A624 to Bakewell. Hotel is on Ecclesall
Road at Hunters Bar roundabout.

Northeast

232 Lindrick Hotel

226 Chippinghouse Road, Sheffield,
South Yorkshire, S7 1DR
Tel: 0114 258 5041 Fax: 0114 255 4758
Email: reception@thelindrick.co.uk
Web: www.thelindrick.co.uk
21 bedrs SB £28 DB £50 D £5.50
CC: MC Vi Am DC Swi Delt

233 Holiday Inn Royal Victoria

Victoria Station Road, Sheffield,
South Yorkshire, S4 7YE
Tel: 0114 276 8822 Fax: 0114 252 6526
Web: www.holiday-inn.com/sheffielduk
100 bedrs SB £125 DB £135 HBS £45
HBD £82.50 B £10.50 L £12.50 D £19.95
CC: MC Vi Am DC Swi Delt JCB

How to get there: Exit J33 M1 to Shefield. At
Park Square roundabout take A61N. At first set
of lights turn right.

Skipton, North Yorkshire

234 Hanover International Hotel & Club Skipton

★★★
Keighley Road, Skipton,
North Yorkshire, BD23 2TA
Tel: 01756 700100 Fax: 01756 700107
Email: hihskipton@totalise.co.uk
Web: www.hanover-international.com
Closed Christmas

HANOVER INTERNATIONAL
HOTELS & CLUBS

Offers stunning views of the Yorkshire Dales,
with a state-registered nursery and extensive
leisure club. Brasserie H2O has an enviable
reputation for mouth-watering cuisine.
75 bedrs SB £85 DB £90
B £7.50 D £16.95
CC: MC Vi Am DC Swi Delt

How to get there: Approach Skipton from A629.
Follow signs for town centre. Hotel is on right-
hand side on entering Skipton.

235 Travelodge Skipton

Travel Accommodation
A65/A59, Gargrave Road, Skipton,
North Yorkshire, BD23 1UD
Tel: 08700 850 950
Web: www.travelodge.co.uk
32 bedrs B £4.25
CC: MC Vi Am DC Swi Delt

236 Skipton Park Guest'otel

2 Salisbury Street, Skipton,
North Yorkshire, BD23 1NQ
Tel: 01756 700640 Fax: 01756 700641
Email: derekchurch@skiptonpark.freeserve.co.uk
Web: www.milford.co.uk/go/skiptonpark.html
7 bedrs SB £35 DB £48
CC: None accepted

South Cave, East Yorkshire

237 Travelodge Hull

Travel Accommodation
A63 East, Beacon Service Area, South Caves
Bypass, Humberside, HU15 1BZ
Tel: 08700 850 950
Web: www.travelodge.co.uk
40 bedrs B £4.25
CC: MC Vi Am DC Swi Delt

238 Rudstone Walk

♦ ♦ ♦ ♦

South Cave, near Beverley,
East Yorkshire, HU15 2AH
Tel: 01430 422230 Fax: 01430 424552
Email: office@rudstone-walk.co.uk
Web: www.rudstone-walk.co.uk
14 bedrs SB £46 DB £59
HBS £64 HBD £47.50
B £4.95 L £15 D £18
CC: MC Vi Am DC Swi Delt JCB

How to get there: Exit J38 M62; through South
Cave to B1230 and turn right to Beverley.
House sign is on the corner.

Stockton-on-Tees, County Durham

239 Swallow Hotel

★ ★ ★ ★ ★ ♨ ♨
10 John Walker Square, Stockton-on-Tees,
County Durham, TS18 1AQ
Tel: 01642 679721 Fax: 01642 601714
Email: info@swallowhotelstockton.co.uk
Web: www.swallowhotelstockton.co.uk
125 bedrs SB £115 DB £120 HBS £135
HBD £80 B £9.95 L £12.50 D £19.95
CC: MC Vi Am DC Swi

How to get there: Follow A19 northbound to
A66 Stockton turning, onto A1130. Over three
roundabouts, turning right to Castlegate car
park.

240 Claireville

★ ★
519 Yarm Road, Easglesclife,
County Durham, TS16 9BG
Tel: 01642 780378 Fax: 01642 784109
Email: reception@clairev.demon.co.uk
Web: www.clairev.demon.co.uk
18 bedrs
CC: MC Vi Am DC Swi Delt

How to get there: On the A135 between the A66
(Stockton-on-Tees) and the A19 at Yarm.
Adjacent to Eaglescliffe Golf Course.

One click does it all

Book RAC inspected hotels and
B&Bs at www.rac.co.uk/hotels

241 Sunnyside Hotel

★ ★
580–582 Yarm Road, Eaglescliffe,
Cleveland, TS16 0DF
Tel: 01642 780075 Fax: 01642 783789
Web: www.sunnysidehotel.co.uk
23 bedrs SB £43 DB £55 HBS £55 HBD £37.50
D £10 CC: MC Vi Am DC Swi Delt

How to get there: Hotel located on A135
between Stockton-on-Tees and Yarm. A135 can
be accessed from A19 and A66.

242 Travelodge Sedgefield

Travel Accommodation
A177/A689, Sedgefield, Stockton-on-Tees,
County Durham, TS21 2JX
Tel: 08700 850 950
Web: www.travelodge.co.uk
40 bedrs B £4.25
CC: MC Vi Am DC Swi Delt

Sunderland, Tyne & Wear

243 Sunderland Marriott Hotel

★ ★ ★ ★
Queens Parade, Seaburn, Sunderland,
Tyne & Wear, SR6 8DB
Tel: 0191 529 2041 Fax: 0191 529 3843
Email: sunderland.marriott@whitbread.com
Web: www.marriotthotels.com
82 bedrs SB £112 DB £125
B £13 L £9.95 D £21.95
CC: MC Vi Am DC Swi Delt

244 Quality Hotel Sunderland

★ ★ ★
Boldon Business Park, Boldon,
near Sunderland, NE35 9PE
Tel: 0191 519 1999 Fax: 0191 519 0655
Email: admin@gb621.u-net.com
Web: www.choicehotels.com
Children minimum age: 14
82 bedrs SB £100.50 DB £110.75 HBS £112.75
HBD £61.38 B £11.75 L £1.50 D £11.95
CC: MC Vi Am DC Swi Delt

How to get there: Hotel is situated on the
junction between A19 and A184, seven miles
from Newcastle train station.

Northeast

Tadcaster, North Yorkshire

245 Hazlewood Castle

★★★★ ® ® ®
Paradise Lane, Hazlewood, Tadcaster,
North Yorkshire, LS24 9NJ
Tel: 01937 535353 Fax: 01937 530630
Email: info@hazlewoodcastle.co.uk
Web: www.hazlewoodcastle.co.uk
21 bedrs SB £110 DB £135 HBD £109 B £12.95
L £12 D £10.86 CC: MC Vi Am DC Swi Delt JCB

246 Travelodge York

Travel Accommodation
A64 East, Wild Man Service Station, Bilborough,
Tadcaster, North Yorkshire, LS24 8EG
Tel: 08700 850 950
Web: www.travelodge.co.uk
62 bedrs B £4.25 CC: MC Vi Am DC Swi Delt

Thirsk, North Yorkshire

247 Angel Inn

★★
Long Street, Topcliffe, Thirsk,
North Yorkshire, YO7 3RW
Tel: 01845 577237 Fax: 01845 578000
15 bedrs SB £45 DB £60 B £7.75 L £10.95
D £14.95 CC: MC Vi Swi Delt

How to get there: Situated just off the A168,
three miles from Junction 49 A1M. Three miles
from A19.

Tynemouth, Tyne & Wear

248 Grand Hotel

★★★
Grand Parade, Tynemouth,
Tyne & Wear, NE30 4ER
Tel: 0191 293 6666 Fax: 0191 293 6665
Email: info@grandhotel-uk.com
Web: www.grandhotel-uk.com
45 bedrs SB £75 DB £80 HBS £91.75
HBD £56.75 B £8.50 L £15.75 D £16.75
CC: MC Vi Am DC Swi Delt

How to get there: From A1 take A19 and then
A1058. Follow the signs for Tynemouth. At the
seafront, turn right. Grand Hotel is approx ½ mile.

249 Park Hotel

★★★
Grand Parade, Tynemouth,
Tyne & Wear, NE30 4JQ
Tel: 0191 257 1406 Fax: 0191 257 1716
49 bedrs SB £55 DB £70
B £5.50 L £9.95 D £12.95
CC: MC Vi Am DC Swi Delt

Wakefield, West Yorkshire

250 Cedar Court Hotel

★★★★
Denby Dale Road, Wakefield,
West Yorkshire, WF4 3QZ
Tel: 01924 276310 Fax: 01924 280221
Email: sales@cedarcourthotels.co.uk
Web: www.cedarcourthotels.co.uk
151 bedrs SB £109 DB £119 HBS £127
HBD £155 B £10 L £14 D £18
CC: MC Vi Am DC Swi Delt

How to get there: Off Junction 39 of M1,
located adjacent to roundabout under
motorway.

251 Hotel St. Pierre

★★★ ®
Barnsley Road, Newmillerdam, Wakefield,
West Yorkshire, WF2 6QG
Tel: 01924 255596 Fax: 01924 252746
Email: res@hotelstpierre.co.uk
Web: www.hotelstpierre.co.uk
54 bedrs SB £81.50 DB £91.50 HBS £95.45
HBD £59.70 B £6.50 L £9.95 D £13.95
CC: MC Vi Am DC Swi Delt

252 Campanile

Travel Accommodation
Monckton Road, Wakefield, West Yorkshire,
Tel: 01924 201054 Fax: 01924 201055

Typical Campanile bedroom

Campanile hotels offer comfortable and
convenient budget accommodation and a
traditional French-style Bistro providing freshly-
cooked food for breakfast, lunch and dinner. All
rooms ensuite with tea/coffee-making facilities,
DDT and TV with Sky channels.
77 bedrs SB £44.45 DB £49.40 HBS £48
HBD £31.10 B £5.95 L £2.95 D £11.95
CC: MC Vi Am DC Swi Delt

How to get there: Junction 39 M1. Towards
Wakefield Centre on A636, hotel is 1 mile from
motorway on left, on Monkton Road Ind. Estate.

253 Travelodge Wakefield

Travel Accommodation
M1, West Bretton, Wakefield,
West Yorkshire, WF4 4LQ
Tel: 08700 850 950
Web: www.travelodge.co.uk
41 bedrs B £4.25 CC: MC Vi Am DC Swi Delt

Warkworth, Northumberland

254 Warkworth House Hotel

★★ ®
16 Bridge Street, Warkworth,
Northumberland, NE65 0XB
Tel: 01665 711276 Fax: 01665 713323
Email: welcome@warkworthhousehotel.co.uk
Web: www.warkworthhousehotel.co.uk
15 bedrs SB £55 DB £90 HBS £69 HBD £54.50
B £10.95 L £10.95 D £17.95
CC: MC Vi Am DC Swi Delt

How to get there: From A1, take the B6345,
follow signs for Warkworth Castle. Hotel is
situated on the B1068 near the bridge.
See advert on follwoing page

Washington, Tyne & Wear

255 Campanile

Travel Accommodation
Emerson Road, District 5, Washington,
Tyne & Wear, NE37 1LE
Tel: 0191 416 5010 Fax: 0191 416 5023
Web: www.envergure.fr

Typical Campanile bistro

Campanile hotels offer comfortable and
convenient budget accommodation and a
traditional French-style Bistro providing freshly-
cooked food for breakfast, lunch and dinner. All
rooms ensuite with tea/coffee-making facilities,
DDT and TV with Sky channels.
78 bedrs SB £48.90 DB £54.85 HBS £54
HBD £34.75 B £5.95 L £4.95 D £5.95
CC: MC Vi Am DC Swi

How to get there: From north or south take
A1M, J64 to Birtley Services. Follow Emerson
Road to arrive at hotel.

Whitby, North Yorkshire

256 Saxonville Hotel

★★★ ®
Ladysmith Avenue, Whitby,
North Yorkshire, YO21 3HX
Tel: 01947 602631 Fax: 01947 820250
Email: newtons@saxonville.co.uk
Web: www.saxonville.co.uk
Closed December to February
22 bedrs SB £42.50 DB £85 HBS £53.50
HBD £53.50 B £9.75 D £21
CC: MC Vi Swi Delt

How to get there: Follow signs for Whitby/West
Cliff. At Metropole Towers turn inland into Argyle
Road. Saxonville first turning on right.

Northeast

Warkworth House Hotel

Set at the heart of the picturesque village of Warkworth. You will experience the very best in comfort and cuisine. Relax, let us take the strain during your well earned rest.

16 Bridge Street, Warkworth, Northumberland NE65 0XB

Tel: 01665 711276   Fax: 01665 713323
welcome@warkworthhousehotel.co.uk
www.warkworthhousehotel.co.uk

257 Old West Cliff Hotel

★★
42 Crescent Avenue, Whitby,
North Yorkshire, YO21 3EQ
Tel: 01947 603292 Fax: 01947 821716
Email: oldwestcliff@telinco.co.uk
Web: www.oldwestcliff.telinco.co.uk
Closed January
12 bedrs SB £33 DB £54 HBS £45 HBD £39
CC: MC Vi Am DC Swi Delt
How to get there: Approaching Whitby, head for West Cliff. Hotel off central exit of Crescent Gardens, opposite Spa and Pavillion complex.

258 White House Hotel

★★
Upgang Lane, Whitby, North Yorkshire, YO21 3JJ
Tel: 01947 600469 Fax: 01947 821600
Web: www.s-h-systems.co.uk/
       hotels/whitehse.html
10 bedrs SB £33 DB £66 HBS £43 HBD £43
B £4 L £6 D £13 CC: MC Vi Swi Delt
How to get there: Follow signs for Westcliff/Sandsend. Hotel located off A174 adjacent to golf course.

259 Glendale Guest House

♦♦♦♦ ✖
16 Crescent Avenue, Whitby,
North Yorkshire, YO21 3ED
Tel: 01947 604242

260 Seacliffe Hotel

♦♦♦♦
North Promenade, West Cliff, Whitby,
North Yorkshire, YO21 3JX
Tel: 01947 603139 Fax: 01947 603139
Email: julie@seacliffe.fsnet.co.uk
Web: www.seacliffe.co.uk
20 bedrs SB £45 DB £69 HBS £57.50
HBD £99 B £7.50 D £15
CC: MC Vi Am DC Swi Delt
How to get there: Follow signs for West Cliff and West Cliff car park. Hotel located on seafront.

261 Heatherdene

♦♦♦
The Common, Goathland, near Whitby,
North Yorkshire, YO22 5AN
Tel: 01947 896334
Email: info@heatherdenehotel.co.uk
Web: www.heatherdenehotel.co.uk
6 bedrs SB £35 DB £60
HBS £50 HBD £45
B £7.50 D £12.50
CC: MC Vi Swi Delt JCB

262 Sandbeck Hotel

♦♦♦
2 Crescent Terrace, West Cliff, Whitby,
North Yorkshire, YO21 3EL
Tel: 01947 604012 Fax: 01947 606402
Email: dysonsandbeck@tesco.net
Closed December
15 bedrs DB £42.
CC: MC Vi Am Swi Delt JCB
How to get there: Take A169/A171 and follow signs for West Cliff.

Whitley Bay, Tyne & Wear

263 Windsor Hotel

★★★

South Parade, Whitley Bay,
Tyne & Wear, NE26 2RF
Tel: 0191 251 8888 Fax: 0191 297 0272
Email: info@windsor-hotel.demon.co.uk
Web: www.windsorhotel-uk.com
70 bedrs SB £65 DB £70 D £14.75
CC: MC Vi Am DC Swi Delt

How to get there: From A1, join A19. Follow
signs for A1058. Once on seafront turn left.
Travel approximately two miles.

Wooler, Northumberland

264 Tankerville Arms Hotel

★★

Cottage Road, Wooler,
Northumberland, NE71 6AD
Tel: 01668 281581 Fax: 01668 281387
Email: enquiries@tankervillehotel.co.uk
Web: www.tankervillehotel.co.uk
16 bedrs SB £45 DB £80 B £5 L £5.95 D £10
CC: MC Vi Swi Delt

How to get there: Situated on northern outskirts
of Wooler on A697. Midway between Edinburgh
and Newcastle upon Tyne.

Yarm, Cleveland

265 Crathorne Hall

Blue Ribbon Winner

★★★★★ ® ® ®
Near Yarm, Crathorne, Cleveland, TS15 0AR
Tel: 01642 700398 Fax: 01642 700814
Email: enquiries@crathornehall.com
Web: www.crathornehall.com

Impressive Edwardian mansion in classical style
with oak-panelled rooms and fine antiques. Set
in 15 acres of wooded grounds.
37 bedrs SB £77.50 DB £135 HBS £90
HBD £80 B £12.50 L £14.50 D £27.50
CC: MC Vi Am DC Swi Delt

How to get there: From A1 north, take A19
Teesside exit. Crathorne is signposted off A19
at Yarm/Teesside airport exit, and is one mile
from slip road.

York, North Yorkshire

266 Royal York Hotel

★★★★

Station Road, York, North Yorkshire, YO24 1AA
Tel: 01904 688617 Fax: 01904 623003
Email: julia.bodmer@principalhotels.co.uk
Web: www.principalhotels.co.uk
166 bedrs SB £142.50 DB £175
B £11.50 L £16 D £26
CC: MC Vi Am DC Swi Delt

How to get there: From M1 take Junction 32
and M18 then Junction 2 onto A1 (north). From
A1, take A64 to York then A1036 to York City
Centre.

267 York Marriott Hotel

★★★★★ ®
Tadcaster Road, York, YO24 1QQ
Tel: 01904 701000 Fax: 01904 702308
Email: york.marriott@whitbread.com
Web: www.marriotthotels.com/qqyyk
108 bedrs SB £101 DB £140
B £12.50 L £14.50 D £21.50
CC: MC Vi Am DC Swi Delt

How to get there: From A64 take exit for York
racecourse. Follow signs for city centre. Hotel is
on right after one mile.

Northeast

Ask the experts

To book a Hotel or Guest
Accommodation, or for help
and advice, call RAC Hotel
Reservations on 0870 603 9109
and quote 'Guide 2002'

268 Aldwark Manor Hotel

★★★★ ⓡ ⓡ

Aldwark, York, North Yorkshire, YO61 1UF
Tel: 01347 838146 Fax: 01347 838867
Email: reception@aldwarkmanor.co.uk
Web: www.aldwarkmanor.co.uk
28 bedrs SB £75 DB £125
B £7.95 L £11 D £29.95
CC: MC Vi Am DC Swi Delt

How to get there: Leave A1(M) onto A59 for York; turn left at Green Hammerton and follow the brown tourist signs.
See advert on facing page

269 Dean Court Hotel

★★★ ⓡ

Duncombe Place, York, North Yorkshire, YO1 7EF
Tel: 01904 625082 Fax: 01904 620305
Email: info@deancourt-york.co.uk
Web: www.deancourt-york.co.uk

Standing in the very shadow of York Minster. Without doubt, the finest location of any hotel in the city. Elegant bedrooms, superb food, friendly service. Regular food and wine and literary events.
39 bedrs SB £85 DB £135
HBS £99 HBD £165
B £8 L £9.75 D £19.75
CC: MC Vi Am DC Swi Delt JCB

How to get there: From outer ring road, take A64 York North, then A1237 A19 Thirsk, then Clifton (inner ring road) to city centre and Minster.

270 Kilima

★★★

129 Holgate Road, York,
North Yorkshire, YO24 4AZ
Tel: 01904 625787 Fax: 01904 612083
Email: sales@kilima.co.uk
Web: www.kilima.co.uk
26 bedrs SB £60 DB £90 HBS £75 HBD £65
B £7.50 L £13.50 D £13.50
CC: MC Vi Am DC Swi Delt

How to get there: Located on west side of city, on A59 Harrogate road.

271 Middlethorpe Hall

Gold Ribbon Winner

★★★★ ⓡ ⓡ ⓡ ⓡ

Bishopthorpe Road, York,
North Yorkshire, YO23 2GB
Tel: 01904 641241 Fax: 01904 620176
Email: info@middlethorpe.com
Web: www.middlethorpe.com
Children minimum age: 8

30 bedrs SB £123.50 DB £189
B £11.50 L £16 D £36 CC: MC Vi Swi Delt

How to get there: Leave A64 to join the A1036 signposted York/Racecourse. Follow smaller signs to Bishopthorpe and Middlethorpe.

272 Monk Fryston Hall Hotel

★★★

Monk Fryston, North Yorkshire, LS25 5DU
Tel: 01977 682369 Fax: 01977 683544
Email: reception@monkfryston-hotel.com
Web: www.monkfryston-hotel.com
30 bedrs SB £84 DB £105 HBD £65
B £9.50 L £13.50 D £24
CC: MC Vi Am DC Swi Delt JCB

How to get there: Situated less than five minutes drive from A1 on the A63 — three miles east off the A1 in North Yorkshire.
See advert on facing page

273 Monkbar Hotel

★★★
Monkbar, York, North Yorkshire, YO31 7JA
Tel: 01904 638086 Fax: 01904 629195
Email: sales@monkbar-hotel.co.uk
Web: www.monkbar-hotel.co.uk

Situated at the heart of York, The Monkbar overlooks the castle walls and Minster. Delightful courtyard garden. Private car parking.
99 bedrs SB £90 DB £130 B £9.50 L £14.50 D £18.50 CC: MC Vi Am DC Swi Delt

How to get there: From A64 take A1079 Hull/York. Left to city centre; right at city walls. Large traffic lights straight ahead. Hotel on the right.

274 Mount Royale

★★★★ ® ®
The Mount, York, North Yorkshire, YO24 1GU
Tel: 01904 628856 Fax: 01904 611171
Email: reservation@mountroyale.co.uk
Web: www.mountroyale.co.uk

The Mount Royale is ideally placed for visitors to the centre of York. With a restaurant overlooking the garden, offering the best of international cuisine.
23 bedrs SB £85 DB £95 B £7.50 D £25 CC: MC Vi Am DC Swi Delt

How to get there: From southbound M1, take A64 to York. Take second turn off for York (A1036 west). At traffic lights turn left. After three miles, Mount Royale is at the top of hill.

275 Novotel York

★★★

Fishergate, York, North Yorkshire, YO10 4FD
Tel: 01904 611660 Fax: 01904 610925
Email: h0949@accor-hotels.com
Web: www.accorhotel.com
124 bedrs
CC: MC Vi Am DC Swi Delt

How to get there: Take A19 exit from the A64.
Follow the A19 towards city centre, following
signs. Novotel York is on left.

276 Parsonage Country House Hotel

★★★★ 🏵🏵🏵

Escrick, York, North Yorkshire, YO19 6LF
Tel: 01904 728111 Fax: 01904 728151
Email: sales@parsonagehotel.co.uk
Web: www.parsonagehotel.co.uk

Set in 6½ acres of landscaped gardens only
minutes from York city centre. Weekend breaks
from £49.50 per person per night. Two AA
rosettes for restaurant, 4-poster, non-smoking
rooms available.
21 bedrs SB £95 DB £110
HBS £110 HBD £140
B £10 L £7 D £19.75
CC: MC Vi Am DC Swi Delt

How to get there: The Parsonage Hotel is
situated in the village of Escrick on the A19
between York and Selby.

277 The Grange Hotel
Blue Ribbon Winner

★★★★ 🏵🏵🏵

1 Clifton, York, North Yorkshire, YO30 6AA
Tel: 01904 644744 Fax: 01904 612453
Email: info@grangehotel.co.uk
Web: www.grangehotel.co.uk

Exclusive Regency townhouse just minutes from
the Minster and city centre. Luxurious
accommodation, three superb restaurants and
award-winning food. Excellent conference
facilities. Private car park.
30 bedrs SB £100 DB £128
HBS £110 HBD £65
B £8.50 L £12 D £26
CC: MC Vi Am DC Swi Delt

How to get there: On A19 York to Thirsk road,
500 yards from city centre.

278 Abbots Mews Hotel

★★

Marygate Lane, Bootham, York,
North Yorkshire, YO30 7DE
Tel: 01904 634866 Fax: 01904 612848

Situated in a quiet location close to the centre
of York, only minutes' walk from the city's
historical attractions. Ensuite accommodation,
restaurant, bar and private car parking.
47 bedrs SB £37.50 DB £65 HBS £50 HBD £90
B £7.50 L £5 D £12.50
CC: MC Vi Am DC Swi Delt

How to get there: Follow A19 into York. Just
before Bootham Bar and traffic lights at
Exhibition Square, turn right into Marygate. At
end of Marygate, turn right and right again.
Hotel overlooking car park.

279 Beechwood Close Hotel

★★
19 Shipton Road, York,
North Yorkshire, YO30 5RE
Tel: 01904 658378 Fax: 01904 647124
Email: bch@selcom.co.uk
Web: www.beechwood-close.co.uk

A warm welcome is assured from Beverley &
Graham and their staff. Set in its own grounds,
the hotel is ideal for visiting the city and
surrounding countryside.
14 bedrs SB £49 DB £80 HBS £55 HBD £47.50
B £6.75 L £8 D £14
CC: MC Vi Am DC Swi Delt JCB
How to get there: From Outer Ring Road
(A1237), turn to city centre at A19 Thirsk
roundabout. Hotel is one mile on right, just
inside 30mph zone.

280 Cottage Hotel

★★
3 Clifton Green, York, North Yorkshire, YO3 6LH
Tel: 01904 643711 Fax: 01904 611230

281 Heworth Court Hotel

★★
Heworth Green, York,
North Yorkshire, YO31 7TQ
Tel: 01904 425156 Fax: 01904 415290
Email: hotel@heworth.co.uk
Web: www.visityork.com

A traditional English hotel within one mile of
York Minster with ensuite hotel accommodation,
four-posters, whisky bar, candle-lit restaurant
and ample parking. Special "short breaks"
available all year.
28 bedrs SB £71 DB £96 B £7.50 L £12 D £12
CC: MC Vi Am DC Swi Delt
How to get there: Use outer ring road (York
bypass) and turn into York from Scarborough
roundabout. Hotel is 12 minutes walk from
Minster

282 Knavesmire Manor Hotel

★★
302 Tadcaster Road, York,
North Yorkshire, YO24 1HE
Tel: 01904 702941 Fax: 01904 709274
Email: enquire@knavesmire.co.uk
Web: www.knavesmire.co.uk
20 bedrs SB £45 DB £65 HBS £57
HBD £44.50 B £3.50 D £15.95
CC: MC Vi Am DC Swi Delt
How to get there: Take the A64 off the A1, near
Tadcaster. Follow signs to York West, then signs
to Bishopthorpe or Racecourse. Hotel opposite
the Knavesmire racecourse.
See advert on following page

283 Minster Hotel

★★
60 Bootham, York, North Yorkshire, YO30 7BZ
Tel: 01904 621267 Fax: 01904 654719
Email: res@minsterhotel.co.uk
Web: www.minsterhotel.co.uk
Children minimum age: 5
31 bedrs SB £55 DB £75
HBS £80 HBD £52.50 B £9.50 D £9.95
CC: MC Vi Am Swi Delt

284 Savages Hotel

★★
St. Peter's Grove, Clifton, York,
North Yorkshire, YO30 3AQ
Tel: 01904 610818 Fax: 01904 627729
21 bedrs SB £25 DB £45 HBS £35
HBD £35 B £7.50 D £11.50
CC: MC Vi Am DC Swi Delt
How to get there: Situated off the A19 to Thirsk,
approximately 10 minutes' walk from York
Minster at the end of St. Peter's Grove.

Northeast

Knavesmire Manor

Once a Rowtree family home, the hotel offers a tropical indoor pool, uninterrupted views of the famous Yorkshire racecourse, comfortable, well-appointed ensuite bedrooms and a 1-Rosette restaurant.

302 Tadcaster Road,
York YO24 1HE
Tel: 01904 702941   Fax: 01904 709274
enquire@knavesmire.co.uk
www.knavesmire.co.uk

Arndale Hotel

A Victorian gem set in beautiful walled grounds overlooking racecourse and within easy walking distance of city, with ample private parking and on main bus route. Lovely bedrooms individually furnished with antiques. Pretty Victorian bathrooms many with whirlpool baths. Spacious drawing room with honesty bar. Also exquisite Garden Rooms.

290 Tadcaster Road, York YO24 1ET
Tel: 01904 702424   Fax: 01904 709800

285 Travelodge York (Central)

Travel Accommodation
90 Piccadilly, York, YO1 9NX
Tel: 08700 850 950
Web: www.travelodge.co.uk
90 bedrs B £4.25
CC: MC Vi Am DC Swi Delt

286 Arndale Hotel

♦ ♦ ♦ ♦
290 Tadcaster Road, York,
North Yorkshire, YO24 1ET
Tel: 01904 702424 Fax: 01904 709800
12 bedrs SB £50 DB £80
CC: MC Vi Swi Delt

How to get there: From A64 take the York West 1036 road. Follow the city centre signs. Hotel situated approximately one mile from A64 on left-hand side overlooking racecourse.
See advert below left

287 Ascot House

♦ ♦ ♦ ♦
80 East Parade, York,
North Yorkshire, YO31 7YH
Tel: 01904 426826 Fax: 01904 431077
Email: j+k@ascot-house-york.demon.co.uk

A family-run Victorian villa 15 minutes' walk from city centre, Castle Museum or York Minster with rooms of character and many four-poster or canopy beds. Traditional English breakfasts. Residential licence, sauna, private enclosed car park.
15 bedrs SB £25 DB £60
CC: MC Vi DC Swi Delt

How to get there: From northeast, junction A1237 and A64 (ringroad) take A1036. Turn left for Heworth after 30mph sign, then right at traffic lights into East Parade.

288 Ashbourne House

139 Fulford Road, York,
North Yorkshire, YO10 4HG
Tel: 01904 639912 Fax: 01904 631332
Email: ashbourneh@aol.com
Web: www.ashbourne-house.com

Family-run Victorian house; ensuite rooms are furnished in a contemporary style and fully equipped. Licensed with a small honesty bar in a comfortable guest lounge. Car parking. Non-smoking.
7 bedrs SB £35 DB £50
CC: MC Vi Am DC Swi Delt
How to get there: On the A19 road south (York to Selby), one mile from the city centre.

289 Curzon Lodge & Stable Cottages

23 Tadcaster Road, Dringhouses, York,
North Yorkshire, YO24 1QG
Tel: 01904 703157 Fax: 01904 703157
Web: www.smoothhound.co.uk/
        hotels/curzon.html
Children minimum age: 7
Closed Christmas

Relax and unwind in a unique atmosphere at this charming 17th-century former farmhouse and stables overlooking York racecourse. Close to centre. Parking in grounds. Personal service.
10 bedrs SB £39 DB £59
CC: MC Vi Swi Delt JCB
How to get there: From A64 take A1036 towards city centre; hotel is two miles on right between York Holiday Inn and York Marriott Hotels.

290 Hazelwood

24–25 Portland Street, York,
North Yorkshire, YO31 7EH
Tel: 01904 626548 Fax: 01904 628032
Email: admin@thehazelwoodyork.com
Web: www.thehazelwoodyork.com
Children minimum age: 8

14 bedrs SB £35 DB £75
CC: MC Vi Swi Delt JCB
How to get there: Situated just 400 yards from York Minster in residential side street, just off inner ring road (Gillygate).
See advert on following page

Northeast

The Hazelwood

Situated in the very heart of York only 400 yards from York Minster yet in an extremely quiet residential area, the award-winning Hazelwood is an elegant Victorian town house with its own car park.

Our individually styled ensuite bedrooms are furnished to the highest standards using designer fabrics.

We offer a wide choice of high quality breakfasts, catering to all tastes including vegetarian.

Completely non-smoking.

RaC ♦♦♦♦ RaC ✠

24–25 Portland Street, York YO31 7EH
Tel: 01904 626548   Fax: 01904 628032
Email: admin@thehazelwoodyork.com
Website: www.thehazelwoodyork.com

---

291 Holly Lodge

♦♦♦♦
204–206 Fulford Road, York,
North Yorkshire, YO1 4DD
Tel: 01904 646005
Web: www.thehollylodge.co.uk

Beautifully appointed Grade II listed building, 10 minutes' stroll to centre. Convenient for all York's attractions. On-site parking. All rooms ensuite overlooking garden or terrace. Booking recommended. 1½ miles from A64/A19 intersection.
5 bedrs SB £58 DB £68 CC: MC Vi Delt
🚫 🖧 💻 📠 📶 🛁 🍴
How to get there: On corner of Fulford Road and Wenlock, 1½ miles towards centre from A19/A64 intersection. 10 minutes' walk along A19 south from centre.

292 Holmwood House Hotel

♦♦♦♦
114 Holgate Road, York,
North Yorkshire, YO24 4BB
Tel: 01904 626183 Fax: 01904 670899
Email: holmwood.house@dial.pipex.com
Web: www.holmwoodhousehotel.co.uk
Children minimum age: 8

Elegant Victorian house.
14 bedrs
CC: MC Vi Am Swi Delt
📠 🚫 🖧 💻 ☎ 📞 📶 🛁 🍴 ♨ 👥
How to get there: On A59 Harrogate to York road, 300 yards past The Fox.

293 Acorn Guest House

 ◆ ◆ ◆ ✳

1 Southlands Road, York,
North Yorkshire, YO23 1NP
Tel: 01904 620081 Fax: 01904 613331
Email: acorn.gh@btinternet.com
5 bedrs DB £46
CC: MC Vi

How to get there: Turn off A64 onto A1036 to
city centre. After ½ mile, turn right into Scarcroft
Road. Then take sixth right. Scott Street leads
to Southlands Road.

294 Blue Bridge Hotel

◆ ◆ ◆

Fishergate, York,
North Yorkshire, YO10 4AP
Tel: 01904 621193 Fax: 01904 671571
Email: info@bluebridgehotel.co.uk
Web: www.bluebridgehotel.co.uk
18 bedrs SB £45 DB £60
HBS £66 HBD £41 D £11
CC: MC Vi Swi JCB

How to get there: On A19 York to Selby road,
two miles from outer ring road on right hand
side. Five minutes' walk from city centre.

295 Georgian Guest House

◆ ◆ ◆

35 Bootham, York,
North Yorkshire, YO3 7BT
Tel: 01904 622874 Fax: 01904 635379
Email: georgian.house@virgin.net
Web: www.georgianhouse.co.uk
Children minimum age: 8
13 bedrs
CC: MC Vi

How to get there: Arriving in York on the A19,
Georgian House is on the left-hand side, in the
city centre.

296 Ivy House Farm

 ◆ ◆ ◆ ✳

Hull Road, Kexby, York,
North Yorkshire, YO41 5LQ
Tel: 01904 489368
Email: ivyhousefarm@faxvia.net

Situated on the A1079 east of York, with easy
access to the Yorkshire wolds, dales, moors and
east coast. Comfortable accommodation with
lounge, dining room and gardens, with TV and
hot and cold water in all rooms.
4 bedrs SB £22 DB £36 CC: None accepted

How to get there: Leaving York on the A1079
Hull Road, about five miles from town centre, Ivy
House Farm is on right-hand side of the road.

297 Linden Lodge Hotel

◆ ◆ ◆

6 Nunthorpe Avenue, Scarcroft Road,
York, North Yorkshire, YO23 1PF
Tel: 01904 620107 Fax: 01904 620985
Email: bookings@lindenlodge.yorks.net
Web: www.yorkshirenet.co.uk/
        stayat/lindenlodge

Linden Lodge is 10 minutes' walk from the city
centre, rail station and racecourse. With a mix of
doubles, singles and family rooms, all with tea-
and coffee-making facilities and colour television.
13 bedrs SB £27.50 DB £52
CC: MC Vi Am DC Swi Delt JCB

Northeast

298 Priory Hotel

126–128 Fulford Road, York,
North Yorkshire, YO10 4BE
Tel: 01904 625280 Fax: 01904 637330
Email: liz@priory-hotelyork.co.uk
Web: www.priory-hotelyork.co.uk
16 bedrs SB £60 DB £80 HBS £65 HBD £45
B £8.95 D £10.95 CC: MC Vi Am DC Swi Delt
🐴🕃🖵☎🅿⚘ℍ👟🏕🏋
How to get there: Situated on the A19 road to
Selby on south side of city. No.9 bus or 1¹/₂
miles from station.

299 St. Denys Hotel

St. Denys Road, York, North Yorkshire, YO1 1QD
Tel: 01904 622207 Fax: 01904 624800
Email: info@stdenyshotel.co.uk
Web: www.stdenyshotel.co.uk
13 bedrs SB £45 DB £60 CC: MC Vi Swi
♿🖂🐴⊘🕃🖵☎🅿⚘ℐ👟🏋
How to get there: Take A1079 for York/Hull, 2¹/₂
miles from outer ring road, through Walmgate
Bar. After ¹/₂ a mile turn left on one way system.
Hotel is on left, two minutes' walk from city
centre.

300 St. Georges Hotel

6 St. Georges Place, York,
North Yorkshire, YO24 1DR
Tel: 01904 625056 Fax: 01904 625009
Email: sixstgeorg@aol.com
Web: members.aol.com/sixstgeorg
10 bedrs SB £30 DB £48 HBS £37 HBD £31 D £7
CC: MC Vi Am DC Swi Delt
♿🖂🐴🕃🖵🅿⚘ℍ👟🏋
How to get there: From south, take A1036. Turn
left as racecourse ends on right. From north, on
A59 turn right after Iron Bridge. Turn right again
and second right.

301 Winston House

4 Nunthorpe Drive, Bishopthorpe Road, York,
North Yorkshire, YO23 1DY
Tel: 01904 653171
Children minimum age: 8
2 bedrs DB £22 CC: None accepted
⊘🕃🖵🅿⚘ℍ
How to get there: 10 minutes walk in direction
of city centre from Railway Station. Take A64 to
York, and Tadcaster road to Bishopthorpe road.

Join RAC from £39

Free £10
Marks and Spencer voucher on joining

- Membership covers you as the driver or passenger, 24 hours a day, 365 days a year

- Our average call out time is under 40 minutes, and our patrols fix 80% of breakdowns at the roadside

- For free travel and motoring information visit us at www.rac.co.uk

- Membership can be paid for monthly

- It's easy to join; call now for instant cover, or visit your local BSM shop, Lex Autocentre or visit our website

For instant cover call
0800 029 029

Quoting HOTEL1

A to B - we RAC to it

Northwest

The Road to the North

In 1936 George Orwell reported that he couldn't find the famous Wigan Pier, and he used this as an example of the decline of the industrial north. In fact, the pier did — and still does — exist, and is now part of a heritage complex (above) — although jokes still abound!

Some of the most beautiful and relaxing landscapes in the UK are found in the Lake District.

Between Bolton and Blackburn, the tiny village of Belmont is dominated by its church spire (below).

Visitors to Chester (below) will find that the city has many Roman remains including the largest Roman amphitheatre in Britain. It also has one of the most unique city centres in England, with a two-tier street system know as The Rows which date back to medieval times.

Adrian's Tower in Lancaster Castle (below) has 8-foot thick walls and a room containing authentic instruments of torture. Part of the castle is still a prison (without torture). Admission to the public section is £3.50.

● Cumbria's Lake District was designated as a National Park in 1951 and is an attractive destination for those who enjoy outdoor pursuits such as walking, climbing and of course boating. The county of Cumbria was itself only created in 1974, from Cumberland, Westmorland and part of Lancashire.

● The Bluebird Café in Coniston is a must for those wishing to find out more about the late Donald Campbell and his speed record attempt on Lake Coniston. The nearby Coniston Boating Centre hires out all kinds of vessels for exploring the lake itself.

● Manchester will be hosting the 2002 Commonwealth Games. The city centre has been redeveloped in recent years and offers superb facilities. Manchester has arguably the best social scene of any English city.

● Liverpool also has a Tate Gallery. Admission is free, except during special exhibitions.

● North of Carlisle is Hadrian's Wall – in fact part of the Roman wall actually runs underneath the city itself. There are various visitor centres and guided tours along the wall's length from coast to coast.

● Nantwich in Cheshire has some of the best examples of timber-framed buildings in the northwest, and a town centre that is compact and a pleasure to walk around.

Blackpool (left) continually re-invents itself to keep the crowds coming, while its famous illuminations remain a favourite. Blackpool Pleasure Beach has the world's fastest roller coaster — the 85mph 'Big One' — with a drop from 235 feet. The Pleasure Beach information number is 01253 341033.

Once one of the most important docks in Britain, Albert Dock (above) went through a slow but inevitable decline in the 20th century, finally closing in 1972. A decade later it was given a complete refurbishment to form Liverpool's Historic Waterfront. A Waterfront Pass is £9.50, or you can visit the attraction's individual museums and pay their admission fee alone. Parking is free.

Manchester's transition from industrial textile centre to cosmopolitan world city is amply demonstrated by the fact it has Britain's largest Chinatown (above). The area is accessed through a traditional Dragon Arch and contributes hugely to the city's vibrant social scene.

Accommodation index

Hotels and Guest Accommodation are indexed by their order of appearance within this region, not by the page. To locate an establishment, note the number to the right of the listing and then find it on the establishment's name bar, as shown here

37 The Turning Mill Hotel

Alderley Edge, Cheshire

1 Alderley Edge

★★★★ 🐾 🐾 🐾

Macclesfield Road, Alderley Edge,
Cheshire, SK9 7BJ
Tel: 01625 583033 Fax: 01625 586343
Email: sales@alderley-edge-hotel.co.uk
Web: www.alderley-edge-hotel.co.uk
46 bedrs SB £119.50 DB £151
B £8.50 L £15.50 D £25.50
CC: MC Vi Am DC Swi Delt

How to get there: Located on B5087, just 400
yards from Alderley Edge village.

Alston, Cumbria

2 Lowbyer Manor Country House Hotel

★★ 🐾

Alston, North Pennines,
Cumbria, CA9 3JX
Tel: 01434 381230 Fax: 01434 382937
Email: stay@lowbyer.com
Web: www.lowbyer.com
11 bedrs SB £36 DB £72 HBS £45 HBD £90
B £12.50 D £19.50
CC: MC Vi Swi Delt

How to get there: From Junction 40 on M6, join
1686. Hotel in wooded location, out of Alston
on A686 towards Newcastle upon Tyne.

Altrincham, Cheshire

3 Best Western Cresta Court Hotel

★★★

Church Street, Altrincham,
Cheshire, WA14 4DP
Tel: 0161 927 7272 Fax: 0161 926 9194
Email: info@cresta-court.co.uk
Web: www.cresta-court.co.uk
136 bedrs SB £87.45 DB £96.40
B £8.95 L £7.50 D £12.50
CC: MC Vi Am DC Swi Delt

How to get there: Situated in Altrincham town
centre on A56. From J19 M6, take A556
towards Manchester. The hotel is on the right.

4 Quality Hotel Altrincham

★★★★ 🐾 🐾

Langham Road, Bowdon, Altrincham,
Cheshire, WA14 2HT
Tel: 0161 928 7121 Fax: 0161 927 7560
Email: admin@gb064.u-net.com
Web: www.choicehotels.com
89 bedrs SB £105.75 DB £115.75 HBS £129.65
HBD £69.83 B £10.75 L £5.95 D £17.95
CC: MC Vi Am DC Swi Delt

How to get there: Exit M6 at Junction 19. Follow
A556 towards Manchester onto A56. Turn left
onto B5161. Hotel one mile on right.

Ambleside, Cumbria

5 Ambleside Salutation Hotel

★★★ 🐾

Lake Road, Ambleside, Cumbria, LA22 9BX
Tel: 01539 432244 Fax: 01539 434157
Email: enquiries@hotelambleside.uk.com
Web: www.hotelambleside.uk.com

Situated in the centre of Ambleside and the
Lake District. Newly refurbished rooms — some
non-smoking. Delightful restaurant and lounge.
42 bedrs SB £41 DB £82 HBS £55.50
HBD £55.50 B £7.50 D £19
CC: MC Vi Am DC Swi Delt

How to get there: M6 Junction 36, A591 into
Ambleside one-way system. Right lane at traffic
lights. Hotel on brow of hill on left corner.

Northwest

The Waterhead Hotel

Lake Road
Ambleside
Cumbria
LA22 0ER

Tel: 015394 32566
Fax: 015394 3i255

waterhead@elhmail.co.uk   www.elh.co.uk

A delightful hotel beautifully situated on the shores of
Lake Windermere. An excellent place from which to explore the Lake
District. A range of drinking and dining facilities are available to suit all
your needs. Bedrooms with Lake Views. Cosy log fires. An informal
and friendly atmosphere. All guests are afforded complimentary use of
the excellent leisure complex at our sister hotel one mile away. Children
very welcome, with seasonal activities available. An ideal place to stay.

6 Langdale Hotel & Country Club

★★★

Langdale Estate, Great Langdale, Ambleside,
Cumbria, LA22 9JD
Tel: 015394 37302 Fax: 015394 37130
Email: marketing@langdale.co.uk
Web: www.langdale.co.uk
65 bedrs SB £130 DB £210 HBS £150
HBD £125 B £8.50 L £12 D £20
CC: MC Vi Am Swi Delt
🖾 🖳 🖵 ☎ 🅿 🛇 🍴 🏌 🏊 ⛲ 🛏 🚻 🆂🅿🅰 ❌ 🚬 🏃 ⛳
🏊 🎿

How to get there: Leave M6 at Junction 36 and
take A591 through Windermere to Ambleside.
Turn left onto B593. At Skelwith Bridge turn
right onto B5343, signposted Langdale.

7 Rothay Manor

★★★★ 👁 👁

Rothay Bridge, Ambleside, Cumbria, LA22 0EH
Tel: 01539 433605 Fax: 01539 433607
Email: hotel@rothaymanor.co.uk
Web: www.rothaymanor.co.uk
Closed 3 January to 8 February

Regency country house hotel with relaxed,
comfortable atmosphere and excellent cuisine.
In beautiful suroundings. Families and disabled
guests welcome. Free use of nearby leisure
centre. Specialised holidays and short breaks
available.
18 bedrs SB £80 DB £125
HBS £105 HBD £90 B £10 L £8.50 D £28
CC: MC Vi Am DC Swi Delt
♿ 🖳 🖵 ☎ 🅿 🛇 🍴 🏌 🍴 🚬 🚻 🏃

How to get there: Exit J36 M6; follow A591 to
Ambleside. Follow signs to Coniston by turning
left at traffic lights, and again $^{1}/_{4}$ mile later.

8 Queens Hotel

★★
Market Place, Ambleside, Cumbria, LA22 9BU
Tel: 01539 432206 Fax: 01539 432721
Email: queenshotel.ambleside@btinternet.com
Web: www.smoothhound.co.uk/hotels/quecum
26 bedrs SB £25 DB £50
CC: MC Vi Am Swi Delt

How to get there: From south, leave M6 at
Junction 36. Take A591 to Windermere and
Ambleside. The hotel is in the town centre.

9 The Waterhead Hotel

★★
Lake Road, Ambleside, Cumbria, LA22 0ER
Tel: 015394 32566 Fax: 015394 31255
Email: waterhead@elhmail.co.uk
Web: www.elh.co.uk
27 bedrs SB £44 DB £88 HBS £54 HBD £54
B £6.50 L £5.95 D £10.95
CC: MC Vi Am DC Swi Delt JCB

How to get there: From north J40 M6, from south
J36; A591 to Windemere, then to Ambleside.
Hotel at Waterhead Bay opposite pier.
See advert on facing page

10 Rowanfield Country House | Little Gem

Kirkstone Road, Ambleside, Cumbria, LA22 9ET
Tel: 01539 433686 Fax: 01539 431569
Email: email@rowanfield.com
Web: www.rowanfield.com
Children minimum age: 8
Closed January to February
Idyllic, quiet countryside location, central
lakeland. Breathtaking lake and mountain views.
Beautiful period house decorated in Laura Ashley
style, every comfort. Award-winning breakfasts,
superb dining locally. Totally non-smoking.
8 bedrs DB £65 HBD £56.50 D £23
CC: MC Vi Swi Delt

How to get there: Exit A591 north of Ambleside
at Button roundabout, signposted Kirkstone
three miles. Rowanfield is ³/₄ mile on the right.

11 Borrans Park Hotel

♦♦♦♦
Borrans Road, Ambleside, Cumbria, LA22 0EN
Tel: 01539 433454 Fax: 01539 433003
Email: info@borranspark.co.uk
Web: www.borranspark.co.uk
Children minimum age: 7
12 bedrs SB £60 DB £70 HBS £80 HBD £55
D £20 CC: MC Vi Swi Delt

How to get there: From Windermere on A591,
left at Waterhead traffic lights. Hotel is situated
¹/₂ mile further, on right opposite rugby field.

12 Elder Grove

♦♦♦♦
Lake Road, Ambleside, Cumbria, LA22 0DB
Tel: 01539 432504 Fax: 01539 432504
Email: info@eldergrove.co.uk
Web: www.eldergrove.co.uk
Closed Christmas
10 bedrs SB £32 DB £68
CC: MC Vi Swi Delt JCB

How to get there: On the south of Ambleside,
A591/Lake Road, opposite BP petrol station at
the start/end of the one-way system.

13 The Samling

Ambleside Road, Windemere, Cumbria, LA23 1LR
Tel: 015394 31922 Fax: 015394 30400
Email: info@thesamling.com
Web: www.@thesamling.com
10 bedrs SB £105 DB £120 B £15 L £25 D £36
CC: MC Vi Am DC Swi Delt

How to get there: A591 to Windemere, on
towards Ambleside. Hotel is in a drive on right.

Northwest

Appleby-in-Westmorland, Cumbria

14 Appleby Manor Country House Hotel

★★★★ ⓡ ⓡ

Roman Road, Appleby-in-Westmorland,
Cumbria, CA16 6JB
Tel: 01768 351571 Fax: 01768 352888
Email: reception@applebymanor.co.uk
Web: www.applebymanor.co.uk
30 bedrs SB £72 DB £104
HBS £82 HBD £62
B £9 L £10 D £17 CC: MC Vi Am Swi Delt

How to get there: Situated ½ a mile from the
town centre on the hill towards A66, Appleby
Manor overlooks the castle.

15 Royal Oak Inn

★★

Bondgate, Appleby-in-Westmorland,
Cumbria, CA16 6UN
Tel: 01768 351463 Fax: 01768 352300
Email: m.m.royaloak@btinternet.com
Web: www.mortal-man-inns.co.uk/royaloak

A lovely genuine old inn, the Royal Oak in
Appleby stands out for its good food and drink,
and above all its atmosphere.
9 bedrs
CC: MC Vi Am Swi Delt

16 Courtfield Hotel

◆ ◆ ◆ ⓡ

Bongate, Appleby-in-Westmorland,
Cumbria, CA16 6UP
Tel: 017683 51394 Fax: 017683 51394

You will find the Courtfield Hotel a real home-
from-home. Set in three acres of lawns and
gardens, a relaxing place to stay, and ideal for
those wishing to enjoy the Eden valley and
explore the Lake District.
11 bedrs SB £30 DB £60 HBS £41 HBD £50
B £8.50 L £10.50 D £15.50 CC: None accepted

Ashton-under-Lyne, Lancashire

17 York House Hotel

★★★ ⓡ

York Place, Ashton-under-Lyne,
Lancashire, OL6 7TT
Tel: 0161 330 5899 Fax: 0161 343 1613
Email: enquiries@yorkhouse-hotel.co.uk
Web: www.yorkhouse-hotel.co.uk
34 bedrs SB £65 DB £80 HBS £80 HBD £55
B £7.50 L £15 D £15
CC: MC Vi Am DC Swi Delt

How to get there: The hotel is situated 10
minutes drive from the motorway network, 15
minutes from Manchester Airport, and a short
distance from Manchester city centre.

18 Welbeck House Hotel

◆ ◆ ◆

324 Katharine Street, Ashton-under-Lyne,
Lancashire, OL6 7BD
Tel: 0161 344 0751 Fax: 0161 343 4278
Email: welbeck5000@breathemail.net
Web: www.smoothhound.co.uk/
hotels/welbeck.html
8 bedrs SB £32 DB £46 D £8
CC: MC Vi DC Delt

29 Travelodge Blackburn

Travel Accommodation
Off J4 M65,
Tel: 08700 850 950
Web: www.travelodge.co.uk
Opens April 2002
48 bedrs B £4.25
CC: MC Vi Am DC Swi Delt

Blackpool, Lancashire

30 Imperial Hotel

★★★★
North Promenade, Blackpool,
Lancashire, FY1 2HB
Tel: 01253 623971 Fax: 01253 751784
Email: imperial-blackpool@paramount-
hotels.co.uk
Web: www.paramount-hotels.co.uk
181 bedrs SB £120 DB £175 HBS £140
HBD £107.50 B £11.50 L £14.75 D £20.50
CC: MC Vi Am DC Swi

How to get there: Exit J4 M55, take A583 North
Shore. Follow signs to North Promenade.

31 Brabyns Hotel

★★
Shaftesbury Avenue, North Shore, Blackpool,
Lancashire, FY2 9QQ
Tel: 01253 354263 Fax: 01253 352915
25 bedrs
CC: MC Vi Am
How to get there: M55 at Junction 4, Preston
New Road to box junction. Turn right into
Whitegate Drive, then onto Devonshire Road.
Third left after island. Hotel on left.

32 Gables Balmoral Hotel

★★
Balmoral Road, Blackpool, Lancashire, FY4 1HP
Tel: 01253 345432 Fax: 01253 406058
60 bedrs SB £45 DB £70
CC: MC Vi Am DC Swi Delt
How to get there: Follow signs off M55 for
Blackpool pleasure beach: the hotel is directly
opposite the Sandcastle Grosvenor Casino.

33 Headlands

★★
611–613 New South Promenade, Blackpool,
Lancashire, FY4 1NJ
Tel: 01253 341179 Fax: 01253 342047
Email: headlands@blackpool.net
Web: www.theheadlands.blackpool.net
Closed 2–16 January
42 bedrs SB £32 DB £64 HBS £38.50
HBD £38.50 B £8.50 L £10.50 D £14.50
CC: MC Vi Am DC Swi

How to get there: Take M6 to M55, turn left at
first roundabout, right at second roundabout (to
Promenade), turn right at Promenade. The
Headlands is ¹/₂ a mile along Promenade.

34 Revill's Hotel

★★
190–194 North Promenade, Blackpool,
Lancashire, FY1 1RJ
Tel: 01253 625768 Fax: 01253 624736
Email: revills.hotel@blackpool.net
Web: www.blackpool.net/www/revills
45 bedrs SB £28 DB £46 HBS £35 HBD £30
CC: MC Vi Swi Delt

How to get there: Three minutes' walk along
north promenade, northwards from Blackpool
Tower.

35 Sheraton

★★
54–62 Queens Promenade, Blackpool,
Lancashire, FY2 9RP
Tel: 01253-352723 Fax: 01253-359549

36 Stretton Hotel

★★
206–214 North Promenade, Blackpool,
Lancashire, FY1 1RU
Tel: 01253 625688 Fax: 01253 752534
Email: strettonhotel@btconnect.com
Web: www.strettonhotel.co.uk
50 bedrs SB £24.50 DB £24.50
HBS £30.50 HBD £30.50
B £4.25 L £6.95 D £7.95
CC: MC Vi Am DC Swi Delt

How to get there: Take the M55 into Blackpool.
Turn right onto promenade. Hotel is 100m past
north pier.

Northwest

37 Warwick

★★

603 New South Promenade, Blackpool,
Lancashire, FY4 1NG
Tel: 01253 342192 Fax: 01253 405776
Closed January
50 bedrs SB £30 DB £60 HBS £40 HBD £40
B £7 D £11
CC: MC Vi Am Swi Delt JCB

How to get there: From the end of the M55
follow the A5230 to South Shore. Turn right at
promenade. Hotel is ½ a mile on right.

38 Manor House Hotel

★★★

Ribby Hall Village, Ribby Road, Wrea Green,
near Blackpool, Lancashire, PR4 2PR
Tel: 01772 688000 Fax: 01772 688036
Email: themanorhousehotel@ribbyhall.co.uk
Web: www.mhhotel.co.uk
29 bedrs SB £65 DB £95
B £3.50 L £8.50 D £14.95
CC: MC Vi Am Swi Delt

How to get there: Two miles from J3 M55.
Follow signs to Wrea Green on A585. Cross the
A583, and Ribby is 200 yards on the left.
See advert on facing page

39 Old Coach House

Little Gem

50 Dean Street, Blackpool, Lancashire, FY4 1BP
Tel: 01253 349195 Fax: 01253 344330
Email: blackpool@theoldcoachhouse.
freeserve.co.uk
Web: www.theoldcoachhouse.freeserve.co.uk
11 bedrs SB £45 DB £60 HBS £57.50
HBD £37.50 B £5 D £12.50
CC: MC Vi Swi

How to get there: M6 Junction 32, M55 to large
roundabout. Straight over, take next right, left at
lights, left at next lights, second right before
Texaco, hotel on right.

Plan your route

Visit www.rac.co.uk for RAC's
interactive route planner, including
up to the minute traffic reports.

40 Burlees Hotel

◆◆◆◆

40 Knowle Avenue, North Shore, Blackpool,
Lancashire, FY2 9TQ
Tel: 01253 354535 Fax: 01253 354535
Email: enquiries@burleeshotel.co.uk
Web: www.burleeshotel.co.uk
Closed November to February
9 bedrs SB £24 DB £48
HBS £33.50 HBD £33.50
CC: MC Vi Swi Delt

How to get there: At 'Uncle Tom's Cabin' on
Queens Promenade, North Shore, turn into
Knowle Avenue. The Burlees is 300 yards on left.

41 Sunray

◆◆◆◆

42 Knowle Avenue, North Shore, Blackpool,
Lancashire, FY2 9TQ
Tel: 01253 351937 Fax: 01253 593307
Email: sun.ray@cwcom.net
Closed December to March
9 bedrs SB £30 DB £60 HBS £43 HBD £86
CC: MC Vi Am

How to get there: 1¾ miles north of Tower along
Promenade. Turn right at Uncle Tom's Cabin.
Sunray is 300 yards on left.

42 Beaucliffe Hotel

◆◆◆

20–22 Holmfield Road, North Shore, Blackpool,
Lancashire, FY2 9TB
Tel: 01253 351663

43 Garville Hotel

◆◆◆ ✉

3 Beaufort Avenue, Bispham, Blackpool,
Lancashire, FY2 9HQ
Tel: 01253 351004 Fax: 01253 351004
Email: garvillehtl@amserve.net
Web: www.smoothhound.co.uk/
hotels/garville.html
Children minimum age: 3
Closed January
7 bedrs SB £22 DB £40
CC: None accepted
How to get there: From Blackpool Tower, 2½
miles north to Red Bank Road. Turn right at the
traffic lights. Beaufort Avenue is first on left.

The Manor House Hotel

Ribby Hall Village
Wrea Green, Near Blackpool

Set on three floors and overlooking an ornamental lake complete with an impressive 50ft high fountain, the magnificent Manor House Hotel is destined to impress. With a range of spacious, sumptuous apartments sleeping between 1–4 guests, the Manor House is ideal for business executives, couples or families searching for something special.

New in 2001, the Manor House contains 29 luxury one and two bedroom apartments including two penthouse suites. Reception area open 24 hours, a residents' lounge bar and ample car parking.

Extensive sport, leisure and entertainment facilities all at walking distance within Ribby Hall Village, including golf, large pool complex, gymnasiums, tennis, horse riding, restaurants and nitespot.

Ribby Road, Wrea Green, near Blackpool. Lancashire PR4 2PR
Tel: 01772 688000 Fax: 01772 688036
themanorhousehotel@ribbyhall.co.uk www.mhhotel.co.uk

MANOR HOUSE HOTEL

44 Harlands Hotel

◆◆◆

298 Queens Promenade, Bispham,
Blackpool, FY2 9AD
Tel: 01253 351895 Fax: 01253 354003

45 Knowlsley Hotel

◆◆◆

68 Dean Street, Blackpool, Lancashire, FY4 1BP
Tel: 01253 343414
11 bedrs SB £20 DB £40 HBS £28 HBD £28
CC: MC Vi Swi Delt
How to get there: Dean Street is situated
opposite South pier. Knowlsley is 400 metres
ahead on the left.

46 Langwood Hotel

◆◆◆

250 Queens Promenade, Bispham, Blackpool,
Lancashire, FY2 9HA
Tel: 01253 351370
Closed January to March
24 bedrs SB £25 DB £50 HBS £30 HBD £60
B £6 L £6 D £8
CC: None accepted
How to get there:

47 Sunny Cliff Hotel

◆◆◆

98 Queens Promenade, Blackpool,
Lancashire, FY2 9NS
Tel: 01253 351155
Closed November to March
9 bedrs SB £22 DB £44
HBS £28 HBD £28 D £8
CC: None accepted
How to get there: 1½ miles from North Pier on
A584, towards Bispham.

48 Westdean Hotel

◆◆◆

59 Dean Street, Blackpool, Lancashire, FY4 1BP
Tel: 01253 342904
Email: mikeball@westdeanhotel.freeserve.co.uk
Web: www.westdeanhotel.freeserve.com
11 bedrs SB £20 DB £40
CC: MC Vi Swi Delt JCB
How to get there: Along Promenade from
Pleasure Beach towards Blackpool Tower. Take
first right after South Pier.

49 Wilmar

◆◆◆

42 Osborne Road, Blackpool,
Lancashire, FY4 1HQ
Tel: 01253 346229
Children minimum age: 11
7 bedrs SB £17.50 DB £35 HBS £24 HBD £48
CC: None accepted
How to get there: On Promenade, pass South
Pier towards Pleasure Beach. Turn left
immediately after pedestrian lights. Wilmar is
approximately 150m on left.

Bolton, Greater Manchester

50 Egerton House Hotel

★★★ ♛♛

Blackburn Road, Egerton, Bolton,
Manchester, BL7 9PL
Tel: 01204 307171 Fax: 01204 593030
Email: info@egerton.macdonald-hotels.co.uk
Web: www.macdonald-hotels.co.uk
32 bedrs SB £60 DB £80 HBS £65 HBD £45
B £10.50 L £13.95 D £20
CC: MC Vi Am DC Swi Delt
How to get there: A666 three miles north of
Bolton town centre.

Borrowdale, Cumbria

51 Borrowdale Gates Country House Hotel

★★★ ♛♛

Grange-in-Borrowdale, Keswick,
Cumbria, CA12 5UQ
Tel: 01768 777204 Fax: 01768 777254
Email: hotel@borrowdale-gates.com
Web: www.borrowdale-gates.com
Closed January

Delightful and charming lakeland house, nestling
in peaceful wooded gardens amidst the
breathtaking scenery of the Borrowdale valley.

Charming and unpretentious hotel with fine food and service. Hotel proprietor-managed.
29 bedrs SB £50 DB £95 HBS £83.50 HBD £87.50 B £12 L £7.50 D £32.50
CC: MC Vi Am Swi Delt

How to get there: From Keswick follow B5289 to Grange. Turn right over the double hump-backed bridge into Grange village. Hotel is through village on right.

52 Borrowdale Hotel

★★★

Borrowdale Road, Borrowdale, Keswick, Cumbria, CA12 5UV
Tel: 01768 777224 Fax: 01768 777338
Email: theborrowdalehotel@yahoo.com
33 bedrs SB £50 DB £120 HBS £60 HBD £140 B £8.50 L £2.50 D £22.25
CC: MC Vi Swi Delt JCB

How to get there: Three miles from the market town of Keswick at the head of Lake Derwent Water.

53 The Leathes Head

★★★★

Borrowdale, Keswick, Cumbria, CA12 5UY
Tel: 017687 77247 Fax: 017687 77363
Email: email@leatheshead.co.uk
Web: www.leatheshead.co.uk
Children minimum age: 7

Set in three acres of grounds in the beautiful Borrowdale Valley. Award-winning cuisine, tranquil surroundings and stunning views. A small, wellcoming hotel offering high quality service and accommodation.
11 bedrs SB £52.50 DB £85 HBS £72.50 HBD £62.50 B £5.95 L £6.95 D £21.50
CC: MC Vi Swi Delt JCB
How to get there: Follow the B5289 Borrowdale road out of Keswick for 3³/₄ miles; we are on the left after the Borrowdale Hotel.

54 Scafell Hotel

★★★

Rosthwaite, Borrowdale, Cumbria, CA12 5XB
Tel: 01768 777208 Fax: 01768 777280
Email: info@scafellhotel.ws
Web: www.scafell.co.uk/hotel
24 bedrs SB £41.50 DB £83.00 HBS £63.50 HBD £127.00 B £8.75 L £10.75 D £21
CC: MC Vi Swi Delt

How to get there: 6¹/₂ miles south of Keswick on B5289
See advert below

55 Greenbank Country House Hotel

◆◆◆◆

Borrowdale, Keswick, Cumbria, CA12 5UY
Tel: 01768 777215
Children minimum age: 2
Closed Christmas and January
10 bedrs SB £32 DB £64 HBS £44 HBD £88
CC: MC Vi Swi
How to get there: Take A66 to Keswick. Follow signs to Borrowdale on B5289 for approximately 3¹/₂ miles.

Northwest

Burnley, Lancashire

56 Higher Trapp Country House Hotel

★★★ ®

Trapp Lane, Simonstone, near Burnley,
Lancashire, BB12 7QW
Tel: 01282 772781 Fax: 01282 772782
Email: reception@highertrapphotel.co.uk
Web: www.highertrapphotel.co.uk
30 bedrs CC: MC Vi Swi Delt

How to get there: M65 at Junction 8 take A678,
head for Clitheroe, through one set of traffic lights
to next. Left following signs to Whalley. A671 for
Clitheroe. Right onto School Lane (this becomes
Trapp Lane). Higher Trapp is one mile on left.

57 Oaks Hotel

★★★★ ®

Colne Road, Reedley, Burnley,
Lancashire, BB10 2LF
Tel: 01282 414141 Fax: 01282 433401
Email: oaks@shireinns.co.uk
Web: www.shireinns.co.uk
50 bedrs SB £96 DB £116 B £11.50 L £5.50
D £22 CC: MC Vi Am DC Swi Delt

How to get there: Leave the M65 at junction 12.
Follow signs for Burnley at next three roundabouts. Oaks is on A682/A56 after about one
mile.

58 Travelodge Burnley

Travel Accommodation
A161/A1679, Calvary Barracks, Barracks Road,
Burnley, Lancashire, BB11 4AS
Tel: 08700 850 950
Web: www.travelodge.co.uk
32 bedrs B £4.25 CC: MC Vi Am DC Swi Delt

Bury, Manchester

59 Bolholt Hotel

★★★

Walshaw Road, Bury, Manchester, BL8 1PU
Tel: 0161 762 4000 Fax: 0161 762 4100
Email: enquiries@bolholt.co.uk
Web: www.bolholt.co.uk
65 bedrs SB £79 DB £94 B £8.95 L £10.95
D £16.95 CC: MC Vi Am DC Swi Delt JCB

See advert on facing page

Buttermere, Cumbria

60 Bridge Hotel

★★★ ®

Buttermere, Lake District, Cumbria, CA13 9UZ
Tel: 01768 770252 Fax: 01768 770215
Email: enquiries@bridge-hotel.com
Web: www.bridge-hotel.com
21 bedrs SB £35 DB £70 HBS £42.50
HBD £42.50 D £21.50
CC: MC Vi Swi

How to get there: Take A66 around Keswick.
Turn off at Braithwaite. Head over "Newlands
Pass". This brings you down into Buttermere
and the hotel.

Carlisle, Cumbria

61 Central Plaza Hotel

★★★

Victoria Viaduct, Carlisle, Cumbria, CA3 8AL
Tel: 01228 520256 Fax: 01228 514657
Email: info@centralplazahotel.co.uk
Web: www.centralplazahotel.co.uk
84 bedrs SB £65 DB £75 HBS £75 HBD £47.50
B £4.50 L £1.95 D £14.95
CC: MC Vi Am DC Swi Delt

How to get there: The Central Plaza Hotel is
situated in the heart of Carlisle.

62 Crown Hotel

★★★ ®

Wetheral, Carlisle, Cumbria, CA4 8ES
Tel: 01282 414141 Fax: 01282 835586
Email: jane@shireinns.co.uk
Web: www.shireinns.co.uk
51 bedrs
CC: MC Vi Am DC Swi

How to get there: Leave M6 at Junction 42 and
follow B6263 to Wetheral, turn right in village.

63 Crown & Mitre Hotel

★★★

4 English Street, Carlisle, Cumbria, CA3 8HZ
Tel: 01228 525491 Fax: 01228 514553
Email: info@crownandmitre-hotel-carlisle-com
Web: www.crownandmitre-hotel-carlisle-com
94 bedrs SB £84 DB £109 HBS £98.50
HBD £69 B £7.95 L £4.95 D £14.50
CC: MC Vi Am DC Swi Delt

How to get there: From M6 Junction 42, take A6
to city centre. Turn left at traffic lights, then
sharp right into Blackfriars Street.

64 Cumbria Park

★★★

32 Scotland Road, Carlisle, CA3 9DG
Tel: 01228 522887 Fax: 01228 514796
Email: enquiries@cumbriaparkhotel.co.uk
Web: www.cumbriaparkhotel.co.uk
Closed Christmas
53 bedrs SB £74 DB £95 HBS £89 HBD £62.50
B £7.50 L £12.50 D £15.95
CC: MC Vi Am DC Swi Delt JCB

How to get there: Leave M6 at Junction 44.
Hotel is 1¹/₂ miles down main road into Carlisle
on left-hand side.

65 Swallow Hilltop Hotel

★★★

London Road, Carlisle, Cumbria, CA1 2PQ
Tel: 01228 529255 Fax: 01228 525238
Email: carlisle-swallow@whitbread.com
Web: www.swallowhotels.com
92 bedrs SB £95 DB £110
B £9.75 L £12 D £18.50
CC: MC Vi Am DC Swi Delt

How to get there: Leave the M6 at Junction 42.
Follow signs for Carlisle on A6. Swallow Hilltop
Hotel two miles on left, up a hill.

66 Graham Arms Hotel

★★

English Street, Longtown, near Carlisle,
The Borders, CA6 5SE
Tel: 01228 791213 Fax: 01228 791213
Email: hotel@cumbria.com
Web: www.cumbria.com
14 bedrs
CC: MC Vi Am Swi

How to get there: Just six miles from Junction
44 of M6. Follow signposts to Galashiels/The
Borders Tourist Route. The Graham Arms is
about 400m on the right as you enter this small
town.

67 Pinegrove Hotel

★★

262 London Road, Carlisle, Cumbria, CA1 2QS
Tel: 01228 524828 Fax: 01228 810941
Closed Christmas Day
31 bedrs SB £48 DB £60 B £6 D £4.75
CC: MC Vi Am DC Swi Delt

How to get there: Leave M6 at Junction 42,
onto A6. Carlisle Hotel is situated 1¹/₂ miles
along this road on left-hand side.

68 Travelodge Carlisle (Southwaite)

Travel Accommodation
M6, Broadfield Site, Carlisle, Cumbria, CA4 0NT
Tel: 08700 850 950
Web: www.travelodge.co.uk
38 bedrs B £4.25
CC: MC Vi Am DC Swi Delt

Northwest

69 Travelodge Caslisle North (Todhills)

Travel Accommodation
A74 South, Todhills, Carlisle,
Cumbria, CA6 4HA
Tel: 08700 850 950
Web: www.travelodge.co.uk
40 bedrs B £4.25
CC: MC Vi Am DC Swi Delt

70 Bessiestown Farm Country Guesthouse

◆ ◆ ◆ ◆ ◆
Catlowdy, Longtown, Carlisle,
Cumbria, CA6 5QP
Tel: 01228 577219 Fax: 01228 577019
Email: bestbb2000@cs.com
Web: www.bessiestown.co.uk
Closed Christmas Day

Featured on TV, Multi Award-Winning Best
Guesthouse. Warm welcome — peace and quiet
— delightful public rooms — beautiful ensuite
bedrooms — delicious real food — indoor
swimming pool — easy access M6 M74 A7.
6 bedrs SB £35 DB £55
HBS £36 HBD £40 D £13
CC: MC Vi

How to get there: M6 exit 44 A7 to Longtown
Road at Bush Hotel 6½ miles to T-junction right
1½ miles to Catlowdy. Bessiestown 1st on left.

71 Vallum House Garden Hotel

◆ ◆ ◆
Burgh Road, Carlisle, Cumbria, CA2 7NB
Tel: 01228 521860
9 bedrs SB £35 DB £50
B £5 L £7 D £10
CC: MC Vi DC Swi Delt

How to get there: On west side of city, 1½ miles
from town centre.

Carnforth, Lancashire

72 Royal Station Hotel

★★
Market Street, Carnforth, Lancashire, LA5 9BT
Tel: 01524 732033 Fax: 01524 720267
Email: royalstation@mitchellshotels.co.uk
Web: www.mitchellshotels.co.uk
13 bedrs SB £40 DB £54
B £5.50 L £2.95 D £4.75
CC: MC Vi DC Swi Delt

How to get there: Leave M6 at J35. Follow signs
for Carnforth. At crossroads turn right into
Market Street. We are on the right.

73 Travelodge Carnforth

Travel Accommodation
M6, Burton West, Carnforth, Lancashire, LA6 1JF
Tel: 08700 850 950
Web: www.travelodge.co.uk
47 bedrs B £4.25
CC: MC Vi Am DC Swi Delt

Chester, Cheshire

74 The Chester Grosvenor

Blue Ribbon Winner

★ ★ ★ ★ ★
56 Eastgate, Chester, CH1 1LT
Tel: 01244 324024 Fax: 01244 313246
Email: chesgrov@chestergrosvenor.co.uk
Web: www.chestergrosvenor.co.uk
Closed Christmas

This deluxe property is set in the heart of historic
Chester. The hotel has 85 individually designed
bedrooms and suites, with two award-winning
restaurants, a leisure suite and car parking.

85 bedrs SB £202.50 DB £311 B £10.50 L £25
D £45 CC: MC Vi Am DC Swi Delt JCB
⚓ ♿ ⊞ ✏ 🐴 ⊗ ⌨ ☎ ✳ ⌕ **P**⊗ ♞ 🕯 ♨ ⚓ ⚏
♨♨ 'Y'
How to get there: Turn off M56 for M53 at
Junction 15; turn off M53 at Junction 12 for A56.
Follow signs for Chester and city centre hotels.

75 Chester Crabwall Manor

★★★★★ ⚘ ⚘ ⚘
Parkgate Road, Mollington, Chester,
Cheshire, CH1 6NE
Tel: 01244 851666 Fax: 01244 851000/400
Email: crabwallmanor@marstonhotels.com
Web: www.marstonhotels.com

48 bedrs SB £129 DB £159 B £12 L £22 D £35
CC: MC Vi Am DC Swi Delt
⚓ ♿ ✏ 🐴 ⊗ ⊙ ⌨ ☎ **P**⊗ ♞ 🕯 ⚓ 🐠 ♨♨ ♨♨
SPA 'Y' ⚡ ⌕ ☑
How to get there: At the end of the M56, follow
signs for Queensferry/North Wales for approx.
$1/2$ a mile, turn left at the roundabout. Crabwall
Manor is $1^3/4$ miles down this road, on the left.

76 De Vere St. David's Park Hotel

★★★★ ⚘ ⚘ ⚘
St. David's Park, Ewloe, near Chester, CH5 3YB
Tel: 01244 520800 Fax: 01244 520930
Email: reservations.stdavidspark
            @devere-hotels.com
Web: www.devereonline.co.uk
145 bedrs B £11.50 L £16.50 D £21
CC: MC Vi Am DC Swi
⚓ ♿ ⊞ ✏ 🐴 ⊗ ⊙ ⌨ ☎ **P**⊗ ♞ 🕯 🐴 ⚓ 👁
♨♨ ♨♨ SPA 'Y' ⚡ ☑
How to get there: From Chester, follow the A55
to North Wales for 12 miles, then follow A494.
Just past the Queensferry junction, take the left
sliproad, B5127 to Buckley.

77 Queen Hotel

★★★★ ⚘
City Road, Chester, Cheshire, CH1 3AH
Tel: 01244 305000 Fax: 01244 318483
Email: reservations.queen@principalhotels.co.uk
Web: www.principalhotels.co.uk
128 bedrs SB £90 DB £110 HBS £68 HBD £68
B £10.95 L £15 D £25 CC: MC Vi Am DC Swi
⚓ ⊞ 🐴 ⊗ ⊙ ⌨ ☎ **P**⊗ ♞ 🕯 ♨♨ ♨♨
How to get there: Follow signs for station, hotel
is opposite.

78 Broxton Hall Country House Hotel

★★★ ⚘
Whitchurch Road, Broxton,
Cheshire, CH3 9JS
Tel: 01829 782321 Fax: 01829 782330
Email: reservations@broxtonhall.com
Web: www.broxtonhall.uk.com
10 bedrs SB £70.00 DB £85.00
HBS £90.00 HBD £70.00
B £6.50 L £17.00 D £26.50
CC: MC Vi Am DC Delt
✏ 🐴 ⌨ ☎ **P** ♞ 🕯 🕯 ♨♨
How to get there: Nine miles south of Chester
on A41 towards Whitchurch.
See advert below

79 Gateway To Wales

★★★
Welsh Road, Sealand, near Chester,
Cheshire, CH5 2HX
Tel: 01244 830332 Fax: 01244 836190
40 bedrs
CC: MC Vi Am DC Swi Delt
♿ ⊞ ⊗ ⊙ ⌨ ☎ **P**⊗ ♞ 🕯 ♨♨ ♨♨ 'Y' ☑
How to get there: From the A55 take the A494.
Four miles from Chester.

Northwest

80 Green Bough Hotel

★★★

60 Hoole Road, Hoole, Chester,
Cheshire, CH2 3NL
Tel: 01244 326241 Fax: 01244 326265
Email: greenboughhotel@cwcom.net
Web: www.smoothhound.co.uk/
 hotels/greenbo.html
Children minimum age: 11
17 bedrs SB £65 DB £85 HBS £85
HBD £62.50 L £10 D £20
CC: MC Vi Am DC Swi Delt

How to get there: Take M53 to Chester. Leave at
Junction 12 and take A56 to Chester city. Hotel
is one mile from motorway.
See advert on facing page

81 Grosvenor Pulford Hotel

★★★

Wrexham Road, Pulford, Chester,
Cheshire, CH4 9DG
Tel: 01244 570560 Fax: 01244 570809
Email: enquiries@grosvenorpulfordhotel.co.uk
Web: www.grosvenorpulfordhotel.co.uk
76 bedrs SB £75 DB £80
CC: MC Vi Am DC Swi Delt

How to get there: Leave M53/A55 at junction
signposted A483 Chester, Wrexham & North
Wales. Turn onto B5445, hotel is two miles on
right.
See advert on facing page

82 Llyndir Hall Hotel

★★★

Llyndir Lane, Rossett, Clwyd, LL12 0AY
Tel: 01244 571648 Fax: 01244 571258
Email: llyndirhall@pageant.co.uk
Web: www.pageant.co.uk
38 bedrs
CC: MC Vi Am Swi Delt

83 Mill Hotel

★★★

Milton Street, Chester, Cheshire, CH1 3NF
Tel: 01244 350035 Fax: 01244 345635
Email: reservations@millhotel.com
Web: www.millhotel.com
129 bedrs SB £55 DB £72 HBS £75 HBD £55
B £8.50 L £10.50 D £18.50

CC: MC Vi Am DC Swi Delt

How to get there: J12 M53 to A56 to city centre,
left at second roundabout (A5268), first left
Sellar Street, second left Milton Street.
See advert on facing page

84 Northop Hall Country House Hotel

★★★

Northop Hall Village, near Mold,
Flintshire, CH7 6HJ
Tel: 01244 816181 Fax: 01244 814661
Email: northop@hotel-chester.com
Web: www.hotel-chester.com

Dating from 1872, steeped in history and set in
acres of tranquil gardens and woodland, offering
the modern comfort and service you would
expect from a lovely Country House Hotel.
27 bedrs SB £59.50 DB £69.50
HBS £75.45 HBD £50.70
B £9.50 L £10.50 D £15.95
CC: MC Vi Am DC Swi Delt JCB

How to get there: A55 Queensferry, take first exit
for Buckley; at roundabout take first exit, then
immediate right to Northop Hall/Ewloe Castle.
Two miles, bear left, hotel is 200 yards on left.

85 The Blossoms

★★★

St. John Street, Chester, Cheshire, CH1 1HL
Tel: 0870 400 8108 Fax: 01244 346433
Email: heritagehotels_chester.blossoms
 @forte-hotels.co.uk
Web: www.heritage-hotels.com
64 bedrs SB £104 DB £129 HBS £122
HBD £82.50 B £14.50 L £6.95 D £18
CC: MC Vi Am DC Swi

How to get there: Leave M53 at Junction 12.
Follow signs for city centre. St. John Street is
off Eastgate Street at centre of shopping area.

Grosvenor Pulford Hotel

18 metre swimming pool • Whirlpool • Sauna Aromatherapy Steam Room • Solarium. Fully equipped gymnasium. Hair and Beauty salon. Snooker Room. 72 ensuite bedrooms with all the modern conveniences.
Bar snacks and à la Carte meals served daily. Conference and Banqueting facilities for between 10 and 240 delegates. Wedding Receptions our speciality. Ideally located only five minutes from Chester city centre.

Wrexham Road, Pulford,
Chester CH4 9DG
Tel: 01244 570560   Fax: 01244 570809
Email: enquiries@grosvenorpulford.co.uk
Website: www.grosvenorpulfordhotel.co.uk

Green Bough Hotel

Non-smoking, traditional, elegant, friendly Victorian townhouse. Lovingly refurbished using luxurious wallpapers and fabrics. Within easy walking distance of historic city centre.
Free car parking. The award-winning restaurant is presided over by our Savoy-trained chef. The daily menu uses fresh local produce and service is attentive yet discreet.

60 Hoole Road, Hoole, Chester,
Cheshire CH2 3NL
Tel:01244 326241   Fax: 01244 326265
greenboughhotel@cwcom.net
www.SmoothHound.co.uk/hotels/
greenbo.html

Northwest

MILL HOTEL

10. Good reasons to discover Chester's Little Venice

1. City centre 130 Bedroom Hotel with parking.
2. 4 classes of rooms. Standard, Business, Premier, and Club (pictured).
3. Chester's waterside "Restaurant Canaletto".
   Friday & Saturday nights' Dine & Dance.
4. Broad Beam 50 seater Restaurant Cruiser.
5. Health Club with 60ft Swimming Pool, Spa Bath, Steam Room, Sauna, Aerobics, Technogym gymnasium.
6. A Beauty Spa using Pevonia Botonica.
   Complete treatments for Men & Women.
7. "Venezia" Cafe Bar.
8. Public Bar serving 15 Traditional Cask Ales.
9. Deli-Bar.
10. Conference Rooms.

** Discover Chester's most innovative Hotel **

Mill Hotel, Milton Street, Chester, Cheshire CH1 3NF   Tel: 01244 350035 Fax: 01244 345635
Email: reservations@millhotel.com   ЯƎC ★★★   www.millhotel.com

86 Chester Court Hotel

★★
48 Hoole Road, Chester, Cheshire, CH2 3NL
Tel: 01244 320779 Fax: 01244 344795
Email: info@chestercourthotel.com
Web: www.chestercourthotel.com
20 bedrs SB £45 DB £70
HBS £61 HBD £51
D £16 CC: MC Vi Am Swi Delt

How to get there: From M53 Junction 12, take
A56 into Chester. Proceed along Hoole Road
(A56), and find Chester Court Hotel on right
opposite All Saints Church.

87 Dene Hotel

★★
95 Hoole Road, Chester, Cheshire, CH2 3ND
Tel: 01244 321165 Fax: 01244 350277
Email: info@denehotel.com
Web: www.denehotel.com
52 bedrs SB £46 DB £59
HBS £53 HBD £36.50
B £6.95 D £7.95
CC: MC Vi Am Swi Delt

How to get there: Take Junction 12 of the M53.
Follow signs for A56 Hoole Road. The Dene
Hotel is about 500 yards on left.

88 Redland Hotel

◆◆◆◆◆ ※
64 Hough Green, Chester,
Cheshire, CH4 8JY
Tel: 01244 671024 Fax: 01244 681309
13 bedrs SB £45 DB £65
CC: None accepted

89 The Guesthouse at Old Hall Country Club

◆◆◆◆◆ ※
Aldford Road, Chester,
Cheshire, CH3 6EA
Tel: 01244 317273 Fax: 01244 313785
Email: info@oldhallcountryclub.com
Web: www.oldhallcountryclub.com
6 bedrs SB £60 DB £100
HBS £75 HBD £65
L £5 D £7.50
CC: MC Vi Swi Delt

How to get there: Call Club reception on 01244
311593 for detailed directions.
See advert on facing page

90 Stone Villa

◆◆◆◆ ※
3 Stone Place, Chester, Cheshire, CH2 3NR
Tel: 01244 345014 Fax: 01244 345015
Email: adam@stonevilla.freeserve.co.uk
Web: www.smoothhound.co.uk
9 bedrs SB £35 DB £28 CC: MC Vi Swi Delt JCB

How to get there: From M5, M6, M53, take A56.
Follow past church on left. Pass through traffic
lights, take second left into Stone Place.
Proceed to bottom of cul-de-sac and through
entrance into car park.

91 Ba Ba Guest House

◆◆◆ ※
65 Hoole Road, Hoole, Chester,
Cheshire, CH2 3NJ
Tel: 01244 315047 Fax: 01244 315046
Email: reservations@babaguesthouse.co.uk
Web: www.babaguesthouse.co.uk

Family-run B&B in large Victorian town house.
Birthplace of Leonard Cheshire V.C. City centre
one mile and railway station ½ mile. On local
bus route. Families welcome.
5 bedrs SB £27 DB £49
CC: MC Vi

How to get there: Exit J12 M53 onto A56, signs
for Chester. The guest house is situated one
mile from the motorway on the left hand side.

92 Glen Garth Guest House

◆◆◆
59 Hoole Road, Chester, Cheshire, CH2 3NJ
Tel: 01244 310260
Email: glengarth@chester63.fsnet.co.uk
5 bedrs SB £27 DB £50 CC: None accepted

How to get there: Leave M53 for A56 and follow
signs for Chester. The guest house is situated
on the right, one mile from the junction.

93 Devonia Guest House

33–35 Hoole Road, Chester,
Cheshire, CH2 3NH
Tel: 01244 322236

Chorley, Lancashire

94 Pines Hotel

★★★
Preston Road, Clayton-le-Woods,
Lancashire, PR6 7ED
Tel: 01772 338551 Fax: 01772 629002
Email: mail@thepines-hotel
Web: www.thepines-hotel.co.uk
34 bedrs SB £70 DB £80 B £7.50 L £10
CC: MC Vi Am DC Swi Delt

How to get there: M6 Junction 29 to Preston
south. Right at roundabout. Follow A6. After
fourth mini roundabout, hotel is immediately on
left.

95 Travelodge Preston (Chorley)

Travel Accommodation
A6, Preston Road, Clayton-le-Woods,
Chorley, Lancashire, PR6 7JB
Tel: 08700 850 950
Web: www.travelodge.co.uk
40 bedrs B £4.25
CC: MC Vi Am DC Swi Delt

96 Parr Hall Farm

♦ ♦ ♦ ♦ ✍
Parr Lane, Eccleston, Chorley,
Lancashire, PR7 5SL
Tel: 01257 451917 Fax: 01257 453749
Email: parrhall@talk21.com
4 bedrs SB £30 DB £50
CC: MC Vi Swi Delt

How to get there: M6 J27, A5209 for Parbold;
immediately right on B5250 for Eccleston. After
five miles Parr Lane on right, property first left.

Clitheroe, Lancashire

97 Brooklyn Guest House

♦ ♦ ♦ ♦ ✍
32 Pimlico Road, Clitheroe, Lancashire, BB7 2AH
Tel: 01200 428268
Email: rg@classicfm.net
4 bedrs SB £27.50 DB £43
HBS £37 HBD £31.50 D £10
CC: MC Vi Swi Delt

How to get there: North of town centre. Close to
roundabout with BP garage: take Waddington
Road, 200 yards. Turn right at smaller
roundabout.

Congleton, Cheshire

98 The Plough At Eaton

♦ ♦ ♦ ♦ ✍
Macclesfield Road, Eaton, Congleton,
Cheshire, CW12 2NR
Tel: 01260 280207 Fax: 01260 298377

Northwest

Coniston, Cumbria

99 Coniston Lodge
Little Gem

♦ ♦ ♦ ♦ ♦ ℛ ✕ ♟

Station Road, Coniston, Cumbria, LA21 8HH
Tel: 01539 441201 Fax: 01539 441201
Email: info@coniston-lodge.com
Web: www.coniston-lodge.com
Children minimum age: 10
Closed January

An RAC Little Gem winner. Beautiful scenery,
peaceful surroundings, fine home cooking and a
very warm welcome.
6 bedrs SB £48.50 DB £84 HBS £67.50
HBD £61 D £19.50 CC: MC Vi Am

How to get there: Leave A593 at the crossroads
close to filling station. Turn up the hill (Station
Road). Hotel is 100m on left. Park under building.

100 Crown Hotel

♦ ♦ ♦ ♦

Coniston, Cumbria, LA21 8EA
Tel: 01539 441243 Fax: 01539 441804
Email: info@crown-hotel-coniston.com
Web: www.crown-hotel-coniston.com
12 bedrs SB £35 DB £60 HBS £50 HBD £45
B £6 L £6 D £15 CC: MC Vi Am DC Swi Delt
How to get there: Leave M6 at Junction 36. Join
the A590 to Windermere and Ambleside. Take
the A593 to Coniston.

Crewe, Cheshire

101 Travelodge Crewe

Travel Accommodation
M6 J16, Barthomley, Crewe, Cheshire, CW2 5PT
Tel: 08700 850 950
Web: www.travelodge.co.uk
42 bedrs B £4.25 CC: MC Vi Am DC Swi Delt

Dalston, Cumbria

102 Dalston Hall Hotel

★ ★ ★ ℛ
Dalston, Cumbria, CA5 7JX
Tel: 01228 710271 Fax: 01228 711273
Email: info@dalston-hall-hotel.co.uk
Web: www.dalston-hall-hotel.co.uk
12 bedrs SB £80 DB £150
HBS £95 HBD £90
B £8.50 L £12 D £25
CC: MC Vi Am DC Swi Delt

Darwen, Lancashire

103 Whitehall Hotel & Restaurant

★ ★ ★
Springbank, Whitehall, Darwen,
Lancashire, BB3 2JU
Tel: 01254 701595 Fax: 01254 773426
Email: hotel@thewhitehallhotel.freeserve.co.uk
17 bedrs SB £55 DB £65 HBS £70.50 HBD £48
B £7.50 L £12.50 D £16.95
CC: MC Vi Am Swi Delt

How to get there: Just off the main A666
between Blackburn and Bolton, close to M65
Junction 4.

Eastham, Merseyside

104 Travelodge Eastham (Wirral)

Travel Accommodation
A41 North, 1408 New Chester Road,
Eastham, Wirral, L62 9AQ
Tel: 08700 850 950
Web: www.travelodge.co.uk
31 bedrs B £4.25
CC: MC Vi Am DC Swi Delt

See the road ahead

Just dial 1740* from any mobile
phone to get up-to-the-minute
RAC traffic information on
motorways and major A roads.
Try it now! *Calls to 1740 are charged
at premium rate.

Ellesmere Port, Cheshire

105 Quality Hotel Chester

★★★
Berwick Road, off Welsh Road, Little Sutton,
Ellesmere Port, Cheshire, CH66 4PS
Tel: 0151 339 5121 Fax: 0151 339 3214
Email: admin@gb066.u-net.com
Web: www.choicehotels.com
53 bedrs SB £104.75 DB £114.75 HBS £123.25
HBD £69.13 B £9.75 L £3.50 D £18.50
CC: MC Vi Am DC Swi Delt

Eskdale, Cumbria

106 Brook House Inn

♦♦♦♦
Boot, Eskdale, Cumbria, CA19 1TG
Tel: 01946 723288 Fax: 01946 723160
Email: stay@brookhouseinn.co.uk
Web: www.brookhouseinn.co.uk
8 bedrs SB £40 DB £60 HBS £55.95
HBD £45.95 B £6.50 L £2.50 D £5.95
CC: MC Vi Swi Delt JCB

How to get there: Located in Boot on the
Ambleside-Eskdale road. Please post/fax/ e-
mail for directions.

Garstang, Lancashire

107 Crofters Hotel

★★★★
A6 Cabus, Garstang, Lancashire, PR3 1PH
Tel: 01995 604128 Fax: 01995 601646
Email: sales@mitchellshotels.co.uk
Web: www.mitchellshotels.co.uk
19 bedrs SB £46 DB £58
B £6 L £10.75 D £16.10
CC: MC Vi Am Swi Delt JCB
How to get there: Situated midway between
Preston and Lancaster, on the A6 trunk road,
near the market town of Garstang.

Gilsland, Cumbria

108 Bush Nook Guest House

♦♦♦♦
Bush Nook, Upper Denton, Gilsland,
Cumbria, CA8 7AF
Tel: 01697 747194 Fax: 01697 747790
Email: paulaibarton@bushnook.freeserve.co.uk
Web: www.hadriansway.co.uk
4 bedrs SB £20 DB £50
HBS £30 HBD £35 D £10
CC: MC Vi Am DC Swi Delt JCB

How to get there: Easy access from A1 or M6.
¹/₂ mile off A69 between Brampton and
Haltwhistle, signposted Birdoswald, Spadeadam
and Bushnook.

Grange-over-Sands, Cumbria

109 Graythwaite Manor Hotel

★★★
Fernhill Road, Grange-over-Sands,
Cumbria, LA11 7JE
Tel: 01539 532001 Fax: 01539 535549
Email: office@graythwaitemanor.co.uk
Web: www.graythwaitemanor.co.uk

A lovely family-run country house set in
extensive gardens and woodland overlooking
bay and hills. Charming bedrooms, some
ground floor, generous lounges with antiques
and log fires. Excellent cuisine and wine cellar.
21 bedrs SB £55 DB £99 HBD £68
B £7.50 L £12 D £18
CC: MC Vi Am Swi Delt JCB
How to get there: Follow B5277 through
Grange. Turn right opposite fire station into
Fernhill Road.

Northwest

110 Netherwood

★★★

Lindale Road, Grange-over-Sands,
Cumbria, LA11 6ET
Tel: 01539 532552 Fax: 01539 534121
Email: blawith@aol.com
Web: www.netherwood-hotel.co.uk
28 bedrs
CC: MC Vi Swi Delt

How to get there: Leave M6 at Junction 36.
Take A590 for Barrow-in-Furness. Follow for
Holker Hall on B5277. Netherwood is on right
just before rail station.

111 Elton Hotel

◆◆◆◆

Windermere Road, Grange-over-Sands,
Cumbria, LA11 6EQ
Tel: 01539 532838 Fax: 01539 532838
Email: chris.crane@btclick.com
Closed January to February
7 bedrs SB £29 DB £48 HBS £40 HBD £35
CC: None accepted

How to get there: 50m after Rail Station, take
right exit at mini roundabout. Hotel 200m on
left.

Grasmere, Cumbria

112 Wordsworth Hotel

★★★★★

Grasmere, Cumbria, LA22 9SW
Tel: 01539 435592 Fax: 01539 435765
Email: enquiry@wordsworth-grasmere.co.uk
Web: www.grasmere-hotels.co.uk

Set in the heart of Lakeland, in magnificent
surroundings, the Wordsworth Hotel has a
reputation for the high quality of its food,
accommodation and hospitality.

37 bedrs SB £90 DB £150 HBS £110 HBD £105
B £12.50 L £19.50 D £32.50
CC: MC Vi Am DC

How to get there: From north M6 J40 for
Keswick, A591 for Grasmere; from south, J36
M6 A590, then A591 as above.

113 Grasmere Red Lion Hotel

★★★

Red Lion Square, Grasmere, Cumbria, LA22 9SS
Tel: 01539 435456 Fax: 01539 435579
Email: enquiries@hotelgrasmere.uk.com
Web: www.hotelgrasmere.uk.com

Beautifully refurbished hotel in the heart of the
Lake District. All rooms ensuite — many with
jacuzzi bath. Good food, friendly staff, leisure
facilities and hairdressing salon.
47 bedrs SB £42 DB £84 HBS £56.50
HBD £56.50 B £7.50 D £19
CC: MC Vi Am DC Swi Delt

How to get there: From South, M6 Junction 36.
Take A591 to Grasmere. From North, M6 J40
and take A66 towards Keswick. Turn left
(signposted Windermere). A591 to Grasmere.

114 Heritage Hotels — The Swan

★★★

Keswick Road, Grasmere, Cumbria, LA22 9RF
Tel: 0870 400 8132 Fax: 01539 435741
Email: heritagehotels-grasmere.swan
        @forte-hotels.com
Web: www.heritage-hotels.com
38 bedrs SB £80 DB £160 HBS £90
HBD £90 B £14 L £14 D £23
CC: MC Vi Am DC Swi JCB

How to get there: From M6 Jct 36 A591 to
Windermere, then through Ambleside to
Grasmere. Hotel on Keswick Road on outskirts
of Grasmere village.

115 Grasmere Hotel

★★

Broadgate, Grasmere, Cumbria, LA22 9TA
Tel: 01539 435277 Fax: 01539 435277
Email: enquiries@grasmerehotel.co.uk
Web: www.grasmerehotel.co.uk
Children minimum age: 12
Closed 2 January to 13 February
12 bedrs SB £30 DB £60
HBS £50 HBD £40 D £22.50
CC: MC Vi Am Swi Delt

116 Moss Grove Hotel

★★

Grasmere, Cumbria, LA22 9SW
Tel: 01539 435251 Fax: 01539 435691
Email: martinw@globalnet.co.uk
Web: www.grasmereccomodation.co.uk
Closed December and January
13 bedrs SB £48 DB £105 HBS £63 HBD £135
B £6 D £13
CC: MC Vi Swi Delt JCB

How to get there: From South, M6 Junction 36, then A591 and left to village. Hotel on right just past church. From North, M6 J40, A66 Keswick, A591 Grasmere and right into village. On left opposite church.

Hampson Green, Lancashire

117 Hampson House Hotel

★★
Galgate, Hampson Green,
Lancashire, LA2 0JB
Tel: 01524 751158 Fax: 01524 751779

Hawkshead, Cumbria

118 Highfield House Country Hotel

★★

Hawkshead Hill, Hawkshead, Cumbria, LA22 0PN
Tel: 01539 436344 Fax: 01539 436793
Email: rooms@highfield-hawkshead.com
Web: www.highfield-hawkshead.com
Closed January

Award-winning family-owned-and-run country house hotel with the best panoramic mountain views in the Lake District. Superb hospitality, service and location. Three acres of gardens, wonderful food.
11 bedrs CC: MC Vi Am Swi Delt

How to get there: Exit J36 M6. Follow signs for Hawkshead. Just outside Hawkshead on B5285.

119 Sawrey House Country Hotel — Little Gem

♦♦♦♦ ® ® ® ⚕ ?
Near Sawrey, Hawkshead, Cumbria, LA22 0LF
Tel: 01539 436387 Fax: 01539 436010
Email: shirley@sawreyhouse.com
Web: www.sawreyhouse.com
Children minimum age: 8
Closed January

Overlooking Esthwaite Waters, in the heart of Beatrix Potter village. Quality comfortable family-run hotel. Excellent food, tranquil setting; a haven for wildlife. Centrally situated.
11 bedrs SB £45 DB £90 HBS £65 HBD £65
B £7.50 D £30 CC: MC Vi Am Swi Delt JCB

How to get there: On B5285 from Hawkshead towards Windermere car ferry.

Northwest

120 Ivy House

◆◆◆◆ ⌀
Ambleside, Hawkshead, Cumbria, LA22 0NS
Tel: 01539 436204 Fax: 01539 436171
Email: david@ivyhousehotel.com
Web: www.ivyhousehotel.com
11 bedrs SB £39 DB £78
HBS £46.50 HBD £46.50
CC: MC Vi Swi Delt JCB
🔥🗑️💻🅿️📠🐾🍴♨️🛗💆
How to get there: M6 J36 or J37, signs for
Kendall, Windemere, Ambleside, Coniston and
then Hawkshead.

Heywood, Lancashire

121 Travelodge Birch (North)

Travel Accommodation
M62, Birch Service Area, Heywood,
Lancashire OL10 2HQ
Tel: 08700 850 950
Web: www.travelodge.co.uk
55 bedrs B £4.25
CC: MC Vi Am DC Swi Delt
🔥🗑️💻🐾

122 Travelodge Birch (South)

Travel Accommodation
M62, Birch Service Area, Heywood,
Lancashire, OL10 2HQ
Tel: 08700 850 950
Web: www.travelodge.co.uk
55 bedrs B £4.25
CC: MC Vi Am DC Swi Delt
🔥🗑️💻🐾

Holmes Chapel, Cheshire

123 Old Vicarage Hotel

★★★★ 🚩🚩
Knutsford Road, Cranage, Holmes Chapel,
Cheshire, CW4 8EF
Tel: 01477 532041 Fax: 01477 535728
Email: oldvichotel@aol.com
29 bedrs SB £73.50 DB £86.50
B £9.50 L £11.50 D £17.50
CC: MC Vi Am DC Swi Delt JCB
♿🗑️💻📠📞🐾🍴♨️🛗🛗
How to get there: Situated on the A50 only one
mile from Junction 18 on the M6.

Holmrook, Cumbria

124 Lutwidge Arms Hotel

★★
Holmrook, Cumbria, CA19 1UH
Tel: 01946 724230 Fax: 01946 724100
Email: ian@lutwidgewestcumbria.co.uk
Web: www.lutwidgewestcumbria.co.uk
19 bedrs SB £41.50 DB £56 HBS £36 HBD £36
B £6 L £5 D £12
CC: MC Vi Swi Delt JCB
♿🔥🗑️💻📠🅿️🐾🍴♨️🛗🛗📶
How to get there: On A595 at Holmrook, three
miles south of Gosforth.

Kendal, Cumbria

125 Heaves Hotel

★★
Heaves, near Kendal, Cumbria, LA8 8EF
Tel: 01539 560396 Fax: 01539 560269
Email: hotel@heaves.freeserve.co.uk
Web: www.heaveshotel.co.uk

Spacious Georgian mansion in 10 acres of
formal gardens and woodland. Four miles from
Exit 36 of M6 and Kendal. Family owned and
run. Library and billiard room.
13 bedrs SB £33 DB £58 HBS £47 HBD £43
B £4.00 L £10 D £14.50
CC: MC Vi Am DC Swi Delt JCB
♨️🍷🔥🗑️💻🅿️🐾🍴♨️🛗🛗♿
How to get there: M6 Junction 36, A590 Barrow
& South Lakes. After three miles follow A590 to
roundabout, again take A590. Second junction
on right (Sizergh), signs on left after turn.

126 Blaven Homestay

♦ ♦ ♦ ♦ ● 🔲 🔲 ❄ 📶

Middleshaw, Old Hutton, Kendall,
Cumbria, LA8 0LZ
Tel: 01539 734394 Fax: 01539 727447
Email: enquiries@blavenhomestay.co.uk
Web: www.blavenhomestay.co.uk

Luxury Lakeland house, quiet streamside
location, lovely garden. Excellent base for M6,
Lakes and Dales. Amiable hosts Janet and
Barry offer gourmet meals, fine wine and every
comfort to guests.
2 bedrs SB £42 DB £64 HBS £72 HBD £62
CC: MC Vi

❄ 🥄 🖵 🅿️

How to get there: From Oxenholme station take
B6254 Kirkby Lonsdale road for approx. 1¹/₂
miles. Left to Ewebank. Blaven 200m on right.

127 Primrose Cottage Guest House

♦ ♦ ♦ ♦

Orton Road, Tebay, Cumbria, CA10 3TL
Tel: 01539 624791
Email: primrosecottebay@aol.com

Adjacent M6 J38. Excellent accommodation, four-
poster, Jacuzzi bath, fruit & flowers, bath-robes,
one acre garden, private parking. Stopover or
short breaks. Pub nearby with restaurant. Pets
welcome. Ground floor bedrooms include
bathroom suitable for disabled person.
5 bedrs SB £25 DB £45 HBS £36 HBD £33.50
CC: None accepted

♿ 🍴 ❄ ⊗ 🥄 🖵 🅿️ ❄ 🔌 ♇

How to get there: Exit M6 J38 take right at
roundabout. We are first on right.

128 Garnett House Farm

♦ ♦ ♦

Burneside, Kendal, Cumbria, LA9 5SF
Tel: 01539 724542 Fax: 01539 724542
Closed Christmas to New Year
5 bedrs DB £40 CC: None accepted

⊗ 🥄 🖵 🅿️ ❄ ♇ 🍴 ♀

How to get there: Exit M6 J36, dual carrigeway
for nine miles. 2nd left at roundabout, A591 for
Windemere. After one mile turn right for Burnside.

Keswick, Cumbria

129 Derwentwater Hotel

★ ★ ★ ®

Portinscale, Keswick, Cumbria, CA12 5RE
Tel: 01768 772538 Fax: 01768 771002
Email: info@derwentwater-hotel.co.uk
Web: www.derwentwater-hotel.co.uk
47 bedrs B £11.95 D £22.50
CC: MC Vi Am DC JCB

♿ ♨ 🍴 ♞ ⊗ 🥄 🖵 ☎ 🅿️ ❄ 🔌 🍴 ⚏ ⚏

How to get there: Exit J40 M6 west on A66. 150
yards past third Keswick junction, left into
Portinscale, then left as road bears right.
See advert on following page

130 Keswick Country House Hotel

★ ★ ★

Station Road, Keswick, Cumbria, CA12 4NQ
Tel: 01768 772020 Fax: 01768 771300
Email: crafferty@principalhotels.co.uk
Web: www.principalhotels.co.uk
74 bedrs SB £73 DB £126 HBS £81 HBD £71
B £8.50 L £11.95 D £18.95
CC: MC Vi Am DC Swi Delt

♨ ♨ 🍴 ♞ 🥄 🖵 ☎ 🅿️ ❄ 🔌 🍴 ♀ ⚏ ⚏ ♿

How to get there: Exit J40 M6; A66 to Keswick;
head for leisure pool/museum; left into Station Rd.

131 The Queens Hotel

★ ★ ★

Main Street, Keswick, Cumbria, CA12 5JF
Tel: 01768 773333 Fax: 01768 771144
Email: book@queenshotel.co.uk
Web: www.queenshotel.co.uk
Closed Christmas
35 bedrs SB £33 DB £66 B £7.50 D £11
CC: MC Vi Am DC Swi Delt JCB

♨ 🍴 🥄 🖵 ☎ 🅿️ ❄ 🍴 ⚏ ⚏

How to get there: From Junction 40 M6 travel
west along A66, take Keswick turnoff, hotel is in
market square.

Northwest

Derwentwater
Hotel

RAC ★★★
RAC Dining Award

"Unique – Unrivalled"

The Derwentwater enjoys a stunning location, standing in 16 acres of conservation grounds on the shore of Lake Derwentwater.

Enjoy panoramic views from our Victorian style conservatory and many bedrooms. For special occasions our Deluxe Rooms with Four-Poster Beds, or separate lounge area, with the very finest of Lake Views, is a must.

The Deer's Leap Restaurant uses the best of local produce with vegetarian options always available.

Award-winning Hospitality, Customer Care, Entry to Leisure Club, Pets Welcome, and Environmental Policy.

A TRANQUIL HAVEN ON THE LAKE SHORE!

Portinscale, Keswick, Cumbria CA12 5RE
Tel: 017687 72538   Fax: 017687 71002
Email: info@derwentwater-hotel.co.uk
Website: www.derwentwater-hotel.co.uk

Best Western

132 Chaucer House Hotel

★★
Derwentwater Place, Keswick,
Cumbria, CA12 4DR
Tel: 01768 772318 Fax: 01768 775551
Email: enquiries@chaucer-house.demon.co.uk
Web: www.chaucer-house.co.uk
Closed December to January
34 bedrs SB £31 DB £62 HBS £45
HBD £90 B £9.50 D £21
CC: MC Vi Am Swi Delt JCB
How to get there: From A591 turn into Manor
Brow. The road is signed Keswick via Manor
Brow. Hotel is opposite church of St. John's at
the bottom of the road.

133 Crow Park Hotel

★★
The Heads, Keswick, Cumbria, CA12 5ER
Tel: 01768 772208 Fax: 01768 774776
28 bedrs SB £30.50 DB £61
HBS £44.50 HBD £89 B £5 D £11
CC: MC Vi Delt
How to get there: Approximately 200 metres
from town centre, overlooking park and lake.

134 Highfield Hotel

★★★ ℛ
The Heads, Keswick, Cumbria, CA12 5ER
Tel: 01768 772508 Fax: 01768 780634
Email: info@highfieldkeswick.co.uk
Web: www.highfieldkeswick.co.uk
Children minimum age: 8
Closed January
18 bedrs SB £37 DB £64
HBS £54 HBD £54
B £5 D £19.50
CC: MC Vi Am Swi Delt
How to get there: From A66 take 2nd exit at
roundabout. Turn left and follow to T-junction.
Turn left again then right at mini roundabout.
The Heads is fourth turning on right.

135 Ladstock Country House Hotel

★★
Thornthwaite, Keswick, Cumbria, CA12 5RZ
Tel: 01768 778210 Fax: 01768 778088
Email: enquiries@keswickhotel.co.uk
Web: www.keswickhotel.co.uk

Ladstock is a fine, grand country house set
amidst beautiful landscaped gardens,
overlooking Skiddaw (3200 ft) and related Fells,
also Bassenthwaite Lake. An ideal centre for
walking, touring or long breaks, also ideal for
weddings or conferences.
19 bedrs SB £45 DB £80 HBS £62 HBD £58
B £10 D £16.50
CC: MC Vi Am
How to get there: Just off the A66, turn left two
miles after Keswick following the signs for
Thornthwaite.

136 Lyzzick Hall

★★★ ℛ
Underskiddaw, Keswick, Cumbria, CA12 4PY
Tel: 01768 772277 Fax: 01768 772278
Email: lyzzickhall@netscapeonline.co.uk
Web: www.lyzzickhall.co.uk
Closed mid-January to mid-February

In a stunning location two miles north of
Keswick, family-run with acclaimed cuisine and
a relaxing atmosphere. Rambling gardens and a
superb indoor swimming pool.
29 bedrs SB £46.50 DB £93 HBS £59 HBD £59
B £7.50 L £12.50 D £24
CC: MC Vi Am Swi Delt JCB
How to get there: Two miles north of Keswick
on the A591, 19 miles west from Junction 40
(Penrith exit) on the M6.

Northwest

137 Middle Ruddings Hotel

★★

Braithwaite, Keswick, Cumbria, CA12 5RY
Tel: 01768 778436 Fax: 01768 778436
Email: middleruddings@aol.com
Web: www.middleruddings.com
11 bedrs SB £30 DB £60 HBS £37.50
HBD £37.50 B £7.50 L £4.25 D £5.95
CC: MC Vi Swi Delt JCB

How to get there: J40 M6, Penrith A66, follow
past Keswick. Pass the turn for Braithwaite,
then turn left after 150 yards — hotel faces you.
See advert below

138 Morrel's Restaurant & Rooms

★★ ℞

34 Lake Road, Keswick, Cumbria, CA12 5DQ
Tel: 01768 772666
Email: info@morrels.co.uk
Web: www.lakedistricthotel.co.uk
14 bedrs SB £30 DB £60 B £5 D £15
CC: MC Vi Swi Delt

How to get there: Leave M6 at Junction 40.
Follow A66 Keswick then take signs to the lake.
Morrel's is on left by roundabout.

139 Thwaite Howe Hotel

★★★ ℞

Thornthwaite, near Keswick, Cumbria, CA12 5SA
Tel: 01768 778281 Fax: 01768 778529
Web: www.thwaitehowe.co.uk
Children minimum age: 12
Closed 1–21 December

Exquisite small country house hotel nestling
against Thornthwaite Forest with views across
Derwent valley to Skidaw and mountains.
Excellent food and good wines.
8 bedrs SB £45 DB £70 HBS £62 HBD £104
CC: MC Vi Swi

How to get there: A66 past Keswick. Left at
Thornthwaite. After Thornthwaite Gallery car
park fork right to hotel at top of hill.

140 Swinside Lodge Hotel
Blue Ribbon Winner

★ ℞ ℞ ℞

Grange Road, Newlands, Keswick,
Cumbria, CA12 5UE
Tel: 01768 772948 Fax: 01768 772948
Email: info@swinsidelodge-hotel.co.uk
Web: www.swinsidelodge-hotel.co.uk
Children minimum age: 10
7 bedrs SB £62 DB £94 HBS £87 HBD £72
D £25
CC: MC Vi Swi Delt

How to get there: Leave Keswick on the A66 to
Cockermouth. Turn left signposted Portinscale.
Continue on this road for two miles, signposted
Grange, not Swinside.
See advert on facing page

Making a booking?

Don't forget to mention RAC
Hotels and Bed & Breakfast 2002.

141 Acorn House Hotel

Ambleside Road, Keswick, Cumbria, CA12 4DL
Tel: 01768 772553 Fax: 01768 775332
Email: info@acornhousehotel.co.uk
Web: www.acornhousehotel.co.uk
Children minimum age: 8
Closed November to February
10 bedrs SB £28.50 DB £52
CC: MC Vi Swi Delt
How to get there: 400m from town centre,
opposite St. John's Church on Ambleside Road.

142 Dalegarth House Country Hotel

Portinscale, Keswick, Cumbria, CA12 5RQ
Tel: 01768 772817 Fax: 01768 772817
Email: john@dalegarth-house.co.uk
Web: www.dalegarth-house.co.uk
Children minimum age: 5
10 bedrs SB £30 DB £60
HBS £43 HBD £43 D £20
CC: MC Vi Swi Delt
How to get there: Approach Portinscale from
A66. Enter village, pass Farmers Arms.
Dalegarth approx 100 yards on left, behind
Dorothy Well.

143 Greystones Hotel

Ambleside Road, Keswick, Cumbria, CA12 4DP
Tel: 01768 773108
Email: greystones@keslakes.freeserve.co.uk
Children minimum age: 10
8 bedrs SB £26 DB £52
CC: MC Vi Delt
How to get there: Leave M6 at Junction 40, take
A66 to Keswick. Then take A591 towards
Windermere. Take first right into Manor Brow.
Greystones is ½ a mile on right.

144 Honister House

1 Borrowdale Road, Keswick,
Cumbria, CA12 5DD
Tel: 017687 73181 Fax: 0870 1202948
Email: philandsueh@aol.com
Web: www.honisterhouse.co.uk

A warm welcome awaits you at our 18th-century home. We are centrally located close to all local amenities. We especially cater for walkers, cyclists and families. Drying room and cycle storage. Special breaks and brochure available.
3 bedrs SB £20 DB £36
CC: None accepted
How to get there: From Tourist Information office we are 400 yards along lake road, on left-hand side, opposite 'George Fisher's'. Credit cards accepted soon.

Northwest

Swinside Lodge Hotel

Beautifully situated in an idyllic location at the foot of Cat Bells and just five minutes walk from Lake Derwentwater, Swinside Lodge offers peace and tranquility. This informal licensed country house hotel provides the highest standards of comfort, service and hospitality, and is renowned both locally and nationally for its superb award-winning cuisine.

Grange Road, Newlands,
Keswick, Cumbria CA12 5UE
Tel: 017687 72948   Fax: 017687 72948
Email: info@swinsidelodge-hotel.co.uk
Website: www.swinsidelodge-hotel.co.uk

145 Parkfield No Smoking Guest House

The Heads, Keswick, Cumbria, CA12 5ES
Tel: 01768 772328
Email: parkfield@kencomp.net
Web: www.kencomp.net/parkfield
8 bedrs SB £32 DB £52 CC: MC Vi Am Swi Delt

How to get there: From A66 or A591, follow road through town and turn left at mini-roundabout. After 500m, turn right onto 'The Heads'. Parkfield is on left.

146 Rickerby Grange

♦♦♦♦ 🙊

Portinscale, near Keswick, Cumbria, CA12 5RH
Tel: 01768 772344 Fax: 01768 775588
Email: val@ricor.demon.co.uk
Web: www.ricor.demon.co.uk
Children minimum age: 5

A small and friendly hotel in the pretty village of Portinscale. Waking distance to Keswick and Lake Derwentwater. Easy access to all parts of the Lakes, ample parking, resident proprietor.
14 bedrs SB £30 DB £60 HBS £43 HBD £43
D £13 CC: MC Vi Swi Delt

How to get there: Bypass Keswick on A66 Cockermouth road. Turn left at Portinscale sign. Pass Farmers Arms Inn on left, and turn down second lane to the right.

147 Shemara Guest House

♦♦♦♦ 🙊

27 Bank Street, Keswick, Cumbria, CA12 5JZ
Tel: 01768 773936
Email: shemaraguesthouse@yahoo.co.uk
Children minimum age: 2
7 bedrs SB £25 DB £22 CC: MC Vi Swi Delt

How to get there: From A66, go into Keswick, over pedestrian crossing. Pass car park on left; guest house is on right.

148 Sunnyside Guest House

♦♦♦♦ 🙊

25 Southey Street, Keswick, Cumbria, CA12 4EF
Tel: 01768 772446 Fax: 01768 774447
Email: raynewton@survey.u-net.com
Web: www.survey.u-net.com
Closed 18–28 December
7 bedrs SB £25 DB £40
CC: None accepted

How to get there: From M6 take A66 west, turn off for Keswick, right at T-junction, left at war memorial. Sunnyside 100 yards on left.

149 Tarn Hows

♦♦♦♦ 🙊

3/5 Eskin Street, Keswick, Cumbria, CA12 4DH
Tel: 01768 773217 Fax: 01768 773217
Email: david@tarnhows40.freeserve.co.uk
Children minimum age: 6
9 bedrs SB £25 DB £42
HBS £37 HBD £66 D £12
CC: None accepted

How to get there: From Penrith or Grasmere follow Keswick Town Centre. After Conservative Club turn left into Greta Street and continue into Eskin Street.

150 Swiss Court Guest House

♦♦♦ 🙊

25 Bank Street, Keswick, Cumbria, CA12 5JZ
Tel: 01768 772637 Fax: 01768 780146
Email: info@swisscourt.co.uk
Web: www.swisscourt.co.uk
7 bedrs SB £20 DB £40
CC: MC Vi Swi Delt

How to get there: Swiss Court is located on the main through road in Keswick, opposite Bell Close car park and the police station.

151 The Paddock Guest House

Wordsworth Street, Keswick, Cumbria, CA12 4HU
Tel: 017687 72510 Fax: 017687 72510
Email: val@keswickonderwentwater.fsnet.co.uk
Web: www.keswickguesthouse.com
6 bedrs DB £40
CC: MC Vi DC Swi Delt

How to get there: A591 to town centre, pass the Dogs Inn, under bridge, third left into Wordsworth Street. Paddock is on the right.

Knutsford, Cheshire

152 Cottons Hotel

★★★★★

Manchester Road, Knutsford,
Cheshire, WA16 0SU
Tel: 01565 650333 Fax: 01565 755351
Email: cottons@shireinns.co.uk
Web: www.shireinns.co.uk
108 bedrs SB £130 DB £150
CC: MC Vi Am DC Swi

How to get there: Just one mile from Junction 19 of M6, on the A50 Knutsford to Warrington road.

153 Mere Court Hotel

★★★★

Warrington Road, Mere, Knutsford,
Cheshire, WA16 0RW
Tel: 01565 831000 Fax: 01565 831001
Email: sales@merecourt.co.uk
Web: www.merecourt.co.uk
34 bedrs SB £99 DB £108 B £9.95 L £14.95
D £22.50
CC: MC Vi Am DC Swi Delt

See advert on this page

154 Longview Hotel

★★

Manchester Road, Knutsford,
Cheshire, WA16 0LX
Tel: 01565 632119 Fax: 01565 652402
Email: enquiries@longviewhotel.com
Web: www.longviewhotel.com
26 bedrs SB £50 DB £69.50 B £6.25 L £5 D £7.95
CC: MC Vi Am DC

How to get there: Leave M6 at Junction 19 and take A556 towards Chester. After one mile turn left at lights. After 1³/₄ miles, turn left at roundabout and hotel is 150 yards on right.

155 Travelodge Knutsford

Travel Accommodation
A556, Chester Road, Tabley, Knutsford,
Cheshire, WA16 0PP
Tel: 08700 850 950
Web: www.travelodge.co.uk
32 bedrs B £4.25 CC: MC Vi Am DC Swi Delt

156 Travelodge Knutsford (M6)

Travel Accommodation
Moto Services Knutsford, J18/J19 M6, Off
Northwich Road, Knutsford, Cheshire, WA16 0TL
Tel: 08700 850 950
Web: www.travelodge.co.uk
54 bedrs B £4.25 CC: MC Vi Am DC Swi Delt

157 Dog Inn

♦♦♦♦

Well Bank Lane, Over Peover, Knutsford,
Cheshire, WA16 8UP
Tel: 01625 861421 Fax: 01625 864800
Web: www.cheshireinns.co.uk
6 bedrs
CC: MC Vi Am Swi Delt

How to get there: From Knutsford, follow A50 Holmes Chapel Road. Turn left at "Whipping Stocks". Proceed for two miles.

Northwest

Mere Court Hotel

This attractive Edwardian country house hotel stands in 7 acres of mature gardens, with an ornamental lake, in the most desirable part of the Cheshire countryside. The 1903 house offers individually designed four-posters, some with double jacuzzi spa baths, and king-size Lakeside rooms furnished to the same standard. The lakeside Arboreum Restaurant, offers du Jour and à la carte menus.

Warrington Road, Mere, Knutsford,
Cheshire WA16 0RW
Tel: 01565 831000 Fax: 01565 831001
Email: sales@merecourt.co.uk
Website: www.merecourt.co.uk

Lancaster, Lancashire

158 Lancaster House Hotel

★★★★★ ☒
Green Lane, Ellel, Lancaster, LA1 4GJ
Tel: 01524 844822 Fax: 01524 844766
Email: lancaster@elhmail.co.uk
Web: www.elh.co.uk
80 bedrs SB £79 DB £79
CC: MC Vi Am DC Swi Delt

How to get there: From Junction 33 on the M6, turn right at roundabout, and travel approx two miles, where it is signposted on right.

159 The Castle Hotel

★★
49 Main street, Hornby, near Lancaster, Lancashire, LA2 8ST
Tel: 015242 21204 Fax: 015242 22258

Family-run hotel with facilities for conferences and weddings. Games room and children's room. Excellent bar food and also an exclusive restaurant are available, all set in the Lune valley.
8 bedrs DB £50 B £7 L £6 D £15
CC: MC Vi Swi Delt

How to get there: J34 M6, follow A683 to Kirkby Lonsdale. Hotel is situated on the A683 in Hornby.

160 Travelodge Lancaster

Travel Accommodation
M6 J32/33, White Carr Lane, Lancaster, Lancashire, LA2 9DU
Tel: 08700 850 950
Web: www.travelodge.co.uk
53 bedrs B £4.25
CC: MC Vi Am DC Swi Delt

Liverpool, Merseyside

161 Liverpool Marriott City Centre

★★★★ ☒
One Queen Square, Liverpool, Merseyside, L1 1RH
Tel: 0151 476 8000 Fax: 0151 474 5000
146 bedrs SB £115 DB £125 HBS £152.95
HBD £95.45 B £9.75 L £10.95 D £25
CC: MC Vi Am DC Swi Delt

How to get there: Follow M62 to end, follow signs for city centre, then Lime Street Station. Turn right when Lime Street is on left: hotel on left.

162 Liverpool Marriott Hotel South

★★★★
Speke Aerodrome, Speke, Liverpool, L24 8QD
Tel: 0151 494 5000 Fax: 0151 494 5050

163 The Gladstone Hotel

★★★
Lord Nelson Street, Liverpool, Merseyside, L3 5QB
Tel: 0151 709 7050 Fax: 0151 707 0352
154 bedrs SB £51 DB £57 HBS £66 HBD £40
B £10.95 L £3.95 D £8.95
CC: MC Vi Am Swi Delt

164 Campanile

Travel Accommodation
Wapping & Cualoner Street, Queens Dock, Liverpool, L3 4AJ
Tel: 0151 709 8104 Fax: 0151 709 8725

Campanile hotels offer comfortable and convenient budget accommodation and a traditional French-style Bistro providing freshly-cooked food for breakfast, lunch and dinner. All rooms ensuite with tea/coffee-making facilities, DDT and TV with Sky channels.

100 bedrs SB £48.90 DB £54.85 HBS £54
HBD £35.40 B £5.95 L £5.25 D £11.25
CC: MC Vi Am DC Swi Delt
& 🚶 ⊗ 🖙 🖵 ☎ 🅿 🖉 🏢 ⚑
How to get there: Follow brown tourist signs for
the Albert Dock. The Campanile Hotel is next to
Queens Dock.

165 Travelodge Liverpool

Travel Accommodation
Manchester Street, Liverpool,
Merseyside
Tel: 08700 850 950
Web: www.travelodge.co.uk
Opens June 2002
105 bedrs B £4.25
CC: MC Vi Am DC Swi Delt
🖉 🖙 🖵 ⚐

166 Aachen Hotel

 ◆ ◆ ◆ ⚐

91 Mount Pleasant, Liverpool,
Merseyside, L3 5TB
Tel: 0151 709 3477 Fax: 0151 709 1126/3633
Email: fpwaachen@netscapeonline.co.uk
Web: www.merseyword.com/aachen
Closed Christmas to New Year
18 bedrs SB £26 DB £40
HBS £47 HBD £74 D £12.75
CC: MC Vi Am DC Swi Delt JCB
& ⊗ 🖙 🖵 ☎ 🅿 🖉 🕸 🏢 ⚑
How to get there: Follow signs city centre to
Mount Pleasant car park.

167 Blenheim Guest House

 ◆ ◆ ◆

37 Aigburth Drive, Sefton Park,
Liverpool, Merseyside, L17 4JE
Tel: 0151 727 7380 Fax: 0151 727 5833

Loweswater, Cumbria

168 Grange Country House Hotel

 ★

Loweswater, near Cockermouth,
Cumbria, CA13 0SU
Tel: 01946 861211
8 bedrs SB £35 DB £60
HBS £50 HBD £45
B £7.50 L £2.50 D £15
CC: None accepted
🖉 🚶 ⊗ 🖙 🖵 🅿 🖉 🕸 🏢 ⚑

How to get there: A66 to Keswick and
Cockermouth; left onto A5086 Lamplugh/
Egremont; travel four miles, left turn Mockerkin
village. Left for Loweswater; hotel at bottom of
hill.

Lymm, Cheshire

169 Travelodge Lymm

Travel Accommodation
Cliffe Lane, Lymm,
Cheshire, WA13 0SP
Tel: 08700 850 950
Web: www.travelodge.co.uk
61 bedrs B £4.25
CC: MC Vi Am DC Swi Delt
🖉 🖙 🖵 ⚐

Lytham St. Annes, Lancashire

170 Clifton Arms Hotel

 ★ ★ ★ ★ 🅡

West Beach, Lytham St. Annes,
Lancashire, FY8 5QJ
Tel: 01253 739898 Fax: 01253 730657
Email: welcome@cliftonarms.com
Web: www.cliftonarms.com

We offer the ultimate experience in luxury at
reasonable prices. We have all the comforts of
home whilst maintaining the tradition of a hotel
with such famous heritage
48 bedrs SB £91 DB £115
HBS £54.50 HBD £44.50
B £10 L £14.50 D £19.50
CC: MC Vi Am DC Swi Delt
🐟 & 🛗 🖉 🚶 ⊗ 🖙 🖵 ☎ 📞 🅿 🖉 🕸 🏢 ⚑ 🏢
🏢
How to get there: From M55 Junction 4, follow
signs for A584. Hotel is situated on the seafront
at Lytham.

171 Chadwick Hotel

★★★

South Promenade, Lytham St. Annes,
Lancashire, FY8 1NP
Tel: 01253 720061 Fax: 01253 714455
Email: sales@thechadwickhotel.com
Web: www.thechadwickhotel.com

Family-run seafront award-winning hotel and
leisure complex providing excellent value for
money. It is renowned for good food, friendly
service and stylish comfort.
75 bedrs SB £47 DB £68 HBS £59
HBD £45.50 B £5.50 L £7.90 D £16
CC: MC Vi Am DC Swi Delt

How to get there: From M6 to M55, then follow
signs to Lytham St. Annes. Hotel is on the
Promenade at St. Annes.

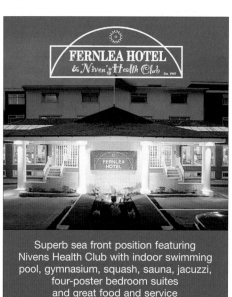
172 Fernlea Hotel

★★★

11–17 South Promenade, Lytham St. Annes,
Lancashire, FY8 1LU
Tel: 01253 726726 Fax: 01253 721561
Email: enquiries@thefernleahotel.co.uk
Web: www.thefernleahotel.co.uk
110 bedrs SB £43 DB £86 HBS £54
HBD £56 B £6.50 D £15.50
CC: MC Vi Am Swi JCB

How to get there: From M6 take M55 to
Blackpool, follow signs to St. Annes. Property is
100 yards south of St. Annes pier on the
promenade.
See advert below left

173 Lindum

★★

63–67 South Promenade, Lytham St. Annes,
Lancashire, FY8 1LZ
Tel: 01253 721534 Fax: 01253 721364
Email: info@lindumhotel.co.uk
Web: www.lindumhotel.co.uk

Holiday or business in St. Annes? You will find
exactly what you are looking for at our popular
seafront hotel, renowned for its excellent food
and warm welcome
78 bedrs SB £37 DB £62 HBS £52
HBD £46 B £8 L £10 D £16
CC: MC Vi Am Swi Delt

How to get there: Situated on the main
promenade (A584) at St. Annes.

174 Endsleigh Hotel

315 Clifton Drive South, Lytham St. Annes,
Lancashire, FY8 1HN
Tel: 01253 725622
15 bedrs SB £23 DB £46 HBS £32 HBD £32 D £9
CC: None accepted

How to get there: Two miles east of Blackpool
on A584. 1st hotel east of St. Anne's Square
shopping centre.

175 Strathmore Hotel

305 Clifton Drive South, Lytham St. Annes,
Lancashire, FY8 1HN
Tel: 01253 725478
Children minimum age: 9
8 bedrs SB £24 DB £48 HBS £29 HBD £58
B £4 L £4 D £5 CC: None accepted

How to get there: Follow signs to St. Annes off
M55. Strathmore Hotel after 200 yards on main
Blackpool to Preston road.

Macclesfield, Cheshire

176 Shrigley Hall Hotel

Shrigley Park, Pott Shrigley, Macclesfield,
Cheshire, SK10 5SB
Tel: 01625 575757 Fax: 01625 573323
Email: shrigleyhall@paramount-hotels.co.uk
Web: www.paramount-hotels.co.uk
150 bedrs CC: MC Vi Am DC Swi Delt

How to get there: 12 miles from Manchester
Airport. Through Macclesfield into Bollington.
Follow signs for Pott Shrigley.

177 Moorhayes House Hotel

27 Manchester Road, Tytherington,
Macclesfield, Cheshire, SK10 2JJ
Tel: 01625 433228 Fax: 01625 429878
Email: helen@moorhayes.co.uk
Web: www.smoothhound.co.uk/
    hotels/moorhaye
8 bedrs CC: MC Vi Swi Delt JCB

How to get there: From Macclesfield, take the
A538 northbound, signposted Tytherington.
Moorhayes is on left, 1/2 a mile from town.

Manchester

178 The Lowry Hotel

50 Dearmans Place, Chapel Wharf, Salford,
Manchester, Greater Manchester, M3 5LH
Tel: 0161 827 4000 Fax: 0161 827 4001
Email: enquiries@thelowryhotel.com
Web: www.rfhotels.com
164 bedrs SB £200 DB £200
B £15.50 L £12 D £22
CC: MC Vi Am DC Swi Delt JCB

How to get there: Manchester City Centre Trinity
Way turn onto Chapel Street, turn right into
Dearmans Place signposted The Lowry Hotel.

179 Copthorne Hotel Manchester

★★★★

Clippers Quay, Salford Quays, Salford,
Manchester, M5 2XP
Tel: 0161 873 7321 Fax: 0161 877 8110
Email: sales.manchester@mill-cop.com
Web: www.stay.with.us.com

At this four-star property guests enjoy spacious
comfort within a peaceful location overlooking
the waterfront. Ideally situated minutes from the
motorway with complementary car parking.
166 bedrs SB £163.95 DB £177.90
HBS £184.95 HBD £102.98 B £13.95 L £17 D £21
CC: MC Vi Am DC Swi Delt

How to get there: From M602 follow A57/A5063
to Salford. A5063 Salford Quays onto Trafford
Road. Turn right into Clippers Quay. Hotel on
right, next to cinema.

Plan your route

Visit www.rac.co.uk for RAC's
interactive route planner, including
up to the minute traffic reports.

Northwest

180 Le Méridien Manchester

★★★★★ ®®

Water Street, Manchester, M3 4JQ
Tel: 0870 400 8585 Fax: 0161 834 2484
Email: frontoffice.manchester@lemeridien.com
Web: www.lemeridien.com
158 bedrs B £14.50 L £9.95 D £14.95
CC: MC Vi Am DC Swi Delt

How to get there: M6, M62, M602 Manchester.
Exit M602 for A57 Manchester, continue through
lights, at 2nd lights turn left onto Water Street.

181 Manchester Airport Marriott Hotel

★★★★ ®

Hale Road, Hale Barns, near Altrincham,
Cheshire, WA15 8XY
Tel: 0161 904 0301 Fax: 0161 980 1787
Web: www.marriotthotels.com/manap
142 bedrs SB £130.50 DB £130.50
CC: MC Vi Am DC Swi Delt JCB

How to get there: M56 junction 6, signposted
Hale.

Stanneylands Hotel

Stanneylands Hotel is a strikingly handsome
house set in beautiful gardens. Dine in
elegance in our award-winning, oak-panelled
dining room, which serves outstanding
cuisine and fine wines.

Stanneylands Road, Wilmslow, Cheshire, SK9 4EY

Tel: 01625 525225   Fax: 01625 537282
enquiries@stanneylandshotel.co.uk

182 Marriott Worsley Park Hotel & Country Club

★★★★ ®®

Worsley Park, Manchester, M28 2QT
Tel: 0161 975 2000 Fax: 0161 799 6341
Web: www.marriotthotels.com/mangs
158 bedrs SB £119 DB £127
HBS £141 HBD £86
CC: MC Vi Am Swi

How to get there: Exit J15 M60, follow signs for
A575 Worsley; hotel is ½ mile on left. From
A580 follow A575 for Worsley.

183 Palace Hotel

★★★★

Oxford Street, Manchester, M60 7HA
Tel: 0161 288 1111 Fax: 0161 288 7792
Web: www.principalhotels.co.uk
252 bedrs SB £165.95 DB £187.90
B £11.95 L £12.95 D £17.95
CC: MC Vi Am DC Swi Delt

How to get there: Follow signs for City centre
Manchester; pick up signs for aquatic centre.
Hotel is two minutes' drive on the same side.

184 Renaissance Manchester Hotel

★★★★

Blackfriars Street, Manchester, M3 2EQ
Tel: 0161 835 2555 Fax: 0161 835 3077
Email: manchester.sales
@renaissancehotels.com
Web: www.renaissancehotels.com
200 bedrs SB £147.50 DB £160
B £12.50 L £12 D £15.50
CC: MC Vi Am DC Swi Delt

How to get there: The hotel is situated at the
junction of Blackfriars Street and Deansgate
close to Kendals store, cathedral and M.E.N.
arena.

185 Bredbury Hall Hotel and Country Club

★★★
Dark Lane, Goyt Valley, Bredbury, Stockport,
Cheshire, SK6 2DH
Tel: 0161 430 7421 Fax: 0161 430 5079
Email: reservations@bredburyhallhotel.co.uk
Web: www.bredburyhallhotel.co.uk

Family-run hotel, one mile M60, seven miles
Manchester Airport. 150 ensuite bedrooms,
corner baths, showers, satellite TV, conference
facilities for up to 150 people. Country Club
weekends. Leisure 2002.
150 bedrs SB £57.50 DB £80.50 HBS £74
HBD £56.75 B £8 L £7.50 D £16.50
CC: MC Vi Am DC Swi Delt
How to get there: Leave M60 at Junction 25.
Follow the Bredbury Hall signs. Turn right at
traffic lights, then turn left after 400 yards into
Osbourne Street.

186 Jurys Inn Manchester

★★★
56 Great Bridgewater Street, Manchester, M1 5LE
Tel: +353(0)1 6070000 Fax: +353(0)1 6316999
Email: bookings@jurysdoyle.com
Web: www.jurysdoyle.com
265 bedrs B £8.50 D £16.95 CC: MC Vi Am DC
How to get there: Located nine miles/14 km
from Manchester Airport. Piccadilly Station one
mile. G-mex Metrolink Station two minutes walk.

187 Novotel Manchester West

★★★
Worsley Brow, Worsley, Manchester, M28 2YA
Tel: 0161 799 3535 Fax: 0161 703 8207
Email: h0907@accor-hotels.com
Web: www.novotel.com
Children minimum age: 16
119 bedrs SB £81.50 DB £91 B £9.50 L £10.50
D £16.50 CC: MC Vi Am DC Swi Delt

188 Stanneylands Hotel

★★★★ RAC RAC RAC
Stanneylands Road, Wilmslow,
Cheshire, SK9 4EY
Tel: 01625 525225 Fax: 01625 537282
Email: enquiries@stanneylandshotel.co.uk
Web: www.stanneylandshotel.co.uk
32 bedrs SB £69.50 DB £103
HBS £94.50 HBD £76.50
CC: MC Vi Am DC Swi Delt

How to get there: Leave M56 at Junction 5,
follow signs to Styal. Follow B5166 and then
B5358, hotel signposted on right-hand side.
See advert on facing page

189 Willow Bank Hotel

★★★
Wilmslow Road, Fallowfield,
Manchester, M14 6AF
Tel: 0161 224 0461 Fax: 0161 257 2561
Email: willowbankhotel@feathers.uk.com
Web: www.feathers.uk.com
120 bedrs SB £59.45 DB £79.95 HBS £69.95
HBD £49.98 B £5.95 D £10.95
CC: MC Vi Am DC Swi Delt JCB
How to get there: M6 M56 Manchester Airport
go to end A5103 dual carriageway; fifth set of
lights turn right; turn second left at lights into
Wilmslow Road; hotel 500 yards on left.

190 Comfort Inn, Manchester

★★
Hyde Road, Birch Street, West Gorton,
Manchester, M12 5NT
Tel: 0161 220 8700 Fax: 0161 220 8848
Email: admin@gb615.u-net.com
Web: www.choicehotels.com
90 bedrs SB £61.25 DB £61.25
HBS £74 HBD £37 B £8.75 D £12.75
CC: MC Vi Am DC Swi Delt
How to get there: Situated just off the A57 Hyde
Road, 2½ miles southeast of city centre. Five
minutes from M60 to Sheffield on A57.

Northwest

191 Monton House Hotel

★★
116–118 Monton Road, Monton, Eccles,
Manchester, Greater Manchester, M30 9HG
Tel: 0161 789 7811 Fax: 0161 787 7609
Email: hotel@montonhousehotel.co.uk
Web: www.montonhousehotel.co.uk

Superbly located hotel with 62 ensuite
bedrooms. Four miles to Manchester city
centre, minutes from M602, M60, M62. Offering
excellent restaurants, bar and conference
facilities at value for money prices.
62 bedrs SB £49.50 DB £59 HBS £59.50
HBD £79 B £5.50 L £6.25 D £10
CC: MC Vi Am DC Swi Delt
How to get there: Exit M602 at J2 turn to
Pendleton and take second left onto Half Edge
Lane. Hotel one mile on right.

192 Campanile

Travel Accommodation
55 Ordsall Lane, Regent Road, Salford,
Manchester, M5 4RS
Tel: 0161 833 1845 Fax: 0161 833 1847

Campanile hotels offer comfortable and
convenient budget accommodation and a
traditional French-style Bistro providing freshly-
cooked food for breakfast, lunch and dinner. All
rooms ensuite with tea/coffee-making facilities,
DDT and TV with Sky channels.

101 bedrs SB £48.90 DB £54.85 HBS £58
HBD £36.50 B £5.95 L £5.95 D £11.25
CC: MC Vi DC Swi Delt
How to get there: Leave M6 Junction 21a onto
M62 to Manchester, then M602 Salford.
Continue over roundabout onto Regent Road.
Hotel on right, after Sainsbury's.

193 Highbury Hotel

♦ ♦ ♦ ♦
113 Monton Road, Monton,
Manchester, M30 9HQ
Tel: 0161 787 8545 Fax: 0161 787 9023
Email: enquiries@highbury-hotel.co.uk
Web: www.highbury-hotel.co.uk
16 bedrs SB £34.50 DB £44.50
CC: MC Vi Am DC Swi Delt
How to get there: M60 Junction 12, then M602
Junction 2. Left for A576 Guilder Brook, second
left Half Edge Lane into Monton Road. Hotel 1/2
mile on left.
See advert on facing page

194 Imperial Hotel

♦ ♦ ♦
157 Hathersage Road, Manchester, M13 0HY
Tel: 0161 225 6500 Fax: 0161 225 6500
Email: imperialhotel.manchester
        @tinyworld.co.uk
Web: www.hotelimperialmanchester.co.uk
Closed Christmas to New Year
27 bedrs SB £35 DB £50 B £5 D £8
CC: MC Vi Am DC Swi Delt
How to get there: 1¼ miles south of city centre.
By Manchester Royal Infirmary and Manchester
University.

195 Victoria Park Hotel

♦ ♦ ♦
4 Park Crescent, Victoria Park,
Manchester, M14 5RE
Tel: 0161 224 1399 Fax: 0161 225 4949
Email: vhp.manchester@claranet.co.uk
Web: www.victoriapark-hotel.co.uk
19 bedrs SB £38 DB £48 B £5
CC: MC Vi Am Swi Delt
How to get there: One mile from city centre.
Follow signs for Manchester University on
Oxford Road, continue until Oxford Road
becomes Wilmslow Road, and we are off this on
Park Crescent.

196 New Central Hotel

144–146 Heywood Street,
Manchester, M8 0PD
Tel: 0161 205 2169 Fax: 0161 205 2169
Email: newcentral@talk21.com
10 bedrs SB £21.50 DB £35 D £4
CC: MC Vi
🐾🕭🖳🅿🐾👪
How to get there: 1½ miles north of city centre,
off Cheetham Hill Road (A665). Look for Esso
service station on right. Heywood Street is
opposite on left.

197 Travelodge Manchester (South)

Travel Accommodation
A34 Kingsway, Didsbury, Manchester
Tel: 08700 850 950
Web: www.travelodge.co.uk
Opens April 2002
62 bedrs B £4.25 CC: MC Vi Am DC Swi Delt
🐾🕭🖳🐾

Maryport, Cumbria

198 The Retreat Hotel

♦ ♦ ♦ ♦ ✗
Birkby, near Maryport, Cumbria, CA15 6RG
Tel: 01900 814056
Email: enquiries@retreathotel.co.uk
Web: www.retreathotel.co.uk
3 bedrs SB £37 DB £50
HBS £56 HBD £41 D £19
CC: MC Vi Delt
🐾🕭🖳🅿🐾👪
How to get there: Situated in the rural hamlet of
Birkley, two miles north of Maryport just off the
A596 road to Carlisle.

Mawdesley, Lancashire

199 Mawdsley's Eating House & Hotel

★★★
Hall Lane, Ormskirk,
Lancashire, L40 2QZ
Tel: 01704 822552 Fax: 01704 822096
Email: mawdsleyeh@aol.com
Web: www.mawdsleyeh.co.uk
55 bedrs SB £45 DB £65 B £5 L £11 D £11
CC: MC Vi Am DC Swi Delt
🕭👌💤🕭🖳☎🅿🐾👘🛡🎄🍴🐾☀📶📶🧖
🍸🎿

How to get there: M6 Junction 27 head to
Parbold. After ¼ mile, right (signed to
Wrightington). Head to Eccleston. At crossroads
turn left, signed to Mawdesley.

Middlewich, Cheshire

200 Travelodge Middlewich

Travel Accommodation
A54, Holmes Chapel Road, Middlewich,
Cheshire, CW10 0JB
Tel: 08700 850 950
Web: www.travelodge.co.uk
32 bedrs B £4.25
CC: MC Vi Am DC Swi Delt
🐾🕭🖳🐾

Northwest

Millom, Cumbria

201 Duddon Pilot Hotel

◆◆◆◆

Devonshire Road, Millom, Cumbria, LA18 4JT
Tel: 01229 774116 Fax: 01229 774116
6 bedrs SB £25 DB £50 B £6.50 L £5 D £10
CC: None accepted

How to get there: Exit M6 at Junction 37. Take the A590 to Greenodd, followed by A5092 and A595 to Millom.

Morecambe, Lancashire

202 Clarendon Hotel

★★★

Marine Road West, Morecambe,
Lancashire, LA4 4EP
Tel: 01524 410180 Fax: 01524 421616
Email: clarendon@mitchellshotels.co.uk
29 bedrs SB £50 DB £70 B £6.50
CC: MC Vi Am DC Swi Delt JCB

How to get there: M6 J34 Morecambe last roundabout by Shrimp pub 1st exit follow road to promenade, turn right. Clarendon on 3rd block.
See advert on facing page

203 The Elms Hotel

★★★

Bare, Morecambe, Lancashire, LA4 6DD
Tel: 01524 411501 Fax: 01524 831979
Email: sales@mitchellshotels.co.uk
Web: www.mitchellshotels.co.uk
40 bedrs SB £61 DB £90
B £7 L £10.25 D £16.95
CC: MC Vi Am DC Swi Delt

How to get there: M6 Junction 34. Follow signs for Morecambe until you reach large roundabout. Take fourth exit onto Hall Drive which adjoins Bare Lane. Follow road, hotel on right.

204 Warwick Non Smoking Hotel

◆◆◆◆

394 Marine Road East, Morecambe,
Lancashire, LA4 5AN
Tel: 01524 418151 Fax: 01524 427235
13 bedrs SB £30 DB £50 CC: None accepted

How to get there: On East Promenade between Broadway and Morecambe town hall.

205 Beach Mount Hotel

◆◆◆

395/6 Marine Road East, Morecambe,
Lancs, LA4 5AN
Tel: 01524 420753 Fax: 01524 420753
Closed November to March
20 bedrs
CC: MC Vi Swi Delt

206 Hotel Prospect

◆◆◆

363 Marine Road East, Morecambe,
Lancashire, LA4 5AQ
Tel: 01524 417819
Closed December to Easter
14 bedrs SB £17 DB £34
HBS £24 HBD £24 B £3 D £7
CC: MC Vi DC Delt

How to get there: Exit M6 Junction 34/35. Follow signs to Lancaster/Morecambe. At Morecambe, follow signs to East Promenade. Turn left at Promenade. Hotel on left.

207 Channings Hotel

◆◆

455 Marine Road East, Bare, Morecambe,
Lancashire, LA4 6AD
Tel: 01524 417925 Fax: 01524 411794
Email: channings.hotel@ukgateway.net
Web: www.channingshotel.co.uk
19 bedrs
CC: MC Vi Am DC Swi Delt

How to get there: From the south, leave M6 at Junction 34. After 3¹/₂ miles, the hotel is situated on the promenade directly opposite Bare Pool and close to Happy Mount Park.

Nantwich, Cheshire

208 Rookery Hall Hotel

★★★★ ⓡ ⓡ ⓡ

Main Road, Worleston, Nantwich,
Cheshire, CW5 6DQ
Tel: 01270 610016 Fax: 01270 626027
Email: rookery@arcadianhotels.co.uk
Web: www.arcadianhotels.co.uk

Award-winning country house hotel set in 38
acres of peaceful countryside, offering 45
luxuriously-appointed bedrooms. Several
elegant lounges and a fine dining restaurant.
45 bedrs SB £95 DB £110 HBS £132.50
HBD £85 L £14 D £37.50
CC: MC Vi Am DC Swi

How to get there: From north, M6 Junction 18,
A54 to Middlewich, then A530 south. Take A51
toward Chester, then B5074. Hotel 1½ miles on
right.

Newby Bridge, Cumbria

209 Whitewater Hotel

★★★
The Lakeland Village, Ulverston, Newby Bridge,
Cumbria, LA12 8PX
Tel: 01539 531133 Fax: 01539 531881
Email: enquiries@whitewater-hotel.co.uk
Web: www.whitewater-hotel.co.uk

In a fantastic location in south Lakeland on the
river, between Windermere and Ulverston, the
Whitewater offers a friendly welcome and
superb leisure facilities, including pool, gym,
and beauty spa.
35 bedrs SB £90 DB £125
HBS £105 HBD £75
B £8 L £7.50 D £21
CC: MC Vi Am DC Swi Delt

How to get there: Exit M6, J36 follow A590
towards Barrow for 16 miles. Hotel is one mile
past Newby Bridge on right.

210 Lyndhurst Country House

♦ ♦ ♦

Lyndhurst, Newby Bridge, Ulverston,
Cumbria, LA12 8ND
Tel: 01539 531245
3 bedrs SB £33 DB £46
CC: None accepted

How to get there: Lyndhurst is situated on A590
at its junction with the A592.

Northwest

211 The Knoll Country House

Lakeside, Newby Bridge, near Ulverston,
Cumbria, LA12 8AU
Tel: 015395 31347 Fax: 015395 30850
Email: info@theknoll-lakeside.co.uk
Web: www.theknoll-lakeside.co.uk

Beautifully-appointed Victorian country house
set amidst woodland, situated near the southern
tip of Lake Windemere. Large ensuite
bedrooms. Open fires. Offering a warm
welcome, excellent cuisine and fine wines.
8 bedrs SB £40 DB £60
HBS £58 HBD £58 D £10
CC: MC Vi Swi Delt
How to get there: A590 to Newby Bridge. Turn
right opposite Newby Bridge Hotel to Lakeside.
300m past the Lakeside Hotel on left.

Northwich, Cheshire

212 Quality Hotel Northwich

★★★

London Road, Northwich, Cheshire, CW9 5HD
Tel: 01606 44443 Fax: 01606 42596
Email: admin@gb618.u-net.com
Web: www.choicehotels.com
60 bedrs SB £85.75 DB £95.75 HBS £100.70
HBD £55.35 B £10.75 D £14.95
CC: MC Vi Am DC Swi Delt
How to get there: M6 at Junction 19 take A556
to Northwich. At Northwich join A533 (London
Road) to hotel.

Oldham, Lancashire

213 Hotel Smokies Park

★★★★

Ashton Road, Bardsley, Oldham,
Lancashire, OL8 3HX
Tel: 0161 785 5000 Fax: 0161 785 5010
Email: sales@smokies.co.uk
Web: www.smokies.co.uk
73 bedrs SB £80 DB £90
HBS £97.50 HBD £62.50
B £7.50 L £6.95 D £17.50
CC: MC Vi Am DC Swi Delt JCB
How to get there: On the A627 midpoint
between Oldham and Ashton-under-Lyne.

214 High Point Hotel

★★

Napier Street East, Oldham, Lancashire, OL8 1TR
Tel: 0161 624 4130 Fax: 0161 627 2757
Email: highpoint-hotel@fsmail.net
Web: highpointhotel.co.uk
19 bedrs SB £42 DB £53
HBS £52 HBD £73
B £5 L £10.95 D £12.95
CC: MC Vi Am Swi Delt
How to get there: Leave M62 at Junction 20.
Follow signs for Oldham and Ashton on A627M.
Take A62 to Manchester. Turn right off
Manchester Street roundabout. Take first left
then right at top and right again.

215 Travelodge Oldham

Travel Accommodation
Tel: 08700 850 950
Web: www.travelodge.co.uk
Opens March 2002
50 bedrs B £4.25
CC: MC Vi Am DC Swi Delt

Penrith, Cumbria

216 North Lakes Hotel

★★★★ ®

Ullswater Road, Penrith, Cumbria, CA11 8QT
Tel: 01768 868111 Fax: 01768 868291
Email: nlakes@shireinns.co.uk
Web: www.shireinns.co.uk
84 bedrs SB £102 DB £122
CC: MC Vi Am DC Swi

How to get there: Leave M6 at Junction 40 and
follow signs for Penrith.

217 Sharrow Bay Hotel
Gold Ribbon Winner

★★★ ® ® ®

Lake Ullswater, Penrith, Cumbria, CA10 2LZ
Tel: 01768 486301 Fax: 01768 486349
Email: enquiries@ sharrow-bay.com
Web: www.sharrow-bay.com
Children minimum age: 13
Closed early December to early March

Nestling on the shores of Ullswater, enjoying
one of the most breathtaking views in the
country. Providing a haven for rest and
relaxation with internationally-renowned cuisine
within idyllic surroundings.
26 bedrs SB £97.75 DB £210 HBS £140
HBD £150 B £17.50 L £36.25 D £47.25
CC: MC Vi Swi Delt JCB

218 Westmorland Hotel

★★★★ ®

Orton, Penrith, Cumbria, CA10 3SB
Tel: 015396 24351 Fax: 015396 24354
Email: westmorelandhotel@aol.com
Web: www.westmorelandhotel.com
53 bedrs SB £60 DB £73
HBS £75 HBD £54.50 B £7.25
CC: MC Vi Am DC Swi Delt

How to get there: The hotel is reched via
Westmoreland motorway services between
junctions 38 and 39 of the M6

219 Travelodge Penrith

Travel Accommodation
A66, Redhills, Penrith, Cumbria, CA11 0DT
Tel: 08700 850 950
Web: www.travelodge.co.uk
54 bedrs B £4.25
CC: MC Vi Am DC Swi Delt

220 Brooklands Guest House

♦ ♦ ♦ ♦

2 Portland Place, Penrith, Cumbria, CA11 7QN
Tel: 01768 863395 Fax: 01768 864895
Email: enquiries@brooklandsguesthouse.com
Web: www.brooklandsguesthouse.com

Charming surroundings await any visitor to
Brooklands, situated in the heart of Penrith.
Brooklands has been totally refurbished
throughout and now offers beautifully-furnished
rooms with luxury ensuite facilities.
6 bedrs SB £25 DB £48 CC: None accepted

How to get there: Exit J40 M6, enter one-way
system, follow town centre signs to Town Hall.
Left into Portland Place; Brooklands is 50m on
left.

Northwest

221 Norcroft Guest House

 ♦ ♦ ♦ ♦ 🦢

Graham Street, Penrith, Cumbria, CA11 9LQ
Tel: 01768 862365 Fax: 01768 862365
Email: info@norcroft-guesthouse.co.uk
Web: www.norcroft-guesthouse.co.uk
Closed Christmas and New Year
9 bedrs SB £22 DB £42
CC: MC Vi Am Swi Delt
🍴 ⊗ 🗢 ⬜ 🅿 🌀 🍽 📺
How to get there: Follow one-way system to
town centre, left at town hall, left again into
Drovers Lane. Norcroft 400 yards.

222 Tymparon Hall

 ♦ ♦ ♦ ♦ 🗡

Newbiggin, Stainton, Penrith,
Cumbria, CA11 0HS
Tel: 017684 83236 Fax: 017684 83236
Email: margaret@tymparon.freeserve.co.uk
Web: www.tymparon.freeserve.co.uk

Close to Lake Ullswater and M6 Junction 40. A
warm welcome, hearty breakfasts and
traditional dinners served. Peaceful rural setting
on village fringe.
3 bedrs SB £25 DB £50 HBS £37 HBD £37
CC: None accepted
🐾 ⊗ 🗢 🅿 🌀 🕯 🍽
How to get there: Leave M6 at Junction 40.
Take A66 to Keswick. Turn right at sign for
Newbiggin. Hotel at extreme end of village on
right.

223 Woodland House Hotel

 ♦ ♦ ♦

Wordsworth Street, Penrith, Cumbria, CA11 7QY
Tel: 01768 864177 Fax: 01768 890152
Email: enquiries@woodlandhouse.co.uk
Web: www.woodlandhouse.co.uk
8 bedrs SB £29.50 DB £48
CC: MC Vi Swi Delt
⊗ 🗢 ⬜ 🅿 🌀 🍽 📺

224 Elm House

 ♣

Pooley Bridge, Penrith, Cumbria, CA10 2NH
Tel: 01768486334 Fax: 01768486851

Preston, Lancashire

225 Preston Marriott Hotel

 ★★★★

Garstang Road, Broughton, Preston,
Lancashire, PR3 5JB
Tel: 01772 866500 Fax: 01772 861327
Email: reservations.preston
          @marriotthotels.co.uk
150 bedrs SB £105 DB £115
CC: MC Vi Am DC Swi Dell JCB
🌊 🔥 🛗 🗲 🍴 ⊗ 🗢 ⬜ ☎ 📞 🅿 🌀 🍽 📺 👁
🎎 📺 SPA 🍷 🗲

226 Novotel Preston

★★★

Reedfield Place, Walton Summit, Preston,
Lancashire, PR5 6AB
Tel: 01772 313331 Fax: 01772 627868
Email: h0838@accor-hotels.com
Web: www.novotel.com
98 bedrs SB £58 DB £63.50 HBS £71.50
HBD £85 B £8.50 L £6 D £13.95
CC: MC Vi Am DC Swi Delt
🌊 🔥 🛗 🐾 ⊗ 🗢 ⬜ ☎ ❄ 📞 🅿 🌀 🍽 🎎 📺
🍷 🗲 🛂
How to get there: Junction 29 off M6. Junction
9 off M61. Junction 1 off M65. Five miles from
Preston railway station. Bus route 125 from
Preston bus station.

227 Swallow Hotel

★★★★ 🦢

Preston New Road, Samlesbury, Preston,
Lancashire, PR5 0UL
Tel: 01772 877351 Fax: 01772 877424
78 bedrs SB £82 DB £105 HBS £97.50
HBD £68 B £9.75 L £12.50 D £19.50
CC: MC Vi Am DC Swi Delt JCB
🛗 🐾 ⊗ 🗢 ⬜ ☎ 📞 🅿 🌀 🍽 🎎 📺 🍷 🗲

228 Brook House Hotel

662 Preston Road, near Chorley,
Clayton-Le-Woods, Lancashire, PR6 7EH
Tel: 01772 336403 Fax: 01772 337369
Email: enquiries@hotel-preston-chorley.co.uk
Web: www.hotel-preston-chorley.co.uk
20 bedrs SB £40 DB £50 B £5 D £10
CC: MC Vi Am DC Swi Delt JCB

How to get there: Brook House is situated on the A6 half a mile from Junction 29 M6, Junction 9 M61 and Junction 2 M65.

229 Claremont Hotel

516 Blackpool Road, Ashton-on-Ribble,
Preston, Lancashire, PR2 1HY
Tel: 01772 729738 Fax: 01772 726274
Email: claremonthotel@btinternet.com
Web: www.claremonthotelpreston.co.uk
15 bedrs SB £39 DB £56 HBS £49 HBD £38
B £5 L £6.50 D £11.95
CC: MC Vi Am DC Swi Delt

How to get there: Leave M6 at Junction 31. Take A59 towards Preston. At roundabout at top of hill turn right. Proceed for approx four miles along Blackpool Road. Hotel on right.

Ramsbottom, Lancashire

230 Old Mill

Springwood Street, Ramsbottom,
Lancashire, BL0 9DS
Tel: 01706 822991 Fax: 01706 822291
Email: oldmillhot@netscapeonline.co.uk
Web: www.oldmillhotel.co.uk
28 bedrs SB £60 DB £80 B £8.95 L £9.95
D £14.95 CC: MC Vi Am DC Swi Delt

How to get there: Close to Junction 1 on M66, five miles from Bury, 15 miles from Manchester city centre.

Ravenglass, Cumbria

231 Muncaster Country Guest House

Muncaster, Ravenglass, Cumbria, CA18 1RD
Tel: 01229 717693 Fax: 01229 717693

Closed December
8 bedrs CC: None accepted

How to get there: Situated on the A595 one mile east of Ravenglass, opposite main entrance to Muncaster Castle.

Runcorn, Cheshire

232 Campanile

Travel Accommodation
Lowlands Road, Runcorn, Cheshire, WA7 5TP
Tel: 01928 581771 Fax: 01928 581730

Campanile hotels offer comfortable and convenient budget accommodation and a traditional French-style Bistro providing freshly-cooked food for breakfast, lunch and dinner. All rooms ensuite with tea/coffee-making facilities, DDT and TV with Sky channels.
53 bedrs SB £46.90 DB £52.85 HBS £55
HBD £34 B £5.95 L £4.95 D £6.35
CC: MC Vi Am DC Swi Delt

How to get there: Exit M56 at Junction 12, joining A557 towards Runcorn. Follow signs for Runcorn railway station.

Rydal, Cumbria

233 Rydal Lodge Hotel

Rydal, Cumbria, LA22 9LR
Tel: 01539 433208
Closed January
SB £31 DB £50 HBS £40 HBD £37 B £10
D £16.50
CC: MC Vi Swi Delt JCB

How to get there: Situated on A591 in Rydal, 1½ miles from Ambleside, three miles from Grasmere.

Salford, Manchester

234 Travelodge Salford

Travel Accommodation
Townbury House, Blackfriars Street, Salford,
Manchester, M3 5AB
Tel: 08700 850 950
Web: www.travelodge.co.uk
171 bedrs B £4.25
CC: MC Vi Am DC Swi Delt

235 Hazeldean Hotel

♦♦♦
467 Bury New Road, Kersal, Salford,
Manchester, M7 3NE
Tel: 0161 792 6667 Fax: 0161 792 6668
Closed Christmas
21 bedrs SB £47 DB £53 D £10
CC: MC Vi Am DC Swi Delt JCB

Sandbach, Cheshire

236 Grove House Hotel & Restaurant

★★ẞẞẞ
Mill Lane, Wheelock, Sandbach,
Cheshire, CW11 4RD
Tel: 01270 762582 Fax: 01270 759465
Closed Christmas

Restaurant with rooms, family-owned and run.
Relaxing ambience, individually-styled rooms.
Excellent restaurant offering ambitious modern
cooking by chef-proprietor. Two miles from Jct
17 on M6.
8 bedrs SB £47.50 DB £75
B £7.50 L £9.25 D £14.50
CC: MC Vi Am Swi Delt

How to get there: Junction 17 M6, then A534.
Through the traffic lights, go left at roundabout.
Follow Wheelock signs.

237 Poplar Mount Guest House

♦♦♦
2 Station Road, Elworth, Sandbach,
Cheshire, CW11 3JG
Tel: 01270 761268 Fax: 01270 761268
Email: popmntgh@aol.co.uk
SB £22 DB £42 D £9 CC: MC Vi Swi Delt JCB

How to get there: Three miles from M6 Junction
17, off A533 Middlewich Road, on B5079.
Opposite Sandbach Railway Station.

Sawrey, Cumbria

238 Sawrey Hotel

★★
Far Sawrey, Ambleside, Cumbria, LA22 0LQ
Tel: 01539 443425 Fax: 01539 443425
Closed Christmas

An attractive two-storey, 18th-century inn built
in traditional Lake District style. Former stables
converted into a bar.
18 bedrs SB £29.50 DB £59 HBS £39.50
HBD £39.50 B £6.50 L £8.50 D £16.50
CC: MC Vi Swi Delt

How to get there: One mile from Windermere
(Bowness) car ferry on B5285 Hawkshead Road.

239 Buckle Yeat

♦♦♦♦
Buckle Yeat, near Sawrey, Hawkshead,
Cumbria, LA22 0LF
Tel: 01539 436446 Fax: 01539 436446
Email: info@buckle-yeat.co.uk
Web: www.buckle-yeat.co.uk
7 bedrs SB £28 DB £60
CC: MC Vi Am Swi Delt

How to get there: Leave M6 at Junction 36.
Proceed to Windermere. Cross Lake. Near
Sawrey is second village.

240 West Vale Country Guest House

 ◆◆◆◆ ✠

Far Sawrey, Ambleside, Sawrey,
Cumbria, LA22 0LQ
Tel: 01539 442817 Fax: 01539 445302
Email: enquiries@westvalecountryhouse.co.uk
Web: www.westvalecountryhouse.co.uk
Children minimum age: 7
7 bedrs SB £40 DB £56
HBS £56 HBD £44 D £16
CC: MC Vi Am Swi Delt JCB
How to get there: West Vale is on the B5285
between Hawkshead and the Ferry at
Windermere.

241 High Green Gate Guest House

 ◆◆◆ ✠

near Sawrey, Ambleside, Cumbria, LA22 0LF
Tel: 01539 436296
Email: highgreengate@amserve,net
Closed November to March
5 bedrs SB £30 DB £54 HBS £39 HBD £74
B £8 D £11 CC: None accepted
How to get there: On B5285 between
Hawkshead and Bowness via Ferry.

Shap, Cumbria

242 Shap Wells Hotel

★★★
Shap, Cumbria, CA10 3QU
Tel: 01931 716628 Fax: 01931 716377
Email: manager@shapwells.com
Web: www.shapwells.com
Closed January to mid-February
98 bedrs SB £60 DB £90 HBS £55 HBD £45
B £7 L £9 D £16 CC: MC Vi Am Swi Delt
How to get there: Exit J39 M6, then A6 for
Kendall. After 1½–2 miles, hotel drive (1 mile
long) on left.

Silloth, Cumbria

243 Golf Hotel

★★
Criffel Street, Silloth, Cumbria, CA5 4AB
Tel: 016973 31438 Fax: 016973 32582

Skelmersdale, Lancashire

244 Quality Hotel Skelmersdale

★★★
Prescott Road, East Pimbo,
Skelmersdale, WN8 9PU
Tel: 01695 720401 Fax: 01695 50953
Email: admin@gb656.u-net.com
Web: www.choicehotels.com
55 bedrs SB £88.75 DB £99.75 HBS £107.50
HBD £58.75 B £10.75 L £5.95 D £17.75
CC: MC Vi Am DC Swi Delt
How to get there: M6 Junction 26, M58
Junction 5. Down to roundabout, turn left, 100
yards further turn left again. Hotel 300 yards on
right.

Southport, Merseyside

245 Scarisbrick

★★★
239 Lord Street, Southport, Merseyside, PR8 1NZ
Tel: 01704 543000 Fax: 01704 533335
Email: scarisbrickhotel@talk21.com
Web: www.scarisbrickhotel.com
90 bedrs
CC: MC Vi Am DC Swi Delt
How to get there: From South, leave M6 at
Junction 26, and take M58 to Ormskirk, then
A570. From North, take M6 to Junction 31, then
A59 through Preston to A565.

Northwest

246 Tree Tops Country House Restaurant and Hotel

★★★★

Southport Old Road, Formby, Southport, Merseyside, L37 0AB
Tel: 01704 572430 Fax: 01704 572430

Ideal for business or pleasure, situated just off the beaten track, in quiet and tranquil surroundings, offering top class dining in our country house restaurant.
11 bedrs SB £58 DB £100 B £7.95 L £11 D £17.95 CC: MC Vi Am DC Swi Delt JCB

How to get there: Follow A565 from Liverpool to Southport. Ignore Formby sign, right at lights after RAF Woodvale onto Southport Old Road.

247 Metropole

★★

Portland Street, Southport, Merseyside, PR8 1LL
Tel: 01704 536836 Fax: 01704 549041
Email: metropole.southport@btinternet.com
Web: www.btinternet.com/~metropole.southport
23 bedrs SB £38.50 DB £66 HBS £50.50 HBD £45 B £6 L £7.75 D £12
CC: MC Vi Am Swi Delt

How to get there: 100m from Southport's Lord Street — a 4-minute walk from the railway station.

248 Ambassador

♦♦♦♦

13 Bath Street, Southport, Merseyside, PR9 0DP
Tel: 01704 543998 Fax: 01704 536269
Email: ambassador.walton@virgin.net
Web: www.ambassadorprivatehotel.co.uk
Closed 23 December to 2 January
8 bedrs SB £36 DB £50 HBS £46 HBD £70 D £10
CC: MC Vi Am Swi Delt

How to get there: Along Lord Street to Cenotaph, turn into Neville Street; take second right into Bath Street; hotel is on left.

249 Rosedale Hotel

♦♦♦♦

11 Talbot Street, Southport, Merseyside, PR8 1HP
Tel: 01704 530604 Fax: 01704 530604
Email: info@rosedalehotelsouthport.co.uk
Web: www.rosedale-hotel.co.uk
Closed late December to early January
9 bedrs SB £25 DB £50
CC: MC Vi Swi Delt JCB

How to get there: Entering the town via A570, follow signs to town centre into Eastbank Street. Talbot Street is on left.

250 White Lodge

♦♦♦

12 Talbot Street, Southport, Merseyside, PR8 1HP
Tel: 01704 536320 Fax: 01704 536320
7 bedrs SB £28 DB £54 HBS £38 HBD £37.50 D £10
CC: None accepted

How to get there: From town centre Tourist Information office, proceed along Eastbank Street. Talbot Street is fourth on the right. First hotel on the right.

251 Whitworth Falls Hotel

♦♦♦

16 Lathom Road, Southport, Merseyside, PR9 0JH
Tel: 01704 530074
Email: whitworthfalls@rapid.co.uk
Web: www.whitworthfallshotel.co.uk
12 bedrs SB £25 DB £50 HBS £32.50 HBD £32.50 B £5 D £7.50
CC: None accepted

How to get there: From Southport town centre, Lord Street, head north to the fire station over the roundabout. Take second left (Alexandra Road), and fourth right (Lathom Road).

St. Helens, Merseyside

252 Travelodge St. Helens

Travel Accommodation
A580, Haydock, St. Helens, Merseyside, WA11 0JZ
Tel: 08700 850 950
Web: www.travelodge.co.uk
62 bedrs B £4.25 CC: MC Vi Am DC Swi Delt

Stockport, Cheshire

253 Travelodge Stockport

Travel Accommodation
A523 London Road, Hope Filling Station,
Adlington, Stockport, Cheshire, SK10 4NA
Tel: 08700 850 950
Web: www.travelodge.co.uk
32 bedrs B £4.25 CC: MC Vi Am DC Swi Delt

Tarporley, Cheshire

254 Willington Hall Hotel

★★★ 🏱
Willington, Tarporley, Cheshire, CW6 0NB
Tel: 01829 752321 Fax: 01829 752596
Email: enquiries@willingtonhall.co.uk
Web: www.willingtonhall.co.uk
Closed Christmas
10 bedrs SB £70 DB £120 B £8 L £12 D £20
CC: MC Vi Am Swi

How to get there: Approaching Chester from
Tarporley on A51, turn right at Bulls Head,
signed Willington. Hall is one mile along on left.

Thornton Hough, Merseyside

255 Thornton Hall Hotel

★★★★ 🏱
Neston Road, Thornton Hough,
Merseyside, CH63 1JF
Tel: 0151 336 3938 Fax: 0151 336 7864
Email: thorntonhallhotel@btinternet.com
Web: www.thorntonhallhotel.com

63 bedrs SB £95 DB £105 B £7.95 L £8.50 D £24
CC: MC Vi Am DC Swi Delt
How to get there: M53 junction 4 take A5151 to
Clatterbridge then B5136 to Neston. Thornton
Hall is after Thornton Hough village on the left

Ullswater, Cumbria

256 Heritage Hotels — Leeming House
Blue Ribbon Winner

★★★★ 🏱 🏱
Watermillock, near Penrith, Ullswater,
Cumbria, CA11 0JJ
Tel: 0870 400 8131 Fax: 01768 486443
Email: heritagehotels_ullswater.leeming_house
@forte-hotels
40 bedrs SB £79 DB £118 HBS £94 HBD £74
B £14 L £13 D £29.50
CC: MC Vi Am DC Swi
How to get there: From M6 J40 follow signs for
Ullswater. At lakeside take right fork for
Windermere. Hotel is 2½ miles further on left.

257 Patterdale Hotel

★★
Patterdale, Penrith, Cumbria, CA11 0NN
Tel: 0845 458 4333 Fax: 01253 754222
Email: reservations@choice-hotels.co.uk
Web: www.patterdalehotel.co.uk
Closed December to April
63 bedrs SB £29 DB £58 HBS £39 HBD £39
B £6.75 D £15
CC: MC Vi Swi Delt
How to get there: From M6 Junction 40, take
A66 towards Keswick, at roundabout take first
exit, signposted Ullswater (A592). Turn right at
T-Junction. Continue through Glenridding to
Patterdale.

Wallasey, Merseyside

258 Grove House Hotel

★★★★ 🏱 🏱
Grove Road, Wallasey, Cheshire, CH43 3HF
Tel: 0151 639 3947 Fax: 0151 639 0028
14 bedrs SB £62.45 DB £62.45
B £6.95 D £8.95
CC: MC Vi Am DC Swi Delt

Northwest

Warrington, Cheshire

259 Hanover International Hotel Warrington

★★★★ ® ®

Stretton Road, Stretton, Warrington,
Cheshire, WA4 4NS
Tel: 01925 730706 Fax: 01925 730740
Web: www.hanover-international.com

HANOVER INTERNATIONAL
HOTELS & CLUBS

Award-winning hotel, set in the heart of Cheshire.
With deluxe bedrooms, an AA rosette restaurant,
conference and banquetting facilities for 400
guests and a super health and leisure spa with
beauty suites.
142 bedrs SB £115 DB £125 B £9.75 L £10.95
D £15.95 CC: MC Vi Am DC Swi Delt
How to get there: Leave M56 at J10 and follow
A49 towards Warrington. At first set of traffic
lights turn right. The hotel is 200 yards on right.

260 Paddington House Hotel

★★

514 Manchester Road, Warrington,
Cheshire, WA1 3TZ
Tel: 01925 816767 Fax: 01925 816651
Email: hotel@paddingtonhouse.co.uk
Web: www.paddingtonhouse.co.uk

Friendly, family-run Georgian house situated in
its own grounds. Conveniently located close to
junction 21 M6 and two miles from Warrington
town centre. Antique-themed bar and
restaurant.
37 bedrs SB £61 DB £70 HBS £69.50 HBD £90
B £6 L £9.50 D £12.50
CC: MC Vi Am DC Swi Delt
How to get there: Exit M6 J-21. Follow signs for
Warrington (A57). Continue along A57 for
approximately one mile.

261 Travelodge Warrington

Travel Accommodation
Kendrick Street, Warrington, Cheshire, WA1 1UR
Tel: 08700 850 950
Web: www.travelodge.co.uk
63 bedrs B £4.25
CC: MC Vi Am DC Swi Delt

Wasdale, Cumbria

262 Wasdale Head Inn

◆ ◆ ◆ ◆ ® ⚔

Wasdale, near Gosforth, Cumbria, CA20 1EX
Tel: 01946 726229 Fax: 01946 726334
Email: wasdaleheadinn@msn.com
Web: www.wasdale.com
13 bedrs SB £45 DB £90 HBS £67 HBD £67
B £7.50 L £5 D £22
CC: MC Vi Am Swi Delt JCB
How to get there: From M6, proceed to West
Cumbria. From A595, turn into Gosforth village
and take left fork for Wasdale. After one mile
bear right to climb steep hill. Inn is another nine
miles along single track road.

Widnes, Cheshire

263 Travelodge Widnes

Travel Accommodation
A562, Fiddlers Ferry Road, Widnes,
Cheshire, WA8 2NR
Tel: 08700 850 950
Web: www.travelodge.co.uk
32 bedrs B £4.25
CC: MC Vi Am DC Swi Delt

Wigan, Lancashire

264 Quality Hotel Wigan

★★★
River Way, Wigan, Greater Manchester, WN1 3SS
Tel: 01942 826888 Fax: 01942 825800
Email: admin@gb058.u-net.com
Web: www.choicehotels.com
88 bedrs SB £95.95 DB £105.95 HBS £111.90
HBD £60.95 B £10.95 L £2.95 D £15.95
CC: MC Vi Am DC Swi Delt

How to get there: From M6 northbound take Junction 25, or from M6 southbound take Junction 27.

265 Bel Air

★★
236 Wigan Lane, Wigan, Lancashire, WN1 2NU
Tel: 01942 241410 Fax: 01942 243967
Email: belair@hotelwigan.freeserve.co.uk
Web: www.belairhotel.co.uk
11 bedrs SB £39.50 DB £49.50 HBS £45
HBD £29.75 B £2.95 L £6.95 D £6.95
CC: MC Vi Am Swi Delt

How to get there: Two miles from Junction 27 of M6. A49 towards Wigan. Bel Air is on right before large roundabout and Cherry Gardens public house.

Wigton, Cumbria

266 Wheyrigg Hall Hotel

◆◆◆
Abbeytown, Wigton, near Carlisle,
Cumbria, CA7 0DH
Tel: 01697 361242 Fax: 01697 361020
12 bedrs SB £40 DB £52 B £5 L £5 D £10
CC: MC Vi Am DC Swi Delt JCB

How to get there: From south M6 J41 to Wigton B5305. From Scotland J44 to Wigton A595/596, B5302 Wigton to Silloth

Windermere, Cumbria

267 Lakeside Hotel

★★★★★ ®®
Lakeside, Newby Bridge, Cumbria, LA12 8AT
Tel: 01539 530001 Fax: 01539 531699
Email: sales@lakesidehotel.co.uk

Web: www.lakesidehotel.co.uk

Overlooking nothing but the lake... Lakeside Hotel is in the perfect location right on the shores of Lake Windemere. Lake cruisers depart from directly outside the hotel.
80 bedrs SB £120 DB £140 HBS £165 HBD £105
B £10 L £10 D £20
CC: MC Vi Am DC Swi Delt JCB

How to get there: Leave M6 at Junction 36 and follow A590 to Newby Bridge or follow signs for Lakeside Steamers.

268 Low Wood Hotel

★★★★ ®
Windermere, Cumbria, LA23 1LP
Tel: 01539 433338 Fax: 01539 434072

269 Beech Hill Hotel

★★★★ ®®
Newby Bridge Road, Bowness-on-Windermere,
Windermere, Cumbria, LA23 3LR
Tel: 01539 442137 Fax: 01539 443745
Email: beechhill@richardsonhotels.co.uk
Web: www.richardsonhotels.co.uk
58 bedrs SB £57 DB £94 HBS £69 HBD £118
B £8.50 L £5 D £27.50
CC: MC Vi Am Swi

How to get there: Leave M6 at Junction 36, take A591 to Windermere. Turn left onto A592 towards Newby Bridge.

270 Craig Manor Hotel

★★★ ®
Lake Road, Windermere,
Cumbria, LA23 3HR
Tel: 015394 88877 Fax: 015394 88878

Northwest

271 Gilpin Lodge Country House Hotel
Gold Ribbon Winner

★★★★ ® ® ®

Crook Road, Windermere, Cumbria, LA23 3NE
Tel: 01539 488818 Fax: 01539 488058
Email: hotel@gilpin-lodge.co.uk
Web: www.gilpin-lodge.co.uk
Children minimum age: 7
14 bedrs SB £80 DB £90 HBS £105 HBD £65
B £12.50 L £10 D £35
CC: MC Vi Am DC Swi Delt JCB

How to get there: Leave M6 at Junction 36.
Take A590/A591 to roundabout north of Kendal,
then B5284 for five miles.
See advert on facing page

272 Heritage Hotels — The Old England

★★★

Church Street, Bowness, Windermere,
Cumbria, LA23 3DF
Tel: 0870 400 8130 Fax: 01539 443432
76 bedrs SB £55 DB £110 HBS £65 HBD £130
B £11.95 L £12.95 D £25
CC: MC Vi Am DC Swi Delt

How to get there: Leave M6 at Junction 36.
Take A592 to Windermere. Hotel is on right,
next to the lake, 18 miles from junction.

273 Hillthwaite House

★★★

Thornbarrow Road, Windermere,
Cumbria, LA23 2DF
Tel: 01539 443636 Fax: 01539 488660
Email: reception@hillthwaite.com
Web: www.hillthwaite.com

An extended 19th-century house, in an elevated
position overlooking lake and fells. Swimming
pool, sauna, steam room, four-poster beds,
jacuzzi baths. Excellent restaurant.
29 bedrs SB £35 DB £70 HBS £49.50
HBD £49.50 B £10 L £10 D £17.50
CC: MC Vi Am DC Swi Delt

How to get there: Halfway between Windermere
and Bowness, turn left into Thornbarrow Road.
Hillthwaite House Hotel can be seen on skyline.

274 Holbeck Ghyll Country House Hotel
Gold Ribbon Winner

★★★★ ® ® ® ®

Holbeck Lane, Windermere, Cumbria, LA23 1LU
Tel: 01539 432375 Fax: 01539 434743
Email: stay@holbeck-ghyll.com
Web: www.holbeck-ghyll.com
19th-century hunting lodge in eight acres with
breathtaking views of Lake Windemere. Art
Nouveau features with log fires, Michelin-star
food and exclusive health spa. Central touring
location, special breaks.
20 bedrs SB £140 DB £220 HBS £175
HBD £320 L £12.50 D £29.50
CC: MC Vi Am DC Swi Delt JCB

How to get there: Leave M6 at Junction 36.
Take A591 to Windermere. Towards Ambleside,
turn right after Brockhole (Holbeck Lane,
signposted Troutbeck). Hotel is ½ a mile on left.

275 Langdale Chase Hotel

★★★★ ® ®

Windermere, Cumbria, LA23 1LW
Tel: 01539 432201 Fax: 01539 432604
Email: sales@langdalechase.co.uk
Web: www.langdalechase.co.uk
27 bedrs SB £45 DB £120 HBD £85 B £8.50
L £14.95 D £30 CC: MC Vi Am DC Swi Delt

How to get there: M6 at Junction 36. head to
Windermere on A591, then sign for Ambleside.
Hotel is ¼ of a mile past Brockhole on left.

276 Lindeth Howe Country House

★★★★ ® ®

Lindeth Drive, Longtail Hill, Windermere,
Cumbria, LA23 3JF
Tel: 01539 445759 Fax: 01539 446368
Email: lindeth.howe@kencomp.net
Web: www.lakes-pages.co.uk
36 bedrs CC: MC Vi Swi Delt

How to get there: Junction 36 of the M6, take
A591 at roundabout, then first left onto B5284.
Travel six miles, drive straight over crossroads
to Longtail Hill. Hotel 200 yards on left (first
drive).

277 Linthwaite House Hotel and Restaurant · Blue Ribbon Winner

★★★ ⓡ ⓡ ⓡ

Crook Road, Windermere, The Lake District, Cumbria, LA23 3JA
Tel: 01539 488600 Fax: 01539 488601
Email: admin@linthwaite.com
Web: www.linthwaite.com

Sublime peaceful location, stunning lake and fell views, 14 acres, log fires, personally run, independently owned, 'unstuffy' staff, good food and eclectic wine list.
26 bedrs SB £85 DB £90 HBS £79 HBD £59
B £13.50 L £10 D £39 CC: MC Vi Am DC Swi Delt
⚓ ♿ 📠 ⊗ ⊙ ▢ ☎ 📞 P 🐾 🛏 ⌇ 😊 ♨ 🍴 ⛵
How to get there: Exit M6 J-36. A591 towards Windermere, then B5284 through Crook. Linthwaite is six miles on left, up private drive.

278 The Famous Wild Boar

★★★★ ⓡ ⓡ

Crook Road, Crook, near Windermere, Cumbria, LA23 3NF
Tel: 015394 45225 Fax: 015394 42498
Email: wildboar@elh.mail.co.uk
Web: www.elh.co.uk

Ideally located for touring the Lake District. Award-winning restaurant. Traditional cuisine and fine wine along with real ales. Free use of leisure facilities at sister hotel. Relaxing, comfortable ambience.
36 bedrs SB £56 DB £112 HBS £65 HBD £65
B £8.95 L £10 D £21.95
CC: MC Vi Am DC Swi Delt JCB
📠 🐎 ⊗ ⊙ ▢ ☎ P 🐾 ⌇ ♨ 😊 ♨ 🍴
How to get there: M6 exit 36 signed A5090/A591 to Windermere. Join B5284 to Crook. Hotel two miles beyond the village of Crook.

Northwest

279 Broadoaks Country House
Blue Ribbon Winner

★★ 🄯 🄯 🄯

Bridge Lane, Troutbeck, Windermere,
Cumbria, LA23 1LA
Tel: 01539 445566 Fax: 01539 488766
Email: trev@broadoaksf9.co.uk
Web: www.broadoaks-lake-district.co.uk
Children minimum age: 5

Award-winning country house set in own grounds.
Superb views, luxury bedrooms with four-posters
and jacuzzis. Exceptional cuisine in our Victorian
dining room. Simply somewhere special.
14 bedrs SB £69.50 DB £99 HBS £99.50
HBD £79.50 B £15 L £14 D £35
CC: MC Vi Delt

How to get there: M6 J36 A590/591 to
Windemere over small roundabout to
Ambleside; through Troutbeck; bridge right, into
Bridge Lane. Property is 1/2 mile on right
See advert on facing page

280 Cedar Manor Hotel

★★ 🄯 🄯

Ambleside Road, Windermere,
Cumbria, LA23 1AX
Tel: 01539 443192 Fax: 01539 445970
Email: cedarmanor@fsbdial.co.uk
Web: www.cedarmanor.co.uk
12 bedrs SB £40 DB £60 HBS £52 HBD £84
B £9 D £19.50 CC: MC Vi

How to get there: 1/4 mile north of Windermere
on A591. Nearest motorway, Junction 36 on M6.
Follow signs for South Lakes.

281 Hideaway Hotel

★★ 🄯

Phoenix Way, Windermere, Cumbria, LA23 1DB
Tel: 01539 443070 Fax: 01539 448664
Email: enquiries@hideaway-hotel.co.uk
Web: www.hideaway-hotel.co.uk

Closed January
15 bedrs SB £35 DB £60 HBS £53 HBD £45
L £6 D £11.50 CC: MC Vi Am Swi Delt

How to get there: Take A591 into Windermere;
turn off into Phoenix Way. The hotel is 100m on
the right down the hill.
See advert on facing page

282 Lindeth Fell Country House Hotel
Blue Ribbon Winner

★★★ 🄯 🄯

Lyth Valley Road, Bowness-on-Windermere,
Cumbria, LA23 3JP
Tel: 01539 443286 Fax: 01539 447455
Email: kennedy@lindethfell.co.uk
Web: www.lindethfell.co.uk
14 bedrs SB £52 DB £90 HBS £69 HBD £70
B £8.50 L £6.95 D £23 CC: MC Vi Swi

How to get there: One mile south of Bowness-
on-Windermere on A5074.
See advert on facing page

283 Miller Howe Hotel
Blue Ribbon Winner

★★★ 🄯 🄯 🄯

Rayrigg Road, Windemere, Cumbria, LA23 1EY
Tel: 015394 42536 Fax: 015394 45664
Email: lakeview@millerhowe.com
Web: www.millerhowe.com
Children minimum age: 8
Closed 3–21 January
Edwardian House with breathtaking views over
Lake Windemere. The house, with antiques,
paintings and objets d'art, boasts a gourmet
cuisine restaurant.
15 bedrs SB £75 DB £150 HBS £95 HBD £65
B £15 L £17.50 D £39.50 CC: MC Vi Am DC Swi

How to get there: On A592 between Windemere
and Bowness. Ring for detailed location map or
visit website.

284 Newstead Guest House

◆◆◆◆◆ 🄯 🄯

New Road, Windermere, Cumbria, LA23 2EE
Tel: 01539 444485
Children minimum age: 7
7 bedrs DB £55
CC: None accepted

How to get there: Leave M6 at Junction 36.
Follow A590/A591 to Windermere village.
Newstead is 1/4 mile on left.

Northwest

285 The Beaumont

◆ ◆ ◆ ◆ ◆ ※ ⚑

Holly Road, Windermere, Cumbria, LA23 2AF
Tel: 01539 447075 Fax: 01539 447075
Email: thebeaumonthotel@btinternet.com
Web: www.lakesbeaumont.co.uk
Children minimum age: 10

The Beaumont enjoys a tranquil location, yet is only a few minutes' walk to Windemere village. Immaculate bedrooms, superb food, genuine hospitality and exceptional value. A five diamond multi-award-winning hotel.
10 bedrs SB £38 DB £34 CC: MC Vi Swi Delt JCB
🖼 ⊗ ⑤ 🖵 P 🕏 iii
How to get there: Follow town centre signs through one-way system, then take 2nd left into Ellerthwaite Road then first left into Holly Road.

286 Blenheim Lodge Hotel

◆ ◆ ◆ ◆ �ℝ ※

Brantfell Road, Bowness-on-Windermere, Windermere, Cumbria, LA23 3AE
Tel: 01539 443440 Fax: 01539 443440
Email: blenheimlodge@supanet.com
Web: www.six-of-the-best.com
Children minimum age: 6
11 bedrs SB £30 DB £50 HBS £52 HBD £47
D £22
CC: MC Vi Am Swi Delt
🖼 ⊗ ⑤ 🖵 P 🕏 ħ iii
How to get there: Leave M6 at Juncion 36. Take A591 to Windermere. Turn left to Bowness Cross mini roundabout, take first left and first left again.

287 Fairfield

◆ ◆ ◆ ◆ ※

Brantfell Road, Bowness-on-Windermere, Cumbria, LA23 3AE
Tel: 01539 446565 Fax: 01539 446565
Email: ray&barb@the-fairfield.co.uk
Web: www.the-fairfield.co.uk
Closed December to January

An attractive 200-year-old house set in a quiet, secluded, well-matured garden. Close to the village, lake, fells & Dales Way. Superb value.
9 bedrs SB £33 DB £66 CC: MC Vi Swi Delt
🖼 ⊗ ⑤ 🖵 P 🕏 ℃ ħ iii
How to get there: From mini roundabout in the centre of Bowness village, take road towards lake, turn left, then left again into Brantfell Road.

288 Fir Trees Guest House

◆ ◆ ◆ ◆

Lake Road, Windermere, Cumbria, LA23 2EQ
Tel: 01539 442272 Fax: 01539 442272

289 Royal Hotel

◆ ◆ ◆

Royal Square, Bowness, Windermere, Cumbria, LA23 3DB
Tel: 01539 443045 Fax: 01539 444990
Web: www.elh.co.uk
Closed 24–25 December

Located in busy Bowness village a warm welcome awaits. Lively setting with two themed bars, McGintys and Circuit Sports Bar. The lake, restaurants and attractions close by. Complementing leisure facilities four miles.
29 bedrs SB £29.50 DB £59.50 B £5.95
CC: MC Vi Am DC Swi Delt JCB
🖼 ☆ ⑤ 🖵 ☎ P 🕏 ℃ ħ 🍴 iii
How to get there: Exit J36 M6, follow signs for Windemere. A591 in to Bowness. In centre of village.

290 The Coppice Guest House and Dining Room

New Road, Windemere,
Cumbria, LA23 2ED
Tel: 015394 88501 Fax: 015394 42148
Email: chris@thecoppice.co.uk
Web: www.thecoppice.co.uk
8 bedrs SB £35 DB £48
HBS £52 HBD £40
B £7 D £18.50
CC: MC Vi Am Swi Delt JCB

How to get there: M6 J36, A590/591 to
Windemere. Left at Windemere Hotel, through
village, down New Road, left into Brook Road
and right into car park.

Workington, Cumbria

291 Cumberland Hotel

★★★
Station Road, Workington,
Cumbria, CA14 2XQ
Tel: 01900 64401 Fax: 01900 872400

Wales

ISLE OF ANGLESEY
Holyhead
Rhyl
Conwy
Bangor
FLINT
Chester
Caernarfon
CONWY
Mold
Nantwich
Ruthin
Betws-y-Coed
DENBIGH-SHIRE
Wrexham
Whitchurch
Criccieth
Porthmadoc
Llangollen
GWYNEDD
Oswestry
Abersoch
Glasgow
Edinburgh
Dolgellau
Shrewsbury
Newcastle
Machynlleth
Welshpool
Church Stretton
Belfast
POWYS
Dublin
Manchester
Newtown
Birmingham
Aberystwyth
Llangurig
Ludlow
Cardiff
London
Rhayader
CEREDIGION
Llandrindod Wells
Leominster
Aberaeron
Cardigan
Builth Wells
Hereford
Fishguard
Llandovery
Brecon
Ross-on-Wye
St David's
PEMBROKESHIRE
CARMARTHENSHIRE
Haverfordwest
Carmarthen
Abergavenny
Monmouth
Milford Haven
Pembroke Dock
Merthyr Tydfil
TORFAEN
MONMOUTH-SHIRE
Llanelli
Neath
RHONDDA, CYNON, TAFF
Cwmbran
Chepstow
Swansea
Port Talbot
Newport
CARDIFF
Bristol
THE VALE OF GLAMORGAN
Western-super-Mare

The city of St David's takes its name from the monastary established by the saint, a place of pilgrimage after the blessing of Pope Calixtus II. The cathedral, begun in 1181, has had its mishaps but its grandeur today is undeniable.

www.stdavidscathedral.org.uk or 01437 720691.

Tredegar House was where the Morgan family once controlled much of Newport, Gwent. It was rebuilt after a fire in the 17th century and was a school in the 1950s, but today houses many fine paintings and furniture. The Orangery and its gardens (below) adjoin the property. Call 01633 815880 or see members.fortunecity.com /tredegarhouse/home.htm.

Encompassing Snowdon and Bardsey Island, the Llyn Peninsula (above) was traversed by pilgrims and supposedly saints until medieval times, now protected by the National Trust. Places to visit include the Victorian copper mine at Beddgelert and the National Centre for Welsh Language & Culture at Nant Gwrtheyrn. Those with an interest in language should visit www.marketsite.co.uk/wlc/.

● The reconstructed Iron Age fort near Newport Castell Henllys, built on original ancient foundations, was used by the BBC for a survival series that made participants live 4,000 years in the past.

● Built for King Edward I, it's not surprising that Caernarfon Castle, Gwynedd, was designed as his administrative Welsh HQ – the huge, hour glass-shaped construction is an imposing sight, and its wall once encompassed the town. www.castlewales.com/caernarf.html for more information.

● Cross the Menai Strait to the Isle of Anglesey and its coastline of outstanding beauty, Sea Zoo, ancient buildings and trout lakes inland.

Tenby harbour (below) sits midway between two marvellous sandy beaches; the remains of 13th century defensive walls add to the town's charms. Boats trips to nearby Caldey Island are available. Visit www.virtualtenby.co.uk.

Easy mountaineering

The Snowdonia National Park (above) covers 840 square miles and offers many walking routes and other outdoor pursuits. Those who cannot face the trek to Snowdon's snowy 3,560-foot peak can catch a train from Llanberis. www.gwynedd.imaginet.co.uk/english/home.html or phone 01341 422888.

Cardiff Arms Park, a legend in Rugby history, was replaced by the 72,500-seater Millennium Stadium (below) in June 1999. Rugby union has been joined by football since the closure of Wembley Stadium. Both benefit — along with the site's established pop concerts — from an impressive retractable roof when weather dictates. Visit www.cardiff-stadium.co.uk; box office 08705 582 582 for sporting events.

The Llyn Brianne reservoir (above) is on the Towy — Carmarthenshire's largest river — in the Cambrian Mountains. This part of Ceredigion has beautiful scenery, passed by horse and pony treks.

● Caerlon, adjacent to Newport, was the site of a Roman fortress for 300 years (its name means "camp of the legion") that, along with Chester and Wroxeter, kept the Welsh subdued — parts of barracks, baths and an amphitheatre remain.

● Skomer Island, off the Pembrokeshire coast, has colonies of puffins, guillemots, peregrines and kittiwakes, among others, and Atlantic grey seals in the autumn.

Accommodation index

Hotels and Guest Accommodation are indexed by their order of appearance within this region, not by the page. To locate an establishment, note the number to the right of the listing and then find it on the establishment's name bar, as shown here

37 The Turning Mill Hotel

Caerphilly, Mid Glamorgan, is the largest castle in Wales (above), its water defences formed by shaping a strip of land between two streams to form an island. Its ruinous state does not diminish the power of the castle and its grounds. www.caerphillycastle.com or 029 2088 0011 for further information.

● The 18th-century estate of Middleton Hall, near Carmarthen, is now the setting for the National Botanic Garden of Wales. Its high-tech single-span glasshouse is the largest in the world, while outside a series of lakes provide a tranquil setting for walks. Call 01558 668768, or go to www.gardenofwales.org.uk.

Music in the valleys

● Llangollen in the Dee Valley, Denbighshire, hosts the Llangollen International Musical Eisteddfod, a choir festival which attracts 6,500 competitors from 47 countries every July. The town developed around its church, originally a tiny wooden one built by Collen; according to legend, this monk was sainted after he defeated an evil fairy king. www.llangollen.org.uk and 01978 860828; www.international-eisteddfod.co.uk and 01978 862000 for International Musical Eisteddfod.

● Cardiff's bay, vital to its success and growth, developed largely from the Marquess of Bute's West Dock; today its many attractions also include the National Museum, Centre for Visual Arts, Church of St John, Techniquest science centre, castle and Alexandra Gardens.

Aberdovey, Gwynedd

1 Trefeddian Hotel

★★★★

Aberdovey, Gwynedd, LL35 0SB
Tel: 01654 767213 Fax: 01654 767777
Email: tref@saqnet.co.uk
Web: www.trefwales.com
Closed January to February
59 bedrs SB £40 DB £55
HBS £59 HBD £79
B £10 L £14 D £22
CC: MC Vi Swi Delt

How to get there: ½ mile north of Aberdovey
village off A493, overlooking golf links and
Cardigan Bay.
See advert on following page

Abergavenny, Monmouthshire

2 Llansantffraed Court Hotel

★★★★

Llanvihangel Gobion, near Abergavenny,
Monmouthshire, NP7 9BA
Tel: 01873 840678 Fax: 01873 840674
Email: mikemorgan@llch.co.uk
Web: www.llch.co.uk

A timeless landscape, steeped in history and
legend awaits at Llansantffraed. This majestic
country house offers the best of Welsh
hospitality. Spoil yourself.
21 bedrs
CC: MC Vi Am DC Swi Delt

How to get there: From convergence of A465
and A40 at Abergavenny, take B4598 to Usk.
Hotel gates are on left after 4½ miles.

Abergele, Conwy

3 Kinmel Manor

★★★

St. Georges Road, Abergele,
Conwy, LL22 9AS
Tel: 01745 832014 Fax: 01745 832014
51 bedrs SB £55 DB £76
HBS £72 HBD £55
B £7.50 L £13 D £17
CC: MC Vi Am DC Swi Delt

How to get there: Travelling west, take Abergele
turn-off to roundabout entrance. Travelling east
A55, take Rhuddlan turn off to roundabout
entrance. We are on the roundabout.

Aberporth, Cardigan

4 Hotel Penrallt

★★★★

Aberporth, Cardigan, SA43 2BS
Tel: 01239 810227 Fax: 01239 811375
Email: info@hotelpenrallt.co.uk
Web: www.hotelpenrallt.co.uk
16 bedrs SB £65 DB £105 HBS £85 HBD £145
B £8.95 L £10.50 D £20
CC: MC Vi Am DC Swi Delt

How to get there: On A487 five miles north of
Cardigan town, take B4333 signed Aberporth.
Hotel Penrallt one mile on right.

Aberystwyth, Ceredigion

5 Belle Vue Royal Hotel

★★★

Marine Terrace, Aberystwyth,
Ceredigion, SY23 2BA
Tel: 01970 617558 Fax: 01970 612190
Email: reception@bellevueroyalhotel.fsnet.co.uk
Web: www.bellevueroyal.co.uk
36 bedrs SB £62 DB £92 HBS £80 HBD £65
B £8.50 L £13 D £22
CC: MC Vi Am DC Swi Delt

How to get there: Situated on promenade
overlooking Cardigan Bay.

Wales

Trefeddian Hotel

Standing prominently overlooking golf links, sand dunes and Cardigan Bay, 1½ miles north of Aberdyfi (Aberdovey) village, Trefeddian is set in its own grounds and suitable for all the family. Trefeddian is renowned for friendly attentive service, excellent meals, an extensive wine list, and spacious lounges, affording relaxing holidays.

The hotel has an indoor swimming pool, tennis court,

9-hole pitch/putt, snooker room, children's indoor/outdoor play areas, sun terraces, and lift.

Trefeddian Hotel
Aberdovey,
Gwynedd LL35 0SB
Tel: 01654 767213
Fax: 01654 767777
Email: tref@saqnet.co.uk

6 Conrah Country House Hotel

★★★★ ☆ ☆
Chancery, Aberystwyth,
Ceredigion, SY23 4DF
Tel: 01970 617941 Fax: 01970 624546
Email: enquiries@conrah.co.uk
Web: www.conrah.co.uk
Children minimum age: 5
Closed Christmas
17 bedrs SB £80 DB £100
HBS £98 HBD £70
B £13 L £15 D £25
CC: MC Vi Am DC Swi Delt

How to get there: 3½ miles south of
Aberystwyth on A487.

7 George Borrow Hotel

★★
Ponterwyd, Aberystwyth, Ceredigion, SY23 3AD
Tel: 01970 890230 Fax: 01970 890587
Email: georgeborrow@clara.net
Web: www.george-borrow.co.uk
9 bedrs SB £25 DB £50
HBS £35 HBD £35
B £5 L £5.50 D £11.95
CC: MC Vi Swi Delt JCB

How to get there: Alongside A44, Aberystwyth
side of village of Ponterwyd, 15 minutes from
Aberystwyth.

8 Glyn-Garth Guest House

♦ ♦ ♦ ♦
South Road, Aberystwyth, Ceredigion, SY23 1JS
Tel: 01970 615050 Fax: 01970 636835
Email: glyn-garth@southroad88.freeserve.co.uk
Children minimum age: 7
Closed Christmas to New Year
10 bedrs SB £21 DB £42
CC: None accepted

How to get there: Close to town centre,
adjacent to South Promenade.

Amlwch, Gwynedd

9 Trecastell Hotel

★★
Bull Bay, Amlwch, Gwynedd, LL68 9SA
Tel: 01407 830651 Fax: 01407 832114

Bala, Gwynedd

10 Plas Coch Hotel

★★
High Street, Bala, Gwynedd, LL23 7AB
Tel: 01678 520309 Fax: 01678 521135

Bangor, Gwynedd

11 Travelodge Bangor

Travel Accommodation
A5/A55, Llandegai, Bangor, Gwynedd, LL57 4BG
Tel: 08700 850 950
Web: www.travelodge.co.uk
62 bedrs B £4.25
CC: MC Vi Am DC Swi Delt

Barmouth, Gwynedd

12 Bontddu Hall Hotel

★★★★ ☆ ☆
Bontddu, Dolgellau, Gwynedd, LL40 2UF
Tel: 01341 430661 Fax: 01341 430284
Email: reservations@bontdduhall.co.uk
Web: www.bontdduhall.co.uk
Closed November to February
20 bedrs
CC: MC Vi Am DC Swi Delt

How to get there: Turn off A470 north of
Dolgellau onto A496 towards Barmouth. Three
miles to Bontddu — hotel is on right-hand side.

Beddgelert, Gwynedd

13 Royal Goat Hotel

★★★
Beddgelert, Gwynedd, LL55 4YE
Tel: 01766 890224 Fax: 01766 890422
Email: info@royalgoathotel.co.uk
Web: www.royalgoathotel.co.uk
32 bedrs SB £45 DB £79 HBS £62.50 HBD £57
B £7 L £10 D £17.50
CC: MC Vi Am DC Swi Delt
How to get there: Situated in the centre of the
village.
See advert on following page

Wales

Royal Goat Hotel

A family owned establishment, The Royal Goat Hotel offers a combination of efficient service, good food and wine and spectacular scenery in the heart of the Snowdonia National Park. The hotel has an excellent reputation for good food and wine. À la carte and table d' hôte menus. Lift to all floors.

Beddgelert, Gwynedd LL55 4YE
Tel: 01766 890224   Fax: 01766 890422
Email: info@royalgoathotel.co.uk
Website: www.royalgoathotel.co.uk

14 Tanronnen Hotel

★★ ℞
Beddgelert, Gwynedd, LL55 4YB
Tel: 01766 890347 Fax: 01766 890606
Email: brewery@frederic-robinson.co.uk
Web: www.frederic-robinson.co.uk
7 bedrs SB £42 DB £80 B £3 L £5 D £9.90
CC: MC Vi Swi Delt
How to get there: Situated in village centre.

Betws-y-Coed, Conwy

15 Royal Oak Hotel

★★★★ ℞
Betws-y-Coed, Conwy, LL24 0AY
Tel: 01690 710219 Fax: 01690 710433
Email: glenn.evans@btinternet.com
Web: www.royaloak@betwsycoed.co.uk
        /acc/royal-oak/default/html
26 bedrs SB £57 DB £86 HBS £73 HBD £59
B £8.50 L £10.50 D £16
CC: MC Vi Am DC Swi Delt
How to get there: The hotel is situated on the main A5 London to Holyhead route, at the village centre.

16 Park Hill Hotel

★★
Llanrwst Road, Betws-y-Coed, Conwy, LL24 0HD
Tel: 01690 710540 Fax: 01690 710540
Email: parkhill.hotel@virgin.net
Web: www.betws-y-coed.co.uk/acc/parkhill
Children minimum age: 6
9 bedrs SB £45 DB £57 HBS £60 HBD £86
  L £5 D £15.50 CC: MC Vi Swi Delt
How to get there: On elevated position on A470 northbound from Betws-y-Coed, 1/2 mile from crossing with A5/Waterloo Bridge.

17 Fron Heulog Country House

♦♦♦♦ ✤ ✿
Betws-y-Coed, Conwy, LL24 0BL
Tel: 01690 710736 Fax: 01690 710920
Email: jean&peter@fronheulog.co.uk
Web: www.fronheulog.co.uk

'The Country House in the village!' Elegant Victorian stone-built south-facing house in peaceful wooded riverside scenery. Excellent modern accommodation — comfort, warmth, style. Jean and Peter Whittingham welcome you to their home.
3 bedrs DB £44.56 CC: None accepted
How to get there: From A5 road in Betwys-y-Coed take B5106 road over picturesque Pont-y-Pair bridge, immediately turn left along riverbank. Fron Heulog is 150 yards up ahead.

Brecon, Powys

18 Peterstone Court Hotel

★★★
Llanhamlach, Brecon, Powys, LD3 7YB
Tel: 01874 665387 Fax: 01874 665376
Closed 26–31 December
12 bedrs SB £89.25 DB £99.75 HBS £118.25
HBD £68.25 B £8.95 L £10.95 D £15.25
CC: MC Vi Am DC Swi Delt

19 Usk Inn

◆ ◆ ◆ ◆ ✕

Station Road, Talybont on Usk, Brecon,
Powys LD3 7JE
Tel: 01874 676251 Fax: 01874 676392
Email: stay@uskinn.co.uk
Web: www.uskinn.co.uk
Closed Christmas

Whether walking, mountain bike riding or
touring in a classic car, good food, wine, beer
and above all rooms combine in an Inn that
continues to exceed guests' expectations.
11 bedrs SB £35 DB £70 B £6.95 D £17.95
CC: MC Vi Am Swi

How to get there: From A40, we are six miles
east of Brecon. Turn into Talybont on Usk. The
Inn is 250 yards from the river bridge.

20 Beacons

◆ ◆ ◆

16 Bridge Street, Brecon, Powys, LD3 8AH
Tel: 01874 623339 Fax: 01874 623339
Email: beacons@brecon.co.uk
Web: www.beacons.brecon.co.uk

This recently-restored listed Georgian house
offers beautifully appointed bedrooms. The
candle-lit restaurant has fine food and wines.
Cosy cellar bar, elegant lounge and private
parking.
14 bedrs SB £25 DB £36 HBS £39.95
HBD £32.95 B £5 D £9.95

CC: MC Vi Swi Delt

How to get there: Following the A40 west
through town centre, turn left. Go downhill at
traffic lights, over bridge, then hotel is 100 yards
on right.

21 Maeswalter

◆ ◆ ◆

Heol Senni, near Brecon,
Powys, LD3 8SU
Tel: 01874 636629
Email: maeswalter@talk21.com
Children minimum age: 10
4 bedrs SB £20 DB £36 HBS £30.50
HBD £28.50 B £5 L £7 D £12
CC: None accepted

How to get there: Take A470 (Brecon to
Merthyr). Turn right onto A4215. After two miles
turn left for Heol Senni. Maeswalter is 1½ miles
on right.

Bridgend

22 Travelodge Bridgend

Travel Accommodation
A473, The Old Mill, Felindre Road, Pencoed,
Bridgend, CF35 5HU
Tel: 08700 850 950
Web: www.travelodge.co.uk
40 bedrs B £4.25
CC: MC Vi Am DC Swi Delt

23 Bryngarw House

◆ ◆ ◆ ◆ ⏚ ⏚ ✕

Bryngarw Country Park, Brynmenyn, near
Bridgend, CF32 8UU
Tel: 01656 729009 Fax: 01656 729007
19 bedrs SB £51 DB £79 B £8.50 L £11.50 D £19
CC: MC Vi Am DC Swi Delt JCB

How to get there: Exit M4 at J36 and follow the
Country Park signs for 2½ mile.

Wales

Burry Port, Carmarthenshire

24 George Hotel

◆◆◆◆

Stepney Road, Burry Port,
Carmarthenshire, SA16 0BH
Tel: 01554 832211
Children minimum age: 7
8 bedrs SB £29 DB £46 L £3.95 D £5.95
CC: None accepted

How to get there: M4 J48, A484 to Burry Port.
Turn at pelican crossing into town centre along
Stepney Road.

Caernarfon, Gwynedd

25 Celtic Royal Hotel

★★★ 🐾

Bangor Street, Caernarfon, Gwynedd, LL55 1AY
Tel: 01286 674477 Fax: 01286 674139
Email: admin@celtic-royal.co.uk
Web: www.celtic-royal.co.uk
110 bedrs SB £65 DB £100 HBS £85 HBD £65
B £8.50 L £6.95 D £15
CC: MC Vi Am Swi Delt

26 Seiont Manor

★★★★ 🐾🐾

Llanrug, Caernarfon, Gwynedd, LL55 2AQ
Tel: 01286 673366 Fax: 01286 672840
Web: www.arcadianhotels.co.uk
28 bedrs SB £95 DB £140 HBS £105
HBD £82.50 B £9.50 L £10.50 D £25
CC: MC Vi Am DC Swi Delt

How to get there: Follow A55 to Caernarfon.
Hotel situated three miles outside Caernarfon
on A4086.

27 Pengwern

◆◆◆◆ 🐾 🦌

Saron, Llanwnda, Caernarfon,
Gwynedd, LL54 5UH
Tel: 01286 831500 Fax: 01286 830741
Email: pengwern@talk21.com
Closed December and January
3 bedrs SB £35 DB £48 HBS £50 HBD £39
CC: MC Vi Am DC Swi Delt JCB

How to get there: From Caernarfon, south on
A487 Porthmadog; over a bridge, turn right for
Saron; two miles, through Saron and over
crossroads; first farm drive on right.

Cardiff

28 The St. David's Hotel & Spa

Blue Ribbon Winner

★★★★★ 🐾🐾

Havannah Street,
Cardiff Bay, CF10 5SD
Tel: 029 2045 4045 Fax: 029 2048 7056
Email: reservations@thestdavidshotel.com
Web: www.rfhotels.com
132 bedrs SB £163.50 DB £207
HBS £193 HBD £118.50
B £10.50 L £14.50 D £25
CC: MC Vi Am DC Swi Delt

How to get there: M4 Junction 33, A4232 for
nine miles. Follow signs to Techniquest. At
roundabout, take first left and immediate right
into Havannah Street.
See advert on facing page

29 Angel

★★★★

Castle Street, Cardiff, CF10 1SZ
Tel: 029 20649200 Fax: 029 20225980
Email: angel@paramount-hotels.co.uk
Web: www.paramount-hotels.co.uk
102 bedrs SB £121 DB £151 HBS £141
HBD £95 B £8.95 L £12 D £19.50
CC: MC Vi Am DC Swi Delt

How to get there: Exit J29 or J32 M4. Situated
in Cardiff city centre, opposite Cardiff Castle.

30 Cardiff Marriott Hotel

★★★★

Mill Lane, Cardiff, CF10 1EZ
Tel: 029 20 399944 Fax: 029 20 395578
Web: www.marriotthotels.co.uk
182 bedrs SB £155 DB £175
HBS £175 HBD £97.50
CC: MC Vi Am DC Swi Delt

How to get there: From M4 J29 or J32 to city
centre. At castle turn into the High Street/St.
Mary Street. Mill Lane is at the top on the left.

31 Copthorne Hotel Cardiff Caerdydd

★★★★ ⓡ

Copthorne Way, Culverhouse Cross,
Cardiff, CF5 6DH
Tel: 029 2059 9100 Fax: 029 2059 9080
Email: sales.cardiff@mill-cop.com
Web: www.millennium-hotels.com

In a picturesque setting just four miles from the
city centre, this luxurious modern lakeside hotel
offers you a warm welcome to Wales.
135 bedrs SB £150 DB £160 HBS £170
HBD £95 B £13.95 L £14.50 D £21.95
CC: MC Vi Am DC Swi

How to get there: J33 M4 take A4232 for three
miles. Take first exit signposted for A48. Fourth
exit off roundabout. Hotel on the left.

32 Hanover International Cardiff

★★★★

Schooner Way, Atlantic Wharf, Cardiff, CF10 4RT
Tel: 029 2047 5000 Fax: 029 2048 1491

HANOVER INTERNATIONAL
HOTELS & CLUBS

Imaginative design with a maritime theme
throughout, this hotel provides quality
accommodation and an exceptional leisure club.
Close to the scenic Brecon Beacons.
156 bedrs SB £95 DB £110
B £11 L £12 D £18
CC: MC Vi Am DC

How to get there: M4 J29, take M48, then
A48(M). Follow signs to Cardiff Bay; or, M4 J33,
A4232 to Cardiff Bay.

33 Jurys Cardiff Hotel

★★★★

Mary Ann Street, Cardiff, CF10 2JH
Tel: +353(0)1 6070000 Fax: +353(0)1 6316999
Email: bookings@jurysdoyle.com
Web: www.jurysdoyle.com
Children minimum age: 12
146 bedrs SB £150.50 DB £161 B £10.50
L £9.95 D £16.95
CC: MC Vi Am DC Swi Delt

How to get there: Located 14 miles from Cardiff
Int'l Airport. Central Station only five minutes
walk. Hotel is adjacent to Cardiff International
Arena.

34 Manor Parc Country Hotel & Restaurant

★★★ ⓡⓡ

Thornhill Road, Thornhill, Cardiff, CF14 9UA
Tel: 029 2069 3723 Fax: 029 2061 4624
12 bedrs SB £65 DB £95 B £9.50 L £18
CC: MC Vi Am Swi

How to get there: Situated on A469 on the
outskirts of the city of Cardiff, going towards
Caerphilly. Manor Parc on the left.

35 Quality Hotel & Suites, Cardiff

★★★

Junction 32/M4 Merthyr Road, Cardiff, CF15 7LD
Tel: 029 2052 9988 Fax: 029 2052 9977
Email: admin@gb629@u-net.com
Web: www.choicehotels.com
95 bedrs SB £98.25 DB £108.95 HBS £113.45
HBD £61.73 B £9.95 L £9.95 D £14.50
CC: MC Vi Am DC Swi Delt

How to get there: Take Junction 32 off the M4.
Follow roundabout through and take the A4054
exit for Tongwynlais. Hotel is located on right.

36 St. Mellons

★★★
Castleton, Cardiff, CF3 2XR
Tel: 01633 680355 Fax: 01633 680399
Email: stmellons@bestwestern.co.uk
Web: www.stmellonshotel.com
41 bedrs SB £100 DB £110
B £10 L £18 D £18
CC: MC Vi Am Swi Delt

How to get there: Leave M4 at Junction 28.
Follow signs to A48 Cardiff. After Castleton
village, hotel is signposted on left-hand side.

37 Sandringham Hotel

★★
21 St. Mary Street, Cardiff, CF10 1PL
Tel: 029 2023 2161 Fax: 029 2038 3998
Email: mm@sandringham-hotel.com
Web: www.sandringham-hotel.com
28 bedrs SB £48 DB £58 HBS £56 HBD £37
B £6 L £3.50 D £6
CC: MC Vi Am DC Swi Delt

38 Campanile

Travel Accommodation
Caxton Place, Pentwyn, Cardiff, CF23 8HA
Tel: 029 2054 9044 Fax: 029 2054 9900

Typical Campanile bistro

A comfortable hotel with 47 ensuite rooms,
colour TV and satellite channels, telephone and
welcome tray. With a friendly restaurant, bar and
free parking for our guests.
47 bedrs SB £41.95 DB £46.90 HBS £52
HBD £34 B £4.95 L £3.95 D £6.25
CC: MC Vi Am DC Swi Delt

How to get there: Exit J30 M4. Follow signs for
city centre.

39 Travelodge Cardiff (Central)

Travel Accommodation
Imperial Gate, St. Marys Street,
Cardiff, CF10 1FA
Tel: 08700 850 950
Web: www.travelodge.co.uk
100 bedrs B £4.25
CC: MC Vi Am DC Swi Delt

40 Travelodge Cardiff (East)

Travel Accommodation
A48, Circle Way East, Llanderyrn,
Cardiff, CF3 7ND
Tel: 08700 850 950
Web: www.travelodge.co.uk
32 bedrs B £4.25
CC: MC Vi Am DC Swi Delt

41 Marlborough Guest House

♦♦♦♦
98 Newport Road, Cardiff, CF2 1DG
Tel: 029 2049 2385

42 Albany Guest House

♦♦♦
191–193 Albany Road, Roath,
Cardiff, CF2 3NU
Tel: 029 2049 4121
Closed Christmas
11 bedrs
CC: None accepted

How to get there: Leave M4 at Junction 29, or
M48 at Cardiff East. Get in lane for city centre.
Turn right at junction with traffic lights, Roath
Court is 500 yards on right.

43 Clare Court Hotel

♦♦♦
46–48 Clare Street, Cardiff, CF11 6RS
Tel: 029 2034 4839
Email: clarecourthotelcardiff@hotmail.com
Web: www.hotelscardiff.net
8 bedrs SB £28.54 DB £40.54
CC: MC Vi Swi Delt

How to get there: Close to city centre, and five
minutes' walk from Cardiff Central rail station,
within reach of M4 motorway.

Wales

Cardigan, Ceredigion

44 Castell Malgwyn

★★

Llechryd, Cardigan, Ceredigion, SA43 2QA
Tel: 01239 682382 Fax: 01239 682644
Email: reception@malgwyn.co.uk
Web: www.castellmalgwyn.co.uk
20 bedrs SB £40 DB £80 HBS £54 HBD £54
B £9 L £14 D £ 20 CC: MC Vi Am DC Swi Delt
How to get there: In Llechryd village, drive over
River Teifi Bridge to hotel entrance.

45 Penbontbren

★★★

Glynarthen, Cardigan, Ceredigion, SA44 6PE
Tel: 01239 810248 Fax: 01239 811129
Closed 22–28 December
10 bedrs
CC: MC Vi Am DC Swi Delt
How to get there: Travelling south from
Aberystwyth on A487, take first left after
Sarnau. Travelling north on A487 from Cardigan
take second right about one mile after Tan-y-
groes (signposted Penbontbren).

The Pembrokeshire Retreat

The Pembrokeshire Retreat is set in a
historic family house of real warmth and
character, located in the Telfi Valley, and
situated in 55 acres of grounds with a tennis
court and walled garden. Relaxed, friendly
atmosphere.

Rhos-y-Gilwen Mansion, Rhos Hill,
Cardigan SA43 2TW
Tel: 01239 841387   Fax: 01239 841387
enquiries@retreat.co.uk
www.retreat.co.uk

46 The Pembrokeshire Retreat

♦ ♦ ♦ ♦

Rhos-y-Gilwen Mansion, Rhos-y-Gilwen Hill,
Cardigan, Ceredigion, SA43 2TW
Tel: 01239 841387 Fax: 01239 841387
Email: enquiries@retreat.co.uk
Web: www.retreat.co.uk
3 bedrs SB £40 DB £70 HBS £55 HBD £42.50
L £5 D £15
CC: MC Vi Am Swi Delt
See advert below left

47 Brynhyfryd Guest House

♦ ♦ ♦

Gwbert Road, Cardigan, Ceredigion, SA43 1AE
Tel: 01239 612861 Fax: 01239 612861
Email: g.arcus@btinternet.com
Children minimum age: 4
7 bedrs SB £18 DB £40 HBS £27 HBD £58
CC: None accepted
How to get there: From town centre drive
through main street. Spar shop on right — turn
left after it. The guest house is opposite tennis
courts.

Carmarthen, Carmarthenshire

48 Travelodge Carmarthen

Travel Accommodation
A40/A4, St. Clears, Carmarthen,
Carmarthenshire, SA32 4JN
Tel: 08700 850 950
Web: www.travelodge.co.uk
32 bedrs B £4.25
CC: MC Vi Am DC Swi Delt

49 Capel Dewi Uchaf Country House

♦ ♦ ♦ ♦

Capel Dewi, Carmarthen,
Carmarthenshire, SA32 8AY
Tel: 01267 290799 Fax: 01267 290003
Email: uchaffarm@aol.com
Web: www.walescottageholidays.uk.com
3 bedrs SB £40 DB £56 D £25
CC: MC Vi Swi Delt JCB
How to get there: Leave M4 at Junction 4. Take
A48 until exit for National Botanic Garden. Take
B4310 to junction with B4300. Turn left. Capel
Dewi is ³/₄ of a mile on right.

Chepstow, Monmouthshire

50 Marriott St. Pierre Hotel & Country Club

★★★★★ ⓡ ⓡ
St. Pierre Park, Chepstow,
Monmouthshire, NP16 6YA
Tel: 01291 625261 Fax: 01291 629975
Email: salesadmin.stpierre@whitbread.com
148 bedrs SB £80 DB £110
HBS £105 HBD £80 B £12.95 D £25
CC: MC Vi Am DC Swi Delt JCB

How to get there: Exit J2 M48, take A466 to
Chepstow. At roundabout, take first exit A48;
hotel is about two miles on the left.

51 Beaufort Hotel Chepstow

★★
Beaufort Square, Chepstow,
Monmouthshire, NP16 5EP
Tel: 01291 622497 Fax: 01291 627389
Email: info@beauforthotel.co.uk
Web: www.beauforthotelchepstow.com
22 bedrs SB £49.95 DB £66.90 B £4 L £6 D £10
CC: MC Vi Am DC Swi Delt

How to get there: From M48, signs to Chepstow.
Stay on A48. Take second left at lights by
church. Hotel car park on Nelson Street.

Chirk, Wrexham

52 Moreton Park Lodge

★★★
Moreton Park, Gledrid, Chirk, LL14 5DG
Tel: 01691 776666 Fax: 01691 776655
Email: reservations@moretonpark.com
Web: www.moretonpark.com
46 bedrs SB £44.95 DB £89.90
B £3.75 L £4.75 D £8
CC: MC Vi Am Swi Delt JCB

How to get there: At intersection of A5 and
B5070, three miles north of Oswestry, eight
miles south of Wrexham.
See advert right

Plan your route

Visit www.rac.co.uk for RAC's
interactive route planner, including
up to the minute traffic reports.

Colwyn Bay, Conwy

53 Hopeside Hotel

★★★
63 Princes Drive, Colwyn Bay, Conwy, LL29 8PW
Tel: 01492 533244 Fax: 01492 532850
Email: hopesidejd@aol.com
14 bedrs SB £49 DB £59
B £4.50 L £2.95 D £9.95
CC: MC Vi Swi Delt JCB

How to get there: From direction of Chester on
A55 — take B5115, turn off for Rhos-on-Sea —
turn left; hotel 100 yards on right.

54 Norfolk House Hotel

★★★
Princes Drive, Colwyn Bay, Conwy, LL29 9PF
Tel: 01492 531757 Fax: 01492 533781

Are you covered?

For competitively priced
travel insurance, buy online at
www.rac.co.uk or call RAC Travel
Sales on 0800 55 00 55.

Wales

55 Quality Hotel Colwyn Bay

★★

Penmaenhead, Old Colwyn, Colwyn Bay,
Conwy, LL29 9LD
Tel: 01492 516555 Fax: 01492 515565
Email: colwynbayhotel@cwcom.net

On a cliff top overlooking the majestic sweep of
the bay, this splendid hotel offers a very high
standard of comfort and service. The Horizon
Restaurant serves excellent cuisine
complemented by panoramic views. Conference
facilities up to 200.
43 bedrs
CC: MC Vi Am DC Swi Delt
How to get there: Hotel stands beside the A547
on cliffs above A55. Leave A55 at Llandulas
exit, follow A547 towards Old Colwyn.

56 Plas Rhos Hotel

◆ ◆ ◆ ◆ ◆ ⚹

53 Cayley Promenade, Rhos-on-Sea,
Colwyn Bay, Conwy, LL28 4EP
Tel: 01492 543698
9 bedrs SB £32 DB £53 HBS £48 HBD £42
CC: MC Vi Swi

57 Northwood Hotel

◆ ◆ ◆ ⚹

47 Rhos Road, Rhos-on-Sea, Colwyn Bay,
Conwy, LL28 4RS
Tel: 01492 549931
Email: mail@northwoodhotel.co.uk
Web: www.northwoodhotel.co.uk
12 bedrs SB £23.50 DB £47
HBS £32 HBD £64 B £6 L £5 D £10
CC: MC Vi Am Swi Delt
How to get there: Opposite Tourist Information
Centre, 150 yards up Rhos Road.

58 Rosehill Manor

◆ ◆ ◆ ⚹ ❧

Queens Avenue, Colwyn Bay, Conwy, LL29 7BE
Tel: 01492 532993
Email: lawrence_ford@hotmail.com
Web: www.rosehillmanor.co.uk
Children minimum age: 12
5 bedrs SB £26 DB £59
CC: None accepted
How to get there: Situated in the west end of
Colwyn Bay immediately to the rear of Rydal
School.

Conwy

59 Old Rectory Country House
Gold Ribbon Winner

★★ ✿ ✿ ✿ ✿

Llanwrst Road, Llansanffraid Glan Conwy,
Conwy, LL28 5LF
Tel: 01492 580611 Fax: 01492 584555
Email: info@oldrectorycountryhouse.co.uk
Web: www.oldrectorycountryhouse.co.uk
Children minimum age: 5

Idyllically situated, beautiful terraced gardens
overlook Conwy Castle, estuary and
Snowdonia beyond. Charming tastefully
decorated, antiques and paintings abound.
Appealing innovative 'Masterchef' cuisine.
Award-winning wine cellar. Relaxing friendly
atmosphere.
6 bedrs SB £99 DB £109 HBS £139
HBD £84 B £9 D £34.90
CC: MC Vi Swi Delt JCB
How to get there: Situated on A470, ½ mile
south of its junction with A55. Gates on left-
hand side just before 30mph sign.

60 Tir-y-Coed Country House Hotel

★★
Rowen, Conwy, LL32 8TP
Tel: 01492 650219 Fax: 01492 650219
Email: tirycoed@btinternet.com
Web: www.tirycoedhotel.co.uk
Closed November to February

Surrounded by magnificent scenery in the peaceful rural setting of a delightful Snowdonia National Park village. Mountains, coast, castles, stately homes and gardens nearby. Well-appointed ensuite bedrooms. Spectacular views.
8 bedrs SB £29 DB £54 HBS £43.50
HBD £41.50 D £14.50 CC: Am
🐾🖥🅿 ⚓ ℵ ℂ ❤ ⛄
How to get there: From B5106, take signposted turning to Rowen (unclassified road). Hotel is on fringe of village, about 60 yards north of post office.

61 Sychnant Pass House
Little Gem

◆◆◆◆◆ ⊗ ✂ ⛱
Sychnant Pass Road, Conwy, LL32 8BJ
Tel: 01492 596868 Fax: 01492 596868
Email: bresykes@sychnant-pass-house.co.uk
Web: www.sychnant-pass-house.co.uk

Our country home is set in 2¹/₂ acres of natural garden, surrounded by National Park land. Large sitting rooms with log fires and comfy sofas. See you soon!
10 bedrs SB £45 DB £65 HBS £60 HBD £47.50
D £16.95 CC: MC Vi Swi Delt
🔄🖥🅿 ⚓ 🐾⊗ ❤ ⛄
How to get there: Go around Conwy system past Visitors' Centre. Take 2nd turn on left into Upper Gate Street: proceed up hill for two miles.

62 Bryn Guest House

◆◆◆ ✂
Sychnant Pass Road, Conwy, Conwy, LL32 8NS
Tel: 01492 592449
Email: b+b@bryn.org.uk
Web: www.bryn.org.uk
5 bedrs SB £23 DB £40
CC: None accepted
🐾⊗🖥🅿 ⚓
How to get there: Against town wall at junction of Sychnant Pass Road, St. Agnes Road and Mount Pleasant, south-west corner of town.

Cowbridge, Vale of Glamorgan

63 Bear Hotel

★★★
High Street, Cowbridge,
Vale of Glamorgan, CF7 2AF
Tel: 01446 774814 Fax: 01446 775425

Criccieth, Gwynedd

64 Bron Eifion Country House Hotel

★★★
Criccieth, Gwynedd, LL52 0SA
Tel: 01766 522385 Fax: 01766 522003
Email: broneifion@criccieth.co.uk
Web: www.broneifion.co.uk

A magnificent baronial mansion set in five acres of glorious gardens and woodlands. Close to the rugged mountains of Snowdonia. Friendly service, fresh cuisine and a well-stocked wine cellar.
19 bedrs SB £75 DB £116 HBS £89 HBD £75
B £12.95 L £12.50 D £23
CC: MC Vi Am Swi
🖥🐾⊗🖥 ☎ ⛱ ⛄
How to get there: On A487 from Porthmadog go through Criccieth. We are ¹/₂ mile outside Criccieth on right-hand side.

Wales

65 Lion Hotel

★★

Y Maes, Criccieth, Gwynedd, LL52 0AA
Tel: 01766 522460 Fax: 01766 523075
Email: info@lionhotelcriccieth.co.uk
Web: www.lionhotelcriccieth.co.uk
46 bedrs SB £36.50 DB £62.50 HBS £53.50
HBD £95.50 B £9.50 L £9.15 D £16.50
CC: MC Vi Am DC Swi Delt JCB

How to get there: The Lion is situated just off
the A497 or B4411 in the centre of Criccieth on
Upper Village Green.

66 Gly-y-Coed Hotel

♦♦♦♦

Portmadoc Road, Criccieth, Gwynedd, LL52 0HL
Tel: 01766 522870 Fax: 01766 523341
Closed Christmas to New Year
10 bedrs CC: MC Vi Am

How to get there: On main A497 Portmadoc to
Pwhelli Road. On right-hand side facing sea,
nearest hotel to shops/village.

67 Min-y-Gaer Hotel

♦♦♦♦

Porthmadog Road, Criccieth,
Gwynedd, LL52 0HP
Tel: 01766 522151 Fax: 01766 523540
Email: info@minygaerhotel.co.uk
Web: www.minygaerhotel.co.uk
Closed November to February

A pleasant licensed hotel with delightful views
of Cardigan Bay coastline. Comfortable, non-
smoking ensuite bedrooms with colour TV and
beverage facilities. An ideal base for touring
Snowdonia. Car parking.
10 bedrs SB £22 DB £44
CC: MC Vi Am Delt

How to get there: Close to Criccieth centre on
A497 Criccieth-Porthmadog road. 300 yards
east of junction with B4411, 300 yards east of
bus stop, 800 yards east of railway station.

Cwmbran, Torfaen

68 Parkway Hotel

★★★★

Cwmbran Drive, Cwmbran, Torfaen, NP44 3UW
Tel: 01633 871199 Fax: 01633 869160
Closed 26–30 December
70 bedrs SB £102.95 DB £123.90 HBS £119.90
HBD £78.90 B £8.95 L £9.50 D £16.95
CC: MC Vi Am DC Swi Delt

How to get there: Leave M4 at Junction 25A
(west). Take A4042. Take first exit at roundabout
onto A4051. Take third exit at next roundabout,
and then next right.

Deganwy, Conwy

69 Deganwy Castle Hotel

★★

Station Road, Deganwy, Conwy, LL31 9DA
Tel: 01492 583555 Fax: 01492 583555
Email: deganwycastlehtl@yahoo.com
Web: www.geocities.com/deganwycastle-htl
31 bedrs SB £35 DB £70 HBS £48 HBD £96
B £8 L £9.50 D £10
CC: MC Vi Am DC Swi Delt

How to get there: Find Deganwy via A55
expressway. A546 to Deganwy leads off second
exit of roundabout after Deganwy Conwy turn-off.

Denbigh, Denbighshire

70 Cayo Guest House

♦♦♦

74 Vale Street, Denbigh, Denbighshire, LL16 3BW
Tel: 01745 812686
6 bedrs SB £19 DB £38
CC: MC Vi Am DC Swi Delt JCB

How to get there: On A525, follow signs to
Denbigh. At the traffic lights turn up the hill into
town. Look for supermarket on right. Hotel is a
little way up on left.

Devil's Bridge, Ceredigion

Hafod Arms Hotel

★★

Devil's Bridge, Aberystwyth,
Ceredigion, SY23 3JL
Tel: 01970 890232 Fax: 01970 890394
Email: enquiries@hafodarms.co.uk
Web: www.hafodarms.co.uk
Children minimum age: 10
Closed 15 December to 15 January
15 bedrs SB £35 DB £55
HBS £50 HBD £42.50 D £15
CC: MC Vi Swi

How to get there: From Aberystwyth take A4120
for 11 miles. From Llangurig travel along A44.
Turn off left at Ponterwyd onto the A4120. Hotel
five miles.

Dolgellau, Gwynedd

Fronoleu Farm Hotel

★★

Tabor, Dolgellau, Gwynedd, LL40 2PS
Tel: 01341 422361 Fax: 01341 422023
11 bedrs
CC: MC Vi Swi

How to get there: From Dolgellau town centre,
follow road past hospital. Proceed up hill.
Follow Restaurant sign.

George III Hotel

★★

Penmaenpool, Dolgellau, Gwynedd, LL40 1YD
Tel: 01341 422525 Fax: 01341 423565
Email: reception@george-3rd.co.uk
Web: www.george-3rd.co.uk

One of the most spectacularly located
waterfront hotels in Wales, standing on the bank

of the Mawddach estuary with 2900-foot Cader
Idris as a backdrop. Ideally located for touring
North Wales.
11 bedrs SB £58 DB £98 B £7.50 L £12.95 D £25
CC: MC Vi Swi Delt

How to get there: Turn left off A470 signposted
Tywyn, after approximately two miles turn right
for toll bridge then first left for hotel.

Royal Ship Hotel

★

Queen's Square, Dolgellau,
Gwynedd, LL40 1AR
Tel: 01341 422209 Fax: 01341 421027
Email: brewery@frederic-robinson.co.uk
Web: www.frederic-robinson.co.uk
24 bedrs SB £38 DB £65 B £4.50 L £5.95
D £9.95
CC: MC Vi Swi

How to get there: Situated in town centre.

Clifton House Hotel

◆◆◆

Smithfield Square, Dolgellau,
Gwynedd, LL40 1ES
Tel: 01341 422554 Fax: 01341 423580
Email: pauline@clifton-hotel.freeserve.co.uk
Web: www.clifton-hotel.freeserve.co.uk
Closed November
6 bedrs SB £38 DB £48
HBS £54 HBD £40 D £15
CC: MC Vi Swi Delt

How to get there: Follow one-way system right
around to come up street facing hotel.

Fishguard, Pembrokeshire

Fishguard Bay Hotel

★★★

Quay Road, Goodwick, Fishguard,
Pembrokeshire, SA64 0BT
Tel: 01348 873571 Fax: 01348 873030
Email: mhar177485@aol.com
59 bedrs
CC: MC Vi Am DC Swi Delt

How to get there: On A40 from Haverfordwest
to Fishguard follow signs for Ferry Port.
Proceed straight over small roundabout, over
railway bridge and hotel is on right.

Wales

77 Abergwaun Hotel

★★

Market Square, Fishguard,
Pembrokeshire, SA65 9HA
Tel: 01348 872077 Fax: 01348 875412
Web: www.abergwaun.com
10 bedrs SB £39.50 DB £58
B £4.50 L £6 D £6
CC: MC Vi Am DC Swi Delt

How to get there: The hotel is situated in the
centre of Fishguard on the A40/A487.

Halkyn, Flintshire

78 Travelodge Halkyn

Travel Accommodation
A55, Halkyn, Flintshire, CH8 8RF
Tel: 08700 850 950
Web: www.travelodge.co.uk
31 bedrs B £4.25
CC: MC Vi Am DC Swi Delt

Harlech, Gwynedd

79 Castle Cottage

◆ ◆ ◆ ◆ ☻ ☻ ☙

Harlech, Gwynedd, LL46 2YL
Tel: 01766 780479 Fax: 01766 780479
Closed February
6 bedrs SB £29 DB £62 D £24
CC: MC Vi Swi Delt

How to get there: Just off Harlech High Street,
behind the Castle.

Haverfordwest, Pembrokeshire

80 Hotel Mariners

★★

Mariner's Square, Haverfordwest,
Pembrokeshire, SA61 2DU
Tel: 01437 763353 Fax: 01437 764258
28 bedrs SB £53.50 DB £73.50 D £19
CC: MC Vi Am DC Swi Delt

How to get there: Follow signs to town centre,
continue up High Steet. Take first turning on
right, Dark Street. This leads to Mariner's Square.

81 Wolf's Castle Country Hotel

★★★ ☻ ☻

Wolf's Castle, Haverfordwest,
Pembrokeshire, SA62 5LZ
Tel: 01437 741688 Fax: 01437 741383
Email: enquiries@wolfscastle.com
Web: www.wolfscastle.com
Closed Christmas

In village of Wolf's Castle, equidistant from
Fishguard and Haverfordwest. Ideal location for
exploring Pembrokeshire National Park and
beaches. Conference facilities and 20 ensuite
bedrooms.
20 bedrs SB £43 DB £77
HBS £65 HBD £106 B £7 L £10 D £16
CC: MC Vi Am Swi Delt

How to get there: Situated in village of Wolf's
Castle, six miles north of Haverfordwest on A40.

82 Highland Grange Farm

◆ ◆ ◆

Robeston Wathen, Narberth,
Pembrokeshire, SA67 8EP
Tel: 01834 860952 Fax: 01834 860952
Email: info@highlandgrange.co.uk
Web: www.highlandgrange.co.uk
3 bedrs
CC: None accepted

How to get there: Take A40 22 miles west of
Carmarthen direct to Robeston. Petrol station
on left, property last on right before Bush Inn.
Seven miles east of Haverfordwest in small
village.
See advert on facing page

Holyhead, Anglesey

83 Bull Hotel

★★
London Road, Valley, Holyhead,
Isle of Anglesey, LL65 3DP
Tel: 01407 740351 Fax: 01407 742328
Web: www.valley-hotel-anglesey.co.uk

Superior ensuite bedrooms with TVs, telephone, tea/coffee makers etc. Our Tudor style lounges serve food and drinks all day. Restaurant open every evening and Sunday lunchtime. Excellent beer garden.
14 bedrs SB £37.50 DB £49.50 B £4.95 D £7.95
CC: MC Vi Am Swi Delt
How to get there: Only four miles from ferries on A5 — just past traffic lights at valley. Take exit marked 'Y Fali' (Valley) from A55

84 Valley Hotel

◆◆◆
London Road, Valley, Holyhead,
Isle of Anglesey, LL65 3DU
Tel: 01407 740203 Fax: 01407 740686
Email: valleyhotel@tinyworld.co.uk
Web: www.valley-hotel-anglesey.co.uk

Ensuite bedrooms with TVs, telephones, tea/coffee makers, hairdryers etc. Our light airy bar lounges serve food and drink all day. Excellent party rooms, gardens with play equipment and snooker room.
20 bedrs SB £37.50 DB £49.50 B £4.95 D £7.50
CC: MC Vi Am Swi Delt
How to get there: Only four miles from ferries on A5. At traffic lights at Valley take exit marked 'Y Fali' (Valley) from A55.

Knighton, Powys

85 Knighton Hotel

★★★
Broad Street, Knighton, Powys, LD7 1BL
Tel: 01547 520530 Fax: 01547 520529
Email: knightonhotel@freeuk.com
Children minimum age: 12
15 bedrs SB £45 DB £68 HBS £61.50
HBD £101 B £7 L £12.50 D £16.50
CC: MC Vi Am Swi JCB
How to get there: Take A4113 off A49 at Ludlow on the A388 or Shrewsbury-Llandrindod Wells road.

Wales

Lampeter, Ceredigion

86 Falcondale Country House Hotel

★★★

Falcondale Drive, Lampeter,
Ceredigion, SA43 7RX
Tel: 01570 422910 Fax: 01570 423559
Web: www.falcondalehotel.com
Closed late January
21 bedrs SB £60 DB £90 HBS £79 HBD £64
B £5.95 L £5 D £21
CC: MC Vi Am Swi Delt

How to get there: The hotel is 500 yards west of
Lampeter centre on the A475 or one mile northwest of Lampeter on the A482.

Llanbedr, Gwynedd

87 Ty Mawr Hotel

★★

Llanbedr, Gwynedd, LL45 2NH
Tel: 01341 241440 Fax: 01341 241440
10 bedrs SB £37 DB £60 HBS £47 HBD £35
B £5 L £5 D £10
CC: MC Vi Swi Delt

How to get there: Llanbedr is situated on A496
between Barmouth and Harlech. Approaching
from Barmouth, turn right after bridge. Ty-Mawr
is 100 yards up on left.

88 Victoria Inn

◆◆◆◆

Llanbedr, Gwynedd, LL45 2LD
Tel: 01341 241213 Fax: 01341 241644
Email: brewery@frederic-robinson.co.uk
Web: www.frederic-robinson.com
5 bedrs SB £35 DB £62 B £4.50 L £4.50 D £6
CC: MC Vi Swi Delt

How to get there: The Victoria stands in the
centre of village of Llandbedr on the A496 coast
road.

Llandrindod Wells, Powys

89 Severn Arms Hotel

★★

Penybont, Llandrindod Wells,
Powys, LD1 5UA
Tel: 01597 851224 Fax: 01597 851693
10 bedrs
CC: MC Vi Swi

How to get there: Located on the junction of the
A488 and A44 in the village of Penybont, east of
Llandrindod Wells.

90 Guidfa House

◆◆◆◆

Cross Gates, Llandrindod Wells,
Powys, LD1 6RF
Tel: 01597 851241 Fax: 01597 851875
Email: guidfa@globalnet.co.uk
Web: www.guidfa-house.co.uk
Children minimum age: 10

Stylish Georgian house with an enviable
reputation for its comfort, good food and
service. Set in the very heart of Wales, offering
an excellent base for touring both Wales and
the Borders.
6 bedrs SB £31.50 DB £53 HBS £49 HBD £44
D £17.50
CC: MC Vi Delt

How to get there: Located in the centre of the
village of Crossgates, where A44 Kington to
Rhayader road crosses A483 Builth Wells to
Newtown road.

91 Hotel Commodore

Spa Road, Llandrindod Wells,
Powys, LD1 5ER
Tel: 01597 822288 Fax: 01597 825737

Llandudno, Conwy

92 Bodysgallen Hall

Gold Ribbon Winner

★★★★ ℞ ℞ ℞ ℞
Llandudno, Conwy, LL30 1RS
Tel: 01492 584466 Fax: 01492 582519
Email: info@bodysgallen.com
Web: www.bodygsgallen.com
Children minimum age: 8
35 bedrs SB £128.50 DB £189 HBS £115
HBD £115 B £11.50 L £16.50 D £34.90
CC: MC Vi Swi Delt
♿🗝🏇⊗🖵☎🅿🐾🦮🐕🎢👪👬🧖🍴🔍
🔥
How to get there: Take A55 to its intersection
with A470. Follow A470 towards Llandudno.
The hotel is two miles on the right.

93 Dunoon Hotel

★★★
Gloddaeth Street, Llandudno, Conwy, LL30 2DW
Tel: 01492 860787 Fax: 01492 860031
Email: reservations@dunoonhotel.co.uk
Web: www.dunoonhotel.co.uk
51 bedrs SB £41 DB £74 HBS £49 HBD £44
B £7.50 L £9 D £14.50
CC: MC Vi Am Swi
♿🛗🕭🖵☎🅿🐾🎢👬👪
How to get there: 200 yards on sea front from
Prince Edward Square on wide street with
centre reservation parking.

94 Imperial Hotel

★★★★ ℞
Vaughan Street, Llandudno, Conwy, LL30 1AP
Tel: 01492 877466 Fax: 01492 878043
Email: imphotel@btinternet.com
Web: www.theimperial.co.uk
CC: None accepted

95 Ambassador Hotel

★★
Grand Promenade, Llandudno, Conwy, LL30 2NR
Tel: 01492 876886 Fax: 01492 876347
57 bedrs SB £32 DB £60 HBS £47 HBD £45
B £8.25 L £6 D £14
CC: MC Vi Am Swi
♿🛗🏇🕭🖵🅿🐾🎢👪👬
How to get there: From A55 road to A470. Turn
to Promenade. Turn left at Promenade junction.
Hotel approx 300 yards from pier.

96 Branksome Hotel

★★
62/64 Lloyd Street, Llandudno, Conwy, LL30 2YP
Tel: 01492 875989 Fax: 01492 875989

97 Epperstone Hotel

★★
15 Abbey Road, Llandudno,
Conwy, LL30 2EE
Tel: 01492 878746 Fax: 01492 871223

Small, select hotel, with car park, in award-
winning gardens. Spacious, comfortable rooms
portraying Edwardian elegance. Bedrooms
ensuite with excellent accessories. Convenient,
level walking. All amenities.
8 bedrs SB £28 DB £56 HBS £41 HBD £40
B £8.50 L £8.50 D £16
CC: MC Vi Am Swi Delt
♿🗝🏇⊗🕭🖵☎🅿🐾🎢🦮🐕🍴👬
How to get there: From A55 follow sign for A470
to Llandudno (Mostyn Street) turn left at
roundabout fourth right into York Road. Hotel on
apex of York Road and Abbey Road.

98 Esplanade Hotel

★★
Central Promenade, Llandudno,
Conwy, LL30 2LL
Tel: 01492 860300 Fax: 01492 860418
Email: info@esplanadehotel.co.uk
Web: www.esplanadehotel.co.uk
59 bedrs SB £15 DB £30
HBS £25 HBD £50
B £6.50 L £3.50 D £12.50
CC: MC Vi Am DC Swi Delt JCB
🛗🏇🕭🖵☎🅿🐾🎢👪👬
How to get there: From A55 follow A470 to
Llandudno. Follow brown tourist signs for
beach: turn towards Great Orme and pier.

Wales

99 Headlands Hotel

★★

Hill Terrace, Llandudno,
Conwy, LL30 2LS
Tel: 01492 877485
Children minimum age: 5
Closed January to February
17 bedrs
CC: None accepted

100 Marlborough Hotel

★★

South Parade, Llandudno, Conwy, LL30 2LN
Tel: 01492 875846 Fax: 01492 876529
Email: nick@marlborough911.freeserve.co.uk
Web: www.northwales.uk.com
40 bedrs
CC: MC Vi Swi Delt

How to get there: On entering Llandudno off the
A55, follow signposts to Promenade. Drive
towards pier and hotel is on left-hand side at
the pier T-junction.

101 Royal Hotel

★★

Church Walks, Llandudno, Conwy, LL30 2HW
Tel: 01492 876476 Fax: 01492 870210

102 Sandringham Hotel

★★

West Parade, West Shore, Llandudno,
Conwy, LL30 2BD
Tel: 01492 876513 Fax: 01492 872753
Email: sandringham@which.net
Web: www.sandringhamhotel-llandudno.co.uk
18 bedrs SB £34 DB £60 HBS £45 HBD £40
B £5 L £4.50 D £14
CC: MC Vi Swi Delt JCB

How to get there: Follow A470 to Llandudno
town centre. Turn left at roundabout by
Woolworths. Proceed approx 1/2 mile; hotel on
left-hand corner.

103 Somerset Hotel

★★

Central Promenade, Llandudno, Conwy, LL30 2LF
Tel: 01492 876540 Fax: 01492 863700
Email: favroy@somerset.freeserve.co.uk
Closed January to February
37 bedrs SB £39 DB £78 HBS £49 HBD £49
B £8.50 L £9.95 D £17.50
CC: MC Vi Swi

104 St. Tudno Hotel & Restaurant
Gold Ribbon Winner

★★ ℞ ℞ ℞

Promenade, Llandudno, Conwy, LL30 2LP
Tel: 01492 874411 Fax: 01492 860407
Email: sttudnohotel@btinternet.com
Web: www.st-tudno.co.uk

Charming seafront hotel with outstanding
reputation for fine food and wine. Elegantly and
lovingly furnished offering the best in service
and hospitality. Host of awards for excellence.
Lift, car park, indoor health pool.
19 bedrs
CC: MC Vi Am DC Swi Delt

How to get there: Directly opposite the pier on
Llandudno's promenade.

105 Min-y-don Hotel

★

North Parade, Llandudno, Conwy, LL30 2LP
Tel: 01492 876511 Fax: 01492 878169
Closed November to February
28 bedrs CC: MC Vi Swi Delt

How to get there: From Chester follow A55 to
Conwy and exit at Llandudno junction, taking
A470. Drive through Martyn Street onto
Promenade. Hotel is on North Parade opposite
the pier entrance.

106 Warwick Hotel

56 Church Walks, Llandudno,
Conwy, LL30 2HL
Tel: 01492 876823

107 Carmel Private Hotel

17 Craig-Y-Don Parade, Promenade,
Llandudno, Conwy, LL30 1BG
Tel: 01492 877643
Children minimum age: 4
9 bedrs SB £16 DB £32 HBS £26 HBD £52
CC: None accepted

How to get there: Take A470 into Llandudno. By
the Links Hotel turn right at roundabout towards
north. At second roundabout turn right. Hotel is
on right-hand side.

108 St. Hilary Hotel

Craig-Y-Don Parade, Promenade,
Llandudno, Conwy, LL30 1BG
Tel: 01492 875551 Fax: 01492 877538
Email: info@sthilaryhotel.co.uk
Web: www.sthilaryhotel.co.uk
Closed December to January
11 bedrs
CC: MC Vi Am Swi Delt

How to get there: Situated on the Promenade,
just 500 yards from the North Wales Theatre,
towards the Little Orme.

109 Minion Hotel

21–23 Carmen Sylva, Llandudno,
Conwy, LL30 1EQ
Tel: 01492 877740
Children minimum age: 3
Closed November to March
10 bedrs
CC: None accepted

110 Rosedene Private Hotel

10 Arvon Avenue, Llandudno,
Conwy, LL30 2DY
Tel: 01492 876491

111 Karden House Hotel

16 Charlton Street, Llandudno, Conwy, LL30 2AN
Tel: 01492 879347 Fax: 01492 879347
10 bedrs SB £15 DB £30 HBS £21 HBD £21
CC: None accepted

How to get there: From Llandudno railway
station head for sea front, turn left after 300
yards onto Charlton Street. Karden House on
left.

112 Gogarth Abbey

Abbey Road, West Shore, Llandudno,
Conwy, LL30 2QY
Tel: 01492 876211 Fax: 01492 875805

Llanelli, Carmarthenshire

113 Hotel Miramar

158 Station Road, Llanelli,
Carmarthenshire, SA15 1YH
Tel: 01554 773607 Fax: 01554 772454
Email: hotelmiramar/@laol.com
Web:
www.smoothhound.co.uk/hotels/hotelmir.html
10 bedrs SB £28 DB £45 L £8.50 D £8.50
CC: MC Vi Am DC Swi Delt

How to get there: M4 Junction 48 to Llanelli.
When in Llanelli look for railway station. The
Miramar is adjacent to Llanelli railway station.

114 Travelodge Llanelli

Travel Accommodation
A48, Cross Hands, Llanelli, Carmarthenshire,
SA14 6NW
Tel: 08700 850 950
Web: www.travelodge.co.uk
32 bedrs B £4.25
CC: MC Vi Am DC Swi Delt

Wales

Llangammarch Wells, Powys

115 Lake Country House Hotel
Gold Ribbon Winner

★★★★ ® ® ®
Llangammarch Wells, Powys, LD4 4BS
Tel: 01591 620202 Fax: 01591 620457
Email: info@lakecountryhouse.co.uk
Web: www.lakecountryhouse.co.uk

This award-winning hotel is calm and comfort
epitomised; the richly furnished sitting rooms
with fine antiques, paintings and sumptuous
sofas beside log fires combine to make visitors
feel like guests in a Welsh country home.
19 bedrs
CC: MC Vi Am DC Swi Delt

How to get there: From Builth Wells head west
on the A483 for six miles to a village called
Garth. Hotel is clearly signposted from here.

Llangollen, Denbighshire

116 Bryn Howel Hotel & Restaurant

★★★ ®
Llangollen, Denbighshire, LL20 7UW
Tel: 01978 860331 Fax: 01978 860119
Web: www.brynhowel.co.uk
36 bedrs SB £80.50 DB £108 HBS £66
HBD £66 B £5 L £9 D £21
CC: MC Vi Am DC Swi Delt None accepted

How to get there: From the east, follow A539
towards Llangollen; two miles after the village of
Trevor, the hotel is signposted.

117 Hand Hotel

★★
Bridge Street, Llangollen,
Denbighshire, LL20 8PL
Tel: 01978 860303 Fax: 01978 861277
58 bedrs SB £40 DB £65
HBS £55 HBD £40
B £5.50 L £8.50 D £14.95
CC: MC Vi Am DC Swi Delt

How to get there: From south follow A5 to
Llangollen. In Llangollen take second right after
Kwik Save. From north follow A539. Left over
bridge, left at traffic lights. Second turning on
left.

118 Tyn-y-Wern Hotel

★★
Maes Mawr Road, Llangollen,
Denbighshire, LL20 7PH
Tel: 01978 860252 Fax: 01978 860252
11 bedrs SB £32 DB £48
B £5 L £3.50 D £3.50
CC: MC Vi Am DC Swi

How to get there: On main A5 approximately ¹/₂
a mile east of town centre.

119 West Arms Hotel

★★ ® ®
Llanarmon-Dyffryn-Ceiriog, Llangollen,
Denbighshire, LL20 7LD
Tel: 01691 600665 Fax: 01691 600622
Email: gowestarms@aol.com
Web: www.hotelwalesuk.com
16 bedrs SB £57.75 DB £104.50
HBS £85.10 HBD £79.60
B £8.95 L £15 D £24.90
CC: MC Vi Swi

How to get there: Follow B4500 from Chirk
through Ceiriog Valley or via Shrewsbury to
Oswestry. Follow signs for Llansilin but bear
right before village.

Llanwddyn, Powys

120 Lake Vyrnwy Hotel

★★★ 🐦🐦
Lake Vyrnwy, Llanwddyn, Powys, SY10 0LY
Tel: 01691 870692 Fax: 01691 870259
Email: res@lakevyrnwy.com
Web: www.lakevyrnwy.com

Classic Victorian sporting elegance, crackling log fires in winter, the view and sunsets of legends in summer. Great gastronomy in an exquisite place. The complete antidote to modern life.
35 bedrs SB £85 DB £115 HBS £108 HBD £75
B £11 L £12.50 D £19.50
CC: MC Vi Am DC Swi Delt

How to get there: From Shrewsbury, take the A458 to Welshpool, then turn right onto B4393 just after Ford (signposted to Lake Vyrnwy 28 miles).

Llanwrtyd Wells, Powys

121 Neuadd Arms Hotel

★
Llanwrtyd Wells, Powys, LD5 4RB
Tel: 01591 610236
20 bedrs SB £29 DB £58 HBS £39 HBD £39
B £5 L £5 D £12 CC: MC Vi Swi

Machynlleth, Powys

122 Ynyshir Hall Hotel
Gold Ribbon Winner

★★★ 🐦🐦🐦🐦
Eglwysfach, Machynlleth, Powys, SY20 8TA
Tel: 01654 781209 Fax: 01654 781366
Email: info@ynyshir-hall.co.uk
Web: www.ynyshir-hall.co.uk
Children minimum age: 9

A small luxury Georgian mansion set in idyllic surroundings betwixt sea and mountains. The perfect place to unwind with award-winning cuisine, a warm welcome and pampered service.
10 bedrs SB £110 DB £150
HBS £148 HBD £115
B £9 L £28 D £39
CC: MC Vi Am DC Swi Delt JCB

How to get there: Six miles from Machynlleth and 11 miles from Aberystwyth on the A487.

123 Wynnstay Hotel

★★★ 🐦
Heol Maengwyn, Machynlleth, Powys, SY20 8AE
Tel: 01654 702941 Fax: 01654 703884
Email: info@wynnstay-hotel.com
Web: www.wynnstay-hotel.com

Rambling coaching inn serving award-winning food, fine wines and real ales in historic market town. Friendly service. Head Chef: Gareth Johns.
23 bedrs SB £45 DB £70
HBS £66 HBD £56
B £5.50 L £6
CC: MC Vi Am DC Swi Delt

Wales

Manorbier, Dyfed

124 Castlemead Hotel

★★★

Manorbier, Dyfed, SA70 7TA
Tel: 01834 871358 Fax: 01834 871358
Email: castlemeadhot@aol.com
Web: www.castlemeadhotel.co.uk
Closed November to February
8 bedrs SB £33 DB £60
HBS £45 HBD £90 D £13
CC: MC Vi Swi Delt

How to get there: Situated at bottom of village, above beach. Car park on left.

Merthyr Tydfil

125 Castle Hotel

★★★

Castle Street, Merthyr Tydfil,
CF47 8BG
Tel: 01685 386868 Fax: 01685 383898
Email: enquiries@castlehotelwales.com
Web: www.castlehotelwales.com
40 bedrs SB £55 DB £69
HBS £51 HBD £40
B £4.95 L £4.95 D £8.95
CC: MC Vi Am Swi Delt

How to get there: Leave A470 at Merthyr junction. Proceed to town centre. Hotel is adjacent to Civic Centre and Law Courts — a prominent five-storey building.

126 The Baverstock Hotel

★★★

The Heads of the Valleys Road, Aberdare, near Merthyr Tydfil, CF44 0LX
Tel: 01685 386221 Fax: 01685 723670
Email: baverstockhotel@btinternet.com

Within easy reach of all coastal towns and cities of South Wales. Adjacent to the beautiful Brecon Beacons. Ideal holiday, business, walking, golfing, fishing, windsurfing, wedding and conference hotel.
50 bedrs SB £55 DB £80 B £5 L £9.95 D £9.95
CC: MC Vi Am DC Swi Delt

How to get there: On the main A465 Heads of the Valleys Road West, past A470 Merthyr Tydfil and opposite the B4276 Aberdare turn.

127 Tredegar Arms Hotel

♦ ♦

66 High Street, Dowlais Top, Merthyr Tydfil, CF48 3PW
Tel: 01685 377467 Fax: 01685 377467

Milford Haven, Pembrokeshire

128 Belhaven House Hotel

♦ ♦

29 Hamilton Terrace (A5076), Milford Haven, Pembrokeshire, SA73 3JJ
Tel: 01646 695983 Fax: 01646 690787
Email: hbruceh@aol.com
Web: www.westwaleshotels.com
Closed 22–29 December
9 bedrs SB £38.50 DB £60 B £5 D £5
CC: MC Vi Am DC Swi Delt

How to get there: Opposite the Cenotaph on the A4076 300 yards from town hall above the marina and waterway.

Mold, Flintshire

129 Bryn Awel Hotel

★★

Denbigh Road, Mold, Flintshire, CH7 1BL
Tel: 01352 758622 Fax: 01352 758625

130 Travelodge Mold

Travel Accommodation
A55, Expressway Eastbound, Northop Hall, near Mold, Flintshire, CH7 6HB
Tel: 08700 850 950
Web: www.travelodge.co.uk
40 bedrs B £4.25
CC: MC Vi Am DC Swi Delt

Monmouth, Monmouthshire

131 Travelodge Monmouth

Travel Accommodation
A40, Monmouth, Monmouthshire,
NP5 4BG
Tel: 08700 850 950
Web: www.travelodge.co.uk
41 bedrs B £4.25
CC: MC Vi Am DC Swi Delt

Morfa Nefyn, Gwynedd

132 Woodlands Hall

★★
Edern, Morfa Nefyn, Gwynedd, LL53 6JB
Tel: 01758 720425

Mumbles, Swansea

133 Coast House

◆◆◆
708 Mumbles Road, Mumbles,
Swansea, SA3 4EH
Tel: 01792 368702
Email: thecoasthouse@aol.com
Closed Christmas
6 bedrs SB £24 DB £44
CC: None accepted

How to get there: M4 Junction 42, A283 to
Swansea, then A4067 to Mumbles Village. Coast
House is ½ mile from shopping area, on right.

Neath, Neath & Port Talbot

134 Aberavon Beach Hotel

★★★
Neath, Port Talbot,
Neath & Port Talbot, SA12 6QP
Tel: 01639 884949 Fax: 01639 897885
Email: sales@aberavonbeach.com
Web: www.aberavonbeach.com

Modern hotel close to M4 and seven miles from
centre of Swansea. Seafront location with views
across Swansea bay. Comfortable bedrooms,
elegant restaurant with fine food, conference
facilities and friendly staff.
52 bedrs SB £72 DB £82 HBS £77 HBD £51
B £5.50 L £8.50 D £11
CC: MC Vi Am DC Swi Delt

How to get there: Leave M4 at Junction 41, take
A48 and follow signs for Aberavon and
Hollywood Park.

135 Castle Hotel

★★
The Parade, Neath,
Neath & Port Talbot, SA11 1RB
Tel: 01639 641119 Fax: 01639 641624
29 bedrs SB £55 DB £65 B £5.50 L £3.50
D £6.50 CC: MC Vi Am DC Swi Delt
How to get there: Leave M4 at J43. Follow
signs for Neath, hotel 200 yards past railway
station on right. Car park 20 yards further on
left.

Wales

New Quay, Ceredigion

136 Brynarfor Hotel

♦ ♦ ♦

New Road, New Quay,
Ceredigion, SA45 9SB
Tel: 01545 560358 Fax: 01545 561204
Email: enquiries@brynarfor.co.uk
Web: www.brynarfor.co.uk
Closed November to February

Superb Victorian house, overlooking beaches
with panoramic views of mountains around
Cardigan Bay. You can spot our resident
dolphins while having breakfast. Visit our
website. Brochure supplied.
7 bedrs SB £32 DB £60 HBS £45 HBD £84
B £8.50 D £8.50
CC: MC Vi Swi Delt
How to get there: A487 to Llanarth, B4342 New
Quay. Hotel left overlooking sea, before town.

Newport

137 The Celtic Manor Resort
Blue Ribbon Winner

★ ★ ★ ★ ★ ★
Coldra Woods, Newport, NP18 1HQ
Tel: 01633 413000 Fax: 01633 412910
Email: postbox@celtic-manor.com
Web: www.celtic-manor.com
400 bedrs SB £191.25 DB £229.75 B £15
L £19.50 D £24.50
CC: MC Vi Am DC Swi Delt
How to get there: Exit M4 at Junction 24. At
roundabout exit A48 towards Newport. Turn
right after Alcatel offices.

138 Kings Hotel

★ ★ ★
High Street, Newport, NP20 1QU
Tel: 01633 842020 Fax: 01633 244667
Email: kingshotel.wales@netscapeonline.co.uk
61 bedrs
CC: MC Vi Am DC Swi Delt
How to get there: From Junction 26 of M4, drive
towards city centre (A4051). At main roundabout
take third exit to the hotel.

139 The Inn At The Elm Tree

♦ ♦ ♦ ♦ ♦
St. Brides, Wentlodge, Newport, NP10 8SQ
Tel: 01633 680225 Fax: 01633 681035
Email: inn@the-elm-tree.co.uk
Web: www.the-elm-tree.co.uk
Children minimum age: 10
10 bedrs SB £70 DB £85 L £8 D £12.50
CC: MC Vi Am Swi Delt JCB
How to get there: Exit M4 at Junction 28. Take
A48 to B4239 two miles along country lane. We
are on S-bend in St. Brides village on left.
See advert on facing page

Newtown, Powys

140 Elephant & Castle Hotel

★ ★
Broad Street, Newtown,
Powys, SY16 2BQ
Tel: 01686 626271 Fax: 01686 622123
Email: info@theelephant.prestel.co.uk
Web: www.elephanthotel.co.uk
Closed Christmas
38 bedrs
CC: MC Vi Am Swi Delt
How to get there: Turn for town centre at traffic
lights by church to reach main street. The hotel
is opposite the junction next to the river bridge.

Pembroke, Pembrokeshire

141 Cleddau Bridge Hotel

★ ★ ★
Essex Road, Pembroke Dock,
Pembrokeshire, SA72 6UT
Tel: 01646 685961 Fax: 01646 685746

142 Lamphey Court Hotel

★★★

Lamphey, Pembroke, Pembrokeshire, SA71 5NT
Tel: 01646 672273 Fax: 01646 672480
Email: info@lampheycourt.co.uk
Web: www.lampheycourt.co.uk

This elegant Georgian mansion, now a deluxe hotel with superb leisure centre, is set in quiet grounds. Ideally situated for the local business area and exploring Pembrokeshire's National Park coast with beautiful beaches.
37 bedrs SB £72 DB £90 HBD £47 B £11.50 L £6.95 D £20 CC: MC Vi Am DC Swi Delt
⟐⟑⬒⬕☎Ⓟ♨✕♨⌂♨✦♨♨♨♨✕⚲✦
How to get there: M4 to Carmarthen and A477 to Pembroke. Left at Milton village. In Lamphey, turn at roadside hotel sign: entrance next to Bishop's Palace.

143 Lamphey Hall Hotel

★★

Lamphey, Pembroke, Pembrokeshire, SA71 5NR
Tel: 01646 672394 Fax: 01646 672369
Web: www.activehotels.com
10 bedrs SB £40 DB £60
CC: MC Vi Am Swi Delt JCB
♿⬒✕⊘⬕⬒☎☏Ⓟ♨✕♨⌂♨♨
How to get there: Near Lamphey Church on Tenby to Pembroke road. Two miles from Pembroke, and Beach, seven miles from Tenby.

144 Wheeler's Old King's Arms

★★

Main Street, Pembroke, Pembrokeshire, SA71 4JS
Tel: 01646 683611 Fax: 01646 682335
Email: reception@oldkingsarmshotel.
　　　freeserve.co.uk
Web: www.oldkingsarmshotel.co.uk
17 bedrs SB £33 DB £48 B £4.50 L £6.95 D £15.95 CC: MC Vi Am Swi Delt JCB
✕⬕⬒☎Ⓟ♨✕♨⌂♨♨
How to get there: M4 to Carmarthen, A477 to Pembroke. Left for Pembroke. At roundabout, head for town centre. Right onto the Parade. Car park is signposted.

The Inn At The Elm Tree

Wales' only Five-Diamond Inn. Only two miles from M4-J28, yet set in a peaceful rural village, close to Capitol. A unique blend of traditional values and understated elegance. Some bedrooms have four-posters, waterbeds, Jacuzzis. Enviable reputation for excellent cuisine. Ideal for short breaks, sightseeing, country pursuits, relaxing, romance, wining and dining.

St. Brides, Wentlooge,
Newport NP10 8SQ

Tel: 01633 680225　　Fax: 01633 681035
inn@the-elm-tree.co.uk
www.the-elm-tree.co.uk　

Wales

Penarth, Glamorgan

145 Glendale Hotel

◆◆◆

10 Plymouth Road, Penarth,
Glamorgan, CF64 3DH
Tel: 029 20706701 Fax: 029 20709269
Web: www.infotel.co.uk

Family-run, well-established, with large menu. Conveniently situated close to town centre and promenade (a two-minute walk).
22 bedrs SB £33 DB £45 L £8 D £14.75
CC: MC Vi Am Swi Delt
⟐♿⬒⬕☎Ⓟ♨♨✕♨⌂♨♨♨
How to get there: One mile off the A40, 2$\frac{1}{2}$ miles west of Crickhowell.

Pontyclun, Rhondda Cynon Taff

146 Travelodge Pontyclun

Travel Accommodation
M4 J33, Pontyclun, CF72 8SA
Tel: 08700 850 950
Web: www.travelodge.co.uk
50 bedrs B £4.25
CC: MC Vi Am DC Swi Delt

Porthmadog, Gwynedd

147 Hotel Portmeirion
Blue Ribbon Winner

★★★★ ❧ ❧
Portmeirion, Gwynedd, LL48 6ET
Tel: 01766 770000 Fax: 01766 771331
Email: hotel@portmeirion-village.com
Web: www.portmeirion-village.com
Closed 4 January to 4 February
51 bedrs SB £91 DB £132 B £11 L £12 D £35
CC: MC Vi Am DC Swi Delt JCB

How to get there: Off the A487 at Minffordd
between Penrhyndeudraeth and Porthmadog.

Ruabon, Wrexham

148 Wynnstay Arms Hotel

★★
Ruabon, Wrexham, LL14 6BL
Tel: 01978 822187 Fax: 01978 820093
6 bedrs SB £32.50 DB £47.50 B £8 L £4 D £8
CC: MC Vi Am DC Swi Delt JCB

Ruthin, Denbighshire

149 Ruthin Castle

★★★
Corwen Road, Ruthin, Denbighshire, LL15 2NU
Tel: 01824 702664 Fax: 01824 705978
Email: reservations@ruthincastle.co.uk
Web: www.ruthincastle.co.uk
58 bedrs SB £83 DB £106 HBD £68.50 B £8
L £7.95 D £19.95 CC: MC Vi Am DC Swi
How to get there: A494 to Ruthin; castle at end
of Castle Street, just off town square

Saundersfoot, Pembrokeshire

150 Merlewood Hotel

★★
St. Bride's Hill, Saundersfoot, Pembrokeshire,
SA69 9NP
Tel: 01834 812421 Fax: 01834 814886
Web: www.merlewood.co.uk
Closed November to February
28 bedrs
CC: MC Vi Swi Delt

How to get there: From Carmarthen, travel west
towards Tenby. At Begelly roundabout take
turning for Saundersfoot. Hotel just out of
Saundersfoot centre, on right as you reach top
of St. Bride's Hill.

151 Rhodewood House Hotel

★★
St. Bride's Hill, Saundersfoot,
Pembrokeshire, SA69 9NU
Tel: 01834 812200 Fax: 01834 815005
Email: relax@rhodewood.co.uk
Web: www.rhodewood.co.uk
Closed January
45 bedrs SB £30 DB £50 HBS £40 HBD £70
B £5.95 L £5.95 D £11.95
CC: MC Vi Am DC Swi Delt

How to get there: From Carmarthen take A40 to
Kilgetty, A477 to B4316. Turn left. Hotel on left
half a mile further on.

152 Woodlands Hotel

◆ ◆ ◆ ✑
St. Bride's Hill, Saundersfoot,
Pembrokeshire, SA69 9NP
Tel: 01834 813338 Fax: 01834 811480
Email: woodlands.hotel@virgin.net
Web: www.woodlands-hotel.net
Closed November to March
10 bedrs SB £25 DB £45
HBS £36 HBD £33.50 D £12.50
CC: MC Vi Swi Delt JCB
How to get there: From centre of village, take
road to Tenby. 500 yards up hill, hotel is on right.

Making a booking?

Don't forget to mention RAC
Hotels and Bed & Breakfast 2002.

153 Bay View Hotel

◆ ◆

Pleasant Valley, Stepaside, Saundersfoot,
Pembrokeshire, SA67 8LR
Tel: 01834 813417
Closed October to March
11 bedrs
CC: None accepted

How to get there: Turn off A477 to Stepaside.
Proceed downhill to flats. Turn left. After 50
yards turn left. ¹/₂ mile on, turn left round chapel.

St. David's, Pembrokeshire

154 Warpool Court

★★★★
St. David's, Pembrokeshire, SA62 6BN
Tel: 01437 720300 Fax: 01437 720676
Email: warpool@enterprise.net
Web: www.warpoolcourthotel.com
Closed January

Unrivalled views and large gardens. Imaginative
and creative food — fish a strong presence on
the menu. Various food awards. Close to
coastal path and sandy beaches.
25 bedrs SB £75 DB £132 HBS £93 HBD £84
B £8.50 L £15.50 D £37
CC: MC Vi Am DC Swi Delt

How to get there: From Cross Square in St.
David's, bear left following hotel signs for
approximately ¹/₂ a mile.

155 Lochmeyler Farm

◆ ◆ ◆ ◆ ◆

Llandeloy, Pen-y-Cwm, near Solva,
St. David's, Pembrokeshire, SA62 6LL
Tel: 01348 837724 Fax: 01348 837622
16 bedrs SB £20 DB £40 HBS £32.50 HBD £65
CC: MC Vi DC Swi Delt

How to get there: From Fishguard, follow A487
St. Davids road to Mathry, turn left and follow
road to Llandeloy. From Haverfordwest, follow
A487 to Pen-y-Cwm, turn right to Llandeloy.

156 Ramsey House

◆ ◆ ◆ ◆

Lower Moor, St. David's,
Pembrokeshire, SA62 6RP
Tel: 01437 720321 Fax: 01437 720025
Email: info@ramseyhouse.co.uk
Web: www.ramseyhouse.co.uk

Mild climate and warm welcome make perfect
climate for year-round breaks. Non-smoking.
Award-winning Welsh cuisine/wines. Quiet,
convenient location for cathedral, coast,
walking, golf.
7 bedrs DB £64 HBD £48 D £16
CC: MC Vi Swi Delt JCB

How to get there: From centre of St. David's,
bear left down hill by HSBC bank, signposted
Porthclais, for ¹/₂ mile. Ramsey is last house on
left.

Wales

157 Y Glennydd Hotel

♦ ♦ ♦

51 Nun Street, St. David's,
Pembrokeshire, SA62 6NU
Tel: 01437 720576 Fax: 01437 720184
Closed December and January
10 bedrs SB £26 DB £45 D £15
CC: MC Vi Swi Delt
⌂ ☐ P ♨ ⑀
How to get there: 800 metres from Cross
Square, next door to fire station.

Swansea

158 Swansea Marriott Hotel

★★★★

Maritime Quarter, Swansea, SA1 3SS
Tel: 01792 642020 Fax: 01792 650345
Web: www.marriotthotels.com/swsdt
117 bedrs SB £115 DB £125 B £13 L £11.95
D £25
CC: MC Vi Am DC Swi Delt JCB
⚓ ♿ ♨ ☓ ⊙ ⌂ ☐ ☎ ❉ ☏ P ● ♨ ⌅ ♩ ☘ ♨ ♨
♩ ⑀
How to get there: Exit J42 M4, then A483
towards the city centre. Follow signs for the
Marina where the hotel is situated.

159 St. Anne's Hotel

★★★

Western Lane, Mumbles,
Swansea, SA3 4EY
Tel: 01792 369147 Fax: 01792 360537
Email: enquiries@stannes-hotel.co.uk

Overlooked by Oystermouth Castle and with
spectacular views over Swansea Bay. Own
grounds, large private car park, quiet location in
the heart of Mumbles village.
33 bedrs
CC: MC Vi Am Swi Delt
⚓ ♿ ♨ ☓ ⊙ ⌂ ☐ ☎ P ● ♨ ⌅ ☘ ♩ ☘ ♨ ♨
How to get there: Leave M4 at Junction 42 and
take A483 to Swansea, then A4067 to Mumbles.

160 Abercrave Inn

★★

145 Heol Tawe, Abercraf,
Swansea, SA9 1XS
Tel: 01639 731002 Fax: 01639 730796

161 Beaumont Hotel

★★★ ⑀

72–73 Walter Road, Swansea, SA1 4QA
Tel: 01792 643956 Fax: 01792 643044
Email: info@beaumonthotel.co.uk
Web: www.beaumonthotel.co.uk
16 bedrs SB £60 DB £70 HBS £85 HBD £50
D £10
CC: MC Vi Am DC Swi Delt
⌨ ♨ ☐ ☎ ☏ P ● ♨ ⌅ ♩ ☘ ♨ ♨
How to get there: M4 J42, A483; right at traffic
lights at Tesco, left at roundabout; first right, top
of the road, turn left.
See advert on facing page

162 Windsor Lodge

★★

Mount Pleasant, Swansea, SA1 6EG
Tel: 01792 642158 Fax: 01792 648996
Web: www.windsor-lodge.co.uk
19 bedrs SB £60 DB £70 HBS £80 HBD £55
B £8 L £15 D £20
CC: MC Vi Am DC Swi Delt
🐾🛏🖥☎📞🅿️♿🍴🛏⛵♨♨♨

How to get there: M4 Junction 42, A483 to
Sainsbury's. Turn right at traffic lights beyond
Sainsbury's. Turn left at railway station, then
immediately right after second lights.

163 Fairyhill

Blue Ribbon Winner

★★

Reynoldston, Swansea, SA3 1BS
Tel: 01792 390139 Fax: 01792 391358
Email: postbox@fairyhill.net
Web: www.fairyhill.net
Children minimum age: 8
Closed 1–18 January
8 bedrs DB £125 HBD £97.50 D £35
CC: MC Vi Am Swi Delt JCB
🐾🛏🖥☎📞🅿️♿♨♨♨

How to get there: Exit J47 M4; follow signs for
Gowerton. Turn right at traffic lights, follow
B4295 for 10½ miles.

164 Travelodge Swansea

Travel Accommodation
M4 J47, Penllergaer, Swansea, SA4 1GT
Tel: 08700 850 950
Web: www.travelodge.co.uk
50 bedrs B £4.25
CC: MC Vi Am DC Swi Delt
🐾🛏🖥♿

165 Grosvenor House

♦♦♦♦ 🕸

Mirador Crescent, Uplands, Swansea, SA2 0QX
Tel: 01792 461522 Fax: 01792 461522
Email: grosvenor@ct6.com
Web: www.ct6.com/grosvenor
Closed Christmas and New Year
7 bedrs SB £30 DB £50
CC: MC Vi Am Swi Delt JCB
🐾⊘🛏🖥📞🅿️♿♨

How to get there: Off A4118, one mile from
Swansea railway station travelling west, take
the third turning on the right, after St. Jame's
Church.

166 Woodside Guest House

♦♦♦♦ 🕸

Oxwich, Gower, Swansea, SA3 1LS
Tel: 01792 390791
Email: woodside@oxwich.fsnet.co.uk
Web: www.oxwich.fsnet.co.uk
5 bedrs SB £30 DB £62 CC: None accepted
🛏🖥🅿️♿♨♨♨

How to get there: M4 at Junction 42 for Swansea.
Take A4118 Swansea to Portegnon. One mile
past Penmaen, take unmarked road to Oxwich.
See advert below

167 Alexander Hotel

♦♦♦ 🕸

3 Sketty Road, Uplands, Swansea, SA2 0EU
Tel: 01792 470045 Fax: 01792 476012
Email: alexander.hotel@swig-online.co.uk
Web: www.swig-online.co.uk/alexanderhotel
Children minimum age: 2
Closed Christmas to New Year
7 bedrs SB £34 DB £54
CC: MC Vi Am DC Swi Delt
⊘🛏🖥☎♿🍴♨♨♨🏧

How to get there: On A4118, in the Uplands
area of Swansea. On left-hand side at the
beginning of Sketty Road, as you leave the
Uplands towards Sketty.

Wales

168 Crescent Guest House

◆◆◆ ⁂

132 Eaton Crescent, Uplands,
Swansea, SA1 4QR
Tel: 01792 466814 Fax: 01792 466814
Email: conveyatthecrescent@compuserve.com
Web: www.crescentguesthouse.co.uk
Closed Christmas to New Year
6 bedrs SB £30 DB £50 CC: MC Vi Swi Delt

How to get there: From railway station, take
A4118 to St. James' Church, then first left, first
right into Eaton Crescent.

169 Rock Villa

◆◆◆

1 George Bank, Southend, Mumbles,
Swansea, SA3 4EQ
Tel: 01792 366794
Email: rockvilla@tinyworld.co.uk
Children minimum age: 2
Closed 21 December to 3 January
6 bedrs SB £24 DB £46 CC: None accepted

How to get there: Approximately 4½ miles from
Leisure Centre down the A483, next to George
restaurant and hotel.

170 Shoreline Hotel

◆◆◆

648 Mumbles Road, Mumbles,
Swansea, SA3 4QZ
Tel: 01792 366233
Web: www.shorelinehotel.co.uk
Closed Christmas

Recently refurbished family run hotel, situated
on the seafront in the beautiful village of
Mumbles, close to the city centre, ferry terminal
and the Gower Peninsula.
12 bedrs CC: MC Vi Am DC Swi Delt

How to get there:M4 at Junction 42, follow signs
for Swansea, then to Mumbles. Situated on main
Mumbles seafront, opposite playground.

Talsarnau, Gwynedd

171 Hotel Maes-y-Neuadd

Blue Ribbon Winner

★★ ® ® ®
Talsarnau, Gwynedd, LL47 6YA
Tel: 01766 780200 Fax: 01766 780211
Email: maes@neuadd.com
Web: www.neuadd.com
16 bedrs
CC: MC Vi Am DC Swi Delt

How to get there: Three miles northeast of
Harlech, signposted on an unclassed road off
B4573.

Tenby, Pembrokeshire

172 Atlantic Hotel

★★★ ®
1 The Esplanade, Tenby,
Pembrokeshire, SA70 7DU
Tel: 01834 842881
Email: enquiries@atlantic-hotel.uk.com
Web: www.atlantic-hotel.uk.com
Closed 21–28 December
42 bedrs SB £62 DB £86 D £16
CC: MC Vi Am Swi Delt JCB

How to get there: Keep town walls on left, then
turn right at Esplanade. Hotel is halfway along
on your right.

173 Fourcroft Hotel

★★★
North Beach, Tenby,
Pembrokeshire, SA70 8AP
Tel: 01834 842886 Fax: 01834 842888
Email: chris@fourcroft-hotel.co.uk
Web: www.fourcroft-hotel.co.uk
42 bedrs SB £33 DB £66
HBS £53 HBD £53
B £9 L £5 D £16
CC: MC Vi Am DC Swi Delt
How to get there: After 'Welcome to Tenby'
signs, fork left towards North Beach. Down a
gentle hill, around a right-handed sweeping
bend, up a gentle hill. At seafront turn sharp left.
Fourcroft is 150 yards along on left.

174 Heywood Mount Hotel

★★★

Heywood Lane, Tenby, Pembrokeshire, SA70 8DA
Tel: 01834 842087 Fax: 01834 842113
Email: reception@heywoodmount.co.uk
Web: www.heywoodmount.co.uk
32 bedrs SB £40 DB £80 HBS £55 HBD £55
B £5 L £5 D £15
CC: MC Vi Am DC Swi Delt JCB
How to get there: Pass 'Welcome to Tenby' sign
and follow sign for Wildlife Park into Heywood
Lane. Hotel third on left.
See advert below right

175 St. Bride's Hotel

★★★

St. Bride's Hill, Saundersfoot,
Pembrokeshire, SA69 9NH
Tel: 01834 812304 Fax: 01834 811766
Email: andrew.evans9@virgin.net
CC: MC Vi Am DC Swi Delt
How to get there: Travel west along M4 to
Carmarthen. Follow A477 towards Tenby.
Saundersfoot is four miles before Tenby. Enter
village: hotel overlooks harbour on a clifftop.

176 Greenhills Country Hotel

★★

St. Florence, Tenby, Pembrokeshire, SA70 8NB
Tel: 01834 871291 Fax: 01834 871948
Email: enquiries@greenhillshotel.co.uk
Web: www.greenhillshotel.co.uk
Closed December to March
28 bedrs SB £27 DB £54 HBS £39 HBD £78
D £12
CC: None accepted
How to get there: In St. Florence, pass church
on right. Turn left at hotel signpost. Hotel 250
yards further on.

177 Kinloch Court Hotel

★★

Queens Parade, Tenby,
Pembrokeshire, SA70 7EG
Tel: 01834 842777 Fax: 01834 843097
14 bedrs SB £3 DB £66 HBS £48 HBD £48
CC: MC Vi Swi Delt

178 Royal Gate House Hotel

★★

North Beach, Tenby, Pembrokeshire, SA70 7ET
Tel: 01834 842255 Fax: 01834 842441
Email: royal_gatehouse@hotmail.com
59 bedrs SB £42 DB £75 HBS £59 HBD £109
B £10 L £5.95 D £17
CC: MC Vi Am Swi Delt JCB
How to get there: From M4, take A478 into Tenby.

179 The Esplanade Hotel

★★

1, The Esplanade, Tenby,
Pembrokeshire, SA70 7DU
Tel: 01834 842760 Fax: 01834 845633
Email: esplanade.tenby@virgin.net
Web: www.esplanadetenby.co.uk
Children minimum age: 6
Closed Christmas, New Year
13 bedrs SB £45 DB £60 HBS £60 HBD £90
D £15
CC: MC Vi Am Swi Delt JCB
How to get there: Keeping town walls on your
left, follow them to the sea; hotel is on the right-
hand corner.

Wales

180 Broadmead Hotel

Heywood Lane, Tenby,
Pembrokeshire, SA70 8DA
Tel: 01834 842641 Fax: 01834 845757
Web: www.broadmeadhotel.com
Closed December to March
20 bedrs SB £31 DB £62
HBS £44 HBD £88 D £14
CC: MC Vi Am Swi Delt

How to get there: On arrival in Tenby, turn right into Serpentine Road, following signs for Wildlife Park. Turn right again into Heywood Lane.

181 Ashby House

24 Victoria Street, Tenby,
Pembrokeshire, SA70 7DY
Tel: 01834 842867
Email: ashbyhouse@yahoo.com
Web: www.ashbyhousetenby.co.uk
Children minimum age: 3
9 bedrs SB £18 DB £32
CC: MC Vi

How to get there: Driving down South Parade, Town Walls will be on your left. Turn right up the Esplanade; Victoria Street is last turning on right.

182 Pen Mar Hotel

♦ ♦ ♦

New Hedges, Tenby, Pembrokeshire, SA70 8TL
Tel: 01834 842435 Fax: 01834 842435
Email: penmar@jhurton.freeserve.co.uk
Web: www.s-h-systems.co.uk/a15498.html
10 bedrs SB £24 DB £48 HBS £35.60
HBD £71.20 B £5.50 D £11.50
CC: MC Vi DC Swi Delt JCB

How to get there: Situated on A478 one mile before Tenby in village of New Hedges.

183 Ripley St. Mary's Hotel

♦ ♦ ♦

St. Mary's Street, Tenby,
Pembrokeshire, SA70 7HN
Tel: 01834 842837 Fax: 01834 842837
Closed November to March
12 bedrs SB £26 DB £52
CC: MC Vi Swi Delt JCB

Trearddur Bay, Gwynedd

184 Trearddur Bay Hotel

★ ★ ★

Lon Isallt, Trearddur Bay, Gwynedd, LL65 2UW
Tel: 01407 860301 Fax: 01407 861181
Email: enquiries@trearddurbayhotel.co.uk
Web: www.trearddurbayhotel.co.uk
42 bedrs SB £82 DB £120
CC: MC Vi Am DC Swi Delt JCB

How to get there: Exit A55 at Valley; take A5 to crossroads, turn left onto B4545. Follow for three miles, turn left at garage.

185 Moranedd Guest House

♦ ♦ ♦

Trearddur Road, Trearddur Bay, Anglesey,
Gwynedd, LL65 2UE
Tel: 01407 860324 Fax: 01407 860324

Moranedd is a lovely guest house with a sun patio overlooking three-quarters of an acre of garden in a quiet cul-de-sac, but only five minutes stroll to the beach, shops, sailing and golf clubs.
6 bedrs SB £20 DB £45
CC: None accepted

How to get there: Take A55 to Valley. Turn left at traffic lights onto B4545 to Trearddur. Continue past Beach Hotel and turn right at second road through village. Moranedd is second house on left in Trearddur Road.

Tyn-y-Groes, Gwynedd

186 The Groes Inn

★ ★ ★

Tyn-y-Groes, near Conwy, Gwynedd, LL32 8TN
Tel: 01492 650545 Fax: 01492 650545

Tywyn, Gwynedd

187 Corbett Arms Hotel

★★
Tywyn, Gwynedd, LL36 9DG
Tel: 01923 822388 Fax: 01923 824906
41 bedrs
CC: MC Vi Am Delt

How to get there: The Corbett Arms Hotel
stands astride the A493 as it passes north to
south from Dolgellau to Machynlleth.

188 Greenfield Hotel

★
High Street, Tywyn, Gwynedd, LL36 9AD
Tel: 01654 710354 Fax: 01654 710354
Email: greentywyn@aol.com
Closed January
8 bedrs SB £21 DB £40
HBS £28 HBD £27
B £3.25 L £3.95 D £6.95
CC: MC Vi Swi Delt
How to get there: Situated in High Street
opposite Leisure Centre and Tourist Information
Centre.

Welshpool, Powys

189 Lane Farm

Criggion, Welshpool, Powys, SY5 9BG
Tel: 01743 884288 Fax: 01743 885126
Email: lane.farm@ukgateway.net
Web: www.smoothhound.co.uk/hotels/lanefarm
4 bedrs SB £25 DB £40
CC: None accepted
How to get there: Situated on B4393 between
Crew Green and Llandrinio, 12 miles from
Shrewsbury, nine miles from Welshpool.

Wrexham

190 Llwyn Onn Hall Hotel

★★★
Cefn Road, Wrexham, LL13 0NY
Tel: 01978 261225 Fax: 01978 363233
Email: llwynonnhall@breathemail.net
13 bedrs SB £64 DB £84
HBS £72 HBD £55
B £6.95 L £8.95 D £17.50
CC: MC Vi Am DC Swi Delt
How to get there: Easily accessible from A483
and ideally situated for Wrexham town centre
and industrial estate.

191 Wynnstay Arms Hotel

★★★
Yorke Street, Wrexham, LL13 8LP
Tel: 01978 291010 Fax: 01978 362138
67 bedrs SB £46.85 DB £53.80
B £6.95 L £9.95 D £12.95
CC: MC Vi Am DC Swi Delt
How to get there: From A438, take left turn at
Ruthin, follow to T-Junction. Left again to
bottom of hill, right onto St. Giles Way. Left at T-
junction, next left at roundabout.

192 Travelodge Wrexham

Travel Accommodation
A483, Wrexham By Pass, Rhostyllen,
Wrexham, LL14 4EG
Tel: 08700 850 950
Web: www.travelodge.co.uk
32 bedrs B £4.25
CC: MC Vi Am DC Swi Delt

Wales

Scotland

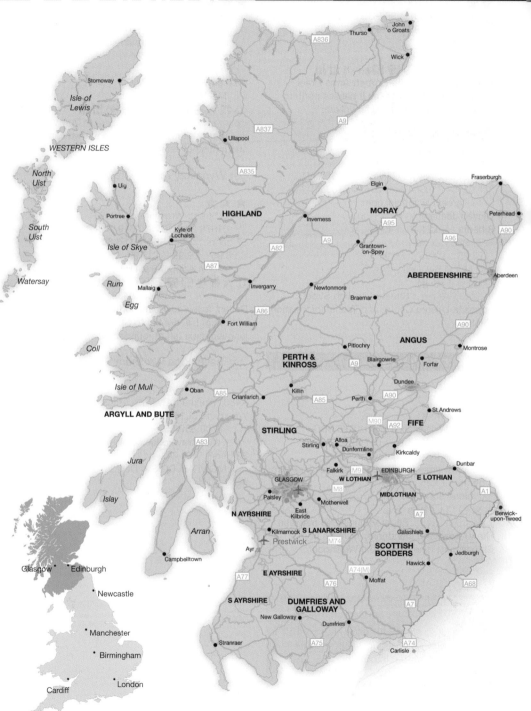

John 'o Groats
Thurso
Wick
A836

Stornoway

Isle of
Lewis

WESTERN ISLES

North
Uist

Uig

South
Uist

Portree

Isle of Skye

Watersay

Rum

Mallaig

Egg

Coll

Isle of Mull

Oban

ARGYLL AND BUTE

Jura

Islay

Arran

Campbelltown

A837

Ullapool

A835

A9

Elgin

HIGHLAND

MORAY

Inverness

Kyle of
Lochalsh

A95

Fraserburgh

Peterhead

A90

A82

A9

Grantown-
on-Spey

A96

A87

ABERDEENSHIRE

Aberdeen

Invergarry

Newtonmore

A86

Braemar

Fort William

A90

ANGUS

Pitlochry

Montrose

PERTH &
KINROSS

Blairgowrie

Forfar

A9

Killin

Dundee

Crianlarich

A85

A85

Perth

A90

St Andrews

M90

A92

FIFE

STIRLING

Alloa

Stirling

Dunfermline

Kirkcaldy

A83

Falkirk

M9

Dunbar

GLASGOW

W LOTHIAN

EDINBURGH

E LOTHIAN

Paisley

M8

MIDLOTHIAN

A1

N AYRSHIRE

East
Kilbride

Motherwell

Berwick-
upon-Tweed

Kilmarnock

S LANARKSHIRE

Galashiels

SCOTTISH
BORDERS

Ayr

Prestwick

M74

E AYRSHIRE

A77

A76

Hawick

Jedburgh

Moffat

A68

S AYRSHIRE

DUMFRIES AND
GALLOWAY

A74(M)

A7

New Galloway

Dumfries

A7

Stranraer

A75

A74

Carlisle

Glasgow

Edinburgh

Newcastle

Manchester

Birmingham

Cardiff

London

Uncovered in 1850 after a violent storm, the Neolothic village of Skara Brae (left) stands on the West Mainland of the Orkneys. Built around 5,000 years ago, it stands in a line with two other major sites, the Standing Stones of Stenness and the Ring of Brodgar.

● The Shetlands, known for their metalcraft, knitwear and small, hardy ponies, is a group of over a hundred small islands dominated by the largest, known simply as Mainland. The islands have many prehistoric sites, notably Jarlshof, which has remains of several settlements, some over 4,000 years ago

ORKNEY ISLANDS

Westray
Sanday
Eday
Rousay
Lady Village
Stronsay
Mainland
Dounby
Shapinsay
Kirkwall
Kirkwall
Stromness
Gritley
Hoy
South Ronaldsay
Burwick

SHETLAND ISLANDS

Haroldswick
Unst
Baltasound
Yell
Fetlar
Whalsay
Mainland
Lerwick
Scalloway
Bressay
Hoswick
Tolob
Sumburgh

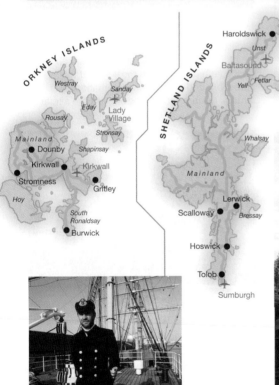

RRS (Royal Research Ship) Discovery, located in Dundee (above), took Captain Scott to the Antarctic in 1901 and was subsequently locked in ice for two years.

Cromarty guards the entrance to Cromarty Firth from the larger Moray Firth. Its Courthouse (above) is a museum with a wealth of information on the North of Scotland. For more details, go to www.cromarty-courthouse.org.uk.

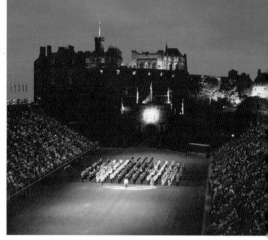

Beating a Tattoo

Situated on a rocky outcrop used as a defensive location since prehistoric times, Edinburgh Castle (left) is Scotland's most visited tourist attraction, and home of the internationally famous Military Tattoo (above); visit the site at www.edinburgh-tattoo.co.uk.

● Burns Cottage, birthplace of the famous poet, is located in the town of Alloway, South Ayrshire. The official site is www.robertburns.org.

The Cairinis (Callanish) Standing Stones, on the Isle of Lewis (below), northernmost of the Western Isles, are arguably the most dramatic megalithic monuments in Scotland, whether viewed close-up or from far across the rugged landscape near Stornoway.

The elegant and historic Royal Exchange building (above) houses Glasgow's Gallery of Modern Art, which displays works by living artists from around the world. Admission is free. Find out more at www.glasgowguide.co.uk.

● Ben Nevis, Scotland's (and Britain's) highest mountain at 4,406 feet, is a granite edifice over half a billion years old. The path up the mountain starts at nearby Fort William.

Accommodation index

Hotels and Guest Accommodation are indexed by their order of appearance within this region, not by the page. To locate an establishment, note the number to the right of the listing and then find it on the establishment's name bar, as shown here

37 The Turning Mill Hotel

Aberdeen

1 Aberdeen Marriott Hotel

★★★★ ℞

Overton Circle, Dyce, Aberdeen, AB21 7AZ
Tel: 01224 770011 Fax: 01224 722347
Web: www.marriotthotels.co.uk/abzap
155 bedrs SB £54 DB £68 HBS £69 HBD £49
B £11 L £12.95 D £18
CC: MC Vi Am DC Swi Delt

2 Copthorne Hotel Aberdeen

★★★★ ℞

122 Huntly Street, Aberdeen, AB10 1SU
Tel: 01224 630404 Fax: 01224 640573
Email: stuart.noble@mill-cop.com
Web: www.millennium-hotels.com
89 bedrs SB £45 DB £50 HBS £65 HBD £45
B £13.50 L £5 D £16.50
CC: MC Vi Am DC Swi Delt

How to get there: Travelling from South, take
second left at roundabout, right at next
roundabout. Follow Holburn Street for two
miles. Turn onto Union Street, and take first left,
second right.

3 Travelodge Aberdeen

Travel Accommodation
9 Bridge Street, Aberdeen, AB11 6JL
Tel: 08700 850 950
Web: www.travelodge.co.uk
97 bedrs B £4.25
CC: MC Vi Am DC Swi Delt

4 Travelodge Aberdeen (West)

Travel Accommodation
A96/A947
Tel: 08700 850 950
Web: www.travelodge.co.uk
Opens March 2002
48 bedrs B £4.25
CC: MC Vi Am DC Swi Delt

Plan your route

Visit www.rac.co.uk for RAC's
interactive route planner, including
up to the minute traffic reports.

5 Jays Guest House

♦♦♦♦

422 King Street, Aberdeen, AB24 3BR
Tel: 01224 638295 Fax: 01224 638295
Email: alice@jaysguesthouse.co.uk
Web: www.jaysguesthouse.co.uk
Children minimum age: 12
10 bedrs CC: MC Vi Swi Delt JCB

How to get there: From East End of Union
Street, turn left onto King Street and the Jays
Guest House is approx ³/₄ mile from this junction.

6 Arkaig Guest House

♦♦♦

43 Powis Terrace, Aberdeen, AB25 3PP
Tel: 01224 638872 Fax: 01224 622189
Email: arkaig@netcomuk.co.uk
Web: www.arkaig.co.uk

The Arkaig is a friendly, family-run guesthouse,
conveniently situated for Old Aberdeen and the
modern city centre. Its fine reputation is
founded on excellent service and facilities, plus
brilliant breakfasts!
9 bedrs SB £25 DB £48 D £12.50
CC: MC Vi Swi Delt

How to get there: Telephone, fax or email for
directions. Easy access from town centre and A96.

7 Bimini Guest House

♦♦♦

69 Constitution Street, Aberdeen, AB24 5ET
Tel: 01224 646912 Fax: 01224 647006
Email: biminiabz@aol.com
Web: www.bimini.co.uk
8 bedrs SB £35 DB £55 CC: MC Vi Am Delt

How to get there: Five minute walk from town
centre, heading towards beachfront.

Scotland

8 Cedars Private Hotel

♦ ♦ ♦

339 Great Western Road, Aberdeen, AB10 6NW
Tel: 01224 583225 Fax: 01224 585050
Email: reservations@cedars-private-hotel.freeserve.co.uk
Web: www.cedars-private-hotel.freeserve.co.uk
13 bedrs SB £38 DB £52
CC: MC Vi Am Delt
🐕😊🍴🖥☎🅿️🛀🍽/.
How to get there: Great Western Road crosses Anderson Drive, which is the city ring road.

Aberfeldy, Perth & Kinross

9 Moness

★ ★ ★

Crieff Road, Aberfeldy,
Perth & Kinross, PH15 2DY
Tel: 01887 820446 Fax: 01887 820062
12 bedrs
CC: MC Vi Swi
🌊😊🖥☎🅿️🛀🐎🏇ⅱ🍽⚿ⅲ/.
How to get there: Follow A9 north from Perth. Turn right at Ballinluig for Aberfeldy. Turn left at the traffic lights in Aberfeldy. Moness is 200m on left.

10 Fortingall Hotel

★ ★

Fortingall, Kenmore, Aberfeldy,
Perth & Kinross, PH15 2NQ
Tel: 01887 830367 Fax: 01887 830367
Email: hotel@fortingall.com
Web: www.fortingall.com
Closed January to February
10 bedrs SB £45 DB £70 HBS £65 HBD £55
CC: MC Vi Swi Delt
🐕😊🍴🖥☎🅿️ⅱⅲ
How to get there: From Aberfeldy take the road to Tummel Bridge. At Coshivielle turn left signed to Fortingall. The hotel is in the village.

Airdrie, North Lanarkshire

11 Tudor Hotel

★ ★ ★

39 Alexandra Street, Airdrie,
North Lanarkshire, ML6 0BA
Tel: 01236 764144 Fax: 01236 747589
20 bedrs CC: MC Vi Am Swi
🌊🐕😊🖥☎🅿️🛀🍴🐎🏇ⅱ🍽ⅲ(€

Anstruther, Fife

12 Smugglers Inn

★ ★

High Street East, Anstruther,
Fife, KY10 3DQ
Tel: 01333 310506 Fax: 01333 312706
Email: smugs106@aol.com
8 bedrs SB £32.90 DB £59 HBS £48 HBD £43
B £5 L £6.50 D £15
CC: MC Vi Swi Delt
🐕😊🖥☎🅿️🛀🍴🐎🍽ⅱ(€
How to get there: On the right of the main A917 through Anstruther after bad bend from west, or turn right at roundabout from St. Andrews.

13 Spindrift

♦ ♦ ♦ ♦ 🐾 🦜

Pittenweem Road, Anstruther,
Fife, KY10 3DT
Tel: 01333 310573 Fax: 01333 310573
Email: info@thespindrift.co.uk
Web: www.thespindrift.co.uk
Children minimum age: 10

The Spindrift has established a growing reputation for its unique brand of comfort, hospitality, freshly prepared food and service. Convenient for golf, walking, bird watching or exploring the picturesque and historic 'Eastneuk'.
8 bedrs DB £60 HBD £45
CC: MC Vi Am Swi Delt JCB
🐕😊🍴🖥☎🅿️🛀ⅲ
How to get there: Approaching Anstruther from the west, the Spindrift is first on the left. From the east, it is last on the right.

Arbroath, Angus

Hotel Seaforth

★★
Dundee Road, Arbroath, Angus, DD11 1QF
Tel: 01241 872232 Fax: 01241 877473
Email: hotelseaforth@ukonline.co.uk
21 bedrs SB £45 DB £58 B £7 L £4.95 D £7.95
CC: MC Vi Am Swi Delt

How to get there: Hotel Seaforth is on the A92, main road from Dundee to Aberdeen, facing the sea.
See advert below right

Arisaig, Highland

Arisaig Hotel

★★
Arisaig, Highland, PH39 4NH
Tel: 01687 450210 Fax: 01687 450310
Email: arisaighotel@dial.pipex.com
Web: www.arisaighotel.co.uk
13 bedrs SB £38 DB £76 B £8.50 L £2.50 D £12
CC: MC Vi Swi Delt

How to get there: Follow A82 through Fort William from south. Turn left onto A830. Arisaig is 35 miles further. Hotel is on right through village.

Auchencairn, Dumfries & Galloway

Balcary Bay Hotel

★★★★
Auchencairn, Dumfries & Galloway, DG7 1QZ
Tel: 01556 640217 Fax: 01556 640272
Email: reservations@balcary-bay-hotel.co.uk
Web: www.balcary-bay-hotel.co.uk
Closed December to February

This 16th-century house occupies a beautifully-secluded location on the shores of the Solway in southwest Scotland. Renowned for fine food and wines, in a unique setting.
20 bedrs SB £61 DB £108 HBS £70 HBD £62 B £12 L £11.50 D £25.75
CC: MC Vi Am Swi Delt JCB

How to get there: The hotel is located off the A711 Dumfries-Kirkudbright road, two miles out of Auchencairn along the shore road.

Aviemore, Highland

Ravenscraig Guest House

◆◆◆
141 Grampian Road, Aviemore,
Highland, PH22 1RP
Tel: 01479 810278 Fax: 01479 812742
Email: ravenscrg@aol.com
Web: www.aviemore.co.uk/ravenscraig
12 bedrs
CC: MC Vi Swi Delt

How to get there: Situated at north end of main street through the village. 300m from Police Station.

Scotland

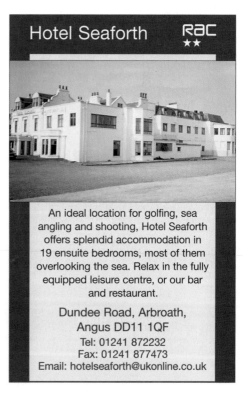

Ayr, South Ayrshire

18 Belleisle House

★★★

Doonfoot, Ayr, South Ayrshire, KA7 4DU
Tel: 01292 442331 Fax: 01292 445325
14 bedrs SB £55 DB £88 B £7.50 L £6 D £18.50
CC: MC Vi Swi

19 Quality Hotel Ayr

★★★

Burns Statue Square, Ayr,
South Ayrshire, KA7 3AT
Tel: 01292 263268 Fax: 01292 262293
Email: admin@gb624.u-net.com
Web: www.choicehotels.com
75 bedrs SB £80.75 DB £92.75 HBS £95.25
HBD £53.63 B £9.75 D £14.50
CC: MC Vi Am DC Swi Delt

How to get there: From A77, take first exit off
Holmston roundabout. Follow one-way system
round to front of hotel.

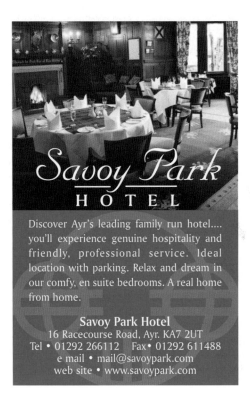

20 Savoy Park Hotel

★★★★

16 Racecourse Road, Ayr,
South Ayrshire, KA7 2UT
Tel: 01292 266112 Fax: 01292 611488
Email: mail@savoypark.com
Web: www.savoypark.com
15 bedrs SB £70 DB £95 HBS £85 HBD £62.50
B £6 CC: MC Vi Am Swi Delt JCB

How to get there: From A77, at A70 crossover
take turning for Ayr South. Follow signs for town
centre then A719 Maidens Road. Hotel is on right.
See advert below left

21 Dunduff Farm

♦♦♦♦♦

Dunure, Ayr, Ayrshire, KA7 4LH
Tel: 01292 500225 Fax: 01292 500222
Email: gemmelldunduff@aol.com
Web: gemmelldunduff.co.uk
Children minimum age: 16
3 bedrs SB £35 DB £50 CC: MC Vi

How to get there: Six miles south of Ayr past
school on 719.

22 Horizon Hotel

♦♦♦♦

Esplanade, Ayr, Ayrshire, KA7 1DT
Tel: 01292 264384 Fax: 01292 264011
Email: mail@horizonhotel.com
Web: www.horizonhotel.com

Situated next to Ayr's sandy beach five minutes
from the vibrant town centre. Meals served in
conservatory. Gourmet two-night breaks from
£99pp, dbb. Golfer's paradise room suitable for
disabled guests. Private parking.
22 bedrs B £6.50 L £4.50 D £10
CC: MC Vi Swi Delt

How to get there: Enter Ayr following seafront
signs. Hotel at north end of esplanade between
pavilion and Citadel Leisure Centre.

Ballachulish, Argyll & Bute

23 Lyn-Leven Guest House

♦ ♦ ♦ ♦ ⚥

West Laroch, Ballachulish, Argyll & Bute,
PH49 4JP
Tel: 01855 811392 Fax: 01855 811600
Email: lynleven@amserve.net
Closed Christmas

A warm Highland welcome awaits you at our
award-winning family-run guest house, only one
mile from lovely Glencoe. We are situated with
attractive gardens overlooking Loch Leven.
Private parking.
12 bedrs SB £30 DB £48 HBS £39 HBD £33
CC: MC Vi Swi Delt
⚱ 🐾 ⊗ ⊜ ▭ P ⚗ ⚬ ⦙⦙⦙
How to get there: Take A82 to Glencoe and
continue for one mile. West Laroch sign on left
to Ballachulish.

Ballater, Aberdeenshire

24 Darroch Learg

Blue Ribbon Winner

★★★★ 🎄 🎄 🎄
Braemar Road, Ballater,
Aberdeenshire, AB35 5UX
Tel: 01339 755443 Fax: 01339 755252
Email: nigel@darrochlearg.co.uk
Web: www.darrochlearg.co.uk
Closed January

Darroch Learg offers relaxing country house
charm, great views over Royal Deeside and a
fine restaurant and wine list. It is close to
Ballater and is the ideal centre for enjoying
Royal Deeside.
18 bedrs SB £62 DB £125 HBS £92 HBD £92
B £9 L £6.50 D £34
CC: MC Vi Am DC Swi Delt
⚱ ⚗ 🐾 ⊗ ⊜ ▭ ☎ P📶 ⚗ ⚬ Ħ ⦙⦙⦙
How to get there: Approaching Ballater on A93
from Braemar, turn left into driveway just past
30mph signs.

25 Monaltrie Hotel

★★
5 Bridge Square, Royal Deeside, Ballater,
Aberdeenshire, AB35 5QJ
Tel: 01339 755417 Fax: 01339 755180
Email: monaltrie.hotel@virgin.net
Web: www.monaltriehotel.freeserve.co.uk
24 bedrs SB £25 DB £50 HBS £35 HBD £35
B £6.95 L £4.95 D £12.50
CC: MC Vi Am DC Swi Delt
⚐ ⚗ 🐱 ⊗ ⊜ ▭ ☎☎ P ⚗ ⚬ Ħ ⦙⦙⦙ ⦙⦙⦙

26 Glen Lui Hotel

♦ ♦ ♦ ♦ 🎄 ⚥ ⚑
Invercauld Road, Ballater, Royal Deeside,
Aberdeenshire, AB35 5RP
Tel: 01339 755402 Fax: 01339 755545
Email: info@glen-lui-hotel.co.uk
Web: www.glen-lui-hotel.co.uk
19 bedrs SB £30 DB £30
HBS £39 HBD £39
L £14 D £14
CC: MC Vi Am Swi Delt
⚱ 🐾 ⊗ ⊜ ▭ ☎ 📶 P📶 ⚗ ⚬ ⦙⦙⦙ ⦙⦙⦙
How to get there: From Aberdeen, turn right into
Ballater. Drive straight through Ballater Town, over
small bridge. Turn left down Invercauld Road.
Drive to bottom of road, hotel is on the right.

27 Inverdeen House B&B

♦ ♦ ♦ ♦ 🎄 ⚑
11 Bridge Square, Ballater, Deeside, AB35 5QJ
Tel: 013397 55759 Fax: 013397 55993
Email: info@inverdeen.com
Web: www.inverdeen.com
3 bedrs SB £22 DB £40
CC: MC Vi Swi Delt
🎄 ⊗ ⊜ ▭ P ⚗
How to get there: At bridge junction coming
from Aberdeen, with village on right, Inverdeen
is opposite the junction.

Scotland

Raemoir House Hotel

This splendid country mansion is set in an idyllic 3,500 acre estate, and situated on beautiful Royal Deeside.
Twenty bedrooms, all ensuite, some with four-poster beds, conference facilities, tennis courts and golf course.

Raemoir House, Raemoir, Banchory
AB31 4ED
Tel: 01330 824884   Fax: 01330 822171
Email: raemoirhse@aol.com

The Burnett Arms Hotel

Historic coaching inn ideally situated for touring Royal Deeside and the northeast of Scotland. 18 miles from Aberdeen and 16 miles from Dyce International Airport (ABZ).

Facilities include two function suites, restaurant, two bars. Surrounding area of Scotland renowned for its breathtaking beauty and golf courses. Golf nearby.

Weekend rates available

25 High Street, Banchory AB31 5TD
Tel: 01330 824944   Fax: 01330 825553
Email: theburnett@totalise.co.uk
Website: www.burnettarms.co.uk

Banchory, Aberdeenshire

28 Banchory Lodge Hotel
Blue Ribbon Winner

★★★ ♛ ♛ ♛
Dee Street, Banchory, Aberdeenshire, AB31 5HS
Tel: 01330 822625 Fax: 01330 825019
Email: banchorylodgeht@btconnect.com
Web: www.banchorylodge.co.uk
Closed two weeks in January

Situated five minutes from Banchory town centre, a Georgian country house hotel in a picturesque and tranquil riverside setting beside the River Dee.
22 bedrs SB £55 DB £90 HBS £70 HBD £55
B £10 L £12.50 D £25
CC: MC Vi Am DC Swi
♿ ⊠ ☎ ⊗ ⊜ ▯ ☎ Ⓟ ● ✗ ✴ ⋔ ♥ ⊞ ⋔ (◄
How to get there: 18 miles inland from Aberdeen. Follow A96 road to Banchory. Left at traffic lights. Signs at end of driveway.

29 Raemoir House Hotel
Blue Ribbon Winner

★★★★ ♛ ♛ ♛
Banchory, Aberdeenshire, AB31 4ED
Tel: 01330 824884 Fax: 01330 822171
Email: raemoirhse@aol.com
Web: www.raemoir.com
20 bedrs SB £60 DB £90 HBS £75 HBD £65
B £10.50 L £5 D £24.50
CC: MC Vi Am DC Swi
◑ ♿ ⊠ ☎ ⊗ ▯ ☎ Ⓟ ● ✗ ✴ ⋔ ♥ ⊞ ⋔ ⊾ ⎍
How to get there: 20 miles west of Aberdeen. From A93 to Banchory, turn right onto A980 Torphins road. After 1½ miles, hotel is opposite T-junction.
See advert above left

30 Burnett Arms Hotel

★★

25 High Street, Banchory,
Aberdeenshire, AB31 5TD
Tel: 01330 824944 Fax: 01330 835553
Email: theburnett@totalise.co.uk
Web: www.burnettarms.co.uk
16 bedrs SB £41 DB £56 HBS £47 HBD £34
B £6 L £8 D £15
CC: MC Vi Am DC Swi Delt

How to get there: On A93 west of Aberdeen in Banchory town centre. Northern side of street.
See advert on facing page

See advert on facing page

Barrhead, East Renfrewshire

31 Dalmeny Park Country House Hotel

★★★★ ₰

Lochilbo Road, Barrhead, Strathclyde, G78 1LG
Tel: 0141 881 9211 Fax: 0141 881 9214
Email: enquiries@maksu-group.co.uk
Web: www.maksu-group.co.uk
20 bedrs SB £70 DB £95 HBS £85 HBD £60
B £6.50 L £9.50 D £14
CC: MC Vi Am DC Swi Delt

How to get there: Follow A736 through Barrhead towards Irvine. Hotel is on the left as you leave Barrhead.

Beauly, Highland

32 Lovat Arms Hotel

★★★★ ₰

Main Street, Beauly, Highland, IV4 7BS
Tel: 01463 782313 Fax: 01463 782862
Email: lovat.arms@cali.co.uk
Web: www.lovatarms.com
28 bedrs SB £39 DB £80 HBS £60 HBD £55
B £6 L £8 D £8
CC: MC Vi DC Swi Delt JCB

How to get there: Take A9 to Inverness, crossing Kessock Bridge. Stay on A9 till Tore roundabout. Take first left on A832 to Muir of Ord, left on A862 to Beauly, hotel at end of square.
See advert right

See advert right

33 Heathmount Guest House

♦♦♦♦ ✍

Station Road, Beauly, Highland, IV4 7EQ
Tel: 01463 782411
Closed Christmas and New Year
5 bedrs SB £20 DB £40 CC: MC Vi

How to get there: 20m from post office on main road through Beauly village.

Biggar, South Lanarkshire

34 Shieldhill Hotel

★★★ ₰ ₰ ₰

Quothquan, Biggar,
South Lanarkshire, ML12 6NA
Tel: 01899 220035
Fax: 01899 221092
Email: enquiries@shieldhill.co.uk
Web: www.shieldhill.co.uk
16 bedrs CC: MC Vi Swi Delt

How to get there: From Biggar take B7016 towards Carnwath. After 3 miles turn left into Shieldhill Road, Castle is 1½ miles on the right.

Scotland

Lovat Arms Hotel

Our Taste of Scotland Kitchen provides an excellent variety of cuisine, much of it produced on our own farm. Our bedrooms are all furnished in clan tartans which adds to the family atmosphere. The Garden and Ceilidh rooms provide excellent areas for small meetings and functions for up to about 60 people.

Beauly, Nr. Inverness IV4 7BS
Tel: 01463 782313   Fax: 01463 782862
Email: lovat.arms@cali.co.uk
Website: www.lovatarms.com

Blairgowrie, Perth & Kinross

35 Angus Hotel

★★★
46 Wellmeadow, Blairgowrie,
Perth & Kinross, PH10 6NQ
Tel: 01250 872455 Fax: 01250 875615
Email: reception@theangushotel.com
Web: www.theangushotel.com
81 bedrs SB £45 DB £90 HBS £65 HBD £55
B £9 L £5 D £18.95 CC: MC Vi Am Swi Delt

How to get there: Situated in the centre of
Blairgowrie on the A93.

Bonar Bridge, Highland

36 Kyle House

♦ ♦ ♦
Dornoch Road, Bonar Bridge, Highland, IV24 3EB
Tel: 01863 766360 Fax: 01863 766360
Email: kyle.hse.@talk21.com
Children minimum age: 4
Closed November to January
6 bedrs SB £20 DB £40 CC: None accepted

How to get there: On A949, fourth house past
newsagents on left northbound. Fourth house
on right entering village from east side.

Bothwell, South Lanarkshire

37 Bothwell Bridge Hotel

★★★
89 Main Street, Bothwell,
South Lanarkshire, G71 8EU
Tel: 01698 852246 Fax: 01698 854686
Email: bothwell-bridge@hotmail.com
Web: www.bothwellbridge-hotel.com

90 bedrs SB £59.50 DB £69.50 L £12 D £14.50
CC: MC Vi Am DC Swi

Braemar, Aberdeenshire

38 Invercauld Arms

★★★
Braemar, Aberdeenshire, AB35 5YR
Tel: 01339 741605 Fax: 01339 741428
68 bedrs SB £85 DB £110 B £9 L £4
CC: MC Vi Am DC Swi Delt

Campbeltown, Argyll & Bute

39 Seafield Hotel

★★★ ☺
Kilkerran Road, Campbeltown,
Argyll & Bute, PA28 6JL
Tel: 01586 554385 Fax: 01586 552741
Web: www.the.seafield.co.uk
9 bedrs SB £50 DB £80 B £8.50 L £5.50 D £15
CC: MC Vi Am Swi
How to get there: From A83 follow signs for
Ballycastle ferry terminal then follow road
around loch for about 500m.

40 Dunvalanree

♦ ♦ ♦ ♦ ♦ ☺ ☺ ☀ ☜
Port Righ, Carradale, Campbeltown,
Argyll & Bute, PA28 6SE
Tel: 01583 431226 Fax: 01583 431339
Email: bookin@dunvalanree.com
Web: www.dunvalanree.com

Dunvalanree is between Port Righ and
Carradale bays and offers the best of local
produce in the dining room after which you can
fall asleep to the sound of the sea.
7 bedrs SB £22 DB £54 HBS £37 HBD £42.50
B £10 D £15 CC: MC Vi Am Swi Delt JCB
How to get there: From Tarbert take A83
towards Campbeltown. Turn left onto B8001
towards Skipness. After 20 miles in Carradale
turn left then right after the bus stop.

41 Westbank Guesthouse

Dell Road, Campbeltown,
Argyll & Bute, PA28 6JG
Tel: 01586 553660 Fax: 01586 553660
7 bedrs
CC: MC Vi Delt

How to get there: Follow signs to Heritage
Centre. 30m past centre travelling in Southend
direction, turn right into Dell Road.

Carnoustie, Angus

42 Letham Grange Hotel

Colliston, Angus, DD11 4RL
Tel: 01241 890373 Fax: 01241 890725
Email: lethamgrange@sol.co.uk
Web: www.lethamgrange.co.uk
42 bedrs
CC: MC Vi Am DC Swi Delt

How to get there: Take A92 to Arbroath, and
then the A933 towards Brechin. Take first right
after Colliston for Letham Grange (follow tourist
board signs).

Castle Douglas, Dumfries & Galloway

43 Douglas Arms Hotel

King Street, Castle Douglas,
Dumfries & Galloway, DG7 1DB
Tel: 01556 502231 Fax: 01556 504000
Email: doughot@aol.com
24 bedrs
CC: MC Vi Am Swi Delt

How to get there: In centre of town on the main
street and close to the town clock tower.

44 Kings Arms Hotel

St. Andrews Street, Castle Douglas,
Dumfries & Galloway, DG7 1EL
Tel: 01556 502626 Fax: 01556 502097
Email: david@galloway-golf.co.uk
Web: www.galloway-golf.co.uk
10 bedrs SB £37 DB £58 HBS £45 HBD £78
B £5.50 L £7.50 D £12.50
CC: MC Vi Swi Delt

How to get there: From A75 turn off at sign for
Castle Douglas. Go down main street to town
clock, turn left. Hotel 100 yards on left.

45 Craigadam
Little Gem

Craigadam, Kirkpatrick Durham, Castle
Douglas, Dumfries & Galloway, DG7 3HU
Tel: 01556 650233 Fax: 01556 650233
Email: inquiry@craigadam.com
Web: www.craigadam.com
11 bedrs SB £40 DB £60
HBS £55 HBD £45 B £5 D £15
CC: MC Vi Swi Delt JCB

How to get there: Leave Dumfries on A75
towards Castle Douglas. At Crocketford (10
miles) turn onto A712: property is two miles on
the right.

Coldstream, Scottish Borders

46 St. Albans

Clouds, Duns, Scottish Borders, TD11 3BB
Tel: 01361 883285 Fax: 01361 884534
Email: st_albans@email.msn.com
Web: www.scotlandbordersbandb.co.uk
Children minimum age: 12

Comfortable, elegant four diamond
accommodation in Georgian house in quiet
small town. Furnished to blend with period.
Walled garden. Varied breakfasts. TV in rooms.
Excellent touring centre. One hour from
Edinburgh.
3 bedrs SB £28 DB £48
CC: MC Vi DC Delt

How to get there: Clouds is a lane immediately
behind the police station which is situated in
Newtown street.

Scotland

Crieff, Perth & Kinross

47 Locke's Acre Hotel

★★

Comrie Road, Crieff, Perth & Kinross, PH7 4BP
Tel: 01764 652526 Fax: 01764 652526
Closed February
6 bedrs SB £30 DB £56 HBS £45 HBD £86
B £6.50 L £5.95 D £7.95
CC: MC Vi Swi Delt

How to get there: Take A9 north, towards Perth.
After Dunblane cut-off, take A822 to Crieff. In
Crieff, take A85 to Comrie, Lochearnhead Road.

48 Gwydyr House Hotel

◆◆◆◆®

Comrie Road, Crieff, Perth & Kinross, PH7 4BP
Tel: 01764 653277 Fax: 01764 653277
Email: george.blackie@iclweb.com
Web: www.smoothhound.co.uk/
        hotels/gwydyr.html
8 bedrs
CC: MC Vi

How to get there: Situated on the A85 Comrie
Road, going west from Crieff, opposite
MacRosty Park.

Crinan, Argyll & Bute

49 Crinan Hotel

★★★★®®®

By Lochgilphead, Crinan,
Argyll & Bute, PA31 8SR
Tel: 01546 830261 Fax: 01546 830292
Email: hryan@crinanhotel.com
Web: www.crinanhotel.com
19 bedrs SB £85 DB £150 HBS £115 HBD £115
B £12.50 L £7.50 D £40
CC: MC Vi Am Swi Delt

Dalmally, Argyll & Bute

50 Rockhill Farm & Guest House

◆◆◆

Rockhill, Ardbrecknish, Dalmally,
Argyll & Bute, PA33 1BH
Tel: 01866 833218

Denny, Falkirk

51 Topps Guest House

◆◆◆®

Topps Farm, Fintry Road, Denny, Falkirk, FK6 5JF
Tel: 01324 822471 Fax: 01324 823099
Email: 2lambs@onetel.net.uk
Web: www.thetopps.com

Scottish farmers Alistair and Jennifer welcome
you to their bungalow farmhouse. Stunning
panoramic views. 'Taste of Scotland' food is our
speciality. Disabled access to the house.
8 bedrs SB £32 DB £46 B £4.50 D £12
CC: MC Vi

How to get there: From Glasgow, A80, A803 to
Denny, then B818, hotel four miles on right.
From Edinburgh, M9, M876, off at Denny sign,
right at lights, third right onto B818.

Dornoch, Highland

52 Dornoch Castle Hotel

✜

Castle Street, Dornoch, Highland, IV25 3SD
Tel: 01862 810216 Fax: 01862 810981

Drymen, Stirling

53 Buchanan Arms Hotel and Leisure Club

★★★®

Main Street, Drymen, Stirling, G63 0BQ
Tel: 01360 660588 Fax: 01360 660943
Email: enquiries@buchananarms.co.uk
Web: www.innscotland.com
52 bedrs HBS £70 HBD £70 L £7 D £22
CC: MC Vi Am DC Swi Delt JCB

How to get there: From Glasgow take A8
Aberfoyle road. At Bearsden cros roundabout,
take A809 to Drymen, signposted from then on.

Dumfries, Dumfries & Galloway

54 Cairndale Hotel

★★★

English Street, Dumfries,
Dumfries & Galloway, DG1 2DF
Tel: 01387 254111 Fax: 01387 250555
Email: sales@cairndale.fsnet.co.uk
Web: www.cairndalehotel.co.uk

Excellent leisure facilities. Regular weekend
entertainment (dinner dances, Ceilidhs, cabaret
nights) and conference facilities make the
Cairndale the number one choice in Dumfries.
Golfers particularly welcome.
91 bedrs SB £85 DB £105 HBS £69.50
HBD £49.50 B £6 L £8.95 D £20
CC: MC Vi Am DC Swi Delt
⬧ ♿ 🕮 ⬧ 🐕 ⊗ ◔ ▢ ☎ 🅿 ♨ ℃ ♒ 💈 ♨ ⚏ ⚌
🇹 🔳
How to get there: Following main routes into
Dumfries, the hotel is on the northeast edge of
the town centre on English Street.

55 Comlongon Castle Hotel

★★★★ 🐾

Clarencefield, Dumfries & Galloway, DG1 4NA
Tel: 01387 870283 Fax: 01387 870266
Web: www.comlongon.com
Closed January
12 bedrs SB £80 DB £110 HBS £113 HBD £88
L £8.50 D £33
CC: MC Vi Am DC Swi
⬧ 🕮 ⊗ ◔ ▢ ☎ 🅿 ♨ ♒ ♨ ⚏ ⚌
How to get there: At England/Scotland border,
take A75 to Annan, then left onto B724. After
eight miles, at Clarencefield turn left down
private drive.

Making a booking?

Don't forget to mention RAC
Hotels and Bed & Breakfast 2002.

56 Hetland Hall Hotel

★★★

Carrutherstown, Dumfries & Galloway, DG1 4JX
Tel: 01387 840201 Fax: 01387 840211
Email: hetlandhallhotel@ic.24.net
Web: www.hetlandhallhotel.ic.24.net

Elegant mansion with glorious views over the
Solway Firth. Pool and leisure club. Mini pitch-
and-putt, satellite TV, superb food, intimate
cocktail bar. Log fires. Ideal for weddings and
short breaks.
30 bedrs SB £58 DB £75 HBS £73 HBD £49.50
B £8.75 L £8.50 D £19.95
CC: MC Vi Am DC Swi Delt
⬧ ♿ 🕮 🐕 ⊗ ◔ ▢ ☎ 🅿 ♨ ℃ ♒ 💈 ♨ ⚏ ⚌ 🇹
🔳
How to get there: On A75 Euroroute, eight miles
east of Dumfries.

57 Huntingdon House Hotel

★★

18 St. Mary's Street, Dumfries,
Dumfries & Galloway, DG1 1LZ
Tel: 01387 254893 Fax: 01387 262553
Email: acame4506@aol.com
Web: www.huntingdonhotel.co.uk
8 bedrs SB £40 DB £59 B £7.95 L £8.95 D £9.95
CC: MC Vi Am DC Swi Delt
⬧ 🐕 ◔ ▢ ☎ 🅿 ♨ ♒ ♨ ⚏ ⚌
How to get there: Travel on M74 to Lockerbie;
take A709 to Dumfries; hotel is first on the left
on entering Dumfries.

58 Travelodge Dumfries

Travel Accommodation
A75, Annan Road, Collin,
Dumfries & Galloway, DG1 3SE
Tel: 08700 850 950
Web: www.travelodge.co.uk
40 bedrs B £4.25
CC: MC Vi Am DC Swi Delt
🐕 ◔ ▢ ♨

Scotland

Dunbar, East Lothian

59 Bayswell Hotel

★★★

Bayswell Park, Dunbar, East Lothian, EH42 1AE
Tel: 01368 862225 Fax: 01368 862225
Email: bayswellhotel@hotmail.com
Web: www.geocities.com/bayswell
18 bedrs SB £58 DB £79 HBS £67.50 HBD £52
B £6.50 L £8.50 D £12.50
CC: MC Vi Am DC Swi Delt JCB

How to get there: Exit the A1 into Dunbar High
Street. At the bottom, turn left (sea on right).
Take the first right to hotel.
See advert on facing page

Dundee

60 Swallow Hotel

★★★★

Kingsway West, Dundee, DD2 5JT
Tel: 01382 641122 Fax: 01382 568340
105 bedrs SB £98 DB £118 HBS £118 HBD £79
B £9.75 L £6 D £22
CC: MC Vi Am DC Swi

How to get there: Off the A90 four miles from
city centre, two miles from Dundee airport.

61 Travelodge Dundee

Travel Accommodation
A90, Kingsway, Dundee Ring Road, Dundee,
Tayside, DD2 4TD
Tel: 08700 850 950
Web: www.travelodge.co.uk
32 bedrs B £4.25
CC: MC Vi Am DC Swi Delt

62 Beach House Hotel

♦♦♦♦

22 Esplanade, Broughty Ferry, Dundee, DD5 2EQ
Tel: 01382 776614 Fax: 01382 420841
5 bedrs SB £38 DB £48
CC: MC Vi JCB

How to get there: From Dundee station, four
miles. 25 minutes drive from St. Andrews, one
hour drive from Edinburgh, one hour 45 minutes
from Aberdeen.

Dunfermline, Fife

63 Elgin Hotel

★★★

Charlestown, Dunfermline, Fife, KY11 3EE
Tel: 01383 872257 Fax: 01383 873044
CC: None accepted

64 King Malcolm Hotel

★★★

Queensferry Road, Wester Pitchorthie,
Dunfermline, Fife, KY11 8DS
Tel: 01383 722611 Fax: 01383 730865
Email: info@kingmalcolm-hotel-dunfermline.com
Web: www.peelhotel.com
48 bedrs SB £90.25 DB £130.50 HBS £106.75
HBD £81.25 B £8.95 L £9.95 D £16.50
CC: MC Vi Am DC Swi Delt

How to get there: Leave M90 at Junction 2.
Take A823 to Dunfermline. Follow A823 and at
third roundabout hotel is situated on right.

65 Pitbauchlie House Hotel

★★★

47 Aberdour Road, Dunfermline,
Fife, KY11 4PB
Tel: 01383 722282 Fax: 01383 620738
Email: info@pitbauchlie.com
Web: www.pitbauchlie.com

Situated in landscaped gardens, minutes from
M90. Conference, banqueting, bars and
restaurant facilities. Excellent food with the chef
taking advantage of Scotland's natural larder.
50 bedrs SB £73 DB £90
B £9 L £11.50 D £22
CC: MC Vi Am DC Swi Delt

How to get there: Leave M90 at Junction 2.
Continue on A823 towards Dunfermline. Turn
right onto B916. Hotel situated 1/2 mile on right.

The Bayswell Hotel

The Bayswell enjoys a stunning location with unrivalled sea views over the Firth of Forth. The hotel is family-owned and is renowned for its friendly hospitality.

On special occasions, our deluxe rooms with jacuzzi baths, power showers, televisions in the bathrooms and sea views are a must. For guests staying on business, we have rooms with desks and computer points. Fax facilities and colour photocopying are available. Two well-stocked bars and a restaurant with beautiful sea views are just the place to relax. We have 18 golf courses nearby. Dunbar is on the A1, with Edinburgh only 30 minutes by car or 20 minutes by train.

Bayswell Hotel, Bayswell Park
Dunbar, East Lothian EH42 1AE
Tel/Fax: 01368 862225
bayswellhotel@hotmail.com   www.geocities.com/bayswell

66 Halfway House Hotel

Main Street, Kingseat, Dunfermline,
Fife, KY12 0TJ
Tel: 01383 731661 Fax: 01383 621274
12 bedrs SB £45 DB £52 HBS £55 HBD £36
L £3 D £5
CC: MC Vi Swi Delt JCB

Dunkeld, Perth & Kinross

67 Kinnaird

Gold Ribbon Winner

Kinnaird Estate, by Dunkeld,
Perth & Kinross, PH8 0LB
Tel: 01796 482440 Fax: 01796 482289
Email: enquiry@kinnairdestate.com
Web: www.kinnairdestate.com
Children minimum age: 12
9 bedrs HBS £300 HBD £345 B £15 L £30
D £45
CC: MC Vi Am Swi

How to get there: Travel north on A9 past Perth
and Dunkeld. Turn left onto B893. Hotel is four
miles along on right.

Dunoon, Argyll & Bute

68 Argyll Hotel

Argyll Street, Dunoon, Argyll & Bute, PA23 7NE
Tel: 01369 702059 Fax: 01369 704483
Email: info@argyll-hotel.co.uk
Web: www.argyll-hotel.co.uk
33 bedrs
CC: MC Vi Am DC Swi Delt

How to get there: From Glasgow, take M8 to
Gourock for ferry to Dunoon. Hotel situated
overlooking town's bandstand area and Firth of
Clyde.

69 Esplanade Hotel

West Bay, Dunoon, Argyll & Bute, PA23 7HU
Tel: 01369 704070 Fax: 01369 702129
Email: relax@ehd.co.uk
Web: www.ehd.co.uk
Closed November to March

Long-established, award-winning family-run
hotel situated on the traffic-free West Bay.
Overlooking the River Clyde with easy access to
the Western Highlands.
63 bedrs SB £41 DB £72 HBS £54 HBD £53
B £5.75 L £6.25 D £15.50
CC: MC Vi DC Swi Delt

70 The Anchorage Hotel & Restaurant

Shore Road, Ardnadam, Sandbank, Dunoon,
Argyll & Bute, PA23 8QG
Tel: 01369 705108 Fax: 01369 705108

71 Ardtully Hotel

297 Marine Parade, Hunters Quay, Dunoon,
Argyll & Bute, PA23 8HN
Tel: 01369 702478
9 bedrs SB £30 DB £60 HBS £47.50
HBD £47.50
CC: None accepted

How to get there: On the coast road between
Dunoon and Sandbank, two miles from Dunoon
overlooking the Firth of Clyde at Hunters Quay.
200 yards from the Western Ferry Terminal.

72 Osborne Hotel

44 Shore Road, Innellan, near Dunoon,
Argyll & Bute, PA23 7TJ
Tel: 01369 830445 Fax: 01369 830445
Email: info@osborne-hotel.co.uk
Web: www.osborne-hotel.co.uk
4 bedrs SB £24.50 DB £45 B £3.50 L £5.50
D £7.50 CC: MC Vi Delt

How to get there: Take ferry from Gourock to
Dunoon, turn left, Innellan is four miles along
the coast; or, via Loch Lomond onto A815.

East Kilbride, Lanarkshire

73 Bruce Hotel

★★★
35 Cornwall Street, East Kilbride,
Lanarkshire, G74 1AF
Tel: 01355 229711 Fax: 01355 242216
Email: enquiries@maksu-group.co.uk
Web: www.maksu-group.co.uk
65 bedrs SB £75 DB £95 B £7.50 L £8 D £16.50
CC: MC Vi Am DC Swi Delt

How to get there: Leave M74 at Junction 5. Take
A725 to East Kilbride. Follow signs to town
centre into Cornwall Street, hotel is 200m on left.

Edinburgh

74 Balmoral Hotel

★★★★★
1 Princes Street, Edinburgh, EH2 2EQ
Tel: 0131 556 2414 Fax: 0131 557 3747
Email: reservations@thebalmoralhotel.com
Web: www.rfhotels.com
188 bedrs SB £219 DB £263 HBS £244
HBD £156.50 B £16.75 L £25 D £25
CC: MC Vi Am DC Swi

How to get there: Follow signs to city centre
and Waverley rail station. The Balmoral is
adjacent to the station.

75 The Scotsman

★★★★★
20 North Bridge, Edinburgh, EH1 1YT
Tel: 0131 556 5565 Fax: 0131 652 3652
Email: reservations@thescotsmanhotel.co.uk
Web: www.thescotsmanhotel.co.uk
68 bedrs SB £164 DB £179 B £15
CC: MC Vi Am DC Swi Delt JCB

How to get there: Next to Waverley train station.

76 Carlton Hotel

★★★★
North Bridge, Edinburgh, EH1 1SD
Tel: 0131 472 3000 Fax: 0131 556 2691
Email: carlton@paramount-hotels.co.uk
Web: www.paramount-hotels.co.uk
189 bedrs B £10 L £12 D £15
CC: MC Vi Am DC Swi Delt

How to get there: Follow signs for Waverley train
station; hotel is situated above north bridge.

77 Marriott Dalmahoy Hotel & Country Club

★★★★★
Near Kirknewton, Edinburgh, EH27 8EB
Tel: 0131 3331845 Fax: 0131 3331433
Email: reservations.dalmahoy
@marriotthotels.com
Web: www.marriott.com/edigs
215 bedrs CC: MC Vi Am DC Swi Delt JCB

78 Royal Terrace Hotel

★★★★
18 Royal Terrace, Edinburgh, EH7 5AQ
Tel: 0131 557 3222 Fax: 0131 557 5339
Email: reservations.royalterrace
@principalhotels.co.uk
108 bedrs SB £135 DB £170
HBS £155 HBD £105
CC: MC Vi Am Swi Delt

How to get there: Northeast from Princes Street,
located off Leith Walk, eight miles from airport,
1/2 mile from Waverley Station on Royal Terrace.

79 Swallow Royal Scot Hotel

★★★★
111 Glasgow Road, Edinburgh, EH12 8NF
Tel: 0131 334 9191 Fax: 0131 316 4507
Email: edinburgh@marriotthotels.com
Web: www.marriotthotels.co.uk
245 bedrs SB £125 DB £145 B £10 L £14 D £19
CC: MC Vi Am Swi

How to get there: Situated next to Gyle
shopping centre and Gogar roundabout on A8
two miles south-west of Edinburgh airport at
end of M8 and A720

80 Barnton Hotel

★★★
562 Queensferry Road, Edinburgh, EH4 6AS
Tel: 0131 339 1144 Fax: 0131 339 5521
50 bedrs
CC: MC Vi Am DC Swi Delt

How to get there: From M8/M9 take A8, then
A902 (Maybury Road). Turn into Queensferry
Road, Barnton on left.

Scotland

81 Braid Hills Hotel

★★★★ ☕ ☕

134 Braid Road, Edinburgh, EH10 6JD
Tel: 0131 447 8888 Fax: 0131 452 8477
Email: bookings@braidhillshotel.co.uk
Web: www.braidhillshotel.co.uk

Magnificently situated only two miles from the city centre, yet a world away from the noise and congestion of the centre itself. An independently owned hotel.
67 bedrs SB £80 DB £135 HBS £95
HBD £82.50 B £8.95 L £8 D £16.95
CC: MC Vi Am DC Swi Delt

How to get there: From city bypass take A702 Lothianburn junction to city centre. Hotel is approximately one mile on right-hand side.

82 Carlton Greens Hotel

★★★ ☕

2 Carlton Terrace, Edinburgh, EH7 5DD
Tel: 0131 556 6570 Fax: 0131 557 6680
Email: carltongreens@british-trust-hotels.com
Web: www.british-trust-hotels.com

Elegant yet friendly accommodation. Quiet location. Few minutes' walk from city centre. Magnificent views across Royal Park and Holyrood Palace. Excellent bar and restaurant. All rooms ensuite.
26 bedrs SB £45 DB £80 HBS £57.50
HBD £52.50 B £8 L £9 D £15
CC: MC Vi DC Swi Delt

83 Johnstounburn House

★★★★ ☕ ☕

Near Dalkeith, Humbie, Edinburgh, EH35 5PL
Tel: 01875 833696 Fax: 01875 833626
20 bedrs
CC: MC Vi Am DC Swi Delt

How to get there: From A68 take B6368, signposted Haddington. Hotel on right.

84 Jurys Inn Edinburgh

★★★

43 Jeffrey Street, Edinburgh, EH1 1DG
Tel: +353(0)1 6070000 Fax: +353(0)1 6316999
Email: bookings@jurysdoyle.com
Web: www.jurysdoyle.com
186 bedrs B £8 L £4.95 D £16
CC: MC Vi Am DC Swi

How to get there: Located nine miles from airport. Just two minutes walk from Waverley Station.

85 Norton House Hotel

Blue Ribbon Winner

★★★★ ☕ ☕ ☕

Ingliston, Edinburgh, EH28 8LX
Tel: 0131 333 1275 Fax: 0131 333 5305
Email: events.nhh@arcadianhotels.co.uk
Web: www.arcadianhotels.co.uk

One of Edinburgh's most stylish country house hotels. Rest assured that a traditional atmosphere without a trace of stuffiness is flawlessly maintained, offering a rare combination of care and comfort.

47 bedrs SB £135 DB £160 HBS £150 HBD £95 B £12.50 L £15.50 D £28
CC: MC Vi Am DC Swi Delt

How to get there: From Edinburgh, take A8 past the airport. Norton House is ½ mile on the left.

86 Old Waverley Hotel

★★★

43 Princes Street, Edinburgh, EH2 2BY
Tel: 0131 556 4648 Fax: 0131 557 6316
Email: oldwaverleyreservations
@paramount-hotels.co.uk
Web: www.paramount-hotels.co.uk
66 bedrs SB £129 DB £169 HBS £145
HBD £92.50 B £9.50 L £3.50 D £9.95
CC: MC Vi Am DC Swi

How to get there: Follow signs to city centre and Waverley Station. Directly opposite Waverley Station & Scott's Monument.

87 Quality Hotel Edinburgh

★★★

Cramond Foreshore, Edinburgh, EH4 5EP
Tel: 0131 336 1700 Fax: 0131 336 4934
Email: admin@gb625.u-net.com
Web: www.choicehotels.com
87 bedrs SB £99.95 DB £109.95 HBS £116.25
HBD £63.13 B £10.95 D £16.30
CC: MC Vi Am DC Swi Delt

88 Allison House Hotel

★★★ ₪

15/17 Mayfield Gardens, Edinburgh, EH9 2AX
Tel: 0131 667 8049 Fax: 0131 667 5001
Email: enquiry@allisonhousehotel.com
Web: www.allisonhousehotel.com
21 bedrs
CC: MC Vi Am DC Swi Delt

How to get there: Situated on the south side of Edinburgh, one mile from city centre on A701.

89 Orwell Lodge Hotel

★★

29 Polwarth Terrace, Edinburgh, EH11 1NH
Tel: 0131 229 1044 Fax: 0131 228 9492
10 bedrs SB £49 DB £75 B £5 L £4 D £12
CC: MC Vi Am Swi

How to get there: From A702 turn into Gilmore Place (opposite Kings Theatre). Hotel is one mile on left.

90 Royal Ettrick Hotel

★★

13 Ettrick Road, Edinburgh, EH10 5BJ
Tel: 0131 622 6800 Fax: 0131 622 6822
Email: ettrick@festival-inns.co.uk
Web: www.festival-inns.co.uk
12 bedrs SB £70 DB £90
CC: MC Vi Am DC Swi Delt JCB

How to get there: From centre, drive up Lothian Road. Turn right on to Gilmore Place. Continue on to Polwarth Gardens. Hotel is on the left.

91 Thrums Hotel

★★ ₪

14 Minto Street, Edinburgh, EH9 1RQ
Tel: 0131 667 5545 Fax: 0131 667 8707
Closed Christmas
14 bedrs SB £35 DB £80 HBS £45 HBD £47.50
B £4.50 L £7.50 D £11.50
CC: MC Vi

How to get there: Follow city bypass to Edinburgh South, then take A7/A701 to Newington.

92 Travelodge Edinburgh (Central)

Travel Accommodation
33 St. Marys Street, Edinburgh, EH1 1TA
Tel: 08700 850 950
Web: www.travelodge.co.uk
193 bedrs B £4.25 CC: MC Vi Am DC Swi Delt

93 Travelodge Edinburgh (East)

Travel Accommodation
A1, Old Craighall, Musselburgh,
Edinburgh, EH21 8RE
Tel: 08700 850 950
Web: www.travelodge.co.uk
45 bedrs B £4.25 CC: MC Vi Am DC Swi Delt

Scotland

94 Travelodge Edinburgh (South)

Travel Accommodation
A720, 46 Dreghorn Link, City Bypass,
Edinburgh, EH13 9QR
Tel: 08700 850 950
Web: www.travelodge.co.uk
72 bedrs B £4.25
CC: MC Vi Am DC Swi Delt

95 Grosvenor Gardens Hotel

◆ ◆ ◆ ◆ ◆ ✖ 🛏
1 Grosvenor Gardens, Edinburgh, EH12 5JU
Tel: 0131 313 3415 Fax: 0131 346 8732
Email: info@stayinedinburgh.com
Web: www.stayinedinburgh.com
8 bedrs SB £40 DB £50
CC: MC Vi Swi Delt

How to get there: Follow A8 from the airport
towards the city centre. Turn left off the A8
(Haymarket Terrace) into Roseberry Crescent.
Grosvenor Gardens is the first street on the left.

96 Lodge Hotel

◆ ◆ ◆ ◆ ◆ ✖ 🛏
6 Hampton Terrace, West Coates,
Edinburgh, EH12 5JD
Tel: 0131 337 3682 Fax: 0131 313 1700
Email: thelodgehotel@btconnect.com
Web: www.thelodgehotel.co.uk

Exclusive West End hotel offering finest quality
accommodation and cuisine. Open fires in
sumptuous lounge and cosy cocktail bar.
Beautifully appointed non-smoking bedrooms.
Car parking.
10 bedrs SB £45 DB £60 B £7.50 D £18.50
CC: MC Vi Am Swi Delt
How to get there: Located on main A8, one mile
west from city centre and railway station. Only
three miles east from Edinburgh airport.

97 Acorn Lodge

◆ ◆ ◆ ◆ 🛏
26 Pilrig Street, Edinburgh, Lothian, EH6 5AJ
Tel: 0131 555 1557 Fax: 0131 555 4475
Email: morag@acornlodge.co.uk
Web: www.acornlodge.co.uk
10 bedrs SB £30 DB £60
CC: MC Vi Am Swi Delt JCB
How to get there: Follow Queens St. in city
centre to top of Leith Walk (East End). Pilrig St.
to left midway down Leith walk.

98 Adam Hotel

◆ ◆ ◆ ◆
19 Lansdowne Crescent, Edinburgh,
Lothian, EH12 5EH
Tel: 0131 337 1148
Email: welcome@adam-hotel.co.uk
Web: www.adam-hotel.co.uk
13 bedrs SB £30 DB £60
CC: MC Vi Am Swi Delt
How to get there: Follow signs for city centre then
to Haymarket Station. Turn up Roseberry
Crescent and fork right into Lansdowne Crescent.

99 Ashlyn Guest House

◆ ◆ ◆ ◆ ✖
42 Inverleith Row, Edinburgh, EH3 5PY
Tel: 0131 552 2954 Fax: 0131 552 2954
Email: reservations@ashlyn-edinburgh.com
Children minimum age: 7
8 bedrs SB £30 DB £70 CC: None accepted

100 Corstorphine Guest House

◆ ◆ ◆ ◆ 🛏
188 St. Johns Road, Edinburgh, EH12 8SG
Tel: 0131 539 4237 Fax: 0131 539 4945
Email: corsthouse@aol.com
Web: www.corstorphineguesthouse.com

Impressive Victorian villa centrally located providing excellent accommodation for a comfortable and relaxed holiday. Excellent amenities. Choice of breakfast, large landscaped gardens. Free parking. Graded three stars STB.

5 bedrs SB £25 DB £39 B £4.95
CC: MC Vi Swi Delt

How to get there: From airport: head for city along A8 into Corstorphine. From city, out on A8 towards airport.

101 Dorstan Hotel
Little Gem

7 Priestfield Road, Edinburgh, EH16 5HJ
Tel: 0131 667 5138 Fax: 0131 668 4644
Email: reservations@dorstan-hotel.demon.co.uk
Web: www.dorstan-hotel.demon.co.uk

Located close to the city centre's many attractions, this tastefully-decorated Victorian house exudes the warm hospitality of its proprietor Mairae Campbell.

14 bedrs SB £32 DB £72 D £17
CC: MC Vi Am Swi Delt

102 Frederick House Hotel

42 Frederick Street, Edinburgh, EH2 1EX
Tel: 0131 226 1999 Fax: 0131 624 7064
Email: frederickhouse@ednet.co.uk
Web: www.townhousehotels.co.uk
Children minimum age: 15

44 bedrs SB £30 DB £50 B £5
CC: MC Vi Am

How to get there: Left from Waverley Station onto Princes Street. Frederick Street is a ten minute walk, third on the right.

103 Ivy Guest House

7 Mayfield Gardens, Edinburgh, EH9 2AX
Tel: 0131 667 3411 Fax: 0131 620 1422
Email: don@ivyguesthouse.com
Web: www.ivyguesthouse.com

Victorian villa; open all year; close to city centre. All rooms have central heating; ensuite or standard rooms, public phone, from £20 per person. Free parking; warm welcome assured.

8 bedrs CC: None accepted

How to get there: Located on A701 just over one mile from Princes Street.

104 Kew House

1 Kew Terrace, Murrayfield, Edinburgh, EH12 5JE
Tel: 0131 313 0700 Fax: 0131 313 0747
Email: kewhouse@ednet.co.uk
Web: www.kewhouse.com

Caring for the more discerning traveller, this immaculate listed building is centrally located with secure parking. Luxurious bedrooms and peaceful residents' bar ensures a memorable stay.

6 bedrs SB £48 DB £80 L £7 D £7
CC: MC Vi Am DC Swi Delt JCB

How to get there: Directly on A8 route one mile west of Princes Street and on main route from airport.

Scotland

105 Kirkland Bed & Breakfast

♦ ♦ ♦ ♦ ✕ ☕

6 Dean Park Crescent, Edinburgh, EH4 1PN
Tel: 0131 332 5017
Email: kirkland.b&b@cableinet.co.uk
Web: www.kirkland.pwp.blueyonder.co.uk
3 bedrs DB £44.58
CC: None accepted
♿ ⊗ ☕ ▭ ☂ ✌
How to get there: Turn north off Queensferry
Road (A90) ½ mile from city centre or ½ mile
after Stuarts Nelville College.

106 The Ben Doran

♦ ♦ ♦ ♦ ✕

11 Mayfield Gardens, Edinburgh, EH9 2AX
Tel: 0131 667 8488 Fax: 0131 667 0076
Email: info@bendoran.com
Web: www.bendoran.com
10 bedrs SB £35 DB £65 D £25
CC: MC Vi DC Delt
⊗ ☕ ▭ P ☂ ✌ ⚏
How to get there: On A701, one mile south of
Princes Street, three miles north of bypass
(A720).
See advert on facing page

107 Thistle Court Hotel

♦ ♦ ♦ ♦ ☕

5 Hampton Terrace, Edinburgh,
Lothian, EH12 5JD
Tel: 0131 313 5500 Fax: 0131 313 5511
Email: info@thistlecourt.co.uk
Web: www.thistlecourt.co.uk
16 bedrs SB £25 DB £50 L £6.50 D £11
CC: MC Vi Am Swi Delt JCB
⌂ ⊔⊔ ⅋ ⊗ ☕ ▭ ☎ P☎ ☂ ☃ ♪ ✌ ⚏ ⊪
How to get there: From city bypass follow for
city centre through Corstorphine past zoo to
Murrayfield under bridge at Roseburn 250
metres on right.

108 Ardleigh Guest House

♦ ♦ ♦

260 Ferry Road, Edinburgh, Lothian, EH5 3AN
Tel: 0131 552 1833 Fax: 0131 552 4951
Email: info@ardleighhouse.com
Web: www.ardleighhouse.com
7 bedrs SB £25 DB £50 D £10
CC: MC Vi Am DC Swi Delt JCB
⅋ ⊗ ☕ ▭ ☎ P☎ ☂ ♪ ✌
How to get there: From city bypass follow A90
from Barnton along Queensferry Road into Ferry
Road towards Leith approximately five miles.

109 Boisdale Hotel

♦ ♦ ♦

9 Coates Gardens, Edinburgh, EH12 5LG
Tel: 0131 337 1134 Fax: 0131 313 0048
10 bedrs SB £25 DB £60
CC: None accepted
🐾 ⊗ ☕ ▭ ☂ ♪ ♫ ✌

110 Cumberland Hotel

♦ ♦ ♦

1 West Coates, Edinburgh, EH12 5JQ
Tel: 0131 337 1198 Fax: 0131 337 1022
Email: cumblhotel@aol.com
Web: www.cumberlandhotel-edinburgh.com
Children minimum age: 6 months

Located on main tourist route into Edinburgh.
Tastefully decorated and furnished to a very
high standard. All ensuite bedrooms with
tea/coffee-making facilities and cable TV.
Attractive cocktail bar and residents' lounge.
SB £29 DB £22
CC: MC Vi Swi
☕ ▭ P ☂ ✌ ⊪
How to get there: From airport: A8 towards
Haymarket. From city centre head for West End
past the Haymarket Station. We are 200 yards
on the right.

111 Galloway Guest House

♦ ♦ ♦

22 Dean Park Crescent,
Edinburgh, EH4 1PH
Tel: 0131 332 3672 Fax: 0131 332 3672
10 bedrs SB £25 DB £40
CC: MC Vi Swi Delt JCB
🐾 ☕ ▭ ☂ ♫ ✌
How to get there: 1km from Princes Street west
end on A9.

112 Maple Leaf

◆ ◆ ◆

23 Pilrig Street, Edinburgh, Lothian, EH6 5AN
Tel: 0131 554 7692 Fax: 0131 554 9919
Email: info@themapleleaf.com
Web: www.themapleleaf.com
11 bedrs SB £30 DB £60 D £10
CC: MC Vi Am Swi Delt JCB

How to get there: Follow Queens St. in city centre to Eastend by John Lewis at Leith Walk. Pilrig St. to left midway down Leith Walk.

113 Newington Guest House

◆ ◆ ◆

18 Newington Road, Edinburgh, EH9 1QS
Tel: 0131 667 3356 Fax: 0131 667 8307
Email: newington.guesthouse@dial.pipex.com
Web: www.newington-gh.co.uk
Children minimum age: 9
9 bedrs SB £32.50 DB £49
CC: MC Vi Swi Delt
How to get there: Centrally situated in south side of city, on A68/A7, main bus route.

114 Quaich Guest House

◆ ◆ ◆

87 St. Johns Road,
Edinburgh, EH12 6NN
Tel: 0131 334 4440 Fax: 0131 476 9002
6 bedrs
CC: MC Vi Am

How to get there: From south, follow M6 to M74 to M8 and A8 to Edinburgh, into Glasgow Road into St. John's Road.

115 Averon City Centre Guest House

◆ ◆

44 Gilmore Place,
Edinburgh, EH3 9NQ
Tel: 0131 229 9932
Email: info@averon.co.uk
Web: www.averon.co.uk
12 bedrs
CC: MC Vi Am DC Swi Delt
How to get there: From Princes Street go up Lothian Road and turn right at the Kings Theatre.

Scotland

116 Kariba Hotel

♦ ♦

10 Granville Terrace, Edinburgh,
Lothian, EH10 4PQ
Tel: 0131 229 3773

117 Park Hotel

♦ ♦

4–6 Alvanley Terrace, Whitehouse Loan,
Edinburgh, EH9 1DU
Tel: 0131 622 6800 Fax: 0131 622 6822
Email: park@festival-inns.co.uk
Web: www.festival-inns.co.uk
19 bedrs SB £70 DB £90
CC: MC Vi Am DC Swi Delt JCB

How to get there: From city centre, walk up
Lothian Road, continue on to Home Street, then
Leven Street. Turn left on to Whitehouse Loan.

118 The Addison

2 Murrayfield Avenue, Edinburgh, EH12 6AX
Tel: 0131 337 4060 Fax: 0131 337 4080
Email: info@addisonedinburgh.com
Web: www.addisonedinburgh.com
10 bedrs SB £30 DB £50 D £10
CC: MC Vi Am Swi Delt JCB

How to get there: From city bypass follow signs
for city centre approx four miles. Left at
Roseburn into Murrayfield Avenue. Just after
BMW garage.

Edzell, Angus

119 Glenesk Hotel

★★★

High Street, Edzell, Angus, DD9 7TF
Tel: 01356 648319 Fax: 01356 647333
Email: gleneskhotel@btconnect.com
Web: www.gleneskhotel.co.uk

Find a warm welcome in picturesque Edzell and
enjoy hunting, fishing, walks, bowling, pony
trekking and golf — all nearby. Fine cuisine,
from traditional Scottish breakfasts to delicious
à la carte dinners.
24 bedrs SB £60 DB £98 B £9 L £16 D £20
CC: MC Vi Am Swi Delt

Erskine, Renfrewshire

120 Erskine Bridge Cosmopolitan Hotel

★★★

Riverside, Erskine, Renfrewshire, PA8 6AN
Tel: 0141 812 0123 Fax: 0141 812 7642
Email: erskineres@cosmopolitan.com
Web: www.cosmopolitan-hotels.com
177 bedrs SB £54.50 DB £109
B £6.50 L £6.95 D £15.95
CC: MC Vi Am DC Swi Delt

How to get there: M8 Junction 30, M898 to first
junction. Turn right at first roundabout, straight
over second, turn left at third, right at fourth.

Falkirk

121 Comfort Inn

★★

Manor Street, Falkirk, FK1 1NT
Tel: 01324 624066 Fax: 01324 611785
Email: admin@gb626.u-net.com
Web: www.choicehotels.com
33 bedrs SB £60.25 DB £60.25 HBS £71
HBD £35.50 B £7.75 D £10.75
CC: MC Vi Am DC Swi Delt

Falkland, Fife

122 Covenanter Hotel

♦ ♦ ♦

The Square, Falkland, Fife, KY15 7BU
Tel: 01337 857224 Fax: 01337 857163
Web: www.covenanterhotel.com
SB £42 DB £54
B £6.50 L £6.50 D £12
CC: MC Vi Am

Forres, Moray

123 Ramnee Hotel

★★★★ ℛ ℛ ℛ

Victoria Road, Forres, Moray, IV36 3BN
Tel: 01309 672410 Fax: 01309 673392
Email: ramneehotel@btconnect.com
20 bedrs SB £70 DB £95 HBS £95.50 HBD £73
B £8.50 L £12.50 D £22.50
CC: MC Vi Am DC Swi Delt JCB

How to get there: From A96 Inverness-Aberdeen road at Forres, turn left onto Forres bypass east of town. Hotel is 500m on right.

124 Park Hotel

★★

Victoria Road, Forres, Moray, IV36 3BN
Tel: 01309 672611 Fax: 01309 672328
12 bedrs SB £45 DB £58 HBS £61 HBD £45
B £10 L £12.50 D £16
CC: MC Vi Am DC

How to get there: Leave A96 bypass at the east end of Forres; we are the first hotel on the right.

Fort William, Highland

125 Inverlochy Castle Hotel
Gold Ribbon Winner

★★★★★ ℛ ℛ ℛ ℛ

Torlundy, Fort William, Highland, PH33 6SN
Tel: 01397 702177 Fax: 01397 702953
Email: info@inverlochy.co.uk
Web: www.inverlochy.co.uk
Closed January to March
17 bedrs SB £255 DB £380
B £17.50 L £23 D £45
CC: MC Vi Am Swi Delt

How to get there: Accessible from the A82 trunk road from Glasgow to Fort William.

126 Moorings Hotel

★★★★ ℛ ℛ ℛ

Banavie, Fort William, Highland, PH33 7LY
Tel: 01397 772797 Fax: 01397 772441
Email: reservations@moorings-fortwilliam.co.uk
Web: www.moorings-fortwilliam.co.uk

Sitting in the shadow of Ben Nevis, this award-winning hotel offers its guests a truly warm welcome, with good food, cosy bedrooms and friendly service. 10 superior rooms also available.
28 bedrs SB £58 DB £48
HBS £83 HBD £73 B £8 D £23
CC: MC Vi Am DC Swi Delt

How to get there: Follow A82 to Fort William and turn onto A830, signposted Mallaig. Past canal bridge, turn right into Banauie.

127 Caledonian Hotel

★★

Achintore Road, Fort William,
Highland, PH33 6RW
Tel: 01397 703117 Fax: 01397 700550
86 bedrs CC: MC Vi Am DC Swi Delt

How to get there: On the A82, two miles south of Fort William.

128 Grand Hotel

★★ ℛ ℛ

Gordon Square, Fort William,
Highland, PH33 6DX
Tel: 01397 702928 Fax: 01397 702928
Email: enquiries@grandhotel.scotland.co.uk
Web: www.grandhotel-scotland.co.uk
Closed January
30 bedrs B £7.95 L £9.95 D £16.95
CC: MC Vi Am DC Swi Delt

How to get there: Located in the town centre at the west end of the pedestrianised high street. Parking is to front and rear of hotel.

Scotland

129 Factor's House

◆ ◆ ◆ ◆ ◆ ☙ ✻ ℘
Torlundy, Fort William, Highland, PH33 6SN
Tel: 01397 702177 Fax: 01397 702953
Email: info@inverlochy.co.uk
Web: www.inverlochy.co.uk
Closed November to March
5 bedrs SB £70 DB £110 B £10 D £15.50
CC: MC Vi Am Swi Delt
🍴🖥☎P☎🏇✻ℵ🐴♒🕯🪑🔍⚓
How to get there: Accessible by the A82 trunk
road from Glasgow to Fort William.

130 Distillery House

◆ ◆ ◆ ◆ ✻
Nevis Bridge, North Road, Fort William,
Highland, PH33 6LH
Tel: 01397 700103 Fax: 01397 702980
Closed December to January
7 bedrs SB £35 DB £60 CC: MC Vi Am Swi
🚫🍴🖥☎P☙
How to get there: From the north, turn right at
second set of traffic lights. From the south, the
hotel is on the left after Glen Nevis roundabout.

Gairloch, Ross-shire

131 Creag Mor Hotel

★ ★ ★ ☙
Charleston, Gairloch, Ross-shire, IV21 2AH
Tel: 01445 712068 Fax: 01445 712044
Email: relax@creagmorhotel.com
Web: www.creagmorhotel.com
17 bedrs SB £47 DB £80 HBS £72 HBD £65
B £10 L £10 D £25
CC: MC Vi Am Swi Delt JCB
♿🏌🐾🚫🍴🖥☎P☙🕯♒🪑🎵
How to get there: First building on the right
entering Gairloch from Inverness.

132 The Old Inn

◆ ◆ ◆ ◆ ☙ ✻ ℘
Gairloch, Ross-shire, IV21 2BD
Tel: 01445 712006 Fax: 01445 712445
Email: nomadscot@lineone.net
Web: www.theoldinn.co.uk
14 bedrs SB £37.50 DB £68 B £7.50 L £8.50
D £17.50 CC: MC Vi Swi
🏌🐾🚫🍴🖥☎P☙🕯🕯♒🪑🎵
How to get there: A9 North of Inverness. Take
A832 at Achnasheen roundabout to Gairloch.
On righthandside of A832 opposite Gairloch
Harbour.

Galashiels, Scottish Borders

133 Kingsknowes Hotel

★ ★ ★ ☙
1 Selkirk Road, Galashiels,
Scottish Borders, TD1 3HY
Tel: 01896 758375 Fax: 01896 750377
Email: enquiries@kingsknowes.co.uk
Web: www.kingsknowes.co.uk
11 bedrs SB £54 DB £80 HBS £66 HBD £52
B £8.50 L £10 D £15
CC: MC Vi Am DC Swi Delt
🏊🐾🚫🍴🖥☎📞P☙🕯🐴♒🪑🎵🎵♣
How to get there: From Edinburgh, or Junction
40 of M6, follow A7 to Glashiels. From
Newcastle, follow A68 to Galashiels.

134 Abbotsford Arms Hotel

★ ★
63 Stirling Street, Galashiels,
Scottish Borders, TD1 1BY
Tel: 01896 752517 Fax: 01896 750744
Email: abb2517@aol.com
Web: abbotsfordarms.co.uk

Family hotel tastefully decorated. Small and
friendly with a reputation for good food, served
all day from 12 noon. Close to town centre.
14 bedrs SB £40 DB £60 B £5 L £9 D £12
CC: MC Vi DC Swi Delt
🍴🖥☎P☙🕯🎵🎵
How to get there: Centrally situated in town.

Gatehouse-of-Fleet, Dumfries & Galloway

135 Bank O'Fleet Hotel

◆ ◆ ◆
47 High Street, Gatehouse-of-Fleet,
Dumfries & Galloway, DG7 2HR
Tel: 01557 814302 Fax: 01557 814302
Email: info@bankofleethotel.co.uk
Web: www.bankofleethotel.co.uk

An attractive hotel, resting in the heart of picturesque and historic Galloway town, Gatehouse of Fleet. The hotel has earned a reputation for good food. Ideal for golf, hillwalking and fishing.
6 bedrs CC: MC Vi Am

Glasgow

136 Glasgow Marriott Hotel

★★★★ 🕮
500 Argyle Street, Glasgow, G3 8RR
Tel: 0141 226 5577 Fax: 0141 221 9202
Web: www.marriotthotels.co.uk
300 bedrs SB £60 DB £80 HBS £78 HBD £49
B £13 L £15 D £18 CC: MC Vi Am DC Swi Delt

137 Millennium Hotel Glasgow

★★★★ 🕮
George Square, Glasgow, G2 1DS
Tel: 0141 332 6711 Fax: 0141 332 4264

In an historic city centre location, this refurbished town house offers a relaxed environment with contemporary interiors, complemented by fashionable conservatories overlooking George Square.
CC: None accepted

138 Glynhill Hotel & Leisure Club

★★★
Paisley Road, Renfrew, PA4 8XB
Tel: 0141 886 5555 Fax: 0141 885 2838
Email: glynhillleisurehotel@msn.com
Web: www.glynhill.com

Ideal, convenient base for business executives and tourists alike. Set in a quiet location with two excellent restaurants, superb leisure club, major conference centre and friendly, efficient staff.
125 bedrs SB £64 DB £69 L £9.50 D £15.25
CC: MC Vi Am DC Swi Delt

How to get there: On M8 towards Glasgow Airport, turn off at Junction 27. Take A741 towards Renfrew Cross. Hotel on right.

139 Jurys Glasgow Hotel

★★★
Great Western Road, Glasgow, G12 0XP
Tel: +353(0)1 6070000 Fax: +353(0)1 6136999
Email: bookings@jurysdoyle.com
Web: www.jurysdoyle.com
137 bedrs SB £124.50 DB £134
B £9.50 L £9.50 D £17.50 CC: MC Vi Am DC

How to get there: Located seven miles from Glasgow Int'l Airport. Central Station three miles, Just 10 minutes from bustling city centre.

140 Kings Park Hotel

★★★★ 🕮 🕮
Mill Street, Rutherglen, Glasgow, G73 2AR
Tel: 0141 647 5491 Fax: 0141 613 3022
Email: enquiries@maksu-group.co.uk
Web: www.maksu-group.co.uk
26 bedrs SB £60 DB £80 HBS £75 HBD £50
B £6.50 L £6.95 D £19.50
CC: MC Vi Am DC Swi Delt

How to get there: Follow A730 from Glasgow towards East Kilbride. Hotel is situated on the left in the suburb on Rutherglen.

Scotland

141 MacDonald Hotel

★★★

Eastwood Toll, Giffnock, Glasgow, G46 6RA
Tel: 0141 638 2225 Fax: 0141 638 6231
55 bedrs
CC: MC Vi Am DC Swi Delt
How to get there: M77 Junction 3, follow A726
eastbound for 1½ miles. Turn right immediately
after second roundabout (Eastwood Toll).

142 Novotel Glasgow

★★★

181 Pitt Street, Glasgow, G2 4JS
Tel: 0141 222 2775 Fax: 0141 204 5438
Email: h3136@accor-hotels.com
Web: www.novotel.com
139 bedrs SB £94.95 DB £104.95 HBS £110.90
HBD £60.45 B £9.35 L £2.50 D £12.95
CC: MC Vi Am DC Swi Delt JCB
How to get there: M8 J8 westbound, veer left to
Sauchiehall Street, Pitt Street on right.
Eastbound, Pitt Street is first on left, follow one-
way signs.

143 Quality Hotel Glasgow

★★★

99 Gordon Street, Glasgow, G1 3SF
Tel: 0141 221 9680 Fax: 0141 226 3948
Email: admin@gb627.u-net.com
Web: www.choicehotels.com
222 bedrs SB £100.75 DB £15.75 HBS £115.25
HBD £65.13 B £10.75 L £9.95 D £14.50
CC: MC Vi Am DC Swi Delt
How to get there: From M8 Westbound take
Junction 19 onto Argyle Street and left onto
Oswald Street. NCP car park on right.

144 Sherbrooke Castle Hotel

★★★★

11 Sherbrooke Avenue, Glasgow, G41 4PG
Tel: 0141 427 4227 Fax: 0141 427 5685
Email: mail@sherbrooke.co.uk
Web: www.sherbrooke.co.uk
21 bedrs SB £65 DB £85 B £6.50 L £12.50 D £20
CC: MC Vi Am DC Swi Delt
How to get there: Close to Junction 1 M77.
Close to Junctions 22 and 23 from City M8.
Close to Junction 27 from Glasgow Aiport.

145 Swallow Hotel

★★★★

517 Paisley Road West,
Glasgow, G51 1RW
Tel: 0141 427 3146 Fax: 0141 427 4059
Email: glasgow.swallow@whitbread.com
Web: www.swallowhotels.com
Children minimum age: 14
117 bedrs SB £70 DB £80
HBS £80 HBD £55
B £9.50 L £9.50 D £18.50
CC: MC Vi Am DC Swi
How to get there: At Junction 23 of M8, turn
right into Paisley Road West. Hotel located 400
yards on right-hand side.

146 Argyll Hotel

★★

973 Sauchiehall Street,
Glasgow, G3 7TQ
Tel: 0141 337 3313 Fax: 0141 337 3283
Email: info@argyllhotelglasgow.co.uk
Web: www.argyllhotelglasgow.co.uk

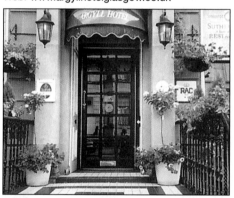

Ideal location half a mile west of city centre.
Minutes' walk to SECC, Kelvingrove art
galleries/museum and Glasgow University.
Traditional bar/restaurant. Good value with
warm Scottish hospitality.
Email: info@argyllhotelglasgow.co.uk,
Website: www.argyllhotel glasgow.co.uk
38 bedrs
CC: MC Vi Am Swi Delt
How to get there: Leave M8 at Junction 18. Go
straight ahead to second set of traffic lights.
Turn right into Berkeley Street, right into
Elderslie Street, then first left into Sauchiehall
Street.

147 Dunkeld Hotel

10/12 Queen's Drive, Glasgow, G42 8BS
Tel: 0141 424 0160 Fax: 0141 423 4437
Email: dunkeldhotel@aol.com
Web: www.dunkeld-hotel.co.uk

Victorian villa set in own grounds overlooking
Glasgow's premier park. Home cooking and a
relaxing atmosphere will make your stay
memorable. All rooms ensuite with
bath/iron/hospitality bar and hairdryer.
21 bedrs SB £39.45 DB £60 HBS £51.95
HBD £42 B £5 L £8 D £12
CC: MC Vi Am Swi Delt JCB
How to get there: From end of M74 follow signs
for Rutherglen, then Mount Florida: through
lights at Asda, turn right at lights into Cathcart
Road. First left is Queen's Drive.

148 Travelodge Glasgow (Central)

Travel Accommodation
Hill Street, Glasgow, G3 6PR
Tel: 08700 850 950
Web: www.travelodge.co.uk
95 bedrs B £4.25 CC: MC Vi Am DC Swi Delt

149 Travelodge Glasgow (Dumbarton)

Travel Accommodation
A82, Milton, Dumbarton, Glasgow, G82 2TZ
Tel: 08700 850 950
Web: www.travelodge.co.uk
32 bedrs B £4.25 CC: MC Vi Am DC Swi Delt

150 Travelodge Glasgow (Paisley Road)

Travel Accommodation
251 Paisley Road, Glasgow, G5 8RA
Tel: 08700 850 950
Web: www.travelodge.co.uk
75 bedrs B £4.25 CC: MC Vi Am DC Swi Delt

151 Angus Hotel

◆◆◆

970 Sauchiehall Street, Glasgow, G3 7TQ
Tel: 0141 357 5155 Fax: 0141 339 9469
Email: info@angushotelglasgow.co.uk
Web: www.angushotelglasgow.co.uk
18 bedrs SB £44 DB £60
CC: MC Vi Am Swi Delt
How to get there: Leave M8 at Junction 18. At
second set of traffic lights, turn right into
Berkeley Street. At end turn right then first left
into Sauchiehall Street.

152 Kelvingrove Hotel

◆◆◆

944 Sauchiehall Street, Glasgow, G3 7TH
Tel: 0141 339 5011 Fax: 0141 339 6566
Email: kelvingrove.hotel@business.ntl.com
Web: www.kelvingrove-hotel.co.uk
25 bedrs SB £38 DB £58
CC: MC Vi Swi
How to get there: M8 Junction 18 follow signs
to Kelvingrove Museum for 1/2 mile west.

153 McLays Guest House

◆◆

264–276 Renfrew Street, Charing Cross,
Glasgow, G3 6TT
Tel: 0141 332 4796 Fax: 0141 353 0422
Email: info@mclays.com
Web: www.mclaysguesthouse.com
62 bedrs SB £27 DB £46
CC: MC Vi Am DC Swi Delt JCB
How to get there: Directly behind Sauchiehall
Street, at the western end of Renfrew Steet. Exit
J18 off the M8 motorway.

154 Smith's Hotel

◆◆

963 Sauchiehall Street,
Glasgow, G3 7TQ
Tel: 0141 339 6363 Fax: 0141 334 1892
Web: www.smiths-hotel.com
33 bedrs SB £20 DB £36
How to get there: 0.75 km from city centre. Next
to the West End (University). Taxi from city
centre approx £4.

Scotland

155 Charing Cross Guest House

♦

310 Renfrew Street, Glasgow, G3 6UW
Tel: 0141 332 2503 Fax: 0141 353 3047
Email: enquiries@charing-x.com
Web: www.charing-x.com
25 bedrs SB £22 DB £38
CC: MC Vi Am DC Swi Delt

How to get there: Exit J18 M8, Charing Cross, take first left for Sauchiehall Street and then two first lefts onto Renfrew Street.

156 Georgian House

29 Buckingham Terrace, Great Western Road, Kelvinside, Glasgow, G12 8ED
Tel: 0141 339 0008
Web: www.thegeorgianhousehotel.com

This restored Georgian town house residence retains many original features to create stylish comfort in the midst of the vibrant West End. Overlooking the Botanic Garden, close to restaurants, theatres and major sights.
12 bedrs SB £28 DB £55
CC: MC Vi Swi Delt

How to get there: M8 J17 onto A82 Great Western Road, about one mile on the right, in a terrace parallel to the Great Western Road.

Glenmoriston, Highland

157 Cluanie Inn

★★★
Glenmoriston, Highland, IV63 7YW
Tel: 01320 340238 Fax: 01320 340293
Email: cluanie@ecosse.net
Web: www.cluanie.co.uk

Lying between Loch Ness and the Isle of Skye, this newly refurbished Highland inn offers a range of facilities and services, the restaurants catering for every requirement. Children welcome. Dogs allowed.
14 bedrs
CC: MC Vi Am Swi

How to get there: The Cluanie Inn lies on the A87 halfway between Loch Ness and the Isle of Skye.

Grantown-on-Spey, Moray

158 Culdearn House Hotel

★★
Woodlands Terrace, Grantown-on-Spey, Moray, PH26 3JU
Tel: 01479 872106 Fax: 01479 873641
Email: culdearn@globalnet.co.uk
Web: www.culdearn.com
Children minimum age: 10
Closed November to February
9 bedrs HBS £75 HBD £150 B £10 D £25
CC: MC Vi Am DC Swi Delt JCB

How to get there: Enter Grantown from southwest on A95. Turn left at 30mph sign.

159 Ardconnel House

Woodlands Terrace, Grantown-on-Spey,
Moray, PH26 3JU
Tel: 01479 872104 Fax: 01479 872104
Email: enquiry@ardconnel.com
Web: www.ardconnel.com
Children minimum age: 8

An elegant and comfortable Victorian house,
furnished with antiques. Excellent 'Taste of
Scotland' dinner prepared by French
owner/chef. 2001 AA guest accommodation of
the year for Scotland. Non-smoking throughout.
6 bedrs SB £35 DB £70 HBS £57 HBD £60
CC: MC Vi Delt

How to get there: On the A95 south-west entry
to town.

160 Ravenscourt House Hotel

Seafield Avenue, Grantown-on-Spey,
Moray, PH26 3JG
Tel: 01479 872286 Fax: 01479 873260
8 bedrs SB £30 DB £60 HBS £47.50 HBD £65
B £5 D £16.50
CC: None accepted

How to get there: Turn left at Bank of Scotland.
Ravenscourt is 200m on right-hand side.

161 The Pines

Little Gem

Woodside Avenue, Grantown-on-Spey,
Moray, PH26 3JR
Tel: 01479 872092
Email: info@thepinesgrantown.co.uk
Web: www.thepinesgrantown.co.uk
Children minimum age: 12
Closed Novermber to February

In its beautiful quiet woodland setting,
experience the comforts of a small hotel in this
historic ancestral Highland home. Two spacious
lounges, two intimate dining rooms, and a small
library.
8 bedrs SB £40 DB £80
HBS £65 HBD £65 D £25
CC: MC Vi Delt

How to get there: On entering the town from the
south take A939 to Tomintoul, then turn first right.

162 Garden Park Guest House

Woodside Avenue, Grantown-on-Spey,
Moray, PH26 3JN
Tel: 01479 873235
Children minimum age: 12
Closed November to February
5 bedrs SB £24 DB £48
HBS £36.50 HBD £73
CC: None accepted

How to get there: Turn off High Street into
Forest Road. Garden Park is at corner of Forest
Road and Woodside Avenue.

163 Bank House

1 The Square, Grantown-on-Spey,
Moray, PH26 3HG
Tel: 01479 873256 Fax: 01479 873256
Email: farleys@breathemail.net
4 bedrs SB £23 DB £46
CC: None accepted

How to get there: From south travel north on
A9, exit at Aviemore, A95 to Grantown.
Entrance to house off Seafield Avenue, beside
Bank of Scotland.

Gretna, Dumfries & Galloway

164 Gretna Chase Hotel

★★★★

Gretna, Dumfries & Galloway, DG16 5JB
Tel: 01461 337517 Fax: 01461 337766
Email: enquiries@gretnachase.co.uk
Web: www.gretnachase.co.uk
20 bedrs SB £65 DB £79 B £8.95 L £9.95
CC: MC Vi Am Swi Delt

How to get there: 6 miles north of J44, take slip road for Gretna. Turn left at junction; hotel is 600 yards on right.

165 Solway Lodge Hotel

★★

Annan Road, Gretna,
Dumfries & Galloway, DG16 5DN
Tel: 01461 338266 Fax: 01461 337791
Web: www.solwaylodge.co.uk
10 bedrs SB £41.50 DB £59 B £8.50
CC: MC Vi Am DC Swi Delt JCB

How to get there: From south, take 2nd exit at roundabout ('Town Centre'). Lodge 200m on right.

166 Royal Stewart Motel

★

Glasgow Road, Gretna,
Dumfries & Galloway, DG16 5DT
Tel: 01461 338210

167 Surrone House Hotel

♦♦♦ ✲

Annan Road, Gretna,
Dumfries & Galloway, DG16 5DL
Tel: 01461 338341 Fax: 01461 338341
Email: surrone@aol.com
Web: www.surrone.co.uk
7 bedrs SB £40 DB £100 D £10.50
CC: MC Vi Am Swi Delt

How to get there: On main road through Gretna (not the bypass).

Haddington, East Lothian

168 Brown's Hotel

Little Gem

♦♦♦♦

1 West Road, Haddington,
East Lothian, EH41 3RD
Tel: 01620 822254 Fax: 01620 822254
Email: info@browns-hotel.com
Web: www.browns-hotel.com
A Georgian-style country house furnished sympathetically with Scottish art hung on the walls. We specialise in fresh fare. Non-residents are welcome to dine and partake from our cellars.
5 bedrs SB £70 DB £105 HBS £99.50
HBD £82.50 B £8.50 L £21.50 D £30
CC: MC Vi Am DC Swi Delt JCB

How to get there: Browns is situated 17 miles east of Edinburgh one mile off route A1 on West road B6471 in Haddington.

Hawick, Scottish Borders

169 Kirklands

★★

West Stewart Place, Hawick,
Scottish Borders, TD9 8BH
Tel: 01450 372263 Fax: 01450 370404
Email: kirklands-hotel@lineone.net
Web: www.kirklandscountryhotel.co.uk
5 bedrs SB £49.50 DB £65 B £4.95 L £6.95
D £10.95 CC: MC Vi Swi Delt

How to get there: ½ mile north of Hawick High Street, 200 yards west of A7.

Helensburgh, Argyll & Bute

170 Kirkton House

Little Gem

♦♦♦♦♦

Darleith Road, Cardross, Argyll & Bute, G82 5EZ
Tel: 01389 841951 Fax: 01389 841868
Email: rac@kirktonhouse.co.uk
Web: www.kirktonhouse.co.uk
Closed December to January

Converted 18th century farmstead, in tranquil country setting with panoramic views of the Clyde. Wine and dine by oil lamplight. In best guides yet informal and unpretentious.
6 bedrs SB £43.50 DB £59 HBS £56.75
HBD £42.75 D £16.25
CC: MC Vi Am DC Swi Delt JCB
How to get there: Turn north off A814 at the west end of Cardross Village, up Darleith Road. Kirkton is ½ mile on right.

Howwood, Renfrewshire

171 Bowfield Hotel & Country Club

★★★★
Lands of Bowfield, Howwood,
Renfrewshire, PA9 1DB
Tel: 01505 705225 Fax: 01505 705230

Innerleithen, Scottish Borders

172 Corner House Hotel

♦ ♦ ♦
1 Chapel Street, Innerleithen, Tweedale,
Scottish Borders, EH44 6HN
Tel: 01896 831181 Fax: 01896 831182
Email: cornerhousehotel@talk21.com
Closed one week in October
6 bedrs SB £23
B £4.95 L £9.50 D £9.50
CC: MC Vi Am DC Swi Delt
How to get there: Follow A703 from Edinburgh to Peebles, then take the A72 to Innerleithen, approximately 25 miles

Inveraray, Argyll & Bute

173 Loch Fyne Hotel

★★★
Inveraray, Argyll & Bute, PA32 8XT
Tel: 01499 302 148 Fax: 01499 302 348
Email: lochfyne@british-trust-hotels.com
Web: www.british-trust-hotels.com

Quiet location. Close to town. Magnificent views across Loch Fyne. Original building over 100 years old. All rooms ensuite. Excellent bar, bistro and restaurant. 15 metre pool with sauna and steam rooms.
80 bedrs SB £55 DB £100 HBS £70 HBD £65
B £8 L £9 D £18 CC: MC Vi DC Swi JCB

Invergarry, Highland

174 Glengarry Castle Hotel

★★★
Invergarry, Highland, PH35 4HW
Tel: 01809 501254 Fax: 01809 501207
Email: castle@glengarry.net
Web: www.glengarry.net
Closed mid-November to mid-March

Fine Victorian mansion in extensive wooded grounds on the shores of Loch Oich. Privately owned and personally managed by the MacCallum family for over 40 years.
26 bedrs SB £55 DB £90 HBS £81 HBD £72
B £8 L £4.50 D £25 CC: MC Vi Swi Delt
How to get there: Located on the A82, overlooking Loch Oich, one mile from Invergarry.

Scotland

Inverness, Highland

175 Inverness Marriott Hotel

★★★★ ®

Culcabock Road, Inverness, Highland, IV2 3LP
Tel: 01463 237166 Fax: 01463 225208
Email: inverness@marriotthotels.co.uk
Web: www.marriott.com/marriott/invkm
82 bedrs SB £120 DB £140
B £4.50 L £8.45 D £15.75
CC: MC Vi Am DC Swi Delt JCB

How to get there: From south (A9) entering
Inverness take the slip road on the left marked
Culduthel and Kingsmills. Follow signs for
Kingsmills. Hotel on left past golf course.

176 Loch Ness House Hotel

★★★ ®

Glenurquhart Road, Inverness, Highland, IV3 6JL
Tel: 01463 231248 Fax: 01463 239327
Email: lnhhchris@aol.com
Web: www.smoothhound.co.uk/
hotels/lochness.html
22 bedrs SB £65 DB £110 HBS £82.50
HBD £70 B £9.50 D £18.50
CC: MC Vi Am DC Swi Delt

How to get there: Situated on A82 (Fort William).
From A9, turn left at Longman roundabout,
follow A82 signs for 2½ miles. Beside Torvean
golf course and Caledonian Canal.

177 Lochardil House Hotel

★★★ ®

Stratherrick Road, Inverness, Highland, IV2 4LF
Tel: 01463 235995 Fax: 01463 713394
Email: lochardil@ukonline.co.uk
12 bedrs SB £82 DB £112 B £10 L £12 D £18
CC: MC Vi Am DC Swi Delt JCB

How to get there: East bank River Ness long
Islans Bank Road, one mile from main bridge left
into Drummond Crescent. ½ a mile, hotel on left.

Ask the experts

To book a Hotel or Guest
Accommodation, or for help
and advice, call RAC Hotel
Reservations on 0870 603 9109
and quote 'Guide 2002'

178 Priory Hotel

★★★

The Square, Beauly, IV4 7BX
Tel: 01463 782309 Fax: 01463 782531
Email: reservations@priory-hotel.com
Web: www.priory-hotel,com
34 bedrs SB £45 DB £85 HBS £52 HBD £99
B £3.50 L £5 D £12.50
CC: MC Vi Am DC Swi Delt JCB

How to get there: A9 bypass Inverness
approximately five miles to Tore roundabout.
Exit first left, follow sign for Beauly. Hotel is in
village square.

179 Royal Highland Hotel

★★★ ®

Station Square, Academy Street,
Inverness, Highland, IV1 1LG
Tel: 01463 231926 Fax: 01463 710705

A popular meeting place, welcomes non-
residents and offers breakfast, morning coffees,
home baking, buffet lunch, afternoon teas, high
teas and dinner in a friendly and restful
atmosphere. Adjacent to railway station and
within easy reach of all major attractions.
69 bedrs
CC: MC Vi Am DC Swi Delt

How to get there: Hotel is in centre of Inverness,
by the railway station.

180 Travelodge Inverness

Travel Accommodation
A9/A96
Tel: 08700 850 950
Web: www.travelodge.co.uk
Opens July 2002
50 bedrs B £4.25
CC: MC Vi Am DC Swi Delt

181 Alban House

Bruce Gardens, Inverness, Highland, IV3 5EN
Tel: 01463 714301 Fax: 01463 714236
6 bedrs SB £30 DB £53 D £15 CC: MC Vi

182 Culduthel Lodge

14 Culduthel Road, Inverness, Highland, IV2 4AG
Tel: 01463 240089 Fax: 01463 240089
Email: rac@culduthel.com
Web: www.culduthel.com
12 bedrs CC: MC Vi Delt

How to get there: Take Castle Street from
Inverness centre. This leads straight into
Culduthel Road — Lodge is on right.

183 Westbourne Guest House

50 Huntly Street, Inverness, Highland, IV3 5HS
Tel: 01463 220700 Fax: 01463 220700
Email: richard@westbourne.org.uk
Web: www.westbourne.org.uk

Situated on the west bank overlooking the River
Ness, five minutes' walk from the city centre,
restaurants, pubs, train and bus stations. Hotel
accommodation at a guesthouse price. Built
1998.
10 bedrs SB £30 DB £46 CC: MC Vi Swi Delt

How to get there: Leave A9 at A82. Proceed
straight over three roundabouts, cross Friars
Bridge. Take 1st left into Wells Street, then into
Huntly Street.

184 Clisham House

43 Fairfield Road, Inverness, Highland, IV3 5QP
Tel: 01463 239965 Fax: 01463 239854

Email: clisham@dircon.co.uk
Web: www.clisham.dircon.co.uk

A non-smoking guest house within walking
distance of the town centre, with a reputation
for good food, warm welcome and Highland
hospitality. All rooms are furnished to a high
standard with guests' comfort a priority.
5 bedrs SB £26 DB £52 CC: None accepted

185 Sunnyholm

12 Mayfield Road, Inverness, Highland, IV2 4AE
Tel: 01463 231336
Email: ago7195587@aol.com
Web: www.invernessguesthouse.com
Children minimum age: 2

Large sandstone bungalow set in a mature,
secluded garden, five minutes walk from the
town centre.
4 bedrs SB £30 DB £42 CC: None accepted

How to get there: From town centre, travel up
Castle Street onto Culduthel Road. At first set of
traffic lights turn left onto Mayfield Road.
Sunnyholm is halfway up on right.

Scotland

Inverurie, Aberdeenshire

186 Strathburn Hotel

★★★

Burghmuir Drive, Inverurie,
Aberdeenshire, AB51 4GY
Tel: 01467 624422 Fax: 01467 625133
Email: strathburn@btconnect.com
Web: www.strathburn-hotel.co.uk
25 bedrs SB £70 DB £95
B £8.75 L £10.95 D £17.75
CC: MC Vi Am Swi Delt

How to get there: From Aberdeen airport turn
right onto A96 towards Inverness for 10 miles.
Then at Blackhall roundabout (Safeway) turn
right. Turn right after 100m.

Isle of Arran, Ayrshire

187 Kinloch Hotel

★★★

Blackwaterfoot, Brodick, Isle of Arran,
Ayrshire, KA27 8ET
Tel: 01770 860444 Fax: 01770 860447
Email: kinloch@cqm.co.uk
Web: www.kinloch-arran.com
43 bedrs SB £49 DB £98 HBS £64 HBD £64
B £9 L £7 D £16.50
CC: MC Vi Am DC Swi Delt

How to get there: Ferry from Ardrossan; take
B880 and follow signs for Blackwaterfoot. Hotel
is in centre of village.

Isle of Bute, Argyll & Bute

188 Ardmory House Hotel

★★ ® ® ®

Ardmory Road, Ardbeg, Isle of Bute,
Argyll & Bute, PA20 0PG
Tel: 01700 502346

189 Avion Bed & Breakfast

◆ ◆ ◆ ◆ ❦

16 Argyle Place, Rothesay,
Isle of Bute, PA20 0BA
Tel: 01700 505897 Fax: 01700 502173

190 Palmyra

◆ ◆ ◆ ◆ ✕ ❦

12 Ardbeg Road, Rothesay,
Isle of Bute, PA20 0NJ
Tel: 01700 502929 Fax: 01700 505712
Web: www.isle-of-bute.com/palmyra
5 bedrs SB £35 DB £60 CC: None accepted

How to get there: Ferry terminal; turn right at
main road; drive ³/₄ of a mile until you see
Palmyra sign.

Isle of Islay, Argyll & Bute

191 Kilmeny Country Guest House

◆ ◆ ◆ ◆ ◆ ✕ ❦

Dining Award awaiting inspection
Ballygrant, Isle of Islay, Argyll & Bute, PA45 7QW
Tel: 01496 840668
Email: info@kilmeny.co.uk
Web: www.kilmeny.co.uk
Closed Christmas and New Year
3 bedrs SB £48 DB £76 HBS £72 HBD £62 D £24
CC: None accepted

How to get there: ¹/₂ mile south of Ballygrant
village. Look for sign on stone pillars. Turn off to
private road for two minutes.

Isle of Mull, Argyll & Bute

192 Western Isles Hotel

★★★★ ® ®

Tobermory, Isle of Mull, Argyll & Bute, PA75 6PR
Tel: 01688 302012 Fax: 01688 302297
Web: www.mullhotel.com

28 bedrs SB £45 DB £96 HBS £70 HBD £73
B £10 L £8 D £25
CC: MC Vi Am Swi Delt

193 Highland Cottage

Blue Ribbon Winner

★★★ 🦋 🦋

Breadalbane Street, Tobermory, Isle of Mull,
Argyll & Bute, PA75 6PD
Tel: 01688 302030 Fax: 01688 302727
Email: davidandjo@highlandcottage.co.uk
Web: www.highlandcottage.co.uk
Closed restricted opening in winter

Cosy family-run hotel in quiet setting in upper
Tobermory conservation area. Four-poster beds
and elegant lounges. Unrivalled hospitality from
resident owners. Wildlife, walking, superb
scenery or just relax!
6 bedrs SB £69.50 DB £85 HBS £91.50
HBD £69 D £26.50
CC: MC Vi Swi Delt JCB

How to get there: From roundabout at top of
town go straight across stone bridge.
Immediately turn right. Hotel is on right opposite
fire station.

194 Gruline Home Farm

Little Gem

♦♦♦♦♦ 🦋 🦋 🦋 ✈

Gruline, Isle of Mull, Argyll & Bute, PA71 6HR
Tel: 01680 300581 Fax: 01680 300573
Email: boo@gruline.com
Web: www.gruline.com

Centrally situated (non-working) Georgian/
Victorian farmhouse, and Mull's finest B&B
offering outstanding levels of hospitality and

superb cuisine, prepared by our chef/proprietor.
Enjoy total luxury and relaxation with us.
2 bedrs SB £62 DB £74
CC: MC Vi DC Swi Delt JCB

How to get there: North on A849 to Salen; take
B8035, drive two miles to fork, go left; past
church, farm is next left.

195 Druimnacroish

♦♦♦♦ 🦋 ✎

Druimnacroish, Dervaig, Isle of Mull,
Argyll & Bute, PA75 6QW
Tel: 01688 400274 Fax: 01688 400274
Email: rac@druimnacroish.co.uk
Web: www.druimnacroish.co.uk
Children minimum age: 5
6 bedrs SB £42 DB £70
CC: MC Vi Am Swi Delt JCB

How to get there: Two miles south of Dervaig,
on road to Salen

196 Old Mill Cottage

♦♦♦♦ 🦋 🦋 ✈ ✎

Lochdon Head, Isle of Mull,
Argyll & Bute, PA64 6AP
Tel: 01680 812442 Fax: 01680 812442

197 Bellachroy Hotel

♦♦♦

Main Street, Dervaig, Isle of Mull,
Argyll & Bute, PA75 6QW
Tel: 01688 400314 Fax: 01688 400314
Email: rac@bellachroy.co.uk
Web: www.bellachroy.co.uk
7 bedrs SB £20 DB £40 HBS £30 HBD £30
B £5 L £3 D £10
CC: MC Vi Swi Delt JCB

How to get there: From Craignure follow
Tobermory road until junction for Dervaig. Take
Dervaig road to end, then turn right. Hotel is
after 100 metres.

Scotland

Isle of Skye, Highland

198 Cuillin Hills Hotel

★★★★ ⓡ ⓡ ⓡ
Portree, Isle of Skye, Highland, IV51 9QU
Tel: 01478 612003 Fax: 01478 613092
Email: office@cuillinhills.demon.co.uk
Web: www.cuillinhills.demon.co.uk

Spectacularly located with breathtaking views over Portree Bay to the Cuillin mountains. Award-winning restaurant; high standards of service and an informal and relaxing atmosphere.
30 bedrs SB £40 DB £80 HBS £66 HBD £66
CC: MC Vi Am Swi Delt

How to get there: Turn right ¼ mile north of Portree off the A855, follow signs for the hotel.

Hotel Eilean Iarmain

This 19th-century Upmarket Country House Hotel, privately owned by Sir Iain & Lady Noble, offers traditional island hospitality, old world character, Victorian charm, panoramic sea views, log fires with a homely atmosphere. Enjoy candlelit dinners in our award-winning AA Rosette restaurant, specialising in Seafood and Game.
An extensive list of rich quality wines. All 12 bedrooms have private bathrooms plus four luxurious suites, furnished with every contemporary comfort.
For over 100 years Hotel Eilean Iarmain has welcomed visitors from around the world.

Open all year, Markets World wide.
Contact: Morag MacDonald (General Manager)

Sleat, Isle of Skye, IV43 8QR
Tel: 01471 833332   Fax: 01471 833275
Email: hotel@eilean-iarmain.co.uk
Website: www.eileaniarmain.co.uk

199 Ardvasar Hotel

★★ ⓡ
Ardvasar, Isle of Skye, Highland, IV45 8RS
Tel: 01471-844223

200 Hotel Eilean Iarmain

★★ ⓡ ⓡ ⓡ
Isleornsay, Sleat, Isle of Skye,
Highland, IV43 8QR
Tel: 01471 833332 Fax: 01471 833275
Email: bookings@eilean-iarmain.co.uk
Web: www.eileaniarmain.co.uk
16 bedrs CC: MC Vi Am Swi Delt

How to get there: Arriving by car, cross the Skye Bridge. Follow A850 for seven miles, turn left onto A851 for eight miles. Turn left at Isleornsay Road sign and drive to the hotel on the harbour front (½ mile).
See advert below right

201 Royal Hotel

★★
Bank Street, Portree, Isle of Skye,
Highland, IV51 9BU
Tel: 01478 612525 Fax: 01478 613198

202 Shorefield House

◆◆◆◆ ⓧ ⓡ
Edinbane, Isle of Skye, Highland, IV51 9PW
Tel: 01470 582444 Fax: 01470 582414
Email: shorefieldhouse@aol.com
Web: www.shorefield.com
5 bedrs SB £28 DB £48 CC: MC Vi Delt

How to get there: From Portree take A87 (U16). After five miles take A850 (Dunvegan). Travel nine miles to Lower Edinbane.

Jedburgh, Scottish Borders

203 Ferniehirst Mill Lodge

◆◆◆
Jedburgh, Scottish Borders, TD8 6PQ
Tel: 01835 863279 Fax: 01835 863279
Email: ferniehirstmill@aol.com
9 bedrs SB £23 DB £46 HBS £37 HBD £37
D £14 CC: MC Vi

How to get there: 2½ miles south of Jedburgh, eight miles north of Scottish border, ⅓ mile off A68 on east side.

Kelso, Scottish Borders

204 Cross Keys Hotel

★★★
36–37 The Square, Kelso,
Scottish Borders, TD5 7HL
Tel: 01573 223303 Fax: 01573 225792
Email: cross-keys-hotel@easynet.co.uk
Web: www.cross-keys-hotel.co.uk
27 bedrs L £4.50 D £10
CC: MC Vi Am DC Swi Delt

205 Ednam House Hotel

★★★
Bridge Street, Kelso, Borders, TD5 7HT
Tel: 01573 224168 Fax: 01573 226319

206 The Queens Head Hotel

★★
24 Bridge Street, Kelso, Borders, TD5 7JD
Tel: 01573 224636 Fax: 01573 224459

Kenmore, Perth & Kinross

207 The Kenmore Hotel

★★★
The Square, Kenmore, Aberfeldy,
Perth & Kinross, PH15 2NU
Tel: 01887 830205 Fax: 01887 830262
Web: www.kenmorehotel.com

Oldest Inn in Scotland (1572), conservation
village in Highland Perthshire on the River Tay.
Famous for golf and fishing, log fires and
genuine Scottish hospitality.
40 bedrs SB £50 DB £80 HBS £75 HBD £65
B £8 L £4 D £10
CC: MC Vi Am Swi Delt

How to get there: On the banks of Loch Tay, at
the mouth of the river.

Kilchrenan, Argyll & Bute

208 Taychreggan Hotel

★★★
Taynuilt, Kilchrenan, Argyll & Bute, PA35 1HQ
Tel: 01866 833211/366 Fax: 01866 833244
Email: info@taychregganhotel.co.uk
Web: www.tacyhregganhotel.co.uk
Children minimum age: 14
19 bedrs SB £105 DB £115
B £10 L £15 D £35
CC: MC Vi Am DC Swi Delt

How to get there: From Glasgow follow M8 to
Erskine Bridge, then A82 to Tyndrum. Take A85
to Taynuilt, then B845 to Kilchrenan.

Killiecrankie, Perth & Kinross

209 Dalnasgadh House

◆ ◆
Pitlochry, Killiecrankie,
Perth & Kinross, PH16 5LN
Tel: 01796 473237

Kilmarnock, East Ayrshire

210 Travelodge Kilmarnock

Travel Accommodation
A71/A76, Riccarton Road, Bellfield Interchange,
Kilmarnock, East Ayrshire, KA1 5LQ
Tel: 08700 850 950
Web: www.travelodge.co.uk
40 bedrs B £4.25
CC: MC Vi Am DC Swi Delt

Kinross, Perth & Kinross

211 Travelodge Kinross

Travel Accommodation
Turfhill Tourist Centre, Kinross,
Perth & Kinross, KY13 7NQ
Tel: 08700 850 950
Web: www.travelodge.co.uk
35 bedrs B £4.25
CC: MC Vi Am DC Swi Delt

Scotland

Kirkcaldy, Fife

212 Dean Park Hotel

★★★ ®

Chapel Level, Kirkcaldy, Fife, KY2 6QW
Tel: 01592 261635 Fax: 01592 261371
Email: info@deanparkhotel.co.uk
Web: www.deanparkhotel.co.uk

Beautifully-appointed and professionally-run hotel with custom-built conference facilities. Well situated for leisure activities (golf, fishing etc). Excellent table (RAC Dining Award) and cellar.
34 bedrs SB £59 DB £89 HBS £80.50 HBD £66
CC: MC Vi Am DC Swi Delt
How to get there: Take A92 Edinburgh-Dunfermline road to Kirkcaldy. Take A910 to first roundabout.

Kyle, Highland

213 Lochalsh Hotel

★★★

Ferry Road, Kyle of Lochalsh,
Highland, IV40 8AF
Tel: 01599 534202 Fax: 01599 534881
Email: mdmacrae@lochalsh-hotel.demon.co.uk

A family-owned hotel overlooking the Isle of Skye. An oasis of comfort and good living in the Scottish highlands, with 38 bedrooms — all ensuite.

38 bedrs SB £45 DB £70 B £9.95 L £10 D £22
CC: MC Vi Am DC Swi Delt
How to get there: From south, turn left at Kyle traffic lights. Hotel 75m from lights.

Laide, Ross-shire

214 The Sheiling

◆◆◆◆

Achgarve, Laide, Ross-shire, IV22 2NS
Tel: 01445 731487 Fax: 01445 731487
Email: annabell.maciver@talk21.com
Closed November to March
2 bedrs SB £24 DB £48
CC: None accepted
How to get there: Take road behind Laide post office and drive for 1½ miles on the Metlon Udricle Road. Turn left at the Sheiling sign.

Largs, Ayrshire

215 Brisbane House Hotel

★★★★ ® ®

14 Greenock Road, Esplanade, Largs,
Ayrshire, KA30 8NF
Tel: 01475 687200
23 bedrs SB £70 DB £90 HBS £90 HBD £55
B £3.75 L £7.50 D £8.99
CC: MC Vi Am DC Swi Delt
How to get there: From Glasgow, follow the Irvine Road and at Loch Winnoch start following signs for Largs. Hotel is on right past main town.

216 Priory House Hotel

★★★★ ® ®

Broomfields, Largs, Ayrshire, KA30 8DR
Tel: 01475 686460 Fax: 01475 689070
Email: enquiries@maksu-group.co.uk
Web: www.maksu-group.co.uk
21 bedrs SB £65 DB £95 HBS £75 HBD £62.50
B £6.50 L £6.50 D £11.50
CC: MC Vi Am DC Swi Delt
How to get there: Entering Largs on A78, take turning into John Street near BP service station. Hotel is at end of road on seafront.

Lochgilphead, Argyll & Bute

217 Stag Hotel and Restaurant

★★

Argyll Street, Lochgilphead,
Argyll & Bute, PA31 8NE
Tel: 01546 602496 Fax: 01546 603549
Email: staghotel@ukhotels.com
Web: www.staghotel.com
18 bedrs SB £39.95 DB £54.95 HBS £49.95
HBD £37.50 B £4.95 L £4.95 D £4.95
CC: MC Vi Swi Delt

How to get there: At junction of Argyll Street
and Lorne Street in town centre.

218 Tigh-Na-Glaic

◆◆◆◆

Crinan, By Lochgilphead,
Argyll & Bute, PA31 8SW
Tel: 01546 830245 Fax: 01546 830266

Lochinver, Sutherland

219 Inver Lodge Hotel

★★★★

Lochinver, Sutherland, IV27 4LU
Tel: 01571 844496 Fax: 01571 844395
Email: stay@inverlodge.com
Web: www.inverlodge.com
Children minimum age: 7
Closed November to March

Our foreground is Lochinver Bay and The
Minch; our backdrop, the great peaks of
Sutherland: Canisp and Suilven. The hotel
combines modern facilities and comforts with
the traditional ambience of a Highland lodge.
20 bedrs SB £80 DB £140 HBS £105 HBD £95
B £12 D £35 CC: MC Vi Am DC Swi Delt

How to get there: On entering Lochinver, head
towards pier/harbour. Take first left after tourist
information centre for private road to hotel.

Lochmaben, Dumfries & Galloway

220 Magdalene House

◆◆◆◆

Bruce Street, Lochmaben,
Dumfries & Galloway, DG11 1PD
Tel: 01387 810439 Fax: 01387 810439
Email: mckerrellofhillhouse@unkonline.co.uk
3 bedrs SB £33 DB £56
HBS £43 HBD £38 D £10
CC: None accepted

How to get there: Take M74 to Lockerbie and
A709 to Lochmaben. Past High Street road
turns left. Magdalene House is first left.

Lockerbie, Dumfries & Galloway

221 Lockerbie Manor Hotel

★★★

Boreland Road, Lockerbie,
Dumfries & Galloway, DG11 2RG
Tel: 01576 202610 Fax: 01576 203046
Email: info@lockerbiemanorhotel.co.uk
Web: www.lockerbiemanorhotel.co.uk
32 bedrs SB £48 DB £68 HBS £60 HBD £90
B £7 L £12 D £17.95
CC: MC Vi Am DC Swi Delt

How to get there: Located half a mile from M74
Junction 17.
See advert on following page

Mallaig, Highland

222 Morar Hotel

★★

Morar, Mallaig, Highland, PH40 4PA
Tel: 01687 462346 Fax: 01687 462212
Email: enquiries@morarhotel.co.uk
Web: www.morarhotel.co.uk
Children minimum age: 14
28 bedrs SB £35 DB £70 HBS £50 HBD £50
CC: MC Vi

How to get there: In the village of Morar on the
A830 Fort William/Mallaig road, three miles from
Mallaig.

Scotland

223 West Highland Hotel

★★

Mallaig, Highland, PH41 4QZ
Tel: 01687 462210 Fax: 01687 462130
Email: westhighland.hotel@virgin.net
Web: www.westhighlandhotel.co.uk
39 bedrs SB £35 DB £70 HBS £49 HBD £49
B £6.50 L £6 D £16
CC: MC Vi

How to get there: From Fort William, turn right at roundabout, then first right uphill. From Skye ferry, turn left at roundabout, then first right uphill.

Markinch, Fife

224 Balbirnie House Hotel
Blue Ribbon Winner

★★★★★ 🏆 🏆 🏆
Balbirnie Park, Markinch,
Fife, KY7 6NE
Tel: 01592 610066 Fax: 01592 610529
Email: balbirnie@breathemail.net
Web: www.balbirnie.co.uk

A quite unique multi-award-winning hotel which combines understated luxury with superb service and outstanding value. Located 30 minutes equidistant from Edinburgh and St. Andrews.
30 bedrs SB £125 DB £185
B £13.75 L £11.50 D £31.50
CC: MC Vi Am DC Swi Delt

How to get there: From Edinburgh, follow signs for Forth Road Bridge (M90). Leave at Junction 2a and take A92. Follow signs to Glenrothes. Across third roundabout, turn right at signs for Balbirnie Park.

Maybole, Ayrshire

225 Ladyburn
Blue Ribbon Winner

★★★ 🏆 🏆 🏆
Ladyburn, Maybole, Ayrshire, KA19 7SG
Tel: 01655 740585 Fax: 01655 740580
Email: jh@ladyburn.demon.co.uk
Web: www.ladyburn.co.uk
5 bedrs SB £100 DB £150
HBS £120 HBD £100 B £10 L £15 D £30
CC: MC Vi Am

How to get there: A77, B7024 to Crosshill. Right at war memorial, left after two miles. After a further 3/4 mile, Ladyburn is on the right.

Melrose, Scottish Borders

226 Dryburgh Abbey Hotel

★★★

St. Boswells, Melrose,
Scottish Borders, TD6 0RQ
Tel: 01835 822261 Fax: 01835 823945
Email: enquiries@dryburgh.co.uk
Web: www.dryburgh.co.uk
38 bedrs SB £55 DB £110 HBS £70 HBD £70
B £12 L £6.50 D £26
CC: MC Vi Am Swi Delt

How to get there: Take A68 to St. Boswells. Turn onto B6404 and head through village. After two miles turn left on to B6356. Continue for two miles to hotel entrance.

227 George & Abbotsford Hotel

★★

High Street, Melrose,
Scottish Borders, TD6 9PD
Tel: 01896 822308 Fax: 01896 823363
Email: enquiries@georgeandabbotsford.co.uk
Web: www.georgeandabbotsford.co.uk
30 bedrs SB £50 DB £85
HBS £55 HBD £110
CC: MC Vi Am DC Swi Delt

How to get there: Use the A7 or A68 trunk road, joined by the A6091 bypass. Hotel is midway up High Street.

228 Braidwood B&B

◆ ◆ ◆ ◆

Buccleuth Street, Melrose,
Scottish Borders, TD6 9LD
Tel: 01896 822488
Email: braidwood.melrose@virgin.net
Web: www.melrose.bordernet/
      traders/braidwood
4 bedrs SB £28 DB £40 CC: None accepted

How to get there: Centrally situated next to Post
Office and close to Abbey.

229 Clint Lodge

◆ ◆ ◆ ◆

Clint Hill, St. Boswells, near Melrose,
Scottish Borders, TD6 0DZ
Tel: 01835 822027 Fax: 01835 822656
Email: clintlodge@aol.om
5 bedrs SB £35 DB £70 HBS £55 HBD £55
B £7.50 D £20
CC: MC Vi

230 The Old Abbey School

◆ ◆ ◆ ◆

Waverley Road, Melrose,
Scottish Borders, TD6 9SH
Tel: 01896 823432
Email: oneill@abbeyschool.fsnet.co.uk
Closed December to February
3 bedrs SB £25 DB £36
CC: None accepted

How to get there: From Melrose High Street
take the main road to Galashiels. The house is
the second on the left on Waverley Road.

Moffat, Dumfries & Galloway

231 Auchen Castle Hotel

★ ★ ★

Beattock, near Moffat,
Dumfries & Galloway, DG10 9SH
Tel: 01683 300407 Fax: 01683 300667
Email: reservations@auchen-castle-hotel.co.uk
Web: www.auchen-castle-hotel.co.uk
25 bedrs SB £75 DB £95 B £10.25 L £7.50 D £25
CC: MC Vi Am DC Swi Delt

How to get there: One mile north on B7076 from
A/M74 Junction 15 (Moffat turn-off).
See advert on following page

Scotland

232 Moffat House Hotel

★ ★ ★

High Street, Moffat,
Dumfries & Galloway, DG10 9HL
Tel: 01683 220039 Fax: 01683 221288
Email: moffat@talk21.com
Web: www.moffathouse.co.uk
Children minimum age: 12
21 bedrs SB £60 DB £94 HBS £84 HBD £148
B £6.50 L £7 D £7 CC: MC Vi Am Swi Delt

How to get there: One mile east off M74 at J15.
Set in Moffat Square.

233 Famous Star Hotel

★★
44 High Street, Moffat,
Dumfries & Galloway, DG10 9EF
Tel: 01683 220156 Fax: 01683 221524
Email: tim@famousstarhotel.com
Web: www.famousstarhotel.com

Although the narrowest hotel, as seen in the
Guinness Book of Records — only 20ft wide —
the interior and welcome are heart-warming.
Excellent accommodation, real ales and good
homecooking restaurant.
8 bedrs SB £40 DB £56 HBS £48 HBD £80
B £4.95 L £4 D £5 CC: MC Vi Am DC Swi Delt
🅂🅂⬚🞈🗔☎🞈🟕🟙🞈
How to get there: Situated one mile off M74
Junction 15. The hotel is on the right-hand side
in the town centre.

234 Well View Hotel

Gold Ribbon Winner

★🎗🎗🎗
Ballplay Road, Moffat,
Dumfries & Galloway, DG10 9JU
Tel: 01683 220184 Fax: 01683 220088
Email: info@wellview.co.uk
Web: www.wellview.co.uk

Mid-Victorian villa set in half an acre of garden
and overlooking the town, with superb views of
surrounding hills.
6 bedrs SB £63 DB £100 HBS £93 HBD £80
B £10 L £15 D £30
CC: MC Vi Am Swi Delt
🞈🞈🞈🞈🗔🅿🞈🞈🞈🞈🞈
How to get there: From Moffat, A708 for Selkirk.
½ mile left into Ballplay Road. then 300 yards
on right.

Monymusk, Aberdeenshire

235 Grant Arms Hotel

◆◆
Monymusk, Aberdeenshire, AB51 7HJ
Tel: 01467 651226 Fax: 01467 651494

Nairn, Highland

236 Alton Burn Hotel

★★
Alton Burn Road, Nairn, Highland, IV12 5ND
Tel: 01667 452051

Nethy Bridge, Highland

237 Nethybridge Hotel

★★
Nethy Bridge, Highland, PH25 3DP
Tel: 01479 821203 Fax: 01479 821686
Web: www.strathmorehotels.com
69 bedrs SB £39 DB £78 HBS £49 HBD £49
B £7.50 D £15
CC: MC Vi Swi Delt JCB
🞈🞈🞈🞈🞈🞈🗔☎🅿🞈🞈🞈🞈🞈🞈

Auchen Castle Hotel

An imposing nineteenth-century country mansion set in 30 acres of beautifully maintained formal gardens and woodland. From the restaurant, enjoy panormaic views over the Moffat Hills and beyond. Ideally located to tour the Border Country or indulge yourself with a round of golf, cycling, horse riding or fishing in our private trout loch. Luxury feature suites with four-poster beds are also available to help turn your stay into a truly memorable occasion.

Beattock, near Moffat, Dumfries & Galloway DG10 9SH

Tel: 01683 300407   Fax: 01683 300667

reservations@auchen-castle-hotel.co.uk

www.auchen-castle-hotel.co.uk

RAC
★★★

Newton Stewart, Dumfries & Galloway

238 Galloway Arms Hotel

★★

54–58 Victoria Street, Newton Stewart, Dumfries & Galloway, DG8 6DB
Tel: 01671 402653 Fax: 01671 401202
Email: information@gallowayarms.fs.net
Web: www.gallowayarmshotel.net

Newton Stewart's oldest hotel established 1750. Now completely refurbished and enlarged by the purchase of building next door. Comfortable hotel specialising in fresh Galloway produce. New bar, lounge and restaurant.
19 bedrs SB £27.50 DB £50 HBS £39.50 HBD £39 B £5 L £5.50 D £12.95

CC: MC Vi Am Swi Delt

How to get there: In centre of Newton Stewart, opposite Town Hall clock. Private parking down lane beside hotel.

Newtonmore, Highland

239 Glen Hotel

★★

Main Street, Newtonmore, Highland, PH20 1DD
Tel: 01540 673203
10 bedrs SB £25 DB £40 HBS £40 HBD £35
B £5 L £5 D £5
CC: MC Vi Am DC Swi Delt JCB

How to get there: One mile off the A9 Perth to Inverness road, 15 miles south of Aviemore.

Plan your route

Visit www.rac.co.uk for RAC's interactive route planner, including up to the minute traffic reports.

North Berwick, East Lothian

240 Heritage Hotels — The Marine

★★★

Cromwell Road, North Berwick,
East Lothian, EH39 4LZ
Tel: 0870 400 8129 Fax: 01620 894480
Email: heritagehotels_north_berwick
@forte-hotels.com
Web: www.heritagehotels.com
83 bedrs SB £60 DB £110 HBS £85 HBD £75
B £13 L £4.95 D £22.50
CC: MC Vi Am DC Swi Delt

How to get there: From A1 City bypass, take
A198 signposted North Berwick. From A198
turn at traffic lights into Hamilton Road, North
Berwick. Hotel is second on right.

Oban, Argyll & Bute

241 Alexandra Hotel

★★★

Corran Esplanade, Oban, Argyll & Bute, PA34 5AA
Tel: 01631 562381 Fax: 01631 564497

242 Royal Hotel

★★★

Argyll Square, Oban, Argyll & Bute, PA34 4BE
Tel: 01631 563021 Fax: 01631 562811
91 bedrs SB £40 DB £80 HBS £60 HBD £120
B £8.50 D £15
CC: MC Vi Am Swi Delt

How to get there: In town centre, five minutes
from ferry/rail/bus terminals.

243 Falls of Lora Hotel

★★

Connel Ferry, by Oban, Oban,
Argyll & Bute, PA37 1PB
Tel: 01631 710483 Fax: 01631 710694
Closed mid-December to January

Overlooking Loch Etive, this owner-run hotel
has inexpensive family rooms to luxury! The
cocktail bar has an open log fire and over 100
brands of whisky; there is an extensive Bistro
menu.
30 bedrs SB £30 DB £39 B £9.50 L £8 D £17.50
CC: MC Vi Am DC Swi Delt

How to get there: A82, A85. Hotel is ½ a mile
past Connel signpost, five miles before Oban.

244 King's Knoll Hotel

★★

Dunollie Road, Oban, Argyll & Bute, PA34 5JH
Tel: 01631 562536 Fax: 01631 566101
Email: info@kingsknollhotel.co.uk
Web: www.kingsknollhotel.co.uk
Closed January to mid-February
15 bedrs SB £32 DB £64 HBS £44 HBD £44
B £8 D £12
CC: MC Vi Swi Delt JCB

How to get there: First hotel on left as you enter
Oban from North/East on A85 main road.

245 Glenbervie Guest House

◆◆◆◆ ※

Dalriach Road, Oban, Argyll & Bute, PA34 5JD
Tel: 01631 564770
8 bedrs SB £20 DB £40 D £12

246 Loch Etive House

◆◆◆◆ ※

Connel, Oban, Argyll & Bute, PA37 1PH
Tel: 01631 710400 Fax: 01631 710680
Closed November to April
6 bedrs SB £25 DB £50
CC: MC Vi

How to get there: Off A85 in Connel between
the village store and St. Oran's Church.

247 Ronebhal Guest House

♦♦♦♦
Connel, by Oban, Argyll & Bute, PA37 1PJ
Tel: 01631 710310/813 Fax: 01631 710310
Email: ronebhal@btinternet.com
Web: www.argyllinternet.co.uk/ronebhal
Children minimum age: 7
Closed December to January
5 bedrs SB £20 DB £40 CC: MC Vi Delt
How to get there: Off A85 in Connel village, 4th house past the Connel Bridge junction.

Onich, Highland

248 Onich Hotel

★★★
Onich, Highland, PH33 6RY
Tel: 01855 821214 Fax: 01855 821484
Email: enquiries@onich-fortwilliam.co.uk
Web: www.onich-fortwilliam.co.uk

Surounded by mountains, lochs and gardens, this hotel offers the perfect setting for a relaxing break. Award-winning cuisine specialising in fresh local produce.
25 bedrs SB £60 DB £120 B £8 L £7.50 D £23
CC: MC Vi Am DC Swi Delt
How to get there: The Onich hotel is situated on the A82 in the village of Onich, overlooking Loch Linnhe, 12 miles south of Fort William.

Peebles, Scottish Borders

249 Lindores Bed & Breakfast

♦♦♦
60 Old Town, Peebles, Borders, EH45 8JE
Tel: 01721 720441
Email: lane.lindores@virgin.net
Web: www.aboutscotland.co.uk/peebles/lindores.html
Closed November
4 bedrs SB £20 DB £32 HBS £29 HBD £25 D £9
CC: None accepted
How to get there: Property is to the west of Peebles, on the A72 next to Millers Farm shop.

Perth, Perth & Kinross

250 Murrayshall House Hotel and Golf Course

★★★
Scone, Perth, Perth & Kinross, PH2 7PH
Tel: 01738 551171 Fax: 01738 552595
Email: info@murrayshall.co.uk
Web: www.murrayshall.co.uk
41 bedrs SB £85 DB £130 HBS £100 HBD £75 B £7.50 D £25.25
CC: MC Vi Am Swi Delt
How to get there: From Perth take A94 to Coupar Angus. Turn right off A94 just before the village of Scone.

251 Quality Hotel Perth

★★★
Leonard Street, Perth, PH2 8HE
Tel: 01738 624141 Fax: 01738 639912
Email: admin@gb628.u-net.com
Web: www.choicehotels.com
70 bedrs SB £89.75 DB £104.75 HBS £104.25 HBD £59.67 B £10.75 L £9.95 D £14.50
CC: MC Vi Am DC Swi Delt
How to get there: From M90/A90, turn left into Marshall Place, which runs into Kings Place, then Leonard Street. Adjacent to railway station.

252 Salutation Hotel

★★★
South Street, Perth, Perth & Kinross, PH2 8PH
Tel: 01738 630066 Fax: 01738 633598
Email: salutation@perth.fsnet.co.uk
Web: www.strathmorehotels.com
84 bedrs SB £45 DB £80 HBS £50 HBD £90 B £5 L £3 D £14.50
CC: MC Vi Am Swi Delt JCB
How to get there: Situated in the centre of Perth, M85 from Dundee, A9 from Inverness, A9 from Stirling/Glasgow, M90 from Edinburgh.

253 Clunie Guest House

◆◆◆ 🕸 ⚕

12 Pitcullen Crescent, Perth,
Perth & Kinross, PH2 7HT
Tel: 01738 623625 Fax: 01738 623238
Email: ann@clunieperth.freeserve.co.uk
Web: www.clunieguesthouse.co.uk
7 bedrs SB £19 DB £38
CC: MC Vi Am

🐾 ⊗ ⑤ 💻 P 🏃 ⚕

How to get there: Situated on A94 Perth/Couper
Angus road. Leave M90 at Junction 11 and
follow signs for A94.

Pitlochry, Perth & Kinross

254 Balrobin Hotel

★★

Higher Oakfield, Pitlochry,
Perth & Kinross, PH16 5HT
Tel: 01796 472901 Fax: 01796 474200
Email: info@balrobin.co.uk
Web: www.balrobin.co.uk
Children minimum age: 5
Closed November to February
15 bedrs SB £25 DB £50 HBS £37 HBD £37
B £inc D £17.50
CC: MC Vi Swi Delt

🐾 ⊗ ⑤ 💻 P 🏃 ⋔

How to get there: From centre of town, follow
brown tourist signs.

255 Knockendarroch House Hotel

★★ 🍴 🍴

Higher Oakfield, Pitlochry,
Perth & Kinross, PH16 5HT
Tel: 01796 473473 Fax: 01796 474068
Email: info@knockendarroch.co.uk
Web: www.knockendarroch.co.uk
Children minimum age: 10
Closed November to February
12 bedrs SB £59 DB £84
HBS £79 HBD £60 B £8.50 D £18
CC: MC Vi Am Swi Delt

♿ 🗐 ⊗ ⑤ 💻 ☎ P 🏃 ⋔

How to get there: Enter Pitlochry from A9 on
main street (Atholl Road), take Bonnethill Road,
Toberargan Road, then Higher Oakfield; three
minutes walk from town centre.

Poolewe, Highland

256 Pool House

★★★ 🍴 🍴

By Inverewe Garden, Poolewe,
Highland, IV22 2LD
Tel: 01445 781272 Fax: 01445 781403
Email: enquiries@poolhousehotel.com
Web: www.poolhousehotel.com
Closed January to February
5 bedrs SB £90 DB £250 HBS £125 HBD £160
B £15 L £12.95 D £28
CC: MC Vi Am Swi Delt JCB

🏊 🗐 🕸 ⊗ ⑤ 💻 ☎ P ⋕ ⋔

How to get there: Six miles north of Gairloch on
the A382, situated by the bridge in Poolewe, by
the River Ewe.

Port Askaig, Argyll & Bute

257 Port Askaig Hotel

★★

Port Askaig, Isle of Islay,
Argyll & Bute, PA46 7RD
Tel: 01496 840 245 Fax: 01496 840 295
Email: hotel@portaskaig.co.uk
Web: www.portaskaig.co.uk
Children minimum age: 5

This 400-year-old inn overlooks the Sound-of-
Islay, the picturesque harbour and lifeboat
station. Situated in own gardens. The best of
home-cooked food. Bars open all day.
8 bedrs
CC: MC Vi Swi

🐾 🐕 ⑤ 💻 P☎ 🏃 ♁ ⋔ 🍴 ⋕ ⋔ ⚗.

How to get there: Harbourside at Port Askaig
ferry terminal. From Port Ellen terminal or from
Islay airport follow straight route through
Bowmore and Bridgend.

Port William, Dumfries & Galloway

258 Corsemalzie House

★★★★ ♟ ♟

Port William, Newton Stewart,
Dumfries & Galloway, DG8 9RL
Tel: 01988 860254 Fax: 01988 860213
Email: corsemalzie@ndirect.co.uk
Web: www.corsemalzie-house.ltd.uk
Closed mid-January to early March
14 bedrs SB £54.50 DB £83 HBS £64.50
HBD £54.50 B £9.75 L £10.95 D £23.75
CC: MC Vi Am Swi Delt

How to get there: From east on A75 turn left at
Newton Steward roundabout onto A714,
bypassing Wigtown. Turn right after crossing
bridge at Bladnoch.

Rosebank, Lanarkshire

259 Popinjay Hotel

★★★★ ♟ ♟

Lanark Road, Rosebank, Lanarkshire, ML8 5QB
Tel: 01555 860441 Fax: 01555 860204
Email: popinjayhotel@attglobal.net
Web: www.popinjayhotel.co.uk
38 bedrs SB £59 DB £75
B £8.50 L £12.50 D £18.50
CC: MC Vi Am DC Swi Delt JCB

How to get there: Four miles from M74, on the
A72 between Hamilton and Lanark.

Rosyth, Fife

260 Gladyer Inn

★★

10 Heath Road, Ridley Drive, Rosyth,
Fife, KY11 2BT
Tel: 01383 419977 Fax: 01383 411728
Email: gladyer@aol.com
21 bedrs
CC: MC Vi Am Swi Delt

How to get there: Leave M90 at Junction 1.
Follow signs into Rosyth. Go straight on at
roundabout. Take first left.

Selkirk, Scottish Borders

261 Ettrickshaws Country House Hotel · Little Gem

♦ ♦ ♦ ♦ ♦ ♟ ♟ ✳ ♞

Ettrickbridge, Selkirk,
Scottish Borders, TD7 5HW
Tel: 01750 52229 Fax: 01750 52229
Email: jenny@ettrickshaws.co.uk
Web: www.ettrickshaws.co.uk
Children minimum age: 12
5 bedrs SB £56 DB £90 HBS £72.50
HBD £62.50 B £10 D £22.50
CC: MC Vi

How to get there: From Selkirk town square
take A708 Moffat road. After ¹/₂ miles turn left
onto B7009 to Ettrickbridge. Ettrickshaws one
mile past village on left hand side (7 miles from
Selkirk).

Shetland Isles

262 Busta House Hotel

★★★ ♟

Brae, Shetland Isles, ZE2 9QN
Tel: 01806 522506 Fax: 01806 522588
Email: reservations@bustahouse.com
Web: www.bustahouse.com
20 bedrs SB £70 DB £95 HBS £95 HBD £140
B £7.50 L £12.95 D £27.50
CC: MC Vi Am DC Swi Delt

How to get there: Travel north on A970; turn left
at Brae onto well-signposted road for
approximately ¹/₂ a mile.

263 Shetland Hotel

★★★ ♟

Holmsgarth Road, Lerwick,
Shetland Isles, ZE1 0PW
Tel: 01595 695515 Fax: 01595 695828
Email: reception@shetlandhotel.co.uk
Web: www.shetlandhotels.com
65 bedrs SB £69 DB £89.95 HBS £84.95
HBD £59.50 B £6.95 L £6.95 D £9.50
CC: MC Vi Am DC Swi

How to get there: Conveniently located opposite
main P&O ferry terminal for Lerwick, and on
main route north out of town.

Scotland

264 Glen Orchy House

♦ ♦ ♦ ♦ ✖ 🍴

20 Knab Road, Lerwick, Shetland Isles, ZE1 0AX
Tel: 01595 692031 Fax: 01595 692031
Email: glenorchy.house@virgin.net
Web: www.guesthouselerwick.com
22 bedrs SB £40 DB £66 D £15
CC: MC Vi Delt JCB

&🐕😊🍵💻❄🅿🛅👬

How to get there: Follow main route until
Church/Knab Road/Annsbrae/Greenfield
junction. Turn right from south, straight ahead
from north, onto Knab Road.
See advert on facing page

Shieldaig, Ross-shire

265 Tigh an Eilean

★ 📻 📻 📻

Shieldaig, by Torridon, Ross-shire, IV54 8XN
Tel: 01520 755251 Fax: 01520 755321
Email: tighaneileanhotel@shieldaig.fsnet.co.uk
Closed mid-October to beginning April

Family-run hotel in unspoilt old fishing village,
amidst Torridon mountains. Glorious views.
Restaurant serves fine local produce, including
seafood delivered daily from jetty to kitchen
door.
11 bedrs SB £49.50 DB £110
HBS £76.50 HBD £82 D £27
CC: MC Vi Swi

🐕😊🛅🎃👬

How to get there: Centre of Quiet village off
A896. Parking opposite. Train: Strathcarron; Bus
connects with lunchtime train, or hotel happy to
meet.

Spean Bridge, Highland

266 Letterfinlay Lodge Hotel

★ ★ ★ 📻

Lochlochy, Spean Bridge, Highland, PH34 4DZ
Tel: 01397 712622
Closed November to mid-March
13 bedrs SB £35 DB £70 HBS £55 HBD £55
B £7.75 L £5.75 D £12
CC: MC Vi Am DC Swi Delt JCB

◁🐕😊💻☎🅿🛅🎃🍴🌊♨👬🎵《✎

How to get there: Seven miles north of Spean
Bridge, on shore of Lochlochy on the A82.

St. Andrews, Fife

267 Heritage Hotels – The Rusacks

★ ★ ★ ★ ★ 📻 📻

Pilmour Links, St. Andrews, Fife, KY16 9JQ
Tel: 01334 474321 Fax: 01334 477896
Email: heritagehotels_standrews.rusacks
@forte-hotels.com
Web: www.heritage-hotels.com

Voted one of the top ten golfing hotels in the
world, our AA rosette-winning restaurant
overlooks the famous old course in St. Andrews
and specialises in local game and seafood.
68 bedrs SB £55 DB £110 HBS £70 HBD £70
B £15 L £4.75 D £35
CC: MC Vi Am DC Swi Delt

◁&⛰🐕😊💻☎📞🅿🛅🎃🍴🌊♨👬

How to get there: Enter St. Andrews on the A91.
Rusacks is 500 yards into town on the left-hand
side.

268 Scores Hotel

★★★

76 The Scores, St. Andrews, Fife, KY16 9BB
Tel: 01334 472451 Fax: 01334 473947
Email: office@scoreshotel.co.uk
30 bedrs SB £93 DB £157 HBS £109
HBD £94.50 B £5.95 L £7.50 D £18.50
CC: MC Vi Am DC Swi Delt

How to get there: M90 J2A, follow A91 to St.
Andrews. Over first small roundabout, then
second. First left and then first right.

269 St. Andrews B&B
Little Gem

♦ ♦ ♦ ♦ ♦ 🖥 ⚛ 🍷

Ladeddie Steading, St. Andrews, Fife, KY15 5TY
Tel: 01334 840514 Fax: 01334 840833
Email: standrewsbb@talk21.com
Web: www.standrewsbb.co.uk
Closed December to January

Delightful, newly-converted 18th-century barn.
Set in idyllic countryside with amazing views,
nearby St. Andrews and the best golf courses in
the world. Luxury restored steading cottage also
available.
4 bedrs SB £28 DB £50 D £20
CC: MC Vi Swi Delt

⊗ 🍵 🖵 🅿 🔌 ⚒

How to get there: From Cupar, B940 to Pitscottie
crossroads, left then next right. After one mile
turn right up hill, entrance right before farm.

St. Fillans, Perth & Kinross

270 The Four Seasons Hotel

★★★★ 🖥 🖥 🖥

St. Fillans, Perth & Kinross, PH6 2NF
Tel: 01764 685333 Fax: 01764 685444
Email: info@thefourseasonshotel.co.uk
Web: www.thefourseasonshotel.co.uk
Closed February

The finest lochside location in the southern
Highlands. Contemporary cuisine using the best
ingredients available from Scotland's natural
larder, catering for the imaginative to more
traditional diner.
12 bedrs SB £41 DB £82 HBS £63.50
HBD £63.50 B £12.50 L £18 D £18
CC: MC Vi Am Swi Delt

How to get there: On the A85 at the west end of
St. Fillans, at the east end of Loch Earn.

Stirling, Stirlingshire

271 Stirling Highland Hotel

★★★★★ ⓡ ⓡ
Spittal Street, Stirling, Stirlingshire, FK8 1DU
Tel: 01786 272727 Fax: 01786 272829
Email: stirling@paramount-hotels.co.uk
Web: www.paramount-hotels.co.uk
96 bedrs SB £110 DB £150 HBS £63 HBD £63
B £8.50 L £11.95 D £22.50
CC: MC Vi Am DC Swi Delt

How to get there: Exit J10 M9; follow ring road and signs to Stirling Castle. Hotel is on left.

272 Royal Hotel

★★★★ ⓡ ⓡ
55 Henderson Street, Bridge of Allan,
Stirlingshire, FK9 4HG
Tel: 01786 832284 Fax: 01786 834377
Email: stay@royal-stirling.co.uk
Web: www.royal-stirling.co.uk
32 bedrs SB £85 DB £130 HBS £105 HBD £80
B £6.95 L £6.95 D £22.50
CC: MC Vi Am DC Swi Delt

How to get there: Leave M9 at Junction 11. At large roundabout, take fourth turning which is signposted Bridge of Allan. Follow this road (A9) into the village centre. Hotel is on left.

273 Travelodge Stirling

Travel Accommodation
Pirnhall, Stirling, FK7 8EU
Tel: 08700 850 950
Web: www.travelodge.co.uk
37 bedrs B £4.25 CC: MC Vi Am DC Swi Delt

Strachur, Argyll & Bute

274 The Creggans Inn

★★★★ ⓡ ⓡ
Strachur, Argyll & Bute, PA27 8BX
Tel: 01369 860279 Fax: 01369 860637
Email: info@creggans-inn.co.uk
Web: www.creggans-inn.co.uk
14 bedrs SB £72 DB £100 HBS £95 HBD £146
B £10 L £6 D £26.50 CC: MC Vi Swi Delt

How to get there: From Glasgow, take the A82 to Arrochar, then A83; turn onto A815 (Dunoon).

Strontian, Argyll & Bute

275 Strontian Hotel

★★ ⓡ
Acharacle, Strontian, Argyll & Bute, PH36 4HZ
Tel: 01967 402029 Fax: 01967 402314
Email: strontianhotel@supanet.com
Web: www.strontianhotel.supanet.com
7 bedrs SB £35 DB £52.50 HBS £47
HBD £38.25 B £5.50 L £5 D £12
CC: MC Vi Swi Delt

How to get there: From A82 take Corran ferry to Ardgour. Turn left off ferry on A861. Hotel on right as you enter Strontian.

Tain, Highland

276 Morangie House Hotel

★★★★ ⓡ
Morangie Road, Tain, Highland, IV19 1PY
Tel: 01862 892281 Fax: 01862 892872
Email: wynne@morangiehotel.com
Web: www.morangiehotel.com
26 bedrs
CC: MC Vi Am DC Swi

How to get there: Turn right off A9 at northern entrance to Tain. Hotel is first building on the right.

277 Royal Hotel

★★
High Street, Tain, Highland, IV19 1AB
Tel: 01862 892013 Fax: 01862 893450
25 bedrs SB £45 DB £70 L £6 D £9
CC: MC Vi Am

Tarbert, Argyll & Bute

278 Stonefield Castle Hotel

★★★★ ⓡ ⓡ
Tarbert, Argyll & Bute, PA29 6YJ
Tel: 01880 820836 Fax: 01880 820929

Making a booking?

Don't forget to mention RAC Hotels and Bed & Breakfast 2002.

279 Columba Hotel

★★★

East Pier Road, Tarbert, Loch Fyne,
Argyll & Bute, PA29 6UF
Tel: 01880 820808 Fax: 01880 820808
Email: columbahotel@fsbdial.co.uk
Web: www.columbahotel.com
Closed Christmas
10 bedrs SB £36.95 DB £73.90 HBS £54.95
HBD £54.98 B £6.50 L £6.50 D £22.50
CC: MC Vi Am Swi Delt

How to get there: As you enter Tarbert on A83,
turn left around the harbour. Columba Hotel is
¹/₂ mile from junction.

280 Victoria Hotel

♦♦♦♦

Barmore Road, Tarbert, Argyll & Bute, PA29 6TW
Tel: 01880 820236 Fax: 01880 820638
Web: www.victoriahoteltarbert.co.uk
5 bedrs SB £29 DB £58 B £7.50 L £6.25 D £10
CC: MC Vi Swi Delt

How to get there: Follow signs to Tarbert. Enter
Tarbert from Lochgilgilphead 200 metres right-
hand side facing harbour.

Thurso, Highland

281 St. Clair Hotel

★★

Sinclair Street, Thurso, Highland, KW14 7AJ
Tel: 01847 896481 Fax: 01847 896481
Web: www.stclairhotel.co.uk
32 bedrs SB £32 DB £60 HBS £40 HBD £40
B £6 L £6 D £13
CC: MC Vi Swi JCB

How to get there: First set of traffic lights
straight on; second set of traffic lights turn
sharp left. Directions from A9 north.

282 Ulbster Arms

★★★

Halkirk, Highland, KW12 6XY
Tel: 01847 831641 Fax: 01847 831641
CC: MC Vi Swi

How to get there: Halkirk is 109 miles north of
Inverness. Follow A9, then turn left onto A895.

Tongue, Highland

283 Ben Loyal Hotel

★★★

Tongue, Highland, IV27 4XE
Tel: 01847 611216 Fax: 01847 611212
Email: benloyalhotel@btinternet.com
Web: www.benloyal.co.uk
11 bedrs SB £38 DB £76 HBS £62.50
HBD £62.50 B £8 L £10 D £24
CC: MC Vi Swi

How to get there: From A9, take road to Bonar
Bridge. Follow A836 north to junction with
A838. Turn left at junction into village.

Torridon, Highland

284 Loch Torridon Country House Hotel
Blue Ribbon Winner

★★★

Torridon By Achnasheen, Highland, IV22 2EY
Tel: 01445 791242 Fax: 01445 791296
Email: enquiries@lochtorridonhotel.com
Web: www.lochtorridonhotel.com
20 bedrs SB £50 DB £88 D £38
CC: MC Vi Am DC Swi Delt

How to get there: From Inverness, follow signs
to Ullapool (A835). At Garve, turn left onto A832.
Follow signs to Kinlochewe. Turn left onto A896:
Torridon 10 miles. Pass Annat: hotel on right.

Troon, South Ayrshire

285 Marine Hotel

★★★★

Crosbie Road, Troon, South Ayrshire, KA10 6HE
Tel: 01292 314444 Fax: 01292 316922
Email: marine@paramount-hotels.co.uk
Web: www.paramount-hotels.co.uk
74 bedrs SB £122.95 DB £186
B £5 L £8 D £18
CC: MC Vi Am DC Swi Delt

How to get there: Take M77/A77 to Prestwick
airport. Turn right at B749 to Troon. Hotel is on
left by Royal Troon golf club.

Scotland

286 South Beach Hotel

★★★
73 South Beach, Troon,
South Ayrshire, KA10 6EG
Tel: 01292 312033 Fax: 01292 318348
Email: info@southbeach.co.uk
Web: www.southbeach.co.uk
34 bedrs SB £55 DB £83 HBS £69.50
HBD £109 B £6 L £6.50
CC: MC Vi Am Swi Delt

Turnberry, South Ayrshire

287 The Westin-Turnberry Resort
Blue Ribbon Winner

★★★★★ R R R
Turnberry, South Ayrshire, KA26 9LT
Tel: 01655 331000 Fax: 01655 331706
Email: turnberry@westin.com
Web: www.turnberry.co.uk
Closed Christmas
221 bedrs SB £135 DB £180 HBS £184
HBD £139 L £15 D £25
CC: MC Vi Am DC Swi Delt JCB

How to get there: Turnberry is located just off
the A77 Glasgow to Stranraer road, 15 miles
south of Ayr.

288 Malin Court Hotel

★★★★ R R R
Girvan, Turnberry, South Ayrshire, KA26 9PB
Tel: 01655 331457 Fax: 01655 331072
Email: info@malincourt.co.uk
Web: www.malincourt.co.uk
18 bedrs SB £72 DB £104 HBS £85 HBD £65
B £6.50 L £5 D £12
CC: MC Vi Am DC Swi Delt

How to get there: On A74 take Ayr exit. From
Ayr, take the A719 to Turnberry and Maidens.

West Wemyss, Fife

289 Belvedere Hotel

★★ R
Coxstool, West Wemyss, Fife, KY1 4SL
Tel: 01592 654167 Fax: 01592 655279

Whitebridge, Highland

290 Whitebridge Hotel

★★ R
Whitebridge, Highland, IV2 6UN
Tel: 01456 486226 Fax: 01456 486413
Email: whitebridgehotel
@southlochness.demon.co.uk
Web: www.southlochness.demon.co.uk
11 bedrs SB £30 DB £50
B £7.50 L £5 D £15
CC: MC Vi Am DC Swi Delt JCB

How to get there: From A82 at Fort Augustus
follow B862 for nine miles. From Inverness,
follow B862 for 24 miles.

Wick, Highland

291 Mackay's Hotel

★★
Union Street, Wick,
Highland, KW1 5ED
Tel: 01955 602323 Fax: 01955 605930
Web: www.mackayshotel.co.uk
30 bedrs B £8.50 L £9.95 D £19.50
CC: MC Vi Am Swi

Commission-free
foreign currency

Your journey can get off to a flying start, thanks to a commission free service RAC has organised with currency experts, Travelex.

Forget standing in long queues, just order your commission free currency and travellers cheques from the comfort of your home and your order will be delivered to your door.

Call RAC Travel Sales
0800 55 00 55
quoting GUI1

A to B - we RAC to it

RAC

Northern Ireland & Republic of Ireland

Coleraine

Londonderry
LONDONDERRY
ANTRIM
A26

Ballymena • Larne

TYRONE
A5
Carrickfergus

Cookstown
M2

Omagh
Belfast International
BELFAST • Bangor

A4

FERMANAGH
M1

A28
Portadown

Armagh
DOWN
A1

ARMAGH

Newry

REPUBLIC OF IRELAND

Glasgow • • Edinburgh

• Newcastle

Belfast •

Dublin •
• Manchester

Birmingham •

Cardiff •
• London

Soft, rounded mountains

The poet William Percy French wrote of "where the Mountains of Mourne sweep down to the sea", a line famous all over the world. The mountains loom over the town of Newcastle and provide a picturesque background to this bustling coastal town.

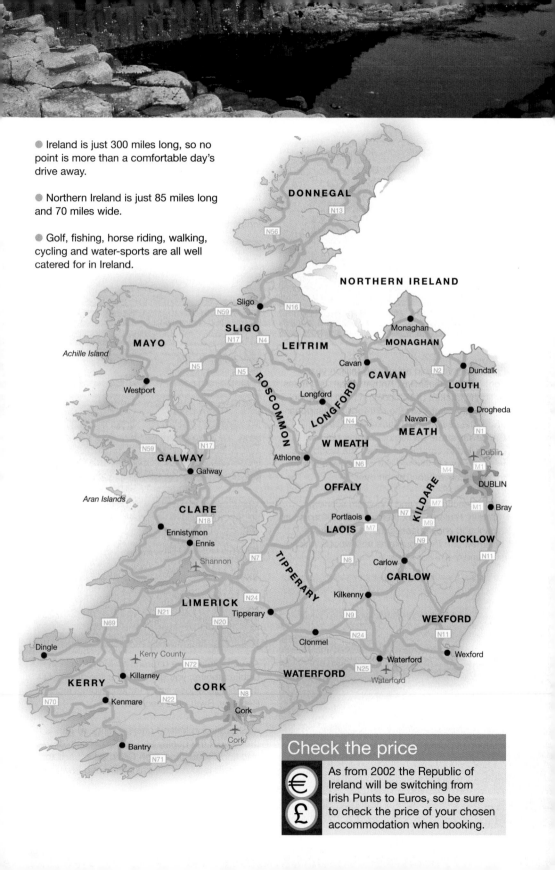

● Ireland is just 300 miles long, so no point is more than a comfortable day's drive away.

● Northern Ireland is just 85 miles long and 70 miles wide.

● Golf, fishing, horse riding, walking, cycling and water-sports are all well catered for in Ireland.

DONNEGAL

NORTHERN IRELAND

Sligo

SLIGO

MAYO

Achille Island

Westport

LEITRIM

Monaghan

MONAGHAN

Cavan

CAVAN

Longford

LONGFORD

Dundalk

LOUTH

Drogheda

Navan

MEATH

Dublin

GALWAY

Aran Islands

Galway

Athlone

W MEATH

OFFALY

KILDARE

DUBLIN

Bray

CLARE

Ennistymon

Ennis

Shannon

LAOIS

Portlaois

WICKLOW

Carlow

CARLOW

TIPPERARY

Kilkenny

LIMERICK

Tipperary

WEXFORD

Dingle

Kerry County

Clonmel

Waterford

Wexford

KERRY

Killarney

CORK

WATERFORD

Waterford

Kenmare

Cork

Bantry

Cork

Check the price

€
£

As from 2002 the Republic of Ireland will be switching from Irish Punts to Euros, so be sure to check the price of your chosen accommodation when booking.

Belfast (left) has a wealth of attractions ranging from botanic gardens to a grand opera house. The city has undergone massive modernisation in recent years and has excellent shopping facilities. During the industrial revolution Belfast was famous for its shipbuilding and linen industries.

Giant's stepping stones

Formed by volcanic activity 60 million years ago, Giant's Causeway, Antrim (right), is a mass of tightly packed basalt columns like stepping stones that lead from the cliff foot to disappear under the sea. Writer Thackerey knew the Causeway's true geological origins but felt compelled to comment: "When the world was moulded and fashioned out of formless chaos, this must have been the bit over."

Set in beautiful lake and mountain scenery, Killarney National Park (below) is 20,000 acres in extent and encompasses the three Lakes of Killarney, and the mountains and woods which surround them. For more: homepage.tinet/~knp.

As you explore the grounds of Trinity College, Dublin (above), you get a feel for the history of the college whose many famous alumni include Berkeley, Swift, and Beckett.

● Shopping in Ireland offers a range of goods that reflect the quality and craftsmanship of the traditional industries. Irish Celtic art is used to ornament lead crystal, chinaware and jewellery.

● To date, 76 nature reserves and five national parks have been established throughout the country.

Accommodation index

Hotels and Guest Accommodation are indexed by their order of appearance within this region, not by the page. To locate an establishment, note the number to the right of the listing and then find it on the establishment's name bar, as shown here

37 The Turning Mill Hotel

Rising up from the Donegal landscape, Mount Errigal is situated in Glenveagh National Park (above). The largest red deer herd in Ireland and possibly in the whole of Europe is scattered among the hills.

● For quieter pleasure there are castles and ancient ruins to explore. Many of Ireland's best gardens are open to visitors.

O'Connell Street (below) is Dublin's main thoroughfare and the starting point for most tourists' exploration of the city. This view shows the famous O'Connell Bridge.

Check the price

As from 2002 the Republic of Ireland will be switching from Irish Punts to Euros, so be sure to check the price of your chosen accommodation when booking. Where establishments provided prices in Euros, these were converted to sterling at the exchange rate prevailing at the time of going to press, and there is some inevitable rounding to avoid "untidy" pricing in the guide.

Built about 3200 BC, the megalithic monument of Newgrange has been designated a World Heritage Site by UNESCO.

NORTHERN IRELAND

Ballycastle, Co. Antrim

1 Portcampley Bed & Breakfast

8 Harbour Road, Ballintoy, Co. Antrim, BT54 6NA
Tel: 028 207 68200 Fax: 028 207 68200
Email: m.donnelly@btclick.com
Web: www.portcampley.8k.com
6 bedrs SB £20 DB £35
CC: MC Vi DC

How to get there: Located along the B15 at
Ballintoy coastal road to Giants Causeway and
Glens of Antrim.
See advert on facing page

Bangor, Co. Down

2 Marine Court Hotel

★★★ 🏮
The Marina, 18-20 Quay Street, Bangor,
Co. Down, BT20 5ED
Tel: 028 9145 1100 Fax: 028 9145 1200
Email: admin@marinecourt.fsnet.co.uk
Web: www.marinecourthotel.net
52 bedrs SB £80 DB £90 B £7.50 L £5.95 D
£8.95
CC: MC Vi Am Swi

How to get there: Located on Quay Street near
central pier on marina.

Belfast, Co. Antrim

3 Culloden

Bangor Road, Holywood, Belfast,
Co. Antrim, BT18 0EX
Tel: 028 9042 5223 Fax: 028 9042 6777
Email: guest@cull.hastingshotels.com
Web: www.hastingshotels.com
79 bedrs SB £165 DB £210 HBS £195
HBD £135 B £15 L £10 D £30
CC: MC Vi Am DC Swi Delt

How to get there: Six miles from Belfast city
centre via A2, signposted Bangor.

4 Dunadry Inn

★★★★ 🏮
2 Islandreagh Drive, Dunadry,
Co. Antrim, BT41 2HA
Tel: 028 9038 5050 Fax: 028 9038 5055
Email: mooneyhotelgroup@talk21.com
Web: www.mooneyhotelgroup.com
83 bedrs SB £120 DB £155 B £10 L £6 D £10
CC: MC Vi Am DC Swi

How to get there: From Belfast take M2, follow
signs to Templepatrick and Belfast International
airport. Take A57 and turn left to Templepatrick.
At roundabout go straight through village of
Templepatrick. Take 2nd turn at next
roundabout. The Dunadry is one mile, on the
lefthandside.

5 Hastings Europa Hotel

★★★★ 🏮
Great Victoria Street, Belfast,
Co. Antrim, BT2 7AP
Tel: 028 9032 7000 Fax: 028 9032 7800
Email: res@eur.hastingshotels.com
Web: www.hastingshotels.com
Closed 24, 25 December
240 bedrs SB £117 DB £174 B £8 L £12 D £15
CC: MC Vi Am DC Swi Delt

6 Hastings Stormont Hotel

★★★★ 🏮🏮
Upper Newtonards Road, Belfast,
Co. Antrim, BT4 1LP
Tel: 028 9065 8621 Fax: 028 9048 0240
Email: res@stor.hastingshotel.com
Web: www.hastingshotel.com
109 bedrs SB £122 DB £169 HBS £140
HBD £102.50 B £12 L £15 D £18
CC: MC Vi Am DC Swi Delt

How to get there: From Belfast city centre,
follow A2 to Newtownards. Turn right at
Stormont Parliament Buildings.

7 McCausland Hotel

★★★★ 🏮
34-38 Victoria Street, Belfast,
Co. Antrim, BT1 3GH
Tel: 028 9022 0200 Fax: 028 9022 0220
Email: info@mccauslandhotel.com
Web: www.mccauslandhotel.com
Closed Christmas

60 bedrs SB £120 DB £150 B £8 L £15 D £20
CC: MC Vi Am DC Swi Delt JCB
How to get there: The hotel is located on Victoria Street between Anne Street and the Albert Clock Tower.

8 Jurys Inn Belfast

★★★
Fisherwick Place, Great Victoria Street,
Belfast, BT2 7AP
Tel: +353(0)1 6070000 Fax: +353(0)1 6316999
Email: bookings@jurysdoyle.com
Web: www.jurysdoyle.com
Children minimum age: 12
190 bedrs B £6.95 D £15.95
CC: MC Vi Am DC Swi Delt
How to get there: Located two miles from Belfast City Airport. Great Victoria Station two minutes walk. Inn is adjacent to Opera House and City Hall.

9 Old Inn

★★★
Main Street, Crawfordsburn, Co. Down, BT19 1JH
Tel: 028 9185 3255 Fax: 028 9185 2775
Email: info@theoldinn.com
Web: www.theoldinn.com
32 bedrs SB £65 DB £85 HBS £88 HBD £65.50
B £8.50 L £5 D £16 CC: MC Vi Am DC Swi Delt
How to get there: Drive along A2 from Belfast towards Bangor. Three miles past Holywood, take the B20 to Crawfordsburn. The hotel is on the main street.

10 Travelodge Belfast

Travel Accommodation
15 Brunswick Street, Belfast,
Co. Antrim, BT2 7GE
Tel: 08700 850 950
Web: www.travelodge.co.uk
76 bedrs B £4.25 CC: MC Vi Am DC Swi Delt

Bushmills, Co. Antrim

11 Bushmills Inn

★★★
9 Dunluce Street, Bushmills,
Co. Antrim, BT57 8QG
Tel: 028 2073 2339 Fax: 028 2073 2048
Email: rac@bushmillsinn.com

Web: www.bushmillsinn.com
32 bedrs SB £68 DB £98 L £10 D £25
CC: MC Vi Am Swi
How to get there: On the A2 Antrim coast road in the village of Bushmills with main entrance as you cross the River Bush.

Carrickfergus, Co. Antrim

12 Dobbins Inn Hotel

★★
6-8 High Street, Carrickfergus,
Co. Antrim, BT38 7AF
Tel: 028 9335 1905 Fax: 028 9335 1905
Email: info@dobbinsinnhotel.co.uk
Web: www.dobbinsinnhotel.co.uk
15 bedrs SB £45 DB £64 HBS £60 HBD £42.50
B £6 L £6 D £12
CC: MC Vi Am Swi Delt
How to get there: Situated approximately 10 miles from Belfast City Airport, 15 miles from Belfast International Airport, 14 miles from port of Larne, 10 miles from port of Belfast.

Northern Ireland

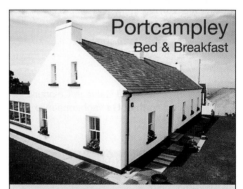

Portcampley
Bed & Breakfast

Spacious six-bedroom modern bungalow with panoramic view of White Park Bay, Rathlin Island and Scottish Coastline. Ideal base for touring Causeway, Coast and Glens. Short walking distance to Ballintoy Harbour and Rope Bridge. Convenient to fishing, walking and golfing. Home cooking and friendly atmosphere assured. Evening meals available. Discount on group bookings – children welcome.

8 Harbour Road, Ballintoy,
Co Antrim BT54 6NA

Tel/Fax: 028 207 68200
Email: m.donnelly@btclick.com
www.portcampley.8k.com

Clogher, Co. Tyrone

13 Corick House

20 Corick Road, Clogher, Co Tyrone, BT76 0BZ
Tel: 028 85 548216 Fax: 028 85 549531

Coleraine, Co. Londonderry

14 Brown Trout Golf & Country Inn

★★

Agivey Road, Aghadowey,
Co. Londonderry, BT51 4AD
Tel: 028 7086 8209 Fax: 028 7086 8878
Email: bill@browntroutinn.com
Web: www.browntroutinn.com
15 bedrs SB £60 DB £85 HBS £75 HBD £52.50
B £5 L £10 D £15
CC: MC Vi Am DC Swi
How to get there: On intersection of A54 B66
seven miles south of Coleraine.

15 Heathfield Farm

31 Drumcroone Road, Killykergan, Coleraine,
Co. Londonderry, BT51 4EB
Tel: 028 295 58245 Fax: 028 295 58245
Email: relax@heathfield.com
Web: www.heathfieldfarm.com
3 bedrs SB £25 DB £45 D £15
CC: MC Vi
How to get there: On A29 Garvagh/Coleraine
road. Two miles north of Garvagh, one mile
south of Coleraine.

Enniskillen, Co. Fermanagh

16 Killyhevlin Hotel

★★★

Killyhevlin, Dublin Road, Enniskillen,
Co. Fermanagh, BT74 6RW
Tel: 028 6632 3481 Fax: 028 6632 4726
Email: info@killyhevlin.com
Web: www.killyhevlin.com
43 bedrs
CC: MC Vi Am DC Swi
How to get there: Situated on A4, due east of
Enniskillen, on main Dublin/Belfast road.

Feeny, Co. Londonderry

17 Drumcovitt House and Barn

704 Feeny Road, Feeny,
Co. Londonderry, BT47 4SU
Tel: 028 7778 1224 Fax: 028 7778 1224
Email: drumcovitt.feeny@btinternet.com
Web: www.drumcovitt.com

Listed Georgian house. Centrally heated. Log
fires, glorious setting. Stroll lanes, hill walk, fish,
golf. Approximately one hour ferries, airports,
Giant's Causeway. 30 minutes Donegal
Sperrins, Derry City. Relax. Enjoy.
9 bedrs SB £24 DB £48 HBS £39 HBD £39 B £5
L £10 D £15
CC: MC Vi Am
How to get there: From A6 Belfast-Derry road, a
quarter-mile west of Dungiven take the B74 to
Feeny. After three miles, Drumcovitt is on right.

Irvinestown, Co. Fermanagh

18 Mahon's Hotel

★★

Enniskillen Road, Irvinestown,
Co. Fermanagh, BT94 1GS
Tel: 028 6862 1656 Fax: 028 6862 8344
Email: info@mahonshotel.co.uk
Web: www.mahonshotel.co.uk
18 bedrs SB £34 DB £70 HBS £49 HBD £47.50
CC: MC Vi Am Swi

Larne, Co. Antrim

19 Hastings Ballygally Castle

★★★

274 Coast Road, Ballygally,
Co. Antrim, BT40 2QZ
Tel: 028 2858 3212 Fax: 028 2858 3681
Email: gm@bgc.hastingshotels.com
Web: www.hastingshotels.com

44 bedrs SB £70 DB £100 HBS £85 HBD £65
B £7 L £5 D £15 CC: MC Vi Am DC Swi Delt

How to get there: 20 miles north of Belfast on
the Antrim coast road (M2 From Belfast, then
A8 to Larne). Four miles north of Larne on
Antrim coast.

20 Derrin Guest House

◆◆◆

2 Princes Gardens, Larne, Co. Antrim, BT40 1RQ
Tel: 028 2827 3269 Fax: 028 2827 3269
Email: info@derrinhouse.co.uk
Web: www.derrinhouse.co.uk
Closed 25, 26 December
6 bedrs SB £20 DB £34 CC: MC Vi Am

How to get there: Turn off Harbour highway (A8)
for A2 coastal route. After traffic lights at main
street take first road on left.

Limavady, Co. Londonderry

21 Radisson Roe Park Hotel & Golf Resort

★★★★★ ® ®

Limavady, Co. Londonderry, BT49 9LB
Tel: 028 7772 2222 Fax: 028 7772 2313
Email: reservations@radissonroepark.com
Web: www.radissonroepark.com
64 bedrs CC: MC Vi Am DC Swi

How to get there: Situated on A2 Londonderry-
Limavady Road, 16 miles from Londonderry,
one mile from Limavady. Resort is 10 miles from
city of Derry and 45 miles from Belfast airport.

Londonderry, Co. Londonderry

22 Hastings Everglades

★★★★ ®

Prehen Road, Waterside, Londonderry,
Londonderry, BT47 2NH
Tel: 028 7134 6722 Fax: 028 7134 9200
Email: res@egh.hastingshotels.com
Web: www.hastingshotels.com
64 bedrs SB £85 DB £110 HBS £100 HBD £72
B £8 L £6 D £18
CC: MC Vi Am DC Swi

How to get there: Follow main A6 route to
Londonderry. Follow signs for Strabane/Omagh.
Go ahead at traffic lights at bridge. Hotel
second left.

23 Travelodge Londonderry

Travel Accommodation
22-24 Strand Road, Derry City,
BT48 7AB
Tel: 08700 850 950
Web: www.travelodge.co.uk
43 bedrs B £4.25
CC: MC Vi Am DC Swi Delt

24 Tower Hotel Derry

❖

The Diamond, Derry, BT48 6HL
Tel: 028 7137 1000 Fax: 028 7137 1234
Web: www.towerhotelgroup.ie
Closed 24-27 December inclusive
95 bedrs SB £75 DB £90
CC: MC Vi Am DC Swi

Newcastle, Co. Down

25 Hastings Slieve Donard Hotel

★★★★ ®

Downs Road, Newcastle, Co. Down, BT33 0AH
Tel: 028 4372 3681 Fax: 028 4372 4830
Email: res@sdh.hastingshotels.com
Web: www.hastingshotels.com
126 bedrs SB £105 DB £160 B £9 L £16 D £23
CC: MC Vi Am DC Swi

How to get there: From Belfast, take A24 and
follow signs to Newcastle. From Dublin, take
R174 to Newry then A2 and follow signs to
Newcastle.

26 Burrendale Hotel & Country Club

★★★ ® ®

51 Castlewellan Road, Newcastle,
Co. Down, BT33 0JY
Tel: 028 4372 2599 Fax: 028 4372 2328
Email: reservations@burrendale.com
Web: www.burrendale.com
69 bedrs SB £65 DB £99 HBS £80 HBD £65
B £4.95 L £9.95 D £16
CC: MC Vi Am DC Swi

How to get there: From Belfast, take A24 to
Newcastle, then A50 Castlewellan Road.

Northern Ireland

REPUBLIC OF IRELAND

Achill Island, Co. Mayo

27 Achill Cliff House Hotel

◆◆◆◆

Keel, Achill Island, Co Mayo
Tel: +353(0)98 43400 Fax: +353(0)98 43007
Email: achillcliff@anu.ie
Web: www.achillcliff.com

Family-run hotel in superb location. Spacious rooms, panoramic views, fresh food, fine wines and good value. Friendly host will advise you what to do. Walking, painting, photography, fishing and golf.
10 bedrs SB £50 DB £70 HBS £70 HBD £50
B £5 L £10 D £20
CC: MC Vi Am Delt

How to get there: Coming from Achill Sound, hotel is on right-hand side of road in village of Keel.

28 Lavelles Sea Side House

◆◆◆

Achill Island, Dooega, Co. Mayo
Tel: +353(01) 2828142
Email: seasidehouse@eircom.net
Closed November to March
14 bedrs SB £30 DB £40 B £6 D £14
CC: MC Vi

It's easier online

For all your motoring and travel needs, www.rac.co.uk

Adare, Co. Limerick

29 Adare Manor Hotel & Golf Resort

★★★★★

Adare, Co. Limerick
Tel: +353(0)61 396566 Fax: +353(0)61 396124
Email: reservations@adaremanor.com
Web: www.adaremanor.com
63 bedrs CC: MC Vi Am DC

How to get there: 30 km from Shannon Airport, 10 km from Limerick City in the Southwest of Ireland.

30 Berkeley Lodge

◆◆◆◆

Station Road, Adare, Co. Limerick
Tel: +353(0)61 396857 Fax: +353(0)61 396857
Email: berlodge@iol.ie
Web: www.adare.org
Children minimum age: 2
6 bedrs SB £40 DB £50
CC: MC Vi

How to get there: Take route N21 (Limerick) via Killarney to Adare. Turn right at roundabout. Hotel is fifth house on the right after petrol station.

31 Coatesland House Bed & Breakfast (Hogans)

◆◆◆◆

Tralee/Killarney Road, Adare, Co. Limerick
Tel: +353(0)61 396372 Fax: +353(0)61 396833
Email: coatesfd@indigo.ie
Web: http://indigo.ie/~coatesfd
Closed 25 December
6 bedrs SB £30 DB £50
CC: MC Vi

How to get there: One km from village centre.
See advert on facing page

Ardmore, Co. Waterford

32 Newtown Farm Guesthouse

◆◆◆◆

Newtown Farm, Grange Via Yougal, Ardmore, Co. Waterford
Tel: +353(0)24 94143 Fax: +353(0)24 94054
Email: newtownfarm@eircom.net
Web: www.newtownfarm.com
SB £30 DB £50
CC: None accepted

Arthurstown, Co. Wexford

33 Dunbrody Country House Hotel

Blue Ribbon Winner

★★★★ ⓡ ⓡ ⓡ

Arthurstown, near Waterford, Co. Wexford
Tel: +353(0)51 389600 Fax: +353(0)51 389601
Email: dunbrody@indigo.ie
Web: www.dunbrodyhouse.com
Children minimum age: 12.
Closed 23–26 December

20 bedrs SB £95 DB £142 HBS £126.50
HBD £102.50 B £10.50 L £25,5 D £31.50
CC: MC Vi Am DC Delt JCB
⬦ & 🍴 ⊗ ⬚ ☎ ⌐ P 🛁 ≋ ⋕ ⦙⦙⦙ ➤
How to get there: From Dublin via M11/N11 to
Wexford and R733 to Arthurstown. From Cork
N25 via Waterford and passage East carferry
Ballyhack.

Athy, Co. Kildare

34 Coursetown Country House
Little Gem

◆ ◆ ◆ ◆ ◆ ✗ ❦

Stradbally Road, Athy, Co. Kildare
Tel: +353(0)507 31101 Fax: +353(0)507 32740
Children minimum age: 8.
Closed Christmas

Large country house in 260 acre farm.
Bedrooms designed for maximum guest
comfort. Tastefully appointed fully accessible
wheelchair-friendly suite. Excellent breakfast
with homemade bread and preserves. Lovely
secluded garden.
4 bedrs SB £48 DB £80
CC: MC Vi Am
& 🍴 ⊗ ⬚ ⬚ ☎ P 🛁
How to get there: Turn off N78 at Athy or N80 at
Stradbally onto R428. Hotel is 3kms from Athy
and 9km from Stradbally.

Ballinamore, Co. Leitrim

35 Riversdale Farm Guesthouse

◆ ◆ ◆ ◆

Ballinamore, Co. Leitrim
Tel: +353(0)78 44122 Fax: +353(0)78 44813
Web: www.riversdalefarmguesthouse.com
Children minimum age: 5
13 bedrs
CC: MC Vi
🍴 ⬚ ☎ P 🛁 ≋ ℂ ♁ ❧ ᛋ ℂ ⦙ ⬀

Ballinasloe, Co. Galway

36 Haydens Gateway Business & Leisure Hotel

★★★★ ®
Dunlo Street, Ballinasloe, Co. Galway
Tel: +353(0)6568 23000 Fax: +353(0)6568 23759
Email: reservations@lynchhotels.com
Web: www.lynchhotels.com
48 bedrs
CC: MC Vi Am DC

How to get there: Located in the heart of Ballinasloe, just 30 minutes from Galway Airport (N6 road).

Ballingeary, Co. Cork

37 Gougane Barra Hotel

★★ ®
Gougane Barra, Ballingeary, Co. Cork
Tel: +353(0)26 47069 Fax: +353(0)26 47226
Email: gouganebarrahotel@eircom.net
Web: www.gouganebarrahotel.com
27 bedrs SB £46 DB £68 L £11.75 D £17.25
CC: MC Vi Am DC

Ballyconnell, Co. Cavan

38 Slieve Russell Hotel Golf & Country Club

★★★★ ®
Ballyconnell, Co. Cavan
Tel: +353(0)49 9526444 Fax: +353(0)49 9526046
Email: slieve-russell@quinn-hotels.com
Web: www.quinnhotels.com
159 bedrs SB £90 DB £153 HBS £118
HBD £104.50 B £8 L £14.50 D £28
CC: MC Vi Am DC

How to get there: N3 to Cavan; take Eniskillen road through Belturbet to Ballyconnell

Ballyheigue, Co. Kerry

39 White Sands Hotel

★★★
Ballyheigue, Co. Kerry
Tel: +353(0)66 33357

Ballylickey, Co. Galway

40 Sea View House Hotel

★★★
Ballylickey, Bantry, Co. Galway
Tel: +353(0)27 50462 Fax: +353(0)27 51555
Email: seaviewhousehotel@eircom.net
Closed mid-November to mid-March
17 bedrs
CC: MC Vi Am DC

How to get there: On main route N71, three miles from Bantry, seven miles from Glengariff.

Ballymacarbry, Co. Waterford

41 Hanoras Cottage

◆◆◆◆◆ ® ✳
Nire Valley, Ballymacarbry, Co. Waterford
Tel: +353 (0)52 36134 Fax: +353 (0)52 36540
Email: hanorascottage@eircom.net
Web: www.hanorascottage.com

Award-winning Hanoras Cottage on the Comeragh mountains has everything for discerning guests. Luxurious lounges and bedrooms, jacuzzi tubs, superior rooms for special occasions. Excellent restaurant. Adults only – sheer bliss – walking, golf, horse-riding...
10 bedrs SB £52 DB £80
CC: MC Vi

How to get there: From Clonmel or Dungarvan take R671 to Ballymacarbry. Turn off at Melody's Pub. We are signposted from there, directly beside the Nire Church.

Making a booking?

Don't forget to mention RAC Hotels and Bed & Breakfast 2002.

Ballyvaughan, Co. Clare

42 Gregans Castle Hotel

Blue Ribbon Winner

★★★★ ⋒ ⋒ ⋒

Ballyvaughan, Co. Clare
Tel: +353(0)65 7077005 Fax: +353(0)65 7077111
Email: res@gregans.ie
Web: www.gregans.ie
Closed 23 December to 13 February

Antique furnishings and turf fires decorate this country house, a family-operated hotel, with views of garden, valley, Burren mountains and Galway Bay. Winner of awards for food, hospitality and service.
22 bedrs SB £107.50 DB £120 HBS £137.25 HBD £90 B £12.20 L £14 D £21
CC: MC Vi Am Delt

How to get there: 3½ miles south of Ballyvaughan village on N67, about one hour from Shannon airport.

43 Hylands Hotel

★★★

Ballyvaughan, Co. Clare
Tel: +353(0)65 7077037 Fax: +353(0)65 7077131
Email: hylands@tinet.ie
Web: www.cmvhotels.com
Closed January
30 bedrs
CC: MC Vi Am DC

How to get there: Situated in the centre of Ballyvaughan village.

44 Rusheen Lodge

♦♦♦♦ ⚘

Knocknagrough, Ballyvaughan, Co. Clare
Tel: +353(0)65 7077092 Fax: +353(0)65 7077152
Email: rusheenl@iol.ie
Web: www.rusheenlodge.com
Closed December to January

8 bedrs SB £50 DB £70 B £7.50
CC: MC Vi

How to get there: From Ballyvaughan village, take N67 south for ¾ km. Rusheen Lodge is on the left-hand side of the road.

Baltimore, Co. Cork

45 Casey's of Baltimore Hotel

★★★ ⋒

Baltimore, Co. Cork
Tel: +353(0)28 20197 Fax: +353(0)28 20509
Email: caseys@eircom.net
Web: www.caseysofbaltimore.com
14 bedrs SB £55.50 DB £74.50 HBS £75 HBD £56.75 B £5.50 L £10.50 D £21.50
CC: MC Vi Am DC Swi

How to get there: From Cork city take the N71 road to Skibbereen. From Skibbereen take the R595 road to Baltimore. Hotel is on the R595 near Baltimore.

Bantry, Co. Cork

46 Westlodge Hotel

★★★

Bantry, Co. Cork
Tel: +353(0)27 50360 Fax: +353(0)27 50438
Email: reservations@westlodgehotel.ie
Web: www.westlodgehotel.ie
90 bedrs SB £48 DB £80 L £12.50 D £22
CC: MC Vi Am DC

How to get there: Situated on Bantry Bay.

47 The Mill

♦♦♦ ⚘

Glengarriff Road, New Town, Bantry, Co. Cork
Tel: +353(0)27 50278 Fax: +353(0)27 50278
Email: bbthemill@eircom.net
6 bedrs SB £18.50 DB £37
CC: None accepted

How to get there: Hotel is on N71, 1km from Bantry town centre towards Glengarriff. Second B&B on left.

Republic of Ireland

Blessington, Co. Wicklow

48 Downshire House Hotel

★★★ ®
Blessington, Co. Wicklow
Tel: +353(0)45 865199 Fax: +353(0)45 865335

Bray, Co. Wicklow

49 Esplanade Hotel

★★★
Bray, Co. Wicklow
Tel: +353(0)1 286 2056 Fax: +353(0)1 286 6496
Email: esplan@regencyhotels.com
Web: www.regencyhotels.com

The Esplanade is on the seafront in Bray, at the gateway to beautiful County Wicklow, but only 30 minutes' drive from Dublin city. This old Victorian hotel oozes with character, charm and open turf fires.
40 bedrs SB £60 DB £80 B £7.95 D £18
CC: MC Vi Am

How to get there: Bray is 19km south of Dublin, off the M11.

50 Royal Hotel & Leisure Centre

★★★
Main Street, Bray, Co. Wicklow
Tel: +353(0)1 2862935 Fax: +353(0)1 2867373
Email: royal@regencyhotels.com
Web: www.regencyhotels.com

The hotel nestles on the main street of the coastal resort of Bray, Co Wicklow. We offer fine dining facilities at the Heritage restaurant and have banquetting facilities for up to 250.
91 bedrs SB £70 DB £90 B £6.95 L £6.95
D £16.95
CC: MC Vi Am

How to get there: As you enter Bray, the hotel is on the top of the hill on the left hand side.

Cappoquin, Co. Waterford

51 Richmond House

♦♦♦♦ ® ®
Cappoquin, Co. Waterford
Tel: +353(0)58 54278 Fax: +353(0)58 54988
Email: info@richmondhouse.net
Web: www.richmondhouse.net
Closed Christmas to mid January

Award-winning 18th century Georgian country house and fully licensed restaurant. Enjoy peace, tranquility and log fires combined with every modern comfort for discerning guests.
9 bedrs SB £60 DB £120
CC: MC Vi Am DC

How to get there: 1/2 mile outside Cappoquin on N72.

Caragh Lake, Co. Kerry

52 Caragh Lodge

Gold Ribbon Winner

★★ ® ® ®
Caragh Lake, Co. Kerry
Tel: +353(0)66 9769115 Fax: +353(0)66 9769316
Email: caraghl@iol.ie
Web: www.caraghlodge.com
Children minimum age: 12
15 bedrs SB £68 DB £98 D £23.50
CC: MC Vi Am DC
☎ P® ⚲ ⋕ ⋔ ⚲ ⟿
How to get there: From Killorglin, take N70
towards Glenbeigh. Turn left after three miles at
signpost 'Caragh Lodge'. Turn left at end of
road. Caragh Lodge is on right.

Carlow Town, Co. Carlow

53 Barrowville Town House

◆◆◆◆◆ ✱ ❧
Kilkenny Road, Carlow Town, Co. Carlow
Tel: +353(0)503 43324 Fax: +353(0)503 41953
Web: www.barrowvillehouse.com

Five diamond Georgian listed town house. Well
appointed bedrooms. Traditional or buffet
breakfast served in conservatory overlooking
gardens. Excellent location for golf or touring
Southeast/Midlands.
7 bedrs SB £30 DB £55
CC: MC Vi Am
☺ ☐ ☎ P
How to get there: On N9 south side of Carlow
Town at fourth traffic light on right travelling
north at first light on left.

It's easier online

For all your motoring and travel
needs, www.rac.co.uk

Carrick-on-Shannon, Co. Leitrim

54 The Landmark Hotel

★★★★
Carrick-on-Shannon, Co. Leitrim
Tel: +353 (0)78 22222 Fax: +353 (0)78 22233
Email: landmarkhotel@eircom.net
Web: www.thelandmarkhotel.com
50 bedrs SB £68 DB £102
CC: MC Vi Am
⟐ ⚅ ⊔ ⚞ ☐ ☎ P ☼ ♬ ⚲ ⋕ ⋔ ⊠ 'Y' ⚡
How to get there: Located on the N4 Sligo-
Dublin road. Approaching Carrick from Dublin,
take the first exit off the roundabout and we are
on the right-hand side.

Carrigaline, Co. Cork

55 Carrigaline Court Hotel & Leisure Centre

★★★★ ®
Main Street, Carrigaline, Co. Cork
Tel: +353(0)21 371300 Fax: +353(0)21 371103

Carrigans, Co. Donegal

56 Mount Royd Country Home

Little Gem

◆◆◆◆ ❧
Carrigans, near Derry, Co. Donegal
Tel: +353(0)74 40163 Fax: +353(0)74 40400
Email: jmartin@mountroyd.com
Web: www.mountroyd.com
Closed Christmas

A warm welcome awaits our guests at our
award-winning family home where every
comfort is assured. Ideal for touring Inishowen,
Giants' causeway and Grianan of Aileach. AA
and RAC winner 2000.
4 bedrs SB £25 DB £40 CC: None accepted
☺ ☐ P® ⚲ ⊱ € ♬
How to get there: Carrigans signposted off N13
and N14 on R236. From Londonderry take A40.
Mount Royd in Carrigans village.

Republic of Ireland

Carrigbyrne, Co. Wexford

57 Woodlands House

◆ ◆ ◆

Carrigbyrne, Co. Wexford
Tel: +353 (0)51 428287 Fax: +353 (0)51 428287
Email: woodwex@eircom.net
Children minimum age: 5
Closed November to February

Beautiful countryside location only 30 minutes from Rosslare. Comfortable, well-equipped rooms. Ideal base for Wexford, Waterford and Kilkenny. Golf, fishing and riding nearby. Guest lounge. Early breakfast available.
4 bedrs SB £24 DB £34 D £11.50 CC: MC Vi
How to get there: Situated on the N25, Rosslare to Waterford/Cork road, 30 minutes from Rosslare, just past the Cedar Lodge Hotel.

Cashel, Co. Galway

58 Cashel House Hotel
Gold Ribbon Winner

★★★ ⚜ ⚜ ⚜
Cashel, Connemara, Co. Galway
Tel: +353(0)95 31001 Fax: +353(0)95 31077
Email: info@cashel-house-hotel.com
Web: www.cashel-house-hotel.com
Children minimum age: 5
Closed January

An oasis of elegance, charm and good food surrounded by 10 acres of one of Irelands' best gardens and 1500 square miles of unspoilt Connemara's mountains and boglands.
32 bedrs SB £68. DB £136 HBS £104 HBD £208 B £17 L £15 D £37
CC: MC Vi Am
How to get there: South of N59 one mile west of Recess.

Castlebar, Co. Mayo

59 Breaffy House Hotel

★★★
Castlebar, Co. Mayo
Tel: +353(0)65 6823000 Fax: +353(0)65 6823759
Email: breaffyhouse@lynchotels.com
Web: www.lynchotels.com
59 bedrs
CC: MC Vi Am DC
How to get there: Take main Roscommon Road out of Castlebar for 3km to Breaffy village.

Cavan, Co. Cavan

60 Hotel Kilmore

★★★★ ⚜
Dublin Road, Cavan, Co. Cavan
Tel: +353(0)49 4332288 Fax: +353(0)49 4332458
Email: kilmore@quinn-hotels.com
Web: www.quinnhotels.com
39 bedrs SB £46 DB £72 HBS £65 HBD £55 B £7 D £20
CC: MC Vi Am DC
How to get there: From Belfast, take A3 to Lisburn. Go to Portadown, Armagh and Monaghan. Take N54 to Clones and Cavan (via bypass). Follow road towards Dublin. Hotel on left.

Clifden, Co. Galway

61 Alcock & Brown Best Western Hotel

★★★★ ⊛ ⊛

The Square, Clifden, Co. Galway
Tel: +353(0)95 21206 Fax: +353(0)95 21842
Email: alcockandbrown@eircom.net
Web: www.alcockandbrown-hotel.com
Closed 23–26 December
19 bedrs SB £80 DB £124 B £14 L £8 D £38
CC: MC Vi Am DC
⟨icons⟩
How to get there: From Dublin take N6 to Galway, then N59 to Clifden. Hotel is in centre of village.

62 Ardagh Hotel & Restaurant

★★★ ⊛ ⊛ ⊛

Ballyconneely Road, Clifden, Co. Galway
Tel: +353(0)95 21384 Fax: +353(0)95 21314
Email: ardaghhotel@eircom.net
Web: www.commerce.ie/ardaghhotel
Closed November to March
21 bedrs SB £80 DB £119 HBS £100 HBD £85
B £10 D £17.50 CC: MC Vi Am DC
⟨icons⟩
How to get there: From Clifden Town follow signs to Ballyconneely. Ardagh Hotel is two miles out of Clifden.

63 Renvyle House Hotel

★★★ ⊛

Renvyle, Connemara, Co. Galway
Tel: +353(0)95 43511 Fax: +353(0)95 43515
Email: renvyle@iol.ie
Web: www.renvyle.com
Closed January to February
65 bedrs SB £70 DB £100 HBS £100 HBD £90
B £15 L £18 D £30 CC: MC Vi Am DC
⟨icons⟩
How to get there: Take N59 west from Galway. At recess turn right, at Kylemore turn left. At Letterfrack turn right. Continue for five miles.
See advert on right

64 Station House Hotel

★★★

Clifden, Connemara, Co. Galway
Tel: +353(0)95 21699 Fax: +353(0)95 21667
Email: station@eircom.net
Web: www.stationhousehotel.com
78 bedrs SB £80 DB £60 HBS £95 HBD £80
B £8 L £8 D £21
CC: MC Vi Am DC
⟨icons⟩
How to get there: N59 from Galway city.

65 Buttermilk Lodge Guest House

◆◆◆◆◆ ⊗ ⊗

Westport Road, Clifden, Co. Galway
Tel: +353(0)95 21951 Fax: +353(0)95 21953
Email: buttermilk@anu.ie
Web: www.buttermilklodge.com
Children minimum age: 5.
Closed January
11 bedrs SB £40 DB £60
CC: MC Vi
⟨icons⟩
How to get there: From Galway, turn right at Esso station; we are 400m on left. From Westport, we are on right 100m after 'Clifden' sign.

Renvyle House Hotel

Renvyle House Hotel is spectacularly located on the west coast of Ireland, nestled between the Twelve Bens and the Atlantic Ocean. It is a place full of old world charm and history, fine food, an extensive wine list and comfortable rooms.
The hotel is situated on 200 acres and offers extensive on-site facilities including Golf and Trout Fishing.

Renvyle, Connemara, Co. Galway
Tel: +353(0)95 43511   Fax: +353(0)95 43515
renvyle@iol.ie
www.renvyle.com

Republic of Ireland

66 Mal Dua House
Little Gem

◆◆◆◆◆
Galway Road, Clifden, Co. Galway
Tel: +353(0)95 21171 Fax: +353(0)95 21739
Email: info@maldua.com
Web: www.maldua.com

In the heart of Connemara, offering luxury in a
relaxed atmosphere, we at Mal Dua House pride
ourselves in providing personalised service to all
our guests. Enjoy spacious bedrooms, pleasant
sitting room, landscaped gardens and stream.
14 bedrs SB £30 DB £60
CC: MC Vi Am DC
& ⊗ ⊜ ◻ ☎ ➰ ℙ☞ ⚒ ⅃ ♰ ﬗ ꕥ ⅲ
How to get there: Located on the Galway Road
(N59), 1¼km from Clifden.

67 Dún Rí Guest House

◆◆◆◆
Hulk Street, Clifden, Co. Galway
Tel: +353(0)95 21625 Fax: +353(0)95 21635
Email: dunri@anu.ie
Web: www.connemara.net/dun-ri
Children minimum age: 4.
Closed November to February
10 bedrs SB £35 DB £50
CC: MC Vi
⊗ ⊜ ◻ ☎ ➰ ℙ ⚒ ⅃ ﬗ ꕥ
How to get there: Entering Clifden on N59, take
left before Statoil Station. Road will bring you
directly to Dún Rí Guesthouse.

68 Kingstown House

◆◆◆
Bridge Street, Clifden, Co. Galway
Tel: +353(0)95 21470 Fax: +353 95 21530
Closed 23 – 28 December
8 bedrs
CC: MC Vi Am
⊗ ⊜ ◻ ⚒ ⅃ ꕥ
How to get there: Enter Clifden on N59; second
B&B on the right at beginning of one way system.

69 Benview House

◆◆
Bridge Street, Clifden, Co. Galway
Tel: +353(0)95 21256 Fax: +353(0)95 21226
Email: benviewhouse@ireland.com
Web: www.connemar.net/benviewhouse
9 bedrs SB £16 DB £28
CC: MC Vi Am
 ◻ ☎ ⚒ ⅃ ♰ ꕥ

Clonakilty, Co. Cork

70 Lodge and Spa at Inchydoney Island
Blue Ribbon Winner

★★★★
Inchydoney Island, Clonakilty, Co. Cork
Tel: +353(0)23 33143 Fax: +353(0)23 35229
Email: reservations@inchydoneyisland.com
Web: www.inchydoneyisland.com
87 bedrs SB £181.50 DB £313.50 HBS £215
HBD £211.75 B £15 L £20 D £50
CC: MC Vi Am DC
& ⅃⅃ ⊗ ⊜ ◻ ☎ ➰ ℙ☞ ⚒ ⅃ ♰ ꕥ ⚘ ﬗ ⅲ SPA
⍍ ⚲ ⊡
How to get there: Take N71 from Cork to
Clonakilty.

Clondrinagh, Co. Limerick

71 Travelodge Limerick

Travel Accommodation
Ennis Road, Clondrinagh, Co. Limerick
Tel: 08700 850 950
Web: www.travelodge.co.uk
40 bedrs B £4.25
CC: MC Vi Am DC Swi Delt
⅄ ⊜ ◻ ⚒

Clonmel, Co. Tipperary

72 Minella Hotel & Leisure Centre

★★★
Coleville Road, Clonmel, Co. Tipperary,
Tel: +353(0) 5222385 Fax: +353(0) 5224381
Email: hotelminella@eircom.net
Web: www.hotelminella.ie
40 bedrs
CC: MC Vi Am DC
⌂ & ⎅ ⅄ ⊗ ⊜ ◻ ☎ ℙ☞ ⚒ ⅃ ♰ ꕥ ﬗ ⅲ
SPA ⍍ ⚲ ⊡ ꕥ

Cobh, Co. Cork

73 Watersedge Hotel

★★★
Next to Cobh Heritage Centre,
Cobh, Co. Cork
Tel: +353(0)21 4815566 Fax: +353(0)21 4812011
Email: watersedge@eircom.net
Web: www.watersedgehotel.ie
19 bedrs SB £50.90 DB £78.30 B £7.04 L £9.40
D £22.
CC: MC Vi DC
How to get there: Cobh is located 12 minutes from Cork city on route R624, which is off the primary road N25. Only 20 minutes from Cork airport and close to ferryport.

Cong, Co. Mayo

74 Ballywarren Country House
Little Gem

♦♦♦♦♦
Cross, Cong, Co Mayo
Tel: +353 (0)92 46989 Fax: +353 (0)92 46989
Email: ballywarrenhouse@iercom.net
Web: www.ballywarrenhouse.com
Children minimum age: 12

Ballywarren is a charming country home with beautiful rooms, large bathrooms, four-poster and hand-carved beds, peat and log fires, and excellent food and wine. Magnificent scenery, plenty of fishing and music.
3 bedrs SB £60 DB £90 D £25
CC: MC Vi Am
How to get there: ¾ of a mile from Cross towards Cong on the right hand side.

Connemara, Co. Galway

75 The Anglers Return

♦♦
Toombeola, Roundstone, Connemara,
Co. Galway
Tel: +353(0)95 31091 Fax: +353(0)95 31091
Email: lynnhill@eircom.net
Web: www.anglersreturn.itgo.com
Children minimum age: 8
Closed December to February
5 bedrs SB £38 DB £26
CC: None accepted
How to get there: From Galway, N59 Galway/Clifden Road, turn left on R341, Roundstone Road, for four miles. The Anglers Return on left.

Cork, Co. Cork

76 Hayfield Manor
Gold Ribbon Winner

★★★★★
Perrott Avenue, College Road, Cork, Co. Cork
Tel: +353(0)21 484 5900 Fax: +353(0)21 431 6839
Email: enquiries@hayfieldmanor.ie
Web: www.hayfieldmanor.ie

Cork's premier 5-star hotel, pleasantly secluded 7km from Cork airport. Luxurious guestrooms, drawing room and library. Private health spa with indoor pool and treatment rooms. Renowned for hospitality.
87 bedrs SB £200 DB £300 B £12.50 L £22.50
D £40 CC: MC Vi Am DC
How to get there: Travelling west from city centre, take N70 for Killarney. Turn left at university gates off Western Road. At top of road turn right and immediately left; hotel at top of avenue.

Republic of Ireland

77 Jurys Cork Hotel

★★★★★ ⛊ ⛊

Western Road, Cork, Co. Cork
Tel: +353(0)1 6070000 Fax: +353(0)1 6316999
Email: bookings@jurysdoyle.com
Web: www.jurysdoyle.com
Children minimum age: 12
185 bedrs SB £129.87 DB £157.16
B £7.92 L £12.55 D £14.34 CC: MC Vi Am DC
⛱♿Ⅲ🍽🖥🖥☎🔌P⛽🐎🐴♨🏇🛏Ⅲ Ⅲ 'X'Ⅾ
🏊

How to get there: Follow signpost for Kerry route. Junction of N22 follow signs city centre. Hotel well signposted from this.

78 Kingsley Hotel

★★★★ 🔘

Victoria Cross, Cork, Co. Cork
Tel: +353(0)21 4800 500 Fax: +353(0)21 4800 527
Web: www.kingsleyhotel.com
69 bedrs SB £105 DB £155 B £7.75 L £12.50
CC: MC Vi Am DC
⛱♿Ⅲ🍽🖥🖥☎❄🔌P⛽🐴🏇🐴Ⅲ
Ⅲ SPA 'X'Ⅾ

79 Silver Springs Moran Hotel

★★★★

Tivoli, Cork, Co. Cork
Tel: +353(0)21 4507533 Fax: +353(0)21 4507641
Email: silversprings@morangroup.ie
Web: www.morangroup.ie

Imposing 4-Star hotel in sylvan grounds. Five minutes drive to city centre, 15 minutes from Cork airport. 109 luxury ensuite bedrooms, choice of bars and restaurants. Excellent cuisine. Leisure centre and 9-hole golf course. 109 bedrs CC: MC Vi Am DC
♿Ⅲ🖥🖥☎P⛽🐴♨🏇🐴Ⅲ Ⅲ SPA 'X'
⛳🏇Ⅾ

How to get there: From airport, follow signs to N25, through Jack Lynch tunnel. Take first left and head for Cork centre. Turn left onto flyover, right at top; hotel is on left.

80 Bayview Hotel

★★★★ ⛊ ⛊

Ballycotton, Co. Cork
Tel: +353(0)21 4646746 Fax: +353(0)21 4646075
Email: bayhotel@iol.ie
Web: www.bayview.net
Closed November to March
35 bedrs SB £101.20 DB £151.30 HBS £135.20
HBD £109.60 B £7 L £16.50 D £34
CC: MC Vi Am DC
⛱♿Ⅲ🍽🖥🖥☎🔌P⛽🐎♨🏇🐴🐴Ⅲ Ⅲ

How to get there: At Castlemantyr on the N25, turn onto the R632. Follow the signs for Ballycotton.

81 Jurys Inn Cork

★★★

Anderson's Quay, Cork, Co. Cork
Tel: +353(0)1 6070000 Fax: +353(0)1 6316999
Email: bookings@jurysdoyle.com
Web: www.jurysdoyle.com
Closed Christmas
133 bedrs B £5.18 D £12.70 CC: MC Vi Am DC
♿Ⅲ🍽🖥🖥☎🔌🐴🏇🐴Ⅲ Ⅲ

How to get there: Located four miles/six kms from airport. Follow signs for City Centre.

82 Travelodge Cork

Travel Accommodation
R600, Frankfield Road, Cork
Tel: 08700 850 950
Web: www.travelodge.co.uk
40 bedrs B £4.25 CC: MC Vi Am DC Swi Delt
🍽🖥🖥🐴

83 Crawford House

♦♦♦♦ ✗

Western Road, Cork, Co. Cork
Tel: +353(0)21 4279000 Fax: +353(0)21 4279927
Email: crawford@indigo.ie
Web: www.crawfordguesthouse.com

This superior guesthouse offers bed and breakfast in a contemporary setting. All rooms furnished with oak wood furniture and king-sized beds. Jacuzzi ensuites with power showers. Enjoy breakfast in the light-filled conservatory.

12 bedrs SB £50 DB £90 CC: MC Vi Am

⊗ ☕ ▢ ☎ ☎ ▣☎ ⌚ ⅄

How to get there: Ten-minute walk from city centre. Located directly across from University College, Cork. N8 from Dublin, N22 from Kerry.

84 Fairy Lawn Guesthouse

◆ ◆ ◆ ◆ ⌖

Western Road, Cork, Co. Cork
Tel: +353(0)21 4543444 Fax: +353(0)21 4544337
Email: fairylawn@holidayhound.com
Web: www.holidayhound.com/fairylawn.htm
14 bedrs
CC: MC Vi

⊗ ☕ ▢ ☎ ▣ ⅄

How to get there: From city centre (Patrick Street) proceed to Capitol cineplex, turn right at lights onto Washington Street. Go straight on past the gates of UCC and hotel is on the right before the next set of traffic lights.

85 Garnish House

◆ ◆ ◆ ◆ ⌖ ⌖

Western Road, Cork City, Co. Cork
Tel: +353(0)21 4275111 Fax: +353(0)21 4273872
Email: garnish@iol.ie
Web: www.garnish.ie

A stay in Garnish House is a memorable one. Tastefully appointed rooms, with optional en-suite jacuzzi and our extensive gourmet breakfast is certain to please, 24 hrs reception for enquiries. Convenient to ferry, airport & bus terminal and five minutes walk to city centre. Ideal base to visit Southern Ireland. Suites and Studios also available.

14 bedrs SB £60 DB £90 B £10
CC: MC Vi Am DC

⌖ ⌖ ⊗ ☕ ▢ ☎ ▣☎ ⌚ ℈ ⌖ ⌖ ⌖ ⌖⌖⌖

How to get there: N8 from Dublin, N22 from Kerry. Close to bus and rail stations, opposite Cork University, 20 min drive from Cork airport.

86 Killarney Guest House

◆ ◆ ◆ ◆ ⌖ ⌖

Western Road, Cork, Co. Cork
Tel: +353(0)21 270290 Fax: +353(0)21 271010
Email: killarneyhouse@iol.ie
Web: killarneyguesthouse.com
19 bedrs SB £45 DB £70
CC: MC Vi Am

⊗ ☕ ▢ ☎ ▣☎ ⅄

How to get there: 10 minutes' walk from city centre and across from Cork University. N8 from Dublin and N22 from Kerry.

87 Lancaster Lodge

◆ ◆ ◆ ◆ ⌖

Lancaster Quay, Western Road, Cork, Co. Cork
Tel: +353(0)21 251125 Fax: +353(0)21 425426
Email: info@lancasterlodge.com
Web: www.lancasterlodge.com
Closed 24-25 December
39 bedrs
CC: MC Vi Am DC Swi Delt

⌖ ⌖ ☕ ▢ ☎ ⌚ ▣☎ ⌖ ⌖

How to get there: Located alongside Jurys Hotel on the western road in Cork. Five minute walk to city centre.

88 Antoine House

◆ ◆ ◆

Western Road, Cork, Co. Cork
Tel: +353(0)21 273494 Fax: +353(0)21 273092

89 Roserie Villa

◆ ◆ ◆

Mardyke Walk, Off Western Road, Cork, Co. Cork
Tel: +353(0)21 272958 Fax: +353(0)21 274087

Republic of Ireland

90 The Gresham Metropole

MacCurtain Street, Cork
Tel: +353(0)21 4508122 Fax: +353(0)21 4506450
Email: info@gresham-metropolehotel.com
Web: www.gresham-hotels.com

113 bedrs SB £170 DB £190 HBS £190
HBD £115 B £8 L £11 D £16
CC: MC Vi Am DC Delt

How to get there: Overlooking the river Lee, the
hotel is directly opposite the central shopping
centre and bus station.

Delgany, Co. Wicklow

91 Glenview Hotel

★★★★★ ☎ ☎

Glen-O-The-Downs, Delgany, Co. Wicklow
Tel: +353(0)1 2873399 Fax: +353(0)1 2877511

Dingle, Co. Kerry

92 Dingle Skellig Hotel

★★★ ☎

Dingle, Co. Kerry
Tel: +353(0)66 9150200 Fax: +353(0)66 9151501
Email: dsk@iol.ie
Web: www.dingleskellig.com
Closed January to mid-February
116 bedrs SB £46.50 DB £76 HBS £67.50
HBD £59 B £7.70 D £25 CC: MC Vi Am DC

How to get there: Hotel on the shores of Dingle
Harbour as you enter the town from the main
Killarney/Tralee road.

93 Alpine House Guest House

Mail Road, Dingle, Co. Kerry
Tel: +353(0)66 9151250 Fax: +353(0)66 9151966
Email: alpinedingle@eircom.net
Web: www.alpineguesthouse.com
Children minimum age: 5

Newly renovated guest house. Beautifully
furnished bedrooms, all with spacious
bathrooms. Non-smoking. Private car park.
Town centre is a two minute walk away.
10 bedrs SB £25 DB £35 CC: MC Vi Am

How to get there: On route N86 at entrance to
Dingle town. Two minutes' walk from town centre.

94 Bambury's Guesthouse

Mail Road, Dingle, Co. Kerry
Tel: +353(0)66 9151244 Fax: +353(0)66 9151786
Email: bamburysguesthouse@eircom.net
Web: www.bamburysguesthouse.com
Children minimum age: 4
12 bedrs SB £25 DB £35 CC: MC Vi

How to get there: On the N86 into Dingle. Hotel
is situated after the Shell station as you enter
Dingle.

95 Cleevaun

Milltown, Dingle, Co. Kerry
Tel: +353(0)66 9151108 Fax: +353(0)66 9152228
Web: www.cleevaun.com
Children minimum age: 8.
Closed mid-November to mid-March
9 bedrs DB £68

How to get there: Route 559. Take first left off
first roundabout. Follow signs for Sleahead.
With water on left, pass marina. Turn left at next
roundabout. Cross bridge. Cleevaun 500m on
left.

96 Doyle's Town House

◆◆◆◆ ✕ ☂

John Street, Dingle, Co. Kerry
Tel: +353(0)66 9151174 Fax: +353(0)66 9151816
Email: cdoyles@iol.ie
Web: www.doylesofdingle.com
Children minimum age: 8.
Closed mid-November to mid-February
8 bedrs SB £60 DB £65
CC: MC Vi Am DC
♿ ⊗ 🖥 💻 ☎ 🍴 ⅲ

97 Greenmount House

◆◆◆◆ ✕ ☂

Upper John Street, Dingle, Co. Kerry
Tel: +353(0)66 9151414 Fax: +353(0)66 9157974
Email: mary@greenmounthouse.com
Web: www.greenmount.com
Children minimum age: 8.
Closed 10-27 December
12 bedrs SB £80 DB £125
CC: MC Vi Swi
♿ ⊗ 🖥 💻 ☎ 🅿 🍴 ⚓
How to get there: On entering Dingle take right
turn at roundabout, right at next junction. The
hotel is situated up hill, 350m on left.

98 Milltown House

◆◆◆◆ ✕ ☂

Dingle, Co. Kerry
Tel: +353(0)66 9151372 Fax: +353(0)66 9151095
Email: milltown@indigo.ie
Web: indigo.ie/~milltown
Children minimum age: 12.
Closed 30 November to 1 February
10 bedrs SB £85 DB £85
CC: MC Vi Am
♿ ✕ ⊗ 🖥 💻 ☎ 🅿 🍴
How to get there: Leave Dingle on Sleahead
Drive Road. Take next two left turns. House less
than one mile west of Dingle town.

Donegal, Co. Donegal

99 Harvey's Point Country Hotel
Blue Ribbon Winner

★★★★ ⓇⓇ Ⓡ
Lough Eske, Donegal, Co. Donegal
Tel: +353(0)73 22208 Fax: +353(0)73 22352

100 Ardeevin

◆◆◆◆ ✕ ☂

Lough Eske, Barnesmore, Donegal, Co. Donegal
Tel: +353(0)73 21790 Fax: +353(0)73 21790
Email: seanmcginty@eircom.net
Web: www.members.tripod.com/nardeevin
Children minimum age: 10
6 bedrs SB £24.50 DB £40 CC: None accepted
🚗 ⊗ 🖥 💻 🍴
How to get there: Take N15 from Donegal Town,
Derry/Letterkenny road for 4km. Turn left at sign
for Ardeevin (past garage).

Dromoland, Co. Clare

101 Clare Inn Golf and Leisure Hotel

★★★
Dromoland, Co. Clare
Tel: +353(0)6568 23000 Fax: +353(0)6568 23759
Email: reservations@lynchhotels.com
Web: www.lynchotels.com
183 bedrs CC: MC Vi Am
🏊 ⛰ 🚗 💻 ☎ 🍴 🅿 🍴 🎠 🏌 ⚓ ⅲ ⅲ SPA Ⲩ
Ⓒ ⚲ 🗐 ⚒ 🏴
How to get there: Located just 10 minutes drive
from Shannon International Airport on the main
Galway Road (N18) on the Dromoland Estate.

Dublin, Co. Dublin

102 Conrad International Dublin

★★★★★ Ⓡ Ⓡ
Earlsfort Hotel, Dublin 2
Tel: +353(0)676 5555 Fax: +353(0)676 5424
Email: sales@conrad-international.ie
191 bedrs CC: MC Vi Am DC
🏊 ♿ ⛰ 💻 ☎ ❄ 🍴 🅿 🍴 🏴 ⅲ Ⲩ
How to get there: Located in the city centre, on
the south side of St. Stephen's Green, at the
end of Leeson Street.

103 Le Méridien Shelbourne

★★★★★ Ⓡ Ⓡ Ⓡ
27 St. Stephens Green, Dublin 2
Tel: +353(0)1 6766471 Fax: +353(0)1 6616006
Email: shelbourneinfo@lemeridien-hotels.com
Web: www.shelbourne.ie
190 bedrs SB £218.50 DB £273 B £13 L £15.50
D £19 CC: MC Vi Am DC
🏊 ⛰ ⊗ 💻 ☎ 🍴 🅿 🍴 🎥 ⅲ ⅲ SPA Ⲩ 🗐
How to get there: In the heart of Dublin city
centre, close to Trinity College.

Republic of Ireland

104 Merrion Hotel

Gold Ribbon Winner

★★★★★ 🏅🏅🏅🏅
Upper Merrion Street, Dublin 2
Tel: +353(0)1 603 0600 Fax: +353(0)1 603 0700
Email: info@merrionhotel.com
Web: www.merrionhotel.com
145 bedrs SB £184.50 DB £214
B £11.75 L £11 D £24.75
CC: MC Vi Am DC Delt

How to get there: Situated at the top of Upper
Merrion Street on left, opposite government
buildings.

105 The Berkeley Court

★★★★★★ 🏅🏅
Lansdowne Road, Dublin 4
Tel: +353(0)1 6090000 Fax: +353(0)1 6316999
Email: bookings@jurysdoyle.com
Web: www.jurysdoyle.com
Children minimum age: 12
188 bedrs SB £231.19 DB £245.93 B £12.75
L £20.31 D £35.85
CC: MC Vi Am DC

How to get there: Follow signs to city centre.
East Link toll, over bridge. Follow signs for RDS.
Turn right at Jurys Hotel. Berkeley is on right.

106 The Westbury Hotel

★★★★★★ 🏅🏅
Grafton Street, Dublin 4
Tel: +353(0)1 6070000 Fax: +353(0)1 6316999
Email: bookings@jurysdoyle.com
Web: www.jurysdoyle.com

107 Alexander Hotel at Merrion Square

★★★★ 🏅
Fenian Street, Dublin 2
Tel: +353 (0)1 607 3700 Fax: +353 (0)1 661 5663
Email: alexanderres@ocallaghanhotels.ie
Web: www.ocallaghanhotels.ie
102 bedrs SB £217 DB £229 HBS £238
HBD £136 B £12.20 L £15.25 D £21.35
CC: MC Vi Am DC

How to get there: The Alexander is located at
the corner of Fenian Street and South
Cumberland Street, just off Merrion Square.

108 Fitzpatrick Castle

★★★★
Killiney, Co. Dublin
Tel: +353(0)1 230 5556 Fax: +353(0)1 230 5466
Email: reservations@fitzpatricks.com
Web: www.fitzpatrickhotels.com
Closed December 24-25
113 bedrs SB £120 DB £150 HBS £150
HBD £110 B £10 L £14.50 D £32.50
CC: MC Vi Am DC

How to get there: Hotel is 1.6km from Dalkey
village. From Castle Street to Dalkey, turn left
onto Dalkey Avenue. Hotel is located on left
side. Dalkey village is 14.4km south of Dublin
city centre.

109 Fitzwilliam Hotel

★★★★ 🏅🏅🏅
St. Stephens Green, Dublin 2
Tel: +353(0)1 4787000 Fax: +353(0)1 4787878

110 Herbert Park Hotel

Blue Ribbon Winner

★★★★ 🏅
Ballsbridge, Dublin 4
Tel: +353(0)1 6672200 Fax: +353(0)1 6672595
Email: reservations@herbertparkhotel.ie
Web: www.herbertparkhotel.ie

This award-winning, contemporary-style hotel is
five minutes from the city centre, with
spectacular views over 48 acre Herbert park.
Adjacent to the RDS. Facilities include gym and
meeting rooms.
153 bedrs SB £145 DB £174 B £12 L £14.35
D £27.50 CC: MC Vi Am DC

How to get there: From Nassau street go
straight out of Mount Street and
Northumberland Road into Ballsbridge; first turn
right after the bridge, next right.

111 Jurys Ballsbridge Hotel

★★★★ ®
Ballsbridge, Dublin 4
Tel: +353(0)1 6070000 Fax: +353(0)1 6316999
Email: bookings@jurysdoyle.com
Web: www.jurysdoyle.com
Children minimum age: 12
303 bedrs SB £181.31 DB £213.94
B £10.36 L £13.14 D £11.55
CC: MC Vi Am DC

How to get there: Follow signs to city centre, then East Link Toll Bridge, go over bridge, follow signs for RDS. Hotel is on left.

112 Red Cow Moran Hotel

★★★★ ®
Naas Road, Dublin 22
Tel: +353(0)1 4593650 Fax: +353(0)1 4591588
Email: sales@morangroup.ie
Web: www.redcowhotel.com
Closed Christmas

Red Cow Moran Hotel combines classic elegance with modern design. Each of the hotel's 123 deluxe bedrooms are fully air-conditioned. Guests have a choice of three restaurants and four bars and a nightclub in the complex. Free parking.
123 bedrs SB £115 DB £160 L £16.50 D £26.50
CC: MC Vi Am DC

How to get there: From Dublin airport – drive towards city on M1; take first exit to M50 southbound and cross toll bridge; take exit 9, N7/The South. Hotel at top of slipway.

Plan your route

Visit www.rac.co.uk for RAC's interactive route planner, including up to the minute traffic reports.

113 The Burlington Hotel

★★★★
Upper Leeson Street, Dublin 4
Tel: +353(0)1 6070055 Fax: +353(0)1 6609625
Email: dorothy_cusack@jurysdoyle.com
Web: www.jurysdoyle.com
504 bedrs CC: MC Vi Am DC Swi Delt

How to get there: Take N7 out of town. Go up Naas Road until you come to Newlands Cross, go right. At second set of lights turn left. Go up that road for ¼ miles and turn left.

114 The Davenport Hotel at Merrion Square

★★★★ ®
Lower Merrion Street, Dublin 2
Tel: +353 (0)1 607 3900 Fax: +353 (0)1 661 5663
Email: davenportres@ocallaghanhotels.ie
Web: www.ocallaghanhotels.ie
115 bedrs SB £217 DB £229 HBS £238
HBD £136 B £12.20 L £15.25 D £21.35
CC: MC Vi Am DC

How to get there: On Lower Merrion Street, just off Merrion Square.

115 The Gresham

★★★★
23 Upper O'Connell Street, Dublin 1
Tel: +353 (0)1 874 6881 Fax: +353 (0)1 878 7175
Email: reservations@thegresham.com
Web: www.gresham-hotels.com

Behind the elegant façade lie luxury bedrooms and spacious suites, an award-winning restaurant and bars.
288 bedrs SB £220 DB £255 B £12.50 L £17
D £23.50 CC: MC Vi Am DC

How to get there: Situated on Dublin's main thoroughfare, O'Connell Street.

116 The Plaza Hotel

★★★★★
Belgard Road, Tallaght, Dublin 24
Tel: +353(0)1 462 4200 Fax: +353(0)1 462 4600

117 Ashling Hotel – Best Western

★★★
Parkgate Street, Dublin 8
Tel: +353(0)1 6772324 Fax: +353(0)1 6793783
Email: info@ashlinghotel.ie
Web: www.ashlinghotel.ie
Closed 23-27 December
150 bedrs DB £67 HBS £88.50
B £6.10 L £9.50 D £14
CC: MC Vi Am DC

How to get there: Easily-found location by car/rail/bus. By car, take city centre route and briefly follow River Liffey westward. Take taxi or 'Airlink' public bus from airport.

118 Cassidy's Hotel

★★★
Cavendish Row, Upper O'Connell Street, Dublin 1
Tel: +353(0)1 8780555 Fax: +353(0)1 8780687
Email: rese@cassidys.iol.ie
Web: www.cassidyshotel.com
Closed December 24-27
88 bedrs SB £85 DB £115 B £7.25 L £5.25
D £13.95 CC: MC Vi Am DC

How to get there: Continue up O'Connell Street away from the river. Cassidy's is located opposite the famous Gate Theatre on Cavendish Row.
See advert on facing page

119 Deer Park Hotel & Golf Courses

★★★
Howth, Co. Dublin
Tel: +353(0)1 8322624 Fax: +353(0)1 8392405
Email: sales@deerpark.iol.ie
Web: www.deerpark-hotel.ie
80 bedrs SB £90 DB £132 HBS £115 HBD £91
B £6 L £15 D £25
CC: MC Vi Am DC

How to get there: Follow coast road via Clontarf. Through Sutton Cross and Deer Park is on your right before Howth Harbour.
See advert on facing page

120 Finnstown Country House Hotel

★★★★
Newcastle Road, Lucan, Dublin
Tel: +353(0)1 601 0700 Fax: +353(0)1 628 1088
Email: manager@finnstown-hotel.ie
Web: www.finnstown-hotel.ie
53 bedrs SB £95 DB £140 HBS £120
HBD £82.50 L £12 D £25
CC: MC Vi Am DC

How to get there: From Dublin, travel along South Quays, passing Heuston Station. Continue on N4. At traffic lights after Texaco garage, turn left. Hotel on right after two roundabouts.
See advert on facing page

121 Hibernian Hotel

★★★★
Eastmoreland Place, Ballsbridge, Dublin 4
Tel: +353(0)1 6687666 Fax: +353(0)1 6602655
Email: info@hibernianhotel.com
Web: www.hibernianhotel.com
Closed Christmas
40 bedrs SB £93 DB £116.50
B £6.20 L £10.80 D £23
CC: MC Vi Am DC Swi Delt JCB

How to get there: Turn right from Mespil Road into Baggot Street Upper, then left into Eastmoreland Place. The Hibernian is at the end on the left.

122 Jurys Green Isle Hotel

★★★
Naas Road, Dublin 22
Tel: +353(0)1 6070000 Fax: +353(0)1 6316999
Email: bookings@jurysdoyle.com
Web: www.jurysdoyle.com
Children minimum age: 12
90 bedrs SB £103.83 DB £119.83
B £5.97 L £11.15 D £15.89
CC: MC Vi Am DC

How to get there: M50 southbound. Exit 9 on to N7 southbound. Right at two lights. 2nd left past garage. Hotel 600 yards on left.

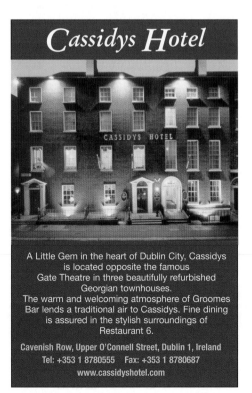

Republic of Ireland

123 Jurys Inn Christchurch

★★★
Christchurch Place, Dublin 8
Tel: +353(0)1 6070000 Fax: +353(0)1 6316999
Email: bookings@jurysdoyle.com
Web: www.jurysdoyle.com
Closed Christmas
182 bedrs B £5.18 D £12.70 CC: MC Vi Am DC

How to get there: Located seven miles/10 kms from airport. Follow signs to city centre. Inn located opposite Christchurch Cathedral at the top of Dame Street.

124 Jurys Inn Custom House

★★★
Custom House Quay, Dublin 1
Tel: +353(0)1 6070000 Fax: +353(0)1 6316999
Email: bookings@jurysdoyle.com
Web: www.jurysdoyle.com
Closed Christmas
239 bedrs B £5.18 D £12.70 CC: MC Vi Am DC
How to get there: Located six miles/10 kms from Dublin airport. Follow signs for city centre. Take left at bridge. Inn is on the left.

125 Jurys Montrose Hotel

★★★
Stillorgan Road, Dublin 4
Tel: +353(0)1 6070000 Fax: +353(0)1 6316999
Email: bookings@jurysdoyle.com
Web: www.jurysdoyle.com
Children minimum age: 12
179 bedrs SB £103.83 DB £119.83 B £5.96 L £10.31 D £15.85
CC: MC Vi Am DC
How to get there: M50 follow signs for N11, cross toll bridge, pass Jurys Tara, take right at lights. Follow road to Woodbine. At the top, take left.

126 Jurys Skylon Hotel

★★★
Upper Drumcondra Road, Dublin 9
Tel: +353(0)1 6070000 Fax: +353(0)1 6316999
Email: bookings@jurysdoyle.com
Web: www.jurysdoyle.com
Children minimum age: 12
88 bedrs SB £103.83 DB £119.83 B £5.97 L £11.15 D £15.89 CC: MC Vi Am DC
How to get there: From airport, M1 to city centre. Three miles on the right.

127 Jurys Tara Hotel

★★★
Merrion Road, Dublin 4
Tel: +353(0)1 6070000 Fax: +353(0)1 6316999
Email: bookings@jurysdoyle.com
Web: www.jurysdoyle.com
Children minimum age: 12
Closed Christmas
113 bedrs SB £103.83 DB £119.83 B £6.32 L £11.11 D £15.89 CC: MC Vi Am DC
How to get there: M50 City Centre. Follow N11 and Ferry signs. Cross toll bridge. Follow Strand Road. Cross Railtrack. Hotel is on the left.

128 Longfields Hotel

★★★★
10 Lower Fitzwilliam Street, Dublin 2
Tel: +353(0)1 6761367 Fax: +353(0)1 6761542
Email: info@longfields.ie
Web: www.longfields.com

A centrally located, charming, intimate hotel with period furnishings and an excellent restaurant.
26 bedrs SB £87 DB £112 B £5.40 L £13.30 D £23.50 CC: MC Vi DC
How to get there: From airport, follow signs for city centre then O'Connell Street. Around front of Trinity College to left, pass Shelbourne Hotel onto Baggot Street. At main junction of Lower and Upper Baggot streets, hotel first on left of Fitzwilliam Street.

129 Marine Hotel

★★★★
Sutton Cross, Sutton, Dublin 13
Tel: +353(0)1 8390000 Fax: +353(0)1 8390442
Email: info@marinehotel.ie
Web: www.marinehotel.ie.
Closed Christmas
48 bedrs SB £91.50 DB £131.15 B £7.65 L £13.50 D £23.20 CC: MC Vi Am DC

130 Mount Herbert Hotel

★★★

Herbert Road, Lansdowne, Dublin 4
Tel: +353(0)1 668 4321 Fax: +353(0)1 660 7077
Email: info@mountherberthotel.ie
Web: www.mountherberthotel.ie

Stately Victorian residence five minutes from city centre in Dublin's exclusive embassy belt. Facilities include 180 modern bedrooms, restaurant, licensed bar, coffee bar, sauna, gift shop, conference centre, private car park and picturesque gardens.
180 bedrs SB £75.50 DB £95 B £5.50 D £16.95
CC: MC Vi Am DC

How to get there: From city centre, Nassau Street at Trinity College along Merrion Square, Mount Street, Northumberland Road. At Lansdowne Road turn left. Cross DART line, pass rugby stadium, cross bridge to hotel.

131 Parliament Hotel

★★★

Temple Bar, Dublin 2
Tel: +353(0)1 670 8777 Fax: +353(0)1 670 8787
Email: parl@regencyhotels.com
Web: www.regencyhotels.com

This brilliantly-located hotel is in Dublin's most fashionable area, opposite Dublin Castle and close to Trinity College and St. Stephen's Green. With an international restaurant and lively pub-style bar.

63 bedrs SB £100 DB £130
B £7 L £14 D £18
CC: MC Vi Am

How to get there: Located in Temple Bar opposite Dublin Castle, two minutes from Trinity College.

132 Regency Airport Hotel

★★★

Swords Road, Whitehall, Dublin 9
Tel: +353(0)1 8373544 Fax: +353(0)1 8373174
Email: regency@regencyhotels.com
Web: www.regencyhotels.com

This superb hotel is located just 3km north of Dublin city centre on the main route to the airport. With exceptional dining facilities, executive rooms and suites, and extensive conference and banquetting facilities.
210 bedrs SB £85 DB £100 B £6 L £10 D £21
CC: MC Vi Am

How to get there: Travelling from Belfast, pass Dublin airport, travel down Airport road towards city centre. At motorway end, go through lights, hotel is on left.

133 Royal Dublin Hotel

★★★

O'Connell Street, Dublin 1, Dublin
Tel: +353(0)1 8733666 Fax: +353(0)1 8733120
Email: enq@royaldublin.com
Web: www.royaldublin.com
117 bedrs SB £85.94 DB £111.31 HBS £104
HBD £73.50 B £8 L £12 D £19.50
CC: MC Vi Am DC

How to get there: In city centre, from O'Connell Bridge go north up O'Connell Street. Hotel is at end of street on left.

134 The Court Hotel

★★★
Killiney Bay, Dublin
Tel: +353(0)1 2851622 Fax: +353(0)1 2852085
Email: book@killineycourt.ie
Web: www.killineycourt.ie
86 bedrs B £10 L £18 D £30
CC: MC Vi Am DC

How to get there: By DART; or take the N11 from Dublin towards Wexford and follow signs for Killiney to the coast and turn left at the coast.

135 The North Star Hotel

★★★
Amien Street, Dublin 1
Tel: +353(0)1 8881600 Fax: +353(0)1 8881604
Email: groupsales@regencyhotels.com
Web: www.regencyhotels.com

The North Star is located ten minutes walk from Temple Bar, Dublin's left bank area, St. Stephens Green and Trinity College. The hotel encompasses 130 newly appointed fully air-conditioned bedrooms, all with modern conveniences.
121 bedrs SB £100 DB £140 B £5 L £14 D £19
CC: MC Vi Am DC

How to get there: The hotel is located in Dublin city centre opposite the International Financial Services Centre, ten minutes from Temple Bar.

136 Uppercross House

★★★
26/30 Upper Rathmines Road 1, Dublin 6
Tel: +353(0)1 4975486 Fax: +353(0)1 4975486

137 White Sands Hotel

★★★
Coast Road, Portmarnock, Co. Dublin
Tel: +353(0)1 8460003 Fax: +353(0)1 8460420

Email: sandshotel@eircom.net
Web: www.whitesandshotel.ie
Closed 24-25 December
32 bedrs SB £70 DB £94 HBS £80 HBD £57
CC: MC Vi Am DC

How to get there: Take Belfast road from Dublin Airport. Turn right at sign for Malahide at 3rd roundabout. Turn left at T-junction and follow through to Portmarnock.
See advert on facing page

138 Wynns Hotel

★★★
35-39 Lower Abbey Street, Dublin 1
Tel: +353(0)1 8745131 Fax: +353(0)1 8741556
Email: info@wynnshotel.ie
Web: www.wynnshotel.com

Ideal city-centre location close to fashionable shops, restaurants, theatres, galleries and places of interest. Conference, banqueting and wedding facilities, small or large groups. Saints and Scholars Bar and Peacock Restaurant.
70 bedrs SB £75 DB £110 B £6 L £12.50 D £16
CC: MC Vi Am DC

139 Travelodge Dublin

Travel Accommodation
N3, Auburn Avenue Roundabout, Navan Road, Castleknock, Dublin
Tel: 08700 850 950
Web: www.travelodge.co.uk
60 bedrs B £4.25 CC: MC Vi Am DC Swi Delt

140 Travelodge Dublin Airport

Travel Accommodation
N1 Belfast Road, Pennock Hill, Swords by-pass, Dublin
Tel: 08700 850 950
Web: www.travelodge.co.uk
100 bedrs B £4.25 CC: MC Vi Am DC Swi Delt

141 Aberdeen Lodge

◆◆◆◆◆

53 Park Avenue, Ballsbridge, Dublin 4
Tel: +353(0)1 2838155 Fax: +353(0)1 2837877
Email: aberdeen@iol.ie
Web: www.halpinsprivatehotels.com
18 bedrs SB £60 DB £80 B £8
CC: MC Vi Am DC

How to get there: Minutes from city centre by DART or car. Take Merrion Road towards Sydney Parade DART station, then first left onto Park Avenue.

142 Butlers Town House

◆◆◆◆◆

44 Lansdowne Road, Ballsbridge, Dublin
Tel: +353(0)1 6674022 Fax: +353(0)1 6673960
Email: info@butlers-hotel.com
Web: www.butlers-hotel.com
19 bedrs SB £90 DB £120 B £10
CC: MC Vi Am DC

How to get there: Hotel is located on the corner of Shelbourne Road and Lansdowne Road in the area of Ballsbridge, just south of the city centre.

143 Cedar Lodge

◆◆◆◆◆

98 Merrion Road, Ballsbridge, Dublin 4
Tel: +353(0)1 6684410 Fax: +353(0)1 6684533
Email: info@cedarlodge.ie
Web: www.cedarlodge.ie
Children minimum age: 12
Closed 23-28 December
16 bedrs SB £48 DB £68 B £6 CC: MC Vi Am

How to get there: From city centre (Nassau Street) continue onto Mount Street. Take Northumberland Road onto Ballsbridge; Jurys Hotel is on left. Cedar lodge opposite British Embassy on Merrion Road.

144 Glenogra

◆◆◆◆◆

64 Merrion Road, Ballsbridge, Dublin 4
Tel: +353(0)1 6683661 Fax: +353(0)1 6683698
Email: glenogra@indigo.ie
Web: www.glenogra.com
Closed Christmas to New Year
13 bedrs SB £49 DB £67.50 B £8 CC: MC Vi Am

How to get there: Situated opposite the Four Seasons Hotel in Ballsbridge on main route from Dun Laoghaire car ferry.

Republic of Ireland

145 Merrion Hall

♦ ♦ ♦ ♦ ♦

54 Merrion Road, Ballsbridge, Dublin 4
Tel: +353(0)1 6681426 Fax: +353(0)1 6684280
Email: merrionhall@iol.ie
Web: www.halpinsprivatehotels.com

Award-winning Edwardian property located just
minutes from downtown Dublin in the leafy
Ballsbridge area. Ideal for visiting Trinity
College, St. Stephen's Green, shopping in
Grafton Street. Private carpark and gardens.
24 bedrs SB £60 DB £80 B £8
CC: MC Vi Am DC
&⊞⊗⊜⬛☎📞🅿️⊗⌂⛱🏃♨⛛🆂🅿️🅰️
How to get there: Located in Ballsbridge, close
to city centre on Merrion Road. Minutes from
city centre by DART or bus.

146 66 Townhouse

♦ ♦ ♦ ♦

66 Northumberland Road, Ballsbridge, Dublin 4
Tel: +353(0)1 6600471 Fax: +353(0)1 6601051
Closed 22 December to 6 January
9 bedrs CC: MC Vi
⊜⬛☎🅿️⊗⌂🕯⌂
How to get there: 66 Townhouse is south of
Trinity College/city centre on Diplomatic centre –
Ballsbridge Lansdowne Road area.

147 Baggot Court

♦ ♦ ♦ ♦

92 Lower Baggot Street, Dublin
Tel: +353(0)66 12819 Fax: +353(0)66 10253
Email: baggot@indigo.ie
Children minimum age: 8.
Closed Christmas and New Year
11 bedrs SB £55 DB £90 CC: MC Vi Am
⌂⊗⊜⬛☎🅿️⊗
How to get there: From O'Connell Street go
south on number 10 bus. Get off at Old
Convent. Directly opposite is Baggot Court.

148 Charleville Lodge

♦ ♦ ♦ ♦

268-272 North Circular Road,
Phisborough, Dublin 7
Tel: +353(0)1 8386633 Fax: +353(0)1 8385854
Email: charleville@indigo.ie
Web: www.charlevillelodge.ie

Charleville Lodge (former home to Lord
Charleville) is a beautifully-restored terrace of
Edwardian houses, offering all the luxury
expected from a large hotel, whilst retaining the
old-world charm.
30 bedrs SB £50 DB £110 B £7.50
CC: MC Vi Am DC
&⬛☎🅿️⊗⌂🕯♨⛛
How to get there: North from city centre
(O'Connell Street) to Phisborough, then take left
fork at St. Peter's Church. 200 metres on the
left; or, take no.60 bus.

149 Eliza Lodge

♦ ♦ ♦ ♦ ☕

23/24 Wellington Quay, Temple Bar, Dublin 2
Tel: +353(0)1 671 8044 Fax: +353(0)1 671 8362
Email: info@dublinlodge.com
Web: www.dublinlodge.com
Closed Christmas
18 bedrs SB £50 DB £90 B £4 CC: MC Vi Am
&⊞⊗⊜⬛☎❄🕯⌂
How to get there: Located at foot of Millennium
Bridge, second bridge after O'Connell Bridge.
25 minutes' drive from Dublin Airport.

150 Glenveagh Town House

♦ ♦ ♦ ♦

31 Northumerland Road, Ballsbridge, Dublin
Tel: +353(0)1 6684612 Fax: +353(0)1 6684559

151 Hedigans

♦ ♦ ♦ ♦ ☕

14 Hollybrook Park, Clontarf
Tel: +353(0)1 8531663 Fax: +353(0)1 8333337
Email: hedigans@indigo.ie

Closed Christmas to mid January
9 bedrs SB £50 DB £70 CC: MC Vi

How to get there: On Clontarf Road turn left after Clontarf Motors. Up Hollybrook Road and Hedigans is at the top.

152 Kilronan House

♦♦♦♦ ⚡ ☞

70 Adelaide Road, Dublin 2
Tel: +353(0)1 4755266 Fax: +353(0)1 4782841
Email: info@dublinn.com
Web: www.dublinn.com

Exclusive Georgian house within walking distance of St. Stephen's Green, Trinity College and most of Dublin's historic landmarks. Under the personal supervision of owner Terry Masterson.
12 bedrs SB £55 DB £90 CC: MC Vi Am DC

How to get there: Drive down St. Stephen's Green east onto Earlsfort Terrace. Proceed onto Adelaide Road. House is on right-hand side.

153 Kingswood Country House

♦♦♦♦ ⚡ ⚡

Kingswood, Naas Road, Clondalkin
Tel: +353(0)1 4592428 Fax: +353(0)1 4592207
Email: kingswoodcountryhse@eircom.net
7 bedrs
CC: MC Vi Am DC

How to get there: From M50 Dublin ring road take N7 exit. Hotel is three miles on N7 heading south, clearly signposted.

154 Trinity Lodge
Little Gem

♦♦♦♦ ⚡ ☞

12 South Frederick Street, Dublin 2
Tel: +353(0)1 6795044 Fax: +353(0)1 6795223
Email: trinitylodge@eircom.net
Closed 22 December to 2 January
13 bedrs CC: MC Vi Am DC

How to get there: Lodge is situated in city centre, beside Trinity College, off Nassau Street.

155 Clifden Guesthouse

♦♦♦

32 Gardiner Place, Dublin 1
Tel: +353(0)18746364 Fax: +353(0)18746122
Email: tnt@indigo.ie
Web: www.clifdenhouse.com
14 bedrs CC: MC Vi

How to get there: From O'Connell Street (North End), drive around three sides of Parnell Square. Exit at the church. Clifden house is 400m further.

156 Fitzwilliam

♦♦♦

41 Upper Fitzwilliam Street, Dublin 2
Tel: +353(0)1 660 0448 Fax: +353(0)1 676 7488

157 Harcourt Inn

♦♦♦

27 Harcourt Street, Dublin
Tel: +353(0)1 4783927

Check the price

£ As from 2002 Ireland will be using Euros, so be sure to check the price of your chosen accommodation when booking.

See the road ahead

Just dial 1740* from any mobile phone to get up-to-the-minute RAC traffic information on motorways and major A roads. Try it now! *Calls to 1740 are charged at premium rate.

Republic of Ireland

158 Redbank Guesthouse & Restaurant

6-7 Church Street, Skerries,
Co. Dublin
Tel: +353(0)1 8490439 Fax: +353(0)1 8491598
Email: redbank@eircom.net
Web: www.redbank.ie
Closed Christmas

Building now listed for protection, confirming
the McCoy's sense of style, having converted
this old bank into one of Ireland's finest
restaurants and guest houses, featuring the
catch of the day at Skerries Pier.
12 bedrs SB £45 DB £74
HBS £70 HBD £140
B £5 L £22 D £28
CC: MC Vi Am DC Swi Delt

How to get there: 20 minutes off the N1 Dublin
to Belfast road. From the south, through the
village of Lusk. From the north, turn to left at
Balbriggan and follow coast road.

159 Saint Andrews House

113 Lambay Road, Drumcondra
Tel: +353(0)1 8374684 Fax: +353(0)1 8570446
Email: andrew@dublinn.com
16 bedrs CC: None accepted

160 Blakes Townhouse

50 Merrion Road, Ballsbridge, Dublin 4
Tel: +353(0)1 6688324 Fax: +353(0)1 6684280
Email: blakestownhouse@iol.ie
Web: www.halpinsprivatehotels.com
13 bedrs SB £60 DB £80 B £8
CC: MC Vi Am DC
How to get there: Located in Ballsbridge, close
to city centre on the Merrion Road. Minutes
from city centre by DART or bus.

161 Temple Bar Hotel

Fleet Stret, Dublin 2
Tel: +353 (0)1 677 3333 Fax: +353 (0)1 677 3088
Email: templeb@iol.ie
Web: www.towerhotelgroup.ie
Closed Christmas
129 bedrs SB £88.50 DB £113
B £7.25 L £7.80 D £15.25 CC: MC Vi Am DC

Dun Laoghaire, Co. Dublin

162 The Gresham Royal Marine

★★★
Dun Laoghaire, Co. Dublin

 Tel: +353(0)1 280 1911 Fax:
+353(0)1 280 1089
Email:
royalmarine@eircom.net
Web: www.gresham-hotels.om

Victorian façade, 103-bedroom hotel set in an
elegant four acres, overlooking Dublin's most
prestigious site.
103 bedrs SB £105 DB £130 HBS £120
B £10 L £12 D £15
CC: MC Vi Am DC Delt
How to get there: Directly opposite Holyhead to
Dun Laoghaire car ferry.

163 Kingston Hotel

★★
Adelaide Street, Dun Laoghaire, Co. Dublin
Tel: +353(0)1 2801810 Fax: +353(0)1 2801237
Email: reserv@kingstonhotel.com
Web: www.kingstonhotel.com
Closed Christmas
53 bedrs SB £60 DB £85 B £6 L £10 D £15
CC: MC Vi Am DC Delt
See advert on facing page

164 Tara Hall

24 Sandycove Road, Dun Laoghaire, Co. Dublin
Tel: +353(0)1 2805120 Fax: +353(0)1 2805120
Email: tarahall@indigo.ie
Children minimum age: 5
8 bedrs SB £22 DB £60 D £11 CC: MC Vi

Dundalk, Co. Louth

165 Ballymascanlon House Hotel

★★★ ®

Ballymascanlon, Dundalk, Co. Louth
Tel: +353(0)42 9371124 Fax: +353(0)42 9371598
Email: info@ballymascanlon.com
Web: www.globalgolf.com/ballymascanlon
Closed 24-27 December
90 bedrs SB £80 DB £114 HBD £80
B £10 L £15 D £28 CC: MC Vi Am DC

How to get there: We are 2 miles north of Dundalk,
off main Belfast Road (on Carlingford Road).

166 Fairways Hotel

★★★

Dublin Road, Dundalk, Co. Louth
Tel: +353(0)42 9321500 Fax: +353(0)42 9321511
Email: info@fairways.ieWeb: www.fairways.ie
101 bedrs SB £55 DB £80 B £6 L £15 D £22
CC: MC Vi Am DC

How to get there: 3 miles south of Dundalk, approx.
one hour 15 minutes from Dublin or Belfast.

Dunfanaghy, Co. Donegal

167 Arnolds Hotel

★★★ ®

Dunfanaghy, Co. Donegal
Tel: +353(0)74 36208 Fax: +353(0)74 36352
Email: arnoldshotel@eircom.net
Web: www.arnoldshotel.com
Closed November to March
30 bedrs SB £55.50 DB £80.50 B £6.75
D £23.20 CC: MC Vi Am DC

How to get there: Take N56 northwest from
Letterkenny. After 23 miles, hotel is on left as
you enter village.
See advert above right

Republic of Ireland

Dungarvan, Co. Waterford

168 Castle Farm

Little Gem

◆ ◆ ◆ ◆ ✕ ☙

Cappagh, Dungarvan, Co. Waterford
Tel: +353(0)58 68049 Fax: +353(0)58 68099
Email: castlefm@iol.ie
Web: www.waterfordfarms.com/castlefarm
Closed November to February

Award winning restored wing of 15th century castle on large dairy farm. Excellent cuisine and elegant decor. Breakfast menu.
5 bedrs CC: MC Vi Swi Delt
✕ ⊕ ☺ ▭ ✳ P ☼ ⅃ℂ ☭ ♬ ☙ ⑾ ‖ ⅃ ⌕
How to get there: Located 15km off N25.

Ennis, Co. Clare

169 Woodstock Hotel

★ ★ ★ ★ ®

Shanaway Road, Ennis, Co. Clare
Tel: +353(0)65 6846600 Fax: +353(0)65 6846611
Email: info@woodstockhotel.com
Web: www.woodstockhotel.com
Closed December 25-26
67 bedrs SB £58.50 DB £112.50
B £6.20 L £10.80 D £21.30
CC: MC Vi Am DC Swi Delt JCB
Ⓖ ⅃ℐ ✕ ⊕ ☺ ▭ ☎ ☏ P☙ ☼ ⅃ℂ ♬ ☜ ⑾ ‖ ⅲ SPA
Ɏ ⅃ ⌕
How to get there: From Limerick, follow N18 to Ennis. Take exit for Lahinch (N85). After 1km, turn left. Woodstock Hotel 1km further.

170 West Country Conference and Leisure

★ ★ ★

Clare Road, Ennis, Co. Clare
Tel: +353(0)6568 23000 Fax: +353(0)6568 23759
Email: reservations@lynchhotels.com
Web: www.lynchhotels.com
152 bedrs CC: MC Vi Am DC

◬ Ⓖ ⅃ℐ ⊕ ☺ ▭ ☎ ☏ P☙ ☼ ☞ ☭ ♬ ☙ ☜ ⑾
ⅲ SPA Ɏ ⌕ ⅃
How to get there: 15km from Shannon Airport, 15 minutes walk from Ennis town Centre. Ideal base for touring the Shannon region.

Ennistymon, Co. Clare

171 Grovemount House

◆ ◆ ◆ ◆

Lahinch Road, Ennistymon, Co. Clare
Tel: +353(0)65 7071431 Fax: +353(0)65 7071823
Email: grovemnt@gofree.indigo.ie
Closed November to April
8 bedrs SB £33 DB £50 CC: MC Vi
Ⓖ ⊕ ☺ ▭ ☎ P☙ ☼ ♬ ☙
How to get there: Take N85 from Ennis to Ennistymon, N67 from Ennistymon to Lahinch. Grovemount House is situated on the outskirts of Ennistymon on the right-hand side.

Faithlegg, Co. Waterford

172 Faithlegg House Hotel

★ ★ ★ ★ ® ®

Faithlegg, Co. Waterford
Tel: +353(0)51 382000 Fax: +353(0)51 380010
82 bedrs SB £113 DB £148 B £10 D £28
CC: MC Vi Am DC
◬ Ⓖ ⅃ℐ ✐ ⊕ ☺ ▭ ☎ ☏ P☙ ☼ ☜ ⑾ ‖ Ɏ ⁄.
⅃ ⌕

Fermoy, Co. Cork

173 Ballyvolane House

◆ ◆ ◆ ◆ ® ✕

Castlelyons, near Fermoy, Co. Cork
Tel: +353(0)25 36349 Fax: +353(0)25 36781
Email: ballyvol@iol.ie
Web: www.ballyvolanehouse.ie

Originally built in 1728, Ballyvolane was remodelled in Italianate style. Bluebell woodland gardens, also formal walled garden. Three small trout lakes and private salmon fishing.

6 bedrs SB £62 DB £100 HBS £86 HBD £73

CC: MC Vi Am

How to get there: From Cork, right off N8 at River Bride, before Rath Cormac (R628). Follow House signs.

Galway, Co. Galway

174 Ardilaun House Hotel Conference Centre and Leisure Club

★★★★

Taylors Hill, Galway, Co. Galway
Tel: +353(0)91 521433 Fax: +353(0)91 521546
Email: ardilaun@iol.ie
Web: www.ardilaunhousehotel.ie
Closed 23-28 December
90 bedrs SB £100 DB £150 HBS £125
HBD £100 B £8.50 L £14.50 D £25
CC: MC Vi Am DC

How to get there: Approaching Galway take N6 to Galway City West.Follow signs for N59 Clifden then the N6 for Salthill. Taylor's Hill is enroute.

175 Galway Bay Golf and Country Club Hotel

★★★★

Oranmore, Co. Galway
Tel: +353(0)65 6823000 Fax: +353(0)65 6823759
Email: reservations@lynchotels.com
Web: www.lynchotels.com
92 bedrs
CC: MC Vi Am DC

How to get there: In Oranmore village follow signs for Maree. At new church take the first exit to the right. Hotel is 5–10 minutes down this road.

176 Glenlo Abbey Hotel

Gold Ribbon Winner

★★★★★

Busheypark, Co. Galway
Tel: +353(0)91 526666 Fax: +353(0)91 527800
Email: info@glenloabbey.ie
Web: www.glenlo.com
46 bedrs B £17 L £19 D £40 CC: MC Vi Am DC

How to get there: Situated four kms from Galway city centre on the N59 to Clifden.
See advert on following page

177 Park House Hotel

★★★★

Forster Street, Eyre Square, Galway, Co. Galway
Tel: +353(0)91 564924 Fax: +353(0)91 569219
Email: parkhousehotel@eircom.net
Web: www.parkhousehotel.ie
57 bedrs SB £95 DB £155
B £8.95 D £26.95
CC: MC Vi Am DC

How to get there: Follow all signs for city centre. Hotel is situated on Forster Street, off Eyre Square. Car park is at rear of hotel.
See advert on following page

178 Westwood House Hotel

★★★★★

Dangan, Upper Newcastle, Galway, Co. Galway
Tel: +353(0)91 521442 Fax: +353(0)91 521400
Email: reservations@westwoodhousehotel.com
Web: www.westwoodhousehotel.com
Closed 24-25 December

The 4-star Westwood House Hotel stands amid a rural landscape of greenery combining a mellow taste of the countryside with the city's cutting edge.

58 bedrs SB £89 DB £109 HBS £114 HBD £67
B £5.50 D £25
CC: MC Vi Am DC

How to get there: When entering Galway, follow signs for N59 Clifden road. We are on this road 1km from the city centre.

Republic of Ireland

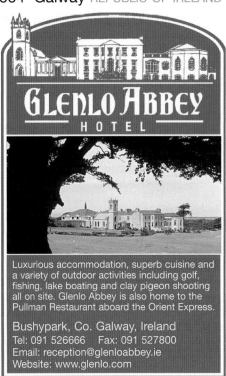

179 Brennans Yard Hotel

★★★

Lower Merchants Road, Galway, Co. Galway
Tel: +353(0)91 568166 Fax: +353(0)91 568262
Email: info@brennansyardhotel.com
Web: www.brennansyardhotel.com
45 bedrs SB £65 DB £105
CC: MC Vi Am DC Swi Delt

How to get there: From Eyre Square, turn left
after the Great Southern Hotel. Turn right. At the
end of the road turn right and stay in right-hand
lane. Turn right and immediately right again.
See advert on facing page

180 Imperial Hotel

★★★

Eyre Square, Galway, Co. Galway
Tel: +353(0)91 63033

181 Jurys Inn Galway

★★★

Quay Street, Galway, Co. Galway
Tel: +353(0)1 6070000 Fax: +353(0)1 6316999
Email: bookings@jurysdoyle.com
Web: www.jurysdoyle.com
Closed Christmas
128 bedrs B £5.18 D £12.70
CC: MC Vi Am DC

How to get there: Located five miles/eight kms
from Galway airport. Train station five minutes
walk. Centrally located beside Spanish Arch and
overlooking Galway Bay.

182 Menlo Park Hotel

★★★

Terryland, Galway
Tel: +353(0) 91 761122 Fax: +3539(0)91 761222

183 The Galway Ryan

★★★

Dublin Road, Galway City East, Galway,
Co. Galway
Tel: +353(0)91 753181 Fax: +353(0)91 753187
Email: enquiries@ryan-hotels.com
Web: www.ryan-hotels.com

A modern hotel, with well-furnished
rooms, situated in the suburbs of Galway
city.
96 bedrs SB £80 DB £120
B £7 L £9.50 D £18.95
CC: MC Vi Am DC

How to get there: Follow the signs for Galway
East when approaching Galway from Dublin.

184 Almara House

◆◆◆◆

2 Merlin Gate, Merlin Park, Dublin Road,
Galway, Co. Galway
Tel: +353 (0)91 755345 Fax: +353 (0)91 771585
Email: matthewkiernan@eircom.net
Web: www.almarahouse.com
Closed one week at Christmas
4 bedrs SB £32 DB £52
CC: MC Vi Am
How to get there: Located on the N6 Dublin
Road beside Corrib Great Southern Hotel and
Merlin Park Hospital.

Glandore, Co. Cork

185 Marine Hotel

★★

Glandore, Co. Cork
Tel: +353(0)28 33366

Republic of Ireland

Glin, Co. Limerick

186 Glin Castle

Blue Ribbon Winner

★★★ ®
Glin, Co. Limerick
Tel: +353(0)68 34173 Fax: +353(0)68 34364
Email: knight@iol.ie
Web: www.glincastle.com
Children minimum age: 10
Closed 1 November to 24 March
15 bedrs SB £148 DB £148 B £15 L £12
D £21.50
CC: MC Vi Am DC

How to get there: 32 miles west of Limerick city on N69, four miles east of Tarbert/Killimar car ferry.

Gorey, Co. Wexford

187 Marlfield House

Gold Ribbon Winner

★★★ ® ® ®
Courtown Road, Gorey, Co. Wexford
Tel: +353(0)55 21124 Fax: +353(0)55 21572
Email: info@marlfieldhouse.ie
Web: www.marlfieldhouse.com
Closed mid December to January

Set in 36 acres of magnificent gardens and filled with numerous antiques, Marlfield's true Irish hospitality and cuisine have gained it world acclaim.
20 bedrs SB £80 DB £152 HBS £112.50
HBD £108 B £11.30 L £20.85 D £32.20
CC: MC Vi Am DC

How to get there: Marlfield House is one mile outside Gorey on the Courtown Road R742.

188 Woodlands Country House

♦ ♦ ♦ ♦ ♦ ⚸ ℱ
Killinierin, Gorey, Co. Wexford
Tel: +353(0)402 37125 Fax: +353(0)402 37133
Email: info@woodlandscountryhouse.com
Web: www.woodlandscountryhouse.com
Closed October to March

Woodlands Country House, built in 1836, is set in 1½ acres of lawns and garden courtyard. Old stone buildings, noted for tranquility, ideal base for touring southeast Ireland. Listed in many quality guides.
6 bedrs SB £31.37 DB £41.41
CC: MC Vi

How to get there: Three miles north of Gorey. One mile off N11 Dublin to Wexford signposted on N11 between Arklow and Gorey.

189 Ashdown Park Hotel

♣
Coach Road, Gorey, Co Wexford
Tel: +353(0)55 80500 Fax: +353(0)55 80777
Email: info@ashdownparkhotel.com
Web: www.ashdownparkhotel.com
Closed closed 24-26 December 2001
60 bedrs SB £64 DB £75.29 HBS £84.07
HBD £57.72 B £7.97 L £11.55 D £19.52
CC: MC Vi Am DC

How to get there: Take M11/N11 southbound from Dublin, pass Ashford Rathnew. Bypass Arklow, Gorey. Before railway bridge turn left. Hotel on left.

Kenmare, Co. Kerry

190 Park Hotel Kenmare
Gold Ribbon Winner

★★★★★ RAC RAC RAC
Kenmare, Co. Kerry
Tel: +353(0)64 41200 Fax: +353(0)64 41402
Email: info@parkkenmare.com
Web: www.parkkenmare.com

Deluxe country house hotel in Ireland's Lake District. Set in 12 acres of terraced gardens overlooking Kenmare Bay, the park is one of Ireland's most luxurious and comfortable retreats. Closed 29 October to 23 December and 2 January to 19 April
46 bedrs SB £121 DB £215 HBS £155 HBD £143 B £13.50 L £7.50 D £35.50
CC: MC Vi Am DC

How to get there: Located at the top of Kenmare.

191 Sheen Falls Lodge
Gold Ribbon Winner

★★★★★ RAC RAC RAC
Kenmare, Co. Kerry
Tel: +353(0)64 41600 Fax: +353(0)64 41386
Email: info@sheenfallslodge.ie
Web: www.sheenfallslodge.ie
Closed December to January

A haven set within 300 acres of magical woodlands and crystal cascading waterfalls. With its luxurious rooms and sumptuous cuisine, the Lodge retains the warm, welcoming atmosphere of a country manor house.
61 bedrs
CC: MC Vi Am DC

How to get there: From Kenmare, take N71 towards Clengarriff. Left after suspension bridge.

192 Dromquinna Manor

★★★
Blackwater Bridge, Kenmare, Co. Kerry
Tel: +353(0)64 41657 Fax: +353(0)64 41791
Email: info@dromquinna.com
Web: www.dromquinna.com
48 bedrs
CC: MC Vi Am DC Swi

How to get there: 3km from Kenmare town on the Sneem Road (Ring of Kerry).

Kilkee, Co. Clare

193 Ocean Cove Business and Leisure Hotel

★★★
Kilkee Bay, Kilkee, Co. Clare
Tel: +353(0)6568 23000 Fax: +353(0)6568 23759
Email: reservations@lynchhotels.com
Web: www.lynchhotels.com
50 bedrs
CC: MC Vi Am

How to get there: Located on the main N67/N68 road, the Ocean Cove Hotel overlooks the Atlantic Ocean and offers commanding views of the bay.

It's easier online

For all your motoring and travel needs, www.rac.co.uk

Check the price

As from 2002 Ireland will be using Euros, so be sure to check the price of your chosen accommodation when booking.

Republic of Ireland

194 Halpins Town House Hotel

♦♦♦♦ ⓡ ⚹

Kilkee, Co. Clare
Tel: +353(0)65 9056032 Fax: +353(0)65 9056317
Email: halpins@iol.ie
Web: www.halpinsprivatehotels.com
Closed December to February

Highly-acclaimed townhouse hotel located in
Victorian Kilkee, close to Shannon airport. Ideal
base for touring the west coast, Cliffs of Moher,
Aran island and the Burren. Close to golf courses.
12 bedrs SB £40 DB £55 B £8
CC: MC Vi Am DC

How to get there: Hotel is in the centre of
Kilkee. Shannon Airport 50-minute drive away
on N67, Killimer Car Ferry 10 miles away.

Kilkenny, Co. Kilkenny

195 Kilkenny Ormonde Hotel

★★★★ ⓡ ⓡ

Ormonde Street, Kilkenny, Co. Kilkenny
Tel: +353(0)56 23900 Fax: +353(0)56 23977
Email: info@kilkennyormonde.com
Web: www.kilkennyormonde.com
118 bedrs SB £76 DB £120
CC: MC Vi Am DC

How to get there: City centre. Just off High
Street, five minutes walk to train station.
See advert below

196 Kilkenny River Court Hotel

★★★★ ⓡ

The Bridge, John Street, Kilkenny, Co. Kilkenny
Tel: +353(0)56 23388 Fax: +353(0)56 23389
Email: reservations@kilrivercourt.com
Web: www.kilrivercourt.com
Closed 25-26 December
90 bedrs SB £120 DB £180 HBS £145
HBD £120 B £8 L £8 D £20 CC: MC Vi Am

The Kilkenny Ormonde Hotel is a new 4★ deluxe property situated in the heart of the medieval city of
Kilkenny. Nestling in the shadows of the historic Kilkenny Castle, this modern stylish hotel has been
designed with the conference client in mind. We have taken time to ensure that our extensive facilities
cater for all conference and banqueting requirements. The Kilkennny Ormonde Hotel is fast becoming
the preferred venue for international companies looking for an alternative vibrant location.

- Self Contained Conference Centre
- 10 Fully Equipped Meeting Rooms
- Capacity for up to 420 delegates
- 118 Luxurious Bedrooms & Suites
- Extensive Leisure Club, largest in Kilkenny
- Fredericks Fine Dining Restaurant
- Earls Bar & Bistro
- Entertainment Venue Bar
- 1½ Hours Drive from Dublin Airport & Port
- City Centre Location
- Secure Car Parking

Tel: +353 56 23900   Fax: +353 56 23977
Email: info@kilkennyormonde.com   Website: www.kilkennyormonde.com

How to get there: Kilkenny Castle is a landmark: the hotel is situated directly opposite across river. Entrance under archways at bridge in city centre.

197 Mount Juliet Hotel
Gold Ribbon Winner

★★★★ ℞ ℞ ℞

Thomastown, Co. Kilkenny
Tel: +353(0)56 73000 Fax: +353(0)56 73019
Email: info@mountjuliet.ie
Web: www.mountjuliet.com
Mount Juliet, a haven of peace so rarely found in today's busy world. Enjoy our outstanding service, friendly staff, delightful cuisine, superb accommodation, championship golf course and new spa and health club.
59 bedrs SB £162.14 DB £253.39
HBS £197.14 HBD £161.70
B £12.50 L £8.50 D £35
CC: MC Vi Am DC

How to get there: Situated in the south-east of Ireland 75 miles from Dublin, 55 from Rosslare. Train services to Thomastown; helipad on site.

198 Hibernian Hotel

★★★

1 Ormonde Street, Kilkenny, Co. Kilkenny
Tel: +353 (0)56 71888 Fax: +353 (0)56 71877
Email: info@hibernian.iol.ie
Web: www.kilkennyhibernianhotel.com
Closed Christmas
42 bedrs SB £122.50 DB £122.50
B £6 L £8.50 D £14
CC: MC Vi Am DC None accepted

How to get there: The hotel is in the city centre.

199 Hotel Kilkenny

★★★

College Road, Kilkenny, Co. Kilkenny
Tel: +353(0)56 62000 Fax: +353(0)56 65984
Web: www.griffingroup.ie
103 bedrs SB £80 DB £140
HBS £105 HBD £85
B £10 L £14 D £27 CC: MC Vi Am DC

How to get there: From city centre, turn onto Patrick Street, then take first right onto Ormonde Road. Hotel is through traffic lights on the left.

200 Shillogher House

◆◆◆◆ ✐

Callan Road, Kilkenny, Co Kilkenny
Tel: +353(0)56 63249 Fax: +353(0)56 64865
6 bedrs CC: None accepted

How to get there: On Callan Road N76 one km from city centre.

201 Belmore Country Home

◆◆◆

Jerpoint Church, Thomastown, Co. Kilkenny
Tel: +353(0)56 24228
Email: belmorehouse@eircom.net
Web: www.belmorehouse.com
Closed Christmas

Charming country home on family farm featuring a warm welcome, spacious ensuite rooms and own fishing for guests. Golf and many other activities and attractions locally. Open all year except Christmas.
3 bedrs SB £26 DB £52 CC: None accepted

How to get there: Off main N9 road near Jerpoint Abbey, towards Stoney Ford/Mount Juliet. House signposted to right – second entrance.

202 Chaplins

◆◆◆

Castlecomer Road, Kilkenny, Co. Kilkenny
Tel: +353(0)56 52236
Email: chaplins@eircom.net
Closed Christmas
Chaplins is a spacious town house located in Ireland's medieval capital where a relaxed and leisurely ambience awaits you. Built in the early 1900s, it captures the charm of that period.
6 bedrs DB £42.70 CC: MC Vi

How to get there: Chaplins is situated in Kilkenny city on the N77 Alhy-Dublin road.

Republic of Ireland

Killarney, Co. Kerry

203 Aghadoe Heights Hotel
Gold Ribbon Winner

★★★★★ ⓡ ⓡ ⓡ
Lakes of Killarney, Killarney, Co. Kerry
Tel: +353(0)64 31766 Fax: +353(0)64 31345
Email: info@aghadoeheights.com
Web: www.aghadoeheights.com

In an idyllic setting with breathtaking views of Killarney Lakes and mountains, this intimate five-star hotel embraces each guest in a gracious and elegant setting.
69 bedrs SB £110 DB £254 HBS £144 HBD £161 B £12.50 L £23 D £34
CC: MC Vi Am DC

How to get there: Take the N22 from Cork to Tralee. On leaving Killarney for Tralee, follow signs for Aghadoe Heights Hotel. Left turn after 2 miles.

204 Dunloe Castle Hotel

★★★★★ ⓡ ⓡ
Beaufort, Killarney, Co. Kerry
Tel: +353(0)64 44111 Fax: +353(0)64 44583
Email: reception.dunloe@kih.liebherr.com
Web: www.iol.ie/khl
Closed October to April
110 bedrs SB £140 DB £140
B £10.50 L £17 D £35 CC: MC Vi Am DC

How to get there: Located six miles outside of Killarney, facing the Gap of Dunloe. Follow signs for Killorglin on entering Killarney.
See advert on facing page

205 Hotel Europe

★★★★
Fossa, Killarney, Co. Kerry
Tel: +353 (0)64 31900 Fax: +353 (0)64 32118
Email: reception.europe@kih.liebherr.com
Web: www.iol.ie/khl
205 bedrs SB £140 DB £140 B £10.50 D £34

CC: MC Vi Am DC Swi Delt

How to get there: From Killarney take the N72 towards Killorglin. Hotel Europe is located in Fossa village.
See advert on facing page

206 Killarney Park Hotel
Blue Ribbon Winner

★★★★ ⓡ ⓡ
Kenmare Place, Killarney, Co. Kerry
Tel: +353 (0)64 35555 Fax: +353 (0)64 35266
Email: info@killarneyparkhotel.ie
Web: www.killarneyparkhotel.ie
Closed December

Superbly located in the heart of Killarney town, this luxury hotel is a place of elegance laced with warmth and hospitality featuring classically designed guestrooms and suites and a magnificent health spa.
73 bedrs SB £210 DB £210 HBS £240 HBD £135 B £12 L £10 D £28 CC: MC Vi Am DC

How to get there: Take N22 from Cork to Killarney. At first roundabout, take the first exit. At second roundabout, take first exit. Killarney Park Hotel is second entrance on left.

207 Killarney Royal

★★★★ ⓡ ⓡ
College Street, Killarney, Co. Kerry
Tel: +353 (0)64 31853
Email: royalhot@iol.ie
Web: www.killarneyroyal.ie
Closed 22-28 December
29 bedrs SB £160 DB £250 B £12 L £20 D £35
CC: MC Vi Am DC

How to get there: Centre of Killarney across from the railway station.

Republic of Ireland

208 Muckross Park Hotel

★★★★ 🏮

Muckross Village, Killarney, Co. Kerry
Tel: +353(0)64 31938

209 Randles Court Hotel

★★★★ 🏮

Muckross Road, Killarney, Co. Kerry
Tel: +353(0)64 35333 Fax: +353(0)64 35206
Email: info@randlescourt.com
Web: www.randlescourt.com
Closed One week at Christmas
50 bedrs SB £90 DB £130
HBS £120 HBD £95 B £8 L £14.50 D £25
CC: MC Vi Am DC

How to get there: Located on the Muckross Road
towards Muckross House. As you leave Killarney,
we are on the left-hand side, ¹⁄₄ of a mile.

210 Holiday Inn Killarney

★★★

Muckross Road, Killarney, Co. Kerry
Tel: +353(0)64 33000 Fax: +353(0)64 33001
Email: holidayinnkillarney@eircom.net
Web: www.holidayinnkillarney.com
Closed Christmas
101 bedrs SB £54 DB £90 HBS £69 HBD £60
B £5.95 L £5 D £18 CC: MC Vi Am DC Swi JCB

How to get there: Follow signs for Killarney town
centre, and then for Muckross Road; hotel is on
the right two minutes' drive from the centre.

211 The Killarney Ryan

★★★

Cork Road, Killarney, Co. Kerry
Tel: +353(0)64 31555 Fax: +353(0)64 32438
Email: enquiries@ryan-hotels.com
Web: www.ryan-hotels.com

A modern hotel set within extensive grounds,
featuring a leisure centre, sports hall, tennis
courts, crazy golf and play areas. An ideal
location from which to enjoy Ireland's
most famed beauty spots.
168 bedrs SB £85 DB £140 B £10 D £20
CC: MC Vi Am DC

How to get there: 2km from Killarney
town centre on N22.

212 White Gates Hotel

★★★

Muckross Road, Killarney, Co. Kerry
Tel: +353(0)64 31164

213 Earls Court House

Little Gem

◆◆◆◆◆ ✳ 🍴

Woodlawn Junction, Muckross Road,
Killarney, Co. Kerry
Tel: +353(0)64 34009 Fax: +353(0)64 34366
Email: earls@eircom.net
Web: www.earlscourt-killarney.ie
Closed December to February
11 bedrs CC: MC Vi Am

How to get there: Take Muckross Road from
Killarney. After Shell petrol station, take a left and
Earls Court House is third house on your left.

214 Foley's Townhouse

◆◆◆◆◆ ✳

23 High Street, Killarney, Co. Kerry
Tel: +353(0)64 31217 Fax: +353(0)64 34683
28 bedrs SB £49.50 DB £82.50 B £8.50 L £9
D £20 CC: MC Vi Am

How to get there: Town centre location on right-
hand side of High Street (when travelling north,
direction Tralee).

215 Fuchsia House

◆◆◆◆◆ ✳ 🍴

Muckross Road, Killarney, Co. Kerry
Tel: +353(0)64 33743 Fax: +353(0)64 36588
Email: fuchsiahouse@eircom.net
Web: www.fuchsiahouse.com
Closed November to end February
10 bedrs SB £35 DB £64
CC: MC Vi DC

How to get there: Take Muckross road from
Killarney. After Shell station third house on the
right.

216 Kathleens Country House

◆◆◆◆◆ ✕ ◟

Tralee Road (N22), Killarney, Co. Kerry
Tel: +353(0)64 32810 Fax: +353(0)64 32340
Email: info@kathleens.net
Web: www.kathleens.net
Children minimum age: 7.
Closed November to February

Set in three acres of award-winning gardens in rural surrounds three km from town. Friendly and attentive. Original paintings and inspirational verses adorn every wall. Easy to get to, hard to leave.
17 bedrs SB £67 DB £79.30 CC: MC Vi Am
&⊗◷▭☎P✗☃❧⋔

217 Ashville Guest House

◆◆◆◆ ✕

Rock Road, Killarney, Co. Kerry
Tel: +353(0)64 36405 Fax: +353(0)64 36778
Email: ashvillehouse@eircom.net
Web: www.ashvillekillarney.com

Spacious, family-run guest house, two minutes' walk from the town centre, situated on the main Tralee road (N22). Private car park. Comfortably furnished ensuite bedrooms. Your ideal touring base.
12 bedrs SB £45 DB £60 CC: MC Vi Am
⊗◷▭☎P✗☃❧
How to get there: On main Tralee road (N22), two minutes walk from town centre.

218 Killarney Villa

◆◆◆◆ ✕

Cork/Mallow Road (N72), Killarney, Co. Kerry
Tel: +353(0)64 31878 Fax: +353(0)64 31878
Email: killarneyvilla@eircom.net
Web: www.killarneyvilla.com
Children minimum age: 6.
Closed November to April
6 bedrs SB £25 DB £37.65
CC: MC Vi
✕⊗◷▭P✗☃⋔❧
How to get there: Take N22 out of Killarney. Travel through two roundabouts on the Cork Mallow road for 1.3 miles. Take left at the Mallow N72 junction for 200 metres, to Killarney Villa on left.

219 Ross Castle Lodge

◆◆◆◆ ✕

Ross Road, Killarney, Co. Kerry
Tel: +353(0)64 36942 Fax: +353(0)64 36942
Email: rosscastlelodge@killarneyb-and-b.com
Web: www.killarneyb-and-b.com
4 bedrs
CC: MC Vi
⊗◷▭P✗
How to get there: 100m past Cineplex Cinema, turn right at Esso garage. House is on left immediately after Ross Golf Club.

220 Purple Heather

◆◆

Gap of Dunloe, Beaufort, Killarney, Co. Kerry
Tel: +353(0)64 44266 Fax: +353(0)64 44266
Email: purpleheather@eircom.net
Web: www.home.eircom.net/~purpleheather
6 bedrs SB £28.50 DB £40
CC: MC Vi
✕⊗◷▭P☃✂⋏☾
How to get there: Killarney N72 to Fossa, left at Fossa to hotel. Dunloe Castle left again and straight ahead for less than one mile.

221 Castlerosse Hotel

✤

Killarney, Co. Kerry
Tel: +353 (0)64 31144 Fax: +353 (0)64 31031
Email: castler@iol.ie
Web: www.towerhotelgroup.ie
Closed 3 November – 14 March
121 bedrs SB £58 DB £80 B £4.70
L £5.50 D £16.50 CC: MC Vi Am DC
⟐&♨✗◷▭☎P✗☃⛵⋏❧♨⋔▥♉☗
♊✍

222 The Cahernane Hotel

Muckross Road, Killarney, Co. Kerry
Tel: +353(0)64 31895 Fax: +353(0)64 34340

Killorglin, Co. Kerry

223 Grove Lodge

Killarney Road, Killorglin, Co. Kerry
Tel: +353(0)66 9761157 Fax: +353(0)66 9762330
10 bedrs
CC: MC Vi DC

How to get there: Located on N72, 300m from
Killorglin Bridge, on the Killarney exit from
Killorglin.

Kilmallock, Co. Limerick

224 Flemingstown House

Kilmallock, Co. Limerick
Tel: +353(0)63 98093 Fax: +353(0)63 98546
Email: flemingstown@keltec.ie
Web: www.ils.ie/flemingstown
Closed December to February

Approached by a long avenue, this 18th-century
farmhouse is the ideal location for relaxation
and gourmet food combined. Ideal base for
touring the south of Ireland.
5 bedrs SB £24.50 DB £42.70
CC: MC Vi

How to get there: On R512 Kilmallock-Kilfinane
road and 4km from R515 Tipperary-Killarney road.

Kinsale, Co. Cork

225 Trident Hotel

★★★
World's End, Kinsale, Co. Cork
Tel: +353(0)21 4772301 Fax: +353(0)21 4774173
Email: info@tridenthotel.com
Web: www.tridenthotel.com
Closed Christmas

On the water's edge in historic Kinsale, the
Trident offers unrivalled panoramic views over
marina and harbour, with award-winning cuisine
and service. Golf, walking tours, scenic cruise,
sailing nearby.
58 bedrs SB £58 DB £38 HBS £83 HBD £63
B £6.50 D £20
CC: MC Vi Am

How to get there: Take the R600 to Kinsale from
Cork City. The Trident is located at the end of
Pier Road on the waterfront.

226 Old Bank House

11 Pearse Street, Kinsale, Co. Cork
Tel: +353(0)21 4774075 Fax: +353(0)21 4774296
Email: oldbank@indigo.ie
Web: www.oldbankhousekinsale.com
Children minimum age: 10.
Closed four days over Christmas.

The Old Bank House is a Georgian residence of great character and charm, which has been consistently voted one of the "Top 100 Places to Stay in Ireland" every year since 1990. Gourmet Irish breakfast cooked to order each morning by Master Chef Michael Riese. A warm welcome awaits you from Michael, Marie and Katy Riese.
17 bedrs SB £120 DB £120
CC: MC Vi Am

How to get there: At start of Kinsale town, on right next to Post Office. 11km on R600 from Cork airport.

227 Long Quay House

◆ ◆ ◆

Long Quay, Kinsale, Co. Cork
Tel: +353(0)21 4774563 Fax: +353(0)21 4773201
Closed December
7 bedrs SB £50 DB £80 B £4.50
CC: MC Vi

How to get there: Take R600 from Cork to Kinsale. Hotel on right as you enter Kinsale, just before supermarket and post office.

Knock, Co. Mayo

228 Belmont Hotel

★★★
Knock, Co. Mayo
Tel: +353(0)94 88122 Fax: +353(0)94 88532
Email: belmonthotel@eircom.net
Web: www.belmonthotel.ie
63 bedrs SB £34 DB £53 B £4.65 L £4.25
D £16.25
CC: MC Vi Am DC

How to get there: Leaving Knock in the direction of Galway, take a left turn and go 200 metres.

Limerick, Co. Limerick

229 Castletroy Park Hotel

★★★★
Dublin Road, Limerick, Co. Limerick
Tel: +353(0)61 335566 Fax: +353(0)61 331117
Email: sales@castletroy-park.ie
Web: www.castletroy-park.ie
107 bedrs SB £119 DB £134 B £7 L £12.20
D £23.20
CC: MC Vi Am DC

How to get there: Situated on main Dublin road (N7), three miles from Limerick city and 25 minutes from Shannon International Airport.

230 Jurys Limerick Hotel

★★★★ ℞ ℞ ℞
Ennis Road, Limerick, Co. Limerick
Tel: +353(0)1 6070000 Fax: +353(0)1 6316999
Email: bookings@jurysdoyle.com
Web: www.jurysdoyle.com
Children minimum age: 12
95 bedrs SB £108.85 DB £141.47 B £6.57
L £10.75 D £15.53 CC: MC Vi Am DC

How to get there: Follow signs for N18.

231 Limerick Inn Hotel

★★★★
Ennis Road, Limerick, Co. Limerick
Tel: +353(0)61 326666 Fax: +353(0)61 326281
Email: limerick-inn@limerick-inn.ie
Web: www.limerick-inn.ie
Closed Christmas
153 bedrs SB £118.50 DB £158 B £7 L £11
D £22
CC: MC Vi Am DC

How to get there: From Dublin to Limerick N7, then N18 towards Shannon, hotel three miles from city centre.

232 South Court Business and Leisure Hotel

★★★★ ℞ ℞ ℞
Adare Road, Raheen, Limerick, Co. Limerick
Tel: +353(0)6 5682 3000 Fax: +353(0)6 5682 3759
Email: reservations@lynchhotels.com
Web: www.lynchhotels.com
65 bedrs
CC: MC Vi Am DC

How to get there: Located on the main Cork/Killarney road (N20), the South Court Hotel offers an ideal base for touring the Shannon region.

Republic of Ireland

233 The Gresham Ardhu

★★★★

Ennis Road, Limerick, Co. Limerick
Tel: +353(0)61 453922 Fax: +353(0)61 326333
Email: ryan@indigo.ie
Web: www.gresham-hotels.com

A Georgian building dating back to 1780 which
has been recently restored to its former elegance.
181 bedrs SB £128 DB £177 HBS £152
HBD £113 B £11 L £8 D £24.50
CC: MC Vi Am DC
&♿🛗⊗☺⌨☎🅿⬚♨ℑ♦♨⚙♨'Y'
How to get there: Limerick Ryan Hotel is
situated on the N18 on the Ennis Road.

234 Jurys Inn Limerick

★★★

Lower Mallow Street, Limerick, Co. Limerick
Tel: +353(0)1 6070000 Fax: +353(0)1 6316999
Email: bookings@jurysdoyle.com
Web: www.jurysdoyle.com
Closed Christmas
151 bedrs B £5.18 D £12.70 CC: MC Vi Am DC
&♿🛗⊗☺⌨☎📞🅿⬚♨♦♨⚙♨
How to get there: Located 15 miles/24 kms
from Shannon Int'l airport. Colbert train station
one mile/two kms. Heart of the city on the
banks of Shannon.

235 Woodfield House Hotel

★★★

Ennis Road, Limerick, Co. Limerick
Tel: +353(0)61 453022 Fax: +353(0)61 326755
Email: woodfield@eircom.net
Web: www.woodfieldhousehotel.com
Closed December 24-25
26 bedrs SB £59 DB £99 CC: MC Vi Am DC
⟨⟩&⊗⌨☎📞🅿⬚♨♦♨⚙♨
How to get there: Situated one mile outside the
city centre on the north side of Limerick city, on
the main Shannon road.

236 Clifton House

♦♦♦

Ennis Road, Limerick, Co. Limerick
Tel: +353(0)61 451166 Fax: +353(0)61 451224
Email: cliftonhouse@eircom.net
16 bedrs
CC: MC Vi
⌨☎🅿♨⚙
How to get there: Clifton House is situated on the
Ennis Road, opposite Woodfield House Hotel,
and near the Gaelic Grounds. Within city limits.

Lisdoonvarna, Co. Clare

237 Kincora Country House Inn and Restaurant

♦♦♦♦ ※🍷

Lisdoonvarna, Co. Clare
Tel: +353(0)65 7074300 Fax: +353(0)65 7074490
Email: kincorahotel@eircom.net
Web: www.kincora-hotel.com
Children minimum age: 12.
Closed November to February

Relax in peace and tranquility at our award-
winning family-run hotel. Enjoy excellent cuisine
in our restaurant/art gallery, set in feature
gardens. Nearby are Cliffs of Moher and Burren.
14 bedrs SB £45 DB £70 B £7 L £8 D £22
CC: MC Vi
⟨⟩&⊗⌨☎📞🅿♨⚙♨
How to get there: From Lisdoonvarna town
centre, take the Doolin Road. Hotel is on the
first junction ¼ km from town centre.

Check the price

As from 2002 Ireland will be
using Euros, so be sure to
check the price of your chosen
accommodation when booking.

Macroom, Co. Cork

238 Castle Hotel and Leisure Centre

★★

Main Street, Macroom, Co. Cork
Tel: +353(0)26 41074 Fax: +353(0)26 41505
Email: castlehotel@eircom.net
Web: www.castlehotel.ie
Closed 25-27 December
42 bedrs SB £50 DB £80 B £4.50 L £8.50
D £18.50 CC: MC Vi Am DC

How to get there: On the N22, 25 miles from
Cork and 30 miles from Killarney.

239 The Mills Inn

◆◆◆

Ballyvourney, Macroom, Co Cork
Tel: +353(0)26 45237 Fax: +353(0)26 45454

Malahide, Co. Dublin

240 Grand Hotel

★★★★ ℝ

Malahide, Co. Dublin
Tel: +353(0)1 8450000 Fax: +353(0)1 8168025
Email: sstone@thegrand.ie
Web: www.thegrand.ie
Closed Christmas
150 bedrs SB £135 DB £175.50 HBS £157.50
HBD £252 B £15 L £18 D £32
CC: MC Vi Am DC

How to get there: From Dublin airport, go
northwards on Belfast road; turn right for
Malahide at appropriate roundabout.

Plan your route

Visit www.rac.co.uk for RAC's
interactive route planner, including
up to the minute traffic reports.

See the road ahead

Just dial 1740* from any mobile
phone to get up-to-the-minute
RAC traffic information on
motorways and major A roads.
Try it now! *Calls to 1740 are charged
at premium rate.

Mallow, Co. Cork

241 Longueville House Hotel

Gold Ribbon Winner

★★★★ ℝ ℝ ℝ

Mallow, Co. Cork
Tel: +353(0)22 47156 Fax: +353(0)22 47459
Email: info@longuevillehouse.ie
Web: www.longuevillehouse.ie
Closed mid-November to mid-March
20 bedrs SB £99 DB £140 HBS £125
HBD £97.50 B £15 L £25 D £37
CC: MC Vi Am DC

How to get there: Three miles west of Mallow,
via the N72 to Killarney. Turn right at
Ballyclough junction.

242 Springfort Hall Country House

★★★

Mallow, Co. Cork
Tel: +353(0)22 21278 Fax: +353(0)22 21557
Email: stay@springfort-hotel.com
Web: www.springfort-hotel.com
49 bedrs SB £70 DB £110 HBS £94 HBD £79
B £6.50 L £12 D £24
CC: MC Vi Am DC

Maynooth, Co. Kildare

243 Moyglare Manor Hotel
Blue Ribbon Winner

★★★★ ℝ ℝ ℝ

Maynooth, Co. Kildare
Tel: +353(0)1 6286351 Fax: +353(0)1 6285405
Email: info@moyglaremanor.ie
Web: www.moyglaremanor.ie
Children minimum age: 12
Experience the atmosphere of this opulent
family-run grade-A hotel. Just 18 miles from
Dublin, this unique 18th-century Georgian
manor is renowned worldwide for its
magnificent decor and cuisine.
16 bedrs SB £110 DB £180
B £9 L £22.50 D £30
CC: MC Vi Am DC

How to get there: Travelling west on N4/M4,
take slip road for Maynooth. Keep right at
Catholic church to Moyglare Road. Hotel is after
2km.

Republic of Ireland

Midleton, Co. Cork

244 Ballymaloe House

Shangarry, Midleton, Co. Cork
Tel: +353(0)21 4652531 Fax: +353(0)21 4652021
Email: res@ballymaloe.ie
Web: www.ballymaloe.ie
Closed 23-27 December
33 bedrs SB £75.29 DB £163.12 HBS £109.79
HBD £116.38 L £24 D £37.50
CC: MC Vi Am DC Swi Delt

How to get there: From Cork, take N25 to
Midleton, then the Ballycotton Road via Cloyne
(signposted from Midleton).

245 Rathcoursey House
Little Gem

Ballinacurra, near Midleton, Co. Cork
Tel: +353(0)21 4613418 Fax: +353(0)21 4613393
Email: beth@rathcoursey.com
Web: www.rathcoursey.com
6 bedrs SB £56.15 DB £104.25 CC: MC Vi

How to get there: At the roundabout for Midleton
on N25 take Whitegate exit. Right after 1 1/2 miles
at crossroads ("East Ferry Scenic Route"). After
1 1/2 miles look out for arrow on left. Entrance is
around next bend. Follow the arrows.

Monasterevin, Co. Kildare

246 Hazel Hotel

Dublin Road, Monasterevin, Co. Kildare
Tel: +353 (0)45 525373 Fax: +353 (0)45 525810
Email: sales@hazelhotel.com
Web: www.hazelhotel.com
22 bedrs SB £30.50 DB £55 CC: MC Vi Am

How to get there: The hotel is situated on the N7
Cork/Limerick road to the west of Monasterevin.
See advert on facing page

Mountshannon, Co. Clare

247 Mountshannon Hotel

Main Street, Mountshannon, Co. Clare
Tel: +353(0)61 927162

Mullingar, Co. Westmeath

248 Crookedwood House

Crookedwood, Mullingar, Co. Westmeath
Tel: +353 (0)44 72165 Fax: +353 (0)44 72166
Email: info@crookedwoodhouse.com
Web: www.crookedwoodhouse.com
Closed Christmas
8 bedrs SB £60 DB £110 L £13.50 D £27
CC: MC Vi Am DC

How to get there: On Mullingar bypass take exit
for Castlepollard and proceed to Crookedwood
village. Turn right at the Wood pub; house is
2km further on.

Naas, Co. Kildare

249 Harbour View Hotel

Limerick Road, Naas, Co. Kildare
Tel: +353(0)45 879145 Fax: +353(0)45 874002
Closed Christmas to New Year
10 bedrs SB £40 DB £70 B £6 L £11 D £15
CC: MC Vi Am DC

250 Ballinagappa Country House

Clane, near Naas, Co. Kildare
Tel: +353 (0)45 892087 Fax: +353 (0)45 892087
Email: ballinagappahouse@eircom.net
Web: www.ballinagappa.com

Ballinagappa Country House is a very spacious
house, built in 1862, where guests can enjoy a
magnificent and secluded location in the rich
green velvet landscape of County Kildare.
3 bedrs SB £30 DB £70 CC: MC Vi

How to get there: From the N4, go towards
Naas; Clane is 6 1/2 miles. Take second right, and
Ballinagappa is 1 1/2 miles on the left.

251 Killashee House Hotel and Spa

Killcullen Road, Naas, Co. Kildare
Tel: +353 45 879277 Fax: +353 45 879266
Email: reservations@killasheehouse.com
Web: www.killasheehouse.com
Closed 25 – 26 December

Originally a Victorian hunting lodge in 1861
Killashee House has 84 luxurious rooms
including suites. Excellent conference and
leisure facilities. Enjoy mouthwatering food in
Turners Restaurant.
84 bedrs SB £110 DB £150 HBS £140
HBD £90 B £12 L £18 D £30
CC: MC Vi Am

How to get there: 30 minutes from Dublin on N7
to Naas then one mile along R448 Killcullen
Road.
See advert on right

Nenagh, Co. Tipperary

252 Abbey Court Hotel
   & Trinity Leisure Club

Dublin Road, Nenagh, Co Tipperary
Tel: +353(0)67 41111 Fax: +353(0)67 41022
Email: abycourt@indigo.ie
Web: www.abbeycourt.ie
82 bedrs SB £39.84 DB £35.85 HBS £54.98
HBD £54.98 B £4.39 L £4.71 D £16.31
CC: MC Vi Am DC Delt

How to get there: The Abbey Court Hotel
located off the main Dublin to Limerick (N7)
road within easy access to Shannon, Cork and
Dublin airports.

New Ross, Co. Wexford

253 Creacon Lodge Hotel

New Ross, Co. Wexford
Tel: +353(0)51 421897 Fax: +353(0)51 422560
Email: info@creaconlodge.com
Web: www.creaconlodge.com

Country House Hotel set amidst the peace and tranquility of the countryside. 45 minutes drive from Rosslare. 10 ensuite bedrooms. Fully licensed bar. Renowned restaurant.
10 bedrs SB £45 DB £70 HBS £60 HBD £50
B £6.95 L £10.95 D £17.50
CC: MC Vi

How to get there: From Wexford take N25 to New Ross. Just before reaching New Ross turn left on R733. After 5km, turn left for Creacon Lodge.

Oranmore, Co. Galway

254 Moorings Restaurant & Guest House

Oranmore, Co. Galway
Tel: +353(0)91 790462 Fax: +353(0)91 790462
Email: themoorings@eircom.net
Web: www.galway.net/moorings
6 bedrs SB £35 DB £50 D £25
CC: MC Vi Am Swi

How to get there: From roundabout on approach road from Dublin/Cork/Limerick into Oranmore village. At T-junction turn right; Moorings is on the right on main street.

One click does it all

Book RAC inspected hotels and B&Bs at www.rac.co.uk/hotels

Oughterard, Co. Galway

255 Ross Lake House Hotel

Rosscahill, Oughterard, Co. Galway
Tel: +353(0)91 550109 Fax: +353(0)91 550184
Email: rosslake@iol.ie
Web: www.rosslakehotel.com
Closed 1 November to 15 March
13 bedrs SB £70 DB £120
HBS £99 HBD £89 D £29
CC: MC Vi Am DC

How to get there: 22km from Galway city on N59, Galway/Clifden road. Turn left after village of Rosscahill.

Portlaoise, Co. Laois

256 Ivyleigh House
Little Gem

Bank Place, Portlaoise, Co. Laois
Tel: +353(0)502 22081 Fax: +353(0)502 63343
Email: dinah@ivyleigh.com
Web: www.ivyleigh.com
Children minimum age: 8.
Closed December 22 to January 2.
4 bedrs SB £55.13 DB £82.69
CC: MC Vi

How to get there: 100 yards from train station.

Portmagee, Co. Kerry

257 Moorings

Portmagee Village, Co. Kerry
Tel: +353(0)66 9477108 Fax: +353(0)66 9477220
Email: moorings@iol.ie
Web: www.moorings.ie
Closed November to February
14 bedrs
CC: MC Vi

How to get there: Follow the Ring of Kerry road – Killarney to Caherciveen. Three miles outside Caherciveen, turn right for Portmagee. The Moorings is in the centre of the village.

Portsalon, Co. Donegal

258 Croaghross

♦♦♦♦ ⚬ ⚬

Portsalon, Letterkenny, Co. Donegal
Tel: +353(0)74 59548 Fax: +353(0)74 59548
Email: jkdeane@croaghross.com
Web: www.croaghross.com
Closed November to February
5 bedrs CC: MC Vi

⚬ ⚬ ⚬ ⚬ ⚬ ⚬ ⚬ ⚬ ⚬ ⚬

How to get there: From Letterkenny, drive to Ramelton, and turn right just before Milford onto R246. Proceed through Kerrykeel to Portsalon. Take small road opposite golf club entrance.

Portumna, Co. Galway

259 Shannon Oaks Hotel and Country Club

★★★★ ⚬

St. Joseph's Road, Portumna, Co. Galway
Tel: +353(0)509 41777 Fax: +353(0)509 41357
Email: sales@shannonoaks.ie
Web: www.shannonoaks.ie
63 bedrs SB £99 DB £125 HBS £124
HBD £86.50 B £7.50 L £11.50 D £22.50
CC: MC Vi Am DC

⚬ ⚬ ⚬ ⚬ ⚬ ⚬ ⚬ ⚬ ⚬ ⚬ ⚬ ⚬ ⚬
⚬ ⚬ ⚬ ⚬ ⚬ ⚬ ⚬ ⚬ ⚬

How to get there: Shannon Oaks Hotel & Country Club is located on St. Joseph's Road in the village of Portumna.
See advert below right

Rathmullan, Co. Donegal

260 Rathmullan House

★★★★ ⚬ ⚬ ⚬

Rathmullan, Letterkenny, Co. Donegal
Tel: +353(0)74 58188 Fax: +353(0)74 58200
Email: info@rathmullanhouse.com
Web: www.rathmullanhouse.com
Closed January to mid-February

This gracious Georgian house stands in lovely tranquil gardens that run down to the shores of Lough Swilly. Superb food and wines served in award-winning Bedouin-style resturant.
24 bedrs SB £54 DB £108 HBS £77.50
HBD £77.50 B £10 L £3.90 D £26
CC: MC Vi Am DC

⚬ ⚬ ⚬ ⚬ ⚬ ⚬ ⚬ ⚬ ⚬ ⚬ ⚬ ⚬ ⚬ ⚬ ⚬ ⚬ ⚬

How to get there: From Belfast airport, follow A6 to Derry. Follow N13 to Letterkenny, and on arrival turn right into Ramelton. After bridge turn right to Rathmullan. Hotel is situated 500m north of village.

Plan your route

Visit www.rac.co.uk for RAC's interactive route planner, including up to the minute traffic reports.

Ask the experts

To book a Hotel or Guest Accommodation, or for help and advice, call RAC Hotel Reservations on 0870 603 9109 and quote 'Guide 2002'

Republic of Ireland

Roscommon, Co. Roscommon

261 Abbey Hotel

★★★

Roscommon, Co. Roscommon
Tel: +353(0)903 26505 Fax: +353(0)903 26021

The Abbey Hotel, set in its own private grounds, is ideally situated for the touring holidaymaker. Excellent restaurant and spacious comfortable accommodation that compare favourably with the best international standards.
25 bedrs SB £60 DB £110 B £7.50 L £17.50 D £27.50 CC: MC Vi Am DC

How to get there: The hotel is on the Galway Road (N63), southern side of Roscommon town in town itself.

Rosslare, Co. Wexford

262 Kelly's Resort Hotel

★★★★ ℞

Rosslare, Co. Wexford
Tel: +353(0)53 32114 Fax: +353(0)53 32222
Email: kellyhot@iol.ie
Web: www.kellys.ie
Closed 8 December to 22 February

Renowned resort hotel. Fine food and wine, indoor/outdoor amenities. Extensive leisure and beauty complex. Special spring–autumn activity midweeks, 2-day weekends and 5-day midweeks.
99 bedrs SB £60 DB £83 L £14 D £26
CC: MC Vi Am

How to get there: From Dublin airport, take N11 to Rosslare, signposted South-East (Gorey, Enniscorthy, Wexford, Rosslare). The hotel is situated in Rosslare Strand.

263 Churchtown House
Little Gem

◆◆◆◆◆ ℞

Tagoat, Rosslare, Co. Wexford
Tel: +353(0)53 32555 Fax: +353(0)52 32577
Email: churchtown.rosslare@indigo.ie
Web: www.churchtown-rosslare.com
Children minimum age: 10
14 bedrs SB £60 DB £120 D £23
CC: MC Vi Am

How to get there: ¼ of a mile from N25 on the R736 at Tagoat. Turn between pub and church in village.

Rosslare Harbour, Co. Wexford

264 Ferryport House

◆◆◆◆

Rosslare Harbour, Co. Wexford
Tel: +353(0)53 33933 Fax: +353(0)53 33033
17 bedrs SB £35 DB £55 CC: MC Vi

265 St. Martins

◆◆◆◆

St. Martins Road, Rosslare Harbour,
Co. Wexford
Tel: +353(0)53 33363 Fax: +353(0)53 33033
Email: thh@iol.ie
Web: www.tuskarhousehotel.com
Closed 23-26 December
8 bedrs SB £25 DB £38
CC: MC Vi Am

How to get there: N11 turn right at church to Rosslare village; first guesthouse on right, opposite Great Southern Hotel.

Roundstone, Co. Galway

266 Roundstone House Hotel

★★★ ℞ ℞
Roundstone, Connemara, Co. Galway
Tel: +353(0)95 35864 Fax: +353(0)95 35944
Email: diar@eircom.net
Closed November to 1 April

12 bedrs SB £50 DB £63 B £6 D £25 CC: MC Vi

267 Heatherglen House

♦ ♦ ♦ ℃
Roundstone, Co. Galway
Tel: +353(0)95 35837 Fax: +353(0)95 35837
Closed November to February
4 bedrs SB £40 DB £45
CC: None accepted

How to get there: N59 Roundstone from Galway.

Sligo, Co. Sligo

268 Tower Hotel

Quay Street, Sligo, Co. Sligo
Tel: +353 (0)71 44000 Fax: +353 (0)71 46888
Email: towersl@iol.ie
Web: www.towerhotelgroup.ie
58 bedrs SB £52 DB £82.50 B £4.30 L £7.40
D £14.50
CC: MC Vi DC

Spiddal, Co. Galway

269 Suan na Mara

♦ ♦ ♦ ♦ ♦ ℞ ⚤ ℃
Stripe, Furbo, Spiddal, Co. Galway
Tel: +353(0)91 591512 Fax: +353(0)91 591632

Straffan, Co. Kildare

270 The K Club

Gold Ribbon Winner

★★★★★ ℞ ℞ ℞
Straffan, Co. Kildare
Tel: +353(0)1 6017200 Fax: +353(0)1 6017299
Email: resortsales@kclub.ie
Web: www.kclub.ie
79 bedrs SB £339 DB £358 HBS £382
HBD £277 B £19 L £25 D £55
CC: MC Vi Am DC Swi

How to get there: Take N7 south as far as the Kill crossing, turn right at traffic lights. Resort is five miles, and is well-signposted from that point.

271 Barberstown Castle

★★★★ ℞ ℞
Straffan, Co Kildare
Tel: +353(0)1 6288157 Fax: +353(0)1 6277027
Email: castleir@iol.ie
Web: www.barberstown.com
Closed 24–26 December and 5–30 January

22 bedrs SB £110 DB £171 HBS £148
HBD £100.50 D £38.50 CC: MC Vi Am DC

How to get there: N4 west from Dublin – exit at Maynooth/Straffan. M50 south from Dublin – exit at "Kill" junction.

Republic of Ireland

Tahilla, Co. Kerry

272 Tahilla Cove Country House

◆ ◆ ◆ ◆

Tahilla, near Sneem, Co. Kerry
Tel: +353(0)64 45204 Fax: +353(0)64 45104
Web: www.tahillacove.com
Closed October to April
9 bedrs SB £45.75 DB £67.10 HBS £61
HBD £48.80 CC: MC Vi Am DC

How to get there: Located just off N70 ring of
Kerry road, five miles east of Sneem, 11 miles
west of Kenmare.

Tralee, Co. Kerry

273 Ballyseede Castle

★ ★ ★

Ballyseede, Tralee, Co. Kerry
Tel: +353(0)66 7125799 Fax: +353(0)66 7125287
Email: ballyseede@eircom.net
Web: www.ballyseedecastle.com
12 bedrs SB £100 DB £180 B £10 D £30
CC: MC Vi DC

How to get there: Located off the N21 from
Limerick and the N22 from Cork.

274 Meadowlands

★ ★ ★

Oakpark, Tralee, Co. Kerry
Tel: +353(0)66 7180444 Fax: +353(0)66 7180964
Email: medlands@iol.ie
Web: www.meadowlandshotel
27 bedrs SB £61 DB £98 HBS £82.50 HBD £70
B £6.10 L £11 D £21.50
CC: MC Vi Am DC

How to get there: 1km from Tralee town centre
on the main N69.

275 Barnagh Bridge Guesthouse

◆ ◆ ◆ ◆

Cappaclogh, Camp, Tralee, Co. Kerry
Tel: +353(0)66 7130145 Fax: +353(0)66 7130299
Email: bbguest@eircom.net
Children minimum age: 10.
Closed November to March
5 bedrs CC: MC Vi Am

How to get there: Leave N86 at Camp. Follow
Conor Pass Road, R560, for one mile.

276 Glenduff House

◆ ◆ ◆ ◆

Tralee, Co. Kerry
Tel: +353(0)66 7137105 Fax: +353(0)66 7137099
Email: glenduffhouse@eircom.net
Web: www.tralee-insight.com/glenduff
Closed November to mid-March
5 bedrs SB £32 DB £64 CC: MC Vi

How to get there: From Tralee take route to race
course off N21 at Clash roundabout and
continue for 4$^1/_2$ miles.

Waterford, Co. Waterford

277 Granville Hotel

★ ★ ★ ★

Meagher Quay, Waterford, Co. Waterford
Tel: +353(0)51 305555 Fax: +353(0)51 305566
Email: stay@granville-hotel.ie
Web: www.granville-hotel.ie
Closed 25-26 December
100 bedrs SB £60 DB £100 B £8.50 L £13.50
D £25 CC: MC Vi Am DC

How to get there: City centre, on the quay
opposite clocktower.
See advert on facing page

278 Dooley's Hotel

★ ★ ★

The Quay, Waterford, Co. Waterford
Tel: +353(0)51 873531 Fax: +353(0)51 870262
Email: hotel@dooleys-hotel.ie
Web: www.dooleys-hotel.ie

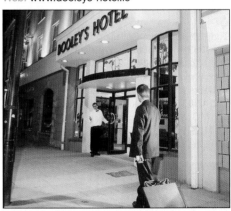

Family-run hotel situated on the quay in
Waterford. High levels of comfort and personal
service. Stay here and you won't be disappointed.

113 bedrs SB £70 DB £93 B £7.50 L £15 D £24
CC: MC Vi Am DC

How to get there: Located in Waterford City on
the quayside. Follow N25 route to the city centre.

279 Jurys Waterford Hotel

★★★
Ferrybank, Waterford, Co. Waterford
Tel: +353(0)1 6070000 Fax: +353(0)1 6316999
Email: bookings@jurysdoyle.com
Web: www.jurysdoyle.com
Closed Christmas
98 bedrs SB £94.73 DB £120.46
B £6.97 L £7.48 D £14.34 CC: MC Vi Am DC

How to get there: Follow sign city centre, drive
along Quay, over bridge take 3rd exit off
roundabout. Hotel is left side of dual carriage way.

280 Travelodge Waterford

Travel Accommodation
N25, Cork Road, Waterford, Co. Wexford
Tel: 08700 850 950
Web: www.travelodge.co.uk
32 bedrs B £4.25 CC: MC Vi Am DC Swi Delt

281 Belmont House

◆◆◆ ⚘ ℮
Belmont Road/Rosslare Road, Ferrybank,
Waterford, Co. Waterford
Tel: +353(0)51 832174
Email: belmonthouse@eircom.net
Children minimum age: 7.
Closed November to April
4 bedrs DB £36 CC: None accepted

How to get there: 2km from Waterford Bridge on
Rosslare Road (N25) – 4th house on right, after
Ferrybank Church.

282 Diamond Hill Country House

◆◆◆
Milepost, Slieverue, Co. Waterford
Tel: +353(0)51 832855 Fax: +353(0)51 832254
Email: diamondhill29@hotmail.com
Closed 24-26 December
18 bedrs SB £30 DB £27.50 CC: MC Vi

How to get there: Situated less than a mile from
Waterford city, off N25 Rosslare-Waterford road.
See advert right

Republic of Ireland

283 Tower Hotel

The Mall, Waterford, Co. Waterford
Tel: +353(0) 51 875801 Fax: +353(0) 51 870129
Email: towerrw@iol.ie
Web: www.towerhotelgroup.ie
140 bedrs SB £78.50 DB £118
B £6.25 L £5.50 D £13.25 CC: MC Vi Am DC

Waterville, Co. Kerry

284 Brookhaven

New Line Road, Waterville, Co. Kerry
Tel: +353(0)66 9474431 Fax: +353(0)66 9474724
Email: brookhaven@esatclear.ie
Web: www.euroka.com/waterville/brookhaven
Closed December to February
5 bedrs SB £40 DB £56 CC: None accepted

How to get there: We are located on the N70
route (Ring of Kerry road), 1km to the north side
of the village of Waterville.

Westmeath, Co. Westmeath

285 Hodson Bay Hotel

★★★★

Athlone, Co. Westmeath
Tel: +353(0)902 80500 Fax: +353(0)902 80520
Email: info@hodsonbayhotel.com
Web: www.hodsonbayhotel.com
133 bedrs SB £90 DB £118 B £9 L £11 D £20
CC: MC Vi Am DC

How to get there: The hotel is located off the
N61 Roscommon road just five minutes from
Athlone Town, 90 minutes from Dublin
International Airport.
See advert on facing page

Westport, Co. Mayo

286 Castlecourt Hotel

★★★

Castlebar Street, Westport, Co. Mayo
Tel: +353(0)98 25444 Fax: +353(0)98 28622
Email: info@castlecourt.ie

Web: www.castlecourthotel.ie
Closed Christmas

Perfectly located in the heart of Westport, a
genuine welcome and a special warm
atmosphere awaits you at this spectacular hotel,
which has been run by the Corcoran family
since 1971.
140 bedrs SB £105 DB £160 HBS £125.95
HBD £100.95 L £13.95 D £20.95
CC: MC Vi Am DC

How to get there: Approaching from the main
Castlebar Road (N5), the Castlecourt Hotel is
located at the first set of traffic lights.

287 Hotel Westport

★★★

Newport Road, Westport, Co. Mayo
Tel: +353(0)98 25122 Fax: +353(0)98 26739
Email: reservations@hotelwestport.ie
Web: www.hotelwestport.ie
129 bedrs SB £66.50 DB £110
B £6.70 L £11 D £19.50
CC: MC Vi Am DC

How to get there: Take N5 to Castlebar, N60 to
Westport. At end of Castlebar Street turn right
before the bridge. Turn right at lights and take
immediate left at hotel signpost. Follow to end
of road.

Wexford, Co. Wexford

288 Ferrycarrig Hotel

★★★★★

Ferrycarrig Bridge, Wexford, Co. Wexford
Tel: +353(0)53 20999 Fax: +353(0)53 20982
Web: www.griffingroup.ie
103 bedrs SB £80 DB £140 HBS £110
HBD £100 B £11 L £15 D £2832
CC: MC Vi Am DC

How to get there: Travelling on N11 from Enniscorthy to Wexford town, the hotel is two miles from Wexford on the Enniscorthy Road, overlooking the River Slavey estuary.

289 Cedar Lodge Hotel

★★★★

Carrigbyrne, Newbawn, New Ross,
Co. Wexford
Tel: +353(0)51 428386 Fax: +353(0)51 428222
Email: cedarlodge@tinet.ie
Web: www.prideofeirehotels.com
Closed January
28 bedrs SB £70 DB £120 HBS £100 HBD £85
B £10 L £15 D £30
CC: MC Vi Am DC

How to get there: We are on the N25 road between Wexford and New Ross.

290 Talbot Hotel

★★★

Trinity Street, Wexford, Co. Wexford
Tel: +353(0)53 22566 Fax: +353(0)53 23377
Email: talbotwx@eircom.net
Web: www.talbothotel.ie

99 bedrs SB £56 DB £89.92 HBS £72.39
HBD £60.20 B £7.62 L £9.91 D £19.81
CC: MC Vi Am

How to get there: From Dublin and Rosslare, take N11, following signs for Wexford. The Hotel is in the town centre, on the quay.
See advert right

Republic of Ireland

291 White's Hotel

★★★
George Street, Wexford, Co. Wexford
Tel: +353(0)53 22311 Fax: +353(0)53 45000

292 Whitford House Hotel

★★★ ⬤
New Line Road, Wexford, Co. Wexford
Tel: +353(0)53 43444 Fax: +353(0)53 46399
Email: whitford@indigo.ie
Web: www.whitford.ie
Closed 23 December to 16 January
36 bedrs SB £55 DB £90 HBS £81.50
HBD £58.25 B £7.95 L £14.95 D £26.50
CC: MC Vi Am

How to get there: Situated two miles from
Wexford Town, 10 miles from Rosslare Port,
easy access to N11 and N25.
See advert on facing page

293 Ballinkeele House

◆◆◆◆ ⬤
Ballymurn, Enniscorthy, Co. Wexford
Tel: +353(0)53 38105 Fax: +353(0)53 38468
Email: info@ballinkeele.com
Web: www.ballinkeele.com
Children minimum age: 5.
Closed 12 November to 28 February

Ballinkeele is an historic house, built in 1840,
surrounded by woodland, ponds and farmland.
A place to unwind with good food, wine and a
tranquil atmosphere. Bicycles and croquet.
5 bedrs SB £57 DB £99
HBS £95 HBD £92 CC: MC Vi

⬤⬤⬤⬤⬤
How to get there: From Wexford take N11 north
to Oilgate village and turn right at signpost.
From Enniscorthy, take N11 south to Oilgate
village and turn left at signpost.

Wicklow, Co. Wicklow

294 The Brooklodge Hotel

★★★★ ⬤⬤⬤
Macreddin Village, Co. Wicklow
Tel: +353(0) 40236444 Fax: +353(0) 40236580
Email: brooklodge@macreddin.ie
Web: www.brooklodge.com
Closed Christmas

The perfect country house hotel, warm, friendly
and relaxed, deep in spectacular countryside
yet only an hour from South Dublin. Featuring
the sublime Strawberry Tree Restaurant.
40 bedrs SB £80 DB £116 HBS £107.50
HBD £85.50 B £8 L £12.50 D £27.50
CC: MC Vi Am DC

⬤⬤⬤⬤⬤⬤⬤⬤⬤⬤⬤⬤⬤
How to get there: South from Dublin Ciry, N11
to Rathnew (29 miles), R752 to Rathdrum (8
miles), R753 to Aughrim (7 miles), follow signs
to Macreddin Village (2 miles).

295 Rathsallagh House Hotel

★★★ ⬤⬤
Dunlavin, Co. Wicklow
Tel: +353(0)45 403112 Fax: +353(0)45 403343
Email: info@rathsallagh.com
Web: www.rathsallagh.com
Children minimum age: 12.
Closed Christmas
29 bedrs SB £110 DB £210
HBS £145 HBD £280
B £18 L £25 D £38.50
CC: MC Vi Am DC Swi

⬤⬤⬤⬤⬤⬤⬤⬤⬤⬤⬤⬤⬤⬤
⬤
How to get there: From Dublin take M7 south,
exit J9 (Carlow). Turn left five miles after Priory
Inn. One hour from Dublin airport.

296 Tinakilly House Hotel
Gold Ribbon Winner

★★★ ⓇⓇⓇ
Rathnew, Wicklow, Co. Wicklow
Tel: +353(0)404 69274 Fax: +353(0)404 67806
Email: reservations@tinakilly.ie
Web: www.tinakilly.ie
51 bedrs SB £96.75 DB £124 D £33.50
CC: MC Vi Am DC

How to get there: Take N11/M11 (Dublin-Wicklow-Wexford road) to Rathnew village. At roundabout, follow R750 to Wicklow Town. Entrance to hotel is 500m from village.

Youghal, Co. Cork

297 Ahernes Seafood Restaurant & Accomodation | Little Gem

◆◆◆◆ ⓇⓇ
163 North Main Street, Youghal, Co. Cork
Tel: +353(0)24 92424 Fax: +353(0)24 93633
Email: ahernes@eircom.net
Web: www.ahernes.com

'Rooms with a seafood view' gourmet hotel in a perfect location to tour the south-east — beautiful beach, numerous golf courses. Fota 1/2 hour, Old Head of Kinsale one hour, Cork airport 40 minutes.
SB £62 DB £85 B £10.50 L £5 D £30
CC: MC Vi Am DC

How to get there: On N25 between Cork and Waterford. From Waterford, take the sign for town centre – Ahernes on left.

Republic of Ireland

Channel Islands & Isle of Man

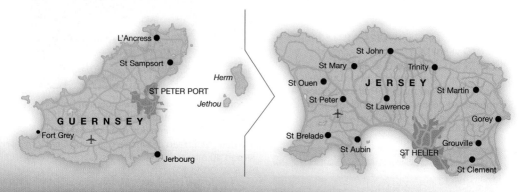

L'Ancress

St Sampsort

ST PETER PORT

Herm

Jethou

GUERNSEY

Fort Grey

Jerbourg

St John

St Mary

St Ouen

Trinity

JERSEY

St Peter

St Martin

St Lawrence

St Brelade

Gorey

St Aubin

Grouville

ST HELIER

St Clement

Alderney

France

Herm

Sark

Guernsey

Jersey

One of Jersey's landmarks stunningly lit-up —
Mont Orgueil at night. The castle sits at the
eastern end of the island near the village of
Gorey on the northern end of the Royal Bay of
Grouville. In 1907 Mont Orgueil was handed
over to the island by the British Crown.

Known as the 'Cup and Saucer' by locals due
to its distinctive white column sticking out of the
dark rock, Fort Grey (below), off the northwest
coast of Guernsey, was once a critical part of
the island defences, especially during the
Napoleonic wars.

Above, a view from one of Guernsey's famous coastal cliff paths.

● It is often said that the Isle of Man landscape combines the most scenic features of England, Scotland, Ireland, and Wales.

● The Isle of Man is a crown dependency belonging neither to the United Kingdom nor to the European Union. Famous for its tailless cats, the island has always been a centre of hospitality for visitors. In unspoiled surroundings, there are still many traditional Manx cottages to be seen (below).

● The Isle of Man offers eight quality golf courses, excellent watersports facilities — particularly diving and sailing — and is home to the infamous TT motorcycle races. The Snaefell Mountain railway travels from the old mining village of Laxey, home to the world's largest waterwheel, to the peak of the island.

The Little Chapel at Les Vauxbelets, Guernsey (below), is decorated with local shells, and reflects the island's small scale.

Nestled between Scarlett Point and Dreswick Point, lies the quiet harbour at Castletown, Isle of Man (above).

● Largely self-governing possessions of the English Crown, the three main "Islands of the Bailiwick" — the Channel Islands — are Guernsey, Alderney and Sark lying in the Gulf of St Malo, approximately 80 miles south of Weymouth and 9–20 miles off the coast of Normandy.

Below, an example of the Isle of Man's industrial heritage (and hilly terrain) — Laxey's hydropump, dominated by a 72-foot (22m) diameter waterwheel, said to be the largest active waterwheel in the world.

The picturesque Saints' Harbour, Guernsey. The climate of the Channel Islands is mild. In winter the mean temperature is 6°C (47°F) and in Summer 17°C (63° F).

Jersey is famous for its sweeping bays and sandy beaches. Portelet Bay below, is at the southwestern end of the island.

Accommodation index

Hotels and Guest Accommodation are indexed by their order of appearance within this region, not by the page. To locate an establishment, note the number to the right of the listing and then find it on the establishment's name bar, as shown here

37 The Turning Mill Hotel

Guernsey

1 Old Government House Hotel

★★★★ ®

Ann's Place, St. Peter Port, Guernsey, GY1 4AZ
Tel: 01481 724921 Fax: 01481 724429
Email: ogh@guernsey.net
Web: www.oghhotelguernsey.com
68 bedrs SB £105 DB £130 HBS £121
HBD £146 B £9.50 L £5 D £18.75
CC: MC Vi Am DC Swi Delt

How to get there: Left out of airport, left at second traffic lights, through two sets of lights, right at next lights. Left at first 'filter', right at next. Through three sets of lights, then right into Ann's Place, just before fourth set.

2 Saint Pierre Park Hotel

★★★★★ ® ® ®

Rohais, St. Peter Port, Guernsey, GY1 1FD
Tel: 01481 728282 Fax: 01481 712041
Email: enquiries@stpierrepark.co.uk
Web: www.stpierrepark.co.uk

Set in 45 acres of its own parkland, 9 hole par 3 golf course designed by Tony Jacklin, three all-weather tennis courts and a wide range of leisure facilities, hair and beauty salon.
131 bedrs SB £130 DB £180
HBS £147 HBD £107
CC: MC Vi Am DC Swi

How to get there: 10 minutes' drive from airport and harbour front. Hire cars provide free maps.

3 Best Western Hotel de Havelet

★★★★ ® ®

Havelet, St. Peter Port, Guernsey, GY1 1BA
Tel: 01481 722199 Fax: 01481 714057
Email: havelet@sarniahotels.com
Web: www.havelet.sarniahotels.com
34 bedrs SB £45 DB £80 HBS £55 HBD £50
B £7 L £12 D £16.50
CC: MC Vi Am DC Swi

How to get there: From the airport, turn left and follow signs for St. Peter Port. At bottom of Val de Terres Hill, turn left up Havelet Hill (signposted). Hotel on right of hill.

4 Green Acres Hotel

★★★ ®

Les Hubits, St. Martins,
Guernsey, GY4 6LS
Tel: 01481 235711 Fax: 01481 235971
Email: greenacres@guernsey.net
Web: www.greenacreshotel.guernsey.net
Closed November to March
47 bedrs SB £33 DB £66 HBS £43.50
HBD £43.50 L £5 D £15
CC: MC Vi Am Swi Delt

How to get there: Follow hotel signs from the three main roads that surround Les Hubits area in the south-east corner of Guernsey.

5 Hotel Bon Port

★★★★ ® ®

Moulin Huet Bay, St. Martins,
Guernsey, GY4 6EW
Tel: 01481 239249 Fax: 01481 239596
Email: mail@bonport.com
Web: www.bonport.com
18 bedrs SB £30 DB £60 HBS £47.50 HBD £95
B £7.50 L £2.55 D £7.50
CC: MC Vi Am Swi Delt

How to get there: From airport follow road to St. Martins village. Follow road signs to Bon Port – blue signs mainly fixed to lamp posts.
See advert on facing page

6 L'Atlantique Hotel

★★★★ ® ®

Perelle Bay, St. Saviours, Guernsey, GY7 9NA
Tel: 01481 264056 Fax: 01481 263800
Email: enquiries@perellebay.com
Web: www.perellebay.com
Closed November to March
23 bedrs SB £45 DB £77 HBS £58 HBD £51
B £6.55 L £13 D £18.50
CC: MC Vi Swi Delt

How to get there: Situated on the west coast. Turn right out of airport. Continue until you reach the west coast. Turn right and follow the coast for 1½ miles.

HOTEL BON PORT

RAC ★★★

Spectacular views over Moulin Huet Bay, the famous Peastacks, Saints Bay and Jersey.

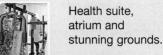

Excellent food and views in the restaurant.

Moulin Huet Bay,
St. Martins,
Guernsey GY4 6EW
Tel: 01481 239249
Fax: 01481 239596
Email: mail@bonport.com
www.bonport.com

Health suite, atrium and stunning grounds.

---

7 La Favorita Hotel

★★★★ ℝ
Fermain Bay, Guernsey, GY4 6SD
Tel: 01481 235666 Fax: 01481 235413
Email: info@favorita.com
Web: www.favorita.com
Closed January to February
37 bedrs SB £57 DB £98 HBS £71.50
HBD £63.50 B £6 L £10.50 D £15.00
CC: MC Vi Am DC Swi Delt
🚿♨☎🛏♿ ... 🎾🏊
How to get there: Follow signs for Fermain Bay at junction of Sausmarez/Fort roads.

8 La Trelade Country House Hotel

★★★
Forest Road, St. Martins, Guernsey, GY4 6UB
Tel: 01481 235454 Fax: 01481 237855
Email: latrelade@guernsey.net
Web: www.latrelade.co.uk
45 bedrs SB £40 DB £80 HBS £52 HBD £52
B £8 L £10 D £16
CC: MC Vi Am DC Swi Delt
How to get there: From airport turn left, hotel one mile. From harbour, follow signs to airport through St. Martins; three miles on left.

9 Le Chalet Hotel

★★★★ ℝ
Fermain Bay, St. Martins, Guernsey, GY4 6SD
Tel: 01481 235716 Fax: 01481 235718
Email: chalet@sarniahotels.com
Web: www.chalet.sarniahotels.com
Closed mid-October to mid-April
41 bedrs SB £40 DB £62 HBS £50 HBD £41
B £6.50 L £10 D £16.50 CC: MC Vi Am DC Swi
How to get there: From Guernsey airport, turn left and follow signs for St. Martins and St. Peter Port. After Sausmarez Manor, follow signs for Fermain Bay and Le Chalet.

10 Les Rocquettes Hotel

★★★ ℝ
Les Gravees, St. Peter Port, Guernsey, GY1 1RN
Tel: 01481 722146 Fax: 01481 714543
Email: rocquettes@sarniahotels.com
Web: www.rocquettes.sarniahotels.com
51 bedrs SB £40 DB £64 HBS £50 HBD £42
B £6.50 L £10 D £16 CC: MC Vi Am DC Swi Delt
How to get there: From airport turn left. At 2nd traffic lights turn left. Straight on next traffic lights, over roundabout. 4th lights turn right. At filter turn left. Next filter left into Les Gravees. Hotel on right.

11 Moores Hotel

★★★★ ☕

Le Pollet, St. Peter Port, Guernsey, GY1 1WH
Tel: 01481 724452 Fax: 01481 714037
Email: moores@sarniahotels.com
Web: www.moores.sarniahotels.com
49 bedrs SB £46 DB £70 HBS £56 HBD £40
B £6.50 L £10.50 D £16.50
CC: MC Vi Am DC Swi
⊔ ※ ⊗ ③ ▭ ☎ ⌖ ⊓ ⌣ ⛁ ♔ 'Υ'
How to get there: From airport follow signs to
St. Peter Port along seafront. On North
Esplanade take left turn into Lower Pollet and
continue to hotel on right.

12 Peninsula Hotel

★★★

Les Dicqs, Vale, Guernsey, GY6 8JP
Tel: 01481 48400 Fax: 01481 48706

13 Saints Bay Hotel & Restaurant

★★★★ ☕ ☕

Icart Point, St. Martins, Guernsey, GY4 6JG
Tel: 01481 238888 Fax: 01481 235558
Email: info@saintsbayhotel.com
Web: www.saintsbayhotel.com
36 bedrs SB £33 DB £60.50 HBS £46.50
HBD £43.50 CC: MC Vi Am DC Swi
③ ▭ ☎ ℙ⊛ ⌖ ⌘ ⊓ ♔ ⌣ ♔ ⛁ ⅏ ⁄⁄ ⌇ ⌕ ☙
How to get there: The Saints Bay Hotel and
Clifftop Restaurant are located at Icart point on
the island's most southerly tip.
See advert below right

14 Grange Lodge Hotel

★★ ☕

The Grange, St. Peter Port, Guernsey, GY1 1RQ
Tel: 01481 725161 Fax: 01481 724211
Email: receptionist@grange-
lodge.hotel.freeserve.co.uk
Web: www.grange-lodge.hotel.freeserve.co.uk
30 bedrs SB £27 DB £54 HBS £33 HBD £33
B £5.50 L £5.50 D £12 CC: MC Vi Swi Delt
◈ ※ ③ ▭ ☎ ℙ ⌖ ⊓ ⁄⁄ ⌇

15 Hotel Hougue du Pommier

Blue Ribbon Winner

★★ ☕ ☕

Castel, Guernsey, GY5 7FQ
Tel: 01481 256531 Fax: 01481 256260
Email: hotel@houguedupommier.guernsey.net
Web: www.hotelhouguedupommier.com

Standing in 10 acres, this 18th century
farmhouse has been carefully developed into a
charming country house hotel. Situated on the
west of the island and five kilometres from the
capital of St. Peter Port.
43 bedrs SB £34 DB £68 HBS £14
L £5.50 D £17.25
CC: MC Vi Am DC Swi
⌗ ※ ⊗ ③ ▭ ☎ ℙ⊛ ⌖ ⌘ ⊓ ♔ ⅏ ⌇
How to get there: From Cobo Bay, take the road
inland to Route de Hougue du Pommier. Ten
minutes' drive from St. Peter Port and 20
minutes from the airport.

16 Sunnycroft Hotel

★★★ ⓡ

5 Constitution Steps, St. Peter Port,
Guernsey, GY1 2PN
Tel: 01481 723008 Fax: 01481 712225
Closed November to March

Situated on an old stepped street in centre of
town, with views of harbour and other islands. A
character hotel with atmosphere and good food.
14 bedrs SB £48 DB £86 HBS £51 HBD £54
B £6 D £13.50
CC: MC Vi

⊗◷⊑□☎ Ⓟ ⅲ

How to get there: Constitution Steps are just
past Salvation Army building in Clifton.

17 Marine Hotel

◆◆◆

Well Road, St. Peter Port, Guernsey, GY1 1WS
Tel: 01481 724978 Fax: 01481 711729
11 bedrs SB £17.95 DB £35.90
CC: MC Vi Swi Delt JCB

⋉⊗◷□ ⌘ ❤

How to get there: Well Road is situated just off
Glategny Esplanade, opposite Queen Elizabeth
II Marina. Just 5 minutes walk from ferry and
town.

18 The Duke of Richmond Hotel

✛

Cambridge Park, St. Peter Port, Guernsey,
Channel Islands, GY1 1UY
Tel: 01481 726221 Fax: 01481 728945
Email: duke@guernsey.net
Web: www.dukeofrichmond.co.uk

Located between 'Candie' Botanical Gardens
and Cambridge Park, the hotel is close to the
town and harbour and makes an ideal centre
from where you can explore the island.
75 bedrs SB £60 DB £80
HBS £75 HBD £52.50 L £9 D £15
CC: MC Vi Am DC Swi Delt JCB

⟨⟩ & ⅲ ⋉⊗◷□☎ ⌐ & ℟ℂ ⌘ ❤ ♨ ⅲ ⌇

How to get there: Located in a residential area
within minutes of town, harbour, 'Candie'
Botanical Gardens and Island's conference and
sports centre.

Jersey

19 Atlantic Hotel

Blue Ribbon Winner

★★★★★ ⓡ ⓡ ⓡ

Le Mont de la Pulente, St. Brelade,
Jersey, JE3 8HE
Tel: 01534 744101 Fax: 01534 744102
Email: info@theatlantichotel.com
Web: www.theatlantichotel.com
Closed 1 January to 7 February

In private local ownership since 1970, this four-
star luxury hotel is the sole Channel Islands
member of Small Luxury Hotels of the World.
50 bedrs SB £140 DB £180 L £17.50 D £30
CC: MC Vi Am DC Swi Delt

ⅲ□☎ ⌐ Ⓟ® & ℟ℂ ⌘ ♨ ⅲ ⍑⌇⍓⌇ ⌇

How to get there: From the A13 take the B35
to Le Mont de la Pulente. Hotel sign is on the
right.

20 Hotel La Place

★★★★®

Route Du Coin, La Haule, St. Brelade,
Jersey, JE3 8BT
Tel: 01534 744261 Fax: 01534 745164
Email: hotlaplace@aol.com
Web: www.jersey.co.uk/hotels/laplace
42 bedrs SB £82 DB £120 HBS £106 HBD £84
B £8.95 L £13.50 D £26
CC: MC Vi Am DC Swi Delt

How to get there: Approaching St. Aubin from
St. Helier, at La Haule Manor turn right. Take
second left then first right. 200 yards on right.

21 L'Horizon

★★★★®®®

St. Brelade's Bay, St. Brelade, Jersey, JE3 8EF
Tel: 01534 743101 Fax: 01534 746269
Email: hotellhorizon@jerseymail.co.uk
Web: www.hotellhorizon.com
107 bedrs SB £110 DB £210 HBS £120
HBD £120 B £12 L £5.50 D £29
CC: MC Vi Am DC Swi Delt

How to get there: Three miles from airport, six
miles from harbour.

22 Longueville Manor
Gold Ribbon Winner

★★★★®®®

St. Saviours, Jersey, JE2 7WF
Tel: 01534 725501 Fax: 01534 731613
Email: longman@itl.net
Web: www.longuevillemanor.com

Stunning 18th Century Norman manor, set in a
16-acre wooded valley. Luxurious bedrooms,
award-winning restaurant and beautiful gardens.
Member of Relais & Châteaux.
30 bedrs SB £175 DB £230 HBS £190
HBD £130 B £12.50 L £21 D £45

CC: MC Vi Am DC Swi Delt

How to get there: From Jersey airport, take A1
to St. Helier and then A3 towards Gorey.
Longueville Manor is situated approximately one
mile on left.

23 St. Brelade's Bay Hotel

★★★★®®

St. Brelade's Bay, St. Brelade, Jersey, JE3 8EF
Tel: 01534 746141 Fax: 01534 747278
Email: info@stbreladesbayhotel.com
Web: www.stbreladesbayhotel.com
Closed October to April
72 bedrs SB £101 DB £202 HBS £116
HBD £116 B £10 L £15 D £25
CC: MC Vi Am Swi JCB

How to get there: Located in the southwest of
the island.

24 Beau Couperon Hotel and Apartments

★★★®®

Rozel Bay, St. Martin, Jersey, JE3 6AN
Tel: 01534 865522 Fax: 01534 865332
Email: beaucouperon@southernhotels.com
Web: www.jerseyhols.com/beaucouperon
Closed November to March
34 bedrs SB £76.65 DB £102.20 HBS £92.65
HBD £67.10 B £4.95 L £10.90 D £16
CC: MC Vi Swi Delt

How to get there: From St. Helier, follow signs
for St. Martin. At St. Martin's church turn right,
directly followed by a left turn. Follow signs
towards Rozel bay.

25 Beausite Hotel

★★★

Grouville Bay, Grouville, Jersey, JE3 9DJ
Tel: 01543 857577 Fax: 01543 857211
Email: beausite@jerseymail.co.uk
Web: www.southernhotels.co.uk
Closed November to February
76 bedrs SB £33.25 DB £66.50 HBS £41
HBD £82 B £inc D £12.95
CC: MC Vi Am DC Swi Delt

How to get there: Follow A1 east to the A17. At
Georgetown take the A3 towards Gorey. The
hotel is on the left at Grouville.

26 Bergerac Hotel

★★★

La Rue Voisin, Portelet Bay, St. Brelade,
Jersey, JE3 8AT
Tel: 01534 745991 Fax: 01534 743010
Email: southern@itl.net
Web: www.southernhotels.com
Closed November to early March
50 bedrs SB £34 DB £68 HBS £43.75
HBD £43.75 B £4.95 D £10.95
CC: MC Vi Am DC Swi Delt

How to get there: From the airport, head
towards St. Brelades then St. Aubin. Turn right
at Woodbine Corner and follow signs to Portelet
and Bergerac hotels.

27 Chateau La Chaire
Gold Ribbon Winner

★★★ ®®®

Rozel, St. Martin, Jersey, JE3 6AJ
Tel: 01534 863354 Fax: 01534 865137
Email: res@chateau-la-chaire.co.uk
Web: www.chateau-la-chaire.co.uk
Children minimum age: 7

CHÂTEAU
LACHAIRE

A charming Victorian house, beautifully
decorated and furnished. Set in terraced,
wooded gardens. 14 bedrooms, all ensuite.
14 bedrs SB £115 DB £165 HBS £135
HBD £97.50 B £7 L £17.50 D £28.50
CC: MC Vi Am DC Swi Delt

28 Chateau Valeuse Hotel

★★★ ®®®

St. Brelade's Bay, Jersey, JE3 8EE
Tel: 01534 746281 Fax: 01534 747110
Email: chatval@itl.net
Web: www.user.super.net.uk/~chatval
Children minimum age: 5.
Closed November to March

Smart central hotel in Jersey's capital. Ideal for
holiday and business. Garden, swimming pool,
waterchute, indoor leisure. Bright new
bedrooms. Fine Food. Free Parking.
34 bedrs SB £34 DB £34 HBS £46 HBD £46
B £6.50 L £12.50 D £19
CC: MC Vi Swi Delt

How to get there: From airport south from
harbour west to St. Brelades Bay. Hotel up lane
to Churchill Memorial Park.

29 Moorings Hotel

★★★★ ®®

Gorey Pier, Gorey, Jersey, JE3 6EW
Tel: 01534 853633 Fax: 01534 857618
5 bedrs SB £42.50 DB £85 HBS £51.50
HBD £51.50 B £7.50 L £15.50 D £20.50
CC: MC Vi Am Swi Delt

How to get there: Situated on the east coast of
the island, near to golf club. Four miles from
town centre and eight miles from airport.

Channel Islands

30 Pomme d'Or Hotel

★★★★ ℜ ℜ

Liberation Square, St. Helier, Jersey, JE1 3UF
Tel: 01534 880110 Fax: 01534 737781
Email: enquiries@pommedorhotel.com
Web: www.pommedorhotel.com

Jersey's best-known hotel is ideally located at the heart of St. Helier's shopping and financial district. The Pomme d'Or overlooks the island's marina and offers outstanding service.
141 bedrs SB £86 DB £142 HBS £100.50
HBD £85.50 B £7 L £10 D £11
CC: MC Vi Am DC Swi Delt

⮐ ♨ 🏠 ⊗ ⛳ ▢ ☎ 📞 ⚱ ⤳ ⅙ ⏰ 🏋 ⛴ ♨♨♨ ♨♨♨

Pontac House Hotel

Pontac House is an elegant old island home that has become a charming hotel combining grace and character and overlooking the spectacular St. Clements Bay. Most of our 27 ensuite rooms have balconies and glorious seaviews. An excellent and varied menu is offered.

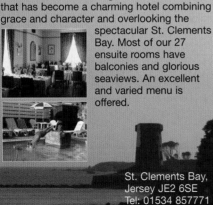

St. Clements Bay,
Jersey JE2 6SE
Tel: 01534 857771
Fax: 01534 857031
pontac@jerseyhols.com
www.jerseyhols.com/pontachouse

31 Pontac House Hotel

★★★

St. Clement's Bay, St. Clements, Jersey, JE2 6SE
Tel: 01534 857771 Fax: 01534 857031
Email: pontac@jerseyhols.com
Web: www.jerseyhols.com/pontachouse
Closed December to February
27 bedrs SB £26 DB £52 HBS £33 HBD £33
B £5 D £12 CC: MC Vi Swi Delt

⮐ 🏠 ⊗ ▢ ☎ 🅿 ⚱ ⅙ ⏰ 🏋 ⛴ ♨♨♨ (€ ⚓

How to get there: From St. Helier follow the A4 coast road to Gorey, approximately 2¹/₂ miles. Entrance to hotel car park is at the rear.
See advert below left

32 Revere Hotel

★★★

Kensington Place, St. Helier, Jersey, JE2 3PA
Tel: 01534 611111 Fax: 01534 611116
Email: reservations@revere.co.uk
Web: www.revere.co.uk
58 bedrs SB £57 DB £114 HBS £70.50
HBD £70.50 B £5 L £4.50 D £13.50
CC: MC Vi Am DC Swi Delt

⮐ 🖃 🏠 ⊗ ⛳ ☎ ⚱ ⏰ 🏋 ⛴ ♨♨♨ ♨♨♨ ⚓

How to get there: 15 min. from the airport by car.

33 Royal Hotel

★★★

David Place, St. Helier, Jersey, JE2 4TD
Tel: 01534 726521 Fax: 01534 811046
Email: royalhotel@itl.net
Web: www.royalhoteljersey.com
88 bedrs SB £69.50 DB £120 HBS £79.50
HBD £70 B £8.50 L £9.95 D £16.95
CC: MC Vi Am DC Swi Delt

♨♨ 🖃 🐾 ⊗ ▢ ☎ ⚱ 🏋 ♨♨♨ ♨♨♨

How to get there: Follow signs for ring road, then Rouge Bouillon A14. Right at roundabout right at traffic lights into Midvale Road. Past two lights, hotel is on left corner at lights.

34 Royal Yacht

★★★

Weighbridge, St. Helier, Jersey, JE2 3NF
Tel: 01534 720511 Fax: 01534 767729
Email: theroyalyacht@mail.com
43 bedrs SB £46.50 DB £93 HBS £59 HBD £59
B £7.50 L £12.50 D £15.50
CC: MC Vi Am Swi Delt

♨♨ 🐾 ⊗ ⛳ ▢ ☎ ⚱ ⏰ 🏋 ⛴ ♨♨♨ ♨♨♨

How to get there: Located in the heart of St. Helier, walking distance to all business houses. Four miles from airport.

35 Silver Springs

★★★
St. Brelade, Jersey, JE3 8DB
Tel: 01534 46401 Fax: 01534 46823

36 Windmills Hotel

★★★
Mont Gras d'Eau, St. Brelade, Jersey, JE3 8ED
Tel: 01534 744201 Fax: 01534 744202
Email: info@windmillshotel.com
Web: www.windmillshotel.com
Closed 18th October

This family-run hotel's tranquil setting enjoys breathtaking views over St. Brelade's bay. Modern facilities compliment its established reputation for personal service and delicious food, making an ideal choice for your Jersey experience.
38 bedrs SB £39 DB £62 HBS £46 HBD £38 B £5.50 D £13.50 CC: MC Vi Am Swi Delt
How to get there: To St. Brelades along A13. Down Mont Gras d'Eau, right next to Hotel Mirimar.

37 Beau Rivage Hotel

★★
St. Brelade's Bay, Jersey, JE3 8EF
Tel: 01534 745983 Fax: 01534 747127
Email: beau@jerseyweb.demon.co.uk
Web: www.jersey.co.uk/hotels/beau
Closed November to March incl.
27 bedrs SB £38 DB £46 HBS £50 HBD £35 B £7 L £14 D £14 CC: MC Vi Am Swi Delt JCB
How to get there: Hotel is located on seaward side of coast road, in centre of St. Brelade's Bay

38 Dolphin Hotel

★★ 🍴 🍴
Gorey Pier, Gorey, Jersey, JE3 6EW
Tel: 01534 853370 Fax: 01534 855343
Email: cavin@itl.net
15 bedrs SB £29 DB £38 HBS £41.50 HBD £41.50 B £7 L £14.50 D £17.50
CC: MC Vi Swi Delt

How to get there: Situated underneath Mont Orgueil Castle, facing harbour of Gorey Pier, 4 miles from town centre, 8 from the airport.

39 Hotel Savoy

★★
Rouge Bouillon, St. Helier, Jersey, JE2 3ZA
Tel: 01534 619916 Fax: 01534 506969
Email: enquiries@hotelsavoyjersey.com
Web: www.hotelsavoyjersey.com
Closed December to January
61 bedrs CC: MC Vi Am DC Swi Delt
How to get there: Located opposite St. Helier police station.

40 Sarum Hotel

★★ 🍴
19-21 New St. John's Road, St. Helier, Jersey, JE2 3LD
Tel: 01534 758163 Fax: 01534 731340
Email: sarum@jerseyweb.demon.co.uk
Web: www.jersey.co.uk/hotels/sarum
Children minimum age: 16
Closed November to March incl.
47 bedrs SB £38.50 DB £62 B £7
CC: MC Vi Am Swi Delt
How to get there: Hotel is located to western side of St. Helier, less than ½ a mile from town centre.

41 White Heather Hotel

★★
Rue de Haut, Millbrook, St. Lawrence, Jersey, JE3 1JQ
Tel: 01534 720978 Fax: 01534 720968
Children minimum age: 3.
Closed November to April

Ideally situated between St. Helier and St. Aubin's beach. Close to all amenities in a quiet location, the hotel offers good catering and comfort in a friendly atmostphere
33 bedrs SB £24 DB £42 HBS £28 HBD £24.50 D £8.25 CC: MC Vi DC

⚃ ▯ ☎ **P** ⚜ ♂ ✿ ⚄ ⦿

How to get there: On A1 between St. Helier and St. Aubin, take the A11, turn right at the school.

42 Bon Air Hotel

◆ ◆ ◆ ◆ ✻ ⚐

Coast Road, Pontac, St. Clements,
Jersey, JE2 6SE
Tel: 01534 855324 Fax: 01534 857801
Closed November to February
18 bedrs CC: None accepted
⚃ ▯ **P** ⚜ ♂ ✿ ⚄ ⦿ ⦿

43 Millbrook House Hotel

◆ ◆ ◆ ◆ ✻

Rue de Trachy, Millbrook, St. Helier,
Jersey, JE2 3JN
Tel: 01534 733036 Fax: 01534 724317
Closed 7 October to 3 May

Peace, quiet and character, where the air is clear and traditional values are maintained. 10 acres of grounds, car park, 27 ensuite rooms, memorable food and wines.
27 bedrs SB £38 DB £76 HBS £44 HBD £88
CC: MC Vi Am Swi Delt
⚌ ⚃ ▯ ☎ **P** ⚜ ⦿ ⦿

How to get there: 1½ miles west from St. Helier off A1.

44 Hotel des Pierres

◆ ◆ ◆

Greve de Lecq Bay, St. Ouen, Jersey, JE3 2DT
Tel: 01534 481858 Fax: 01534 485273
Email: despierres@jerseyhols.com
Web: www.jerseyhols.com
Closed December 15 to January 11
16 bedrs SB £25.50 DB £51
HBS £35 HBD £35 B £4.85 D £10.85
CC: MC Vi Swi Delt
⊗ ⚃ ▯ **P** ♂ ✿ ⚄ ⦿ 'T'

Sark

45 Aval Du Creux Hotel

★ ★ ★ ⦿

Harbour Hill, Sark, GY9 0SB
Tel: 01481 832036 Fax: 01481 832368

Set in secluded south-facing gardens close to the village with all amenities on our doorstep; internationally renowned for superb cuisine and regularly visited by yachtsmen. All rooms are ensuite.
20 bedrs SB £62.50 DB £85 HBS £80.45
HBD £60.45 B £4.95 L £4.95 D £17.95
CC: MC Vi Am Swi Delt JCB
⚌ ⚃ ▯ ☎ ⦿ **P** ⦿ ♂ ✿ ⚄ ⦿ ⦿ ⚐

How to get there: Hotel is situated on the right at the top of Harbour Hill.

46 Dixcart Bay Hotel

★ ★

Sark, GY9 0SD
Tel: 01481 832015 Fax: 01481 832164
Email: dixcart@itl.net
Web: www.dixcart.guernseyci.com
15 bedrs SB £45 DB £90 HBS £61 HBD £61
B £5.50 L £7.50 D £16
CC: MC Vi Am DC Swi Delt JCB
⦿ ⚃ ▯ ☎ ♂ ✿ ⚄ ⦿ ⦿

How to get there: From top of Harbour Hill take avenue through centre of village. Turn left, following signs to Dixcart Hotel.
See advert on facing page

47 Hotel Petit Champ

◆ ◆ ◆ ◆ ⦿ ⦿ ⚐

Sark, GY9 0SF
Tel: 01481 832046 Fax: 01481 832469
Email: hpc@island-of-sark.co.uk
Web: www.island-of-sark.co.uk
Children minimum age: 6.
Closed October – Easter
13 bedrs SB £49.50 DB £87 HBS £60 HBD £58
L £3 D £19.25 CC: MC Vi Am DC Swi Delt
⚐ ⚜ ✿ ⚄ ⦿ ⚌

How to get there: Follow the sign-posted lane towards the sea from the Methodist chapel.

Isle of Man

48 Mount Murray Hotel and Country Club

★★★★★ 🏵🏵

Santon, Isle of Man, IM4 2HT
Tel: 01624 661111 Fax: 01624 611116
Email: hotel@mountmurray.com
Web: www.mountmurray.com
90 bedrs SB £85 DB £105 B £8.50 L £6.95
D £18.95 CC: MC Vi Am DC Swi Delt

How to get there: From airport take main road to Douglas. Turn left at Santon, hotel is signposted.

49 Ascot Hotel

★★★ 🏵

7 Empire Terrace, Douglas, Isle of Man, IM2 4LE
Tel: 01624 675081 Fax: 01624 661512

50 Port Erin Royal Hotel

★★★

Promenade, Port Erin, Isle of Man, IM9 6LH
Tel: 01624 833116 Fax: 01624 835402
Email: rac@porterinhotels.com
Web: www.porterinhotels.com
Closed December to January
79 bedrs SB £28 DB £56 HBS £38 HBD £38
B £5.95 D £13.95 CC: MC Vi Swi Delt

How to get there: Follow signs from either sea terminal or airport marked 'Port Erin and the South'. Hotel on upper promenade facing sea.

51 The Empress Hotel

★★★

Central Promenade, Douglas, Isle of Man, IM2 4RA
Tel: 01624 661155 Fax: 01624 673554

52 Port Erin Imperial Hotel

★★

Promenade, Port Erin, Isle of Man, IM9 6LH
Tel: 01624 832122 Fax: 01624 835402
Email: rac@porterinhotels.com
Web: www.porterinhotels.com
Closed December to January
51 bedrs SB £25 DB £50 HBS £33 HBD £33
B £5.95 D £12.95 CC: MC Vi Swi Delt

How to get there: Follow directions from either sea terminal or airport marked 'Port Erin and the South'. Hotel on upper promenade facing sea.
See advert right

Channel Islands

National Accessible Standard for the UK

If your accommodation requirements include access for a wheelchair user, or a guest with impaired mobility look out for the disability access symbol ♿ shown throughout this guide*. This symbol indicates that the accommodation in question offers some disability access. The nature of this access may vary between properties and we recommend that you check with the property concerned that they are able to cater for your exact requirements.

Alternatively, the following list shows RAC Accredited properties that have been assessed for access for guests with a disability. The assessment has been undertaken by either the English Tourism Council, Visit Scotland, the Wales Tourist Board and Northern Ireland Tourist Board or Holiday Care.

These organisations inspect properties for accessibility under the National Accessible Standard within the UK. Properties are shown by region and by location to make it as easy as possible for you to find suitable accommodation.

The National Accessible Standard comprises 3 levels of accessibility:

Category 1: Accessible to a wheelchair user travelling independently

Category 2: Accessible to a wheelchair user travelling with assistance

Category 3: Accessible to someone with limited mobility but able to stand, walk a few paces, and (in some circumstances) up a maximum of three steps

Additional help and guidance on the National Accessible Standard and on finding suitable accommodation for those with specific access requirements can be obtained from:

Holiday Care
2nd Floor, Imperial Buildings
Victoria Road
Horley RH6 7P7

Tel 01293 774535   Fax 01293 784647
Minicom 01293 776943

* Please note that where a wheelchair symbol is displayed in the guide, this is based on data which has been provided to RAC by the hotel or guest accommodation and does not indicate that the property has been assessed for disabled access. Please note RAC does not assess for disabled accessibility and cannot be held liable for any loss (whether direct, indirect, special or consequential) suffered through reliance by guests on the accuracy of this information.

London

Berners Hotel	3
Bonnington in Bloomsbury	2
Conrad London	3
Copthorne Tara Hotel London Kensington	1
Holiday Inn London Kensington South	3
London Bridge Hotel	3
Novotel London Waterloo	3
Novotel London West	3
Sheraton Park Tower Hotel	3

Southeast

Andover, Hampshire
Fifehead Manor Hotel	3

Basildon, Essex
Campanile Hotel	3

Basingstoke, Hampshire
Hanover International Hotel & Club Basingstoke	3

Bexleyheath, Kent
Bexleyheath Marriott Hotel	3

Billingshurst, West Sussex
Travelodge Billinghurst	3

Botley, Hampshire
MacDonald Botley Park	1

Bracknell, Berkshire
Coppid Beech Hotel	1

Brentwood, Essex
Heybridge Hotel	3

Brighton, East Sussex
Quality Hotel Brighton	3

Brockenhurst, Hampshire
Watersplash Hotel	3

Broxbourne, Herts
Cheshunt Marriott Hotel	1

Colchester, Essex
Five Lakes Hotel Golf Country Club	3
Rose & Crown Hotel	3

Crawley, West Sussex
Travelodge Crawley	3

Eastbourne, East Sussex
Congress Hotel	3
Grand Hotel	3
Langham Hotel	3
York House Hotel	2

Egham, Surrey
Runnymede Hotel & Spa	3

Fareham, Hampshire
Avenue House Hotel	3
Solent Hotel	3

Gatwick Airport
Copthorne Hotel Effingham Park Gatwick	3
Copthorne Hotel London Gatwick	3
Langshott Manor	3
Renaissance London Gatwick Hotel	3

Harlow, Essex
Swallow Churchgate	3

Southwest

East Anglia

East Midlands

West Midlands

Wales

Scotland

Northern Ireland

To find the distance from one town to another, follow the horizontal and vertical columns until they intersect.

The upper figures are miles and the lower *italic* figures are kilometres - for example the distance from Perth to York is 249 miles or *401* kilometres

Aberdeen	445	420	493	471	505	221	588	125	569	149	145	439	105	327	383	341	517	340	235	496	686	82	360	547	228	319
	716	*676*	*793*	*758*	*813*	*356*	*947*	*201*	*916*	*240*	*233*	*707*	*169*	*526*	*616*	*549*	*832*	*547*	*378*	*798*	*1104*	*132*	*579*	*880*	*367*	*513*
Aberystwyth	114	125	214	105	224	292	320	201	430	320	111	486	169	199	104	211	129	257	276	317	386	159	201	325	195	
	183	*201*	*344*	*169*	*360*	*478*	*515*	*323*	*692*	*515*	*179*	*782*	*272*	*320*	*167*	*340*	*208*	*414*	*444*	*510*	*621*	*256*	*323*	*523*	*314*	
BIRMINGHAM	81	100	103	196	194	292	157	392	292	148	458	113	90	93	117	80	207	166	275	337	76	128	297	130		
	130	*161*	*166*	*315*	*312*	*470*	*253*	*631*	*470*	*238*	*737*	*182*	*145*	*150*	*188*	*129*	*333*	*267*	*443*	*542*	*122*	*206*	*478*	*209*		
Bristol	169	45	277	202	373	76	486	373	206	539	194	183	161	122	161	299	252	185	419	161	76	378	222			
	272	*72*	*466*	*325*	*600*	*122*	*782*	*600*	*332*	*867*	*312*	*295*	*259*	*196*	*259*	*481*	*406*	*298*	*674*	*259*	*122*	*608*	*357*			
Cambridge	190	264	125	345	249	479	372	270	505	145	85	194	54	165	241	62	337	390	120	148	379	165				
	306	*425*	*201*	*555*	*401*	*771*	*599*	*435*	*813*	*233*	*137*	*312*	*87*	*266*	*388*	*100*	*543*	*628*	*193*	*238*	*610*	*266*				
CARDIFF	289	238	385	121	485	385	216	549	232	208	165	157	183	325	262	233	440	194	121	390	244					
	465	*383*	*620*	*195*	*781*	*620*	*348*	*884*	*373*	*335*	*272*	*253*	*295*	*523*	*422*	*375*	*708*	*312*	*195*	*628*	*393*					
Carlisle	389	96	353	206	96	231	262	119	191	120	301	119	57	289	461	144	152	324	101	121						
	626	*154*	*568*	*332*	*154*	*372*	*422*	*192*	*307*	*193*	*484*	*192*	*92*	*465*	*742*	*232*	*245*	*521*	*163*	*195*						
Dover	462	248	596	488	360	622	260	202	299	71	276	358	174	356	534	245	143	496	282							
	744	*399*	*959*	*786*	*580*	*1001*	*418*	*325*	*481*	*114*	*444*	*576*	*280*	*573*	*859*	*394*	*230*	*798*	*454*							
EDINBURGH	450	144	44	333	158	202	258	216	390	215	110	366	559	43	235	438	124	194								
	724	*232*	*71*	*536*	*254*	*325*	*415*	*348*	*628*	*346*	*177*	*589*	*900*	*69*	*378*	*705*	*200*	*312*								
Exeter	560	449	282	618	270	247	237	181	236	364	308	112	492	237	105	454	287									
	901	*723*	*454*	*995*	*435*	*398*	*381*	*291*	*380*	*586*	*496*	*180*	*792*	*381*	*169*	*731*	*462*									
Fort William	101	438	66	329	399	329	510	329	253	504	661	97	348	541	195	330										
	163	*705*	*106*	*530*	*642*	*530*	*821*	*530*	*407*	*811*	*1064*	*156*	*560*	*871*	*314*	*531*										
Glasgow	330	166	215	291	216	397	215	148	385	556	50	248	433	84	217											
	531	*267*	*346*	*468*	*348*	*639*	*346*	*238*	*620*	*895*	*80*	*399*	*697*	*135*	*349*											
Holyhead	474	176	216	102	269	124	272	311	403	371	168	293	338	204												
	763	*283*	*348*	*164*	*433*	*200*	*438*	*501*	*649*	*597*	*270*	*472*	*544*	*328*												
Inverness	360	427	382	550	373	268	529	720	116	393	598	262	352													
	579	*687*	*615*	*885*	*600*	*431*	*852*	*1159*	*187*	*632*	*963*	*422*	*566*													
Leeds	68	75	189	40	92	176	401	254	33	232	220	24														
	109	*121*	*304*	*64*	*148*	*283*	*645*	*409*	*53*	*373*	*354*	*39*														
Lincoln	129	131	84	159	105	367	312	46	204	298	75															
	208	*211*	*135*	*256*	*169*	*591*	*502*	*74*	*328*	*480*	*121*															
Liverpool	202	35	168	220	366	266	72	239	221	99																
	325	*56*	*270*	*354*	*589*	*428*	*116*	*385*	*356*	*159*																
LONDON	185	286	114	285	433	159	77	402	207																	
	298	*460*	*183*	*459*	*718*	*256*	*124*	*647*	*333*																	
MANCHESTER	132	185	354	263	38	221	220	64																		
	212	*298*	*570*	*423*	*61*	*356*	*354*	*103*																		
Newcastle upon Tyne	264	484	155	125	324	158	84																			
	425	*779*	*249*	*201*	*521*	*254*	*135*																			
Norwich	436	430	146	206	403	181																				
	702	*692*	*235*	*332*	*649*	*291*																				
Penzance	604	368	223	569	410																					
	974	*592*	*359*	*916*	*661*																					
Perth	306	479	154	249																						
	492	*771*	*248*	*401*																						
Sheffield	199	263	217																							
	320	*423*	*349*																							
Southampton	445	258																								
	716	*415*																								
Stranraer	222																									
	357																									
York																										

Inverness

Aberdeen

Fort William
Perth

Glasgow
EDINBURGH

Stranraer
Newcastle upon Tyne

Londonderry
Carlisle

Donegal
BELFAST

York

Sligo
Leeds

Galway
Liverpool   MANCHESTER

Athlone
DUBLIN   Holyhead   Sheffield   Lincoln

Limerick
Norwich

Rosslare   BIRMINGHAM
Killarney   Cork   Waterford   Aberystwyth   Cambridge

LONDON

CARDIFF   Bristol

Southampton   Dover

Exeter

Penzance

KEY TO MAPS

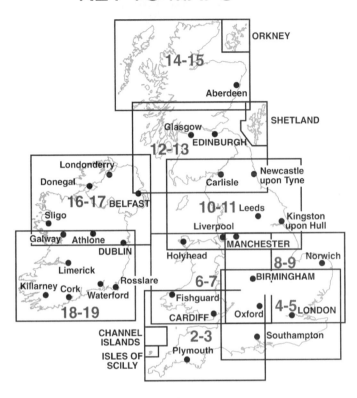

LEGEND

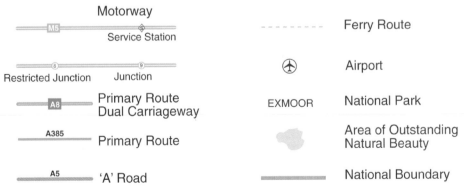

Motorway — Service Station	- - - - - - Ferry Route
Restricted Junction Junction	✈ Airport
Primary Route Dual Carriageway	EXMOOR National Park
Primary Route	Area of Outstanding Natural Beauty
'A' Road	National Boundary

● denotes location of RAC Inspected property/properties

 Ordnance Survey®

This product includes mapping data licensed from Ordnance Survey® with the permission of the Controller of Her Majesty's Stationary Office. © Crown copyright. All rights reserved. Licence No: 39856X

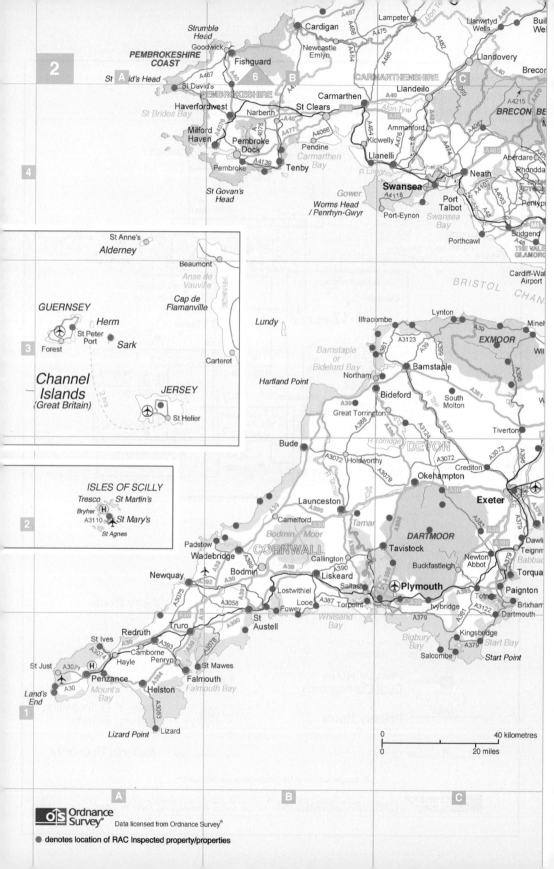

2

PEMBROKESHIRE
COAST

Strumble
Head
Goodwick
St A id's Head
Fishguard
6
Cardigan
Lampeter
Llanwrtyd
Wells
Buil
Wel
Newcastle
Emlyn

CARMARTHENSHIRE
Llandovery
Brecor

St David's
PEMBROKESHIRE
St Brides Bay
Haverfordwest
Narberth
Carmarthen
St Clears
Llandeilo
BRECON BE
A4215
M

Milford
Haven
Pembroke
Dock
Pendine
Carmarthen
Bay
Afon Tywi
Ammanford
Kidwelly
Aberdare
Rhondda

Pembroke
Tenby
Llanelli
R Loughor
Neath
Port
Talbot
Pontyp

St Govan's
Head
St Govan's
Head
Gower
Worms Head
/ Penrhyn-Gwyr
Port-Eynon
Swansea
A4118
SWANSEA
Swansea
Bay
Porthcawl
Bridgend
THE VALE
GLAMORG

4

Cardiff-Wal
Airport
BRISTOL
CHAN

St Anne's
Alderney

Beaumont
Anse de
Vauville

Lundy
Ilfracombe
Lynton
Mine
EXMOOR
Wil

GUERNSEY
Herm
Cap de
Flamanville
Forest
St Peter
Port
Sark

Barnstaple
or
Bideford Bay
Northam
A3123
A39
A361
Barnstaple
South
Molton
A361
W

3

Channel
Islands
(Great Britain)
Carteret
JERSEY
St Helier

Hartland Point
Bideford
Great Torrington
A39
A388
H Taw
Tiverton
A3072
A396

R Torridge
DEVON
A3072
Crediton
A396

Bude
A3072
Holsworthy
Okehampton
A30
Exeter
A376

ISLES OF SCILLY
Tresco   St Martin's
Bryher   St Mary's
A3110
St Agnes
Launceston
A395
Tamar
DARTMOOR
Tavistock
Newton
Abbot
Dawli
Teignm
Babbac
Torqua

2

Camelford
A30
Bodmin Moor
Buckfastleigh
Paignton
Brixham
Dartmouth

Newquay
Padstow
Wadebridge
CORNWALL
Bodmin
Liskeard
Saltash
Plymouth
Ivybridge
Totnes
A3122
A379

A3075
A392
A30
A389
A391
Callington
A390
Lostwithiel
Looe
Fowey
Torpoint
Whitsand
Bay
A379
Kingsbridge
A379
Start Bay

Redruth
Truro
A390
St
Austell
Bigbury
Bay
Salcombe
Start Point

St Ives
A3071
A30
A393
A39
A3076
St Mawes
Falmouth
Falmouth Bay

St Just
A3071
Camborne
Hayle
Penryn
Helston
A394
A3083

Penzance
A30
Mount's
Bay

Land's
End

1

Lizard Point   Lizard

0   40 kilometres
0   20 miles

A   B   C

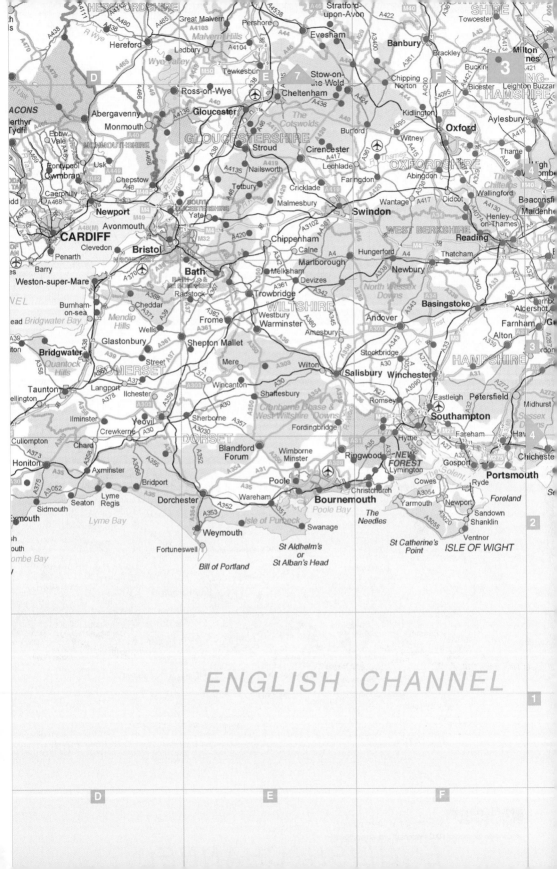

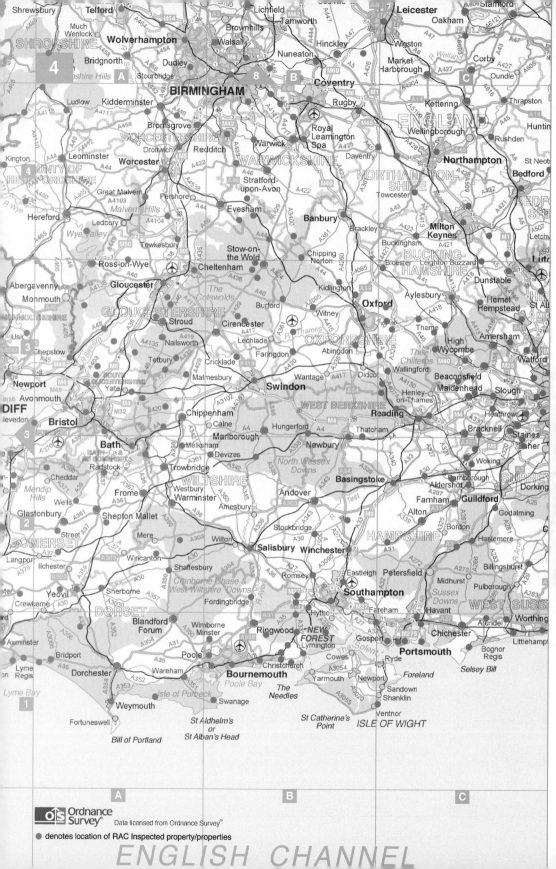

denotes location of RAC Inspected property/properties

ENGLISH CHANNEL

IRISH SEA

6

A   B   C

4

3

2

1

Amlwch

A5025

ISLE OF ANGLESEY
ANGLESEY

Benllech

Llandudno

Holyhead

Llangefni

Menai Bridge

Beaumaris

Conwy

A55

Colwyn Bay

A545

Rhosneigor

A5

Bangor

A54

Bethesda

A4080

A4086

Llanrwst

Caernarfon

A487

A4085

A498

CONWY

Betws-y-Coed

Blaenau Ffestiniog

A4212

A470

Nefyn

Porthmadog

A499

A497

Criccieth

Ffestiniog

SNOWDONIA

GWYNEDD

A494

Pwllheli

Llŷn

A499

Harlech

A496

Abersoch

A487

Dolgellau

Barmouth

A493

A487

A470

Machynlleth

A489

Tywyn

A493

Caernarfon Bay

CARDIGAN BAY / BAE CEREDIGION

WA

Aberystwyth

A44

A4120

CAMBRIAN MO

A485

Aberaeron

CEREDIGION

Rhaya

New Quay

Tregaron

A482

A487

Lampeter

Llanwrtyd Wells

Strumble Head

Goodwick

Cardigan

A486

A475

A485

A482

Llandover

Newcastle Emlyn

A484

A40

PEMBROKESHIRE COAST

Fishguard

A487

St David's Head

A40

St David's

A478

CARMARTHENSHIRE

Llandeilo

A483

A40

BRE

PEMBROKESHIRE

Haverfordwest

Narberth

St Clears

Carmarthen

Afon Tywi

A48

St Brides Bay

A4076

A40

A4075

Pendine

A4066

Ammanford

A483

A476

A474

A465

Ab

Kidwelly

Milford Haven

Pembroke Dock

A477

Carmarthen Bay

Llanelli

R. Loughor

Neath

A4139

Tenby

Swansea

A4118

Port Talbot

A48

Pembroke

St Govan's Head

Gower

Worms Head / Penrhyn-Gwyr

Port-Eynon

Swansea Bay

Porthcawl

2

BRISTOL

Ordnance Survey®   Data licensed from Ordnance Survey®

● denotes location of RAC Inspected property/properties

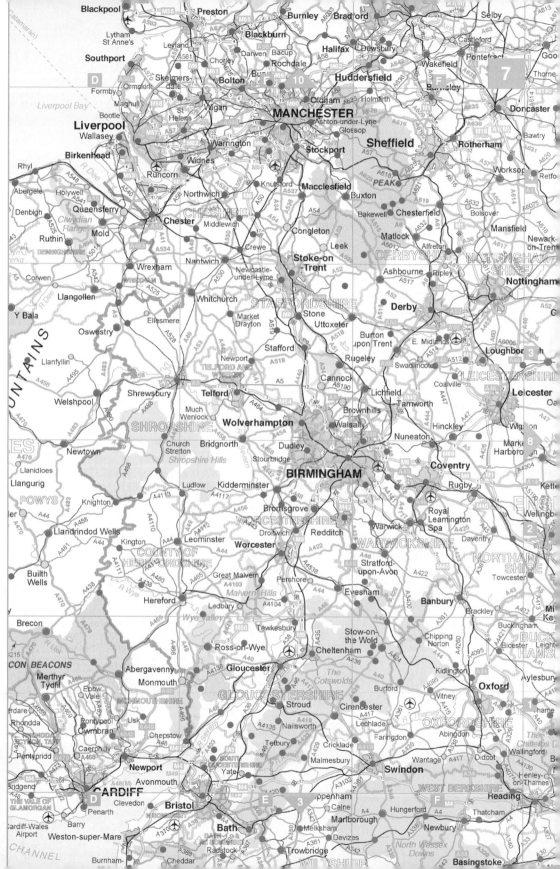

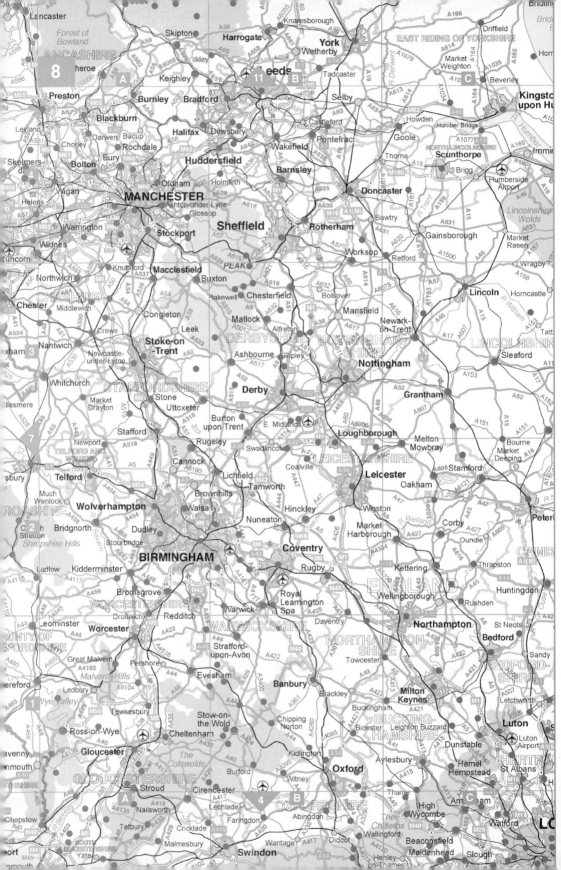

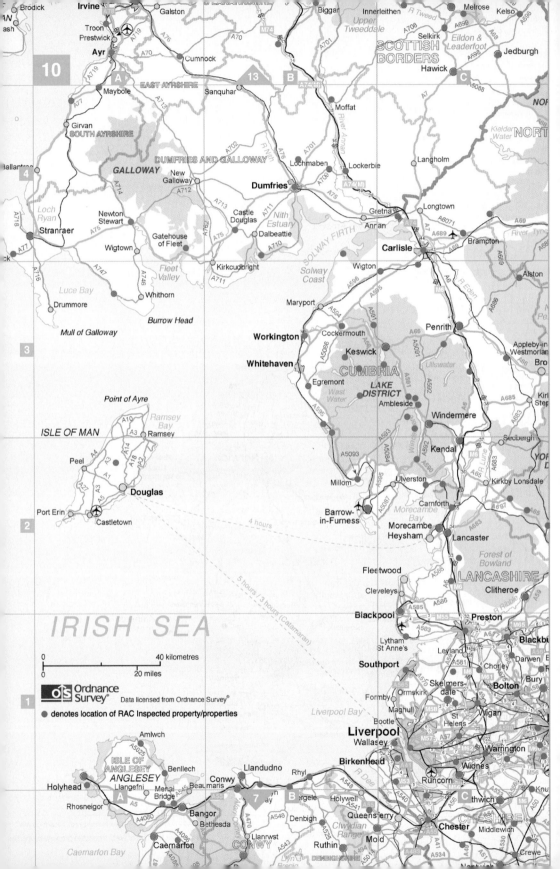

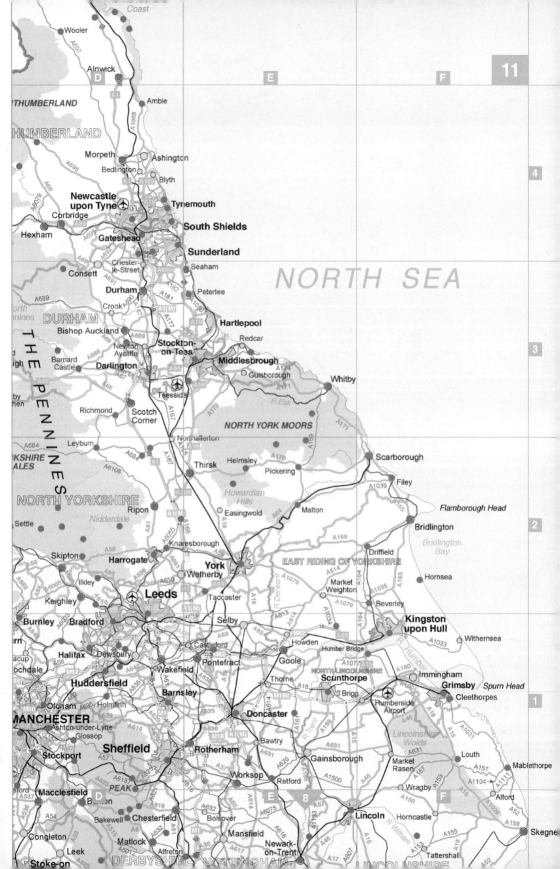

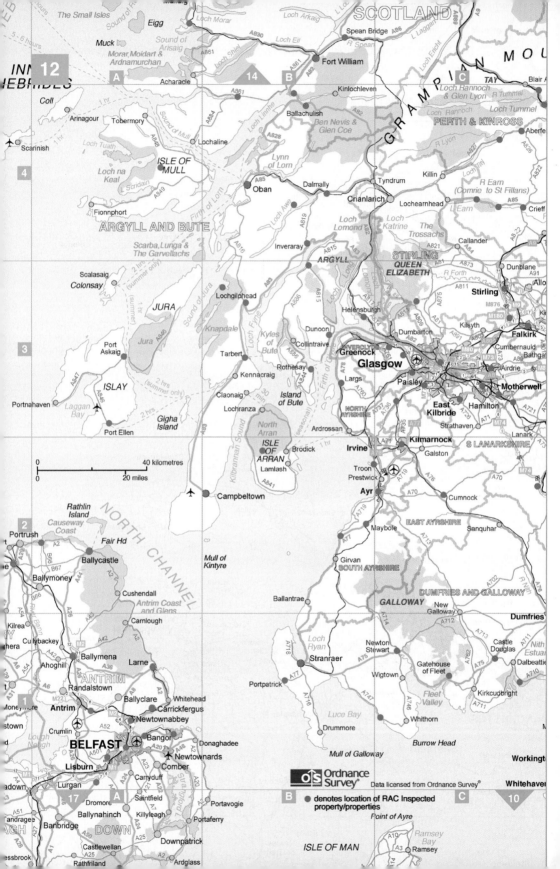

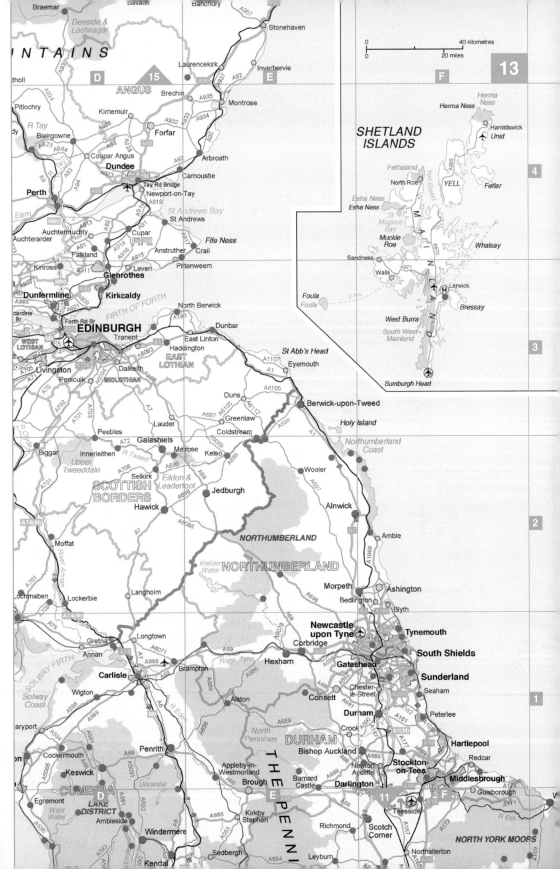

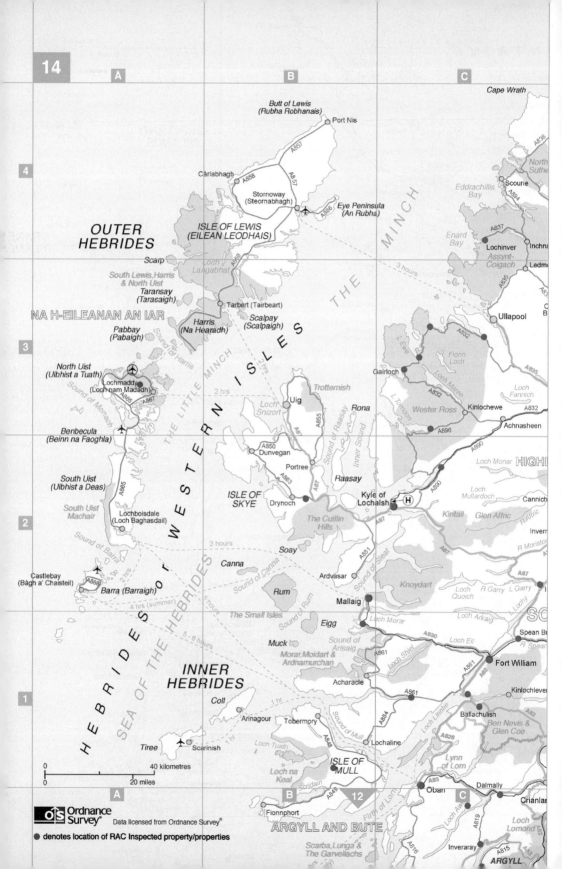

A   B   C

Cape Wrath

Butt of Lewis
(Rubha Robhanais)

Port Nis

A857

North
Suthe

Scourie

Cārlabhagh   A858   Eddrachillis
Bay

Stornoway
(Steornabhagh)   Eye Peninsula
(An Rubha)   Enard
Bay   Lochinver   Inchna

A866

OUTER
HEBRIDES   ISLE OF LEWIS
(EILEAN LEODHAIS)   Assynt-
Coigach   Ledmo

Scarp   Loch
Langabhat   A835

A896   Ledm

South Lewis, Harris
& North Uist   Ullapool   C
B

NA H-EILEANAN AN IAR   Taransay
(Tarasaigh)   Tarbert (Tairbeart)

Harris
(Na Hearadh)   Scalpay
(Scalpaigh)   Fionn
Loch   A832

Pabbay
(Pabaigh)   A832   Gairloch   Loch
Fannich

North Uist
(Uibhist a Tuath)   Trotternish   Wester Ross   Kinlochewe   A832

Lochmaddy
(Loch nam Madadh)   Loch
Snizort   Uig   A832   Achnasheen

A865   A867   2 hrs   A855   Rona   A896

Benbecula
(Beinn na Faoghla)   Dunvegan   Sound of Raasay   Loch Monar   HIGHL

A850   Portree   Loch
Mullardoch   Cannich

South Uist
(Uibhist a Deas)   A863   Raasay   Inver

A865   ISLE OF
SKYE   Kyle of
Lochalsh   (H)   Kintail   Glen Affric   R Affric

Lochboisdale
(Loch Baghasdail)   Drynoch   The Cuillin
Hills   A87   Loch
Quoich   R Garry L Garry

South Uist
Machair   3 hours   Soay   A851   Knoydart   SO

Sound of Barra   Canna   Ardvasar   A87

Castlebay
(Bàgh a' Chaisteil)   Rum   Mallaig   A830   Loch Arkaig   Spean Br

Barra (Barraigh)   A888   Eigg   Loch Morar   R Spean

The Small Isles   Sound of Rum   A830   Loch Eil   Fort William

Muck   Sound of
Arisaig   A861   Kinlochleve

Morar, Moidart &
Ardnamurchan   Acharacle   A861   Ballachulish   A82

INNER
HEBRIDES   A861   Ben Nevis &
Glen Coe

Coll   A884   Loch
Linnhe   A828

Arinagour   Tobermory   Sound of Mull   Lynn
of Lorn

Tiree   Scarinish   A848   Lochaline   Dalmally

Loch Tuath   ISLE OF
MULL   A85   A819

Loch na
Keal   A849   Oban   Loch
Lomond

0   40 kilometres
0   20 miles   Scridain   Firth of Lorn   C   Crianlar

A   B   12   Fionnphort   Inveraray   A815

ARGYLL AND BUTE   A816   ARGYLL

Scarba, Lunga &
The Garvellachs

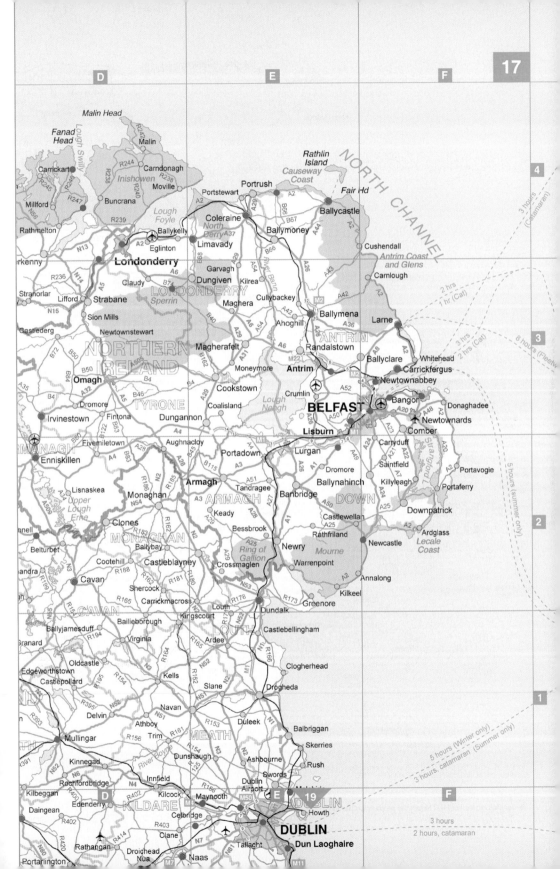

denotes location of RAC Inspected property/properties

Ireland based on the Ordnance Survey by permission of the
Government of the Irish Republic. Permit No. 7195

0   40 kilometres
0   20 miles

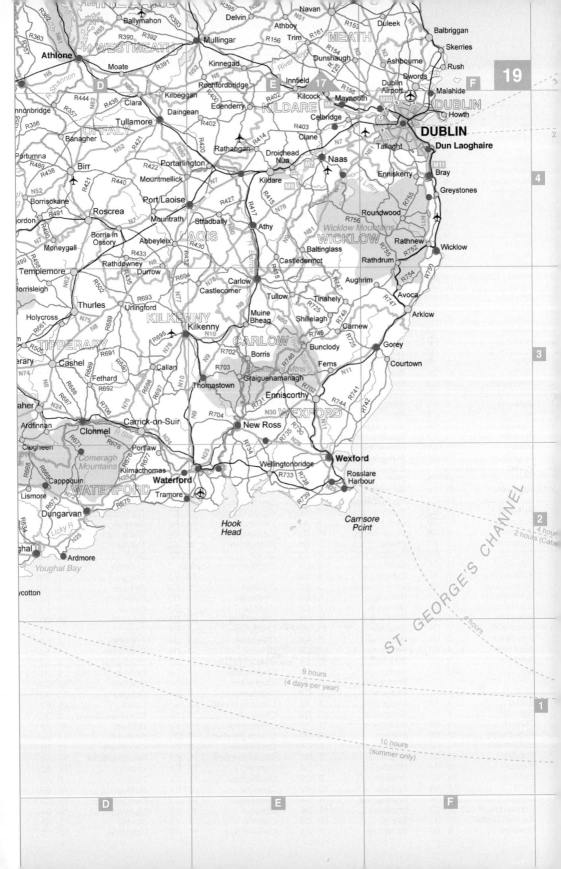

INDEX TO GREAT BRITAIN

INDEX TO IRELAND

Notes

Notes